BIOMARKERS IN CANCER DETECTION AND MONITORING OF THERAPEUTICS

VOLUME TWO

BIOMARKERS IN CANCER DETECTION AND MONITORING OF THERAPEUTICS

Volume 2: Diagnostic and Therapeutic Applications

Edited by

R.C. SOBTI
Department of Biotechnology, Panjab University, Chandigarh, India

M. WATANABE
Department of Oncologic Pathology, Mie University School of Medicine, Tsu, Mie, Japan

AASTHA SOBTI
Department of Immunotechnology, University of Lund, Lund, Sweden

ELSEVIER

ACADEMIC PRESS
An imprint of Elsevier

Academic Press is an imprint of Elsevier
125 London Wall, London EC2Y 5AS, United Kingdom
525 B Street, Suite 1650, San Diego, CA 92101, United States
50 Hampshire Street, 5th Floor, Cambridge, MA 02139, United States
The Boulevard, Langford Lane, Kidlington, Oxford OX5 1GB, United Kingdom

Notices
Knowledge and best practice in this field are constantly changing. As new research and experience broaden our understanding, changes in research methods, professional practices, or medical treatment may become necessary.

Practitioners and researchers must always rely on their own experience and knowledge in evaluating and using any information, methods, compounds, or experiments described herein. In using such information or methods they should be mindful of their own safety and the safety of others, including parties for whom they have a professional responsibility.

To the fullest extent of the law, neither the Publisher nor the authors, contributors, or editors, assume any liability for any injury and/or damage to persons or property as a matter of products liability, negligence or otherwise, or from any use or operation of any methods, products, instructions, or ideas contained in the material herein.

ISBN 978-0-323-95114-2

For information on all Academic Press publications
visit our website at https://www.elsevier.com/books-and-journals

Publisher: Stacy Masucci
Acquisitions Editor: Rafael E. Teixeira
Editorial Project Manager: Matthew Mapes
Production Project Manager: Sajana Devasi P K
Cover Designer: Vicky Pearson

Typeset by STRAIVE, India

Working together
to grow libraries in
developing countries

www.elsevier.com • www.bookaid.org

Contents

Contributors   xiii
Preface   xxi

1. Oral squamous cell carcinoma   1
Anubha Gulati and R.C. Sobti

1. Oral cancer   1
2. Oral squamous cell carcinoma   2
3. Epidemiology   3
4. Etiology   5
5. Precursor lesions   12
6. Oral epithelial dysplasia   16
7. Pathogenesis   18
8. Cancer stem cells   23
9. Tumor microenvironment   25
10. Epithelial–mesenchymal transition   32
11. Metastasis   33
12. Oral bacteria in oral carcinogenesis   34
13. Clinical features   35
14. Diagnosis   37
15. Histopathological features   51
16. Treatment   56
17. Prognosis   65
References   71

2. Genetic predisposition and pathophysiology of oral squamous cell carcinoma   89
Selvaraj Jayaraman, Duraj Sekar, Ponnulakshmi Rajagopal, Veerakumar Ramachandran,
Ramya Sekar, JH Shazia Fathima, Dhayasankar Prabhu Shankar, and
Gowtham Kumar Subbaraj

1. Introduction   90
2. Oral squamous cell carcinoma and glucose transporters   97
3. Oral squamous cell carcinoma and methylated genes   98
References   100

3. Molecular biomarkers in gastric cancer   105
Kazuki Kanayama and Yoshifumi S. Hirokawa

1. Introduction   105

    2. RNF43   105
    3. APC   106
    4. ARID1A   106
    5. ARID2   106
    6. MSI   107
    7. MALTA1-GLT1 fusion   108
    8. TP53   108
    9. RB1   108
   10. ERBB2   109
   11. C-MET   109
   12. EGFR   109
   13. PD-L1   110
   14. Epstein–Barr virus   110
   15. VEGF-A   111
   16. CD44   111
   17. E-cadherin   112
   18. Matrix metalloproteinases (MMPs)   113
   19. Conclusions   114
   References   114

4. Recent advancement in molecular markers of pancreatic cancer   121

L. Tharrun Daniel Paul, Ganesh Munuswamy-Ramanujam,

Rajappan Chandra Satish Kumar, Vasukidevi Ramachandran,

Dhanavathy Gnanasampanthapandian, and Kanagaraj Palaniyandi

    1. Introduction   121
    2. Blood markers   122
    3. DNA and RNA markers   123
    4. Serum markers   124
    5. Serum carbohydrate antigen (CA) CA19-9   124
    6. Glycosylation   125
    7. Mucins   126
    8. Genetic markers   127
    9. Oncogenic KRAS   127
   10. Tumor suppressor genes   129
   11. CDKN2A   130
   12. TP53   131
   13. SMAD4   131
   14. Epigenetic markers   132
   15. DNA methylation changes   133
   16. Micro RNA modification   134
   17. Pancreatic tumor juice markers   135
   18. Proteomics   136
   19. Growth factors and receptors   137

20. Mitochondrial mutations   138
21. Telomerase   138
22. M2-pyruvate kinase   138
23. Microarray   139
24. Pancreatic tumor tissue markers   139
25. Precancerous lesions   140
26. Cystic fluid   141
27. Screening and diagnosis of pancreatic cancer   142
28. Recent imaging strategies   143
29. Conclusion   143
Acknowledgment   144
References   144

5. Molecular biomarkers in pancreatic ductal adenocarcinoma   151

Junya Tsuboi, Reiko Yamada, and Yoshifumi S. Hirokawa

1. Introduction   151
2. Metabolic reprograming   151
3. Biomarkers for diagnosis   155
4. Prognostic biomarkers   159
5. Targeted therapy   163
6. Conclusions   166
References   166

6. Biomarkers in endocrine diseases   175

Dhritiman Maitra, Sunil Chumber, and R.C. Deka

1. Introduction   175
2. Basic biomarkers   175
3. Modern biomarkers (including molecular markers)   186
References   197

**7. Cancer immunotherapy-associated endocrine complications
and treatment strategies   199**

Koushik Sen, Madhuchhanda Adhikari, Chayan Biswas, Sukhendu Maity,

Ankit Chatterjee, and Kousik Pramanick

1. Introduction   199
2. Immune checkpoints and its function   200
3. Immune checkpoint inhibitors   202
4. Functional mechanism and efficacy of immune checkpoint inhibitors   203
5. Cancer immunotherapy with ICIs and associated endocrinopathies   205
6. Screening, management and treatment strategies   212
7. Conclusion and future directions   214
References   215

8. **Shared and distinct aspects of hematopoietic malignancies such as leukemia and lymphoma**   223

   Iyshwarya B.K. and Ramakrishnan Veerabathiran

   1. Introduction   223
   2. Leukemia   224
   3. Lymphoma   228
   4. Conclusion   231
   Acknowledgment   232
   References   232

9. **Molecular diagnosis, drivers, and treatment modalities for chronic lymphocytic leukemia**   235

   Saurabh Yadav and Balraj Mittal

   1. Introduction   235
   2. Diagnosis/detection of CLL   236
   3. Molecular drivers of CLL   237
   4. Treatment modalities for the CLL disease   242
   5. Intratumor heterogeneity and clonal evolution of CLL   244
   6. Future directions   246
   Acknowledgments   246
   References   246

10. **Myelodysplastic syndrome: A challenging entity**   249

    Anshu Palta and Manveen Kaur

    1. Pathogenesis   250
    2. Clinical presentation   252
    3. Classification   253
    4. Approach to diagnosis of MDS   260
    References   271

11. **Multiple myeloma**   273

    Vijay Goni, Vikas Bachhal, Deepak Negi, and Mohak Kataria

    1. Etiopathogenesis   273
    2. Clinical features   273
    3. Diagnosis   274
    4. Radiographic evaluation   275
    5. Histology   276
    6. Prognosis   277
    7. Treatment   277
    References   279

12. Role of biomarkers in assessing response to immune checkpoint inhibitors in cancer treatment   **281**

Kriti Jain, Nirmal Kumar Ganguly, and Shyam Aggarwal

1. Introduction   281
2. Predictive biomarkers to assess response to checkpoint inhibitor therapy   285
3. Summary   297
References   298
Further reading   302

13. Molecular biomarkers in prostate cancer   **305**

Remi Semba and Katsunori Uchida

1. Introduction   305
2. Molecular biomarkers used for diagnosis   305
3. Molecular biomarkers used for treatment   307
4. Future prospects   310
5. Conclusion   311
References   311

14. Biomarkers in endometrial and cervical cancer   **313**

Navdeep Kaur Mangat, Ritu Aggarwal, and Aashima Arora

1. Endometrial cancer   313
2. Biomarkers in EC   313
3. Cervical cancer   315
References   319

15. Skin cancer biology and its biomarkers: Recent trends and prospective   **321**

Himani Sharma, Davinder Parsad, and Ravinder Kumar

1. Introduction   321
2. Etiopathogenesis of skin cancer   323
3. Biomarkers of skin cancer   324
4. Biomarkers for melanoma skin cancer   324
5. Biomarkers for nonmelanoma skin cancers (NMSCs)   328
6. Conclusion   331
References   331

16. Genetics of neuronal and glioneuronal cancers   **339**

Pooja, Varunvenkat M. Srinivasan, and Anshika Srivastava

1. Introduction   340
2. Brain development   340
3. Tumors of the central nervous system   341

4. Conclusion   361
References   362

17. Therapeutic potential of melatonin in glioblastoma: Current knowledge and future prospects   371

Nithar Ranjan Madhu, Bhanumati Sarkar, Paramita Biswas, Shubhadeep Roychoudhury,

Biplab Kumar Behera, and Chandan Kumar Acharya

1. Introduction   371
2. Melatonin's structure, physiology, and functions   374
3. Tumor growth suppression and melatonin   374
4. Conclusion   382
Conflict of interest   382
References   382

18. Genotype influenced pharmacokinetics of anticancer medicine: A connecting link   387

Monika Kadian, Kritika Sharma, Kanishka Shrivasatava, Shivani Pandita,

Anusha Rana, Preeti Jaiswal, Ramica Sharma, and Anil Kumar

1. Introduction   387
2. Cancer types and linked genetic mutations   388
3. Influence of enzymes on the pharmacokinetics of drugs   391
4. Drug transporters   396
5. Cancer derived immunoglobulins vs B-cell derived immunoglobulins   403
6. Concluding remarks   405
Conflict of interest   405
References   405

19. Emergence of metal-based anticancer therapeutics: A promising perspective   411

Priyatosh Nath, Abhijit Datta, Tanushree Sen, and Suman Adhikari

1. Introduction   413
2. Platinum-based drugs from past to present   415
3. Mechanism of action of platinum drugs   421
4. Toxicity and related side effects of platinum drugs   423
5. Ruthenium anticancer compounds   424
6. Gold anticancer compounds   428
7. Fluorescent metal-based complexes: Bioimaging tool   431
8. Metal-based nanoparticles in cancer therapy   434
9. Conclusions and future directions   438
Acknowledgment   439
References   439

20. Nanoparticles for drug delivery in cancer therapy   **451**

Adeniyi S. Ohunayo, Olusola O. Elekofehinti, Olorunfemi R. Molehin,

Ajibade O. Oyeyemi, and Tiwa M. Ogunleye

1. Introduction   451
2. Limitation of chemotherapy   453
3. Nanoparticle in cancer research   454
4. Mechanism of activities of nanoparticle   456
5. Advantages of nanoparticles in cancer therapy   457
References   457

21. Near-infrared (NIR) responsive nanomaterial–liposome nanohybrids
for cancer photothermal therapy   **459**

Animesh Pan, Chiranjib Banerjee, and Md Golam Jakaria

1. Introduction   459
2. Strategically design and surface modification of hybrid nanostructures using
   liposomes   460
3. Different kind of nanomaterial–liposome nanohybrids (NLHs)   462
4. Application of NLHs   464
5. Future perspective and challenges   466
References   467

22. Anticancer activities of macromolecules of marine origin: Clinical
evidence   **471**

Aryaman Patwardhan, Moin Merchant, Smit Bhavsar, Harpal S. Buttar,

and Maushmi S. Kumar

1. Introduction   471
2. Anticancer agents—Current scenario   471
3. Clinical trials with fucoidans   478
4. Conclusion   481
Acknowledgment   481
Conflict of interest   481
References   481

23. Therapeutic potential of microalgae and their prospects
in targeted delivery in cancer management   **485**

Dhruv S. Gupta, Vaishnavi Gadi, and Maushmi S. Kumar

1. Introduction   485
2. Sources and distribution of microalgae   487
3. Molecular pathways of microalgae in cancer management   489

    4. Nanotechnology to overcome the limitations of microalgal delivery   490
    5. Challenges and future perspectives   494
    6. Conclusion   495
    Acknowledgment   495
    References   495

24. Prospects of mangrove-derived phytochemicals in cancer research   499
    Sayantani Mitra, Nabanita Naskar, Arijit Reeves, and Punarbasu Chaudhuri

    1. Introduction   500
    2. Mangrove's distribution and diversity   503
    3. Bioactivities of mangroves   506
    4. Application of mangroves in in vitro cancer research   516
    5. Bibliometric analysis of mangrove-derived phytochemicals in cancer research   519
    Acknowledgment   527
    References   527

**25. Impact of pesticides on immune-endocrine disorders and its relationship
    to cancer development   533**
    Tatiane Renata Fagundes, Aedra Carla Bufalo Kawassaki, Virginia Marcia Concato,
    João Paulo Assolini, Taylon Felipe Silva, Manoela Daiele Gonçalves,
    Elaine da Silva Siqueira, Claudia Stoeglehner Sahd, Fabrício Seidy Ribeiro Inoue,
    Thais Peron da Silva, Debora Messagi de Lima, Mariane Okamoto Ferreira,
    Ivete Conchon-Costa, Wander Rogério Pavanelli, and Carolina Panis

    1. Introduction   535
    2. Pesticides as immune-endocrine disruptors   536
    3. Agricultural poisons as immunological disruptors   543
    4. Implications of pesticide-induced immune-endocrine deregulation in cancer
        development   547
    Acknowledgments   558
    Funding   558
    Authors' contributions   558
    Competing interests   558
    References   558

Index   565

Contributors

Chandan Kumar Acharya
Department of Botany, Bajkul Milani Mahavidyalaya, Kismat Bajkul, West Bengal, India

Madhuchhanda Adhikari
Integrative Biology Research Unit (IBRU), Department of Life Sciences, Presidency University, Kolkata, West Bengal, India

Suman Adhikari
Department of Chemistry, Govt. Degree College, Dharmanagar, Tripura, India

Ritu Aggarwal
Department of Immunopathology, Post Graduate Institute of Medical Education and Research, Chandigarh, India

Shyam Aggarwal
Department of Medical Oncology, Sir Ganga Ram Hospital, New Delhi, India

Aashima Arora
Department of Immunopathology, Post Graduate Institute of Medical Education and Research, Chandigarh, India

João Paulo Assolini
Laboratory of Immunoparasitology of Neglected Diseases and Cancer, State University of Londrina, Londrina, Paraná, Brazil

Iyshwarya B.K.
Human Cytogenetics and Genomics Laboratory, Faculty of Allied Health Sciences, Chettinad Hospital and Research Institute, Chettinad Academy of Research and Education, Kelambakkam, Tamil Nadu, India

Vikas Bachhal
Postgraduate institute of Medical Education and Research, Chandigarh, India

Chiranjib Banerjee
Department of Biological Science, University of Northwestern, Evanston, IL, United States

Biplab Kumar Behera
Department of Zoology, Siliguri College, Siliguri, West Bengal, India

Smit Bhavsar
Shobhaben Pratapbhai Patel School of Pharmacy and Technology Management SVKM's NMIMS Mumbai, Mumbai, Maharashtra, India

Chayan Biswas
Integrative Biology Research Unit (IBRU), Department of Life Sciences, Presidency University, Kolkata, West Bengal, India

Paramita Biswas
Department of Agronomy, Faculty of Agriculture, Uttar Banga Krishi Viswavidyalaya, Cooch Behar, West Bengal, India

Harpal S. Buttar
Department of Pathology and Laboratory Medicine, University of Ottawa, Ottawa, ON, Canada

Ankit Chatterjee
Integrative Biology Research Unit (IBRU), Department of Life Sciences, Presidency University, Kolkata, West Bengal, India

Punarbasu Chaudhuri
Department of Environmental Science, University of Calcutta, Kolkata, India

Sunil Chumber
Department of Surgery, AIIMS, New Delhi, India

Virginia Marcia Concato
Laboratory of Immunoparasitology of Neglected Diseases and Cancer, State University of Londrina, Londrina, Paraná, Brazil

Ivete Conchon-Costa
Laboratory of Immunoparasitology of Neglected Diseases and Cancer, State University of Londrina, Londrina, Paraná, Brazil

Thais Peron da Silva
Laboratory of Immunoparasitology of Neglected Diseases and Cancer, State University of Londrina, Londrina, Paraná, Brazil

Elaine da Silva Siqueira
Laboratory of Immunoparasitology of Neglected Diseases and Cancer, State University of Londrina, Londrina, Paraná, Brazil

Abhijit Datta
Department of Botany, Ambedkar College, Fatikroy, Tripura, India

Debora Messagi de Lima
Laboratory of Immunoparasitology of Neglected Diseases and Cancer, State University of Londrina, Londrina, Paraná, Brazil

R.C. Deka
Department of ENT, AIIMS, New Delhi, India

Olusola O. Elekofehinti
Bioinformatics and Molecular Biology Unit, Department of Biochemistry, Federal University of Technology Akure, Akure, Nigeria

Tatiane Renata Fagundes
Laboratory of Immunoparasitology of Neglected Diseases and Cancer, State University of Londrina, Londrina, Paraná, Brazil

Mariane Okamoto Ferreira
Laboratory of Tumor Biology, State University of Western Paraná, Francisco Beltrão, Paraná, Brazil

Vaishnavi Gadi
Shobhaben Pratapbhai Patel School of Pharmacy & Technology Management, SVKM's NMIMS, Mumbai, India

Nirmal Kumar Ganguly
Department of Research, Sir Ganga Ram Hospital, New Delhi, India

Dhanavathy Gnanasampanthapandian
Cancer Science Laboratory, Department of Biotechnology, School of Bioengineering, SRM Institute of Science and Technology, Kattankulathur, Chengalpattu, India

Manoela Daiele Gonçalves
Laboratory of Biotransformation and Phytochemistry, State University of Londrina, Londrina, Paraná, Brazil

Vijay Goni
Postgraduate institute of Medical Education and Research, Chandigarh, India

Anubha Gulati
H S Judge Institute of Dental Sciences, Panjab University, Chandigarh, India

Dhruv S. Gupta
Shobhaben Pratapbhai Patel School of Pharmacy & Technology Management, SVKM's NMIMS, Mumbai, India

Yoshifumi S. Hirokawa
Department of Oncologic Pathology, Mie University Graduate School of Medicine, Tsu, Mie, Japan

Fabrício Seidy Ribeiro Inoue
Laboratory of Immunoparasitology of Neglected Diseases and Cancer, State University of Londrina, Londrina, Paraná, Brazil

Kriti Jain
Department of Research, Sir Ganga Ram Hospital, New Delhi, India

Preeti Jaiswal
University School of Pharmaceutical Sciences, Rayat Bahra University, Mohali, Punjab, India

Md Golam Jakaria
Department of Chemical Engineering, University of Rhode Island, Kingston, RI, United States

Selvaraj Jayaraman
Centre for Molecular Medicine and Diagnostics (COMManD), Department of Biochemistry, Saveetha Dental College & Hospitals, Saveetha Institute of Medical & Technical Sciences (Deemed to be University), Chennai, India

Monika Kadian
Pharmacology Division, University Institute of Pharmaceutical Sciences, UGC Centre of Advanced Study, Panjab University, Chandigarh, India

Kazuki Kanayama
Department of Clinical Nutrition, Suzuka University of Medical Science, Suzuka, Mie, Japan

Mohak Kataria
Postgraduate institute of Medical Education and Research, Chandigarh, India

Manveen Kaur
Department of Pathology, Government Medical College and Hospital, Chandigarh, India

Aedra Carla Bufalo Kawassaki
Laboratory of Tumor Biology, State University of Western Paraná, Francisco Beltrão, Paraná, Brazil

Anil Kumar
Pharmacology Division, University Institute of Pharmaceutical Sciences, UGC Centre of Advanced Study, Panjab University, Chandigarh, India

Maushmi S. Kumar
Somaiya Institute of Research and Consultancy, Somaiya Vidyavihar University, Vidya Vihar East, Mumbai, Maharashtra, India

Rajappan Chandra Satish Kumar
Interdisciplinary Institute of Indian System of Medicine, SRM Institute of Science and Technology, Kattankulathur, Chengalpattu, India

Ravinder Kumar
Department of Zoology, Panjab University, Chandigarh, Punjab, India

Nithar Ranjan Madhu
Department of Zoology, Acharya Prafulla Chandra College, New Barrackpore, West Bengal, India

Dhritiman Maitra
Department of Surgery, Medical College Kolkata, Kolkata, India

Sukhendu Maity
Integrative Biology Research Unit (IBRU), Department of Life Sciences, Presidency University, Kolkata, West Bengal, India

Navdeep Kaur Mangat
Department of Immunopathology, Post Graduate Institute of Medical Education and Research, Chandigarh, India

Moin Merchant
Shobhaben Pratapbhai Patel School of Pharmacy and Technology Management SVKM's NMIMS Mumbai, Mumbai, Maharashtra, India

Sayantani Mitra
Department of Environmental Science, University of Calcutta, Kolkata, India

Balraj Mittal
Sanjay Gandhi Postgraduate Institute of Medical Sciences, Lucknow, India

Olorunfemi R. Molehin
Department of Biochemistry, Faculty of Science, Ekiti State University, Ado-Ekiti, Nigeria

Ganesh Munuswamy-Ramanujam
Interdisciplinary Institute of Indian System of Medicine, SRM Institute of Science and Technology, Kattankulathur, Chengalpattu, India

Nabanita Naskar
Department of Botany, Diamond Harbour Women's University, Kolkata, India

Priyatosh Nath
Faculty of Allied Health Sciences, The ICFAI University Tripura, Mohanpur; Department of Human Physiology, Tripura University, Suryamaninagar, Tripura, India

Deepak Negi
Postgraduate institute of Medical Education and Research, Chandigarh, India

Tiwa M. Ogunleye
Oklahoma State University, Stillwater, OK, United States

Adeniyi S. Ohunayo
Department of Science Laboratory Technology, Faculty of science, Ekiti State University, Ado-Ekiti, Nigeria

Ajibade O. Oyeyemi
Department of Biochemistry, Faculty of Science, Ekiti State University, Ado-Ekiti, Nigeria

Kanagaraj Palaniyandi
Cancer Science Laboratory, Department of Biotechnology, School of Bioengineering, SRM Institute of Science and Technology, Kattankulathur, Chengalpattu, India

Anshu Palta
Department of Pathology, Government Medical College and Hospital, Chandigarh, India

Animesh Pan
Department of Chemical Engineering, University of Rhode Island, Kingston, RI, United States

Shivani Pandita
Pharmacology Division, University Institute of Pharmaceutical Sciences, UGC Centre of Advanced Study, Panjab University, Chandigarh, India

Carolina Panis
Laboratory of Tumor Biology, State University of Western Paraná, Francisco Beltrão, Paraná, Brazil

Davinder Parsad
Department of Dermatology, PGIMER, Chandigarh, Punjab, India

Aryaman Patwardhan
Shobhaben Pratapbhai Patel School of Pharmacy and Technology Management SVKM's NMIMS Mumbai, Mumbai, Maharashtra, India

Wander Rogério Pavanelli
Laboratory of Immunoparasitology of Neglected Diseases and Cancer, State University of Londrina, Londrina, Paraná, Brazil

Pooja
Department of Medical Genetics, Sanjay Gandhi Post Graduate Institute of Medical Sciences, Lucknow, India

Kousik Pramanick
Integrative Biology Research Unit (IBRU), Department of Life Sciences, Presidency University, Kolkata, West Bengal, India

Ponnulakshmi Rajagopal
Department of Central Research Laboratory, Meenakshi Ammal Dental College and Hospitals, Chennai, India

Vasukidevi Ramachandran
Department of Microbiology and Biotechnology, Bharath Institute of Higher Education and Research, Selaiyur, Chennai, India

Veerakumar Ramachandran
Department of Pedodontics and Preventive Dentistry, Priyadharshini Dental College, Thiruvallur, India

Anusha Rana
University School of Pharmaceutical Sciences, Rayat Bahra University, Mohali, Punjab, India

Arijit Reeves
Department of Environmental Science, University of Calcutta, Kolkata, India

Shubhadeep Roychoudhury
Department of Life Science and Bioinformatics, Assam University, Silchar, India

Claudia Stoeglehner Sahd
Laboratory of Immunoparasitology of Neglected Diseases and Cancer, State University of Londrina, Londrina, Paraná, Brazil

Bhanumati Sarkar
Department of Botany, Acharya Prafulla Chandra College, New Barrackpore, West Bengal, India

Duraj Sekar
RNA Biology Lab, Saveetha Dental College & Hospitals, Saveetha Institute of Medical & Technical Sciences (Deemed to be University), Chennai, India

Ramya Sekar
Centre for Molecular Medicine and Diagnostics (COMManD), Department of Biochemistry, Saveetha Dental College & Hospitals, Saveetha Institute of Medical & Technical Sciences (Deemed to be University), Chennai, India

Remi Semba
Department of Pathology, Kuwana City Medical Center, Kuwana, Mie, Japan

Koushik Sen
P.G. Department of Zoology, Jhargram Raj College, Jhargram, West Bengal, India

Tanushree Sen
Department of Chemistry, Jagannath Kishore College, Purulia, West Bengal, India

Dhayasankar Prabhu Shankar
Department of Oral & Maxillofacial Surgery, Meenakshi Ammal Dental College, Chennai, India

Himani Sharma
Department of Zoology, Panjab University, Chandigarh, Punjab, India

Kritika Sharma
Pharmacology Division, University Institute of Pharmaceutical Sciences, UGC Centre of Advanced Study, Panjab University, Chandigarh, India

Ramica Sharma
University School of Pharmaceutical Sciences, Rayat Bahra University, Mohali, Punjab, India

JH Shazia Fathima
Centre for Molecular Medicine and Diagnostics (COMManD), Department of Biochemistry, Saveetha Dental College & Hospitals, Saveetha Institute of Medical & Technical Sciences (Deemed to be University), Chennai, India

Kanishka Shrivasatava
Pharmacology Division, University Institute of Pharmaceutical Sciences, UGC Centre of Advanced Study, Panjab University, Chandigarh, India

Taylon Felipe Silva
Laboratory of Immunoparasitology of Neglected Diseases and Cancer, State University of Londrina, Londrina, Paraná, Brazil

R.C. Sobti
Department of Biotechnology, Panjab University, Chandigarh, India

Varunvenkat M. Srinivasan
Department of Medical Genetics, Sanjay Gandhi Post Graduate Institute of Medical Sciences, Lucknow, India

Anshika Srivastava
Department of Medical Genetics, Sanjay Gandhi Post Graduate Institute of Medical Sciences, Lucknow, India

Gowtham Kumar Subbaraj
Faculty of Allied Health Sciences, Chettinad Hospital and Research Institute, Chettinad Academy of Research and Education (Deemed to be University), Kelambakkam, India

L. Tharrun Daniel Paul
Cancer Science Laboratory, Department of Biotechnology, School of Bioengineering, SRM Institute of Science and Technology, Kattankulathur, Chengalpattu, India

Junya Tsuboi
Department of Gastroenterology and Hepatology, Mie University Graduate School of Medicine, Tsu, Mie, Japan

Katsunori Uchida
Department of Pathology, Mie University Hospital, Tsu, Mie, Japan

Ramakrishnan Veerabathiran
Human Cytogenetics and Genomics Laboratory, Faculty of Allied Health Sciences, Chettinad Hospital and Research Institute, Chettinad Academy of Research and Education, Kelambakkam, Tamil Nadu, India

Saurabh Yadav
Department of Medical Oncology, Dana Farber Cancer University/Harvard Medical School, Boston, MA, United States

Reiko Yamada
Department of Gastroenterology and Hepatology, Mie University Graduate School of Medicine, Tsu, Mie, Japan

Preface

Early cancer detection has immense potential for increasing cancer diagnosis, monitoring response to therapy, and predicting recurrence. Cancer biomarkers are transformative tools that offer a wide array of applications. These applications include, but are not limited to, detection and diagnosis, prognosis, selection of treatment, monitoring the efficacy of the treatment and the need for adjustment, predicting toxicity and delivering tailored medicine, also known as personalized medicine, and predicting the likelihood of recurrence. Biomarkers are essential tools in cancer drug development by identifying potential therapeutic targets and treatment efficacy. They aid in discovering new avenues for novel therapeutic interventions by providing insight into the underlying cellular mechanism. The conventional clinical assessment might not be able to identify residual cancer after treatment, whereas biomarker expression may be an essential tool to detect residual cancer cells and help in predicting therapeutic efficacy.

Cancer biomarkers are transformative tools with immense potential and application that have been briefly explained in this book. With the advancement in research and technology, the potential for cancer biomarkers to revolutionize cancer management remains a promising frontier in oncology.

This volume of *Biomarkers in Cancer* includes chapters on the use of various biomarkers for diagnosis and for developing treatment protocols for various cancers.

R.C. Sobti and Aastha Sobti are thankful to Dr. Vipin Sobti, Er. Aditi, Er. Vineet, Er. Ankit, and Irene for their full support in preparing the book.

R.C.S. acknowledges Indian National Science Academy, New Delhi, for providing a platform as Senior Scientist to continue the academic pursuits.

Editors
R.C. Sobti
M. Watanabe
Aastha Sobti

CHAPTER ONE

Oral squamous cell carcinoma

Anubha Gulati[a] and R.C. Sobti[b]
[a]H S Judge Institute of Dental Sciences, Panjab University, Chandigarh, India
[b]Department of Biotechnology, Panjab University, Chandigarh, India

1. Oral cancer

Head and neck cancer is a broad term used to describe a variety of neoplasms occurring in different anatomical structures including oral cavity, oropharynx and the larynx (Hussein et al., 2017). It is typically regarded as a disease of the elderly and is predominantly seen in men in their sixth and seventh decades after many years of tobacco and alcohol abuse (Llewellyn et al., 2004). However, the incidence of patients being diagnosed with head and neck squamous cell carcinoma at a younger age (<40–45 years old) has been on the rise worldwide over the last 3 decades (Majchrzak et al., 2014). This new trend of high incidence among young patients was primarily observed in oropharyngeal cancer involving the areas of the base of the tongue, tonsil and oropharynx and cancers affecting the body of the tongue (Shoboski et al., 2005). In their systematic review, Hussein et al. found that oral tongue was the most common site of occurrence of oral squamous cell carcinoma among the younger age group, especially in females (Hussein et al., 2017).

The world over is afflicted by oral cancer which is an aggressive tumor with poor response to chemotherapy and resistance to most standards of care therapies (Chi et al., 2015). The annual report of new cases of oral cancer is about 405,000 cases. The prevalence of this disease varies widely in different parts of the world or even within the minorities or subpopulations of the same countries. Sri Lanka, India, Pakistan, Bangladesh, Hungary and France attribute to the main burden of oral cancer. Head and neck cancer is known to be the sixth most common malignancy in the world; its occurrence in South-central Asia is much more common with it being the third most common type of cancer here (Warnakulasuriya, 2009).

This complex disease reveals a marked variation in the trends and patterns of mortality between countries and across specific cancer types that are linked to differences in changing lifestyles and in local exposures to known or presumptive determinants, as well as an altering environment. The recent few decades have shown the evolution of cancer as the first or second leading cause of premature death (i.e., at ages 30–69 years) in most countries (WHO, 2018). Specifically, cancer is currently the leading cause of premature death in most of the countries with high or very high HDI. This epidemiological transition based on Omran's theory (Omran, 1971) is owed to dramatic decline in mortality from infectious diseases due to better sanitation and the development of vaccines and antibiotics and the improving primary and secondary prevention for cardiovascular diseases. The differences in levels of medical practice and health infrastructure also influence the diverging patterns and trends in cancer mortality (World Cancer Report, 2020).

2. Oral squamous cell carcinoma

Squamous cell carcinoma represents the most common form of head and neck cancer—representing around 90% of all head and neck malignancies (Warnakulasuriya, 2009). Squamous cell carcinomas can originate from any part of the lining of the upper aerodigestive tract—nasopharynx, lip vermilion, oral cavity, oropharynx, and larynx (Hussein et al., 2017). Of all these anatomic locations, squamous cell carcinomas most commonly arise within the oral cavity. Recently, oral squamous cell carcinoma (OSCC) has emerged as the sixth most common malignancy in the world (as of 2016) (Seigel et al., 2016).

In the 2017 WHO classification of tumors, oral squamous cell carcinoma was defined as "the carcinoma with squamous differentiation arising from the mucosal epithelium" (WHO, 2017). The 21st century has evidenced a rise in the morbidity and mortality associated with oral squamous cell carcinoma especially in younger patients. Over 300,000 new cases are reported each year contributing to the global impact of this malignancy. Despite sizable advances in diagnosis and management, 50% of patients suffering from oral squamous cell carcinoma die within 5 years. Even with the relatively easy visualization of the tumor in the clinic and/or successful treatment intervention, the long-term prognosis is compromised due to late initial presentation of advanced tumors and widespread, multifocal presentation throughout the upper aerodigestive tract (Thomson, 2018).

Early diagnosis of oral squamous cell carcinoma plays a crucial role in saving a patient's life as well as minimizing the negative impact on quality of life linked to invasive surgical intervention. A vast array of diagnostic tools are available for screening and visual devices that can substantively improve the ability of the clinician to characterize any suspicious lesion. Additionally, with the advent of salivary biomarkers and liquid biopsy, recognition of the risk of malignant transformation has been made easier. Although surgical biopsy and histology are still considered the mainstay of diagnosis, auxiliary methods should be considered during objective clinical examination. The scientific community is constantly devising preventive measures and screening methods for early detection of oral cancer with the aim of reducing the diagnostic delay to help save the patient's life (Abati et al., 2020).

3. Epidemiology

One of the key variables in the occurrence of oral cancer is geographic location with low socioeconomic status group in developing countries being at a higher risk of developing oral squamous cell carcinoma attributable to their self-neglect and lack of advertence to the consequences of exposure to the avoidable risk factors such as tobacco and alcohol (Conway et al., 2018). A diversity in reporting of oral cancer in epidemiological studies is related to the several anatomical subsites of its presentation (Conway et al., 2006). There is a lack of consensus regarding the sites that can be included in cancers of the oral cavity and oropharynx which has been detrimental for the understanding and comparison of the actual disease prevalence across the globe. Conway et al. proposed a "compromise" way of describing oral squamous cell carcinoma and oropharyngeal cancers distinctly in concurrence with the International Classification of Diseases for Oncology (ICD-O) coding. According to them, the oral cavity cancer comprises of the involvement of the labial mucosa, dorsal surface of the tongue, gingiva, hard and soft palate, buccal mucosa, floor of the mouth and other unspecified parts of the mouth, while oropharyngeal cancer is cancer involving base of the tongue, tonsils including lingual tonsil, anterior surface of the epiglottis, lateral wall of the oropharynx and pharynx unspecified involving Waldeyer's ring/overlapping sites of oral cavity and pharynx (Conway et al., 2018).

The incidence rate, mortality rate and survival rate within the specific population help gauge the impact of oral cancer. Globally there has been a substantial rise in incidence rates of cancer owing to the development of advanced technologies in cancer detection even in the subclinical stages. GLOBOCAN 2018 by the International Association of Cancer Registries (IACR) provides the global picture of different cancers, including oral cancer. Approximately 354,864 newly diagnosed cases of lip and oral cavity cancer and around 92,8887 new cases of oropharynx cancer were reported accounting for about 2% and 0.5% of all the malignancies. In 2018, 4.0 per 100,000 was the projected age-standardized incidence rate of lip and oral cavity cancer worldwide. Similarly, a mortality rate of 177,384 was reported across the globe for oral cancer in 2018, with an age-standardized mortality rate of 2.0 per 100,000 individuals (Bray et al., 2018) (Fig. 1).

The global age-standardized rates (ASR) of incidence of oral cancer are consistently higher in males (5.8 per 100,000) as compared to females (2.3 per 100,000). Some studies show an inverse trend with greater incidence in women. This change in trend could be ascribed to increasing habits of tobacco use, especially the smoking form, among women as compared to the traditional days (Jemal et al., 2018).

The highest burden of oral cancer is linked to cultural practices like tobacco chewing, alcohol consumption, and extreme use of betel quid in Asia. According to GLOBOCAN 2018, oral cancer is the eleventh most common cancer in Asia, with a projected 227,906 newly diagnosed cases. The Asian population presented with a mortality rate and a 5-year prevalence of the disease of 129,939 and 536,185, respectively (Bray et al., 2018).

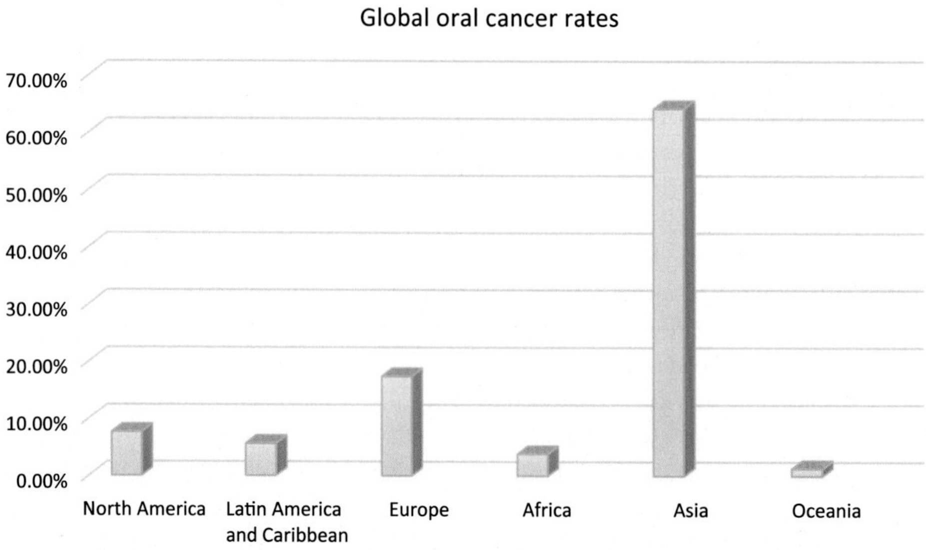

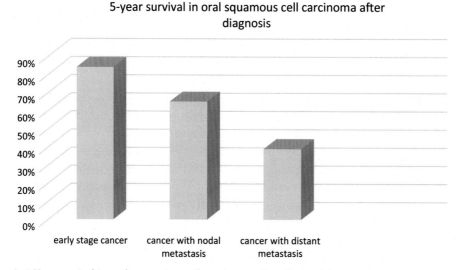

Fig. 1 Global oral cancer rates.

Fig. 2 5-Year survival in oral squamous cell carcinoma after diagnosis.

Differing population habits, life expectancies, preventive education, and the quality of medical records in various countries (poverty, illiteracy, advanced stage at presentation, lack of access to health care, and poor treatment infrastructure) are major contributors for the differences in oral cancer between the developing world and the Western world (Inchingolo et al., 2020). However, as the rural populations are not well represented in the cancer registries so the GLOBOCAN data may not be reflective of the true incidence of oral squamous cell carcinoma (Fig. 2).

4. Etiology

Tobacco smoking which was once prevalent mostly among men in high-income countries is now much more prevalent among women in many countries. Asia, Africa, and South America account for the highest tobacco use (World Cancer Report, 2020).

1. Tobacco

Tobacco which is available in many forms has a long-established cause relationship with multiple types of cancer and other major noncommunicable diseases. Cigarette smoking has been found to result in at least 20 different types of cancer (US Department of Health and Human Services, 2014). An estimated 1.3 billion people use tobacco products worldwide (WHO, 2019). Together, cigarettes and other tobacco products are estimated to cause 2.4 million tobacco-related cancer deaths worldwide every year (Stanaway et al., 2017).

Tobacco is used in the following forms:

Smoked (Fig. 3)

Smokeless (Fig. 4)

E-cigarettes

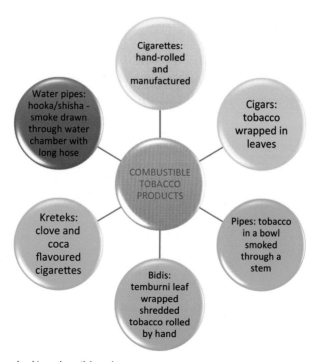

Fig. 3 Forms of smoked/combustible tobacco.

Fig. 4 Forms of smokeless tobacco products across the world.

Heated tobacco products
- E-cigarettes and other electronic nicotine delivery systems (ENDS)—An aerosol is produced by heating a nicotine-containing solution.
- Heated tobacco products—tobacco sticks are heated to produce an aerosol (World Cancer Report, 2020).

Impact of tobacco products

The most predominant form of tobacco consumption worldwide is in the smoked form as cigarettes, manufactured or hand-rolled ones. The carcinogenicity of smoked and smokeless tobacco products (US Department of health and human services, 2014) includes enzymatic and nonenzymatic transformations of nitrosamines, benzopyrenes, and aromatic amines into molecules covalently bound to various regions of DNA. This results in various mutations and the formation of DNA adducts. High oxidative stress is also generated by tobacco smoke due to its high concentration of free radicals (oxygen and nitrogen species) which deplete the enzymatic and nonenzymatic cellular antioxidants causing cell damage which in turn leads to cancer (Choudhari et al., 2013). Tobacco also impacts nonmalignant diseases, and the harmful effects of second-hand smoke have been widely studied (US Department of health and human services, 2014).

Smoke from cigarettes comprises more than 8000 compounds, which include over 70 carcinogens, including tobacco-specific nitrosamines, polycyclic aromatic hydrocarbons, and aromatic amines. Over the past 5 years, cigarette smoking has been linked to altered patterns of circulating inflammatory markers, altered DNA methylation patterns, altered airway gene expression patterns, an altered oral microbiome, specific mutational signatures, and Y chromosome loss. Almost all the carcinogens found in cigarette smoke are also produced by other combustible products, including bidis, cigars, and pipes.

The levels of specific carcinogens vary across the different products, but smokeless tobacco has been shown to contain at least 30 carcinogens and release high levels of tobacco-specific nitrosamines (World Cancer Report, 2020).

ENDS have emerged only during the past decade. Contents of ENDS products are nicotine, propylene glycol, glycerine, and flavors mixed in a solution, which is then evaporated to produce an aerosol. They are available in fruit and caramel flavors. Laboratory studies have shown that ENDS devices generally heat to a lower temperature and have lower levels of most carcinogens than combusted cigarettes (Shahab et al., 2017).

Patterns and trends in tobacco use

The most common pattern of smoked tobacco use is daily smoking. In 2015, an estimated 1.3 billion people worldwide used tobacco products and 1.1 billion people smoked, of which more than 80% smoked daily. The prevalence of smoking is higher in men than in women. About 25% of men in the world are daily smokers, compared with about 5% of women. Geographical patterns of smoking prevalence also differ by sex. Among men, the prevalence of daily smoking is highest in central and eastern Europe and South-East Asia; among women, the prevalence is highest in selected countries in eastern and western Europe.

The prevalence of daily smoking in both men and women has declined from 1990 to 2015. The Global Burden of Disease collaboration surveyed 195 countries and found estimated reductions in smoking of 28% in men and 34% in women since 1990. Other studies report similar reductions in smoking prevalence. The reductions were largest in high-income countries and in Latin America with the largest reduction in smoking prevalence occurring in Brazil, where the prevalence dropped by more than 50%. Pakistan, Panama, and India have implemented numerous tobacco controls that have led to large declines in daily smoking prevalence since 2005.

Nevertheless, the worldwide prevalence of tobacco use remains high. Low- and middle-income countries are home to about 80% of the world's smokers with more than 50% of the world's male smokers living in three countries: China, India, and Indonesia. Due to the size and the growth of populations and the aging of long-term, continuing smokers, the disease burden from tobacco use continues to increase rapidly in low- and middle-income countries despite a decrease in smoking prevalence.

Use of smokeless tobacco products

WHO has estimated that worldwide there are more than 367 million smokeless tobacco users aged 15 years or older with more men (237 million) than women (129 million). Smokeless tobacco accounts for an estimated more than 101,000 cancer deaths per year. Comparable results of 76,000 cancer deaths per year from the use of smokeless tobacco have been reported by the Global Burden of Disease project. An estimated 82% of users (301 million users) are in the South-East Asia Region with an estimated 87% of cancer deaths from smokeless tobacco occurring in this region.

In much of the world, 13- to 15-year-old children use smokeless tobacco. The highest prevalence in this age group is in the South-East Asia Region (7.3% overall; 9.5% in boys and 4.8% in girls), which accounts for almost 60% of smokeless tobacco use in this age group worldwide (World Cancer Report, 2020).

2. Alcohol

   Alcoholic beverages contain numerous carcinogenic compounds, but most of the risk relationship between alcohol consumption and the development of cancer is due to ethanol. Alcohol-induced carcinogenesis is not fully understood. However, the postulated main pathophysiological carcinogenic mechanisms of ethanol include its breakdown into the carcinogenic metabolite acetaldehyde, its one-carbon metabolism pathway inhibition, and DNA methylation (especially in people with lower intake of dietary folate), and its effect on elevation of serum levels of endogenous estrogens. Ethanol is also said to increase the risk of cancer via the production of reactive oxygen species and polar metabolites; through the conversion of procarcinogens in the metabolic pathway of ethanol; by peroxidation of lipids; by prostaglandin production; by alteration of the insulin-like growth factor 1 pathway; and by acting as a solvent for cellular penetration of environmental carcinogens (e.g., tobacco) (Pflaum et al., 2016). There is a site-specific difference in the biological pathways involved, and the relative contributions of these pathways to carcinogenesis. There are dose–response relationships, with almost linear gradients of relative risks and no apparent lower risk threshold. The level of lifetime exposure to alcohol is said to impact risk relationships. Alcohol was responsible for 26.4% of all cancers of the lip and oral cavity, 30.5% of all other pharyngeal cancers (excluding nasopharyngeal cancers), 21.6% of all laryngeal cancers, and 16.9% of all esophageal cancers (Rehm et al., 2017). These findings reflect the stronger associations—i.e., the higher gradients of the dose-response curves—between levels of alcohol consumption and cancers of the upper aero-digestive tract compared with cancers of the colorectum, liver, and breast (World Cancer Report, 2020).

3. Human papillomavirus

   Human papillomavirus (HPV) has a strong affinity for the epithelium and infects the basal epithelial cells of stratified squamous epithelium in both skin and mucous membranes. It causes lesions that include common warts and invasive neoplasia.

Based on their potential oncogenic activity, HPV subtypes have been divided into high-risk and low-risk groups. The high-risk Human papilloma viruses are associated with the development of cancer and are called "oncogenic" viral types and belong to 16, 18, 31, 33, 35, 45, 51, 52, 56, 58, 59, 68, 73, and 82 subtypes of which types 16 and 18 have been particularly associated with cervical carcinoma, anogenital neoplasia, and oropharyngeal lesions (Bouvard et al., 2009; Bernard et al., 2010). Benign epithelial lesions result from infection with the low-risk HPV, such as types 6, 11, 42, 43, and 44. The early region of the HPV genome encodes 7 proteins of which E6 induces DNA synthesis, prevents cell differentiation, and interacts with tumor suppressors and DNA repair factors and E7 protein that induces cell proliferation by interacting with negative regulators of cell cycle proteins and tumor suppressors are considered oncoproteins which result in carcinogenesis. E6 is a transforming protein that functions to promote p53 degradation which is a tumor suppressor protein; E7, on the other hand, is a transforming protein that has an affinity for the retinoblastoma protein (Valencia et al., 2008). Oral sexual practices have been associated with HPV transmission to the oral mucosa in both young and adult populations, because this sexual behavior is associated with a greater number of partners, especially in men. Sharing of smoking devices, lipstick, or toothbrushes has been reported as an alternate route of transmission that needs further validation. Occasionally, HPV can be transmitted to the oral mucosa by vertical transmission from mother to son.

HPV 16 and 6 are the most persistent viruses associated with HPV infection of the oral mucosa. Other factors linked to the persistence of HPV infection include smoking, patients over the age of 40 years, HIV patients treated with highly active antiretroviral therapy (HAART), and a CD4 count of 500 (Lafaurie et al., 2018).

HPV infects the basal cells by entering through wounds in the epithelial layer. The virus then resides in the nucleus of the infected cell where 1000 virus particles are produced per cell and maintain a high number of copies in squamous cells following which the viral progenies are subsequently released into the microenvironment. HPV protein E7 degrades all members of the Rb family by binding to them, thus resulting in the release and activation of the transcription factor E2F and deregulation of the G1/S checkpoint; E7 of high-risk HPV bind with higher affinity (Gage et al., 1990). A p53-dependent inhibition of cell growth and apoptosis occurs from the interaction of E7 with Rb. In addition, E6 proteins target the p53 tumor suppressor that leads to degradation, prevention of the inhibition of growth in differentiated and undifferentiated cells (Cooper et al., 2003). Cancer develops many years later when the immune system fails to clear persistent HPV infections. Two forms of HPV viral genome persist in the infected cells—the stable/episomal form that is responsible for latent disease and the integrated form present within the host DNA. A growth advantage is conferred to the cell through viral integration, which contrasts with harboring copies of viral episomal DNA. An important step in carcinogenesis associated with

HPV is the coexistence of episomes with integrated copies (Kadaja et al., 2009; Lafaurie et al., 2018).

Oncogenic HPVs are responsible for approximately 60% of oropharyngeal cancer in North America; 36%–45% in Asia, Oceania, and Europe; and 15% in South and Central America. An increase in HPV-associated oropharyngeal cancers from 16% in the 1980s to the current 60% has been reported in the United States with increases in Europe mirroring this trend. This dramatic rise in HPV-related oropharyngeal cancer points to the emergence of a cancer epidemic. Of all oncogenic forms, HPV-16 is responsible for 90% of HPV-related oropharyngeal cancer (Chi et al., 2015). A subgroup analysis of oral potentially malignant disorders revealed an HPV association for oral leukoplakia (OR: 4.03, 95% CI: 2.34–6.92), oral lichen planus (OR: 5.12, 95% CI: 2.40–10.93), and epithelial dysplasia (OR: 5.10, 95% CI: 2.03–12.80) (Lafaurie et al., 2018).

4. Other microbes/microbial infections

Syphilis—It is a systemic bacterial infection caused by *Treponema pallidum*. The incubation period of the infection is usually 21–30 days after contact, although it can vary from 10 to 90 days, depending on the number and virulence of the host to the causative agent. One of the clinical presentations of syphilis in the oral cavity is Syphilitic leukoplakia which involves the dorsum of the tongue and presents as a homogenous white patch. Both clinically- and serology-based studies have suggested an increased prevalence of syphilis in patient groups with squamous cell carcinoma of the tongue (up to 60% in one study), the association is stronger in males than females. A relatively recent study of 16,420 people with syphilis, resident in the United States, found a significantly raised frequency of cancer of the tongue (and Kaposi's sarcoma) in males (Leão et al., 2006).

Candida albicans—It is the most common opportunistic organism residing in the oral cavity as a normal commensal. A complex process involving factors related to yeast cells, host cells, and environmental factors exists which contributes to the virulence of the organism with a predisposition to infection, causing several clinical manifestations.

Candida infection was first recognized and introduced as "candidal leukoplakia" by Jepsen and Winther. They mentioned the adherent white patch which is infected by Candida. This tends to undergo malignant transformation (Jepsen and Winther, 1965). In his study, Cawson found that 6 out of 10 tissue biopsies initially diagnosed as chronic hyperplastic candidiasis underwent a malignant transformation to oral squamous cell carcinoma (Cawson, 1966). McCullough et al. postulated that the progression of chronic hyperplastic candidiasis to dysplasia is advanced by *Candida albicans*. It is due to the higher nitrosation potential of certain species which elaborate nitrosamine compounds which play a role in the initiation of carcinogenesis (McCullough et al., 2002).

5. Chronic irritation

   The constant action of a deleterious agent in the oral cavity (defective restorations, broken tooth, constant biting of the oral mucosa, or ill-fitting dentures with sharp or retentive edges) results in chronic mechanical irritation which can also be another cause of oral cancer. These agents maintain a chronic state of inflammation that invokes epigenetic transformation of these affected cells (Piemonte et al., 2018).

6. Oral cancer can be caused by genetic factors, epigenetic modifications (such as histones modifications; nucleosome integrity, DNA methylation and expression of noncoding RNAs (ncRNAs) (World Cancer Report, 2020).

   Genetic alterations—Studies have revealed that oral carcinoma is not genetically stable as there is an accumulation of genetic variations in proto-oncogenes and tumor suppressor genes that leads to the development of oral squamous cell carcinoma through a multistep process (Califano et al., 1996). Two important observations were made in the Cancer Genome Atlas (TCGA) project (2006) while analyzing 10,000 samples from 20 different types of tumors.

   (1) Genetic variations exist in tumors with an equivalent origin, and

   (2) Similar patterns of genomic variations are shown by tumors with different origins.

   Tumor cells acquire genetic instability by defects in segregation of chromosomes, copy number alterations, loss of heterozygosity, telomere stabilities, regulation of cell-cycle checkpoints, Notch signaling pathway, and DNA damage repairs (Ali et al., 2017; World Cancer Report, 2020).

   Epigenetic modifications—Epigenetic modifications include hypermethylation within the promoter region of genes, posttranslational histone modifications, and posttranscriptional regulation by microRNAs. Epigenetic regulation occurs early in the process of oral carcinogenesis. The concept of genetic control of cancer has paved the way for a more comprehensive picture where DNA methylation, (Sharma et al., 2010) modifications of histones and nucleosome positioning are now considered to play an important role. Also, the expression of noncoding RNAs (ncRNAs), especially microRNAs (miRNAs), could also influence the epigenetic mechanisms (Irimie et al., 2018). The basic characterization of the epigenetic concept states that these mechanisms are reversible changes that are not associated with modifications within the structure of DNA and may be inherited and preserved for multiple generations (Sharma et al., 2010).

7. Others

   A variety of suspected risk factors such as poor oral hygiene, occupational exposure, and malnutrition as well as low fruit and vegetable diets, have been proposed for the development of oral cancer (WHO, 2017; World Cancer Report, 2020).

5. Precursor lesions

WHO termed the pathologies that are associated with an increased risk of transforming into cancer as potentially malignant disorders. These include leukoplakia, erythroplakia, oral submucous fibrosis, oral lichen planus, palatal changes due to reverse smoking, discoid lupus erythematosus, actinic cheilosis, epidermolysis bullosa, and dyskeratosis congenita (Warnakulasuriya et al., 2007). All these arise either from genetic aberrations, immune disorders, or exposure to exogenous agents like tobacco. Some may arise as a rare inherited disease.

Ganesh et al. grouped these disorders according to their etiology as

a. Genetically acquired disorders: leukoplakia, erythroplakia, actinic cheilitis.

b. Tobacco-induced disorders: oral submucous fibrosis, palatal keratosis associated with reverse smoking.

c. Immune-mediated disorders: oral lichen planus, discoid lupus erythematosus.

d. Genetically inherited disorders: dyskeratosis congenita, epidermolysis bullosa (Ganesh et al., 2018).

5.1 Genetically acquired potentially malignant disorders

Leukoplakia—It is a diagnosis of exclusion. Leukoplakia has been defined as, "white plaque of questionable risk having excluded (other) known diseases" by WHO (WHO, 2017). Two clinical forms exist: homogeneous and nonhomogeneous. A uniform pattern of the white lesion is exhibited in homogenous leukoplakia. In the nonhomogeneous forms, a speckled (mixture of red and white with a predominance of white), nodular (red or white polypoid outgrowths), or verrucous (wrinkled or corrugated) appearance is seen at the time of presentation. Etiologic factors include the use of tobacco, alcohol, betel quid, and genetic abnormalities. Leukoplakia arising from the latter are termed Idiopathic leukoplakia.

Middle-aged or older men are most affected by leukoplakia. A rare form of nonhomogeneous leukoplakia is proliferative verrucous leukoplakia. It is most frequent on the gingiva and buccal mucosa and rapidly progresses to involve surrounding areas, both contiguous and noncontiguous (Warnakulasuriya et al., 2007).

The malignant transformation rate of leukoplakia has been reported to range between 0.13% and 34% in different studies. Sixty-one percent of patients with proliferative verrucous leukoplakia transform into malignancy up to 7 years postdiagnosis (Warnakulasuriya and Ariyawardana, 2016).

Hyperorthokeratosis or hyperparakeratosis with acanthosis is the typical histological presentation. Different degrees of dysplasia are also reported. Diagnosis of leukoplakia requires correlation between clinical presentation and histopathological findings.

Erythroplakia—WHO defined it as, "a fiery red patch that cannot be characterized clinically or pathologically as any definable disease" (WHO, 2017). This too is a diagnosis of exclusion like leukoplakia. It is strongly associated with the use of tobacco and alcohol. A mean global prevalence of 0.1% (range: 0.01%–0.21%) has been reported (Villa et al., 2011). Males in the 6th to 8th decades are most frequently affected by erythroplakia (WHO, 2017). A malignant transformation rate of 51% has been reported (Shafers and Waldron, 1975) with a range of 14%–50% reported in the literature (WHO, 2017). Thus, early diagnosis and immediate treatment are desired.

Histopathology reveals mild to moderate dysplasia in about 9% of cases of erythroplakia and carcinoma in situ in 40% cases. At times frank invasive carcinoma may be the histopathologic picture of a case clinically diagnosed as erythroplakia (Shafers and Waldron, 1975).

Actinic cheilitis—It is characterized by mottled lips with atrophic or erosive areas along with scaly, rough, flaky, keratotic patches on the exposed portion of lips. Wrinkling of the vermilion border has also been reported. The lower lip is more commonly affected but both lips may be involved in patients with bimaxillary protrusion. Labial mucosa of the lower lip may also be involved when the lip is everted due to exposure to UV radiations of the sun (Schwartz et al., 2008).

Pathogenesis involves UVA- and UVB-induced damage to collagen resulting in the aging of skin, breakdown of vitamin A and release of hydroxyl and oxygen radicals due to ionization which damage the DNA (Matsumura and Ananthaswamy, 2004).

There is a high risk of transformation of actinic cheilitis of the lower lip into squamous cell carcinoma of the lip. A malignant transformation rate of 6% to 10% has been reported. A study by Kwon et al. revealed a higher risk of malignant transformation of these lesions compared to other parts of the lip (Kwon et al., 2011).

Histopathologic presentation is in the form of atrophy or hyperplasia of the epithelium along with drop-shaped rete ridges, cytological atypia, and keratinization in the vermilion border. The underlying connective tissue exhibits UV radiation-induced basophilic degeneration (Warnakulasuriya et al., 2007).

5.2 Tobacco-induced potentially malignant disorders

Oral submucous fibrosis—It is a chronic disease involving the oral mucosa, pharynx, and esophagus at times. The patient presents with rigidity of the oral mucosa brought upon by fibroelastic changes in the juxta-epithelial connective tissue which leads to progressive trismus.

Etiologic factors include nutritional deficiencies, consumption of chillies, tobacco, areca nut, collagen disorder and genetic susceptibility (Murti et al., 1995). 20- to 40-year-old Indians are commonly affected by this condition. These patients are more likely to undergo malignant transformation than healthy adults. The transformation is generally reported in the 5th decade with an almost 32 times higher incidence in males. This malignancy is more invasive and with a higher metastatic potential than oral squamous cell carcinoma arising elsewhere. A 2% to 8% malignant transformation risk exists for patients with oral submucous fibrosis (Ray et al., 2016).

Atrophic epithelium and juxta-epithelial hyalinization along with collagen of differing densities are seen on histopathological examination (Warnakulasuriya et al., 2007).

Palatal keratosis associated with reverse smoking—A practice of keeping the lit end of a rolled tobacco leaf in the mouth (reverse of the conventional form of smoking) has been reported in people from India and Philippines (Asia), Columbia, Venezuela, Panama, and the Caribbean islands (South America) as well as Sardinia (Europe). This is termed reverse smoking and is associated with palatal and tongue changes of which the palatal changes have a malignant transformation potential ascribed to them (Ramesh et al., 2014; Ganesh et al., 2018).

Most patients are women belonging to the lower socioeconomic status. Clinical presentation on the palate ranges from keratosis, excrescences, white patches, ulcerations to even frank malignancy. 83% of these lesions present with some form of epithelial dysplasia while 13% exhibit oral squamous cell carcinoma (Gómez et al., 2008).

The histopathology reveals atypia of the epithelium, papules with umbilication at the ductal orifices resulting from hyperplastic changes in the mucous salivary gland, and microinvasive cancer (Warnakulasuriya et al., 2007).

5.3 Immune-mediated potentially malignant disorders

Oral lichen planus—It is a chronic immune-mediated disease that affects the skin and mucous membranes. Six clinical forms exist: reticular, papular, plaque, erosive, bullous, and atrophic with Wickham's Striae (lacy white network of fine lines) being its hallmark feature. A viral etiology has been proposed, citing an association with Epstein–Barr virus, hepatitis C and even human papilloma virus (Warnakulasuriya et al., 2007).

Approximately 0.5%–2.6% of prevalence has been reported. Middle-aged females are most afflicted with lichen planus. Controversy exists regarding the premalignant nature of this lesion. Approximately 0.4%–3.7% malignant transformation rate risk exists for oral lichen planus (Epstein et al., 2003).

A histopathological diagnosis is made based on the findings of hyperkeratosis with saw-tooth rete ridges, basement membrane degeneration, along with basal cell degeneration and intraepithelial T-cell migration. The underlying connective tissue shows a band lymphocytic infiltrate subepithelially (Warnakulasuriya et al., 2007; Epstein et al., 2003).

Discoid lupus erythematosus—It is a chronic immunological disorder that results in scarring of the involved mucocutaneous region (Warnakulasuriya et al., 2007). These patients present characteristic keratinized plaques exhibiting elevated borders, white radiating striae, and telangiectasia (Lourenço et al., 2006). Females are more commonly affected, and this disorder rarely transforms to malignancy unless it displays epithelial dysplasia (high-risk dysplastic lesions are at 19.25 times higher risk of transformation) or there is prolonged UV exposure (Liu et al., 2011).

Histopathological features include atrophic epithelium with hyperkeratosis, inflammatory cell infiltrate within the underlying connective tissue along with edema. PAS staining reveals thick (patchy or continuous) deposits along the basal lamina (Lourenço et al., 2006).

5.4 Genetically inherited potentially malignant disorders

Dyskeratosis congenita—It is a very rare inherited disease which is alternatively termed Cole–Engman syndrome or Zinsser–Cole–Engman syndrome. Patients present with a classic triad of reticular pigmentation of the skin, dystrophy of the nails, and oral leukoplakia (87% cases) (Auluck, 2007; Bongiorno et al., 2017). The most common form of inheritance is an X-linked recessive trait where the affected males are usually between the ages of 5 and 13 (Bongiorno et al., 2017). Mutation of DKC1 (dyskerin pseudouridine synthase 1) gene is seen on Xq28 locus (Kirwan and Dokal, 2008).

Oral manifestations include hypodontia with remaining teeth exhibiting short, blunted roots and hypocalcification. Gingival recession and inflammation, gingival bleeding, bone loss, extensive caries, leukoplakia, and lichen planus are other presentations (Auluck, 2007). This disease is associated with an increased malignant transformation potential (Bongiorno et al., 2017).

Epidermolysis bullosa—It is a rare inherited disease that presents as blistering of skin and mucous membranes. Four major forms exist: simplex (intraepidermal), junction, dystrophic (dermolytic), and mixed (Kindler syndrome) which are associated with different mutations.

Form of epidermolysis bullosa	Type of mutation
Epidermolysis bullosa simplex	plakophilin1, desmoplakin, keratin 5, 14, plectin, integrin subunit 6 genes
Epidermolysis bullosa junctional	Laminin subunit α3, beta 3, γ3, collagen type XVII α1 chain, integrin α6a, and integrin subunit beta 4 genes
Epidermolysis bullosa dystrophic	Collagen type VII α1 chain gene
Epidermolysis bullosa mixed	Fermentin family 1 gene

(Fine et al., 2008; Ganesh et al., 2018).

Oral blistering which heals with scarring, enamel defects, and microstomia are common oral manifestations (Wright, 2011). The junctional form has a 25% malignant

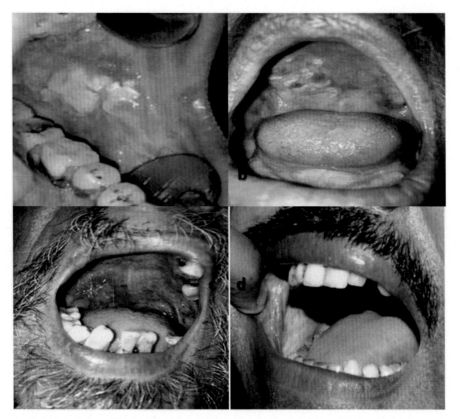

Fig. 5 Clinical images: (A) Oral leukoplakia. (B) Erythroleukoplakia. (C) Erythroplakia. (D) Oral submucous fibrosis.

transformation risk (Yuen and Jonkman, 2011). In addition, these patients show a higher risk of developing basal cell carcinoma or malignant melanoma (Fine and Mellerio, 2009) (Fig. 5).

6. Oral epithelial dysplasia

WHO in 2017 defined dysplasia as "a spectrum of architectural and cytological epithelial changes caused by accumulation of genetic changes, associated with an increased risk of progression to squamous carcinoma." In dysplasia the epithelial cell undergoes abnormal proliferation, maturation, and differentiation. The epithelium may be atrophic or show acanthosis and may or may not be keratinized.

WHO listed the dysplastic features of oral epithelium as architectural changes and cytological changes. Irregular stratification of the epithelium, loss of basal cell polarity, drop-shaped rete ridges, increased mitosis or presence of abnormally superficial mitotic figures, individual cell keratinization, keratin pearl formation, and loss of cellular cohesion make up the architectural dysplastic changes. The cytological abnormalities in dysplasia include altered cell size or shape, altered nuclear size or shape, increased nuclear:cytoplasmic ratio, presence of atypical mitotic figures, increase in number or size of nucleoli, and hyperchromasia of cells. The grading of epithelial dysplasia is then done based on the third affected with the involvement of the basal one-third of epithelium is allotted a mild grade, involvement up to the middle third is termed moderate dysplasia and in severe dysplasia epithelial involvement up to the upper third is noted (WHO, 2017). In the 1997 WHO classification, Pindborg et al., defined carcinoma in situ as "a lesion in which the full thickness, or almost the full thickness, of squamous epithelium shows the cellular features of carcinoma without stromal invasion" (Pindborg et al., 1997) (Fig. 6).

In 2017, WHO pointed out that architectural and cytological atypia alone can form the basis for grading dysplasia. Marked atypia in the basal third can be used to give a diagnosis of severe dysplasia. Dysplasia grading, however, has a lower predictive value in cases of high malignant transformation. In HPV oral potentially malignant disorders, there is epithelial hyperplasia with marked karyorrhexis and apoptosis. Presence of these features warrants an assignment of severe grade of dysplasia (WHO, 2017).

Risk factors for malignant transformation of oral potentially malignant disorders include old age, large size of lesion, long duration of disease, presence of epithelial dysplasia, erythroplakia or speckled leukoplakia presentation, female gender, multifocal lesion, involvement of the tongue, and occurrence in nonsmokers. Of these, the presence of epithelial dysplasia is said to be the best predictor for malignant change (Reibel, 2003).

Fig. 6 Photomicrographs (A) Mild dysplasia (4×, H&E), (B) moderate dysplasia (10×, H&E), (C) severe dysplasia (10×, H&E) (D) carcinoma in situ (4×, H&E).

7. Pathogenesis

The normal oral epithelium undergoes transformation into first a premalignant and then a malignant tissue as a part of a complex, multistep process that is affected by multiple factors. There is an accumulation of genetic alterations that result in disruption of the normal functioning of oncogenes and tumor suppressor genes. In its earliest phase, the cell cycle is disrupted by dysregulation, increased proliferation and alterations in differentiation, DNA repair, apoptosis and cellular immunity (Thomson, 2012).

Any genetic, phenotypic and/or functional alterations acquired in oral stem cells result in loss of a cell cycle regulatory mechanism and causes abnormal cell proliferation. These seem to be the core mechanisms that drive the process of carcinogenesis (Thomson, 2018).

Several genes are involved in the pathogenesis of oral cancers via four major groups: regulatory genes involved in response to DNA damage, genes controlling the cell cycle, those that control growth inhibition and apoptosis, as well as the genes involved in signal transduction and cell–cell collaboration. In their systematic review, Khattak et al. concluded that tumor protein 53 (TP53) is the protein with the highest degree (maximum number of neighbor proteins for interactions), TSPO is the protein with the largest betweenness centrality (BC) value, and EGFR is the protein with the highest closeness centrality (CC) values. However, TP53 has a key position in the network due to its degree, BC, and CC values, thus indicating that TP53 is centrally localized in the network and plays a significant role in the protein–protein interaction in oral cancer. Based on these findings, the authors suggested that in pathogenesis of oral cancer, variation was carried out via an integrated network of protein-to-protein interaction that centered around TP53. Through its functions of regulating cell division and restriction of uncontrolled growth and division of cells, TP53 executes the function of at least one of the gene groups in oral cancer (Khattak et al., 2021).

Progression of dysplasia to carcinoma was initially explained as follows: there was a sequential progression from one stage to the other via a series of mutations and chromosomal changes that occurred until several genetic changes that were required for the development of cancer had accumulated (Califano et al., 1996) (Fig. 7).

In the Progressive mutation or selective sweep model, it was suggested that clones of cells that undergo dysplastic changes have a growth advantage over the normal cells. Through continuous growth, these dysplastic cells replace the normal cells of epithelium. Exposure of amplifying cells (parabasal cells that have the capability of undergoing mitotic divisions) to carcinogens which are modulated through factors such as stem cell quiescence, metabolic insults, telomere loss, error in DNA replication, epigenetic changes and/or inflammation leads to the daughter cells receiving the genetic effects of these carcinogens. The mature cells that have exited the cell cycle, however, cannot pass on these

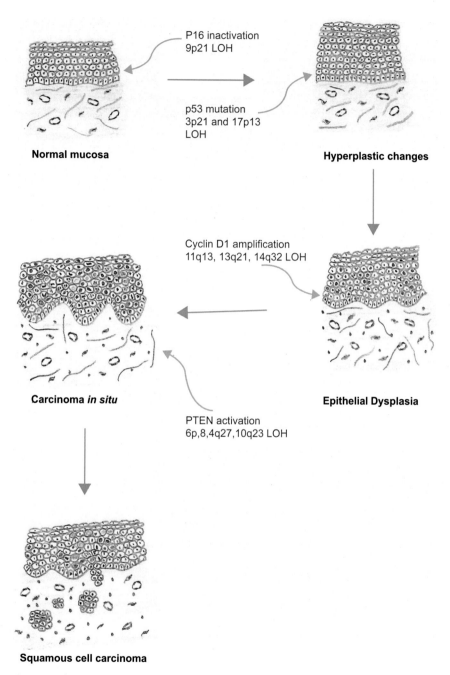

Fig. 7 Sequential progression to carcinoma.

genetic changes to any other cell. Clones of cells that are actively dividing and have undergone genetic changes start taking over the entire epithelium due to their growth advantage and proliferation. A repeated exposure to carcinogens would further accumulate more mutations in these altered surviving clones. These clones lead to the production of a plethora of altered stem cells resulting from clonal divergence and selection. They, however, share the same clonal origin. It is understood that with each increasing growth advantage, these altered cells start becoming closer to a carcinoma and ultimately take over the entire epithelium (Mohan and Jagannathan, 2014).

An alternate hypothesis has been proposed by Cross et al., where evolutionary stasis is seen in dysplastic or precursor lesions. They are genetically stable and remain unchanged for long periods. Dysplasia is more common than cancer, so only a minority of dysplastic lesions undergo malignant transformation. Most of the mutations found in cancer also exist in dysplastic lesions (Cross et al., 2016). It is now thought that carcinoma arises because of chromothripsis and chromoplexy, which are catastrophic events where sudden chromosomal rearrangements are seen in the cells. Oral cancers are molecularly diverse with few driver genes. Carcinoma evolves in dysplasia and not due to progression of dysplasia. Thus, no predictive pathway exists for cancer (Makarev et al., 2017).

Punctuated equilibrium theory (based on other body sites but fits the oral cavity) states that small clones of altered cells are formed within the actively dividing cell populations that are exposed to carcinogens. Their genetic pathways are inhibited. Some of these clones are unable to survive in a solid population and require intermingling with normal cells as they require signaling and obtain their nutrients from these normal cells. Ultimately, genetically abnormal clones of cells are found in the altered epithelium (Gould and Eldredge, 1993).

Henry Wood et al. stated that there was a rare mutation in the known cancer genes found only in the dysplasia samples. This suggests that much of the evolution of dysplasia is related to accumulation of passenger events. It is probable that these gene mutations in cancer were likely to be shared. Dysplasia seems to develop through accumulation of random nonsignificant mutations in cells. A separate unconnected event leads to the development of cancer in these dysplastic lesions. TP53 mutations, however, were almost always common to both lesions, presaging that, where displayed, they were essentially early events in the development of squamous cell carcinoma in the head and neck region. Thus, making p53 the most promising marker of field cancerization as there is a strong positive correlation with tumor progression from a benign to a malignant state (Wood et al., 2017).

7.1 Autophagy

Autophagy is natural cell-housekeeping which functions to remove damaged or senescent cell proteins and/or organelles. Cellular components are degraded by sequestration

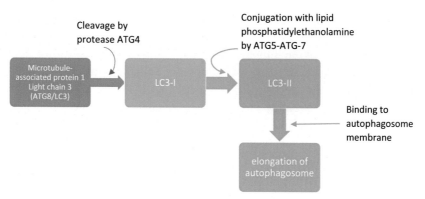

Fig. 8 Autophagy cascade.

in vesicles (autophagosomes) which eventually fuse with lysosomes. At low pH in these organelles, now termed autolysosomes, the hydrolytic enzymes degrade the sequestered material (Feng et al., 2014; Yang and Klionsky, 2020). By virtue of this survival-promoting pathway, autophagy prevents the buildup of toxic cellular waste products and provides substrates required for sustenance of metabolism during starvation (Alexandra et al., 2020). Stress up-regulates autophagy for coping with the damage in the cell. Autophagy-related proteins (ATGs) participate in autophagy (Feng et al., 2014) (Fig. 8).

ATG1 serves as an on/off switch for autophagy (Peña-Oyarzún et al., 2020). ATG1 also termed ULK1 (Unc-51-like autophagy activating kinase) is activated by AMPK (AMP-activated protein kinase) and inactivated by mTOR (mechanism target of rapamycin). The nutritional status of a cell is kept under check by AMPK and mTOR. mTOR is elevated in normal nutritional conditions where it suppresses autophagy. On the other hand, starvation leads to activation of AMPK which in turn promotes autophagy (Li et al., 2013; Meijer et al., 2015).

Inflammatory pathways like transcription factor nuclear factor -Kappa B (NF-κB) also regulate the process of autophagy. NF-κB is translocated to the nucleus on the degradation of its inhibitors. This results in an increase in the expression of genes that control inflammation, the proliferation of cells, cell survival, an epithelial–mesenchymal transition which in turn leads to invasion, angiogenesis as well as metastasis (Liu et al., 2017). Thus, activation of NF-κB leads to increased autophagy via ATG5 and LC3 expression (Copetti et al., 2009). Another effect of NF-κB is to promote mTOR expression through which autophagy is repressed (Lee et al., 2007).

For cancers to progress, autophagy modulation is to be carried out. Autophagy not only results in tumor formation due to its inhibition in normal cells but is also increased in frank tumors such that their growth is facilitated by enabling the tumor cells to survive microenvironmental stress. These cancer cells then exhibit an increase in both growth and aggressiveness (Singh et al., 2018). Mechanisms that include suppression of the P53 tumor suppressor protein by autophagy promote cancer development. Autophagy also helps to maintain the metabolic function of mitochondria. Genetics, tumor microenvironment, type of tumor, and its stage of development influence autophagy which in turn affects the process of carcinogenesis (Sakakura et al., 2015).

In oral squamous cell carcinoma, impaired autophagy is linked to a poor prognosis. Advanced cases of oral squamous cell carcinoma show high levels of SQSTM1/p62. As a result, there is absence of fusion of lysosomes in the tumor cells with autophagosomes (Liu et al., 2014). Immune infiltration of T lymphocytes and tumor associated macrophages along with the accumulation of SQSTM1 and LC3 portray inhibition of autophagy during these advanced stages. These help to establish a tumor immune niche (Sakakura et al., 2015). Downregulation of autophagy through activation of AMPK results in the transformation of normal fibroblasts to tumor-associated fibroblasts that release chemokines which promote epithelial–mesenchymal transition in cancer cells (Zhang et al., 2019) (Fig. 9).

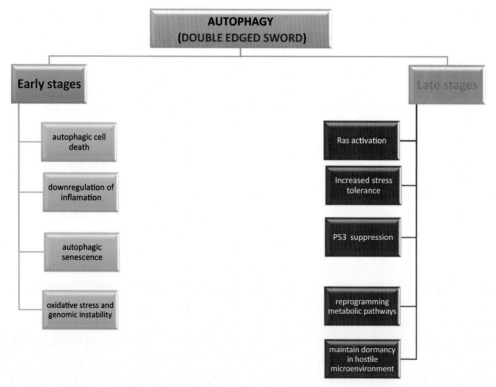

Fig. 9 Bidirectional role of autophagy in cancer.

8. Cancer stem cells

"Cancer Stem Cells" are a rare population of cancer cells that are tolerant to therapy and have the properties of long-term self-renewability, progeny differentiation and tumorigenicity (Naik et al., 2017). The regenerated tumor represents a phenocopy of the parent tumor, and it arises from a limited number of cells (Patel et al., 2014). Additionally, this subpopulation of cancer cells has enhanced DNA damage responses, possesses the ability to evade apoptosis, has an active drug efflux potential and readily undergoes epithelial to mesenchymal transition enabling these cells the distinction to tumorigenesis, sustained growth, and resistance to therapy (Costea et al., 2006).

According to the American Association of Cancer Research Workshop on cancer stem cells, these cells are defined as "cells within a tumor that possess the capacity to self-renew and to cause the heterogeneous lineages of cancer cells that comprise the tumor" (Clarke et al., 2006). The tumor cells face adverse growth conditions, limited resources for survival and are targeted by the host immune surveillance provided in the tumor microenvironment. The fate of the disease progression is dependent upon the ability of the tumor cells to modify the microenvironment making it conducive to allow these cells to evade the harsh factors that they are exposed to (McGranahan and Swanton, 2017). The cancer stem cells can form tumor spheres that are clusters of clonally derived cells under the influence of growth factors which drive them from their undifferentiated state toward proliferation (Shah et al., 2014).

Intratumor heterogeneity is said to exist which is evident by the phenotypic features of variations in cell morphology, genetic heterogeneity, proliferative capacity, angiogenic potential, immunogenic response, and metastatic potential. This variability within the same tumor results from a combination of genetic and nongenetic influences (Meacham and Morrison, 2013). These properties of cancer stem cells set them apart from other stem cells (Patel et al., 2014).

Two models have been used to describe the heterogeneity within a tumor: the "Clonal Evolution Model" and the "Cancer Stem Cells Model." In the Clonal Evolution model, Peter Nowell documented that a tumor arises due to stepwise mutational events occurring in the clone of single tumor cells that allow tenacious subclones to be selected sequentially leading to the evolution of the tumor and its progression (Nowell, 1976). The Cancer Stem Cell model disputed this theory by emphasizing that the variability in genetic, environmental, and epigenetic factors resulted in the phenotypic and functional heterogeneity of the tumor (Shackleton et al., 2009). With the improved understanding of the role the tumor microenvironment plays in a developing cancer, an alternate cancer plasticity model has been proposed to explain the heterogeneity of tumors. Cancer evolves and displays intratumor heterogeneity because of the microenvironment interactions (Marusyk et al., 2012). According to this model, microenvironmental signals boost self-renewal mechanisms to foster cancer stem cell characteristics. This is a reversible process that allows the interconversion of cancer stem cells to noncancer stem cells. The bidirectional model explains the intratumor heterogeneity through the interconversion of tumorigenic and nontumorigenic cells. Both these cell populations readily switch between these two states on receiving suitable microenvironmental signals displaying their highly adaptable nature (Cabrera et al., 2015).

Prince et al. were the first to isolate cancer stem cells in head and neck squamous cell carcinoma in 2007. They sequestered a group of cells expressing a high level of *CD44* with stem cell-like characteristics of self-renewal, ability to generate differentiated progeny, lack of differentiation markers, and expression of immature cell markers. These cells showed tumorigenic capacity when inoculated in immunosuppressed mice (Prince et al., 2007). Oral cancer stem cells may arise from normal adult epithelial stem cells rather than developing new self-renewal pathways like Notch, Hedgehog and Wnt signaling (Reya and Clevers, 2005; Naik et al., 2017). Additionally, the differentiation process may be initiated by the oncogenic mutations which are followed by self-renewal in progenitors or partly differentiated cells (Zhou et al., 2009). Moreover, the terminally differentiated adult oral epithelial cells may acquire stem-like mutations which may lead to de-differentiation resulting in the development of cancer stem cells (Zhang et al., 2013).

Nutrient starvation, hypovascularity, mild therapeutic stress, hypoxia, and challenged microenvironment have been shown to reprogram the genetic and epigenetic landscapes that help acquire an adapted inheritable state of drug-resistance and/or stem-like state. The niche of cancer stem cells provides a special microhabitat for survival and maintenance of stem cell-like property as well as the repropagation of the tumor posttherapy (Pisco and Huang, 2015) (Fig. 10).

The cancer stem cells contribute to resistance to the therapeutic modalities currently practiced by promoting recurrences and metastasis. To achieve a better success of treatment outcomes, the therapeutic applications require modifications.

These cells are prospective biomarkers and targets for therapy, so their isolation and characterization are being widely carried out by employing flow cytometry and anchorage-dependent culture assays (Naik et al., 2017; Patel et al., 2014).

Markers for cancer stem cells in oral squamous cell carcinoma include *CD44* [expression correlated with poor 5-year survival. However, as it is also expressed in normal epithelial cells, its applicability as a marker is debated] (Prince et al., 2007); *CD133* (prominin-1) [its expression is associated with increased clonability, epithelial–mesenchymal transition, self-renewability, and higher tumorigenicity] (Wu and Wu, 2009); *ALDH* (aldehyde dehydrogenase) [expression correlated with tumor formation, increased invasive capacity, self-renewal, and resistance to chemotherapy. A correlation between ALDH levels and cancer staging and poor patient outcome also exists] (Clay et al., 2010) and *c-Met*, proto-oncogene [encodes for hepatocyte growth factor tyrosine kinase receptor. Normally expressed in normal stem cells and progenitor cells. Their expression in cancer stem cells is associated with metastatic and invasive

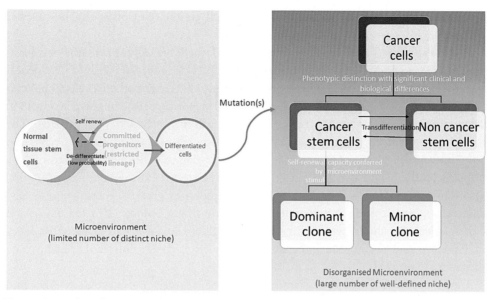

Fig. 10 Hierarchy of normal and cancer cells.

potential as well as heterogeneity in the phenotype of oral squamous cell carcinoma] (Sun and Wang, 2011).

Further investigations are required to validate the use of these as markers for cancer stem cells in oral squamous cell carcinoma. By comparing the genetic profile of the cancer stem cell with the tumor cells in oral squamous cell carcinoma, a characteristic pattern of gene profile can be established for the oral squamous cell carcinoma stem cells (Patel et al., 2014).

9. Tumor microenvironment

Oral squamous cell carcinoma is no longer studied as just a mass of malignant keratinocytes but is viewed as a baroque tumor microenvironment where, with cancer progression, these malignant cells modulate the adjacent stroma to form a self-reliant biological niche by inhibiting the host antitumoral responses (Peltanova et al., 2019).

The tumor environment varies in terms of the nutrients, oxygen, growth factors, cytokines, pH, extracellular matrix as well as its cellular components (Naik et al., 2017). The cellular component of squamous cell carcinoma includes malignant and normal keratinocytes, fibroblasts, endothelial cells, melanocytes, Langerhans cells, macrophages, mast cells, plasmacytoid, dendritic cells, myeloid-derived suppressor cells, natural killer cells, and CD4 and CD8 cells. These cells interact with the cancer cells and with each other through the elaboration of cytokines, growth factors, chemokines, and extracellular matrix proteins to exert pro- and/or antitumoral effects (Peltanova et al., 2019). The dynamic tumor microenvironment exhibits variation in the proportion of these cells which seems to be influenced by both genetic and other intrinsic factors (Ji et al., 2020).

Endothelial cells—The stromal population of endothelial cells along with the fibroblasts provide a niche conducive for angiogenesis which plays an essential role in cancer development (Florence et al., 2011). The expression of CD200 on endothelial cells along with its ligand, CD200R (present in macrophages and dendritic cells), might play a role in immunosuppression within the tumor microenvironment (Belkin et al., 2013). The release of factors from the stromal endothelial cells probably contribute to the increase in the invasive migration of tumor cells and their resistance to anoikis (induction of cell apoptosis on the loss of attachment to neighboring cells and extracellular matrix) in oral squamous cell carcinoma (Neiva et al., 2009). Epidermal growth factors expressed by these cells induce epithelial–mesenchymal transition by a reduction in the expression of desmoglein, β-catenin, cytokeratin 18 and E-cadherin and elevated levels of fibronectin, vimentin, and N-cadherin and enable the tumor cells to develop stem cell-like characteristics (Yang et al., 2013).

Cancer-associated fibroblasts—Transformation of normal oral fibroblasts first into dysplasia-associated fibroblasts and ultimately into cancer-associated fibroblasts results in progression of tumor and invasion. In a cancer microenvironment, the cancer-associated fibroblasts predominate and create a niche suitable for tumor proliferation and growth. There is phenotypic and genotypic diversity in these cells (Costea et al., 2013). Data reveals that the interplay of cytokines, extracellular matrix proteins and enzymes between tumor and stromal cells results in the development and progression of tumors (Amôr et al., 2021).

An important feature of oral squamous cell carcinoma is the acquisition of α-smooth muscle actin (α-SMA)–positive fibroblasts termed myofibroblasts or carcinoma-associated fibroblasts (CAF) that promote cancer cell proliferation and invasion (Kabir et al., 2016). For this transformation, the oral squamous cell carcinoma cells release interleukin 1 β which activates the NF-κB pathway. This then leads to the release of chemokine ligand 1 (CXCL1). The CXCL1 transforms normal fibroblasts to cancer-associated fibroblasts that express α-smooth muscle actin (α–SMA), (Peña-Oyarzún et al., 2020) fibroblast-activation protein α (FAPα), and ferroptosis suppressor protein 1 (FSP-1) (Öhlund et al., 2014).

These fibroblasts are said to directly impact the behavior of tumor cells through an increase in the expression of the laminin-332 γ2 chain in tumor cells by activation of the TGF-β signaling that subsequently results in enhanced cell invasion (Siljamäki et al., 2020). In vitro studies have shown a higher migration rate in cancer-associated fibroblasts in comparison to the normal fibroblasts. This may be linked to epithelial–mesenchymal transition which facilitates the progression of cancer (Costea et al., 2013). The epithelial–mesenchymal transition appears to be associated with an elevation in levels of platelet-derived growth factor receptor β which is responsible for the activation of STAT3 (signal transducer and activator of transcription protein 3) and JAK2

(Janus kinase 2). Activation of this pathway involving JAK2/STAT3 further leads to the release of epidermal growth factor that in turn promotes the above mentioned epithelial–mesenchymal transition (Peña-Oyarzún et al., 2020). Zhang et al. demonstrated that these cells protect epithelial cells from DNA damage thus preventing tumor formation in carcinogen-exposed tissue (Zhang et al., 2013a).

In the advanced stages of oral squamous cell carcinoma, the cancer-associated fibroblasts also generate microRNA contained exosomes which have been suggested to reduce tumor suppressor gene expression in cancer. Studies have also revealed that the cancer-associated fibroblasts in oral squamous cell carcinoma facilitate the release of microRNAs with protumor activity in favor of antitumoral microRNAs (Li et al., 2018). The stromal cancer-associated fibroblasts also release chemokines such as interleukin 1 β which is responsible for the infiltration of immune cells or altering the phenotype of oral cancer to one which favors migration and proliferation of tumor cells or release of CCL-2 (also termed monocyte chemoattractant protein 1) which shows a strong association with metastasis to lymph nodes (Peña-Oyarzún et al., 2020).

Based on their experimental studies, Daniele et al. found that the population of cancer-associated fibroblasts is heterogeneous with a subset of these cells possessing tumor-restraining ability while the other subset consists of tumor-promoting cancer-associated fibroblasts. The latter population makes up the bulk of the cancer-associated fibroblasts. Their study also revealed diverse gene expression signatures in these cells setting them apart from the normal oral fibroblasts or even dysplasia-associated fibroblasts. An upregulation of transcription factors that modulate the bioactivity of TGF-β1 was found in the cancer-associated fibroblasts. Two subgroups of cancer-associated fibroblasts were found based on cluster arrangements of 3-D cultures. CAF 1–4 clustered closer to normal oral fibroblasts (in genetic profiling and secretory activity) and were termed CAF-N while the other subset CAF 5–7 displayed transcriptional divergence so were termed CAF—D. CAF-N showed greater effectiveness in supporting the deeper invasion of the cancer cells compared to the CAF-D subgroup. However, compared to the normal oral fibroblasts or dysplasia-associated fibroblasts both types of cancer-associated fibroblasts supported a greater depth of tumor invasion. Increased synthesis of TGF-β1, TNF-α, keratinocyte growth factor, and fibroblast growth factor were seen in CAF-N while the normal oral fibroblasts secreted VEGF and hepatocyte growth factor (the latter suppresses the secretion of TGF-β1). It is a known fact that TGF-β1 aids in tumor cell invasion and expression of extracellular matrix markers in the malignant keratinocytes. It also facilitates the migration of the tumor cells. Even the motility of CAF-N was found to be greater than that of the other types of fibroblasts probably associated with increased hyaluronan production by these cells. Elevated hyaluronan levels support the deeper invasion of malignant oral keratinocytes (Costea et al., 2013).

In their study on cancer-associated fibroblasts, Patel AK et al. found two subsets of these cells based on the level of α-SMA stress fiber expression where they found that subset 1 termed C1-type CAF showed lower levels of expression than in C2-type CAF. The

C1-type CAF expressed higher levels of BMP, Ki-67, and ALDH levels. BMP4 expression suppresses the self-renewal growth potential of the cancer stem cells. They concluded that an inverse relation exists between α-SMA expression in the cancer-associated fibroblasts and proliferative capacity of cancer cells while increased expression positively correlated with the presence of cancer stem cells in oral squamous cell carcinoma patients. The α-SMA rich cancer-associated fibroblasts (C2-type CAF) provide an environment conducive for tumor growth by downregulation of BMP4 which provides deregulated self-renewal capability of cancer stem cells that facilitate tumor progression (Patel et al., 2018).

Inflammatory mediators—The microenvironment of oral squamous cell carcinoma is dominated by both proinflammatory and antiinflammatory mediators. The increased tumor features in the initial epithelial insult are accompanied by underlying inflammation. To sustain proliferation, migration, and invasion, the cancer cells elaborate proinflammatory cytokines that convert normal fibroblasts to cancer-associated fibroblasts. The latter facilitates metastasis of cancer cells to lymph nodes (Peña-Oyarzún et al., 2020).

a. *Tumor-associated neutrophils*—Neutrophils are among the first phagocytes to be recruited during inflammation in the malignant stroma, mostly through chemokine-mediated chemotaxis and they predominate at the invasive front (Khou et al., 2020). These cells can also play an antitumoral effect in squamous cell carcinoma (Amôr et al., 2021). Challacombe et al. (2006) showed that depletion of neutrophils increases squamous cell carcinoma development, suggesting that they mediate antitumor responses. Additionally, their experimental studies have revealed that neutrophils were essential for the antitumoral effects of Ingenol 3-angelate (Challacombe et al., 2006). The tumor-associated neutrophils may acquire either an antitumor activity (termed N1 neutrophils), and/or a protumoral activity (termed N2 neutrophils) that are mediated by TGF-β signaling (Fridlender et al., 2009) and elaborate vascular endothelial growth factor (VEGF) and MMP-9 that are angiogenesis and tumor invasion promoting factors. The presence of interferon β or the blockade of TGF-β1 converts the N2 neutrophils back into the cytotoxic N1 cells (Peltanova et al., 2019).

b. *Tumor-associated macrophages*—Macrophages are important immune cells required for tissue homeostasis and for generating an immune response against pathogens (Peltanova et al., 2019). Tumor-associated macrophages also form a significant percentage of the population of the infiltrating phagocytes in squamous cell carcinoma (Amôr et al., 2021), and their depletion inhibits tumor growth (Takahashi et al., 2009). The recruitment of monocytes into squamous cell carcinoma is mediated by chemokines such as CCL2 and are then polarized toward either an M1 or M2 phenotype. On activation by T helper type 1 cytokine interferon-ϒ, M1 macrophages produce proinflammatory cytokines such as IL-2, IL-23, Chemokines

CCL-5, CXCL-5, and CXCL-9. They provide Th1 response to infection and thus confer antitumor immunity. Through their cytotoxic activity they inhibit cell proliferation. Abundance of Th2-related cytokines such as IL-13, IL-4, and IL-10 promotes a predominance of M2 macrophages evoking an antiinflammatory response (Linde et al., 2012). The secretion of tumor-derived exosomes may also result in polarization toward M2-phenotype (Pang et al., 2020). These cells also facilitate the progression of tumor by producing metalloproteinases (MMPs) and increasing angiogenesis, which aid in tumor cells dissemination (Linde et al., 2012) via growth factors like vascular endothelial growth factor and platelet-derived growth factor. The tumor-associated macrophages express epidermal growth factor which is responsible for cell proliferation in oral squamous cell carcinoma (Peña-Oyarzún et al., 2020).

c. *Dendritic cells*—Dendritic cells are often thought to be the first immune cells to be exposed to tumor antigens from squamous cell carcinoma (Valladeau and Saeland, 2005). Squamous cell carcinoma-derived dendritic cells greatly induce the proliferation of $CD4^+$ and $CD8^+$ T cells as well as the production of IFN-γ, both of which promote an antitumoral response (Fujita et al., 2012). A significant reduction in the infiltration of these cells has been reported in squamous cell carcinoma and it seems to be an important mechanism for tumor escape. In squamous cell carcinoma, migration of the dendritic cells is inhibited by TGF-β1 secretion and interferes with the ability of these dendritic cells to undergo maturation into a potent T-cell activators (Weber et al., 2005).

d. *T cells*—T-cell regulation is carried out by the CD28-related inhibitory receptors, namely cytotoxic T-lymphocyte–associated protein 4 (CTLA-4) and programmed cell-death protein-1 (PD-1). These receptors show a high expression in human squamous cell carcinoma samples and are associated with cancer progression (Welsh et al., 2009; Gambichler et al., 2017).

  $CD8^+$ T cells play a crucial role in directly eliminating the tumor cells via release of cytolytic enzymes, which are essential mediators of the antitumoral response. There is a low frequency of these CD8+ T lymphocytes in squamous cell carcinoma lesions. TGF-β inhibits the infiltration of $CD8^+$ T cells and induces the expression of T-cell exhaustion markers such as Tim-3, CTLA-4, and PD-1 (Weber et al., 2005). Experimental studies in CD4+ cell-deficient mice who have been exposed to carcinogenic UVB radiation have revealed that there is higher tumor growth associated with elevated inflammation and increased number of p53+ tumor cells. This demonstrates that this subset of T cells play an important role in controlling inflammation-associated carcinogenesis (Hatton et al., 2007).

e. *Tregs (regulatory T cells)* —These cells form a unique subgroup of T cells that suppress excessive immune response and regulate the other immune cells including T cells, B cells, NK cells, and macrophages. They influence the immune system through either a contact-dependent mechanism or one which is contact-independent (Lahl et al., 2007).

f. *Myeloid-derived suppressor cells*—These cells are immature inhibitory immune cells that play a critical role in cancers and inflammation by negatively regulating the immune response. They deplete the amino acids in the microenvironment and thereby modulate the inflammation here (Lechner et al., 2010). They also inhibit T-cell activation and NK cell activity. Recent evidence suggests that these cells are linked to tumor angiogenesis and degradation of the extracellular matrix through release of proangiogenic factors and MMPs such as MMP-9. Through these actions they form a niche prior to metastasis of the tumor (Du et al., 2008).

g. *Platelets*—they also serve as one of the first responders during injury. Platelets contain three types of granules through which they regulate the tumor microenvironment (Peltanova et al., 2019). When activated the platelets release the mediators in these granules to cause aggregation of platelets, vasoconstriction and regulation of cell proliferation through release of growth factors. The dense granules contain 5-HT, ADP, ATP, membrane protein CD63 and P-selectin (Shah et al., 2001). The lysosomes contain acid hydrolases which remodel the extracellular matrix and blood vasculature (Metzelaar et al., 1991). α-granules are the third and most abundant group of granules in platelets that contain factors such as thrombospondin, von Willebrand factor that are important for hemostasis. These granules also release growth factors, chemokines and MMPs thus promoting tumor cell growth and angiogenesis (King and Reed, 2002).

h. *Mast cells*—Mast cells generate both innate and acquired immune responses. From their site of origin in the bone marrow, they migrate to the target tissue and undergo maturation there under the influence of the microenvironment. Activated mast cells release histamine, heparin, prostaglandin 2, TNF-α, and a variety of interleukins. In cancers, the tumor-associated mast cells are formed which can exert either protumoral or antitumoral effects. The protumor effects of these cells include release of VEGF and FGF-2 which aid in angiogenesis and release of MMPs and proteases that degrade the matrix (Norrby et al., 1989). These facilitate tumor invasion and migration. Histamine induces tumor cell proliferation while release of chemotactic factors engages other immune cells into the tumor. On the other hand, through tumor rejection and promotion of tumor cell apoptosis by IL-4 and TNF-α production, the tumor-associated mast cells exert a tumor-suppressive action (Lätti et al., 2003).

i. *Natural killer cell*—quick detection and killing of malignant or viral-infected cells is carried out by Natural killer cells. They express surface markers CD16 or CD56 and release important cytokines IFN-Υ and TNF-α (Lanier et al., 1986). Once these cells recognize the malignant cells, they induce apoptosis of the target cells. They do not require a prior sensitization (Topham and Hewitt, 2009) (Fig. 11).

Tumor microenvironment

Protumor	Antitumor
Endothelial cells	
SMA rich CAF and CAF-N	CAF-D
N2 tumor-associated neutrophils	N1 tumor-associated neutrophils
M2 tumor-associated macrophages	M1 tumor-associated macrophages
	Dendritic cells
Tregs	
Myeloid derived suppressor cells	
Mast cells	
Platelets	
	Natural killer cells

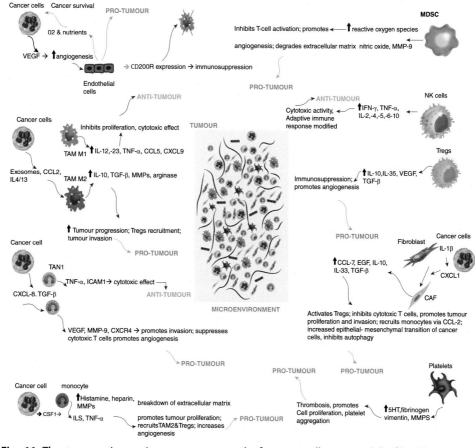

Fig. 11 The tumor microenvironment composed of cancer cells, neutrophils, fibroblasts, macrophages, monocytes, endothelial cells, cytotoxic T cells, natural killer cells (NK cells), T-regulatory cells (Tregs), platelets, cancer-associated fibroblasts (CAFs), tumor-associated macrophages (TAMs), tumor-associated neutrophils (TANs), and myeloid-derived suppressor cells (MDSC).

Extracellular matrix—it is a network of macromolecules comprising of fibers, ground substance, and growth factors that support the surrounding cells. In cancer, deregulation and disorganization of the extracellular matrix stimulates the transformation of the malignant cells. High levels of MMPs expression degrade the basement membrane proteins thus helping the tumor cells in migrating to local and distant locations. MMPs also activate growth factors in the matrix and help in the initiation and proliferation of tumors (Egeblad and Werb, 2002). They also promote angiogenesis through activation of FGF and VEGF (Bergers et al., 2000). MMPs are not only produced by the tumor cells but also by stromal cells in the tumor microenvironment (Rosenthal et al., 2004).

Collagen, fibronectin, laminin, and elastin make up the proteins of the matrix and provide a medium for the migration of cells in and out of the matrix. Increased production of these proteins leads to stiffness of the tumor which impacts cancer production by the activation of oncogenic pathways as well as inhibition of tumor suppressor genes (Chaudhuri et al., 2014). The stiffness also promotes the conversion of normal oral fibroblasts into cancer-associated fibroblasts. An increase in fibronectin levels is associated with tumor progression, invasion, and reduction in response to therapy (Knowles et al., 2013; Pontiggia et al., 2012).

Hypoxia within the tumor stimulates upregulation of VEGF which is responsible for the formation of new vessels that have an impaired function due to high leakage and irregular structure (Blouw et al., 2003). This hypoxic microenvironment is an important contributor of resistance to radiation and multidrug chemotherapy by means of hypoxia-inducible factor 1. This factor adapts cell response to hypoxic levels in this microenvironment (Teicher, 1994). This triggers the Warburg effect in which the tumor cells produce ATP by metabolizing glucose into lactate by aerobic glycolysis (Warburg, 1956). Through this, the tumor microenvironment is made conducive for proliferation, survival, and invasion of cancer cells. Increased levels of lactate and protons released by tumor cells acidify the tumor microenvironment promoting metastasis of tumor and therapy resistance (Estrella et al., 2013).

10. Epithelial–mesenchymal transition

In the epithelial–mesenchymal transition, the keratinocytes acquire a mesenchymal phenotype by losing cell adhesion (through loss of proteins E-cadherin and β-catenin of the cell junctions) and upregulation of extracellular matrix components (α-SMA, vimentin and N-cadherin). This in turn increases the migration and invasion of tumor cells (Myong, 2012). These have been implicated in tumor progression and metastases in head and neck squamous cells carcinoma cases (Nijkamp et al., 2011).

Degradation of the basement membrane and subjacent connective tissue matrix is essential for tumor cell migration. These migrating tumor cells develop protrusions called invadopodia that exhibit actin regulators, adhesion proteins and many MMPs (Jacob et al.,

2013). These invadopodia expedite the degradation of the extracellular matrix by regulating MMPs (mainly MMP-2, MMP-9 and MMP-14) through the action of Tissue inhibitors of MMPs (TIMPs) (Herrmann et al., 2014). Increased levels of neural precursor cell expressed developmentally downregulated 9 (NEDD9) can be used as a biomarker for gauging the aggressiveness of the tumor as it is required for VEGF-stimulated tumor cell migration and invasion in head and neck squamous cell carcinoma patients (Grauzam et al., 2018). Invadopodia formation is also enhanced by M2 macrophages and neutrophils in the tumor microenvironment (Gao et al., 2016).

By targeting the pathways that affect tumor metabolism, it is possible to impair epithelial–mesenchymal transition, migration, and invasion of oral squamous cell carcinoma (Peltanova et al., 2019). Li et al. in their study revealed that migration and invasion of cancer cells in head and neck squamous cell carcinoma patients can be suppressed by blocking glycolysis which in turn inhibits the formation of invadopodia (Li et al., 2017).

11. Metastasis

It is a multistep process that involves detachment of some cancer cells from the parent tumor, their invasion into the blood vessels or lymphatics and migration to a new site where they adhere to the local tissue at that site, form micrometastases, show angiogenesis and grow into a gross and clinical metastatic deposit (Chambers et al., 2002; Pantel and Brakenhoff 2004). This spread of disease from the original site to a distant one is driven by cancer stem cells. The stationary cancer stem cells acquire cancer stemness and undergo epithelial–mesenchymal transition and then develop into a mobile cancer stem cell population (Brabletz et al., 2005).

The primary tumor alters the microenvironment at the site of metastasis prior to the dissemination of the tumor cells into blood or lymphatics. This results in the development of a premetastasis niche at this site by the release of cytokines and growth factors like VEGF, TGF-β and TNF-α into circulation so that other supporting cells can be engaged to prepare the microenvironment at the secondary site for promoting the formation of metastatic tumor (Peinado et al., 2017). The recruitment of myeloid-derived suppressor cells and reduction in cytotoxicity of natural killer cells play a defining role in the establishment of this premetastatic niche which is conducive for supporting the growth of the disseminated cancer cells at the site of metastasis (Sceneay et al., 2012).

Invasion and survival in circulation—To survive and proliferate, normal keratinocytes need direct contact with the basement membrane through integrins. In the absence of such a contact these epithelial cells undergo anoikis (programmed cell death). This prevents the development of metastasis.

Anoikis must be evaded by the tumor cells to disseminate from the primary site, survive in circulation and then extravasate at the site for metastasis and form a tumor there (Peltanova et al., 2019). Release of IL-6, IL-8, and EGF by endothelial cells activates the

STAT3/Akt pathway in head and neck squamous cell carcinoma cells to abet survival and migration of malignant cells (Neiva et al., 2009). Hepatocyte growth factor released by cancer-associated fibroblasts also confer resistance to anoikis by ERK and Akt pathways as their blockade leads to tumor cell apoptosis (Knowles et al., 2013). Type 1 collagen delays anoikis in cancer cells by upregulating cytokine expression which activates MMP-2 and MMP-9. These MMPs boost tumor cell invasion in oral squamous cell carcinoma (Richter et al., 2010).

Once the tumor cells reach the circulation, they employ various means to evade an immune response. They survive circulation by aggregation of platelets to form a "platelet cloak" which protects the circulating cells from immune cells like natural killer cells (Nieswandt et al., 1999). This "cloak" allows the adhesion of tumor cells to the vascular endothelium, thereby aiding in their extravasation (Rickles and Falanga, 2001). It also confers protection to the tumor cells in circulation from shear forces in the vascular channels. The "platelet cloak" also provides growth factors for the use of cancer cells (Takagi et al., 2014). Huang et al. found an increased aggregation of platelets in patients with head and neck squamous cell carcinoma and demonstrated its correlation with the stage of tumor in these patients (Huang et al., 2009a, b).

Extravasation—Once the cancer cells metastasize to the secondary site, they extravasate into the tissue to escape the hostile intravascular/intralymphatic environment. This requires trans-endothelial migration by altering the cell-to-cell attachment of endothelial cells. Tumor-promoting immune cells such as platelets and neutrophils also facilitate this migration. Little is known about the impact of the microenvironment on the extravasation of tumor cells from the lymph vessels in oral squamous cell carcinoma (Peltanova et al., 2019).

Mesenchymal–epithelial transition—this is the reverse of epithelial–mesenchymal transition. In this process, the cancer cells revert from their induced mesenchymal phenotype which was required for their survival during intravasation and dissemination. To persist in this new environment and form tumor colonies resembling the primary tumor, this transition back to epithelial phenotype is required. Reexpression of E-cadherin has been shown to be an important factor for the development of a metastatic tissue. The impact of the microenvironment at the metastatic site on the tumor cells is yet to be investigated in oral squamous cell carcinoma (Hong et al., 2009).

12. Oral bacteria in oral carcinogenesis

Oral bacteria offer a beneficial ecological environment in the oral cavity. Dysbiosis alters the balanced, healthy oral ecosystem and facilitates the colonization of the oral cavity by pathogens that lead to diseases such as dental caries and periodontal diseases (Baker et al., 2017). Oral bacterial microflora plays an important role in the process of oral carcinogenesis. Studies reveal that oral microflora can enhance cell proliferation, exert an antiapoptotic effect, and abet tumor invasion and metastasis (Groeger et al., 2017). *Porphyromonas gingivalis* modifies the expression levels of oncogenic-relevant α-defensin genes (Hoppe et al., 2016) or regulates genes that downstream signaling pathway of the proinflammatory active transcription factor NF-κB thus impacting the cell proliferation (Groeger et al., 2017). Additionally, this bacterium induces the apoptosis of immune cells providing protection to cancer cells from an immune attack and inhibits the apoptosis of keratinocytes (Yao et al., 2010). *Fusobacterium nucleatum* has also been found to inhibit tumor cell apoptosis by activation of TLR2 (toll-like receptor 2) which aids in the expression of miR-146a-5p that in turn affects apoptosis (Ikehata et al., 2018). However, *Lactobacillus plantarum* plays an antitumoral role by inducing apoptosis in oral cancer cells by upregulating PTEN and downregulating MAPK signaling pathways (Asoudeh-Fard et al., 2017). In vitro studies reveal that *P. gingivalis* and *F. nucleatum* trigger the epithelial–mesenchymal transition signaling pathway that in turn leads to the release of proinflammatory mediators like TGF-β1, EGF and TNF-α in oral squamous cell carcinoma cell lines. They also upregulate the expression of MMPs (Abdulkareem et al., 2018). Angiogenesis promotion in oral squamous cell carcinoma is carried out by these bacteria through the release of IL-6 and IL-8 (Huang et al., 2016). IL-6 and IL-8 induce cancer-associated fibroblasts to release VEGF that is required for neovascularization through JAK/STAT signaling (Gallimidi et al., 2015). IL-6 and IL-8 also provide a suitable proinflammatory environment for cancer stem cells. Reduction in expression of IL-6 and IL-8 could lead to inhibition of growth and invasion of cancer cells (Li et al., 2020) (Fig. 12).

13. Clinical features

In its early stages, oral squamous cell carcinoma requires biopsy and histopathological examination to arrive at a definitive diagnosis since the clinical characteristics alone are insufficient. However, in the advanced stages, the characteristic clinical presentation is enough to raise suspicion of malignancy. The presentation of the oral squamous cell carcinoma is variable with the smaller lesion being asymptomatic or bearing resemblance to other nonmalignant oral lesions while the more advanced cases present with pain, discomfort, reduced movement of tongue, or inability to wear dentures in many cases. The clinical appearance may be endophytic or exophytic with the color of the involved mucosa being white, erythematous or a combination of the two. Raised, indurated margins of a nonhealing ulcer are a hallmark of malignancy.

Oral squamous cell carcinoma can involve any oral site with the most frequent involvement of the tongue, the floor of the mouth and gingiva in over half of the diagnosed cases (WHO, 2017). Thomson PJ et al. found that the S phase of DNA synthesis showed elevated and prolonged activity in the floor of the mouth and along the ventrolateral tongue. This could help explain the increased frequency of involvement of these

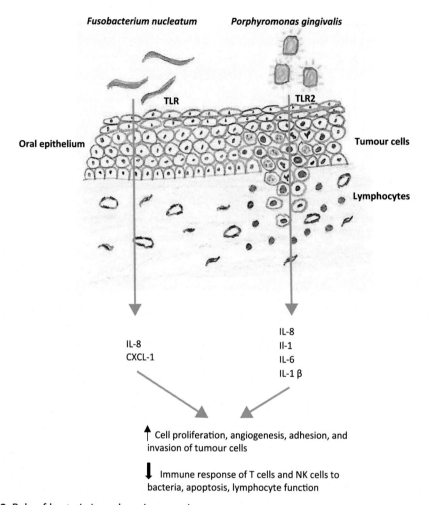

Fig. 12 Role of bacteria in oral carcinogenesis.

locations (Thomson, 2018). In the South–East Asian subcontinent, the gingiva and the buccal mucosa are the commonly involved locations for oral squamous cell carcinoma. Contrastingly, the tongue and the floor of the mouth are more commonly affected subsites in Western countries. This variation in the site distribution is probably attributed to the habit/risk factor prevailing in these regions (WHO, 2017; Dhanuthai et al., 2018). In children aged 16 and below, the 6 commonest sites for carcinoma in descending order of frequency are the mandible (17.9%), palate (14.9%), gingiva (13.4%), alveolar mucosa (11.9%), maxilla and tongue (10.4% each) (Dhanuthai et al., 2018).

The afflicted sites are closely related to the prevalence of risk factors and lifestyle conditions. These follow the "field cancerization concept" (Mohan and Jagannathan, 2014). Tongue cancers that generally develop in elderly patients because of chronic exposure to alcohol and tobacco are more aggressive and are associated with a higher rate of relapse

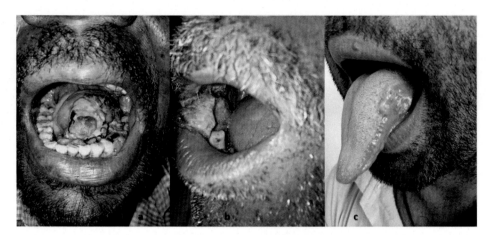

Fig. 13 Clinical photographs. (A) Exophytic growth on the left side of the tongue and the floor of the mouth. (B) Exophytic growth on the right buccal mucosa involving the commissure. (C) Ulceroproliferative growth on the left lateral border of the tongue posteriorly.

and greater invasiveness (Paderno et al., 2018). Lower lip cancers mainly result from environmental factors such as solar radiation, smoking and viral infections (Kerawala et al., 2016) (Fig. 13).

Salient features specific to subsite

 Floor of the mouth/tongue
- Aggressive biologic behavior
- High likelihood of neural and lymphovascular invasion and spread
- Submucosal spread is common
- Metastasis to regional nodes and distant sites

 Buccal mucosa/gingiva, buccal vestibule/mandible
- Associated with tobacco chewing and prevalent in the Indian subcontinent
- Requires analysis of the involvement of the masticator space and infratemporal fossa
- Retromolar trigone area may be involved in posteriorly located tumors

 Lip
- Majority are squamous cell carcinoma on histological evaluation
- Esthetics and function are affected in cases with the involvement of oral commissure (Gupta et al., 2019).

14. Diagnosis

Cancer screening which is defined as the process by which a healthcare provider evaluates an asymptomatic patient to detect malignancy, has been shown to reduce cancer-associated morbidity and premature mortality due to early diagnosis made for many patients. Currently, oral cancer is diagnosed through clinical history and physical examination followed by a biopsy (Epstein et al., 2008a, b). The American Dental Association in 2017 recommended that clinicians should remain alert for oral cancer while carrying out routine visual and tactile examinations in all patients, but particularly in those who use tobacco or consume alcohol heavily (Boing et al., 2011).

Features that raise suspicion of malignancy include sharp or distinct margins, a red component or variation in color, a nonhomogenous white component with an irregular surface, and large-sized or persistent ulceration. Special attention should be directed toward any persistent or progressive lesion found on the ventrolateral tongue or the floor of the mouth as both these areas are high-risk sites for oral squamous cell carcinoma (Chi et al., 2015).

Early detection and intervention are very challenging as premalignant lesions are not readily apparent and there is a limited ability to accurately discriminate oral potentially malignant disorders from abnormal mucosa using visual inspection alone (Baron, 2012). The physical examination is subjective and not very accurate. It has a sensitivity of 64% and a 31%–76% specificity (Basu et al., 2018). Moreover, as OPMDs may regress on cessation of tobacco use, it makes it possible to teach the patients to cease the use of tobacco and alcohol which is critical for oral cancer prevention (WHO, 2017).

Other causes that result in the delay in detection of oral squamous cell carcinoma in primary settings include poor awareness of cancer-related symptoms, lack of easy access to health facilities, and preference to taking alternative medicine including herbal medicines. All these highlight the necessity of imparting cancer education to the communities as well as to the healthcare providers to improve awareness and thus avoid delays in catching oral cancer early. Speight et al. studied the cost-effectiveness of oral screening in dental practices and found that in contrast to population screening or invitational mass screening programs, screening in dental practice was more cost-effective (Speight et al., 2006).

A screening test should be repeated at regular intervals to be beneficial for the screened population. In a study by Nagao and Samarnayake, repeat oral examinations were carried out on a cohort of 6340 subjects in Tokoname, Japan which revealed that annual screening allows detection of new cancers and potentially malignant disorders (Nagao and Warnakulasuriya, 2003).

Seventeen to 35% of oral leukoplakias transform into squamous cell carcinoma. Thus, early detection of oral leukoplakia aids in secondary prevention of oral cancer, although some cancers may arise de novo, and not all leukoplakias transform to cancer. Moreover, at present, the detection of oral epithelial dysplasia following biopsy remains the gold standard for distinguishing high-risk from low-risk leukoplakia (Napier and Speight, 2008).

Recently, in Sri Lanka, Amarasinghe et al. derived and validated a risk-factor model suitable for selecting subjects who may present with undiagnosed oral potentially malignant disorders where they studied the age, socio-economic status, betel quid chewing, smoking, and alcohol use. This study yielded a sensitivity (95.5%) and specificity (75.9%) for positive detection (Amarasinghe et al., 2010).

14.1 Adjunctive aids for early detection

Screening for early detection of disease or diagnosis of an occult lesion of oral potentially malignant disorders or oral squamous cell carcinoma can be aided by the use of adjunctive chairs-side techniques such as vital tissue staining (Epstein et al., 2008a, b), oral brush biopsy, and cytology (Husain et al., 2018), fluorescent instruments (Tiwari et al., 2019) and narrow-band imaging (Piazza et al., 2010) and making the tissue aceto-white (Epstein et al., 2008a, b).

In addition to oral examination and chair-side adjunctive methods, basic diagnostic procedures such as oral cytology, histopathological evaluation of biopsy specimen, ELISA, immunohistochemistry, PCR, flow cytometry, and in-situ hybridization can also be employed to characterize oral squamous cell carcinoma. Recent years have seen the advent of advanced diagnostic procedures such as nano-diagnostics, lab-on-chip/microfluidics, liquid biopsy, microarray technology, next-generation sequencing, and omics that include genomics, proteomics, transcriptomics, and metabolomics (Madhura et al., 2020).

Nano-diagnostics

This is an upcoming system of detection that is linked to several advantages over conventional imaging contrast agents including convenience, cost-effectiveness, ease in synthesizing the nano-particles, ability to target specific surface molecules, better biocompatibility, higher image resolution and contrast, and real-time diagnosis. They are thus employed by clinicians or surgeons for the detection and monitoring of oral squamous cell carcinomas (Chen et al., 2018).

This system is employed in:

1. Magnetic resonance imaging (MRI)—the nano-contrast agents have a longer half-life in the blood and possess higher relaxivity in comparison to conventional contrast agents. However, the higher cost is its disadvantage (Aryal et al., 2014).
2. Quantum dots (QDs) imaging—quantum dots offer a better intensity of fluorescence, exhibit lower nonspecific binding and higher stability against photobleaching than conventional agents. In vivo biodegradability and cytotoxicity are its limitations (Liu et al., 2013).
3. Photoacoustic imaging—there is an enhancement in the signals provided by the nanosensors used, especially in cancers exhibiting micro-metastasis. The difficulty in capturing real time imaging is its disadvantage (Luke et al., 2014).
4. Optical coherence tomography (OCT)—advantages offered by the nano-contrast agents include higher biocompatibility as well as superior contrast levels. Limited

depth of penetration and complex procedure, however, limit its use currently (Oldenburg et al., 2006).

5. Nano-based ultrasensitive biomarker detection systems offer higher sensitivity in the detection of biomarkers at lower concentrations in the tissue fluid studied (Janissen et al., 2017).

6. Diffusion reflection imaging—good results are provided while screening oral cancers when gold nano-rods are used. They also aid in the detection of any residual disease during surgery (Ankri et al., 2016).

7. Surface plasmon resonances—nano-particles are responsible for the generation of focal surface plasmon resonances close to visible and infrared wavelengths. The instability of targeted nano-particles is however an issue (Oldenburg et al., 2006).

8. Surface-enhanced Raman spectroscopy (SERS)—it provides a high index sensitivity by employing nanorods. Disadvantages include complicated preparation of probes and limited types of nanomaterials that produce the SERS effect (Harmsen et al., 2017).

These nano-based diagnostic techniques provide molecular targeted imaging, allow detection of surgical margins intraoperatively and act as prognostic markers (Chen et al., 2018; Madhura et al., 2020).

Lab-on-chip/microfluidics

Lab-on-chip technology which encompasses the use of chemical and biotechnology skills involves the system of microfluidics in which a single device/chip is incorporated with miniaturized integrated and automated laboratory procedures. This is employed to study the living cells in their respective biological environments.

In oral precancer/cancers, salivary analysis is carried out on lab-on-chip by utilizing the technology of microfluidics. In this, membrane-associated proteins are used for the diagnosis of pathology. The profiles thus measured are then compared to archival gene profiles to type and stage the malignancy (Ziober et al., 2008). Tumor cell migration can be studied through microfluidics by targeting the cell membrane. Circulating tumor cells are also isolated by microfluidics (Chaw et al., 2006).

Coculture techniques using microfluidics help to study the tumor microenvironment, proliferation of cells, progression of cancer cells as well as the signal exchanges between cancer cells and the mesenchymal cells (Huang et al., 2009a, b). These techniques, therefore, provide a platform for testing of drugs and to evaluate targeting. To isolate pure cancer cells, immunomagnetic separation, hydrodynamic focusing, and dielectrophoresis are carried out (Song et al., 2017).

This method is well established for prostate, breast, colon, ovary, brain, lung, and other cancers but is in the exploratory stages for screening and diagnosis of oral cancers (Madhura et al., 2020).

Liquid biopsy

In 1869, Australian physician Thomas R. Ashworth first described a treasure trove of information in the form of circulating tumor cells (CTCs) in one of his patients. He suggested that these cells that were found in the blood that resembled cancer itself could provide an insight into the mode of origin of multiple tumors in the same patient (Ashworth, 1869).

Pantel and Alix-Panabiéres were the first to introduce the procedure for analyzing the cancer cells and their products in blood and other body fluids. This procedure was termed liquid biopsy (Pantel and Alix-Panabières, 2010). Saliva, urine, plasma, sputum, CSF, pleural effusions and stool samples and blood provide a rich resource for biomarkers to diagnose and evaluate premalignancies and cancers at an early stage through liquid biopsy.

Ease of access, low cost, minimal invasion, and ability to take multiple samples for disease monitoring provide liquid biopsy with an edge over tissue biopsies for screening, diagnosing, and monitoring a premalignant or malignant tumor (Peng et al., 2017). Apoptosis and necrosis of cancer cells result in the release of these tumor markers into the tumor microenvironment from where they enter the blood and other biofluids (Choi et al., 2005). Analysis of these markers can be helpful in studying the development and progression of cancer. It offers an advantage over imaging methods as well due to a reduction in exposure to harmful radiations and by offering a more convenient method to monitor disease progression as well as response to therapy by repeat tests.

mRNA biomarkers, metabolites, proteins, circulating tumor RNA, circulating cell-free tumor DNA, circulating tumor cells, exosomes, and proinflammatory cytokines have been evaluated in patients with oral squamous cell carcinoma (Madhura et al., 2020, Arantes et al., 2018). Tumor-educated platelets are the latest liquid biopsy analyte of interest (Veld and Wurdinger, 2019) (Fig. 14).

By the 1990s, technology was developed to capture circulating tumor cells in the blood, and later, CellSearch became the first FDA-approved diagnostic device, which could separate and quantify these cells that serve as a prognostic tool to predict survival of patients with prostate, colorectal, and breast cancers (Millner et al., 2013). OncoDiscover Liquid Biopsy technology in 2017 became India's first indigenously developed technology to receive approval from DCGI under new Medical Device Rules 2017 (www.octorius.co.in/OncoDiscover/).

Molecular profiling of the cancer patients through liquid biopsy provides a snapshot of the primary and metastatic tumor. It aids in detecting recurrences of cancer early, enhances risk assessment which impacts tumor staging and helps in evaluating therapy resistance which is then employed in future therapeutic decision-making (Madhura et al., 2020). Real-time monitoring of therapies can also be carried out through liquid biopsy. Additionally, prognostic information is also provided by liquid biopsy as it can be used to estimate the risk of progression of metastasis or its relapse. If circulating tumor cells are revealed in a

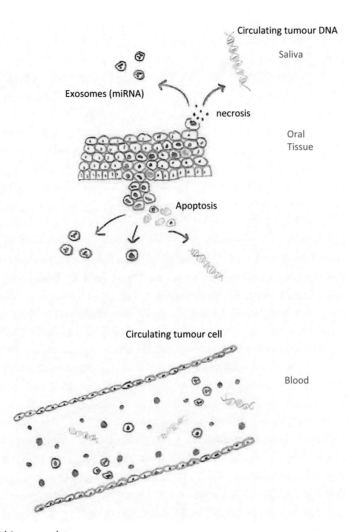

Fig. 14 Liquid biopsy analytes.

liquid biopsy sample of a patient who has completed adjuvant therapy, it is a predictor of relapse of metastasis and is associated with poor survival (WHO, 2017).

Circulating tumor DNA arises from apoptotic or necrotic tumor cells and shows somatic mutations specific to the tumor. Analysis of these unique genetic changes can accentuate the diagnostic accuracy of these analytes. Wang et al. (2015) demonstrated circulating tumor DNA in plasma and salivary samples when screening a cohort of 93 head and neck cancer for somatic mutations (TP53, PIK3CA, NOTCH1, FBXW7, CDKN2A, NRAS, and HRAS) and human papillomaviruses (HPV16 and 18). According to them, the sensitivity of circulating tumor DNA as a salivary biomarker was higher than that in plasma for oral cancers with 100% expression of salivary circulating tumor DNA in contrast to 80% in plasma. The proximity of the tumor to saliva is responsible for this (Wang et al., 2015).

Circulating tumor cells are released from both primary and metastatic tumors into the blood. In 2012, Buglione et al. found a more frequent expression of circulating tumor cells in advanced cases of head and neck cancer than in early stages (Buglione et al., 2012). Epithelial-to-mesenchymal transition is found once there is dissemination of these cancer tumor cells. This can lead to the formation of an additional tumor in a distant organ resulting in metastatic tumors following extravasation. Validation of the genotyping and phenotyping of cancers is required. Surveillance of cancer tumor cells is important to monitor the treatment outcome and as a follow-up measure in these patients (WHO, 2017). While detecting early cancers, the sensitivity of circulating tumor cells is lesser than that of circulating tumor DNA. Nichols et al. (2012) reported only 1–2 circulating tumor cells/7.5 mL of blood (Nichols et al., 2012).

Exosomes are small membrane-bound vesicles of size 40–150 nm. They possess DNA, RNA, surface proteins in the form of heat shock proteins, integrins, fusion and transport proteins as well as tetraspanins from the parent tumor cell. Their expression in the tumor microenvironment highlights their importance in initiation, progression, invasiveness, and metastasis of the tumor. The most relevant constituents of exosomes for cancer diagnosis are miRNAs since they represent regulatory molecules of both oncogenes and tumor suppressor genes (Chen et al., 2012) with their profiles correlating with the miRNA profiles of parent tumor (Mitchell et al., 2008). In oral squamous cell carcinoma, these exosomes have been found to be linked to cancer progression through increased levels of TGF-beta as well as in drug resistance (Fernandez et al., 2018; Siravegna et al., 2017). However, systemic or local inflammation may upset the expression of miRNA and affect its reproducibility even in the same patient so its diagnostic relevance in head and neck cancers is inconsistent (Pritchard et al., 2012).

The first detection and characterization of circulating cell-free salivary miRNAs were carried out by Park et al. in 2009. They found that these miRNAs were relatively stable, and the degradation of endogenous salivary miRNAs occurs at a slower pace than exogenous miRNAs (Park et al., 2009). Elevated miR-27b and miR-31 were reported in saliva obtained from oral cancer patients (Liu et al., 2012; Momen-Heravi et al., 2014) compared with that obtained from controls and the levels of these miRNAs reverted to baseline following surgery (Duz et al., 2016). This is suggestive of their utility as potential diagnostic biomarkers.

Up until 5 years back, tissue biopsy has long been the gold standard for testing and is well understood whereas the tools for a liquid biopsy were yet to achieve applications in routine diagnostic procedures due to its armamentarium and high cost. There was also an issue regarding relevant material being present in the fluid analyzed and the quantity of these cells evident for analysis. Liquid biopsy is paving its way in the diagnosis of malignancies. However, it is yet to prove its validity and clinical utility as a diagnostic and monitoring tool in oral cancer diagnosis. The need of the hour is to determine whether all types of circulating biomarkers (circulating tumor DNA, circulating tumor cells, and exosomal miRNAs) are representative of the whole tumor, especially for those that display heterogeneity.

Multiple body fluids analysis of the circulating biomarkers could provide complementary information and help establish the use of liquid biopsies in personalized medicine. An important future challenge is to develop simple, rapid, and affordable technologies for the analysis of circulating biomarkers. Larger sample size-based studies are required to identify target-oriented biomarkers that can help differentiate the high-risk population from the low risk one.

Microarray technology

This technique is employed for studying gene expression in a variety of cancers. Messenger RNA is used as a surrogate marker for this technique where DNA spots are collected on a solid surface for representing the DNA microarray. The procedure involves cutting the unknown DNA fragments through enzyme restriction endonucleases followed by reacting fluorescent markers with the DNA chip probes. This results in the binding of target DNA fragments to the probes and their identification by emission of fluorescence.

All coding (mRNA) and noncoding (small nuclear RNAs, small nucleolar RNAs, miRNAs and long noncoding RNAs) transcripts make up a transcriptome. These are found at a particular developmental stage or physiological condition in a cell. Transcriptome provides information about the functional elements of the genome as well as molecular components of cells and tissues, development, and disease. It therefore is a potential biomarker that is mainly analyzed through microarray (Bumgarner, 2013; Kuo et al., 2002; Arantes et al., 2018).

Microarrays are used for analyzing gene expression, binding of transcription factors as well as for genotyping. In oral squamous cell carcinoma, study of the gene mutations, detection of cancer biomarkers, single-nucleotide polymorphism identification as well as detection of genes responsible for chemoresistance have been carried out through microarray. Gene microarrays are employed to compare genetic hybridization.

Microarrays, however, come with a set of limitations that include: 1. Linear signal production over a limited range of concentration. 2. Indirect measure of relative concentration. 3. They can only represent the genomes that have been annotated (Madhura et al., 2020).

Next generation sequencing

Sanger et al. (1977) were the first to perform DNA sequencing (Sanger et al., 1977). The second generation of sequencing was introduced in 2005 as next-generation sequencing. Large sequence data is obtained via DNA extraction. It also furnishes percipience of genomic pathways which endorse our understanding of the development of disease and its progression.

Several methods of next-generation sequencing have been devised to characterize the genome, code it, and analyze alterations in DNA copy number, any translocation or mRNA abundance.

A single molecule real-time system has been introduced by Oxford Nanopore which is being referred to as third generation sequencing (Madhura et al., 2020).

Oral squamous cell carcinoma is heterogeneous in nature and displays a complex molecular interplay. Next-generation sequencing has helped improve our knowledge about the genetic variations found in oral squamous cell carcinoma that include alterations in HRAS, TP53, CDKN2A, STST3, TGF-α, PIK3CA, and EGFR pathways (Rizzo et al., 2015). They have also been used to study the differential expression of noncoding RNAs like miR-193-3p, miR370, and miR1307 (Pedersen et al., 2018). To evaluate the progression of oral leukoplakia to oral squamous cell carcinoma, nextgeneration sequencing has been employed by evaluating the alteration in the expression of miR-150 (Chang et al., 2018).

Omics

Oral cancers exhibit molecular diversity and are associated with few driver genes. Malignant transformation does not occur in every single lesion of oral potentially malignant disorders, and neither are all these disorders receptive to curative treatment. Therefore, the biomarkers that signal malignant transformation need to be validated (Coletta and Salo 2018).

Saliva is a body fluid that reflects the current physiological state of an individual. It is abounding with biomarkers for not only diseases but also for gauging the presymptomatic and health status. Thus, saliva acts as a substantial reservoir of molecules and microbes providing information on disease anywhere in the body (Lee and Wong, 2009; Schafer et al., 2014).

This has led scientists the world over to explore various biomarkers that can aid in detection of oral cancer, since both oral cancer and potentially malignant disorders are physically exposed to the oral cavity. Ease of collection, low cost, painless and noninvasive procedure offer advantages of using saliva as a diagnostic tool for stress-free sample collection which can be easily stored and transported. Additionally, using saliva as a diagnostic medium offers better patient compliance in providing samples and is associated with minimal risk of infection when compared to traditional blood or tissue-based biochemical analysis (Nunes et al., 2015).

Once unstimulated saliva is collected for analysis, volumetric measurement is performed. Following this, biomarker evaluation is done using either ELISA or Chromatography or 2-D electrophoresis or Liquid chromatography and mass spectroscopy.

The concept of "salivaomics" put forward by Kaczor-Urbanowicz et al. includes six diagnostic parameters: salivary genomics, transcriptomics, proteomics, metabolomics, microbiomics, and microRNA (miRNA) (Kaczor-Urbanowicz et al., 2017). Cellular and molecular heterogeneity of oral squamous cell carcinoma and the vast array of genes potentially involved in the process of oral carcinogenesis deem it important to study the changes in gene expression through proteomics. Diagnosis and treatment of oral squamous cell carcinoma can be carried out by targeting multiple proteins (pathways) (Hu et al., 2008). The evolution and advancement in the fields of salivary proteomic, metabolomic, genomic, and transcriptomic research has led to the improvement in the diagnostic and detection proficiency for oral cancer and precancer. Upward of 120 biomarkers in saliva (salivary constituents, proteomic, transcriptomic, genomic, and metabolomic analyses) have been discovered over the past 30 years via 100 plus studies suggesting their role as potential diagnostic adjuncts for the diagnosis of oral cancer and precancer (Kaur et al., 2018).

Individual salivary proteins have been studied in different set-ups to ascertain their use as potential diagnostic markers for oral cancer. Elevation in salivary soluble CD44 levels have been found in most of the patients with oral squamous cell carcinoma. It offers a distinction between cancer and benign disease with high specificity (Franzmann et al., 2007). Significant rise in levels of salivary cytokeratin 19 fragment (Cyfra21–1), cancer antigen 125, and tissue polypeptide antigen have been reported in oral squamous cell carcinoma with comparable levels in the sera of these patients (Nagler et al., 2006). Positive correlation has also been found in the levels of p53 autoantibody in saliva with those in serum of oral squamous cell carcinoma patients and detection of p53 antibody in saliva may provide a specific method for detection of a subset of p53 aberrations associated with oral squamous cell carcinoma (Tavassoli et al., 1998). The discovery of these candidate biomarkers on an individual basis, however, limits their predicting power for oral squamous cell carcinoma detection.

High-throughput technologies have been utilized to shed light on the molecular mechanisms (genetic and epigenetic changes) driving the process of carcinogenesis in oral squamous cell carcinoma (Madhura et al., 2020).

Genomics

Intra- and intertumor heterogeneity exist in oral squamous cell carcinoma making it necessary to conduct genetic profiling for these tumors. Oral squamous cell carcinoma involves many chromosomal alterations such as loss at 3p, 9p, and 17p. Gains at chromosomes 3q, 6p, 8q, 11q, 16q, 16p, 17q, 17p, 19q, 2q, 4q, and of myc have also been reported. Next-generation sequencing, genome wide association studies and/or candidate gene signatures are employed to study the altered chromosomal loci. Extensive data on 264 identified loci associated with oral cancer is available on the web-based link "ORNATE". Of these, validation has been provided for 28 loci (Sharma et al., 2017).

Tight regulation of miRNA expression and correspondent DNA methylation patterns exist in normal oral mucosa. However, aberrant epigenetic and miRNA expression are noted in patients with oral squamous cell carcinoma. miR 375 is repressed and miR-127 activated in these patients. Epigenetic activation of miR 200 and miR 205 is also reported (Wiklund et al., 2011).

lncRNAs have gained importance in cancer biology in the last decade. They are non-protein coding RNAs of >200 nucleotides length. Dysregulation of these lncRNAs has been reported in oral squamous cell carcinoma which directly/indirectly affects the transcriptional translation of a target gene. LncRNA-UCA1 is said to play an oncogenic role through Wnt/β-catenin pathway (Lei et al., 2019) while lncRNA-MALAT1 has been proposed to promote tumor growth and metastasis via epithelial–mesenchymal transition (Tang et al., 2013).

Transcriptomics

The study of the entire set of RNA transcripts produced by the genome (transcriptome) is termed Transcriptomics. It is done by high-throughput techniques such as microarray technology, polymerase chain reaction, and next-generation sequencing. Transcriptomics can be carried out to study microRNAs and lncRNAs.

Levels of numerous probe sets for lncRNAs expressed in oral squamous cell carcinoma have been evaluated to elucidate the role they play in oral carcinogenesis. Differentially expressed lncRNA transcripts have been validated in three independent datasets from the Gene Expression Omnibus repository. These have further been verified by quantitative reverse transcriptase polymerase chain reaction (Feng et al., 2017).

Proteomics

A proteome represents the entire array of intracellular and secreted proteins expressed by a tissue or cell population. Protein analysis through testing biofluids like plasma, serum and saliva have aided in cancer diagnosis, prognostication, and ascertaining treatment response (Arantes et al., 2018).

Upregulation or downregulation of candidate genes is seen in the initiation and progression of oral squamous cell carcinoma by facilitating cell proliferation, cell differentiation, and evading cell death. Proteomics provides an accurate prediction of the altered marker protein functions. Salivary proteomics offers advantages over other biofluids as discussed earlier in the text.

Proteomic analysis is based on sublocalization of cellular proteins and their posttranslational modifications. The proteins related to the cell structure, motility, metabolism, signal transduction, and cell attachment are altered in oral squamous cell carcinoma. There is also upregulation of oncoprotein expression. It utilizes enzyme-linked immunosorbent assay, high-performance liquid chromatography, radioimmunoassay, mass spectrometry, two-dimensional gel electrophoresis, and liquid chromatography for the analysis to name a few.

Glutathione, TNF-α, interleukins (1a, 1b, 6, 8), IgG, p53 antibodies, CD44, CD59, Mac2 binding protein, S100 calcium-binding protein, transferrin, fibrin, MRP14 (a calcium binding protein), profilin, cancer antigen-125, albumin, cofilin-1, endothelin-1, telomerase, and α-amylase have been identified as proteomes in patients with oral squamous cell carcinoma (Lo et al., 2007; Hu et al., 2008).

Metabolomics

Metabolic pathways of tumors have been studied through Metabolomics in the biological system. A comparison between the metabolic profile of tumor and normal tissue is carried out. The metabolites commonly reported in cancers include sugars, polyamines, amino acids, nucleotides, bile, and organic acids. Changes in cell kinetics and genetic regulation are studied by analyzing small molecular weight compounds. This provides an insight into the cellular state in metabolomics (World Cancer Report, 2020).

Nuclear magnetic resonance spectroscopy, ultrahigh performance liquid chromatography-mass spectrometry and/or flight-liquid chromatography–mass spectrometry are the universal analytical tools used to detect and diagnose oral cancer and other metabolic disorders.

Serum metabolomic profile revealed an upregulation of 4–hydroxy penbutolol glucuronide, putrescine, 5,6–dihydrouridine, and 8–hydroxy adenine in oral leukoplakia and oral squamous cell carcinoma with a more significant rise seen in cancer patients when compared to those in oral leukoplakia.

8-Hydroxyadenine, Lysine, L-carnitine, putrescine, 2–methyl citric acid, 17–estradiol, and 5,6-dihydrouridine have served as diagnostic markers in oral precancer and oral cancer. Elevation in levels of 5,6-dihydrouridine, 8-hydroxyadenine, and putrescine in oral squamous cell carcinoma is a predictive marker for malignant transformation of oral leukoplakia (Sridharan et al., 2017).

Wang Q et al. reported an upregulation of eight metabolites in the saliva of oral squamous cell carcinoma patients that include lactic acid, hydroxyphenyl lactic acid, N-nonanoyl glycine, 5-hydroxymethyl uracil, succinic acid, ornithine, hexanoyl carnitine, and propionyl choline. While a downregulation of six metabolites namely carnitine, 4-hydroxy-L-glutamic acid, acetyl phenylalanine, sphinganine, phytosphingosine, and S-carboxymethyl-L-cysteine was reported by them. In their study, they found that 5 of these metabolites -propionyl choline, acetyl phenylalanine, sphinganine, phytosphingosine, and S-carboxymethyl-L-cysteine have a high clinical value in the early detection of oral squamous cell carcinoma (in stages I and II) (Wang et al., 2014).

Metabolomics provides important insights into cancer metabolism. However, more research in the field of metabolomics in oral cancer is required for a better understanding of cancer etiology.

Staging of oral squamous cell carcinoma

The size and extent of spread of the tumor are used to categorize patients such that they can be assigned to separate prognostic groups that help in planning the therapy for them.

In the 8th edition of the American Joint Committee on Cancer Staging Manual significant modifications were done from the previous edition of 2010 to provide uniformity across all sites. The major changes that were made in the staging of oral squamous cell carcinoma include:

1. The depth of invasion was added to the T category of oral squamous cell carcinoma for the primary tumor. Any T2 tumor with the depth of invasion beyond 10 mm was shifted to the T3 category (Kim and Lee, 2019). According to this, the tumors portraying a larger depth of invasion are associated with an enhanced risk of metastasis to

lymph nodes and a poorer prognosis. Also, it better reflected the invasive potential of the malignancy than the maximum dimension of the tumor.

2. A separate staging system was also added for the HPV+ve oral squamous cell carcinoma patients who were younger and healthier than the HPV−ve oral squamous cell carcinoma patients and had little or no tobacco exposure. A better response to therapy and thus a better prognosis was attached to cases of HPV+ve oral squamous cell carcinoma.

3. Extranodal extension (earlier known as extracapsular spread) is the spread of tumor beyond the lymph nodes. It was included to upstage the cases of oral squamous cell carcinoma that showed nodal metastasis adding one more category to Node classification. The extranodal extension seems to be an important prognostic factor in oral squamous cell carcinoma.

TNM classification for HPV−ve oral squamous cell carcinoma patients essentially stayed unchanged but for the removal of T0 from T classification—Nonviral T0 tumors can be from any site and thus cannot localize to oropharynx; N Classification was assigned a division of N3 based on extranodal extension (ENE) with N3a for lymph node >6 cm in dimension, no ENE and N3b was lymph node involvement with any ENE. In the M Classification: as ENE was now classified as N3b therefore there is a higher proportion of patients in the stage IVb group (Kim and Lee, 2019; Moeckelmann et al., 2018).

Moeckelmann et al. evaluated the prognostic capability of this new staging of oral squamous cell carcinoma and found that even though the new staging system improved the prognostication, its clinical relevance was still limited (Moeckelmann et al., 2018).

Eigth edition of tumor staging for lip and oral cavity cancers by the American Joint Committee on Cancer.

T classification

Tx	Tis	T1	T2	T3	T4
Primary tumor cannot be assessed	Carcinoma in situ	Size ≤2 cm and DOI ≤5 mm	Size ≤2 cm and DOI 5-≤10 mm or size 2-≤4 cm and DOI ≤10 mm	Size >4 cm or any tumor >10 mm DOI	Moderately advanced or very advanced disease T4a: moderately advanced disease with tumor invading adjacent structures only (cortical bone of maxilla or mandible or maxillary sinus or skin of the face) T4b: very advanced disease with tumor invading the masticator space, pterygoid plates, or skull base or encases internal carotid artery

DOI: Depth of invasion.

N classification

Clinical							Pathological
							Criteria for pathologic ENE (+): Oral cavity: only macroscopic (>2 mm)
N0	N1		N2			N3	
		N2a	N2b	N2c	N3a	N3b	
No LN involved and ENE (−)	Single ipsilateral LN ≤3 cm in size and ENE (−)	Single ipsilateral LN, 3-≤6 cm in size and ENE (−)	Multiple ipsilateral LNs, all ≤6 cm in size and ENE (−)	Any bilateral or contralateral LNs, all ≤6 cm in size and ENE (−)	LN >6 cm in size and ENE (−)	Any ENE (+), either clinical or radiographic	N1 and N2 are the same as previous and ENE (−) with exception: N2a includes lymph nodes ≤3 cm, ENE (+) LN. N3 now with subcategories: N3a is previous N3 (size >6 cm) and ENE (−) N3b: ≥3 cm and ENE (+) LN or >1 ENE (+) LNs

LN: Lymph Node; ENE: Extranodal Extension; Nx: regional lymph nodes cannot be assessed.

Distant metastasis (M)

M0	M1
No distant metastasis	Distant metastasis

cM1: metastasis found on imaging
pM1: biopsy-proven metastasis
Prognostic stage grouping for oral cavity cancers:

Stage	T	N	M categories
0	Tis	N0	M0
I	T1	N0	M0
II	T2	N0	M0
III	T3	N0	M0
	T1–3	N0–1	M0
IVA	T4a	N0–1	M0
	T1–4a	N2	M0
IVB	Any T	N3	M0
	T4b	any N	M0
IVC	Any T	any N	M1

A histologic grading was also issued for the cancers as
Gx: cannot be assessed
G1: well differentiated
G2: moderately differentiated
G3: poorly differentiated

15. Histopathological features

Subcategorization of squamous cell carcinoma is based on the differentiation status of the epithelium, and the presence of metastatic lesions as evidenced microscopically (Amôr et al., 2021). Oral squamous cell carcinoma exhibits different degrees of differentiation of the tumor cells where the well-differentiated form displays tumor cells closely resembling the normal squamous epithelial cells. This form, however, displays destruction of the basement membrane by the invading tumor cells and may reveal dyskeratosis, loss of polarity, disorganized growth, prominent nucleoli, increased nuclear–cytoplasmic ratio as features of dysplasia. At the other end of the spectrum, the poorly differentiated increased atypical mitosis and increased necrosis are displayed. The subepithelial connective tissue exhibits a lymphoplasmacytic infiltrate and a dense fibrous stroma. The presence of perineural invasion is an indicator of the tumor's metastatic potential (Ahmed et al., 2019).

The histological grading is a crucial adjunct in predicting the general biological behavior of the tumor. Generally, tumors that more closely resemble their native tissues are well-differentiated and tend to possess a far better long-term prognosis. In contrast, tumors with abundant amounts of cellular and nuclear alterations with little or no resemblance to the squamous epithelium or lacking keratin production could also be classified as poorly differentiated tumors. These lesions, also termed anaplastic or high grade, have an increased propensity for regional metastasis and correlate with a poor prognosis. Additional features that favor a more aggressive nature include perineural spread, lymphatic invasion, and tumor extension beyond the lymph gland capsule (WHO, 2017).

The one advantage of grading a tumor is that the grade reflects the anaplasticity of the lesion, which successively indicates the overall rapidity of growth, the rapidity of metastatic spread, the overall reaction to be expected after X-ray radiation and therefore, the prognosis.

Many models and scoring systems have been developed for predicting the biological behavior of oral squamous cell carcinoma. Broders' system (1920) was first established on the idea of the proportion of highly differentiated cells within the tumor.

Parameter	Characteristics
Grade I	0%–25% undifferentiated cells
Grade II	25%–50% undifferentiated cells
Grade II	50%–75% undifferentiated cells
Grade IV	75%–100% undifferentiated cells

This grading system is a poor predictor of growth, outcome, and survival of the patient (Broders, 1920).

Anneroth et al. (1987) gave a new grading system for oral cancer based on the characteristics of the tumor cell population and the tumor–host relationship where there highlighted the need for inclusion of parameters such as pattern of invasion as it displays the invasive characteristics of the malignancy. They also suggested that analysis of the lymphoplasmacytic infiltration should be done in an area away from ulceration and close to the frontline of the growing tumor cell population (Anneroth et al., 1987).

Histologic grading of malignancy of tumor cell population

Morphologic parameter	Points			
	1	2	3	4
Degree of keratinization	Highly keratinized (> 50% of the cells)	Moderately keratinized (20%–50% of the cells)	Minimal keratinization (5%–20% of the cells)	No keratinization (0%–5% of the cells)
Nuclear pleomorphism	Little nuclear polymorphism (>75% mature cells)	Moderately abundant nuclear polymorphism (50%–75% mature cells)	Abundant nuclear polymorphism (25%–50% mature cells)	Extreme nuclear polymorphism (0%–25% mature cells)
Number of mitotic figures/high power field (HPF)	0–1	2–3	4–5	>5

Histologic grading of malignancy of tumor–host relationship

Morphologic parameter	Points			
	1	2	3	4
Pattern of invasion	Pushing, well-delineated infiltrating borders	Infiltrating, solid cords, bands and/or strands	Small groups or cords of infiltrating cells ($n > 15$)	Marked and widespread cellular dissociation in small groups of cells [$n < 15$] and/or in single cells
Stage of invasion (depth)	Carcinoma in situ and/or questionable invasion	Distinct invasion, but involving lamina propria only	Invasion below lamina propria adjacent to muscles. salivary gland tissues and periosteum	Extensive and deep invasion replacing most of the stromal tissue and infiltrating jaw bone
Lymphoplasmacytic infiltration	Marked	Moderate	Slight	None

(Anneroth et al., 1987).

Bryne et al. (1992) presented a hypothesis suggesting that the molecular and morphological characteristics at the invasive front area of different squamous cell carcinomas may reflect tumor prognosis better than other parts of the tumor. Several molecular events of importance exist for tumor spread like gains and losses of adhesion molecules, secretion of proteolytic enzymes, increased cell proliferation and initiation of angiogenesis occur at the tumor–host interface. Consequently, there was a need to develop an easy morphological malignancy grading system that restricts the evaluation to the deep invasive front of the tumor. Several studies have shown that this technique may be a significantly better predictor of prognosis (Fig.15).

Morphometric parameters	1	2	3	4
Degree of keratinization	Highly (>50%)	Moderately (20%–50%)	Minimal (5%–20%)	None (0%–5%)
Nuclear pleomorphism	Little	Moderately	Abundant	Extreme
Number of mitosis	0–1	2–3	4–5	>5
Pattern of invasion	Pushing borders	Infiltrating cords/bands or strands	Small cell groups (number > 15)	Single cell/tiny groups (number < 15)
Lymphocytic infiltrate	Marked	Moderate	Small	None

(Bryne et al., 1992).

Brandwein-Gensler et al. put forward a highly predictive histologic risk scoring scheme which presented a rationale for adjuvant radiation therapy (RT) at the primary tumor site. They studied the pattern of invasion as proposed by Bryne et al. and added a type 5 for tumor infiltrate exhibiting a widely dispersed pattern. This pattern includes tumor satellites (of any size) at the tumor/host interface that showed a 1 mm or greater distance of intervening normal tissue (not exhibiting fibrosis).

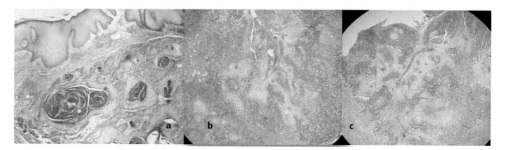

Fig. 15 Photomicrographs of oral squamous cell carcinoma (A) Well differentiated (4×, H&E) (B) Moderately differentiated (4×, H&E) (C) Poorly differentiated (4×, H&E).

Variable	Grade
Pattern of invasion	Type 1: pushing border
	Type 2: finger-like growth pattern
	Type 3: large separate islands, >15 cells/island
	Type 4: small tumor islands, ≤ 15 cells/island
	Type 5: tumor satellites, ≥ 1 mm intervening normal tissue not exhibiting any fibrosis
Lymphocytic infiltrate	Pattern 1: continuous and dense rim of lymphoid tissue at tumor–host interface.
	Pattern 2: patches of dense lymphoid infiltrate at tumor–host interface with discontinuities along the interface. (Any lymphoid patch warranted a lymphocyte pattern 2)
	Pattern 3: limited response without any lymphoid patches/no lymphoid response.
Perineural invasion	None
	Small nerves (<1 mm diameter)
	Large nerves (≥ 1 mm diameter)
	Not evaluated
Keratinization	Most (>50%)—1
	Intermediate (<50%)—2
	Least (<10%)—3
Nuclear grade	Well—1
	Intermediate—2
	Poor—3
Foreign body reaction	None
	Any (1 or more High Power Field)
	Not evaluated
Eosinophilia	None
	Any (1 or more High Power Field)
	Not evaluated
Lymphatic or vascular tumor emboli	None
	1 or 2 vessels
	3 or more vessels
	Not evaluated
Carcinoma in situ in mucosa adjacent to tumor	No slides
	1 slide
	More than 1 slide
	Not evaluated

Local recurrence and overall survival were strongly associated with the worst pattern of invasion (assigned as the highest score for the pattern of invasion found, no matter how focal), perineural invasion, and lymphocytic response. The worst pattern of invasion exhibited a significant association with the N status at the time of presentation. Local recurrence was common in patients with a limited/weak lymphocytic response. A significant association was found between overall survival and perineural invasion involving small and large nerves while local recurrence was more common with a peri-neural invasion of large nerves (Brandwein-Gensler et al., 2005).

In their study of the evaluation of the prognostic value of common histopathological variables, Bjerkli et al. proposed a new grading system for squamous cell carcinoma of the tongue. Tumor differentiation and lymphocytic infiltration were used to create a combined score which they termed histoscore with the lowest score being given as 2 and highest as 6.

Variables with original and alternative grading proposed by Bjerkli et al.

Tumor Characteristics	Original grading	Alternative grading
1.0 Differentiation whole tumor	Well	1.1 Low-grade
	Moderate	
	Poorly	High-grade
2.0 Differentiation worst pattern	Well	2.1 Low-grade
	Moderate	
	Poorly	High-grade
3.0 Keratinization in whole tumor	High	3.1 Low-grade
	Moderate	
	Minimal	High-grade
	None	
4.0 Keratinization at tumor front (as per Bryne classification)	High	4.1 Low-grade
	Moderate	
	Minimal	High-grade
	None	
5.0 Polymorphism in whole tumor	Little/none	5.1 Low-grade
	Moderate	
	Abundant	High-grade
	Extreme	
6.0 Polymorphism at tumor front (as per Bryne classification)	Little/none	6.1 Low-grade
	Moderate	
	Abundant	High-grade
	Extreme	
7.0 Perineural invasion	None	7.1 No
	Invasive front	
	Tumor center	Yes
8.0 Lymphocytic infiltrate	Marked	8.1 Marked/Abundant
	Moderate	Not Marked/Little
	Little/none	
9.0 Worst pattern of invasion (as per Brandwein-Gensler classification	Type 1: pushing border	9.1 Low grade
	Type 2: finger-like growth pattern	
	Type 3: large separate islands, >15 cells/island	
	Type 4: small tumor islands, ≤15 cells/island	High grade
	Type 5: tumor satellites, ≥1 mm from main tumor/satellite	

They studied the 5 years of disease-specific survival by correlating with the clinico-pathological characteristics of gender, age group, pT, and N status of the patient (based on the 8th edition of AJCC staging of cancers) as well as the stage of malignancy. Results revealed an overall 64.8% disease-specific survival with 82.8% survival in the low-stage group and 44.6% in the high-stage group. A significant association was found between disease-specific survival and differentiation of the whole tumor (original and alternate grading), nuclear polymorphism whole tumor (original and alternate grading), nuclear polymorphism at tumor front (alternate grading), and lymphocytic infiltrate (original and alternate grading) in low stage cancer patients (Bjerkli et al., 2020).

16. Treatment

Treatment of oral squamous cell carcinoma is governed by the basic principles of oncology, despite the disease subsite and pathology. Stages I and II disease should be addressed with single modality treatment, whereas Stages III and IV warrant a combined modality approach. Choice of modality (surgical versus nonsurgical) depends on the intent of treatment, chances of cure, accessibility, and resectability of the disease, impact on quality of life, and the patient's general health profile.

Surgery is usually recommended for the initial management of patients with early-stage oral squamous cell carcinoma, but many patients present with locally advanced disease that precludes resection. This is often a common presentation in cancers of other subsites also.

16.1 Surgical resection

Surgery is the mainstay for treating oral cancers. The aim of surgery is a complete removal of the primary tumor and appropriate clearance of regional lymph nodes, without compromising the integrity of the uninvolved structures.

Management of primary lesion

The surgical plan should involve a wide excision of the tumor with adequate margins to account for histopathological shrinkage (approximately 25%). The following table shows the adequacy of margins for resection of oral primary:

Negative margin	>5 mm
Close margin	1–5 mm
Positive margin	<1 mm/tumor cut through (Gupta et al., 2019)

An intraoperative frozen section evaluation is an effective means to evaluate removal of the entire lesion prior to closure at the time of surgical intervention. They provide instant pathological information to guide intraoperative surgical decision-making like adequacy of margins, and identification of nodal metastases (Byers et al., 1978).

Management of neck nodes

Five-year survival rates fall by 50% in the presence of lymphatic metastases from an 80% survival seen in early-stage localized disease. A further reduction of survival by 50% exists in cases with extranodal extension (Pantvaidya et al., 2020).

An elective neck dissection is now the standard procedure for treating all oral cancers. Regional metastases risk correlates with the thickness of the tumor, site, size, and histological features. The involvement of regional lymph nodes in primary oral cancers occurs in a predictable and sequential fashion (Spiro et al., 1986). The initial spread from carcinoma occurs to node levels I, II, III. Involvement of Level IV nodes is usually implicated in the tongue and the floor of the mouth cancers. Isolated skip metastases to Level V are quite rare and usually seen in tongue cancers. Lateral neck dissection is required in some patients. A selective (supraomohyoid) neck dissection clearing Levels I, II, III and IV is considered appropriate for many primary oral cancers with clinicoradiological N0 neck. The extent of neck dissection varies consistently with the clinicoradiological staging of nodal disease (Shah, 1990).

Surgical management of cervical nodes is linked to two main controversies—the role played by prophylactic neck dissections in N0 early oral cancers, and the extent of neck dissection done for both N+ and N0 patients.

Sentinel node biopsy has gained much interest as an alternative to prophylactic neck dissection in N0 patients. It is reliable and oncologically safe and is associated with reduced morbidity when compared to elective neck dissection. Its wider applicability has been limited for want of resources, expertise, and a steep learning curve for accurate result interpretation (Schilling et al., 2015).

Tumor subsite and pattern of nodal metastasis dictate the extent of neck dissection done in oral squamous cell carcinoma. Patients with large nodes and extranodal extension are managed by radical neck dissections (Ferlito et al., 2010). Selective neck dissections are preferred over modified neck dissections in patients with clinicoradiologic N0 necks (Brentani et al., 1999). However, no consensus exists on the extent of the neck dissection and the need to dissect level IV while performing a prophylactic neck dissection (Pantvaidya et al., 2020).

16.2 Chemotherapy

Adjuvant chemotherapy

The primary treatment modality for patients with carcinoma is surgery, when possible, without undue morbidity. Adjuvant chemotherapy is given postsurgery for reducing the incidence of metastatic recurrence.

Adjuvant chemoradiotherapy

Studies are being conducted to validate the use of concurrent chemotherapy and radiation. In this form of therapy, chemotherapy is given as a radiation sensitizer to reduce radiation resistance. This approach has been found to be superior to the use of radiation alone in patients with an increased risk of recurrence.

The utilization of chemoradiation should be considered on a case-by-case basis for patients with 1 or more high-risk features aside from extracapsular extension of nodal metastases or positive margins. Significant risks include renal failure, deafness, tinnitus, nausea, vomiting, and peripheral neuropathy. Furthermore, data clearly indicates that radiation complications (both acute and chronic) are more common in patients treated with chemotherapy. Because of these issues, considerable interest has been generated in alternatives to high-dose cisplatin.

Cetuximab (antibody directed against the epidermal protein receptor) given with the chemotherapy agent, docetaxel (prescribed as a weekly schedule) is being currently investigated as a primary treatment of locally advanced unresectable carcinoma. Currently, there is no standard treatment optimization for use with adjuvant chemoradiation (Hartner, 2018).

Primary chemoradiation

The utilization of combined chemotherapy and radiation has been studied extensively for the treatment of locally advanced oral and other head and neck cancer. Primary chemoradiation plays a major role in the management of unresectable oral squamous cell carcinoma. Compared with radiation alone, it improves survival and reduces the danger of recurrence (Stenson et al., 2010).

Induction chemotherapy

Induction chemotherapy is the chemotherapy administered before definitive local therapy. This is prescribed as combination chemotherapy, the advantages of which include reduction in metastatic recurrence and downsizing the primary tumor to enhance locoregional control. Studies have shown the efficacy of using cisplatin, 5-FU, docetaxel, carboplatin, and hydroxyurea. Further validation is required to clearly define the role of induction chemotherapy in patients with locally advanced oral squamous cell carcinomas (Vermorken et al., 2007).

In the management of metastatic disease

Significant changes have been made in the management of metastatic oral carcinoma over the past several years. Although metastatic disease is an uncommon occurrence in patients, classically, treatment options are limited, and favorable responses are not common.

Treatment regimens involving use of cisplatin or carboplatin are considered standard chemotherapy for the treatment of metastatic disease. These drugs are generally used as single agents, but within the front-line setting, these are mostly used in combination with other chemotherapy agents like 5-FU, docetaxel, and paclitaxel (Gibson et al., 2005). No convincing evidence exists that supports any efficacy difference between these two agents, although there are clear differences in their side effects. Myelosuppression is a complication that is more commonly seen with carboplatin than cisplatin and cisplatin-related complications of neuropathy, hearing toxicity, and acute kidney injury have also been reported. For these reasons, carboplatin is usually utilized in the treatment of patients with metastatic disease (Hartner, 2018).

A study by Vermorken et al. revealed that a platinum-based combination chemotherapy regimen has a higher response rate with combination therapy but there is no evidence that its use improves survival compared with the use of single-agent chemotherapy. In addition to its role as a radiation sensitizer for patients with locally advanced disease, cetuximab has been studied within the treatment of metastatic disease. To improve treatment outcomes within the first-line treatment setting, study was conducted by combining cetuximab with platinum-based combination chemotherapy regimens in previously untreated patients (Vermorken et al., 2008).

Panitumumab, a human antibody also directed against the epidermal protein receptor, has been studied for treatment efficacy in metastatic head and neck cancers in combination with chemotherapy with cisplatin and fluorouracil. Currently, this agent does not have a significant role in improving the overall survival of recurrent or metastatic head and neck cancers. It, however, has an acceptable toxicity profile that improves the progression-free survival in these patients (Vermorken et al., 2013).

Many options for therapy exist for patients who exhibit progression following front-line chemotherapy. These include cytotoxic chemotherapy, programmed necrobiosis (PD)-1 inhibitors, cetuximab, and little molecule tyrosine kinase inhibitors. Choice of treatment depends on prior treatment history, performance status, and therefore the presence or absence of serious medical comorbid illnesses. Out of those, PD-1 inhibitors are found to enhance survival during this treatment setting.

Approved agents so far include nivolumab, pembrolizumab, and atezolizumab. Both nivolumab and pembrolizumab have been shown to be effective in treating recurrent and metastatic head and neck cancers and both are currently FDA approved.

As there are no comparative studies to guide treatment decisions, the choice of agent depends on previous treatment history and differences in expected toxicity between the agents. Recurrent and metastatic head and neck cancer carry the potential for considerable morbidity combined with short survival. Comfort care and hospice should be preferred overactive therapy when appropriate (Hartner, 2018).

16.3 Nanotechnology in carcinoma therapy

The aim of cancer therapy is to exert cytotoxic effect on the cancer cells without deleterious effects on normal healthy cells. The interaction of nanotechnology with medicine, physics, mathematics, and biology has given rise to the new field of nanomedicine.

Nanotechnology-based systems are emerging in cancer therapy to optimize oral, buccal, and intravenous treatment routes. Nanoparticle systems have demonstrated high drug carrier capabilities and site-specific drug accumulation in tumors.

Nanoparticles are reported as suitable carriers of chemotherapeutic compounds, nucleic acids, and diagnostic agents for both diagnostic and therapeutic purposes. These can provide better stability to the chemotherapeutic agent and control its delivery to the target site, enabling a constant and uniform concentration of the drug at the site of a lesion. They also facilitate drug extravasation into the tumor system, thus reducing side effects (Calixto et al., 2014).

Targeted delivery to cervical lymph nodes via perioral cancer submucosal injection of cucurbitacin BE polylactic acid nanoparticles (CuBE-PLA-NPs) was evaluated along with the efficacy of this clinical therapy by Yang et al. in 2003. Their study revealed that the drug concentrations in cervical lymph nodes after CuBE-PLA-NP injection were much higher than those in the control group. Also, the blood drug concentrations in the CuBE-PLA-NP group were much lower than those in the control group (Yang et al., 2003).

Chemoprevention using nanoparticles

Chemoprevention for oral squamous cell carcinoma employs drugs to reverse, prevent or suppress malignant transformation of preneoplastic cells. Natural plant compounds like flavonoids and stilbenes have received great attention. Curcumin, genistein (Aditya et al., 2013), and naringenin (Sulfikkarali et al., 2013) hold promising antitumor activity in a preclinical setup. However, bioactive plant compounds have poor bioavailability and poor solubility, which reduces their efficacy in clinical studies. To overcome this problem, nanoparticle-based chemoprevention is being explored preclinically (Calixto et al., 2014).

16.4 Radiotherapy

Radiotherapy (radiation therapy) is a localized treatment employed alone for early-stage tumors or for patients who cannot have surgery. It can be used presurgery to kill cancer cells and shrink the tumor or postsurgery to destroy cancer cells left behind in the treated area.

Radiotherapy works by damaging the DNA of rapidly dividing cells such that the standard mechanisms of DNA repair (which are usually less effective in cancer cells compared to normal cells) cannot work and therefore the cells die. However, normal cells that proliferate rapidly such as hair, salivary glands, and oral mucosa are also adversely affected by therapeutic radiation. Conventional radiotherapy uses high-energy photons to kill cancer cells.

Radiotherapy is commonly used as teletherapy, where the radiation is produced by an external beam (linear accelerator) machine. A 5 days-a-week regimen of radiotherapy is done for several weeks as an outpatient procedure. Alternatively, radiotherapy can be given in the form of brachytherapy (implant therapy) where the radiation is delivered by seeds, needles, or carried via thin plastic tubes and put directly into the tissue. The patient must stay in the hospital for the duration of the implant therapy, typically several days. Some patients require both types, i.e., External Beam Radiotherapy and Brachytherapy for the same cancer (Glenny et al., 2010).

Use of immunotherapies, super-selective intra-arterial chemotherapy, and photo-immunotherapy have recently been added to the treatment regimen. However, some unresolved issues exist with respect to therapy resistance and metastasis. To overcome these issues, using tumoroids, saliva biopsies, genomics, and epigenomics are currently key approaches (Eguchi, 2020).

16.5 Immunotherapy

The introduction of immunotherapy as a treatment option in recent years for oral squamous cell carcinoma is based on the ability of the immune system to suppress the cancer cells thus aiding in patient recovery. (Adams et al., 2015) Immunotherapy approvals were first given for the treatment of recurrent and metastatic oral squamous cell carcinomas (Zandberg et al., 2019). Later neoadjuvant immunotherapy was added to the preoperative treatment regimen (Schoenfeld et al., 2020).

Cancer immunotherapy is considered an important pillar of treatment for cancers. The understanding of the immune system–tumor cells interplay has facilitated the development of pathbreaking treatment strategies (Rothschild et al., 2015).

Cytokines

A cell-derived mixture of cytokines, IRX-2, is a combination of interleukins-1β, IL-2, IL-6 and IL-8, tumor necrosis factor-α, interferon-γ, and granulocyte as well as granulocyte-macrophage colony-stimulating factors (G-CSF and GM-CSF). Preclinical study models have revealed morphologic, functional, and phenotypic changes with IRX-2 treatment of human monocyte-derived dendritic cells with development of the mature activated dendritic cells that can stimulate T cells and enhance interleukin-12 production (Egan et al., 2007; Schilling et al., 2013). This cytokine mixture has also been found to decrease levels of immunosuppressive cytokines (interleukin-10, transforming growth factor-β) within the tumor and increase levels of interferon-γ (Schilling et al., 2013). In an early clinical trial, preoperative peritumoral injection of IRX-2 was administered in 27 patients where these subcutaneous immunotherapy injections were given over a period of 10 days as two bilateral injections in the mastoid region of the left and right neck, close to the regional nodes. This therapy was combined with a single infusion of a noncytotoxic dose of cyclophosphamide ($300\,mg/m^2$) on day 1, daily zinc gluconate (24 mg once daily) and oral indomethacin (25 mg three times daily). Minimal toxicity was produced with this neoadjuvant immunotherapy regimen that was well tolerated and resulted in a reduction in tumor size in 45.8% of patients. An overall survival rate of 92% was reported at 12 months and the survival rate at 24 and 36 months was 73% and 69% respectively.

A randomized phase II trial [INSPIRE trial (NCT02609386)] by Gregory T Wolf as principal investigator is currently underway for investigating the neoadjuvant IRX-2 regimen in patients with stage II to IVA resectable oral squamous cell carcinoma in Switzerland (Wolf et al., 2011).

Promising results have been seen with cytokine immunotherapeutic strategies in HNSCC patients. Targeted cytokine therapy with chimeric constructs is a more tumor-specific treatment modality that is potentially less toxic as lower doses of cytokines are required. This approach is currently being tested in early phase clinical trials (Uta et al., 2018).

Toll-like receptors

Pattern-recognition receptors, Toll-like receptors (TLRs) function to recognize pathogen-associated molecules and play a major role in mediating the immune response. These receptors are found on immune cells, and they elicit a local protective inflammatory response to binding pathogenic molecules like lipopolysaccharide and double-stranded RNA. In certain circumstances the toll-like receptors may induce cell proliferation as well as activation of NF-κB signaling pathway acting as promoter of tumor progression. They also prompt resistance to natural killer cells (Szczepanski et al., 2009). Preclinical models have demonstrated profound immune stimulatory effects of the agonists of toll-like receptors (Uta et al., 2018). A small molecule TLR-8 agonist, Motolimod (VTX-2337), activates monocytes, dendritic cells and natural killer cells (Dietsch et al., 2016). In their phase Ib study in patients with HNSCC, Chow et al. combined motolimod with cetuximab and validated a 50% disease control rate and an overall response rate of 17% (Chow et al., 2017). Based on these data and preclinical work a randomized phase II trial for evaluating the additional benefit of motolimod with the EXTREME regimen (NCT01836029) is currently under investigation (Uta et al., 2018).

Immune checkpoint inhibitors

Monoclonal antibodies targeting a broad range of immune checkpoint receptors have been investigated in clinical trials for the treatment of cancers. Immune checkpoint inhibitors do not target cancer cells directly, instead, they bind with the receptors or their ligands on immune cells. This helps them in modulating the activity of these cells. This action is quite contrasting to that of the conventional tumor cell–directed antibodies or chemotherapeutic agents (Uta et al., 2018). Interestingly, these immune checkpoint inhibitors might induce long-lasting remissions in advanced and metastatic solid tumors even after discontinuation of therapy (Robert et al., 2017).

The exact role of CTLA-4 inhibitors in squamous cell carcinoma of the head and neck region is still under investigation. In a study by Jie et al., cetuximab was shown to increase CTLA-4 expression in the majority of intratumoral Tregs. Also, the CTLA-4 inhibitor, ipilimumab resulted in decreasing the suppression of natural killer cells from Tregs (Jie et al., 2015). Investigation of a combinant therapy using Ipilimumab and tremelimumab with cetuximab and radiotherapy in patients with advanced cases of head and neck squamous cell carcinoma is going on.

Immune checkpoint activators

Immune checkpoint activators produce an immunostimulatory effect by activating the TNF- receptors on T cells. Their action contrasts with that of the inhibitory checkpoint receptor antibodies (Croft et al., 2013). The stimulatory checkpoint receptors along with their ligands that have been studied extensively include CD137 (4-1BB ligand), OX40 (OX40-ligand), and CD27 (CD70). Activated T cells express OX40, the activating antibody stimulation of which suppresses the apoptosis carried out by T cells. Cytokines with an immunostimulatory action are also produced. In their clinical trial in head and neck squamous cell carcinoma patients in stage II-IVA, Duhen et al. found it safe to administer an anti-OX40 antibody (MEDI6469) at various intervals preoperatively. They found that elevation of peripheral blood CD4+ and CD8$^+$ T-cell activation and proliferation was found in majority of these patients. Few patients showed the expansion of CD103+ CD39+ CD8+ tumor immune lymphocytes. These correlate with greater disease-free survival. Clinical trial testing of humanized OX40 agonist (MEDI0562) in the neo-adjuvant setting in head and neck squamous cell carcinoma and melanoma patients is currently being conducted to assess the agonist activity of an anti-OX40 antibody independent of antidrug immune responses (Duhen et al., 2021). Agonistic antibody against CD137, Urelumab that is expressed on the surface of different immune cells including natural killer cells is being investigated in a phase I study in combination with cetuximab in patients with squamous cell carcinoma of the head and neck region and colorectal carcinoma (NCT02110082). Srivastava et al. have already shown that urelumab enhances cetuximab-activated natural killer cell survival, dendritic cell maturation, and tumor antigen cross-presentation in their preclinical study (Srivastava et al., 2017). Ongoing investigations included one with Varlilumab (a CD27 agonist) in combination with nivolumab (NCT02335918), as well as with atezolizumab (NCT02543645) and the JAVELIN Medley trial (NCT02554812) [phase Ib/II trial] where inhibitory antibody against PD-L1 avelumab is being studied with different cancer immunotherapies including PF-04518600 and the anti–4-1BB antibody utomilumab (Uta et al., 2018).

Identification of markers predictive of immunotherapy response will play a pivotal role in the future as they would enable better characterization of patients who would benefit from these medications. Different phases of immune response can be targeted by combining different immunotherapeutic approaches. This would eventually lead to improved response and better outcome as opposed to monotherapy.

16.6 Therapeutic markers

Circulating tumor *cells* have been used to determine the therapy targets as well. Positive cell surface expression of the epidermal growth factor receptor has shown promising results with cetuximab therapy in head and neck cancer (Tinhofer et al., 2012).

Circulating tumor *DNA* could be used reliably to monitor tumor dynamics due to its ability to provide insight into rapid changes in tumor size in cancer patients undergoing chemotherapy and/or surgery. Their levels have also been used to detect the minimal residual disease following surgery and predict relapse in oral squamous cell carcinoma (Hamana et al., 2005). Large clinical trials need to be carried out to determine whether the identification of minimal residual disease-positive patients could help improve patient outcomes by early therapeutic interventions (Nonaka and Wong, 2018).

Many *miRNAs* have been evaluated in patients with oral squamous cell carcinoma. Study reports reveal that elevated levels of miRNA-31, miRNA-139-5p, and miRNA-184 found in oral cancer patients were greatly reduced postsurgery, indicative of these biomarkers being expressed by the tumor tissue (Liu et al., 2012; Duz et al., 2016; Wong et al., 2008).

Nonmetastatic oral squamous cell carcinoma samples exhibit upregulation of MiR-130b, while metastatic tumors displayed miR-296 expression. These were confirmed in the plasma of these respective patients (Severino et al., 2015). A worse prognosis is assigned to those patients with head and neck cancers who express high levels of miR-142-3p, miR-186-5p, miR-195-5p, miR-374b-5p, and miR-574-3p (Summerer et al., 2015).

Vermorken et al. found that levels of *p16 expression* acted as prognostic and predictive markers in patients treated with panitumumab and chemotherapy, but it requires further validation (Vermorken et al., 2013).

Evasion of the immune response: development and progression of squamous cell carcinoma can be checked by eliciting an appropriate immune response. Thus, the evasion of immune response can be used as a target for immune therapy.

  a. A potent antitumoral response was generated by blocking PD-1 (required for T-cell activation) in a chemically induced squamous cell carcinoma model in mice where the infiltration of activated CD4$^+$ and CD8$^+$ T cells, IFN-γ levels, and reduction in the levels of the immunosuppressive cytokine TGF-β was reported (Belai et al., 2014). Currently, two immunotherapies for squamous cell carcinoma (i.e., pembrolizumab and cemiplimab) have received approval from the FDA that target the interaction between PD-1/PD-L1 molecules (Amôr et al., 2021).

  b. Another relevant strategy for immunotherapy is the inhibition of Tregs recruitment or their differentiation through antagonistic antibodies against CCR5 or neutralizing antibodies against TGF-β. Dodagatta-Marri et al. found complete regression in established tumors in 60% cases with a combination of α-PD-1 therapy and anti–TGF-β therapy. Their study highlighted the beneficial effects of combinatory immunotherapies for cutaneous squamous cell carcinomas (Dodagatta-Marri et al., 2019).

c. Macrophage-based therapies pose a challenge because of the plasticity of these cells (as M1 macrophages easily switch for M2 phenotype when stimulated) (Linde et al., 2012). A sustained M1 differentiation is required to overcome this. It has been found that nanoparticles containing IL-12 foster conversion of M2 macrophage to the M1 phenotype in the tumor microenvironment (Amôr et al., 2021).

Autophagy: Targeting autophagy is showing promising results in improving the outcomes of cancer therapy. Autophagy may enhance the efficacy of some anticancer agents; conversely, it could also promote cell survival by maintaining bioenergetics following exposure to chemotherapeutic agents (Carew et al., 2007). The study by Carew JS et al. has revealed that the disruption of autophagy amplifies the effectiveness of anticancer agents (Carew et al., 2008). In order to devise new and efficient therapeutic strategies for oral cancer, more detailed exploration is required into the autophagy landscape to identify novel targets (Alexandra et al., 2020). Autophagy inhibition would also help in reversing chemoresistance in cancer therapy. Sulfasalazine, Tetrandrine, and thymoquinone have been shown to induce cell death via autophagic cell death induction in oral cancer cells, thus providing an alternative approach to therapy (Han et al., 2014; Huang et al., 2013; Chu et al., 2014).

Cancer stem cells: According to the cancer stem cell hypothesis, for effective treatment of cancer, the cancer stem cells should be eliminated by targeting the signal pathways involved in their formation that include Notch (Pannuti et al., 2010), Wnt (Takahashi-Yanaga and Kahn, 2010), and Hedgehog (Takezaki et al., 2011). Pharmaceutical drug formulations are being devised that would selectively target the cancer stem cells and spare the normal stem cells. This could be crucial for the future application of cancer stem cell therapy. By altering the intracellular environment through modification of the ROS status of cancer stem cells, apoptotic signals can be generated (Smith et al., 2000). Knockdown of *CD44* can help make the cancer stem cells more chemosensitive (Thomson et al., 1998). Also, selectively targeting tumor angiogenesis can also reduce the fraction of the cancer stem cells (Krishnamurthy et al., 2010). More research is required in these spheres.

Shah et al. proposed a multistrategic approach to improve morbidity and mortality in oral squamous cell carcinoma patients. Debulking of the tumor through conventional therapy must be combined with therapy to target the cancer stem cells. This could help prevent recurrence and metastasis (Shah et al., 2014).

17. Prognosis

At present, the clinical and histopathological parameters are mostly employed for designing the treatment strategies also as determining the prognosis of carcinoma patients. The poor prognosis of oral squamous cell carcinoma is attributed to lower response rate to conventional therapy, diagnosis in advanced stages, high risk of recurrence of the primary tumor, aggressive regional lymph node metastasis. All these warrant improvements in the existing diagnostic and therapeutic modalities (Patel et al., 2014).

17.1 Clinical factors

a. Ethnicity:

A disproportionately poorer survival is linked to certain ethnic groups, specifically African Americans in whom the mortality rates from oral cancer are nearly twice as high as in whites. Also, black males usually present with more advanced, aggressive forms of disease and a lower percentage of HPV-positive disease compared to their white counterparts. Patients with HPV-associated oropharyngeal cancer have a better prognosis than patients with HPV-negative oropharyngeal cancer or oral cavity cancer (Moeckelmann et al., 2018; World Cancer Report, 2020).

b. Anatomic location:

There exists regional variation in histology, vascular supply, and lymphatic networks within the mouth. Ease of visual examination of the location may also influence the diagnosis. It is a general belief that anterior sites in the oral cavity generally have a better prognosis ascribed to them. This is related to the nodal drainage and the surgical management at the local site. The posterior third of the tongue has bilateral drainage whereas the anterior part has a unilateral one. Also, the anterior region of the oral cavity drains to the upper cervical nodes as associated with a better prognosis when compared to the posterior part of the oral cavity which drains to the deeper cervical nodes (Omar, 2013).

c. TNM staging:

Studies have demonstrated a decisive role of TNM staging in the prognostic outcome and long-term survival of carcinoma cases. Diagnosis at an earlier stage (I, II) compared with that at a late or advanced stage (III, IV) would improve survival (Warnakulasuriya, 2014). A replacement staging system was proposed by Lee et al. which has shown better disease-free survival discrimination and skill to spot high-risk group patients with oral squamous cell carcinoma. They proposed an integer-based weighted point system for categorize the 5-year disease-specific survival. The reference normal for each variable was allotted a value of 0. Individual scores were given by adding up the individual risk factor points (perineural invasion—1 point; neutrophil-lymphocyte ratio—1 point; advanced pT—1 point; and advanced pN—3 points). The new staging category thus created was as follows: new stage I (score of 0), new stage II (score of 1), new stage III (score of 2 or 3) and new stage IV (score of 4–6). In comparison with the American Joint Committee on Cancer staging system, the new staging categories showed a far better discriminatory ability for a 5-year disease-specific survival (Lee et al., 2017).

d. Tumor volume (tumor thickness):

Tumor volume is often assessed by imaging scans or by macroscopically measuring the surgical specimen. This reflects the aggressiveness of the tumor proliferation. It was possible to predict disease-free and overall survival of patients based on tumor volume in advanced cases(T4a) of oral squamous cell carcinoma. Lymph node metastasis is closely linked to tumor volume. Metastasis to ipsilateral nodes is associated with a better prognosis compared to that to contralateral ones (Omar, 2013).

17.2 Histopathological factors

a. Histopathological differentiation:

Tumor differentiation influences the prognostic outcome. Higher differentiation often indicates a poorer prognosis. Kolokythas et al. showed that the grade of differentiation also as a degree of keratin expression in carcinomas of the tongue was associated with poor outcomes (Kolokythas et al., 2015).

Bjerkli et al. found that the differentiation of the whole tumor (alternate grading) and perineural infiltration (original grading) were the only prognostic indicators for disease-specific survival in high stage patients. (Bjerkli et al., 2020).

b. Histopathological grading systems:

The prognostic significance of the different grading systems used for oral squamous cell carcinoma are varied. Broders' was the primary grading system proposed for determining the prognosis of oral squamous cell carcinoma. However, a scarcity of correlation between Broders' grades and prognosis has been observed as the malignant squamous cells usually exhibit a heterogeneous population with differences in the degree of differentiation and tumor–host relationship is not considered in Broders' grading. Bryne's grading system was found to possess a prognostic significance in a study by Dissanayake (Dissanayake, 2017).

c. Tumor thickness:

Tumor thickness measured in pathology specimens has been used as a prognostic factor. T1 and T2 cancers generally present a median tumor thickness of 1.5–8 mm (Warnakulasuriya, 2014). The ratio of tumor margin to tumor thickness ratio was proposed as an independent predictor of regional recurrence and disease-specific mortality by Ganly et al. In their study they revealed that low-risk, pT1-T2N0 squamous cell carcinoma of oral tongue had a greater than expected rate of neck failure, with contralateral recurrence accounting for close to 40% of recurrences. A failure occurred predominantly in patients with primary tumors of thickness ≥ 4 mm (Ganly et al., 2013).

d. Depth of invasion:

Depth of invasion (DOI) is the distance between the basement membrane of the normal mucosa closest to malignancy and the deepest point of tumor invasion. In their study, Kane et al. revealed that microscopic tumor depth is a critical histologic predictor of cervical lymph node metastasis in early oral cancers. Patients with early cancers with a tumor depth ≥ 5 mm were found to have a greater risk of harboring neck node metastasis associated with them (Kane et al., 2006). The 8th Edition of the American Joint Committee on Cancer Staging Manual has incorporated depth of invasion in the staging of oral cancers.

Gupta NK et al. found a poor prognosis in patients with greater depth of invasion and involvement of the extrinsic tongue muscles (Gupta et al., 2019).

e. Surgical margins:

A space of 5 mm or more that is clear from the invasive tumor cells is assigned as clear surgical margins by the UK Royal College of Pathologists. A clearance of 1–5 mm is termed close and < 1 mm is considered a positive or involved margin (Luryi et al., 2014). There is a significant increase in the risk of local recurrence in cases of incomplete resection where the margins are involved or show signs of dysplasia (Warnakulasuriya, 2014). Garzino-Demo et al. demonstrated that 5-year survival in patients with positive margins was 48% in contrast to the 65% survival rate seen in patients with negative margins (Garzino-Demo et al., 2006).

f. Tumor invasion:

The invasive front of a tumor is of great importance as the tumor cells at the invading edge are relatively more proliferative compared to those in the superficial part. The correlation between survival and invasive front revealed that a better invasive front grading (tumor islands with >15 versus <15 tumor cells) was related to overall poor survival (Brandwein-Gensler et al., 2005).

g. Tumor budding:

A pattern of aggressive growth of carcinomas at the invasive front is seen with single or small clusters of tumor cells. This feature is significantly related to the general survival of the oral squamous cell carcinoma patients and has been proposed as an independent prognostic indicator (Almangush et al., 2014). Tumor budding is found to be a good predictor of clinically node-negative oral squamous cell carcinoma cases. Angadi et al. reported high-intensity tumor budding to be a robust independent prognostic factor for the prediction of lymph gland metastasis (Angadi et al., 2015).

h. Perineural and vascular invasion:

Vascular invasion is characterized by the presence of neoplastic cells within the lumen or wall of lymphatics and blood vessels, while perineural invasion denotes a tropism of neoplastic cells for nerve bundles. Literature supports this claim that both perineural and vascular invasion are the known predictors of poor outcomes (Matsushita et al., 2015).

In their study, Bjerkli et al. found perineural invasion to be a prognostic indicator for high stage disease, related to larger sized tumors which invade deeper into the mucosa where the nerve bundles are found. They also found that using fewer histopathological variables improved the reproducibility of assigning a grade score (Bjerkli et al., 2020).

i. Sialadenotrophism:

Dysplastic changes are sometimes noted along the lumen of the exocrine gland ducts. Mohan et al. studied changes in minor salivary glands in 250 patients with oral squamous cell carcinoma. The alterations observed in excretory ducts included simple hyperplasia, squamous metaplasia, mucous metaplasia, oncocytic metaplasia, moderate and severe dysplasia and malignant cell infiltration into the duct. Within the gland, ductal proliferation, ductal metaplasia, dysplastic changes, and infiltration by malignant squamous cells were noted. Presently, the prognostic role of those findings in oral squamous cell carcinoma is uncertain. Nevertheless, the glands that have undergone dysplastic changes/malignant cell infiltration should be excised, as there are reports of recurrence of oral squamous cell carcinoma due to inadequate removal of such exocrine gland tissues (Mohan et al., 2016).

j. Cancer-associated inflammation:

A good antitumor response is associated with a favorable prognosis. Anneroth et al. (1987) proposed the inclusion of the assessment of the inflammatory cell response in the grading system of oral squamous cell carcinoma (Anneroth et al., 1987). Many proposals have been received for the incorporation of immune response into the grading system of oral squamous cell carcinoma citing its utility since then. This, however, is yet to be implemented in reporting practice.

According to Almangush et al., tumor-infiltrating lymphocytes provide a significant tool to prognosticate the overall survival as well as disease-free survival (Almangush et al., 2021). Sievilainen et al. carried out a systematic review on oral squamous cell carcinoma and found that 7 immune checkpoints exist which predict worse survival. These include PD-L1, FKBP51, B7-H4, B7-H6, ALHD1, IOD1, and B7-H3 (Sievilainen et al., 2019). In their meta-analysis, Huang et al. found that dense infiltration of CD8$^+$, CD45RO$^+$, and CD57$^+$ tumor-infiltrating lymphocytes signal improved survival. On the other hand, the presence of CD68$^+$ and CD163$^+$ macrophages were linked with a poor prognosis (Huang et al., 2019). Zhou et al. revealed promising predictor value for expression of CD3, CD45 RO, and FOXP3 in the central areas and invasive front of oral squamous cell carcinoma and evaluation of CD8 in the center of the lesion (Zhou et al., 2020). Further validation is required for incorporating these prognostic markers into practice. In addition to the immune biomarkers, tumor mutational burden which is the number of somatic mutations in each coding area of the tumor genome has also been found to be a favorable predictor for longer survival in patients treated with pembrolizumab as per the study of Cristescu et al. (2018).

Bjerkli et al. found that tumor differentiation and lymphocytic infiltration were found to be independent prognosticators of survival both for the entire cohort studied and for low-stage cancer patients. Little infiltration of lymphocytes in tumor stroma was associated with a more aggressive clinical course. According to them, patients with poorly differentiated who exhibited a weak lymphocytic response should be categorized as high-risk patients even if the tumor size was small and no nodal metastasis was found (Bjerkli et al., 2020).

k. Cellular cannibalism:

It is speculated that nutritional supply to tumor cells is not in pace with the high proliferation–related tumor load. This might lead to increased nutritional demand in tumor mass, which could probably initiate cannibalism in tumor cells. Cellular cannibalism in oral squamous cell carcinoma has also shown a good correlation with TNM stages and nodal metastasis, making it a perfect histopathological prognosticator (Sarode et al., 2012).

l. Liquid biopsy analytes:

The quantification of circulating tumor cells was found to correlate with a higher incidence of regional metastasis in head and neck cancer (Hristozova et al., 2011).

High expression of circulating miR–142, miR–186, miR–195, miR–374b, and miR–574 have been found to be of prognostic utility in head and neck cancer (Summerer et al., 2015).

17.3 Metastasis

a. Lymph node metastasis:

It is one of the foremost consistent prognosticators in head and neck carcinoma. The 5-year disease-specific survival was found to be 42.0% for patients with the level I, II or III involvement, whereas for the level IV group it was 30.6% and for the level V group it had been 26.4%. Involvement of the level IV and V nodes was associated with a worse prognosis. Studies have also shown that the amount, size also as occult node metastasis has a big impact on the survival rates (Yamada et al., 2016).

b. Lymph node ratio:

The lymph node ratio has been used as a prognostic indicator for various carcinomas and is defined as the ratio of the amount of tumor-positive lymph nodes to the entire number of lymph nodes removed. High-risk patients have a higher than 6% lymph node ratio. The ratio proved to be a good prognostic tool in patients with pN0–pN2b lymph node status (Chen et al., 2015).

c. Distant metastasis:

Although the incidence of distant metastasis has decreased with the advent of advanced and combined therapies, it is considered a crucial parameter for prognosis within the patients. A clinicopathological study by Takahashi et al. revealed 54 out of 102 cases positive for distant metastasis. The survival period of the patients ranged from 1 to 21 months with a median of 3 months, after confirmation of metastasis. Additionally, locoregional recurrence was also noted in 29 of 54 cases (Takahashi et al., 2014).

Since many factors impact prognosis, an accurate staging system is important to design customized treatment strategies.

References

Abati, S., Bramati, C., Bondi, S., Lissoni, A., Trimarchi, M., 2020. Oral cancer and precancer: a narrative review on the relevance of early diagnosis. Int. J. Environ. Res. Public Health 17, 9160. https://doi.org/10.3390/ijerph17249160.

Abdulkareem, A.A., Shelton, R.M., Landini, G., Cooper, P.R., Milward, M.R., 2018. Periodontal pathogens promote epithelial-mesenchymal transition in oral squamous carcinoma cells in vitro. Cell Adhes. Migr. 12, 127–137.

Adams, J.L., Smothers, J., Srinivasan, R., Hoos, A., 2015. Big opportunities for small molecules in immuno-oncology. Nat. Rev. Drug Discov. 14, 603–622. https://doi.org/10.1038/nrd4596.

Aditya, N., Shim, M., Lee, I., Lee, Y., Im, M.H., Ko, S., 2013. Curcumin and genistein coloaded nano-structured lipid carriers: in vitro digestion and antiprostate cancer activity. J. Agric. Food Chem. 61 (8), 1878–1883.

Ahmed, S.P., Jayan, L., Dineshkumar, T., Raman, S., 2019. Oral squamous cell carcinoma under microscopic vision: a review of histological variants and its prognostic indicators. SRM J. Res. Dent. Sci. 10, 90–97.

Alexandra, T., Marina, I.M., Daniela, M., Ioana, S.I., Maria, B.Z., Radu, R., et al., 2020. Autophagy—a hidden but important actor on Oral cancer scene. Int. J. Mol. Sci. 21, 9325. https://doi.org/10.3390/ijms21239325.

Ali, J., Sabiha, B., Jan, H.U., Haider, S.A., Khan, A.A., Ali, S.S., 2017. Genetic etiology of oral cancer. Oral Oncol. 2017 (70), 23–28. https://doi.org/10.1016/j.oraloncology.2017.05.004.

Almangush, A., Salo, T., Hagström, J., Leivo, I., 2014. Tumour budding in head and neck squamous cell carcinoma – a systematic review. Histopathology 65 (5), 587–594.

Almangush, A., Leivo, I., Mäkitie, A.A., 2021. Biomarkers for immunotherapy of oral squamous cell carcinoma: current status and challenges. Front. Oncol. 11, 6616629.

Amarasinghe, H.K., Johnson, N.W., Lalloo, R., Kumaraarachchi, M., Warnakulasuriya, S., 2010. Derivation and validation of a risk factor model for detection of oral potentially malignant disorders in populations with high prevalence. Br. J. Cancer 103 (3), 303–309.

Amôr, N.G., Santos, P.S.S., Campanelli, A.P., 2021. The tumor microenvironment in SCC: mechanisms and therapeutic opportunities. Front. Cell Dev. Biol. 9, 636544. https://doi.org/10.3389/fcell.2021.636544.

Angadi, P.V., Patil, P.V., Hallikeri, K., Mallapur, M.D., Hallikerimath, S., Kale, A.D., 2015. Tumor budding is an independent prognostic factor for prediction of lymph node metastasis in oral squamous cell carcinoma. Int. J. Surg. Pathol. 23 (2), 102–110.

Ankri, R., Ashkenazy, A., Milstein, Y., Brami, Y., Olshinka, A., Goldenberg-Cohen, N., et al., 2016. Gold nanorods based air scanning electron microscopy and diffusion reflection imaging for mapping tumor margins in squamous cell carcinoma. ACS Nano 10, 2349–2356.

Anneroth, G., Batsakis, J., Luna, M., 1987. Review of the literature and a recommended system of malignancy grading in oral squamous cell carcinomas. Scand. J. Dent. Res. 95, 229–249. https://doi.org/10.1111/j.1600-0722.1987.tb01836.x.

Arantes, L.M.R.B., Carvalho, A.C.D., Melendez, M.E., Carvalho, A.L., 2018. Serum, plasma and saliva biomarkers for head and neck cancer. Expert. Rev. Mol. Diagn. 18 (1), 85–112. https://doi.org/10.1080/14737159.2017.1404906.

Aryal, S., Key, J., Stigliano, C., Landis, M.D., Lee, D.Y., Decuzzi, P., 2014. Positron emitting magnetic nanoconstructs for PET/MR imaging. Small 10, 2688–2696.

Ashworth, T.R., 1869. A case of cancer in which cells similar to those in the tumours were seen in the blood after death. Med. J. Aust. 14, 146–147 (Cross ref 1 Qiagen).

Asoudeh-Fard, A., Barzegari, A., Dehnad, A., Bastani, S., Golchin, A., Omidi, Y., 2017. Lactobacillus plantarum induces apoptosis in oral cancer KB cells through upregulation of PTEN and downregulation of MAPK signalling pathways. Bioimpacts 7, 193–198.

Auluck, A., 2007. Dyskeratosis congenita report of a case with literature review. Med. Oral Patol. Oral Cir. Bucal. 12, 369–373.

Baker, J.L., Bor, B., Agnello, M., Shi, W., He, X., 2017. Ecology of the oral microbiome: beyond bacteria. Trends Microbiol. 25, 362–374.

Baron, J.A., 2012. Screening for cancer with molecular markers: progress comes with potential problems. Nat. Rev. Cancer 12 (5), 368–371. https://doi.org/10.1038/nrc3260. 22495319.

Basu, P., Ponti, A., Anttila, A., Ronco, G., Senore, C., Vale, D.B., et al., 2018. Status of implementation and organization of cancer screening in the European Union member states – summary results from the second European screening report. Int. J. Cancer 142 (1), 44–56. https://doi.org/10.1002/ijc.31043. 28940326.

Belai, E.B., de Oliveira, C.E., Gasparoto, T.H., Ramos, R.N., Torres, S.A., Garlet, G.P., et al., 2014. PD-1 blockage delays murine squamous cell carcinoma development. Carcinogenesis 35, 424–431. https://doi.org/10.1093/carcin/bgt305.

Belkin, D.A., Mitsui, H., Wang, C.Q., Gonzalez, J., Zhang, S., Shah, K.R., et al., 2013. CD200 upregulation in vascular endothelium surrounding cutaneous squamous cell carcinoma. JAMA Dermatol. 149, 178–186. https://doi.org/10.1001/jamadermatol.2013.1609.

Bergers, G., Brekken, R., McMahon, G., Vu, T.H., Itoh, T., Tamaki, K., et al., 2000. Matrix metalloproteinase-9 triggers the angiogenic switch during carcinogenesis. Nat. Cell Biol. 2, 737.

Bernard, H.U., Burk, R.D., Chen, Z., van Doorslaer, K., Zur Hausen, H., de Villiers, E.M., 2010. Classification of papillomaviruses (PVs) based on 189 PV types and proposal of taxonomic amendments. Virology 401, 70–79.

Bjerkli, I.H., Hadler-Olsen, E., Nginamau, E.S., Laurvik, H., Soland, T.M., Costea, D.E., et al., 2020. A combined histo-score based on tumor differentiation and lymphocytic infiltrate is a robust prognostic marker for mobile tongue cancer. Virchows Arch. 477 (6), 865–872. https://doi.org/10.1007/s00428-020-02875-9.

Blouw, B., Song, H., Tihan, T., Bosze, J., Ferrara, N., Gerber, H.-P., et al., 2003. The hypoxic response of tumors is dependent on their microenvironment. Cancer Cell 4 (2), 133–146.

Boing, A.F., Antunes, J.L., de Carvalho, M.B., Filho, J.F.G., Kowalski, L.P., Michaluart Jr., P., et al., 2011. How much do smoking and alcohol consumption explain socioeconomic inequalities in head and neck cancer risk? J. Epidemiol. Community Health 65 (8), 709–714.

Bongiorno, M., Rivard, S., Hammer, D., Kentosh, J., 2017. Malignant transformation of oral leukoplakia in a patient with dyskeratosis congenita. Oral Surg. Oral Med. Oral Pathol. Oral Radiol. 124 (4), e239–e242. https://doi.org/10.1016/j.oooo.2017.08.001.

Bouvard, V., Baan, R., Straif, K., Grosse, Y., Secretan, B., Ghissassi, F.E., Cogliano, V., et al., 2009. A review of human carcinogens—part B: biological agents. Lancet Oncol. 10 (4), 321–322. https://doi.org/10.1016/s1470-2045(09)70096-8.

Brabletz, T., Jung, A., Spaderna, S., Hlubek, F., Kirchner, T., 2005. Migrating cancer stem cells—an integrated concept of malignant tumour progression. Nat. Rev. Cancer 5 (9), 744–749.

Brandwein-Gensler, M., Teixeira, M.S., Lewis, C.M., Lee, B., Rolnitzky, L., Hille, J.J., et al., 2005. Oral squamous cell carcinoma: histologic risk assessment, but not margin status, is strongly predictive of local disease-free and overall survival. Am. J. Surg. Pathol. 29 (2), 167–178.

Bray, F., Ferlay, J., Soerjomataram, I., Siegel, R.L., Torre, L.A., Jemal, A., 2018. Global cancer statistics 2018: GLOBOCAN estimates of incidence and mortality worldwide for 36 cancers in 185 countries. CA Cancer J. Clin. https://doi.org/10.3322/caac.21492.

Brentani, R.R., Kowalski, L.P., Soares, J.F., Torloni, H., Principal investigators of Brazilian Head and Neck Cancer Study Group, 1999. End results of a prospective trial on elective lateral neck dissection vs type III modified radical neck dissection in the management of supraglottic and transglottic carcinomas. Head Neck 21 (8), 694–702.

Broders, A.C., 1920. Squamous cell carcinoma of the lip: a study of five hundred and thirty-seven cases. JAMA 74, 656–664.

Bryne, M., Koppang, H.S., Lilleng, R., Kjærheim, Å., 1992. Malignancy grading of the deep invasive margins of oral squamous cell carcinomas has high prognostic value. J. Pathol. 166 (4), 375–381. https://doi.org/10.1002/path.1711660409.

Buglione, M., Grisanti, S., Almici, C., Mangoni, M., Polli, C., Consoli, F., et al., 2012. Circulating tumour cells in locally advanced head and neck cancer: preliminary report about their possible role in predicting response to non-surgical treatment and survival. Eur. J. Cancer 48 (16), 3019–3026. https://doi.org/10.1016/j.ejca.2012.05.007.

Bumgarner, R., 2013. DNA microarrays: types, applications and their future. Curr. Protoc. Mol. Biol., 22. January Unit–22.1 https://doi.org/10.1002/0471142727.mb2201s101.

Byers, R.M., Bland, K.I., Borlase, B., Luna, M., 1978. The prognostic and therapeutic value of frozen section determinations in the surgical treatment of squamous carcinoma of the head and neck. Am. J. Surg. 136 (4), 525–528.

Cabrera, M.C., Hollingsworth, R.E., Hurt, E.M., 2015. Cancer stem cell plasticity and tumor hierarchy. World J. Stem Cells 7, 27–36.

Califano, J., van der Riet, P., Westra, W., Nawroz, H., Clayman, G., Piantadosi, S., et al., 1996. Genetic progression model for head and neck cancer: implications for field cancerization. Cancer Res. 56 (11), 2488–2492.

Calixto, G., Bernegossi, J., Fonseca-Santos, B., Chorilli, M., 2014. Nanotechnology-based drug delivery systems for treatment of oral cancer: a review. Int. J. Nanomedicine 9, 3719–3735. https://doi.org/10.2147/IJN.S61670.

Carew, J.S., Nawrocki, S.T., Cleveland, J.L., 2007. Modulating autophagy for therapeutic benefit. Autophagy 3 (5), 464–467.

Carew, J.S., Nawrocki, S.T., Giles, F.J., Cleveland, J.L., 2008. Targeting autophagy: a novel anticancer strategy with therapeutic implications for imatinib resistance. Biologics 2 (2), 201–204.

Cawson, R.A., 1966. Chronic oral candidiasis and leukoplakia. Oral Surg. Oral Med. Oral Pathol. 22 (5), 582–591. https://doi.org/10.1016/0030-4220(66)90161-7.

Challacombe, J.M., Suhrbier, A., Parsons, P.G., Jones, B., Hampson, P., Kavanagh, D., et al., 2006. Neutrophils are a key component of the antitumor efficacy of topical chemotherapy with ingenol-3-angelate. J. Immunol. 177, 8123–8132. https://doi.org/10.4049/jimmunol.177.11.8123.

Chambers, A.F., Groom, A.C., MacDonald, I.C., 2002. Dissemination and growth of cancer cells in metastatic sites. Nat. Rev. Cancer 2 (8), 563–572.

Chang, Y.A., Weng, S.L., Yang, S.F., Chou, C.H., Huang, W.C., Tu, S.J., et al., 2018. A three-microRNA signature as a potential biomarker for the early detection of oral cancer. Int. J. Mol. Sci. 19, 758. https://doi.org/10.3390/ijms19030758.

Chaudhuri, O., Koshy, S.T., da Cunha, C.B., Shin, J.-W., Verbeke, C.S., Allison, K.H., et al., 2014. Extracellular matrix stiffness and composition jointly regulate the induction of malignant phenotypes in mammary epithelium. Nat. Mater. 13, 970.

Chaw, K.C., Manimaran, M., Tay, F.E.H., Swaminathan, S., 2006. A quantitative observation and imaging of single tumor cell migration and deformation using a multi-gap microfluidic device representing the blood vessel. Microvasc. Res. 72 (3), 153–160.

Chen, X., Liang, H., Zhang, J., Zen, K., Zhang, C.Y., 2012. Secreted microRNAs: a new form of intercellular communication. Trends Cell Biol. 22 (3), 125–132.

Chen, C.C., Lin, J.C., Chen, K.W., 2015. Lymph node ratio as a prognostic factor in head and neck cancer patients. Radiat. Oncol. 10 (1), 181.

Chen, X.J., Zhang, X.Q., Liu, Q., Zhang, J., Zhou, G., 2018. Nanotechnology: a promising method for oral cancer detection and diagnosis. J. Nanobiotechnol. 16, 52. https://doi.org/10.1186/s12951-018-0378-6.

Chi, A.C., Day, T.A., Neville, B.W., 2015. Oral cavity and oropharyngeal squamous cell carcinoma—an update. CA Cancer J. Clin. 65 (5), 401–421.

Choi, J.J., Reich 3rd, C.F., Pisetsky, D.S., 2005. The role of macrophages in the in vitro generation of extracellular DNA from apoptotic and necrotic cells. Immunology 115, 55–62.

Choudhari, S.K., Chaudhary, M., Gadbail, A.R., Sharma, A., Takad, S., 2013. Oxidative and antioxidative mechanisms in oral cancer and precancer: a review. Oral Oncol. 50 (1), 10–18. https://doi.org/10.1016/j.oraloncology.2013.09.001.

Chow, L.Q.M., Morishima, C., Eaton, K.D., Baik, C.S., Goulart, B.H., Anderson, L.N., et al., 2017. Phase Ib trial of the toll-like receptor 8 agonist, Motolimod (VTX-2337), combined with cetuximab in patients with recurrent or metastatic SCCHN. Clin. Cancer Res. 23 (10), 2442–2450. https://doi.org/10.1158/1078-0432.CCR-16-1934 (PubMed).

Chu, S.C., Hsieh, Y.S., Yu, C.C., Lai, Y.Y., Chen, P.N., 2014. Thymoquinone induces cell death in human squamous carcinoma cells via caspase activation-dependent apoptosis and LC3-II activation-dependent autophagy. PLoS One 9, e101579.

Clarke, M.F., Dick, J.E., Dirks, P.B., et al., 2006. Cancer stem cells-perspectives on current status and future directions: AACR workshop on cancer stem cells. Cancer Res. 66 (19), 9339–9344.

Clay, M.R., Tabor, M., Owen, J.H., et al., 2010. Single-marker identification of head and neck squamous cell carcinoma cancer stem cells with aldehyde dehydrogenase. Head Neck 32, 1195–1201.

Coletta, R.D., Salo, T., 2018. Myofibroblasts in oral potentially malignant disorders: is it related to malignant transformation? Oral Dis. 24, 84–88. https://doi.org/10.1111/odi.12694.

Conway, D.I., Stockton, D.L., Warnakulasuriya, K.A., Ogden, G., Macpherson, L.M., 2006. Incidence of oral and oropharyngeal cancer in United Kingdom (1990-1999) – recent trends and regional variation. Oral Oncol 42 (6), 586–592.

Conway, D.I., Purkayastha, M., Chestnutt, I.G., 2018. The changing epidemiology of oral cancer: definitions, trends, and risk factors. Br. Dent. J. 225 (9), 867–873. https://doi.org/10.1038/sj.bdj.2018.922.

Cooper, B., Schneider, S., Bohl, J., Jiang, Y., Beaudet, A., Pol, S.V., 2003. Requirement of e6ap and the features of human papillomavirus e6 necessary to support degradation of p53. Virology 306 (1), 87–99. https://doi.org/10.1016/s0042-6822(02)00012-0.

Copetti, T., Bertoli, C., Dalla, E., Demarchi, F., Schneider, C., 2009. p65/RelA modulates BECN1 transcription and autophagy. Mol. Cell. Biol. 29 (10), 2594–2608. https://doi.org/10.1128/MCB.01396-08.

Costea, D., Tsinkalovsky, O., Vintermyr, O., Johannessen, A., Mackenzie, I., 2006. Cancer stem cells – new and potentially important targets for the therapy of oral squamous cell carcinoma. Oral Dis. 12 (5), 443–454. https://doi.org/10.1111/j.1601-0825.2006.01264.x.

Costea, D.E., Hills, A., Osman, A.H., Thurlow, J., Kalna, G., Huang, X., et al., 2013. Identification of two distinct carcinoma-associated fibroblast subtypes with differential tumour promoting abilities in oral squamous cell carcinoma. Cancer Res. 73 (13), 3888–3901.

Cristescu, R., Mogg, R., Ayers, M., Albright, A., Murphy, E., Yearley, J., et al., 2018. Pan- tumor genomic biomarkers for PD-1 checkpoint blockade-based immunotherapy. Science 362 (6411), 362. https://doi.org/10.1126/science.aar3593.

Croft, M., Benedict, C.A., Ware, C.F., 2013. Clinical targeting of the TNF and TN-FR superfamilies. Nat. Rev. Drug Discov. 12 (2), 147–168. https://doi.org/10.1038/nrd3930 (PubMed).

Cross, W.C., Graham, T.A., Wright, N.A., 2016. New paradigms in clonal evolution: punctuated equilibrium in cancer. J. Pathol. 240 (2), 126–136. https://doi.org/10.1002/path.4757.

Dhanuthai, K., Rojanawatsirivej, S., Thosaporn, W., Kintarak, S., Subarnbhesaj, A., Darling, M., et al., 2018. Oral cancer: a multicenter study. Med. Oral Patol. Oral Cir. Bucal. 23 (1), e23–e29.

Dietsch, G.N., Lu, H., Yang, Y., Morishima, C., Chow, L.Q., Disis, M.L., et al., 2016. Coordinated activation of toll-like Receptor8 (TLR8) and NLRP3 by the TLR8 agonist, VTX-2337, ignites tumoricidal natural killer cell activity. PLoS One 11 (2), e0148764. https://doi.org/10.1371/journal.pone.0148764 (PubMed).

Dissanayake, U., 2017. Malignancy grading of invasive fronts of oral squamous cell carcinomas: correlation with overall survival. Transl. Res. Oral Oncol. 2, 1–8.

Dodagatta-Marri, E., Meyer, D.S., Reeves, M.Q., Paniagua, R., To, M.D., Binnewies, M., et al., 2019. α-PD-1 therapy elevates Treg/Th balance and increases tumor cell pSmad3 that are both targeted by α-TGFβ antibody to promote durable rejection and immunity in squamous cell carcinomas. J. Immunother. Cancer 7, 62. https://doi.org/10.1186/s40425-018-0493-9.

Du, R., Lu, K.V., Petritsch, C., Liu, P., Ganss, R., Passegué, E., et al., 2008. HIF1α induces the recruitment of bone marrow-derived vascular modulatory cells to regulate tumor angiogenesis and invasion. Cancer Cell 13 (3), 206–220.

Duhen, R., Ballesteros-Merino, C., Frye, A.K., Tran, E., Rajamanickam, V., Chang, S.C., et al., 2021. Neoadjuvant anti-OX40 (MEDI6469) therapy in patients with head and neck squamous cell carcinoma activates and expands antigen-specific tumor-infiltrating T cells. Nat. Commun. 12 (1), 1047. https://doi.org/10.1038/s41467-021-21383-1. 33594075. PMCID: PMC7886909.

Duz, M.B., Karatas, O.F., Guzel, E., Turgut, N.F., Yilmaz, M., Creighton, C.J., et al., 2016. Identification of miR-139-5p as a saliva biomarker for tongue squamous cell carcinoma: a pilot study. Cell. Oncol. (Dordr.) 39 (2), 187–193.

Egan, J.E., Quadrini, K.J., Santiago-Schwarz, F., Hadden, J.W., Brandwein, H.J., Signorelli, K.L., 2007. IRX-2, a novel in vivo immunotherapeutic, induces mat- uration and activation of human dendritic cells in vitro. J. Immunother. 30 (6), 624–633. https://doi.org/10.1097/CJI.0b013e3180691593 (PubMed).

Egeblad, M., Werb, Z., 2002. New functions for the matrix metalloproteinases in cancer progression. Nat. Rev. Cancer 2, 161.

Eguchi, T., 2020. Organoids and liquid biopsy in oral cancer research. J. Clin. Med. 9, 3701. https://doi.org/10.3390/jcm9113701.

Epstein, J.B., Wan, L.S., Gorsky, M., Zhang, L., 2003. Oral lichen planus: progress in understanding its malignant potential and implications for clinical management. Oral Surg. Oral Med. Oral Pathol. 96, 32–37.

Epstein, J.B., Gorsky, M., Day, T., Gonsalves, W., 2008a. Screening for and diagnosis of oral premalignant lesions and oropharyngeal squamous cell carcinoma. Can. Fam. Physician 54 (6), 870–875.

Epstein, J.B., Silverman Jr., S., Epstein, J.D., Lonky, S.A., Bride, M.A., 2008b. Analysis of oral lesion biopsies identified and evaluated by visual examination, chemiluminescence and toluidine blue. Oral Oncol. 44 (6), 538–554.

Estrella, V., Chen, T., Lloyd, M., Wojtkowiak, J., Cornnell, H.H., Ibrahim-Hashim, A., et al., 2013. Acidity generated by the tumor microenvironment drives local invasion. Cancer Res. 73 (5), 1524–1535.

Feng, Y., He, D., Yao, Z., Klionsky, D.J., 2014. The machinery of macroautophagy. Cell Res. 24 (1), 24–41. https://doi.org/10.1038/cr.2013.168.

Feng, L., Houck, J.R., Lohavanichbutr, P., Chen, C., 2017. Transcriptome analysis reveals differentially expressed lncRNAs between oral squamous cell carcinoma and healthy oral mucosa. Oncotarget 8, 31521–31531.

Ferlito, A., Robbins, K.T., Shah, J.P., Medina, J.E., Silver, C.E., Al-Tamimi, S., et al., 2010. Proposal for a rational classification of neck dissections. Head Neck. https://doi.org/10.1002/hed.21614 (Editorial).

Fernandez, F.L., Gonzalez, O.R., Cedrun, J.L.L., Lopez, R.L., Romay, L.M., Cunqueiro, M.M.S., 2018. Liquid biopsy in Oral cancer. Int. J. Mol. Sci. 19, 1704. https://doi.org/10.3390/ijms19061704.

Fine, J.D., Mellerio, J.E., 2009. Extracutaneous manifestations and complications of inherited epidermolysis bullosa: part II: other organs. J. Am. Acad. Dermatol. 61, 387–402.

Fine, J.D., Eady, R.A., Bauer, E.A., Bauer, J.W., Bruckner-Tuderman, L., Heagerty, A., et al., 2008. The classification of inherited epidermolysis bullosa (EB): report of the third international consensus meeting on diagnosis and classification of EB. J. Am. Acad. Dermatol. 58, 931–950 (CR Ganesh 67).

Florence, M.E., Massuda, J.Y., Bröcker, E.B., Metze, K., Cintra, M.L., Souza, E.M., 2011. Angiogenesis in the progression of cutaneous squamous cell carcinoma: an immunohistochemical study of endothelial markers. Clinics 66, 465–468. https://doi.org/10.1590/s1807-59322011000300018.

Franzmann, E.J., Reategui, E.P., Pedroso, F., Pernas, F.G., Karakullukcu, B.M., Carraway, K.L., et al., 2007. Soluble CD44 is a potential marker for the early detection of head and neck cancer. Cancer Epidemiol. Biomark. Prev. 16, 1348–1355.

Fridlender, Z.G., Sun, J., Kim, S., Kapoor, V., Cheng, G., Ling, L., et al., 2009. Polarization of tumor-associated neutrophil phenotype by TGF-beta: "N1" versus "N2" TAN. Cancer Cell 16, 183–194. https://doi.org/10.1016/j.ccr.2009.06.017.

Fujita, H., Suárez-Fariñas, M., Mitsui, H., Gonzalez, J., Bluth, M.J., Zhang, S., et al., 2012. Langerhans cells from human cutaneous squamous cell carcinoma induce strong type 1 immunity. J. Invest. Dermatol. 132, 1645–1655. https://doi.org/10.1038/jid.2012.34.

Gage, J.R., Meyers, C., Wettstein, F.O., 1990. The E7 proteins of the nononcogenic human papillomavirus type 6b (HPV-6b) and of the oncogenic HPV-16 differ in retinoblastoma protein binding and other properties. J. Virol. 64, 723–730.

Gallimidi, A.B., Fischman, S., Revach, B., Bulvik, R., Maliutina, A., Rubinstein, A.M., et al., 2015. Periodontal pathogens Porphyromonas gingivalis and fusobacterium nucleatum promote tumor progression in an oral-specific chemical carcinogenesis model. Oncotarget 6, 22613–22623.

Gambichler, T., Gnielka, M., Rüddel, I., Stockfleth, E., Stücker, M., Schmitz, L., 2017. Expression of PD-L1 in keratoacanthoma and different stages of progression in cutaneous squamous cell carcinoma. Cancer Immunol. Immunother. 66, 1199–1204. https://doi.org/10.1007/s00262-017-2015-x.

Ganesh, D., Sreenivasan, P., Öhman, J., Wallström, M., Braz-Silva, P.H., Giglio, D., et al., 2018. Potentially malignant oral disorders and cancer transformation. Anticancer Res. 38, 3223–3229.

Ganly, I., Goldstein, D., Carlson, D.L., Patel, S.G., O'Sullivan, B., Lee, N., et al., 2013. Long-term regional control and survival in patients with "low-risk," early-stage oral tongue cancer managed by partial glossectomy and neck dissection without postoperative radiation: the importance of tumour thickness. Cancer 119, 1168–1176.

Gao, L., Wang, F.-q., Li, H.-m., Yang, J.-g., Ren, J.-G., He, K.-f., et al., 2016. CCL2/EGF positive feedback loop between cancer cells and macrophages promotes cell migration and invasion in head and neck squamous cell carcinoma. Oncotarget 7 (52), 87037–87051.

Garzino-Demo, P., Dell'acqua, A., Dalmasso, P., Fasolis, M., La Terra Maggiore, G.M., Ramieri, G., et al., 2006. Clinicopathological parameters and outcome of 245 patients operated for oral squamous cell carcinoma. J. Cranio-Maxillofac. Surg. 34 (6), 344–350. https://doi.org/10.1016/j.jcms.2006.04.004.

Gibson, M.K., Li, Y., Murphy, B., DeConti, R.C., Ensley, J., Forastiere, A.A., 2005. Randomized phase III evaluation of cisplatin plus fluorouracil versus cisplatin plus paclitaxel in advanced head and neck cancer (E1395): an intergroup trial of the eastern cooperative oncology group. J. Clin. Oncol. 23, 3562–3567.

Glenny, A.M., Furness, S., Worthington, H.V., Conway, D.I., Oliver, R., Clarkson, J.E., et al., 2010. The CSROC expert panel. Interventions for the treatment of mouth and oropharyngeal cancer: radiotherapy. Cochrane Database Syst. Rev. (12), CD006387. https://doi.org/10.1002/14651858.cd006387.pub2.

Gómez, A.G.J., Martínez, A.E., Gómez, J.R., Silva, M.Y., Núñez, G.A.M., Agudelo, G.A., et al., 2008. Reverse smokers's and changes in oral mucosa Department of Sucre, Colombia. Med. Oral Patol. Oral Cir. Bucal. 13, 1–8.

Gould, S.J., Eldredge, N., 1993. Punctuated equilibrium comes of age. Nature 366, 223–227 (CR Cross 6).

Grauzam, S., Brock, A.M., Holmes, C.O., Tiedeken, J.A., Boniface, S.G., Pierson, B.N., et al., 2018. NEDD9 stimulated MMP9 secretion is required for invadopodia formation in oral squamous cell carcinoma. Oncotarget 9 (39), 25503–25516.

Groeger, S., Jarzina, F., Domann, E., Meyle, J., 2017. Porphyromonas gingivalis activates NFκB and MAPK pathways in human oral epithelial cells. BMC Immunol. 18, 1.

Gupta, N.K., Mahajan, M., Hore, A., 2019. Management strategies for Oral cancer subsites. Prevention, detection and Management of Oral. Cancer. https://doi.org/10.5772/intechopen.81555.

Hamana, K., Uzawa, K., Ogawara, K., Shiiba, M., Bukawa, H., Yokoe, H., et al., 2005. Monitoring of circulating tumour-associated DNA as a prognostic tool for oral squamous cell carcinoma. Br. J. Cancer 92 (12), 2181–2184.

Han, H.Y., Kim, H., Jeong, S.H., Lim, D.S., Ryu, M.H., 2014. Sulfasalazine induces autophagic cell death in oral cancer cells via Akt and ERK pathways. Asian Pac. J. Cancer Prev. 15, 6939–6944.

Harmsen, S., Wall, M.A., Huang, R.M., Kircher, M.F., 2017. Cancer imaging using surface-enhanced resonance Raman scattering nanoparticles. Nat. Protoc. 12, 1400–1414.

Hartner, L., 2018. Chemotherapy for oral cancer. Dent. Clin. N. Am. 62 (1), 87–97. https://doi.org/10.1016/j.cden.2017.08.006.

Hartner, L., 2018. Chemotherapy for Oral cancer. Dent. Clin. N. Am. 62 (1), 87–97. https://doi.org/10.1016/j.cden.2017.08.006.

Hatton, J.L., Parent, A., Tober, K.L., Hoppes, T., Wulff, B.C., Duncan, F.J., et al., 2007. Depletion of CD4 + cells exacerbates the cutaneous response to acute and chronic UVB exposure. J. Invest. Dermatol. 127, 1507–1515. https://doi.org/10.1038/sj.jid.5700746 (CR Amor).

Herrmann, D., Conway, J.R.W., Vennin, C., Magenau, A., Hughes, W.E., Mortan, J.P., et al., 2014. Three-dimensional cancer models mimic cell-matrix interactions in the tumour microenvironment. Carcinogenesis 35 (8), 1671–1679.

Hong, K.-O., Kim, J.-H., Hong, J.-S., Yoon, H.-J., Lee, J.-I., Hong, S.-P., et al., 2009. Inhibition of Akt activity induces the mesenchymal-to- epithelial reverting transition with restoring E-cadherin expression in KB and KOSCC-25B oral squamous cell carcinoma cells. J. Exp. Clin. Cancer Res. 28 (1), 28.

Hoppe, T., Kraus, D., Novak, N., Probstmeier, R., Frentzen, M., Wenghoefer, M., et al., 2016. Oral pathogens change proliferation properties of oral tumor cells by affecting gene expression of human defensins. Tumour Biol. 37, 13789–13798.

Hristozova, T., Konschak, R., Stromberger, C., Fusi, A., Liu, Z., Weichert, W., et al., 2011. The presence of circulating tumor cells (CTCs) correlates with lymph node metastasis in nonresectable squamous cell carcinoma of the head and neck region (SCCHN). Ann. Oncol. 22 (8), 1878–1885.

Hu, S., Arellano, M., Boontheung, P., Wang, J., Zhou, H., Jiang, J., et al., 2008. Salivary proteomics for Oral cancer biomarker discovery. Clin. Cancer Res. 14, 6246–6252.

Huang, G.-W., Nong, H.-T., Yu, Q.-S., Kinjoh, K., Nakamura, M., Kosug, T., 2009a. Platelet aggregation in head and neck Tumors in China. Laryngoscope 107 (8), 1142–1145.

Huang, C.P., Lu, J., Seon, H., Lee, A.P., Flanagan, L.A., Kim, H.-Y., et al., 2009b. Engineering microscale cellular niches for three-dimensional multicellular cocultures. Lab Chip 9 (12), 1740–1748.

Huang, A.C., Lien, J.C., Lin, M.W., Yang, J., Wu, P., Chang, S., et al., 2013. Tetrandrine induces cell death in SAS human oral cancer cells through caspase activation- dependent apoptosis and LC3-I and LC3-II activation-dependent autophagy. Int. J. Oncol. 43, 485–494.

Huang, J.S., Yao, C.J., Chuang, S.E., Yeh, C.T., Lee, L.M., Chen, R.M., et al., 2016. Honokiol inhibits sphere formation and xenograft growth of oral cancer side population cells accompanied with JAK/ STAT signaling pathway suppression and apoptosis induction. BMC Cancer 16, 245.

Huang, Z., Xie, N., Liu, H., Wan, Y., Zhu, Y., Zhang, M., et al., 2019. The prognostic role of tumour-infiltrating lymphocytes in oral squamous cell carcinoma: a meta- analysis. J. Oral Pathol. Med. 48, 788–798. https://doi.org/10.1111/jop.12927.

Husain, A., Kujan, O., Farah, C.S., 2018. The utility of oral brush cytology in the early detection of oral cancer and oral potentially malignant disorders: a systematic review. J. Oral Pathol. Med. 47 (2), 104–116.

Hussein, A.A., Helder, M.N., de Visscher, J.G., Leemans, C.R., Braakhuis, B.J., de Vet, H.C.W., Forouzanfar, T., 2017. Global incidence of oral and oropharynx cancer in patients younger than 45 years versus older patients: a systematic review. Eur. J. Cancer 82, 115–127.

Ikehata, N., Takanashi, M., Satomi, T., Watanabe, M., Hasegawa, O., Kono, M., et al., 2018. Toll-like receptor 2 activation implicated in oral squamous cell carcinoma development. Biochem. Biophys. Res. Commun. 495, 2227–2234.

Inchingolo, F., Santacroce, L., Ballini, A., Topi, S., Dipalma, G., Haxhirexha, K., et al., 2020. Oral cancer: a historical review. Int. J. Environ. Res. Public Health 17, 3168.

Irimie, A.I., Ciocan, C., Gulei, D., Mehterov, N., Atanasov, A.G., Dudea, D., Berindan-Neagoe, I., 2018. Current insights into Oral cancer epigenetics. Int. J. Mol. Sci. 19, 670. https://doi.org/10.3390/ijms19030670.

Jacob, A., Jing, J., Lee, J., Schedin, P., Gilbert, S.M., Peden, A.A., et al., 2013. Rab40b regulates trafficking of MMP2 and MMP9 during invadopodia formation and invasion of breast cancer cells. J. Cell Sci. 126, 4647–4658.

Janissen, R., Sahoo, P.K., Santos, C.A., da Silva, A.M., von Zuben, A.A.G., Souto, D.E.P., et al., 2017. InP nanowire biosensor with tailored biofunctionalization: ultrasensitive and highly selective disease bio-marker detection. Nano Lett. 17, 5938–5949.

Jemal, A., Miller, K.D., Ma, J., Seigal, R.L., Fedewa, S.A., Islami, F., et al., 2018. Higher lung cancer incidence in young women than young men in the United States. N. Engl. J. Med. 378, 1999–2009.

Jepsen, A., Winther, J.E., 1965. Mycotic infection in Oral Leukoplakia. Acta Odontol. Scand. 23 (3), 239–256. https://doi.org/10.3109/00016356509007513.

Ji, A.L., Rubin, A.J., Thrane, K., Jiang, S., Reynolds, D.L., Meyers, R.M., et al., 2020. Multimodal analysis of composition and spatial architecture in human squamous cell carcinoma. Cell 182, 497.e–514.e. https://doi.org/10.1016/j.cell.2020.05.039.

Jie, H.-B., Schuler, P.J., Lee, S.C., Srivastava, R.M., Argiris, A., Ferrone, S., et al., 2015. CTLA-4+ regulatory T cells increased in cetuximab-treated head and neck cancer patients suppress NK cell cytotoxicity and correlate with poor prognosis. Cancer Res. 75 (11), 2200–2210. https://doi.org/10.1158/0008-5472.CAN-14-2788 (PubMed).

Kabir, T.D., Leigh, R.J., Tasena, H., Mellone, M., Coletta, R.D., Parkinson, E.K., et al., 2016. A miR-335/COX-2/PTEN axis regulates the secretory phenotype of senescent cancer-associated fibroblasts. Aging (Albany NY) 8, 1608–1624.

Kaczor-Urbanowicz, K.E., Carreras-Presas, C.M., Kaczor, T., Tu, M., Wei, F., Garcia-Godoy, F., et al., 2017. Emerging technologies for salivaomics in cancer detection. J. Cell. Mol. Med. 21 (4), 640–647.

Kadaja, M., Isok-Paas, H., Laos, T., Ustav, E., Ustav, M., 2009. Mechanism of genomic instability in cells infected with the high-risk human papillomaviruses. PLoS Pathog. 5, e1000397.

Kane, S.V., Gupta, M., Kakade, A.C., Cruz, A.D.'., 2006. Depth of invasion is the most significant histological predictor of subclinical cervical lymph node metastasis in early squamous carcinomas of the oral cavity. Eur. J. Surg. Oncol. 32, 795–803.

Kaur, J., Jacobs, R., Huang, Y., Salvo, N., Politis, C., 2018. Salivary biomarkers for oral cancer and precancer screening: a review. Clin. Oral Investig. 22 (2), 633–640. https://doi.org/10.1007/s00784-018-2337-x.

Kerawala, C., Roques, T., Jeannon, J.P., Bisase, B., 2016. Oral cavity and lip cancer: United Kingdom National Multidisciplinary Guidelines. J. Laryngol. Otol. 130, S83–S89.

Khattak, F.W., Alhwaiti, Y.S., Ali, A., Faisal, M., Siddiqi, M.H., 2021. Protein-protein interaction analysis through network topology (Oral cancer). J. Healthc. Eng., 6623904. 9 pages https://doi.org/10.1155/2021/6623904.

Khou, S., Popa, A., Luci, C., Bihl, F., Meghraoui-Kheddar, A., Bourdely, P., et al., 2020. Tumor-associated neutrophils dampen adaptive immunity and promote cutaneous squamous cell carcinoma development. Cancers 12, 12071860. https://doi.org/10.3390/cancers12071860.

Kim, K., Lee, D.J., 2019. Editorial: the updated AJCC/TNM staging system (8th edition) for oral tongue cancer. Transl. Cancer Res. 8 (Suppl 2), S164–S166.

King, S.M., Reed, G.L., 2002. Development of platelet secretory granules. Semin. Cell Dev. Biol. 13 (4), 293–302.

Kirwan, M., Dokal, I., 2008. Dyskeratosis congenita: a genetic disorder of many faces. Clin. Genet. 73, 103–112.

Knowles, L.M., Gurski, L.A., Engel, C., Gnarra, J.R., Maranchie, J.K., Pilch., 2013. J integrin αvβ3 and fibronectin upregulate slug in cancer cells to promote clot invasion and metastasis. Cancer Res. 73 (20). https://doi.org/10.1158/0008-5472.CAN-13-0602.

Kolokythas, A., Park, S., Schlieve, T., Pytynia, K., Cox, D., 2015. Squamous cell carcinoma of the oral tongue: histopathological parameters associated with outcome. Int. J. Oral Maxillofac. Surg. 44 (9), 1069–1074.

Krishnamurthy, S., Dong, Z., Vodopyanov, D., Imai, A., Helman, J.I., Prince, M.E., et al., 2010. Endothelial cell-initiated signaling promotes the survival and self-renewal of cancer stem cells. Cancer Res. 70 (23), 9969–9978.

Kuo, W.P., Jenssen, T.K., Park, P.J., Lingen, M.W., Hasina, R., Machado, L.O., 2002. Gene expression levels in different stages of progression in oral squamous cell carcinoma. Proc. AMIA Symp., 415–419.

Kwon, N.H., Kim, S.Y., Kim, G.M., 2011. A case of metastatic squamous cell carcinoma arising from actinic cheilitis. Ann. Dermatol. 23, 101–103.

Lafaurie, G.I., Perdomo, S.J., Buenahora, M.R., Amaya, S., Díaz-Báez, D., 2018. Human papilloma virus: an etiological and prognostic factor for oral cancer? J. Investig. Clin. Dent. 9, e12313. https://doi.org/10.1111/jicd.12313.

Lahl, K., Loddenkemper, C., Drouin, C., Freyer, J., Arnason, J., Eberl, G., et al., 2007. Selective depletion of Foxp3+ regulatory T cells induces a scurfy-like disease. J. Exp. Med. 204 (1), 57–63. 10.1084/jem.20061852.

Lanier, L.L., Le, A.M., Civin, C.I., Loken, M.R., Phillips, J.H., 1986. The relationship of CD16 (Leu-11) and Leu-19 (NKH−1) antigen expression on human peripheral blood NK cells and cytotoxic T lymphocytes. J. Immunol. 136 (12), 4480 (CR Peltanova 131).

Lätti, S., Leskinen, M., Shiota, N., Wang, Y., Kovanen, P.T., Lindstedt, K.A., 2003. Mast cell-mediated apoptosis of endothelial cells in vitro: a paracrine mechanism involving TNF-α-mediated down-regulation of bcl-2 expression. J. Cell. Physiol. 195 (1), 130–138.

Leão, J.C., Gueiros, L.A., Porter, S.R., 2006. Oral manifestations of syphilis. Clinics 61 (2), 161–166.

Lechner, M.G., Liebertz, D.J., Epstein, A.L., 2010. Characterization of cytokine-induced myeloid-derived suppressor cells from normal human peripheral blood mononuclear cells. J. Immunol. 185 (4), 2273–2284.

Lee, Y.H., Wong, D.T., 2009. Saliva: an emerging biofluid for early detection of diseases. Am. J. Dent. 22 (4), 241–248.

Lee, D.F., Kuo, H.P., Chen, C.T., Hsu, J.M., Chou, C.K., Wei, Y., et al., 2007. IKK beta suppression of TSC1 links inflammation and tumor angiogenesis via the mTOR pathway. Cell 130 (3), 440–455. https://doi.org/10.1016/j.cell.2007.05.058.

Lee, C.C., Huang, C.-Y., Lin, Y.-S., Chang, K.-P., Chi, C.C., Lin, M.Y., et al., 2017. Prognostic performance of a new staging category to improve discrimination of disease-specific survival in non-metastatic oral cancer. JAMA Otolaryngol. Head Neck Surg. 143, 395–402.

Lei, Z., Xiang, M., Xin-wei, Z., Deng-Cheng, Y., Ran, C., Yong, J., et al., 2019. Long non coding RNAs in oral squamous cell carcinoma: biologic function, mechanisms and clinical implications. Mol. Cancer 18, 102.

Li, L., Chen, Y., Gibson, S.B., 2013. Starvation-induced autophagy is regulated by mitochondrial reactive oxygen species leading to AMPK activation. Cell. Signal. 25 (1), 50–65. https://doi.org/10.1016/j.cellsig.2012.09.020 (CR Daniel Pena 65).

Li, H.-M., Yang, J.-G., Liu, Z.-J., Wang, W.-M., Yu, Z.-L., Ren, J.-G., et al., 2017. Blockage of glycolysis by targeting PFKFB3 suppresses tumor growth and metastasis in head and neck squamous cell carcinoma. J. Exp. Clin. Cancer Res. 36 (1), 7.

Li, Y.Y., Tao, Y.W., Gao, S., Li, P., Zheng, J.M., Zhang, S.E., et al., 2018. Cancer-associated fibroblasts contribute to oral cancer cells proliferation and metastasis via exosome-mediated paracrine miR-34a-5p. EBioMedicine 36, 209–220. https://doi.org/10.1016/j.ebiom.2018.09.006.

Li, Q., Hu, Y., Zhou, X., Liu, S., Han, Q., Cheng, L., 2020. Role of Oral bacteria in the development of Oral squamous cell carcinoma. Cancer 12, 2797. https://doi.org/10.3390/cancers12102797.

Linde, N., Gutschalk, C.M., Hoffmann, C., Yilmaz, D., Mueller, M.M., 2012. Integrating macrophages into organotypic co-cultures: a 3D in vitro model to study tumor-associated macrophages. PLoS One 7, e40058. https://doi.org/10.1371/journal.pone.0040058.

Liu, W., Shen, Z.Y., Wang, L.J., Hu, Y.H., Shen, X.M., Zhou, Z.T., Li, J., 2011. Malignant potential of oral and labial chronic discoid lupus erythematosus: a clinicopathological study of 87 cases. Histopathology 59, 292–298. https://doi.org/10.1111/j.1365-2559.2011.03934.x.

Liu, C.J., Lin, S.C., Yang, C.C., Cheng, H.W., Chang, K.W., 2012. Exploiting salivary miR-31 as a clinical biomarker of oral squamous cell carcinoma. Head Neck 34 (2), 219–224.

Liu, L., Miao, Q., Liang, G., 2013. Quantum dots as multifunctional materials for tumor imaging and therapy. Materials 6, 483–499.

Liu, J.L., Chen, F.F., Lung, J., Lo, C.H., Lee, F.H., Lu, Y.C., et al., 2014. Prognostic significance of p62/SQSTM1 subcellular localization and LC3B in oral squamous cell carcinoma. Br. J. Cancer 111 (5), 944–954. https://doi.org/10.1038/bjc.2014.355.

Liu, T., Zhang, L., Joo, D., Sun, S.C., 2017. NF-kB signaling in inflammation. Signal Transduct. Target. Ther. 2, 17023. https://doi.org/10.1038/sigtrans.2017.23.

Llewellyn, C.D., Linklater, K., Bell, J., Johnson, N.W., Warnakulasuriya, S., 2004. An analysis of risk factors for oral cancer in young people: a case-control study. Oral Oncol. 40 (3), 304–313.

Lo, W.Y., Tsai, M.H., Tsai, Y., Hua, C.H., Tsai, F.J., Huang, S.Y., et al., 2007. Identification of overexpressed proteins in oral squamous cell carcinoma (OSCC) patients by clinical proteomic analysis. Clin. Chim. Acta 376 (1–2), 101–107.

Lourenço, S.V., Sotto, N.M., Vilela, C.M.A., de Carvalh, R.G.F., Rivitti, E.A., Nico, M.S.M., 2006. Lupus erythematosus: clinical and histopathological study of oral manifestations and immunohistochemical profile of epithelial maturation. J. Cutan. Pathol. 33 (10), 657–662. https://doi.org/10.1111/j.1600-0560.2006.00518.x [CR Ganesh 58].

Luke, G.P., Myers, J.N., Emelianov, S.Y., Sokolov, K.V., 2014. Sentinel lymph node biopsy revisited: ultrasound-guided photoacoustic detection of micro- metastases using molecularly targeted plasmonic nanosensors. Cancer Res. 74, 5397–5408.

Luryi, A.L., Chen, M.M., Mehra, S., Roma, S.A., Sosa, J.A., Judson, B.L., 2014. Positive surgical margins in early stage oral cavity cancer: an analysis of 20,602 cases. Otolaryngol. Head Neck Surg. 151 (6), 984–990.

Madhura, M.G., Rao, R.S., Patil, S., Fageeh, H.N., Alhazmi, A., Habib Awan, K., 2020. Advanced diagnostic aids for oral cancer. Dis. Mon. 5, 51.

Majchrzak, E., Szybiak, B., Wegner, A., Pienkowski, P., Pazdrowski, J., Luczewski, L., et al., 2014. Oral cavity and oropharyngeal squamous cell carcinoma in young adults: a review of the literature. Radiol. Oncol. 48 (1), 1–10.

Makarev, E., Schubert, A.D., Kanherkar, R.R., London, N., Teka, M., Ozerov, I., et al., 2017. In silico analysis of pathways activation landscape in oral squamous cell carcinoma and oral leukoplakia. Cell Death Dis. 3, 17022. https://doi.org/10.1038/cddiscovery.2017.22.

Marusyk, A., Almendro, V., Polyak, K., 2012. Intra-tumour heterogeneity: a looking glass for cancer? Nat. Rev. Cancer 12, 323–334.

Matsumura, Y., Ananthaswamy, H.N., 2004. Toxic effects of ultraviolet radiation on the skin. Toxicol. Appl. Pharmacol. 195, 298–308 (Cross Ref Ganesh 28).

Matsushita, Y., Yanamoto, S., Takahashi, H., Yamada, S., Naruse, T., Sakamoto, Y., et al., 2015. A clinicopathological study of perineural invasion and vascular invasion in oral tongue squamous cell carcinoma. Int. J. Oral Maxillofac. Surg. 44 (5), 543–548.

McCullough, M., Jaber, M., Barrett, A., Bain, L., Speight, P., Porter, S., 2002. Oral yeast carriage correlates with presence of oral epithelial dysplasia. Oral Oncol. 38 (4), 391–393. https://doi.org/10.1016/s1368-8375(01)00079-3.

McGranahan, N., Swanton, C., 2017. Clonal heterogeneity and tumor evolution: past, present, and the future. Cell 168, 613–628.

Meacham, C.E., Morrison, S.J., 2013. Tumour heterogeneity and cancer cell plasticity. Nature 501, 328–337.

Meijer, A.J., Lorin, S., Blommaart, E.F., Codogno, P., 2015. Regulation of autophagy by amino acids and MTOR-dependent signal transduction. Amino Acids 47 (10), 2037–2063. https://doi.org/10.1007/s00726-014-1765-4.

Metzelaar, M.J., Wijngaardg, P.L.J., Petersll, P.J., Sixma, J.J., Nieuwenhuis, H.K., Clevers, H.C., CD63 antigen., 1991. A novel lysosomal membrane glycoprotein, cloned by a screening procedure for intracellular antigens in eukaryotic cells. J. Biol. Chem. 266 (5), 3239–3245.

Millner, L.M., Linder, M.W., Valdes Jr., R., 2013. Circulating tumor cells: a review of present methods and the need to identify heterogeneous phenotypes. Ann. Clin. Lab. Sci. 43 (3), 295–304.

Mitchell, P.S., Parkin, R.K., Kroh, E.M., Fritz, B.R., Wyman, S.K., Pogosova-Agadjanyan, E.L., et al., 2008. Circulating microRNAs as stable blood-based markers for cancer detection. Proc. Natl. Acad. Sci. U. S. A. 105 (30), 10513–10518.

Moeckelmann, N., Ebrahimi, A., Tou, Y.K., Gupta, R., Low, T.-H., Ashford, B., et al., 2018. Prognostic implications of the 8th edition of American joint committee on cancer (AJCC) staging system in oral cavity squamous cell carcinoma. Oral Oncol. 85, 82–86.

Moeckelmann, N., Ebrahimi, A., Tou, Y.K., Gupta, R., Low, T.-H., Ashford, B., et al., 2018. Prognostic implications of the 8th edition of American Joint Committee on Cancer (AJCC) staging system in oral cavity squamous cell carcinoma. Oral Oncol. 85, 82–86.

Mohan, M., Jagannathan, N., 2014. Oral field cancerization: an update on current concepts. Oncol. Rev. 8, 244.

Mohan, S.P., Chitturi, R.T., Ragunathan, Y.T., Lakshmi, S.J., Mallusamy, J., Joseph, I., 2016. Minor salivary gland changes in oral epithelial dysplasia and oral squamous cell carcinoma—a histopathological study. J. Clin. Diagn. Res. 10 (7), ZC12–ZC15. https://doi.org/10.7860/JCDR/2016/20218.8116.

Momen-Heravi, F., Trachtenberg, A.J., Kuo, W.P., Cheng, Y.S., 2014. Genomewide study of salivary microRNAs for detection of oral cancer. J. Dent. Res. 93 (7 Suppl), 86S–93S.

Murti, P.R., Bhonsle, R.B., Gupta, P.C., Daftary, D.K., Pindborg, J.J., Mehta, F.S., 1995. Etiology of oral submucous fibrosis with special references to the role of areca nut chewing. J. Oral Pathol. Med. 24, 145–152.

Myong, N.H., 2012. Loss of E-cadherin and Acquisition of Vimentin in epithelial-mesenchymal transition are Noble indicators of uterine cervix cancer progression. Korean J. Pathol. 46 (4), 341 (2092-8920).

Nagao, T., Warnakulasuriya, S., 2003. Annual screening for oral cancer detection. Cancer Detect. Prev. 27 (5), 333–337.

Nagler, R., Bahar, G., Shpitzer, T., Feinmesser, R., 2006. Concomitant analysis of salivary tumor markers—a new diagnostic tool for oral cancer. Clin. Cancer Res. 12, 3979–3984.

Naik, P.P., Panda, P.K., Bhutia, S.K., 2017. Oral cancer stem cells microenvironment. In: Birbrair, A. (Ed.), Stem Cell Microenvironments and beyond, Advances in Experimental Medicine and Biology. Vol. 1041, pp. 207–233, https://doi.org/10.1007/978-3-319-69194-7_11 (Chapter 11).

Napier, S.S., Speight, P.M., 2008. Natural history of potentially malignant oral lesions and conditions: an overview of the literature. J. Oral Pathol. Med. 37 (1), 1–10.

Neiva, K.G., Zhang, Z., Miyazawa, M., Warner, K.A., Karl, E., Nör, J.E., 2009. Cross talk initiated by endothelial cells enhances migration and inhibits anoikis of squamous cell carcinoma cells through STAT3/Akt/ERK signaling. Neoplasia 11, 583IN12–593IN14.

Nichols, A.C., Lowes, L.E., Szeto, C.C., Basmaji, J., Dhaliwal, S., Chapeskie, C., et al., 2012. Detection of circulating tumor cells in advanced head and neck cancer using the CellSearch system. Head Neck 34 (10), 1440–1444.

Nieswandt, B., Hafner, M., Echtenacher, B., Männel, D.N., 1999. Lysis of tumor cells by natural killer cells in mice is impeded by platelets. Cancer Res. 59 (6), 1295–1300.

Nijkamp, M.M., Span, P.N., Hoogsteen, I.J., van der Kogel, A.J., Kaanders, J.H.A.M., Bussink, J., 2011. Expression of E-cadherin and vimentin correlates with metastasis formation in head and neck squamous cell carcinoma patients. Radiother. Oncol. 99 (3), 344–348.

Nonaka, T., Wong, D.T.W., 2018. Liquid biopsy in head and neck cancers: promises and challenges. J. Dent. Res. 97 (6), 701–708.

Norrby, K., Jakobsson, A., Sörbo, J., 1989. Mast-cell secretion and angiogenesis, a quantitative study in rats and mice. Virchows Arch. B Cell Pathol. Incl. Mol. Pathol. https://doi.org/10.1007/bf02899089 (0340-6075 (Print)).

Nowell, P.C., 1976. The clonal evolution of tumor cell populations. Science 194, 23–28.

Nunes, L.A.S., Mussavira, S., Bindhu, O.S., 2015. Clinical and diagnostic utility of saliva as a non-invasive diagnostic fluid: a systematic review. Biochem. Med. 25, 177–192. https://doi.org/10.11613/BM.2015.018.

Öhlund, D., Elyada, E., Tuveson, D., 2014. Fibroblast heterogeneity in the cancer wound. J. Exp. Med. 211, 1503–1523. https://doi.org/10.1084/jem.20140692.

Oldenburg, A.L., Hansen, M.N., Zweifel, D.A., Wei, A., Boppart, S.A., 2006. Plasmon- resonant gold nanorods as low backscattering albedo contrast agents for optical coherence tomography. Opt. Express 14, 6724–6738.

Omar, E., 2013. The outline of prognosis and new advances in diagnosis of oral squamous cell carcinoma (OSCC). J. Oral Oncol. 2013, 519312. 13 pages https://doi.org/10.1155/2013/519312.

Omran, A.R., 1971. The epidemiologic transition. A theory of the epidemiology of population change. Milbank Mem. Fund Q. 49 (4), 509–538. https://doi.org/10.2307/3349375. 5155251.

Paderno, A.R., Morello, C., Piazza, C., 2018. Tongue carcinoma in young adults: a review of the literature. Acta Otorhinolaryngol. Ital. 38, 175–180.

Pang, X., Wang, S.S., Zhang, M., Jiang, J., Fan, H.-Y., Wu, J.-S., et al., 2020. OSCC cell-secreted exosomal CMTM6 induced M2-like macrophages polarization via ERK1/2 signaling pathway. Cancer Immunol. Immunother. 2741–2742. https://doi.org/10.1007/s00262-020-02741-2.

Pannuti, A., Foreman, K., Rizzo, P., Osipo, C., Golde, T., Osborne, B., et al., 2010. Targeting notch to target cancer stem cells. Clin. Cancer Res. 16 (12), 3141–3152.

Pantel, K., Alix-Panabières, C., 2010. Circulating tumour cells in cancer patients: challenges and perspectives. Trends Mol. Med. 16 (9), 398–406. https://doi.org/10.1016/j.molmed.2010.07.001. 20667783.

Pantel, K., Brakenhoff, R.H., 2004. Dissecting the metastatic cascade. Nat. Rev. Cancer 4 (6), 448–456.

Pantvaidya, G., Rao, K., D'Cruz, A., 2020. Management of the neck in oral cancers. Oral Oncol 100, 104476. https://doi.org/10.1016/j.oraloncology.2019.104476.

Park, N.J., Zhou, H., Elashoff, D., Henson, B.S., Kastratovic, D.A., Abemayor, E., et al., 2009. Salivary microRNA: discovery, characterization, and clinical utility for oral cancer detection. Clin. Cancer Res. 15 (17), 5473–5477.

Patel, S.S., Shah, K.A., Shah, M.J., Kothari, K.C., Rawal, R.M., 2014. Cancer stem cells and stemness markers in Oral squamous cell carcinomas. Asian Pac. J. Cancer Prev. 15 (20), 8549–8556. https://doi.org/10.7314/APJCP.2014.15.20.8549.

Patel, A.K., Vipparthi, K., Thatikonda, V., Arun, I., Bhattacharjee, S., Sharan, R., et al., 2018. A subtype of cancer-associated fibroblasts with lower expression of alpha-smooth muscle actin suppresses stemness though BMP4 in oral carcinoma. Oncogene 7, 78.

Pedersen, N.J., Jensen, D.H., Lelkaitis, G., Kiss, K., Charabi, B.W., Ullum, H., et al., 2018. MicroRNA-based classifiers for diagnosis of oral cavity squamous cell carcinoma in tissue and plasma. Oral Oncol. 83, 46–52.

Peinado, H., Zhang, H., Matei, I.R., Costa-Silva, B., Hoshino, A., Rodrigues, G., et al., 2017. Pre-metastatic niches: organ-specific homes for metastases. Nat. Rev. Cancer 17, 302.

Peltanova, B., Raudenska, M., Masarik, M., 2019. Effect of tumour microenvironment on pathogenesis of head and neck squamous cell carcinoma: a systematic review. Mol. Cancer 18, 63.

Peña-Oyarzún, D., Reyes, M., Hernández-Cáceres, M.P., Kretschmar, C., Morselli, E., Ramirez-Sarmiento, C.A., et al., 2020. Role of autophagy in the microenvironment of Oral squamous cell carcinoma. Front. Oncol. 10, 602661. https://doi.org/10.3389/fonc.2020.602661.

Peng, M., Chen, C., Hulbert, A., Brock, M.V., Yu, F., 2017. Non-blood circulating tumor DNA detection in cancer. Oncotarget 8, 69162–69173.

Pflaum, T., Hausler, T., Baumung, C., Ackermann, S., Kuballa, T., Rehm, J., Lachenmeier, D.W., 2016. Carcinogenic compounds in alcoholic beverages: an update. Arch. Toxicol. 90 (10), 2349–2367. https://doi.org/10.1007/s00204-016-1770-3.

Piazza, C., Cocco, D., Del Bon, F., Mangili, S., Nicolai, P., Majorana, A., 2010. Narrow band imaging and high definition television in evaluation of oral and oropharyngeal squamous cell cancer: a prospective study. Oral Oncol. 46 (4), 307–310.

Piemonte, E.J., Lazos, P., Belardinelli, D., Secchi, M., Brunotto, H., Lanfranchi-Tizeira, H., 2018. Oral cancer associated with chronic mechanical irritation of the oral mucosa. Med. Oral Patol. Oral Cir. Bucal. 23, e151–e160.

Pindborg, J.J., Reichart, P., Smith, C.J., van der Waal, I., 1997. World Health Organization: Histological Typing of Cancer and Precancer of the Oral Mucosa. Springer-Verlag, Berlin.

Pisco, A., Huang, S., 2015. Non-genetic cancer cell plasticity and therapy-induced stemness in tumour relapse: 'what does not kill me strengthens me'. Br. J. Cancer 112, 1725–1732.

Pontiggia, O., Sampayo, R., Raffo, D., Motter, A., Xu, R., Bissel, M.J., et al., 2012. The tumor microenvironment modulates tamoxifen resistance in breast cancer: a role for soluble stromal factors and fibronectin through β1 integrin. Breast Cancer Res. Treat. 133 (2), 459–471.

Prince, M., Sivanandan, R., Kaczorowski, A., Wolf, G., Kaplan, M., Dalerba, P., et al., 2007. Identification of a subpopulation of cells with cancer stem cell properties in head and neck squamous cell carcinoma. Proc. Natl. Acad. Sci. U. S. A. 104, 973–978.

Pritchard, C.C., Kroh, E., Wood, B., Arroyo, J.D., Dougherty, K.J., Miyaji, M.M., et al., 2012. Blood cell origin of circulating microRNAs: a cautionary note for cancer biomarker studies. Cancer Prev. Res. (Phila.) 5 (3), 492–497.

Ramesh, T., Reddy, R.S., Kiran, C.H., Lavanya, R., Kumar, B.N., 2014. Palatal changes in reverse and conventional smokers. A clinical comparative study in South India. Indian. J. Dent. 5, 34–38 (cross ref Ganesh 38).

Ray, J.G., Ranganathan, K., Chattopadhyay, A., 2016. Malignant transformation of oral submucous fibrosis: overview of histopathological aspects. Oral Surg. Oral Med. Oral Pathol. Oral Radiol. 122, 200–209.

Rehm, J., Gmel Sr., G.E., Gmel, G., Hasan, O.S.M., Imtiaz, S., Popova, S., et al., 2017. The relationship between different dimensions of alcohol use and the burden of disease – an update. Addiction 112 (6), 968–1001. https://doi.org/10.1111/add.13757. 28220587.

Reibel, J., 2003. Prognosis of oral pre-malignant lesions: significance of clinical, histopathological and molecular biological characteristics. Crit. Rev. Oral Biol. Med. 14, 47–62.

Reya, T., Clevers, H., 2005. Wnt signalling in stem cells and cancer. Nature 434, 843–850.

Richter, P., Umbreit, C., Franz, M., Berndt, A., Grimm, S., Uecker, A., et al., 2010. EGF/TGFβ1 co-stimulation of oral squamous cell carcinoma cells causes an epithelial–mesenchymal transition cell phenotype expressing laminin 332. J. Oral Pathol. Med. 40 (1), 46–54.

Rickles, F.R., Falanga, A., 2001. Molecular basis for the relationship between thrombosis and cancer. Thromb. Res. 102 (6), V215–V224.

Rizzo, G., Black, M., Mymryk, J.S., Barrett, J.W., Nichols, A.C., 2015. Defining the genomic landscape of head and neck cancers through next-generation sequencing. Oral Dis. 21, e11–e24.

Robert, C., Ribas, A., Hamid, O., Daud, A., Wolchok, J.D., Joshua, A.M., et al., 2017. Durable complete response after discontinuation of pembrolizumab in patients with metastatic melanoma. J. Clin. Oncol. 75, JCO2017756270 (PubMed).

Rosenthal, E.L., McCrory, A., Talbert, M., Carroll, W., Magnuson, J.S., Peters, G.E., 2004. Expression of proteolytic enzymes in head and neck cancer–associated fibroblasts. Arch. Otolaryngol. Head Neck Surg. 130 (8), 943–947.

Rothschild, S.I., Thommen, D.S., Moersig, W., Müller, P., Zippelius, A., 2015. Cancer immunology—development of novel anticancer therapies. Swiss Med. Wkly. 145, w14066. https://doi.org/10.4414/smw.2015.14066.

Sakakura, K., Takahashi, H., Kaira, K., Toyoda, M., Oyama, T., Chikamatsu, K., 2015. Immunological significance of the accumulation of autophagy components in oral squamous cell carcinoma. Cancer Sci. 106, 1–8.

Sanger, F., Nicklen, S., Coulson, A.R., 1977. DNA sequencing with chain-terminating inhibitors. Proc. Natl. Acad. Sci. U. S. A. 74 (12), 5463–5467.

Sarode, G.S., Sarode, S.C., Karmarkar, S., 2012. Complex cannibalism: an unusual finding in oral squamous cell carcinoma. Oral Oncol. 48 (2), e4–e6.

Sceneay, J., Chow, M.T., Chen, A., Halse, H.M., Wong, C.S.F., Andrews, D.M., et al., 2012. Primary tumor hypoxia recruits CD11b+/Ly6Cmed/Ly6G+ immune suppressor cells and compromises NK cell cytotoxicity in the premetastatic niche. Cancer Res. 72 (16), 3906–3911. https://doi.org/10.1158/0008-5472.CAN-11-3873.

Schafer, C.A., Schafer, J.J., Yakob, M., et al., 2014. Saliva diagnostics: utilizing oral fluids to determine health status. Monogr. Oral Sci. 24, 88–98.

Schilling, B., Harasymczuk, M., Schuler, P., Egan, J., Ferrone, S., Whiteside, T.L., 2013. IRX-2, a novel immunotherapeutic, enhances functions of human dendritic cells. PLoS One 8 (2), e47234. https://doi.org/10.1371/journal.pone.0047234 (PubMed).

Schilling, C., Stoeckli, S.J., Haerle, S.K., Broglie, M.A., Huber, G.F., Sorensen, J.A., et al., 2015. Sentinel European node trial (SENT): 3-year results of sentinel node biopsy in oral cancer. Eur. J. Cancer 51 (18), 2777–2784.

Schoenfeld, J.D., Hanna, G.J., Jo, V.Y., Rawal, B., Chen, Y.H., Catalano, P.S., et al., 2020. Neoadjuvant nivolumab or nivolumab plus ipilimumab in untreated oral cavity squamous cell carcinoma: a phase 2 open-label randomized clinical trial. JAMA Oncol. 6, 1563–1570. https://doi.org/10.1001/jamaoncol.2020.2955.

Schwartz, R.A., Bridges, T.M., Butani, A.K., Ehrlich, A., 2008. Actinic keratoses: an occupational and environmental disorder. J. Eur. Acad. Dermatol. Venerol. 22, 606–615.

Severino, P., Oliveira, L.S., Andreghetto, F.M., Torres, N., Curioni, O., Cury, P.M., et al., 2015. Small RNAs in metastatic and non-metastatic oral squamous cell carcinoma. BMC Med. Genet. 8, 31.

Shackleton, M., Quintana, E., Fearon, E.R., Morrison, S.J., 2009. Heterogeneity in cancer: cancer stem cells versus clonal evolution. Cell 138, 822–829.

Shafers, W.G., Waldron, C.A., 1975. Erythroplakia of the oral cavity. Cancer 36, 1021–1028.

Shah, J.P., 1990. Patterns of nodal metastasis from squamous cell carcinomas of the upper aerodigestive tract. Am. J. Surg. 160, 405–409.

Shah, B.H., Rasheed, H., Rahman, I.H., Shariff, A.H., Khan, F.L., Rahman, H.B., et al., 2001. Molecular mechanisms involved in human platelet aggregation by synergistic interaction of platelet-activating factor and 5-hydroxytryptamine. Exp. Mol. Med. 33, 226.

Shah, A., Patel, S., Pathak, J., Swain, N., Kumar, S., 2014. The evolving concept of cancer stem cells in head and neck squamous cell carcinoma. Sci. World J., 842491. https://doi.org/10.1155/2014/842491.

Shahab, L., Goniewicz, M.L., Blount, B.C., Brown, J., McNeill, A., Alwis, K.U., et al., 2017. Nicotine, carcinogen and toxicant exposure in long-term ecigarette and nicotine replacement therapy users: a crosssectional study. Ann. Intern. Med. 166 (6), 390–400. https://doi.org/10.7326/M16-1107.

Sharma, S., Kelly, T.K., Jones, P.A., 2010. Epigenetics in cancer. Carcinogenesis 31 (1), 27–36.

Sharma, V., Nandan, A., Sharma, A.K., Singh, H., Bharadwaj, M., Sinha, D.N., et al., 2017. Signature of genetic associations in oral cancer. Tumor Biol. 39 (10), 1010428317725923. https://doi.org/10.1177/1010428317725923.

Shiboski, C.H., Schmidt, B.L., Jordan, R.C., 2005. Tongue and tonsil carcinoma: increasing trends in the U.S. population ages 20-44 years. Cancer 103 (9), 1843–1849.

Siegel, R.L., Miller, K.D., Jemal, A., 2016. Cancer statistics, 2016. CA Cancer J. Clin. 66 (1), 7–30.

Sievilainen, M., Almahmoudi, R., Al-Samadi, A., Salo, T., Pirinen, M., Almangush, A., 2019. The prognostic value of immune checkpoints in oral squamous cell carcinoma. Oral Dis. 25, 1435–1445. https://doi.org/10.1111/odi.12991.

Siljamäki, E., Rappu, P., Riihilä, P., Nissinen, L., Kähäri, V.M., Heino, J., 2020. H-Ras activation and fibroblast-induced TGF-β signaling promote laminin-332 accumulation and invasion in cutaneous squamous cell carcinoma. Matrix Biol. 87, 26–47. https://doi.org/10.1016/j.matbio.2019.09.001.

Singh, S.S., Vats, S., Chia, A.Y., Tan, T.Z., Deng, S., Ong, M.S., et al., 2018. Dual role of autophagy in hallmarks of cancer. Oncogene 37 (9), 1142–1158. https://doi.org/10.1038/s41388-017-0046-6.

Siravegna, G., Marsoni, S., Siena, S., Bardelli, A., 2017. Integrating liquid biopsies into the management of cancer. Nat. Rev. Clin. Oncol. 14, 531–548.

Smith, J., Ladi, E., Mayer-Pröschel, M., Noble, M., 2000. Redox state is a central modulator of the balance between self-renewal and differentiation in a dividing glial precursor cell. Proc. Natl. Acad. Sci. U. S. A. 97 (18), 10032–10037.

Song, Y., Tian, T., Shi, Y., Liu, W., Zou, Y., Khajvand, T., et al., 2017. Enrichment and single-cell analysis of circulating tumor cells. Chem. Sci. 8, 1736–1751.

Speight, P.M., Palmer, S., Moles, D.R., Smith, D.H., Henriksson, M., Augustoviski, F., 2006. The cost-effectiveness of screening for oral cancer in primary care. Health Technol. Assess. 10 (14), 1–144.

Spiro, R.H., Huvos, A.G., Wong, G.Y., Spiro, J.D., Gnecco, C.A., Strong, E.W., 1986. Predictive value of tumor thickness in squamous cancer confined to the tongue and floor of mouth. Am. J. Surg. 152, 345–350.

Sridharan, G., Ramani, P., Patankar, S., 2017. Serum metabolomics in oral leukoplakia and oral squamous cell carcinoma. J. Can. Res. Ther. 13, 556–561.

Srivastava, R.M., Trivedi, S., Concha-Benavente, F., Gibson, S.P., Reeder, C., Ferrone, S., et al., 2017. CD137 stimulation enhances cetuximab-induced Nat- ural killer: dendritic cell priming of antitumor T-cell immunity in patients with head and neck cancer. Clin. Cancer Res. 23 (3), 707–716. https://doi.org/10.1158/1078-0432.CCR-16-0879 (Pub).

Stanaway, J.D., Afshin, A., Gakidou, E., Lim, S.S., Abate, D., Abate, K.H., et al., 2017. Global, regional, and national comparative risk assessment of 84 behavioural, environmental and occupational, and metabolic risks or clusters of risks for 195 countries and territories, 1990–2017: a systematic analysis for the Global Burden of Disease Study 2017. Lancet 392 (10159), 1923–1994. https://doi.org/10.1016/s0140-6736(18)32225-32226.

Stenson, K.M., Kunnavakkam, R., Cohen, E.E., Portugal, L.D., Blair, E., Haraf, D.J., et al., 2010. Chemoradiation for patients with advanced oral cavity cancer. Laryngoscope 120, 93–99.

Sulfikkarali, N., Krishnakumar, N., Manoharan, S., Nirmal, R.M., 2013. Chemopreventive efficacy of naringenin-loaded nanoparticles in 7,12-dimethylbenz(a)anthracene induced experimental oral carcinogenesis. Pathol. Oncol. Res. 19 (2), 287–296.

Summerer, I., Unger, K., Braselmann, H., Schuettrumpf, L., Maihoefer, C., Baumeister, P., et al., 2015. Circulating microRNAs as prognostic therapy biomarkers in head and neck cancer patients. Br. J. Cancer 113 (1), 76–82.

Sun, S., Wang, Z., 2011. Head neck squamous cell carcinoma c- met+ cells display cancer stem cell properties and are responsible for cisplatin-resistance and metastasis. Int. J. Cancer 129, 2337–2348.

Szczepanski, M.J., Czystowska, M., Szajnik, M., Harasymczuk, M., Boyiadzis, M., Kruk-Zagajewska, A., et al., 2009. Triggering of toll-like receptor 4 expressed on human head and neck squamous cell carcinoma promotes tumor development and protects the tumor from immune attack. Cancer Res. 69 (7), 3105–3113. https://doi.org/10.1158/0008-5472.CAN-08-3838 (PubMed).

Takagi, S., Takemoto, A., Takami, M., Oh-hara, T., Fujita, N., 2014. Platelets promote osteosarcoma cell growth through activation of the platelet-derived growth factor receptor-Akt signaling axis. Cancer Sci. 105 (8), 983–988.

Takahashi, T., Ibata, M., Yu, Z., Shikama, Y., Endo, Y., Miyauchi, Y., et al., 2009. Rejection of intradermally injected syngeneic tumor cells from mice by specific elimination of tumor-associated macrophages with liposome-encapsulated dichloromethylene diphosphonate, followed by induction of CD11b(+)/CCR3(−)/gr-1(−) cells cytotoxic again. Cancer Immunol. Immunother. 58, 2011–2023. https://doi.org/10.1007/s00262-009-0708-5 (CR Amor).

Takahashi, M., Aoki, T., Nakamura, N., Kajiwara, H., Kumaki, N., Inomot, C., et al., 2014. Clinicopath-ological analysis of 502 patients with oral squamous cell carcinoma with special interest to distant metas-tasis. Tokai J. Exp. Clin. Med. 39 (4), 178–185.

Takahashi-Yanaga, F., Kahn, M., 2010. Targeting Wnt signaling: can we safely eradicate cancer stem cells? Clin. Cancer Res. 16 (12), 3153–3162.

Takezaki, T., Hide, T., Takanaga, H., Nakamura, H., Kuratsu, J., Kondo, T., 2011. Essential role of the hedgehog signaling pathway in human glioma-initiating cells. Cancer Sci. 102 (7), 1306–1312.

Tang, H., Wu, Z., Zhang, J., Su, B., 2013. Salivary lncRNA as a potential marker for oral squamous cell carcinoma diagnosis. Mol. Med. Rep. 7 (3), 761–766.

Tavassoli, M., Brunel, N., Maher, R., Johnson, N.W., Soussi, T., 1998. p53 antibodies in the saliva of patients with squamous cell carcinoma of the oral cavity. Int. J. Cancer 78, 390–391 (Letter to Editor).

Teicher, B.A., 1994. Hypoxia and drug resistance. Cancer Metastasis Rev. 13, 139–168.

Thomson, P.J., 2012. Oral carcinogenesis. In: Thomson, P.J. (Ed.), Oral Precancer – Diagnosis and Man-agement of Potentially Malignant Disorders. Wiley-Blackwell, Chichester, pp. 31–47.

Thomson, P.J., 2018. Perspectives on oral squamous cell carcinoma prevention-proliferation, position, pro-gression and prediction. J. Oral Pathol. Med. 47 (9), 803–807. https://doi.org/10.1111/jop.12733. Epub 2018 May 27 29752860.

Thomson, J.A., Itskovitz-Eldor, J., Shapiro, S.S., Waknitz, M.A., Swiergiel, J.J., Marshall, V.S., et al., 1998. Embryonic stem cell lines derived from human blastocysts. Science 282 (5391), 1145–1147 (Cross ref Shah A 64).

Tinhofer, I., Hristozova, T., Stromberger, C., Keilhoiz, U., Budach, V., 2012. Monitoring of circulating tumor cells and their expression of EGFR/phospho-EGFR during combined radiotherapy regimens in locally advanced squamous cell carcinoma of the head and neck. Int. J. Radiat. Oncol. Biol. Phys. 83 (5), e685–e690.

Tiwari, L., Kujan, O., Farah, C.S., 2019. Optical fluorescence imaging in oral cancer and potentially malig-nant disorders: a systematic review. Oral Dis., 1–20. https://doi.org/10.1111/odi.13071.

Topham, N.J., Hewitt, E.W., 2009. Natural killer cell cytotoxicity: how do they pull the trigger? Immu-nology 128 (1), 7–15.

U.S. Department of Health and Human Services, 2014. The Health Consequences of Smoking – 50 Years of Progress: A Report of the Surgeon General. U.S. Department of Health and Human Services, Centers for Disease Control and Prevention, National Center for Chronic Disease Prevention and Health Pro-motion, Office on Smoking and Health, Atlanta (GA), USA. Available from: https://www.ncbi.nlm. nih.gov/books/NBK179276/. (CrossRef-World cancer report Tobacco ch 2).

Uta, R., Laurent, M., Axel, L., Hans, A.S., Dirk, B., Heinz, L., et al., 2018. Immunotherapy in head and neck cancer –scientific rationale, current treatment options and future directions. Review article: biomedical intelligence. Swiss Med. Wkly. 148, w14625. https://doi.org/10.4414/smw.2018.14625 (Cite this as).

Valencia, C., Bonilla-Delgado, J., Oktaba, K., Ocádiz-Delgado, R., Gariglio, P., Covarrubias, L., 2008. Human papillomavirus E6/E7 oncogenes promote mouse ear regeneration by increasing the rate of wound re-epithelization and epidermal growth. J. Investig. Dermatol. 128 (12), 2894–2903. https:// doi.org/10.1038/jid.2008.156.

Valladeau, J., Saeland, S., 2005. Cutaneous dendritic cells. Semin. Immunol. 17, 273–283. https://doi.org/ 10.1016/j.smim.2005.05.009 (CR Amor).

Veld, S.G.J.G.I., Wurdinger, T., 2019. Tumor-educated platelets. Blood 133 (22), 2359–2364.

Vermorken, J.B., Remenar, E., van Herpen, C., Gorlia, T., Mesia, R., Degardin, M., et al., 2007. Cisplatin, fluorouracil, and docetaxel in unresectable head and neck cancer. N. Engl. J. Med. 357, 1695–1704.

Vermorken, J.B., Mesia, R., Rivera, F., Remenar, E., Kawecki, A., Rottey, S., et al., 2008. Platinum-based chemotherapy plus cetuximab in head and neck cancer. N. Engl. J. Med. 359, 1116–1127.

Vermorken, J.B., Stohlmacher-Williams, J., Davidenko, I., Licitra, L., Winquist, E., Villanueva, C., et al., 2013. Cisplatin and fluoro- uracil with or without panitumumab in patients with recurrent or metastatic squamous-cell carcinoma of the head and neck (SPECTRUM): an open-label phase 3 randomised trial. Lancet Oncol. 14, 697–710.

Villa, A., Villa, C., Abati, S., 2011. Oral cancer and oral erythroplakia: an update and implication for clini-cians. Aust. Dent. J. 56, 253–256.

Wang, Q., Gao, P., Wang, X., Duan, Y., 2014. The early diagnosis and monitoring of squamous cell carcinoma via saliva metabolomics. Sci. Rep. 4, 6802.

Wang, Y., Springer, S., Mulvey, C.L., Silliman, N., Schaefer, J., Sausen, M., et al., 2015. Detection of somatic mutations and HPV in the saliva and plasma of patients with head and neck squamous cell carcinomas. Sci. Transl. Med. 7 (293) (293ra104).

Warburg, O., 1956. On respiratory impairment in cancer cells. Science, 0036–8075 (CR Peltanova 192).

Warnakulasuriya, S., 2009. Global epidemiology of oral and oropharyngeal cancer. Oral Oncol. 45 (4–5), 309–316. https://doi.org/10.1016/j.oraloncology.2008.06.002.

Warnakulasuriya, S., 2014. Prognostic and predictive markers for oral squamous cell carcinoma: the importance of clinical, pathological and molecular markers. Saudi J. Med. Med. Sci. 2 (1), 12.

Warnakulasuriya, S., Ariyawardana, A., 2016. Malignant transformation of oral leukoplakia: a systematic review of observational studies. J. Oral Pathol. Med. 45 (3), 155–166. https://doi.org/10.1111/jop.12339.

Warnakulasuriya, S., Johnson, N.W., van der Waal, I., 2007. Nomenclature and classification of potentially malignant disorders of the oral mucosa. J. Oral Pathol. Med. 36, 575–580.

Weber, F., Byrne, S.N., Le, S., Brown, D.A., Breit, S.N., Scolyer, R.A., et al., 2005. Transforming growth factor-beta1 immobilises dendritic cells within skin tumours and facilitates tumour escape from the immune system. Cancer Immunol. Immunother. 54, 898–906. https://doi.org/10.1007/s00262-004-0652-3.

Welsh, M.M., Applebaum, K.M., Spencer, S.K., Perry, A.E., Karagas, M.R., Nelson, H.H., 2009. CTLA4 variants, UV-induced tolerance, and risk of non-melanoma skin cancer. Cancer Res. 69, 6158–6163. https://doi.org/10.1158/0008-5472.can-09-0415.

WHO, 2017. WHO Classification of Head and Neck Tumours. In: El-Naggar, A.K., Chan, J.K.C., Grandis, J.R., Takata, T., Slootweg, P.J. (Eds.), WHO Classification of Tumours, 4th. Vol. 9. WHO. https://publications.iarc.fr/Book-And-Report-Series/Who-Classification-Of-Tumours/WHO-Classification-Of-Head-And-NEck-Tumous-2007.

WHO, 2018. Global Health Estimates 2016: Deaths by Cause, Age, Sex, by Country and by Region, 2000–2016. World Health Organization, Geneva, Switzerland. (1 of World cancer book 2020). Available from: https://www.who.int/healthinfo/global_burden_disease/en/.

WHO, 2019. WHO Global Report on Trends in Prevalence of Tobacco Use 2000–2025, third ed. World Health Organization, Geneva, Switzerland. Available from: https://www.who.int/publications-detail/who-global-report-on-trends-in-prevalence-of-tobacco-use-2000-2025-third-edition. (world cancer report 2020 CR).

Wiklund, E.D., Gao, S., Hulf, T., Sibbritt, T., Nair, S., Costea, D.E., et al., 2011. MicroRNA alterations and associated aberrant DNA methylation patterns across multiple sample types in oral squamous cell carcinoma. PLoS One 6 (11), e27840.

Wolf, G.T., Fee Jr., W.E., Dolan, R.W., Moyer, J.S., Kaplan, M.J., Spring, P.M., et al., 2011. Novel neoadjuvant immunotherapy regimen safety and survival in head and neck squamous cell cancer. Head Neck 33 (12), 1666–1674. https://doi.org/10.1002/hed.21660. PubMed.

Wong, T.S., Liu, X.B., Wong, B.Y., Ng, R.W.-M., Yuen, A.P.-W., Wei, W.I., 2008. Mature miR-184 as potential oncogenic microRNA of squamous cell carcinoma of tongue. Clin. Cancer Res. 14 (9), 2588–2592.

Wood, H.M., Daly, C., Chalkley, R., Senguven, B., Ross, L., Egan, P., et al., 2017. The genomic road to invasion—examining the similarities and differences in the genomes of associated oral pre-cancer and cancer samples. Genome Med. 9, 53. https://doi.org/10.1186/s13073-017-0442-0.

World Cancer Report, 2020. Cancer Research for Cancer Prevention. In: Wild, C.P., Weiderpass, E., Stewart, B.W. (Eds.), International Agency for Research on Cancer. https://www.iarc.int/cards_page/world-cancer-report/.

Wright, J.T., 2011. Oral manifestations in the epidermolysis bullosa spectrum. Dermatol. Clin. 28, 159–164.

Wu, Y., Wu, P.Y., 2009. CD133 as a marker for cancer stem cells: progresses and concerns. Stem Cells Dev. 18, 1127–1134.

Yamada, S., Yanamoto, S., Otani, S., Hasegawa, T., Miyakoshi, M., Minamikawa, T., et al., 2016. Evaluation of the level of progression of extracapsular spread for cervical lymph node metastasis in oral squamous cell carcinoma. Int. J. Oral Maxillofac. Surg. 45 (2), 141–146.

Yang, Y., Klionsky, D.J., 2020. Autophagy and disease: unanswered questions. Cell Death Differ 27 (3), 858–871. https://doi.org/10.1038/s41418-019-0480-9.

Yang, K., Wen, Y., Wang, C., 2003. Clinical application of anticancer nanoparticles targeting metastasis foci of cervical lymph nodes in patients with oral carcinoma. Hua Xi Kou Qiang Yi Xue Za Zhi 21 (6), 447–450 (Chinese. Cross ref Calixto 204).

Yang, C.C., Zhu, L.F., Xu, X.H., Ning, T.Y., Ye, J.H., Liu, L.K., 2013. Membrane type 1 matrix metalloproteinase induces an epithelial to mesenchymal transition and cancer stem cell-like properties in SCC9 cells. BMC Cancer 13, 171.

Yao, L., Jermanus, C., Barbetta, B., Choi, C., Verbeke, P., Ojcius, D.M., et al., 2010. Porphyromonas gingivalis infection sequesters pro-apoptotic bad through Akt in primary gingival epithelial cells. Mol Oral Microbiol 25, 89–101.

Yuen, W.Y., Jonkman, M.F., 2011. Risk of squamous cell carcinoma in junctional epidermolysis bullosa, non-Herlitz type: report of 7 cases and a review of the literature. J. Am. Acad. Dermatol. 65, 780–789.

Zandberg, D.P., Algazi, A.P., Jimeno, A., Good, J.S., Fayette, J., Bouganim, N., et al., 2019. Durvalumab for recurrent or metastatic head and neck squamous cell carcinoma: results from a single-arm, phase II study in patients with >/=25% tumour cell PD-L1 expression who have progressed on platinum- based chemotherapy. Eur. J. Cancer 107, 142–152. https://doi.org/10.1016/j.ejca.2018.11.015.

Zhang, H., Wu, H., Zheng, J., Yu, P., Xu, L., Jiang, P., et al., 2013. Transforming growth factor β1 signal is crucial for dedifferentiation of cancer cells to cancer stem cells in osteosarcoma. Stem Cells 31, 433–446.

Zhang, J., Chen, L., Liu, X., Kammertoens, T., Blankenstein, T., Qin, Z., 2013a. Fibroblast-specific protein 1/S100A4-positive cells prevent carcinoma through collagen production and encapsulation of carcinogens. Cancer Res. 73, 2770–2781. https://doi.org/10.1158/0008-5472.CAN-12-3022.

Zhang, Z., Liang, X., Fan, Y., Gao, Z., Bindoff, L.A., Costea, D.E., et al., 2019. Fibroblasts rescue oral squamous cancer cell from metformin-induced apoptosis via alleviating metabolic disbalance and inhibiting AMPK pathway. Cell Cycle 18 (9), 949–962. https://doi.org/10.1080/15384101.2019.1598727.

Zhou, B.B., Zhang, H., Damelin, M., Geles, K.G., Grindley, J.C., Dirks, P.B., 2009. Tumour-initiating cells: challenges and opportunities for anticancer drug discovery. Nat. Rev. Drug Discov. 8, 806–823.

Zhou, C., Diao, P., Wu, Y., Wei, Z., Jiang, L., Zhang, W., et al., 2020. Development and validation of a seven-immune-feature-based prognostic score for oral squamous cell carcinoma after curative resection. Int. J. Cancer 146, 1152–1163. https://doi.org/10.1002/ijc.32571.

Ziober, B.L., Mauk, M.G., Falls, E.M., Chen, Z., Ziober, A.F., Bau, H.H., 2008. Lab-on-a-Chip for oral cancer screening and diagnosis. Head Neck. https://doi.org/10.1002/hed.

CHAPTER TWO

Genetic predisposition and pathophysiology of oral squamous cell carcinoma

Selvaraj Jayaraman[a,*], Duraj Sekar[b,*], Ponnulakshmi Rajagopal[c,*], Veerakumar Ramachandran[d,*], Ramya Sekar[a,*], JH Shazia Fathima[a,*], Dhayasankar Prabhu Shankar[e,*], and Gowtham Kumar Subbaraj[f,*]

[a]Centre for Molecular Medicine and Diagnostics (COMManD), Department of Biochemistry, Saveetha Dental College & Hospitals, Saveetha Institute of Medical & Technical Sciences (Deemed to be University), Chennai, India
[b]RNA Biology Lab, Saveetha Dental College & Hospitals, Saveetha Institute of Medical & Technical Sciences (Deemed to be University), Chennai, India
[c]Department of Central Research Laboratory, Meenakshi Ammal Dental College and Hospitals, Chennai, India
[d]Department of Pedodontics and Preventive Dentistry, Priyadharshini Dental College, Thiruvallur, India
[e]Department of Oral & Maxillofacial Surgery, Meenakshi Ammal Dental College, Chennai, India
[f]Faculty of Allied Health Sciences, Chettinad Hospital and Research Institute, Chettinad Academy of Research and Education (Deemed to be University), Kelambakkam, India

Abbreviations

5-FU	fluorouracil
5-NQO	4-nitroquinoline-1-oxide
ATP	adenosine triphosphate
COVID-19	coronavirus disease-19
DNA	deoxyribonucleic acid
FDG	fluorodeoxyglucose
GLUTs	glucose transporters
HPV	human papillomavirus
OSCCC	oral squamous cell carcinoma
pRB	retinoblastoma protein
PVL	proliferative verrucous leukoplakia
rRNA	ribosomal ribonucleic acid
SCC	squamous cell carcinomas
SGLTs	sodium-glucose cotransporters

* Authors contributed equally.

Biomarkers in Cancer Detection and Monitoring of Therapeutics
https://doi.org/10.1016/B978-0-323-95114-2.00004-2

1. Introduction

Human microbiomes contain hundreds of pathogenic, commensal, and symbiotic microorganisms. Diverse groups of microorganisms are found in the environment, such as viruses, fungi, viruses, bacteria, protozoa, archaea, protozoa, and other microbes. The microbiota of a human body is abundant and plays a critical role in its health. The skin contains many microorganisms that are beneficial for the immune system and for wound healing. Based on the environmental conditions and accessibility to nutrients, various positions in the body support various microbial communities. Further, composition of each individual's microbiome can be unpredictable and fluctuate depending on a range of factors, including their current health, lifestyle, genetics, and other influential factors. In this review, we focus on the oral microbiome, specifically its interaction with oral cancer, namely squamous cell carcinomas.

1.1 Microbial flora

In the oral microbiome, there are 1500 genomes and 32 taxa recognized, making it the second largest microbial environment in the body (Deo and Deshmukh, 2020). There are three anatomical sites where the oral microbiome can be found: the oral cavity which contains teeth, gums, soft and hard palates, saliva, buccal mucosa, saliva, supragingival, and subgingival plaques; the oropharynx which contains base of tongue, tonsils, mid-pharynx, larynx, posterior, and hypopharynx. The oral microbiome has eight sub sites, each of them has a distinctive structure and creates a distinct microenvironment in which the microbiome can thrive (An et al. 2020).

1.2 Oral microbial flora

A significant portion of the oral microbiota lives on the tongue, and by using saliva, it then colonizes other oral mucosal surfaces, including *Selenomonas* spp., *Porphyromonas gingivalis, Prevotella intermedia, Capnocytophaga* spp.*, Actinobacillus actinomycetemcomitans,* and others. As well as saliva, the next subsite, the oropharynx, produces mucus that aids digestion and is colonized with pathogenic bacteria, including *Streptococcus pyogenes, Haemophilus para influenzae,* and *Haemophilus influenza* (An et al. 2020) (Fig. 1).

It is essential to have pathogenic and mutualistic bacteria which can be isolated from healthy individuals in order to maintain balance (Ramya et al., 2022). People with a chronic illness are at high risk of developing ventilator-associated pneumonia because their oral microbiome shifts from gram-positive to gram-negative organisms (Hull and Chow, 2007). A detailed information review on the indigenous microbial communities of the neck and head is provided by Hull and Chow (2007) which highlights how the oral microbiome is highly adapted to the biology and physiology and of the head and neck.

Fig. 1 Effect of smoking on oral (subgingival plaque) microbial flora.

Despite the sterility of the womb, the oral microbiome begins to form in utero, and extant species such as *Streptococcus salivarius* become colonized before birth (An et al., 2020; Sampaio-Maia and Monteiro-Silva, 2014). The microbial succession process plays a crucial role in the evolution of the oral microbiome fueled by *S. salivarius*. It utilizes sucrose as an extracellular polymer source to allow other bacteria, such as *Actinomyces*, to attach to them and grow. As teeth emerge in the mouth, a new adhesion surface is formed, along with a new oral microbiome (Sampaio-Maia and Monteiro-Silva, 2014). The development of dental caries goes hand in hand with the development of dentition, a chronic condition that almost everyone experiences. Among the most important factors contributing to dental caries are Actinomyces, *Streptococcus mutans*, *Lactobacillus*, and other nonmutagenic *Streptococcus* strains (Fig. 2).

1.3 Oral microbial flora and cancer

In addition, the oral microbiome has been shown to influence oral diseases such as periodontitis and esophageal and oral cancer as well as systemic diseases such as cystic fibrosis, diabetes, colorectal cancer. Currently, oral microbiome are not fully understood as to their role in neck and head cancer formation. Various factors, including oral hygiene

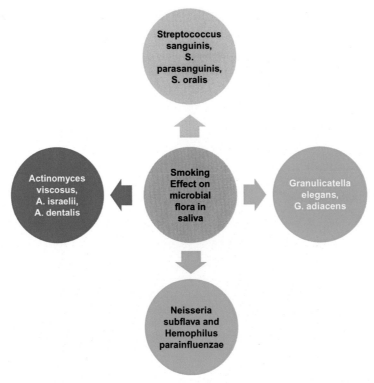

Fig. 2 Effect of smoking on oral (saliva) microbial flora.

practices (Zarco et al. 2012), alcohol consumption, and tobacco consumption (Fan et al., 2018; O'Grady et al., 2020), can influence the amount and type of oral microbial flora fluctuations, which may cause changes to squamous cell carcinomas in the neck and head. The socioeconomic conditions around the world are another complicating factor. Further complicating the study of how mouth microbes affect disease pathogenesis, specifically of neck and head cancer, is the age of the mouth microbes. The scope of microbiome research was previously limited because researchers were unable to culture many microorganisms in the laboratory using their methods and techniques. In addition to culture-independent techniques, metagenomic approaches, and the latest technology researchers have studied the diversity of oral bacteria (An et al. 2020; Torralba et al. 2020; Shay et al. 2020; Sarkar et al. 2021). The oral microbiota may trigger a wide range of local and systemic diseases, including Down syndrome, cardiovascular disease, periodontal disease, and obesity. 16S rRNA sequencing, next-generation sequencing, and phylogenetic DNA microarrays provide insight into this possibility (Fig. 3).

A correlation has been demonstrated between a compromised oral microbiome and COVID-19 infection, particularly in the pharynx and the nasopharynx (Sulaiman et al.

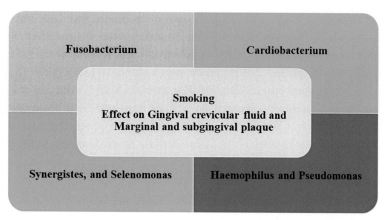

Fig. 3 Effect of smoking on oral (gingival crevicular fluid and marginal and subgingival plaque) microbial flora.

2021; Nardelli et al., 2021; Budding et al., 2020). In ventilated COVID-19, oral microbes (*Mycoplasma salivarium*) adversely affect clinical outcomes (Sulaiman et al., 2021). Since it is associated with these diseases, the oral microbiome could provide a target for developing new diagnostic and therapeutic tools in a wide range of clinical settings. Studies have found that oral microbiota may play a more significant role in controlling immune responses in the body, viral and bacterial infections, and the development of squamous cell carcinomas of the neck and then previously thought (Sharma et al., 2020; Chen et al., 2021; Sulaiman et al., 2021; Hayes et al., 2018). It may be possible to develop new diagnostic tools and novel therapeutics by understanding the interactions between host-oral microbes and the development of head and neck cancer.

As a result of its association with these diseases, the oral microbiome might be useful for developing new diagnostic and therapeutic tools. A disruption, out of balance, or eradication of the oral microorganisms may result in chronic inflammation and suppression of the normal host immune system, ultimately leading to head and neck cancer (Rai et al., 2021; Perera et al., 2018; Kleinstein et al., 2020; Chen et al., 2020). Gram-negative anaerobic bacteria are commonly found in periodontitis. Gram-negative anaerobes that cause chronic oral inflammation and cancer, such as *Porphyromonas gingivalis, Tannerella forsythia*, and *Treponema denticola*, are often found in periodontal disease (Kakabadze et al., 2020; Malinowski et al., 2019; Wen et al., 2020; Teles et al., 2020). In a variety of ways, oral microbiomes contribute to cancer development, but their mechanisms are not fully understood. Periodontal disease manifested in poor oral hygiene is thought to influence the development of oral cancer. Researchers have not addressed the mechanism by which periodontal disease stimulates neck and head cancer. Prospective studies indicate the microbes associated with periodontal disease may not play a role in the development of oral cancer based on their results (Colonia-García et al., 2020).

The first prospective study examining the oral microbiome and neck and head squamous cell carcinoma by Hayes et al. found that *Actinobacteria* were associated with a higher risk of squamous cell carcinoma, while *Corynebacterium* and *Kingella* were associated with a lower risk (Hayes et al., 2018). Furthermore, no incidence of tooth decay (*S. mutans*) or periodontal disease (*P. gingivalis*, *T. forsythia*, *P. aeruginosa*, and *T. denticola*) was associated with a higher risk of squamous cell carcinoma of the head and neck. Hayes et al. suggest that toxins found in tobacco products may play a role in the protective mechanisms that *Corynebacterium* and *Kingella* provide in colonization. According to a study by Sharma et al., smokers with head and neck squamous cell carcinoma and those without exhibited significantly different oral microbiome (Sharma et al., 2020). It was found that the *Stenotrophomonas* and *Comamonadaceae* species were abundant among smokers with squamous cell carcinomas of the head and neck, as well as bacterial pathways that engaged in the degradation of xenobiotics (e.g., hydroxyacetone, phenol, toluene, and vanillin), amino acids, amine utilization (histidine, arginine, putrescence, and polygenic amines), and antibiotic resistance. Evidence suggests that smokers with cancer have different oral microbiomes than that without. Squamous cell carcinoma of the head and neck is not related to these differences.

The development of oropharyngeal squamous cell carcinoma is related to viruses such as HPV in recent years. The oral microbiome is largely unknown as to whether it promotes or suppresses HPV infection within the oropharynx, and the available studies are limited. There has been evidence that HPV status influences the composition of the oral microbiome, including an increase in *Actinomyces*, *Selenomonas noxia*, *Campylobacter genera*, *Granulicatella*, *Rothia mucilaginosa*, *Oribacterium*, *H. parainfluenzae*, and *Veillonella disparand* in patients with HPV-positive oropharynx cancer, as compared with patients without HPV. Several metabolic pathways are altered in the body when HPV positive patients are present, including glutamate metabolism and metal transport. On the basis of observations that type 2 transglutaminase inhibits HPV E7 binding to pRB, glutamine metabolism is increased in HPV-positive oropharynx tumors suggest that type 2 transglutaminase catalytic activity promotes HPV infection in part through the oral microbiome (Bazzo Goulart et al., 2017).

Translational research models that include the oral microbiome are insufficiently described in head and neck cancer research. Based on a germ-free murine model, Stashenko et al. characterized oral squamous cell cancer development. This study showed that 4-nitroquinoline-1-oxide (5-NQO) caused oral squamous cell carcinoma. By injecting germ-free recipient mice with the microbiome of either tumor-bearing or healthy tumor-free mice, the desired outcomes were obtained. The tumor burden of mice inoculated with "healthy microbiomes" was significantly higher than mice inoculated with tumor-derived microbiomes. The abundances of *Parabacteroides* and *Corynebacterium* both changed reciprocally (Stashenko et al., 2019). When mice developed oral squamous cell carcinomas, *Parabacteroides* increased and *Corynebacterium* decreased. The odds for carrying *Corynebacterium* and *Kingella* decrease in patients with esophageal squamous cell carcinoma, while the odds for carrying *Corynebacterium* and *Kingella* decrease in patients with head and neck cancer (Hayes et al., 2018; Stashenko et al., 2019). *Rodentibacter pneumotropicus* was enriched in both cohorts at different times, but it occurred more rapidly in the healthy microbiome group at an earlier point in time. Among laboratory rodents, *R. pneumotropicus* colonizes the urogenital tract and respiratory tract. It is highly contagious among rodents (Fingas et al., 2019). While Stashenko et al. may not be completely clear regarding their results; these findings suggest that *R. pneumotropicus* might be involved in the development of oral squamous cell carcinoma in mice. Metatranscriptome analysis of mice treated with 4-NQO compared to mice not treated revealed that the treatment increased organic/nitrogen substance transport, stress response, and interspecies interaction functions, including cell wall biosynthesis, amino acid metabolism, and interspecies interactions.

1.4 Squamous cell carcinoma of the head and neck

Squamous cell carcinoma of the head and neck is most commonly caused by smoking and alcohol consumption. The condition of dysbiosis is caused by an imbalance between commensal and harmful microbes. *Actinomyces, Leptotrichia, Cardiobacterium*, and *Neisseria* have all been detected in the oral microbiomes of heavy drinkers (Fan et al., 2018). The carcinogen acetaldehyde is produced by *Neisseria* when colonized with ethanol. This bacterium produces 100 times more acetaldehyde than most other bacteria, even though *Neisseria mucosa* is considered a good indicator of good oral health (O'Grady et al., 2020). It is possible, therefore, that *N. mucosa* may play a protective role in tobacco users due to a lower colonization rate. In addition to illustrating the scope of the oral microbiome, the study of oral mucosa provides insight into the importance of certain bacteria in colonizing that region of the mouth for both health and disease.

Additionally, tobacco use causes dysbiosis in the oral cavity. An analysis of oral microbiomes revealed that smokers had fewer microbes that metabolize carbohydrates and energy, whereas they had more microbes that metabolize xenobiotic. The microenvironment of a smoker is acidic, allowing anaerobes to colonize (Wu et al., 2016). As a result of a slow carbohydrate metabolism, the oral microbiome of smokers seems to facilitate xenobiotic pathway degrading of phenyl compounds, aromatic amines, and toluene that are thought to cause head and neck cancers. There is a need for further investigation into whether smoking changes the oral microbiome in a way that promotes the release of various xenobiotics or whether people at higher risk of developing head and neck cancer have an oral microbiome that contributes to the release of these toxins. Former smokers apparently have microbes more similar to those of nonsmokers after stopping smoking, indicating that tobacco has reversible effects on dysbiosis (Wu et al., 2016).

Head and neck cancer is not associated with changes in the oral microbiome of smokers. People who smoke are more likely to have periodontal disease and head and neck cancer than those who have never smoked. There was less of an association with changes in oral health variables in smokers as compared to nonsmokers for cancers of the aero digestive tract (Gholizadeh et al., 2016). There is evidence that betel nut consumption alters the oral microbiome in Asia and the Pacific, but it is rare in the United States. *Streptococcus infantis* colonization was four-fold more common in betel nut chewers, and *Streptococcus anginosus* colonization was multiple fold more common in chewers with premalignant oral lesions (Hernandez et al., 2017). As of now, it is only speculation about how changes in the oral microbiome of chewers may increase their risk for oral cancer.

Squamous cell carcinoma in the head and neck is typically advanced and may require concurrent chemotherapy and radiation. Dysbiosis is a potential cause of side effects and poor treatment outcomes for patients with head and neck cancer. Patients can be negatively affected by radiation or chemotherapy systemic toxicities. Mucositis of the mouth and oropharynx can cause patients to experience dizziness, pain, and dysphagia, requiring hospitalization and potentially feeding tubes. A severe, grade 3 or 4 mucositis was associated with *Fusobacterium, Porphyromonas, Treponema,* and *Prevotella.* There is no evidence that many oral antibiotic rinses work in preventing oral mucositis (Hou et al., 2018). There is no evidence that many oral antibiotic rinses work in preventing oral mucositis. In fact, they may encourage early dysbiosis due to their ineffectiveness to kill intracellular bacteria. A number of chemotherapeutic agents, including 5-FU and cisplatin, are known to alter the bacterial communities while not altering the fungal communities, causing dysbiosis. The reasons for the development of oral mucositis in these patients may be related to this. Interestingly, the drug itself did not possess an antibacterial effect on oral commensals as did the dose. Chemotherapy administration results in the rapid reduction of salivary 5-FU (5-fluorouracil) levels and their absence 22 h after infusion, as well as oral mucositis within days (Hong et al., 2019). A placebo-controlled double-blind, randomized study did not show improvement in mucositis following treatment with gram-negative bacteria when compared to controls.

It is difficult to manage head and neck squamous cell carcinomas because of the wide heterogeneity of their pathology and response to treatment. Viral infections, tobacco use, alcohol, and the use of betel nuts can all cause cancer of the head and neck. It is expected that from the initiation of cancer up to the response to treatment, the oral microbiome plays an important role. Through the development of molecular techniques, the oral microbiome can be better characterized, allowing experiments to be developed to gain a deeper understanding of the mechanism of gene expression changes within the microbiome. A better understanding of how oral microbiomes change may lead to earlier detection of premalignant conditions. The propagation of commensal homeostasis may reduce severe mucositis in patients who are undergoing chemotherapy and radiation therapy. It may be possible to improve outcomes and quality of life by better understanding the role oral microbiota play in health and disease, such as head and neck cancer.

2. Oral squamous cell carcinoma and glucose transporters

Squamous cell carcinomas (SCC) of the mouth are prevalent malignancies with poor prognoses. In OSCCs, the Warburg effect is evident, with cancer cells requiring a strong glucose concentration. Multiple malignancies are associated with overexpression of sodium–glucose cotransporters (SGLTs) and glucose transporters (GLUTs), which are associated with resistance of treatment and deprived survival (Pao et al., 1998).

2.1 Human glucose transporters

Humans have more than 400 glucose transporters, which are members of the Major Facilitator Superfamily of solute carriers. Glucose transporter 1 is frequently expressed in Squamous cell carcinomas and is overexpressed compared to NOK, with high expression associated with advanced disease stages, treatment resistance, and poor prognosis. GLUT-1 does not appear to be associated with FDG uptake, metastasis, or tumor grade. GLUT-3 has been studied narrowly, but was detected in most samples and is generally overexpressed when compared to NOK. Data on correlations with other clinical factors were not available, but GLUT-3 negatively associated with general existence. Studies evaluating expression of GLUT-1, GLUT-2, GLUT-4, GLUT-8, and SGLT-13 found no differences in expression. OSCC has never evaluated GLUT 7 or 14. These data indicate that GLUT-3 as well as GLUT-1 play a significant part in the progression of OSCC and can serve as significant biomarkers for prognosis and diagnosis. Further GLUTs are relatively understudied and should be examined further considering their potential for improving patient care (Hediger et al., 2013; Burant et al., 1992; Rumsey et al., 1997).

The hydrophobic cell membrane facilitates diffusion of other metabolites, nutrients and soluble ions. The GLUT family of transporters consists of 14 transmembrane peptides and are primarily responsible for transporting glucose and molecules like fructose. Additionally, they transport myoinositol, ascorbate, uric acid, glucosamine, and other similar substrates. The tissue distribution of GLUTs, their affinity for substrates, and their turnover rates vary widely. Despite advances in treatment, the survival rate for oral squamous cell carcinoma (OSCC) remains unchanged over the last few decades. In 2018, 354,864 oral squamous cell carcinoma cases were diagnosed, and 177,384 individuals died. Cancer is characterized by dysregulation of metabolic pathways, and OSCCs use aerobic glycolysis for ATP synthesis. In various types of cancer cells, glycolytic enzymes are upregulated and GLUTs are often overexpressed. As a result, rapid growth and proliferation are fueled by a steady supply of glucose (Mazurek et al., 2002; Macheda et al., 2005).

2.2 Glucose transporters (GLUT 1) and its expression

A poor prognosis has been associated with GLUT expression in numerous tumors, together with oral squamous cell carcinoma. The expression of GLUT-1 has been linked with both chemo resistant tumors as well as radioresistant tumors, including oral squamous cell carcinoma. Due to the increased glycolysis process, DNA repair mechanisms and antiapoptotic genes may be upregulated, resulting in these associations. A higher expression level of GLUT has been found in tumors of progressive stages and high grades of tumor. GLUT-1 was repeatedly implicated in clinical factors and clinical outcomes. In most of studies, increased expression of GLUT-1 is related to deprived survival. Furthermore, GLUT-1 was considered to be a self-determining predictive factor in these studies, accounting for clinical factors such as grade, stage, size of the tumor, as well as the status of the lymph node. It was surprising that GLUT-1 did not specify a relationship with disease-free existence (Kim et al., 2017; Huang et al., 2014; Haber et al., 1998; Ayala et al., 2010).

Information on clinical staging suggest that expression of GLUT-1 is clearly associated with stage with only a single study contradicting this. A positive correlation was found in only few patients of the study, while 231 patients were involved in the other studies. It is unclear what role GLUTs play in tumor differentiation and grading. GLUT-1 was positively correlated with grading and tumor differentiation in half of the studies, while the other half found no association. Likewise, a significant consensus was lacking among studies on metastasis, which made it difficult to draw any conclusions. Previous reports also correlated GLUT-1 levels with both lymph node metastasis and grade in a wide range of cancer types. In that there were significant differences between studies, the findings on the relationship among fluorodeoxyglucose (FDG) consumption by tumors and expression of GLUT-1 were analogous. Therefore, it is possible that glucose metabolism is not limited by GLUT-1 expression in OSCC (Han et al., 2012; Yu et al., 2017; Kraus et al., 2016, 2018).

3. Oral squamous cell carcinoma and methylated genes

Globally, oral cancer represents the sixth most common form of cancer with an increasing incidence. Additionally, late diagnosis and delayed management contribute to dramatically low five-year survival rates. The use of early screening process of asymptomatic cancer is important to diminish mortality from OSCC, because most oral carcinomas have visible lesions preceding them, such as proliferative verrucous leukoplakia (PVL). Studies have shown that a visual investigation of oral of increased risk individuals may be a current screening approach, but biomarkers and related aids are essential to develop the clinical detection of oral premalignant lesions (Hansen et al., 1985; Campisi et al., 2004).

Among these, methylation of DNA investigation has been shown to be a significant method for recognizing oral cancer lesions at the initial stage, and related methodologies are already being developed to detect lung cancer lesions. A methylation differential analysis was conducted between individuals with and without PVL lesions, meanwhile PVL is the most forceful form of leukoplakia, with a cancer conversion rate ranging from 70% to 100%. From the previous findings, PVL and healthy donors exhibit distinct patterns of methylation, with PVL patients exhibiting markedly higher rates of methylation across the board compared to healthy donors. Approximately 600 proteins-coding genes were affected, which played a significant role in the response of persons to the treatment and disease, as well as in PVL progression and the development of cancer. Morandi and his colleagues have previously reported epigenetic modifications in PVL, display patterns of methylation that are similar to those of OSCC than normal persons. Some cancer types have already been treated with this approach, such as hepatocellular carcinoma and cervical cancer (Silverman and Gorsky, 1997; Gandolfo et al., 2009; Upadhyaya et al., 2018; Bagan et al., 2011).

3.1 Variation of methylated genes in cancer conditions

The following genes (SPOCK2, ARTN, CD8A, GATA3, PCLB1, OSR2, and MYO7A) were found to be highly methylated and were also considerably over expressed in PVL, and these genes are significantly related with cancer. It has been proposed that proteins encoded by PLCB1, OSR2, and ARTN may be involved in oral cancer oncogenesis and pain medication. Furthermore, GATA3 and CD8A appear to be related to immune responses to tumors. Hypermethylated SPOCK2 was found to be a probable candidate biomarker in head and neck cancer. Upregulation of HOXD10 was linked with augmented migration and proliferation. Deregulated expression of MYO7A has been shown to promote tumor progression (Turhani et al., 2006; Ogawa et al., 2020).

Additionally, hyper methylated genes such as DLG2, PITX2, ZNF736, ANKRD6 and GPX3 were significantly lesser expressed in PVL. It has been reported that GPX3 and DLG2 are downregulated in OSCC and are suggested as probable candidate biomarkers for this type of tumor. Using both epigenomic and transcriptomic data, a combination investigation of the oral masticatory mucosa found a link between smoking and absence of expression of ANKRD6, a key WNT pathway regulator. Additional tumor candidate biomarkers earlier identified as part of PVL are studied. To evaluate their potential value in predicting the development of oral cancer, their gene expression patterns were assessed in TCGA patients with OSCC. As in PVL, deregulation was also observed in OSCC, indicating that the genomic changes begun at PVL continue at OSCC (Guo et al., 2016; Pedro et al., 2018).

TCGA patients with OSCC were evaluated for the expression of genes associated with these markers. As in PVL, deregulation was also observed in OSCC, indicating that genomic changes initiated during PVL are additionally observed during OSCC. PVL lesions are a precancer niche for malignant transformation and OSCC development, and studies such as these are particularly valuable because they validate the notion that PVL lesions represent an important precancer niche. Patients with potentially malignant disorders need to be better classified as oral cancer patients, since early detection of oral cancer would improve treatment outcomes. As a result of recent breakthroughs in technology, new approaches are making it possible to classify unique biomarkers for prognostics, pathological diagnostics, and monitoring of patient health (Katoh, 2005; Richter et al., 2019; Farah, 2021).

3.2 DNA methylation modifications and its implications

As a result, patients with insignificant results may be treated adjuvantly or closely monitored, since they are at greater risk of developing cancer or dying. It was found that methylation analysis is an effective method for identifying possible malignant markers in PVL. In addition to formative variations already present in precancerous lesions, these markers could be used as an early detection method for asymptomatic carcinomas. The study revealed the importance of epigenetic modification and unusual DNA methylation status in PVL that might be used as oral malignant biomarkers in the future. The quick and prompt oral cancer diagnosis can be significant for high-risk group of people's management. These candidate markers could be an influential tool for understanding PVL's molecular events. The previous studies revealed the possible use of methylation modifications for the diagnosis of oral cancer and this could lead to the improvement of novel epigenetic remedies in the future (Herreros-Pomares et al., 2021).

References

An, R., Gowda, M., Rey, F.E., Thibeault, S.L., 2020. Selective bacterial colonization of the murine larynx in a gnotobiotic model. Front. Microbiol. 11, 594617.

Ayala, F.R.R., Rocha, R.M., Carvalho, K.C., Carvalho, A., Da Cunha, I.W., Lourenço, S.V., Soares, F.A., 2010. Glut1 and Glut3 as potential prognostic markers for Oral squamous cell carcinoma. Molecules 15, 2374–2387.

Bagan, J.V., Jiménez-Soriano, Y., Diaz-Fernandez, J.M., Murillo-Cortés, J., Sanchis Bielsa, J.M., Poveda-Roda, R., Bagan, L., 2011. Malignant transformation of proliferative verrucous leukoplakia to oral squamous cell carcinoma: a series of 55 cases. Oral Oncol. 47 (8), 732–735.

Bazzo Goulart, K.O., Guerra Godoy, A.E., Litvin, I.E., Firmbach Pasqualotto, F., 2017. Expression analysis of transglutaminase 2 in premalignant lesions of the cervix. Appl. Cancer Res. 37, 27.

Budding, A., Sieswerda, E., Wintermans, B., Bos, M., 2020. An age dependent pharyngeal microbiota signature associated with SARS-CoV-2 infection. SSRN Electron. J.

Burant, C., Takeda, J., Brot-Laroche, E., Bell, G., Davidson, N., 1992. Fructose transporter in human spermatozoa and small intestine is GLUT5. J. Biol. Chem. 267, 14523–14526.

Campisi, G., Giovannelli, L., Ammatuna, P., Capra, G., Colella, G., Di Liberto, C., et al., 2004. Proliferative verrucous vs conventional leukoplakia: no significantly increased risk of HPV infection. Oral Oncol. 40 (8), 835–840.

Chen, Z., Wong, P.Y., Ng, C.W.K., Lan, L., Fung, S., Li, J.W., Cai, L., Lei, P., Mou, Q., Wong, S.H., et al., 2020. The intersection between oral microbiota, host gene methylation and patient outcomes in head and neck squamous cell carcinoma. Cancers 12, 3425.

Chen, S.-H., Hsiao, S.-Y., Chang, K.-Y., Chang, J.-Y., 2021. New insights into oral squamous cell carcinoma: from clinical aspects to molecular tumorigenesis. Int. J. Mol. Sci. 22, 2252.

Colonia-García, A., Gutiérrez-Vélez, M., Duque-Duque, A., de Andrade, C.R., 2020. Possible association of periodontal disease with oral cancer and oral potentially malignant disorders: a systematic review. Acta Odontol. Scand. 78, 553–559.

Deo, P.N., Deshmukh, R., 2020. Oral microbiome and oral cancer—the probable nexus. J. Oral Maxillofac. Pathol. 24, 361–367.

Fan, X., Peters, B.A., Jacobs, E.J., Gapstur, S.M., Purdue, M.P., Freedman, N.D., Alekseyenko, A.V., Wu, J., Yang, L., Pei, Z., et al., 2018. Drinking alcohol is associated with variation in the human oral microbiome in a large study of American adults. Microbiome 6, 59.

Farah, C.S., 2021. Molecular, genomic and mutational landscape of oral leukoplakia. Oral Dis 27 (4), 803–812.

Fingas, F., Volke, D., Hassert, R., Fornefett, J., Funk, S., Baums, C.G., Hoffmann, R., 2019. Sensitive and immunogen-specific serological detection of Rodentibacter pneumotropicus infections in mice. BMC Microbiol. 19, 43.

Gandolfo, S., Castellani, R., Pentenero, M., 2009. Proliferative verrucous leukoplakia: a potentially malignant disorder involving periodontal sites. J. Periodontol. 80 (2), 274–281.

Gholizadeh, P., Eslami, H., Yousefi, M., Asgharzadeh, M., Aghazadeh, M., Kafil, H.S., 2016. Role of oral microbiome on oral cancers, a review. Biomed. Pharmacother. 84, 552–558.

Guo, T., Gaykalova, D.A., Considine, M., Wheelan, S., Pallavajjala, A., Bishop, J.A., Califano, J.A., 2016. Characterization of functionally active gene fusions in human papillomavirus related oropharyngeal squamous cell carcinoma. Int. J. Cancer 139 (2), 373–382.

Haber, R.S., Rathan, A., Weiser, K.R., Pritsker, A., Itzkowitz, S.H., Bodian, C., Slater, G., Weiss, A., Burstein, D.E., 1998. GLUT1 glucose transporter expression in colorectal carcinoma: a marker for poor prognosis. Cancer 83, 34–40.

Han, M.W., Lee, H.J., Cho, K.J., Kim, J.S., Roh, J.L., Choi, S.H., Nam, S.Y., Kim, S.Y., 2012. Role of FDG-PET as a biological marker for predicting the hypoxic status of tongue cancer. Head Neck 34 (10), 1395–1402.

Hansen, L.S., Olson, J.A., Silverman, S.J., 1985. Proliferative verrucous leukoplakia. A longterm study of thirty patients. Oral Surg. Oral Med. Oral Pathol. 60 (3), 285–298.

Hayes, R.B., Ahn, J., Fan, X., Peters, B.A., Ma, Y., Yang, L., Agalliu, I., Burk, R.D., Ganly, I., Purdue, M.-P., et al., 2018. Association of oral microbiome with risk for incident head and neck squamous cell cancer. JAMA Oncol. 4, 358–365.

Hediger, M.A., Clémençon, B., Burrier, R.E., Bruford, E.A., 2013. The ABCs of membrane transporters in health and disease (SLC series): introduction. Mol. Asp. Med. 34, 95–107.

Hernandez, B.Y., Zhu, X., Goodman, M.T., Gatewood, R., Mendiola, P., Quinata, K., Paulino, Y.C., 2017. Betel nut chewing, oral premalignant lesions, and the oral microbiome. PLoS One 12, e0172196.

Herreros-Pomares, A., Llorens, C., Soriano, B., Bagan, L., Moreno, A., Calabuig-Fariñas, S., Bagan, J., 2021. Differentially methylated genes in proliferative verrucous leukoplakia reveal potential malignant biomarkers for oral squamous cell carcinoma. Oral. Oncol. 116, 105191.

Hong, B.-Y., Sobue, T., Choquette, L., Dupuy, A.K., Thompson, A., Burleson, J.A., Salner, A.L., Schauer, P.K., Joshi, P., Fox, E., et al., 2019. Chemotherapy-induced oral mucositis is associated with detrimental bacterial dysbiosis. Microbiome 7, 66.

Hou, J., Zheng, H., Li, P., Liu, H., Zhou, H., Yang, X., 2018. Distinct shifts in the oral microbiota are associated with the progression and aggravation of mucositis during radiotherapy. Radiother. Oncol. 129, 44–51.

Huang, X.-Q., Chen, X., Xie, X.-X., Zhou, Q., Li, K., Li, S., Shen, L.-F., Su, J., 2014. Co-expression of CD147 and GLUT-1 indicates radiation resistance and poor prognosis in cervical squamous cell carcinoma. Int. J. Clin. Exp. Pathol. 7, 1651.

Hull, M.W., Chow, A.W., 2007. Indigenous microflora and innate immunity of the head and neck. Infect. Dis. Clin. N. Am. 21, 265–282.

Kakabadze, M.Z., Paresishvili, T., Karalashvili, L., Chakhunashvili, D., Kakabadze, Z., 2020. Oral microbiota and oral cancer: review. Oncol. Rev. 14, 476.

Katoh, M., 2005. WNT/PCP signalling pathway and human cancer. Oncol. Rep. 14 (6), 1583–1588.

Kim, Y.H., Jeong, D.C., Pak, K., Han, M.-E., Kim, J.-Y., Liangwen, L., Kim, H.J., Kim, T.W., Kim, T.H., Hyun, D.W., 2017. SLC2A2 (GLUT2) as a novel prognostic factor for hepatocellular carcinoma. Oncotarget 8, 68381.

Kleinstein, S.E., Nelson, K.E., Freire, M., 2020. Inflammatory networks linking oral microbiome with systemic health and disease. J. Dent. Res. 99, 1131–1139.

Kraus, D., Reckenbeil, J., Wenghoefer, M., Stark, H., Frentzen, M., Allam, J.P., Novak, N., Frede, S., Götz, W., Probstmeier, R., Meyer, R., 2016. Ghrelin promotes oral tumor cell proliferation by modifying GLUT1 expression. Cell. Mol. Life Sci. 73 (6), 1287–1299.

Kraus, D., Reckenbeil, J., Veit, N., Kuerpig, S., Meisenheimer, M., Beier, I., Stark, H., Winter, J., Probstmeier, R., 2018. Targeting glucose transport and the NAD pathway in tumor cells with STF-31: a re-evaluation. Cell. Oncol. (Dordr.) 41 (5), 485–494.

Macheda, M.L., Rogers, S., Best, J.D., 2005. Molecular and cellular regulation of glucose transporter (GLUT) proteins in cancer. J. Cell. Physiol. 202, 654–662.

Malinowski, B., Wesierska, A., Zalewska, K., Sokolowska, M.M., Bursiewicz, W., Socha, M., Ozorowski, M., Pawlak-Osinska, K., Wicinski, M., 2019. The role of Tannerella forsythia and Porphyromonas gingivalis in pathogenesis of esophageal cancer. Infect. Agent Cancer 14, 3.

Mazurek, S., Grimm, H., Boschek, C., Vaupel, P., Eigenbrodt, E., 2002. Pyruvate kinase type M2: a crossroad in the tumor metabolome. Br. J. Nutr. 87, S23–S29.

Nardelli, C., Gentile, I., Setaro, M., Di Domenico, C., Pinchera, B., Buonomo, A.R., Zappulo, E., Scotto, R., Scaglione, G.L., Castaldo, G., et al., 2021. Nasopharyngeal microbiome signature in COVID-19 positive patients: can we definitively get a role to fusobacterium periodonticum? Front. Cell. Infect. Microbiol. 11, 625581.

O'Grady, I., Anderson, A., O'Sullivan, J., 2020. The interplay of the oral microbiome and alcohol consumption in oral squamous cellcarcinomas. Oral Oncol. 110, 105011.

Ogawa, H., Nakashiro, K.-I., Tokuzen, N., Kuribayashi, N., Goda, H., Uchida, D., 2020. MicroRNA361-3p is a potent therapeutic target for oral squamous cell carcinoma. Cancer Sci. 111 (5), 1645–1651.

Pao, S.S., Paulsen, I.T., Saier, M.H., 1998. Major facilitator super family. Microbiol. Mol. Biol. Rev. 62, 1–34.

Pedro, N.F., Biselli, J.M., Maniglia, J.V., de Santi-Neto, D., Pavarino, É.C., Goloni-Bertollo, E.M., Biselli-Chicote, P.M., 2018. Candidate biomarkers for oral squamous cell carcinoma: differential expression of oxidative stress-related genes. Asian Pac. J. Cancer Prev. 19 (5), 1343.

Perera, M., Al-Hebshi, N.N., Perera, I., Ipe, D., Ulett, G.C., Speicher, D.J., Chen, T., Johnson, N.W., 2018. Inflammatory bacteriome and oral squamous cell carcinoma. J. Dent. Res. 97, 725–732.

Rai, A.K., Panda, M., Das, A.K., Rahman, T., Das, R., Das, K., Sarma, A., Kataki, A.C., Chattopadhyay, I., 2021. Dysbiosis of salivary microbiome and cytokines influence oral squamous cell carcinoma through inflammation. Arch. Microbiol. 203, 137–152.

Ramya, S., Preethi, M., Mohammed, J., 2022. Quantification of Helicobacter pylori and its oncoproteins in the oral cavity: a cross-sectional study. Oral Dis. https://doi.org/10.1111/odi.14141. In this issue.

Richter, G.M., Kruppa, J., Munz, M., Wiehe, R., Häsler, R., Franke, A., Schaefer, A.S., 2019. A combined epigenome-and transcriptome-wide association study of the oral masticatory mucosa assigns CYP1B1 a central role for epithelial health in smokers. Clin. Epigenetics 11 (1), 1–18.

Rumsey, S.C., Kwon, O., Xu, G.W., Burant, C.F., Simpson, I., Levine, M., 1997. Glucose transporter isoforms GLUT1 and GLUT3 transport dehydroascorbic acid. J. Biol. Chem. 272, 18982–18989.

Sampaio-Maia, B., Monteiro-Silva, F., 2014. Acquisition and maturation of oral microbiome throughout childhood: an update. Dent. Res. J. 11, 291–301.

Sarkar, P., Malik, S., Laha, S., Das, S., Bunk, S., Ray, J.G., Chatterjee, R., Saha, A., 2021. Dysbiosis of oral microbiota during oral squamous cell carcinoma development. Front. Oncol. 11, 614448.

Sharma, A.K., DeBusk, W.T., Stepanov, I., Gomez, A., Khariwala, S.S., 2020. Oral microbiome profiling in smokers with and without head and neck cancer reveals variations between health and disease. Cancer Prev. Res. (Phila.) 13, 463–474.

Shay, E., Sangwan, N., Padmanabhan, R., Lundy, S., Burkey, B., Eng, C., 2020. Bacteriome and mycobiome and bacteriome-mycobiome interactions in head and neck squamous cell carcinoma. Oncotarget 11, 2375–2386.

Silverman, S.J., Gorsky, M., 1997. Proliferative verrucous leukoplakia: a follow-up study of 54 cases. Oral Surg. Oral Med. Oral Pathol. Oral Radiol. Endod. 84 (2), 154–157.

Stashenko, P., Yost, S., Choi, Y., Danciu, T., Chen, T., Yoganathan, S., Kressirer, C., Ruiz-Tourrella, M., Das, B., Kokaras, A., et al., 2019. The oral mouse microbiome promotes tumorigenesis in oral squamous cell carcinoma. mSystems 4 (4), e00323–19.

Sulaiman, I., Chung, M., Angel, L., Tsay J-CJ, W.B.G., Yeung, S.T., Krolikowski, K., Li, Y., Duerr, R., Schluger, R., et al., 2021. Microbial Signatures in the Lower Airways of Mechanically Ventilated COVID19 Patients Associated with Poor Clinical Outcome. Cold Spring Harbor Laboratory (2021).

Teles, F.R.F., Alawi, F., Castilho, R.M., Wang, Y., 2020. Association or causation? Exploring the oral microbiome and cancer links. J. Dent. Res. 99, 1411–1424.

Torralba, M.G., Aleti, G., Li, W., Moncera, K.J., Lin, Y.-H., Yu, Y., Masternak, M.M., Golusinski, W., Golusinski, P., Lamperska, K., et al., 2020. Oral microbial species and virulence factors associated with oral squamous cell carcinoma. Microb. Ecol. 82, 1030–1046 (110).

Turhani, D., Krapfenbauer, K., Thurnher, D., Langen, H., Fountoulakis, M., 2006. Identification of differentially expressed, tumor-associated proteins in oral squamous cell carcinoma by proteomic analysis. Electrophoresis 27 (7), 1417–1423.

Upadhyaya, J.D., Fitzpatrick, S.G., Islam, M.N., Bhattacharyya, I., Cohen, D.M., 2018. A retrospective 20-year analysis of proliferative verrucous Leukoplakia and its progression to malignancy and association with high-risk human papillomavirus. Head Neck Pathol. 12 (4), 500–510.

Wen, L., Mu, W., Lu, H., Wang, X., Fang, J., Jia, Y., Li, Q., Wang, D., Wen, S., Guo, J., et al., 2020. Porphyromonas gingivalis promotes oral squamous cell carcinoma progression in an immune microenvironment. J. Dent. Res. 99, 666–675.

Wu, J., Peters, B.A., Dominianni, C., Zhang, Y., Pei, Z., Yang, L., Ma, Y., Purdue, M.P., Jacobs, E.J., Gapstur, S.M., et al., 2016. Cigarette smoking and the oral microbiome in a large study of American adults. ISME J. 10, 2435–2446.

Yu, M., Yongzhi, H., Chen, S., Luo, X., Lin, Y., Zhou, Y., Jin, H., Hou, B., Deng, Y., Tu, L., Jian, Z., 2017. The prognostic value of GLUT1 in cancers: a systematic review and meta-analysis. Oncotarget 8 (26), 43356–43367.

Zarco, M.F., Vess, T.J., Ginsburg, G.S., 2012. The oral microbiome in health and disease and the potential impact on personalized dental medicine. Oral Dis. 18, 109–120.

CHAPTER THREE

Molecular biomarkers in gastric cancer

Kazuki Kanayama[a] and Yoshifumi S. Hirokawa[b]
[a]Department of Clinical Nutrition, Suzuka University of Medical Science, Suzuka, Mie, Japan
[b]Department of Oncologic Pathology, Mie University Graduate School of Medicine, Tsu, Mie, Japan

1. Introduction

Gastric cancer (GC) is the fifth most common cancer and the fourth most common cause of cancer-related death in the world (Rawla and Barsouk, 2019). Gastric carcinomas account for 5.6% of all new cancer cases and 7.7% of all cancer deaths worldwide (Rawla and Barsouk, 2019). The reduction of GC incidence has been observed worldwide over the past 50 years, due to treatment of *H. pylori* infection and changing of food processing (Erdman et al., 2014). Recent advances in the earlier detection of GC, surgical treatment, achievements in chemotherapy and targeted therapy, and mortality have decreased in recent decades. However, the overall survival of GC remains low, because the majority of GC patients are usually not diagnosed until an advanced stage (Zheng et al., 2021).

Evaluation of the new strategies to detect GC at an early stage or to predict the chemotherapy response contains enormous clinical value for benefits patient's qualities of life. Biomarkers are playing a crucial role in these strategies.

This chapter describes molecular biomarkers for gastric cancer with reference to the publication that categorized gastrointestinal tissue-based molecular biomarkers from the 2019 World Health Organization classification of tumors Digestive system tumors, fifth ed. (Board WC of TE, n.d.).

2. RNF43

RNF43, negative feedback loop of the Wnt signaling pathway, expression is significantly higher in adenomas and lower in GC. *RNF43* mutations were present in both the adenoma and carcinoma portions in 63.6% of the cases, and were present in only the carcinoma portion in 36.4% of the cases. These results suggest that *RNF43* mutation is the key tumorigenic drivers in early gastric carcinogenesis during adenoma–carcinoma sequence (Min et al., 2016). RNF43, the integral membrane E3 ubiquitin ligase, targets

Biomarkers in Cancer Detection and Monitoring of Therapeutics
https://doi.org/10.1016/B978-0-323-95114-2.00005-4

Wnt receptors, thereby inactivating mutations of the gene sensitizing cells to Wnt (Koo et al., 2012). Therefore, RNF43 is a potential target of the Wnt-β-catenin signaling (Tsukiyama et al., 2015).

3. APC

The Adenomatous polyposis coli (APC) gene is a tumor suppressor gene located chromosome 5q. The APC protein acts on β-catenin and regulates cell proliferation (Regimbald-Dumas and He, 2011). Deletion of APC function is thought to contribute to carcinogenesis (Powell et al., 1992). *APC* mutations have been reported in gastric adenomas (Lim et al., 2016). Moreover, loss of heterozygosity on chromosome 5q has been found in gastric carcinoma of well differentiated type (Sano et al., 1991). Thus, inactivation of the APC gene is involved in the development and progression of gastric tumors, and it is also positioned as a biomarker for disease progression.

4. ARID1A

The AT-rich interaction domain 1A (ARID1A) is one of subunits that compose SWI/SNF, a family of chromatin remodeling complex (Jiang et al., 2020). *ARID1A* mutations are found in many cancers (Wu and Roberts, 2013; Karachaliou et al., 2018). PD-L1 inhibitor resulted in reduced tumor volume and better survival in mice with ARID1A-deficient ovarian cancer (Shen et al., 2018). In gastric cancer, *ARID1A* alterations were associated with markedly high immune infiltrates (Jiang et al., 2020). *ARID1A* alterations have been suggested to be predictive biomarkers for immune checkpoint inhibitors.

5. ARID2

The AT-rich interaction domain-containing protein (ARID) family is a superfamily of 15 members, one of which is ARID2. ARID2 are highly mutated and show loss of expression in certain cancer type (Aso et al., 2015). In gastric dysplasia, *ARID2* mutations have been reported to always cooccur with *APC* mutations (Rokutan et al., 2019). In addition, *ARID1A* aberrations might be connected to EBV-associated gastric cancer via MLH1 status and hypermethylation, whereas have been suggested that *ARID2* aberrations were not related to EBV status (Aso et al., 2015). The effects of EBV may differ among ARID family.

6. MSI

Microsatellites are regions repeating 1–6 nucleotide of DNA sequences that can be detected in both noncoding and protein coding sequences of DNA (Ellegren, 2004). MSI has been reported to occur in about 15%–30% of gastric cancers. The mismatch repair (MMR) is a system that detects and corrects DNA replication errors. Protein complexes of hMSH2/hMSH6 and hMSH2/hMSH3 detect the replication errors by DNA polymerase and hMLH1/hPMS2 removes the mismatched base and allows DNA resynthesis (Yuza et al., 2017). Mutation or DNA promoter methylation of the MMR genes leads to a deficiency in mismatch repair function and an accumulating number of mutations (Ratti et al., 2018) (Fig. 1).

MSI is mainly caused by epigenetic silencing via promoter hypermethylation of the *MLH1* (Pinto et al., 2000). Patients with MSI-high who underwent surgery and perioperative chemotherapy have been shown to shorter prognosis than patients with MSI-low (Smyth et al., 2017). Whereas, MSI-high gastroesophageal tumors are characterized by high degrees infiltration of CD8-positive T cells (Angell et al., 2019). Patients with MSI-high gastroesophageal tumors can substantially benefit of immune checkpoint inhibitor and MSI may be a beneficial predictive and prognostic biomarker in patients with gastric cancers. MSI is usually assessed by polymerase chain reaction (PCR) of microsatellite

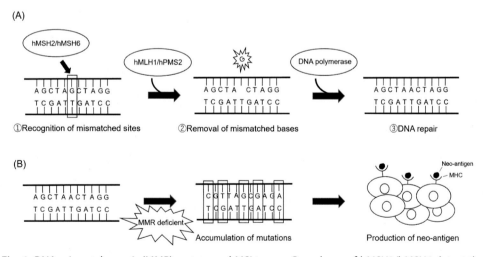

Fig. 1 DNA mismatch repair (MMR) system and MSI tumor. Complexes of hMSH2/hMSH6 detect the mismatched sites. hMLH1/hPMS2 removes the mismatched bases and allows DNA resynthesis (A). In the presence of deficient MMR, DNA replications errors are not repaired and lead to a tumor with high mutational burden. Hyper-mutated tumor cells produce several neo-antigens (B). *(Adapted from article Ratti, M., Lampis, A., Hahne, J.C., Passalacqua, R., Valeri, N., 2018. Microsatellite instability in gastric cancer: molecular bases, clinical perspectives, and new treatment approaches. Cell. Mol. Life Sci. 75(22), 4151–62.)*

regions or MMR protein expression by immunohistochemical staining (Shia, 2008). Recent studies have reported that MSI can also be identified in next-generation sequencing (NGS) and may be even more sensitive than PCR (Middha et al., 2017).

7. MALTA1-GLT1 fusion

MALTA1-GLT1 fusion gene shown to harbor in 15%–20% of rare gastric spindle cell neoplasms (Spans et al., 2016). The fusion gene results in overexpression of GLT1 protein and activation of the Sonic hedgehog pathway (Graham et al., 2017). *MALTA1-GLT1* fusion gene was identified as oncogenic gene and may serve as a diagnostic marker in gastroblastoma. Reverse transcriptase-PCR (RT-PCR) and fluorescence in situ hybridization (FISH) are used as detection of *MALTA1-GLT1* fusion gene, but GLT1 Immunohistochemistry (IHC) is effective as a screening method (Graham et al., 2017).

8. TP53

TP53 is an extremely important tumor suppressor gene which has function including growth arrest and apoptosis, DNA damage, and aberrant proliferative signals (Lamb and Crawford, 1986; Levine, 1997). Over 50% of human cancers show inactivated TP53 due to loss of functional mutations (Ozaki and Nakagawara, 2011). The loss of function of *TP53* gene usually occurs through loss heterozygosity (LOH), mutations, and rarely by DNA methylation. In gastric cancer, *TP53* mutation is detected often in the intestinal type (Endoh et al., 2000). *TP53* mutational spectrum was wide, including in codons 175, 248, 273, 282, 245, and 213, all of which are CpG sites (Bellini et al., 2012). *TP53* codon 72 single nucleotide polymorphism (SNP) Arg72Pro was associated with a shorter outcome in patients with gastric cancer, and was shown to predict the response to chemotherapy (Li et al., 2010).

9. RB1

Retinoblastoma tumor suppressor gene 1 (*RB1*) is the first tumor suppressor gene to be molecularly defined and is a key target molecule in tumor progression. Its gene product, RB1 (pRB), negatively regulates the cell cycle by regulating transcription. *RB1* mutations has been detected in all familial and sporadic retinoblastoma. Inactivation of RB1 due to *RB1* mutation contributes to tumor progression in retinoblastoma (Dimaras et al., 2015). In gastric cancer, miR-215 has been suggested to suppress *RB1* expression via 3'-UTR of *RB1* (Deng et al., 2014). MiR-215 may be a candidate molecular biomarker of gastric cancer. In addition, overexpression of RB1 has been reported to enhance 5-fluorouracil (5-FU) chemosensitivity in gastric cancer cells by regulating cell autophagy through SDF-1/CXCR4 pathway (Tang et al., 2021). RB1 might useful as a therapeutic target or predictive biomarker for gastric cancer.

10. ERBB2

Human epidermal growth factor receptor 2 (HER2) is proto-oncogene encoded by ERBB2 on chromosome 17q and is a cell membrane surface-bound receptor tyrosine kinase. HER2 is promote cell proliferation and suppress apoptosis via mitogen-activated protein kinase (MAPK), phosphoinositide 3-kinase (PI3K), phospholipase C, protein kinase C, which may facilitate excessive/uncontrolled cell growth and tumorigenesis. In breast cancer, HER2 overexpression is a powerful prognostic factor. In addition, HER2 overexpression with ductal carcinoma in situ has been reported to be associated with tumor progression (Bartkova et al., 1990; Roses et al., 2009). Overexpression of HER2 protein in association with *HER2* gene amplification has been detected in 7%–34% of gastric cancers by FISH and IHC (Hofmann et al., 2008; Lee et al., 2011). HER2-positive gastric cancer has characteristics that are often found in the intestinal subtype. HER2 overexpression in advanced gastric cancer have been suggested to be important for the treatment and prognosis of this disease (Sawaki et al., 2012). Moreover, *HER2* gene amplification occurred in early gastric cancer and have been suggested to be involved in tumor progression (Kanayama et al., 2018).

11. C-MET

Receptor tyrosine kinase Met is a promising target for *Met* aberration gastric cancers. Met overexpression and gene amplification have been reported to be found in 7%–39% of advanced gastric cancers (Peng et al., 2015). The pathways activated by *Met* aberrations are involved in invasion, metastasis and survival of gastric cancers (Kawakami and Okamoto, 2016). Therefore, amplification of *Met* has been suggested as a therapeutic predictive marker for Met tyrosine kinase inhibitors (Met-TKI). Additionally, Met-TKIs induced protective autophagy via Met/mTOR/ULK1 cascade and Met-TKIs combined with autophagy inhibitors increased antitumor effect in *Met*-amplified gastric cancers (Lin et al., 2019). Autophagy may be a new biomarker for *Met*-amplified gastric cancers.

12. EGFR

Epithelial growth factor receptor (EGFR) is one of the HER family that, unlike HER2, is activated by the binding of specific ligands, including EGF and TGF-α, and is encoded by *EGFR*. Gene amplification of EGFR has been detected in 4.9%–7.7% of gastric cancer by FISH (Deng et al., 2012). EGFR protein overexpression has been reported to be an important prognostic factor (Kim et al., 2008). However, a meta-analysis found that EGFR was not an independent predictor for survival in patients with gastric cancers (Hong et al., 2013). EGFR inhibitors have been tested in several clinical trials, but the results in gastric cancers have been disappointing (Waddell et al., 2013; Lordick et al., 2013).

13. PD-L1

The programmed cell death 1 (PD-1) and 2 (PD-2) are key receptors of immune checkpoint expressed on activated T and B lymphocytes, natural killer T cells, and monocytes (Sharpe et al., 2007). Programmed death ligands (PD-Ls) 1 and 2 are its two ligands, binding to PD-1 on activated T cells leads to downregulation of cytotoxic T-cell activity and induce immune tolerance to cancer. The expression of PD-L1 in patients with gastric cancer is ranged in 15%–70% of cases. Moreover, gastric cancer patient with EBV-positive and MSI tend to show PD-L1 expression, which demonstrated that specifically status of EBV and MSI may be show therapy candidates for immune check inhibitors (Gu et al., 2017). Pembrolizumab and nivolumab are an anti-PD-1 monoclonal antibody, and they promoted the ability of the immune system. A phase II study (KEYNOTE-059) demonstrated that pembrolizumab showed clinical efficacy in advanced gastric cancer (Curea et al., 2017). Targeting the PD-1 pathway and immune checkpoint blockade has proved to be a novel treatment for gastric cancer.

14. Epstein–Barr virus

Epstein–Barr virus (EBV), a gamma-herpes virus of double-stranded DNA, is the most common human herpes viruses. More than 90% of the world's population establishes latent infections. EBV caused a number of different human malignancies including lymphoproliferative disorders of immunocompromised hosts. The first case of the association between EBV and gastric adenocarcinoma was reported by Burke et al in 1990 based on PCR techniques (Burke et al., 1990). EBV infection is maintained in a latent form in B-lymphocytes or epithelial cells. Latent EBV infection is demonstrated by the three distinct expression patterns of latent genes (Shinozaki-Ushiku et al., 2015). The common antigen expressed in all latency types are EBER-1 and 2, EBV-determined nuclear antigen (EBNA)-1, *Bam*HI A region rightward transcripts (BARTs), and BART miRNAs. Because *EBER*s are the most abundant viral transcripts in latently EBV-infected cells, *EBER*-in situ hybridization (ISH), detection in the tissue serves as the standard molecular biomarker detection technology of EBV-associated gastric carcinoma

(EBVaGC) (Shibata and Weiss, 1992). Recent advances in genetic and molecular analysis provide new technologies to detect EBV in EBVaGC. Gastric cancers with EBV-positive were accurately identified by quantifying virus DNA in whole genome sequence data (Camargo et al., 2016). Droplet digital PCR (ddPCR), the highly sensitive and quantitative method, was applied to diagnose EBVaGC from tissue samples (Shuto et al., 2019).

The EBV have more than 40 miRNAs in the virus genome and infected cells express those viral miRNAs. Involvement in cancer development and progression, miRNAs potentiate as molecular biomarkers in EBVaGC (Sun et al., 2020). For example, BART10-3p and BART22 promote EBVaGC metastasis through Wnt signaling activation by targeting APC and Dkk1 (Dong et al., 2020).

15. VEGF-A

The growth of new blood vessels support cancer progression and one of the primary modulators is vascular endothelial growth factor-A (VEGF-A) produced from tumors and host mesenchymal cells. Angiogenic effect of VEGF-A is conducted mainly through its receptor VEGF receptor 2 (VEGFR2) expressed in vascular endothelial cells (Apte et al., 2019).

Increased VEGF-A levels were correlated with decreased overall survival, and serum VEGF-A was independent prognostic factor in a multivariate analysis (Park et al., 2014).

A meta-analysis revealed that VEGF-A overexpression indicates a poor prognosis for overall survival and disease-free survival in patients with GC (Ji et al., 2014).

16. CD44

A cell surface adhesion molecule CD44 is expressed on gastric epithelial cells as well on a variety of cells (Zavros, 2017). Especially, cancer stem cell, including gastric cancer, express CD44 as a cell surface marker. The subpopulation of CD44-positive cells presented the ability to initiate tumor growth and sustain tumor self-renewal (Takaishi et al., 2009). The *CD44* standard isoform (*CD44s*) consists of all 20 exons, wherein gene encoding the proximal extracellular domain is the site of alternative mRNA splicing, which results in multiple variant isoforms (*CD44v2–v10*) (Zavros, 2017). The patients with CD44v6-positive cancers were associated with metastasis and poor prognosis than CD44v6–negative cancers (Yamaguchi et al., 2002). The invasive front of tumors has important characters associated with prognostic measure. The expressions of CD44s, CD44v6, and CD44v9 revealed poor survival of the patients and distal organ recurrence (Kodama et al., 2017). CD44v9 interacts with and stabilizes the glutamate-cysteine transporter SLC7A11 (xCT), increased intracellular levels of reduced glutathione, and thereby potentiates defense against reactive oxygen species (Ishimoto et al., 2011). Thus, giving the involvement of CD44 and its splice variants with the progression of GC, they play important roles in the diagnosis, therapy, and prognosis of the disease.

17. E-cadherin

Cadherin is a calcium dependent intercellular adhesion molecule localize with extracellular, transmembrane and intracellular domains. E-cadherin (CDH1) contains extracellular domains (ECD) composed of five cadherin repeats and intracellular domains (ICD), both domains mediate the adhesion function of E-cadherin. One of the cadherin repeats in ECD mediates cell–cell adhesion by homodimerizing in trans with same repeats of neighboring cells. ICD binds with alfa-, beta-catenin, and other catenin family members. Catenins and their binding molecules make connection to the cytoskeleton of actin, which maintain the stability of cell structure, and participating in cell signal transduction (Venhuizen et al., 2020).

A meta-analysis has shown that the low E-cadherin expression was a predictive factor of poor prognosis for gastric cancer particularly in Asian population. On the contrary, low or abnormal E-cadherin expression has no significant relation on patient survival in other ethnic group (Xing et al., 2013; Gamboa-Dominguez et al., 2005; Corso et al., 2013). The precise reason for this discrepancy has not been elucidated but different ethnic background could be involved. The decreased expression of E-cadherin results from several molecular mechanisms, including CDH1 germline inactivating mutations of the hereditary diffuse GC (HDGC) (Guilford et al., 1998; Richards et al., 1999; Oliveira et al., 2004), promoter hypermethylation of the gene (Qian et al., 2008), and posttranscriptional regulation by microRNA (Mei et al., 2019).

The full length, membrane-bound E-cadherin is cleaved by several extracellular proteases, soluble forms are generated and released from plasma membrane. The major form is soluble E-cadherin (sE-cad), an N-terminus product of 80 kDa molecule with all 5 EC domains. Generation of sE-cad is induced by proteolytic activities of alfa-secretase and coactivities of matrix metalloproteases (MMPs), members of the a disintegrin, and metalloproteases (ADAMs) family, kallikreins and plasmin (Hu et al., 2016). The functional properties of sE-cad are the disruption of cell–cell adhesion, decreased cell aggregation and increased migration and invasion, the representative actions of oncogenic ability. Interestingly sE-cad functions as a ligand for HER2 and HER3 in the MCF-7 breast cancer cell line, that is recombinant human E-cadherin/Fc chimeric protein enhances HER2-HER3 heterodimerization, and activate downstream extracellular signal-regulated kinases 1 and 2 (ERK1/2) (Najy et al., 2008). In skin cancers, sE-cad activates the MAPK and PI3K/Akt/mTOR signaling pathways via HER/IGF-1 receptor families, promoting cancer cell proliferation, migration and invasion facilitated by MMPs (Brouxhon et al., 2014). Consequence of the sE-cad generation, adhesion-competent

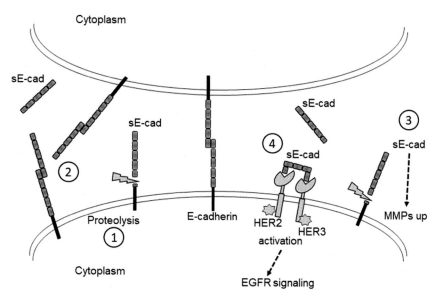

Fig. 2 Soluble E-cadherin fragment. Proteolysis of full-length E-cadherin generate sE-cad (1). Oncogenic functions of the sE-cad. sE-cad disrupts adhesion competent full-length E-cadherin (2), activates the expression of MMPs (3) to increase extracellular domain shedding, and activates EGFR signaling pathway (4). *(Adapted from articles Najy, A.J., Day, K.C., Day, M.L., 2008. The ectodomain shedding of E-cadherin by ADAM15 supports ErbB receptor activation. J. Biol. Chem. 283(26), 18393–401; David, J.M., Rajasekaran, A.K., 2012. Dishonorable discharge: the oncogenic roles of cleaved E-cadherin fragments. Cancer Res. 72(12), 2917–23.)*

E-cadherin in the plasma membrane is reduced, full-length E-cadherin homodimers between adjacent cells is blocked. Major MMPs (MMP-2, MMP-9, and MT1-MMP), induced by sE-cad could degrade the basement membrane to allow tumor invasion into the stroma (David and Rajasekaran, 2012; Nawrocki-Raby et al., 2003). Giving that shedded sE-cad serve as cancer promoting molecule, allows for its possible detection in blood of patients, making it a clinically valuable prognostic biomarker. Indeed, pretherapeutic serum sE-cad is an independent factor predicting long-term survival in GC (Chan et al., 2003), serum sE-cad levels is a predictor of disease recurrence after surgery in the patients with gastric carcinoma (Chan et al., 2005) (Fig. 2).

18. Matrix metalloproteinases (MMPs)

Reciprocal interactions between malignant cells and their microenvironment influence the tumorigenesis that these interactions continue from a relatively early stage of tumor progression to both local invasion and distant metastasis (Brown and Murray, 2015; Quail and Joyce, 2013). ECM consists of variety types of collagen and undergoes tightly regulated during tissue remodeling processes (Bonnans et al., 2014). A central process of tissue remodeling is proteolysis of the ECM mainly conducted by MMPs, the most important in the context of tumor invasion and metastasis (Shay et al., 2015). The subgroups of MMPs are categorized by a combination of amino acid sequence, peptide domain structure, and substrate specificity. The main groups of MMPs are the collagenases, gelatinases, stromelysins, and membrane-associated MMPs. The MMPs can also modulate cellular processes including cell proliferation, cell differentiation, and apoptosis by activating growth factors or by releasing cytokines from the ECM (Mannello et al., 2005). Regulation of ECM through MMPs has a key factor in tumor progression and poor prognosis of GC (Abbaszadegan et al., 2020). An apparent relation has been observed between T allele of –1562C/T promoter polymorphism of MMP9 and advanced-stage with lymph node metastasis of GC (Matsumura et al., 2005). MMP2 overexpression has an unfavorable overall survival, association with higher TNM stage, advanced depth of invasion, lymph node metastasis, and distant metastasis (Shen et al., 2014). A meta-analysis from 3 studies shows that MMP14, one of the membrane-bound MMPs, the overexpression was a significantly poor prognostic factor (Dong et al., 2015). Furthermore, the high serum levels of MMP14 has been determined as an independent prognostic factor of GC (Kasurinen et al., 2018).

Laminin subunit gamma 2 (LAMC2) is expressed in gastric cancer cells at invading front (Koshikawa et al., 1999). Advanced T grade, N grade and tumor stage have been associated with expression of MMP-7, cytoplasmic LAMC2 and EGFR (Sentani et al., 2014).

19. Conclusions

Accumulating knowledge of the molecular markers of gastric cancers help to understand molecular pathogenesis, to develop new therapeutic molecules, and to improve patients' survival. Although there are relatively few biomarkers with fulfilled clinical performance, WHO characterized molecular markers are reliable, and can be reassessed with compositive way when new information becomes available in the future.

References

Abbaszadegan, M.R., Mojarrad, M., Moghbeli, M., 2020. Role of extra cellular proteins in gastric cancer progression and metastasis: an update. Genes Environ. 42, 18.
Angell, H.K., Lee, J., Kim, K.-M., Kim, K., Kim, S.-T., Park, S.H., et al., 2019. PD-L1 and immune infiltrates are differentially expressed in distinct subgroups of gastric cancer. OncoImmunology 8 (2), e1544442.
Apte, R.S., Chen, D.S., Ferrara, N., 2019. VEGF in Signaling and disease: beyond discovery and development. Cell 176 (6), 1248–1264.
Aso, T., Uozaki, H., Morita, S., Kumagai, A., Watanabe, M., 2015. Loss of ARID1A, ARID1B, and ARID2 expression during progression of gastric cancer. Anticancer Res. 35 (12), 6819–6827.
Bartkova, J., Barnes, D.M., Millis, R.R., Gullick, W.J., 1990. Immunohistochemical demonstration of c-erbB-2 protein in mammary ductal carcinoma in situ. Hum. Pathol. 21 (11), 1164–1167.

Bellini, M.F., Cadamuro, A.C.T., Succi, M., Proença, M.A., Silva, A.E., 2012. Alterations of the *TP53* gene in gastric and Esophageal carcinogenesis. J. Biomed. Biotechnol. 2012, 1–13.

Board WC of TE, Digestive System Tumours. (Internet). (Cited 12 January 2022). Available from: https://publications.iarc.fr/Book-And-Report-Series/Who-Classification-Of-Tumours/Digestive-System-Tumours-2019.

Bonnans, C., Chou, J., Werb, Z., 2014. Remodelling the extracellular matrix in development and disease. Nat. Rev. Mol. Cell Biol. 15 (12), 786–801.

Brouxhon, S.M., Kyrkanides, S., Teng, X., Athar, M., Ghazizadeh, S., Simon, M., et al., 2014. Soluble E-cadherin: a critical oncogene modulating receptor tyrosine kinases, MAPK and PI3K/Akt/mTOR signaling. Oncogene 33 (2), 225–235.

Brown, G.T., Murray, G.I., 2015. Current mechanistic insights into the roles of matrix metalloproteinases in tumour invasion and metastasis. J. Pathol. 237 (3), 273–281.

Burke, A.P., Yen, T.S., Shekitka, K.M., Sobin, L.H., 1990. Lymphoepithelial carcinoma of the stomach with Epstein-Barr virus demonstrated by polymerase chain reaction. Mod. Pathol. 3 (3), 377–380.

Camargo, M.C., Bowlby, R., Chu, A., Pedamallu, C.S., Thorsson, V., Elmore, S., et al., 2016. Validation and calibration of next-generation sequencing to identify Epstein-Barr virus-positive gastric cancer in the cancer genome atlas. Gastric Cancer 19 (2), 676–681.

Chan, A.O.-O., Chu, K.-M., Lam, S.-K., Wong, B.C.-Y., Kwok, K.-F., Law, S., et al., 2003. Soluble E-cadherin is an independent pretherapeutic factor for long-term survival in gastric cancer. J. Clin. Oncol. 21 (12), 2288–2293.

Chan, A.O.O., Chu, K.-M., Lam, S.K., Cheung, K.L., Law, S., Kwok, K.-F., et al., 2005. Early prediction of tumor recurrence after curative resection of gastric carcinoma by measuring soluble E-cadherin. Cancer 104 (4), 740–746.

Corso, G., Carvalho, J., Marrelli, D., Vindigni, C., Carvalho, B., Seruca, R., et al., 2013. Somatic mutations and deletions of the E-cadherin gene predict poor survival of patients with gastric cancer. J. Clin. Oncol. 31 (7), 868–875.

Curea, F.G., Hebbar, M., Ilie, S.M., Bacinschi, X.E., Trifanescu, O.G., Botnariuc, I., et al., 2017. Current targeted therapies in HER2-positive gastric adenocarcinoma. Cancer Biother. Radiopharm. 32 (10), 351–363.

David, J.M., Rajasekaran, A.K., 2012. Dishonorable discharge: the oncogenic roles of cleaved E-cadherin fragments. Cancer Res. 72 (12), 2917–2923.

Deng, N., Goh, L.K., Wang, H., Das, K., Tao, J., Tan, I.B., et al., 2012. A comprehensive survey of genomic alterations in gastric cancer reveals systematic patterns of molecular exclusivity and co-occurrence among distinct therapeutic targets. Gut 61 (5), 673–684.

Deng, Y., Huang, Z., Xu, Y., Jin, J., Zhuo, W., Zhang, C., et al., 2014. MiR-215 modulates gastric cancer cell proliferation by targeting RB1. Cancer Lett. 342 (1), 27–35.

Dimaras, H., Corson, T.W., Cobrinik, D., White, A., Zhao, J., Munier, F.L., et al., 2015. Retinoblastoma. Nat. Rev. Dis. Primers 1 (1), 1–23.

Dong, Y., Chen, G., Gao, M., Tian, X., 2015. Increased expression of MMP14 correlates with the poor prognosis of Chinese patients with gastric cancer. Gene 563 (1), 29–34.

Dong, M., Gong, L.-P., Chen, J.-N., Zhang, X.-F., Zhang, Y.-W., Hui, D.-Y., et al., 2020. EBV-miR-BART10-3p and EBV-miR-BART22 promote metastasis of EBV-associated gastric carcinoma by activating the canonical Wnt signaling pathway. Cell. Oncol. (Dordr.) 43 (5), 901–913.

Ellegren, H., 2004. Microsatellites: simple sequences with complex evolution. Nat. Rev. Genet. 5 (6), 435–445.

Endoh, Y., Sakata, K., Tamura, G., Ohmura, K., Ajioka, Y., Watanabe, H., et al., 2000. Cellular phenotypes of differentiated-type adenocarcinomas and precancerous lesions of the stomach are dependent on the genetic pathways. J. Pathol. 191 (3), 257–263.

Erdman, J.W., Jeffery, E., Hendrickx, M., Cross, A.J., Lampe, J.W., 2014. Can food processing enhance cancer protection? Nutr. Today 49 (5), 230–234.

Gamboa-Dominguez, A., Dominguez-Fonseca, C., Chavarri-Guerra, Y., Vargas, R., Reyes-Gutierrez, E., Green, D., et al., 2005. E-cadherin expression in sporadic gastric cancer from Mexico: exon 8 and 9 deletions are infrequent events associated with poor survival. Hum. Pathol. 36 (1), 29–35.

Graham, R.P., Nair, A.A., Davila, J.I., Jin, L., Jen, J., Sukov, W.R., et al., 2017. Gastroblastoma harbors a recurrent somatic MALAT1–GLI1 fusion gene. Mod. Pathol. 30 (10), 1443–1452.

Gu, L., Chen, M., Guo, D., Zhu, H., Zhang, W., Pan, J., et al., 2017. PD-L1 and gastric cancer prognosis: a systematic review and meta-analysis. Katoh M, editor, PLoS One 12 (8), e0182692.

Guilford, P., Hopkins, J., Harraway, J., McLeod, M., McLeod, N., Harawira, P., et al., 1998. E-cadherin germline mutations in familial gastric cancer. Nature 392 (6674), 402–405.

Hofmann, M., Stoss, O., Shi, D., Büttner, R., van de Vijver, M., Kim, W., et al., 2008. Assessment of a HER2 scoring system for gastric cancer: results from a validation study. Histopathology 52 (7), 797–805.

Hong, L., Han, Y., Yang, J., Zhang, H., Jin, Y., Brain, L., et al., 2013. Prognostic value of epidermal growth factor receptor in patients with gastric cancer: a meta-analysis. Gene 529 (1), 69–72.

Hu, Q.-P., Kuang, J.-Y., Yang, Q.-K., Bian, X.-W., Yu, S.-C., 2016. Beyond a tumor suppressor: soluble E-cadherin promotes the progression of cancer. Int. J. Cancer 138 (12), 2804–2812.

Ishimoto, T., Nagano, O., Yae, T., Tamada, M., Motohara, T., Oshima, H., et al., 2011. CD44 variant regulates redox status in cancer cells by stabilizing the xCT subunit of system xc(−) and thereby promotes tumor growth. Cancer Cell 19 (3), 387–400.

Ji, Y., Wang, Q., Li, Y., Wang, Z., 2014. Prognostic value of vascular endothelial growth factor a expression in gastric cancer: a meta-analysis. Tumour Biol. 35 (3), 2787–2793.

Jiang, T., Chen, X., Su, C., Ren, S., Zhou, C., 2020. Pan-cancer analysis of *ARID1A* alterations as biomarkers for immunotherapy outcomes. J. Cancer 11 (4), 776–780.

Kanayama, K., Imai, H., Usugi, E., Shiraishi, T., Hirokawa, Y.S., Watanabe, M., 2018. Association of HER2 gene amplification and tumor progression in early gastric cancer. Virchows Arch. 473 (5), 559–565.

Karachaliou, N., Paulina Bracht, J.W., Rosell, R., 2018. ARID1A gene driver mutations in lung adenocarcinomas. J. Thorac. Oncol. 13 (12), e255–e257.

Kasurinen, A., Tervahartiala, T., Laitinen, A., Kokkola, A., Sorsa, T., Böckelman, C., et al., 2018. High serum MMP-14 predicts worse survival in gastric cancer. PLoS One 13 (12), e0208800.

Kawakami, H., Okamoto, I., 2016. MET-targeted therapy for gastric cancer: the importance of a biomarker-based strategy. Gastric Cancer 19 (3), 687–695.

Kim, M.A., Lee, H.S., Lee, H.E., Jeon, Y.K., Yang, H.K., Kim, W.H., 2008. EGFR in gastric carcinomas: prognostic significance of protein overexpression and high gene copy number. Histopathology 52 (6), 738–746.

Kodama, H., Murata, S., Ishida, M., Yamamoto, H., Yamaguchi, T., Kaida, S., et al., 2017. Prognostic impact of CD44-positive cancer stem-like cells at the invasive front of gastric cancer. Br. J. Cancer 116 (2), 186–194.

Koo, B.-K., Spit, M., Jordens, I., Low, T.Y., Stange, D.E., van de Wetering, M., et al., 2012. Tumour suppressor RNF43 is a stem-cell E3 ligase that induces endocytosis of Wnt receptors. Nature 488 (7413), 665–669.

Koshikawa, N., Moriyama, K., Takamura, H., Mizushima, H., Nagashima, Y., Yanoma, S., et al., 1999. Overexpression of laminin gamma2 chain monomer in invading gastric carcinoma cells. Cancer Res. 59 (21), 5596–5601.

Lamb, P., Crawford, L., 1986. Characterization of the human p53 gene. Mol. Cell. Biol. 6 (5), 1379–1385.

Lee, S., de Boer, W.B., Fermoyle, S., Platten, M., Kumarasinghe, M.P., 2011. Human epidermal growth factor receptor 2 testing in gastric carcinoma: issues related to heterogeneity in biopsies and resections. Histopathology 59 (5), 832–840.

Levine, A.J., 1997. p53, the cellular gatekeeper for growth and division. Cell 88 (3), 323–331.

Li, Q.-F., Yao, R.-Y., Liu, K., Lv, H.-Y., Jiang, T., Liang, J., 2010. Genetic polymorphism of GSTP1: prediction of clinical outcome to oxaliplatin/5-FU-based chemotherapy in advanced gastric cancer. J. Korean Med. Sci. 25 (6), 846.

Lim, C.-H., Cho, Y.K., Kim, S.W., Choi, M.-G., Rhee, J.-K., Chung, Y.-J., et al., 2016. The chronological sequence of somatic mutations in early gastric carcinogenesis inferred from multiregion sequencing of gastric adenomas. Oncotarget 7 (26), 39758–39767.

Lin, X., Peng, Z., Wang, X., Zou, J., Chen, D., Chen, Z., et al., 2019. Targeting autophagy potentiates antitumor activity of met-TKIs against met-amplified gastric cancer. Cell Death Dis. 10 (2), 139.

Lordick, F., Kang, Y.-K., Chung, H.-C., Salman, P., Oh, S.C., Bodoky, G., et al., 2013. Capecitabine and cisplatin with or without cetuximab for patients with previously untreated advanced gastric cancer (EXPAND): a randomised, open-label phase 3 trial. Lancet Oncol. 14 (6), 490–499.

Mannello, F., Luchetti, F., Falcieri, E., Papa, S., 2005. Multiple roles of matrix metalloproteinases during apoptosis. Apoptosis 10 (1), 19–24.

Matsumura, S., Oue, N., Nakayama, H., Kitadai, Y., Yoshida, K., Yamaguchi, Y., et al., 2005. A single nucleotide polymorphism in the MMP-9 promoter affects tumor progression and invasive phenotype of gastric cancer. J. Cancer Res. Clin. Oncol. 131 (1), 19–25.

Mei, J.-W., Yang, Z.-Y., Xiang, H.-G., Bao, R., Ye, Y.-Y., Ren, T., et al., 2019. MicroRNA-1275 inhibits cell migration and invasion in gastric cancer by regulating vimentin and E-cadherin via JAZF1. BMC Cancer 19 (1), 740.

Middha, S., Zhang, L., Nafa, K., Jayakumaran, G., Wong, D., Kim, H.R., et al., 2017. Reliable Pan-cancer microsatellite instability assessment by using targeted next-generation sequencing data. JCO Precis. Oncol. 2017 (1), 1–17.

Min, B.-H., Hwang, J., Kim, N.K., Park, G., Kang, S.Y., Ahn, S., et al., 2016. Dysregulated Wnt signalling and recurrent mutations of the tumour suppressor RNF43 in early gastric carcinogenesis. J. Pathol. 240 (3), 304–314.

Najy, A.J., Day, K.C., Day, M.L., 2008. The ectodomain shedding of E-cadherin by ADAM15 supports ErbB receptor activation. J. Biol. Chem. 283 (26), 18393–18401.

Nawrocki-Raby, B., Gilles, C., Polette, M., Bruyneel, E., Laronze, J.-Y., Bonnet, N., et al., 2003. Upregulation of MMPs by soluble E-cadherin in human lung tumor cells. Int. J. Cancer 105 (6), 790–795.

Oliveira, C., de Bruin, J., Nabais, S., Ligtenberg, M., Moutinho, C., Nagengast, F.M., et al., 2004. Intragenic deletion of CDH1 as the inactivating mechanism of the wild-type allele in an HDGC tumour. Oncogene 23 (12), 2236–2240.

Ozaki, T., Nakagawara, A., 2011. p53: the attractive tumor suppressor in the cancer research field. J. Biomed. Biotechnol. 2011, 1–13.

Park, D.J., Yoon, C., Thomas, N., Ku, G.Y., Janjigian, Y.Y., Kelsen, D.P., et al., 2014. Prognostic significance of targetable angiogenic and growth factors in patients undergoing resection for gastric and gastroesophageal junction cancers. Ann. Surg. Oncol. 21 (4), 1130–1137.

Peng, Z., Li, Z., Gao, J., Lu, M., Gong, J., Tang, E.-T., et al., 2015. Tumor MET expression and gene amplification in Chinese patients with locally advanced or metastatic gastric or gastroesophageal junction cancer. Mol. Cancer Ther. 14 (11), 2634–2641.

Pinto, M., Oliveira, C., Machado, J.C., Cirnes, L., Tavares, J., Carneiro, F., et al., 2000. MSI-L gastric carcinomas share the hMLH1 methylation status of MSI-H carcinomas but not their clinicopathological profile. Lab. Investig. 80 (12), 1915–1923.

Powell, S.M., Zilz, N., Beazer-Barclay, Y., Bryan, T.M., Hamilton, S.R., Thibodeau, S.N., et al., 1992. APC mutations occur early during colorectal tumorigenesis. Nature 359 (6392), 235–237.

Qian, X., Huang, C., Cho, C.H., Hui, W.M., Rashid, A., Chan, A.O.O., 2008. E-cadherin promoter hypermethylation induced by interleukin-1beta treatment or H. pylori infection in human gastric cancer cell lines. Cancer Lett. 263 (1), 107–113.

Quail, D.F., Joyce, J.A., 2013. Microenvironmental regulation of tumor progression and metastasis. Nat. Med. 19 (11), 1423–1437.

Ratti, M., Lampis, A., Hahne, J.C., Passalacqua, R., Valeri, N., 2018. Microsatellite instability in gastric cancer: molecular bases, clinical perspectives, and new treatment approaches. Cell. Mol. Life Sci. 75 (22), 4151–4162.

Rawla, P., Barsouk, A., 2019. Epidemiology of gastric cancer: global trends, risk factors and prevention. Przeglad Gastroenterol. 14 (1), 26–38.

Regimbald-Dumas, Y., He, X., 2011. Wnt signalling: what the X@# is WTX? EMBO J. 30 (8), 1415–1417.

Richards, F.M., McKee, S.A., Rajpar, M.H., Cole, T.R., Evans, D.G., Jankowski, J.A., et al., 1999. Germline E-cadherin gene (CDH1) mutations predispose to familial gastric cancer and colorectal cancer. Hum. Mol. Genet. 8 (4), 607–610.

Rokutan, H., Abe, H., Nakamura, H., Ushiku, T., Arakawa, E., Hosoda, F., et al., 2019. Initial and crucial genetic events in intestinal-type gastric intramucosal neoplasia: early mutations of gastric intramucosal neoplasia. J. Pathol. 247 (4), 494–504.

Roses, R.E., Paulson, E.C., Sharma, A., Schueller, J.E., Nisenbaum, H., Weinstein, S., et al., 2009. HER-2/neu overexpression as a predictor for the transition from in situ to invasive breast cancer. Cancer Epidemiol. Biomark. Prev. 18 (5), 1386–1389.

Sano, T., Tsujino, T., Yoshida, K., Nakayama, H., Haruma, K., Ito, H., et al., 1991. Frequent loss of heterozygosity on chromosomes 1q, 5q, and 17p in human gastric carcinomas. Cancer Res. 51 (11), 2926–2931.

Sawaki, A., Ohashi, Y., Omuro, Y., Satoh, T., Hamamoto, Y., Boku, N., et al., 2012. Efficacy of trastuzumab in Japanese patients with HER2-positive advanced gastric or gastroesophageal junction cancer: a subgroup analysis of the trastuzumab for gastric cancer (ToGA) study. Gastric Cancer 15 (3), 313–322.

Sentani, K., Matsuda, M., Oue, N., Uraoka, N., Naito, Y., Sakamoto, N., et al., 2014. Clinicopathological significance of MMP-7, laminin γ2 and EGFR expression at the invasive front of gastric carcinoma. Gastric Cancer 17 (3), 412–422.

Sharpe, A.H., John Wherry, E., Ahmed, R., Freeman, G.J., 2007. The function of programmed cell death 1 and its ligands in regulating autoimmunity and infection. Nat. Immunol. 8 (3), 239–245. https://doi.org/10.1038/ni1443.

Shay, G., Lynch, C.C., Fingleton, B., 2015. Moving targets: emerging roles for MMPs in cancer progression and metastasis. Matrix Biol. 44–46, 200–206.

Shen, W., Xi, H., Wei, B., Chen, L., 2014. The prognostic role of matrix metalloproteinase 2 in gastric cancer: a systematic review with meta-analysis. J. Cancer Res. Clin. Oncol. 140 (6), 1003–1009.

Shen, J., Ju, Z., Zhao, W., Wang, L., Peng, Y., Ge, Z., et al., 2018. ARID1A deficiency promotes mutability and potentiates therapeutic antitumor immunity unleashed by immune checkpoint blockade. Nat. Med. 24 (5), 556–562.

Shia, J., 2008. Immunohistochemistry versus microsatellite instability testing for screening colorectal cancer patients at risk for hereditary nonpolyposis colorectal cancer syndrome. J. Mol. Diagn. 10 (4), 293–300.

Shibata, D., Weiss, L.M., 1992. Epstein-Barr virus-associated gastric adenocarcinoma. Am. J. Pathol. 140 (4), 769–774.

Shinozaki-Ushiku, A., Kunita, A., Fukayama, M., 2015. Update on Epstein-Barr virus and gastric cancer (review). Int. J. Oncol. 46 (4), 1421–1434.

Shuto, T., Nishikawa, J., Shimokuri, K., Yanagi, A., Takagi, T., Takagi, F., et al., 2019. Establishment of a screening method for Epstein-Barr virus-associated gastric carcinoma by droplet digital PCR. Microorganisms 7 (12), E628.

Smyth, E.C., Wotherspoon, A., Peckitt, C., Gonzalez, D., Hulkki-Wilson, S., Eltahir, Z., et al., 2017. Mismatch repair deficiency, microsatellite instability, and survival: an exploratory analysis of the Medical Research Council adjuvant gastric Infusional chemotherapy (MAGIC) trial. JAMA Oncol. 3 (9), 1197–1203.

Spans, L., Fletcher, C.D., Antonescu, C.R., Rouquette, A., Coindre, J.-M., Sciot, R., et al., 2016. Recurrent MALAT1-GLI1 oncogenic fusion and GLI1 up-regulation define a subset of plexiform fibromyxoma: GLI1 up-regulation in plexiform fibromyxoma. J. Pathol. 239 (3), 335–343.

Sun, K., Jia, K., Lv, H., Wang, S.-Q., Wu, Y., Lei, H., et al., 2020. EBV-positive gastric cancer: current knowledge and future perspectives. Front. Oncol. (10), 583463.

Takaishi, S., Okumura, T., Tu, S., Wang, S.S.W., Shibata, W., Vigneshwaran, R., et al., 2009. Identification of gastric cancer stem cells using the cell surface marker CD44. Stem Cells 27 (5), 1006–1020.

Tang, H., Long, Q., Zhuang, K., Han, K., Zhang, X., Guo, H., et al., 2021. Retinoblastoma tumor suppressor gene 1 enhances 5-fluorouracil chemosensitivity through SDF-1/CXCR4 axis by regulating autophagy in gastric cancer. Pathol. Res. Pract. 224, 153532.

Tsukiyama, T., Fukui, A., Terai, S., Fujioka, Y., Shinada, K., Takahashi, H., et al., 2015. Molecular role of RNF43 in canonical and noncanonical Wnt Signaling. Mol. Cell. Biol. 35 (11), 2007–2023.

Venhuizen, J.-H., Jacobs, F.J.C., Span, P.N., Zegers, M.M., 2020. P120 and E-cadherin: double-edged swords in tumor metastasis. Semin. Cancer Biol. 60, 107–120.

Waddell, T., Chau, I., Cunningham, D., Gonzalez, D., Okines, A.F.C., Wotherspoon, A., et al., 2013. Epirubicin, oxaliplatin, and capecitabine with or without panitumumab for patients with previously untreated advanced oesophagogastric cancer (REAL3): a randomised, open-label phase 3 trial. Lancet Oncol. 14 (6), 481–489.

Wu, J.N., Roberts, C.W.M., 2013. *ARID1A* mutations in cancer: another epigenetic tumor suppressor? Cancer Discov. 3 (1), 35–43.

Xing, X., Tang, Y.-B., Yuan, G., Wang, Y., Wang, J., Yang, Y., et al., 2013. The prognostic value of E-cadherin in gastric cancer: a meta-analysis. Int. J. Cancer 132 (11), 2589–2596.

Yamaguchi, A., Goi, T., Yu, J., Hirono, Y., Ishida, M., Iida, A., et al., 2002. Expression of CD44v6 in advanced gastric cancer and its relationship to hematogenous metastasis and long-term prognosis. J. Surg. Oncol. 79 (4), 230–235.

Yuza, K., Nagahashi, M., Watanabe, S., Takabe, K., Wakai, T., 2017. Hypermutation and microsatellite instability in gastrointestinal cancers. Oncotarget 8 (67), 112103–112115.

Zavros, Y., 2017. Initiation and maintenance of gastric cancer: a focus on CD44 variant isoforms and cancer stem cells. Cell. Mol. Gastroenterol. Hepatol. 4 (1), 55–63.

Zheng, X., Wu, Y., Zheng, L., Xue, L., Jiang, Z., Wang, C., et al., 2021. Disease-specific survival of AJCC 8th stage II gastric cancer patients after D2 gastrectomy. Front. Oncol. 11, 2871.

CHAPTER FOUR

Recent advancement in molecular markers of pancreatic cancer

L. Tharrun Daniel Paul[a], Ganesh Munuswamy-Ramanujam[b], Rajappan Chandra Satish Kumar[b], Vasukidevi Ramachandran[c], Dhanavathy Gnanasampanthapandian[a], and Kanagaraj Palaniyandi[a]

[a]Cancer Science Laboratory, Department of Biotechnology, School of Bioengineering, SRM Institute of Science and Technology, Kattankulathur, Chengalpattu, India
[b]Interdisciplinary Institute of Indian System of Medicine, SRM Institute of Science and Technology, Kattankulathur, Chengalpattu, India
[c]Department of Microbiology and Biotechnology, Bharath Institute of Higher Education and Research, Selaiyur, Chennai, India

1. Introduction

Pancreatic cancer has been predicted to be the second leading cause of cancer deaths in the year 2030, although it is the fourth leading cause at present. It is the most aggressive and deadliest disease with a survival rate of only 5 years, and the chance of survival is merely 9% (Siegel et al., 2020). Pancreatic cancers are irresponsive to therapies as most of them are detected only at the advanced stages of the disease. Thus, an early detection strategy is in demand to tackle the disease with therapeutics and prevent mortality rates. Although pancreatic cancer is fatal, its incidence is low, which should be considered when developing biomarkers for pancreatic cancers. Screening the general public for signs of pancreatic cancer and screening for familial history can help in the prognosis of the disease at an earlier stage, but this strategy is not feasible for a large population. Individuals with a familial history are at ninefold increased risk if they are the first-degree relatives of pancreatic cancer patients. Most importantly, apart from the familial history, germline mutations in certain genes, namely *BRCA1*, *CDKN2A*, *APC*, *ATM*, *MLH1*, *PALB2*, and so on, have been associated with an increase in the number of pancreatic cancer cases. In addition, the prediction of germline mutations helps in assessing the response of patients to therapies (Kato and Honda, 2020), as 85% of the patients pose with unresectable pancreatic cancer. Usually, patients, who have been diagnosed incidentally with this disease without symptoms, have a longer survival rate when compared with patients who get diagnosed after experiencing symptoms (Garg and Chari, 2020). Other risk factors may include lifestyle habits (such as drinking and smoking), increasing age, male, and diabetes mellitus, which are independent of lifestyle factors, yet these are manageable (Schizas et al., 2020).

Biomarkers in Cancer Detection and Monitoring of Therapeutics
https://doi.org/10.1016/B978-0-323-95114-2.00025-X

Gemcitabine has been the preferred drug of choice after 5-fluorouracil (5-FU) for pancreatic cancer patients in the first stage and in the advanced stages of the disease. However, the disease started gaining resistance to gemcitabine and, therefore, treatment strategies have shifted toward using combinations of different drugs along with gemcitabine. Drugs, such as FOLFIRINOX (a combination of oxaliplatin, irinotecan, and leucovorin) and nanoparticle bound albumin-paclitaxel (nab-paclitaxel), have been tested clinically along with gemcitabine, and the patient outcomes have improved when compared with the administration of gemcitabine alone (Kieler et al., 2020). Nanoliposomal irinotecan along with 5-FU/leucovorin has been approved as the treatment for metastatic PDAC after a phase 3 clinical trial positive results in a gemcitabine-based therapy (NAPOLI-1) (Wang-Gillam et al., 2016).

Pancreatic cancer patients experience least symptoms before the disease progresses to the advanced stage; moreover, the symptoms are nonspecific, such as nausea, abdominal pain, bloating, back pain, and change in consistency of the stool. Approximately 40%–60% of the cases present with abdominal pain, 13%–20% of the cases present with sudden onset of diabetes, 12% with back pain, and 10% with weight loss. These symptoms also depend on the location of the tumor, as 60%–70% of the tumors occur at the head portion of the pancreas. Other symptoms include anorexia, gastric outlet, obstruction in bowel, depression, venous thrombosis, pancreatitis, fat absorption disorder, and inadequate pancreatic enzyme production (Mizrahi et al., 2020; Walter et al., 2016).

Although various signs and symptoms are present to diagnose pancreatic cancer, it is well known that early detection of the cancer alone can help in improving patient survival and treatment response. This textual content contains the recent findings and strategies of early pancreatic cancer diagnosis by means of available signatures of the microenvironment and residing biomarkers.

2. Blood markers

In perspective of the prognosis of pancreatic cancer, blood serves as an effective source to be analyzed. Owing to the ease of acquirement and minimally invasive technique to draw blood, biomarker analysis from peripheral blood can provide more benefits than any other source. Various circulating biomarkers have been identified till date in plasma and serum components of the blood. Blood circulation accommodates in it the circulating tumor cells (CTC) that have been released by the primary tumors. These CTC can serve as a marker for predicting survival rates of patients. In a meta-analysis study, it has been discovered that patients with CTC have reduced overall survival (OS) and progression-free survival (PFS) (Wang et al., 2020a). Even after chemotherapy or chemoradiotherapy treatments for a period of 3 months, the overall survival was low in CTC-positive patients when compared with CTC negative patients

(Okubo et al., 2017). Protein biomarkers, TIMP1 and LRG1 in blood, have improved the detection of early-stage pancreatic cancer in combination with CA19–9 and have found to be statistically significant (Capello et al., 2017).

3. DNA and RNA markers

Circulating tumor DNA (ctDNA) arises from dead somatic cells and has been released into the circulation. ctDNA can be a direct reflection of the tumor burden as to whether the tumor is metastatic or in a minimally residual disease state. In addition, the threshold ratio of normal DNA to ctDNA is 10,000:1, which makes it a sensitive target and an effective biomarker of patient cancer stage prognosis. ctDNA was found in postoperative samples with the recurrence of disease even after gemcitabine-based adjuvant therapy (Lee et al., 2019). A detailed review on CTC and cell-free DNA (cfDNA) with the emphasis on pancreatic cancer has been published by Gall et al. (2019). Circulating free tumor DNA (cftDNA) obtained from the plasma can serve as a marker to estimate the treatment response and the progression of disease in pancreatic cancer patients. cftDNA with mutant KRAS expression was found to be increased in patients after 15 days of combinational chemotherapy, consisting of 5-FU, FOLFIRINOX, Gemcitabine, and nab-paclitaxel, and the disease seems to be progressed (Del Re et al., 2017). In a clinical study, ctDNA was found even before surgery and the amount of ctDNA decreased after surgical resection of pancreatic cancer. During the follow-up, ctDNA analysis was able to predict the recurrence of the disease with a sensitivity of 90% and a specificity of 88%. Postsurgery follow-up and ctDNA analysis predicted an overall survival period of 17 months (Groot et al., 2019). In another clinical study, 135 patients, including 31 resectable patients, 36 locally advanced patients, and 68 metastatic patients, were analyzed for ctDNA (Pietrasz et al., 2017). The presence of ctDNA was correlated with the reduced overall survival rate and disease-free survival among six patients who had curative intent resection (Pietrasz et al., 2017). Preoperative and postoperative KRAS transitions (from wild type to mutant) are associated with the overall survival of the patients and helps in deciding the treatment regimen (Nakano et al., 2018). Mutant *KRAS* were also found in circulating exosomes of pancreatic cancer patients (Allenson et al., 2017). Various studies have been performed on ctDNA and cfDNA that actually correlate with pancreatic cancer, which can predict the disease state, survival rate, and treatment responses of patients, and can serve as a potential prognostic marker in the diagnosis of pancreatic cancer patients (Perets et al., 2018).

Apart from the DNA circulating in the blood, various noncoding RNAs have also been linked to the diagnosis and prognosis of pancreatic cancer (Previdi et al., 2017). A recent study found out that, based on the comparison studies of various mRNAs with CA19–9, WASF2 mRNA presence correlated effectively with the pancreatic cancer risk

(Kitagawa et al., 2019). Other types of RNAs, such as circular RNA (circ-LDLRAD3) (Yang et al., 2017), long noncoding RNA (lncRNA) from plasma extracellular vesicle (Yu et al., 2020), plasma microRNAs (miR) miR-22-3p, 642b-3p, 885-5p (Hussein et al., 2017), and plasma exosomal miR-196a and miR-1246 (Zhou et al., 2018) have also been documented to play vital role as prognostic and diagnostic biomarkers in pancreatic cancer.

4. Serum markers

Serum markers for the detection of pancreatic cancer are advantageous than biomarkers from other sources, such as a tissue or a pancreatic cancer juice, because the detection can be carried out by using a single blood test report. In a recent study, serum analysis using antibody array technology in a follow-up study has produced an area under curve (AUC) value of 0.96 with a sensitivity of 94% and a specificity of 95% (Carmicheal et al., 2019). Exosome-based spectrometric analysis has been reported to yield an accuracy of 90% in diagnosis. It is significant to note that an outstanding AUC value of 1.0 was achieved during the mass spectrometric analysis of exosomal biomarker Glypican-1 (Ansari et al., 2019).

5. Serum carbohydrate antigen (CA) CA19-9

CA19–9 is also known as Sialyl Lewis A antigen or carbohydrate antigen 19–9. It was isolated 30 years ago when murine splenocytes were immunized with human cancer cells. Generally, it is synthesized by stepwise addition of fucose moieties to type 1 precursor chains of proteins and other molecules, thereby creating an α1,4 linkage between fucose and N-acetylglucosamine and the whole reaction being FUT3 catalyzed by fucosyltransferase, which adds the fucose moieties. It is significant to note that mice lack this enzyme. CA19–9 is present in 75% of the pancreatic cancer patients. Pancreatic intraepithelial neoplasms, a precursor of pancreatic ductal adenocarcinoma, have increased levels of this antigen. CA19–9 has known to play various biological roles. Being an embedded ganglioside or a mucin in the epithelial cells of pancreatic duct, biliary tract, prostate, and stomach, it regulates apoptosis, signal transduction, cell growth, and differentiation (Goh et al., 2017; Engle et al., 2019). It has been shown that rather than using CA19–9 alone as a biomarker, the combination of CEA and CA19–9 has increased the specificity to about 84% and even when combines with CA125 markers. Therefore, it has been suggested that the combination test screening for CA19–9 with CA242 or CA19–9 with *KRAS* gene mutation can provide better diagnosis of the disease. Further screening of CA19–9 with miRNA provides much more improved and accurate results (Ge et al., 2017).

In pancreatic cancer, CA19–9, known to have high sensitivity and specificity, functions as a biomarker of abnormal glycosylation. Although CA19–9 has a considerable sensitivity of 80%, it has limitations in terms of false positive in the case of inflammation and nonpancreatic cancers and false negatives in the case of Lewis negative patient groups. Lewis blood group individuals with Le (a+b−) and Le (a − b+) types express CA19–9, whereas individuals of Le (a − b−) type do not express fucosyltransferase even in the presence of tumor. Only 5%–7% of the population belong to this Le (a − b−) type.

In a clinical study performed by Azizian et al. (2020), it has been shown that a 1.35-fold increase in the CA19–9 can be used to predict the recurrence with 100% sensitivity, 67% specificity, 83% positive predictive value, and 100% negative predictive value. At the same time, a 2.45-fold increase in CA19–9 can be used to predict recurrence with 90% sensitivity, 83.33% specificity, and an AUC with 95% (Azizian et al., 2020). In another clinical study performed with 375 patients, the CA19–9 levels >305 U/mL had a positive predictive value of 73.6% in the presence of advanced PDAC conditions (van Manen et al., 2020). In another study of 200 advanced pancreatic cancer patients, an interaction among CA19–9 levels, overall survival, and platelet count was studied. Patients after two cycles of chemotherapy, who had ≥20% decrease in the CA19–9 levels, had significant overall survival rate and progression-free survival in conditions of low platelet count only. Therefore, low platelet count with decreased CA19–9 values in the pancreatic cancer patient is a prognostic marker (Chen et al., 2019). Fujimoto et al. have provided combination screening of CA19–9 and methylated RUNX3 by using combined restriction digital PCR assay (CORD) and recorded a sensitivity of 77.8% for pancreatic stage I cancer (Fujimoto et al., 2021). Another glycan named TRA antigen has been found to be activated in pancreatic cancer patients. During the development of the disease, the stem-like populations expressing nonsialylated TRA antigen modify it with sialylation and/or fucosylation reactions; therefore, providing them characterized functions. Sialylated TRA antigens are similar to CA19–9 antigens in terms of specificity to pancreatic cancers (Barnett et al., 2017). In addition, CA19–9 remains as the standard biomarker of choice for the comparison of novel biomarker potential to the prognosis of pancreatic cancer.

6. Glycosylation

Glycosylation, a posttranslational modification process involving the addition of sugar groups to membrane proteins, is required by the pancreas to lubricate and protect the ducts. In the case of pancreatic cancer, glycosylation is abnormal leading to disease progression. Glycome profile alterations can be attributed to the modifications in Sialyl Lewis antigens, truncated O-glycans, branched fucosylated N-glycans, particular proteoglycans and galectins, and O-GlnNAcylations. Glycosylation modes and profiles differ in various conditions of the disease. In a clinical study conducted among 200 patients, various glycans were profiled. Three glycans, namely sLe^x, CA19–9, and DUPAN-2 (sialylated LacNAc), were found to be increased; therefore, targeting these antigens may help in better disease prognosis and categorization. An enzyme GALNT3, involved in abnormal O-linked glycosylation, is increased in well-differentiated tumors but not in poorly differentiated tumor tissues. Glypican-1, a heparin sulfate glycoprotein, is found in the exosomes in circulation, hence it can act as a biomarker for diagnosis (Munkley, 2019). CA19–9, a glycan, can increase the levels of EGFR in pancreatic cancer of mice (Engle et al., 2019). Fucosylation is a type of glycosylation in which fucose molecules are added to O-glycans, N-glycans, and glycolipids. Fucosyltransferase is the enzyme catalyzing the fucosylation reaction. Specifically, fucosyltransferase 8 (FUT8) has been upregulated in pancreatic cancers and is involved in lymph node metastasis and prevents disease recurrence. In addition, FUT8 knockdown reduced invasion in pancreatic cancer cell lines and in xenograft it reduced the peritoneal metastasis. Thus, FUT8 can serve as an effective therapeutic biomarker targeting posttranslational process (Bastian et al., 2021). ST6GAL1, an enzyme catalyzing the addition of α-2,3-linked sialic acids to the N-glycans, has been found to be upregulated in various cancers. In pancreatic cancer, ST6GAL1 is upregulated and causes advanced metastasis, thereby reducing the relapse free intervals and overall survival rate. In contrast, ST6GAL1 in bladder cancer has known to have a tumor suppressive role (Collisson et al., 2019). High-glycosylated CD133 obtained from ascites-derived exosomes has been studied in pancreatic cancer patients and has increased the overall survival rate. Thus, it can serve as an effective biomarker for patient prognosis of the advanced state of the disease (Sakaue et al., 2019).

7. Mucins

Mucins are glycoproteins of high molecular weight containing a sugar moiety associated with a protein. There are various kinds of mucins that present as biomarkers in pancreatic cancer patients' sera. MUC1, MUC4, MUC5AC, and MUC16 have been reported to be present in pancreatic cancer. Mucins have functional domains that are targeted during the development and progression of the disease. MUC16 has gained its significance as a tumor-associated antigen (Smid et al., 2019) for immunotherapy targeting. MUC4, on the other hand, is not expressed in normal pancreas but only during the development and progression of the disease. MUC4 is also an effective immunotherapeutic target due to its multifunctional role in several processes occurring during the course of the pancreatic cancer tumorigenesis. MUC4 is known to be expressed on the pancreatic cancer stem cells, thus maintaining the development of pancreatic cancer cells and responsible for the gemcitabine resistance (Gautam et al., 2020). It was found in a study that mucin-secreting pancreatic cancer cell line (Capan-1) was sensitive to bortezomib treatment, whereas the mucin-silenced cells were sensitive to gemcitabine treatment; thus, serves as a biomarker in aiding pancreatic cancer classification for appropriate chemotherapies based on its secretory capability (Wissniowski et al., 2012). $\alpha 1,4$-linked N-acetylglucosamine (αGlcNAc) residues, found usually on the mucin core unit of MUC6, are expressed in normal amount in intraductal papillary mucinous neoplasms (IPMNs) and pancreatic intraepithelial neoplasias (PanINs). During the course of the development of the disease, the level of αGlcNAc was found to be decreasing in gastric glands, thus marking the start of the cancer. Therefore, the prognosis of αGlcNAc along with MUC6 for reduced expression can detect the disease at an earlier stage and determine its metastatic stage (Yamanoi and Nakayama, 2018). In order to differentiate between malignant tumors and chronic pancreatitis, Wiktorowicz et al. have demonstrated the use of RT-PCR for profiling mucins (such as MUC1, MUC2, MUC3, MUC4, MUC5AC, and MUC6) present in fine needle aspiration biopsies (FNAB) of patients (Wiktorowicz et al., 2018). Mucins are effective immunotherapeutic and genetic targets as well, which can elicit specific responses by functioning either as an antibody or as a vaccine against pancreatic cancer (Nagata et al., 2007).

8. Genetic markers

Genetic markers have been the focus of research in prognosis and in the diagnosis of the disease. However, one genetic alteration cannot be targeted for therapy in order to provide better efficacy. Therefore, one genetic target in a disease state cannot be used to target another disease effectively, which will be much variable. Hence, figuring out the type of genetic alterations occurring at different frequencies, various sites, and periods of disease development can help to categorize disease toward an effective treatment (Collisson et al., 2019).

Genetic mutations have been said to occur in a vast majority of cancers, in that, which include aberrations in oncogenic *KRAS* genes and involved suppression of the tumor suppression genes, such as *SMAD4*, *TP53*, and *CDKN2A*. Apart from these genes, a large number of genes have known to be mutated in pancreatic cancer in a low frequency of $\leq 10\%$. Mutations in these genes have been pertained and channelized to certain important pathways, such as Notch, Wnt, KRAS, TGF-β, and hedgehog signaling. In addition, S-phase entry, axon guidance, remodeled chromatin structure, DNA repair, and RNA processing contribute to genetic mutations (Grant et al., 2016) (Fig. 1).

9. Oncogenic *KRAS*

The *KRAS* is a molecular switch that controls various cellular functions by associating intracellular signaling pathways and transcription factors to cell membrane

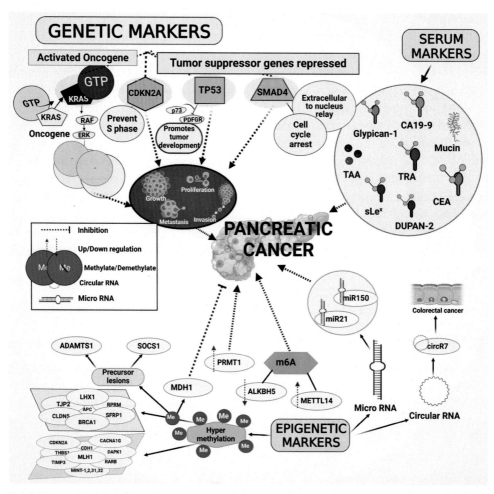

Fig. 1 Various markers of pancreatic cancer pertaining to genetic, epigenetic, and serum origin have been portrayed. Major genetic markers are oncogenic *KRAS* and tumor suppressor *TP53*, *SMAD4*, and *CDKN2A*. Most probably, epigenetic markers involve in methylation and demethylation mechanisms and the regulation by noncoding RNAs. Serum markers contain glycosylated molecules circulating in the blood and the most common marker being the cancer antigen 19-9 (CA19-9).

growth factor receptor. KRAS induces cell proliferation in the development of cancer through a series of cellular pathways. Briefly, KRAS is a GTPase that when bound to GTP is in "on" state and when bound to GDP is in "off" state. Although in the case of cancer, KRAS is bound constant to GTP, thereby promoting proliferation. When KRAS is in an activated state, it binds to RAF family members (RAF1, BRAF, and ARAF) and activates them. Activated RAFs induce MEK 1/2 kinases activation, which in turn activate ERK1/2 kinases via phosphorylation. Finally, ERKs phosphorylate cell and nuclear proteins that increase cell proliferation, such as ELK-1 and c-JUN. These series of events that lead to KRAS activation cause the development and progression of cancer. The *KRAS* mutations occur as point mutations in codon 12, which is the first initiating step in pancreatic cancer (Cicenas et al., 2017).

Pancreatic cancer has been noted for possessing the highest rate of *KRAS* mutations between ~95% and 99% that occur in the exon G12, one among G12, G13, or Q61, which are associated commonly with activated KRAS (Cicenas et al., 2017). It was found in a study that out of the 136 patients with pancreatic adenocarcinoma, 71 patients (52%) had point mutations in G12 and Q61. Mutated *KRAS* shows higher resistance to gemcitabine than the wild-type variant. Gemcitabine in combination with erlotinib was able to provide survival benefits that gemcitabine alone could not. On the other hand, erlotinib alone did not provide survival benefits in 121 patients out of the 173 patients (Cicenas et al., 2017). In addition, the activation of KRAS leads to simultaneous genetic inactivation of other tumor suppressor gene pathways, such as TP53, INK4A-ARF, and DPC4-SMAD4, in most of the pancreatic cancers. Precursor lesions, such as PanINs and IPMNs, contain *KRAS* mutations prior to pancreatic cancer progression.

Numerous studies on KRAS have been conducted using transgenic mice KRAS^{G12D}. These transgenic mice express KRAS from the beginning of the embryonic development of pancreas and PanIN was found after a period of weaning and developed in stages and grades. KRAS diagnosis involves molecular biology techniques, mostly implying PCR-based assays, that amplify mutated regions of *KRAS* specifically, exons 2 and 3 where mutation occurs, and differentiating from the wild-type variants by analyzing the codons 12 and 13. Wild-type *KRAS* status is a marker of benign state of the disease (Cicenas et al., 2017). The diagnostic sensitivity (0.94) of KRAS has been shown to improve when the analysis was performed along with the telomerase activity and decreased heterogeneity (O'Neill and Stoita, 2021). Exosomes capable of targeting oncogenic *KRAS* were developed using shRNA and was found to be an effective treatment against pancreatic cancer in orthotopic mice models and has improved the overall survival rate. Exosomal activity was efficient as it has been protected by CD47 present on the exosome membrane by means of CD47-SIRP signaling and they were able to penetrate the stroma through macropinocytosis (McWilliams et al., 2018).

10. Tumor suppressor genes

Tumor suppressor genes, as their name implies, prevent the cell proliferation induced by oncogenes through mechanisms, such as cell-cycle arrest, apoptosis, and senescence. When considering PDAC, three genes (*CDKN2A*, *TP53*, and *SMAD4/*

DPC4) are suppressed most commonly leading to tumorigenesis. The inactivation of tumor suppressor genes occurs with the simultaneous activation of oncogenic *KRAS* sequentially. The p16/*INK4A* genes encoded by *CDKN2A* brings about senescence but deteriorates with the induction of *KRAS*. Functionally, the *CDKN2A* is lost in 95% of the PDACs. Thus, deactivation of tumor suppressor genes and induction of *KRAS* occurs simultaneously leading to progressive disease. In addition, *CDKN2A* codes for the p14/ARF, which induced apoptosis by inhibiting MDM2-dependent p53 proteolytic degradation. Apart from this, p14 has also been shown to decrease PDAC condition by means of repressing RNA processing, NF-κB, and hyper proliferation induced by c-Myc (Grant et al., 2016). Gu et al. conducted meta-analysis on the tumor suppressor genes and found out that the overexpression of P53, loss of SMAD4 and CDKN2A/P16, and mutation of *KRAS* in pancreatic cancer tissues have resulted in decreased overall survival rate (Gu et al., 2020).

11. CDKN2A

CDKN2A, also known as *INK4A/P16*, functions as a senescence initiator for preventing the cell from the S phase in cell-cycle by means of inhibiting cyclin D-CDK4/6. The mutation of CDKN2A leads to continuous cell growth. *CDKN2A* mutation occurs spontaneously after *KRAS* has been mutated, thus circumventing the senescence. *P16* loss also leads to *P14/ARF* loss, which is another tumor suppressor gene encoded by CDKN2A; nonetheless, it is not correlated significantly with disease progression. However, p14 expression is controlled by an independent promoter that is not affected by epigenetic modifications, which happens in the case of p16. In addition, the loss of *p16* leads to the loss of *p14* and that is unpreventable. CDKN2A can act as a prognostic marker, the claims of which can be derived from several studies.

In a clinical study involving 88 pancreatic cancer patients, among which 68 of them have undergone surgical resection, a change in the genotype between CC and CT/TT variations present in C580T of 3′ UTR has shown important results portraying a disease-free survival. Targeted deep sequencing assay used for finding *CDKN2A* mutations showed significant results for mutations in 0–2 and 3 as a prognostic and improved overall survival rate. CDKN2A might have no significant relationship with clinicopathological criteria but can be related inversely to tumor size; that is, low levels of this protein expression can promote tumor size to be large than normal levels. *CDKN2A* loss can be attributed to promoter hypomethylation, mutation due to a loss of gene or its deletion, which can lead to a large tumor size and poor survival rates. An epidemiological study conducted by McWilliams et al. (2018) has concluded that CDKN2A rare coding variants (RCV) were frequent in African-Americans, a rare minority group, whose CDKN2A RCVs require much characterization (Grant et al., 2016).

12. TP53

TP53 is a gene that encodes the transcription factor p53. A study carried out on mice tumor cells demonstrates that a tumor-associated mutated variant of the p53, known to repress the expression of platelet-derived growth factor receptor (PDGFR) by means of binding to p73, and PDGFR expression are known to promote invasiveness, metastasis, and migration of cancer cells. In addition, TP53 promotes cancer progression through PDGFR-independent mechanisms by inhibiting genes that prevent cell migration and epithelial-to-mesenchymal transition (EMT) (Grant et al., 2016). Mutation rate of *TP53* in pancreatic cancers is 70%. *TP53* has been known to have a good prognostic value (Gu et al., 2020).

Low TP53 mRNA expression has been correlated with poor prognosis and that of wild-type variant showed good prognosis of the disease in a study conducted among 57 patients. A study was conducted with tumor samples from 50 pancreatic cancer patients, among which 4 (8%) of them had complete loss of *TP53*, 20 (40%) of them had regular expression, and 26 (52%) of them had overexpression, and patients with regular expression of TP53 had a better progression free survival when compared with those with total loss (Cicenas et al., 2017). P53 induces cell-cycle arrest via its target gene *p21*. A study brings out that cyclin B1 (*CCNB1*) gene knockdown reduces the expression of p53 and p21 along with Bax and caspases 3 and 9. P53 inhibition alone has been shown to bring down the expression of Bax, caspase 3/9, p53, and p21, but increased MDM2 expression of oncoprotein inhibiting p53 transactivation (Zhang et al., 2018). In addition, TP53 carries out the activation of ARF6 (a small GTPase involved in invasion and metastasis) and associated AMAP1 through the PDGFR and upregulates the mevalonate pathway. Furthermore, ARF6-AMAP1 pathways drives RTK activation which induces PD-L1 recycling and cell surface expression (Gu et al., 2020).

13. SMAD4

SMAD4 is another important tumor suppressor protein involved in cell-cycle control via signal transduction between extracellular components and nucleus. SMAD4 is also known as DPC4/MADH4. SMAD4 controls the cell to sustain in the G1 phase itself, thereby arresting cell-cycle. SMAD4 is one among the three categories of SMAD proteins, namely, SMAD 1/2/3/5/8 (receptor mediator SMAD), SMAD4 (Co-mediator SMAD), and SMAD 6/7 (inhibitory SMAD). SMAD 2/3 regulates TGF-β signaling and SMAD 1/5/8 regulates signaling from bone morphogenic proteins (BMPs). SMAD4 regulates the signals from both TGF-β and BMPs, thereby behaving as an intermediate mediator. SMAD 6/7 inhibits the phosphorylation of regulatory SMAD, thus preventing

SMAD4 complex formation. SMAD4 is known to have cross-talks with several pathways, which include MAPK, ERK, JNK, P38, PI3K/AKT, and WNT/β-catenin pathways (Zhao et al., 2018).

Gradual and increased expression of SMAD4 in pancreatic cancer patients has been a better prognostic marker for analyzing the operative conditions. SMAD4 mutation analysis using sequencing was effective than immunohistochemistry (IHC) in the case of organoid invasive phenotypic models, as IHC cannot differentiate between genetic subtypes such as homo/heterozygous deletions. Furthermore, SMAD4 requires TGF-β to function as an apoptotic inducer and inhibit cell proliferation. In addition, the loss of SMAD4 leads to collective invasion induced by TGF-β signaling via RAC1 and CDC42 (Rho-like GTPases) noncanonically. Phosphoglycerate kinase 1 (PGK1) has been known to affect the metastatic and proliferative potential of pancreatic cancer in the case of *SMAD4* loss (Huang et al., 2020). SMAD4 depletion in vivo is known to make pancreatic cancer resistant to ionizing radiation through mechanisms of autophagy and reactive oxygen species (ROS). From 55% of the PDAC cases, 30% of the PanIN3 (late lesions) and only 10% of IPMNs show the presence of SMAD4 loss, insisting SMAD4 can act as a potent biomarker for in part PDACs; added, further studies need to be performed to improve the efficacy of the screening methods (Wang et al., 2018). SMAD4 loss is known to increase HNF4G expression. *HNF4G* is an oncogene that is reported to modulate invasion and metastasis in pancreatic cancer. However, a study performed on mice models and clinical subjects has shown that the *SMAD4* loss-induced expression of HNF4G can be reversed by treatment with metformin (Wang et al., 2021).

14. Epigenetic markers

Epigenetics regulates the transcriptional processes by using various mechanisms that modify the genomic integrity, chromatin marking, and the formation of histones via DNA packaging. The most implied mechanisms involve DNA modifications, such as methylation, hydroxylation, formylation, nucleosome occupancy, positioning and its subsequent modifications, and noncoding RNA mediated gene silencing. Although epigenetic changes establish a stable cell phenotype, they tend to adapt to changing developmental and genetic conditions and this mechanism is harnessed by the cancer cells to initiate and progress the tumorigenesis (Dumitrescu, 2018). Potential applications of the epigenetic markers are found most probably in three areas of cancer therapy, namely, detection, prognosis, and predicting treatment responses. Epigenetic markers are present in body fluids, such as serum/plasma, urine, vaginal fluid, and nipple fluid aspirate, and DNA methylation signatures being the significant one among them. Circulating cfDNA serves as the main source of markers, usually found in higher amount in cancer subjects

(Lomberk et al., 2018). Analysis of the tumor tissue-specific DNA methylation patterns has enormous advantages when compared with general methylation patterns.

Epigenomic mapping studies have brought out two different subtypes of the PDAC, namely, the classical tumors and the basal tumors. The classical subtypes are correlated with the regulation of transcription factors involved in the development of PDAC and also in the regulation of metabolism and Ras signaling. The basal subtypes are associated with the transcriptional nodes downstream of *MET* oncogene, which is involved in the proliferation and EMT. This information states that the downregulation of *MET* genes can mark a shift from the basal to classical transcriptomic signatures, thereby providing new insight into epigenome and the related genes as a potent marker for pancreatic cancer and for choosing an appropriate treatment regimen (Lomberk et al., 2018).

15. DNA methylation changes

DNA methylation of CpG islands was identified to be occurring preferentially in pancreatic tumor samples. The genes, such as *CACNA1G*, *CDH1*, *CDKN2A*, *DAPK1*, *MGMT*, *MINT1-2-31-32*, *MLH1*, *RARB*, *THBS1*, and *TIMP3*, were analyzed from the pancreatic tumor xenografts. This was the first study to compare the methylation status of DNA in normal and cancer subjects. Aberrant DNA methylation was found in all the genes in at least at one locus except for *MGMT*, where no methylation was observed either in neoplastic or in normal samples. *MINT 1*, *MINT-28*, and *MINT-32* were the most recurring methylations. DNA methylation can be a predictive marker of the disease stage, namely, ADAMTS1 or SOCS1 in PanINs and IPMNs.

On the other hand, few genes might show high methylation that may subside with the progress of the disease. Particularly, seven genes were found to be highly methylated in invasive disease stage, namely *LHX1*, *BRCA1*, *APC*, *RPRM*, *CLDN5*, *TJP2*, and *SFRP1* (Natale et al., 2019). However, single gene targets cannot confirm precisely the disease stage and a collection of targeted biomarkers are required to stage the pancreatic cancer and improve the treatment mechanism. Alkylation repair protein homolog 5 (ALKBH5), a demethylase that reverses m6A methylations, is said to be downregulated in pancreatic cancer and is known to render the PDAC xenograft resistant to gemcitabine, leading to cancer proliferation, migration, and invasion via the regulation of the Wnt signaling pathway and respective m6A-mediated Wnt inhibitory factor 1 (WIF-1) (Tang et al., 2020). METTL14, a methylase, is upregulated in pancreatic cancer and is responsible for the migration and invasion in vitro and in vivo through the regulation of m6A-mediated p53 effector related to PMP-22 (PERP) targeting (Wang et al., 2020b). Protein arginine methyltransferase 1 (PRMT1), responsible for the methylation of arginine residues, is found to be expressed highly in PDAC tissue samples, as studied by using RT-PCR and tissue microarray analysis. PRMT1 was responsible for the growth of tumor both in vitro and in vivo, via increased expression of β-catenin levels in cells. It is found to be a prognostic marker for tumor size and postoperative pancreatic cancer subjects (Song et al., 2020). Histone acetylases, such as H3K14ac, H3K27ac, and H4K5ac, are known to be upregulating at a faster pace and confined space and involved in mediating inflammatory processes in acute pancreatitis (Negoi et al., 2019).

Methylation status of genes is vital clinically for diagnostic and for prognostic purposes. DNA methylations are dependent on histone modifications, especially histone methylases and demethylases. When considerable studies have been carried out on histone methyltransferases, more research works are yet to be carried out on histone demethylases. Histone demethylase 3A an important role in progression of pancreatic cancer (Dandawate et al., 2019). On the other hand, histone arginine demethylases, rather than histone lysine demethylase, are less explored (Liu et al., 2021). The methylation of arginine residue (R248) of malate dehydrogenase (MDH1) is known to disrupt the glutamine metabolism and suppress pancreatic cancer, inducing oxidative stress; in addition, it has been analyzed that MDH1 is demethylated in PDAC clinical samples (Wang et al., 2016).

16. Micro RNA modification

miRNAs function by either disrupting the mRNA or preventing the translation process. miRNA aberrant expression has been linked to various attributes that contribute to tumorigenesis of pancreatic cancer. This leads to unrestricted cell proliferation and growth, delay in cell death, bypassing actions of tumor suppressor genes, invasion, metastasis, and increased vasculature. In addition, miRNAs can have tumor suppressive roles and the types of miRNA expression vary for different types of cancer; thus, making the treatment a noninvasive one. Recently, in mice models and clinical subjects, miR342-3p was found to possess a tumor suppressor role in hepatocellular carcinoma, which was due to the modulation of the lactate transport machinery of monocarboxylic acid transporter 1 (Komoll et al., 2021). miR-92b, -10a, and -7 were found to be decreased in acute pancreatitis; miR-126-5p, -148-3p, -216a-5p, -551b-5p, and -375 were found in higher concentration; and miR-216a-5p, -551b-5p, and -375 were found in mild cases of acute pancreatitis. Among this, miR-21 is an effective biomarker for pancreatic cancer and in regulating inflammatory responses. The upregulation of miR-142-5p and -320c is known to induce gemcitabine resistance and miR-142-5p downregulation improved the patient survival. Four miRNAs, such as miR-155, miR-203, miR-210, and miR-222, were found to increase fatality by 6.2-fold in patients with PDAC; and another set of six miRNAs, such as miR-45, miR-105, miR-127, miR-187, miR-309-3p, and miR-518-a-2, were analyzed for their prognostic value in long-term survivors and patients with positive nodes. miR-21 is another important biomarker involved in reduced survival rates and increased metastasis to lymph nodes and gemcitabine resistance. A clinical study carried out among 200 PDAC patient samples has shown that miRNA-574-5p, -1244, and -4474-5p are upregulated and miR-574-5p, -1244, -145-, -328, -26b, and -4321 are related with overall survival (OS) and disease-free survival (DFS) of patients. Another study put forward that the overexpression of miR-155, -203, -222, and -210 correlated with the decrease in the overall survival rate and poor prognosis, the same condition which occurred when miR-217 was downregulated. miR-21 is known to be directed against various targets, such as PTEN, PDCD4, IL-6R, and CDK6, and its upregulation has less effect on the survival rates in pancreatic cancer patients. miR-let7 family (a,b), -126, -143, -193b, -206, -217, -3923, and -145 with tumor suppressive effect target the *KRAS* oncogene and its pathways (Daoud et al., 2019). miR-30a-3p, -105, -127, -187, -452, and -518a-2 can better prognosis 2-year survival and above on PDAC patients. miR-7 analysis in serum of pancreatic cancer patients has shown that a decrease in the expression was associated with chemoresistance of PDAC to gemcitabine, which was attributed to the repression of the Warburg effect to reduce glucose uptake to bring about autophagy; hence, acting as a prognostic and diagnostic marker (Ye et al., 2020). miR-150 is known to downregulate MUC4, an oncoprotein resulting in the repression of growth (Rawat et al., 2019).

Apart from miRNAs, there are noncoding RNAs similar to long noncoding circular RNAs (lncRNA) and circular RNAs (circRNA) involved in gene silencing. Circular RNA (human serum albumin) is upregulated in PDAC patients and when inhibited, it disrupts PDAC cell proliferation through cell-cycle arrest, interacts with miR-874-3p, and induces the expression of polo-like kinase 1 (PLK1) (Yamanoi and Nakayama, 2018). circRNA-7 is known to capture miR-7 by acting as a molecular sponge and, therefore, may be a potential prognostic marker in colorectal cancer; thus, paving a path into experimental studies in this area (Ye et al., 2020).

Given the enormous roles of miRNA in regulating pancreatic cancer tumorigenesis and metastasis, the research performed on this area is less, requiring much experimental trials to bring out their potential roles and to channelize their use as an effective noninvasive prognostic biomarker.

17. Pancreatic tumor juice markers

Pancreatic juice is a direct reflection of the functional properties of the pancreas and, therefore, can act as a suitable source for the identification of biomarkers. Pancreatic cancer juice was first known to be extracted by using endoscopic retrograde cholangiopancreatography (ERCP). Although the purity has been the highest till now, ~25% of the patients experienced pancreatitis post-ERCP. Therefore, this technique was discontinued. Another technique invented by Raimondo et al. (2003) implied the combination of routine upper endoscopy, secretin administration, and collection of the pancreatic cancer juice using an aspiration catheter (Ideno et al., 2020). Conwell et al. (2003) proposed another method involving the direct aspiration of the juice through endoscope channel.

Pancreatic cancer juice analysis can also differentiate the metabolome of normal and diseased subjects as well as improve the prognostic accuracy when compared with plasma samples based on different metabolic variations of specific diseases. H NMR analysis of 18 metabolites from pancreatic cancer juice has identified lactate accumulation to be higher with a decrease in essential amino acids, such as glycine and acetoacetate, which marks a shift in the metabolism toward aerobic glycolysis and an increase in nucleotide and lipid biosynthesis, respectively (Cortese et al., 2020). In addition, pancreatic cancer juice contains methylated DNA markers that were distinguishable from normal subjects. Approximately 83% sensitivity was achieved for analysis from any of the cancer stages and for stages of 1 and 2, and for IPMN–high grade dysplasia 80% sensitivity was achieved. It was significant that three methylated DNA markers were identified that discriminate between cancer and normal subjects with an area under receiver operating characteristic (ROC) curve of 0.9 pancreatic cancer (Majumder et al., 2020). Pancreatic cancer juice samples also contained extracellular vesicles linked with proteins, such as MUC1, MUC 4, MUC 5 AC, MUC 6, MUC 16, CFTR, and MDR-1 (Osteikoetxea et al., 2018) (Fig. 2).

18. Proteomics

Carcinoembryonic antigen (CEA) is one of the significant proteins that has been used as a biomarker in pancreatic cancer and is known to be present in the pancreatic cancer juice (Wang et al., 2021). Actually, CEA is present in higher amounts in the pancreatic cancer juice when compared with normal subjects. Similarly, a calcium-binding protein, S100P, has been reported to be present in an increased amount in pancreatic cancer juice samples when compared with normal subjects. Both these proteins have the potential to be used as an effective biomarker in the diagnosis of pancreatic cancer (Ideno et al., 2020). In a study performed among patients with gallstone disease, it was found that pancreatic juice proteins have a modulation due to gallstone disease. A collection of analytical techniques was performed to analyze the pancreatic cancer juice samples to bring out the effective proteomic markers, such as lithostathine 1α, A1BG, Caldecrin, DJ-1, FGB, MMP9, L1CAM, plasminogen, S100A8, and S100A9. However, the markers, such as CEA, S100-A6, A8, A9, and plasminogen, were regulated differentially among the cancer patients and benign variants (Ansari et al., 2019).

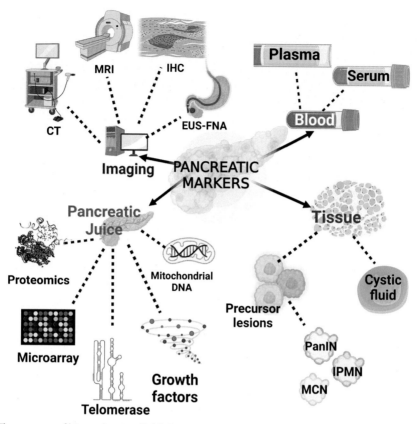

Fig. 2 The sources of biomarkers available for pancreatic cancer prognosis and diagnosis are depicted. They are categorized into four different sources, namely, blood, tissue, pancreatic juice, and imaging.

19. Growth factors and receptors

There are several growth factors that the cancer cells hijack from the normal cells' machinery to aid to their growth and progression. Some of the growth factors having significance with regard to most of the cancers are transforming growth factor (TGF), vascular endothelial growth factor (VEGF), fibroblast growth factor-10 (FGF-10)/ keratinocyte growth factor-2 (KGF-2), platelet-derived growth factor (PDGF), and tumor-specific growth factor (TSGF) (O'Neill and Stoita, 2021). Growth factors lead to the formation of new blood vessels (neovascularization) and, thus, contribute to the development of tumor and its progression (Bournet et al., 2016).

20. Mitochondrial mutations

The pancreatic acinar cells and the ductal cells are powered by the mitochondria as their energy demand is met by the processes of oxidative phosphorylation. Acinar cells control the release of Ca^{2+} for mitochondrial functioning; thereby, any misfunction can lead to pathological conditions, such as acute pancreatitis. *KRAS* mutations are known to alter the mitochondrial metabolism in pancreatic cancer (Fu et al., 2021). Mitochondrial damage induces the release of mitochondrial DNA (mtDNA), the copy number of which when is low can interfere with the metabolism, and is known to increase tumorigenesis, progression, and affect drug resistance (Sanyal et al., 2018).

21. Telomerase

Telomere shortening marks the senescence of cells and impaired telomere shortening occurs in cancer conditions that lead to unwanted mutations and, thereby, immortality of the cells. Telomerase has been known to indulge in the tumorigenesis of pancreatic cancer. Enhanced telomere transcriptase expression and activation of epidermal growth factor receptor (EGFR) caused by CD133 has led to the development of stem-like phenotype in pancreatic cancer cell lines. Telomerase reverse transcriptase (TERT) has been found to be associated with the development of pancreatic cancer. TERT variants, rs401681 and rs2853677 caused due to single nucleotide polymorphisms, were associated with a high probability of pancreatic cancer neoplasia. Thus, making TERT an effective genetic and prognostic biomarker (Sansone et al., 2020). A meta-analysis study conducted by Hata et al. (2017) showed that the telomerase activity was an effective biomarker among KRAS, CDKN2A/p16, and TP53SMAD4/DPC4. In addition, the diagnostic value was even higher when the analysis was performed using telomerase and cytology together with a sensitivity of 0.88 and sensitivity of 1.00 rather than telomerase activity alone (O'Neill and Stoita, 2021; Springer et al., 2019).

22. M2-pyruvate kinase

Pyruvate kinase (PK), an enzyme involved in the conversion of phosphoenolpyruvate to pyruvate in glycolysis, is involved in the poor prognosis of pancreatic cancer and decreased overall survival rate. The role of PK in caners is disturbed, thus result in incomplete glycolysis and lead to an accumulation of side metabolites, which favors the production of lipids, nucleic acids, and proteins for cancer progression and growth.

Pyruvate kinase M2 (PKM2) can differentiate advanced pancreatic cancers from initial stage pancreatic cancers; however, the sensitivity and specificity are not up to the mark for it to be used as a biomarker unlike CA19–9 (Mohammad et al., 2019).

23. Microarray

A recent study was carried out on pancreatic cancer juice clinical samples by using the MitoChip array-based sequencing. From the study, it was identified that similar to the primary tumor DNA, heteroplasmic mutations were found in 50% of the juice samples. Another microarray study performed on pancreatic cancer juice for 17 genes selected through RT-PCR showed that mesothelin was found to have a good correlation in both the juice and the tissue samples. IPMN and matrix metalloproteinase 7 (MMP7) have shown good correlation in both tissue and juice samples (Sanyal et al., 2018). Microarray analysis of mucin cystic fluid have shown modulation in glycosylation patterns and glycoproteins in clinical samples and certain glycoproteins, such as ACTB, YWHAQ, YWHAZ, LDHA, S100A11, YWHAG, HSPA5, KRT18, and LAMC1, have increased in the mucinous cystic neoplasia (MCN) and these were correlated with increased mucin expression in the invasive subtypes (Wang et al., 2019).

24. Pancreatic tumor tissue markers

It can be put in a way that tumorigenesis and cancer progression originate as a result of uncontrolled tissue fibrosis due to a damaged epithelia leading to aberrant changes in the molecular mechanisms and, thereby, a remodeled extracellular matrix (ECM) accommodating factors and precursors that trigger cancer development. Therefore, markers in tissues are indispensable to study the biology of pancreatic cancer for better diagnosis and prognosis of the disease in an earlier stage. Generally, epithelial marker E-cadherin and mesenchymal markers, such as N-cadherin, vimentin, and Snail, are expressed highly in cancer accommodating stem cells. However, specific markers need to be targeted in order to classify the cancers precisely according to their respective stages to improve treatment strategies and to segregate patients with the possibility of surgical resection (Thomas and Radhakrishnan, 2019).

Apart from morphological markers that mark the stage of the disease, pancreatic cancer also harbors various genetic and molecular signatures. Genetic alteration (mainly in the *KRAS*, *CDKN2aA*, *SMAD4*, and *TP53*), epigenetic modulations performed by tissue-specific noncoding RNAs, and various other markers such as exosomes, metabolic components, the residing microbiome, and proteomic profiles together contribute for better diagnosis of the various stages of pancreatic cancer (Zhou et al., 2017).

25. Precancerous lesions

PanINs, IPMNs, and MCN are the precursor lesions that develop into pancreatic cancers. Among the three, the most common precancerous lesion is the PanINs. PanINs can be low grade (PanIN-1A, 1B subtypes), intermediate (PanIN-2), or high grade (PanIN-3).

As far as initial stages of PanINs are concerned, the major important genetic modulations that occur are the telomere shortening and mutations associated with *KRAS*, *CDKI2A*, and *p21WAF/CIP1*. Among these, the telomere shortening events contribute up to 90% of the PanIN-1 cases. Especially, all these alterations are expressed in PanINs. In addition, MMP7 is also expressed in PanINs that imparts resistance to apoptosis in cancer cells. Prostate stem cell antigen is expressed in 60% of the different PanIN subtypes. MUC1, which is overexpressed in PDAC, is expressed in less quantity in PanIN unlike MUC5 that is overexpressed in all stages of PanINs. Similarly, in intermediate and late stages of PanINs, alterations can be found in SMAD4, TP53, COX-2, and cyclin-D1. PSCA-5, SOX17, MMP-7, Fascin, and Mucin-5 have been expressed in all the stages of PanINs (Guo et al., 2016).

IPMNs remain to be the most common type of cystic precursor lesion of the PDAC. Although the sensitivity gained by the diagnostic techniques in detecting invasive IPMN is good enough, further studies have to be undertaken to improve the specificity of the diagnosis. IPMNs also accommodate 90% of the *KRAS* mutations in the high grade and 40% to 90% in low-grade dysplasia. Mutation analysis of KRAS along with GNAS has improved the sensitivity (90%) and specificity (50%) with a positive and negative predictive value of 71% and 81%, respectively (Tulla and Maker, 2018). GNAS mutations found with higher incidence rate in IPMNs and, especially, in fluids that reflect the tissue condition but not in other pancreatic cystic lesions (Kadayifci et al., 2017). Apart from these aberrations, other oncogenic mutations (such as in *PI3Ks*, *BRAF/MAPK* pathways), expression of Telomerase reverse transcriptase TERT, hedgehog signaling pathways, and mutations in tumor suppressor genes (such as *TP53*, *CDKN2A/p16*, *SMAD4/DPC4*, *RNF43/Wnt* pathway/β-catenin, and *BRG1/SMARCA4*), occur in the IPMNs. Apart from these genetic changes, other molecular changes in glycoproteins (such as CEA, CA19–9, and mucins) and cytokine expression (such as IL-5, IL-8, IL-1 β, CD4+, and CD8+) have also been known to be expressed in IPMNs (Tulla and Maker, 2018).

Mucinous cystic neoplasm is another precursor lesion of the pancreatic cancer. Although it is less common than the IPMNs, it accommodates markers of good diagnostic and prognostic values. Microarray analysis of MCN fluid showed glycoproteins that are expressed highly, which also correlates with the increase in mucin expression (Wang et al., 2019).

26. Cystic fluid

Pancreatic cancer cyst fluids are an effective way for biomarker prediction as they link the condition of precancerous stage. Pancreatic cyst can be either of IPMNs or of MCN variant that have the potential to develop into a pancreatic cancer. The fluid from these cysts is aspirated using the combined EUS and FNA techniques. On the basis of the fluid biomarkers, patients can be categorized into surgical treatments. When compared with proteins, CEA and VEGF-A in cystic fluids have more potential to differentiate cancerous subtypes from the benign ones. Recently, a machine learning algorithm was developed (Compcyst), which actually portrays the clinical features of the pancreatic cysts, such as imaging and genetic and biochemical markers, and the authors suggested for the discovery of more effective ways to classify cysts for surgical treatments to prevent invasive procedures (Springer et al., 2019). Another group developed an AI-based algorithm to differentiate benign and cancerous tumors with a high sensitivity of 95.7%, specificity of 91.1%, and an accuracy of 92.9% (Kurita et al., 2019). These values were higher when compared with CEA and cytology analysis (Kurita et al., 2019).

After surgical resection of pancreatic cancer, cystic fluid was analyzed for DNA methylation signatures by using methylation-specific droplet digital PCR. The results of this study have shown that the genes (*SOX17*, *FOXE3*, *BNIP3*, *SLIT2*, *EYA4*, *PTCHD2*, and *SFRP1*) were able to distinguish invasive cancer subtypes independently. Among these, methylated SOX17 combined with cytology was able to predict the grade of neoplasia accurately (Hata et al., 2017). Targeted next-generation sequencing (NGS) was performed for cystic fluids obtained from the endoscopic ultrasound (EUS) combined with fine needle aspiration (FNA) method. *KRAS* and *GNAS* were detected in mucinous neoplasms but not in high grade dysplasia, yet there is a need for an effective biomarker. This is the reason why genetic markers (*CDKN2A/TP53/SMAD4*) are unable to be detected even in combinational techniques of NGS and cytology even when the markers' presence is confirmed through histopathology. Yet this study identified TP53 in high grade dysplasia but not in benign subtypes (Haeberle et al., 2021).

Faias et al. have put forward in a study that glucose levels correlate well with CEA levels in differentiating mucinous cysts from nonmucinous ones, and that a commercial glucometer can be used to measure the glucose levels in cystic fluids (Jabbar et al., 2018). In a phase II clinical study, the accuracy of tandem mass spectrometry, for the purpose of differential diagnosis of precancerous lesions, was performed by analyzing the peptides from mucin-5 AC and mucin-2 and comparing it with that of cystic fluid CEA and cytology. The accuracy of tandem mass spectrometry was seen to be 97%, whereas for CEA and cytology analysis it was 61% and 84%, respectively. Whereas in the case of identifying high grade dysplasia, analysis using mucin-5 AC and prostate stem cell antigen combination had an accuracy of 96% when compared with the accuracy of CEA (35%)

and cytology (50%) (Jabbar et al., 2018). Prostaglandin E2 residing in IPMNs cystic fluid served as a marker for IPMNs dysplasia in patients with the preoperative cystic fluid level of >192 ng/mL. A sensitivity of 78%, specificity of 100%, and an accuracy of 86% were achieved when the PGE2 threshold level was 0.5 pg/mL (Yip-Schneider et al., 2017).

The analysis of the cyst fluid is important in discriminating between invasive and noninvasive cyst types and also helps in classifying the patients for surgical treatments. Cystic fluid analysis may serve as a source of biomarker identification and targeting in pancreatic cancer provided more advances are yet to be made to improve the sensitivity and specificity to different grades of the preinvasive tumors (García et al., 2021).

27. Screening and diagnosis of pancreatic cancer

The pancreatic cancer is known to have an incidence rate of 1.49%, that is, 1 in 67 cases is a pancreatic cancer and occurs in the people between the age range of 60–80 years (Ansari et al., 2016). PDAC is a dense, rigid, debilitate, and a poorly differentiated tumor. Usually, most of the pancreatic cancer patients present at the late stage of locally advanced or metastatic condition. Almost 80%–85% of the pancreatic cancers are unresectable and surgery being the only best cure for the disease, it is still uncertain that the disease would not recur after operation. A well to moderately differentiated PDAC will have penetration of the ductal and gland-like structure into the parenchymatous regions, whereas poorly differentiated tumors possess small glandular structures. A visual characteristic of the tumors is that they produce sialo-type and sulfated acid mucins which stain with Alcian blue and periodic acid-Schiff (McGuigan et al., 2018). The stages of pancreatic adenocarcinoma have been classified based on the location, size, surrounding vessels, and metastatic condition of the tumor. The TNM staging system has been designed by the American joint committee on cancer staging system. The T stage is based on the size of tumor and to what extent the lesions come in contact with the nearby vessels. The other two N (node) and M (distant metastasis) stages are based on to what extend the tumor has metastasized to the regional lymph nodes and other distant sites. Magnetic resonance imaging (MRI) and computed tomography (CT) have been the most preferred imaging systems of choice for the detection of the pancreatic cancer. CT is preferred mostly in determining the resectability of the disease, whereas MRI is preferred for screening cystic precursor lesions (Chu et al., 2017).

Approximately 60%–70% of the pancreatic cancers occur on the head portion of the pancreas. It then spreads to the remaining portions of the tissues and the nodes during which it is diagnosed (Luchini et al., 2016). Although patients present during the development of disease, it has been too late to proceed with therapies and treatments. In this regard, concerning an aggressive disease, such as pancreatic cancer, prognosis of the disease may help to treat the cancer and its symptoms. Pancreatic cancer possesses considerable genomic heterogeneity and, thus, predicting the genomic instability and targeting multiple pathways may help control the progression of disease. Genomic targets, such as *KRAS*, *SMAD4*, *TP53*, and *CDKN2A*, have been the most common and preferred markers even though no drug has been known to target them (McGuigan et al., 2018).

28. Recent imaging strategies

Imaging techniques used for pancreatic screening range from conventional MRI screening to molecular tracer-based screenings. Generally, MRI is preferred as a second line imaging method and has a high contrast for tissue imaging. In cases of high-risk subjects screening, MRI has an advantage of detecting cystic precursor lesion and the lack of ionizing radiations. CT is superior to MRI when local staging is performed due to its well-defined spatial resolution and three-dimensional reconstructions, which occur as a result of multiplanar arrangements to depict the vascular implication. MRI is considered superior to CT in terms of tissue characterization and the characterization of metastatic minor liver lesions (Chu et al., 2017). Currently, EUS-FNA has been proved to be an effective diagnosing method. EUS-FNA can be used to diagnose even primary tumors; however, the presence of a dense stroma or necrotic tissues and null vasculation in the tumor area may make the diagnosis tedious. The EUS-FNA techniques has a sensitivity range of 65%–95% with a mean accuracy of 85%. In spite of improvements made on the technology side for the sake of EUS-FNA, its limitations of negative results for a patient population of 20% has made it challenging to image the disease. Furthermore, differential diagnosis between PDAC and chronic pancreatitis and other forms of the benign PDAC tumors require histopathological and tissue biopsy analysis along with EUS-FNA to grade the tumors for treatment aspects appropriately (Kamerkar et al., 2017).

29. Conclusion

As a fatal disease, pancreatic cancer still remains challenging to treat and to predict. Treatment strategies are being optimized in every study for better prognosis of the disease. Further studies are carried out to predict the molecular markers specific to pancreatic cancer with improved sensitivity and accuracy. However, from an individual's point of view the best precaution to be followed is to get diagnosed as soon as possible if records of familial pancreatic cancer are found or equip a healthy lifestyle so as to prevent pancreatic cancer and keep a check on the specific symptoms.

Acknowledgment

We would like to thank Mr. M. Vijayaraman for English language edition.

Author contributions: T.D.P.L. and other authors written the manuscript, D.G. and K.P. were edited the manuscript.

References

Allenson, K., Castillo, J., San Lucas, F.A., Scelo, G., Kim, D.U., Bernard, V., et al., 2017. High prevalence of mutant KRAS in circulating exosome-derived DNA from early-stage pancreatic cancer patients. Ann. Oncol. 28 (4), 741–747. https://doi.org/10.1093/annonc/mdx004.

Ansari, D., Tingstedt, B., Andersson, B., Holmquist, F., Sturesson, C., Williamsson, C., et al., 2016. Pancreatic cancer: yesterday, today and tomorrow. Future Oncol. 12 (16), 1929–1946. https://doi.org/10.2217/fon-2016-0010.

Ansari, D., Torén, W., Zhou, Q., Hu, D., Andersson, R., 2019. Proteomic and genomic profiling of pancreatic cancer. Cell Biol. Toxicol. 35 (4), 333–343. https://doi.org/10.1007/s10565-019-09465-9.

Azizian, A., Rühlmann, F., Krause, T., Bernhardt, M., Jo, P., König, A., et al., 2020. CA19-9 for detecting recurrence of pancreatic cancer. Sci. Rep. 10 (1), 1332. https://doi.org/10.1038/s41598-020-57930-x.

Barnett, D., Liu, Y., Partyka, K., Huang, Y., Tang, H., Hostetter, G., et al., 2017. The CA19-9 and sialyl-TRA antigens define separate subpopulations of pancreatic cancer cells. Sci. Rep. 7 (1), 4020. https://doi.org/10.1038/s41598-017-04164-z.

Bastian, K., Scott, E., Elliott, D.J., Munkley, J., 2021. FUT8 alpha-(1,6)-fucosyltransferase in cancer. Int. J. Mol. Sci. 22 (1). https://doi.org/10.3390/ijms22010455.

Bournet, B., Vignolle-Vidoni, A., Grand, D., Roques, J., Breibach, F., Cros, J., et al., 2016. Endoscopic ultrasound-guided fine-needle aspiration plus KRAS and GNAS mutation in malignant intraductal papillary mucinous neoplasm of the pancreas. Endosc. Int. Open 4 (12), E1228–E1235. https://doi.org/10.1055/s-0042-117216.

Capello, M., Bantis, L.E., Scelo, G., Zhao, Y., Li, P., Dhillon, D.S., et al., 2017. Sequential validation of blood-based protein biomarker candidates for early-stage pancreatic cancer. J. Natl. Cancer Inst. 109 (4). https://doi.org/10.1093/jnci/djw266.

Carmicheal, J., Hayashi, C., Huang, X., Liu, L., Lu, Y., Krasnoslobodtsev, A., et al., 2019. Label-free characterization of exosome via surface enhanced Raman spectroscopy for the early detection of pancreatic cancer. Nanomedicine 16, 88–96. https://doi.org/10.1016/j.nano.2018.11.008.

Chen, Y., Wang, Y.R., Deng, G.C., Dai, G.H., 2019. CA19-9 decrease and survival according to platelet level in patients with advanced pancreatic cancer. BMC Cancer 19 (1), 860. https://doi.org/10.1186/s12885-019-6078-2.

Chu, L.C., Goggins, M.G., Fishman, E.K., 2017. Diagnosis and detection of pancreatic cancer. Cancer J. 23 (6), 333–342. https://doi.org/10.1097/ppo.0000000000000290.

Cicenas, J., Kvederaviciute, K., Meskinyte, I., Meskinyte-Kausiliene, E., Skeberdyte, A., Cicenas, J., 2017. KRAS, TP53, CDKN2A, SMAD4, BRCA1, and BRCA2 mutations in pancreatic cancer. Cancers 9 (5), 42. https://doi.org/10.3390/cancers9050042.

Collisson, E.A., Bailey, P., Chang, D.K., Biankin, A.V., 2019. Molecular subtypes of pancreatic cancer. Nat. Rev. Gastroenterol. Hepatol. 16 (4), 207–220. https://doi.org/10.1038/s41575-019-0109-y.

Conwell, D.L., Zuccaro Jr., G., Vargo, J.J., Morrow, J.B., Obuchowski, N., Dumot, J.A., et al., 2003. An endoscopic pancreatic function test with cholecystokinin-octapeptide for the diagnosis of chronic pancreatitis. Clin. Gastroenterol. Hepatol. 1 (3), 189–194. https://doi.org/10.1053/cgh.2003.50028.

Cortese, N., Capretti, G., Barbagallo, M., Rigamonti, A., Takis, P.G., Castino, G.F., et al., 2020. Metabolome of pancreatic juice delineates distinct clinical profiles of pancreatic cancer and reveals a link between glucose metabolism and PD-1(+) cells. Cancer Immunol. Res. 8 (4), 493–505. https://doi.org/10.1158/2326-6066.Cir-19-0403.

Dandawate, P., Ghosh, C., Palaniyandi, K., Paul, S., Rawal, S., Pradhan, R., et al., 2019. The histone demethylase KDM3A, increased in human pancreatic tumors, regulates expression of DCLK1 and promotes tumorigenesis in mice. Gastroenterology 157 (6), 1646–1659.e11. https://doi.org/10.1053/j.gastro.2019.08.018.

Daoud, A.Z., Mulholland, E.J., Cole, G., McCarthy, H.O., 2019. MicroRNAs in pancreatic cancer: biomarkers, prognostic, and therapeutic modulators. BMC Cancer 19 (1), 1130. https://doi.org/10.1186/s12885-019-6284-y.

Del Re, M., Vivaldi, C., Rofi, E., Vasile, E., Miccoli, M., Caparello, C., et al., 2017. Early changes in plasma DNA levels of mutant KRAS as a sensitive marker of response to chemotherapy in pancreatic cancer. Sci. Rep. 7 (1), 7931. https://doi.org/10.1038/s41598-017-08297-z.

Dumitrescu, R.G., 2018. Early epigenetic markers for precision medicine. Methods Mol. Biol. 1856, 3–17. https://doi.org/10.1007/978-1-4939-8751-1_1.

Engle, D.D., Tiriac, H., Rivera, K.D., Pommier, A., Whalen, S., Oni, T.E., et al., 2019. The glycan CA19-9 promotes pancreatitis and pancreatic cancer in mice. Science 364 (6446), 1156–1162. https://doi.org/10.1126/science.aaw3145.

Fu, Y., Ricciardiello, F., Yang, G., Qiu, J., Huang, H., Xiao, J., et al., 2021. The role of mitochondria in the chemoresistance of pancreatic cancer cells. Cells 10 (3). https://doi.org/10.3390/cells10030497.

Fujimoto, Y., Suehiro, Y., Kaino, S., Suenaga, S., Tsuyama, T., Matsui, H., et al., 2021. Combination of CA19-9 and blood free-circulating methylated RUNX3 may be useful to diagnose stage I pancreatic cancer. Oncology 99 (4), 234–239. https://doi.org/10.1159/000511940.

Gall, T.M.H., Belete, S., Khanderia, E., Frampton, A.E., Jiao, L.R., 2019. Circulating tumor cells and cell-free DNA in pancreatic ductal adenocarcinoma. Am. J. Pathol. 189 (1), 71–81. https://doi.org/10.1016/j.ajpath.2018.03.020.

García, G., de Paredes, A., Gleeson, F.C., Rajan, E., Vázquez-Sequeiros, E., 2021. Current clinical and research fluid biomarkers to aid risk stratification of pancreatic cystic lesions. Rev. Esp. Enferm. Dig. 113 (10), 714–720. https://doi.org/10.17235/reed.2021.7948/2021.

Garg, S.K., Chari, S.T., 2020. Early detection of pancreatic cancer. Curr. Opin. Gastroenterol. 36 (5), 456–461. https://doi.org/10.1097/mog.0000000000000663.

Gautam, S.K., Kumar, S., Dam, V., Ghersi, D., Jain, M., Batra, S.K., 2020. MUCIN-4 (MUC4) is a novel tumor antigen in pancreatic cancer immunotherapy. Semin. Immunol. 47, 101391. https://doi.org/10.1016/j.smim.2020.101391.

Ge, L., Pan, B., Song, F., Ma, J., Zeraatkar, D., Zhou, J., et al., 2017. Comparing the diagnostic accuracy of five common tumour biomarkers and CA19-9 for pancreatic cancer: a protocol for a network meta-analysis of diagnostic test accuracy. BMJ Open 7 (12), e018175. https://doi.org/10.1136/bmjopen-2017-018175.

Goh, S.K., Gold, G., Christophi, C., Muralidharan, V., 2017. Serum carbohydrate antigen 19-9 in pancreatic adenocarcinoma: a mini review for surgeons. ANZ J. Surg. 87 (12), 987–992. https://doi.org/10.1111/ans.14131.

Grant, T.J., Hua, K., Singh, A., 2016. Molecular pathogenesis of pancreatic cancer. Prog. Mol. Biol. Transl. Sci. 144, 241–275. https://doi.org/10.1016/bs.pmbts.2016.09.008.

Groot, V.P., Mosier, S., Javed, A.A., Teinor, J.A., Gemenetzis, G., Ding, D., et al., 2019. Circulating tumor DNA as a clinical test in resected pancreatic cancer. Clin. Cancer Res. 25 (16), 4973–4984. https://doi.org/10.1158/1078-0432.Ccr-19-0197.

Gu, Y., Ji, Y., Jiang, H., Qiu, G., 2020. Clinical effect of driver mutations of KRAS, CDKN2A/P16, TP53, and SMAD4 in pancreatic cancer: a meta-analysis. Genet. Test. Mol. Biomarkers 24 (12), 777–788. https://doi.org/10.1089/gtmb.2020.0078.

Guo, J., Xie, K., Zheng, S., 2016. Molecular biomarkers of pancreatic intraepithelial neoplasia and their implications in early diagnosis and therapeutic intervention of pancreatic cancer. Int. J. Biol. Sci. 12 (3), 292–301. https://doi.org/10.7150/ijbs.14995.

Haeberle, L., Schramm, M., Goering, W., Frohn, L., Driescher, C., Hartwig, W., et al., 2021. Molecular analysis of cyst fluids improves the diagnostic accuracy of pre-operative assessment of pancreatic cystic lesions. Sci. Rep. 11 (1), 2901. https://doi.org/10.1038/s41598-021-81065-2.

Hata, T., Dal Molin, M., Hong, S.-M., Tamura, K., Suenaga, M., Yu, J., et al., 2017. Predicting the grade of dysplasia of pancreatic cystic neoplasms using cyst fluid DNA methylation markers. Clin. Cancer Res. 23 (14), 3935–3944. https://doi.org/10.1158/1078-0432.CCR-16-2244.

Huang, W., Navarro-Serer, B., Jeong, Y.J., Chianchiano, P., Xia, L., Luchini, C., et al., 2020. Pattern of invasion in human pancreatic cancer organoids is associated with loss of SMAD4 and clinical outcome. Cancer Res. 80 (13), 2804–2817. https://doi.org/10.1158/0008-5472.Can-19-1523.

Hussein, N.A., Kholy, Z.A., Anwar, M.M., Ahmad, M.A., Ahmad, S.M., 2017. Plasma miR-22-3p, miR-642b-3p and miR-885-5p as diagnostic biomarkers for pancreatic cancer. J. Cancer Res. Clin. Oncol. 143 (1), 83–93. https://doi.org/10.1007/s00432-016-2248-7.

Ideno, N., Mori, Y., Nakamura, M., Ohtsuka, T., 2020. Early detection of pancreatic cancer: role of biomarkers in pancreatic fluid samples. Diagnostics 10 (12). https://doi.org/10.3390/diagnostics10121056.

Jabbar, K.S., Arike, L., Verbeke, C.S., Sadik, R., Hansson, G.C., 2018. Highly accurate identification of cystic precursor lesions of pancreatic cancer through targeted mass spectrometry: a phase IIc diagnostic study. J. Clin. Oncol. 36 (4), 367–375. https://doi.org/10.1200/jco.2017.73.7288.

Kadayifci, A., Atar, M., Wang, J.L., Forcione, D.G., Casey, B.W., Pitman, M.B., et al., 2017. Value of adding GNAS testing to pancreatic cyst fluid KRAS and carcinoembryonic antigen analysis for the diagnosis of intraductal papillary mucinous neoplasms. Dig. Endosc. 29 (1), 111–117. https://doi.org/10.1111/den.12710.

Kamerkar, S., LeBleu, V.S., Sugimoto, H., Yang, S., Ruivo, C.F., Melo, S.A., et al., 2017. Exosomes facilitate therapeutic targeting of oncogenic KRAS in pancreatic cancer. Nature 546 (7659), 498–503. https://doi.org/10.1038/nature22341.

Kato, S., Honda, K., 2020. Use of biomarkers and imaging for early detection of pancreatic cancer. Cancers (Basel) 12 (7), 1965. https://doi.org/10.3390/cancers12071965.

Kieler, M., Unseld, M., Bianconi, D., Schindl, M., Kornek, G.V., Scheithauer, W., et al., 2020. Impact of new chemotherapy regimens on the treatment landscape and survival of locally advanced and metastatic pancreatic cancer patients. J. Clin. Med. 9 (3). https://doi.org/10.3390/jcm9030648.

Kitagawa, T., Taniuchi, K., Tsuboi, M., Sakaguchi, M., Kohsaki, T., Okabayashi, T., et al., 2019. Circulating pancreatic cancer exosomal RNAs for detection of pancreatic cancer. Mol. Oncol. 13 (2), 212–227. https://doi.org/10.1002/1878-0261.12398.

Komoll, R.M., Hu, Q., Olarewaju, O., von Döhlen, L., Yuan, Q., Xie, Y., et al., 2021. MicroRNA-342-3p is a potent tumour suppressor in hepatocellular carcinoma. J. Hepatol. 74 (1), 122–134. https://doi.org/10.1016/j.jhep.2020.07.039.

Kurita, Y., Kuwahara, T., Hara, K., Mizuno, N., Okuno, N., Matsumoto, S., et al., 2019. Diagnostic ability of artificial intelligence using deep learning analysis of cyst fluid in differentiating malignant from benign pancreatic cystic lesions. Sci. Rep. 9 (1), 6893. https://doi.org/10.1038/s41598-019-43314-3.

Lee, B., Lipton, L., Cohen, J., Tie, J., Javed, A.A., Li, L., et al., 2019. Circulating tumor DNA as a potential marker of adjuvant chemotherapy benefit following surgery for localized pancreatic cancer. Ann. Oncol. 30 (9), 1472–1478. https://doi.org/10.1093/annonc/mdz200.

Liu, X.-Y., Guo, C.-H., Xi, Z.-Y., Xu, X.-Q., Zhao, Q.-Y., Li, L.-S., et al., 2021. Histone methylation in pancreatic cancer and its clinical implications. World J. Gastroenterol. 27 (36), 6004–6024. https://doi.org/10.3748/wjg.v27.i36.6004.

Lomberk, G., Blum, Y., Nicolle, R., Nair, A., Gaonkar, K.S., Marisa, L., et al., 2018. Distinct epigenetic landscapes underlie the pathobiology of pancreatic cancer subtypes. Nat. Commun. 9 (1), 1978. https://doi.org/10.1038/s41467-018-04383-6.

Luchini, C., Capelli, P., Scarpa, A., 2016. Pancreatic ductal adenocarcinoma and its variants. Surg. Pathol. Clin. 9 (4), 547–560. https://doi.org/10.1016/j.path.2016.05.003.

Majumder, S., Raimondo, M., Taylor, W.R., Yab, T.C., Berger, C.K., Dukek, B.A., et al., 2020. Methylated DNA in pancreatic juice distinguishes patients with pancreatic cancer from controls. Clin. Gastroenterol. Hepatol. 18 (3), 676–683.e3. https://doi.org/10.1016/j.cgh.2019.07.017.

McGuigan, A., Kelly, P., Turkington, R.C., Jones, C., Coleman, H.G., McCain, R.S., 2018. Pancreatic cancer: a review of clinical diagnosis, epidemiology, treatment and outcomes. World J. Gastroenterol. 24 (43), 4846–4861. https://doi.org/10.3748/wjg.v24.i43.4846.

McWilliams, R.R., Wieben, E.D., Chaffee, K.G., Antwi, S.O., Raskin, L., Olopade, O.I., et al., 2018. CDKN2A germline rare coding variants and risk of pancreatic cancer in minority populations. Cancer Epidemiol. Biomark. Prev. 27 (11), 1364–1370. https://doi.org/10.1158/1055-9965.Epi-17-1065.

McWilliams, R.R., Wieben, E.D., Chaffee, K.G., Antwi, S.O., Raskin, L., Olopade, O.I., Li, D., Highsmith Jr., W.E., Colon-Otero, G., Khanna, L.G., et al., 2018. CDKN2A germline rare coding variants and risk of pancreatic cancer in minority populations. Cancer Epidemiol. Biomarkers Prev. 27 (11), 1364–1370. https://doi.org/10.1158/1055-9965.Epi-17-1065.

Mizrahi, J.D., Surana, R., Valle, J.W., Shroff, R.T., 2020. Pancreatic cancer. Lancet 395 (10242), 2008–2020. https://doi.org/10.1016/s0140-6736(20)30974-0.

Mohammad, G.H., Vassileva, V., Acedo, P., Olde Damink, S.W.M., Malago, M., Dhar, D.K., et al., 2019. Targeting pyruvate kinase M2 and lactate dehydrogenase a is an effective combination strategy for the treatment of pancreatic cancer. Cancers 11 (9). https://doi.org/10.3390/cancers11091372.

Munkley, J., 2019. The glycosylation landscape of pancreatic cancer. Oncol. Lett. 17 (3), 2569–2575. https://doi.org/10.3892/ol.2019.9885.

Nagata, K., Horinouchi, M., Saitou, M., Higashi, M., Nomoto, M., Goto, M., et al., 2007. Mucin expression profile in pancreatic cancer and the precursor lesions. J. Hepato-Biliary-Pancreat. Surg. 14 (3), 243–254. https://doi.org/10.1007/s00534-006-1169-2.

Nakano, Y., Kitago, M., Matsuda, S., Nakamura, Y., Fujita, Y., Imai, S., et al., 2018. KRAS mutations in cell-free DNA from preoperative and postoperative sera as a pancreatic cancer marker: a retrospective study. Br. J. Cancer 118 (5), 662–669. https://doi.org/10.1038/bjc.2017.479.

Natale, F., Vivo, M., Falco, G., Angrisano, T., 2019. Deciphering DNA methylation signatures of pancreatic cancer and pancreatitis. Clin. Epigenetics 11 (1), 132. https://doi.org/10.1186/s13148-019-0728-8.

Negoi, I., Beuran, M., Hostiuc, S., Sartelli, M., El-Hussuna, A., De-Madaria, E., 2019. Glycosylation alterations in acute pancreatitis and pancreatic cancer: CA19-9 expression is involved in pathogenesis and maybe targeted by therapy. Ann. Transl. Med. 7 (Suppl 8), S306. https://doi.org/10.21037/atm.2019.10.72.

Okubo, K., Uenosono, Y., Arigami, T., Mataki, Y., Matsushita, D., Yanagita, S., et al., 2017. Clinical impact of circulating tumor cells and therapy response in pancreatic cancer. Eur. J. Surg. Oncol. 43 (6), 1050–1055. https://doi.org/10.1016/j.ejso.2017.01.241.

O'Neill, R.S., Stoita, A., 2021. Biomarkers in the diagnosis of pancreatic cancer: are we closer to finding the golden ticket? World J. Gastroenterol. 27 (26), 4045–4087. https://doi.org/10.3748/wjg.v27.i26.4045.

Osteikoetxea, X., Benke, M., Rodriguez, M., Pálóczi, K., Sódar, B.W., Szvicsek, Z., et al., 2018. Detection and proteomic characterization of extracellular vesicles in human pancreatic juice. Biochem. Biophys. Res. Commun. 499 (1), 37–43. https://doi.org/10.1016/j.bbrc.2018.03.107.

Perets, R., Greenberg, O., Shentzer, T., Semenisty, V., Epelbaum, R., Bick, T., et al., 2018. Mutant KRAS circulating tumor DNA is an accurate tool for pancreatic cancer monitoring. Oncologist 23 (5), 566–572. https://doi.org/10.1634/theoncologist.2017-0467.

Pietrasz, D., Pécuchet, N., Garlan, F., Didelot, A., Dubreuil, O., Doat, S., et al., 2017. Plasma circulating tumor DNA in pancreatic cancer patients is a prognostic marker. Clin. Cancer Res. 23 (1), 116–123. https://doi.org/10.1158/1078-0432.Ccr-16-0806.

Previdi, M.C., Carotenuto, P., Zito, D., Pandolfo, R., Braconi, C., 2017. Noncoding RNAs as novel biomarkers in pancreatic cancer: what do we know? Future Oncol. 13 (5), 443–453. https://doi.org/10.2217/fon-2016-0253.

Raimondo, M., Imoto, M., DiMagno, E.P., 2003. Rapid endoscopic secretin stimulation test and discrimination of chronic pancreatitis and pancreatic cancer from disease controls. Clin. Gastroenterol. Hepatol. 1 (5), 397–403. https://doi.org/10.1053/s1542-3565(03)00182-4.

Rawat, M., Kadian, K., Gupta, Y., Kumar, A., Chain, P.S.G., Kovbasnjuk, O., et al., 2019. MicroRNA in pancreatic cancer: from biology to therapeutic potential. Genes 10 (10), 752. https://doi.org/10.3390/genes10100752.

Sakaue, T., Koga, H., Iwamoto, H., Nakamura, T., Ikezono, Y., Abe, M., et al., 2019. Glycosylation of ascites-derived exosomal CD133: a potential prognostic biomarker in patients with advanced pancreatic cancer. Med. Mol. Morphol. 52 (4), 198–208. https://doi.org/10.1007/s00795-019-00218-5.

Sansone, V., Le Grazie, M., Roselli, J., Polvani, S., Galli, A., Tovoli, F., et al., 2020. Telomerase reactivation is associated with hepatobiliary and pancreatic cancers. Hepatobiliary Pancreat. Dis. Int. 19 (5), 420–428. https://doi.org/10.1016/j.hbpd.2020.04.007.

Sanyal, S., Siriwardena, A.K., Byers, R., 2018. Measurement of indicator genes using global complementary DNA (cDNA) amplification, by polyadenylic acid reverse transcriptase polymerase chain reaction (poly A RT-PCR): a feasibility study using paired samples from tissue and ductal juice in patients undergoing pancreatoduodenectomy. Pancreatology 18 (4), 458–462. https://doi.org/10.1016/j.pan.2018.03.003.

Schizas, D., Charalampakis, N., Kole, C., Economopoulou, P., Koustas, E., Gkotsis, E., et al., 2020. Immunotherapy for pancreatic cancer: a 2020 update. Cancer Treat. Rev. 86, 102016. https://doi.org/10.1016/j.ctrv.2020.102016.

Siegel, R.L., Miller, K.D., Jemal, A., 2020. Cancer statistics, 2020. CA Cancer J. Clin. 70 (1), 7–30. https://doi.org/10.3322/caac.21590.

Smid, M., Wilting, S.M., Uhr, K., Rodríguez-González, F.G., de Weerd, V., Prager-Van der Smissen, W.-J.C., et al., 2019. The circular RNome of primary breast cancer. Genome Res. 29 (3), 356–366. https://doi.org/10.1101/gr.238121.118.

Song, C., Chen, T., He, L., Ma, N., Li, J.A., Rong, Y.F., et al., 2020. PRMT1 promotes pancreatic cancer growth and predicts poor prognosis. Cell. Oncol. (Dordr.) 43 (1), 51–62. https://doi.org/10.1007/s13402-019-00435-1.

Springer, S., Masica, D.L., Dal Molin, M., Douville, C., Thoburn, C.J., Afsari, B., et al., 2019. A multimodality test to guide the management of patients with a pancreatic cyst. Sci. Transl. Med. 11 (501). https://doi.org/10.1126/scitranslmed.aav4772.

Tang, B., Yang, Y., Kang, M., Wang, Y., Wang, Y., Bi, Y., et al., 2020. M(6)a demethylase ALKBH5 inhibits pancreatic cancer tumorigenesis by decreasing WIF-1 RNA methylation and mediating Wnt signaling. Mol. Cancer 19 (1), 3. https://doi.org/10.1186/s12943-019-1128-6.

Thomas, D., Radhakrishnan, P., 2019. Tumor-stromal crosstalk in pancreatic cancer and tissue fibrosis. Mol. Cancer 18 (1), 14. https://doi.org/10.1186/s12943-018-0927-5.

Tulla, K.A., Maker, A.V., 2018. Can we better predict the biologic behavior of incidental IPMN? A comprehensive analysis of molecular diagnostics and biomarkers in intraductal papillary mucinous neoplasms of the pancreas. Langenbeck's Arch. Surg. 403 (2), 151–194. https://doi.org/10.1007/s00423-017-1644-z.

van Manen, L., Groen, J.V., Putter, H., Vahrmeijer, A.L., Swijnenburg, R.J., Bonsing, B.A., et al., 2020. Elevated CEA and CA19-9 serum levels independently predict advanced pancreatic cancer at diagnosis. Biomarkers 25 (2), 186–193. https://doi.org/10.1080/1354750x.2020.1725786.

Walter, F.M., Mills, K., Mendonça, S.C., Abel, G.A., Basu, B., Carroll, N., et al., 2016. Symptoms and patient factors associated with diagnostic intervals for pancreatic cancer (SYMPTOM pancreatic study): a prospective cohort study. Lancet Gastroenterol. Hepatol. 1 (4), 298–306. https://doi.org/10.1016/s2468-1253(16)30079-6.

Wang, Y.P., Zhou, W., Wang, J., Huang, X., Zuo, Y., Wang, T.S., et al., 2016. Arginine methylation of MDH1 by CARM1 inhibits glutamine metabolism and suppresses pancreatic cancer. Mol. Cell 64 (4), 673–687. https://doi.org/10.1016/j.molcel.2016.09.028.

Wang, F., Xia, X., Yang, C., Shen, J., Mai, J., Kim, H.C., et al., 2018. SMAD4 gene mutation renders pancreatic cancer resistance to radiotherapy through promotion of autophagy. Clin. Cancer Res. 24 (13), 3176–3185. https://doi.org/10.1158/1078-0432.Ccr-17-3435.

Wang, Y., Sun, Y., Feng, J., Li, Z., Yu, H., Ding, X., et al., 2019. Glycopatterns and glycoproteins changes in MCN and SCN: a prospective cohort study. Biomed. Res. Int. 2019, 2871289. https://doi.org/10.1155/2019/2871289.

Wang, Y., Yu, X., Hartmann, D., Zhou, J., 2020a. Circulating tumor cells in peripheral blood of pancreatic cancer patients and their prognostic role: a systematic review and meta-analysis. HPB (Oxford) 22 (5), 660–669. https://doi.org/10.1016/j.hpb.2019.11.003.

Wang, M., Liu, J., Zhao, Y., He, R., Xu, X., Guo, X., et al., 2020b. Upregulation of METTL14 mediates the elevation of PERP mRNA N(6) adenosine methylation promoting the growth and metastasis of pancreatic cancer. Mol. Cancer 19 (1), 130. https://doi.org/10.1186/s12943-020-01249-8.

Wang, C., Zhang, T., Liao, Q., Dai, M., Guo, J., Yang, X., et al., 2021. Metformin inhibits pancreatic cancer metastasis caused by SMAD4 deficiency and consequent HNF4G upregulation. Protein Cell 12 (2), 128–144. https://doi.org/10.1007/s13238-020-00760-4.

Wang-Gillam, A., Li, C.P., Bodoky, G., Dean, A., Shan, Y.S., Jameson, G., et al., 2016. Nanoliposomal irinotecan with fluorouracil and folinic acid in metastatic pancreatic cancer after previous gemcitabine-based therapy (NAPOLI-1): a global, randomised, open-label, phase 3 trial. Lancet 387 (10018), 545–557. https://doi.org/10.1016/s0140-6736(15)00986-1.

Wiktorowicz, M., Mlynarski, D., Pach, R., Tomaszewska, R., Kulig, J., Richter, P., et al., 2018. Rationale and feasibility of mucin expression profiling by qRT-PCR as diagnostic biomarkers in cytology specimens of pancreatic cancer. Pancreatology 18 (8), 977–982. https://doi.org/10.1016/j.pan.2018.09.008.

Wissniowski, T.T., Meister, S., Hahn, E.G., Kalden, J.R., Voll, R., Ocker, M., 2012. Mucin production determines sensitivity to bortezomib and gemcitabine in pancreatic cancer cells. Int. J. Oncol. 40 (5), 1581–1589. https://doi.org/10.3892/ijo.2012.1337.

Yamanoi, K., Nakayama, J., 2018. Reduced αGlcNAc glycosylation on gastric gland mucin is a biomarker of malignant potential for gastric cancer, Barrett's adenocarcinoma, and pancreatic cancer. Histochem. Cell Biol. 149 (6), 569–575. https://doi.org/10.1007/s00418-018-1667-8.

Yang, F., Liu, D.-Y., Guo, J.-T., Ge, N., Zhu, P., Liu, X., et al., 2017. Circular RNA circ-LDLRAD3 as a biomarker in diagnosis of pancreatic cancer. World J. Gastroenterol. 23 (47), 8345–8354. https://doi.org/10.3748/wjg.v23.i47.8345.

Ye, Z.-q., Zou, C.-l., Chen, H.-b., Jiang, M.-j., Mei, Z., Gu, D.-n., 2020. MicroRNA-7 as a potential biomarker for prognosis in pancreatic cancer. Dis. Markers 2020, 2782101. https://doi.org/10.1155/2020/2782101.

Yip-Schneider, M.T., Carr, R.A., Wu, H., Schmidt, C.M., 2017. Prostaglandin E2: a pancreatic fluid biomarker of intraductal papillary mucinous neoplasm dysplasia. J. Am. Coll. Surg. 225 (4), 481–487. https://doi.org/10.1016/j.jamcollsurg.2017.07.521.

Yu, S., Li, Y., Liao, Z., Wang, Z., Wang, Z., Li, Y., et al., 2020. Plasma extracellular vesicle long RNA profiling identifies a diagnostic signature for the detection of pancreatic ductal adenocarcinoma. Gut 69 (3), 540–550. https://doi.org/10.1136/gutjnl-2019-318860.

Zhang, H., Zhang, X., Li, X., Meng, W.B., Bai, Z.T., Rui, S.Z., et al., 2018. Effect of CCNB1 silencing on cell cycle, senescence, and apoptosis through the p53 signaling pathway in pancreatic cancer. J. Cell. Physiol. 234 (1), 619–631. https://doi.org/10.1002/jcp.26816.

Zhao, M., Mishra, L., Deng, C.-X., 2018. The role of TGF-β/SMAD4 signaling in cancer. Int. J. Biol. Sci. 14 (2), 111–123. https://doi.org/10.7150/ijbs.23230.

Zhou, B., Xu, J.W., Cheng, Y.G., Gao, J.Y., Hu, S.Y., Wang, L., et al., 2017. Early detection of pancreatic cancer: where are we now and where are we going? Int. J. Cancer 141 (2), 231–241. https://doi.org/10.1002/ijc.30670.

Zhou, X., Lu, Z., Wang, T., Huang, Z., Zhu, W., Miao, Y., 2018. Plasma miRNAs in diagnosis and prognosis of pancreatic cancer: a miRNA expression analysis. Gene 673, 181–193. https://doi.org/10.1016/j.gene.2018.06.037.

CHAPTER FIVE

Molecular biomarkers in pancreatic ductal adenocarcinoma

Junya Tsuboi[a], Reiko Yamada[a], and Yoshifumi S. Hirokawa[b]
[a]Department of Gastroenterology and Hepatology, Mie University Graduate School of Medicine, Tsu, Mie, Japan
[b]Department of Oncologic Pathology, Mie University Graduate School of Medicine, Tsu, Mie, Japan

1. Introduction

Pancreatic cancer remains one of the most lethal cancers and the seventh leading cause of cancer death worldwide (Sung et al., 2021). In the United States, pancreatic cancer has become the third leading cause of cancer death with a 5-year relative survival rate of 11%, and the incidence of pancreatic cancer continues to rise (Siegel et al., 2022). PDAC is the most common type of pancreatic cancer, representing approximately 90% of pancreatic cancers (Wang et al., 2021). Although surgical resection is the curative therapy for PDAC, most patients present with locally advanced (30%–35%) or metastatic (50%–55%) disease at diagnosis due to lack of effective screening (Park et al., 2021), and there is no effective treatment options for advanced disease (Kuehn, 2020). Therefore, it is crucial to develop the effective biomarkers for early diagnosis and targeted therapy to improve the prognosis of patients of PDAC. In this review, we first describe the metabolic reprogramming of PDAC, and we then describe current findings about molecular biomarkers for PDAC screening, prognosis, and targeted therapy.

2. Metabolic reprograming

Metabolic reprogramming and/or pathway reconstruction is a fundamental biological alteration in cancer, and it provides energy and macromolecular precursors essential for the survival and growth of cancer cells (Hanahan and Weinberg, 2011). The feature of pancreatic cancer is highlighted by hypovascularization, desmoplasia, or dense fibrous stroma, thus creating a severe hypoxic and nutrient low microenvironment (Sousa and Kimmelman, 2014; Yang et al., 2020). In the course of malignant progression, such as distant organ metastasis, cancer cells are required to satisfy their energy and metabolites demand which rely on shift to anabolic reactions for de novo synthesis of proteins, nucleic acids and lipids (Ward and Thompson, 2012). Myc and KRAS-driven cancer

Biomarkers in Cancer Detection and Monitoring of Therapeutics
https://doi.org/10.1016/B978-0-323-95114-2.00016-9

cells change their metabolism to elevation of glutamine uptake and to shift from catabolic to anabolic utilization of glutamine (Dejure and Eilers, 2017; Son et al., 2013).

The Warburg effect is the hallmark of metabolic reprograming for cancer cells survive and proliferation in the microenvironments, which is consist of increase glucose uptake, enhance glycolysis and lactate production by including glycolytic enzyme overexpression and increased lactate production (Yang et al., 2020). Oncogenic KRAS promotes glycolysis by enhancing glucose uptake and rate-limiting glycolytic enzymes, including hexokinase 1 and 2, phosphofructokinase-1, and lactate dehydrogenase A, the enzyme responsible for converting pyruvate to lactate (Bryant et al., 2014). In the consequence of KRAS mutation, activated glycolysis generates biosynthetic precursors for anabolic pathways, including the hexosamine biosynthesis pathway (HBP) and the nonoxidative arm of the pentose phosphate pathway (PPP). HBP provides biosynthetic precursors required for protein glycosylation and the synthesis of proteoglycans, glycolipids, and glycosyl phosphatidylinositol anchors (Taparra et al., 2018). These precursors syntheses, both increased glycolysis and glutamine fructose-6-phosphate transaminase 1 elevation, are required (Ying et al., 2012). KRAS mutant enhances the generation of ribose-5-phosphate for de novo nucleotide biosynthesis through nonoxidative arm of the PPP (Santana-Codina et al., 2018).

Aberrant amino acids metabolism propels proliferation of cancer cells (Xu et al., 2020). Even though one of a nonessential amino acid (NEAA), glutamine serves as a fundamental amino acid through cell division (Bernfeld and Foster, 2019). In standard tissue culture medium, glutamine concentration is at tenfold higher levels than other amino acids and is the most abundant amino acid in human plasma (Zhang et al., 2017a). Glutamine achieves roles in many biosynthesis process during cell division, when it is supplied in nucleotide, amino acid, protein and lipid biosynthesis. Glutamine metabolism (glutaminolysis) generating α-ketoglutarate (α-KG) supports those anabolic reaction as a source of carbon in cancer cells. α-KG in the mitochondria drive the TCA cycle, which is converted generally from glutamate by glutamate dehydrogenase (GLUD1) (Yoo et al., 2020). By contrast, PDCA cell lines do not rely on GLUD1, but they utilize the aspartate transaminase (GOT2) to generate anaplerotic α-KG in the mitochondria. The process generates aspartate from oxaloacetate (OAA), which is released into the cytoplasm. Cytoplasmic aspartate is converted into OAA by aspartate transaminase (GOT1). OAA is converted into malate, pyruvate and then converted into NADPH (Fig. 1). The increased NADPH/NADP(+) ratio generated by this pathway is critical to maintain the cellular redox state (Son et al., 2013; Gorrini et al., 2013).

The mammalian target of rapamycin (mTOR) plays an important role as a regulator of late G1 cell cycle progression. Several nutrients and growth factors are necessary for mTOR complex 1 (mTORC1) activation and subsequent cell cycle progression from late G1 into S phase (Saqcena et al., 2013). Once mTORC1 is activated, protein, lipid, and nucleotide biosynthesis are stimulated and all of which are under control of glutamine (Altman et al., 2016).

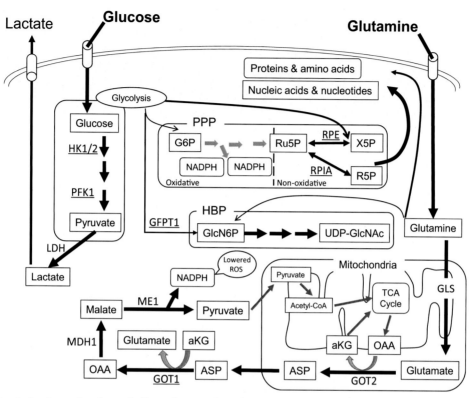

Fig. 1 A schematic of metabolic pathways altered in pancreas carcinogenesis. The enzymes with underline indicate their expression is elevated by KRAS. Increased uptake of glucose propagates glycolysis, anabolic pathways of the nonoxidative arm of the PPP (producing ribose for nucleotide biosynthesis) and the HBP (producing precursors for glycosylation). Another key metabolite in PDCA is glutamine which stimulates the metabolism in the TCA cycle and maintains redox homeostasis with a novel pathway that through in and out of mitochondria. *HK1/2*, hexokinase 1 and 2; *PFK1*, phosphofructokinase 1; *ME1*, malic enzyme; *GOT1/GOT2*, aspartate aminotransferase 1 and 2; *MDH1*, malate dehydrogenase; *GLS*, glutaminase; *GFPT1*, glutamine fructose-6-phosphate amidotransferase; *RPIA*, ribose 5-phosphate isomerase A; *RPE*, ribulose-5-phosphate-3-epimerase; *Asp*, aspartate; *OAA*, oxaloacetate; *G6P*, glucose 6-phosphate; *Ru5P*, ribulose 5-phosphate; *R5P*, ribose 5-phosphate; *X5P*, xylulose 5-phosphate. *LDH*, lactate dehydrogenase; *αKG*, alpha ketoglutarate; *GlcN6P*, glucosamine-6-phosphate; *UPD-GlcNAc*, uridine diphosphate N-acetylglucosamine. *(Adapted from articles Sousa, C.M., Kimmelman, A.C., 2014. The complex landscape of pancreatic cancer metabolism. Carcinogenesis 35,1441–50; Bryant, K.L., Mancias, J.D., Kimmelman, A.C., Der, C.J., 2014. KRAS: feeding pancreatic cancer proliferation. Trends Biochem. Sci. 39, 91–100.)*

Cancer cells with wild-type KRAS arrest in G1 on Glutamine deprivation, however mutant KRAS cancer cells arrest in S or G2 phase in the absence of Glutamine (Saqcena et al., 2015). This phenomenon presents an opportunity of drug induced lethal intervention for mutant KRAS cancer cells with S-phase-specific cytotoxic drugs such as

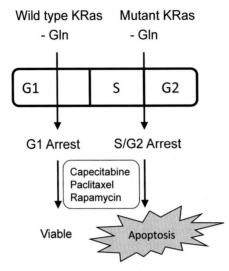

Fig. 2 Chemosensitivity is influenced by KRAS status under glutamine deprivation. Glutamine deprivation creates a synthetic lethal phenotype in KRAS-driven cancer cells when administrated S phase specific cytotoxic drugs such as capecitabine, paclitaxel, or rapamycin. *(Adapted from article Bernfeld, E., Foster, D.A., 2019. Glutamine as an essential amino acid for KRas-driven cancer cells. Trends Endocrinol. Metab. 30, 357–68.)*

capecitabine, paclitaxel, or rapamycin. When these drugs administrated to wild-type KRAS cancer cells in the absence of Glutamine, they are stalled at G1 (Fig. 2).

Although the altered glutamine metabolism, CB-839 the small molecular inhibitors targeting the initiating enzyme in glutamine metabolism glutaminase (GLS), has not shown significant tumor growth suppression in mouse models of pancreas cancer (Biancur et al., 2017). And the idea of treatment regimen with GLS inhibition plus ROS induction was investigated. The concomitant administration of CB-389 and inhibitor of which is related to antioxidant glutathione resulted in decreased cancer cell growth in vitro and in vivo (Biancur et al., 2017). But no clinical studies have been conducted with targeting combination of glutamine metabolism and ROS induction.

Asparagine is also an important amino acid for cancer cell proliferation. A phase IIb clinical trial (NCT02195180) has been completed, which include the asparaginase encapsulated in erythrocytes in combination with chemotherapeutic drugs gemcitabine or FOLFOX. This trial revealed clinical efficacy associated with improvements in overall survival (OS) and progression-free survival (PFS) when used in the second-line treatment of advanced pancreas cancer (Hammel et al., 1990).

Arginine is also a critical amino acid for metabolic functions of pancreas cancer including synthesis of other amino acids, proteins, polyamines, and NO. Arginine is physiologically synthesized from aspartate and citrulline by argininosuccinate synthetase

(ASS). The arginine-depleting enzyme arginine deiminase is pegylated, namely ADI-PEG20 selectively targets ASS-deficient pancreas cancer cells. A clinical trial of phase 1/1B (NCT02101580) to assess ADI-PEG20 in combination with gemcitabine and nab-paclitaxel has been completed. These drug administration was well-tolerated in some patients with advanced pancreas cancer, and a further phase 2 trial is under planning (Lowery et al., 2017).

Arginase 1 is a fundamental factor of the urea cycle catalyzing L-arginine to urea and L-ornithine, which is further metabolized into proline and polyamides that facilitate the collagen synthesis and bioenergetic products critical for cell proliferation. The immunosuppression of myeloid-derived suppressor cells (MDSCs) is regulated with the arginine metabolism. MDSCs of high arginase and iNOS inhibit T cells functions via arginine depletion and NO generation, consequence of decreased T cell proliferation and inducing T cells apoptosis (Gabrilovich and Nagaraj, 2009). Given that maintain and/or enhance antitumor immune response, arginase has been an attractive potential target in cancer immunotherapy, but clinical trial for pancreas cancer has not been conducted.

Another immunosuppressive molecule, indoleamine 2,3-dioxygenase (IDO), is a potential target of immunochemotherapy. IDO converts tryptophan to kynurenine, suppress CD8+ T effector cells and natural killer cells as well as induction of Tregs and MDSCs (Prendergast et al., 2014). IDO is overexpressed in pancreas cancer of poor prognosis (Zhang et al., 2017b). Several clinical trials with IDO inhibitors have been conducted including concomitant treatment with GVAX pancreas vaccine (NCT02077881, NCT03006302, and NCT03085914).

3. Biomarkers for diagnosis
3.1 Carbohydrate antigen 19-9 (CA19-9)

Carbohydrate antigen 19-9 (CA19-9) is a glycoprotein complex expressed on the cell surface. H Koprowski et al. first described about this antigen defined by a mouse monoclonal antibody in human colorectal carcinoma cell line (Koprowski et al., 1979).

CA19-9 is commonly used in the diagnosis and monitoring of PDAC, and its utility has been broadly validated (Ballehaninna and Chamberlain, 2012). Goonetilleke et al. evaluated with pooled data from 2283 patients of pancreatic cancer in their systematic review (Yang et al., 2020). In symptomatic patients, the median sensitivity and specificity of CA 19-9 for diagnosis were 79% and 82%, respectively (Goonetilleke and Siriwardena, 2007). Other meta-analyses of CA19-9 in the diagnosis of PDAC have shown similar results (Xing et al., 2018; Zhang et al., 2015a). However, in asymptomatic patients, CA 19-9 is not a useful diagnostic biomarker of pancreatic cancer because of its low positive predictivity when cut-off value was set at 37 U/mL (Kim et al., 2004; Chang et al., 2006).

On the other hand, there are several problems about interpretation of CA19-9 levels. Firstly, CA 19-9 levels may increase in benign diseases such as acute pancreatitis, non-malignant respiratory diseases, benign ovarian tumor, chronic liver disease, liver cirrhosis, and obstructive jaundice due to benign disease (Binicier and Pakoz, 1992; Kodama et al., 2007; Pandey et al., 2017; Bertino et al., 2013; Kim et al., 2017; Giannis et al., 2021; Sturm et al., 2022). Secondary, CA19-9 levels can be elevated with other malignant tumor such as ovarian cancer, colorectal cancer, and cholangiocarcinoma (Pandey et al., 2017; Zhang et al., 2015b; Lumachi et al., 2014). Finally, CA19-9 is absent in Lewis antigen negative individuals (5%–10% of the population), and therefore CA19-9 is not useful for diagnosis of PDAC in these individuals (Luo et al., 2017; Kannagi, 2007).

3.2 Micro-RNAs

Micro-RNAs (miRNAs) are small noncoding RNAs that have an important role to regulate gene expression, and contribute to tumorigenesis by affecting oncogenic or tumor suppressing pathways (Ventura and Jacks, 2009). Because miRNAs profiling is related to tumor growth or response to treatment, and miRNAs have been detected in various tissue or body fluids, such as pancreatic parenchyma, pancreatic secretions, saliva, urine, blood, stool, breast milk, and peritoneal cavity fluid, these molecules have potential to be cancer biomarkers including PDAC (Iorio and Croce, 2012; O'Brien et al., 2018; Lekchnov et al., 2016; Yonemori et al., 2017; Gablo et al., 2019) . Bloomston et al. analyzed miRNAs in benign pancreatic tissue, chronic pancreatitis tissue and PDAC tissue, and identified distinct miRNAs patterns that can distinguish PDAC from benign pancreas and chronic pancreatitis. Moreover, they described that miRNAs expression patterns can distinguish between long and short term survivors (Bloomston et al., 2007). Debernardi et al. described the efficacy of urine miRNA as biomarkers of Stage I PDAC. In their study, miRNA-143, miRNA-223, and miRNA-30e were significantly highly expressed in stage I PDAC patients compared to healthy population, and miRNA-143, miRNA-223 and miRNA-204 were also highly expressed compared to stage II-IV PDAC patients. Moreover, miRNA-223 and miRNA-204 could distinguish early stage PDAC from chronic pancreatitis (Debernardi et al., 2015). Humeau et al. reported analysis of salvia from patients with pancreatic cancer ($n = 7$), pancreatitis ($n = 4$), intraductal papillary mucinous neoplasm (IPMN) ($n = 2$), and healthy controls ($n = 4$). They identified that hsa-miRNA-21, hsa-miRNA-23a, hsa-miRNA-23b, and miRNA-29c were significantly highly expressed in patients of pancreatic cancer compared to controls, and hsa-miRNA-23a and hsa-miRNA23b were highly expressed in patients with pancreatic cancer precursor lesions (Humeau et al., 2015). Yang et al. analyzed stool samples from patients with PDAC ($n = 30$), chronic pancreatitis ($n = 10$), and healthy controls ($n = 15$). They reported that miRNA-21 and miRNA-155 levels were significantly higher, and miRNA-216 was significantly lower in patients of PDAC compared to controls (Yang et al., 2014). Other several studies described the efficacy of miRNAs as a biomarker for early detection of pancreatic cancer (Habbe et al., 2009; Ryu et al., 2010; Slater et al., 2014; Xue et al., 2013).

3.3 Cell-free DNA (cfDNA) or circulating tumor DNA (ctDNA)

Cell-free DNA (cfDNA) or circulating tumor DNA (ctDNA) assays as a liquid biopsy have a potential to diagnose PDAC in early stage (Takai and Yachida, 2016; Martini et al., 2019; Nagrath et al., 2016; Gall et al., 2019). Although it is described that the sensitivity of cfDNA or ctDNA to detect pancreatic cancer in early stage is low (Cohen et al., 2017; Jung et al., 2010), the combined assays of cfDNA or ctDNA and protein biomarkers such as CA19-9 or assays for genetic alteration such as KRAS mutations have a potential to increase the sensitivity for early stage pancreatic cancer (Cohen et al., 2017; Berger et al., 2019). Berger et al. reported the efficacy of combination biomarker panel (cfDNA, CA19-9, and thrombospondin-2), that is, this biomarker panel could significantly ameliorate the diagnostic power of CA19-9, particularly in the recognition of stage I PDAC (Berger et al., 2019). A meta-analysis by Zhu et al. revealed that the pooled sensitivity and specificity of ctDNA in detecting pancreatic cancer were 64% and 92%, respectively. (Zhu et al., 2020a).

3.4 Extracellular vesicles (EVs)

Extracellular vesicles (EVs) are cell-derived bilayer phospholipid membrane-structured nanosize vesicles, and various molecules are contained such as proteins, lipids and nucleic acids (Eguchi et al., 2019). EVs are categorized into three types, microvesicles, exosomes and apoptotic bodies (Lässer et al., 2018). As the component of EVs reflect pathophysiology in various type of cancers including PDAC, and they can be isolated from various body fluids or tissues, they have potential to be biomarkers for diagnosis of PDAC (Yee et al., 2020). Kitagawa et al. analyzed the expression of serum pancreatic cancer exosomal RNAs. In their study, four exosomal mRNAs (CCDC88A, ARF6, Vav3, and WASF2) and five exosomal small nucleolar RNAs (snoRNAs: SNORA14B, SNORA18, SNORA25, SNORA74A, and SNORD22) in serum from 27 pancreatic cancer patients and 13 healthy controls were analyzed, and reported that the area under the receiver operating characteristic curves (AUCs) of WASF2, ARF6, SNORA74A, and SNORA25 in serum from early stage pancreatic cancer patients were > 0.9 (Kitagawa et al., 2019). Melo et al. identified exosomal glypican-1 (GPC1) that is a cell surface proteoglycan, and reported that GPC1 positive circulating exosomes showed a sensitivity of 100% and specificity of 100% when comparing pancreatic cancer patients (stage I to stage IV) with healthy controls and benign pancreatic disease. On the other hand, CA19-9 could not distinguish between pancreatic cancer patients and healthy controls. Therefore, they concluded that circulating GPC1 positive exosomes have a potential to detect pancreatic cancer in early stage (Melo et al., 2015). Lai et al. reported that high exosomal levels of miRNA-10b, −21, −30c, and -181a and low let7a had 100% sensitivity and 100% specificity when comparing pancreatic cancer patients with healthy controls (Lai et al., 2017). Recently, our group investigated EV proteins isolated from endoscopic ultrasound–guided fine needle aspiration (EUS-FNA) samples in PDAC, and found that several EV proteins fluctuated depending on the cancer stage. That is, eukaryotic elongation factor 2 (EEF2), charged multivesicular body protein 4b (CHMP4B), RALB, and RALA increased as cancer stage progressed; L–lactate dehydrogenase A chain (LDHA), 14-3-3 protein sigma (SFN), phospholipid scramblase 1 (PLSCR1), and syntaxin-3 (STX3) increased up to stage III and decreased at stage IV; moesin (MSN), CD55, radixin (RDX), ras-related protein rap-1A (RAP1A), and Dipeptidyl peptidase 4 (DPP4) increased up to stage II and decreased at stage III-IV (Inoue et al., 2021). For the diagnosis of PDAC, meta–analysis analyzed 19 studies including cumulative 1872 patients with respect to ctDNA, circulating tumor cells and exosomes, and exosomes showed highest sensitivity and specificity (0.93 and 0.92 respectively) (Zhu et al., 2020a). Based on these results, it is considered that exosomes are one of the most promising biomarkers to diagnose PDAC in early stage.

3.5 DNA methylation

DNA methylation is an epigenetic modification involving the addition of a methyl group onto the cytosine, and which regulates the gene expression and stable gene silencing (Kulis and Esteller, 2010). Aberrant DNA methylation is associated with various types of cancer including PDAC through activating oncogenes and inactivating tumor suppressor genes (Baylin and Jones, 2016; Tan et al., 2009). Matsubayashi et al. analyzed methylated genes in pancreatic secretions, and the result showed that the sensitivity of methylated *NPTX2* and *SPARC* genes was more than 90%, and the specificity was more than 70% in terms of discrimination between patients with PDAC and patients without PDAC (Matsubayashi et al., 2006). Kisiel et al. also analyzed hyper methylated regions in pancreatic secretions derived DNA from 61 pancreatic cancer patients, 22 chronic pancreatitis patients and 19 healthy controls, and reported that the AUC of *CD1D* was 0.92 for pancreatic cancer compared with healthy control or chronic pancreatitis (Kisiel et al., 2015). Li et al. investigated serum cfDNA methylation of PDAC patients, and reported that eight markers (*TRIM73, FAM150A, EPB41L3, SIX3, MIR663, MAPT, LOC100128977,* and *LOC100130148*) might serve as potential biomarkers for detecting PDAC in early stage (Li et al., 2020). Promoter DNA methylation of *BNC1* and *ADAMTS1* might be promising biomarkers of early stage PDAC. *BNC1* and *ADAMTS1* showed high rate of occurrence of methylation in early stage PDAC including pancreatic intraepithelial neoplasia (PanIN), whereas little to no DNA methylation was seen in chronic pancreatitis and normal pancreas (Yi et al., 2013; Eissa et al., 2019; Brancaccio et al., 2019).

3.6 PAM4

PAM4 is a murine monoclonal antibody which has high specificity for PDAC including its precursor lesions, and which is able to distinguish between normal or benign pancreatic tissue and PDAC including PanIN (Gold et al., 2013a). PAM4 shows a reaction to the MUC5AC, which is a secretory mucin expressed in PanIN and retained during disease progression, therefore, PAM4 can detect early stage PDAC (Gold et al., 2013b; Liu et al., 2015). Gold et al. reported that the overall sensitivity for detection of PDAC was 76%, with 64% and 85% sensitivity in patients with stage I and advanced diseases, respectively. Additionally, PAM4 and CA19-9 combination assay improved the sensitivity to 84%, and the specificity was 82% (Gold et al., 2013a). Shi et al. described the efficacy of PAM4 in distinguishing PDAC from chronic pancreatitis. Although PAM4 labeled 19% of chronic pancreatitis tissues, the reactivity was due to coexistence of PanIN (Shi et al., 2014).

3.7 Leukemia inhibitory factor (LIF)

LIF is a cytokine participate in various physiological processes such as regulation of cell proliferation, differentiation and survival (Wrona et al., 2021). In PDAC, LIF is secreted by cancer associated fibroblasts into the tumor microenvironment (Bressy et al., 2018), and bind on the surface of cancer cells, and eventually stimulate PDAC progression through STAT3 phosphorylation (Albrengues et al., 2014; Shi et al., 2019). Shi et al. analyzed LIF expression in 77 patients of PDAC, and reported that expression of LIF in PDAC tissue was significantly higher than in healthy pancreatic tissue. Moreover, LIF concentrations in serum of PDAC patients were also significantly higher than that of healthy controls (Shi et al., 2019). Bressy et al. described that PanIN expressed low levels of LIF by immunohistochemical staining (Bressy et al., 2018). Although further clinical study is needed, LIF might be a promising biomarker for PDAC and has a potential to diagnose PDAC in early stage.

4. Prognostic biomarkers
4.1 CA19-9

CA19-9 has been utilized for diagnostic biomarker of PDAC as shown in the previous section. On the other hand, it is also utilized as prognostic biomarker.

In patients with resectable pancreatic cancer, high levels of preoperative CA 19-9 was associated with shorter overall survival (OS) (Palmquist et al., 2020). In a cohort of 111

PDAC patients who underwent surgical resection, increase in postoperative serum CA 19-9 and postoperative CA 19-9 > 200 U/mL were significantly associated with poor survival (Ferrone et al., 2006). Other study reported that preoperative CA19-9 levels >52 U/mL and postoperative CA19-9 levels >37 U/mL were significantly associated with early recurrence of resectable and borderline resectable PDAC after surgery (Imamura et al., 2021). A recent meta-analysis by Ye et al. investigated the prognostic value of CA19-9 response after neoadjuvant treatment in pancreatic cancer patients, and revealed that post neoadjuvant CA19-9 response >50% or CA19-9 normalization was significantly associated with higher OS (Ye et al., 2020a).

4.2 microRNA

Various miRNAs have been reported as prognostic biomarkers of pancreatic cancer. Ohuchida et al. reported that elevated expression of miRNA 142-5p was significantly associated with better survival in pancreatic cancer patients treated with gemcitabine after surgery (Ohuchida et al., 2011). In other study, Yu et al. reported that elevated expression of miRNA-200c was significantly associated with better survival (Yu et al., 2010). On the other hand, elevated expression of miRNA-196a-2, miRNA-155, miRNA-203, miRNA-210, miRNA-222, and miRNA-21, or lower expression of miRNA-7 were associated with poor survival after surgery (Bloomston et al., 2007; Greither et al., 2010; Dillhoff et al., 2008; Ye et al., 2020b). Namkung et al. analyzed 200 PDAC tissue samples, and reported that higher expression of miRNA-574-5p, miRNA-1244 and lower expression of miRNA-145-star, miRNA-328, miRNA-26b-star, and miRNA-4321 were significantly associated with poor OS and disease-free survival (DFS), and these miRNAs had a potential as prognostic biomarkers of PDAC (Namkung et al., 2016).

4.3 Circulating tumor cells (CTCs), cell-free DNA (cfDNA), and circulating tumor DNA (ctDNA)

A meta-analysis by Wang et al. investigated the prognostic role of CTCs in pancreatic cancer patients, and reported that CTCs-positive status was significantly associated with poor OS and progression-free survival (PFS) (Wang et al., 2020). A systematic meta-analysis by Chen et al. assessed 18 articles with 1243 pancreatic cancer patients regarding cfDNA, and reported that cfDNA was significantly associated with OS and PFS. Specifically, the mutation, ctDNA existence, hypermethylation, and elevated expression of cfDNA were associated with poor survival (Chen et al., 2018). A recent meta-analysis by Guven et al. revealed the association between ctDNA and prognosis in pancreatic cancer patients. In the analysis, positive preoperative or postoperative ctDNA was significantly associated with poor relapse-free survival (RFS), PFS, and OS. Additionally, ctDNA-positive status was significantly associated with poor RFS, PFS, and OS in advanced pancreatic cancer patients (Guven et al., 2021).

4.4 Extracellular vesicles (EVs)

As shown in the previous section, EVs are one of the most promising biomarker to detect PDAC in early stage. Whereas, EVs have a potential as a prognostic biomarker. Circulating GPC-1 positive exosomes levels had a correlation with tumor burden and was associated with survival (Melo et al., 2015). Other study reported that GPC-1 overexpression by immunohistochemical staining of PDAC tissue was an independent prognostic factor of poor survival (Duan et al., 2013). Bernard et al. analyzed *KRAS* mutation in plasma exosomal DNA of PDAC patients, and revealed that 5% or more of *KRAS* mutant allele fractions in exosomal DNA were significantly associated with poor PFS and OS (Bernard et al., 2019). Higher exosomal miRNA-451a is also related to poor OS and DFS of PDAC patients (Takahasi et al., 2018; Kawamura et al., 2019). Recently, a meta-analysis by Bunduc et al. assessed 11 studies with 634 PDAC patients regarding exosomes, positive exosomal biomarkers was significantly associated with higher risk of mortality among various PDAC stages, and preoperative positive exosomal biomarkers was significantly associated with higher risk of mortality in resectable PDAC patients. Additionally, positive exosomal miRNAs were associated with poor OS (Bunduc et al., 2022).

4.5 DNA methylation

Henriksen et al. found that PDAC patients with more than 10 hypermethylated genes in the circulating cfDNA had significantly worse OS compared to patients with fewer hypermethylated genes. Additionally, their subgroup analysis revealed that the hypermethylation of *SFRP1*, *BMP3*, and *TFPI2* in circulating cfDNA was significantly associated with worse prognosis in stage IV PDAC patients (Henriksen et al., 2017). Yang et al. analyzed the relationship between the DNA methylation levels of Pumilio homologous protein 1 (PUM1) and prognosis of PDAC patients. PUM1 is involved in promoting invasion and migration in various cancers including PDAC, and lower methylation level of PUM1 was significantly associated with poor survival (Yang et al., 2021). Yokoyama et al. investigated the mucin gene methylation status in pancreatic tissue obtained from neoplastic and nonneoplastic areas of 191 patients, and revealed that hypomethylation of *MUC1* and *MUC4* genes were significantly associated with poor prognosis (Yokoyama et al., 2020).

4.6 Human equilibrative nucleoside transporter 1 (hENT1)

Human equilibrative nucleoside transporter 1 (hENT1) is an integral membrane transporter, and that is the major mediators of gemcitabine uptake into human cells.

Therefore, it has been studied as a potential biomarker to predict the response to gemcitabine based chemotherapy (Spratlin et al., 2004; Farrell et al., 2009; Giovannetti et al., 2006; Mori et al., 2007; Aoyama et al., 2017). Yamada et al. investigated hENT1 expression in EUS-FNA samples from resectable and unresectable PDAC patients before preoperative gemcitabine-based chemoradiotherapy, and reported that median survival time was significant longer in hENT1 positive patients than in hENT1 negative patients (Yamada et al., 2016). In an analysis of the ESPAC-3 trial cohort including 434 patients of PDAC, hENT1 expression levels were significantly associated with the prognosis of PDAC patients treated with gemcitabine, that is, median OS for patients with low hENT1 expression was 17.1 months and that for patients with high hENT1 expression was 26.2 months (Greenhalf et al., 2014). A systematic review by Bird et al. revealed that higher expression of hENT1 detected by immunohistochemistry of PDAC tissues was significantly associated with extended DFS and OS in patients treated with gemcitabine (Bird et al., 2017).

4.7 Human concentrative nucleoside transporters 3 (hCNT3)

In addition to hENT1, the human concentrative nucleoside transporters 3 (hCNT3) is also associated with intracellular uptake of gemcitabine. Higher expression of hCNT3 detected by immunohistochemistry in PDAC patients treated with gemcitabine based chemoradiation after surgery was significantly associated with extended OS. Additionally, patients with both higher expression of hENT1 and higher expression of hCNT3 had a significant longer median OS (94.8 months) compared to patients with higher expression of only one biomarker (18.7 months) (Maréchal et al., 2009).

4.8 Deoxycytidine kinase (dCK), ribonucleotide reductase M1 (RRM1)

Deoxycytidine kinase (dCK) plays a key role in the transformation of nucleoside analogues including gemcitabine. Therefore, expression of dCK seems necessary to improve therapeutic efficacy of gemcitabine. Lower expression of dCK detected by immunohistochemistry was significantly associated with poor PFS and OS in pancreatic cancer patients treated with gemcitabine (Sebastiani et al., 2006). Conversely, lower expression of tumor ribonucleotide reductase M1 (RRM1) was significantly associated with prolonged OS in pancreatic cancer patients treated with gemcitabine (Nakahira et al., 2007).

4.9 Dihydropyrimidine dehydrogenase (DPD)

Dihydropyrimidine dehydrogenase (DPD) is an enzyme catalyzing the degradation of 5-FU. As DPD catabolizes most of the administered 5-FU, partial or complete deficiency of DPD leads to severe or lethal toxicities with 5-FU exposure (Ogura, 2006). On the other hand, lower expression of intra-tumoral DPD is associated with favorable prognosis. Elander et al. assessed intra-tumoral DPD expression by immunohistochemistry from 238 pancreatic cancer patients, and reported that higher expression of DPD was significantly associated with reduced OS in patients treated with 5FU but not in patients treated with gemcitabine (Elander et al., 2018).

4.10 Carboxylesterase 2 (CES2)

The FOLFIRINOX regimen (5-FU, leucovorin, irinotecan, and oxaliplatin) is current standard chemotherapy of advanced pancreatic cancer, and recently, meta-analysis revealed the efficacy of neoadjuvant FOLFIRINOX in pancreatic cancer patients (Janssen et al., 2019). Irinotecan is activated by carboxylesterases into SN-38, and carboxylesterase 2 (CES2) is the important isoform for activating irinotecan. Therefore, CES2 expression in PDAC tissue may affect the therapeutic effect of irinotecan-based chemotherapy including FOLFIRINOX. Capello et al. revealed that higher expression of CES2 in PDAC tissues was associated with prolonged OS in patients treated with neoadjuvant FOLFIRINOX chemotherapy (Capello et al., 2015).

5. Targeted therapy
5.1 PARP

Poly (adenosine diphosphate–ribose) polymerase (PARP) is a nuclear enzyme which plays an important role in single-strand DNA break repair such as base excision repair. PARP binds to sites of DNA damage, and synthesizes poly (adenosine diphosphate-ribose) chains on the damaged sites in the domain of DNA and PARP itself. This attachment enables the recruitment of DNA repair proteins to achieve the repair process (Desai et al., 2021; Zhu et al., 2020b). On the other hand, the *breast cancer susceptibility gene 1 and 2 (BRCA1/2)* are tumor suppressor genes involved in double-strand DNA break repair through homologous recombination, therefore *BRCA1/2* mutant cells are not able to undergo double-strand DNA break repair. As base excision repair is a primary back-up system for homologous recombination deficiency, and PARP inhibition disrupts the base excision repair, PARP inhibitor could effectively induce *BRCA1/2* mutated tumor cell death (Zhu et al., 2020b). Several studies have shown the efficacy of PARP inhibitor in PDAC patients harboring mutations affecting DNA repair mechanisms (Qian et al., 2020; Singh and O'Reilly, 2020; Nevala-Plagemann et al., 2020; Schlick et al., 2021). A phase III randomized clinical trial revealed the efficacy of olaparib (PARP inhibitor) in metastatic pancreatic cancer patients with germline *BRCA1/2* mutation. The study reported that the median PFS was significant longer in the patients treated with olaparib compared to the patients treated with placebo (7.4 months vs 3.8 months). However, there was no benefit regarding OS (Golan et al., 2019).

5.2 PD-1

The cancer growth is promoted by various immune subversion mechanisms including expression of immune checkpoint molecules such as PD-1. PD-1 predominantly expressed on T cells interacts with the ligand, PD-L1 and PD-L2 expressed on antigen-presenting cells and tumor cells, resulting in T-cell exhaustion. Immune checkpoint inhibitors can block these molecules, and leads to T-cell-mediated antitumor responses (Dyck and Mills, 2017). Tumors with high microsatellite instability (MSI-H) or mismatch-repair deficiency (dMMR) are susceptible to immune checkpoint inhibitors, because the increased neoantigen expression by the tumor cells can be targeted by reinvigorated T-cells (Zhao et al., 2019; Lee et al., 2016; Dudley et al., 2016; Subudhi et al., 2020). In the phase II studies, the PD-1 inhibitor pembrolizumab showed apparent efficacy in treatment of dMMR/MSI-H solid tumors including pancreatic cancer (Le et al., 2017; Marabelle et al., 2020). Therefore, current guidelines recommend dMMR and MSI-H testing in locally advanced or metastatic PDAC patients. However, dMMR/MSI-H phenotype is very rare (about 1%) in PDAC patients (Eso et al., 2020).

5.3 EGFR

Erlotinib is the epidermal growth factor receptor (EGFR) tyrosine kinase inhibitor and the first approved targeted therapy for PDAC patients (Schlick et al., 2021). A phase III study revealed that the benefit of gemcitabine plus erlotinib versus gemcitabine plus placebo was greater in patients with unresectable, locally advanced, or metastatic pancreatic cancer. Specifically, the OS in gemcitabine plus erlotinib arm was significantly longer than in gemcitabine plus placebo arm (6.24 months vs 5.91 months). Additionally, PFS was also significantly longer (3.75 months vs 3.55 months) and one-year survival rate was significantly greater with gemcitabine plus erlotinib (23% vs 17%) (Moore et al., 2007). However, in the phase III LAP07 study, there was no statistically significant difference in OS between the groups treated with gemcitabine plus erlotinib and the groups treated with gemcitabine alone for patients with locally advanced pancreatic cancer (Hammel et al., 2016).

5.4 KRAS

Oncogenic KRAS plays a central role in the initiation and progression of PDAC, and nearly 90% of PDAC patients have the activating mutation (Eser et al., 2014). For a long time, various attempts to inhibit KRAS have failed and therefore this target was considered to be undruggable (Gorfe and Cho, 2021). Recently, KRAS^{G12C} have been demonstrated to be successfully targeted and covalent inhibitors of mutant KRAS^{G12C} have been developed. In a phase I trial, the KRAS^{G12C} inhibitor sotorasib demonstrated encouraging antitumor activity in patients with various advanced solid tumors harboring

$KRAS^{G12C}$ mutation (Hong et al., 2020a). In other phase I/IB trial, the $KRAS^{G12C}$ inhibitor adagrasib also exhibited antitumor activity in patients with $KRAS^{G12C}$ mutant solid tumors (Ou et al., 2022). Unfortunately, $KRAS^{G12C}$ mutation occur in only 3% of pancreatic cancer (Zeitouni et al., 2016).

5.5 NTRK

The tropomyosin receptor kinase (TRK) encoded by neurotrophic tropomyosin receptor kinase (*NTRK*) gene plays an essential role in the development and function of the nervous system. Fusions involving *NTRK* and various genes that act as fusion partners, which are present in <5% of PDAC, are oncogenic and activate various signal transduction pathways such as MAPK, PI3K, and PKC pathways (Amatu et al., 2016; Cocco et al., 2018). Recently, TRK inhibitors, larotrectinib and entrectinib, have been approved for patients with advanced or metastatic solid tumors harboring *NTRK* gene fusion without an acquired resistance mutation (Drilon et al., 2018; Delgado et al., 2021; Scott, 2019). A pooled analysis of three phase I/II trials for larotrectinib including 159 patients with locally advanced or metastatic solid tumors harboring TRK fusion showed that the objective response rate and the complete response rate were 79% and 16%, respectively. In this trial, two patients with pancreatic cancer were included, and one had a positive response (Hong et al., 2020b). Similarly, an integrated analysis of three phase I/II clinical trials for entrectinib including 54 patients with locally advanced or metastatic solid tumors harboring *NTRK* gene fusion demonstrated that the objective response rate was 57%, and responses were recorded in two of three patients with pancreatic cancer (Doebele et al., 2020).

5.6 ALK

The anaplastic lymphoma kinase (*ALK*) fusion genes resulting from chromosomal rearrangements play an important role in tumorigenesis, and have been identified in several cancers including PDAC (Singhi et al., 2017). In a small cohort of four patients with locally advanced or metastatic PDAC harboring *ALK* fusion gene, three of four patients had stable disease, radiographic response, and/or normalization of CA19-9 levels after the treatment with ALK inhibitor (Singhi et al., 2017). Although *ALK* fusion genes are extremely uncommon in PDAC (<1%), ALK fusion proteins would be a potential therapeutic target for PDAC (Sturm et al., 2022).

5.7 CDKN2A

CDKN2A tumor suppressor gene encodes the p16-INK4a protein which plays an important role in regulation of the cell cycle progression by inhibiting cyclin D-CDK4, and cyclin D–CDK6 complexes (Cicenas et al., 2017). As *CDKN2A* gene is frequently inactivated in PDAC patients, CDK4/6 can be a potential target in PDAC (Nevala-Plagemann et al., 2020). However, exploration of CDK4/6 inhibitors in PDAC is limited to preclinical studies (Chou et al., 2018).

6. Conclusions

Accumulating knowledge of the molecular biomarkers of PDAC can help to understand molecular pathogenesis and might contribute to develop novel diagnostic biomarker, prognostic biomarker, and therapeutic targets. It is expected that progress in the study of molecular biology of PDAC can lead to improve prognosis of PDAC patients in the near future.

References

Albrengues, J., Bourget, I., Pons, C., Butet, V., Hofman, P., Tartare-Deckert, S., et al., 2014. LIF mediates proinvasive activation of stromal fibroblasts in cancer. Cell Rep. 7, 1664–1678.

Altman, B.J., Stine, Z.E., Dang, C.V., 2016. From Krebs to clinic: glutamine metabolism to cancer therapy. Nat. Rev. Cancer 16, 619–634.

Amatu, A., Sartore-Bianchi, A., Siena, S., 2016. NTRK gene fusions as novel targets of cancer therapy across multiple tumour types. ESMO Open 1, e000023.

Aoyama, T., Kazama, K., Miyagi, Y., Murakawa, M., Yamaoku, K., Atsumi, Y., et al., 2017. Predictive role of human equilibrative nucleoside transporter 1 in patients with pancreatic cancer treated by curative resection and gemcitabine-only adjuvant chemotherapy. Oncol. Lett. 14, 599–606.

Ballehaninna, U.K., Chamberlain, R.S., 2012. The clinical utility of serum CA 19-9 in the diagnosis, prognosis and management of pancreatic adenocarcinoma: an evidence based appraisal. J. Gastrointest. Oncol. 3, 105–119.

Baylin, S.B., Jones, P.A., 2016. Epigenetic determinants of cancer. Cold Spring Harb. Perspect. Biol. 8, a019505.

Berger, A.W., Schwerdel, D., Reinacher-Schick, A., Uhl, W., Algül, H., Friess, H., et al., 2019. A blood-based multi marker assay supports the differential diagnosis of early-stage pancreatic cancer. Theranostics 9, 1280–1287.

Bernard, V., Kim, D.U., San Lucas, F.A., Castillo, J., Allenson, K., Mulu, F.C., et al., 2019. Circulating nucleic acids are associated with outcomes of patients with pancreatic cancer. Gastroenterology 156, 108–118.e4.

Bernfeld, E., Foster, D.A., 2019. Glutamine as an essential amino acid for KRas-driven cancer cells. Trends Endocrinol. Metab. 30, 357–368.

Bertino, G., Ardiri, A.M., Calvagno, G.S., Malaguarnera, G., Interlandi, D., Vacante, M., et al., 2013. Carbohydrate 19.9 antigen serum levels in liver disease. Biomed. Res. Int. 2013, 531640.

Biancur, D.E., Paulo, J.A., Małachowska, B., Quiles Del Rey, M., Sousa, C.M., Wang, X., et al., 2017. Compensatory metabolic networks in pancreatic cancers upon perturbation of glutamine metabolism. Nat. Commun. 8, 15965.

Binicier, O.B., Pakoz, Z.B., 1992. CA 19-9 levels in patients with acute pancreatitis due to gallstone and metabolic/toxic reasons. Rev. Assoc. Med. Bras. 2019 (65), 965–970.

Bird, N.T.E., Elmasry, M., Jones, R., Psarelli, E., Dodd, J., Malik, H., et al., 2017. Immunohistochemical hENT1 expression as a prognostic biomarker in patients with resected pancreatic ductal adenocarcinoma undergoing adjuvant gemcitabine-based chemotherapy. Br. J. Surg. 104, 328–336.

Bloomston, M., Frankel, W.L., Petrocca, F., Volinia, S., Alder, H., Hagan, J.P., et al., 2007. MicroRNA expression patterns to differentiate pancreatic adenocarcinoma from normal pancreas and chronic pancreatitis. JAMA 297, 1901–1908.

Brancaccio, M., Natale, F., Falco, G., Angrisano, T., 2019. Cell-free DNA methylation: the new frontiers of pancreatic cancer biomarkers' discovery. Genes 11, E14.

Bressy, C., Lac, S., Nigri, J., Leca, J., Roques, J., Lavaut, M.N., et al., 2018. LIF drives neural Remodeling in pancreatic cancer and offers a new candidate biomarker. Cancer Res. 78, 909–921.

Bryant, K.L., Mancias, J.D., Kimmelman, A.C., Der, C.J., 2014. KRAS: feeding pancreatic cancer proliferation. Trends Biochem. Sci. 39, 91–100.

Bunduc, S., Gede, N., Váncsa, S., Lillik, V., Kiss, S., Juhász, M.F., et al., 2022. Exosomes as prognostic biomarkers in pancreatic ductal adenocarcinoma-a systematic review and meta-analysis. Transl. Res. S1931-5244 (22), 00001–00009.

Capello, M., Lee, M., Wang, H., Babel, I., Katz, M.H., Fleming, J.B., et al., 2015. Carboxylesterase 2 as a determinant of response to irinotecan and neoadjuvant FOLFIRINOX therapy in pancreatic ductal adenocarcinoma. J. Natl. Cancer Inst. 107, djv132.

Chang, C.Y., Huang, S.P., Chiu, H.M., Lee, Y.C., Chen, M.F., Lin, J.T., 2006. Low efficacy of serum levels of CA 19-9 in prediction of malignant diseases in asymptomatic population in Taiwan. Hepato-Gastroenterology 53, 1–4.

Chen, L., Zhang, Y., Cheng, Y., Zhang, D., Zhu, S., Ma, X., 2018. Prognostic value of circulating cell-free DNA in patients with pancreatic cancer: a systemic review and meta-analysis. Gene 679, 328–334.

Chou, A., Froio, D., Nagrial, A.M., Parkin, A., Murphy, K.J., Chin, V.T., et al., 2018. Tailored first-line and second-line CDK4-targeting treatment combinations in mouse models of pancreatic cancer. Gut 67, 2142–2155.

Cicenas, J., Kvederaviciute, K., Meskinyte, I., Meskinyte-Kausiliene, E., Skeberdyte, A., Cicenas, J., 2017. KRAS, TP53, CDKN2A, SMAD4, BRCA1, and BRCA2 mutations in pancreatic cancer. Cancers 9, E42.

Cocco, E., Scaltriti, M., Drilon, A., 2018. NTRK fusion-positive cancers and TRK inhibitor therapy. Nat. Rev. Clin. Oncol. 15, 731–747.

Cohen, J.D., Javed, A.A., Thoburn, C., Wong, F., Tie, J., Gibbs, P., et al., 2017. Combined circulating tumor DNA and protein biomarker-based liquid biopsy for the earlier detection of pancreatic cancers. Proc. Natl. Acad. Sci. U. S. A. 114, 10202–10207.

Debernardi, S., Massat, N.J., Radon, T.P., Sangaralingam, A., Banissi, A., Ennis, D.P., et al., 2015. Noninvasive urinary miRNA biomarkers for early detection of pancreatic adenocarcinoma. Am. J. Cancer Res. 5, 3455–3466.

Dejure, F.R., Eilers, M., 2017. MYC and tumor metabolism: chicken and egg. EMBO J. 36, 3409–3420.

Delgado, J., Pean, E., Melchiorri, D., Migali, C., Josephson, F., Enzmann, H., et al., 2021. The European medicines agency review of entrectinib for the treatment of adult or paediatric patients with solid tumours who have a neurotrophic tyrosine receptor kinase gene fusions and adult patients with non-small-cell lung cancer harbouring ROS1 rearrangements. ESMO Open 6, 100087.

Desai, D., Khandwala, P., Parsi, M., Potdar, R., 2021. PARP inhibitors: shifting the paradigm in the treatment of pancreatic cancer. Med. Oncol. 38, 61.

Dillhoff, M., Liu, J., Frankel, W., Croce, C., Bloomston, M., 2008. MicroRNA-21 is overexpressed in pancreatic cancer and a potential predictor of survival. J. Gastroinest. Surg. 12, 2171–2176.

Doebele, R.C., Drilon, A., Paz-Ares, L., Siena, S., Shaw, A.T., Farago, A.F., et al., 2020. Entrectinib in patients with advanced or metastatic NTRK fusion-positive solid tumours: integrated analysis of three phase 1-2 trials. Lancet Oncol. 21, 271–282.

Drilon, A., Laetsch, T.W., Kummar, S., DuBois, S.G., Lassen, U.N., Demetri, G.D., et al., 2018. Efficacy of Larotrectinib in TRK fusion-positive cancers in adults and children. N. Engl. J. Med. 378, 731–739.

Duan, L., Hu, X.Q., Feng, D.Y., Lei, S.Y., Hu, G.H., 2013. GPC-1 may serve as a predictor of perineural invasion and a prognosticator of survival in pancreatic cancer. Asian J. Surg. 36, 7–12.

Dudley, J.C., Lin, M.T., Le, D.T., Eshleman, J.R., 2016. Microsatellite instability as a biomarker for PD-1 blockade. Clin. Cancer Res. 22, 813–820.

Dyck, L., Mills, K.H.G., 2017. Immune checkpoints and their inhibition in cancer and infectious diseases. Eur. J. Immunol. 47, 765–779.

Eguchi, A., Kostallari, E., Feldstein, A.E., Shah, V.H., 2019. Extracellular vesicles, the liquid biopsy of the future. J. Hepatol. 70, 1292–1294.

Eissa, M.A.L., Lerner, L., Abdelfatah, E., Shankar, N., Canner, J.K., Hasan, N.M., et al., 2019. Promoter methylation of ADAMTS1 and BNC1 as potential biomarkers for early detection of pancreatic cancer in blood. Clin. Epigenetics 11, 59.

Elander, N.O., Aughton, K., Ghaneh, P., Neoptolemos, J.P., Palmer, D.H., Cox, T.F., et al., 2018. Expression of dihydropyrimidine dehydrogenase (DPD) and hENT1 predicts survival in pancreatic cancer. Br. J. Cancer 118, 947–954.

Eser, S., Schnieke, A., Schneider, G., Saur, D., 2014. Oncogenic KRAS signalling in pancreatic cancer. Br. J. Cancer 111, 817–822.

Eso, Y., Shimizu, T., Takeda, H., Takai, A., Marusawa, H., 2020. Microsatellite instability and immune checkpoint inhibitors: toward precision medicine against gastrointestinal and hepatobiliary cancers. J. Gastroenterol. 55, 15–26.

Farrell, J.J., Elsaleh, H., Garcia, M., Lai, R., Ammar, A., Regine, W.F., et al., 2009. Human equilibrative nucleoside transporter 1 levels predict response to gemcitabine in patients with pancreatic cancer. Gastroenterology 136, 187–195.

Ferrone, C.R., Finkelstein, D.M., Thayer, S.P., Muzikansky, A., Fernandez-delCastillo, C., Warshaw, A.L., 2006. Perioperative CA19-9 levels can predict stage and survival in patients with resectable pancreatic adenocarcinoma. J. Clin. Oncol. 24, 2897–2902.

Gablo, N.A., Prochazka, V., Kala, Z., Slaby, O., Kiss, I., 2019. Cell-free microRNAs as non-invasive diagnostic and prognostic bio-markers in pancreatic cancer. Curr. Genomics 20, 569–580.

Gabrilovich, D.I., Nagaraj, S., 2009. Myeloid-derived suppressor cells as regulators of the immune system. Nat. Rev. Immunol. 9, 162–174.

Gall, T.M.H., Belete, S., Khanderia, E., Frampton, A.E., Jiao, L.R., 2019. Circulating tumor cells and cell-free DNA in pancreatic ductal adenocarcinoma. Am. J. Pathol. 189, 71–81.

Giannis, D., Moris, D., Barbas, A.S., 2021. Diagnostic, predictive and prognostic molecular biomarkers in pancreatic cancer: an overview for clinicians. Cancers 13, 1071.

Giovannetti, E., Del Tacca, M., Mey, V., Funel, N., Nannizzi, S., Ricci, S., et al., 2006. Transcription analysis of human equilibrative nucleoside transporter-1 predicts survival in pancreas cancer patients treated with gemcitabine. Cancer Res. 66, 3928–3935.

Golan, T., Hammel, P., Reni, M., Van Cutsem, E., Macarulla, T., Hall, M.J., et al., 2019. Maintenance Olaparib for germline BRCA-mutated metastatic pancreatic cancer. N. Engl. J. Med. 381, 317–327.

Gold, D.V., Gaedcke, J., Ghadimi, B.M., Goggins, M., Hruban, R.H., Liu, M., et al., 2013a. PAM4 enzyme immunoassay alone and in combination with CA 19-9 for the detection of pancreatic adenocarcinoma. Cancer 119, 522–528.

Gold, D.V., Newsome, G., Liu, D., Goldenberg, D.M., 2013b. Mapping PAM4 (clivatuzumab), a monoclonal antibody in clinical trials for early detection and therapy of pancreatic ductal adenocarcinoma, to MUC5AC mucin. Mol. Cancer 12, 143.

Goonetilleke, K.S., Siriwardena, A.K., 2007. Systematic review of carbohydrate antigen (CA 19-9) as a biochemical marker in the diagnosis of pancreatic cancer. Eur. J. Surg. Oncol. 33, 266–270.

Gorfe, A.A., Cho, K.J., 2021. Approaches to inhibiting oncogenic K-Ras. Small GTPases 12, 96–105.

Gorrini, C., Harris, I.S., Mak, T.W., 2013. Modulation of oxidative stress as an anticancer strategy. Nat. Rev. Drug Discov. 12, 931–947.

Greenhalf, W., Ghaneh, P., Neoptolemos, J.P., Palmer, D.H., Cox, T.F., Lamb, R.F., et al., 2014. Pancreatic cancer hENT1 expression and survival from gemcitabine in patients from the ESPAC-3 trial. J. Natl. Cancer Inst. 106, djt347.

Greither, T., Grochola, L.F., Udelnow, A., Lautenschläger, C., Würl, P., Taubert, H., 2010. Elevated expression of microRNAs 155, 203, 210 and 222 in pancreatic tumors is associated with poorer survival. Int. J. Cancer 126, 73–80.

Guven, D.C., Sahin, T.K., Yildirim, H.C., Aktepe, O.H., Dizdar, O., Yalcin, S., 2021. A systematic review and meta-analysis of the association between circulating tumor DNA (ctDNA) and prognosis in pancreatic cancer. Crit. Rev. Oncol. Hematol. 168, 103528.

Habbe, N., Koorstra, J.B.M., Mendell, J.T., Offerhaus, G.J., Ryu, J.K., Feldmann, G., et al., 2009. MicroRNA miR-155 is a biomarker of early pancreatic neoplasia. Cancer Biol. Ther. 8, 340–346.

Hammel, P., Fabienne, P., Mineur, L., Metges, J.P., Andre, T., De La Fouchardiere, C., et al., 1990. Erythrocyte-encapsulated asparaginase (eryaspase) combined with chemotherapy in second-line treatment of advanced pancreatic cancer: an open-label, randomized phase IIb trial. Eur. J. Cancer 2020 (124), 91–101.

Hammel, P., Huguet, F., van Laethem, J.L., Goldstein, D., Glimelius, B., Artru, P., et al., 2016. Effect of chemoradiotherapy vs chemotherapy on survival in patients with locally advanced pancreatic cancer controlled after 4 months of gemcitabine with or without erlotinib: the LAP07 randomized clinical trial. JAMA 315, 1844–1853.

Hanahan, D., Weinberg, R.A., 2011. Hallmarks of cancer: the next generation. Cell 144, 646–674.

Henriksen, S.D., Madsen, P.H., Larsen, A.C., Johansen, M.B., Pedersen, I.S., Krarup, H., et al., 2017. Cell-free DNA promoter hypermethylation in plasma as a predictive marker for survival of patients with pancreatic adenocarcinoma. Oncotarget 8, 93942–93956.

Hong, D.S., Fakih, M.G., Strickler, J.H., Desai, J., Durm, G.A., Shapiro, G.I., et al., 2020a. KRASG12C inhibition with Sotorasib in advanced solid Tumors. N. Engl. J. Med. 383, 1207–1217.

Hong, D.S., DuBois, S.G., Kummar, S., Farago, A.F., Albert, C.M., Rohrberg, K.S., et al., 2020b. Larotrectinib in patients with TRK fusion-positive solid tumours: a pooled analysis of three phase 1/2 clinical trials. Lancet Oncol. 21, 531–540.

Humeau, M., Vignolle-Vidoni, A., Sicard, F., Martins, F., Bournet, B., Buscail, L., et al., 2015. Salivary MicroRNA in pancreatic cancer patients. PLoS One 10, e0130996.

Imamura, M., Nagayama, M., Kyuno, D., Ota, S., Murakami, T., Kimura, A., et al., 2021. Perioperative predictors of early recurrence for Resectable and borderline-Resectable pancreatic cancer. Cancers 13, 2285.

Inoue, H., Eguchi, A., Kobayashi, Y., Usugi, E., Yamada, R., Tsuboi, J., et al., 2021. Extracellular vesicles from pancreatic ductal adenocarcinoma endoscopic ultrasound-fine needle aspiration samples contain a protein barcode. J. Hepatobiliary Pancreat. Sci.

Iorio, M.V., Croce, C.M., 2012. MicroRNA dysregulation in cancer: diagnostics, monitoring and therapeutics. A comprehensive review. EMBO Mol. Med. 4, 143–159.

Janssen, Q.P., Buettner, S., Suker, M., Beumer, B.R., Addeo, P., Bachellier, P., et al., 2019. Neoadjuvant FOLFIRINOX in patients with borderline Resectable pancreatic cancer: a systematic review and patient-level meta-analysis. J. Natl. Cancer Inst. 111, 782–794.

Jung, K., Fleischhacker, M., Rabien, A., 2010. Cell-free DNA in the blood as a solid tumor biomarker—a critical appraisal of the literature. Clin. Chim. Acta 411, 1611–1624.

Kannagi, R., 2007. Carbohydrate antigen sialyl Lewis a—its pathophysiological significance and induction mechanism in cancer progression. Chang Gung Med. J. 30, 189–209.

Kawamura, S., Iinuma, H., Wada, K., Takahashi, K., Minezaki, S., Kainuma, M., et al., 2019. Exosome-encapsulated microRNA-4525, microRNA-451a and microRNA-21 in portal vein blood is a high-sensitive liquid biomarker for the selection of high-risk pancreatic ductal adenocarcinoma patients. J. Hepatobiliary Pancreat. Sci. 26, 63–72.

Kim, J.E., Lee, K.T., Lee, J.K., Paik, S.W., Rhee, J.C., Choi, K.W., 2004. Clinical usefulness of carbohydrate antigen 19-9 as a screening test for pancreatic cancer in an asymptomatic population. J. Gastroenterol. Hepatol. 19, 182–186.

Kim, M.S., Jeon, T.J., Park, J.Y., Choi, J., Shin, W.C., Park, S.E., et al., 2017. Clinical interpretation of elevated CA 19-9 levels in obstructive jaundice following benign and malignant pancreatobiliary disease. Korean J. Gastroenterol. 70, 96–102.

Kisiel, J.B., Raimondo, M., Taylor, W.R., Yab, T.C., Mahoney, D.W., Sun, Z., et al., 2015. New DNA methylation markers for pancreatic cancer: discovery, tissue validation, and pilot testing in pancreatic juice. Clin. Cancer Res. 21, 4473–4481.

Kitagawa, T., Taniuchi, K., Tsuboi, M., Sakaguchi, M., Kohsaki, T., Okabayashi, T., et al., 2019. Circulating pancreatic cancer exosomal RNAs for detection of pancreatic cancer. Mol. Oncol. 13, 212–227.

Kodama, T., Satoh, H., Ishikawa, H., Ohtsuka, M., 2007. Serum levels of CA19-9 in patients with non-malignant respiratory diseases. J. Clin. Lab. Anal. 21, 103–106.

Koprowski, H., Steplewski, Z., Mitchell, K., Herlyn, M., Herlyn, D., Fuhrer, P., 1979. Colorectal carcinoma antigens detected by hybridoma antibodies. Somatic Cell Genet. 5, 957–971.

Kuehn, B.M., 2020. Looking to long-term survivors for improved pancreatic cancer treatment. JAMA 324, 2242–2244.

Kulis, M., Esteller, M., 2010. DNA methylation and cancer. Adv. Genet. 70, 27–56.

Lai, X., Wang, M., McElyea, S.D., Sherman, S., House, M., Korc, M., 2017. A microRNA signature in circulating exosomes is superior to exosomal glypican-1 levels for diagnosing pancreatic cancer. Cancer Lett. 393, 86–93.

Lässer, C., Jang, S.C., Lötvall, J., 2018. Subpopulations of extracellular vesicles and their therapeutic potential. Mol. Asp. Med. 60, 1–14.

Le, D.T., Durham, J.N., Smith, K.N., Wang, H., Bartlett, B.R., Aulakh, L.K., et al., 2017. Mismatch-repair deficiency predicts response of solid tumors to PD-1 blockade. Science 357, 409–413.

Lee, V., Murphy, A., Le, D.T., Diaz, L.A., 2016. Mismatch repair deficiency and response to immune checkpoint blockade. Oncologist 21, 1200–1211.

Lekchnov, E.A., Zaporozhchenko, I.A., Morozkin, E.S., Bryzgunova, O.E., Vlassov, V.V., Laktionov, P.P., 2016. Protocol for miRNA isolation from biofluids. Anal. Biochem. 499, 78–84.

Li, S., Wang, L., Zhao, Q., Wang, Z., Lu, S., Kang, Y., et al., 2020. Genome-wide analysis of cell-free DNA methylation profiling for the early diagnosis of pancreatic cancer. Front. Genet. 11, 596078.

Liu, D., Chang, C.H., Gold, D.V., Goldenberg, D.M., 2015. Identification of PAM4 (clivatuzumab)-reactive epitope on MUC5AC: a promising biomarker and therapeutic target for pancreatic cancer. Oncotarget 6, 4274–4285.

Lowery, M.A., Yu, K.H., Kelsen, D.P., Harding, J.J., Bomalaski, J.S., Glassman, D.C., et al., 2017. A phase 1/1B trial of ADI-PEG 20 plus nab-paclitaxel and gemcitabine in patients with advanced pancreatic adenocarcinoma. Cancer 123, 4556–4565.

Lumachi, F., Lo Re, G., Tozzoli, R., D'Aurizio, F., Facomer, F., Chiara, G.B., et al., 2014. Measurement of serum carcinoembryonic antigen, carbohydrate antigen 19-9, cytokeratin-19 fragment and matrix metalloproteinase-7 for detecting cholangiocarcinoma: a preliminary case-control study. Anticancer Res. 34, 6663–6667.

Luo, G., Liu, C., Guo, M., Cheng, H., Lu, Y., Jin, K., et al., 2017. Potential biomarkers in Lewis negative patients with pancreatic cancer. Ann. Surg. 265, 800–805.

Marabelle, A., Le, D.T., Ascierto, P.A., Di Giacomo, A.M., De Jesus-Acosta, A., Delord, J.P., et al., 2020. Efficacy of pembrolizumab in patients with noncolorectal high microsatellite instability/mismatch repair-deficient cancer: results from the phase II KEYNOTE-158 study. J. Clin. Oncol. 38, 1–10.

Maréchal, R., Mackey, J.R., Lai, R., Demetter, P., Peeters, M., Polus, M., et al., 2009. Human equilibrative nucleoside transporter 1 and human concentrative nucleoside transporter 3 predict survival after adjuvant gemcitabine therapy in resected pancreatic adenocarcinoma. Clin. Cancer Res. 15, 2913–2919.

Martini, V., Timme-Bronsert, S., Fichtner-Feigl, S., Hoeppner, J., Kulemann, B., 2019. Circulating tumor cells in pancreatic cancer: current perspectives. Cancers 11, E1659.

Matsubayashi, H., Canto, M., Sato, N., Klein, A., Abe, T., Yamashita, K., et al., 2006. DNA methylation alterations in the pancreatic juice of patients with suspected pancreatic disease. Cancer Res. 66, 1208–1217.

Melo, S.A., Luecke, L.B., Kahlert, C., Fernandez, A.F., Gammon, S.T., Kaye, J., et al., 2015. Glypican-1 identifies cancer exosomes and detects early pancreatic cancer. Nature 523, 177–182.

Moore, M.J., Goldstein, D., Hamm, J., Figer, A., Hecht, J.R., Gallinger, S., et al., 2007. Erlotinib plus gemcitabine compared with gemcitabine alone in patients with advanced pancreatic cancer: a phase III trial of the National Cancer Institute of Canada clinical trials group. J. Clin. Oncol. 25, 1960–1966.

Mori, R., Ishikawa, T., Ichikawa, Y., Taniguchi, K., Matsuyama, R., Ueda, M., et al., 2007. Human equilibrative nucleoside transporter 1 is associated with the chemosensitivity of gemcitabine in human pancreatic adenocarcinoma and biliary tract carcinoma cells. Oncol. Rep. 17, 1201–1205.

Nagrath, S., Jack, R.M., Sahai, V., Simeone, D.M., 2016. Opportunities and challenges for pancreatic circulating tumor cells. Gastroenterology 151, 412–426.

Nakahira, S., Nakamori, S., Tsujie, M., Takahashi, Y., Okami, J., Yoshioka, S., et al., 2007. Involvement of ribonucleotide reductase M1 subunit overexpression in gemcitabine resistance of human pancreatic cancer. Int. J. Cancer 120, 1355–1363.

Namkung, J., Kwon, W., Choi, Y., Yi, S.G., Han, S., Kang, M.J., et al., 2016. Molecular subtypes of pancreatic cancer based on miRNA expression profiles have independent prognostic value. J. Gastroenterol. Hepatol. 31, 1160–1167.

Nevala-Plagemann, C., Hidalgo, M., Garrido-Laguna, I., 2020. From state-of-the-art treatments to novel therapies for advanced-stage pancreatic cancer. Nat. Rev. Clin. Oncol. 17, 108–123.

O'Brien, J., Hayder, H., Zayed, Y., Peng, C., 2018. Overview of MicroRNA biogenesis, mechanisms of actions, and circulation. Front. Endocrinol. 9, 402.

Ogura, K., 2006. Dihydropyrimidine dehydrogenase activity and its genetic aberrations. Gan To Kagaku Ryoho 33, 1041–1048.

Ohuchida, K., Mizumoto, K., Kayashima, T., Fujita, H., Moriyama, T., Ohtsuka, T., et al., 2011. Micro-RNA expression as a predictive marker for gemcitabine response after surgical resection of pancreatic cancer. Ann. Surg. Oncol. 18, 2381–2387.

Ou, S.H.I., Jänne, P.A., Leal, T.A., Rybkin, I.I., Sabari, J.K., Barve, M.A., et al., 2022. First-in-human phase I/IB dose-finding study of Adagrasib (MRTX849) in patients with advanced KRASG12C solid Tumors (KRYSTAL-1). J. Clin. Oncol., JCO2102752.

Palmquist, C., Dehlendorff, C., Calatayud, D., Hansen, C.P., Hasselby, J.P., Johansen, J.S., 2020. Prediction of Unresectability and prognosis in patients undergoing surgery on suspicion of pancreatic cancer using carbohydrate antigen 19-9, interleukin 6, and YKL-40. Pancreas 49, 53–61.

Pandey, D., Sharma, R., Sharma, S., Salhan, S., 2017. Unusually high serum levels of CA 19-9 in an ovarian tumour: malignant or benign? J. Clin. Diagn. Res. 11, QD08–QD10.

Park, W., Chawla, A., O'Reilly, E.M., 2021. Pancreatic cancer: a review. JAMA 326, 851–862.

Prendergast, G.C., Smith, C., Thomas, S., Mandik-Nayak, L., Laury-Kleintop, L., Metz, R., et al., 2014. Indoleamine 2,3-dioxygenase pathways of pathogenic inflammation and immune escape in cancer. Cancer Immunol. Immunother. 63, 721–735.

Qian, Y., Gong, Y., Fan, Z., Luo, G., Huang, Q., Deng, S., et al., 2020. Molecular alterations and targeted therapy in pancreatic ductal adenocarcinoma. J. Hematol. Oncol. 13, 130.

Ryu, J.K., Hong, S.M., Karikari, C.A., Hruban, R.H., Goggins, M.G., Maitra, A., 2010. Aberrant MicroRNA-155 expression is an early event in the multistep progression of pancreatic adenocarcinoma. Pancreatology 10, 66–73.

Santana-Codina, N., Roeth, A.A., Zhang, Y., Yang, A., Mashadova, O., Asara, J.M., et al., 2018. Oncogenic KRAS supports pancreatic cancer through regulation of nucleotide synthesis. Nat. Commun. 9, 4945.

Saqcena, M., Menon, D., Patel, D., Mukhopadhyay, S., Chow, V., Foster, D.A., 2013. Amino acids and mTOR mediate distinct metabolic checkpoints in mammalian G1 cell cycle. PLoS One 8, e74157.

Saqcena, M., Mukhopadhyay, S., Hosny, C., Alhamed, A., Chatterjee, A., Foster, D.A., 2015. Blocking anaplerotic entry of glutamine into the TCA cycle sensitizes K-Ras mutant cancer cells to cytotoxic drugs. Oncogene 34, 2672–2680.

Schlick, K., Kiem, D., Greil, R., 2021. Recent advances in pancreatic cancer: novel prognostic biomarkers and targeted therapy-a review of the literature. Biomol. Ther. 11, 1469.

Scott, L.J., 2019. Larotrectinib: first global approval. Drugs 79, 201–206.

Sebastiani, V., Ricci, F., Rubio-Viqueira, B., Rubio-Viquiera, B., Kulesza, P., Yeo, C.J., et al., 2006. Immunohistochemical and genetic evaluation of deoxycytidine kinase in pancreatic cancer: relationship to molecular mechanisms of gemcitabine resistance and survival. Clin. Cancer Res. 12, 2492–2497.

Shi, C., Merchant, N., Newsome, G., Goldenberg, D.M., Gold, D.V., 2014. Differentiation of pancreatic ductal adenocarcinoma from chronic pancreatitis by PAM4 immunohistochemistry. Arch. Pathol. Lab. Med. 138, 220–228.

Shi, Y., Gao, W., Lytle, N.K., Huang, P., Yuan, X., Dann, A.M., et al., 2019. Targeting LIF-mediated paracrine interaction for pancreatic cancer therapy and monitoring. Nature 569, 131–135.

Siegel, R.L., Miller, K.D., Fuchs, H.E., Jemal, A., 2022. Cancer statistics, 2022. CA Cancer J. Clin. 72, 7–33.

Singh, R.R., O'Reilly, E.M., 2020. New treatment strategies for metastatic pancreatic ductal adenocarcinoma. Drugs 80, 647–669.

Singhi, A.D., Ali, S.M., Lacy, J., Hendifar, A., Nguyen, K., Koo, J., et al., 2017. Identification of targetable ALK rearrangements in pancreatic ductal adenocarcinoma. J. Natl. Compr. Cancer Netw. 15, 555–562.

Slater, E.P., Strauch, K., Rospleszcz, S., Ramaswamy, A., Esposito, I., Klöppel, G., et al., 2014. MicroRNA-196a and -196b as potential biomarkers for the early detection of familial pancreatic cancer. Transl. Oncol. 7, 464–471.

Son, J., Lyssiotis, C.A., Ying, H., Wang, X., Hua, S., Ligorio, M., et al., 2013. Glutamine supports pancreatic cancer growth through a KRAS-regulated metabolic pathway. Nature 496, 101–105.

Sousa, C.M., Kimmelman, A.C., 2014. The complex landscape of pancreatic cancer metabolism. Carcinogenesis 35, 1441–1450.

Spratlin, J., Sangha, R., Glubrecht, D., Dabbagh, L., Young, J.D., Dumontet, C., et al., 2004. The absence of human equilibrative nucleoside transporter 1 is associated with reduced survival in patients with gemcitabine-treated pancreas adenocarcinoma. Clin. Cancer Res. 10, 6956–6961.

Sturm, N., Ettrich, T.J., Perkhofer, L., 2022. The impact of biomarkers in pancreatic ductal adenocarcinoma on diagnosis, surveillance and therapy. Cancers 14, 217.

Subudhi, S.K., Vence, L., Zhao, H., Blando, J., Yadav, S.S., Xiong, Q., et al., 2020. Neoantigen responses, immune correlates, and favorable outcomes after ipilimumab treatment of patients with prostate cancer. Sci. Transl. Med. 12, eaaz3577.

Sung, H., Ferlay, J., Siegel, R.L., Laversanne, M., Soerjomataram, I., Jemal, A., et al., 2021. Global cancer statistics 2020: GLOBOCAN estimates of incidence and mortality worldwide for 36 cancers in 185 countries. CA Cancer J. Clin. 71, 209–249.

Takahasi, K., Iinuma, H., Wada, K., Minezaki, S., Kawamura, S., Kainuma, M., et al., 2018. Usefulness of exosome-encapsulated microRNA-451a as a minimally invasive biomarker for prediction of recurrence and prognosis in pancreatic ductal adenocarcinoma. J. Hepatobiliary Pancreat. Sci. 25, 155–161.

Takai, E., Yachida, S., 2016. Circulating tumor DNA as a liquid biopsy target for detection of pancreatic cancer. World J. Gastroenterol. 22, 8480–8488.

Tan, A.C., Jimeno, A., Lin, S.H., Wheelhouse, J., Chan, F., Solomon, A., et al., 2009. Characterizing DNA methylation patterns in pancreatic cancer genome. Mol. Oncol. 3, 425–438.

Taparra, K., Wang, H., Malek, R., Lafargue, A., Barbhuiya, M.A., Wang, X., et al., 2018. O-GlcNAcylation is required for mutant KRAS-induced lung tumorigenesis. J. Clin. Invest. 128, 4924–4937.

Ventura, A., Jacks, T., 2009. MicroRNAs and cancer: short RNAs go a long way. Cell 136, 586–591.

Wang, Y., Yu, X., Hartmann, D., Zhou, J., 2020. Circulating tumor cells in peripheral blood of pancreatic cancer patients and their prognostic role: a systematic review and meta-analysis. HPB 22, 660–669.

Wang, S., Zheng, Y., Yang, F., Zhu, L., Zhu, X.Q., Wang, Z.F., et al., 2021. The molecular biology of pancreatic adenocarcinoma: translational challenges and clinical perspectives. Signal Transduct. Target. Ther. 6, 249.

Ward, P.S., Thompson, C.B., 2012. Metabolic reprogramming: a cancer hallmark even Warburg did not anticipate. Cancer Cell 21, 297–308.

Wrona, E., Potemski, P., Sclafani, F., Borowiec, M., 2021. Leukemia inhibitory factor: a potential biomarker and therapeutic target in pancreatic cancer. Arch. Immunol. Ther. Exp. 69, 2.

Xing, H., Wang, J., Wang, Y., Tong, M., Hu, H., Huang, C., et al., 2018. Diagnostic value of CA 19-9 and carcinoembryonic antigen for pancreatic cancer: a meta-analysis. Gastroenterol. Res. Pract. 2018, 8704751.

Xu, R., Yang, J., Ren, B., Wang, H., Yang, G., Chen, Y., et al., 2020. Reprogramming of amino acid metabolism in pancreatic cancer: recent advances and therapeutic strategies. Front. Oncol. 10, 572722.

Xue, Y., Abou Tayoun, A.N., Abo, K.M., Pipas, J.M., Gordon, S.R., Gardner, T.B., et al., 2013. MicroRNAs as diagnostic markers for pancreatic ductal adenocarcinoma and its precursor, pancreatic intraepithelial neoplasm. Cancer Gene Ther. 206, 217–221.

Yamada, R., Mizuno, S., Uchida, K., Yoneda, M., Kanayama, K., Inoue, H., et al., 2016. Human Equilibrative nucleoside transporter 1 expression in endoscopic ultrasonography-guided fine-needle aspiration biopsy samples is a strong predictor of clinical response and survival in the patients with pancreatic ductal adenocarcinoma undergoing gemcitabine-based chemoradiotherapy. Pancreas 45, 761–771.

Yang, J.Y., Sun, Y.W., Liu, D.J., Zhang, J.F., Li, J., Hua, R., 2014. MicroRNAs in stool samples as potential screening biomarkers for pancreatic ductal adenocarcinoma cancer. Am. J. Cancer Res. 4, 663–673.

Yang, J., Ren, B., Yang, G., Wang, H., Chen, G., You, L., et al., 2020. The enhancement of glycolysis regulates pancreatic cancer metastasis. Cell. Mol. Life Sci. 77, 305–321.

Yang, Y., Su, X., Shen, K., Zhang, C., Dai, H., Ma, H., et al., 2021. PUM1 is upregulated by DNA methylation to suppress antitumor immunity and results in poor prognosis in pancreatic cancer. Transl. Cancer Res. 10, 2153–2168.

Ying, H., Kimmelman, A.C., Lyssiotis, C.A., Hua, S., Chu, G.C., Fletcher-Sananikone, E., et al., 2012. Oncogenic Kras maintains pancreatic tumors through regulation of anabolic glucose metabolism. Cell 149, 656–670.

Zhang, J., Pavlova, N.N., Thompson, C.B., 2017a. Cancer cell metabolism: the essential role of the non-essential amino acid, glutamine. EMBO J. 36, 1302–1315.

Yoo, H.C., Yu, Y.C., Sung, Y., Han, J.M., 2020. Glutamine reliance in cell metabolism. Exp. Mol. Med. 52, 1496–1516.

Zhang, T., Tan, X.L., Xu, Y., Wang, Z.Z., Xiao, C.H., Liu, R., 2017b. Expression and prognostic value of indoleamine 2,3-dioxygenase in pancreatic cancer. Chin. Med. J. 130, 710–716.

Zhang, Y., Yang, J., Li, H., Wu, Y., Zhang, H., Chen, W., 2015a. Tumor markers CA19-9, CA242 and CEA in the diagnosis of pancreatic cancer: a meta-analysis. Int. J. Clin. Exp. Med. 8, 11683–11691.

Zhang, S.Y., Lin, M., Zhang, H.B., 2015b. Diagnostic value of carcinoembryonic antigen and carcinoma antigen 19-9 for colorectal carcinoma. Int. J. Clin. Exp. Pathol. 8, 9404–9409.

Yonemori, K., Kurahara, H., Maemura, K., Natsugoe, S., 2017. MicroRNA in pancreatic cancer. J. Hum. Genet. 62, 33–40.

Zhu, Y., Zhang, H., Chen, N., Hao, J., Jin, H., Ma, X., 2020a. Diagnostic value of various liquid biopsy methods for pancreatic cancer: a systematic review and meta-analysis. Medicine (Baltimore) 99, e18581.

Yee, N.S., Zhang, S., He, H.Z., Zheng, S.Y., 2020. Extracellular vesicles as potential biomarkers for early detection and diagnosis of pancreatic cancer. Biomedicine 8, E581.

Yi, J.M., Guzzetta, A.A., Bailey, V.J., Downing, S.R., Van Neste, L., Chiappinelli, K.B., et al., 2013. Novel methylation biomarker panel for the early detection of pancreatic cancer. Clin. Cancer Res. 19, 6544–6555.

Ye, C., Sadula, A., Ren, S., Guo, X., Yuan, M., Yuan, C., et al., 2020a. The prognostic value of CA19-9 response after neoadjuvant therapy in patients with pancreatic cancer: a systematic review and pooled analysis. Cancer Chemother. Pharmacol. 86, 731–740.

Yu, J., Ohuchida, K., Mizumoto, K., Sato, N., Kayashima, T., Fujita, H., et al., 2010. MicroRNA, hsa-miR-200c, is an independent prognostic factor in pancreatic cancer and its upregulation inhibits pancreatic cancer invasion but increases cell proliferation. Mol. Cancer 9, 169.

Ye, Z.Q., Zou, C.L., Chen, H.B., Jiang, M.J., Mei, Z., Gu, D.N., 2020b. MicroRNA-7 as a potential biomarker for prognosis in pancreatic cancer. Dis. Markers 2020, 2782101.

Yokoyama, S., Hamada, T., Higashi, M., Matsuo, K., Maemura, K., Kurahara, H., et al., 2020. Predicted prognosis of patients with pancreatic cancer by machine learning. Clin. Cancer Res. 26, 2411–2421.

Zhu, H., Wei, M., Xu, J., Hua, J., Liang, C., Meng, Q., et al., 2020b. PARP inhibitors in pancreatic cancer: molecular mechanisms and clinical applications. Mol. Cancer 19, 49.

Zhao, P., Li, L., Jiang, X., Li, Q., 2019. Mismatch repair deficiency/microsatellite instability-high as a predictor for anti-PD-1/PD-L1 immunotherapy efficacy. J. Hematol. Oncol. J. Hematol. Oncol. 12, 54.

Zeitouni, D., Pylayeva-Gupta, Y., Der, C.J., Bryant, K.L., 2016. KRAS mutant pancreatic cancer: no lone path to an effective treatment. Cancers 8, E45.

CHAPTER SIX

Biomarkers in endocrine diseases

Dhritiman Maitra[a], Sunil Chumber[b], and R.C. Deka[c]
[a]Department of Surgery, Medical College Kolkata, Kolkata, India
[b]Department of Surgery, AIIMS, New Delhi, India
[c]Department of ENT, AIIMS, New Delhi, India

1. Introduction

Biomarkers or biological markers are quantifiable indicators of some biological state or condition. They may be measured in biological samples like blood, urine, saliva, soft tissues etc. (Hirsch and Watkins, 2020; Biomarkers Definitions Working Group, 2001). Digital biomarkers are a completely new concept on the horizon and are software based and measured by biosensors as for example certain mobile phone based health applications based on measuring heart rate, amount of exercise and calories burnt (Babrak et al., 2019).

Biomarkers are classified as molecular markers, cellular markers or imaging markers. However, when it is not otherwise specified, by biomarkers we loosely mean molecular markers only. Molecular markers are further classified as genetic markers, epigenetic markers, and immunocytochemical markers.

The biomarkers help to arrive at a pin-point diagnosis by ruling out the differentials, to predict response to different therapeutic measures and to subclassify diseases into various subgroups with similar prognosis and so on. Accordingly, they are classified as diagnostic, predictive and prognostic biomarkers.

2. Basic biomarkers

2.1 Thyroid

Hypothyroidism is reliably diagnosed since ages by elevated serum TSH (thyroid stimulating hormone) levels. If a patient, with clinical features of hypothyroidism, has a low serum level of TSH, then one has to think of pituitary hypofunction. Sometimes hypothyroidism may occur due to autoimmune destruction of thyroid (as in autoimmune thyroiditis) whence anti-TPO (antithyroid peroxidase) antibodies may be raised.

Hyperthyroidism states are diagnosed by a combination of serum-free T3, free T4, and TSH levels. Patients with suppressed TSH are subjected to radioactive iodine or technetium nuclear scans. Anti-TSH antibody/thyroid receptor autoantibodies (TRAb) are raised in Grave's disease or autoantibody mediated thyroid hyperfunction.

Biomarkers in Cancer Detection and Monitoring of Therapeutics
https://doi.org/10.1016/B978-0-323-95114-2.00026-1

All these parameters may be dubbed as biomarkers so to speak.

The role of markers in thyroid cancer will be discussed in detail in the segment on modern biomarkers. For the uninitiated, thyroglobulin is an important marker to monitor treatment response and recurrence in patients with differentiated thyroid cancer (DTC). Calcitonin and carcinoembryonic antigen (CEA) are markers for medullary thyroid cancer (MTC) used for screening kindreds of known cases, follow-up of known cases and for treatment planning. Risk stratification for development of MTC is also done by identifying the specific codons bearing carcinogenic mutations. There is a bouquet of marker-based studies/gene-based assays/miRNA-based microarrays to predict the malignant potential of thyroid nodules which are indeterminate on FNAC (Fine Needle Aspiration Cytology) as well. Targeted therapy is also customized on the basis of different biomarkers (Kline and Sadrzadeh, 2017) (Figs. 1–4).

2.2 Disorders related to calcium and bone metabolism

The endocrine glands chiefly responsible for bone and calcium metabolism are the parathyroid glands. Parathyroid hyperfunction may be due to adenoma, hyperplasia or carcinoma. However, often in spite of parathyroid hyperfunction, patients are hypercalcemic yet asymptomatic. Some of them may be normocalcemic as well with

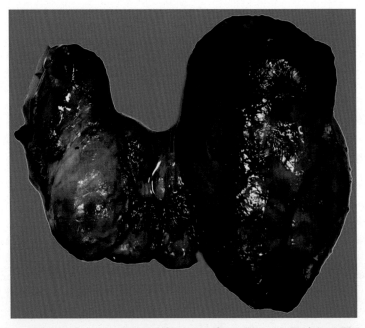

Fig. 1 Total thyroidectomy for toxic multinodular goiter (fT4 ↑, TSH ↓↓↓, TRAb/anti-TSH Ab −ve, multiple nodules on both lobes of thyroid on ultrasonography).

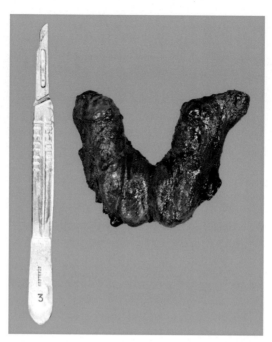

Fig. 2 Total thyroidectomy for Graves disease (fT4 ↑. TSH ↓↓↓, TRAb/anti-TSH Ab +ve, diffuse uptake in thyroid on radio-iodine scintigraphy, both lobes of thyroid diffusely enlarged on ultrasonography).

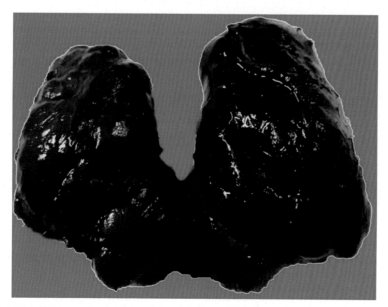

Fig. 3 Total thyroidectomy for nodular Graves disease—Marine-Lenhart syndrome (fT4 ↑. TSH ↓↓↓, TRAb/anti-TSH Ab +ve, multiple nodules on both lobes of thyroid on ultrasonography).

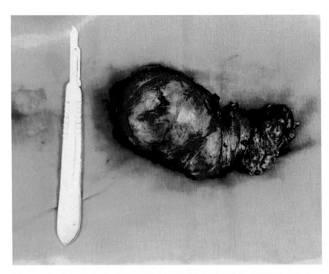

Fig. 4 Total thyroidectomy for toxic goiter (fT4 ↑,TSH ↓↓↓, TRAb/anti-TSH Ab −ve, anti-TPO Ab +ve, multiple nodules on both lobes of thyroid on ultrasonography, final diagnosis after histopathological examination was Hashitoxicosis).

or without symptoms. Loss of parathyroids after thyroid surgery or their agenesis and hypofunction may lead to hypocalcemia.

The role of evaluation of serum calcium, vitamin D, inorganic phosphate, FGF-23 (Fibroblast Growth Factor-23), parathormone assay, magnesium, albumin, chloride, bicarbonate in finding the "corrected calcium levels" and to narrow down to the most probable etiological diagnosis for disorders of calcium is widely accepted. Biomarkers further help to detect syndromic associations (like MEN1, MEN2a), hereditary conditions (HPT-JT syndrome/HRPT2 mutation) and help to differentiate parathyroid cancer from adenoma and hyperplasia. Disease severity can be ascertained using several biomarkers as well. Some conditions like familial hypocalciuric hypercalcemia (FHH) need to be ruled out before surgery (24-h urinary calcium <100 g) as patients with these conditions are usually not benefitted by surgery. Decision-making regarding the need of surgery in asymptomatic primary hyperparathyroidism patients is also dependent on a battery of marker based criteria including several imaging biomarkers. The CaxP (calcium and phosphate product), in addition to other parameters, is an important tool for decision-making regarding need of parathyroidectomy in patients with secondary hyperparathyroidism. The possibility of a patient for developing hungry bone syndrome following parathyroidectomy can also be predicted by the use of a number of biomarkers including alkaline phosphatase levels in serum in the preoperative setting (Symonds and Buse, 2017).

Bone mineral density is measured by dual energy X-Ray absorptiometry (DEXA scan) and findings are reported as normal, osteopenia and osteoporosis. In hyperparathyroidism, osteoporosis at the wrist is sort of pathognomonic. Bone metabolic biomarkers are classified as those pertaining to osteoclastic bone resorption (N or C terminal telopeptides) or those related to osteoblastic bone formation (alkaline phosphatase, procollagen type-1 N/C propeptide, etc.). Sclerostin, osteopontin, and osteocalcin are also being explored for potential clinical uses. Bone histomorphometry is also emerging as an essential tool for bone health assessment (Kline et al., 2017).

The imaging modalities for preoperative localization of parathyroids have evolved from high resolution ultrasound to sestamibi biplanar images, sestamibi SPECT CT hybrid images, 4-dimensional CT scan (4D-CT), 4D-MRI, fluorocholine PET, etc. with specific characteristics on these images which are considered as imaging biomarkers. Intraoperative localization measures like FNA-PTH, iOPTH, fluorescence using indocyanine green, autofluorescence [due to expression of Calcium Sensing Receptors(CASR)] are all based on the evaluation of various biomarkers. The "Miami criteria" states that a minimum fall of iOPTH of more than 50% from preincision or preexcision level (whichever is higher) may predict successful removal of criminal gland(s) and has almost become an essential tool for parathyroid surgery, especially focused parathyroidectomy (Figs. 5–8).

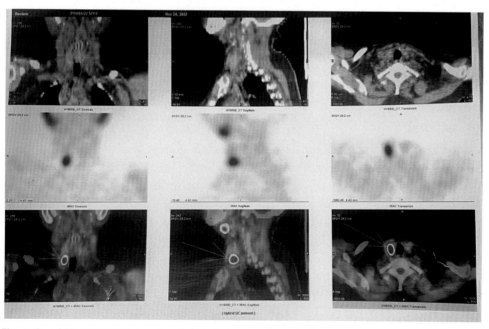

Fig. 5 SestaMIBI SPECT CT showing right inferior parathyroid adenoma.

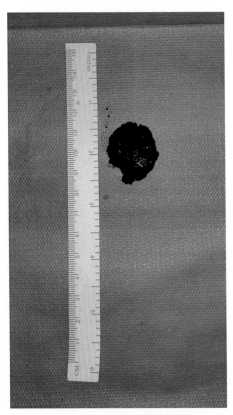

Fig. 6 Focused parathyroidectomy for right inferior parathyroid adenoma, iOPTH dropped to 20% of preincision value 15 min after excision.

2.3 Adrenal

Adrenal hypofunction or Addisonian crisis may occur after bilateral adrenalectomy, miliary tuberculosis, or Waterhouse Friderichsen syndrome due to destruction of the adrenal cortex whence adrenal cortical hormonal levels drop with a concomitant rise of the corresponding trophic hormone secreted by the pituitary gland (ACTH). If there is a drop in both ACTH and cortisol levels, then the hypoadrenal state is presumptively due to hypopituitarism. ACTH/cosyntropin stimulation followed by cortisol estimation is also helpful in this context.

Cushing's syndrome occurs as a result of hypercortisolemia due to Cushing's disease (adrenal hyperplasia secondary to a pituitary adenoma secreting excessive ACTH), ectopic sources secreting ACTH (some cancers) or due to primary hyperfunctioning adenoma/hyperplasia of the adrenal cortex leading to excess cortisol secretion. The cortisol hypersection is first confirmed by measuring evening salivary cortisol, loss of diurnal variation of serum cortisol levels, 24-h urine free cortisol or overnight low dose

Fig. 7 Preoperatively, right inferior parathyroid adenoma was diagnosed. But after focused parathyroidectomy, iOPTH value did not drop below 50% of preincision value at 15 min postexcision. Right superior gland was also found to be enlarged and removed, following which there was satisfactory drop in Sr. PTH value. So the other side of the neck was not explored—a case of double adenoma.

dexamethasone suppression test. ACTH levels help in ascertaining adrenal or pituitary cause as mentioned before. High dose dexamethasone suppression test, in cases with elevated ACTH, helps to differentiate between pituitary and ectopic sources of increased ACTH. Selective venous sampling from inferior petrosal sinus is also done in some cases.

Aldosteronoma or Conn's syndrome leads to aldosterone excess. It is diagnosed by measuring serum electrolytes (sodium and potassium), direct rennin concentration, plasma renin activity to aldosterone ratio, saline loading followed by measurement of aldosterone levels etc. Localization of Conn's adenoma and lateralization (diagnosing unilateral versus bilateral) are done by selective venous sampling and measuring the gradient between the right and left sides. This is essential for planning surgery.

In adrenocortical carcinoma (ACC), there may be a rise of all the cortical hormones in combination including dihydro-epiandrosterone sulfate (DHEAS). The modern biomarkers of ACC including histopathological criteria and modern molecular subclassification have been described in a later segment of this chapter.

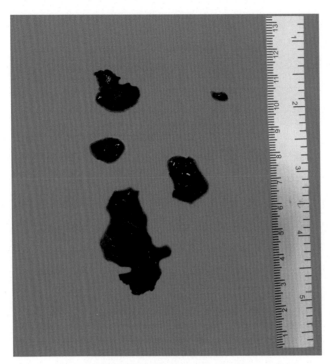

Fig. 8 Subtotal parathyroidectomy along with excision of cervical horn of thymus in a case of MEN-I associated parathyroid hyperplasia. Patient had positive family history and menin gene mutation. Pituitary and pancreatic endocrine tumors were ruled out by appropriate biomarkers.

Congenital abnormalities in the steroidogenesis pathway may lead to abnormal levels of different sex steroids leading to virilization, feminization and precocious puberty. All these hormones and metabolic intermediates and end-products can be measured by modern sensitive assays.

The commonest disease affecting the adrenal medulla is pheochromocytoma. Extra-adrenal pheochromcytomas are called paragangliomas. The extra-adrenal ones secrete more of noradrenaline and those arising from the adrenal medulla predominantly secrete adrenaline. Thoracic paraganglioma mostly secrete dopamine. Head and neck paragangliomas are parasympathetic. These are diagnosed by measuring catecholamine levels and the levels of their metabolites in body fluids. Estimation of plasma metanephrines, 24-h urinary fractionated catecholamines, metanephrines, normetanephrines, and vanillyl mandelic acid is widely practiced. Clonidine suppression test is also employed sometimes. Chromogranin A (CgA) is also found to be raised in pheochromocytoma. All the above are biomarker based investigations. The modern molecular marker based classification of pheochromocytoma will be discussed with the modern biomarkers in a later segment.

Imaging for diagnosis and precise localization of adrenal tumors has evolved from USG of abdomen to present day thin slice multidetector CT scans with adrenal protocol, MRI, MIBG scan, NP-59 scan, bifunctional chelate–based nuclear scans like Gallium 68–DOTANOC, DOTATOC, DOTATATE scans, and metabolic scans like 18F-FDG PET CT scan (including hybrid ones like DOPA PET) (Kline and Chin, 2017) (Figs. 9–11).

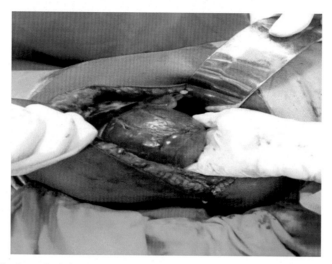

Fig. 9 Nonfunctioning adrenal cyst.

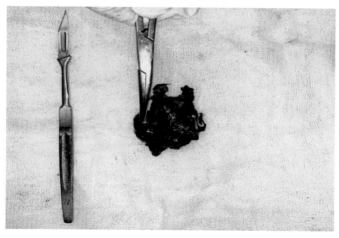

Fig. 10 Left adrenalectomy for Conn's adenoma (raised plasma aldosterone:renin ratio and refractory hypokalemia.

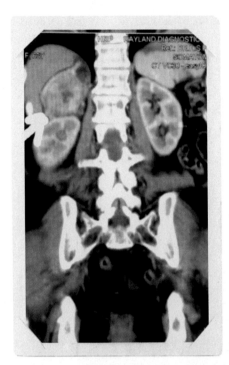
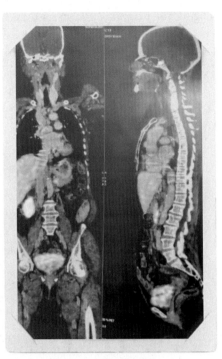
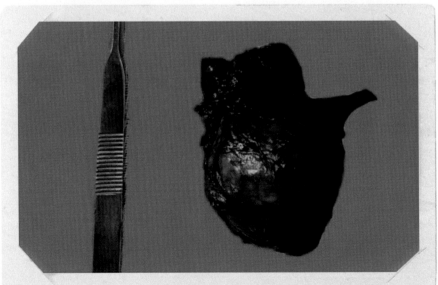

Fig. 11 (A) CECT showing right suprarenal mass; (B) 68Ga DOTANOC PET-CT showing significant right suprarenal uptake; (C) Specimen of right adrenalectomy (both plasma and 24-h urinary metanephrines and normetanephrines were raised).

2.4 Endocrine pancreas including diabetes and neuroendocrine tumors (NET) of gastrointestinal tract

Diabetes is caused either due to insulin deficiency secondary to autoimmune destruction of the Islet of Langerhans (type I) located in the endocrine pancreas or due to insulin resistance (type 2) leading to relative insulin deficiency. Leptin, adiponectin, and several other hormones have been implicated in modulating insulin resistance. Diabetic status is ascertained by measuring fasting and postprandial blood glucose levels. Long-term glycemic control is monitored by HbA1C levels (glycated hemoglobin). Complications of diabetes mellitus like ketoacidosis can be predicted beforehand by detecting ketone bodies in urine by dipstick tests and so on (Venos and Koning, 2017).

Neuroendocrine tumors (NET) arise from enterochromaffin cells, Kulchitsky cells, APUD (Amine precursor uptake and degradation) cells and other endocrine tissues in the pancreas, gastrointestinal tract and parts of the airway.

Chromogranin A, synaptophysin, neuron-specific enolase, neurophysin, pancreastatin, and pancreatic polypeptide are general biomarkers secreted nonspecifically from majority of NETs and are detected in blood or by immunohistochemical tumor staining or both. Patients with serotonin secreting carcinoid tumors have elevated urinary 5-hydroxy indole acetic acid levels(5-HIAA).

Previously gastrinoma used to be detected by measurement of basal and maximal (stimulated) acid output on the nasogastric aspirate of suspected patients. Insulinoma used to be detected by Whipple's triad which involved measurement of serial fasting blood glucose levels to document hypoglycemia and reversal of hypoglycemia by administration of glucose. Now all these conditions including glucagonoma, somatostatinoma, VIPoma, etc. can be diagnosed by elevated hormone levels(basal or stimulated) due to availability of sophisticated assays. Biomarker based imaging modalities, also dubbed as functional and hybrid scans have also been added to the armamentarium of diagnostic tools for NETs. The modern biomarkers employed for the diagnosis of some of these conditions have been dealt with in the next segment of this chapter (Rorstad, 2017).

2.5 Others (pituitary and reproductive glands)

Endocrine dysfunctions are broadly classified as "secondary"/"central" resulting from pituitary diseases and "primary" which result from abnormalities of the end-organs. Pituitary disease may involve decreased pituitary secretions or hypersecretion. Both conditions may be associated with pituitary tumors. Other conditions affecting the pituitary gland are hemorrhage or infarction. Accordingly, there may be increased or decreased blood levels of adrenocorticotrophic hormone (ACTH), prolactin, thyroid stimulating hormone (TSH), growth hormone and gonadotropins (Luteinizing hormone and Follicular stimulating hormone), all of which are secreted from the anterior pituitary. Since GH is an unstable hormone, IGF-1 is measured in serum as its surrogate in suspected cases of gigantism and acromegaly. In inflictions of the posterior pituitary, there may be abnormalities of oxytocin and ADH (antidiuretic hormone)/arginine vasopressin levels (Corenblum and Flynn, 2017).

Sexual development, sexual function and reproduction may be affected by any abnormality of the hypothalamo-pituitary-gonadal axis which are detected by altered levels of different hormones. Inhibin A levels have also become part of routine hormonal evaluation along with estrogen, progesterone, testosterone, LH, FSH, and prolactin. Anti-Mullerian hormone (AMH), along with the above form an important part of assessment for primary infertility. Epithelial tumors of ovaries are associated with elevated CA-125 levels. Human epididymal protein 4 (HE4) has also become an important part of ROMA(Ovarian Malignancy Risk Algorithm) panel. Testicular tumors are associated with elevation of serum markers like LDH, beta-HCG, and alpha-fetoprotein. Some tumors also secrete placental alkaline phosphatase (PLAP) (Corenblum and Boyd, 2017).

3. Modern biomarkers (including molecular markers)

3.1 Thyroid

Thyroid cancer presents mostly as thyroid nodules. Ultrasonography is riddled with significant interobserver variation. To overcome this, standard lexicons based on parameters like echogenicity, margins, shape, composition, echogenic foci are followed to assign a specific TIRADS (Thyroid Imaging Reporting and Data Systems) score to a nodule. The American College of Radiologists (ACR) and Korean TIRADS are widely followed. Depending on size and TIRADS score, it is decided which nodules need FNAC and for which only follow-up would suffice. FNAC findings are also reported as per the universally accepted Bethesda System. Bethesda 1 implies inconclusive result, Bethesda 2 means benign findings, Bethesda 3 means atypia of unknown significance/follicular lesion of unknown significance, Bethesda 4 includes follicular neoplasm, Bethesda 5 implies suspicion of malignancy and Bethesda 6 means malignant (Crippa et al., 2010). However Bethesda 3 and 4 represent a "gray zone" in which molecular markers in conjunction with FNAC can help in treatment planning. If molecular markers predictive of cancer are negative, a patient with a Bethesda 3 solitary thyroid nodule can just be followed up without the need of diagnostic lobectomy. If on the other hand, the molecular markers of cancer are positive, then aggressive treatment can be undertaken at the very outset to avoid sequential surgeries(lobectomy and then a completion thyroidectomy) for Bethesda 3 and 4 lesions. Most commonly studied genetic biomarkers for differentiated thyroid cancer(DTC) include a seven-gene panel of mutations (including BRAF, RAS, RET/PTC, PAX8/PPAR-gamma), a gene expression classifier (mRNA-expression of 167 genes) and galectin-3 immunohistochemistry. These tests have been shown to rule out malignancy in indeterminate cytology specimens or to guide surgical procedures (Alexander et al., 2012; Bartolazzi et al., 2008; Nikiforov et al., 2011).

Some commercially available tests are there, viz., Afirma (microarray for expression analysis of 167 mRNA, 25 for screening and 142 as classifier), ThyroSeq (DNA and RNA targeted 56 gene NGS to detect mutations, gene fusions and gene expressions), ThyGenX/ThyraMir (NGS for mutations[5 genes], 3 gene fusions and expression analysis of 10 miRNA) and Rossetta GX reveal (expression analysis of 24 miRNAs by qRTPCR).

Apart from diagnosis, markers are helpful for surveillance too. Diagnostic and therapeutic/ablative radioiodine scans are helpful in patients with differentiated thyroid cancer. Such patients are also followed up by thyroglobulin (Tg) levels in the postoperative period. Radioiodine scan and Tg measurement are performed in postoperative patients after stopping thyroxine replacement, thereby allowing TSH levels to rise above 30 mIU/L or by using recombinant TSH. Sometimes, in course of time, in spite of elevated thyroglobulin levels, the iodine scan results may turn negative in spite of presence of recurrent or residual disease. This entity is called TENIS (thyroglobulin elevated negative iodine scan) and results due to loss of NIS (sodium iodide symporters) leading to de-differentiation. Such patients can be followed up by 18F-FDG PET scan. Sometimes Tg levels may be falsely low due to presence of antiTg antibodies. Detection of TSHR-mRNA and peripheral BRAF mutation can act as additional postoperative indicators of persistent or recurrent thyroid cancer.

WHO and other thyroid authorities/associations have classified thyroid cancer into many subtypes on the basis of histopathological criteria. Of those, the poorly differentiated and anaplastic varieties do not express NIS and are hence radioiodine resistant. Common mutations in the MAP (mitogen-activated protein) kinase pathway are BRAF (T1799A or V600E), RAS, and RET/PTC rearrangements. BRAF mutation is seen in association with papillary thyroid cancer and RAS mutation is more common in follicular thyroid carcinoma and FVPTC (follicular variant of papillary thyroid cancer). BRAF mutation is associated with aggressiveness, tumor invasion, metastasis, recurrence and loss of radioiodine uptake. Anaplastic carcinoma is associated with p53 mutation. Follicular carcinoma is differentiated from follicular adenoma on the basis of vascular and capsular invasion. Also, the presence of PAX8/PPARgamma mutation favors a diagnosis of follicular carcinoma over adenoma.

Mutation commonly affecting the PI3K pathway is PTEN (phosphatase and tensin on chromosome 10) mutation and is present in Cowden's syndrome. There are quite a few aberrant gene methylations detected in thyroid cancer. These DNA methylation markers can be measured both in the serum and by FNAC.

Apart from Galectin-3 or Gal-3, which has been already mentioned, the other immunocytochemical markers are Hector Battifora mesothelial cell (HBME-1) and cytokeratin 19. These two, when used together can help to differentiate papillary carcinoma from nonpapillary lesions. Vascular endothelial growth factor (VEGF) expression is another important marker associated with higher incidence of distant metastasis and lymph node involvement.

Epigenetic markers are related to pathways of DNA methylation, histone protein modification, nucleosome positioning and microRNA silencing.

Epigenetic modulators including SAHA (suberoyl anilide hydroxamic acid) have been described for use as targeted therapy. Efatutazone, a PPAR-gamma agonist has been used in anaplastic cancer along with paclitaxel chemotherapy. Selumetinib and ATRA (*all-trans* retinoic acid) have been used for redifferentiation therapy to overcome RAI resistance. Sunitinib, Axitinib, and other tyrosine kinase inhibitors have been used in advanced differentiated thyroid carcinoma. The DECISION trial led to US-FDA approval of Sorafenib for being used in advanced radioiodine refractory disease. SELECT trial established Lenvatinib as being effective in DTC. Vemurafenib is a small molecule TKI(tyrosine kinase inhibitor) effective in BRAF mutation positive cancers. Larotractinib is recommended in NTRK gene fusion positive anaplastic cancer and dabrafenib/trametinib in BRAF mutation positive anaplastic carcinoma (George et al., 2016; NCCN Guidelines: Thyroid Carcinoma. Version3.2018, 2018).

Coming to medullary thyroid cancer(MTC), role of biomarkers is supreme in identifying the degree of risk of development of MTC in patients with MEN 2A, MEN 2B, and FMTC syndromes. Risk stratification is done by detecting specific codons bearing the RET mutation. Depending on risk stratification, the age and extent of prophylactic surgery is decided. Calcitonin levels help for screening as well as follow-up. The extent of lymph node dissection is also governed by calcitonin level along with other factors. Another marker for MTC is CEA. Amyloid is detected on FNAC in MTC. Calcitonin expressing MTCs are expected to be well-differentiated. For patients with elevated calcitonin levels, 68-Ga DOTANOC scan is advised for postoperative follow-up and to detect distant metastases. Patients with significant uptake on DOTANOC scan may be treated by Lutetium (177Lu)-based PRRT (peptide receptor radiotherapy). Those with elevated CEA are relatively de-differentiated and are followed up by 18F-FDG PET CT scans. Vandetinib has been used for targeted therapy in advanced MTC. Anti-CEA antibodies have also been used with limited success (Jin and Moley, 2016) (Figs. 12–15).

3.2 Parathyroid

Most of the modern markers in parathyroid diseases have been relegated to the status of basic biomarkers due to their rampant and almost routine usage and have been discussed in the previous section. Here, we shall discuss the markers employed for diagnosis of parathyroid carcinoma (PCa). PCa may be sporadic or hereditary(with HRPT2 mutation) associated with ossifying fibromas of the jaw and positive family history. Patients with carcinoma have very high calcium levels(>1.35 times the upper limit of normal). The

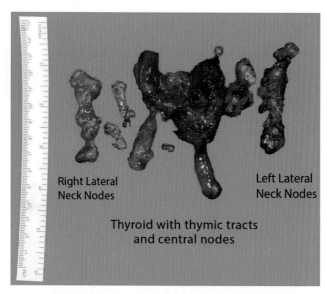

Fig. 12 Total thyroidectomy with bilateral central and lateral neck dissection in a case of sporadic medullary thyroid cancer. Postoperative follow up was done with Sr. Calcitonin and CEA levels. Since Sr. Calcitonin levels were found to be high, whole body 68Ga DOTANOC PET-CT was done to look for distant metastasis. Liver metastases were picked up and patient was subjected to Lutetium-based peptide receptor radiotherapy.

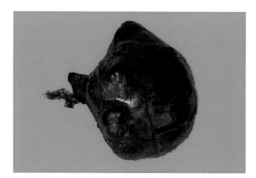

Fig. 13 Diagnostic left lobectomy in a case of Bethesda-IV STN of left lobe of thyroid with a negative 7-gene mutation panel. Hence unnecessary total thyroidectomy was avoided. Final histopathology was consistent with follicular adenoma.

carcinomatous gland may be palpable in contrast to the cases of adenoma/hyperplasia. PTH levels are generally more than 10 times the upper limit of normal with the third generation: second generation PTH ratio > 1. Alkaline phosphatase is markedly raised (usually above 285 IU/L). Raised urinary HCG levels indicate a more aggressive stage of PCa with higher fracture risk.

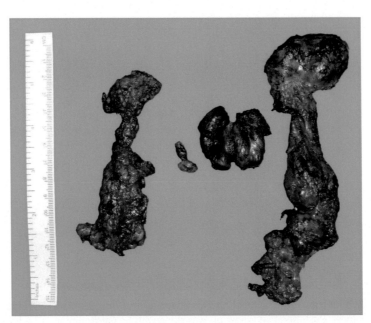

Fig. 14 Total thyroidectomy with bilateral central and lateral neck dissection in a case of papillary thyroid cancer. Postoperative follow up was done with Sr. Thyroglobulin, Anti-TG antibodies and TSH-stimulated radioiodine scan. Finally, patient was put on TSH suppressive L-thyroxine therapy.

Preoperative imaging for localization is of utmost importance as in other parathyroid conditions as already described. Preoperative FNAC is avoided to prevent rupture of the tumor otherwise parathyromatosis may result. As far as histopathological examination of the postoperative specimen is considered, several characteristics have been described to be suggestive of cancer. These include fibrous bands, trabecular growth, capsular invasion, vascular invasion, mitotic activity, necrosis and nuclear atypia (Schantz and Castleman, 1973; Bondeson et al., 1993). Though aneuploidy was previously touted as an important marker, current evidence states otherwise.

Loss of parafibromin staining on IHC (absence in more than 99% cells), Ki67 overexpression (>5%) and Galectin-3 positivity as standalone markers or in combination are very helpful in the diagnosis of PCa. The balance of proapoptotic and antiapoptotic markers is retained in adenoma but lost in carcinoma. There are studies showing cyclin D1/PRAD1 overexpression, human telomerase reverse transcriptase (hTERT) expression, loss of retinoblastoma gene, loss of APC gene, and underexpression of p27 to be associated with PCa. Loss of E-cadherin with concomitant overexpression of Snail and Twist indicate tumor progression and ongoing metastatic process. MicroRNA profiling has revealed that miR 126 downregulation is consistent with PCa. Protein Gene Product 9.5(PGP 9.5), a protein product of ubiquitin carboxyl terminal esterase L1

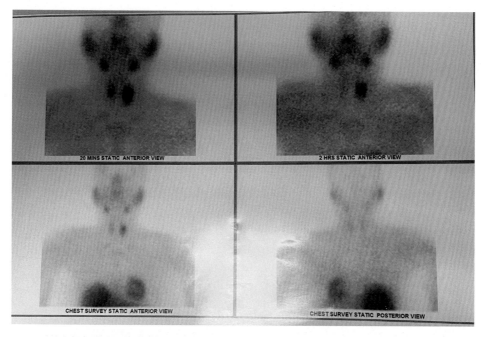

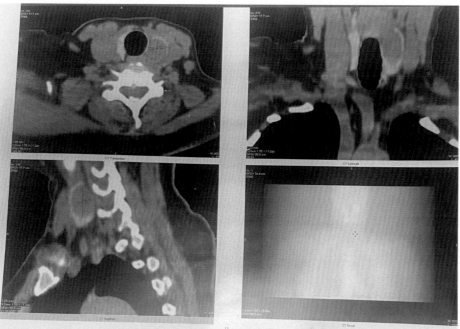

Fig. 15 SestaMIBI SPECT CT scan showing enlarged left superior parathyroid. En bloc excision of enlarged parathyroid along with ipsilateral lobe of thyroid done. Final histopathology was suggestive of parathyroid carcinoma. *(Continued)*

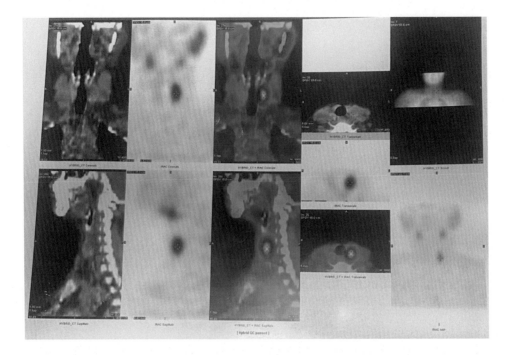

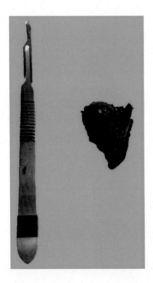

Fig. 15, cont'd

(UCHL1) is a complimentary marker for PCa. Immunotherapy by inducing acquired immunity with PTH protein fragments is being experimented with, over and above the standard available treatment modalities (Ranvier and Chau, 2016).

3.3 Adrenal

The routine diagnostics for adrenal diseases have been discussed in the previous section on adrenal gland. In this section, we will describe the recent advances in diagnosis, prognosis and management of pheochromocytoma and ACC based on modern markers.

Cells from adrenal medulla give characteristic color reactions determined by their content of catecholamines. With dichromate salts, they give the brown chromaffin reaction. With ferric chloride, they give a green Vulpian reaction and with silver salts, an argentaffin reaction.

With histochemical staining reactions, two kinds of chromaffin cells can be distinguished between (1) those storing norepinephrine, which have a low affinity for the dye azocarmine, are autofluorescent, give argentaffin and potassium iodide reactions, and are free for acid phosphatase; and (2) those storing epinephrine with opposite features. The normal adrenal medulla has cells in which epinephrine is predominant (85%) because of the high activity of PNMT (phenylethanolamine *N*-methyltransferase) (Fawcett and Raviola, 1994).

Pheochromocytoma and paraganglioma are often present simultaneously. The surest sign of malignancy is the presence of metastasis. In addition, markers of proliferation and mitotic index on histopathology may be helpful to stamp cases as malignant. Pheochromocytoma may be associated with MEN 2A (bilateral, parathyroid hyperplasia and MTC) or MEN 2B (bilateral, marfanoid habitus, mucocutaneous neuromas, MTC). Both are due to RET protoncogene mutation in Chromosome 10. Other heritable syndromes associated with pheochromocytoma/paraganglioma are (a) Von Hippel Lindau (VHL)-type 2: associated with CNS hemangioblastoma, renal cell carcinoma, pNET and endolymphatic sac tumors, (b) Neurofibromatosis 1(NF1), (c) Carney Stratakis and Carney triad, (d) PGL1(-SDHD mutation), PGL2 (SDHAF1), PGL3 (SDHC) and PGL4 (SDHB). The molecular subclassification on the basis of SDH (succinate dehydrogenase) mutation is of prime importance, as each subgroup has a specific predilection for a particular location, secrete different catcholamines and have different rates of malignancy and consequently different prognosis. The peculiarity of VHL and SDHB mutation associated adrenal pheochromocytomas is that they predominantly secrete norepinephrine unlike other pheochromcytomas of adrenal origin. SDHB mutation is also related to higher rates of malignancy. CT, MRI and I-131Metaiodobenzyl Guanidine (MIBG) scans are crucial to localize the tumors and to rule out metastasis. 111-Indium pentereotide/octreo-scan and 99mTc Hynic TOC scan have been found to be useful. Gallium 68 DOTANOC scan is fast replacing all other scans. 18F-FDG PET is a better modality for detecting metastases and for SDHB mutation positive cases. 18F-FDG DOPA PET is good for head and neck paraganglioma and SDHB mutation negative cases. For metastatic disease following debulking surgery and for locally unresectable tumors, HAS Iobenguane I131 or I131 MIBG therapy may be used if the metastases/tumor showed MIBG uptake on prior scans. PRRT with 177Lu-DOTATATE can be used when somatostatin receptor imaging shows positive uptake (Frunzac and Grant, 2016; NCCN Guidelines: Neuroendocrine and Adrenal Tumors. Version 4.2018, 2019).

Adrenocortical cancers may be nonfunctioning or functioning with hypersecretion of more than one hormone. The most important parameter for predicting cancer from preoperative images is the size of the tumor. Preoperative FNAC is not mandatory. Other markers of malignancy on imaging are: (a) heterogeneous pattern, (b) irregular surface, (c) stippled calcification, (d) areas of necrosis, (e) contrast enhancement $>+10$ Hounsfeld Units (HU) on CT, and (f) lymphadenopathy. Bone scintigraphy is recommended in all patients of ACC.

A method of defining malignancy histologically has been relatively simply described by Weiss. Presence of more than 3 of the following features is indicative of malignancy:

(a) high nuclear grade, (b) mitotic rate $>5/50$ high power fields, (c) atypical mitoses, (d) eosinophilic tumor cytoplasm ($>75\%$ of tumor cells), (e) diffuse architectural pattern ($>33\%$ of tumor) with fibrous and trabecular bands, (f) foci of confluent necrosis, (g) venous invasion, (h) sinusoidal invasion, and (i) capsular invasion. High mitotic index is more prognostic than diagnostic. In small tumors without obvious capsular invasion and with weak mitotic activity, markers like vimentin are helpful to rule out cancer as the latter is negative in cancer. Synaptophysin and MIB-1, on the other hand, are expressed more often in cancers (Weiss, 1995; Proye et al., 2016).

The 8th edition AJCC–TNM staging for ACC has incorporated grade as well. Low grade cancers have <20 mitoses/ 50 high power fields. High grade ones have >20 mitoses/50 hpf and are positive for p53 and CTNNB mutation. Testing for gene mutations present in Lynch syndrome is also recommended. Pembrolizumab should be considered for mismatch repair gene deficient(dMMR) or microsatellite instability–high(MSI-H) unresectable/metastatic ACC that have progressed following prior treatment or have no suitable alternatives left (NCCN Guidelines: Neuroendocrine and Adrenal Tumors. Version 4.2018, 2019) (Figs. 16–17).

3.4 NET

In 1980, WHO described the entity "carcinoid," which was modified in 2000 to cover WDET (well–differentiated endocrine tumors), WDEC (well–differentiated endocrine carcinoma), and PDEC (poorly differentiated endocrine carcinoma). However, the current classification of NET includes a) Well differentiated Neuroendocrine Tumors (low grade and intermediate grade) and b) Poorly differentiated Neuroendocrine Tumors

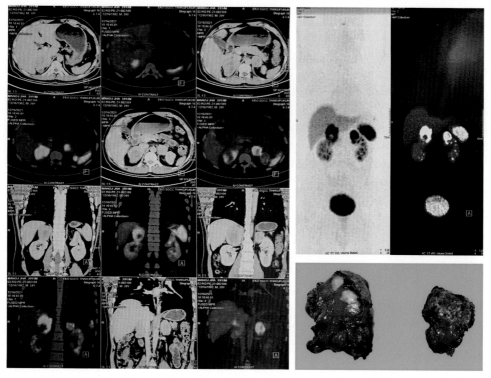

Fig. 16 68Ga DOTANOC PET-CT scan showing uptake in bilateral suprarenal region in a hypertensive patient with raised plasma and urinary metanephrines. Genetic mutations relevant for MEN, VHL and SDH were found to be negative. No other endocrinopathy was present. Bilateral subcortical adrenalectomy was done.

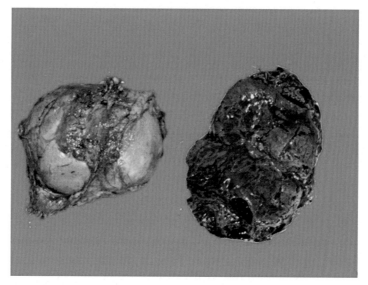

Fig. 17 Specimen of right adrenalectomy in a patient with sporadic adrenocortical cancer. The patient had raised levels of serum cortisol and DHEAS. Though there was minimal uptake on 68Ga DOTANOC PET scan, the tumor showed significant uptake in 18F FDG PET scan.

(high grade). Apart from their appearance and behavior, two important markers, viz., Ki67 expression and mitotic index form the basis of this classification.

The most reliable marker of malignancy is presence of metastasis. High-grade/poorly differentiated NETs are sometimes referred to as "neuroendocrine carcinoma". Well-differentiated tumors still have malignant potential, but the differences in behavior persist, even in patients with metastatic disease.

Inherited mutations have only been identified in tumor-suppressor genes (MEN1, VHL, TSC, NF-1) and occur in <5% of all NETs. Three main pathways of mutations have been identified in sporadic NETs as well, viz., MEN1, DAXX (Death Domain Associated Protein), or ATRX and mTOR (mammalian Target of Rapamycin). Abnormal MEN1 and DAXX/ATRX expression are present in approximately half of the well-differentiated tumors and are associated with improved survival. DAXX/ATRX mutations are absent in poorly differentiated tumors. High incidence of abnormal p53 and Rb (retinoblastoma) gene expression along with over-expression of the antiapoptotic protein Bcl-2 are associated with poorly differentiated tumors. VHL-associated tumors are indolent.

The routine markers used in diagnosis and prognostication have been discussed in the previous section on NETs. Here, we shall discuss the modern diagnostic tools for different NETs. The modern biochemical diagnosis of insulinoma includes measurement of serum glucose, insulin levels, proinsulin levels, C-peptide levels, insulin:glucose ratio, insulin:C-pepide ratio, blood levels of sulfonylureas/meglitinides, antiinsulin autoantibodies and betahydroxy butyrate. Along with these, several functional and structural imaging (somatostatin receptor scintigraphy, CT, MRI, 68-Gallium-DOTA-Exendin PET CT/SPECT CT, Endoscopic Ultrasound, etc.), timing of hypoglycemia (fasting versus postprandial) and angiography or selective venous sampling with or without calcium stimulation help in confirming the diagnosis and localization of insulinomas thereby ruling out the differential diagnoses (noninsulinoma pancreatogenous hypoglycemia, surreptitious insulin administration/OHA intake, nesidioblastosis, etc.). Insulinomas do not express somatostatin receptors as much as other NETs. So, for imaging of insulinomas exendin (GLP-1 receptor agonist) based nucleopharmaceuticals are being used more and more.

For diagnosis of gastrinoma, serum gastrin levels have replaced erstwhile gastric acid output measurement. The other causes of hypergastrinemia (chronic PPI use, *H. pylori* infection, atrophic gastritis, etc.) have to be kept in mind. Imaging modalities to localize these tumors include CT, MRI, EUS (± FNAC), Somatostatin Receptor Scintigraphy/Octreoscan, 111-Indium Pentetreotide scan, 68-Ga DOTANOC, and other hybrid scans. Use of fluorescence technology, transillumination and intraoperative ultrasound for intraoperative localization of gastrinoma and GI-NETS is well known.

Direct hormonal analysis can be done for diagnosing VIPomas, somatostatinomas, and glucagonomas also. The nonfunctional NETs of pancreas may secrete substances like PP but due to lack of symptoms they may present very late with obstructive jaundice.

Surgery is the mainstay of treatment (enucleation, Whipple's procedure, triple bypass, distal pancreatectomy, GI resection, and anastomosis) depending on tumor location, size and resectability. Symptoms due to insulinomas may be treated with drugs like diazoxide. Liver transplant is also an option for limited liver metastases from NETs. For metastatic or unresectable disease, apart from cytotoxic chemotherapy, targeted therapy using long acting somatostatin analogues like Lanreotide (depot injection)/Sandostatin have been used for cases with positive expression of somatostatin receptors. Everolimus (mTOR) and Sunitinib (TKI) have also been approved by USFDA for targeted therapy. Lutetium based PRRT is also being tried in select cases with positive somatostatin receptor expression (White and Riall, 2016).

3.5 Others

Important molecular markers for pituitary carcinoma are Ki-67, p53, cytokeratin, epithelial membrane antigen, glial fibrillary acidic protein, CgA, hTERT, HER-2/neu (Human epidermal receptor), COX-2, FGFR4 (fibroblast growth factor receptor), and MMP (Matrix metalloproteinase). The hormonal markers are adrenocorticotropic hormone (ACTH), prolactin (PRL), etc. Genetic mutational biomarkers are Gsp, Ras, H-RAS, Rb, Chromosome 11 deletion, and PTTG. In imaging, 111In-DPTA-octreotide SRS and MIB-1 staining index play an important role. Immunohistochemistry is of utmost importance (Luo et al., 2018).

For testicular cancer, apart from the serum markers mentioned in the previous section on testes, XIST gene expression and miR-371-3/miR-302/367 evaluation are useful (Luo et al., 2018).

For ovarian cancer, over and above CA-125 and HE4, the following markers are quite useful: Inhibin, AFP, Beta-HCG, LDH, CEA, cytokeratin 7 (CK7), PAX8, and estrogen receptor (ER). Genetic mutational markers of importance are BRCA1/BRCA2 and miRNA-based microarrays (Luo et al., 2018).

References

Alexander, E.K., Kennedy, G.C., Baloch, Z.W., Cibas, E.S., Chudova, D., Diggans, J., et al., 2012. Preoperative diagnosis of benign thyroid nodules with indeterminate cytology. N. Engl. J. Med. 367, 705–715.

Babrak, L.M., Menetski, J., Rebhan, M., Nisato, G., Zinggeler, M., Brasier, N., et al., 2019. Traditional and digital biomarkers: two worlds apart? Digit. Biomark. 3 (2), 92–102.

Bartolazzi, A., Orlandi, F., Saggiorato, E., Volante, M., Arecco, F., Rossetto, R., et al., 2008. Galectin-3-expression analysis in the surgical selection of follicular thyroid nodules with indeterminate fine-needle aspiration cytology: a prospective multicentre study. Lancet Oncol. 9, 543–549.

Biomarkers Definitions Working Group, 2001. Biomarkers and surrogate endpoints: preferred definitions and conceptual framework. Clin. Pharmacol. Ther. 69 (3), 89–95. as cited in Siderowf A, Aarsland D, Mollenhauer B, Goldman JG, Ravina B (April 2018). "Biomarkers for cognitive impairment in Lewy body disorders: Status and relevance for clinical trials". Movement Disorders (Review). 33 (4): 528–536.

Bondeson, L., et al., 1993. Histopathological variables and DNA cytometry in parathyroid carcinoma. Am. J. Surg. Pathol. 17 (8), 820–829.

Corenblum, B., Boyd, J., 2017. Endocrinology and disorders of the reproductive system. In: Kline, G., Sadrzadeh, H. (Eds.), Endocrine Biomarkers: Clinical Aspects and Laboratory Determination. Elsevier, Canada, pp. 351–397.

Corenblum, B., Flynn, E., 2017. Pituitary disorders. In: Kline, G., Sadrzadeh, H. (Eds.), Endocrine Bio-markers: Clinical Aspects and Laboratory Determination. Elsevier, Canada, pp. 301–349.

Crippa, S., Mazzucchelli, L., Cibas, E.S., Ali, S.Z., 2010. The Bethesda system for reporting thyroid fine-needle aspiration specimens. Am. J. Clin. Pathol. 134, 343–344.

Fawcett, D.W., Raviola, E., 1994. The adrenal glands. In: Fawcett, D.W. (Ed.), Bloom and Fawcett: A Textbook of Histology, 12th ed. Chapman & Hall, New York, p. 503.

Frunzac, R.W., Grant, C.S., 2016. Pheochromocytoma. In: Clarke, O.H., et al. (Eds.), Textbook of Endo-crine Surgery, third ed. Jaypee, USA, pp. 1047–1067.

George, N., Sabaretnam, M., Agarwal, A., 2016. Molecular markers in thyroid cancer. In: Puneet (Ed.), Roshan Lall Gupta's Recent Advances in Surgery: Edition 1. vol. 14. Jaypee, India, pp. 1–14.

Hirsch, M.S., Watkins, J., 2020. A comprehensive review of biomarker use in the gynecologic tract includ-ing differential diagnoses and diagnostic pitfalls. Adv. Anat. Pathol. 27 (3), 164–192.

Jin, X.L., Moley, J.F., 2016. Medullary thyroid cancer. In: Clarke, O.H., et al. (Eds.), Textbook of Endo-crine Surgery, third ed. Jaypee, USA, pp. 193–200.

Kline, G., Chin, A.C., 2017. Adrenal disorders. In: Kline, G., Sadrzadeh, H. (Eds.), Endocrine Biomarkers: Clinical Aspects and Laboratory Determination. Elsevier, Canada, pp. 181–249.

Kline, G., Sadrzadeh, H., 2017. Thyroid disorders. In: Kline, G., Sadrzadeh, H. (Eds.), Endocrine Bio-markers: Clinical Aspects and Laboratory Determination. Elsevier, Canada, pp. 41–93.

Kline, G., Orton, D., Sadrzadeh, H., 2017. Bone metabolism. In: Kline, G., Sadrzadeh, H. (Eds.), Endocrine Biomarkers: Clinical Aspects and Laboratory Determination. Elsevier, Canada, pp. 157–180.

Luo, Y., Zhu, H., Tan, T., He, J., 2018. Current standards and recent advances in biomarkers of major endo-crine tumors. Front. Pharmacol. 9, 963.

Anon., January 2019. NCCN Guidelines: Neuroendocrine and Adrenal Tumors. Version 4.2018.

Anon., Dec 2018. NCCN Guidelines: Thyroid Carcinoma. Version3.2018.

Nikiforov, Y.E., Ohori, N.P., Hodak, S.P., Carty, S.E., LeBeau, S.O., Ferris, R.L., et al., 2011. Impact of mutational testing on the diagnosis and management, of patients with cytologically indeterminate thy-roid nodules: a prospective analysis of 1056 FNA samples. J. Clin. Endocrinol. Metab. 96, 3390–3397.

Proye, C.A.G., Armstrong, J.D., Pattou, F.N., 2016. Adrenocortical carcinoma: nonfunctioning and func-tioning. In: Clarke, O.H., et al. (Eds.), Textbook of Endocrine Surgery, third ed. Jaypee, USA, pp. 1025–1032.

Ranvier, G.G.F., Chau, A.H., 2016. Molecular tests for parathyroid carcinomas. In: Clarke, O.H., et al. (Eds.), Textbook of Endocrine Surgery, third ed. Jaypee, USA, pp. 939–953.

Rorstad, O.P., 2017. Neuroendocrine tumours. In: Kline, G., Sadrzadeh, H. (Eds.), Endocrine Biomarkers: Clinical Aspects and Laboratory Determination. Elsevier, Canada, pp. 399–437.

Schantz, A., Castleman, B., 1973. Parathyroid carcinoma. A study of 70 cases. Cancer 31 (3), 600–605.

Symonds, C., Buse, J., 2017. Disorders related to calcium metabolism. In: Kline, G., Sadrzadeh, H. (Eds.), Endocrine Biomarkers: Clinical Aspects and Laboratory Determination. Elsevier, Canada, pp. 95–155.

Venos, E., Koning, L., 2017. Endocrine markers of diabetes and cardiovascular disease risk. In: Kline, G., Sadrzadeh, H. (Eds.), Endocrine Biomarkers: Clinical Aspects and Laboratory Determination. Elsevier, Canada, pp. 251–299.

Weiss, L.M., 1995. Comparative histological study of 43 metastasizing and nonmetastasizing adrenocortical tumors. Am. J. Surg. Pathol. 8, 163.

White, R., Riall, T.S., 2016. Endocrine pancreas. In: Townsend, C.M., et al. (Eds.), Sabiston Testbook of Surgery: The Biological Basis of Modern Surgical Practice, first ed. Elsevier, South Asia, pp. 941–962.

CHAPTER SEVEN

Cancer immunotherapy-associated endocrine complications and treatment strategies

Koushik Sen[a], Madhuchhanda Adhikari[b], Chayan Biswas[b], Sukhendu Maity[b], Ankit Chatterjee[b], and Kousik Pramanick[b]

[a]P.G. Department of Zoology, Jhargram Raj College, Jhargram, West Bengal, India
[b]Integrative Biology Research Unit (IBRU), Department of Life Sciences, Presidency University, Kolkata, West Bengal, India

1. Introduction

The advent of immunotherapy uses the features of immune system as an armamentarium to facilitate the control or elimination of neoplastic cells which has revolutionized the field of cancer treatment (Martins et al., 2019). Novel therapeutic approaches that manipulate the immune system to treat cancer include the use of cytokines, innovative vaccines, monoclonal antibodies and drugs that target the immune cell signaling to modulate immune response against tumor cells (Iglesias, 2018). Among these, immune checkpoint inhibitors (ICIs) are immunomodulatory monoclonal antibody molecules (mAbs) that accelerate host antitumor immunity and have demonstrated efficacy in eliminating multiple tumor malignancies. ICIs target certain immune checkpoints through controlling the T-cell interaction with antigen-presenting cells (APCs) and leads to the T-cell activation and antitumor activity (Chang et al., 2019). ICIs exerts its effect through acting on the receptor—T lymphocyte-associated antigen-4 (CTLA4), programmed cell death protein-1 (PD1), and programmed death ligand 1 and 2 (PD-L1 and PD-L2), resulting the upregulation of the immune response to malignant cells, restricting the usual inhibitory pathways of T-cell regulation (Castinetti and Borson-Chazot, 2018). Since its initial approval for the cancer treatment by US Drug Administration (FDA) in 2011, ICIs become an integral part of several cancer therapeutic regimens. Currently, seven ICIs, targeting CTLA-4, PD1, and PD-L1 are the only inhibitory molecules approved for cancer treatment (Chang et al., 2019). Although scientists are trying to develop newer therapies by targeting some other molecules such as lymphocyte activation gene (LAG)-3, T cell immunoglobulin and mucin-domain containing (TIM)-3, and T cell immunoreceptor with immunoglobulin and ITIM domains (TIGIT) (Chen and Mellman, 2017).

Immune checkpoints are important to maintain immunological self-tolerance and preventing autoimmune disorders. Initiation of immunotherapy with ICIs greatly improves the survival rates in patients with several forms of cancer such as melanoma, lung cancer, renal cell carcinoma, squamous cell carcinoma of the head and neck, urothelial carcinoma, advanced gastric cancer but alteration of immune signaling trigger several types of immune-related adverse events (irAEs) ranging from mild biochemical abnormalities to life-threatening events. The degree of irAEs varies in terms of tissue damage, severity and time of irAE appearance relative to the cancer treatment. Most irAE induced immune toxicity affect multiple organs including the skin, gastrointestinal system, lungs, endocrine organs; renal system, cardiovascular system, ocular system, neural system may rarely be affected (Brahmer et al., 2018; Haanen et al., 2017).

Among these, one of the most common irAE associated with ICI therapy are endocrinopathies including hypophysitis, thyroiditis, diabetes mellitus (DM) and primary adrenal insufficiency (PAI). The association of ICIs with hypoparathyroidism has also been reported (Chang et al., 2019; Ntali et al., 2017; Okura et al., 2020). Specific endocrinopathies appear due to clinical application of specific ICIs, while combination of such therapies seems to elevate the risk of such endocrine complications. The appearance of these endocrine associated adverse events generally ranges from weeks to months after starting the initial dose of immunotherapy. Although most of the irAEs are manageable and curable with the prompt cessation of ICI agents and with use of corticosteroid or the immunosuppressive medications, endocrinopathies commonly persist and require continuous and life-long treatment (Barroso-Sousa et al., 2018; Okura et al., 2020). Both CTLA-4 and PD1 inhibitors promote thyroiditis, hypophysitis, adrenal insufficiency, and diabetes mellitus. Why endocrine tissue is particularly vulnerable to Immunotherapeutic agents is still remain undefined, several hypotheses have been proposed including that the CTLA-4 expression in pituitary tissue and the role of PD1/PD-L1 in immune tolerance disruption in the pathogenesis of endocrinopathy. Furthermore, endocrine cells are nonregenerative and very low volume, so immune toxicity has greatly affected the essential hormone secretion. Society for Endocrinology, UK, provides a practical guideline but this is only useful when general physicians consider the differential diagnosis process. Awareness should be raised to warn physicians regarding such effects of ICIs in cancer patients in order to avoid preventable morbidity and mortality (Hattersley et al., 2021).

2. Immune checkpoints and its function

Immune checkpoints are receptor molecules residing on the surface of T-lymphocyte that binds their ligand and play crucial role in maintaining immune homeostasis and self-tolerance by modulating the time period and amplitude of immune response (Chang et al., 2019). Immune checkpoints may enhance or attenuate T-cell activity; such as CD28, ICOS, CD137, OX40, and CD27 send stimulatory signals to enhance T-cell activity (Pardoll, 2012), whereas CTLA-4 and PD1 are the main two inhibitory control points that reduce the T-cell response (Ott et al., 2013).

2.1 CTLA-4

CTLA-4 is a glycoprotein molecule expressed on the surface of both activated CD 4+ and CD 8+ cells. CTLA-4 is CD28 homolog that binds to B7 ligands on APC with much higher affinity and inhibits T-lymphocyte activation. Instead of CD28, Binding of CTLA-4 results in inhibition of IL-2 production, IL-2 receptor expression, and cell cycle progression of activated T-cells and leads to inhibition of T-cell activation (Walunas et al., 1996). CTLA-4 also blockade prevents the induction of energy (Perez et al., 1997). Regulatory T cells (Tregs) that govern the effectors T cell function, constitutively express CTLA-4 and seems to be crucial for their inhibitory effect. The mechanism behind the inhibitory role of CTLA-4 is yet to be fully known. Both intrinsic and extrinsic pathways have been proposed. In intrinsic fashion, CTLA-4 inhibit conventional T-cell activation through ligand dependent or independent fashion by competing with CD28 for B7 ligand binding, increasing adhesion or impeding stop signals. In extrinsic pathway, CTLA-4 on a T-cell imped the activation of CTLA-4 deficient cell. In addition to that, CTLA-4 promotes signal reversal its CD80 and CD86 on APCs. The reversal of signal activates tryptophan degrading enzyme indoleamine-2,3-dioxygenase (IDO) in APCs leads to the production of regulatory cytokines and promote the inhibition of APCs or T cells. Soluble form of CTLA-4 can bind with CD80 and CD86, limiting ligand availability to CD28. CTLA-4 can also occupy CD80 and CD86 from APC and inactivated them by the process of endocytosis, thereby lowering their concentration for CD28 binding.

2.2 PD1

In 1992, PD1 was discovered in by Dr. Honjo and his team as a gene that encodes a protein belonging to the immunoglobulin superfamily (Ishida et al., 1992). The PD1 glycoprotein resembles CD28 and is a cell surface receptor (Francisco et al., 2010; Parry et al., 2005). Normally basal level of PD1 expression is observed on B cells but not in naïve T-cells; the PD1 expression is increased after upon T-cell or B-cell activation. Apart from that PD1 also expressed on NKT cells, Tregs and myeloid dendritic cells. PD1 has specific ligands, viz., PD-L1 and PD-L2. PD-L2 mainly expressed on macrophages and dendritic cells (Francisco et al., 2009; Latchman et al., 2001), whereas PD-L1 expression is almost universal and found in both immune and nonimmune cells, such as hepatocytes, pancreatic islet cells, vascular endothelial cells, fibroblastic reticular cells, epithelial cells, thyroid cells, muscle cells, and neurons (Latchman et al., 2001; Keir et al., 2008; Francisco et al., 2010). Interestingly many types of tumor cells can synthesize and express elevated level of PD-L1 which enables them to inhibit T cell activity and escape from the host immune response.

After binding with their ligands PD1 inhibit cell division, cytokine production, and cytotoxic ability of effectors T cells (Carreno et al., 2000). PD1 also reduces the threshold for apoptosis and stimulates energy through blunted T cell receptor signaling pathway results in T cell depletion (Iwai et al., 2002). Moreover, PD1 upon ligand binding induces intracellular biochemical alteration that promotes reduction in glucose uptake and gluconeogenesis of T-cells. This phenomenon induces T-cell exhaustion and interruption of co-stimulatory pathways. So, various solid tumor cells such as renal cell carcinoma, thymoma, ovarian cancer cells and colorectal cancer cells express PD-L1 as a shield to generate immunosuppressive microenvironment for avoiding T-cell attack (Harding et al., 1992; Bynoe et al., 2005).

3. Immune checkpoint inhibitors

Immune checkpoint inhibitors are monoclonal IgG antibodies that bind to immune checkpoint proteins (CTLA-4, PD1) to overcome cancer induced T-cell inhibition. In 2011, US FDA first approved Ipilimumab (CTLA-4 antibodies) for the treatment of advanced melanoma (Hodi et al., 2010). Since then, a number of ICIs have been approved for the treatment of several types of cancer. The anti–CTLA-4 (ipilimumab and tremelimumab), anti-PD1 (pembrolizumab, nivolumab, and pidilizumab), and anti-PD-L1 (atezolizumab, durvalumab, and avelumab) antibodies are in focus of current clinical use. These drugs are now used for the treatment of 17 different cancer types including melanoma, lung carcinoma, and cancer of head, neck, upper aerodigestive tract and many more. Response rates varies from 15% to 25% (most solid tumors including lung carcinoma), 40%–60% (Mismatch repair defect cancer, Skin cancer including Melanoma) to 90% (Hodgkin's lymphoma) (Yarchoan et al., 2017). In most cases, responses are long-lasting and, in a few cases, it may cure some patients, though long-term follow up and more data is required before making a conclusive comment, as use of these drugs has just become popular in last 5–7 years.

Ipilimumab, a recombinant human monoclonal (IgG-1κ) antibody, was the first artificially designed inhibitor of immune checkpoints and reported to have efficacy against advanced melanoma. In 2011, it was approved by the FDA and the European Medicines Agency (EMA) for the treatment of melanoma (Hodi et al., 2010; Maio et al., 2015). Moreover, ipilimumab used as an adjuvant, for treating advanced stage of melanoma and reported to associate with significantly higher rates of relapse-free survival (Eggermont et al., 2016). Its efficacy has also been tested and found positive against renal cell carcinoma (Atkins et al., 2017). Tremelimumab, anti-CTLA-4 monoclonal antibody (IgG2b) that although has not reported to have any positive effect on survival rate on chemotherapy in patients with advanced melanoma (Ribas et al., 2013), now being tasted against other tumors like malignant mesothelioma and renal cell carcinoma (Calabrò et al., 2015; Comin-Anduix et al., 2016).

The main anti-PD1 antibodies, pembrolizumab and nivolumab, are humanized monoclonal antibodies that produced complete or partial responses in nonsmall-cell lung cancer (NSCLC), renal–cell carcinoma and melanoma, in clinical trials; these have been approved in 2014 by the FDA and in 2015 by the EMA to fight against metastatic melanoma. In addition to that, pembrolizumab and nivolumab have shown their efficacy in other tumors including non-small cell lung cancer and recurrent head and neck squamous cell carcinoma respectively (Reck et al., 2013; Ferris et al., 2016). Pidilizumab, another anti-PD1 antibody, has shown assuring efficacy in patients with diffuse large B-cell lymphoma after hematopoietic stem cell transplantation (Armand et al., 2013). ICI-based combined therapy has also shown promising effect. The combined therapy using ipilimumab and nivolumab reported to have remarkable synergistic effect with increased response rate in melanoma, renal cell carcinoma, mismatch repair-defect colon cancer compared to monotherapy (Larkin et al., 2019; Motzer et al., 2018; Hellmann et al., 2019). Anti-PD1 or anti-PD-L1 drugs along with chemotherapy reported to have higher response rate and survival in lung cancer, head and neck squamous cell cancer and in triple negative breast cancer (Horn et al., 2018; Schmid et al., 2020; Burtness et al., 2019). Other combined therapeutic strategies such as radiotherapy with ICIs, angiogenic agents with ICIs and ICIs along with oncolytic viruses are used to treat several types of solid and hematologic tumors (Hwang et al., 2018; Gao et al., 2019). In this context, it is notable that ICI based combined therapy has greater efficacy but it comes at the cost of increased incidence of severe therapeutic toxicities. Some of the FDA approved ICIs and their role in the type of cancer treatment along with the type of endocrine complications associated with them is given here. (Table 1).

4. Functional mechanism and efficacy of immune checkpoint inhibitors

Immune checkpoints act to limit the immune response and allow self-tolerance by turning off the cytotoxic T-cell. Through expressing specific surface ligands, cancer cells interact with receptors on cytotoxic T-cells and exploit these checkpoints to evade host immune response. ICIs interfere between T-cell and cancer cell interaction and allow T-cells to remain activated against the cancer cells. As mentioned earlier in this chapter, current ICIs target CTLA-4, PD1 and PD-L1 because these are over expressed in certain tumor microenvironments.

How CTLA-4 blockade initiate antitumor effect is still remain undefined. It is thought that CTLA-4 blockade may enhance differentiation and expansion of naive T cells into tumor antigen–specific T cells from direct sequestration of CD80 and CD86 during effector T cell activation (Chen et al., 2009; Fehlings et al., 2017;

Table 1 Immune checkpoint inhibitors and the type of cancer treated with its associated endocrine toxicities and occurrence rates.

Target immune checkpoints	Immune checkpoint inhibitors/drugs	ICI mAbs Types	Cancer treated	Endocrinopathy	Rate of irAE
(1) Anti-CTLA-4	Ipilimumab	IgG-1κ	Advanced melanoma, Renal cell carcinoma, colorectal carcinoma	Hypophysitis PAI Thyroiditis	11% (0.3–1.5)% (6–16)%
	Tremelimumab	IgG-2b	Malignant mesothelioma, Renal cell carcinoma	Hypophysitis Thyroiditis PAI	(1–2)% (2–5)% (0.3–1.5)%
(2) Anti-PD1	Nivolumab	IgG-4A	Stage III / IV Melanoma, Ovarian carcinoma, Urothelial carcinoma	Hypophysitis Thyroiditis	< 1% (20–40)%
	Pembrolizumab	IgG-4Aκ	NSC lung carcinoma, Metastatic melanoma	Hypophysitis Thyroiditis PAI	(< 1–1.5)% (20–40)% (1–2)%
(3) Anti-PD-L1	Atezolizumab	IgG1	Breast cancer, Squamous cell carcinoma, NSC lung carcinoma	PAI Other endocrinopathies	
	Avelumab	IgG1	Merkel carcinoma, Renal carcinoma	Diabetes mellitus PAI	1% 1%
	Durvalumab	IgG-1κ	Lung carcinoma	Diabetes mellitus PAI Thyroiditis	1% 1%
(4) Anti-CTLA-4/PD1 (combination therapy)	Nivolumab + Ipilimumab	IgG-4A-IgG-1κ combination	Stage III / IV Melanoma, NSC lung carcinoma	Hypophysitis PAI Parathyroiditis	6% (5–8)% 20%

Liakou et al., 2008; Tang et al., 2013) and exhaustion of inhibitory Treg cells mediated via antibody-dependent cellular cytotoxicity (ADCC) due to continuous expression of CTLA-4 on Tregs (Vargas et al., 2018; Romano et al., 2015). Impediment of PD1 or PDL-1 using ICIs, revive fatigued cytotoxic T-cells that have been continuously stimulated by antigens present on tumor cells. ICIs targeting PD1 or PDL-1 acts through inhibiting T cell receptor (TCR) thereby amplifying the function of cytotoxic T cells (Huang et al., 2017). Moreover, blockade of PD1 or PD-L1 may partly reverse the impaired metabolic activity of cytotoxic T cells, which contribute to exhaustion revival (Gubin et al., 2014; Patsoukis et al., 2015).

5. Cancer immunotherapy with ICIs and associated endocrinopathies

Inhibition of immune checkpoint proteins by ICIs for cancer immunotherapy interferes in the maintenance of self-tolerance and prevention of autoimmune diseases (Haanen et al.,2017; Brahmeret al., 2018). Thus the use of ICIs often induces adverse events of immune toxicities, of which the endocrine complications or endocrinopathies are most common adverse outcome of immunotherapy. Hypopituitarism, adrenocortical dysfunction, thyroid dysfunction, and type 1 diabetes mellitus are common endocrinopathies triggered by ICI treatment. Moreover, ICI therapy may rarely trigger hypoparathyroidism. Onset of endocrine dysfunction maybe present as a clinical biomarker for ICI therapy response (Chang et al., 2019; Okura et al., 2020). Some endocrine complications associated with different types of ICI monotherapy as well as combination therapy, their prevalence rate and associated clinical complications are given below (Table 2).

Table 2 The prevalence rate of different ICIs on endocrine complications and associated pathological changes.

Endocrine complications	Anti-CTLA-4	Anti-PD1/ PD-L1	Anti-CTLA-4/pd-1 (combination therapy)	Pathophysiology
Hypophysitis	(0.4–17)%	(0.5–5)%	(8.5–9)%	Enlargement and inflammation of pituitary cells
Thyroiditis	(4.3–11)%	(5–10) %	(17–22)%	Thyrotoxicosis and thyroid hormonal imbalance
Type-1 diabetes mellitus	0%	1%	NA	Destruction of pancreatic β-cells, Insulin deficiency
Primary adrenal insufficiency (PAI)	1%	<2%	(5–7)%	Destruction and damage of adrenal cortex cells, low aldosterone and elevated renin levels

5.1 Hypophysitis

Hypophysitis refers to inflammation of the pituitary gland (Caturegli et al., 2005; Faje, 2016a). It has been reported that patients receiving anti–CTLA-4-based therapy, either with ipilimumab or more commonly found in Anti-CTLA4-PD1 combination therapy, hypophysitis is more common. The occurrence of hypophysitis ranges from 0.4% to 17%. Hypophysitis is rarely found in patients with anti-PD1 or anti-PD-L1 monotherapy, occurring in 0.5%–1% patients. The frequency of ICI-induced hypophysitis is higher in men, though in generally hypophysitis mainly affects women in higher rates (Torino et al., 2012). The onset of ICI induced hypophysitis typically occur approximately within 9 weeks, with a range of 5–36 weeks after the initiation of ICI therapy (Gao et al., 2015; Min et al., 2015) but it has been reported as late as 19 months later after first cycle with ipilimumab (Ryder et al., 2014). Hypophysitis can be asymptomatic or appear with precise symptoms. The autoimmune inflammation of the hypophysitis alters the pituitary gland structure and induce enlargement of pituitary, leading to structural changes and initiation of headache and fatigue, the most common primary symptoms often reported (Dillard et al., 2010; Marlier et al., 2014). Along with these, some other symptoms are confusion, dizziness, weakness, hallucinations, nausea, weight loss, memory loss, labile mood, anorexia, decreased libido and hyponatremia; visual disturbances are rare, may be found after impingement of the optic chiasm (Haanen et al., 2017; Cukier et al., 2017). The patients suffering from ICI induced hypophysitis represent with numerous symptoms, due to deficiency in one or more pituitary hormones, can be diagnosed by clinical symptoms or blood test. Among them, the most frequently observed deficiencies are central hypothyroidism, central adrenal insufficiency, hypogonadotropic, and hypogonadism. Approximately 80% of patients with ICI associated hypophysitis represent one or more of the above three deficiencies (Barroso-Sousa et al., 2018; Chang et al., 2019). Low or elevated level of prolactin (Cukier et al., 2017), low levels of insulin–like growth factor 1 (IGF1) has also been reported (Byun et al., 2017); diabetes insipidus is extremely rare (Cukier et al., 2017). Male gender and increasing age are considered as risk factors for ICI induced hypophysitis (Faje, 2016b).

A low or subnormal level of free thyroxine (FT4) along with low or normal level of TSH is indicative of central hypothyroidism (Fleseriu et al., 2016). This condition of thyroid axis is transient and, in most cases, recovers spontaneously. Central adrenal insufficiency is often reported in ICI induced hypophysitis and may be representing with hypotension and hyponatremia. A low morning serum cortisol level <250 nmol/L or random cortisol <150 nmol/L is indicative of adrenal insufficiency (Ferrari et al., 2019). Adrenal crisis may be fatal without early detection and initiation of treatment with corticosteroid. Hyponatremia is mediated by the elevated secretion of antidiuretic hormone (ADH), resulting in water retention and a decrease in plasma sodium concentration. The elevation in ADH secretion is caused due to increased hypothalamic secretion of corticotropin releasing hormone (CRH) which stimulates the pituitary cells to secrete ADH (Chang et al., 2019). The clinical manifestations of hypogonadotropic hypogonadism are low or inappropriately normal FSH and LH along with low morning testosterone levels in men (Bhasin et al., 2018) and low estradiol levels in premenopausal women; The level of FSH and LH are generally elevated in postmenopausal women, inappropriately low FSH and LH indicates hypogonadotropic hypogonadism in them (Chang et al., 2019).

It is sometimes difficult to differentiate from functional hypogonadism due to advanced underlying malignant disease or ongoing therapy. Hypogonadotropic hypogonadism is temporary and often recovers spontaneously. The level of IGF1 levels may be low or within reference range. Prolactin level is often below the normal reference range and Hyperprolactinemia is rarely found (Faje et al., 2014; Min et al., 2015; Albarel et al.,2015). Posterior pituitary (neurohypophysis) is rarely affected and diabetes insipidus (DI) has rarely been reported (Dillard et al., 2010; Nallapaneni et al., 2014; Zhao et al., 2018; Gunawan et al., 2018).

The proposed mechanism of hypophysitis associated to type II hypersensitivity reaction. Laboratory experiment with wild-type C57BL/6 mice, repeatedly injected with anti–CTLA-4 develop hypophysitis, manifested by lymphocytic infiltration into the pituitary tissues and circulating antipituitary autoantibodies specific to thyrotropin-secreting cells, gonadotropin-secreting cells, and corticotropin-secreting cells (Iwama et al., 2014). Interestingly, pituitary Glands cells of C57BL/6 mice expressed CTLA4 were targets for CTLA4 antibody binding, and lead to complement deposition. This finding may explain why only anti-CTLA-4 therapy, but rarely PD1–PD-L1 monotherapy, results in hypophysitis (Tahir et al., 2019) (Fig. 1).

The diagnosis of ICI induced hypophysitis involves appropriate biochemical analyses of hypothalamic–hypophysis axis and brain imaging with magnetic resonance imaging (MRI). Test to measure the circulating levels of pituitary hormones should be performed. MRI before and after intravenous infusion of paramagnetic contrast medium is the best technique to assess the pituitary gland in a patient, suspected to develop ICI induced hypophysitis. MRI is also suitable for confirming the diagnosis and allows to identify new brain metastases, cerebrovascular events, or leptomeningeal disease. Moreover, it is pertinent to differentiate central pituitary dysfunction from other immune endocrinopathies, such as pituitary macro-adenomas, autoimmune thyroiditis, etc. (Castillero et al., 2019).

5.2 Thyroiditis

Thyroid gland dysfunction is one of the most common adverse events reported after treatment with ICIs; though acute thyroid dysfunction is rare. Immunotherapy induced

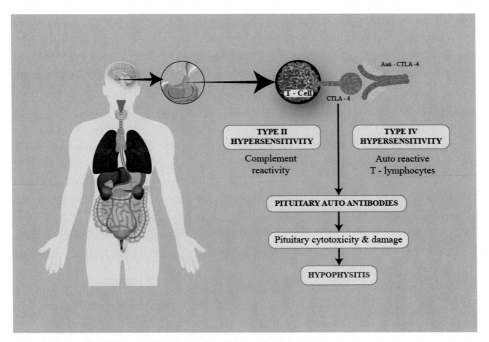

Fig. 1 Mechanism of ICI (anti-CTLA4) mediated hypophysitis.

thyroid dysfunction can be evident as hyperthyroidism or thyrotoxicosis, either subclinically or overt. However, the most frequent pathophysiological outcome perhaps to be thyroiditis (Orlov et al., 2015; de Filette et al., 2016; Morganstein et al., 2017; Lee et al., 2017; Osorio et al., 2017; O'Malley et al., 2017; Yamazaki et al., 2017; Guaraldi et al., 2018). The incidence and prevalence of hypo or hyperthyroidism varies depending on the type of antibody used, the route of administration and therapeutic strategy (monotherapy or combination therapy), and the degree of thyroid dysfunction (Larkin et al., 2015; Morganstein et al., 2017). Nearly 10% patients suffer from thyroid dysfunction after treating with anti-PD1 or anti-PD-L1 agents and up to 15%–20% of those after receiving combined therapy with ipilimumab and nivolumab. Thyroid adverse events are less common in patients receiving anti-CTLA 4 monotherapy (Larkin et al., 2019; De Filette et al., 2019). A large number of patients receiving immunotherapy develop hypothyroidism, which is gradually preceded by destructive thyroiditis in 30%–40% of patients undergoing anti-PD1 or anti-PD-L1 therapy, and approximately 66% patients with combination therapy-induced hypothyroidism. Graves' disease is rare in patient under ICI treatment (Brancatella et al., 2019). Thyroid dysfunction commonly arises within a few weeks after initiating immunotherapy. However, it can also be occur as early as within 7 days, just after a single dose of ICI, or as late as 3 years after initiating ICI therapy (Ryder et al., 2014; Lee et al., 2017).

Clinical symptoms of ICI induced hypothyroidism is similar to classical hypothyroid condition and can be manifested with fatigue, cold intolerance, depressed mood, weakness, mild weight gain and constipation, as well as altered cognitive ability in severe hypothyroidism, although many patients have few or no symptoms. On the other hand, hyperthyroidism leading to the thyrotoxicosis may be asymptomatic but can be present with typical symptom such as heat intolerance, diarrhea, tremor, diaphoresis, heat intolerance, anxiety, atrial fibrillation (Yu et al., 2015; Yonezaki et al., 2018; Chang et al., 2019). Thyroid storm as a consequence of thyrotoxicosis is rare in patient treated with ICIs (Yu et al., 2015; McMillen et al., 2016). Elevated level of thyroid peroxidase auto antibodies (anti-TPO) and thyroglobulin antibodies (anti-Tg) has been detected in some patients those develop thyroid dysfunction after receiving ICIs. Generally, the evidence reported so far in this field indicates that thyroid auto antibodies are not vital, but they represent a risk factor. Stimulating auto antibodies for the TSH receptors were negative in the majority of patients (Orlov et al., 2015; de Filette et al., 2016; Morganstein et al., 2017; Lee et al., 2017; Osorio et al., 2017; O'Malley et al., 2017; Yamazaki et al., 2017; Guaraldi et al., 2018) (Fig. 2).

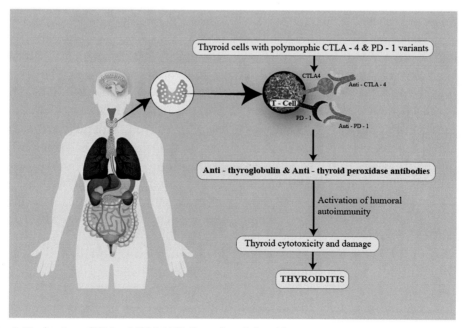

Fig. 2 Mechanism of ICI (anti-CTLA4/PD-1) mediated thyroiditis.

In patients treated with ICIs, thyroid function test screening through measuring TSH and free T4 level should be done in every 8 weeks or more frequently. Many clinicians suggest these tests after every cycle of treatment with ICIs (Thompson et al., 2019). Patients having mild or no symptoms do not require separate treatment and can be managed by the oncologist and sometimes require a little gap between the cycles of their immunotherapy with blood tests to monitor thyroid function. Those with symptoms or severe abnormalities must be consulting with an endocrinologist for initiating the treatment. Sometimes in such cases, immunotherapy may need to be paused and resumed after normalization of the symptoms (Higham et al., 2018; Chang et al., 2019; Trinh et al., 2019a). Management of hypothyroidism should be involved thyroid hormone supplementation after adrenal insufficiency has been ruled out. Thyroiditis should be managed conservatively during the thyrotoxic phase. Other causes of thyrotoxicosis, including Graves' disease can be kept under control through routine laboratory tests, imaging and with proper medications after consulting with an endocrinologist. Patients having symptoms of thyrotoxicosis along with tachycardia and tremor should be kept under control through symptom-directed management with β blockers (Kennedy and Salama, 2020).

5.3 Diabetes mellitus

The onset of Diabetes Mellitus (DM) is rare but severe, potentially life-threatening endocrine complication associated with ICI therapy. ICI-associated Diabetes Mellitus (ICI-DM) is reported in less than 1% patients those receiving ICI therapy; more than 95% of total cases that have been observed so far mostly occur due to anti-PD1 or anti–PD-L1 therapy (Chang et al., 2019), either onset of type 1 DM or exacerbation of type 2 DM (De Filette et al., 2019; Quandt et al. 2020). The ICI-DM may develop just after a single or as many as after 17 doses and ranging from a 1 week to 12 months (Paschou et al., 2021). Destruction of the β-cells due to ICI therapy leads to the development of ICI-DM appears nearly similar to the permanent autoimmune process of Type 1 DM (Wright et al., 2021). The ICI induced DM characterized by hyperglycemia, polyuria, polydipsia, weight loss, insulin deficiency, and high risk of diabetic ketoacidosis (DKA). The clinical symptoms of DKA include nausea, vomiting, abdominal pain, tachypnea or lethargy and coma (Barroso-Sousa et al., 2018; Chang et al., 2019; Okura et al., 2020). Patients with ICI associated DM often represents with slightly elevated level of glycated hemoglobin (HbA1c) with low or undetectable serum level of C peptide, indicating the rapid destruction of pancreatic β cells (De Filette et al., 2019; Quandt et al., 2020).

The exact mechanism of ICI induced β cell destruction is still unclear. T-lymphocyte activation due to PD-1 receptor blockade followed by the production of anti-GAD and anti-IA2 antibodies together with T-cell infiltration into the pancreatic islets contribute to the development of ICI-DM (Chae et al., 2017). Genetic factors may also contribute to the ICI-DM susceptibility. HLA haplotypes associated with classic T1DM are also over expressed among patients receiving ICI therapy; especially there is a strong relationship is found between ICI-DM and HLA-DR4 (Stamatouli et al., 2018) (Fig. 3).

Due to β cell destruction and rapid onset of insulin deficiency, continuous monitoring for early detection and rapid initiative to start treatment is important for controlling ICI-DM. Blood glucose monitoring after each therapeutic cycle is an important strategy for early detection of ICI-DM (Brahmer et al., 2018). Patients developed signs and symptoms of hyperglycemia, blood glucose, C-peptide, HbA1c, electrolytes, urine or serum ketones, anion gap, and islet autoantibodies (anti–GAD65, antiislet cell, antiinsulin, anti–IA2, anti–ZnT8) should be measured (Clotman et al., 2018; Quandt et al., 2021). These values can assist to diagnose DKA and help to distinguish the etiology of hyperglycemia due to other causes such as, T2DM, stress hyperglycemia or steroid-induced hyperglycemia. Patients with DKA, primarily treated according to standard therapy for DKA, whereas, patients with new onset hyperglycemia without DKA, insulin therapy should be started.

Unlike other ICI induced endocrinopathies, glucocorticoids are not recommended to treat ICI-DM. Like classic DM, patients with ICI-DM also require lifelong insulin

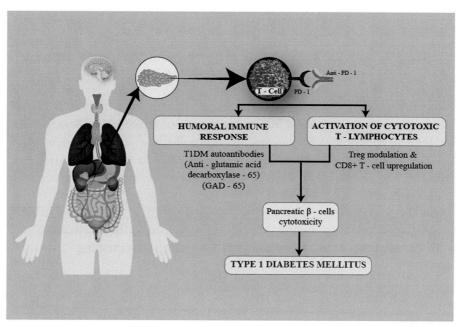

Fig. 3 Mechanism of ICI (anti-PD-1) mediated type 1 diabetes mellitus.

replacement therapy but management of hyperglycemia is more challenging in ICI-DM (Hansen et al., 2016; Trinh et al., 2019b).

5.4 Primary adrenal insufficiency (PAI)

Primary adrenal insufficiency(PAI) after immunotherapy for cancer management is less common. PAI has been reported in 1% of patients treated with anti–CTLA-4 monotherapy, and 5%–7% cases in anti-TLA-4–PD1 combination therapy (Barroso-Sousa et al., 2018). The symptoms are often nonspecific, such as anorexia, fatigue, dizziness, fever, nausea, malaise, abdominal pain and altered mental status (Quandt et al., 2021). Adrenal insufficiency is a common complication in cancer patients, and efforts must be made for early-stage detection. Decreased morning cortisol levels along with elevated ACTH levels in laboratory assessment indicate PAI and also differentiate PAI from secondary adrenal insufficiency due to hypophysitis. Moreover, ICI induced adrenal crisis is often represented with low aldosterone and elevated renin levels, as all zones of the adrenal cortex are affected (Bornstein et al., 2016).

If mineralocorticoid producing cells are affected, metabolic acidosis and hyperkalemia might also be present, which are attributed to the life-threatening nature of both primary and secondary adrenal insufficiency; hypoglycemia and hypocalcaemia can rarely be seen (Bornstein et al., 2016). In few patients, high levels of adrenal autoantibodies have also been reported (Paepegaey et al., 2017) (Fig. 4).

Diagnosis can be done from a low morning cortisol with elevated morning ACTH along with poor response to synthetic ACTH. Computer-assisted tomography Scan (CT scan) of the adrenal glands may demonstrate atrophy or adrenalitis and facilitate exclusion of other causes (Higham et al., 2018; Brahmer et al., 2018).

Morbidity and mortality rates appear to be high in patients having ICI induced PAI. PAI management requires prompt initiation of hormone replacement therapy with glucocorticoids (prednisone or hydrocortisone) and mineralocorticoids (fludrocortisone). The ICI therapy should be withheld in severe condition and similar to ICI induced hypophysitis, the immunotherapy can be resumed following stabilization of acute symptoms (Brahmer et al., 2018).

6. Screening, management and treatment strategies

Patients going to undertake cancer immunotherapy are at high risk of developing endocrine disorders and should be kept in appropriate considerations and utmost care. The endocrine complications associated with cancer immunotherapy are severe as well as nonspecific; hence attention must be paid on the screening strategies for the diagnosis and proper management of such endocrine complications. American Society of Microbiology, Society of Endocrinology and European Society of Medical Oncology have set

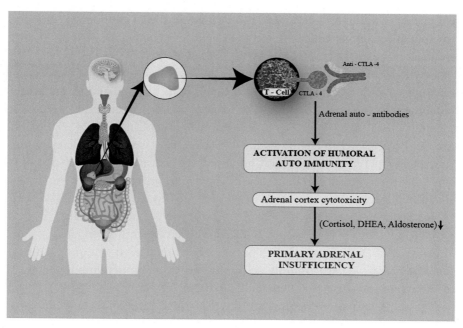

Fig. 4 Mechanism of ICI (anti-CTLA4) mediated primary adrenal insufficiency.

up several guidelines for the proper management of such cancer immunotherapy associated endocrine complications (Brahmer et al., 2018; Haanen et al., 2017).

Prior of initiating the cancer immunotherapeutic regimen, it is always essential and advisable to perform a hormonal evaluation of thyroid (TSH and free T4 serum) levels and estimation of blood glucose level at the baseline and also after the immunotherapy regimen (Higham et al., 2018). Patients with advanced melanoma enduring treatment with ipilimumab must be considered for periodic evaluation and proper monitoring of ACTH level and serum cortisol level. If observed for unusual plasma ACTH level and serum cortisol level, major steps must be taken for further screening and clinical evaluation of PAI. Common physiological symptoms of patients undertaking cancer immunotherapy such as headache, fatigue and vision aberrations should not be neglected and further considered for diagnosis of hypophysitis. If suspected for hypophysitis, anterior pituitary dysfunctioning must be tested by hormonal monitoring. After the hormonal analysis is found to be compatible with any of the endocrine complications, complete central hormone axis monitoring along with MRI-based pituitary imaging must be done. Pre and post hormonal analysis of TSH and free T4 levels must be done following pembrolizumab and nivolumab administration. In the extent of thyroid hormone level analysis, there lies an extra role on the period measurement of thyroperoxidase (TPO) level. Patients positive for TPO antibodies prior to advent of cancer immunotherapy are at a higher risk of developing thyroiditis. Also the possibility of developing

Type-1 diabetes mellitus in patients undergoing nivolumab and ipilimumab combination therapy should be considered strictly and must be recommended for periodic evaluation of glycaemia.

Patients undergoing cancer immunotherapy, if diagnosed with primary level of endocrine complications must readily be started with hormone therapy; such as, initial cases of thyroiditis must sooner be started with levothyroxine and there is no need for terminating immunotherapeutic regimen for carcinoma treatment (Topalian et al., 2012). Hyperthyroidism can be managed efficiently with β-blockade (propanolol) as well as thionanide (carbimazole) at the initial stages until suspected for Graves's disease. In case of PAI, use of glucocorticoid and mineralocorticoid can be relied upon and thereafter immunotherapeutic regimen can be resumed (Juszczak et al., 2012); as in hypophysitis where hormonal replacement therapy is helpful. Onset of type-1 diabetes mellitus by cancer immunotherapy must be immediately initiated with proper insulin therapy.

Along with this, multiple guidelines have been recommended with proper dosage of immunosuppressor and corticosteroid use for the management of immunotherapy associated endocrine complications (Petrelli et al., 2020).

For grade 3 and 4 endocrinopathies, ICI-based immunotherapeutic regimen must be permanently stopped and rapidly initiated with higher dosage of corticosteroid (mainly prednisone at 1–2 mg/kg. of body wt./day).

For grade 2 endocrinopathies, ICI-based immunotherapeutic regimen must be withheld and not resumed till toxicity resolves within a period of 1 or 2 weeks after corticosteroid (mainly prednisone at 0.5 mg/kg. of body wt./day) use.

For grade 1 endocrinopathies or less, corticosteroids can be administered for 1–2 months with periodic stoppage.

If patients are still reported with endocrine complications and its pathophysiological observations, infliximab (at the dosage of 5 mg. /kg. of body wt.) can be administered intravenously rather than further continuing with administration of higher doses of corticosteroids.

7. Conclusion and future directions

Along with chemotherapy and radiation therapy, cancer immunotherapy has revolutionized the treatment strategies for numerous melanomas and malignancies. FDA-approved immune checkpoint inhibitors (ICIs) play vital roles in inhibiting the inhibitory molecules present over the cancer cells thereby allowing the T cells to propagate and initiate the innate immune system toward the cancer cells. However, the ICIs in turn are associated with several mild to severe irAEs, of which the most fatal ones are endocrine complications viz. hypophysitis, thyroiditis, Diabetes mellitus and PAI, which usually onset at 7–10 weeks usage of ipilimumab, nivolumab and other ICIs.

The risk factors and clinical complications associated with endocrinopathies are not fully understood, so its proper screening must be preceded with multidisciplinary approaches, imaging and hormone replacement based therapy. It is utmost necessary to do more advanced research in the field of ICI associated endocrine complications to further understand its mechanism and standardize some advanced and essential clinical guidelines that can help in the decision making while using ICI, which in turn are associated with endocrine complications. Awareness must be spread among worldwide population about the multifaceted management strategies of these endocrine complications such as long term follow up during the therapeutic regimen. Recommendations must be provided for patient counseling regarding clinical signs, symptoms, treatment and management ways.

References

Albarel, F., Gaudy, C., Castinetti, F., Carré, T., Morange, I., Conte-Devolx, B., Grob, J.J., Brue, T., 2015. Long-term follow-up of ipilimumab-induced hypophysitis, a common adverse event of the anti-CTLA-4 antibody in melanoma. Eur. J. Endocrinol. 172 (2), 195–204.

Armand, P., Nagler, A., Weller, E.A., Devine, S.M., Avigan, D.E., Chen, Y.B., Kaminski, M.S., Holland, H.K., Winter, J.N., Mason, J.R., Fay, J.W., 2013. Disabling immune tolerance by programmed death-1 blockade with pidilizumab after autologous hematopoietic stem-cell transplantation for diffuse large B-cell lymphoma: results of an international phase II trial. J. Clin. Oncol. 31 (33), 4199.

Atkins, M.B., Clark, J.I., Quinn, D.I., 2017. Immune checkpoint inhibitors in advanced renal cell carcinoma: experience to date and future directions. Ann. Oncol. 28 (7), 1484–1494.

Barroso-Sousa, R., Barry, W.T., Garrido-Castro, A.C., Hodi, F.S., Min, L., Krop, I.E., Tolaney, S.M., 2018. Incidence of endocrine dysfunction following the use of different immune checkpoint inhibitor regimens: a systematic review and meta-analysis. JAMA Oncol. 4 (2), 173–182.

Bhasin, S., Brito, J.P., Cunningham, G.R., Hayes, F.J., Hodis, H.N., Matsumoto, A.M., Snyder, P.J., Swerdloff, R.S., Wu, F.C., Yialamas, M.A., 2018. Testosterone therapy in men with hypogonadism: an Endocrine Society clinical practice guideline. J. Clin. Endocrinol. Metabol. 103 (5), 1715–1744.

Bornstein, S.R., Allolio, B., Arlt, W., Barthel, A., Don-Wauchope, A., Hammer, G.D., Husebye, E.S., Merke, D.P., Murad, M.H., Stratakis, C.A., Torpy, D.J., 2016. Diagnosis and treatment of primary adrenal insufficiency: an endocrine society clinical practice guideline. J. Clin. Endocrinol. Metabol. 101 (2), 364–389.

Brahmer, J.R., Lacchetti, C., Schneider, B.J., Atkins, M.B., Brassil, K.J., Caterino, J.M., Chau, I., Ernstoff, M.S., Gardner, J.M., Ginex, P., Hallmeyer, S., 2018. Management of immune-related adverse events in patients treated with immune checkpoint inhibitor therapy: American Society of Clinical Oncology Clinical Practice Guideline. J. Clin. Oncol. Off. J. Am. Soc. Clin. Oncol. 36 (17), 1714.

Brancatella, A., Viola, N., Brogioni, S., Montanelli, L., Sardella, C., Vitti, P., Marcocci, C., Lupi, I., Latrofa, F., 2019. Graves' disease induced by immune checkpoint inhibitors: a case report and review of the literature. Eur. Thyroid J. 8 (4), 192–195.

Burtness, B., Harrington, K.J., Greil, R., Soulières, D., Tahara, M., de Castro Jr, G., Psyrri, A., Basté, N., Neupane, P., Bratland, Å., Fuereder, T., 2019. Pembrolizumab alone or with chemotherapy versus cetuximab with chemotherapy for recurrent or metastatic squamous cell carcinoma of the head and neck (KEYNOTE-048): a randomised, open-label, phase 3 study. Lancet 394 (10212), 1915–1928.

Bynoe, M.S., Viret, C., Flavell, R.A., Janeway Jr., C.A., 2005. T cells from epicutaneously immunized mice are prone to T cell receptor revision. Proc. Natl. Acad. Sci. 102 (8), 2898–2903.

Byun, D.J., Wolchok, J.D., Rosenberg, L.M., Girotra, M., 2017. Cancer immunotherapy—immune checkpoint blockade and associated endocrinopathies. Nat. Rev. Endocrinol. 13 (4), 195–207.

Calabrò, L., Morra, A., Fonsatti, E., Cutaia, O., Fazio, C., Annesi, D., Lenoci, M., Amato, G., Danielli, R., Altomonte, M., Giannarelli, D., 2015. Efficacy and safety of an intensified schedule of tremelimumab for chemotherapy-resistant malignant mesothelioma: an open-label, single-arm, phase 2 study. Lancet Respir. Med. 3 (4), 301–309.

Carreno, B.M., Bennett, F., Chau, T.A., Ling, V., Luxenberg, D., Jussif, J., Baroja, M.L., Madrenas, J., 2000. CTLA-4 (CD152) can inhibit T cell activation by two different mechanisms depending on its level of cell surface expression. J. Immunol. 165 (3), 1352–1356.

Castillero, F., Castillo-Fernández, O., Jiménez-Jiménez, G., Fallas-Ramírez, J., Peralta-Álvarez, M.P., Arrieta, O., 2019. Cancer immunotherapy-associated hypophysitis. Future Oncol. 15 (27), 3159–3169.

Castinetti, F., Borson-Chazot, F., 2018. Introduction to expert opinion on endocrine complications of new anticancer therapies. Ann. Endocrinol. 79 (5), 535–538. Elsevier Masson.

Caturegli, P., Newschaffer, C., Olivi, A., Pomper, M.G., Burger, P.C., Rose, N.R., 2005. Autoimmune hypophysitis. Endocr. Rev. 26 (5), 599–614.

Chae, Y.K., Chiec, L., Mohindra, N., Gentzler, R., Patel, J., Giles, F., 2017. A case of pembrolizumab-induced type-1 diabetes mellitus and discussion of immune checkpoint inhibitor-induced type 1 diabetes. Cancer Immunol. Immunother. 66 (1), 25–32.

Chang, L.S., Barroso-Sousa, R., Tolaney, S.M., Hodi, F.S., Kaiser, U.B., Min, L., 2019. Endocrine toxicity of cancer immunotherapy targeting immune checkpoints. Endocr. Rev. 40 (1), 17–65.

Chen, D.S., Mellman, I., 2017. Elements of cancer immunity and the cancer–immune set point. Nature 541 (7637), 321–330.

Chen, H., Liakou, C.I., Kamat, A., Pettaway, C., Ward, J.F., Tang, D.N., Sun, J., Jungbluth, A.A., Troncoso, P., Logothetis, C., Sharma, P., 2009. Anti-CTLA-4 therapy results in higher CD4+ ICOShi T cell frequency and IFN-γ levels in both nonmalignant and malignant prostate tissues. Proc. Natl. Acad. Sci. U. S. A. 106 (8), 2729–2734.

Clotman, K., Janssens, K., Specenier, P., Weets, I., De Block, C.E., 2018. Programmed cell death-1 inhibitor–induced type 1 diabetes mellitus. J. Clin. Endocrinol. Metabol. 103 (9), 3144–3154.

Comin-Anduix, B., Escuin-Ordinas, H., Ibarrondo, F.J., 2016. Tremelimumab: research and clinical development. Onco. Targets. Ther. 9, 1767.

Cukier, P., Santini, F.C., Scaranti, M., Hoff, A.O., 2017. Endocrine side effects of cancer immunotherapy. Endocr. Relat. Cancer 24 (12), T331–T347.

de Filette, J., Jansen, Y., Schreuer, M., Everaert, H., Velkeniers, B., Neyns, B., Bravenboer, B., 2016. Incidence of thyroid-related adverse events in melanoma patients treated with pembrolizumab. J. Clin. Endocrinol. Metabol. 101 (11), 4431–4439.

De Filette, J., Andreescu, C.E., Cools, F., Bravenboer, B., Velkeniers, B., 2019. A systematic review and meta-analysis of endocrine-related adverse events associated with immune checkpoint inhibitors. Horm. Metab. Res. 51 (03), 145–156.

Dillard, T., Yedinak, C.G., Alumkal, J., Fleseriu, M., 2010. Anti-CTLA-4 antibody therapy associated autoimmune hypophysitis: serious immune related adverse events across a spectrum of cancer subtypes. Pituitary 13 (1), 29–38.

Eggermont, A.M., Chiarion-Sileni, V., Grob, J.J., Dummer, R., Wolchok, J.D., Schmidt, H., Hamid, O., Robert, C., Ascierto, P.A., Richards, J.M., Lebbé, C., 2016. Prolonged survival in stage III melanoma with ipilimumab adjuvant therapy. N. Engl. J. Med. 375 (19), 1845–1855.

Faje, A., 2016a. Hypophysitis: evaluation and management. Clin. Diabetes Endocrinol. 2 (1), 1–8.

Faje, A., 2016b. Immunotherapy and hypophysitis: clinical presentation, treatment, and biologic insights. Pituitary 19 (1), 82–92.

Faje, A.T., Sullivan, R., Lawrence, D., Tritos, N.A., Fadden, R., Klibanski, A., Nachtigall, L., 2014. Ipilimumab-induced hypophysitis: a detailed longitudinal analysis in a large cohort of patients with metastatic melanoma. J. Clin. Endocrinol. Metabol. 99 (11), 4078–4085.

Fehlings, M., Simoni, Y., Penny, H.L., Becht, E., Loh, C.Y., Gubin, M.M., Ward, J.P., Wong, S.C., Schreiber, R.D., Newell, E.W., 2017. Checkpoint blockade immunotherapy reshapes the high-dimensional phenotypic heterogeneity of murine intratumoural neoantigen-specific CD8+ T cells. Nat. Commun. 8 (1), 1–12.

Ferrari, S.M., Fallahi, P., Elia, G., Ragusa, F., Ruffilli, I., Patrizio, A., Galdiero, M.R., Baldini, E., Ulisse, S., Marone, G., Antonelli, A., 2019. Autoimmune endocrine dysfunctions associated with cancer immunotherapies. Int. J. Mol. Sci. 20 (10), 2560.

Ferris, R., Blumenschein, G., Fayette, J., Guigay, J., Colevas, A., Licitra, L., Harrington, K., Kasper, S., Vokes, E., Even, C., Worden, F., Saba, N., Iglesias Docampo, L., Haddad, R., Rordorf, T., Kiyota, N., Tahara, M., Monga, M., Lynch, M., Geese, W., Kopit, J., Shaw, J., Gillison, M., 2016. Nivolumab for recurrent squamous-cell carcinoma of the head and neck. N. Engl. J. Med. 375 (19), 1856–1867.

Fleseriu, M., Hashim, I.A., Karavitaki, N., Melmed, S., Murad, M.H., Salvatori, R., Samuels, M.H., 2016. Hormonal replacement in hypopituitarism in adults: an endocrine society clinical practice guideline. J. Clin. Endocrinol. Metabol. 101 (11), 3888–3921.

Francisco, L.M., Salinas, V.H., Brown, K.E., Vanguri, V.K., Freeman, G.J., Kuchroo, V.K., Sharpe, A.H., 2009. PD-L1 regulates the development, maintenance, and function of induced regulatory T cells. J. Exp. Med. 206 (13), 3015–3029.

Francisco, L.M., Sage, P.T., Sharpe, A.H., 2010. The PD-1 pathway in tolerance and autoimmunity. Immunol. Rev. 236 (1), 219–242.

Gao, J., He, Q., Subudhi, S., Aparicio, A., Zurita-Saavedra, A., Lee, D.H., Jimenez, C., Suarez-Almazor, M., Sharma, P., 2015. Review of immune-related adverse events in prostate cancer patients treated with ipilimumab: MD Anderson experience. Oncogene 34 (43), 5411–5417.

Gao, L., Yang, X., Yi, C., Zhu, H., 2019. Adverse events of concurrent immune checkpoint inhibitors and antiangiogenic agents: a systematic review. Front. Pharmacol. 10, 1173.

Guaraldi, F., La Selva, R., Samà, M.T., D'Angelo, V., Gori, D., Fava, P., Fierro, M.T., Savoia, P., Arvat, E., 2018. Characterization and implications of thyroid dysfunction induced by immune checkpoint inhibitors in real-life clinical practice: a long-term prospective study from a referral institution. J. Endocrinol. Invest. 41 (5), 549–556.

Gubin, M.M., Zhang, X., Schuster, H., Caron, E., Ward, J.P., Noguchi, T., Ivanova, Y., Hundal, J., Arthur, C.D., Krebber, W.J., Mulder, G.E., 2014. Checkpoint blockade cancer immunotherapy targets tumour-specific mutant antigens. Nature 515 (7528), 577–581.

Gunawan, F., George, E., Roberts, A., 2018. Combination immune checkpoint inhibitor therapy nivolumab and ipilimumab associated with multiple endocrinopathies. Endocrinol. Diabetes Metab. Case Rep. 2018 (1).

Haanen, J.B.A.G., Carbonnel, F., Robert, C., Kerr, K.M., Peters, S., Larkin, J., Jordan, K., 2017. Management of toxicities from immunotherapy: ESMO clinical practice guidelines for diagnosis, treatment and follow-up. Ann. Oncol. 28, iv119–iv142.

Hansen, E., Sahasrabudhe, D., Sievert, L., 2016. A case report of insulin-dependent diabetes as immune-related toxicity of pembrolizumab: presentation, management and outcome. Cancer Immunol. Immunother. 65 (6), 765–767.

Harding, F.A., McArthur, J.G., Gross, J.A., Raulet, D.H., Allison, J.P., 1992. CD28-mediated signalling co-stimulates murine T cells and prevents induction of anergy in T-cell clones. Nature 356 (6370), 607–609.

Hattersley, R., Nana, M., Lansdown, A.J., 2021. Endocrine complications of immunotherapies: a review. Clin. Med. 21 (2), e212.

Hellmann, M.D., Paz-Ares, L., Bernabe Caro, R., Zurawski, B., Kim, S.W., Carcereny Costa, E., Park, K., Alexandru, A., Lupinacci, L., de la Mora Jimenez, E., Sakai, H., 2019. Nivolumab plus ipilimumab in advanced non–small-cell lung cancer. N. Engl. J. Med. 381 (21), 2020–2031.

Higham, C.E., Olsson-Brown, A., Carroll, P., Cooksley, T., Larkin, J., Lorigan, P., Morganstein, D., Trainer, P.J., 2018. SOCIETY FOR ENDOCRINOLOGY ENDOCRINE EMERGENCY GUIDANCE: acute management of the endocrine complications of checkpoint inhibitor therapy. Endocr. Connect. 7 (7), G1–G7.

Hodi, F.S., O'Day, S.J., McDermott, D.F., Weber, R.W., Sosman, J.A., Haanen, J.B., Gonzalez, R., Robert, C., Schadendorf, D., Hassel, J.C., Akerley, W., 2010. Improved survival with ipilimumab in patients with metastatic melanoma. N. Engl. J. Med. 363 (8), 711–723.

Horn, L., Mansfield, A.S., Szczęsna, A., Havel, L., Krzakowski, M., Hochmair, M.J., Huemer, F., Losonczy, G., Johnson, M.L., Nishio, M., Reck, M., 2018. First-line atezolizumab plus chemotherapy in extensive-stage small-cell lung cancer. N. Engl. J. Med. 379 (23), 2220–2229.

Huang, A.C., Postow, M.A., Orlowski, R.J., Mick, R., Bengsch, B., Manne, S., Xu, W., Harmon, S., Giles, J.R., Wenz, B., Adamow, M., 2017. T-cell invigoration to tumour burden ratio associated with anti-PD-1 response. Nature 545 (7652), 60–65.

Hwang, W.L., Pike, L.R., Royce, T.J., Mahal, B.A., Loeffler, J.S., 2018. Safety of combining radiotherapy with immune-checkpoint inhibition. Nat. Rev. Clin. Oncol. 15 (8), 477–494.

Iglesias, P., 2018. Cancer immunotherapy-induced endocrinopathies: clinical behavior and therapeutic approach. Eur. J. Intern. Med. 47, 6–13.

Ishida, Y., Agata, Y., Shibahara, K., Honjo, T., 1992. Induced expression of PD-1, a novel member of the immunoglobulin gene superfamily, upon programmed cell death. EMBO J. 11 (11), 3887–3895.

Iwai, Y., Ishida, M., Tanaka, Y., Okazaki, T., Honjo, T., Minato, N., 2002. Involvement of PD-L1 on tumor cells in the escape from host immune system and tumor immunotherapy by PD-L1 blockade. Proc. Natl. Acad. Sci. U. S. A. 99 (19), 12293–12297.

Iwama, S., De Remigis, A., Callahan, M.K., Slovin, S.F., Wolchok, J.D., Caturegli, P., 2014. Pituitary expression of CTLA-4 mediates hypophysitis secondary to administration of CTLA-4 blocking antibody. Sci. Transl. Med. 6 (230), 230ra45.

Juszczak, A., Gupta, A., Karavitaki, N., Middleton, M.R., Grossman, A.B., 2012. Ipilimumab: a novel immunomodulating therapy causing autoimmune hypophysitis: a case report and review. Eur. J. Endocrinol. 167 (1), 1–5.

Keir, M.E., Butte, M.J., Freeman, G.J., Sharpe, A.H., 2008. PD-1 and its ligands in tolerance and immunity. Annu. Rev. Immunol. 26, 677–704.

Kennedy, L.B., Salama, A.K., 2020. A review of cancer immunotherapy toxicity. CA Cancer J. Clin. 70 (2), 86–104.

Larkin, J., Chiarion-Sileni, V., Gonzalez, R., Grob, J.J., Cowey, C.L., Lao, C.D., Schadendorf, D., Dummer, R., Smylie, M., Rutkowski, P., Ferrucci, P.F., 2015. Combined nivolumab and ipilimumab or monotherapy in untreated melanoma. N. Engl. J. Med. 373 (1), 23–34.

Larkin, J., Chiarion-Sileni, V., Gonzalez, R., Grob, J.J., Rutkowski, P., Lao, C.D., Cowey, C.L., Schadendorf, D., Wagstaff, J., Dummer, R., Ferrucci, P.F., 2019. Five-year survival with combined nivolumab and ipilimumab in advanced melanoma. N. Engl. J. Med. 381 (16), 1535–1546.

Latchman, Y., Wood, C.R., Chernova, T., Chaudhary, D., Borde, M., Chernova, I., Iwai, Y., Long, A.J., Brown, J.A., Nunes, R., Greenfield, E.A., 2001. PD-L2 is a second ligand for PD-1 and inhibits T cell activation. Nat. Immunol. 2 (3), 261–268.

Lee, H., Hodi, F.S., Giobbie-Hurder, A., Ott, P.A., Buchbinder, E.I., Haq, R., Tolaney, S., Barroso-Sousa, R., Zhang, K., Donahue, H., Davis, M., 2017. Characterization of thyroid disorders in patients receiving immune checkpoint inhibition therapy. Cancer Immunol. Res. 5 (12), 1133–1140.

Liakou, C.I., Kamat, A., Tang, D.N., Chen, H., Sun, J., Troncoso, P., Logothetis, C., Sharma, P., 2008. CTLA-4 blockade increases IFNγ-producing CD4+ ICOShi cells to shift the ratio of effector to regulatory T cells in cancer patients. Proc. Natl. Acad. Sci. U. S. A. 105 (39), 14987–14992.

Maio, M., Grob, J.J., Aamdal, S., Bondarenko, I., Robert, C., Thomas, L., Garbe, C., Chiarion-Sileni, V., Testori, A., Chen, T.T., Tschaika, M., 2015. Five-year survival rates for treatment-naive patients with advanced melanoma who received ipilimumab plus dacarbazine in a phase III trial. J. Clin. Oncol. 33 (10), 1191.

Marlier, J., Cocquyt, V., Brochez, L., Van Belle, S., Kruse, V., 2014. Ipilimumab, not just another anticancer therapy: hypophysitis as side effect illustrated by four case-reports. Endocrine 47 (3), 878–883.

Martins, F., Sofiya, L., Sykiotis, G.P., Lamine, F., Maillard, M., Fraga, M., Shabafrouz, K., Ribi, C., Cairoli, A., Guex-Crosier, Y., Kuntzer, T., 2019. Adverse effects of immune-checkpoint inhibitors: epidemiology, management and surveillance. Nat. Rev. Clin. Oncol. 16 (9), 563–580.

McMillen, B., Dhillon, M.S., Yong-Yow, S., 2016. A rare case of thyroid storm. Case Rep. 2016, bcr2016214603.

Min, L., Hodi, F.S., Giobbie-Hurder, A., Ott, P.A., Luke, J.J., Donahue, H., Davis, M., Carroll, R.S., Kaiser, U.B., 2015. Systemic high-dose corticosteroid treatment does not improve the outcome of ipilimumab-related hypophysitis: a retrospective cohort study. Clin. Cancer Res. 21 (4), 749–755.

Morganstein, D.L., Lai, Z., Spain, L., Diem, S., Levine, D., Mace, C., Gore, M., Larkin, J., 2017. Thyroid abnormalities following the use of cytotoxic T-lymphocyte antigen-4 and programmed death receptor protein-1 inhibitors in the treatment of melanoma. Clin. Endocrinol. (Oxf) 86 (4), 614–620.

Motzer, R.J., Tannir, N.M., McDermott, D.F., Frontera, O.A., Melichar, B., Choueiri, T.K., Plimack, E.R., Barthélémy, P., Porta, C., George, S., Powles, T., 2018. Nivolumab plus ipilimumab versus sunitinib in advanced renal-cell carcinoma. N. Engl. J. Med. 378 (14), 1277–1290.

Nallapaneni, N.N., Mourya, R., Bhatt, V.R., Malhotra, S., Ganti, A.K., Tendulkar, K.K., 2014. Ipilimumab-induced hypophysitis and uveitis in a patient with metastatic melanoma and a history of ipilimumab-induced skin rash. J. Natl. Compr. Canc. Netw. 12 (8), 1077–1081.

Ntali, G., Kassi, E., Alevizaki, M., 2017. Endocrine sequelae of immune checkpoint inhibitors. Hormones 16 (4), 341–350.

Okura, N., Asano, M., Uchino, J., Morimoto, Y., Iwasaku, M., Kaneko, Y., Yamada, T., Fukui, M., Takayama, K., 2020. Endocrinopathies associated with immune checkpoint inhibitor cancer treatment: a review. J. Clin. Med. 9 (7), 2033.

O'Malley, G., Lee, H.J., Parekh, S., Galsky, M.D., Smith, C.B., Friedlander, P., Yanagisawa, R.T., Gallagher, E.J., 2017. Rapid evolution of thyroid dysfunction in patients treated with nivolumab. Endocr. Pract. 23 (10), 1223–1231.

Orlov, S., Salari, F., Kashat, L., Walfish, P.G., 2015. Induction of painless thyroiditis in patients receiving programmed death 1 receptor immunotherapy for metastatic malignancies. J. Clin. Endocrinol. Metabol. 100 (5), 1738–1741.

Osorio, J.C., Ni, A., Chaft, J.E., Pollina, R., Kasler, M.K., Stephens, D., Rodriguez, C., Cambridge, L., Rizvi, H., Wolchok, J.D., Merghoub, T., 2017. Antibody-mediated thyroid dysfunction during T-cell checkpoint blockade in patients with non-small-cell lung cancer. Ann. Oncol. 28 (3), 583–589.

Ott, P.A., Hodi, F.S., Robert, C., 2013. CTLA-4 and PD-1/PD-L1 blockade: new immunotherapeutic modalities with durable clinical benefit in melanoma patients. Clin. Cancer Res. 19 (19), 5300–5309.

Paepegaey, A.C., Lheure, C., Ratour, C., Lethielleux, G., Clerc, J., Bertherat, J., Kramkimel, N., Groussin, L., 2017. Polyendocrinopathy resulting from pembrolizumab in a patient with a malignant melanoma. J. Endocr. Soc. 1 (6), 646–649.

Pardoll, D.M., 2012. The blockade of immune checkpoints in cancer immunotherapy. Nat. Rev. Cancer 12 (4), 252–264.

Parry, R.V., Chemnitz, J.M., Frauwirth, K.A., Lanfranco, A.R., Braunstein, I., Kobayashi, S.V., Linsley, P.-S., Thompson, C.B., Riley, J.L., 2005. CTLA-4 and PD-1 receptors inhibit T-cell activation by distinct mechanisms. Mol. Cell. Biol. 25 (21), 9543–9553.

Paschou, S.A., Stefanaki, K., Psaltopoulou, T., Liontos, M., Koutsoukos, K., Zagouri, F., Lambrinoudaki, I., Dimopoulos, M.A., 2021. How we treat endocrine complications of immune checkpoint inhibitors. ESMO Open 6 (1), 100011.

Patsoukis, N., Bardhan, K., Chatterjee, P., Sari, D., Liu, B., Bell, L.N., Karoly, E.D., Freeman, G.J., Petkova, V., Seth, P., Li, L., 2015. PD-1 alters T-cell metabolic reprogramming by inhibiting glycolysis and promoting lipolysis and fatty acid oxidation. Nat. Commun. 6 (1), 1–13.

Perez, V.L., Van Parijs, L., Biuckians, A., Zheng, X.X., Strom, T.B., Abbas, A.K., 1997. Induction of peripheral T cell tolerance in vivo requires CTLA-4 engagement. Immunity 6 (4), 411–417.

Petrelli, F., Signorelli, D., Ghidini, M., Ghidini, A., Pizzutilo, E.G., Ruggieri, L., Cabiddu, M., Borgonovo, K., Dognini, G., Brighenti, M., De Toma, A., 2020. Association of steroids use with survival in patients treated with immune checkpoint inhibitors: a systematic review and meta-analysis. Cancers 12 (3), 546.

Quandt, Z., Young, A., Anderson, M., 2020. Immune checkpoint inhibitor diabetes mellitus: a novel form of autoimmune diabetes. Clin. Exp. Immunol. 200 (2), 131–140.

Quandt, Z., Young, A., Perdigoto, A.L., Herold, K.C., Anderson, M.S., 2021. Autoimmune endocrinopathies: an emerging complication of immune checkpoint inhibitors. Annu. Rev. Med. 72, 313–330.

Reck, M., Bondarenko, I., Luft, A., Serwatowski, P., Barlesi, F., Chacko, R., Sebastian, M., Lu, H., Cuillerot, J.M., Lynch, T.J., 2013. Ipilimumab in combination with paclitaxel and carboplatin as first-line therapy in extensive-disease-small-cell-lung cancer: results from a randomized, double-blind, multicenter phase 2 trial. Ann. Oncol. 24 (1), 75–83.

Ribas, A., Kefford, R., Marshall, M.A., Punt, C.J., Haanen, J.B., Marmol, M., Garbe, C., Gogas, H., Schachter, J., Linette, G., Lorigan, P., 2013. Phase III randomized clinical trial comparing tremelimumab with standard-of-care chemotherapy in patients with advanced melanoma. J. Clin. Oncol. 31 (5), 616.

Romano, E., Kusio-Kobialka, M., Foukas, P.G., Baumgaertner, P., Meyer, C., Ballabeni, P., Michielin, O., Weide, B., Romero, P., Speiser, D.E., 2015. Ipilimumab-dependent cell-mediated cytotoxicity of regulatory T cells ex vivo by nonclassical monocytes in melanoma patients. Proc. Natl. Acad. Sci. U. S. A. 112 (19), 6140–6145.

Ryder, M., Callahan, M., Postow, M.A., Wolchok, J., Fagin, J.A., 2014. Endocrine-related adverse events following ipilimumab in patients with advanced melanoma: a comprehensive retrospective review from a single institution. Endocr. Relat. Cancer 21 (2), 371–381.

Schmid, P., Rugo, H.S., Adams, S., Schneeweiss, A., Barrios, C.H., Iwata, H., Diéras, V., Henschel, V., Molinero, L., Chui, S.Y., Maiya, V., 2020. Atezolizumab plus nab-paclitaxel as first-line treatment for unresectable, locally advanced or metastatic triple-negative breast cancer (IMpassion130): updated efficacy results from a randomised, double-blind, placebo-controlled, phase 3 trial. Lancet Oncol. 21 (1), 44–59.

Stamatouli, A.M., Quandt, Z., Perdigoto, A.L., Clark, P.L., Kluger, H., Weiss, S.A., Gettinger, S., Sznol, M., Young, A., Rushakoff, R., Lee, J., 2018. Collateral damage: insulin-dependent diabetes induced with checkpoint inhibitors. Diabetes 67 (8), 1471–1480.

Tahir, S.A., Gao, J., Miura, Y., Blando, J., Tidwell, R.S., Zhao, H., Subudhi, S.K., Tawbi, H., Keung, E., Wargo, J., Allison, J.P., 2019. Autoimmune antibodies correlate with immune checkpoint therapy-induced toxicities. Proc. Natl. Acad. Sci. U. S. A. 116 (44), 22246–22251.

Tang, D.N., Shen, Y., Sun, J., Wen, S., Wolchok, J.D., Yuan, J., Allison, J.P., Sharma, P., 2013. Increased frequency of ICOS+ CD4 T cells as a pharmacodynamic biomarker for anti-CTLA-4 therapy. Cancer Immunol. Res. 1 (4), 229–234.

Thompson, J.A., Schneider, B.J., Brahmer, J., Andrews, S., Armand, P., Bhatia, S., Budde, L.E., Costa, L., Davies, M., Dunnington, D., Ernstoff, M.S., 2019. Management of immunotherapy-related toxicities, version 1.2019, NCCN clinical practice guidelines in oncology. J. Natl. Compr. Canc. Netw. 17 (3), 255–289.

Topalian, S.L., Hodi, F.S., Brahmer, J.R., Gettinger, S.N., Smith, D.C., McDermott, D.F., Powderly, J.D., Carvajal, R.D., Sosman, J.A., Atkins, M.B., Leming, P.D., 2012. Safety, activity, and immune correlates of anti–PD-1 antibody in cancer. N. Engl. J. Med. 366 (26), 2443–2454.

Torino, F., Barnabei, A., De Vecchis, L., Salvatori, R., Corsello, S.M., 2012. Hypophysitis induced by monoclonal antibodies to cytotoxic T lymphocyte antigen 4: challenges from a new cause of a rare disease. Oncologist 17 (4), 525.

Trinh, S., Le, A., Gowani, S., La-Beck, N.M., 2019a. Management of immune-related adverse events associated with immune checkpoint inhibitor therapy: a minireview of current clinical guidelines. Asia Pac. J. Oncol. Nurs. 6 (2), 154.

Trinh, B., Donath, M.Y., Läubli, H., 2019b. Successful treatment of immune checkpoint inhibitor–induced diabetes with infliximab. Diabetes Care 42 (9), e153–e154.

Vargas, F.A., Furness, A.J., Litchfield, K., Joshi, K., Rosenthal, R., Ghorani, E., Solomon, I., Lesko, M.H., Ruef, N., Roddie, C., Henry, J.Y., 2018. Fc effector function contributes to the activity of human anti-CTLA-4 antibodies. Cancer Cell 33 (4), 649–663.

Walunas, T.L., Bakker, C.Y., Bluestone, J.A., 1996. CTLA-4 ligation blocks CD28-dependent T cell activation. J. Exp. Med. 183 (6), 2541–2550.

Wright, J.J., Powers, A.C., Johnson, D.B., 2021. Endocrine toxicities of immune checkpoint inhibitors. Nat. Rev. Endocrinol. 17 (7), 389–399.

Yamazaki, H., Iwasaki, H., Yamashita, T., Yoshida, T., Suganuma, N., Yamanaka, T., Masudo, K., Nakayama, H., Kohagura, K., Rino, Y., Masuda, M., 2017. Potential risk factors for nivolumab-induced thyroid dysfunction. In Vivo 31 (6), 1225–1228.

Yarchoan, M., Hopkins, A., Jaffee, E.M., 2017. Tumor mutational burden and response rate to PD-1 inhibition. N. Engl. J. Med. 377 (25), 2500.

Yonezaki, K., Kobayashi, T., Imachi, H., Yoshimoto, T., Kikuchi, F., Fukunaga, K., Sato, S., Ibata, T., Yamaji, N., Lyu, J., Dong, T., 2018. Combination therapy of ipilimumab and nivolumab induced thyroid storm in a patient with Hashimoto's disease and diabetes mellitus: a case report. J Med Case Reports 12 (1), 1–5.

Yu, C., Chopra, I.J., Ha, E., 2015. A novel melanoma therapy stirs up a storm: ipilimumab-induced thyrotoxicosis. Endocrinol. Diabetes Metab. Case Rep. 2015 (1).

Zhao, C., Tella, S.H., Del Rivero, J., Kommalapati, A., Ebenuwa, I., Gulley, J., Strauss, J., Brownell, I., 2018. Anti–PD-L1 treatment induced central diabetes insipidus. J. Clin. Endocrinol. Metabol. 103 (2), 365–369.

CHAPTER EIGHT

Shared and distinct aspects of hematopoietic malignancies such as leukemia and lymphoma

Iyshwarya B.K. and Ramakrishnan Veerabathiran
Human Cytogenetics and Genomics Laboratory, Faculty of Allied Health Sciences, Chettinad Hospital and Research Institute, Chettinad Academy of Research and Education, Kelambakkam, Tamil Nadu, India

Abbreviation

ALL	acute lymphoid leukemia
AML	acute myeloid leukemia
CLL	chronic lymphoid leukemia
CML	chronic myeloid leukemia
DNA	deoxyribonucleic acid
DS	down syndrome
EBV	Epstein–Barr virus
HCs	hematopoietic cancers
HL	Hodgkin's lymphoma
HRS	Hodgkin and Reed–Sternberg
IGFRS	insulin like growth factor receptors
MRD	minimum residual disease
NHL	non-Hodgkin lymphoma
NK	natural killer cells
RS	Reed–Sternberg
t-AMLs	therapy-related AMLs
TKIs	tyrosine kinase inhibitors

1. Introduction

Blood cell regeneration is sustained by the hematopoietic system, which involves self-renewal and differentiation of hematopoietic stem cells (HSCs). Through an evolutionary process, adult mammals' HSCs remain multipotent, and they can become any kind of mature blood cell through self-renewal. The balance between self-renewal and differentiation is controlled by either internal or external elements such as niche-associated factors, signal transduction pathways, transcription factors, or chromatin modifiers. Hematological diseases may result from the disruption of these processes

(Baron et al., 2012; Cullen et al., 2014; Doulatov et al., 2012). Blood cell production and function can be affected at any stage during hematological cancers, leaving patients unable to fight infections or prone to bleeding excessively. A patient's bone marrow contains HSCs that can produce myeloid and lymphoid progenitors. Immune responses are initiated by cells of the lymphoid lineage, which produce B and T lymphocytes, followed by the cells of the myeloid lineage, which include erythrocytes, platelets, neutrophils, eosinophils, dendritic cells, and macrophages. Leukemia, lymphoma, and myeloma may develop when normal hematopoietic differentiation is interrupted (Hu and Shilatifard, 2016).

2. Leukemia

Leukemia is caused by defects in rise in the formation of white blood cells in bone marrow, which leads to the existence of circulatory leukemic cells throughout the body. The majority of leukemias are categorized based on whether the transformed cell is myeloid or lymphoid in origin, and whether the illness develops promptly or persistently. Based on the origin of the malignant cells and the clinical history, leukemia is classified as acute myeloid leukemia (AML), acute lymphocytic leukemia (ALL), chronic myeloid leukemia (CML), and chronic lymphoid leukemia (CLL) (Baliakas et al., 2015). Leukemia with altered erythroid, megakaryocytic, or NK cell lineages are examples of other forms of leukemia. Acute leukemia may afflict both adults and children, whereas chronic leukemia typically affects those over the age of 50. In contrasted to NHCs, the overall incidence of leukemia is quite low, comprising for about 3% of all malignancies. Consequently, acute leukemia is the most dangerous disease among people under the age of 20 (Koestler et al., 2012).

2.1 Acute myeloid leukemia (AML)

Acute myeloid leukemia (AML), a rare but deadly malignancy, occurs when immature hematopoietic cells multiply and divide in the blood and bone marrow. During their growth, these malignant tissues overpower the normal progenitors of erythroid, myeloid, and megakaryocytes. Over the past decade, AML clinic assessments and prognoses have made substantial advances. Cytogenetic, immunologic, and molecular research have improved the etiology and prognosis of AML. The new WHO AML classification system is used to examine regional heterogeneity in AML by integrating molecular markers with morphology and immunophenotyping. In determining the minimum residual disease (MRD), genetic abnormalities provide important predictive information (Harris, 2008). The prevalence of AML has significantly increased in the United States over the past decade, with around 8000–9000 new cases diagnosed every year. It affects mostly adults in the United States, with a median age at diagnosis of 65 years, accounting for approximately 1.2% of all cancer-related deaths. Approximately 90% of all acute leukemia in adults is AML, which becomes increasingly common as one age. Over 50 years old, AML is commonly diagnosed and its incidence rates are 3, 15, and 22 per hundred thousand for 50, 70, and 80 year-olds, respectively (Appelbaum et al., 2006). The progress of leukemia is thought to be a result of genetic, environmental and occupational exposures. The sensitivity of hematopoietic progenitor cells to inductive stimuli changes as leukemogenesis progresses. Certain single-gene mutations are intensely allied with hereditary AML, such as Li-Fraumeni syndromes, down syndromes (DS), and bone marrow failure syndromes. It is caused by highly penetrant mutations in leukemia susceptibility genes. Several prenatal diseases have been exposed to be linked with hereditary vulnerability to AML (Massey et al., 2006).

AML is thought to be largely influenced by environmental factors and family history, even though it is unclear why AML develops. Occupational chemical exposure, chemotherapy drugs, and ionizing radiation have all been linked to a greater prevalence of AML. As a result of ionizing radiation, chromosomes can be broken, making mutations, deletions, and translocations possible (Delsol et al., 2001; Garratty, 2007). A variety of factors affect the degree of tissue damage caused by radiation. Radiation exposure factors include the type, amount, and rate of absorption, as well as the frequency and duration. Radiation is also associated with an increased risk of AML when administered in conjunction with chemotherapy for malignancies like Hodgkin's lymphoma and thyroid cancer (Schilling et al., 1998). The most significant chemical factors in the development of acute leukemia are alkylating agents and topoisomerase type II inhibitors, which account for most of the WHO subtype of therapy-related AMLs (t-AMLs) (Greene et al., 2006; Bennett et al., 2005). Patients with immune-related diseases and transplant patients may be at greater risk of AML after immunosuppressive medication (Natelson, 2007). Organic solvents and solvent-like compounds such as benzene, pesticides, and other organic chemicals can increase AML risk (Van Maele-Fabry et al., 2007). Over 60s are at greater risk for developing AML when they smoke cigarettes (Lichtman, 2007) (Fig. 1).

2.2 Acute lymphoid leukemia (ALL)

Leukemia is a malignancy caused by the presence of basic hematopoietic progenitor cells. Acute lymphocytic leukemia (ALL) is also known as acute lymphoblastic leukemia. ALL accounts for 20% of adult acute leukemia, even though it is most common in pediatric patients. There are several types of the disease, which are categorized by morphology and immunology. ALL is a condition characterized by the clonal reproduction of malignantly altered lymphoid progenitor cells in the bone marrow. Bone marrow failure is caused by malignant cells that are responsible for over 30% of the bone marrow content (Silverman, 2009). There is no known cause for acute lymphocytic leukemia, but genetic, social, and environmental factors could be involved. Only a small fraction of newborns gets leukemia because of a genetic tendency, with at least three-quarters of acute leukemia caused by acquired changes in hematological tissues (Cortes and Kantarjian, 1995). Cancers,

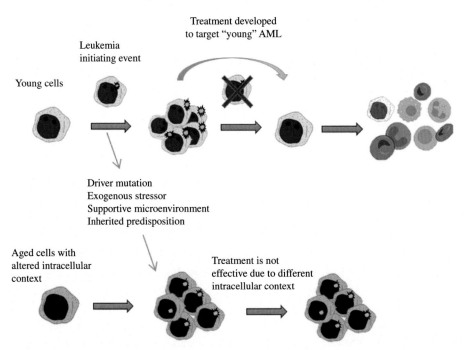

Fig. 1 A diagram depicting the variables that resulted to cells in acute myeloid leukemia.

such as leukemia, have a clonal component. Cancer is caused by molecular modifications that disrupt the signaling system, causing proliferative signals to be released even when there is no more cell growth required, causing DNA replication and cell division to occur incorrectly. The encoded protein of an oncogene undergoes structural changes and sometimes displays heightened transformative activity, retaining the ability to transmit signals via tyrosine kinase interactions and staying in an active state. This leads to cell proliferation and survival (Gallegos-Arreola et al., 2013). ALL is characterized by numerical chromosomal abnormalities as well as structural rearrangements (translocations). B cell progenitors with abnormal chromosomal structures, such as t (9; 22) or chromosome 22, have a poor prognosis for ALL, and their frequency increases as they get older (Rix et al., 2013). ALL is associated with genetic abnormalities found in oncogene regions, such as MLL oncogene, which is linked to ALL in children (Ayton and Cleary, 2001), deletions and inversions, such as deletions of the transcription factor PAX5, seen in at least 30% of B cell precursor ALL (Heltemes-Harris et al., 2011).

2.3 Chronic myeloid leukemia (CML)

CML is an aggressive, life-threatening form of blood cancer caused by BCRABL1 in cells with an inherent or acquired tendency to develop leukemia (Goldman and Melo, 2001). BCRABL1 encodes a 210 KD chimeric protein with constitutive tyrosine kinase activity

(P210BCRABL1) (Ren, 2005). A proliferation regulation mechanism has been developed in chronic-phase CML, providing leukemia cells with the capacity to grow and respond to normal regulatory factors such as granulocyte colony-stimulating and macrophage colony-stimulating factors (G-CSF and G/M-CSF) and infection (Clarkson et al., 2003). Initially, BCRABL1 forms chronic phase CML in CML stem cells. The progeny of these cells may also recur in CML if they have stem cell characteristics, such as a capacity to induce recurrence. Because CML may have multiple LSCs, especially when the interval is long, someone can have more than one LSC (Shi et al., 2017). People with chronic phase CML have been treated with tyrosine kinase inhibitors (TKIs) that inhibit P210BCRABL1. Among those with CML who have received proper treatment, most deaths are caused by causes other than leukemia, such as cardiovascular disease and new forms of cancer (Savona and Saglio, 2013). Despite inhibiting CML clone proliferation, TKIs do not affect CML LSCs, as considered by significant conceptual and experimental evidence (Graham et al., 2002). TKI resistance can be caused by mutations in the ATP-binding site or adjacent regions of P210BCRABL1 or through PI3K/AKT, WNT/catenin, Hedgehog, and JAK/STAT signaling (Soverini et al., 2011). Stem cells are unable to self-renew or remain alive over the long term without β-catenin. When serially transplanting CML LSCs from β-catenin deficient animals onto secondary recipients, this causes self-renewal problems. Advanced CML is also associated with increased expression of β-catenin (Zhao et al., 2007). For those whose illness does not respond to any of the numerous treatments currently available, it is now possible to discontinue the use of tyrosine kinase inhibitors, a treatment once considered to be lifelong. New medications are also emerging for those whose illness does not respond to the presently available options. The cure for chronic myeloid leukemia might become a reality in the majority of cases if these discoveries reach all patients (Cortes et al., 2021).

2.4 Chronic lymphoid leukemia (CLL)

A lymphoproliferative disorder, chronic lymphocytic leukemia (CLL) explains approximately 30% of all adult leukemia and 25% of all non-Hodgkin lymphomas (Knittel et al., 2015). Approximately 10% of CLL patients are under the age of 40, while the median age of diagnosis is 72 years (Hallek and Pflug, 2010). The mechanism by which CLLs differ from other cancers is that they are very dependent on external stimuli including (auto-)antigen signaling through (stereotyped) BCRs, stimulation of CD40/CD40L by interactions with insulin-like growth factor receptors (IGFRs), VEGF receptors, chemokine receptors, and toll-like receptor (TLR) signaling as illustrated in Fig. 2 (Seiffert et al., 2012; Schattner, 2000; Burger, 2010; Muzio et al., 2009; Lee et al., 2005). Many cellular responses are triggered by the signals received through these receptor molecules, including the progression of the cell cycle and activation of critical intracellular survival pathways that inhibit apoptosis (Packham and Stevenson, 2005). Among all cancers characterized by apoptosis

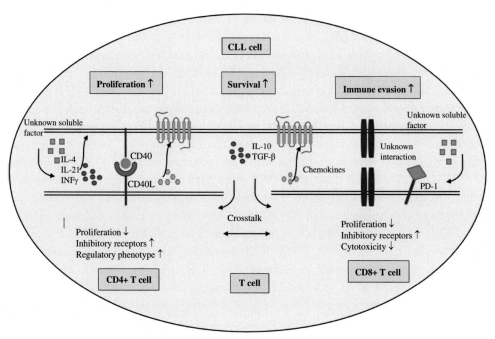

Fig. 2 Chronic lymphoid leukemia.

failure, CLL is often considered a model (Keating, 1999) because it is characterized by relatively few proliferating cells in the G0/G1 phases of the cell cycle. The inevitable increase in white blood cell numbers in some patients is explained by the division of cells, most likely in proliferation centers in specific niches, as shown by the shortening of telomeres in CLL cells (Damle et al., 2004). The disruption of normal B-cell homeostasis occurs in all subgroups of this cancer due to apoptosis. Cell autonomy and nonautonomous pathways play a role in CLL cells' apoptosis resistance. Cells resistant to CD95- and TRAIL-mediated death become overexpressed with X-linked inhibitors of apoptosis protein (XIAP) and acyl-protein thioesterases (APTs) 1 and 2 (Frenzel et al., 2011; Berg et al., 2015). As a consequence, various fundamental biological properties of CLL cells may be connected to the coordinated failure of critical cellular DNA damage-sensing and cell death systems (Zenz et al., 2010a; Longo et al., 2008; Contri et al., 2005). The spread of these leukemias may be at least in part explained by the impact of a multitude of changes in these regulatory pathways (Zenz et al., 2010b; Guipaud et al., 2003). A novel CLL therapy could be designed by targeting each of these physiological systems.

3. Lymphoma

The term "lymphoma" refers to a category of hematological neoplasms that develop from B and T cells. Hodgkin lymphoma (HL), non-Hodgkin lymphoma (NHL), plasma cell neoplasms, and lymphoid leukemia are the sixth most frequent malignancies in the United States, respectively. There are variations among lymphoma subtypes in relation to changing demographics, according to epidemiological data, indicating etiological differences in conjunction with analytical findings of the research. The genesis of lymphomas is difficult to pinpoint owing to the diversity of lymphoma subtypes and difficulties in separating disease categories (Turner et al., 2010). Both NHL and HL have various manifestations depending on which lymphocytic tissue is implicated. When a disease originally begins, it is isolated within the lymphatic system and spreads through contiguity. The swelling of a single lymph node, commonly in the neck, groin or underarm, is most prevalent indication in most occurrences. As the condition progresses, a systemic symptom may arise, resembling an infectious process. Common symptoms include shortness of breath, tiredness, nocturnal sweats, and skin itching. These symptoms can cause the diagnosis to be delayed due to their widespread nature. A lymphoma is diagnosed by examining the tissue based on a pathological examination (Amador-Ortiz et al., 2011). Phenotypically differentiated lymphocytes are produced by hematopoietic stem cells. They participate in the immune response that protects the body from invasion and foreign agents, as well as the secondary lymphoid organs. Lymphocytic cell growth, cell signaling, programmed cell death, and immune elimination all play a part in immunological regulation. An imbalance in this intricate system may initiate molecular pathways that promote lymphocyte malignancy and increase neoplastic cell proliferation; however, these mechanisms are poorly understood. Normal B- and T-cell development needs complicated B-cell immunoglobulin and T-cell receptor gene rearrangements, both of which are prone to error. Chromosome translocations are observed in up to 90% of lymphoid cancers. Certain oncogenic viruses and environmental pollutants may also induce genomic alterations. Normal cells can become malignant, self-replicating cells when they are infected with a virus. These chromosomal translocations, deletions, and mutations may impair cell recognition, precipitate oncogene activation, and inhibit repair mechanisms, permitting malignant B or T-cell clonal growth. According to a new lymphomagenesis paradigm, chronic antigenic stimulation, or a protracted inflammatory process, enhances B-cell proliferation, which raises the probability of random genetic errors. A protracted state of external or autoantigenic stimulation is typical in these patients, resulting in a chronic inflammatory response that includes a cascade of cellular and cytokine responses that may induce tissue damage, compensatory immunosuppression, and tumor formation. Other immunosuppressive exposures may operate as cofactors in lymphomagenesis by preventing a malignant cell from being identified and destroyed (Nayak and Deschler, 2003).

3.1 Hodgkin lymphoma

Hodgkin lymphoma (HL) has developed from a malformed cryptic illness to advanced cancer with complex biology that may hold the key to its treatment (Swerdlow et al., 2016). The expanded lymph nodes of "Hodgkin's disease" patients contained a few multinucleated cells, which were surrounded by normal-looking cells. Reed–Sternberg (RS) cells are named after their discoverers since they have multinucleated cytoplasm. The proliferation pattern of RS cells was later determined to be clonal, which indicated that these cells were altered. As RS cells are the cancer cells of a malignant mass instead of Hodgkin's disease, the diagnosis of the disease was later confirmed to be a hematopoietic cancer. Reed–Sternberg cells (RS cells) are pathognomonic cells that show multi-nucleation in all subtypes but are deficient in CD19 and CD20, as well as CD15 and CD30. They are also infrequent among the total number of cells within the affected tissue and show EBV positive and negative forms. The aggressive illness, which affects children, adolescents, adults, and seniors, has attracted experts for nearly two centuries. The disease has a grim prognosis whether diagnosed early or refractory (Piccaluga et al., 2011). Tumors with cancerous cells are often surrounded by an inflammatory milieu including lymphocytes, eosinophils, neutrophils, histiocytes, and plasma cells. They are also known as Hodgkin and Reed–Sternberg (HRS) cells, which are polynucleated, multinucleated, or large mononuclear cells (Shanbhag and Ambinder, 2018). The hallmarks of HRS have been illustrated in Fig. 3.

3.2 Non-Hodgkin lymphoma

Several lymphoid tissues are affected by non-Hodgkin lymphoma (NHL), which begins as progenitors of B cells and progresses to mature B cells, precursors of T cells, and mature T cells. They are divided into subgroups with different epidemiology, etiology, immunophenotypic, genetic, and clinical characteristics. According to its prognosis, the illness is categorized as 'indolent' or 'aggressive' (Armitage and Weisenburger, 1998).

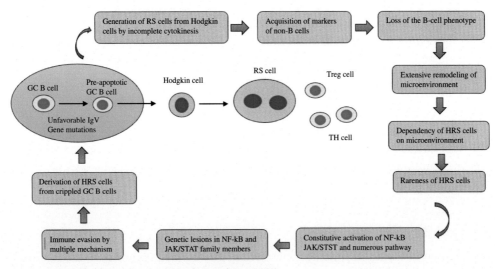

Fig. 3 Hallmarks of Hodgkin and Reed–Sternberg (HRS).

In contrast to Hodgkin's lymphomas, NHL is a multitype of lymphoproliferative malignancy with a higher tendency to migrate to extranodal sites. More than 25% of NHL cases occur in areas other than the node (Bowzyk Al-Naceb et al., 2018); however, most cases involve both node and extranodal locations. There are about 30% of NHL subtypes in rich countries, most commonly diffuse large B cell lymphomas and follicular lymphomas. The prevalence of all other NHL subtypes is less than 10% (Ekstrom-Smedby, 2006). Among the leading causes of cancer-related death in the United States, NHL is sixth behind prostate, breast, lung, colorectal, and bladder cancer. Oropharyngeal lymphomas are second to squamous cell carcinomas in terms of common malignancies of the oral cavity (Kolokotronis et al., 2005). To understand how lymphomas develop, we must understand how B-cells mature in the body. An immunoglobulin heavy chain gene is recombined with an immunoglobulin light chain gene during normal B-cell development, where enzymes that break double-stranded DNA facilitate that process. Chromosome translocations can be caused by DNA strand breaks in lymphoma cells (Jung et al., 2006). Activation of proto-oncogenes often occurs with translocations of this type. As B lymphocytes mature, they migrate to peripheral lymphoid tissues. When antibodies bind to antigens in lymph nodes, mature B cells are activated since T lymphocytes transmit signals through them (Allen et al., 2007). An antigen-specific T cell and follicular dendritic cell carrying antigen multiply in response to centroblasts, which develop rapidly and have a noncleaved nucleus. Centroblasts become centrocytes when they reach the germinal center light zone, which ingests antigen and transports it to T cells. Upon reverting to centroblast form or developing into memory B and plasma cells, centrocytes may become centroblast. During B cell development, two DNA modifications take place: class-switch recombination, in which the immune system switches from IgM to IgG, IgA, or IgE, and somatic hypermutation, in which the light chain of variable immunoglobulin (IgV) mutates as a result of antigen exposure, which changes the affinity of B cells to that antigen (Lenz and Staudt, 2010).

4. Conclusion

Each hematological malignancy arises from a distinct stage in lymphocyte ontogenesis, making the epidemiology, clinical presentation, and appropriate treatment very diverse. It is important to understand that diseases in this category typically present in early or late stages, a variety of staging methods can be used in lymphoma patients to assess the prognosis, such as cross-sectional imaging, functional imaging, and evaluations of the bone marrow and cerebrospinal fluid. There are also a variety of treatment options, ranging from observation to combination therapies or high-dose therapy using autologous or allogeneic stem cells. The proper management of lymphomas requires an appreciation of the unique aspects of the natural history of specific types of lymphoma, as well as an understanding of lymphoma principles, such as the need for comprehensive diagnostic evaluations and staging. Lymphoma cancers represent a diverse group of diseases concerning their clinical behavior and genetic characteristics. We can gain a better understanding of the clinical heterogeneity underlying these challenging tumors from genomic research, which sheds new light on their molecular heterogeneity. Progress has been made in identifying subgroups with unique genomes and therapeutic responses among the traditionally broad category of lymphomas, as well as finding diagnostic and prognostic gene expression patterns. Several aspects of treatment are improved by this work, including diagnosis, prognosis counseling for patients, selecting patients most likely to benefit from therapy, and conducting clinical trials to expand current knowledge.

Acknowledgment

The authors thank the Chettinad academy of research and education for the constant support and encouragement during the study.

References

Allen, C.D., Okada, T., Cyster, J.G., 2007. Germinal-center organization and cellular dynamics. Immunity 27, 190–202.

Amador-Ortiz, C., Chen, L., Hassan, A., et al., 2011. Combined core needle biopsy and fine-needle aspiration with ancillary studies correlate highly with traditional techniques in the diagnosis of nodal-based lymphoma. Am. J. Clin. Pathol. 135, 516–524.

Appelbaum, F.R., Gundacker, H., Head, D.R., Slovak, M.L., Willman, C.L., Godwin, J.E., Anderson, J.E., Petersdorf, S.H., 2006. Age and acute myeloid leukemia. Blood 107 (9), 3481–3485.

Armitage, J.O., Weisenburger, D.D., 1998. New approach to classifying non-Hodgkin's lymphomas: clinical features of the major histologic subtypes. Non-Hodgkin's Lymphoma Classification Project. J. Clin. Oncol. 16 (8), 2780–2795.

Ayton, P.M., Cleary, M.L., 2001. Molecular mechanisms of leukemogenesis mediated by MLL fusion proteins. Oncogene 20 (40), 5695–5707.

Baliakas, P., Hadzidimitriou, A., Sutton, L.A., Rossi, D., Minga, E., Villamor, N., Larrayoz, M., Kmínková, J., Agathangelidis, A., Davis, Z., Tausch, E., 2015. Recurrent mutations refine prognosis in chronic lymphocytic leukemia. Leukemia 29 (2), 329–336.

Baron, M.H., Isern, J., Fraser, S.T., 2012. The embryonic origins of erythropoiesis in mammals. Blood 119, 4828–4837.

Bennett, J.M., Kaminski, M.S., Leonard, J.P., Vose, J.M., Zelenetz, A.D., Knox, S.J., Horning, S., Press, O.W., Radford, J.A., Kroll, S.M., Capizzi, R.L., 2005. Assessment of treatment-related myelodysplastic syndromes and acute myeloid leukemia in patients with non-Hodgkin lymphoma treated with tositumomab and iodine I131 tositumomab. Blood 105, 4576–4582.

Berg, V., Rusch, M., Vartak, N., et al., 2015. miRs-138 and -424 control palmitoylation-dependent CD95-mediated cell death by targeting acyl protein thioesterases 1 and 2 in CLL. Blood 125, 2948–2957.

Bowzyk Al-Naeeb, A., Ajithkumar, T., Behan, S., Hodson, D.J., 2018. Non-Hodgkin lymphoma. BMJ 362, k3204.

Burger, J.A., 2010. Chemokines and chemokine receptors in chronic lymphocytic leukemia (CLL): from understanding the basics towards therapeutic targeting. Semin. Cancer Biol. 20, 424–430.

Clarkson, B., Strife, A., Wisniewski, D., Lambek, C.L., Liu, C., 2003. Chronic myelogenous leukemia as a paradigm of early cancer and possible curative strategies. Leukemia 17, 1211–1262.

Contri, A., Brunati, A.M., Trentin, L., Cabrelle, A., Miorin, M., Cesaro, L., Pinna, L.A., Zambello, R., Semenzato, G., Donella-Deana, A., 2005. Chronic lymphocytic leukemia B cells contain anomalous Lyn tyrosine kinase, a putative contribution to defective apoptosis. J. Clin. Invest. 115, 369–378.

Cortes, J.E., Kantarjian, H.M., 1995. Acute lymphoblastic leukemia. A comprehensive review with emphasis on biology and therapy. Cancer 76, 2393–2417.

Cortes, J., Pavlovsky, C., Saußele, S., 2021. Chronic myeloid leukaemia. Lancet 398 (10314), 1914–1926.

Cullen, S.M., Mayle, A., Rossi, L., Goodell, M.A., 2014. Hematopoietic stem cell development: an epigenetic journey. Curr. Top. Dev. Biol. 107, 39–75.

Damle, R.N., Batliwalla, F.M., Ghiotto, F., et al., 2004. Telomere length and telomerase activity delineate distinctive replicative features of the B-CLL subgroups defined by immunoglobulin V gene mutations. Blood 103, 375–382.

Delsol, G., Ralfkiaer, E., Stein, H., Wright, D., Jaffe, E.S., 2001. Anaplastic large cell lymphoma. In: Jaffe, E.S., Harris, N.L., Stein, H., Vardiman, J.W. (Eds.), World Health Organization Classification of Tumours. Pathology and Genetics of Tumours of Haematopoietic and Lymphoid Tissues. IARC Press, Lyon, pp. 230–235.

Doulatov, S., Notta, F., Laurenti, E., Dick, J.E., 2012. Hematopoiesis: a human perspective. Cell Stem Cell 10, 120–136.

Ekstrom-Smedby, K., 2006. Epidemiology and etiology of non-Hodgkin lymphoma-A review. Acta Oncol. 45, 258–271.

Frenzel, L.P., Patz, M., Pallasch, C.P., et al., 2011. Novel X-linked inhibitor of apoptosis inhibiting compound as sensitizer for TRAIL-mediated apoptosis in chronic lymphocytic leukaemia with poor prognosis. Br. J. Haematol. 152, 191–200.

Gallegos-Arreola, M.P., Borjas-Gutie´rrez, C., Zu´n˜iga-Gonza´lez, G.M., Figuera, L.E., Puebla-Pe´rez, A.M., Garci´a-Gonza´lez, J.R., 2013. Pathophysiology of acute lymphoblastic leukemia. In: Mejia-Arangue, J.M. (Ed.), Clinical Epidemiology of Acute Lymphoblastic Leukemia—From the Molecules to the Clinic. Mexican Social Security Institute, Mexico, ISBN: 978-953-51-0990-7, pp. 43–73.

Garratty, G., 2007. Sir John Dacie, MD, FRCP, FRCPath, FRS (1912-2995). Transfus. Med. Rev. 21 (1), 72–74.

Goldman, J.M., Melo, J.V., 2001. Targeting the BCR-ABL tyrosine kinase in chronic myeloid leukemia. N. Engl. J. Med. 344, 1084–1086.

Graham, S.M., Jorgensen, H.G., Allan, E., Pearson, C., Alcorn, M.J., Richmond, L., et al., 2002. Primitive, quiescent, Philadelphia-positive stem cells from patients with chronic myeloid leukemia are insensitive to STI571 in vitro. Blood 99, 319–325.

Greene, M.H., Boice Jr., J.D., Greer, B.E., Blessing, J.A., Dembo, A.J., Knoche, E., McLeod, H.L., Graubert, T.A., 2006. Pharmacogenetics of alkylatorassociated acute myeloid leukemia. Pharmacogenomics 7, 719–729.

Guipaud, O., Deriano, L., Salin, H., et al., 2003. B-cell chronic lymphocytic leukaemia: a polymorphic family unified by genomic features. Lancet Oncol. 4, 505–514.

Hallek, M., Pflug, N., 2010. Chronic lymphocytic leukemia. Ann. Oncol. 21 (Suppl7), vii154–vii164.

Harris, N.L., 2008. Introduction to the WHO classification of tumours of haematopoietic and lymphoid tissues. In: WHO Classification of Tumours of Haematopoietic and Lymphoid Tissues. IARC Press, Lyon, pp. 14–15.

Heltemes-Harris, L.M., et al., 2011. Ebf1 or Pax5 haploinsuffciency synergizes with STAT5 activation to initiate acute lymphoblastic leukemia. J. Exp. Med. 208 (6), 1135–1149.

Hu, D., Shilatifard, A., 2016. Epigenetics of hematopoiesis and hematological malignancies. Genes Dev. 30 (18), 2021–2041.

Jung, D., Giallourakis, C., Mostoslavsky, R., Alt, F.W., 2006. Mechanism and control of V(D)J recombination at the immunoglobulin heavy chain locus. Annu. Rev. Immunol. 24, 541–570.

Keating, M.J., 1999. Chronic lymphocytic leukemia. Semin. Oncol. 26 (Suppl 14), 107–114.

Knittel, G., Liedgens, P., Reinhardt, H.C., 2015. Targeting ATM-deficient CLL through interference with DNA repair pathways. Front. Genet. 6, 207.

Koestler, D.C., Marsit, C.J., Christensen, B.C., Accomando, W., Langevin, S.M., Houseman, E.A., Nelson, H.H., Karagas, M.R., Wiencke, J.K., Kelsey, K.T., 2012. Peripheral blood immune cell methylation profiles are associated with nonhematopoietic cancers. Cancer Epidemiol. Biomarkers Prev. 21 (8), 1293–1302.

Kolokotronis, A., Konstantinou, N., Christakis, I., Papadimitriou, P., Matiakis, A., Zaraboukas, T., et al., 2005. Localized B-cell non-Hodgkin's lymphoma of oral cavity and maxillofacial region: a clinical study. Oral Surg. Oral Med. Oral Pathol. Oral Radiol. Endod. 99, 303–310.

Lee, Y.K., Shanafelt, T.D., Bone, N.D., et al., 2005. VEGF receptors on chronic lymphocytic leukemia (CLL) B cells interact with STAT 1 and 3: implication for apoptosis resistance. Leukemia 19, 513–523.

Lenz, G., Staudt, L.M., 2010. Aggressive lymphomas. N. Engl. J. Med. 362, 1417–1429.

Lichtman, M.A., 2007. Cigarette smoking, cytogenetic abnormalities, and acute myelogenous leukemia. Leukemia 21, 1137–1140.

Longo, P.G., Laurenti, L., Gobessi, S., et al., 2008. The Akt/Mcl-1 pathway plays a prominent role in mediating antiapoptotic signals downstream of the B-cell receptor in chronic lymphocytic leukemia B cells. Blood 111, 846–855.

Massey, G.V., Zipursky, A., Chang, M.N., et al., 2006. A prospective study of the natural history of transient leukemia (TL) in neonates with Down syndrome (DS): Children's Oncology Group (COG) study POG-9481. Blood 107, 4606–4613.

Muzio, M., Scielzo, C., Bertilaccio, M.T., et al., 2009. Expression and function of toll like receptors in chronic lymphocytic leukaemia cells. Br. J. Haematol. 144, 507–516.

Natelson, E.A., 2007. Benzene-induced acute myeloid leukemia: a clinician's perspective. Am. J. Hematol. 82, 826–830.

Nayak, L.M., Deschler, D.G., 2003. Lymphomas. Otolaryngol. Clin. North Am. 36 (4), 625–646.

Packham, G., Stevenson, F.K., 2005. Bodyguards and assassins: Bcl-2 family proteins and apoptosis control in chronic lymphocytic leukaemia. Immunology 114, 441–449.

Piccaluga, P.P., Agostinelli, C., Gazzola, A., Tripodo, C., Bacci, F., Sabattini, E., Sista, M.T., Mannu, C., Sapienza, M.R., Rossi, M., et al., 2011. Pathobiology of hodgkin lymphoma. Adv. Hematol. 2011, 920898.

Ren, R., 2005. Mechanisms of BCR-ABL in the pathogenesis of chronic myelogenous leukaemia. Nat. Rev. Cancer 5, 172–183.

Rix, U., et al., 2013. A target-disease network model of secondgeneration BCR-ABL inhibitor action in Ph+ ALL. PLoS One 8 (10), e77155.

Savona, M.R., Saglio, G., 2013. Identifying the time to change BCR-ABL inhibitor therapy in patients with chronic myeloid leukemia. Acta Haematol. 130, 268–278.

Schattner, E.J., 2000. CD40 ligand in CLL pathogenesis and therapy. Leuk. Lymphoma 37, 461–472.

Schilling, V.R., Abellan, P.F., Dominguez, E., Gonzalez, C.R., Barbera, E.M., Cendra, R.C., 1998. Acute leukemias after treatment with radioiodine for thyroid cancer. Laematologica 83 (8), 767–768.

Seiffert, M., Dietrich, S., Jethwa, A., et al., 2012. Exploiting biological diversity and genomic aberrations in chronic lymphocytic leukemia. Leuk. Lymphoma 53, 1023–1031.

Shanbhag, S., Ambinder, R.F., 2018. Hodgkin lymphoma: a review and update on recent progress. CA Cancer J. Clin. 68 (2), 116–132.

Shi, Y., Inoue, H., Wu, J.C., Yamanaka, S., 2017. Induced pluripotent stem cell technology: a decade of progress. Nat. Rev. Drug Discov. 16, 115–130.

Silverman, L.B., 2009 Jan 1. Acute lymphoblastic leukemia. In: Vora, A. (Ed.), Oncology of Infancy and Childhood. WB Saunders, pp. 295–330.

Soverini, S., Hochhaus, A., Nicolini, F.E., Gruber, F., Lange, T., Saglio, G., et al., 2011. BCR-ABL kinase domain mutation analysis in chronic myeloid leukemia patients treated with tyrosine kinase inhibitors: recommendations from an expert panel on behalf of European LeukemiaNet. Blood 118, 1208–1215.

Swerdlow, S.H., Campo, E., Pileri, S.A., Harris, N.L., Stein, H., Siebert, R., Advani, R., Ghielmini, M., Salles, G.A., Zelenetz, A.D., et al., 2016. The 2016 revision of the World Health Organization classification of lymphoid neoplasms. Blood 127, 2375–2390.

Turner, J.J., Morton, L.M., Linet, M.S., et al., 2010. InterLymph hierarchical classification of lymphoid neoplasms for epidemiologic research based on the WHO classification (2008): update and future directions. Blood 116, e90–e98.

Van Maele-Fabry, G., Duhayon, S., Lison, D., 2007. A systematic review of myeloid leukemias and occupational pesticide exposure. Cancer Causes Control 18, 457–478.

Zenz, T., Vollmer, D., Trbusek, M., et al., 2010a. TP53 mutation profile in chronic lymphocytic leukemia: evidence for a disease specific profile from a comprehensive analysis of 268 mutations. Leukemia 24, 2072–2079.

Zenz, T., Mertens, D., Stilgenbauer, S., 2010b. Biological diversity and risk-adapted treatment of chronic lymphocytic leukemia. Haematologica 95, 1441–1443.

Zhao, C., Blum, J., Chen, A., Kwon, H.Y., Jung, S.H., Cook, J.M., et al., 2007. Loss of beta-catenin impairs the renewal of normal and CML stem cells in vivo. Cancer Cell 12, 528–541.

CHAPTER NINE

Molecular diagnosis, drivers, and treatment modalities for chronic lymphocytic leukemia

Saurabh Yadav[a] and Balraj Mittal[b]

[a]Department of Medical Oncology, Dana Farber Cancer University/Harvard Medical School, Boston, MA, United States
[b]Sanjay Gandhi Postgraduate Institute of Medical Sciences, Lucknow, India

1. Introduction

Chronic lymphocytic leukemia (CLL) is a blood malignancy in which bone marrow overproduces a type of white blood cells known as lymphocytes. In normal physiological homeostatic conditions, the bone marrow produces blood (hematopoietic) stem cells that maintain their numbers and give rise to other blood cells over time. Hematopoietic stem cells may become a lymphoid stem cell or myeloid stem cell, however in the case of CLL, they mainly convert into high numbers of abnormal B lymphocytes also known as leukemia cells (Slager and Zent, 2014). B lymphocytes make antibodies to help fight infection. The abnormal monoclonal leukemia cells are not effective in fighting infections. The overproduction of these cells leads to overcrowding in the blood and bone marrow, leaving less room for critical role-playing various blood cells such as red blood cells and platelets. Thus, this overcrowding condition leads to high infection and anemia and easy bleeding in CLL patients. In the early stages, CLL remains asymptomatic and is mainly found using a routine blood test (Stevenson et al., 2011). Later signs and symptoms may include painless swelling of the lymph nodes in the neck, weakness or feeling tired for unusually longer durations, pain or a feeling of fullness below the ribs, fever and infection, easy bruising or bleeding, petechiae, weight loss for no known reason, and drenching night sweats.

CLL is the most frequently diagnosed adult leukemia in the Western world. It is characterized by remarkable populational heterogeneity. Its incidences are higher in Caucasians from North America, Europe and Russia as compared to African Americans. On the other hand, the incidence rate of CLL is significantly lower in South Asian countries, particularly in Japan, India, and China (Nabhan and Rosen, 2014). However, such high variability in the incidence rates can't be explained by a single factor. But genetic predisposition seems to be one of the main contributing factors since the pattern in incidences remains the same in the next generations after migration to other geographical

Biomarkers in Cancer Detection and Monitoring of Therapeutics
https://doi.org/10.1016/B978-0-323-95114-2.00014-5

235

locations. In addition, other studies have reported that approximately 10% of CLL patients have a family history of the disease (Slager and Zent, 2014).

2. Diagnosis/detection of CLL

In general, the diagnosis of CLL occurs in old age as CLL development is a multistep process that takes place over decades. The median age of diagnosis of CLL in the United States, Europe, and Australia is about 72 years, with about one-quarter of patients aged <65 years. However, the incidences of CLL disease in patients younger than 50 years at diagnosis are relatively rarer (Parikh et al., 2014). CLL is diagnosed incidentally as part of the routine blood test known as a complete blood count (CBC). In the CBC, various types of cells that constitute blood are measured in the sample from the person. People who may have CLL have too many WBCs in their blood. According to the recent guidelines for the diagnosis of CLL, the number of lymphocytes should increase more than 5000 B cells/μL of the peripheral blood (Eichhorst et al., 2021).

High CBC count is followed by morphological and clinical investigations of the patients and clonality of the cells is determined **using flow cytometry and cytochemistry**. Chemicals or dyes are used to get expression information about the leukemia cells and their associated subtypes. CLL cells express different cell surface markers/proteins compared to other cell types of blood. The pattern of expression of these proteins is called the immunophenotype. Immunophenotyping distinguishes B-cell from T-cell disease; in addition, it also identifies CLL cells as positive for CD20, CD5 and CD23 with low expressions of IgM/IgD and CD79b when compared to normal B cells. Fluorescence in situ hybridization assays and other genetic tests such as sequencing and PCR are used to find genetic changes in the CLL specimens. Some of the genetic changes that occur in CLL include deletion of the long arm of chromosome 13 [del(13q)], found in about half of CLL patients. Other chromosomal abnormalities such as deletion of 11q or 17p, and an extra copy of chromosome 12 (trisomy 12) can also be detected in CLL patients at diagnosis. In addition, the number of RBCs is lower, thus resulting in anemia and low platelets resulting in thrombocytopenia. The detection of CLL in the advanced stage is presented with lymphadenopathy of cervical, marginal, or axillary lymph nodes or, splenomegaly, and thrombocytopenia. Secondary infections result in most of the morbidities and mortalities in CLL patients due to weak immunity. Humoral immuno-depression causes a high susceptibility to bacterial infections (Nosari, 2012).

Rai et al. and Binet et al. proposed clinical staging systems to categorize CLL patients. Both systems utilize clinical features of the CLL patients that are presented at the time of initial examination and are currently in use in the clinics (Rai et al., 1975; Binet et al., 1981). These systems determine the initial prognosis of CLL patients and treatment strategy. Rai staging system has been modified (Table 1), it categorizes the cases into five stages starting from stage 0 (low risk), stage I and II (intermediate risk), and stage III and IV (high risk) (Rai et al., 2004). Binet staging system has three stages A, B, C.

Table 1 Rai CLL staging systems.
Rai staging modified

Rai stages	Clinical features	RBC and platelet counts
Low risk	Lymphocytosis; no lymphadenopathy (enlargement of the lymph nodes), spleen, or liver	RBC: Hb >11 g/dL Platelets: >100 × 10⁹/L
Intermediated risk	Lymphocytosis and lymphadenopathy in any site and splenomegaly (enlarged spleen) and/or hepatomegaly (enlarged liver)	RBC: Hb >11 g/dL Platelets: >100 × 10⁹/L
High risk	Disease-related anemia or thrombocytopenia.[a] May or may not have lymph nodes, splenomegaly or hepatomegaly	RBC: Hb <11 g/dL or Platelets: <100 × 10⁹/L

Binet stating system

Binet stages	Clinical features	RBC and platelet counts
A	Up to two of the areas of involvement[b]	Hb ≥10 g/dL Platelets ≥100 × 10⁹/L
B	Three or more areas of nodal or organ enlargement[b]	Hb ≥10 g/dL Platelets ≥100 × 10⁹/L
C	Disease-related anemia or thrombocytopenia	Hb <10 g/dL and/or Platelet <100 × 10⁹/L

Based on Binet, J.L., et al., 1981. A new prognostic classification of chronic lymphocytic leukemia derived from a multivariate survival analysis. Cancer 48, 198–206; Rai, K.R., et al., 1975. Clinical staging of chronic lymphocytic leukemia. Blood 46, 219–234; Rai, K.R., 1987. A critical analysis of staging in CLL. In: Gale, R.P., Rai, K.R. (Eds.), Chronic Lymphocytic Leukemia: Recent Progress and Future Direction. 1987 UCLA Symposia on Molecular and Cellular Biology, New Series, vol. 59. Alan R Liss, New York, p. 253; Hallek, M., Cheson, B.D., Catovsky, D., et al., 2018. iwCLL guidelines for diagnosis, indications for treatment, response assessment, and supportive management of CLL. Blood 131 (25), 2745–2760.
[a]Anemia and thrombocytopenia due to medullar infiltration. Need to exclude auto immune cytopenia.
[b]The areas of involvement considered are (1) head and neck, including the Waldeyer ring (this counts as one area, even if more than one group of nodes is enlarged); (2) axillae (involvement of both axillae counts as one area); (3) groins, including superficial femoral (involvement of both groins counts as one area); (4) palpable spleen; and (5) palpable liver (clinically enlarged).

The median survival time for CLL patients categorized as Rai 01 and Binet A is 12 years, and which are considered low risk patients. On the other hand, the median survival time for Rai IV and Binet C is less than 3 years and these cases are the high-risk category. The remaining patients are put into the intermediate risk category (Nabhan and Rosen, 2014).

3. Molecular drivers of CLL

The development of CLL is a complex process that can't be attributed to a single genetic aberration. Monoclonal B-cell lymphocytosis is a premalignant stage that occurs prior to CLL, later CLL can transform into a more aggressive lymphoma, known as Richter transformation (Bosch and Dalla-Favera, 2019). Fluorescence in situ hybridization (FISH) can detect the most common recurrent genetic abnormalities in more than 80% of CLL patients. Some patients harbor more than one cytogenetic abnormality, indicating toward heterogenic nature of the disease. The most common somatic chromosomal deletions occur in the chromosome regions 13q14, 11q22–23, and 17p13 (Bosch and Dalla-Favera, 2019). Döhner et al. showed that the presence of these deletions influences median overall survival (Döhner et al., 2000). Recent progress in the next generation sequestering techniques has made it possible to sequence the whole genome, whole exome, and whole transcriptome in an unbiased, cost and time-effective manner, thus making it possible to identify the molecular drivers of the CLL oncogenesis. In general, driver somatic mutations are acquired mutations over time that provide the cells with an advantageous survival phenotypes, these mutations are present in the genome of the cancer cells and are absent from the normal noncancerous cells in the body (Vogelstein et al., 2013). The acquisition of somatic mutations is one of requisites of the cancer evolution in addition to the epigenetic cell state that is amenable to cancer growth. However, the majority of the somatic mutations do not make any significant change in the cells' ability to grow and survive. These mutations are known as passenger mutations as these mutations simply co-occur with the driver mutations in the cancer cells. To differentiate between the driver and passenger mutations remains a challenge in the field of functional cancer genomics.

The mutation status of the immunoglobulin heavy chain gene (IGHV) has now become an important factor in deciding the treatment strategies and is recommended to be carried out before beginning any therapy (Crombie and Davids, 2017). Based on the mutation status of the IGHV, the CLL patients are categorized as IGHV-unmutated if the homology is more than 98% with the germline heavy-chain sequence, patients with this profile have a poorer clinical prognosis. On the other hand, CLL patients with 2% or more difference from the germline heavy-chain sequence due to somatic hypermutation are categorized as IGHV mutated and are associated with better clinical prognosis and increased overall survival. The reasons behind the difference in clinical prognosis between IGHV unmutated and mutated remain largely enigmatic. Whole-exome sequencing of the more than 1000 CLL specimens and whole-genome sequencing of the 200 patient samples with CLL has revealed that there are ∼0.9 somatic mutations per megabase, including point mutations, copy number aberrations, and rare chromosomal translocations (Bosch and Dalla-Favera, 2019). In addition, there is a load of ∼10–30 nonsilent mutations per patient, with a higher number frequency of somatic substitutions in IGHV-mutated CLL (∼2800) than in IGHV-unmutated CLL (∼2000) (Lazarian et al., 2017). In CLL, the mutation load is lower than in other most epithelial tumors and lymphoid neoplasms (that is, diffuse large B-cell lymphoma, Burkitt lymphoma, and multiple myeloma) and is like that in the acute leukemias and pediatric tumors. Some of the IGHV mutated CLL patients lack any driver mutations thus making it tedious to explain carcinogenesis in these patients(Knisbacher et al., 2022). The recurrently mutated genes that drive CLL development have been identified using next generation sequencing studies and these are listed in Table 2 and shown in Fig. 1. The

Table 2 Somatic mutations in CLL patients identified using next generation sequencing studies, data collected from intOGen (https://www.intogen.org/) (Martínez-Jiménez et al., 2020).

Symbol	Mutations	Samples	Samples (%)	Cohorts
SF3B1	71	69	9.48	3
NOTCH1	15	58	7.97	2
ATM	51	41	5.63	4
TP53	42	34	4.67	3
MYD88	33	32	4.4	3
LRP1B	36	26	3.57	2
CHD2	23	26	3.57	3
FAT4	24	21	2.88	3
POT1	20	18	2.47	3
XPO1	18	15	2.06	3
BRAF	14	13	1.79	2
SPEN	12	12	1.65	3
FAT1	18	12	1.65	2
DDX3X	14	12	1.65	2
MGA	16	11	1.51	1
FAT3	12	11	1.51	2
DTX1	10	9	1.24	1
IRF4	9	9	1.24	2
EGR2	13	8	1.1	1
NFKBIE	2	8	1.1	2
BCOR	6	8	1.1	2
NXF1	9	8	1.1	2
FBXW7	11	8	1.1	2

Fig. 1 The somatic mutation driver cloud represents the most recurrently mutated **cancer driver genes in CLL.** The size of the gene symbol is relative to the count of samples with mutation in that gene, collected from intOGen (https://www.intogen.org/) (Martínez-Jiménez et al., 2020).

clonality of the somatic alterations can be used to reconstruct the phylogeny of the tumors. Thus, clonal mutations are somatic events that occur earlier and may drive the tumor initiation. On the other hand, subclonal mutations are acquired at later stages of the tumor development. In the case of the CLL, chromosomal alterations (del(13q), tri12, and del(11q)) are acquired clonal and initiating events. Later, CLL cells acquire sub-clonal driver mutations in *SF3B1*, *TP53*, *ATM*, *BIRC3*, *NOTCH1*, *POT1*, and others (Nadeu et al., 2020).

Deletions of the 13q14 chromosomal region are the most common genetic lesion that is associated with CLL disease (~50%–60% of patients), these deletions are mostly monoallelic (~80%) and frequently observed in IGHV-mutated CLLs. 13q14 deletions are often sole cytogenetic aberration, indicating its role in the initiation of CLL development (Bosch and Dalla-Favera, 2019; Parker and Strout, 2011). Studies using mouse models have shown that the deletion of 13q14 plays a critical role in CLL development. Around 20% of CLL patients have deletions in the 11q22–23 chromosomal region (11q–) at diagnosis and 11q deletions are associated with the IGHV-UM subtype of CLL disease (Bosch and Dalla-Favera, 2019). The genetic deletion of the 11q lesion is large (>20 Mb) and mostly monoallelic, and it includes the ataxia telangiectasia mutated (*ATM*) gene which is a well-known tumor suppressor. *ATM* gene encodes a protein that plays a crit-ical role in the cellular response to DNA damage. Disruption of the *ATM* gene is asso-ciated with genomic instability in CLL, and chemoresistance. In addition to the ATM gene, 11q deletions may also target *BIRC3* gene, which acts as a negative regulator of the noncanonical NF-κB pathway.

The deletions in the 17p13 chromosomal region (17p–) are relatively less frequent in the CLL patients at diagnosis, this deletion is more commonly found in those of the IGHV-unmutated subgroup (Bosch and Dalla-Favera, 2019). 17p losses invariably encompass the loss of the TP53 gene which is another well-known tumor suppressor gene and one of the most widely mutated across different cancer types. The p53 protein plays important roles in inducing cell apoptosis and arrest of the cell cycle when the DNA is damaged. Deletion of one copy of *TP53* gene is followed by the mutational disruption of the second allele in ~80% of 17q– CLL patients. The deletion of *TP53* leads to higher genomic instability thus the 17p– CLLs patients show higher genomic complexity and poor overall survival when compared TP53 wild-type patients. *TP53* mutations that lack 17p deletions of the second allele are also associated with poor responses to chemother-apeutic regimens, indicating their dominant-negative function.

Trisomy12 is found to be associated with early progression in CLL. Recurrent dupli-cation in the 12q13 region is found and there is ongoing speculation of an oncogene playing a pathogenic role (Stilgenbauer et al., 2002). The *MDM2* (murine double minute 2) an oncogene is reported to be overexpressed in CLL and is in the same region as the amplification unit of chromosome 12. However, *MDM2* overexpression is not associated with trisomy 12 aberration. CLL up-regulated gene (CLLU1) is highly up-regulated in

CLL cells and located in the same chromosome 12 region, but as for MDM2, the expression does not correlate with trisomy12 (Buhl et al., 2006). So far, the role of trisomy12 and associated genes involved is unsolved. Additionally, it is recently reported that *NOTCH1* (chromosome 9q34) mutations in CLL are associated with trisomy12 and together confer an unfavorable prognosis (del Giudice et al., 2012; Balatti et al., 2012). Somatic point mutations in the *NOTCH1* gene are found in ~12% of CLL patients at diagnosis, these mutations are mainly found in CLL IGHV-unmutated patient subgroup (Bosch and Dalla-Favera, 2019). It has been also noted that nearly 40% of the *NOTCH1* mutated CLL cases also have trisomy 12, suggesting functional synergistic relationship between these two genetic alterations. Other sequencing studies of the CLL samples have identified recurrent somatic mutations affecting components of the spliceosome machinery, with splicing factor 3b subunit 1 (*SF3B1*) mutations being the most frequent event (~10% of cases, mainly of the IGHV-unmutated subgroup). *SF3B1* is also one of the most highly recurrent somatically mutated genes in CLL, it encodes for a component of the U2snRNP and plays role in initiation of RNA splicing (Bosch and Dalla-Favera, 2019). The somatic events in the *SF3B1* gene are heterozygous missense mutations mapping to its highly conserved C terminus of the SF3B1 protein. *SF3B1*-K700E mutation alone accounts for half of all the mutations in the gene. The mutations in the *SF3F1* genes have been predicted to alter the interaction between RNA and *SF3B1*. In addition to the impact of *SF3B1* mutations on splicing, some of them are also thought to play a role in DNA damage responses.

BIRC3 is a negative regulator of NF-κB, and thus disruption of *BIRC3* through mutation or deletion may constitutively activate the NF-κB pathway and upregulate NF-κB target genes, e.g., numerous antiapoptotic genes in CLL cells (Bosch and Dalla-Favera, 2019; Rossi et al., 2012). Alterations in the *NOTCH1*, *SF3B1* and *BIRC3* genes are associated with poor survival and resistance to fludarabine treatment in patients harboring wild-type *TP53*. Additionally, low frequency of mutations in the *MYD88* gene, intracellular transducer of cytokine signaling, and toll-like receptor activation are also identified in CLL and described to alter the NF-κB inflammatory pathway (Landau et al., 2015; Puente et al., 2015). The *POT1* (protection of telomeres 1) gene is mutated in 3% to 7% of CLL patients with advanced disease at diagnosis (Bosch and Dalla-Favera, 2019). *POT1* encodes a component of the Shelterin protein complex and is involved in telomere protection. Most *POT1* mutations are represented by missense or truncating events that map to the two N-terminal Oligonucleotide/Oligosaccharide Binding OB1 and OB2 folds, which mediate interaction with single-strand TTAGGG sequences. These lesions were shown to result in destabilized binding to telomeric DNA, chromosomal breaks, and structural aberrations, without evidence of initiation of a DNA damage response (Ramsay et al., 2013). Other genetic lesions with functional consequences relevant to CLL pathogenesis include events affecting the chromatin remodeler chromodomain helicase DNA binding protein 2 (*CHD2*), which results in altered nuclear distribution and defective association with active chromatin, and mutations of the deoxynucleoside triphosphate triphosphohydrolase SAM domain and HD domain 1 (*SAMHD1*) (Bosch and Dalla-Favera, 2019).

In addition to the genomic, epigenomic alterations also play a key role in CLL development. Epigenomic studies have shed light on the clear reprogramming of regulatory regions in CLL tumor cells in comparison to the normal B cells (Nadeu et al., 2020). All epigenetic aberrations modulate heterogeneous biological and clinical behavior of the subsets of the CLL disease. The interaction between genomic and epigenomic alterations remains largely unknown in CLL. Tumors with subclonal mutations show higher heterogeneity in their methylation profile, and both methylation and subclonal changes evolve in parallel. In addition, studies have reported that rare somatic mutations in the genes involved in chromatin remodeling such as *CHD2* may lead to change in epigenomic landscape of the CLL cells. *CHD2* is mutated in ~4% of CLL patients and it binds to H3K4me3 histone marks that play a critical role in transcriptional regulation. The somatic mutations are loss of function mutations that either affect the functional domains or are truncating that alter the normal nuclear localization of the *CHD2* protein thus leading to affecting the transcriptomic profile of the cells with the mutations. Other examples of the genes that alter the epigenetic landscape of the CLL cells include *SETD2* (2%–5% CLLs) and *ARID1A* (2% CLLs) (Nadeu et al., 2020). Taken together these findings suggest somatic mutations and epigenetic alterations and their cross-interactions play a key role in CLL development.

4. Treatment modalities for the CLL disease

There are different types of treatment for patients with different degrees of severity and cancer growth for CLL patients. The choice of the treatment regimen for each CLL patient will depend on the stage of the disease, the clinical symptoms that are presented at the time of diagnosis, the age and overall health of the patient, and the benefits versus side effects of treatment. Treatment choice may also vary depending on whether the patient's lymphoma cells are missing parts of certain chromosomes called genomic deletions. One possible deletion in CLL is found in the smaller arm of chromosome 17 (called a 17p deletion). While 17p is one of the most commonly occurring deletions, other deletions may affect treatment options. In general, early-stage CLL patients who are asymptomatic, are not treated and are considered for "wait and watch" before the disease is in progression. A previous study reported that early asymptomatic patients who underwent treatment did not show any long-term benefits in comparison to patients for whom the treatment was started when the disease symptoms presented (Hallek et al., 2008).

Targeted therapy drugs or other substances are used to specifically eliminate cancer cells. Since these targeted therapies have minor harmful effects on normal cells in comparison to conventional chemotherapy or radiation therapies, these are expected to be less toxic and more effective. Different targeted treatment modalities are used to treat CLL. Tyrosine kinase inhibitors (TKI) treatment inhibitors are used to block cancer-driving enzymes, tyrosine kinases such as Bruton Tyrosine Kinases (BTK) or PI3 Kinase isoforms. TKIs such as ibrutinib, acalabrutinib, idelalisib, and duvelisib are used to treat symptomatic or progressive, recurrent, or refractory CLL. Idelalisib and ibrutinib both are approved for the treatment of CLL patients and target the BCR signaling pathway (Bosch and Dalla-Favera, 2019). More specifically, ibrutinib is an irreversible BTK inhibitor that abrogates BCR signaling, resulting in slowing CLL proliferation and overall growth. Idelalisib is a selective small molecule inhibitor of PI3Kδ isoform (PI3Kδ), PI3Kδ is specifically expressed in the hematopoietic cells. Idelalisib has been used alone and in combination with rituximab (O'Brien et al., 2015; Furman et al., 2014). Duvelisib is FDA approved PI3K inhibitor that specifically is used as a PI3Kδ/γ (PI3K delta and gamma isoforms) dual inhibitor (Brown, 2019). In the case of idelalisib and Duvelisib, toxicities were reported thus limiting their use to suitable CLL cases only. The BCL2 inhibitor therapy blocks a protein known as BCL2 which is present in the leukemia cells. In CLL, BCL2 prevents apoptosis using molecular mechanisms that are not very well understood (Bosch and Dalla-Favera, 2019). Targeting the BCL2 protein using Venetoclax kills the leukemia cells and makes them more prone to cell death induced by other anticancer drugs. Venetoclax is used for the treatment of symptomatic or progressive, recurrent, or refractory CLL.

Chemotherapeutic drugs stop the growth of cancers, either by stopping the cancer cells from dividing or by killing them. **Purine analogs such as** fludarabine, pentostatin, and cladribine are also used to treat CLL patients. Fludarabine is given as one of the first drugs for the treatment alongside cyclophosphamide and rituximab. This combination is also known as FCR. The CLL patients without the deletion of 17p and mutations in P53 genes who are relatively fit and have no renal-related problems, FCR or FC is the first line of therapy against the cancer (Hallek et al., 2010). FCR has better response rates than FC, however, has lower levels of toxicity. In the case of the overall survival rate, both perform well and have almost similar rate and complete remission (CR) is observed in 47%–70% of patients when they are given FCR or FC (Eichhorst et al., 2014). Immunotherapy induces the patient's immune system to get rid of the cancer cells. In this kind of treatment regimen, different molecules synthesized by the body or made in the laboratories are used to boost or reestablish the body's natural immunity against cancer. Immunomodulating agents such Lenalidomide stimulates T cells to eliminate CLL cells. It is used as a single therapy or given with rituximab to treat CLL patients. CAR T-cell therapy utilizes manipulated T cells that are called chimeric antigen receptor (CAR)-T cells. These T cells from the cancer patients are collected and genetically engineered to express anti-CD19 chimeric T-cell receptors. After this, these are infused back into patients' blood. These genetically engineered cells then proliferate in the patient's blood and attack the cancerous cells. In recent years, CAR-T cells have been given to the CLL patients (Kalos, 2016; Porter et al., 2011;

Turtle et al., 2017). These studies show that CAR-T-cell therapy is a good therapeutic regimen to consider for relapsed and refractory CLL patients who have been previously treated with other treatment modalities.

The combination of chemotherapy and immune therapy is known as chemo-immunotherapy. The therapy was found to result in better therapeutic response and progression free survival. **Alkylating agents such as** chlorambucil, bendamustine, and cyclophosphamide are often prescribed alongside monoclonal antibodies. Monoclonal antibodies are produced in the laboratory to create treatment regimens against many diseases, including CLL. These antibodies can attach to a specific target on cancer cells or other cells that may be helping cancer cells grow. The antibodies can then kill the cancer cells, block their growth, or keep them from spreading. Monoclonal antibodies are given by infusion. They may be used alone or to carry drugs, toxins, or radioactive material directly to cancer cells. Rituximab, ofatumumab, and obinutuzumab alone and in combination with chemotherapy are used to treat symptomatic or progressive, recurrent, or refractory CLL. Ofatumumab is an anti-CD20 monoclonal antibody that has been used in combination with FC and FCR as front-line therapy and it improves the CLL patient's outcomes. On the hand when Alemtuzumab (anti-CD52) was given in combination with FCR to CLL patients with 17p deletions and TP53 mutations, it resulted in overall efficacy, but major toxicities were reported, thus it was removed from the clinical trial (Rai and Jain, 2016).

In some of the cases that receive chemotherapy, tumor lysis syndrome is observed. In general, it happens during the first cycle of chemotherapy due to the presence of remarkably high number of CLL cells also known as bulky disease. In bulky disease condition, the chemotherapy kills lots of CLL cells and cell waste accumulate in the patient's blood. The kidneys are unable to filter out this waste, resulting in kidney failure and change in heart rhythm. This is generally treated by giving extra fluids to the patients to help clear the cell waste from the kidneys.

Despite a lot of progress in treating and managing CLL, the cancer type remains incurable. The cure for CLL patients remains a challenge due to the highly heterogeneous nature of cancer limiting the success of single target therapeutics. Thus, there is an urgent need for the development of novel therapies that have low toxicity and show high efficacy resulting in better prognosis.

5. Intratumor heterogeneity and clonal evolution of CLL

Most of cancers are driven by genetic alterations or oncogenic events in the genomes. It has been long recognized that the tumor cell populations within a cancer patient show great genetic diversity, this is known as tumors displaying genetic intratumor heterogeneity (ITH). In recent years, the advancement of more sophisticated single cell techniques such as scRNA sequencing and scATAC sequencing has shed light on tumors being IT heterogeneous in not only genetic but also nongenetic abnormalities, leading to phenotypic characteristics of the cancers. The nongenetic deviations can lead to changes in proteomes of the cells thus reshaping the phenotypic states of cancer and cancer-microenvironmental cells. Just like somatic mutation-driven tumor evolution of the tumors, phenotypic evolution and tumor plasticity is feasible due to nongenetic factors. High intratumor heterogeneity confers poor treatment prognosis and outcome in cancer patients. ITH leads to therapeutic resistance against cancer targeted treatments that were considered the panacea for the disease. This is because high intratumor heterogeneity means presence of various cellular phenotypes/states of the cancer cells that have different sensitivities to various therapies. High ITH makes it more challenging to select patients for the targeted therapies to accomplish the goals of precision medicine (Marusyk et al., 2020).

In general, cancerous cells employ various approaches to resist the treatment, these mainly include inactivating mutations in the target genes affecting the binding with the drugs, activating mutations in cellular signaling pathways, and overexpression of an unrelated cell survival pathway. Resistance to ibrutinib in CLL patients occurs mainly due to the presence of somatic mutations of its target gene *BTK* (C481S), or mutations in its direct downstream gene *PLCG2,* thus driving CLL by autonomously stimulating B-cell receptor activity (Sedlarikova et al., 2020). Scientists have investigated whether the therapeutic resistance in CLL patients was driven by the acquisition of de novo mutations, or whether the resistant clones were already present at a lower frequency in the pretreatment samples. It has been revealed that rare resistance-driving mutations already existed in the cancer patients (Bosch and Dalla-Favera, 2019; Burger et al., 2016). Like ibrutinib, resistance to venetoclax (an inhibitor of BCL2) is also a result of active selection. Of note, although somatic point mutations in genes involved in apoptosis (including the drug target *BCL2*) have recently been reported, relapse clones also use various other potential resistance mechanisms (Kapoor et al., 2020). Herling et al. reported 8 patients with CLL characterized by WES and methylation profiling before and after relapse to venetoclax These studies demonstrated signs of accumulating genomic instability (copy number alterations or aneuploidy); recurrent mutations in *BTG1, NOTCH1,* and *TP53*; and infrequent alterations in *BRAF, CD274 (PD-L1), NOTCH1, RB1, SF3B1,* and *TP53* (divergent evolution) (Herling et al., 2018).

Chronic lymphocytic leukemia patients that underwent Idelalisib therapy didn't respond to the targeted therapy. Ishwarya et al. reported that 60% of the Idelalisib nonresponders (6/10 CLLs) harbor baseline activating somatic mutations in *MAP2K1, BRAF,* and *KRAS* genes that belong to the MAPK pathway. They concluded that the MAPK/ERK pathway activation leads to resistance to idelalisib in CLL and thus suggested inhibition of ERK in combination with PI3Kδ. In the rest 40% of nonresponders (4/10 CLLs), they did not find any potential somatic mutations that can explain the resistance observed in CLL (Murali et al., 2021). Upregulation of the PI3Kδ or other isoforms may serve as a possible mechanism to PI3K inhibition using idelalisib and duvelisib (Skånland and Mato, 2021).

6. Future directions

Significant progress has been made in the last couple of decades toward understanding the genetic landscape of the IGHV mutated and unmutated CLL patients, identification of the novel molecular drivers of CLL development. The great depth of interpatient and intrapatient heterogeneity exists in CLLs, complicating the strategies of CLL treatments. The next goal is to utilize this generated knowledge to tailor better treatment modalities with higher efficacy and lower overall toxicities. Revealing functional implications and molecular mechanisms by which the majority of nonrecurrent and low-frequency identified genetic and epigenetic alterations drive CLL development remains a key goal in the CLL biology. Highly sensitive single cell sequencing technologies will shed light on the subclonal genetic and epigenetic changes and their role in disease progression and treatment resistance. This may help the clinicians in predicting cancer progression and possibly better managing the disease over time, resulting in better patient outcomes. The promise of targeted therapies against BCR and PI3K signaling and BCL2 have yielded good results but failed to confer advantages in unresponsive patients. Moreover, cancer recurrence in these therapeutic regimens has not been resolved because molecular mechanisms that drive such recurrence remain largely unknown. Identifying the genetic and epigenetic determinants of resistance to targeted therapies using single cell approaches should be the next frontier in CLL.

Acknowledgments

We feel grateful to the scientific community for generating plethora of knowledge in CLL biology in last few decades. We are also thankful to the patients who have made the clinical investigations possible by participating in the novel drug trials and biological studies by donating the precious patient samples.

References

Balatti, V., et al., 2012. NOTCH1 mutations in CLL associated with trisomy 12. Blood 119, 329–331.

Binet, J.L., et al., 1981. A new prognostic classification of chronic lymphocytic leukemia derived from a multivariate survival analysis. Cancer 48, 198–206.

Bosch, F., Dalla-Favera, R., 2019. Chronic lymphocytic leukaemia: from genetics to treatment. Nat. Rev. Clin. Oncol. 16, 684–701.

Brown, J.R., 2019. Phosphatidylinositol 3 kinase δ inhibitors: present and future. Cancer J. 25, 394–400.

Buhl, A.M., et al., 2006. Identification of a gene on chromosome 12q22 uniquely overexpressed in chronic lymphocytic leukemia. Blood 107, 2904–2911.

Burger, J.A., et al., 2016. Clonal evolution in patients with chronic lymphocytic leukaemia developing resistance to BTK inhibition. Nat. Commun. 7, 11589.

Crombie, J., Davids, M.S., 2017. IGHV mutational status testing in chronic lymphocytic leukemia. Am. J. Hematol. 92, 1393–1397.

del Giudice, I., et al., 2012. NOTCH1 mutations in +12 chronic lymphocytic leukemia (CLL) confer an unfavorable prognosis, induce a distinctive transcriptional profiling and refine the intermediate prognosis of +12 CLL. Haematologica 97, 437–441.

Döhner, H., et al., 2000. Genomic aberrations and survival in chronic lymphocytic leukemia. N. Engl. J. Med. 343, 1910–1916.

Eichhorst, B., et al., 2014. Frontline chemoimmunotherapy with fludarabine (F), cyclophosphamide (C), and rituximab (R) (FCR) shows superior efficacy in comparison to bendamustine (B) and rituximab (BR) in previously untreated and physically fit patients (pts) with advanced chronic lymphocytic leukemia (CLL): final analysis of an international, randomized study of the German CLL Study Group (GCLLSG) (CLL10 study). Blood 124, 19.

Eichhorst, B., et al., 2021. Chronic lymphocytic leukaemia: ESMO clinical practice guidelines for diagnosis, treatment and follow-up. Ann. Oncol. 32, 23–33.

Furman, R.R., et al., 2014. Idelalisib and rituximab in relapsed chronic lymphocytic leukemia. N. Engl. J. Med. 370, 997–1007.

Hallek, M., et al., 2008. Guidelines for the diagnosis and treatment of chronic lymphocytic leukemia: a report from the International Workshop on Chronic Lymphocytic Leukemia updating the National Cancer Institute-Working Group 1996 guidelines. Blood 111, 5446–5456.

Hallek, M., et al., 2010. Addition of rituximab to fludarabine and cyclophosphamide in patients with chronic lymphocytic leukaemia: a randomised, open-label, phase 3 trial. Lancet 376, 1164–1174.

Herling, C.D., et al., 2018. Clonal dynamics towards the development of venetoclax resistance in chronic lymphocytic leukemia. Nat. Commun. 9, 727.

Kalos, M., 2016. Chimeric antigen receptor-engineered T cells in CLL: the next chapter unfolds. J. Immunother. Cancer 4, 5.

Kapoor, I., Bodo, J., Hill, B.T., Hsi, E.D., Almasan, A., 2020. Targeting BCL-2 in B-cell malignancies and overcoming therapeutic resistance. Cell Death Dis. 11, 941.

Knisbacher, B.A., Lin, Z., Hahn, C.K., Nadeu, F., Duran-Ferrer, M., Stevenson, K.E., Tausch, E., Delgado, J., Barbera-Mourelle, A., Taylor-Weiner, A., Bousquets-Muñoz, P., Diaz-Navarro, A., Dunford, A., Anand, S., Kretzmer, H., Gutierrez-Abril, J., López-Tamargo, S., Fernandes, St.M., Sun, C., Sivina, M., Rassenti, L.Z., Schneider, C., Li, S., Parida, L., Meissner, A., Aguet, F., Burger, J.-A., Wiestner, A., Kipps, T.J., Brown, J.R., Hallek, M., Stewart, C., Neuberg, D.S., Martín-Subero, J.I., Puente, X.S., Stilgenbauer, S., Wu, C.J., Campo, E., Getz, G., 2022. Molecular map of chronic lymphocytic leukemia and its impact on outcome. Nat. Genet. 54 (11), 1664–1674. https://doi.org/10.1038/s41588-022-01140-w.

Landau, D.A., et al., 2015. Mutations driving CLL and their evolution in progression and relapse. Nature 526, 525–530.

Lazarian, G., Guièze, R., Wu, C.J., 2017. Clinical implications of novel genomic discoveries in chronic lymphocytic leukemia. J. Clin. Oncol. 35, 984–993.

Martínez-Jiménez, F., et al., 2020. A compendium of mutational cancer driver genes. Nat. Rev. Cancer 20, 555–572.

Marusyk, A., Janiszewska, M., Polyak, K., 2020. Intratumor heterogeneity: the rosetta stone of therapy resistance. Cancer Cell 37, 471–484.

Murali, I., et al., 2021. Activation of the MAPK pathway mediates resistance to PI3K inhibitors in chronic lymphocytic leukemia. Blood 138, 44–56.

Nabhan, C., Rosen, S.T., 2014. Chronic lymphocytic leukemia: a clinical review. JAMA 312, 2265–2276.

Nadeu, F., Diaz-Navarro, A., Delgado, J., Puente, X.S., Campo, E., 2020. Genomic and epigenomic alterations in chronic lymphocytic leukemia. Annu. Rev. Pathol. 15, 149–177.

Nosari, A., 2012. Infectious complications in chronic lymphocytic leukemia. Mediterr. J. Hematol. Infect. Dis. 4, e2012070.

O'Brien, S.M., et al., 2015. A phase 2 study of idelalisib plus rituximab in treatment-naïve older patients with chronic lymphocytic leukemia. Blood 126, 2686–2694.

Parikh, S.A., et al., 2014. Chronic lymphocytic leukemia in young (≤ 55 years) patients: a comprehensive analysis of prognostic factors and outcomes. Haematologica 99, 140–147.

Parker, T.L., Strout, M.P., 2011. Chronic lymphocytic leukemia: prognostic factors and impact on treatment. Discov. Med. 11, 115–123.

Porter, D.L., Levine, B.L., Kalos, M., Bagg, A., June, C.H., 2011. Chimeric antigen receptor-modified T cells in chronic lymphoid leukemia. N. Engl. J. Med. 365, 725–733.

Puente, X.S., et al., 2015. Non-coding recurrent mutations in chronic lymphocytic leukaemia. Nature 526, 519–524.

Rai, K.R., Jain, P., 2016. Chronic lymphocytic leukemia (CLL)-then and now. Am. J. Hematol. 91, 330–340.

Rai, K.R., et al., 1975. Clinical staging of chronic lymphocytic leukemia. Blood 46, 219–234.

Rai, K.R., et al., 2004. Clinical staging and prognostic markers in chronic lymphocytic leukemia. Hematol. Oncol. Clin. North Am. 18, 795–805. vii.

Ramsay, A.J., et al., 2013. POT1 mutations cause telomere dysfunction in chronic lymphocytic leukemia. Nat. Genet. 45, 526–530.

Rossi, D., et al., 2012. Disruption of BIRC3 associates with fludarabine chemorefractoriness in TP53 wild-type chronic lymphocytic leukemia. Blood 119, 2854–2862.

Sedlarikova, L., Petrackova, A., Papajik, T., Turcsanyi, P., Kriegova, E., 2020. Resistance-associated mutations in chronic lymphocytic leukemia patients treated with novel agents. Front. Oncol. 10, 894.

Skånland, S.S., Mato, A.R., 2021. Overcoming resistance to targeted therapies in chronic lymphocytic leukemia. Blood Adv. 5, 334–343.

Slager, S.L., Zent, C.S., 2014. Genetic risk of chronic lymphocytic leukemia: a tale of two cities. Leuk. Lymphoma 55, 735–736.

Stevenson, F.K., Krysov, S., Davies, A.J., Steele, A.J., Packham, G., 2011. B-cell receptor signaling in chronic lymphocytic leukemia. Blood 118, 4313–4320.

Stilgenbauer, S., Bullinger, L., Lichter, P., Döhner, H., German CLL Study Group (GCLLSG). Chronic lymphocytic leukemia, 2002. Genetics of chronic lymphocytic leukemia: genomic aberrations and V(H) gene mutation status in pathogenesis and clinical course. Leukemia 16, 993–1007.

Turtle, C.J., et al., 2017. Durable molecular remissions in chronic lymphocytic leukemia treated with CD19-specific chimeric antigen receptor-modified T cells after failure of ibrutinib. J. Clin. Oncol. 35, 3010–3020.

Vogelstein, B., et al., 2013. Cancer genome landscapes. Science 339, 1546–1558.

CHAPTER TEN

Myelodysplastic syndrome: A challenging entity

Anshu Palta and Manveen Kaur
Department of Pathology, Government Medical College and Hospital, Chandigarh, India

Myelodysplastic syndrome (MDS) is a clonal hematopoietic stem cell disorder which is heterogeneous in its pathogenesis and clinical presentation and is characterized by (i) peripheral cytopenias (Table 1), (ii) usually normocellular or hypercellular bone marrow, (iii) ineffective myelopoiesis [ineffective erythropoiesis and/ineffective granulopoiesis and/ineffective megakaryopoiesis], (iv) morphological features of dysplasia in one or more lineages, (v) cytogenetic abnormalities with the inherent risk of transformation to AML in 25%–33% of cases, thus becoming one of an important differential diagnosis of bone marrow failure syndromes (Arber et al., 2016; Hoffman et al., 2000; Tefferi and Vardiman, 2009; Vardiman et al., 2009). MDS predominantly affects older adults with a median age of 70 years and has a male predilection. Overall annual incidence is 3–5/100,000 but rising to >20/100,000 among those >70 years. The incidence rate is quite low in individuals aged <40 years of age, i.e., ~0.1 per 100,000 people per year. Age of onset is almost a decade younger in India. In one study of 150 cases of MDS, the median age was 55.5 (range 2–87 years). MDS accounts for < 5% of all hematopoietic neoplasms in patients aged less than 14 years of age (Naqvi et al., 2011; Tefferi and Vardiman, 2009).

Features of dysplasia may be associated with an increase in the number of myeloblasts in the peripheral blood and/or bone marrow, but the **blast percentage is always <20%, which is the prerequisite WHO threshold recommended for the diagnosis of AML**.

Tracing the history, first in 1938 hundred patients with refractory anemia were described. Subsequently, the terms "preleukemic anemia" and "preleukemia" were used. In 1963, a variant of acute leukemia was described, characterized by a prolonged and often benign clinical course, with a comparatively lower but variable percentage of bone marrow blasts; the authors termed this condition "smoldering acute leukemia." In the 1970s, chronic myelomonocytic leukemia (CMML) was recognized as a unique preleukemic syndrome. In 1976, the French-American-British (FAB) Cooperative Group initially defined refractory anemia with excess blasts (RAEB) and CMML as preleukemic states. These disorders and other entities of the MDS were subsequently defined by the WHO (Tefferi and Vardiman, 2009; Vardiman et al., 2009).

Biomarkers in Cancer Detection and Monitoring of Therapeutics
https://doi.org/10.1016/B978-0-323-95114-2.00003-0

Table 1 WHO criteria for cytopenias (Vardiman et al., 2009).

Hemoglobin	$<10\,\text{g/dL}$
Platelet count	$<100 \times 10^9/\text{L}$
Absolute neutrophil count	$<1.8 \times 10^9/\text{L}$

MDS is a disease with a remarkable impact on every-day life due to associated cytopenias leading to frequent infections and thus episodes of bleeding. Here it needs to be emphasized that a majority of patients with MDS have devastating morbidities and complications, requiring unique treatment strategies.

However, a diagnosis of MDS may still be made in patients with milder degrees of anemia (hemoglobin $<13\,\text{g/dL}$ in men or $<12\,\text{g/dL}$ in women) or thrombocytopenia (platelets $<150 \times 10\text{o}9/\text{L}$) if "definitive morphologic and/or cytogenetic findings are present."

1. Pathogenesis

Occurrence of MDS is a multistep process and involves changes within the hematopoietic progenitor stem cell, the bone marrow microenvironment and the immune system. Akin to the heterogeneous clinical presentation of MDS, its pathogenesis is also governed by varied and heterogeneous factors. Both heritable and nonheritable (acquired) factors are implicated in the pathogenesis of MDS, although majority of the cases are due to acquired abnormalities in the hematopoietic progenitors. Among heritable MDS, important conditions include genetic disorders such as Down's syndrome, Familial monosomy 7, and trisomy 8 mosaicism. Others are neurofibromatosis 1 and disorders of DNA repair such as Fanconi's anemia, Ataxia telangiectasia, Bloom syndrome, and Xeroderma pigmentosum (Neukirchen et al., 2011).

Most cases of MDS are due to nonheritable causes including environmental exposures to tobacco, smoking, alcohol, benzene, various infections and autoimmune disorders. Also included in this category is therapy-related MDS (t-MDS) or secondary MDS, which is caused by treatment with alkylating agents or topoisomerase inhibitors or radiation exposure. An increased risk of developing MDS is also seen in patients with acquired aplastic anemia and paroxysmal nocturnal hemoglobinuria. All these exposures ultimately lead to DNA damage and genetic alterations. MDS has been historically considered a disease of old age and accumulation of an increasing number of genetic and epigenetic alterations have been recently identified to be responsible for causing MDS. Apart from initiation of the disease, these changes are also involved in progression of MDS. Genetic defects include cytogenetic abnormalities, gene mutations and abnormal gene expression. Epigenetic events such as DNA methylation and histone modification result in silencing of the affected gene in the absence of any identifiable mutation. Both genetic and epigenetic alterations ultimately result in clonal hematopoiesis which is the common underlying event in all subtypes of MDS (Tefferi and Vardiman, 2009).

Chromosomal abnormalities can be detected in as many as 50%–60% cases of primary MDS and almost 80% to 90% of secondary (treatment-related) MDS (Bains et al., 2011; Bejar et al., 2011; Papaemmanuil et al., 2011). In addition to conventional cytogenetics, application of FISH further improves their identification, which is important not only in the diagnosis but also in the prognostication and in deciding the treatment regimens (Malcovati et al., 2011). Important chromosomal abnormalities and their prognostic relevance is shown in Table 2.

- Clonal hematopoiesis evidenced by karyotyping &/or molecular genetics is the key event in pathogenesis of MDS

- Abnormalities of chromosome 7 and complex karyotypes are associated with high risk of leukemic transformation

- del5(q), del20(q) and chromosome Y abnormalities are associated with low risk of leukemic transformation

With the advent of advanced technologies such as next-generation sequencing, somatic mutations have been detected in 80%–90% of patients of MDS. Following gene

Table 2 Cytogenetic abnormalities and their prognostic significance.

Cytogenetic abnormalities	Prognosis
del(5q)	Good
del(12p)	Good
del(20q)	Good
del(7q)	Intermediate
gain of chromosome 8 or 19	Intermediate
Isochromosome 17q	Intermediate
Loss of chromosome 7	Poor
inv(3), t(3q)or del(3q)	Poor
Complex karyotype (≥3 abnormalities)	Poor
Loss of Y chromosome	Very good
del(11q)	Very good

mutations are common and notable in the pathogenesis of MDS (Godley, 2021a; Goldberg et al., 2011; Hosono, 2019; Lindsley et al., 2017; Pellagatti and Boultwood, 2015; Sperling et al., 2017).

1. *Mutations in RNA splicing protein*s: SF3B1, SRSF2, U2AF1, ZRSR2
2. *Epigenetic modifications*:
    a. DNA methylation defects: TET2, DNMT3A, IDH1/IDH2
    b. Histone modification: ASXL1, EZH2
3. *Mutations in genes encoding transcription factors*: RUNX1, NRAS, BCOR
4. *Mutations in signaling proteins*: CBL
5. *Mutations in tumor suppressor genes*: TP53 mutation
6. *Mutations in Cohesin complex*: STAG2

From the above discussion, it is clear that the pathogenesis of MDS is complex and involves a plethora of somatic mutations. It is important, however, to note that these mutations are not mutually exclusive and more than one mutation could be found in any given case of MDS. Additionally, the detection of these mutations alone is insufficient for the diagnosis of MDS and only one genetic abnormality (SF3B1 mutation) has been given consideration in MDS subtype assignment according to the latest classification (WHO 2016 Update). SF3B1 is a recently described mutation in about 80% of MDS cases with ring sideroblasts (MDS-RS) and is associated with a favorable prognosis.

2. Clinical presentation

MDS is heterogeneous in its clinical presentation. Most of the clinical features are attributed to associated cytopenias (Foran and Shammo, 2012; Steensma, 2012). Nevertheless a few patients are asymptomatic and come to attention because of abnormalities revealed on routine complete blood count (CBC).

Anemia: MDS patients most commonly present with anemia which result in weakness, fatigue, postural dizziness and cardiovascular signs and symptoms like dyspnea on exertion, angina and sometimes congestive heart failure. All these contribute to poor quality of life and some of these patients become transfusion dependent.

Leucopenia: Leucopenia mainly associated with neutropenia along with defects in chemotaxis leads to increased risk of infections. Bacterial infections are the most common and mainly involve skin. However viral, fungal and mycobacterial infections can also occur, although more common in immunosuppressed individuals.

Thrombocytopenia: Patients have increased predisposition to bruising, petechiae, purpura, ecchymosis, and bleeding because of decreased platelet counts and defects in platelet function.

Neutropenia and thrombocytopenia are relatively less common as compared to anemia which is the most common cytopenia.

"It is noteworthy that refractory anemia refers to anemia that is non-responsive to hematinics given for 3 months."

Organomegaly: Lymphadenopathy, hepatomegaly and splenomegaly are extremely uncommon. Mild splenomegaly can, however, occur in cases of hemolysis.

Autoimmune manifestations: Nearly 25% patients of MDS can present with auto-immune abnormalities like Rheumatoid arthritis, chronic rheumatic heart disease, Per-nicious anemia, Psoriasis, Polymyalgia rheumatica, iritis, peripheral neuropathy, etc. These autoimmune phenomena can occur prior to the diagnosis or can follow (Lindsley et al., 2017).

3. Classification

MDS was first classified into five subgroups, based on the FAB (French American British) system. In 1999, WHO gave classification for MDS which was updated three times; in 2001, 2008, and 2016 (Arber et al., 2016; Tefferi and Vardiman, 2009; Vardiman et al., 2009) (Table 3).

FAB classification worked for a few years but there was a need for better classification because

- *Each FAB subgroup was heterogeneous.*
- *Guidelines for RA & RARS were ambiguous & resulted in different interpretation by different observers.*
- *Patients categorized as RAEB differed in prognosis according to the degree of increase in blasts.*
- *Controversy started rising whether CMML, particularly those with high TLC should be classified as MDS or MPD.*
- *Some cases were unclassifiable.*
- *FAB classification ignores other information of prognostic significance* (Tables 4 and 5).

The various subtypes of MDS are classified according to the number of cytopenias at presentation, the number of myeloid lineages exhibiting dysplasia, the presence of ring sideroblasts, and the percentages of blasts in the peripheral blood and bone marrow.

Table 3 FAB classification, 1982.
Refractory anemia

Refractory anemia with ring sideroblasts
Refractory anemia with excess of blasts
Refractory anemia with excess of blasts in
transformation (now AML)
Chronic myelomonocytic leukemia

Table 4 WHO classification, 2001; WHO classification, 2008.

Refractory anemia	Refractory cytopenia with unilineage dysplasia
Refractory cytopenia with multilineage dysplasia	Refractory cytopenia with multilineage dysplasia
5q(−) syndrome	Myelodysplastic syndrome with isolated del(5q)
Myelodysplastic syndrome, not otherwise specified	Myelodysplastic syndrome, unclassifiable
Refractory anemia with ringed sideroblasts	Refractory anemia with ring sideroblasts
Refractory anemia with excess of blasts	Refractory anemia with excess of blasts
Type I	Type 1
Type II	Type 2
	Childhood myelodysplastic syndrome

Table 5 WHO 2016 update.

MDS with single lineage dysplasia (MDS-SLD)
MDS with multiple lineage dysplasia (MDS-MLD)
MDS with ring sideroblasts(MDS-RS-)
MDS with ring sideroblasts with single lineage dysplasia (MDS-RS-SLD)
MDS with ring sideroblasts with multiple lineage dysplasia (MDS-RS-MLD)
MDS with excess of blasts
MDS with excess of blasts1(MDS-EB-1)
excess of blasts2(MDS-EB-2)
MDS with isolated del(5q)
MDS-U
With 1% blood blasts
With single lineage dysplasia and pancytopenia
Based on defining cytogenetic abnormality

3.1 MDS with single lineage dysplasia (MDS-SLD)

MDS-SLD comprises 7%–20% of all cases of MDS. It is characterized by refractory cytopenia or bicytopenia along with dysplasia in one myeloid lineage which is responsive to growth factors but not to hematinics.

Genetics

Cytogenetic abnormalities can be detected in nearly 50% of cases and include del(20q), +8 and abnormalities of 5 and/or 7. Patients with MDS SLD and MDS MLD with thrombocytopenia often show del(20q) and is useful to distinguish this entity from ITP. Somatic driver mutations have been found in 60%–70% cases of MDS-SLD.

Prognosis

Most of the patients have an indolent clinical course. Overall median overall survival is 66 months. The rate of progression to acute myeloid leukemia at 5 years is 10%. Approximately 90%–95% of patients with MDS-SLD have a low or intermediate 1 IPSS risk score (Table 6).

3.2 MDS with multiple lineage dysplasia (MDS-MLD)

MDS-MLD accounts for approximately 30% of cases and is characterized by one or more cytopenias along with dysplastic features in two or more of the lineages (erythroid, granulocytic, and megakaryocytic). The blast percentage is <1% in the peripheral blood and <5% in the bone marrow. Auer rods are absent, and the monocyte count in the peripheral blood is $<1 \times 10^9$/L.

Genetics

Clonal cytogenetic abnormalities are detected in approximately 50% of patients with MDS which include +8, −7, −5, del(20q), del(7q), and del(5q). More than 50% cases of MDS-MLD carry mutations in genes that are also mutated in MDS with excess blasts and acute myeloid leukemia; STAG2, ASXL1, RUNX1, TET2, CBL and TP53.

Prognosis

Median survival is approximately 36 months. Progression to AML is approximately 15% at 2 years and 28% at 5 years. Complex karyotypes associated with worse survival (10–18 months) similar to MDS-EB (Table 7).

3.3 MDS with ring sideroblasts (MDS-RS)

MDS-RS-SLO accounts for 3%–11% of all MDS cases. MDS-RS-MLO is relatively more common, accounting for about 13% of MDS cases. MDS with ring sideroblasts

Table 6 MDS with single lineage dysplasia.

Name	Dysplastic lineages	Cytopenia(s)	Ring sideroblasts	PB blasts	BM blasts
MDS with single lineage dysplasia (MDS-SLD)	1	1 or 2	<15% ring sideroblasts or <5% if SF3B1 mutation present	Blasts <1%; No Auer rods	Blasts <5%; No Auer rods

Table 7 MDS with multilineage dysplasia.

Name	Dysplastic lineages	Cytopenia (s)	Ring sideroblasts	PB blasts	BM blasts
MDS with multilineage dysplasia (MDS-MLD)	2 or 3	1 or 3	<15% ring sideroblasts or <5% if SF3B1 mutation present	Blasts <1%; No Auer rods	Blasts <5%; No Auer rods

(MDS-RS) is characterized by cytopenias, morphological features of dysplasia and ≥15% ring sideroblasts on Perl's stain.

Genetics

Chromosomal abnormalities are seen in approximately 5%–20% of MDS-RS-SLD and typically involve a single chromosome, −7. Spliceosome gene mutation, i.e., *SF3B1* is frequent in 80%–90% of MDS-RS-SLD cases and 30%–70% of MDS-RS-MLD cases. Mutations in genes affecting DNA methylation (TET2 and DNMT3A) are associated with SF3B1 mostly in MDS RS.

In the presence of *SF3B1* mutation, ≥5% ring sideroblasts are sufficient for the diagnosis. Myeloblasts count is <5% of the nucleated bone marrow cells and <1% in peripheral blood. Auer rods are absent. In MDS with ring sideroblasts and single lineage dysplasia (MDS-RS-SLD), there is anemia along with dysplasia limited to the erythroid lineage only. In MDS with ring sideroblasts and multilineage dysplasia (MDS-RS-MLD), there are any number of cytopenias and dysplasia is present in two or three hematopoietic lineages.

Prognosis

Overall median survival is 69 to 108 months in MDS-RS-SLD and 28 months in MDS-RS -MLD. Rate of progression to AML is 1%–2% in cases of MDS-RS-SLD and 8% in MDS-RS-MLD.

Adverse prognostic factors include MDS RS MLD, absence of SF3B1 mutation, thrombocytopenia and RUNX1 mutations (Table 8).

3.4 MDS with excess of blasts

It accounts for approximately 40% of all cases of MDS. On the basis of number of blasts, this entity is classified into two subtypes:
- *MDS with excess of blasts 1 (MDS-EB-1)*
- *MDS with excess of blasts 2 (MDS-EB-2)*

MDS with excess of blasts 1 (MDS-EB-1) is defined by or 2%–4% blasts in the peripheral blood and 5%–9% blasts in the bone marrow. MDS with excess of blasts 2(MDS-EB-2) is

Table 8 MDS with ring sideroblasts.

Name	Dysplastic lineages	Cytopenia(s)	Ring sideroblasts	PB blasts	BM blasts
MDS with ring sideroblasts(MDS-RS) MDS with ring sideroblasts with single lineage dysplasia (MDS-RS-SLD)	1	1 or 2	≥15% ring sideroblasts or ≥5% if SF3B1 mutation present	<1% blasts	Blasts <5% No Auer rods
MDS with ring sideroblasts with single lineage dysplasia (MDS-RS-SLD)	2 or 3	1 or 3	≥15% ring sideroblasts or ≥5% if SF3B1 mutation present	<1% blasts	Blasts <5% No Auer rods

defined by 10%–19% blasts in the bone marrow or 5%–19% blasts in the peripheral blood. **The presence of Auer rods in blasts marks any case of MDS as MDS-EB-2 irrespective of the percentage of blasts.**

Genetics

Thirty to 50% of cases of MD-EB have clonal cytogenetic abnormalities like +8, −5, del(5q), and −7, del(7q). Somatic. Mutations include splicing genes, SRSF2 (in both EB1 and EB2). Other mutations include IDH1/ IDH2, ASXL1, CBL, RUNX1, RAS. In addition, complex karyotypes may also be detected.

Prognosis

Median survival in cases with MDS-EB-1 is 16 months and in cases with MDS-EB-2 is 9 months. Nearly 25% cases of MDS-EB-1 and 33% of cases of MOS-EB-2 progress to AML (Table 9).

3.5 MDS with isolated del(5q)

MDS with isolated del(5q) mutation has a female predilection and is characterized by predominant presentation of anemia. It can be accompanied by other cytopenias and thrombocytosis. On the contrary thrombocytopenia is uncommon. Blast percentage is <5% in bone marrow and <1% in the peripheral blood. Auer rods are absent. Progression to AML is seen in <10% of cases.

Table 9 MDS with excess of blasts.

Name	Dysplastic lineages	Cytopenia(s)	Ring sideroblasts	PB blasts	BM blasts
MDS with excess of blasts (MDS-EB)					
MDS with excess of blasts (MDS-EB-1)	0–3	1–3	None or any	2%–4% blasts	Blasts 5%–9% No Auer rods
MDS with excess of blasts (MDS-EB-2)	0–3	1–3	None or any	5%–19% blasts	Blasts 10%–19% Auer rods+

Table 10 MDS with isolated del(5q).

Name	Dysplastic lineages	Cytopenia (s)	Ring sideroblasts	PB blasts	BM blasts
MDS with isolated del(5q)	1–3	1–2	None or any	Blasts <1%; No Auer rods	Blasts <5%; No Auer rods

Genetics

Cytogenetic abnormality is del(5q), i.e., deletion between bands q31 and q33 on chromosome 5. Size of deletion and breakpoints are variable. Any additional cytogenetic abnormality excludes placement in this category.

Prognosis

Good long-term survival. Progression to AML is seen in <10% of cases (Table 10).

3.6 MDS-U

All the cases of MDS that initially lack diagnostic criteria for classification into any the defined MDS category can be grouped into MDS-U. Exact incidence is not known. Few studies have estimated its incidence at approximately 6.3%. Diagnosis can be made in the following instances:

Patients with findings of MDS-SLD or MDS-MLD but with 1% blasts in the PB on two successive evaluations

- Cases of MDS-SLD which are associated with pancytopenia
- Patients with persistent cytopenia(s) with 1% or fewer blast in PB and <5%
- In the BM, unequivocal dysplasia in <10% of cells in one or more myeloid lineages and which have cytogenetic abnormalities considered as presumptive evidence of MDS

Genetics

May be normal or may have clonal abnormalities as in other MDS syndromes.

Prognosis

Patients in this category have unknown heterogeneous clinical behavior. Occasionally defining characteristics develop and subsequently the case is reclassified (Table 11).

3.7 Refractory cytopenia of childhood (RCC)

RCC accounts for approximately 50% of all cases of childhood myeloid neoplasm and is defined by <5% blasts in the bone marrow and <2% blasts in the peripheral blood. In nearly 80% cases bone marrow is hypocellular, thus posing a challenge to differentiate it from other causes of hypocellular bone marrow like acquired aplastic anemia, inherited bone marrow failure disorders and hypocellular acute leukemias.

Genetics

Cytogenetic abnormalities are present in approximately 20% of the cases and Monosomy 7 is the most common cytogenetic abnormality seen (20%). Although rare, spontaneous disappearance of cytopenia with monosomy 7 and del (7q) has been reported in some infants. Patients with trisomy 8 or a normal karyotype may experience a long, stable course of disease. In a small percentage of patients, GATA2 mutations can be seen. The risk of transformation to AML in various MDS subtypes is shown in Table 12.

Table 11 MDS-unclassified.

Name	Dysplastic lineages	Cytopenia(s)	Ring sideroblasts	PB blasts	BM blasts
MDS-Unclassified(MDS–UC)					
– With 1% blood blasts	1–3	1–3	None or any	=1% (counted on two separate occasions)	Blasts <5%; No Auer rods
– With single lineage dysplasia and pancytopenia	1	3	None or any	1% blasts No Auer rods	Blasts <5%; No Auer rods
– Based on defining cytogenetic abnormality	0	1–3	<15%	1% blasts No Auer rods	Blasts <5%; No Auer rods

MDS
- It is noteworthy that the myeloid lineages which are affected by cytopenias are not essentially the same as those manifest dysplasia accounting for the replacement of word cytopenias with MDS in the latest classification

MDS
- MDS-RS with *SF3B1* mutations need special attention as patients showing *SF3B1* mutations need >/=5% ring sideroblasts as compared to >15% criteria required for the diagnosis of MDS with RS . Moreover these patients have more favourable course and relatively lesser risk of leukemic transformation but at the same time have higher risk of becoming transfusion dependent

MDS
- Excess blasts define a distinct disease phenotype and requires careful verification of the bone marrow and blood blast counts
- [Text]

Table 12 Risk of transformation to AML in various MDS subtypes.

Subtype	Risk
MDS with single lineage dysplasia (MDS-SLD)	2%
MDS with ring sideroblasts(MDS-RS)MDS with multilineage dysplasia (MDS-MLD)	1%–2%
MDS with multilineage dysplasia (MDS-MLD)	10%
MDS with excess of blasts (MDS-EB-1)	25%
MDS with excess of blasts (MDS-EB-2)	33%
MDS -U	Unknown
MDS with isolated del(5q)	<10%

4. Approach to diagnosis of MDS

Establishment of diagnosis of MDS requires an extensive evaluation of the clinical history, physical examination, peripheral blood film analysis, biochemical studies and finally a thorough bone marrow aspiration and biopsy examination.

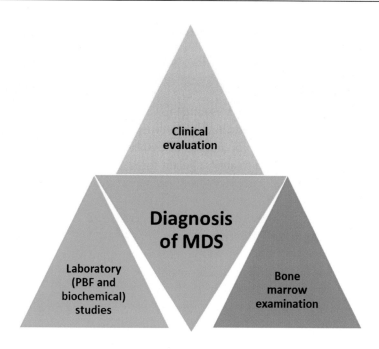

The diagnosis and classification of MDS depends on the morphologic assessment of the peripheral blood (PB) and bone marrow (BM), with presence of cytopenia and dysplasia (in >10% of cells) in at least one hematopoietic lineage, increase in number of PB/BM blasts, and/or MDS-defining cytogenetic abnormality (Arber et al., 2016; Naqvi et al., 2011). The initial investigation in a patient presenting with clinical features suggestive of myelodysplasia is complete blood count with reticulocyte count and peripheral blood film examination.

4.1 Complete blood count (CBC)

CBC with leucocyte differential consistently reveals anemia in most of the cases of MDS. However, the presence of neutropenia and thrombocytopenia is variable and around 50% cases have pancytopenia.

Monocytosis is also considered an important finding on CBC. Leucocyte differential might also show a shift to the left with presence of immature cells and increase in number of blasts. Few cases demonstrate thrombocytosis, which might be indicative of an isolated del5q or a specific category of MDS/MPN known as MDS/ MPN with ringed sideroblasts and thrombocytosis (harboring SF3B1 mutation).

Anemia is associated with an inadequate reticulocyte response with usual reticulocyte count being less than 1% in most of the cases. RBC indices reveal macrocytosis with

MCV >100 fl and usually a normal MCHC. Red cell distribution width is increased reflecting anisopoikilocytosis.

4.2 Peripheral blood film (PBF)

An analysis of peripheral blood film is essential for blast count and to look at features of dysplasia in the various hematopoietic lineages before proceeding to bone marrow examination. WHO recommends that for analysis of dysplasia on PBF,

- fresh blood which is exposed to anticoagulant for not more than 2 h should be used.
- All slides should be stained with May Grunwald Giemsa (MGG) stain for establishing features of dysplasia.

Important morphologic abnormalities characteristic of dysplasia in different hematopoietic lineages on PBF are:

RBCs: Red blood cells (RBCs) in MDS are macrocytic and often show megaloblastic morphology. However, alone this feature is nonspecific and many other differentials (discussed later) must be excluded.

WBCs: Granulocytic dysplasia is particularly better appreciated on PBF as compared to bone marrow. Features of dysplastic neutrophils are small or unusually large size, nuclear hyposegmentation and reduced granularity (known as Pseudo-Pelger Huet anomaly, Fig. 1A), nuclear hypersegmentation (Fig. 1B) and even abnormally large granules (Pseudo-Chediak Higashi granules). Nonlobated nuclei and abnormal clumping of chromatin may be apparent. At least 200 leucocyte differential count on freshly prepared and adequately stained PBF to analyze blast percentage is important in categorizing the MDS subtype. Buffy coat can be prepared for differential count in cases with severe cytopenia.

Platelets: Dysplastic platelets could be smaller or larger than normal and have a hypogranular cytoplasm.

4.3 Bone marrow examination

Bone marrow examination is an essential component of the evaluation, diagnosis, and classification of MDS. Most MDS cases typically show a markedly increased marrow cellularity for the patient's age. Hypocellularity is more frequent in pediatric MDS, following prior aplastic anemia, and in therapy related MDS. Cases may have single lineage or multilineage (bilineage or trilineage) dysplasia depending on the number of lineages with ≥10% dysplastic cells. An adequate bone marrow aspirate should provide material for a 500 cell differential count and a cytologic evaluation of the blasts and other cells. Additionally, staining with Perl's Prussian Blue stain is required to detect ring sideroblasts and Periodic acid–Schiff (PAS) staining proves helpful in detecting dyserythropoiesis. Cytochemical staining with Myeloperoxidase (MPO) and Sudan Black B (SBB) highlights abnormal myeloid differentiation and is useful in counting the number of blasts.

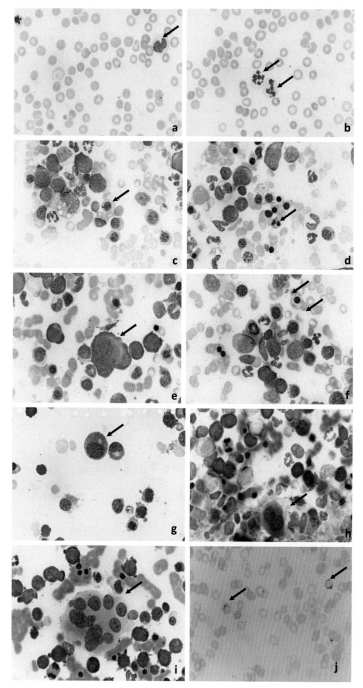

Fig. 1 (A) Photomicrograph of peripheral blood smear showing Pseudo Pegler-Huet anomaly (MGG, X1000). (B) Photomicrograph of peripheral blood smear showing hypersegmentation of neutrophils (MGG, X1000). (C) Bone marrow aspirate showing dyserythropoiesis in the form of multinucleation (MGG, X1000). (D) Bone marrow aspirate showing dyserythropoiesis in the form of nuclear bridging (MGG, X1000). (E) Bone marrow aspirate showing dyserythropoiesis in the form of nuclear budding (MGG, X1000). (F) Bone marrow aspirate showing dyserythropoiesis in the form of megaloblastoid features(MGG, X1000). (G) Bone marrow aspirate showing dysgranulopoiesis in the form of hypogranulation(MGG, X1000). (H) Bone marrow aspirate showing dysmegakaryopoiesis in the form of hypolobation (MGG, X1000). (I) Bone marrow aspirate showing dysmegakaryopoiesis in the form of nuclear separation (MGG, X1000). (J) Bone marrow aspirate showing dyserythropoiesis in the form of ring sideroblasts (Prussian Blue, X1000).

Table 13 Morphologic features of MDS in bone marrow.

Hematopoietic lineage	Dysplastic features
Erythroid	Nuclear multilobation (Fig. 1C)
	Nuclear bridging (Fig. 1D)
	Internuclear budding (Fig. 1E)
	Megaloblastoid features (Fig. 1F)
	Cytoplasmic vacuolization
	Coarse or fine Periodic acid–Schiff-positive granule
	Ring sideroblasts (Fig. 1J)
Myeloid	Impaired myeloid maturation
	Maturation arrest at the myelocyte stage
	Hypogranulated myelocytes (Fig. 1G)
	Abnormal localization of immature precursors
	Increased Myeloblasts
	Auer rods (Diagnostic of MDS with excess blasts, regardless of blast percentage)
Megakaryocytic	Increased in number, sometimes in clusters
	Micromegakaryocytes or "dwarf megakaryocytes"
	Non-lobulated or mononuclear megakaryocytes, (associated with del5q-) (Fig. 1H)
	Megakaryocytes with multiple dispersed nuclei ("pawn ball megakaryocytes") (Fig. 1I)

Characteristic morphologic features of MDS on bone marrow examination are shown in the following table (Table 13).

4.4 Bone marrow biopsy

The usefulness of bone marrow biopsy in evaluation of a suspected case of MDS cannot be overemphasized. It allows better appreciation of the bone marrow cellularity, blast percentage and distribution of various cells in the marrow spaces. Most of the cases of MDS have a hypercellular marrow with the presence of immature cells in variable numbers. Approximately 10% cases of MDS have a hypocellular marrow for age, a feature more often encountered in pediatric patients. Normally, immature cells are seen at either paratrabecular or perivascular locations. Presence of aggregates or clusters of immature cells in the central portion of bone marrow spaces away from their normal location is known as Abnormal localization of immature precursors (ALIP), which is a pointer toward diagnosis of MDS. Apart from that, presence of bone marrow fibrosis (on reticulin staining) and lymphoid aggregates also requires bone marrow biopsy.

Immunohistochemical stains such as CD34 can be applied on bone marrow for delineating blast percentage, particularly in cases of hypocellular MDS. Megakaryocyte markers such as CD41, CD61 can be used to identify micromegakaryocytes which could be difficult to discern on bone marrow biopsy. Bone marrow biopsy is of great importance in identifying megakaryocytic dysplasia, features of which are better appreciated than on aspiration. For diagnosis of megakaryocytic dysplasia, WHO recommends that at least 30 megakaryocytes should be counted, out of which at least 10% should be dysplastic to fulfill the diagnostic criteria.

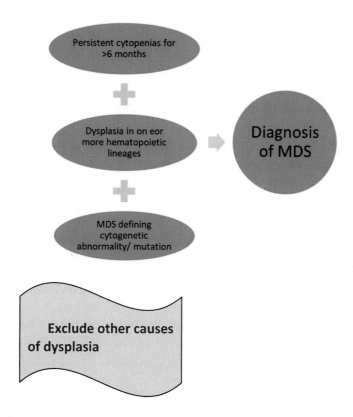

4.5 Differential diagnoses

Making a diagnosis of MDS is a daunting task and has significant implications, both for the patient, as well as the treating physician. It requires a careful and thorough evaluation to distinguish it from a long list of differential diagnoses, which includes both hematologic and nonhematologic conditions. These mimics could be associated with one or more features of MDS, i.e., dysplasia, cytopenias, and/or clonality (Hosono, 2019).

Clinical features of MDS are nonspecific and the diagnosis is suspected in an elderly patient if anemia, thrombocytopenia, or neutropenia are detected on routine CBC. In cases of isolated anemia, it is reasonable to rule out nonhematologic conditions such as gastrointestinal bleeding, cardiac cause and nutritional deficiencies before proceeding to further hematologic work-up. Organomegaly is uncommon in MDS and should raise suspicion of a hematologic cause, i.e., a myeloproliferative or lymphoproliferative neoplasm, particularly if associated with leucocytosis.

Important differential diagnoses of MDS include the following (Godley, 2021a; Goldberg et al., 2011):

A. **Nonhematologic conditions:**

1. **Nutritional deficiencies**—Megaloblastic anemia caused by the deficiency of Vitamin B12 or folic acid or both is the most common condition that needs to be considered in the differential diagnosis of MDS. Severe deficiency can lead to cytopenias affecting all hematopoietic lineages and is associated with dysplasias which could be difficult to distinguish from MDS. Testing for serum B12 and folate levels should be done and patients should be given a trial of hematinics before subjecting them to bone marrow examination. Other than megaloblastic anemia, copper deficiency can also cause dysplasia and should be excluded by clinical examination and laboratory testing.

2. **Exposure to toxins and drugs**—Heavy metal poisoning (arsenic, lead, zinc) can lead to development of dysplastic features in various lineages. Also, excessive alcohol intake has been seen to lead to cytopenias and dysplasia. Certain drugs used for both hematologic and nonhematologic conditions are also known to cause dysplasia. Important ones include chemotherapeutic agents, antibiotics (such as cotrimoxazole, tacrolimus, and mycophenolate mofetil), antiepileptics like valproic acid, antitubercular drugs (isoniazid), antivirals (ganciclovir), alemtuzumab, and granulocyte colony-stimulating factor. Therefore, a thorough clinical history should be taken to rule out such exposures before considering a diagnosis of MDS. removal of the offending agent often leads to reversal of dysplastic changes.

3. **Infections**—Infection with HIV can cause cytopenias as well as dysplasia in one or more lineages, due to the direct effect of virus on hematopoietic progenitor cells or by indirect effect of drugs used for the treatment as well as due to the associated opportunistic infections. A proper history and laboratory testing for HIV status is therefore essential. Another infection which could lead to dysplasia, particularly affecting the erythroid lineage is Parvovirus B19, which could be diagnosed by associated features like reticulocytopenia, erythroblastopenia, and giant pronormoblasts. Kala azar and Plasmodium (vivax and falciparum) infection could also result in dysplasia affecting predominantly erythroid lineage.

B. **Hematologic conditions:**

1. **Congenital dyserythropoietic anemia (CDA)**—It can cause dysplasia in the erythroid lineage, however, it is usually detected in younger age and is associated

with a hypercellular bone marrow, in contrast with hypocellular MDS in children. Also, presence of hepatosplenomegaly and jaundice are pointers toward a diagnosis of CDA.

2. **Pelger-Huët anomaly**—A benign autosomal dominant condition characterized by presence of hyposegmented neutrophils. However, the neutrophils have normal phagocytic activity.

3. **Sideroblastic anemia**—Sideroblastic anemias comprise a spectrum of acquired and heritable erythropoietic disorders caused by various abnormalities of heme synthesis and mitochondrial function. Detection of ring sideroblasts requires exclusion of other causes of acquired sideroblastic anemia (e.g., copper deficiency, medications, excessive alcohol use).

4. **Myeloproliferative neoplasms (myelofibrosis)**—Mild to moderate bone marrow fibrosis is common in patients with MDS, and a small percentage display marked fibrosis that is similar to that in patients with primary myelofibrosis (PMF). Both conditions are associated with pancytopenia, but fibrotic MDS can be distinguished from PMF by the presence of significant dysplasia, diagnostic chromosomal abnormalities, lack of splenomegaly, and absence of mutations that are characteristic for PMF such as mutations of *JAK2*, *CALR*, or *MPL* which are present in >90% of patients with PMF, whereas only *JAK2* mutations could be found in MDS (in only 5% of cases).

5. **Aplastic anemia (AA)/paroxysmal nocturnal hemoglobinuria (PNH)**—Most patients with MDS have hypercellular bone marrow, but a minority have hypoplastic MDS that can resemble AA. MDS can generally be distinguished from AA by the characteristic dysplasia, ring sideroblasts, and/or karyotypic/molecular abnormalities.

6. **MDS/MPN syndromes**—The myelodysplastic/myeloproliferative neoplasms (MDS/MPN) include disorders where both dysplastic and proliferative features coexist. Cases with prominent dysplastic and myeloproliferative features should be classified as MDS/MPN rather than MDS. Myeloproliferative features include thrombocytosis (i.e., platelet count $\geq 450 \times 10^9$/L), megakaryocytic proliferation, and leukocytosis (white blood cell count $\geq 13 \times 10^9$/L) with or without prominent splenomegaly.

7. **Acute myeloid leukemia (AML)**—AML and MDS lie along a disease continuum. The distinction between MDS and AML is based on the blast percentage and/or the presence of certain cytogenetic/molecular features that are diagnostic of AML.

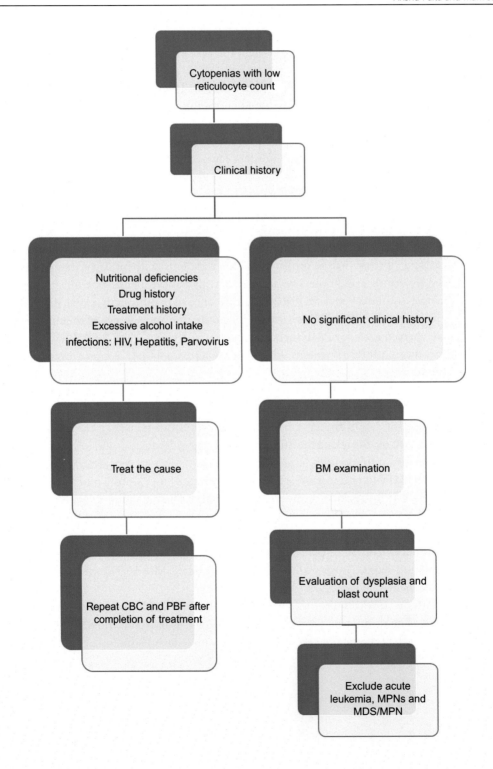

4.6 MDS scoring system

MDS is scored according to Revised International Prognostic Scoring System (IPSS-Revised) (Godley, 2021b; Valent et al., 2017).

Significance: MDS scoring system has been developed to predict outcomes in an individual case in terms of survival and risk of transformation to AML. It also helps to make treatment decisions (To treat or not to treat) (Table 14).

Key factors:

- MDS subtype
- Percent of blast cells
- Chromosome changes

> **Case study**
>
> A 68-year-old female presented with a hemoglobin 9 gm% and a platelet count that fell slowly from 2,30,000 to 97,000 over the past 3 years. Bone marrow reveals 1% blast cells with ANC of 0.6; cytogenetic study revealed del (20q).
>
> Diagnosis: MDS with single lineage dysplasia.
>
> IPSS-R scoring system
>
> | Parameter | Score |
> | --- | --- |
> | Hb 9.9 g% | 1 |
> | Platelet count 97,000/l | 0.5 |
> | Bone marrow Blast 1% | 0.5 |
> | del 20q | 1 |
>
> **So score is 3 with estimated survival of approximately 5.3 years.**

Table 14 IPSS-R scoring system.

	0	0.5	1	1.5	2	3	4
Cytogenetics	Very good		Good		Intermediate	Poor	Very Poor
BM BLAST %	<2%	>2%–<5%		5%–10%		>10%	
Hb	>10		8–10	<8			
Platelet count	100,000	50,000–100,000					
ANC	>0.8	<0.8					

Cytogenetics risk grouping	Cytogenetics
Very Good	Del 11q, –Y
Good	Normal, del 5q, del 12p, del 20q, double, including del 5q
Intermediate	del 7q, +8, +19, isochromosome 17q, any single or other double independent clones

Continued

Table 14 IPSS-R scoring system—cont'd

Cytogenetics risk grouping	Cytogenetics
Poor	−7, inv(3), t3q, del 3q, double independent including-7 /del 7q, complex = 3 abnormalities
Very Poor	Complex > 3 abnormalities

Score	<1.5 Very low	1.5–3 low	>3–4.5 intermediate	>4.5–6 High	>6 Very high
Survival	8.8	5.3 years	3	1.6	0.8
Risk of AML in 25% of cases	No risk	10.8 years	3.2	1.4	0.73

4.7 Treatment of MDS

Different therapeutic strategies are available for the management of patients with MDS. Considering the highly heterogeneous nature of this disease, accurate classification and assessment of prognosis is of utmost importance to provide individualized treatment to the patients. Risk assessment according to IPSS-R is important before starting treatment. Also important in the decision to treat are factors such as age, comorbidities, HLA status and availability of donors. For many low-risk MDS patients, particularly those with no symptoms, only watchful observation with regular follow-up is indicated.

Standard treatment regimes for MDS can be categorized as given below:

1. Supportive management

    Supportive management is indicated for low-risk MDS patients with mild cytopenias, no excess of blasts and no adverse cytogenetics (Manero, 2014). It includes:

    a. Treatment of anemia with repeated RBC transfusions (with concomitant iron chelation),

    b. Administration of growth factors such as erythropoietin (erythropoiesis stimulating agent) and granulocyte colony-stimulating factor (G-CSF).

    c. Thrombopoietin receptor agonists such as eltrombopag and romiplostim— important first-line options for patients with significant thrombocytopenia.

2. Suppression of MDS clone (Jabbour et al., **2015**; Lindberg and TobiassonM, **2020**)

    Hypomethylating agents (HMAs): 5-azacitidine and decitabine:

    • Cornerstone of treatment in higher-risk MDS cases (increased blasts, severe cytopenias, and/or adverse-risk cytogenetics)

    • Improve cytopenias for some patients and prolong survival

    • Act as a bridge before stem cell transplant

3. **Immunosuppressive agents (Mohammad, 2018)**

    Antithymocyte globulin (ATG) and cyclosporine have been used in MDS because of the underlying role of immune dysregulation in the pathogenesis of MDS.

4. **Lenalidomide:** It is a thalidomide analog used for low-risk MDS patients with isolated del5(q). It acts by exerting an antiproliferative effect on blasts and also has an immunomodulatory effect on bone marrow microenvironment (Lindberg and TobiassonM, 2020).

5. **Curative treatment**: **Allogeneic hematopoietic stem cell transplantation is the only potentially curative therapy for MDS patients (Lindberg and TobiassonM, 2020; Vardiman et al., 2009).**

Novel treatment strategies (including targeted therapy) (Arslan et al., 2021; Brunner and Steensma, 2018; Pagliuca et al., 2021; Weinberg and Hasserjian, 2019)

1. **Erythropoiesis-maturating agents (EMAs):** Luspatercept and sotatercept are specific activin receptor fusion proteins that act as ligand traps to neutralize negative regulators of late-stage erythropoiesis. These have been found very useful to treat anemia in patients harboring SF3B1 mutation.

2. **Hypoxia-inducible factor and telomerase modulation:** Roxadustat is an orally administered hypoxia-inducible factor prolyl hydroxylase inhibitor which promotes erythropoiesis by increasing endogenous EPO levels and modulating hepcidin levels. Imetelstat is a telomerase inhibitor targeting cells with short telomere lengths and hyperactive telomerase. These drugs are currently under clinical trials.

3. **Targeted molecular therapies-**
   a. **Venetoclax** is a B-cell leukemia/lymphoma-2 (BCL-2) inhibitor. It is one of the most potent antiapoptotic inhibitors, and represents a novel promising agent for the treatment of MDS.
   b. **IDH inhibitors and FLT-3 inhibitors**—currently in clinical trials
   c. **Drugs targeting p53 pathway**
   d. **Immune checkpoint inhibitors**—such as Pembrolizumab (Programmed death ligand-1 inhibitor) are currently being investigated for their potential role in management of MDS.

References

Arber, D.A., Orazi, A., Hasserjian, R., Thiele, J., Borowitz, M.J., Le Beau, M.M., et al., 2016. The 2016 revision to the World Health Organization classification of myeloid neo- plasms and acute leukemia. Blood 127 (20), 2391–2405S5.

Arslan, S., Khaled, S., Nakamura, R., 2021. Current management and new developments in the treatment of myelodysplastic syndrome. Cancer Treat. Res. 181, 115–132.

Bains, A., Luthra, R., Medeiros, L.J., Zuo, Z., 2011. FLT3 and NPM1 mutations in myelodysplastic syndromes: frequency and potential value for predicting progression to acute myeloid leukemia. Am. J. Clin. Pathol. 135, 62–69.

Bejar, R., Levine, R., Ebert, B.L., 2011. Unraveling the molecular pathophysiology of myelodysplastic syndromes. J. Clin. Oncol. 29 (5), 504–515.

Brunner, A.M., Steensma, D.P., 2018. Recent advances in the cellular and molecular understanding of myelodysplastic syndromes and implications for new therapeutic approaches. Clin. Adv. Hematol. Oncol. 16, 56–66.

Foran, J.M., Shammo, J.M., 2012. Clinical presentation, diagnosis, and prognosis of myelodysplastic syndromes. Am. J. Med. 125, S6–13.

Godley, L.A., 2021a. Germline mutations in MDS/AML predisposition disorders. Curr. Opin. Hematol. 28, 86–93.

Godley, L.A., 2021b. Germline mutations in MDS/AML predisposition disorders. Curr. Opin. Hematol. 28, 86–93.

Goldberg, S.L., Chen, E., Corral, M., Guo, A., Mody-Patel, N., Pecora, A.L., et al., 2011. Incidence and clinical complications of myelodysplastic syndromes among United States Medicare beneficiaries. J. Clin. Oncol. 28 (17), 2847–2852.

Hoffman, R., Benz, E., Shattil, S.J., Furie, B., Cohen, H.J., Silberstein, L.E., et al. (Eds.), 2000. Hematology: Basic Principle and Practice, third ed. Churchill Livingstone, New York, pp. 1106–1129.

Hosono, N., 2019. Genetic abnormalities and pathophysiology of MDS. Int. J. Clin. Oncol. 24, 885–892.

Jabbour, E.J., Garcia-Manero, G., Strati, P., Mishra, A., Al Ali, N.H., Padron, E., et al., 2015. Outcome of patients with low-risk and intermediate-risk myelodysplastic syndrome after hypomethylating agent failure: a report on behalf of the MDS clinical research consortium. Cancer 121 (6), 876–882.

Lindberg, E.H., TobiassonM, G.P., 2020. Myelodysplastic syndromes: moving towards personalized management. Haematologica 105, 1765–1779.

Lindsley, R.C., Saber, W., Mar, B.G., Redd, R., Wang, T., Haagenson, M.D., et al., 2017. Prognostic mutations in myelodysplastic syndrome after StemCell transplantation. N. Engl. J. Med. 376 (6), 536–547.

Malcovati, L., Papaemmanuil, E., Bowen, D.T., Boultwood, J., Della Porta, M.G., Pascutto, C., 2011. Clinical significance of SF3B1 mutations in myelodysplastic syndromes and myelodysplastic/myeloproliferative neoplasms. Blood 118 (24), 6239.

Manero, G.G., 2014. The myelodysplastic syndromes. In: Greer, J.P., Forester, J., Rodgers, G.M., Paraskevas, F., Glader, B., Arber, D.A. (Eds.), Wintrobe's Clinical Haematology 13ed. Lippincott Williams and Wilkins, Philadelphia, pp. 1673–1687.

Mohammad, A., 2018. Myelodysplastic syndrome from theoretical review to clinical application view. Oncol. Rev. (12), 134–142.

Naqvi, K., Garcia-Manero, G., Sardesai, S., Oh, J., Vigil, C.E., Pierce, S., et al., 2011. Association of comorbidities with overall survival in myelodysplastic syndrome: development of a prognostic model. J. Clin. Oncol. 29, 2240–2246.

Neukirchen, J., Schoonen, W.M., Strupp, C., Gattermann, N., Aul, C., Haas, R., et al., 2011. Incidence and prevalence of myelodysplastic syndromes: data from the Dusseldorf MDS-registry. Leuk. Res. 35 (12), 1591–1596.

Pagliuca, S., Gurnari, C., Visconte, V., 2021. Molecular targeted therapy in myelodysplastic syndromes: new options for tailored treatments. Cancers (Basel) 13 (4), 784.

Papaemmanuil, E., Cazzola, M., Boultwood, J., Malcovati, L., Vyas, P., Bowen, D., et al., 2011. Somatic SF3B1 mutation in myelodysplasia with ring sideroblasts. N. Engl. J. Med. 365 (15), 1384–1395.

Pellagatti, A., Boultwood, J., 2015. The molecular pathogenesis of the myelodysplastic syndromes. Eur. J. Haematol. 95, 3–15.

Sperling, S.A., Gibson, C.J., Ebert, B.L., 2017. The genetics of myelodysplastic syndrome: from clonal hematopoiesis to secondary leukemia. Nat. Rev. Cancer 17 (1), 5–19.

Steensma, D.P., 2012. Dysplasia has a differential diagnosis: distinguishing genuine myelodysplastic syndromes (MDS) from mimics, imitators, copycats and impostors. Curr Hematol Malig Rep. 7 (4), 310–320.

Tefferi, A., Vardiman, J.W., 2009. Myelodysplastic syndromes. N. Engl. J. Med. 361, 1872–1885.

Valent, P., Orazi, A., Steensma, D.P., Ebert, B.L., Haase, D., Malcovati, L., et al., 2017. Proposed minimal diagnostic criteria for myelodysplastic syndromes (MDS) and potential pre-MDS conditions. Oncotarget 8 (43), 73483–73500.

Vardiman, J.W., Thiele, J., Arber, D.A., Brunning, R.D., Borowitz, M.J., Porwit, A., et al., 2009. The 2008 revision of the WHO classification of myeloid neoplasms and acute leukemia: ratio- nale and important changes. Blood 114 (5), 937–951.

Weinberg, O.K., Hasserjian, R.P., 2019. The current approach to the diagnosis of myelodysplastic syndromes. Semin. Hematol. 56 (1), 15–21.

CHAPTER ELEVEN

Multiple myeloma

Vijay Goni, Vikas Bachhal, Deepak Negi, and Mohak Kataria
Postgraduate institute of Medical Education and Research, Chandigarh, India

Multiple myeloma is one of the plasma cell disorders characterized by a malignant proliferation of plasma cells derived from a single clone. It is the most common primary malignancy of the bone. The tumor results in a myriad of symptoms and dysfunctions like pathologic fractures, renal failure, hypercalcemia, increased risk of infections, and neurologic symptoms.

1. Etiopathogenesis

The etiology of multiple myeloma is not known, however various hypothesis suggest involvement of occupational, environmental and genetic causes. Radiation is known to increase the risk of myeloma. It is associated with a variety of chromosomal alterations particularly those involving the immunoglobulin heavy chain (IgH) locus and a variety of protooncogenes.

It is the second most common hematological malignancy after non-Hodgkin lymphoma, occurring usually in older age group (40–70 years). Males are more commonly affected.

The survival and multiplication of myeloma cells is dependent on Interleukin-6 (IL-6), which is synthesized by the myeloma cells themselves. Higher levels of IL-6 indicate an active disease and poorer prognosis. Myeloma cells bind to the bone marrow stromal cells, which leads to tumor cell growth and survival in the bone marrow. Bone destruction is mediated by the various factors released by the neoplastic cells as well as due to the direct infiltration of the stroma by the myeloma cells.

2. Clinical features

The symptoms depend on the stage of disease and may have various manifestations. Bone pain is the most frequently encountered complaint. Persistent pain is usually due to pathologic fracture. The bony destruction occurs due to tumor cell proliferation and activation of osteoclasts leading to bone resorption. Osteoclast activation occurs due to various factors released by myeloma cells. The bone lesions are osteolytic with no reactive bone formation due to inactivation of osteoblasts by the tumor cells. Significant bone resorption leads to hypercalcemia which could manifest as confusion, fatigue, frequent headaches, irritability and nausea.

Another significant problem in myeloma patients is susceptibility to infections, such as pneumonia and pyelonephritis/urinary tract infection. Recurrent infections may be the presenting complaint in some patients. The causes of susceptibility to infection include decreased production and increased destruction of normal antibodies, altered complement functions, and reduced granulocyte migration. Another possible cause could be the use of immunosuppressants in the treatment of multiple myeloma.

Renal failure occurs in about one fourth of the patients. Hypercalcemia, recurrent glomerulonephritis, and frequent use of NSAIDs due to pain all contribute to renal pathology. Rarely, there could be infiltration of renal tubules by myeloma cells. Excessive presentation of light chains to the kidney tubules leads to tubular damage manifesting as Fanconi's syndrome (proximal renal tubular acidosis) which leads to excretion of glucose and amino acids in urine, and inability to acidify urine.

Normocytic normochromic anemia is seen in many patients due to infiltration of marrow by tumor cells. Factors secreted by tumor cells inhibit erythropoiesis. Anemia also occurs due to effects of long-term therapy.

Neurological features are rarely seen which are mostly due to hypercalcemia or hyperviscosity. Vertebral body collapse due to pathologic fracture may lead to cord compression and neurologic symptoms such as radiculopathy and Cauda equina symptoms.

3. Diagnosis

The following are required for multiple myeloma diagnosis:
1. Bone marrow plasmacytosis >10%,
2. Serum/urine M protein,
3. At least one myeloma defining event.

Myeloma defining events: End-organ damage attributable to myeloma cell infiltration:
a. Hypercalcemia >11 mg/dL
b. Anemia <10 g/dL
c. Renal insufficiency (serum creatinine >2 mg/dL)
d. One or more osteolytic lesion
e. Any one or more of the following biomarkers of malignancy:
   • Clonal bone marrow plasma cell percentage ≥ 60%.
   • Involved: uninvolved serum free light chain ratio ≥ 100.
   • >1 focal lesions on MRI studies (Fig. 1).

Workup for multiple myeloma

a.

For establishing diagnosis
Bone marrow aspirate and biopsy for histology
Serum and 24-h urine electrophoresis

b.

For end organ damage evaluation
Hemogram, serum electrolytes and Renal function
Skeletal Survey

c.

For risk stratification
β-2 microglobulin and serum albumin
Lactate dehydrogenase

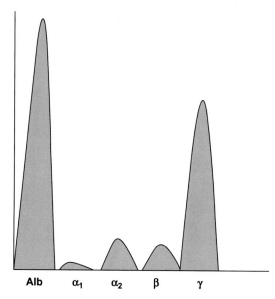

Fig. 1 Serum electrophoresis, densitometric tracing of agarose gel. Sharp spike seen in gamma globulin is characteristic of multiple myeloma.

4. Radiographic evaluation

A significant number of patients have bone pains/pathological fracture as their presenting complaint. Whenever multiple myeloma is in the differential diagnosis, a skeletal survey should be performed for evaluation of the bony lesions. There are multiple, osteolytic punched-out lesions with no reactive new bone (Fig. 2), commonly in the

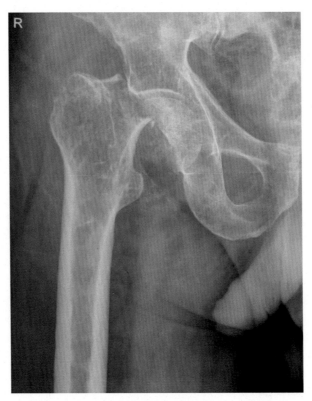

Fig. 2 Multiple lytic punched out lesions with pathological fracture of neck femur in a known case of multiple myeloma.

skull, spine, ribcage, and pelvis, although they can occur in any bone. Before the development of these well-defined lytic lesions, diffuse osteopenia develops due to infiltration of bone by myeloma cells.

5. Histology

Malignant plasma cells are seen in bone marrow aspirate. They have a perinuclear clear space due to prominent Golgi apparatus and eccentric nucleus (Fig. 3). These cells infiltrate the marrow of bone and sometimes completely replace the bony structure. Other cytologic variants such as flame cell and Mott cell could be seen.

Peripheral blood smear sometimes shows rouleaux formation.

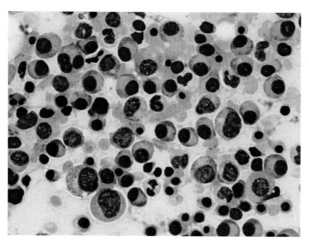

Fig. 3 Plasma cells with eccentric nucleus and perinuclear halo.

6. Prognosis

Serum β_2 microglobulin is the most important prognostic marker of myeloma disease activity and can be used for estimating survival. Serum albumin and lactate dehydrogenase are also predictors of disease activity.

7. Treatment

7.1 There are two purposes of the therapy

1. To control disease
2. Supportive treatment for symptomatic care.

Treatment for newly diagnosed multiple myeloma consists of initial therapy followed by maintenance therapy and management of relapse.

A combination of lenalidomide, bortezomib, and dexamethasone is used as initial therapy (induction regimen). Lenalidomide 20 mg oral once daily for days 1–21 every 28 days, with bortezomib injection 1.3 mg/m^2 once weekly (iv/sc) and dexamethasone 40 mg once weekly is the most commonly used induction regimen. Four cycles of this therapy are given, followed by autologous stem cell transplantation in eligible patients. In stem cell transplant ineligible patients, 8 more cycles of lenalidomide, bortezomib and dexamethasone are given followed by lenalidomide maintenance therapy (Rajkumar and Kumar, 2016).

Patients who are above 75 years of age or are frail do not tolerate triple therapy, and hence are given lenalidomide and dexamethasone therapy.

The treatment of relapsed multiple myeloma consists of triple therapy or sometimes only lenalidomide and dexamethasone. Multiple myeloma is a relapsing remitting disease with each remission lasting lesser than the previous one (Kumar et al., 2004). New agents approved for the treatment of relapsed multiple myeloma include carfilzomib, pomalidomide, and panobinostat.

The median survival of these patients is 8 years. Younger patients might survive longer. The major causes of death are progressive disease, renal complications and recurrent infections.

The treatment algorithm for multiple myeloma is outlined in Fig. 4.

7.2 Supportive treatment

1. Skeletal lesions: The most important part of treatment is the use of bisphosphonates to decrease the number of lesions. Zoledronate once per month for first 1–2 years is given to all patients with evidence of skeletal disease. Vertebroplasty and kyphoplasty

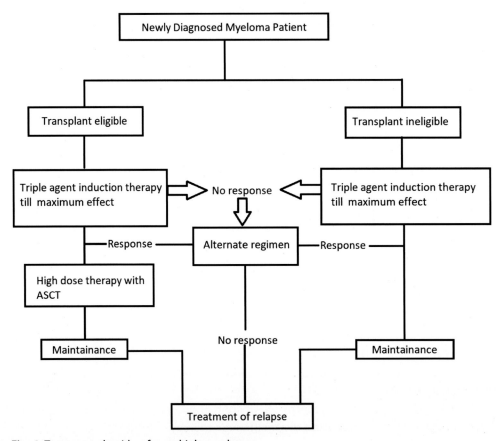

Fig. 4 Treatment algorithm for multiple myeloma.

are used to reduce the pain from vertebral involvement. Prophylactic fixation is done in impending fractures as per Mirel's criteria. Pathological fracture fixation is done using standard principles for fracture fixation (Berenson et al., 2001).

2. Hypercalcemia: The most important part of the therapy is hydration, steroids and bisphosphonates. Calcitonin is used in refractory cases (Major et al., 2001).

3. Prevention of infection: Recurrent infections occur due to severe hypogammaglobulinemia, which can be prevented by administering gamma globulins intravenously once every month. Influenza and pneumococcus vaccinations should be given to all multiple myeloma patients. Low-dose dexamethasone should be used for treatment to prevent infections.

4. Hyperviscosity syndrome: rarely develops in some patients. Plasmapheresis is the treatment of choice.

References

Berenson, J.R., Rosen, L.S., Howell, A., Porter, L., Coleman, R.E., Morley, W., et al., 2001. Zoledronic acid reduces skeletal-related events in patients with osteolytic metastases. Cancer 91 (7), 1191–1200.

Kumar, S.K., Therneau, T.M., Gertz, M.A., Lacy, M.Q., Dispenzieri, A., Rajkumar, S.V., et al., 2004. Clinical course of patients with relapsed multiple myeloma. Mayo Clin. Proc. 79 (7), 867–874.

Major, P., Lortholary, A., Hon, J., Abdi, E., Mills, G., Menssen, H.D., et al., 2001. Zoledronic acid is superior to pamidronate in the treatment of hypercalcemia of malignancy: a pooled analysis of two randomized, controlled clinical trials. J. Clin. Oncol. Off. J. Am. Soc. Clin. Oncol. 19 (2), 558–567.

Rajkumar, S.V., Kumar, S., 2016. Multiple myeloma: diagnosis and treatment. Mayo Clin. Proc. 91 (1), 101–119.

CHAPTER TWELVE

Role of biomarkers in assessing response to immune checkpoint inhibitors in cancer treatment

Kriti Jain[a], Nirmal Kumar Ganguly[a,*], and Shyam Aggarwal[b,*]
[a]Department of Research, Sir Ganga Ram Hospital, New Delhi, India
[b]Department of Medical Oncology, Sir Ganga Ram Hospital, New Delhi, India

1. Introduction

1.1 Immune checkpoint inhibitors

Immune checkpoints are crucial regulators of the immune system. These pathways are important for self-tolerance because they prevent the immune system from attacking cells indiscriminately. However, some types of cancer possess the ability to protect themselves from attack by stimulation of the immune checkpoint targets (Pardoll, 2012).

Programmed death-1 (PD-1) is an immune checkpoint that is responsible for limiting excessive immune responses to antigens and thereby preventing autoimmunity. It is expressed on various immune cells, such as T lymphocytes, B lymphocytes, natural killer T cells (NKT), activated monocytes, and dendritic cells. PD-1 has two known ligands, PD-L1 and PD-L2. Human activated T lymphocytes, dendritic cells, monocytes, and myeloid cells express PD-L1 (Nguyen and Ohashi, 2015). PD-L1 expression can be induced by type I and type II interferons. The interaction of PD-1 with its ligands also inhibits CD8[+] T-cell cytolytic effector functions. In addition to binding to PD-1, PD-L1 can bind to B7-1 on the surface of T cells and induce inhibitory signals in those cells (Butte et al., 2007). A plethora of agents targeting PD-1 or PD-L1 are in clinical development in various phases. Nivolumab (OPDIVOTM, Bristol-Myers Squibb Company) and Pembrolizumab (KeytrudaTM, Merck & Co., Inc.) are humanized PD-1-blocking monoclonal antibodies (mAbs) that have already received approval from the US Food and Drug Administration (FDA) and the European Medical Agency (EMA) (Medina and Adams, 2016). Both drugs have been registered for the treatment of patients with unresectable or advanced malignant melanoma (MM), nonsmall cell lung cancer (NSCLC) with progression on or after platinum-based chemotherapy, and recurrent

---

* Nirmal Kumar Ganguly and Shyam Aggarwal contributed equally.

Biomarkers in Cancer Detection and Monitoring of Therapeutics
https://doi.org/10.1016/B978-0-323-95114-2.00023-6
281

or metastatic squamous cell carcinoma of the head and neck (SCCHN) with disease progression on or after platinum-based therapy.

CTLA-4 (cytotoxic T-lymphocyte–associated protein 4) is also known as CD152 (cluster of differentiation 152). It is a protein receptor that acts as an immune checkpoint and down regulates immune responses. CTLA-4 is expressed on regulatory T cells and unregulated in conventional T cells after activation. It acts as an "off" switch when bound to CD80 or CD86 on the surface of antigen-presenting cells (dendritic cells). CTLA-4 is a member of the immunoglobulin superfamily that is expressed by activated T cells and also transmits an inhibitory signal to T cells. CTLA-4 is homologous to the T-cell co-stimulatory protein, CD28, and both molecules bind to CD80 and CD86, also called B7-1 and B7-2, respectively, on antigen-presenting cells. CTLA-4 binds CD80 and CD86 with greater affinity and avidity than CD28, thus enabling it to outcompete CD28 for its ligands. It is to be noted that T-cell activation through the T-cell receptor and CD28 leads to increased expression of CTLA-4.

Specifically, CTLA-4 primarily affects cellular proliferation and PD-1 signaling in T cells predominantly modifies cytokine production such as IFN-γ, TNF-α, and IL-2 (Buchbinder and Desai, 2016). Nivolumab has also received approval for the treatment of advanced renal cell carcinoma (RCC) progressing after previous therapy and relapsed or progressive classical Hodgkin's lymphoma after autologous hematopoietic stem cell transplantation (HSCT). Pembrolizumab has recently received approval for the first-line treatment of patients with 50 percent or more PD-L1 expression (Reck et al., 2016). The FDA has also recently granted approval to atezolizumab (Tecentriq, Roche-Genentech), a mAb against PD-L1, for the treatment of patients with locally advanced or metastatic urothelial carcinoma (Medina and Adams, 2016) who had disease progression during or following platinum-based chemotherapy, and for the treatment of patients with locally advanced or metastatic NSCLC (Rittmeyer et al., 2017) who had disease progression during or following platinum-containing chemotherapy, and have progressed on an appropriate FDA-approved targeted-therapy if their tumor has EGFR or ALK gene abnormalities. Other drugs in this class, such as durvalumab (Astra-Zeneca) and avelumab (Merck KGaA-Pfizer), were granted breakthrough therapy designation by the US FDA for treatment of patients with PD-L1 positive urothelial bladder cancer and metastatic Merkel Cell Carcinoma, respectively. Effective patient selection tools have not accompanied this impressive development of anti-PD-1/PD-L1 inhibitors and their recent arrival in the clinic. The results of the major clinical studies reveal that despite the remarkable survival benefit obtained with checkpoint inhibition immunotherapy in certain populations, around 40%–60% of patients will not benefit from these therapies. Additionally, these treatments are costly and might have some associated toxicities. Thus, it is imperative to identify valid biomarkers of response that help us optimize patient selection. Given the dynamic nature of the immune system and the multiple elements involved in the complex immune response against cancer, developing biomarkers for immunotherapeutics is more challenging than developing biomarkers for targeted therapy. This review presents the current evidence regarding biomarkers of response to PD-1/PD-L1 and CTLA-4 inhibition, analyzing factors related to the tumor and those related to the host immune system.

Inhibitory checkpoint molecules are the major targets for cancer immunotherapy because of their impending use in multiple types of solid cancers. Presently, the checkpoint inhibitors that are approved are the ones that block CTLA-4 and PD-1 and PD-L1. Immune checkpoints are the molecules that modulate the signals of the immune system by increasing or decreasing them, and they are known to be critical factors in treating infections, cancers, and autoimmune diseases. Currently, immune checkpoint therapy is seen as a pillar of cancer therapy. Immune checkpoints play an important role in immune regulation, and the blocking of immune checkpoints on the cell membrane is a potential strategy in the treatment of various types of cancer. Based on this, monoclonal antibodies are developing rapidly, such as those against PD-1 (programmed cell death protein 1). However, the cost involved in the preparation of monoclonal antibodies is too high and their therapeutic effect is still not fully understood. Among the different checkpoint therapies, those involving PD-1 are currently considered the most effective. The PD-1 pathway suppresses activated T cells at the late stage of an immune response, typically in peripheral tissues (Abbas et al., 2014; Addeo et al., 2019).

Immune checkpoint inhibitor (ICI) therapy is one of the types of cancer immunotherapy. This therapy targets immune checkpoints, which are the key regulators of the immune system and, when they are stimulated, can generate an immune response to an immunologic stimulus. Tumors protect themselves and escape the immune cells by stimulating the immune checkpoint targets. Immune checkpoint therapy can block inhibitory checkpoints, in order to restore immune system function (Patel and Kurzrock, 2015). Ipilimumab-a CTLA-4 blocker, is the first anticancer drug targeting an immune checkpoint, approved in the United States in 2011 (Cameron et al., 2011).

ICIs herald a new era in cancer therapy by increasing antitumor responses and providing significant survival advantages in multiple tumors. Gong et al. (2018) describe how antitumor responses are increased and significant survival advantages are provided in multiple tumors. PD1/PD-L1 therapies are approved for second-line or first-line treatment in a variety of malignant neoplasm, including melanoma, lung cancer, renal cell carcinoma (RCC), head and neck squamous cell carcinoma (HNSCC), and gastroesophageal cancer (Gong et al., 2018).

However, despite the huge breakthroughs observed in clinical treatment with ICIs, only 30%–40% of patients get benefit. Hence, it is crucial to comprehend the determinants that drive response, resistance, and adverse effects. During the past few years, it has been an area of potential research for scientists for the identification and development of predictive biomarkers for assessing response to ICIs. However, in recent years, large amounts of data and comprehensive understanding have been obtained, including new sets of data on tumor genome biomarkers, blood-based biomarkers, gremlin genetics, tumor microenvironment, and host-related factors. Advancements in the improvement of multiplex immunohistochemical technology, next-generation sequencing, and a variety of combinational biomarker strategies have emerged during recent years in order to develop multifactorial synergistic predictive biomarkers for ICIs. Development of a set of these predictive biomarkers will not only provide us a better understanding of the mechanisms of ICIs but also assist in disease management, in achieving decision-making in personalized antitumor immunotherapy, monitoring efficacy, tumor prognosis, guiding clinical trial design, as well as for deeper understanding of drug resistance mechanisms. A better knowledge of how these variables interact to affect tumor-host interactions is required to optimize the implementation of checkpoint inhibitor therapy (Akinleye and Rasool, 2019).

In this book chapter, we summarize the current status of pretreatment and posttreatment biomarkers and also focus on recently identified molecular and cellular determinants of response that may assist in predicting response to ICIs (Fig. 1).

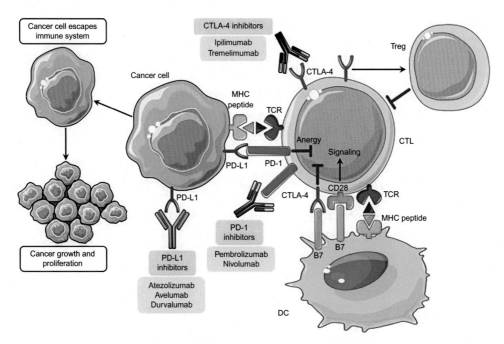

Fig. 1 Immune checkpoint inhibitor. Inability to activate CD8-T cells in tumor microenvironment through the suppressive effect of Tregs or through immune checkpoints allows cancer cells to escape immune attack, survive, and grow. B7 ligands expressed on antigen-presenting cells bind to CD28 receptor on CD8-T cells leading to T-cell amplification and immune response. Alternatively, binding of B7 ligands to CTLA-4 expressed on T cells suppresses their activity. CTLA-4 also enhances the activity of Tregs leading to immunosuppressive activity. PD-1 is expressed on activated T cells. PD-1 binds to its PD-L1 leading to the energy of CTLs further promoting inhibitory signals. Pharmacological inhibition of immune checkpoints with monoclonal antibodies restores CTL antitumor activity and relieves immunosuppression).

1.2 Approved checkpoint inhibitors

CTLA-4, PD-1, and PD-L1 are currently approved checkpoint inhibitors across the world. PD-1 is known as the transmembrane programmed cell death 1 protein, which interacts with PD-L1 (PD-1 ligand 1, or CD274). PD-L1 on the cell surface binds to PD-1 on an immune cell surface, which inhibits the immune system from generating response (Karwacz et al., 2011). It is a known phenomenon that up regulation of PD-L1 on the cell surface inhibits T cells to attack the tumor and as a result tumor escapes immune response. Therefore, antibodies that bind to either PD-1 or PD-L1 block this interaction and therefore allow the T-cells to restore its function to attack the tumor (Butte et al., 2007).

James P. Allison and Tasuku Honjo won Nobel Prize in the discoveries in basic science of checkpoint inhibitor therapies in 2018 (Devlin and James, 2018) (Table 1).

2. Predictive biomarkers to assess response to checkpoint inhibitor therapy

Tumor cells express antigens that are recognized by the immune system and hence trigger an immune response, which is known as immune surveillance. These antigens can be tumor specific or host specific, or antigens associated with the tumor that are also expressed on normal cells. There are multiple mechanisms by which the tumor escapes immune surveillance, such as loss of antigen presentation, loss of antigen expression, and inhibition of immune response through expression of molecules such as the immune checkpoint control modulators PD-1/PD-L1, which have immune suppressive effects (Abbas et al., 2021). It has been proven that blocking the checkpoint pathways restores CD8 T-cell function, promotes T-cell responses, and promotes tumor regression. Blockade of checkpoint pathways (like PD-1/PD-L1) enhances antitumor immune responses by decreasing the number and/or suppressive activity of regulatory T cells and by rescuing the activity of effector T cells in tissues and the tumor microenvironment, therefore, generating an immune response against tumors. Herein, we elaborate on the established research progress of predictive biomarkers that can be utilized for enhancing the efficacy of checkpoint inhibitor therapies in cancer.

2.1 Pretreatment biomarkers

Tissue biomarkers

PD-L1 expression on tumor cells

Immunohistochemistry (IHC) detection of PD-L1 (B7-H1) is the most common and well-established clinical predictive biomarker for predicting response to checkpoint inhibitor therapy (Patel and Kurzrock, 2015). Overexpression of PD-L1 on tumor cells facilitates immune evasion by inhibiting cytotoxic T-cell functions. Therefore, it is considered that overexpression of PD-L1 on tumor correlates with a poor prognosis (Nduom et al., 2015). Multiple studies in various cancer types have demonstrated a positive

Table 1 List of approved checkpoint inhibitors till 2021.

S. no.	Name	Brand name	Marketing rights	Target	Approved	Indications (April 2021)
1	Ipilimumab	Yervoy	Bristol-Myers Squibb	CTLA-4	2011	Metastatic melanoma, renal cell carcinoma, colorectal cancer, hepatocellular carcinoma, nonsmall cell lung cancer, and malignant pleural mesothelioma
2	Nivolumab	Opdivo	Bristol-Myers Squibb (North America) + Ono Pharmaceutical (other countries)	PD-1	2014	Metastatic melanoma, nonsmall cell lung cancer, renal cell carcinoma, Hodgkin's lymphoma, head and neck cancer, urothelial carcinoma, colorectal cancer, hepatocellular carcinoma, small cell lung cancer, esophageal carcinoma, and malignant pleural mesothelioma
3	Pembrolizumab	Keytruda	Merck Sharp & Dohme	PD-1	2014	Metastatic melanoma, nonsmall cell lung cancer, head and neck cancer, Hodgkin's lymphoma, urothelial carcinoma, gastric cancer, cervical cancer, hepatocellular carcinoma, Merkel cell carcinoma, renal cell carcinoma, small cell lung cancer, esophageal carcinoma, endometrial cancer, and squamous cell carcinoma
4	Atezolizumab	Tecentriq	Genentech/Roche	PD-L1	2016	Bladder cancer, nonsmall cell lung cancer, breast cancer, small cell lung cancer, hepatocellular carcinoma, and metastatic melanoma
5	Avelumab	Bavencio	Merck KGaA and Pfizer	PD-L1	2017	Merkel cell carcinoma, urothelial carcinoma, and renal cell carcinoma
6	Durvalumab	Imfinzi	Medimmune/AstraZeneca	PD-L1	2017	Nonsmall cell lung cancer and small cell lung cancer
7	Cemiplimab	Libtayo	Regeneron	PD-1	2018	Squamous cell carcinoma, basal cell carcinoma, and nonsmall cell lung cancer

correlation between PD-L1 expression and response to ICIs, and now some studies have also used it in first-line combination therapy (Wolchok et al., 2016; Rouquette et al., 2019). Pembrolizumab is presently approved by the FDA for NSCLC, in which PD-L1 expression ≥50% of tumor cells in first-line treatment and ≥1% in second-line treatment (Topalian et al., 2016; Gibney et al., 2016).

However, because PD-L1 expression on tumor cells may be the result of IFN production by tumor-infiltrating T cells, which are associated with responders, PD-L1 alone cannot always be a positive predictive marker in all cancers (Li et al., 2016; Sabatier et al., 2015). Some studies have reported that PD-L1 negative patients also benefit clinically with treatment with ICI or combination treatment with ICI (Carbone et al., 2017). Therefore, PD-L1 is not yet a comprehensive and independent biomarker in clinical practice to assess the responses to ICIs, with the following challenges presently. First, no standard definition of the cut-off range of PD-L1 expression across cancer types has been established. Several different cut-offs are considered. Second, PD-L1 expression on tumor cells and immune cells is a dynamic process due to which the evaluation at a particular time point (from formalin-fixed, paraffin-embedded tissue samples) is usually insufficient to predict response to ICI therapy (Mukherji et al., 2016). The predictive value of PD-L1 at different biopsy sites varied, which also created discrepancies in results (Hong et al., 2020). In addition to these, there are multiple assays for performing the PD-L1 test and antibodies are not standardized because of which the results are not always directly comparable (Hansen and Siu, 2016). Currently, the tumor proportion score (TPS) is used to calculate the PD-L1 positive score, which is based primarily on PD-L1 expression on tumor cells. But PD-L1 is also expressed on immune cells such as lymphocytes, macrophages, and stromal cells, and thus comes the concept of "combined positive score" (CPS), which is the proportion score of the sum of PD-L1 expressed by tumor cells and tumor-associated immune cells (Nishino et al., 2017). In addition, PD-L1 expression on immune cells is also considered separately as one of the biomarkers to distinguish the population that is going to benefit, called the immune positive score (IPS). Finally, prior cancer therapies such as radiation, chemotherapy, and others may alter PD-L1 expression via tumor-infiltrating lymphocytes that secrete IFN (Wimberly et al., 2015).

These limitations explain the diversity of results obtained from PD-L1 expression and also refer to a huge clinical need to develop a set of more sensitive and specific biomarkers that can predict response to ICI therapy. Nevertheless, overexpression of PD-L1 definitely assists in patient selection and approved biomarker prediction for a better response to checkpoint inhibition.

Tumor mutation burden
Tumor mutation burden is defined as the number of noninherited mutations per million bases (Mb) of an investigated genomic sequence, and its measurement is performed by

next-generation sequencing (Merino et al., 2020). Tumor mutational burden (TMB) is known as a genetic characteristic of tumor tissue and is relevant in cancer research and treatment. TMB has shown immense potential as a predictive biomarker with numerous applications, including patient response to immune checkpoint inhibitor (ICI) therapy in a variety of solid cancers. Tumor mutational burden (TMB) is a potential biomarker which is associated with response to immune checkpoint inhibitor therapies. It has been shown to differ distinctly among tumor types and also among patients within tumor types. Higher TMB is commonly observed in cancers associated with mutagens such as ultraviolet light exposure in melanoma and smoking in nonsmall-cell lung cancer (NSCLC) (Hellmann et al., 2018a, b).

High TMB is associated with increased expression of tumor-specific neoantigens, a subset of which can be recognized by the immune system. Higher numbers of somatic mutations in tumor DNA have been hypothesized to increase the probability of the immune system recognizing and eliminating tumor cells during treatment with check-point inhibitor therapy. One of the main survival and escape mechanisms in tumors, among others, is to increase the expression of immune checkpoint molecules that can bind to tumor-specific T-cells and inactivate them, preventing tumor cells from being detected and killed (Kim et al., 2019). ICIs have the potential to improve patients' responses and survival rates by helping the immune system target tumor cells. Various studies on TMB have shown an association between the survival of patients and TMB values (Merino et al., 2020). Apart from being a predictive biomarker for response to therapy, TMB also assists in identifying individuals that can benefit from ICI therapy with cancers that generally have low TMB values. Furthermore, it has been shown that tumors with higher TMB values usually result in a higher number of neoantigens, the antigens that are presented on the tumor cell surface and are usually a result of missense mutations. So, TMB is considered a good predictor of neoantigen load and also helps in finding patients who may benefit from ICI therapy by enhancing the possibility of detecting the neoantigens. However, it is important to note that different sequencing platforms and bioinformatics pipelines have been used to estimate TMB and it is important to harmonize TMB quantification protocols and procedures before it can be used as a reliable biomarker (Addeo et al., 2019). There have been some efforts to standardize these methods. Significant correlations between TMB and patients' response to therapy have been proven in several cancer types, including small cell lung cancer (SCLC), NSCLC, melanoma, urothelial carcinoma, and human papilloma virus (HPV)-negative HNSCC. However, there are studies which suggest that TMB alone cannot clearly distinguish responders and predict nonresponders to ICI therapy in cancer types, but as per approval given in April 2020 by the Food and Drug Administration (FDA), TMB can be used as a companion diagnostic biomarker for ICI therapy. TMB cut-off values differ depending on cancer type and assay platform (Goodman et al., 2017). However, according to the NCCN and FDA guidelines Version 2.2021, a TMB score of 10 is considered TMB-high, and checkpoint inhibitor therapies are an option, such as ultraviolet light exposure in melanoma and smoking in nonsmall-cell lung cancer (NSCLC) (Hellmann et al., 2018a, b). High TMB is associated with increased expression of tumor-specific neoantigens, a subset of which can be recognized by the immune system. Higher numbers of somatic mutations in tumor DNA have been hypothesized to increase the probability of the immune system recognizing and eliminating tumor cells during treatment with checkpoint inhibitor therapy. One of the main survival and escape mechanisms in tumors, among others, is to increase the expression of immune checkpoint molecules that can bind to tumor-specific T-cells and inactivate them, preventing tumor cells from being detected and killed (Kim et al., 2019). ICIs have the potential to improve patients' responses and survival rates by helping the immune system target tumor cells. Various studies on TMB have shown an association between the survival of patients and TMB values (Merino et al., 2020). Apart from being a predictive biomarker for response to therapy, TMB also assists in identifying individuals that can benefit from ICI therapy with cancers that generally have low TMB values. Furthermore, it has been shown that tumors with higher TMB values usually result in a higher number of neoantigens, the antigens that are presented on the tumor cell surface and are usually a result of missense mutations. So, TMB is considered a good predictor of neoantigen load and also helps in finding patients who may benefit from ICI therapy by enhancing the possibility of detecting the neoantigens. However, it is important to note that different sequencing platforms and bioinformatics pipelines have been used to estimate TMB and it is important to harmonize TMB quantification protocols and procedures before it can be used as a reliable biomarker (Addeo et al., 2019). There have been some efforts to standardize these methods. Significant correlations between TMB and patients' response to therapy have been proven in several cancer types, including small cell lung cancer (SCLC), NSCLC, melanoma, urothelial carcinoma, and human papilloma virus (HPV)-negative HNSCC. However, there are studies which suggest that TMB alone cannot clearly distinguish responders and predict nonresponders to ICI therapy in cancer types, but as per approval given in April 2020 by the Food and Drug Administration (FDA), TMB can be used as a companion diagnostic biomarker for ICI therapy. TMB cut-off values differ depending on cancer type and assay platform (Goodman et al., 2017). However, according to the NCCN and FDA guidelines Version 2.2021, a TMB score of 10 is considered TMB-high, and checkpoint inhibitor therapies are an option.

TMB cannot predict therapy response alone due to the complexity of tumor-immune interactions and tumor heterogeneity, and its clinical applicability is limited due to the difficulty in obtaining tissue samples and the high cost of the test involved when compared to other tests.

Microsatellite instability (MSI) and DNA mismatch repair (MMR)
Microsatellites are repeated sequences of DNA that are made up of repeating units of one to six base pairs in length. The length of these microsatellites is extremely variable from person to person and contributes to the individual's DNA "fingerprint," so each

individual has microsatellites of a particular length. The condition of genetic hyper-mutability resulting from impaired DNA mismatch repair (MMR) is called microsatellite instability (MSI) (Zhang et al., 2017). The presence of MSI shows phenotypic evidence that MMR is not functioning normally. The role of MMR is to correct the errors that spontaneously occur during the process of DNA replication, such as single-base mis-matches or short insertions and deletions. DNA polymerase errors are corrected by the proteins involved in MMR by inserting the appropriate sequence in their place. Cells with abnormal MMR function are unable to correct errors that occur during DNA rep-lication and, as a result, accumulate errors. This results in the formation of novel micro-satellite fragments. Polymerase chain reaction-based assays can disclose these novel microsatellites and provide evidence for the presence of MSI (Overman et al., 2018).

Microsatellite instability is connected with colon cancer, gastric cancer, endometrium cancer, ovarian cancer, hepatobiliary tract cancer, urinary tract cancer, brain cancer, and skin cancers. MSI is most prevalent in colon cancers. There are over 500,000 colon can-cer cases worldwide each year. Based on findings from over 7000 patients stratified for MSI-high (MSI-H), MSI-low (MSI-L), or microsatellite stable (MSS) colon cancers, those with MSI-H tumors had a more positive prognosis by 15% compared to MSI-L or MSS tumors. Lynch syndrome is associated with MSI-H tumors, but MSI-H can also occur in patients without Lynch syndrome, and confirmation of Lynch syndrome requires testing of germline DNA.

MMR is a key DNA repair mechanism for identifying and repairing erroneous dele-tions and insertions of bases that might occur during DNA replication and recombination (Iyer et al., 2006). MMR deficiency is a positive predictive biomarker for response to ICI in colorectal cancer (Li et al., 2015). These findings are indicative of the greater number of mutations that are unresolved by MMR, which would make the tumor more immu-nogenic. In a recent publication, it has been shown that MMR/MSI markers will guide treatment decisions for ICI in multiple tumor types. However, cases with MSS and intact MMR tumors have also shown favorable responses to ICI, making it an indefinite bio-marker and further studies are required for its real predictive value. In May 2017, two immune checkpoint inhibitors for PD1 and PD-L1, which are pembrolizumab (Keytruda) and nivolumab (Opdivo), got approval by the Food and Drug Administration (FDA) for patients with metastatic CRC with MMR-D or MSI-H, denoting significant survival benefit. This finding is considered independent of PD-L1 expression assessment, tissue type, and tumor location. According to NCCN guidelines, MSI-H must be 40% unstable, MSI-L 20% unstable, and MSS 5% stable. All other markers are stable. Studies have shown a sustained clinical response to immune checkpoint inhibitors with remark-able clinical improvement in patients with MSI-H or MMR in solid cancers. Addition-ally, disease progression after an initial positive response to ICIs indicates acquired resistance mechanisms. A paradigm shift in cancer diagnosis and treatment strategies based on next-generation sequencing is generation sequencing is currently under way.

The approval of anti-PD-1 therapy for the treatment of MSI-H/dMMR tumors has marked the first step toward revolutionizing cancer treatment strategies including checkpoint inhibitor therapy. MSI status is currently considered as a sensible surrogate marker for predicting immunotherapeutic response; however, further studies are needed to investigate more precise biomarkers which will significantly advance precision cancer medicine.

Tumor-infiltrating lymphocytes (TIL)

Tumor immune infiltration is classified as immune-inflamed, immune-excluded, and immune-desert (Chen and Mellman, 2017). Inflammation is described by the presence of $CD8^+$ and $CD4^+$ T cells in the tumor microenvironment and also by the expression of immune checkpoint molecules (Llosa et al., 2015), which indicates a potential antitumor immune response to ICIs treatment (Herbst et al., 2016). Joyce and Fearon (2015) found that immune-excluded tumors have different immune cell types in the aggressive margin but cannot infiltrate into the tumor parenchyma, whereas immune-desert tumors have an absence of abundant T cells in the tumor parenchyma or stroma and a poor response to ICI-treatment (Herbst et al., 2016). The presence of TILs in different tumor types and stages has been shown to have remarkable prognostic potential. A high abundance of $CD8^+$ T cells at the invasive margin as well as tumor environment have been observed in responders. Recently, the immunoscore concept (Galon et al., 2015) was established on the basis of the tumor microenvironment (TME), which differentiates between responders and nonresponders based on the density of two lymphocyte populations ($CD8^+$ and $CD45RO^+$ memory T cells). In studies done on colorectal cancer, multivariate analysis and immunoscore significantly showed relevance in predicting ICI efficacy and survival (Mlecnik et al., 2011). The value of immunoscore for predicting ICI efficacy is also being validated internationally in clinical trials of melanoma and NSCLC (Galon et al., 2015). A deeper assessment of active immune responses within the TME by immune gene-expression profiling is essential to predict the clinical benefit of ICIs therapies. Expression of cytotoxic T-cell markers such as CD8A, perforin 1, granzyme B, Th1 cytokines, chemokines, and other immune-related genes (NGK7, IDO1) in tumor microenvironment of tumor biopsies was remarkably different in subsets of responders and nonresponders, making them a potential candidate to be established as a biomarker (Ji et al., 2012). In a study by Ascierto et al. (2012), more than 299 immune-related genes were compared in patients with recurrent breast cancer 1–5 years posttreatment and those without recurrence post 7 years and later, and they found that five genes (IGK, GBP1, STAT1, IGLL5, and OCLN) were highly overexpressed in patients with recurrence-free survival. In addition to this, IFN-γ-induced immune gene signatures may be effective biomarkers for predicting the clinical benefit of treatment with ICIs. Based on the receiver operating characteristic curve (ROC curve), optimized cut-off values for

IFN-scores can achieve a positive predictive value of 59% for responders and a negative predictive value of 90% for nonresponders (Ribas et al., 2015).

Host germline genetics

Pathogens are the strongest selective forces in human evolution, and the continuous interaction between humans and microorganisms leads to a huge amount of immunologically associated gene variation found in humans. One of the major mechanisms of immune escape is dysfunction in the antigen presentation pathway, which in-turn promotes tumor progression. For example, tumors down regulate HLA-I expression by acquiring damaging mutations in HLA-I genes or harboring loss of heterozygosity (LOH) of HLA-I genes, wherein the HLA-I halotype is somatically lost (Aptsiauri et al., 2007). Some patients with germline heterozygous HLA-I loci can harbor somatic LOH in their tumors which is associated with a reduced response to ICI therapy. Immune gene variation also impacts the efficacy of ICI therapy. The HLA genes in the human genome encode the key components of immune genicity and are known as the most polymorphic genes. HLA class I (HLA-I) diversity is characterized by a remarkable sequence variation in the peptide binding region (Parham et al., 1989). Studies have found that the more diverse array of HLA-I molecules was associated with good response and survival to ICI (Havel et al., 2019). It is possibly due to the broader presentation of tumor antigens to the T cells. Additionally, the association of HLA-I heterozygosity with extended survival was increased when correlated with the TMB (Chowell et al., 2018). Patients treated with ICI therapy who expressed heterozygosity at HLA-I loci were able to undergo better clonal expansion of their TCR repertoires. Additionally, specific HLA-I super types (HLAB44) are associated with survival after ICI therapy (Hillen et al., 2008).

The present findings indicate that small differences in the number of available HLA-I molecules influence the strength of antitumor T-cell responses after ICI.

Host-related biomarkers
General characteristics Several studies have shown that immune responses can also be gender-specific. A meta-analysis of a large number of melanoma and NSCLC patients has reported that gender differences in efficacy of ICIs were significantly higher in males as compared to females. A significant correlation has also been observed between age and immune response. Aging is associated with a decline in immune response and has significant effects on both innate and adaptive immune responses (Fulop et al., 2011). However, several studies done in melanoma patients have reported a significantly higher tumor response in patients over 60 as compared to lower-aged patients treated with ICI therapy (Kugel et al., 2018). Obesity and inadequate fat distribution in the body have also been shown to affect tumor prognosis and response to ICI. It has been shown that the

phenomenon of T-cell exhaustion is promoted by obesity, which leads to immune ageing and also promotes tumor growth (Wang et al., 2020).

Presently, there is no substantial evidence to support the mechanisms by which general characteristics at baseline level influence the efficacy of ICI therapy. However, this could be used for patient selection and stratification in the future by further studies.

2.2 Posttreatment biomarkers

Blood biomarkers

Peripheral blood is a noninvasive method to explore potential biomarkers to predict response to ICI. In several studies, a substantial association with clinical benefit and response has been observed and validated.

Lactate dehydrogenase (LDH)

LDH is a housekeeping enzyme that is released by metastatic tumors. Therefore, serum LDH correlated positively with tumor mutation burden. Most studies have observed no correlation between baseline values of LDH and response. Nevertheless, dynamic changes in LDH from baseline to week 12 were observed to be correlated with response in several studies (Dick et al., 2016). Hence, elevated serum LDH may be one of the prognostic biomarkers for exclusion of patients from ICI treatment.

C-reactive protein (CRP)

Acute-phase protein C reactive protein (CRP) correlates favorably with TMB. It is a prognostic biomarker in cases of melanoma and its elevated serum concentrations are associated with no response to ICI (Fang et al., 2015). In malignancies such as gastrointestinal, renal, pancreas, bladder, and hepatocellular cancer, CRP has been shown to affect the prognosis. In some studies, elevated CRP levels are shown to be associated with poor response in NSCLC (Oya et al., 2017).

Differential blood count markers

Since ICI therapy works by activating the T lymphocytes of the host, the number of lymphocytes and other circulating immune cells has been shown to affect its efficacy. Increased counts of neutrophils are found in the peripheral blood of cancer patients and have been correlated with worse overall survival and no response to ICI therapy in melanoma patients (Ferrucci et al., 2016). An increase in the count of lymphocytes is correlated with a response to ICI therapy (Simeone et al., 2014). It has been reported in several studies that neutrophil-to-lymphocyte ratio (NLR) is also used as a prognostic biomarker for predicting response to therapy (Chasseuil et al., 2018). High baseline NLR is associated with poor response to ICI therapy in the case of melanoma, NSCLC, and RCC (Jeyakumar et al., 2017). NLR is considered to be a good prognostic biomarker, but it is not treatment specific and, alone, cannot be used as a predictive biomarker. Some studies have found that a high eosinophil count correlates with response to ICI therapy. Myeloid-derived suppressor cells (MDSCs) also play an important role in melanoma and other malignant tumors. Immunosuppressive, particularly for T cells, MDSCs, and granulocytic and monocytic (mo-MDSCs) are immunosuppressive. A higher number of mo-MDSCs were negatively correlated with response to ICI in melanoma patients (Weber et al., 2015). All these differential blood count biomarkers have the potential to be used as predictive markers for ICI, but further studies are required to investigate their predictive cut-off values in different malignancies.

Peripheral T-cell biomarkers

Peripheral blood analysis provides us with deep knowledge regarding the immune responses that are induced by blocking the PD-1 pathway. T cells are known as the effector cells of ICI treatment. Therefore, a detailed analysis of the T cells and their subsets in the peripheral blood can be beneficial and serve as a potential biomarker for ICI. Several studies have shown that the increase in the cytotoxic CD8 T cells post ICI therapy, as compared to the baseline, has been shown to be responders to therapy (Tietze et al., 2017). Proliferation of the PD-1$^+$ CD8 T cells in the peripheral blood of lung cancer patients has also been shown to correlate with response to ICI therapy. CyTOF analysis performed on melanoma patients in several studies has demonstrated the increase in natural killer cells and their subsets posttherapy as compared to the baseline level (before the initiation of therapy) and can therefore serve as potential biomarkers for ICI treatment after validation in a larger cohort of patients with various malignant conditions (Krieg et al., 2018). Additionally, high levels of circulating T regulatory cells at baseline level were also associated with responders to therapy. T-cell costimulatory markers such as inducible T-cell costimulator (ICOS), which is expressed by activated T cells and Tregs, have also been shown to be enhanced post-ICI in responders, clearly showing the activation of T cells posttherapy, which is required (Liakou et al., 2008). Apart from these, studies have reported and correlated the presence of circulating tumor cells (CTCs) in the peripheral blood with the metastatic process in tumors, and PD-L1 is a highly expressed ion in CTCs from patients with advanced head and neck cancer, which shows that PD-L1$^+$ CTCs may be considered as a predictive biomarker of response to ICI (Kulasinghe et al., 2017).

To summarize, T cells, being the effector cells of ICI, are the current focus of biomarker research in the field of advanced malignant conditions eligible to receive ICI therapy. The approaches toward it appear to be promising, but no biomarkers have yet been established to be used in clinical practice, and hence larger studies are required for it to be validated.

Soluble serum biomarkers (cytokines)

The relationship between inflammatory cells, cancer, and proinflammatory proteins such as chemokines (which regulate tumor growth and angiogenesis) are well known in the field of cancer. These inflammatory chemokines are also involved in metastasis (Coussens and Werb, 2002). Soluble serum biomarkers, which include immune regulatory molecules such as cytokines and soluble checkpoint receptors with their binding partners, also correlate with the clinical benefit of ICI treatment. Interferons (IFNs) are cytokines that activate the immune cells and increase MHC-I expression on cancer cells, thereby improving cytotoxic CD8$^+$ T-cell recognition and tumor cell destruction and this interaction assists in the use of IFN gene signatures for selecting the appropriate ICI therapy in various malignant conditions. These cytokines are produced and act on both cancer cells and immune cells. Some studies have shown serum IFN-, IL-6, and IL-10 levels were significantly higher in nonresponders as compared to responders (Yamazaki et al., 2017). Recently, in a study, it was shown that mutations in the IFN receptor signaling pathway are responsible for acquired resistance to anti–PD-1 therapy in melanoma (Zaretsky et al., 2016). In another study, resistance to CTLA-4 inhibition was demonstrated by genomic alterations in the IFN-γ pathway genes. These findings support the relevance of tumor genomic data about IFN-related genes as a predictor of response as well as patient selection for ICI therapy (Gao et al., 2016). Hence, tumor genetic signatures of IFN-γ, may be used in the predictive model of response to ICI therapy in the near future.

Liquid biopsy biomarkers
Biomarkers of circulating tumor DNA (ctDNA)
Circulating tumor DNA (ctDNA) is found in the blood of the human body and is defined as the DNA that arises from cancerous cells and tumors. Most DNA is inside a cell's nucleus. Cell death occurs and they are replaced by new cells when the tumor progresses. The DNA of broken cells with their contents is thereafter released into the bloodstream. ctDNA basically comprises small fragments of DNA which usually comprise fewer than 200 nucleotides in length. The genomic information related to the response to ICIs can be obtained from ctDNA. Numerous studies have found that a high number of ctDNA mutations are associated with improved overall survival and a poor response in cancer patients treated with ICI. ctDNA can also be a useful marker for the identification of pseudoprogression during ICI therapy. The association of TMB based on ctDNA levels and clinical benefit was also validated in tumor patients, confirming it to be a promising predictive biomarker. An association was also observed between high hypermutated ctDNA levels and nonresponders to therapy for diverse malignancies treated by ICI (Khagi et al., 2017). To summarize, dynamic monitoring of ctDNA can predict response to ICI therapy during the course of the treatment process in a noninvasive manner, thereby improving the sensitivity and specificity of predicting response.

Other circulating molecular biomarkers
Exosomes are single-membrane organelles that are secreted by many types of cells, including cancer cells and immune cells. The main molecular components of exosomes are

cell-derived proteins; lipids, glycoconjugates, and nucleic acids. Exosomes show a variety of activities, such as remodeling the extracellular matrix (ECM) as well as mediating the intercellular transmission of signals and molecules. There have been multiple studies demonstrating the variety of roles of exosomes in cancer progression as well as suppression. As cell-derived nanovesicles, exosomes have potential uses in ICI because of their immunogenicity and molecular transfer functions. Moreover, some new studies suggest that tumor cell-derived exosome DNA (ExoDNA) activates the immune cells and can act as a key regulator of checkpoint immunotherapy as well as regulate tumor immunity. In ongoing clinical trials, exosomes are considered immunotherapeutic vaccines, markers of cancer diagnosis, prognosis, recurrence, and metastasis, or drug delivery carriers for cancer treatment. Plasma exosomes can also provide relevant information about the tumor and ICI therapy.

2.3 Stool biomarkers

Gut microbiome profile

As shown in several studies (Routy et al., 2018), the microbiota profile also plays a significant role in stimulating and inhibiting the immune response. The gut microbiome is significantly associated with improved responses to ICI therapy in several cancers such as melanoma, NSCLC, RCC, and urothelial carcinoma (Gopalakrishnan et al., 2018; Chaput et al., 2017; Matson et al., 2018). It has been reported that commensal bifidobacteria enhanced PD-1/anti-PD-1 antibody response by enhancing the function of dendritic cells. Also, baseline microbiota enriched with Faecalibacterium species and other fermicutes generated a better response in patients treated with ICI as compared to microbiota enriched with bacteroides (Chaput et al., 2017). A significant correlation was also observed between the response to ICI and microbiota enriched with *Akkermansia muciniphilia*. Another analysis found that the enrichment of bacteroides caccae in all ICI responders, and specifically *Faecalibacterium prausnitzii*, *Bacteroides thetaiotaomicron*, and *Holdemania filiformis* when treated with anti-PD-1 therapy. *Collinsella aerofaciens*, *Enterococcus faecium*, and *Bifidobacterium longum* relative abundance have also been linked to melanoma responders (Matson et al., 2018). All the studies reported that an imbalance in gut microbiota is associated with immune dysfunction in nonresponders. It is to be noted that the efficacy of ICI as per microbiota profiling is associated with geographical location, antibiotic treatment, different cancer types, dietary habits, and microbial sequencing technique. The present studies indicate a relevant association between response and microbiome profile. However, further prospective studies are required to establish gut microbiota as a predictive biomarker to be used across different cancer types.

2.4 Immune-related adverse events (irAEs)

The various spectrums of side effects caused by the ICI therapy are known as irAEs. irAEs affect almost every organ of the body, including the skin, gastrointestinal tract, lung,

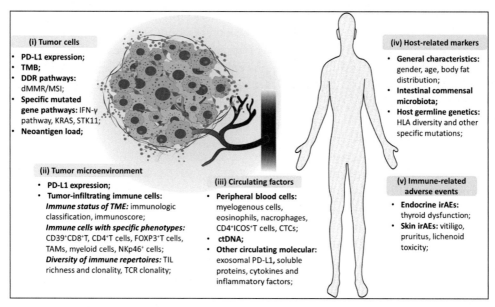

Fig. 2 A comprehensive overview of predictive biomarkers to assess response to immune checkpoint inhibitor therapy.

endocrine, musculoskeletal, and various other systems. Different types of irAEs are associated with different tumor types. ICIs cause tumor regression and irAEs through enhanced immune response. Several studies have shown a relevant association between these two. In a multivariate analysis, it was shown that low grade irAEs were associated with better response to ICI therapy in nonmelanoma patients and that early development of overall irAEs was associated with better survival in NSCLC patients receiving ICI therapy (Teraoka et al., 2017). In addition to this, an association was also observed between endocrine irAEs and vitiligo and a better prognosis in melanoma patients; thyroid dysfunction was associated with a better response in NSCLC patients receiving ICI therapy. Additional studies are required to confirm certain irAEs' ability to be used as a prognostic biomarker to predict response to ICI (Fig. 2).

3. Summary

To conclude, we are yet to establish a predictive model for ICIs efficacy. The current mechanisms and understanding of how to assess the clinical response to ICI therapy are unambiguously indicative of the fact that there cannot be a single biomarker to predict the response to this therapy. Since these therapies are highly expensive and effective only for 30%–40% of total patients, it is imperative to develop biomarkers that can predict and assess response to therapy. Therefore, the development of a comprehensive predictive biomarker model that takes different components into consideration is primarily essential for utilizing ICI therapy to its full strength. Importantly, this type of predictive model will provide a one-of-a-kind opportunity to assess confounding factors and the individual contributions of each of these factors to the response to ICIs. Comprehensive predictive models will need a permutation of different types of data sets for training and constant evaluation. These variables include DNA sequencing data for calculation of TMB, genetic alterations, RNA sequencing data to evaluate whether the immune phenotype will favor sensitivity to ICIs, germline DNA sequencing data for HLA diversity, IHC for PD-L1 expression, TME, commensal microbiota, and expression of other checkpoint molecules. Furthermore, as more knowledge about the molecular determinants of response to ICIs becomes available, these predictive models will require a continuous process of model update and reevaluation. For precision immunooncology, such biomarker models for response to ICIs will have profound implications in the area of checkpoint inhibitors. Ultimately, clinical use will be governed not just by the science but also by feasibility and reproducibility in the "real world" clinical setting, as well as cost and investment to establish prospective validation. The ongoing, intensive work to establish and understand biomarkers for ICI response prediction holds great promise for maximizing patient benefit from these transformative therapies.

References

Abbas, A.K., Lichtman, A.H., Pillai, S., 2014. Cellular and molecular immunology e-book. Elsevier Health Sciences.

Abbas, A., Lichtman, A., Pillaie, S., 2021. Cellular and Molecular Immunology, tenth ed. Elsevier. Book ISBN: 9780323757508, Paperback ISBN: 9780323757485.

Addeo, A., Banna, G.L., Weiss, G.J., 2019. Tumor mutation burden—from hopes to doubts. JAMA Oncol. 5 (7), 934–935.

Akinleye, A., Rasool, Z., 2019. Immune checkpoint inhibitors of PD-L1 as cancer therapeutics. J. Hematol. Oncol. 12 (1), 1–3.

Aptsiauri, N., Cabrera, T., Mendez, R., Garcia-Lor, A., Ruiz-Cabello, F., Garrido, F., 2007. In: Shurin, M.R., Smolkin, Y.S. (Eds.), Immune-Mediated Diseases. Advances in Experimental Medicine and Biology. 601. Springer, New York, NY. https://doi.org/10.1007/978-0-387-72005-0_13.

Ascierto, M.L., Kmieciak, M., Idowu, M.O., Manjili, R., Zhao, Y., Grimes, M., Dumur, C., Wang, E., Ramakrishnan, V., Wang, X.Y., Bear, H.D., 2012. A signature of immune function genes associated with recurrence-free survival in breast cancer patients. Breast Cancer Res. Treat. 131 (3), 871–880.

Buchbinder, E.I., Desai, A., 2016. CTLA-4 and PD-1 pathways: similarities, differences, and implications of their inhibition. Am. J. Clin. Oncol. 39 (1), 98–106. https://doi.org/10.1097/COC.0000000000000239.

Butte, M.J., Keir, M.E., Phamduy, T.B., Sharpe, A.H., Freeman, G.J., 2007. Programmed death-1 ligand 1 interacts specifically with the B7-1 costimulatory molecule to inhibit T cell responses. Immunity 27 (1), 111–122.

Cameron, F., Whiteside, G., Perry, C., 2011. Ipilimumab. Drugs 71 (8), 1093–1104.

Carbone, D.P., Reck, M., Paz-Ares, L., Creelan, B., Horn, L., Steins, M., Felip, E., van den Heuvel, M.M., Ciuleanu, T.E., Badin, F., Ready, N., 2017. First-line nivolumab in stage IV or recurrent non-small-cell lung cancer. N. Engl. J. Med. 376 (25), 2415–2426.

Chaput, N., Lepage, P., Coutzac, C., Soularue, E., Le Roux, K., Monot, C., Boselli, L., Routier, E., Cassard, L., Collins, M., Vaysse, T., 2017. Baseline gut microbiota predicts clinical response and colitis in metastatic melanoma patients treated with ipilimumab. Ann. Oncol. 28 (6), 1368–1379.

Chasseuil, E., Saint-Jean, M., Chasseuil, H., Peuvrel, L., Quereux, G., Nguyen, J.M., Gaultier, A., Varey, E., Khammari, A., Dréno, B., 2018. Blood predictive biomarkers for nivolumab in advanced melanoma. Acta Derm. Venereol. 98 (4), 406–410.

Chen, D.S., Mellman, I., 2017. Elements of cancer immunity and the cancer-immune set point. Nature 541 (7637), 321–330.

Chowell, D., Morris, L.G., Grigg, C.M., Weber, J.K., Samstein, R.M., Makarov, V., Kuo, F., Kendall, S.M., Requena, D., Riaz, N., Greenbaum, B., 2018. Patient HLA class I genotype influences cancer response to checkpoint blockade immunotherapy. Science 359 (6375), 582–587.

Coussens, L.M., Werb, Z., 2002. Inflammation and cancer. Nature 420 (6917), 860–867.

Devlin, H., James, P., 2018. Allison and Tasuku Honjo win Nobel prize for medicine. Guardian 15, 27.

Dick, J., Lang, N., Slynko, A., Kopp-Schneider, A., Schulz, C., Dimitrakopoulou-Strauss, A., Enk, A.H., Hassel, J.C., 2016. Use of LDH and autoimmune side effects to predict response to ipilimumab treatment. Immunotherapy 8 (9), 1033–1044.

Fang, S., Wang, Y., Sui, D., Liu, H., Ross, M.I., Gershenwald, J.E., Cormier, J.N., Royal, R.E., Lucci, A., Schacherer, C.W., Gardner, J.M., 2015. C-reactive protein as a marker of melanoma progression. J. Clin. Oncol. 33 (12), 1389.

Ferrucci, P.F., Ascierto, P.A., Pigozzo, J., Del Vecchio, M., Maio, M., Cappellini, G.A., Guidoboni, M., Queirolo, P., Savoia, P., Mandalà, M., Simeone, E., 2016. Baseline neutrophils and derived neutrophil-to-lymphocyte ratio: prognostic relevance in metastatic melanoma patients receiving ipilimumab. Ann. Oncol. 27 (4), 732–738.

Fulop, T., Larbi, A., Kotb, R., de Angelis, F., Pawelec, G., 2011. Aging, immunity, and cancer. Discov. Med. 11 (61), 537–550.

Galon, J., Fox, B.A., Bifulco, C.B., Masucci, G., Rau, T., Botti, G., Marincola, F.M., Ciliberto, G., Pages, F., Ascierto, P.A., Capone, M., 2015. Immunoscore and Immunoprofiling in Cancer: An Update From the Melanoma and Immunotherapy Bridge.

Gao, J., Shi, L.Z., Zhao, H., Chen, J., Xiong, L., He, Q., Chen, T., Roszik, J., Bernatchez, C., Woodman, S.E., Chen, P.L., 2016. Loss of IFN-γ pathway genes in tumor cells as a mechanism of resistance to anti-CTLA-4 therapy. Cell 167 (2), 397–404.

Gibney, G.T., Weiner, L.M., Atkins, M.B., 2016. Predictive biomarkers for checkpoint inhibitor-based immunotherapy. Lancet Oncol. 17 (12), e542–e551.

Gong, J., Chehrazi-Raffle, A., Reddi, S., Salgia, R., 2018. Development of PD-1 and PD-L1 inhibitors as a form of cancer immunotherapy: a comprehensive review of registration trials and future considerations. J. Immunother. Cancer 6 (1), 1–8.

Goodman, A.M., Kato, S., Bazhenova, L., Patel, S.P., Frampton, G.M., Miller, V., Stephens, P.J., Daniels, G.A., Kurzrock, R., 2017. Tumor mutational burden as an independent predictor of response to immunotherapy in diverse cancers. Mol. Cancer Ther. 16 (11), 2598–2608.

Gopalakrishnan, V., Spencer, C.N., Nezi, L., Reuben, A., Andrews, M.C., Karpinets, T.V., Prieto, P.A., Vicente, D., Hoffman, K., Wei, S.C., Cogdill, A.P., 2018. Gut microbiome modulates response to anti-PD-1 immunotherapy in melanoma patients. Science 359 (6371), 97–103.

Hansen, A.R., Siu, L.L., 2016. PD-L1 testing in cancer: challenges in companion diagnostic development. JAMA Oncol. 2 (1), 15–16.

Havel, J.J., Chowell, D., Chan, T.A., 2019. The evolving landscape of biomarkers for checkpoint inhibitor immunotherapy. Nat. Rev. Cancer 19 (3), 133–150.

Hellmann, M.D., Callahan, M.K., Awad, M.M., Calvo, E., Ascierto, P.A., Atmaca, A., Rizvi, N.A., Hirsch, F.R., Selvaggi, G., Szustakowski, J.D., Sasson, A., 2018a. Tumor mutational burden and efficacy of nivolumab monotherapy and in combination with ipilimumab in small-cell lung cancer. Cancer Cell 33 (5), 853–861.

Hellmann, M.D., Ciuleanu, T.E., Pluzanski, A., Lee, J.S., Otterson, G.A., Audigier-Valette, C., Minenza, E., Linardou, H., Burgers, S., et al., 2018b. Nivolumab plus ipilimumab in lung cancer with a high tumor mutational burden. N. Engl. J. Med. 378 (22), 2093–2104.

Herbst, R.S., Baas, P., Kim, D.W., Felip, E., Pérez-Gracia, J.L., Han, J.Y., Molina, J., Kim, J.H., Arvis, C.D., Ahn, M.J., Majem, M., 2016. Pembrolizumab versus docetaxel for previously treated, PD-L1-positive, advanced non-small-cell lung cancer (KEYNOTE-010): a randomised controlled trial. Lancet 387 (10027), 1540–1550.

Hillen, F., Baeten, C.I., van de Winkel, A., Creytens, D., van der Schaft, D.W., Winnepenninckx, V., Griffioen, A.W., 2008. Leukocyte infiltration and tumor cell plasticity are parameters of aggressiveness in primary cutaneous melanoma. Cancer Immunol. Immunother. 57 (1), 97–106. https://doi.org/10.1007/s00262-007-0353-9.

Hong, L., Negrao, M.V., Dibaj, S.S., Chen, R., Reuben, A., Bohac, J.M., Liu, X., Skoulidis, F., Gay, C.M., Cascone, T., Mitchell, K.G., 2020. Programmed death-ligand 1 heterogeneity and its impact on benefit from immune checkpoint inhibitors in NSCLC. J. Thorac. Oncol. 15 (9), 1449–1459.

Iyer, R.R., Pluciennik, A., Burdett, V., Modrich, P.L., 2006. DNA mismatch repair: functions and mechanisms. Chem. Rev. 106 (2), 302–323.

Jeyakumar, G., Kim, S., Bumma, N., Landry, C., Silski, C., Suisham, S., Dickow, B., Heath, E., Fontana, J., Vaishampayan, U., 2017. Neutrophil lymphocyte ratio and duration of prior anti-angiogenic therapy as biomarkers in metastatic RCC receiving immune checkpoint inhibitor therapy. J. Immunother. Cancer 5 (1), 1–8.

Ji, R.R., Chasalow, S.D., Wang, L., Hamid, O., Schmidt, H., Cogswell, J., Alaparthy, S., Berman, D., Jure-Kunkel, M., Siemers, N.O., Jackson, J.R., 2012. An immune-active tumor microenvironment favors clinical response to ipilimumab. Cancer Immunol. Immunother. 61 (7), 1019–1031.

Joyce, J.A., Fearon, D.T., 2015. T cell exclusion, immune privilege, and the tumor microenvironment. Science 348 (6230), 74–80.

Karwacz, K., Bricogne, C., MacDonald, D., Arce, F., Bennett, C.L., Collins, M., Escors, D., 2011. PD-L1 co-stimulation contributes to ligand-induced T cell receptor down-modulation on CD8+ T cells. EMBO Mol. Med. 3 (10), 581–592.

Khagi, Y., Kurzrock, R., Patel, S.P., 2017. Next generation predictive biomarkers for immune checkpoint inhibition. Cancer Metastasis Rev. 36 (1), 179–190. https://doi.org/10.1007/s10555-016-9652-y.

Kim, J.Y., Kronbichler, A., Eisenhut, M., Hong, S.H., van der Vliet, H.J., Kang, J., Shin, J.I., Gamerith, G., 2019. Tumor mutational burden and efficacy of immune checkpoint inhibitors: a systematic review and meta-analysis. Cancer 11 (11), 1798.

Krieg, C., Nowicka, M., Guglietta, S., Schindler, S., Hartmann, F.J., Weber, L.M., Dummer, R., Robinson, M.D., Levesque, M.P., Becher, B., 2018. High-dimensional single-cell analysis predicts response to anti-PD-1 immunotherapy. Nat. Med. 24 (2), 144–153.

Kugel, C.H., Douglass, S.M., Webster, M.R., Kaur, A., Liu, Q., Yin, X., Weiss, S.A., Darvishian, F., Al-Rohil, R.N., Ndoye, A., Behera, R., 2018. Age correlates with response to anti-PD1, reflecting age-related differences in intratumoral effector and regulatory T-cell populations. Clin. Cancer Res. 24 (21), 5347–5356.

Kulasinghe, A., Perry, C., Kenny, L., Warkiani, M.E., Nelson, C., Punyadeera, C., 2017. PD-L1 expressing circulating tumour cells in head and neck cancers. BMC Cancer 17 (1), 1–6.

Li, Y., Liang, L., Dai, W., Cai, G., Xu, Y., Li, X., Li, Q., Cai, S., 2016. Prognostic impact of programed cell death-1 (PD-1) and PD-ligand 1 (PD-L1) expression in cancer cells and tumor infiltrating lymphocytes in colorectal cancer. Mol. Cancer 15 (1), 1–5.

Li, W., Wildsmith, S., Ye, J., Si, H., Morsli, N., He, P., Shetty, J., Yovine, A.J., Holoweckyj, N., Raja, R., Real, K., 2015. Plasma-based tumor mutational burden (bTMB) as predictor for survival in phase III EAGLE study: Durvalumab (D)±tremelimumab (T) versus chemotherapy (CT) in recurrent/metastatic head and neck squamous cell carcinoma (R/M HNSCC) after platinum failure. J. Clin. Oncol. 38 (15_suppl), 6511.

Liakou, C.I., Kamat, A., Tang, D.N., Chen, H., Sun, J., Troncoso, P., Logothetis, C., Sharma, P., 2008. CTLA-4 blockade increases IFNγ-producing CD4+ ICOShi cells to shift the ratio of effector to regulatory T cells in cancer patients. Proc. Natl. Acad. Sci. 105 (39), 14987–14992.

Llosa, N.J., Cruise, M., Tam, A., Wicks, E.C., Hechenbleikner, E.M., Taube, J.M., Blosser, R.L., Fan, H., Wang, H., Luber, B.S., Zhang, M., 2015. The vigorous immune microenvironment of microsatellite instable colon cancer is balanced by multiple counter-inhibitory checkpoints. Cancer Discov. 5 (1), 43–51.

Matson, V., Fessler, J., Bao, R., Chongsuwat, T., Zha, Y., Alegre, M.L., Luke, J.J., Gajewski, T.F., 2018. The commensal microbiome is associated with anti-PD-1 efficacy in metastatic melanoma patients. Science 359 (6371), 104–108.

Medina, P.J., Adams, V.R., 2016. PD-1 pathway inhibitors: immuno-oncology agents for restoring anti-tumor immune responses. Pharmacotherapy 36 (3), 317–334. https://doi.org/10.1002/phar.1714.

Merino, D.M., McShane, L.M., Fabrizio, D., Funari, V., Chen, S.J., White, J.R., Wenz, P., Baden, J., Barrett, J.C., Chaudhary, R., Chen, L., 2020. Establishing guidelines to harmonize tumor mutational burden (TMB): in silico assessment of variation in TMB quantification across diagnostic platforms: phase I of the Friends of Cancer Research TMB Harmonization Project. J. Immunother. Cancer 8 (1).

Mlecnik, B., Tosolini, M., Kirilovsky, A., Berger, A., Bindea, G., Meatchi, T., Bruneval, P., Trajanoski, Z., Fridman, W.H., Pagès, F., Galon, J., 2011. Histopathologic-based prognostic factors of colorectal cancers are associated with the state of the local immune reaction. J. Clin. Oncol. 29 (6), 610–618.

Mukherji, D., Jabbour, M.N., Saroufim, M., Temraz, S., Nasr, R., Charafeddine, M., Assi, R., Shamseddine, A., Tawil, A.N., 2016. Programmed death-ligand 1 expression in muscle-invasive bladder cancer cystectomy specimens and lymph node metastasis: a reliable treatment selection biomarker? Clin. Genitourin. Cancer 14 (2), 183–187.

Nduom, E.K., Wei, J., Yaghi, N.K., Huang, N., Kong, L.Y., Gabrusiewicz, K., Ling, X., Zhou, S., Ivan, C., Chen, J.Q., Burks, J.K., 2015. PD-L1 expression and prognostic impact in glioblastoma. Neuro Oncol. 18 (2), 195–205.

Nguyen, L.T., Ohashi, P.S., 2015. Clinical blockade of PD1 and LAG3—potential mechanisms of action. Nat. Rev. Immunol. 15 (1), 45–56. https://doi.org/10.1038/nri3790.

Nishino, M., Ramaiya, N.H., Hatabu, H., Hodi, F.S., 2017. Monitoring immune-checkpoint blockade: response evaluation and biomarker development. Nat. Rev. Clin. Oncol. 14 (11), 655–668.

Overman, M.J., Lonardi, S., Wong, K.Y., Lenz, H.J., Gelsomino, F., Aglietta, M., Morse, M.A., Van Cutsem, E., McDermott, R., Hill, A., Sawyer, M.B., 2018. Durable clinical benefit with nivolumab plus ipilimumab in DNA mismatch repair-deficient/microsatellite instability-high metastatic colorectal cancer. J. Clin. Oncol. 36 (8), 773–779.

Oya, Y., Yoshida, T., Kuroda, H., Mikubo, M., Kondo, C., Shimizu, J., Horio, Y., Sakao, Y., Hida, T., Yatabe, Y., 2017. Predictive clinical parameters for the response of nivolumab in pretreated advanced non-small-cell lung cancer. Oncotarget 8 (61), 103117.

Pardoll, D.M., 2012. The blockade of immune checkpoints in cancer immunotherapy. Nat. Rev. Cancer 12 (4), 252–264. https://doi.org/10.1038/nrc3239. PMID: 22437870; PMCID: PMC4856023.

Parham, P., Benjamin, R.J., Chen, B.P., Clayberger, C., Ennis, P.D., Krensky, A.M., Lawlor, D.A., Littman, D.R., Norment, A.M., Orr, H.T., Salter, R.D., 1989. Diversity of class I HLA molecules: functional and evolutionary interactions with T cells. In: Cold Spring Harbor Symposia on Quantitative Biology. vol. 54. Cold Spring Harbor Laboratory Press, pp. 529–543.

Patel, S.P., Kurzrock, R., 2015. PD-L1 expression as a predictive biomarker in cancer immunotherapy. Mol. Cancer Ther. 14 (4), 847–856.

Reck, M., Rodríguez-Abreu, D., Robinson, A.G., Hui, R., Csőszi, T., Fülöp, A., Gottfried, M., Peled, N., Tafreshi, A., Cuffe, S., O'Brien, M., Rao, S., Hotta, K., Leiby, M.A., Lubiniecki, G.M., Shentu, Y., Rangwala, R., Brahmer, J.R., 2016. KEYNOTE-024 Investigators. Pembrolizumab versus chemotherapy for PD-L1-positive non-small-cell lung cancer. N. Engl. J. Med. 375 (19), 1823–1833. https://doi.org/10.1056/NEJMoa1606774.

Ribas, A., Robert, C., Hodi, F.S., Wolchok, J.D., Joshua, A.M., Hwu, W.J., Weber, J.S., Zarour, H.M., Kefford, R., Loboda, A., Albright, A., 2015. Association of response to programmed death receptor 1 (PD-1) blockade with pembrolizumab (MK-3475) with an interferon-inflammatory immune gene signature. J. Clin. Oncol. 33 (15_suppl), 3001.

Rittmeyer, A., Barlesi, F., Waterkamp, D., Park, K., Ciardiello, F., von Pawel, J., Gadgeel, S.M., Hida, T., Kowalski, D.M., Dols, M.C., Cortinovis, D.L., Leach, J., Polikoff, J., Barrios, C., Kabbinavar, F., Frontera, O.A., De Marinis, F., Turna, H., Lee, J.S., Ballinger, M., Kowanetz, M., He, P., Chen, D.S., Sandler, A., Gandara, D.R., OAK Study Group, 2017. Atezolizumab versus docetaxel in patients with previously treated non-small-cell lung cancer (OAK): a phase 3, open-label, multicentre randomised controlled trial. Lancet 389 (10066), 255–265. https://doi.org/10.1016/S0140-6736(16)32517-X.

Rouquette, I., Taranchon-Clermont, E., Gilhodes, J., Bluthgen, M.V., Perallon, R., Chalabreysse, L., De Muret, A., Hofman, V., Marx, A., Parrens, M., Secq, V., 2019. Immune biomarkers in thymic epithelial tumors: expression patterns, prognostic value and comparison of diagnostic tests for PD-L1. Biomarker Res. 7 (1), 1–2.

Routy, B., Le Chatelier, E., Derosa, L., Duong, C.P., Alou, M.T., Daillère, R., Fluckiger, A., Messaoudene, M., Rauber, C., Roberti, M.P., Fidelle, M., 2018. Gut microbiome influences efficacy of PD-1-based immunotherapy against epithelial tumors. Science 359 (6371), 91–97.

Sabatier, R., Finetti, P., Mamessier, E., Adelaide, J., Chaffanet, M., Ali, H.R., Viens, P., Caldas, C., Birnbaum, D., Bertucci, F., 2015. Prognostic and predictive value of PDL1 expression in breast cancer. Oncotarget 6 (7), 5449.

Simeone, E., Gentilcore, G., Giannarelli, D., Grimaldi, A.M., Caracò, C., Curvietto, M., Esposito, A., Paone, M., Palla, M., Cavalcanti, E., Sandomenico, F., 2014. Immunological and biological changes during ipilimumab treatment and their potential correlation with clinical response and survival in patients with advanced melanoma. Cancer Immunol. Immunother. 63 (7), 675–683.

Teraoka, S., Fujimoto, D., Morimoto, T., Kawachi, H., Ito, M., Sato, Y., Nagata, K., Nakagawa, A., Otsuka, K., Uehara, K., Imai, Y., 2017. Early immune-related adverse events and association with outcome in advanced non-small cell lung cancer patients treated with nivolumab: a prospective cohort study. J. Thorac. Oncol. 12 (12), 1798–1805.

Tietze, J.K., Angelova, D., Heppt, M.V., Reinholz, M., Murphy, W.J., Spannagl, M., Ruzicka, T., Berking, C., 2017. The proportion of circulating CD45RO+ CD8+ memory T cells is correlated with clinical response in melanoma patients treated with ipilimumab. Eur. J. Cancer 75, 268–279.

Topalian, S.L., Taube, J.M., Anders, R.A., Pardoll, D.M., 2016. Mechanism-driven biomarkers to guide immune checkpoint blockade in cancer therapy. Nat. Rev. Cancer 16 (5), 275–287.

Wang, Z., Duan, J., Wang, G., Zhao, J., Xu, J., Han, J., Zhao, Z., Zhao, J., Zhu, B., Zhuo, M., Sun, J., 2020. Allele frequency-adjusted blood-based tumor mutational burden as a predictor of overall survival for patients with NSCLC treated with PD-(L) 1 inhibitors. J. Thorac. Oncol. 15 (4), 556–567.

Weber, J.S., D'Angelo, S.P., Minor, D., Hodi, F.S., Gutzmer, R., Neyns, B., Hoeller, C., Khushalani, N.I., Miller Jr., W.H., Lao, C.D., Linette, G.P., 2015. Nivolumab versus chemotherapy in patients with advanced melanoma who progressed after anti-CTLA-4 treatment (CheckMate 037): a randomised, controlled, open-label, phase 3 trial. Lancet Oncol. 16 (4), 375–384.

Wimberly, H., Brown, J.R., Schalper, K., Haack, H., Silver, M.R., Nixon, C., Bossuyt, V., Pusztai, L., Lannin, D.R., Rimm, D.L., 2015. PD-L1 expression correlates with tumor-infiltrating lymphocytes and response to neoadjuvant chemotherapy in breast cancer. Cancer Immunol. Res. 3 (4), 326–332.

Wolchok, J.D., Chiarion-Sileni, V., Gonzalez, R., Rutkowski, P., Grob, J.J., Cowey, C.L., Lao, C., Schadendorf, D., Ferrucci, P.F., Smylie, M., Dummer, R., 2016. Updated Results From a Phase III Trial of Nivolumab (NIVO) Combined With Ipilimumab (IPI) in Treatment-Naive Patients (PTS) With Advanced Melanoma (MEL) (CheckMate 067).

Yamazaki, N., Kiyohara, Y., Uhara, H., Iizuka, H., Uehara, J., Otsuka, F., Fujisawa, Y., Takenouchi, T., Isei, T., Iwatsuki, K., Uchi, H., Ihn, H., Minami, H., Tahara, H., 2017. Cytokine biomarkers to predict antitumor responses to nivolumab suggested in a phase 2 study for advanced melanoma. Cancer Sci. 108 (5), 1022–1031. https://doi.org/10.1111/cas.13226.

Zaretsky, J.M., Garcia-Diaz, A., Shin, D.S., Escuin-Ordinas, H., Hugo, W., Hu-Lieskovan, S., Torrejon, D.Y., Abril-Rodriguez, G., Sandoval, S., Barthly, L., Saco, J., 2016. Mutations associated with acquired resistance to PD-1 blockade in melanoma. N. Engl. J. Med. 375 (9), 819–829.

Zhang, Y., Sun, Z., Mao, X., Wu, H., Luo, F., Wu, X., Zhou, L., Qin, J., Zhao, L., Bai, C., 2017. Impact of mismatch-repair deficiency on the colorectal cancer immune microenvironment. Oncotarget 8 (49), 85526.

Further reading

Bindea, G., Mlecnik, B., Angell, H.K., Galon, J., 2014. The immune landscape of human tumors: implications for cancer immunotherapy. Onco. Targets. Ther. 3 (2), e27456.

Fuchs, C.S., Özgüroğlu, M., Bang, Y.J., Di Bartolomeo, M., Mandala, M., Ryu, M.H., Vivaldi, C., Olesinski, T., Caglevic, C., Chung, H.C., Muro, K., 2020. The association of molecular biomarkers with efficacy of pembrolizumab versus paclitaxel in patients with gastric cancer (GC) from KEYNOTE-061. J. Clin. Oncol. 38, 4512.

Hanna, G.J., Lizotte, P., Cavanaugh, M., Kuo, F.C., Shivdasani, P., Frieden, A., Chau, N.G., Schoenfeld, J. D., Lorch, J.H., Uppaluri, R., MacConaill, L.E., 2018. Frameshift events predict anti–PD-1/L1 response in head and neck cancer. JCI Insight 3 (4).

Jin, J., 2014. FDA approval of new drugs. JAMA 311 (9), 978.

Klein, J., Sato, A., 2000. The HLA system. First of two parts. N. Engl. J. Med. 343 (10), 702–709. https://doi.org/10.1056/NEJM200009073431006. PMID: 10974135.

Legrand, F.A., Gandara, D.R., Mariathasan, S., Powles, T., He, X., Zhang, W., Jhunjhunwala, S., Nickles, D., Bourgon, R., Schleifman, E., Paul, S.M., 2018. Association of high tissue TMB and atezolizumab efficacy across multiple tumor types. JCO 36 (15_suppl), 12000.

Li, W., Matakidou, A., Ghazoui, Z., Si, H., Wildsmith, S., Morsli, N., Mann, H., Wrona, M., de Los, R.M., Raja, R., Barker, C., 2020. Molecular biomarkers to identify patients (pts) who may benefit from durvalumab (D; anti-PD-L1)±tremelimumab (T; anti-CTLA-4) in recurrent/metastatic head and neck squamous cell carcinoma (R/M HNSCC) from HAWK and CONDOR studies. J. Clin. Oncol. 38 (15_suppl), 6548.

Luheshi, N., Coates-Ulrichsen, J., Harper, J., Davies, G., Legg, J., Wilkinson, R., et al., 2016. The combination of CD40 agonism and PD-L1 blockade enhances anti-tumor immunity in a mouse syngeneic orthotopic pancreatic tumor model. Oncotarget 7 (14), 18508–18520.

Miao, D., Margolis, C.A., Gao, W., Voss, M.H., Li, W., Martini, D.J., Norton, C., Bossé, D., Wankowicz, S.M., Cullen, D., Horak, C., 2018. Genomic correlates of response to immune checkpoint therapies in clear cell renal cell carcinoma. Science 359 (6377), 801–806.

Parham, P., Ohta, T., 1996. Population biology of antigen presentation by MHC class I molecules. Science 272 (5258), 67–74.

Riaz, N., Havel, J.J., Makarov, V., Desrichard, A., Urba, W.J., Sims, J.S., Hodi, F.S., Martín-Algarra, S., Mandal, R., Sharfman, W.H., Bhatia, S., 2017. Tumor and microenvironment evolution during immunotherapy with nivolumab. Cell 171 (4), 934–949.

Rosenberg, J.E., Hoffman-Censits, J., Powles, T., Van Der Heijden, M.S., Balar, A.V., Necchi, A., Dawson, N., O'Donnell, P.H., Balmanoukian, A., Loriot, Y., Srinivas, S., 2016. Atezolizumab in patients with locally advanced and metastatic urothelial carcinoma who have progressed following treatment with platinum-based chemotherapy: a single-arm, multicentre, phase 2 trial. Lancet 387 (10031), 1909–1920.

Shen, C., Chen, Y., 2015. Immune checkpoint blockade therapy: the 2014 Tang prize in biopharmaceutical science. Biom. J. 38 (1), 5.

Shitara, K., Özgüroğlu, M., Bang, Y.J., Di Bartolomeo, M., Mandalà, M., Ryu, M.H., Vivaldi, C., Olesinski, T., Chung, H.C., Muro, K., Van Cutsem, E., 2020. The association of tissue tumor mutational burden (tTMB) using the Foundation Medicine genomic platform with efficacy of pembrolizumab versus paclitaxel in patients (pts) with gastric cancer (GC) from KEYNOTE-061. J. Clin. Oncol. 38 (15 suppl), 4537.

Singal, G., Miller, P.G., Agarwala, V., Li, G., Kaushik, G., Backenroth, D., Gossai, A., Frampton, G.M., et al., 2019. Association of patient characteristics and tumor genomics with clinical outcomes among patients with non-small cell lung cancer using a clinicogenomic database. JAMA 321 (14), 1391–1399.

Yarchoan, M., Hopkins, A., Jaffee, E.M., 2017. Tumor mutational burden and response rate to PD-1 inhibition. N. Engl. J. Med. 377 (25), 2500.

CHAPTER THIRTEEN

Molecular biomarkers in prostate cancer

Remi Semba[a] and Katsunori Uchida[b]
[a]Department of Pathology, Kuwana City Medical Center, Kuwana, Mie, Japan
[b]Department of Pathology, Mie University Hospital, Tsu, Mie, Japan

1. Introduction

For the past decade, various molecular biomarkers for diagnosis and treatment of prostate cancer (PCa) have been studied and developed. The usefulness of prostate-specific antigen (PSA) based on blood serum has been validated, and the addition of the various specimen tests listed below (Tables 1, 2) has improved the accuracy of diagnosis and made it possible to tailor treatment to individual patients. In this chapter, we will review the molecular biomarkers that affect the diagnosis and treatment of PCa, focusing on those that are currently included in the National Comprehensive Cancer Network (NCCN) (National Comprehensive Cancer Network, n.d.), the European Association of Urology (EAU) (European Association of Urology, n.d.), and the American Urological Association (AUA) (American Urological Association, n.d.) guidelines, and suggest promising biomarkers.

2. Molecular biomarkers used for diagnosis (Table 1)
2.1 Blood-based molecular biomarkers

Blood-based molecular biomarkers used in the diagnosis of PCa include PSA isoform and its related proteins. PSA is a glycoprotein encoded by the Kallikrein 3 (KLK3) gene located on chromosome 19q 13.3–13.4. Since the approval of the PSA test by the FDA in 1986, it has been widely used to screen for PCa, determine treatment response, and predict recurrence and prognosis. Although the PSA test has been shown to be useful in reducing the mortality rate from PCa, it has also been associated with overdiagnosis in about 40% of screened patients (Schröder et al., 2014). In recent years, PSA isoform has been attracting attention for its potential to further improve the accuracy of PCa detection and treatment. PrePro-PSA produced by prostate luminal epithelial cells is converted to active PSA by human kallikrein-2, and most of it is bound to ACT and exists in the blood as complexed PSA (cPSA) (Özen and Sözen, 2006). The total PSA (tPSA), which is the sum of cPSA and free PSA (fPSA), is conventionally referred to as PSA.

Biomarkers in Cancer Detection and Monitoring of Therapeutics
https://doi.org/10.1016/B978-0-323-95114-2.00019-4

Table 1 Biomarker tests for diagnosis.

Biomarker test	Molecular markers	Available as	Sample
PSA(tPSA)	Total PSA	FDA	Blood
PHI	tPSA, fPSA, [−2]proPSA	FDA	Blood
4K	tPSA, fPSA, intact PSA, and hK2	FDA	Blood
ExoDx Prostate	PCA3, SPDEF, ERG	FDA	Urine
Progensa PCA3	PCA3	FDA	Urine
SelectMDx	HOXC6, DLX1	−	Urine
ConfirmMDx	GSTP1, APC, RASSF1	−	Tissue

There are three different isoforms of fPSA: BPSA, inactive PSA (iPSA), and proPSA. BPSA is associated with benign prostatic hyperplasia, while iPSA is reduced in PCa. The last isoform, proPSA, can be further divided into [−7]proPSA, [−5]proPSA, [−4]proPSA, and [−2]proPSA, among which [−2]proPSA is the most effective in detecting PCa (Mikolajczyk et al., 2004) and is used in various assays. In addition, the usefulness of age-adjusted PSA, PSA kinetics, PSA density, PSA velocity, and PSA doubling time, which comprehensively consider clinical information and PSA levels, has been reported.

2.2 Urine-based molecular biomarkers

Urine contains a variety of PCa-derived molecular markers, including PCa cells, DNA, RNA, and proteins, which have recently attracted attention for their usefulness and are being developed as new biomarkers. Among them, those that have been approved by the FDA for assay and listed in all guidelines will be outlined.

PCA3, a long noncoding RNA mapping to chromosome 9q21–22, was first reported by Bussemakers et al. (1999) in 1999 to be significantly overexpressed in PCa compared to normal prostate tissue. PCA3 promotes cell proliferation by down-regulating PRUNE2, a tumor suppressor gene (Salameh et al., 2015). PCA3 has been evaluated in various assays. On the other hand, a PCa-specific fusion gene between TMPRSS2 and ETS family genes was reported by Tomlins et al. (2005). TMPRSS2 is one of the androgen-responsive genes expressed in normal prostate cells and PCa cells, and it forms fusion genes by translocating with transcription factors belonging to the ETS family genes. Among these fusion genes, the most frequent is TMPRSS2:ERG, which is found in about 50% of PCa and is known to be highly specific (Mosquera et al., 2009). The TMPRSS2:ERG fusion gene upregulates the expression of ERG, and in PCa, high expression of ERG has been reported to be associated with advanced stage, high Gleason score, metastasis, and shortened survival (Hägglöf et al., 2014). In addition to the above biomarkers, microarray analysis of PCa has identified 39 other PCa biomarkers, from which HOXC6, TDRD1, and DLX1 can be used in panels to improve the prediction accuracy of PCa (Leyten et al., 2015), and are now being applied clinically.

2.3 Tissue-based molecular biomarkers

It is known that methylation of promoter regions of tumor suppressor genes and DNA repair genes suppresses the expression of these genes. In PCa, the frequency of hypermethylation and its role have been studied in more than 30 genes (Park, 2010). Among them, an assay to evaluate hypermethylation of three genes, GSTP1 (corticosteroid hormonal response gene), APC (gatekeeper gene), and RASSF1 (cell-cycle gene), using tissue samples, has been used to improve stratification of men considering rebiopsy (MDxHealth, n.d.). The assay is performed on men with negative biopsies to determine if the negative results are true negatives or false negatives due to sampling errors. The negative predictive value is reported to be 88%–96% (Van Neste et al., 2016; Partin et al., 2014; Stewart et al., 2013), which may reduce the need for unnecessary rebiopsies. This assay has not been approved by the FDA at this time.

3. Molecular biomarkers used for treatment (Table 2)

3.1 Gatekeeper-type tumor suppressor genes

It has been reported that some clinically aggressive PCa have molecular similarities (Aparicio et al., 2016). These cases were characterized by complex mutations in the Gatekeeper-type tumor suppressor genes PTEN, RB1, and TP53, which were associated with resistance to AR inhibitors and sensitivity to chemotherapy (Aparicio et al., 2013). These genetic defects are identified by immunostaining using FFPE specimens or by genomic analysis of circulating tumor DNA (ctDNA) in the blood (Corn et al., 2019). The NCCN states that combination therapy with cabazitaxel and carboplatin may be considered for patients with metastatic castration-resistant prostate cancer (mCRPC) who have abnormalities in at least two of the three tumor suppressor genes. Incidentally, AKT inhibitors for PTEN deficiency are currently undergoing clinical trials (European Association of Urology, n.d.).

3.2 Caretaker-type tumor suppressor genes

In recent years, companion diagnostics and diagnostic systems for caretaker-type tumor suppressor genes that are involved in DNA damage and replication error repair, especially homologous recombination gene mutations (HRRm) and mismatch repair gene deficient (dMMR), have been developed one after another and are now commercially available. DNA damaged by external or internal factors is repaired using various pathways, and disorders in the repair mechanisms are known to lead to cancer. The major DNA repair defects are homologous recombination repair defects caused by gene mutations such as BRCA1/2, and dMMR caused by MLH1, MSH2, MSH6, and PMS2 mutations. DNA repair mutations have been reported to occur in 19% of localized PCa (Cancer Genome Atlas Research Network, 2015) and 23% of mCRPC (Robinson et al., 2015). The all

Table 2 Biomarker tests for treatment.

Biomarker test	Molecular markers	Available as	Sample	Medicine
BRACAnalysis	Germline BRACA1/2	FDA	Blood	Olaparib
FoundationOne	BRCA1, BRCA2, ATM, BARD1, BRIP1, CDK12, CHEK1, CHEK2, FANCL, PALB2, RAD51B, RAD51C, RAD51D, and RAD54L	FDA	Tissue	Olaparib
	MSI-H	FDA	Tissue	Pembrolizumab
	TMB-H	FDA	Tissue	Pembrolizumab
	NTRK1/2/3	FDA	Tissue	Larotrectinib
FoundationOne Liquid	BRACA1/2, ATM BRACA1/2	FDA FDA	Blood blood	Olaparib Rucaparib
VENTANA MMR RxDx panel	MLH1, PMS2, MSF2, MSH6	FDA	Tissue	Dostarlimab-gxly
Prolaris	mRNA expression; 31 genes (cell-cycle progression)	FDA	Tissue	Active surveillance or not
Oncotype Dx	mRNA expression; 17 genes	–	Tissue	Active surveillance or not
Decipher	mRNA expression; 22 genes	–	Tissue	Active surveillance or not After radical prostatectomy
Oncotype DX AR-V7 Nucleus Detect test	AR-V7	FDA	Blood	Taxanes

guidelines recommend genetics and molecular/biomarker analysis based on family history, presence of metastases, histology, and other factors (National Comprehensive Cancer Network, n.d.; European Association of Urology, n.d.; American Urological Association, n.d.). Tests for HRRm and dMMR are listed in Table 2. Olaparib, a PARP inhibitor, is approved by the FDA for mCRPC patients with HRRm, and rucaparib is approved for BRCA-mutated mCRPC patients (U.S. Food & Drug, n.d.-a; U.S. Food & Drug, n.d.-b). Other PARP inhibitors (niraparib and talazoparib) are currently undergoing clinical trials (Teyssonneau et al., 2021). In addition to PARP inhibitors, the NCCN (National Comprehensive Cancer Network, n.d.) and AUA (American Urological Association, n.d.) guidelines states that early platinum-based chemotherapy may be considered for patients with HRRm. On the other hand, dMMR can be analyzed by immunohistochemistry or next-generation sequencing (NGS) assay. The use of pembrolizumab, an anti–PD-1 antibody, was approved by the FDA in 2017 for unresectable or metastatic cases with microsatellite instability-high or dMMR (U.S. Food & Drug, n.d.-c). In addition, pembrolizumab has been approved for use in patients with tumor mutation burden-high (TMB-H).

3.3 mRNA-based genomic biomarkers

In addition to existing prognostic factors and nomograms, numerous kinds of mRNA-based genomic biomarkers have been studied, but it is difficult to select just one. Therefore, assays that combine multiple mRNAs have been developed and used for risk stratification. The risk classification determines the treatment strategy, including active surveillance (AS), but none are currently recommended as routine tests and are clearly stated in the EAU guidelines (European Association of Urology, n.d.). The NCCN guidelines (National Comprehensive Cancer Network, n.d.) state that it may be considered for initial risk stratification in men diagnosed with PCa who are at low to high risk and have a life expectancy of 10 years or more. The following three tests are listed in both guidelines, but only prolaris is approved by the FDA.

    Prolaris: Prolaris, developed by Myriad Genetics, Inc. (n.d.), measures the expression of 31 genes related to cell-cycle progression (CCP) in biopsy specimens by RT-PCR and calculates the CCP score. The CCP score has been reported to be an independent predictor of biochemical recurrence, metastatic disease, and prostate cancer–specific mortality (Bishoff et al., 2014; Cuzick et al., 2012). The clinical cell-cycle risk (CCR) score, which combines CCP risk with clinicopathologic risk from the Cancer of the Prostate Risk Assessment (CAPRA) model, can be used to classify AS candidates into high-risk and low-risk groups for 10-year PCM, with a 100% negative predictive value for the low-risk group (Lin et al., 2018). It was suggested that the CCR score could be used to more accurately select patients for AS.

    Oncotype Dx: The Oncotype DX Genomic Prostate Score test (GPS), developed by Genomic Health, Inc. (n.d.), is a biopsy tissue-based test that measures expression levels of 12 PCa-related genes and 5 control housekeeping genes. In a cohort study of men in the very low, low, and intermediate risk groups, GPS showed a strong correlation with biochemical relapse (BCR), metastasis, and poor prognostic factors in pathology (primary Gleason pattern 4 or any pattern 5 and/or pT3 disease) (Cullen et al., 2015). It may be useful in stratifying patients for AS because it may predict high invasiveness of PCa.

    Decipher: The Decipher test, developed by GenomeDx (Veracyte, Inc., n.d.), is an assay that quantifies the RNA expression levels of 22 genes involved in cell adhesion and migration, cell-cycle regulation, immune system regulation, cell differentiation, and androgen signaling in FFPE tissue. The addition of the Decipher test to the Cancer of the Prostate Risk Assessment and the NCCN risk classification has improved the ability to predict metastasis and PCa-specific mortality (Nguyen et al., 2017). Furthermore, a study of the Decipher test using RP specimens reported that it is an independent prognostic predictor of PCa-specific mortality (Cooperberg et al., 2015) and can assist in determining the timing of postoperative irradiation (Den et al., 2014).

3.4 Androgen receptor splice variant 7 (AR-v7)

AR-v7 is a splice variant of the androgen receptor that is upregulated in CRPC patients. Because it lacks a ligand-binding domain but remains permanently active (Shafi et al., 2013), CRPC patients with overexpression of AR-v7 are resistant to hormone therapy. On the other hand, it has been reported to be sensitive to taxane (Scher et al., 2018). For patients with disease progression after secondary hormone therapy, the NCCN (National Comprehensive Cancer Network, n.d.) states that AR-v7 testing in circulating tumor cells can be considered. The blood-based Oncotype DX AR-v7 Nucleus Detect test was approved by the FDA in 2018 for AR-v7 testing.

4. Future prospects

Although not included in the guidelines, there are promising biomarkers for clinical application.

4.1 micro-RNA (miRNA)

miRNAs are short noncoding RNAs of about 21–25 nucleotides that have the effect of suppressing gene expression and are mainly involved in posttranscriptional modification of mRNAs. In the prostate, Mitchell et al. (2008) first reported the presence of miRNAs in the plasma of PCa patients in 2008, and since then, various studies on miRNAs have been conducted. However, at this stage, miRNAs have not yet been applied clinically due to difficulties in reproducibility and conflicting research results in some papers (Abramovic et al., 2020).

4.2 Biomarkers for antibody–drug conjugates (ADCs)

ADCs are compounds consisting of a monoclonal antibody conjugated with a cytotoxic agent (payload). To date, 12 ADCs have been approved by the FDA, but the indication for PCa is still under investigation. The development of ADCs targeting the antigens STEAP1, TROP2, PSMA, CD46, and B7-H3 is underway (Rosellini et al., 2021).

> ## 5. Conclusion

Molecular biomarkers and assays related to diagnosis and treatment, as described in all three guidelines, were outlined. Recently, combinations of multiple molecular biomarkers have been applied for diagnostic and therapeutic purposes and are becoming clinically available. It is important to pay attention to the latest information. In addition, it is advisable to use the latest biomarkers in an appropriate and timely manner in accordance with various guidelines, rather than blindly incorporating them into diagnosis and treatment.

References

Abramovic, I., Ulamec, M., Katusic Bojanac, A., Bulic-Jakus, F., Jezek, D., Sincic, N., 2020. miRNA in prostate cancer: challenges toward translation. Epigenomics 12 (6), 543–558.

American Urological Association, Prostate Cancer Guidelines. https://uroweb.org/guideline/prostate-cancer/. Accessed 08.02.22.

Aparicio, A.M., Harzstark, A.L., Corn, P.G., et al., 2013. Platinum-based chemotherapy for variant castrate-resistant prostate cancer. Clin. Cancer Res. 19 (13), 3621–3630.

Aparicio, A.M., Shen, L., Tapia, E.L., et al., 2016. Combined tumor suppressor defects characterize clinically defined aggressive variant prostate cancers. Clin. Cancer Res. 22 (6), 1520–1530.

Bishoff, J.T., Freedland, S.J., Gerber, L., et al., 2014. Prognostic utility of the cell cycle progression score generated from biopsy in men treated with prostatectomy. J. Urol. 192 (2), 409–414.

Bussemakers, M.J., van Bokhoven, A., Verhaegh, G.W., et al., 1999. DD3: a new prostate-specific gene, highly overexpressed in prostate cancer. Cancer Res. 59 (23), 5975–5979.

Cancer Genome Atlas Research Network, 2015. The molecular taxonomy of primary prostate Cancer. Cell 163 (4), 1011–1025.

Cooperberg, M.R., Davicioni, E., Crisan, A., Jenkins, R.B., Ghadessi, M., Karnes, R.J., 2015. Combined value of validated clinical and genomic risk stratification tools for predicting prostate cancer mortality in a high-risk prostatectomy cohort. Eur. Urol. 67 (2), 326–333.

Corn, P.G., Heath, E.I., Zurita, A., et al., 2019. Cabazitaxel plus carboplatin for the treatment of men with metastatic castration-resistant prostate cancers: a randomised, open-label, phase 1-2 trial [published correction appears in lancet Oncol. 2020 Jan;21(1):e14]. Lancet Oncol. 20 (10), 1432–1443.

Cullen, J., Rosner, I.L., Brand, T.C., et al., 2015. A biopsy-based 17-gene genomic prostate score predicts recurrence after radical prostatectomy and adverse surgical pathology in a racially diverse population of men with clinically low- and intermediate-risk prostate Cancer. Eur. Urol. 68 (1), 123–131.

Cuzick, J., Berney, D.M., Fisher, G., et al., 2012. Prognostic value of a cell cycle progression signature for prostate cancer death in a conservatively managed needle biopsy cohort. Br. J. Cancer 106 (6), 1095–1099.

Den, R.B., Feng, F.Y., Showalter, T.N., et al., 2014. Genomic prostate cancer classifier predicts biochemical failure and metastases in patients after postoperative radiation therapy. Int. J. Radiat. Oncol. Biol. Phys. 89 (5), 1038–1046.

European Association of Urology, Oncology Guidelines, Prostate Cancer. https://uroweb.org/guideline/prostate-cancer/. Accessed 08.02.22.

Genomic Health, Inc. https://www.oncotypeiq.com/. Accessed 01.02.22.

Hägglöf, C., Hammarsten, P., Strömvall, K., et al., 2014. TMPRSS2-ERG expression predicts prostate cancer survival and associates with stromal biomarkers. PLoS One 9 (2), e86824 (Published 2014 Feb 5).

Leyten, G.H., Hessels, D., Smit, F.P., et al., 2015. Identification of a candidate gene panel for the early diagnosis of prostate Cancer. Clin. Cancer Res. 21 (13), 3061–3070.

Lin, D.W., Crawford, E.D., Keane, T., et al., 2018. Identification of men with low-risk biopsy-confirmed prostate cancer as candidates for active surveillance. Urol. Oncol. 36 (6), 310.e7–310.e13.

MDxHealth. https://mdxhealth.com; Accessed 01.02.22.

Mikolajczyk, S.D., Catalona, W.J., Evans, C.L., et al., 2004. Proenzyme forms of prostate-specific antigen in serum improve the detection of prostate cancer. Clin. Chem. 50 (6), 1017–1025.

Mitchell, P.S., Parkin, R.K., Kroh, E.M., et al., 2008. Circulating microRNAs as stable blood-based markers for cancer detection. Proc. Natl. Acad. Sci. U.S.A. 105 (30), 10513–10518.

Mosquera, J.M., Mehra, R., Regan, M.M., et al., 2009. Prevalence of TMPRSS2-ERG fusion prostate cancer among men undergoing prostate biopsy in the United States. Clin. Cancer Res. 15 (14), 4706–4711.

Myriad Genetics, Inc. https://myriad.com. Accessed 08.02.22.

National Comprehensive Cancer Network, NCCN Guidelines Version 3.2022 Prostate Cancer. https://www.nccn.org/professionals/physician_gls/pdf/prostate.pdf. Accessed 08.02.22.

Nguyen, P.L., Haddad, Z., Ross, A.E., et al., 2017. Ability of a genomic classifier to predict metastasis and prostate Cancer-specific mortality after radiation or surgery based on needle biopsy specimens. Eur. Urol. 72 (5), 845–852.

Özen, H., Sözen, S., 2006. PSA isoforms in prostate cancer detection. Eur. Urol. Suppl. 5 (6), 495–499.

Park, J.Y., 2010. Promoter hypermethylation in prostate cancer. Cancer Control 17 (4), 245–255.

Partin, A.W., Van Neste, L., Klein, E.A., et al., 2014. Clinical validation of an epigenetic assay to predict negative histopathological results in repeat prostate biopsies. J. Urol. 192 (4), 1081–1087.

Robinson, D., Van Allen, E.M., Wu, Y.M., et al., 2015. Integrative clinical genomics of advanced prostate cancer [published correction appears in cell. 2015 Jul 16;162(2):454]. Cell 161 (5), 1215–1228.

Rosellini, M., Santoni, M., Mollica, V., et al., 2021. Treating prostate Cancer by antibody-drug conjugates. Int. J. Mol. Sci. 22(4):1551 (Published 2021 Feb 4).

Salameh, A., Lee, A.K., Cardó-Vila, M., et al., 2015. PRUNE2 is a human prostate cancer suppressor regulated by the intronic long noncoding RNA PCA3. Proc. Natl. Acad. Sci. U. S. A. 112 (27), 8403–8408.

Scher, H.I., Graf, R.P., Schreiber, N.A., et al., 2018. Assessment of the validity of nuclear-localized androgen receptor splice variant 7 in circulating tumor cells as a predictive biomarker for castration-resistant prostate Cancer. JAMA Oncol. 4 (9), 1179–1186.

Schröder, F.H., Hugosson, J., Roobol, M.J., et al., 2014. Screening and prostate cancer mortality: results of the European randomised study of screening for prostate Cancer (ERSPC) at 13 years of follow-up. Lancet 384 (9959), 2027–2035.

Shafi, A.A., Yen, A.E., Weigel, N.L., 2013. Androgen receptors in hormone-dependent and castration-resistant prostate cancer. Pharmacol. Ther. 140 (3), 223–238.

Stewart, G.D., Van Neste, L., Delvenne, P., et al., 2013. Clinical utility of an epigenetic assay to detect occult prostate cancer in histopathologically negative biopsies: results of the MATLOC study. J. Urol. 189 (3), 1110–1116.

Teyssonneau, D., Margot, H., Cabart, M., et al., 2021. Prostate cancer and PARP inhibitors: progress and challenges. J. Hematol. Oncol. 14(1):51 (Published 2021 Mar 29).

Tomlins, S.A., Rhodes, D.R., Perner, S., et al., 2005. Recurrent fusion of TMPRSS2 and ETS transcription factor genes in prostate cancer. Science 310 (5748), 644–648.

U.S. Food & Drug. https://wayback.archive-it.org/7993/20201222063036/https://www.fda.gov/drugs/drug-approvals-and-databases/fda-approves-olaparib-hrr-gene-mutated-metastatic-castration-resistant-prostate-cancer. Accessed 08.02.22.

U.S. Food & Drug. https://wayback.archive-it.org/7993/20201222063117/https://www.fda.gov/drugs/fda-grants-accelerated-approval-rucaparib-brca-mutated-metastatic-castration-resistant-prostate. Accessed 08.02.22.

U.S. Food & Drug. https://www.fda.gov/news-events/press-announcements/fda-approves-first-cancer-treatment-any-solid-tumor-specific-genetic-feature. Accessed 08.02.22.

Van Neste, L., Partin, A.W., Stewart, G.D., Epstein, J.I., Harrison, D.J., Van Criekinge, W., 2016. Risk score predicts high-grade prostate cancer in DNA-methylation positive, histopathologically negative biopsies. Prostate 76 (12), 1078–1087.

Veracyte, Inc. https://decipherbio.com. Accessed 01.02.22.

CHAPTER FOURTEEN

Biomarkers in endometrial and cervical cancer

Navdeep Kaur Mangat, Ritu Aggarwal, and Aashima Arora
Department of Immunopathology, Post Graduate Institute of Medical Education and Research, Chandigarh, India

1. Endometrial cancer

Endometrial cancer (EC) is the 6th most prevalent cancer in females globally with highest frequency among the malignancies of female genital tract. The GLOBOCAN 2018 reported ASR (age standardized incidence rate) and mortality rate of 8.4 and 1.8 per 100,000 respectively. ASR increases with the increase in human development index.

Histologically EC is classified as Type I (low grade with favorable prognosis, linked to estrogen and obesity) and Type II (high grade and estrogen independent). Molecular classification includes microsatellite instable, polymerase-epsilon (POLE) ultramutated, low and high copy number (Njoku et al., 2020).

2. Biomarkers in EC
2.1 Tumor markers in clinical use
CA125

It is reported in literature that CA125 levels was raised in 26.2% of uterine ECs. With a limit level of 20 U/mL (specificity: 74%, sensitivity: 69%), it could detect the invasiveness of uterine carcinoma. Others found that a high CA125 level (>40 U/mL) was linked to a higher stages of EC and increased depth of invasiveness along with metastases (Chen et al., 2011).

HE4

Increased levels of HE4 are also reported in EC. When it came to recognizing advanced stage disease, HE4 was found to be more sensitive in comparison to CA125. Furthermore, a link was discovered between HE4 and tumor diameter along with profound myometrial invasion. HE4 was found to be a stronger predictive factor of outer-half myometrial invasion than CA125 in a population-based investigation, especially in patients with initial stage endometrioid tumors (Brennan et al., 2014).

Biomarkers in Cancer Detection and Monitoring of Therapeutics
https://doi.org/10.1016/B978-0-323-95114-2.00006-6
313

2.2 Predictive genomic markers

Various studies have reported that mutations in ERα (estrogen receptor alpha) could be an important prognostic biomarker in EC. This biomarker has been found to explain the progression of EC in women with low BMI. Microsatellite instability (MSI) is a malfunction in the DNA-MMR system that manifests as an error in DNA replication of trinucleotide repeat regions in around 25% of ECs. MSI tumors develop either due to EPCAM deletions or due to deficiency in MMR genes (MLH1, MSH2, MSH6) (Howitt et al., 2015).

Other important genomic markers in EC include tumor suppressor genes (PTEN and TP53), Ki-67 (marker for proliferation), adhesion molecules (L1CAM and E Cadherin), and Erb-B2 receptor tyrosine kinase 2 (Howitt et al., 2015).

2.3 Epigenetic markers

DNA methylation

Hypermethylation of tumor suppressor genes has been recognized in atypical endometrial hyperplasia suggesting that abnormal DNA methylation occurs not only early in EC, but also in the precancerous stage. As a result, DNA methylation, which affects gene expression, is expected to be involved in EC cell development, proliferation, and death.

There is a difference in observed methylation patterns in type I and type II EC which explains the histology and pathological disparities between these malignancies.

DNMT1 and DNMT3B are reported to be upregulated in type I EC due to which hypermethylation at the promoter regions of MLH1 and PTEN is frequently seen. However, downregulation is reported in type II EC leading to global hypomethylation and genomic instability. Promoters of more than 50 tumor suppressor genes are reported to be hypermethylated, comprising the familiar tumor suppressor genes like MLH1, PR, CDH, PTEN, RASSF1A, and MGMT (Stampoliou et al., 2016).

This hypermethylation at the promoter region of MLH1 is reported in nearly 35% of cases of EC and is positively co related from pre-cancerous stage to EC.

Recently some studies claimed the use of hypermethylation markers as diagnostic tool in EC. Presence of hypermethylated genes in serum samples is comparatively less invasive than traditional methods. Hypermethylation in at least three genes out of a combination of five genes (*HSPA2, SOCS2, MLH1, CDH13*, and *RASSF1A*) has been proposed as less invasive diagnostic tool for EC (sensitivity: 100% and specificity: 91%) (Jones and Baylin, 2007).

Histone modification

In EC, the literature is limited on histone acetyltransferases (HATs); however, histone deacetylases (HDACs), in comparison to HATs, have been widely studied in EC. Various physiological activities like cell proliferation, cell death, and cellular differentiation are regulated by HDACs due to which HDACs dysregulation plays a role in carcinogenesis. As a result, HDAC inhibitors are beneficial in a variety of malignancies.

HDACs are upregulated in EC, HDAC1–3 expression levels are more significant in EC compared to normal endometrium, and these levels are linked to a bad prognosis. Even though numerous HDACs are overexpressed in EC, expression of SIRT6 is down-regulated, causing apoptosis through suppressing survivin. SIRT1, 2, 4, and 5 levels show downregulation; in contrast, SIRT7 is overexpressed (Stampoliou et al., 2016). Apart from histone acetylation, aberrant methylation patterns on histone proteins are also associated with the progression of EC. H3K4me2 and H3K4me3 are found to be upregulated and linked with the degree of malignancy in EC. Additionally some components of histone methyltransferase complex like ASH2L and EZH2 were also reported to be overexpressed in EC (Stampoliou et al., 2016).

Noncoding RNAs

In EC, MiR-205 was consistently found to be elevated, with more than 10 studies reporting differential expression and a mean fold change of 198.08. In endometrial cancer, MiR-205 regulates PTEN expression, which leads to a reduction in cell apoptosis. MiR-205 also suppresses the tumor suppressor gene JPH4, increasing carcinogenesis and progression. MiR-205, on the other hand, is increased not just in endometrial cancer but also in other cancers such as lung and ovarian cancer. As a result, miR-205 appears to be inadequate as a diagnostic test for endometrial cancer on its own (Jones and Baylin, 2007).

The distinct miRNA panel which is identified as consistently dysregulated in most of the research studies in EC comprises of miR-135b, -182, -183, miR-205, and the miR-200 family.

As a result, miRNAs could be intriguing biomarker in management of EC, but there isn't enough high-quality evidence to establish firm conclusions. To increase the accuracy of employing these miRNAs in diagnosing EC in the future, additional research with standardized methodologies are needed to test the discovered miRNAs (Egger et al., 2004).

3. Cervical cancer

As per the GLOBOCON report 2018, cervical cancer is the 4th most frequent malignancy among women, accounting for 6.6% of all cancer diagnoses and 7.5% of all cancer deaths (Global Cancer Statistic, 2018). Additionally, it is also the principal cause of death in females of reproductive age. The change from normal epithelium to cervical carcinoma can take many years. The overall survival rate of cervical cancer is 70%–90% in the early stages, but it drops to 15% in the late stages. Cervical cancer (CC) has a high fatality rate because it is asymptomatic and remains undiagnosed in its early stages, making early identification extremely difficult. There are a various treatment options available, if risk of cancer progression is predicted in initial stages, making the disease curable. The most popular methods for cervical cancer screening are the Pap smear (specificity: 98% and sensitivity: 51%) and colposcopy. Cervical cancer in situ and adenocarcinoma are difficult to detect with a Pap test, although colposcopy and biopsy could be proficient to detect some early-stage cervical malignancies. Both practices are intrusive and can result in management delays as well as increased expenses and hazards. There hasn't been a precise and reliable serologic marker for screening rationales until now.

3.1 Tumor markers in clinical use

Squamous cell carcinoma antigen

It is a serum tumor antigen for squamous cell carcinoma and found to be aberrant in 28% to 88% of individuals. It is positively correlated with the progression and stages of disease along with relapse and survival rate (Kato and Torigoe, 1977; Charakorn et al., 2018).

Serum fragments of cytokeratin

Cytokeratin 19 is a component of cytokeratin which is found in both normal epithelia and cervical carcinoma. The fragments of cytokeratin 19 in serum samples are measured using CYFRA 21-1. It is upregulated in 26%–63% of cervical cancer patients. It is found to be positively associated with tumor size and stage in the majority of patients (Gadducci et al., 2008).

CA125

CA125 levels are elevated in 20%–75% of patients with squamous cell cervical cancer and adenocarcinoma. It is high in 75% of adenocarcinoma against only 25% of squamous cell carcinoma (Lehtovirta et al., 1990).

CA19

Upregulated CA19-9 in the blood indicates an inflammation and a poor prognosis. It aids in the diagnosis of tumor relapse in CC patients undergoing radiotherapy. Despite the fact that CA-125 is substantially connected with CC, CA19-9 is a helpful measure in cases when CA-125 readings are negative in serum (Borras et al., 1995).

3.2 Tumor markers under investigation

Increased insulin-like growth factor II (IGF-II) expression aids in the early detection of CC, while upregulation of vascular endothelial growth factor–C (VEGF-C) in blood depicts CC metastasis (Mathur et al., 2005). With a sensitivity of 68%, serum YKL-40 (tyrosine [Y], lysine [K], and leucine [L]) discriminates among cervical cancer and controls. Furthermore, people with CC have been found to have increased amounts of thymidine kinase (TK) and macrophage colony-stimulating factor (M-CSF) (Lawicki et al., 2008).

3.3 Predictive genomic markers

Multiple research studies have demonstrated that specific genetic changes are involved in the initiation and progression of cervical cancer. The genome characterization of a significant number of cervical patients showed the vast complexity of molecular abnormalities, including somatic aberrations and copy number alterations.

Several investigations have demonstrated the association of somatic mutations in **TP53, EP300, PIK3CA, FBXW7, STK11, and HLA-B** with cervical cancer. Recently, significant recurrent mutations in **MUC16 (**19%), **TTN** (33%), and **MUC4** (31%) have been discovered. However, little is known about the patterns of cellular changes and virus integrations in cervical lesions, particularly in cervical intraepithelial neoplasia (CIN) (Gerull et al., 2002; Munro et al., 2009; Li et al., 2008; Yang et al., 2006).

3.4 Epigenetic markers

DNA methylation

Hypermethylation has been shown in several studies to inactivate tumor suppressor genes, resulting in cervical cancer. Furthermore, the epigenetic marks on HPV genome, leading to cervical cancer, are also well studied.

Methylation levels were also linked to the severity of histopathological grading. Methylation expression increased from precancerous stage to invasive carcinoma, though it was indiscernible in normal cervix. As a result, these indicators could be used as a novel form of biomarker for CC diagnosis, prognosis, and screening (Zhao and Cui, 2015; Laengsri et al., 2018). Tumor suppressor genes consistently reported hypermethylated in CC are **adenylate cyclase 8 (ADCY8), cadherin 8 type 2 (CDH8), zinc finger protein 582 (ZNF582), breast cancer metastasis suppressor 1 (BRMS1), p16, p53, Ras association domain family 1 isoform A (RASSF1A), and chromosome 13 open reading frame 18 (C13ORF18) (Laengsri et al., 2018)**.

Hypomethylated proto oncogenes include **Wolf–Hirschhorn syndrome candidate 1 (WHSC1) and cyclin A1 (CCNA1) (de la Cruz-Hernández et al., 2007)**.

Histone modifications

Understanding the pattern of HDAC expression in different cancers could aid in predicting prognosis. Histone deacetylation in tumor suppressor genes also contributes to cancer development. Valproate, a histone deacetylase inhibitor, has an inhibitory effect on CC cell lines and primary tumors by inducing hyperacetylation of p53, but has no effect on the production of oncoproteins like E6 and E7 (Lin et al., 2009). Furthermore, a synergistic effect of bortezomib, a proteasome inhibitor, and trichostatin A (TSA) or vorinostat, an HDAC inhibitor, has been shown to be efficient in lysis of HPV–positive cervical cancer cells. As a result, an HDAC inhibitor is considered as an epigenetic phenomenon to target CC (Beyer et al., 2017).

Commonly reported histone modification markers of cervical cancer are p53, H3K9ac, H3K4RARB2, p21Cip1/WAF1, hTERT, SOCS, MMP2, MMP9, and MGMT (Beyer et al., 2017; Zhang et al., 2007; Huang et al., 2005; Wu et al., 2005; Kim et al., 2015; Sasi et al., 2014).

miRNA

Various studies reported the link between progression of cervical cancer and altered miRNA expression (Nahand et al., 2019).

Circulating miRNAs, such as miRNA-20a, miRNA-21, miRNA-203, miRNA-205, and miRNA-485-5, as well as tissue-specific miRNAs, such as miR-7, miR-10a, miR135b, and miR-149, have been found to be upregulated in cervical cancer studies (Hasanzadeh et al., 2019).

MiR-944 is another miRNA that has been found in high levels in cervical cancer. While several studies claim it acts as an oncogene in many cancers, including cervical cancer, by encouraging the tumor growth processes, others claim it has tumor suppressor capabilities in cancers of the colon, stomach, and breast. MiR-944 expression was shown to be considerably upregulated in cervical carcinoma tissues. Presence of MiR-944 is also linked to a higher FIGO stage, a larger tumor, lymph node metastases, and a lower survival rate. In light of the foregoing, miR-944 could be used as a predictive biomarker (He et al., 2016; Park et al., 2019).

Other miRNAs, including miR-195, miR-138, miR-214, and miR-148b, are reported with repressed expression in CC, indicating that they may act as tumor suppressors. As previously indicated, miR-138 is downregulated and functions as a tumor suppressor by inducing the tumor progression. It has the potential to be employed as a predictive biomarker because it is adversely related with lymph node metastases and advanced FIGO stage. Downregulation of miR-34a and miR-206 has been positively correlated with advanced stages of CC and metastasis and poor survival rate (Zhou et al., 2016; Li et al., 2017).

The development of chemotherapy resistance is a key issue in cancer treatments. As previously indicated, miRNA expression levels appear to influence the tumor cell's treatment sensitivity/resistance. MiR-34a, miR-375, and miR-664 are some of the miRNAs discovered to influence the cells' response to chemotherapy. Increased expression of miR-664 in HeLa cells, on the other hand, resulted in increased cisplatin sensitivity and decreased cell motility in cervical cancer cells (Yu et al., 2015; Shen et al., 2013).

Despite the fact that numerous researches have been undertaken, many miRNA signatures still lack consistency. miRNA source (serum or cervical tissue), sample size, study subjects with various comorbidities that may affect the miRNA expression could explain these disparities.

There is a critical need for rapid techniques to predict cervical cancer risk at an initial stage, especially given that the vast majority of cases are diagnosed in later stages. Despite current limitations, miRNAs as biomarkers can meet this need, making this a promising research field.

References

Beyer, S., Zhu, J., Mayr, D., et al., 2017. Histone H3 acetyl K9 and histone H3 tri methyl K4 as prognostic markers for patients with cervical cancer. Int. J. Mol. Sci. 18, 3.

Borras, G., Molina, R., Xercavins, J., Ballesta, A., Iglesias, J., 1995. Tumor antigens CA 19.9, CA 125, and CEA in carcinoma of the uterine cervix. Gynecol. Oncol. 57 (2), 205–211.

Brennan, D.J., Hackethal, A., Metcalf, A.M., Coward, J., Ferguson, K., Oehler, M.K., et al., 2014. Serum HE4 as a prognostic marker in endometrial cancer—a population based study. Gynecol. Oncol. 132 (1), 159–165.

Charakorn, C., Thadanipon, K., Chaijindaratana, S., Rattanasiri, S., Numthavaj, P., Thakkinstian, A., 2018. The association between serum squamous cell carcinoma antigen and recurrence and survival of patients with cervical squamous cell carcinoma: a systematic review and meta-analysis. Gynecol. Oncol. 150 (1), 190–200.

Chen, Y.L., Huang, C.Y., Chien, T.Y., Huang, S.H., Wu, C.J., Ho, C.M., 2011. Value of pre-operative serum CA125 level for prediction of prognosis in patients with endometrial cancer. Aust. N. Z. J. Obstet. Gynaecol. 51 (5), 397–402.

de la Cruz-Hernández, E., Pérez-Cárdenas, E., Contreras-Paredes, A., et al., 2007. The effects of DNA methylation and histone deacetylaseinhibitors on human papillomavirus early gene expression in cervical cancer, an in vitro and clinical study. Virol. J. 4, 18.

Egger, G., Liang, G., Aparicio, A., Jones, P.A., 2004. Epigenetics in human disease and prospects for epigenetic therapy. Nature 429, 457–463.

Gadducci, A., Tana, R., Cosio, S., Genazzani, A.R., 2008. The serum assay of tumour markers in the prognostic evaluation, treatment monitoring and follow-up of patients with cervical cancer: a review of the literature. Crit. Rev. Oncol. Hematol. 66 (1), 10–20.

Gerull, B., Gramlich, M., Atherton, J., McNabb, M., Trombitas, K., Sasse-, K.S., et al., 2002. Mutations of TTN, encoding the giant muscle filament titin, cause familial dilated cardiomyopathy. Nat. Genet. 30, 201–204.

Global Cancer Statistics 2018: GLOBOCAN Estimates of Incidence and Mortality Worldwide for 36 Cancers in 185 Countries, 2018.

Hasanzadeh, M., Movahedi, M., Rejali, M., Maleki, F., Moetamani-Ahmadi, M., Seifi, S., et al., 2019. The potential prognostic and therapeutic application of tissue and circulating microRNAs in cervical cancer. J. Cell. Physiol. 234, 1289–1294.

He, H., Tian, W., Chen, H., Jiang, K., 2016. MiR-944 functions as a novel oncogene and regulates the chemoresistance in breast cancer. Tumour Biol. 37, 1599–1607.

Howitt, B.E., Shukla, S.A., Sholl, L.M., Ritterhouse, L.L., Watkins, J.C., Rodig, S., et al., 2015. Association of polymerase e-mutated and microsatellite-instable endometrial cancers with neoantigen load, number of tumor-infiltrating lymphocytes, and expression of PD-1 and PD-L1. JAMA Oncol. 1 (9), 1319–1323.

Huang, B.H., Laban, M., Leung, C.H., 2005. Inhibition of histone deacetylase 2 increases apoptosis and p21Cip1/WAF1 expression, independent of histone deacetylase. Cell Death Differ. 12 (4), 395–404.

Jones, P.A., Baylin, S.B., 2007. The epigenomics of cancer. Cell 128, 683–692.

Kato, H., Torigoe, T., 1977. Radioimmunoassay for tumor antigen of human cervical squamous cell carcinoma. Cancer 40 (4), 1621–1628.

Kim, M.H., Kim, M.S., Kim, W., 2015. Suppressor of cytokine signaling (SOCS) genes are silenced by DNA hypermethylation and histone deacetylation and regulate response to radiotherapy in cervical cancer cells. PLoS One 10 (4), e0123133.

Laengsri, V., Kerdpin, U., Plabplueng, C., Treeratanapiboon, L., Nuchnoi, P., 2018. Cervical cancer markers: epigenetics and microRNAs. Lab. Med. 49 (2), 97–111.

Lawicki, S., Bedkowska, E., Gacuta-Szumarska, E., Knapp, P., Szmitkowski, M., 2008. The plasma levels and diagnostic utility of stem cell factor (SCF) and macrophage-colony stimulating factor (M-CSF) in cervical cancer patients. Pol. Merkur. Lekarski 25 (145), 38–42.

Lehtovirta, P., Viinikka, L., Ylikorkala, O., 1990. Comparison between squamous cell carcinoma- associated antigen and CA-125 in patients with carcinoma of the cervix. Gynecol. Oncol. 37 (2), 276–278.

Li, X., Pasche, B., Zhang, W., Chen, K., 2008. Association of MUC16 mutation with tumor mutation load and outcomes in patients with gastric cancer. JAMA Oncol. 4, 1691–1698.

Li, H., Sheng, Y., Zhang, Y., Gao, N., Deng, X., Sheng, X., 2017. MicroRNA-138 is a potential biomarker and tumor suppressor in human cervical carcinoma by reversely correlated with TCF3 gene. Gynecol. Oncol. 145, 569–576.

Lin, Z., Bazzaro, M., Wang, M.C., Chan, K.C., Peng, S., Roden, R.B., 2009. Combination of proteasome and HDAC inhibitors for uterine cervical cancer treatment. Clin. Cancer Res. 15 (2), 570–577.

Mathur, S.P., Mathur, R.S., Gray, E.A., Lane, D., Underwood, P.G., Kohler, M., Creasman, W.T., 2005. Serum vascular endothelial growth factor C (VEGF-C) as a specific biomarker for advanced cervical cancer: relationship to insulin-like growth factor II (IGF-II), IGF binding protein 3 (IGF-BP3) and VEGF-A. Gynecol. Oncol. 98 (3), 467–483.

Munro, G., Jain, M., Oliva, E., Kamal, N., Lele, S.M., Lynch, M.P., et al., 2009. Upregulation of MUC4 in cervical squamous cell carcinoma: pathologic significance. Int. J. Gynecol. Pathol. 28, 127–133.

Nahand, J.S., Taghizadeh-boroujeni, S., Karimzadeh, M., Borran, S., Pourhanifeh, M.H., Moghoofei, M., Bokharaei-Salim, F., Karampoor, S., Jafari, A., Asemi, Z., 2019. microRNAs: new prognostic, diagnostic, and therapeutic biomarkers in cervical cancer. J. Cell. Physiol. 234, 17064–17099.

Njoku, K., Chiasserini, D., Jones, E.R., Barr, C.E., O'Flynn, H., Whetton, A.D., et al., 2020. Urinary biomarkers and their potential for the non-invasive detection of endometrial cancer. Front. Oncol. 10, 559016.

Park, S., Kim, J., Eom, K., Oh, S., Kim, S., Kim, G., et al., 2019. microRNA-944 overexpression is a biomarker for poor prognosis of advanced cervical cancer. BMC Cancer. 19, 419.

Sasi, W., Sharma, A.K., Mokbel, K., 2014. The role of suppressors of cytokine signalling in human neoplasms. Mol. Biol. Int. 2014, 630797.

Shen, Y., Wang, P., Li, Y., Ye, F., Wang, F., Wan, X., et al., 2013. miR-375 is upregulated in acquired paclitaxel resistance in cervical cancer. Br. J. Cancer. 109, 92–99.

Stampoliou, A., Arapantoni-Dadioti, P., Pavlakis, K., 2016. Epigenetic mechanisms in endometrial cancer. J BUON 21 (2), 301–306.

Wu, P., Meng, L., Wang, H., 2005. Role of hTERT in apoptosis of cervical cancer induced by histone deacetylase inhibitor. Biochem. Biophys. Res. Commun. 335 (1), 36–44.

Yang, Y.X., Yang, A.H., Yang, Z.J., Wang, Z.R., Xia, X.H., 2006. Involvement of tumor suppressor in lung cancer 1 gene expression in cervical carcinogenesis. Int. J. Gynecol. Cancer 16 (5), 1868–1872.

Yu, L., Xiong, J., Guo, L., Miao, L., Liu, S., Guo, F., 2015. The effects of lanthanum chloride on proliferation and apoptosis of cervical cancer cells: involvement of let-7a and miR-34a microRNAs. Biometals 28, 879–890.

Zhang, Z., Joh, K., Yatsuki, H., 2007. Retinoic acid receptor beta2 is epigenetically silenced either by DNA methylation or repressive histone modifications at the promoter in cervical cancer cells. Cancer Lett. 247 (2), 318–327.

Zhao, X., Cui, Y., 2015. Li Y significance of TSLC1 gene methylation and TSLC1 protein expression in the progression of cervical lesions. Zhonghua Zhong Liu Za Zhi 37 (5), 356–360.

Zhou, N., Fei, D., Zong, S., Zhang, M., Yue, Y., 2016. MicroRNA-138 inhibits proliferation, migration and invasion through targeting hTERT in cervical cancer. Oncol. Lett. 12, 3633–3639.

CHAPTER FIFTEEN

Skin cancer biology and its biomarkers: Recent trends and prospective

Himani Sharma[a], Davinder Parsad[b], and Ravinder Kumar[a]
[a]Department of Zoology, Panjab University, Chandigarh, Punjab, India
[b]Department of Dermatology, PGIMER, Chandigarh, Punjab, India

1. Introduction

Human skin is mainly composed of three layers, outermost epidermis, dermis, and inner hypodermis. Cancer can develop in any of these three skin layers (Silverberg et al., 1990). The incidence of skin cancer is highest among all cancers. Despite various advancements and high-end technologies available, the treatment of skin cancer still remains one of the greatest challenges. Unrepairable DNA damage in the skin cells is the mainly reported in the development of cancer. Multiplication of damaged cells ultimately leads to tumor formation (Gloster and Brodland, 1996). Skin cancer occurs on the basis of type and color of skin, but it is more frequent in sun-exposed areas of the skin (Miller and Weinstock, 1994). It is also reported that heredity plays a crucial role in the advancement of skin cancer (Holme et al., 2000; Buettner and Raasch, 1998). Skin cancer is a group of heterogeneous malignancies and is classified into following types (Jemal et al., 2008; Kavoussi et al., 2012):

1. **Nonmelanoma skin cancer (NMSC)**: NMSC is a group of cancers that develops in upper layers of the skin. It mainly arises from epidermal keratinocytes of skin. NMSC originates due to combined interplay of genetic, environmental, and phenotypic factors (Samarasinghe and Madan, 2012). The most common forms of NMSC involve squamous cell carcinoma (SqCC) and basal cell carcinoma (BCC) (Kavoussi et al., 2012). BCC arises from basal round cells found in lower epidermis of skin. This form of cancer accounts for about 80% of skin cancers. BCC grows at slower pace and rarely spreads to other parts of the body. SqCC accounts for 20% of total skin malignancies (AlZou et al., 2016). It has 2%–5% probability of spreading to other parts of the body.

2. **Melanoma skin cancer (MSC)**: Melanoma is the most fatal form of skin cancer which develops from epidermal skin melanocytes. The incidence rate of melanoma is higher than all other forms of skin cancer (Riker et al., 2010). The exact cause of melanoma is not clear but the most common environmental risk factor for the

Biomarkers in Cancer Detection and Monitoring of Therapeutics
https://doi.org/10.1016/B978-0-323-95114-2.00015-7

melanoma development is UV radiations. Melanoma is most common in persons with light skin phenotypes as compared to the dark phenotypic individuals because of the presence of sun protecting pigment melanin in the dark skin (Orthaber et al., 2017) (Fig. 1).

International status: The incidence of skin cancers is high worldwide depending upon racial and geographical pattern variations. It was observed that highest cases of melanoma incidence were in the five regions, i.e., Eastern Europe, Central Europe, Western Europe, North America, and Australia (Labani et al., 2020). In United States, it is estimated that skin cancer is one among every five individuals (Guy Jr et al., 2015). According to the annual reports of United States, there occur 5.4 million cases of basal and squamous cell carcinomas (Rogers et al., 2015) and 76,380 cases of malignant

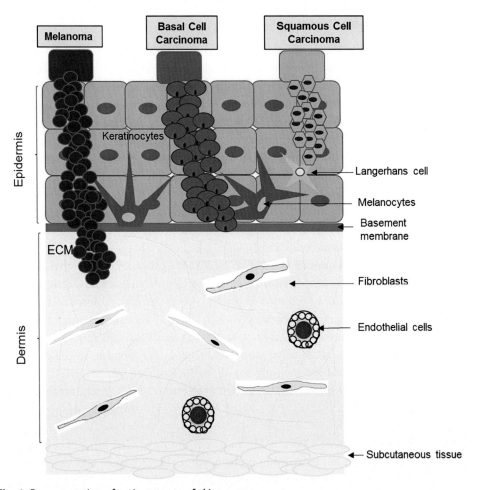

Fig. 1 Representation of various types of skin cancers.

melanoma (National Cancer Institute, 2016; Linos et al., 2016). Due to high skin cancer incidences, there is a burden on the health care system as well as on economy of these countries. The incidence of skin cancers was highest in western pacific region in the world. The incidence rate of skin cancer is dramatically expanding, whereas the mortality rate shows a stable or decreasing trend all over the world (Fabbrocini et al., 2010). In United States, melanoma skin cancer is sixth dominant cause of malignancy (Stubblefield and Kelly, 2014).

National status: The incidence of skin cancer is less common in India and it is reported to be less than 1% of all cancers in Indian population (Mahajan et al., 2000). Although various reports and studies proposed that nowadays non melanoma skin cancers may be on rise in India (Panda, 2010). Worldwide, the most common type of skin cancer is basal cell carcinoma but in India the most prevalent form of skin cancer is squamous cell carcinoma (Godbole et al., 1968). In India, skin cancer constitutes a significant proportion of skin cancer patients. This attributes to the presence of natural sun protection pigment, i.e., melanin in the skin of Indian population. According to a study conducted on Malwa Region of Punjab, it was found that the use of pesticides leads to accumulation of arsenic in drinking water which further contributes to skin cancer along with exposure to UV radiation which is another major cause for the skin cancer development (Lal et al., 2016).

2. Etiopathogenesis of skin cancer

The etiopathogenesis of skin cancer is diverse as various factors are responsible for its occurrence and progression. Various epidemiological studies identified the interactions between environment and host factors which determine the development and progression of disease. The most common factor responsible for the induction of skin cancer is exposure to sunlight and UV radiations (Leiter and Garbe, 2008; Mutti, 2012). In today's world, the atmospheric ozone layer depletion leads to increase in extent of UV radiations reaching the earth which ultimately results in escalating the risk of skin cancer. Mathematical models suggest that there is an increase in the incidence of tumors to the extent of 2%–4% for each 1% depletion of the ozone layer (Fears and Scotto, 1983). Basal cell carcinoma (BCC) is most common malignant skin cancer occurring in fair skin individuals. The incidence of BCC is higher in immunosuppressant individuals (Leiter and Garbe, 2008; Mutti, 2012). Cutaneous squamous cell carcinoma (cSCC) is the second most common form of skin cancer elucidating 20% of all cutaneous malignancies. The affected sites include all body parts including genital areas and mucosae but it mainly affects those areas which are exposed to UV radiations such as head, ears, neck and dorsal hands. Various other factors contributing to its development includes exposure to chemical products like arsenic-contaminated water, uses of herbicides, pesticides, and consumption of tobacco. Chronic ulcers and some types of HPV (human papillomavirus) are also considered carcinogenic (Howley and Pfister, 2015).

Melanoma skin cancer is the deadliest form of skin cancer. Major risk factors which contribute to melanoma are high exposure to sunlight and chronic cumulative exposure to UV radiations. Host susceptibility factors include fair complexion, freckling, blonde hair, and family history of melanoma. The high-risk individuals include those having family history of multiple skin cancers and melanoma (Linos et al., 2016). Melanoma can be treated in its initial stages but if left untreated, it metastasizes and then it is very challenging to treat this disease (Bray et al., 2020).

3. Biomarkers of skin cancer

Various technologies have been emerged which help in early detection of cancer. Clinical, biological, and histological methods provide insights for detection of non-melanoma cancer in initial stages, and still melanoma skin cancer is unpredictable disease. In its initial stages it is easy to cure but one it gets metastasize and spread to other body parts, it become hard to treat it. The disease burden continues to rise worldwide despite screening campaigns and intensive public health programs. This is mainly due to ageing population and various environmental factors such as changing climate, habits of sun exposure, contaminations of natural resources with carcinogens (Tandler et al., 2012; De Giorgi et al., 2012). Therefore, more techniques are needed in order to find suitable and reliable biomarkers which improve its early-stage diagnosis and accurate staging (Belter et al., 2017). Biomarkers not only help in detection and diagnosis of the disease but also give information about the biological behavior of tumor and metastasis, mechanism of resistance and sensitivity to therapy. For a cancer biomarker to be effective, it must possess following properties:

a) It must detect and cure melanoma at early stages before it becomes clearly visible or patient becomes symptomatic.
b) It must expedite easy perception without surgical intervention.
c) It must help for screenings based on population.
d) It must be metabolically and analytically stable in order to detect in blood or any other body fluid.
e) It must exhibit sufficient specificity and sensitivity so as to minimize false negative and false positive results.

4. Biomarkers for melanoma skin cancer

At present there is no ideal biomarker exists for melanoma skin cancer. The important prognostic markers/factors for melanoma detection include pathological characteristics of melanoma such as thickness of tumor and rate of its division (Balch et al., 2009).

4.1 Diagnostic biomarkers

Immunohistochemical diagnostic markers

The histological identification of melanoma is difficult due to its different cytomorphic forms (Banerjee and Harris, 2000). Human melanoma Black-45 (*HMB-45*), *tyrosinase, Melan-A, microphthalmia transcription factor (MITF)*, and *S100* are the main histological markers which are helpful in detection of melanoma.

   i. *HMB-45* encodes for premelanosome protein (*Pmel*) which is an important component for polymerization of eumelanin (Theos et al., 2005). The sensitivity of *HMB-45* has been presented to be 66%–97% with declined sensitivity in metastatic areas compared to primary lesions (Hofbauer et al., 1998; Jing et al., 2013). *HMB-45* exhibits poor sensitivity for detection of desmoplastic malignant melanoma (Granter et al., 2001; Miettinen et al., 2001).

  ii. *S100* exhibit low specificity to distinguish melanoma from other malignancies but due to its greater sensitivity, it is used in the case of detection of desmoplastic malignant melanoma (Busam et al., 2001, 2005).

 iii. *Melan-A*, also known as melanoma antigen is reported to be superior to S-100 having 93% sensitivity and 98% specificity for distinguishing melanoma and non-melanocytic neoplasms (Coulie et al., 1994; Kawakami et al., 1994; Jing et al., 2013). But *Melan-A* is found to be sensitive to detect primary melanomas but is less sensitive for metastatic melanomas (Miettinen et al., 2001; Gajjar et al., 2004).

  iv. *Tyrosinase* is an enzyme responsible for melanin synthesis. Presence of enzyme tyrosinase in the peripheral blood is an indicator of circulating melanoma cells and enhanced possibility of metastases. It is highly sensitive for primary melanoma and its sensitivity goes on decreasing for later stages (Kaufmann et al., 1998; Miettinen et al., 2001; Gajjar et al., 2004). It is highly sensitive for distinguishing between melanoma and nonmelanocytic neoplasms but not suitable for detection of desmoplastic malignant melanoma (Miettinen et al., 2001; Gajjar et al., 2004).

   v. *Microphthalmia transcription factor (MITF)* is a key regulator for the development and differentiation of melanocytes. Various studies suggested that *MITF* is found to control the transcriptional activity of *Pmel, Melan-A*, and *tyrosinase* (Tachibana et al., 1996; Du et al., 2003). It is found to be highly sensitive for distinguishing between melanoma and nonmelanocytic carcinomas but lacks sensitivity and specificity for desmoplastic melanomas (King et al., 2001).

  vi. *SM5-1* is a mouse IgG1 monoclonal antibody targeted against two fibronectin isoforms that are involved in cell migration and cell adhesion (Trefzer et al., 2006). It possesses high specificity and sensitivity for the discriminating different type of tumors, thus it is much better than other available biomarkers (Reinke et al., 2005).

 vii. Chondroitin sulfate proteoglycan 4 (*CSPG4*), also known as melanoma-associated antigen (HMw-MAA). It is a membrane-bound proteoglycan also found on melanocytes (Campoli et al., 2010). It promotes cell motility, cell adhesion, and growth of cells and may aid in invasion and metastasis. It is found to be highly sensitive for melanoma and less sensitivity toward benign melanocytic lesions (Natali et al., 1983). According to recent studies, *CSPG4* is significantly higher sensitive for detection of both primary and metastatic desmoplastic melanoma as compared to *HMB-45* and *Melan-A* (Goto et al., 2010). *CSPG4* is also known for its potential in immunotherapy for melanoma (Schmidt et al., 2011; Torisu-Itakura et al., 2011).

viii. *p16* has been found to assist in discriminating melanoma from spitz nevi. Diminishing immunohistochemical staining of *p16* has been correlated with melanoma detection (George et al., 2010; Al Dhaybi et al., 2011). Several other biomarkers for melanoma diagnosis are currently under examination including *MUM-1*, *Mel-5*, *melanocortin-1*, and *PNL2* (Ohsie et al., 2008).

4.2 Prognostic biomarkers

In order to find out which patient is more likely to develop the disease and need therapy, prognostic markers play an important role. Some of the prognostic markers for melanoma can be explained as follows.

Immunohistochemical biomarkers

i. Breslow depth, or tumor thickness: On histopathological examination of tumorous tissue, this attribute is the most authentic prognostic marker in initial stages of cutaneous melanoma (Thompson et al., 2011).

ii. Mitotic rate is one of the important criteria as it correlates with survival of the patient. It is the second most significant marker in the case of localized primary cutaneous melanoma (Thompson et al., 2011).

iii. Ki-67, a nuclear antigen and is very important proliferation marker (Vereecken et al., 2007). It has been reported that in thicker melanomas, Ki-67 is preferred over mitotic count as a prognostic factor (Ladstein et al., 2010).

iv. Melanoma cell adhesion molecule (MCAM), also known as MUC18 and CD146, is expressed on endothelial and smooth muscle cells (Mintz–Weber and Johnson, 2000). It is highly expressed in advanced primary and metastatic melanoma and diminishes in other types of carcinomas (Shih et al., 1997; Bar-Eli, 1999).

v. Metallothioneins are small cysteine-rich, heavy metal-binding proteins (Thirumoorthy et al., 2011). Various reports have revealed that higher expression of metallothioneins in primary melanoma is analogous to progression of disease and metastasis (Weinlich et al., 2007; Emri et al., 2013).

vi. Melanoma skin cancer expresses a number of MMPs and most important among them is *MMP-2* and *MMP-9* (Lugowska et al., 2015; Thakur and Bedogni, 2016). Kamyab-Hesari et al., 2014 found that there is a correlation between *MMP-2* expression and tumor thickness in melanoma. In contrast, according to Rotte et al. (2012), the expression of *MMP-2* is related to poorer survival of melanoma patients but is not dependent on tumor thickness. The concentration of *MMP-9* in the serum was also elevated in melanoma patients as compared to controls. However, there is no association found between the level of *MMP-9* and overall survival (Lugowska et al., 2015). *MMP-12* and *MMP-23* expression were also correlated with the melanoma (Zhang et al., 2015; Moogk et al., 2014).

vii. *Cyclooxygenase-2* is an enzyme whose overexpression results in inflammation processes involved in tumor, its metastasis and angiogenesis (Tondera et al., 2015). Recently a prognostic and predictive role of this enzyme was also reported in melanoma (Kim et al., 2016).

viii. Recently, the biomarker *CD10* a zinc dependent endopeptidase has been found to be significantly correlated to progression and prognosis in patients with melanoma (Bertucci et al., 2007; Oba et al., 2011).

Serologic biomarkers

i. Lactate dehydrogenase (LDH): This enzyme is responsible for conversion of pyruvate to lactate which is a common condition in rapid growing tumors (Alegre et al., 2015). The level of LDH increases due to necrosis of tumor cells causing spillover of the enzyme into the bloodstream (Agarwala et al., 2009). Moreover, it is nonspecific for melanoma and its elevated concentration is found in many other malignant tumors.

ii. C-reactive protein (CRP): It is a nonspecific marker for infection, inflammation and tissue injury (Pepys and Hirschfield, 2003). Furthermore, increased levels of CRP are related with advancement from stage I, II, or III to stage IV melanoma (Deichmann et al., 2004).

iii. Melanoma-inhibiting activity (MIA): It is an autocrine growth factor and despite its name, it increases the metastasis of melanoma cells (Guba et al., 2000). Higher levels of MIA are reported in melanoma than the normal healthy skin (Bosserhoff et al., 1996). Its expression correlates with the disease progression and patient's response to the therapy (Cao et al., 2007).

iv. Vascular endothelial growth factor (VEGF): It is an angiogenic cytokine that coordinated endothelial differentiation, proliferation, and survival (Connolly et al., 1989). Angiogenesis is one of the main phenomena responsible for tumor growth, migration, and metastasis (Redondo et al., 2003). VEGF shows low specificity toward melanoma as it is secreted by various cells (Shellman et al., 2003). According to some other studies the level of VEGF is higher in melanoma as compared to control but there is no association of VEGF with tumor progression and therapeutic response (Pelletier et al., 2005).

v. S100: It is used both as immunological and serological biomarker for melanoma diagnosis. In the patients with advanced melanoma, increased level of S100 contributes to treatment response, metastasis, relapse, and overall survival (Tarhini et al., 2009; Kruijff et al., 2012).

vi. Osteopontin: It is a secreted integrin-binding glycol-phosphoprotein reported to exhibit various properties such as reduction of apoptosis and enhancement of tumor growth (Perrotta et al., 2010). Though it is not a specific biomarker for melanoma, according to a recent study, osteopontin serves as an important biomarker in combination with S100B in order to distinguish the patients who have probability to develop metastatic cancer (Maier et al., 2012).

vii. Galectin-3: This is produced predominantly by inflammatory cells and plays role in progression of tumor and metastasis in melanoma (Buljan et al., 2011). Brown et al. (2012) reported that there is an inverse relationship between tumor size and galectin-3.

viii. Tumor-associated antigen 90 immune complex (TA90IC): It is the earliest elevated marker in the case of recurrence of melanoma in 57% cases (Gogas et al., 2009).

ix. YKL-40: It is a protein secreted by several cancer cells and immune cells including macrophages and neutrophils (Johansen et al., 2006; Schultz and Johansen, 2010). As a biomarker YKL-40 can give false-negative results if the patient is taking immunomodulatory drugs treatment (Krogh et al., 2010).

x. Progenitor and stem cell like markers: Akiyama et al. (2013) reported an association between stem cell marker nestin expression and advanced disease. According to immunohistological studies, *SOX10* (*Sry-related HMG-Box gene*) is used to detect metastatic melanoma. It is highly sensitive, specific and is a reliable marker for augmenting other immunohistochemical diagnostics markers (Willis et al., 2015), but this marker cannot discriminate between metastatic melanoma and nodal nevi. On the contrary, *SOX-2* effectively distinguishes between melanocytic nevus and metastatic melanomas (Chen et al., 2013) (Table 1).

5. Biomarkers for nonmelanoma skin cancers (NMSCs)

The incidence of nonmelanoma skin cancer (NMSC) is rising worldwide so there is a great demand of efficient biomarker for detection of these malignant tumors. NMSCs are mainly of two types: squamous cell carcinoma (SCC) and basal cell carcinoma (BCC). These two types of tumors can be easily distinguishable based on their morphological characteristics (Rajabi et al., 2007). However, in some cases, when the sample is very small or injured, it becomes very difficult to distinguish them. In order to distinguish between these two types of NMSCs, B-cell lymphoma 2, carcinoembryonic antigen, cluster of differentiation 10 (*CD10*), and epithelial membrane, antigen biomarkers play

Table 1 Different types of biomarkers for melanoma skin cancer.

Type of skin cancer	Diagnostic biomarkers	Prognostic biomarkers	
Melanoma skin cancer	Immunohistochemical biomarkers *HMB-4, S100, Melan-A, microphthalmia transcription factor (MITF), Tyrosinase, SM5-1, p16*	Immunohistochemical biomarkers Breslow depth or tumor thickness, mitotic rate, *Ki-67*, melanoma cell adhesion molecule (*MCAM*), metallothioneins, *MMP-2, MMP-9, MMP-12, MMP-23, Cyclooxygenase-2, CD10*	Serological biomarkers C-reactive protein (CRP), lactate dehydrogenase (LDH), melanoma-inhibiting activity (MIA), vascular endothelial growth factor (VEGF), *S100*, osteopontin, galectin-3, tumor-associated antigen 90 immune complex (TA90IC), *YKL-40, SOX-10, SOX-2*

an important role. B-cell lymphoma 2 and cluster of differentiation 10 are specific biomarkers for BCC, whereas carcinoembryonic antigen and epithelial membrane antigen are the biomarkers specific for SCC (Ramezani et al., 2016). It is a challenge for clinicians to identify and detect tumor before it gets metastasize. So, there is an obvious demand for prognostic biomarkers that can be used at initial stages of tumor. Various biomarkers have been identified for detection and treatment of SCC which can be explained as follows.

5.1 Biomarkers for squamous cell carcinoma (SCC)

- **Matrix metalloproteinase-7 (MMP-7)**: Increase in the expression of *MMP-7* can be found in various cancerous conditions including SCCs (Kerkelä and Saarialho-Kere, 2003). Immunohistochemical studies revealed that the expression of *MMP-7* is higher in the invasive edges of the cSCC tumors (Kivisaari et al., 2008).
- **Serine peptidase inhibitor clade A member 1**: Serine peptidase inhibitors (Serpins) constituted largest family of peptidase inhibitors found in humans (Silverman et al., 2001; Law et al., 2006). According to a study conducted by Farshchian et al. (2011), it was found that the expression of Serpin A1 increased in SCCs which is correlated with tumorigenic potential of transformed keratinocytes and disease progression (Farshchian et al., 2011).
- ***p53* tumor suppressor gene**: According to the molecular studies, it is found that the gene involved during the initial stages of Ultraviolet radiations effect is *p53* tumor suppressor gene which has important role in cell proliferation, DNA differentiation, apoptosis, and repair process. Any type of mutation in this gene leads to uncontrolled

proliferation of cells resulting in formation of cancerous cells (Bode and Dong, 2004; Nelson et al., 1994).

- Several other biomarkers such as *E-cadherin*, *Ki-67*, and *Cyclin D1* play an important role in diagnosis of NMSC (Møller et al., 1979). *E-cadherin* is an intercellular adhesion molecule whose decreased concentration in primary lesion in case of cSCC correlates with increased potential of metastasis and tumor invasiveness (Koseki et al., 1999). Mutation in another tumor suppressor gene APC leads to induction of *β-catenin* destruction which leads to activation of transcription of oncogenes (*Cyclin-D1* and *MYC*) (Wang et al., 2011a).

- Another important biomarker associated with development of skin cancers is CD_{133} (González-Herrero et al., 2013). It correlates with advanced stages of poorly differentiated tumor. Various evidences confirmed that CD_{133+} cancer stem cells exhibit resistance to apoptosis induced through action on *TGF-β*. Thus, there is a need of therapeutic agents which target CD_{133} in order to stop the metastatic spread of tumor (Ding et al., 2009; Hay, 2005). cSCC is a heterogeneous group of tumors, so a single biomarker for its detection will not be sufficient. Therefore, there is a need for a group of biomarkers for its early detection and treatment.

5.2 Biomarkers for basal cell carcinoma (BCC)

Basal cell carcinoma (BCC) accounts for nearly 75% of skin cancers (Ballester-Sanchez et al., 2016). The recurrence of BCC is frequent as it involves local cell destruction but it rarely metastasizes or results into death (Tanese, 2019). Available treatments are not satisfactory to cure BCC, so there is a need to promote assuring approach which aids in early detection and prevention of BCC.

- Three BCC-correlated genes have been identified by Yunoki et al. (2018), which include *BCL2* (B-cell lymphoma 2), *PTCH1* (Patched 1), and *SOX9* (SRY-box 9) associated with tumorigenesis. According to a study, it was also suggested that the genes *CDC20*, *MARCKSL*, *PTPN3*, *CYFIP2*, *PTCH1*, and *HOXB5* had superior diagnostic values for BCC prognosis (Liu et al., 2020).

- *PTCH1* encodes for a receptor of hedgehog pathway which involved in cell development and tumorigenesis (Stone et al., 1996). It was proposed that *PTCH1* mRNA is overexpressed in BCC infected cells as compared to the normal epidermal cells (Undén et al., 1997). Various studies reported that about 90% of functional mutations in *PTCH1* lead to development and progression of BCC (Bresler et al., 2016).

- FAS is undetectable and under expressed in BCC, but the concentration of FAS ligand is higher owing to the cancerous condition (Gutierrez-Steil et al., 1998). Some studies revealed that the expression of mRNA and protein levels of FAS/FASL was deceased in the BCC as compared to the normal healthy skin (Wang et al., 2011b) (Table 2).

Table 2 Different biomarkers for nonmelanoma skin cancer.

Types of nonmelanoma skin cancer	Biomarkers
Biomarkers for squamous cell carcinoma (SCC)	*MMP-7*, serine peptidase inhibitor clade A member 1, *p53* tumor suppressor gene, *Ki-67*, *E-cadherin* and *Cyclin D1*, *CD133*
Biomarkers for basal cell carcinoma (BCC)	*BCL2* (B-cell lymphoma 2), *PTCH1* (patched 1), and *SOX9* (SRY-box 9), *CDC20, MARCKSL, PTPN3, CYFIP2, HOXB5, FAS/FASL*

6. Conclusion

Preliminary detection and prompt management of skin cancer are of pivotal importance to prevent the destruction of local tissue and subsequent disfigurement. All the above explained markers exhibit potential for diagnosis and treatment of skin cancers but these are associated with some limitations. The major limitation is nonspecificity, nonsensitivity, and lack of accuracy of these markers. A number of potential biomarkers are available which are cellular or immunological proteins but they can be found in both healthy as well as diseased conditions which results in reducing their specificity. There is very complex interplay between immune cells and cancer cells. Therefore it is very challenging to establish correlation between immunological parameters and clinical outcomes for accurate prognosis. Use of different markers in combination would be an ideal diagnostic approach which offers much higher specificity and sensitivity. Thus, the main target of new interventions known as "multimarker profiling" is the identification of multiple coexpressed biomarkers which leads to early detection and prognostic predictions of the disease. Validation and establishment of optimal combination of biomarkers is the main challenge which needs intensive research in the field of skin cancer.

References

Agarwala, S.S., Keilholz, U., Gilles, E., Bedikian, A.Y., Wu, J., Kay, R., Stein, C.A., Itri, L.M., Suciu, S., Eggermont, A.M., 2009. LDH correlation with survival in advanced melanoma from two large, randomised trials (Oblimersen GM301 and EORTC 18951). Eur. J. Cancer 45 (10), 1807–1814.

Akiyama, M., Matsuda, Y., Ishiwata, T., Naito, Z., Kawana, S., 2013. Nestin is highly expressed in advanced-stage melanomas and neurotized nevi. Oncol. Rep. 29 (4), 1595–1599.

Al Dhaybi, R., Agoumi, M., Gagné, I., McCuaig, C., Powell, J., Kokta, V., 2011. p16 expression: a marker of differentiation between childhood malignant melanomas and Spitz nevi. J. Am. Acad. Dermatol. 65 (2), 357–363.

Alegre, E., Sammamed, M., Fernández-Landázuri, S., Zubiri, L., González, Á., 2015. Circulating biomarkers in malignant melanoma. Adv. Clin. Chem. 69, 47–89.

AlZou, A.B., Thabit, M.A.B., AlSakkaf, K.A., Basaleem, H.O., 2016. Skin cancer: ClinicoPathological study of 204 patients in southern Governorates of Yemen. Asian Pac. J. Cancer Prev. 17 (7), 3195–3199.

Balch, C.M., Gershenwald, J.E., Soong, S.J., Thompson, J.F., Atkins, M.B., Byrd, D.R., Buzaid, A.C., Cochran, A.J., Coit, D.G., Ding, S., Sondak, V.K., 2009. Final version of 2009 AJCC melanoma staging and classification. J. Clin. Oncol. 27 (36), 6199.

Ballester-Sanchez, R., Pons-Llanas, O., Candela-Juan, C., Celada-Álvarez, F.J., Barker, C.A., Tormo-Mico, A., Perez-Calatayud, J., Botella-Estrada, R., 2016. Electronic brachytherapy for superficial and nodular basal cell carcinoma: a report of two prospective pilot trials using different doses. J. Contemp. Brachyther. 8 (1), 48.

Banerjee, S.S., Harris, M., 2000. Morphological and immunophenotypic variations in malignant melanoma. Histopathology 36 (5), 387–402.

Bar-Eli, M., 1999. Role of AP-2 in tumor growth and metastasis of human melanoma. Cancer Metastasis Rev. 18 (3), 377–385.

Belter, B., Haase-Kohn, C., Pietzsch, J., 2017. Biomarkers in malignant melanoma: recent trends and critical perspective. Exon Pub., 39–56.

Bertucci, F., Pages, C., Finetti, P., Rochaix, P., Lamant, L., Devilard, E., Nguyen, C., Houlgatte, R., Birnbaum, D., Xerri, L., Brousset, P., 2007. Gene expression profiling of human melanoma cell lines with distinct metastatic potential identifies new progression markers. Anticancer Res 27 (5A), 3441–3449.

Bode, A.M., Dong, Z., 2004. Post-translational modification of p53 in tumorigenesis. Nat. Rev. Cancer 4 (10), 793–805.

Bosserhoff, A.K., Hein, R., Bogdahn, U., Buettner, R., 1996. Structure and promoter analysis of the gene encoding the human melanoma-inhibiting protein MIA (*). J. Biol. Chem. 271 (1), 490–495.

Bray, F., Ferlay, J., Soerjomataram, I., Siegel, R.L., Torre, L.A., Jemal, A., 2020. Erratum: global cancer statistics 2018: GLOBOCAN estimates of incidence and mortality worldwide for 36 cancers in 185 countries. CA Cancer J. Clin. 70 (4), 313.

Bresler, S.C., Padwa, B.L., Granter, S.R., 2016. Nevoid basal cell carcinoma syndrome (Gorlin syndrome). Head Neck Pathol. 10 (2), 119–124.

Brown, E.R., Doig, T., Anderson, N., Brenn, T., Doherty, V., Xu, Y., Bartlett, J.M., Smyth, J.F., Melton, D.W., 2012. Association of galectin-3 expression with melanoma progression and prognosis. Eur. J. Cancer 48 (6), 865–874.

Buettner, P.G., Raasch, B.A., 1998. Incidence rates of skin cancer in Townsville, Australia. Int. J. Cancer 78 (5), 587–593.

Buljan, M., Šitum, M., Tomas, D., Milošević, M., Krušlin, B., 2011. Prognostic value of galectin-3 in primary cutaneous melanoma. J. Eur. Acad. Dermatol. Venereol. 25 (10), 1174–1181.

Busam, K.J., Iversen, K., Coplan, K.C., Jungbluth, A.A., 2001. Analysis of microphthalmia transcription factor expression in normal tissues and tumors, and comparison of its expression with S-100 protein, gp100, and tyrosinase in desmoplastic malignant melanoma. Am. J. Surg. Pathol. 25 (2), 197–204.

Busam, K.J., Kucukgöl, D., Sato, E., Frosina, D., Teruya-Feldstein, J., Jungbluth, A.A., 2005. Immunohistochemical analysis of novel monoclonal antibody PNL2 and comparison with other melanocyte differentiation markers. Am. J. Surg. Pathol. 29 (3), 400–406.

Campoli, M., Ferrone, S., Wang, X., 2010. Functional and clinical relevance of chondroitin sulfate proteoglycan 4. Adv. Cancer Res. 109, 73–121.

Cao, M.G., Auge, J.M., Molina, R., Marti, R., Carrera, C., Castel, T., Vilella, R., Conill, C., Sanchez, M., Malvehy, J., Puig, S., 2007. Melanoma inhibiting activity protein (MIA), beta-2 microglobulin and lactate dehydrogenase (LDH) in metastatic melanoma. Anticancer Res 27 (1B), 595–599.

Chen, P.L., Chen, W.S., Li, J., Lind, A.C., Lu, D., 2013. Diagnostic utility of neural stem and progenitor cell markers nestin and SOX2 in distinguishing nodal melanocytic nevi from metastatic melanomas. Mod. Pathol. 26 (1), 44–53.

Connolly, D.T., Heuvelman, D.M., Nelson, R., Olander, J.V., Eppley, B.L., Delfino, J.J., Siegel, N.R., Leimgruber, R.M., Feder, J., 1989. Tumor vascular permeability factor stimulates endothelial cell growth and angiogenesis. J. Clin. Invest. 84 (5), 1470–1478.

Coulie, P.G., Brichard, V., Van Pel, A., Wölfel, T., Schneider, J., Traversari, C., Mattei, S., De Plaen, E., Lurquin, C., Szikora, J.P., Boon, T., 1994. A new gene coding for a differentiation antigen recognized by autologous cytolytic T lymphocytes on HLA-A2 melanomas. J. Exp. Med. 180 (1), 35–42.

De Giorgi, V., Gori, A., Grazzini, M., Rossari, S., Oranges, T., Longo, A.S., Lotti, T., Gandini, S., 2012. Epidemiology of melanoma: is it still epidemic? What is the role of the sun, sunbeds, Vit D, betablocks, and others? Dermatol. Ther. 25 (5), 392–396.

Deichmann, M., Kahle, B., Moser, K., Wacker, J., Wüst, K., 2004. Diagnosing melanoma patients entering American Joint Committee on cancer stage IV, C-reactive protein in serum is superior to lactate dehydrogenase. Br. J. Cancer 91 (4), 699–702.

Ding, W., Mouzaki, M., You, H., Laird, J.C., Mato, J., Lu, S.C., Rountree, C.B., 2009. CD133+ liver cancer stem cells from methionine adenosyl transferase 1A-deficient mice demonstrate resistance to transforming growth factor (TGF)-β-induced apoptosis. Hepatology 49 (4), 1277–1286.

Du, J., Miller, A.J., Widlund, H.R., Horstmann, M.A., Ramaswamy, S., Fisher, D.E., 2003. MLANA/MART1 and SILV/PMEL17/GP100 are transcriptionally regulated by MITF in melanocytes and melanoma. Am. J. Pathol. 163 (1), 333–343.

Emri, E., Egervari, K., Varvolgyi, T., Rozsa, D., Miko, E., Dezso, B., Veres, I., Mehes, G., Emri, G., Remenyik, E., 2013. Correlation among metallothionein expression, intratumoural macrophage infiltration and the risk of metastasis in human cutaneous malignant melanoma. J. Eur. Acad. Dermatol. Venereol. 27 (3), e320–e327.

Fabbrocini, G., Triassi, M., Mauriello, M.C., Torre, G., Annunziata, M.C., De Vita, V., Pastore, F., D'Arco, V., Monfrecola, G., 2010. Epidemiology of skin cancer: role of some environmental factors. Cancer 2 (4), 1980–1989.

Farshchian, M., Kivisaari, A., Ala-Aho, R., Riihilä, P., Kallajoki, M., Grénman, R., Peltonen, J., Pihlajaniemi, T., Heljasvaara, R., Kähäri, V.M., 2011. Serpin peptidase inhibitor clade A member 1 (SerpinA1) is a novel biomarker for progression of cutaneous squamous cell carcinoma. Am. J. Pathol. 179 (3), 1110–1119.

Fears, T.R., Scotto, J., 1983. Estimating increases in skin cancer morbidity due to increases in ultra-violet radiation exposure. Cancer Invest. 1, 119–126.

Gajjar, N.A., Cochran, A.J., Binder, S.W., 2004. Is MAGE-1 expression in metastatic malignant melanomas really helpful? Am. J. Surg. Pathol. 28 (7), 883–888.

George, E., Polissar, N.L., Wick, M., 2010. Immunohistochemical evaluation of p16INK4A, E-cadherin, and cyclin D1 expression in melanoma and Spitz tumors. Am. J. Clin. Pathol. 133 (3), 370–379.

Gloster, H.M., Brodland, D.G., 1996. The epidemiology of skin cancer. Dermatol. Surg. 22, 217–226.

Godbole, V.K., Toprani, H.T., Shah, H.H., 1968. Skin cancer in Saurashtra. Indian J. Pathol. Bacteriol. 11 (3), 183–189.

Gogas, H., Eggermont, A.M.M., Hauschild, A., Hersey, P., Mohr, P., Schadendorf, D., Spatz, A., Dummer, R., 2009. Biomarkers in melanoma. Ann. Oncol. 20, vi8–vi13.

González-Herrero, I., Romero-Camarero, I., Cañueto, J., Cardeñoso-Álvarez, E., Fernández-López, E., Pérez-Losada, J., Sánchez-García, I., Román-Curto, C., 2013. CD 133+ cell content correlates with tumour growth in melanomas from skin with chronic sun-induced damage. Br. J. Dermatol. 169 (4), 830–837.

Goto, Y., Arigami, T., Murali, R., Scolyer, R.A., Tanemura, A., Takata, M., Turner, R.R., Nguyen, L., Nguyen, T., Morton, D.L., Hoon, D.S., 2010. High molecular weight–melanoma-associated antigen as a biomarker of desmoplastic melanoma. Pigment Cell Melanoma Res. 23 (1), 137.

Granter, S.R., Weilbaecher, K.N., Quigley, C., Fletcher, C.D., Fisher, D.E., 2001. Microphthalmia transcription factor: not a sensitive or specific marker for the diagnosis of desmoplastic melanoma and spindle cell (non-desmoplastic) melanoma. Am. J. Dermatopathol. 23 (3), 185–189.

Guba, M., Bosserhoff, A.K., Steinbauer, M., Abels, C., Anthuber, M., Buettner, R., Jauch, K.W., 2000. Overexpression of melanoma inhibitory activity (MIA) enhances extravasation and metastasis of A-mel 3 melanoma cells in vivo. Br. J. Cancer 83 (9), 1216–1222.

Gutierrez-Steil, C., Wrone-Smith, T., Sun, X., Krueger, J.G., Coven, T., Nickoloff, B.J., 1998. Sunlight-induced basal cell carcinoma tumor cells and ultraviolet-B-irradiated psoriatic plaques express Fas ligand (CD95L). J. Clin. Invest. 101 (1), 33–39.

Guy Jr., G.P., Thomas, C.C., Thompson, T., Watson, M., Massetti, G.M., Richardson, L.C., 2015. Vital signs: melanoma incidence and mortality trends and projections—United States, 1982–2030. Morb. Mortal. Wkly. Rep. 64 (21), 591.

Hay, E.D., 2005. The mesenchymal cell, its role in the embryo, and the remarkable signaling mechanisms that create it. Dev. Dynam. 233 (3), 706–720.

Hofbauer, G.F., Kamarashev, J., Geertsen, R., Böni, R., Dummer, R., 1998. Tyrosinase immunoreactivity in formalin-fixed, paraffin-embedded primary and metastatic melanoma: frequency and distribution. J. Cutan. Pathol. 25 (4), 204–209.

Holme, S.A., Malinovszky, K., Roberts, D.L., 2000. Changing trends in non-melanoma skin cancer in South Wales, 1988–98. Br. J. Dermatol. 143 (6), 1224–1229.

Howley, P.M., Pfister, H.J., 2015. Beta genus papillomaviruses and skin cancer. Virology 479, 290–296.

Jemal, A., Siegel, R., Ward, E., Hao, Y., Xu, J., Murray, T., Thun, M.J., 2008. Cancer statistics, 2008. CA Cancer J. Clin. 58 (2), 71–96.

Jing, X., Michael, C.W., Theoharis, C.G., 2013. The use of immunocytochemical study in the cytologic diagnosis of melanoma: evaluation of three antibodies. Diagn. Cytopathol. 41 (2), 126–130.

Johansen, J.S., Jensen, B.V., Roslind, A., Nielsen, D., Price, P.A., 2006. Serum YKL-40, a new prognostic biomarker in cancer patients? Cancer Epidemiol. Prev. Biomark. 15 (2), 194–202.

Kamyab-Hesari, K., Mohtasham, N., Aghazadeh, N., Biglarian, M., Memar, B., Kadeh, H., 2014. The expression of MMP-2 and Ki-67 in head and neck melanoma, and their correlation with clinicpathologic indices. J. Cancer Res. Ther. 10 (3), 696.

Kaufmann, O., Koch, S., Burghardt, J., Audring, H., Dietel, M., 1998. Tyrosinase, melan-A, and KBA62 as markers for the immunohistochemical identification of metastatic amelanotic melanomas on paraffin sections. Mod. Pathol. 11 (8), 740–746.

Kavoussi, H., Rezaei, M., Ebrahimi, A., Hossaini, S., 2012. Epidemiological incidences of non-melanoma skin cancer in Kermanshah-Iran. J. Pak. Assoc. Dermatol. 22, 112–117.

Kawakami, Y., Eliyahu, S., Delgado, C.H., Robbins, P.F., Sakaguchi, K., Appella, E., Yannelli, J.R., Adema, G.J., Miki, T., Rosenberg, S.A., 1994. Identification of a human melanoma antigen recognized by tumor-infiltrating lymphocytes associated with in vivo tumor rejection. Proc. Natl. Acad. Sci. 91 (14), 6458–6462.

Kerkelä, E., Saarialho-Kere, U., 2003. Matrix metalloproteinases in tumor progression: focus on basal and squamous cell skin cancer. Exp. Dermatol. 12 (2), 109–125.

Kim, S.H., Hashimoto, Y., Cho, S.N., Roszik, J., Milton, D.R., Dal, F., Kim, S.F., Menter, D.G., Yang, P., Ekmekcioglu, S., Grimm, E.A., 2016. Microsomal PGE 2 synthase-1 regulates melanoma cell survival and associates with melanoma disease progression. Pigment Cell Melanoma Res. 29 (3), 297–308.

King, R., Googe, P.B., Weilbaecher, K.N., Mihm Jr., M.C., Fisher, D.E., 2001. Microphthalmia transcription factor expression in cutaneous benign, malignant melanocytic, and nonmelanocytic tumors. Am. J. Surg. Pathol. 25 (1), 51–57.

Kivisaari, A.K., Kallajoki, M., Mirtti, T., McGrath, J.A., Bauer, J.W., Weber, F., Königová, R., Sawamura, D., Sato-Matsumura, K.C., Shimizu, H., Kähäri, V.M., 2008. Transformation-specific matrix metalloproteinases (MMP)-7 and MMP-13 are expressed by tumour cells in epidermolysis bullosa-associated squamous cell carcinomas. Br. J. Dermatol. 158 (4), 778–785.

Koseki, S., Aoki, T., Ansai, S., Hozumi, Y., Mitsuhashi, Y., Kondo, S., 1999. An immunohistochemical study of E-cadherin expression in human squamous cell carcinoma of the skin: relationship between decreased expression of E-cadherin in the primary lesion and regional lymph node metastasis. J. Dermatol. 26 (7), 416–422.

Krogh, M., Christensen, I.J., Bouwhuis, M., Johansen, J.S., Schmidt, H., Hansson, J., Aamdal, S., Testori, A., Eggermont, A.M., Bastholt, L., Nordic Melanoma Group and EORTC Melanoma Group, 2010. Prognostic value of serum YKL-40 in stage IIB-III melanoma patients receiving adjuvant interferon therapy. J. Clin. Oncol. 28 (15_suppl), 8587.

Kruijff, S., Bastiaannet, E., Brouwers, A.H., Nagengast, W.B., Speijers, M.J., Suurmeijer, A.J.H., Hospers, G.A., Hoekstra, H.J., 2012. Use of S-100B to evaluate therapy effects during bevacizumab induction treatment in AJCC stage III melanoma. Ann. Surg. Oncol. 19 (2), 620–626.

Labani, S., Asthana, S., Rathore, K., Sardana, K., 2020. Incidence of melanoma and nonmelanoma skin cancers in Indian and the global regions. J. Cancer Res. Ther. 17 (4), 906.

Ladstein, R.G., Bachmann, I.M., Straume, O., Akslen, L.A., 2010. Ki-67 expression is superior to mitotic count and novel proliferation markers PHH3, MCM4 and mitosin as a prognostic factor in thick cutaneous melanoma. BMC Cancer 10 (1), 1–15.

Lal, S.T., Banipal, R.P.S., Bhatti, D.J., Yadav, H.P., 2016. Changing trends of skin cancer: a tertiary care hospital study in Malwa region of Punjab. J. Clin. Diagn. Res. 10 (6), PC12.

Law, R.H., Zhang, Q., McGowan, S., Buckle, A.M., Silverman, G.A., Wong, W., Rosado, C.J., Langendorf, C.G., Pike, R.N., Bird, P.I., Whisstock, J.C., 2006. An overview of the serpin superfamily. Genome Biol. 7 (5), 1–11.

Leiter, U., Garbe, C., 2008. Epidemiology of melanoma and nonmelanoma skin cancer—the role of sunlight. In: Sunlight, Vitamin D and Skin Cancer, pp. 89–103.

Linos, E., Katz, K.A., Colditz, G.A., 2016. Skin cancer—the importance of prevention. JAMA Intern. Med. 176 (10), 1435–1436.

Liu, Y., Liu, H., Bian, Q., 2020. Identification of Potential Biomarkers Associated With Basal Cell Carcinoma. BioMed Research International.

Lugowska, I., Kowalska, M., Fuksiewicz, M., Kotowicz, B., Mierzejewska, E., Koseła-Paterczyk, H., Szamotulska, K., Rutkowski, P., 2015. Serum markers in early-stage and locally advanced melanoma. Tumor Biol. 36 (11), 8277–8285.

Mahajan, M.K., Lal, P., Biswal, B.M., Mohanti, B.K., 2000. Text book of radiation oncology: principles and practice. In: Rath, G.K., Mohanti, B.K. (Eds.), Cancer of Skin. B. I. Churchill Livingstone, New York, pp. 223–237.

Maier, T., Laubender, R.P., Sturm, R.A., Klingenstein, A., Korting, H.C., Ruzicka, T., Berking, C., 2012. Osteopontin expression in plasma of melanoma patients and in melanocytic tumours. J. Eur. Acad. Dermatol. Venereol. 26 (9), 1084–1091.

Miettinen, M., Fernandez, M., Franssila, K., Gatalica, Z., Lasota, J., Sarlomo-Rikala, M., 2001. Microphthalmia transcription factor in the immunohistochemical diagnosis of metastatic melanoma: comparison with four other melanoma markers. Am. J. Surg. Pathol. 25 (2), 205–211.

Miller, D.L., Weinstock, M.A., 1994. Nonmelanoma skin cancer in the United States: incidence. J. Am. Acad. Dermatol. 30 (5), 774–778.

Mintz-Weber, C.S., Johnson, J.P., 2000. Identification of the elements regulating the expression of the cell adhesion molecule MCAM/MUC18: loss of AP-2 is not required for MCAM expression in melanoma cell lines. J. Biol. Chem. 275 (44), 34672–34680.

Møller, R., Reymann, F., Hou-Jensen, K., 1979. Metastases in dermatological patients with squamous cell carcinoma. Arch. Dermatol. 115 (6), 703–705.

Moogk, D., da Silva, I.P., Ma, M.W., Friedman, E.B., de Miera, E.V.S., Darvishian, F., Scanlon, P., Perez-Garcia, A., Pavlick, A.C., Bhardwaj, N., Krogsgaard, M., 2014. Melanoma expression of matrix metalloproteinase-23 is associated with blunted tumor immunity and poor responses to immunotherapy. J. Transl. Med. 12 (1), 1–10.

Mutti, S.T., 2012. Pattern of skin cancer among patients who attended King Abdulaziz University between Jan 2000-2010. J. Saudi Soc. Dermatol. Surg. 16. 13-08.

Natali, P.G., Giacomini, P., Russo, C., Steinbach, G., Fenoglio, C., Ferrone, S., 1983. Antigenic profile of human melanoma cells. Analysis with monoclonal antibodies to histocompatibility antigens and to melanoma-associated antigens. J. Cutan. Pathol. 10 (4), 225–237.

National Cancer Institute, 2016. SEER stat fact sheets: melanoma of the skin. In: Surveillance, Epidemiology, and End Results Program. National Cancer Institute (Accessed July 14, 2016).

Nelson, M.A., Einspahr, J.G., Alberts, D.S., Balfour, C.A., Wymer, J.A., Welch, K.L., Salasche, S.J., Bangert, J.L., Grogan, T.M., Bozzo, P.O., 1994. Analysis of the p53 gene in human precancerous actinic keratosis lesions and squamous cell cancers. Cancer Lett. 85 (1), 23–29.

Oba, J., Nakahara, T., Hayashida, S., Kido, M., Xie, L., Takahara, M., Uchi, H., Miyazaki, S., Abe, T., Hagihara, A., Furue, M., 2011. Expression of CD10 predicts tumor progression and unfavorable prognosis in malignant melanoma. J. Am. Acad. Dermatol. 65 (6), 1152–1160.

Ohsie, S.J., Sarantopoulos, G.P., Cochran, A.J., Binder, S.W., 2008. Immunohistochemical characteristics of melanoma. J. Cutan. Pathol. 35 (5), 433–444.

Orthaber, K., Pristovnik, M., Skok, K., Perić, B., Maver, U., 2017. Skin cancer and its treatment: novel treatment approaches with emphasis on nanotechnology. J. Nanomater. 2017.

Panda, S., 2010. Nonmelanoma skin cancer in India: current scenario. Indian J. Dermatol. 55 (4), 373.

Pelletier, F., Bermont, L., Puzenat, E., Blanc, D., Cairey-Remonnay, S., Mougin, C., Laurent, R., Humbert, P., Aubin, F., 2005. Circulating vascular endothelial growth factor in cutaneous malignant melanoma. Br. J. Dermatol. 152 (4), 685–689.

Pepys, M.B., Hirschfield, G.M., 2003. C-reactive protein: a critical update. J. Clin. Invest. 111 (12), 1805–1812.

Perrotta, R., Bevelacqua, Y., Malaguarnera, G., Paladina, I., Giordano, M., Malaguarnera, M., 2010. Serum markers of cutaneous melanoma. Front. Biosci. (Elite Ed.) 2, 1115–1122.

Rajabi, P., Aboutalebdokht, M., Heidarpour, M., Asilian, A., Rajabi, F., 2007. Evaluation of diagnostic values of EMA and Ber-Ep4 in distinction between basal cell carcinoma and squamous cell carcinoma of the skin. Iran. J. Pathol. 2 (1), 7–10.

Ramezani, M., Mohamadzaheri, E., Khazaei, S., Najafi, F., Vaisi-Raygani, A., Rahbar, M., Sadeghi, M., 2016. Comparison of EMA, CEA, CD10 and Bcl-2 biomarkers by immunohistochemistry in squamous cell carcinoma and basal cell carcinoma of the skin. Asian Pac. J. Cancer Prev. 17 (3), 1379–1383.

Redondo, P., Sánchez-Carpintero, I., Bauzá, A., Idoate, M., Solano, T., Mihm Jr., M.C., 2003. Immunologic escape and angiogenesis in human malignant melanoma. J. Am. Acad. Dermatol. 49 (2), 255–263.

Reinke, S., Königer, P., Herberth, G., Audring, H., Wang, H., Ma, J., Guo, Y., Sterry, W., Trefzer, U., 2005. Differential expression of MART-1, tyrosinase, and SM5-1 in primary and metastatic melanoma. Am. J. Dermatopathol. 27 (5), 401–406.

Riker, A.I., Zea, N., Trinh, T., 2010. The epidemiology, prevention, and detection of melanoma. Ochsner J. 10 (2), 56–65.

Rogers, H.W., Weinstock, M.A., Feldman, S.R., Coldiron, B.M., 2015. Incidence estimate of non-melanoma skin cancer (keratinocyte carcinomas) in the US population, 2012. JAMA Dermatol. 151 (10), 1081–1086.

Rotte, A., Martinka, M., Li, G., 2012. MMP2 expression is a prognostic marker for primary melanoma patients. Cell. Oncol. 35 (3), 207–216.

Samarasinghe, V., Madan, V., 2012. Nonmelanoma skin cancer. J. Cutan. Aesthet. Surg. 5 (1), 3.

Schmidt, P., Kopecky, C., Hombach, A., Zigrino, P., Mauch, C., Abken, H., 2011. Eradication of melanomas by targeted elimination of a minor subset of tumor cells. Proc. Natl. Acad. Sci. 108 (6), 2474–2479.

Schultz, N.A., Johansen, J.S., 2010. YKL-40—a protein in the field of translational medicine: a role as a biomarker in cancer patients? Cancer 2 (3), 1453–1491.

Shellman, Y.G., Park, Y.L., Marr, D.G., Casper, K., Xu, Y., Fujita, M., Swerlick, R., Norris, D.A., 2003. Release of vascular endothelial growth factor from a human melanoma cell line, WM35, is induced by hypoxia but not ultraviolet radiation and is potentiated by activated Ras mutation. J. Investig. Dermatol. 121 (4), 910–917.

Shih, L.M., Hsu, M.Y., Palazzo, J.P., Herlyn, M., 1997. The cell-cell adhesion receptor Mel-CAM acts as a tumor suppressor in breast carcinoma. Am. J. Pathol. 151 (3), 745.

Silverberg, E., Boring, C.C., Squires, T.S., 1990. Cancer statistics 1990. CA Cancer J. Clin. 40, 9–26.

Silverman, G.A., Bird, P.I., Carrell, R.W., Church, F.C., Coughlin, P.B., Gettins, P.G., Irving, J.A., Lomas, D.A., Luke, C.J., Moyer, R.W., Whisstock, J.C., 2001. The serpins are an expanding superfamily of structurally similar but functionally diverse proteins. J. Biol. Chem. 276 (36), 33293–33296.

Stone, D.M., Hynes, M., Armanini, M., Swanson, T.A., Gu, Q., Johnson, R.L., Scott, M.P., Pennica, D., Goddard, A., Phillips, H., Rosenthal, A., 1996. The tumour-suppressor gene patched encodes a candidate receptor for Sonic hedgehog. Nature 384 (6605), 129–134.

Stubblefield, J., Kelly, B., 2014. Melanoma in non-Caucasian populations. Surg. Clin. North Am. 94 (5), 1115–1126.

Tachibana, M., Takeda, K., Nobukuni, Y., Urabe, K., Long, J.E., Meyers, K.A., Aaronson, S.A., Miki, T., 1996. Ectopic expression of MITF, a gene for Waardenburg syndrome type 2, converts fibroblasts to cells with melanocyte characteristics. Nat. Genet. 14 (1), 50–54.

Tandler, N., Mosch, B., Pietzsch, J., 2012. Protein and non-protein biomarkers in melanoma: a critical update. Amino Acids 43 (6), 2203–2230.

Tanese, K., 2019. Diagnosis and management of basal cell carcinoma. Curr. Treat. Options Oncol. 20 (2), 13.

Tarhini, A.A., Stuckert, J., Lee, S., Sander, C., Kirkwood, J.M., 2009. Prognostic significance of serum S100B protein in high-risk surgically resected melanoma patients participating in Intergroup Trial ECOG 1694. J. Clin. Oncol. 27 (1), 38.

Thakur, V., Bedogni, B., 2016. The membrane tethered matrix metalloproteinase MT1-MMP at the forefront of melanoma cell invasion and metastasis. Pharmacol. Res. 111, 17–22.

Theos, A.C., Truschel, S.T., Raposo, G., Marks, M.S., 2005. The silver locus product Pmel17/gp100/Silv/ME20: controversial in name and in function. Pigment Cell Res. 18 (5), 322–336.

Thirumoorthy, N., Sunder, A.S., Kumar, K.M., Ganesh, G.N.K., Chatterjee, M., 2011. A review of metallothionein isoforms and their role in pathophysiology. World J. Surg. Oncol. 9 (1), 1–7.

Thompson, J.F., Soong, S.J., Balch, C.M., Gershenwald, J.E., Ding, S., Coit, D.G., Flaherty, K.T., Gimotty, P.A., Johnson, T., Johnson, M.M., Sondak, V.K., 2011. Prognostic significance of mitotic rate in localized primary cutaneous melanoma: an analysis of patients in the multi-institutional American Joint Committee on Cancer melanoma staging database. J. Clin. Oncol. 29 (16), 2199.

Tondera, C., Ullm, S., Laube, M., Meister, S., Neuber, C., Mosch, B., Kniess, T., Pietzsch, J., 2015. Optical imaging of COX-2: Studies on an autofluorescent 2,3-diaryl-substituted indole-based cyclooxygenase-2 inhibitor. Biochem. Biophys. Res. Commun. 458 (1), 40–45.

Torisu-Itakura, H., Schoellhammer, H.F., Sim, M.S., et al., 2011. redirected lysis of human melanoma cells by a MCSP/CD3-bispecific BiTe antibody that engages patient-derived T cells. J. Immunother. 34 (8), 597–605.

Trefzer, U., Chen, Y., Herberth, G., Hofmann, M.A., Kiecker, F., Guo, Y., Sterry, W., 2006. The monoclonal antibody SM5-1 recognizes a fibronectin variant which is widely expressed in melanoma. BMC Cancer 6 (1), 1–12.

Undén, A.B., Zaphiropoulos, P.G., Bruce, K., Toftgård, R., Ståhle-Bäckdahl, M., 1997. Human patched (PTCH) mRNA is overexpressed consistently in tumor cells of both familial and sporadic basal cell carcinoma. Cancer Res. 57 (12), 2336–2340.

Vereecken, P., Laporte, M., Heenen, M., 2007. Significance of cell kinetic parameters in the prognosis of malignant melanoma: a review. J. Cutan. Pathol. 34 (2), 139–145.

Wang, N.J., Sanborn, Z., Arnett, K.L., Bayston, L.J., Liao, W., Proby, C.M., Leigh, I.M., Collisson, E.A., Gordon, P.B., Jakkula, L., Cho, R.J., 2011a. Loss-of-function mutations in Notch receptors in cutaneous and lung squamous cell carcinoma. Proc. Natl. Acad. Sci. 108 (43), 17761–17766.

Wang, X.Y., Zhang, R., Lian, S., 2011b. Aberrant expression of Fas and FasL pro-apoptotic proteins in basal cell and squamous cell carcinomas. Clin. Exp. Dermatol. 36 (1), 69–76.

Weinlich, G., Topar, G., Eisendle, K., Fritsch, P.O., Zelger, B., 2007. Comparison of metallothionein-overexpression with sentinel lymph node biopsy as prognostic factors in melanoma. J. Eur. Acad. Dermatol. Venereol. 21 (5), 669–677.

Willis, B.C., Johnson, G., Wang, J., Cohen, C., 2015. SOX10: a useful marker for identifying metastatic melanoma in sentinel lymph nodes. Appl. Immunohistochem. Mol. Morphol. 23 (2), 109–112.

Yunoki, T., Tabuchi, Y., Hirano, T., Miwa, S., Imura, J., Hayashi, A., 2018. Gene networks in basal cell carcinoma of the eyelid, analyzed using gene expression profiling. Oncol. Lett. 16 (5), 6729–6734.

Zhang, Z., Zhu, S., Yang, Y., Ma, X., Guo, S., 2015. Matrix metalloproteinase-12 expression is increased in cutaneous melanoma and associated with tumor aggressiveness. Tumor Biol. 36 (11), 8593–8600.

CHAPTER SIXTEEN

Genetics of neuronal and glioneuronal cancers

Pooja, Varunvenkat M. Srinivasan, and Anshika Srivastava
Department of Medical Genetics, Sanjay Gandhi Post Graduate Institute of Medical Sciences, Lucknow, India

Abbreviations

NSCs	neural stem cells
SVZ	subventricular zone
CNS	central nervous system
WHO	World Health Organization
N-Myc	N-myc proto-oncogene
TP53	tumor protein 53
PDGF	platelet-derived growth factor
mTOR	mammalian target of rapamycin
PTEN	phosphatase and tensin homolog
MAPKs	mitogen-activated protein kinases
PI3K	phosphatidylinositol 3-kinase
ERK	extracellular regulated kinase
IGF1	insulin growth factor 1
IGF-2	insulin-like growth factor 2
EGFR	epidermal growth factor receptor
PDGF-D	platelet-derived growth factor D
PACAP	pituitary adenylate-cyclase-activating polypeptide
CNs	central neurocytomas
GTR	gross total resection
cLNC	cerebellar liponeurocytomas
PGNT	papillary glioneuronal tumors
RGNTs	rosette-forming glioneuronal tumors
DNET	dysembryoplastic neuroepithelial tumor
DGONC	diffuse glioneuronal tumor with oligodendroglioma like features and nuclear clusters
MGTs	myxoid glioneuronal tumors

Biomarkers in Cancer Detection and Monitoring of Therapeutics
https://doi.org/10.1016/B978-0-323-95114-2.00022-4

1. Introduction

Brain development is a complex process. Enormous amount of work has identified a fundamental image of the developing brain as the consequence of a complex set of networks of vigorous and adaptable mechanisms operating in a very confined but frequently evolving environment. For neurologists striving to know the underlying processes which accelerate the cognitive and social development, neural systems regulating them, the perspective of neurophysiology on the literature of brain development presents both difficulties and opportunities. In line to this, discovery of certain tumors as a genetic disorder has opened up the probability of classifying them on the basis of genetic mutation that can determine their pathogenesis and thereby controlling their destructive behavior. While the particular pathways driving the tumor characteristics are still being identified, identification of the genetic alterations that can define specific tumor type permits the opportunities for developing more effective therapies.

The present chapter highlights the basic understanding of the cellular, molecular mechanism and genetic alterations leading to the development of neuronal tumors.

2. Brain development

The intricacy of the human brain is astounding. Within a confined volume, a large population of around 250 billion brain cells including neurons and neuroglia are compacted. Brain development begins during the third week of pregnancy in humans along with the differentiation occurring in neural progenitor cells. The neural stem cells (NSCs) are self-renewing, multipotent progenitor cells of the brain which get differentiated into the fully functional neurons by the process of neurogenesis required. NSCs are found in hippocampus, subcortical white matter and dentate gyrus along with subventricular zone (SVZ) of the lateral ventricles which is the major source of NSCs during human development.

Earlier it was believed that the brain tumors are primarily caused by mutations in neuronal or glial cells. However, the existence of brain tumor stem cells has been recently identified with their involvement in tumor initiation and proliferation. Although SVZ is the reservoir for tumor stem cells, the specific type of cells within the tumor mass responsible for tumorigenesis and its progression remains debatable.

The developing brain is reported to be influenced by both the molecular mechanisms of gene expression and certain sets of physical, biological, chemical, and environmental factors, and disruption in either, can possess a significant impact on the neural development. Experimental studies using animals as a model system, has contributed a lot of the foundational understanding about the developing brain and will definitely provide further deeper insights in the future as well.

3. Tumors of the central nervous system

Neuronal tumors are the rare tumors of central nervous system (CNS) that contain aberrant neuronal components, and contributes for nearly 1% of all the tumors arising in brain. Their origin is mainly neuronal or has a mixed neuronal and glial component, together comprising the subgroup of glioneuronal tumors. They differ from pure glial tumors in that neuronal tumors have favorable clinical results and may usually be treated with surgery alone, but gliomas generally require the radiation therapy or chemotherapy based on their histologic grade.

The 2021 WHO classification for CNS tumors has included 14 distinct tumors in their list thereby reflecting the discovery of genetic alterations underlying various tumors of CNS (Bale and Rosenblum, 2022). With the use of novel technologies in molecular diagnostics, the following substantial changes have been made in the CNS tumor classification:

A) Pure neuronal tumors
- **(i)** Central neurocytoma
- **(ii)** Extraventricular neurocytoma
- **(iii)** Cerebellar liponeurocytoma
- **(iv)** Dysplastic cerebellar gangliocytoma
- **(v)** Gangliocytoma
- **(vi)** Multinodular and vacuolating neuronal tumors

B) Mixed neuronal tumors
- **(i)** Gangliogliomas
- **(ii)** Desmoplastic infantile ganglioglioma/desmoplastic infantile astrocytoma (DIG/DIA)
- **(iii)** Papillary glioneuronal tumor (PGNT)
- **(iv)** Rosette-forming glioneuronal tumor (RGNT)
- **(v)** Dysembryoplastic neuroepithelial tumor (DNET)
- **(vi)** Diffuse glioneuronal tumor with oligodendroglioma-like features and nuclear clusters (DGONC)
- **(vii)** Myxoid glioneuronal tumor (MGT)
- **(viii)** Diffuse leptomeningeal glioneuronal tumor (DLGNT)

3.1 Pure neuronal tumors

Central neurocytoma

Central neurocytomas (CNs), firstly identified in 1982 by Hassoun et al., are the tumors which arise from ventricles and account for nearly 0.1%–0.5% of all the primary brain cancers (Hassoun et al., 1982; Kim et al., 2015). It is recognized as a noninvasive tumor of CNS, classified as grade II tumor by World Health Organization (WHO) (Louis et al., 2016). CN's biological origins is still unclear; but it is proposed to arise from the neuronal progenitor cells, neural multipotent stem cells as well as neuronal cells (Lee et al., 2016; Choudhari et al., 2009). It is generally located intraventricularly and manifested by hydrocephalus and elevated intracranial pressure (AbdelBari Mattar et al., 2021).

Age, sex distribution, and location
Approximately 65%–70% of affected individuals are in between 20 and 40 years with even distribution among both the sexes (Hassoun et al., 1993). CNs are most commonly found in the foramen of Monro, anterior half of lateral ventricle, the corpus callosum, slightly adjacent to the septum pellucidum, third and fourth ventricle (Schmidt et al., 2004).

Immunohistochemical markers
Staining with synaptophysin usually performed in the fibrillar zones as well as perivascular areas of CN indicates its neuronal origin. Positive staining with NeuN also indicates the neuronal nature of CN and its neoplasms and is also considered to be among the important markers for clear cell neoplasms of the CNS (Bonney et al., 2015).

Genetic alteration
Molecular genetics of CNs has not been fully characterized till now, however, studies have shown loss of chromosome 17, 1p, 2q, 5q, 13q, 15q, 17p, and 20p and gain of chromosomes 7, 2p, 10q, 11q, 12p, 15q, 18q, and 20q, respectively (Cerda-Nicolas et al., 1993; Jay et al., 1999; Korshunov et al., 2007; Taruscio et al., 1997; Sander et al., 2019) (Table 1).

Korshunov et al. and Kane et al. have reported *N-Myc* and *PTEN* overexpression in CNs (Korshunov et al., 2007; Kane et al., 2011). A tumor suppressor gene encoding Myc box-dependent-interacting protein 1 (BIN-1), has shown under expression and is negatively associated with the N-Myc levels (Korshunov et al., 2007). These studies indicate the promising role of relevant upregulation and under expression of N-Myc and BIN-1 for initiating CNs as this tumor might be caused by a genetic alteration in the pathway which encompasses both BIN-1 and N-Myc (Stupp and Hegi, 2007). The upregulation of *PTEN* and *N-Myc* has also been suggested to be a probable reason for the complete loss of neuronal differentiation in patients suffering from CN (Kane et al., 2011).

Furthermore, Sim et al. discovered the upregulation of neuregulin 2 (NRG2), insulin-like growth factor 2 (IGF-2), platelet-derived growth factor D (PDGF-D) and Pituitary adenylate-cyclase-activating polypeptide (*PACAP*) thereby suggesting their critical role in neurocytoma cell proliferation (Sim et al., 2006). Aghajan et al. have

Table 1 Summary of the genetic/chromosomal aberrations involved in neurocytoma.

S. no.	Gene/Chromosome	References
1.	*Chromosomal gain*: 1p36.33-p36.31, 1q44, 2p22.3-p22.1, 2p24.1, 2q37.1-q37.3, 6q27, 7, 10q23.3, 11p11.2, 11q23, 11q25, 12p13.33-p13.31, 14q32.33, 15q11-q13, 15q26 *Chromosomal loss*: 1p34.3, 2q14, 5p15.2, 5q21-q22, 6p12.1-p21.1, 7q21.3-q22, 11p15.5, 12q23, 13q14, 13q34, 15q12, 16q23.2, 17q11.2-q12, 17p13.3, 19p13.2, 19p13.3-p12, 20pter, 20p12.1-p11.2	Cerda-Nicolas et al. (1993), Korshunov et al. (2007), Taruscio et al. (1997), and Sander et al. (2019)
2.	Overexpression of *IGF-2, PACAP, PDGFD, NRG2*	Sim et al. (2006)
3.	Overexpression of *PTEN* and *N-Myc* Downregulation of *BIN1*	Korshunov et al. (2007)
4.	*EWSR1-ATF1* fusion and *MUTYH* mutation	Aghajan et al. (2019)

recently reported *EWSR1-ATF1* fusion and *MUTYH* mutation in a pediatric atypical CN (Aghajan et al., 2019).

Extraventricular neurocytoma

Neurocytomas originating from the cerebral parenchyma, spinal cord, outside the ventricles have been termed as extraventricular neurocytomas (EVNs) (Brat et al., 2001). EVNs are of two types—typical and atypical EVNs, primarily based on the severity and their histological characteristics. The typical EVNs reflect the less intrusive form of disease. Atypical EVNs, on the other hand, are aggressive tumors with a high mitotic and proliferative index, as well as extensively high angiogenesis and necrosis (Choi et al., 2011).

Ferreol et al. and Nishio et al. were the first to report the unusual incidences of extraventricular neurocytomas (EVNs) (Ferreol et al., 1989; Nishio et al., 1990, 1992) previously thought to be one of the types of CN. EVNs, reported as a separate entity in the WHO classification of tumors of the CNS have been considered as the grade II tumors (Louis et al., 2016).

Age, sex distribution, and location

EVN seems to have no preference over sex, with males occasionally displaying a little predominance, and appears to be spread evenly throughout all the age groups (Gaggiotti et al., 2021). They are usually observed in the frontal, occipital, parietal and the temporal lobes (Brat et al., 2001). Other less commonly reported regions are thalamus (Mallick et al., 2018), sellar region (Kawaji et al., 2014), spine (Hu et al., 2015), cerebellum (Enam et al., 1997), ovary (Yu et al., 2015), and pelvis region (Friedrichs et al., 2003).

Immunohistochemical markers

A consistent positive synaptophysin expression in immunohistochemistry, indicate their origin of neuronal differentiation. Other specific markers for EVNs including MAP-2 and NeuN have also been identified. Focal expression of chromogranin-A and glial fibrillary acidic protein (GFAP) has been observed in rarely exceptional cases (Brat et al., 2001).

Genetic alterations

Despite their close resemblance to CN, EVNs additionally show 1p/19q chromosomal deletions which have not been found in any cases of CN (Rodriguez et al., 2009).

Cerebellar liponeurocytoma

Cerebellar liponeurocytomas (cLNC) are the rare type of adult cerebellar tumors which usually affect people in their adulthood (Khatri et al., 2018). cLNC have an identical histology and immunological profile to that of central neurocytomas except the presence of fat component in cLNC only. The affected individuals experience vomiting along with progressive vision loss because of the increased cranial pressure (Jenkinson et al., 2003; Alkadhi et al., 2001). cLNC has a low Ki-67/MIB-1 proliferation index with a mean range of 3.73%±4.01% (Gembruch et al., 2018).

Age, sex distribution, and location

The peak incidence has generally been reported in the fifth and sixth decades. Men and women are affected almost equally with no sex predominance (Nishimoto and Kaya, 2012). The cerebellar hemispheres, fourth ventricle, posterior fossa and cerebellar vermis are the most common sites at which cLNC develops (Khatri et al., 2018; Gembruch et al., 2018).

Immunohistochemical markers

cLNCs immunohistochemical profile shows positive expression profile for Synaptophysin, MAP-2, neuron-specific enolase (NSE), and glial fibrillary acidic protein (GFAP) (Borekci et al., 2018; Cai et al., 2018; Tucker et al., 2017; Hirono et al., 2021). Enhanced levels of transcription factor Neurogenin 1 (NEUROG1) which has been associated with adipocytes and fatty acid-binding protein 4 (*FABP4*) have also been described in cLNCs (Anghileri et al., 2012).

Genetic alterations

The genetic spectra of cLNC has not yet been thoroughly elucidated. Horstmann et al. reported *TP53* mutation as the common genetic cause in cLNC, with a 20% frequency (Horstmann et al., 2004). Studies have shown the upregulation of *FABP4* gene expressed in adipocytes and macrophages (Tucker et al., 2017). Hirono et al. reported a splice site mutation of G→A transversion at the first base of the 3′-acceptor splice site of intron 30 (c.6850–1 G→A) of the *ATRX* gene in a patient with cLNC (Hirono et al., 2021). Broggi et al. have identified various genetic alterations, summarized in Table 2.

Table 2 Summary of the genetic/chromosomal aberrations involved in cLNCs.

S. No.	Gene/Chromosome	Variation	References
1	TP53	• c.711G>A (exon 7) • c.856G>A (exon 8)	Tucker et al. (2017)
2	ATRX	• c.6850-1 G>A	Hirono et al. (2021)
3	**a. Missense variants**		
	• TP53	c.215C>G (exon 4)	
	• APC	c.3949G>C (exon 16)	
	• PIK3CA	c.1173A>G	
	• KDR	c.1416A>T (exon 11)	
	b. Synonymous variants		
	• FGFR3	c.1953G>A (p.T651=)	Broggi et al. (2022)
	• PDGFRA	c.1701A>G (p.P567=)	
	• APC	c.4479G>A (p.T1493=)	
	• EGFR	c.2361G>A (p.Q787=)	
	• IDH1	c.315C>T (p.G105=)	
	• RETR	c.2307G>T (p.L769=)	
	• FBXW7	p.D400=	
	• RAS	p.H27=	
	c. Intronic variants		
	• KDR	c.798 + 54G>A, c.3849-24C>A	
	• PIK3CA	c.352 + 40A>G	
	• FLT3	c.1310-3 T>C	
	• STK11	c.465-51 T>C)	
	• SMARCB1	c.1119-41G>A	
	• CSF1R (3′-UTR)	c.*1841TG>GA	

Treatment

A complete removal has been suggested as a cure for most of the neurocytomas, but unusual cytology and location at extraventricular sites often necessitates additional therapy after the primary treatment to minimize the risk (Mallick et al., 2015).

The preferred approach for treating EV and cLNC is surgery, but the gross total resection (GTR) should be considered as an ultimate goal for absolute treatment because GTR has previously shown better controlling tumor rate as compared with subtotal resection (STR) (Mpairamidis et al., 2009; Kane et al., 2012).

Dysplastic cerebellar gangliocytoma

Dysplastic cerebellar gangliocytoma also termed as Lhermitte Duclos disease (LDD) was first described by Lhermitte and Duclos. These benign tumors have been found in nearly 35% of Cowden syndrome (CS) patients, hence considered to be an important indicator of CS in adults (Lok et al., 2005). LDD is hamartomatous in nature in which ganglion cells have been overgrown resulting in cerebellar folia thickening (Nowak and Trost, 2002).

Patients manifest cerebellar dysfunction, obstructive hydrocephalus (Kulkantrakorn et al., 1997) and experience mass effect changes in posterior fossa along with visual abnormalities, headache, and nausea. Because CT has limitations in examining the posterior fossa, noncontrast MRI has been used for the diagnosis.

Age, sex distribution, and location

The age at presentation can range from birth to sixth decade with predominance in the third decade with no gender predilection (Roessmann and Wongmongkolrit, 1984; Gessaga, 1980). The tumor usually originates from the cerebellar cortex (Nowak and Trost, 2002).

Immunohistochemistry

Immunohistochemical analysis revealed the involvement of *PTEN/AKT/mTOR* pathway in pathogenesis among most of the cases (Zhou et al., 2003). Robust activation of S6 (downstream of mTOR) has also been identified. These findings strongly suggest that mTOR inhibitors, such as CCI-779 54, could be used as a novel medication for LDD (Abel et al., 2005).

Genetic variation

Because *PTEN* is the only known susceptibility gene in LDD, Zhou et al. revealed that LDD patients may be harboring germline variants in genes belonging to the PTEN signaling pathway (Zhou et al., 2003). Later on, Colby et al. (2016) observed four missense heterozygous variants in genes that are upstream of or downstream from *PTEN*, i.e., *EGFR* p.Cys326Phe, *NSRR* p.Arg87Cys, *ILK* p.Arg59Trp, and *MET* p.Ile247Val, respectively. Further structural modeling predicted that the *EGFR* p.Cys326Phe variant has a severe impact on protein structure because of breakage of a disulfide bond in the

Table 3 Summary of the genetic/chromosomal aberrations involved in LDD.

S. no.	Gene/ Chromosome	Variation	References
1.	PTEN	16–18 del AA, c.737C>T (p.P246L), 53 del A, 347–51del ACAAT, c.262T>C (p.Y88H), c.950_953delTACT (p.L318fs*2)	Zhou et al. (2003) and Chen et al. (2014)
2.	EGFR	c.977G>T (p.C326F) p.Cys326Ph	Colby et al. (2016)
3.	INSRR	c.259C>T (p.R87C)	Colby et al. (2016)
4.	ILK	c.175C>T (p.R59W)	Colby et al. (2016)
5.	MET	p.I247V	Colby et al. (2016)
6.	PALB2	c.1273G > A (p.V425M)	Jiang et al. (2020)

extracellular receptor domain and replacement of a 100% conserved cysteine with a phenylalanine residue (Colby et al., 2016). Their findings suggest that activating mutations in *EGFR* contribute to the pathogenesis of *PTEN* wild-type LDD. *PTEN* mutation analysis showed a heterozygous c.950_953delTACT (or p.L318fs*2) mutation in exon 8 of the *PTEN* gene in both germline and somatic DNA (Chen et al., 2014) (Table 3).

Treatment
With symptom management, unless the mass effect symptoms are problematic enough to warrant surgical resection is the suggested treatment of LDD (Savardekar et al., 2012). Complete surgical resection is associated with low rates of postoperative recurrence (Masmoudi et al., 2011). mTOR inhibitors may be an effective alternative or adjunct to surgical intervention (Abel et al., 2005).

Gangliocytomas
Gangliocytomas (GCs) are benign neuroepithelial tumors primarily made up of a group of nonuniform mature neoplastic ganglionic cells without a component of glia. GCs have been categorized as grade I tumors in 1979 by WHO classification for CNS tumors (Fuller and Scheithauer, 2007). Characterized as slow-growing tumors, GCs do not become malignant. Large, mature ganglion cells that are binucleated or multinucleated with conspicuous nucleoli having the dense cytoplasm and Nissl bodies eventually comprise the gangliocytomas (Cossu et al., 2019).

Age, sex distribution, and location
Gangliocytomas have been widely observed in the pediatric and young adult populations with an average age of diagnosis from 8.5 to 25 years (Wolf et al., 1994; Hirose et al., 1997). The most common sites for presentation are temporal lobe, cerebral hemispheres, cerebellum, third ventricle, and medullary oblongata (Jacob et al., 2005; Takahashi et al., 2016; Wakao and Imagama, 2012; Mhatre et al., 2020). Spinal gangliocytomas are exceedingly rare, comprising less than 10% of all gangliocytomas.

Genetic alterations

The protein kinase B (*PKB*)/*AKT* system has recently been identified as a tumorigenic pathway in pediatric ganglioneuroma hence the *AKT*/mTOR/S6 mechanism is mostly linked to ganglioneuroma rather than neuroblastoma (Tao et al., 2021). In aggressive ganglioneuromas, the transcription factor insulinoma-associated protein 1 (INSM1) has been reported to be positive, however its role as a prognostic marker still has to be determined (Wang et al., 2019).

Tao et al. have created a zebrafish model by coexpressing mCherry and a constitutively active, myristoylated murine Akt2 (myr-Akt2) in the PSNS under the control of the zebrafish dopamine—hydroxylase (dh) gene promoter (Tao et al., 2021). Their results identified that sirolimus and everolimus could be used to treat pediatric ganglioneuromas before surgery, allowing the tumors to be removed more safely. They also concluded that *AKT* and its downstream mTOR-S6 pathway are activated more frequently in ganglioneuroma and the expression of *SOX10*, a master transcription factor expressed by mature, differentiated ganglion cells and Schwann cells (Delfino-Machin et al., 2017) was remarkably upregulated in human and zebrafish ganglioneuromas suggesting its role in regulating neuronal progenitor cells differentiation.

The molecular mechanism of gangliocytoma is still unclear but might have a genetic link to gangliogliomas. In some cases, a certain neural migratory abnormality, hemimegalencephaly, has been associated with cytological abnormalities (Alarifi et al., 2022). Gupte et al. have presented a novel molecular finding in which fusion of breakpoint cluster region and neurotropic receptor tyrosine kinase 2 (BCR-NTRK2) and overexpression of *BRAF* has been discovered in a pediatric patient with spinal gangliocytoma (Gupte et al., 2021).

Treatment

Maximal safe resection is the mainstay of treatment, as this tumor does not respond to irradiation or traditional chemotherapy. Very little is known about the molecular makeup or the role of targeted therapy in this tumor (Jacob et al., 2005). In general, the prognosis of gangliocytoma and ganglioglioma is considered favorable; the 5-year survival rate of even brainstem ganglioglioma was reported as 78% after surgical treatment (Lang et al., 1993).

Multinodular and vacuolating neuronal tumor

Multinodular and vacuolating neuronal tumors (MVNT) are rare benign brain lesions first reported in 2013 (Huse et al., 2013). The patients are usually asymptomatic with very few showing seizures as a major clinical manifestation (Nunes et al., 2017).

Age, sex distribution, and location

Studies have found MVNTs to be two times more common in females than the males with an average age of 42 years at diagnosis. The tumor has been commonly found in middle-aged populations with neurological symptoms including headaches and seizures (Buffa et al., 2020). They are usually located in left hemisphere, in the frontal and parietal lobes of left hemisphere, slightly inclined toward subcortex and deep white matter (Nunes et al., 2017; Arbuiso et al., 2021).

Immunohistochemical markers

MVNTs tumor cells showed immunopositivity for CD34 in adjacent parenchyma, neuronal marker synaptophysin and glial marker OLIG2 but negative for NeuN and GFAP (Pekmezci et al., 2018). Immunohistochemical analysis with antibodies against phospho-ERK revealed robust staining in neoplastic neurons and some smaller glial cells, similar to that seen in other tumors having genetic alterations within the MAP kinase signaling pathway, implying that they are characterized by the pathogenic alterations that activate Ras-Raf-MAP kinase signaling pathway.

Genetic alterations

The genetic basis for MVNT is different from many other neuronal and glioneuronal tumors. Pekmezci et al. reported *BRAF* missense mutation (p.L597R and p.G469S) in two cases, *MAP2K1* missense mutation in exon2 (p.Q56P) in five cases, and *FGFR2-INA* in-frame gene fusion in one case (Pekmezci et al., 2018) (Table 4).

Treatment

Surgical intervention is often indicated in case of seizures.

3.2 Mixed glioneuronal tumors

Gangliogliomas

Gangliogliomas (GG) are infrequent, well-differentiated, slow-growing benign neuroepithelial neoplasms consisted of neoplastic glial and neuronal cells (Pandita et al., 2007). They account for roughly 1%–10% of all the pediatric CNS lesions (Zhang et al., 2008) and are commonly referred to as the pediatric neoplasms. In more than 60% of the instances, epileptic seizures is associated with this disease condition, half of which are uncontrollable (Huang et al., 2014).

Table 4 Summary of the genetic/chromosomal aberrations involved in MVNT.

S. no.	Gene/Chromosome	Variation	Reference
1.	*BRAF* missense mutation *MAP2K1* *FGFR2-INA* in-frame gene fusion	c.1790T>G (p.L597R) & c.1405_1406delinsTC (p.G469S), [MAP2K1] c.167A>C(p.Q56P), exon 2	Pekmezci et al. (2018)

Age, sex distribution, and location

GG affects mainly the children and young adults, with a peak incidence age of 10–25 years (Demierre et al., 1986) and is more slightly spread in males as compared to the females (Koeller and Henry, 2001). These tumors can arise anywhere within the central nervous system, with the temporal lobe being the most frequently affected area (>70%), and the infratentorial compartment contributing for about 15% of the total GGs (Tandon et al., 2016; Hakim et al., 1997).

Immunohistochemical markers

Immunohistochemistry revealed cells with the increased synaptophysin expression, indicating their neuronal origin (Kang et al., 2007). The cells have also been reported to be positive for neurofilament protein (NF), neuronal class III β-tubulin (TuJ1), neuronal specific nuclear protein (NeuN) and GFAP (Yano et al., 2013).

CD34, a stem cell epitope, has positive staining in gangliomas which otherwise is not expressed in normal healthy brain (Blumcke and Wiestler, 2002).

Genetic alterations

In 60% of the total gangliogliomas, *BRAFV600E* mutation has been discovered in deformed astroglial tumor cells as well as in atypical neuronal and neoplastic cells (Koelsche et al., 2013). The most prevalent *BRAFV600E* mutation discovered is a substitution of thymidine for adenosine at c.1799 (c.1799T > A) (Donson et al., 2014).

The Akt/mTOR pathway get activated in individuals with *BRAF* V600E-positive GGs (Rak et al., 2013; Prabowo et al., 2014). Cases-Cunillera et al. have discovered the presence of phospho-ribosomal protein S6 (pS6) as a downstream effector of the Akt/mTOR signaling cascade in GGs (Cases-Cunillera et al., 2021).

Several studies based on animal model systems have been performed to understand the genetic basis of GGs and the role of specific genes and gene mutations in their occurrence.

In 2018, Koh et al. developed a mouse model of GGs with somatic mutation of *BRAFV637E* in the NPCs during early neurogenesis and brain development and discovered that BRAFV637E mutation mainly affects the elevated CD34 intensity in the cortical areas and intractable epilepsy has been caused by the *BRAFV600E* mutation, which induce an increase in REST expression in developing neurons, which appear to be controlled and driven by *MYC* (Koh et al., 2018).

In 2021, Cases-Cunillera et al. developed mouse model by manipulating *BRAFV600E* and Akt/mTOR-pathway signaling and revealed phosphorylation of numerous critical downstream targets, including ERK1/2, BRAF, and MEK1/2 due to mutation and also the elevated amount of pS6 expression in mice electroporated with *BRAFV600E/pAkt IU*, indicating the activation of Akt/mTOR signaling pathway in these lesions. The oncofetal protein CD34 has also been substantially expressed in the BRAFV600E tumor region in *BRAFV600E* mice (Cases-Cunillera et al., 2021).

In 2021, Ahmad et al. used rabbit brain as a model system and revealed elevated level of AKT, H Ras, GFAP and Ki 67 and reduced level of p53 expression in the tumor location (Ahmad et al., 2021) which shed light on the pathophysiology of this rare brain tumor.

Treatment

The literature has argued the role of radiation therapy and chemotherapy. Gross total resection (GTR) is the therapy of choice for GGs for long-term results. Gangliogliomas have an 82%–93% 10-year survival rate following full excision. However, both histologically and physiologically, gangliogliomas appear to be heterogeneous, and tumor recurrence or anaplastic progression occurs in a small percentage of patients (Hakim et al., 1997; Matsumoto et al., 1999). These tumors have limited options for the treatment, particularly if they develop in the brainstem (BS), where total surgical resection is not really achievable. Furthermore, as compared to cerebellar or cerebral GGs, BS-GGs have a shorter prodrome of clinical symptoms, a higher mortality rate, and a lower progression-free survival rate (Lang et al., 1993; Donson et al., 2014).

Anaplastic ganglioglioma

Anaplastic gangliogliomas (AGG) is a rare, epileptogenic malignant form of ganglioglioma (GG) (Giulioni et al., 2005, 2006) accounting for nearly 1.3% of all primary CNS neoplasm (Kalyan-Raman and Olivero, 1987). The World Health Organization (WHO) categorized AGG into Grade III form with a poor survival rate of about 29 months (Louis et al., 2016). The survival of the individuals varies from 1% to 6% of GG (Zanello et al., 2016) with an incidence rate of roughly 0.02 cases per million individuals (Selvanathan et al., 2011). Glial section is commonly affected by anaplastic transformation that comprises cellular and vascular expansion together with regional necrosis (Niemeyer and Marchiori, 2018). AGG can develop as a by-product of a de novo lesion, and approximately 10% are the result of a WHO grade 1 GG's malignant transformation (Vlachos et al., 2021).

Age, sex distribution, and location

Since AGG is a severe form of GG so its occurrence would definitely be similar to the GG and there have been very few cases reported for AGG. Retrospective data are available on some cases of AGG with different sex distribution but at the time of manifestation, patients are generally children or young adults so it comes under the category of the pediatric tumor, with a slight predilection of gender causing male to be much more affected than female (Selvanathan et al., 2011). AGGs are usually supratentorial and unifocal and spread throughout the temporal lobes and spinal cord. However, primary spinal AGGs are extremely rare, and only few cases have been reported till date (Schneider et al., 2012; Vlachos et al., 2021).

Immunohistochemistry

Immunostaining for synaptophysin, neurofilament, CD34, NSE, vimentin, and chromogranin A reveals neuronal origin of tumor (Chretien et al., 2007; Ghosal et al., 2010; Kuten et al., 2012).

For the identification of the neoplastic glial cells, three markers, Olig-2, glial fibrillary acidic protein (GFAP), and S-100, have been generally used (Chretien et al., 2007; Ghosal et al., 2010; Kuten et al., 2012). AGGs have also shown positive staining for Ki-67.

Genetic alterations

Although any specific mutation has not been recognized as the sole cause of the disease, a mutation in the *BRAF*V600E gene has been found in a number of individuals (Koelsche et al., 2013; Dahiya et al., 2013; Rush et al., 2013).

Immunohistochemistry revealed that the p.K27M H3F3A mutant protein has a high expression of the Histone H3.3 gene mutation, correlated with a loss of H3K27 trimethylation (Zanello et al., 2016). Immunostaining has demonstrated positive staining in both glial and neuronal populations for the *BRAF*V600E mutant protein (Zanello et al., 2016). Both the glial and neuronal components of the brain showed a loss of *ATRX* staining according to Zanello et al. (2016).

Mistry et al. described two cases of secondary AGG, one mutation with a p.K27M H3F3A and double *BRAF*V600E of the midline and another mutation with an hTERT promoter and a *BRAF*V600E in the hemisphere (Mistry et al., 2015). Even in the initial phase, these cancers may include a p.K27M H3F3A mutation or a *BRAF*V600E mutation, indicating that such mutations are acquired early and not always after malignant growth (Table 5).

To evaluate the underlying pathogenic impact of loss-of-function of the Trp53 mutations in human AGGs, Cases-Cunillera et al. have created a mouse model with *BRAF*V600E, pAkt, and Cre co-IU-electroporated at E14 in Trp53loxP/loxP mice (Cases-Cunillera et al., 2021) and concluded that *Trp53* loss does not really evoke AGG-like tumors in a manner independent of *BRAF*V600E/pAkt, but rather acts as a modifier that finally led to the acquisition of anaplastic tumor features.

Table 5 Summary of the genetic/chromosomal aberrations involved in AGGs.

S. no.	Gene/Chromosome	Variation	References
1.	Loss of K27M trimethylation, K27M H3.3 mutation, *hTERT* promoter mutation, loss of *ATRX*, *BRAF* V600E (c.1799T>A) mutation	p.K27M (H3F3A)	Zanello et al. (2016) and Mistry et al. (2015)

Treatment

AGG has a wide range of therapy options and prognosis. While the basic treatment for anaplastic gangliogliomas is the maximal safe excision, the role of chemotherapy and radiation is yet to be established in randomized clinical trials and is rarely reported in existing case reports (Varlet et al., 2004).

Desmoplastic infantile astrocytoma and ganglioglioma (DIA/DIG)

This uncommon kind of neuroepithelial tumor can have completely astrocytic differentiation (DIA) or be made up of astrocytic and neuronal differentiation tumor cells (DIG). DIA and DIG are continuous spectrum of the same tumor which show relatively homogeneous molecular architecture based on the copy number and DNA methylation profiling (Gessi et al., 2013). They are categorized as WHO grade I tumors because of their benign nature accounting for approximately 0.5%–1.0% of the total intracranial tumors.

Age, sex distribution, and location

The first description of the tumor was a superficial cerebral astrocytoma attached to dura (Taratuto et al., 1984). Typically, massive, enhancing, cystic and solid, supratentorial DIA/DIG are usually seen in the cerebral hemisphere with mean age of onset at 6 months with major manifestation in less than 24 months of age (Louis et al., 2016). Until now, only a limited number of noninfantile DIA/DIGs have been reported.

Genetic alterations

Gessi et al. carried a genome-wide evaluation of DNA copy number variations and identified focused recurring losses of genomic material in both DIA and DIG, within distinct discrete loci such as 5q13.3, 10q21.3, and 21q22.11. At 13q14 (TPT1), there had been focal gains (Gessi et al., 2013). One case each from the series which were either DIA/DIG positive for *BRAF*V600E have been reported (Gessi et al., 2013; Koelsche et al., 2014; Karabagli et al., 2014; Dougherty et al., 2010). *BRAF* fusion and V600D have been identified in one case each (Koelsche et al., 2014; Greer et al., 2017) (Table 6).

Treatment

The treatment involves total resection and has a good prognosis. Sometimes in large tumors or deep locations, the total resection is not possible and may require radiotherapy or chemotherapy (Gelabert-Gonzalez et al., 2010; Hummel et al., 2012). In case of *BRAF*V600E mutation positivity the tumor is amenable to treatment with specific agents.

Papillary glioneuronal tumor

Papillary glioneuronal tumors (PGNT) are newly-discovered grade I primary brain tumors that prefer to grow in the periventricular and supratentorial areas of the brain.

Table 6 Summary of the genetic/chromosomal aberrations involved in DIA/DIG.

S. no.	Gene/Chromosome	Variation	References
1.	*Chromosome gain*: 1q31.1–31.3 (*MET*), 5p13.1–13.3, 7q31 (*MET*), 4q12 (*KDR, KIT, PDGFR* loci), 12q14.3 (*MDM2*) *Chromosome loss*: 17q24.3–25.3, 9q33.3–34.3, 7q22.1, 19p (*MET, BRAF, KDR, KIT, MDM2* gain), 8p22-pter		Gessi et al. (2013) and Kros et al. (2002)
2.	*FXR1–BRAF* fusion		Zhang et al. (2013)
3.	*EML4–ALK* fusion, *ATRX* deletion, *TP53*		
4.	Somatic *BRAF* gene mutation	c.1799T>A (p.V600E), c.1799_1800delinsAC (p.V600D)	Chatterjee et al. (2018)

PGNTs are the members of a wider family of glioneuronal cancers along with DNET, GGs and AGGs. Since Komori et al. originally described them in 1998 (Komori et al., 1998), several cases have been reported in the literature.

Patients experience headaches or seizures as the most common clinical manifestation. These tumors usually proceed in a benign manner with a 5-year progression-free survival rate.

Age, sex distribution, and location
These tumors are more common in the population of young adults with mean age of 23 years but can occur at any age with no sexual preferences (Louis et al., 2016). The tumor is reported to be found supratentorial, periventricular (Carangelo et al., 2015).

Immunohistochemical markers
The glial part is positive for GFAP, S100 and nestin and the neuronal component is positive for synaptophysin, neuron specific enolase, and class 111 beta tubulin.

Epigenetics and genetic alterations
Pages et al. (2015) and Hou et al. (2019) identified *SLC44A1-PRKCA* gene fusions in PGNT specimens and concluded that specimens missing such fusions belonged invariably to other tumor types. Because of the *SLC44A1* fusion, *PRKCA* expression is deregulated and thereby MAPK signaling pathway also gets deregulated (Dougherty et al., 2010). *BRAF*V600E mutations have also been described in PGNT (Dougherty et al., 2010). Ki-67 indices have always been low for PGNTs.

Several cases demonstrating the canonical fusion, and a single case demonstrating *NOTCH1-PRKCA* fusion has been noted (Hou et al., 2019; Pages et al., 2015;

Table 7 Summary of the genetic/chromosomal aberrations involved in PGNT.

S. no.	Gene/Chromosome	Variation	References
1.	Fusions of *SLC4A1-PRKCA*	–	Pages et al. (2015) and Hou et al. (2019)
2.	*FGFR1* mutation2	c.1638C>A (p.N546K)	Gessi et al. (2014a)
3.	*BRAF*	c.1799T>A (p.V600E)	Dougherty et al. (2010)
4.	*TERT* promoter mutation *FGFR3-TACC3* fusion Loss of copy number in *CDKN2A/CDKN2B*	–	Goethe et al. (2019)

Nagaishi et al., 2016). Gain and structural abnormalities of chromosome 7 have also been reported in the literature (Faria et al., 2008). Gessi et al. has described an *FGFR1* mutation by pyrosequencing (*FGFR1N546K*) (Gessi et al., 2014a). The recurrence of PGNT in one patient identified an *FGFR3-TACC3* oncogenic fusion, a *TERT* promoter mutation and a copy number loss in *CDKN2A/CDKN2B* (Goethe et al., 2019) (Table 7).

Treatment
The treatment involves total resection and has a good prognosis. Sometimes in large tumors or deep locations, the total resection is not possible and may require radiotherapy or chemotherapy.

Rosette forming glioneuronal tumor
Rosette-forming glioneuronal tumors (RGNTs) are the unusual glioneuronal tumors of fourth ventricle that affect predominantly the young adults (Gessi et al., 2014b). They have been identified by rosettes of neurocytic cells features having similar features to pilocytic astrocytoma (PA), which include piloid cytology and, in certain cases, rosenthal strands and eosinophilic granular aggregates (Nair et al., 2014).

Age, sex distribution, and location
The major affected population is young adults, with an average age of 23 years. Female predominance has been noted for this tumor type (Komori et al., 2002). Primarily located in the fourth ventricle (Gessi et al., 2014b) RGNTs have also been identified in cerebellum, spinal cord and pineal gland (Xu et al., 2012).

Immunohistochemical markers
Synaptophysin has been shown to be significantly expressed in the rosettes' centers while GFAP has been highly expressed in spindle cells that resemble pilocytic astrocytoma (Wilson et al., 2020).

Genetic alterations

FGFR1 K656E and N546K mutations have been reported by Gessi et al. (2014b). Recurrent *FGFR1* missense mutations may coexist with mutations in oncogene *PIK3CA* (Gessi et al., 2014b) or *PIK3R1*. Amplification of Exons 9 and 20 of *PIK3CA* have been reported earlier (Hartmann et al., 2006) with hotspot codons E542, E545, and H1047 (Thommen et al., 2013; Ellezam et al., 2012). *FGFR1* K687E (Zehir et al., 2017) and *PIK3R1* H450del (Lucas et al., 2020a) alterations were previously identified in a patient having RGNT of the fourth ventricle. Besides activating *FGFR1* and *PIK3CA* mutations, missense or damaging mutations in *NF1* tumor suppressor gene or *PTPN11* have also been reported in the literature (Sievers et al., 2019) (Table 8).

Treatment

Surgery is still the therapy of choice, with gross total resection (GTR) being the preferred method and subtotal resection (STR) as an alternative.

Dysembryoplastic neuroepithelial tumor

Dysembryoplastic neuroepithelial tumor (DNET) is a rare and newly detected kind of brain tumor that was originally described roughly about 3 decades ago by Daumas-Duport (1993). It has been defined as a mixed glial-neuronal neoplasm with a multinodular architecture, cortical supratentorial location, and association with focal cortical dysplasia (Daumas-Duport et al., 1988). It was categorized as a Grade I1 tumor in 2016 by WHO Classification of tumors of the CNS (Louis et al., 2016) and can be frequently visible enough on MRI to make a diagnosis of its occurrence (Chassoux et al., 2012).

There have been about 30 intraventricular DNET cases reported so far. They have been usually linked to the supratentorial middle line structures. Intraventricular DNET tumors of the septum pellucidum, third ventricle and caudate nucleus are the most commonly observed types (Yuan et al., 2011; Chiang et al., 2019).

Table 8 Summary of the genetic/chromosomal aberrations involved in RGNTs.

S. no.	Gene/ Chromosome	Variation	References
1.	*FGFR1*	c.1638C>A (p.N546K) c.1966A>G (p.K656E)	Gessi et al. (2014b)
2.	*FGFR1-PIK3CA*	PIK3CA c.3140A>G (p.H1047R) along with FGFR1- c.1638C>A (p.N546K)	Gessi et al. (2014b) and Ellezam et al. (2012)
3.	*FGFR1-PIK3R1*	FGFR1 c.2059A>G (p.K687E) and *PIK3R1* c.1348_1350del (p.H450del)	Lucas et al. (2020a)
4.	*NF1, PTPN11*	–	Sievers et al. (2019)

Location

DNETs are prevalent in the cortex of the brain and usually affecting one gyrus with neuronal components forming columnar formations perpendicular to the cortical surface (Sontowska et al., 2017). Although intraventricular DNETs are quite uncommon they are frequently found near the third ventricle, and the patients are sometimes manifested with hydrocephalus (Ahluwalia et al., 2020).

Epigenetic modification

When compared to the control group, miR-3138 has been found to be down-regulated in the DNET cohort. The DNET cohort had significantly higher levels of expression of miR-1909*, suggesting that it may have carcinogenic properties when overexpressed (Rivera et al., 2016).

Genetic alterations

The genetic basis of DNETs still not clearly understood. Overactivation of the *NF1* aberrations (Barba et al., 2013) and mTOR pathway (Blumcke et al., 2014) have been suggested as probable etiology of DNET, while BRAF p.V600E mutation is detected in approximately 50% of all the DNETs cases (Chappe et al., 2013). A single *TERT* promoter mutation (Killela et al., 2013), three *IDH1* mutations (Thom et al., 2011), and some reports of a *FGFR1* intragenic tyrosine kinase domain duplication have also been reported (Zhang et al., 2013; Slegers and Blumcke, 2020). There have been gains on chromosomes 5, 6, and 7, as well as LOH of 1p/19q and 10q (Barba et al., 2013; Prabowo et al., 2015).

There has been one example of a mixed DNET/RGNT with a verified *PIK3CA* mutation (Eye et al., 2017). A mutation in exon 9 (E545K, c.1633G > A) has been discovered by PCR analysis in exons 1, 9, and 20 of *PIK3CA*, which could be further altering cell proliferation, survival, differentiation, motility, and intracellular trafficking (Stone et al., 2018).

Many tumors, particularly DNET-GG spectrum tumors, have been found to have somatic *ATM* mutations. Stone et al. found three *ATM* mutations in DNT-GG tumors, two of which have been at variant allele frequencies proposing somatic alterations (R2461C at 20% in a GG and R1039L at 9% in a DNT), whereas the third variant (V2696L) has been discovered in a "glioneuronal tumor NOS" at 48%, implying it might be a germline alteration (Blumcke et al., 2014) (Table 9).

Table 9 Summary of the genetic/chromosomal aberrations involved in DNETs.

S. no.	Gene/Chromosome	Variation	References
1.	*IDH1* mutation combined LOH 1p/19q and 10q (*PTEN* locus), *FGFR1* intragenic tyrosine kinase domain duplication		Suh (2015), Zhang et al. (2013), Slegers and Blumcke (2020)
2.	*PIK3CA and BRAF* mutation	c.1633G>A (p.E545K) [PIK3CA], c.1799T>A (p.V600E)	Eye et al. (2017), Chappe et al. (2013)

Diffuse glioneuronal tumor with oligodendroglioma like features and nuclear clusters (DGONC)

DGONCs has been recently identified as a glioneuronal tumor entity with the characteristics including oligodendroglioma-like perinuclear halos and nuclear clusters having a clear cell appearance with vascular proliferation. This represents WHO grade II tumor with limited data (Deng et al., 2020). Nuclear clusters have been arranged narrowly with little cytoplasm surrounding them, suggesting "pennies on a plate." The presence of focal lymphocytic infiltrations, perivascular pseudo-rosettes, neutrophil-like islands, macrophages and calcifications have been observed in many cases.

Age, sex distribution, and location

DGONCs commonly arise in the pediatric population with a median age of 9 years. No gender predilection has been observed because of the limited number of cases (Deng et al., 2020). DGONCs are generally located in the cerebral hemispheres, with more frequency in the temporal lobes (Deng et al., 2020).

Immunohistochemical markers

The neuronal and oligodendrocyte markers OLIG2, Synaptophysin, and MAP2 all revealed favorable expression profiles for DGONCs (Deng et al., 2020).

Genetic alteration

Recurrent monosomy of chromosome 14 (the major molecular hallmark of DGONCs), gain of 1q and 17q, loss of 19q have been discovered on a genetic level, but no additional defining pathogenic genetic abnormalities have been detected (Pickles et al., 2021). Deng et al. observed gain of *FGFR1* on the copy number profile, but RNA sequencing for *FGFR1* fusions was undetectable.

Treatment

Surgical resection has been widely used. After resection, all patients might receive craniospinal radiation as well as chemotherapy for better survival.

Myxoid glioneuronal tumor

Myxoid glioneuronal tumors (MGTs) are newly recognized tumors with low grade proliferation, similar to DNET but located in the septum pellucidum and are classified as grade I tumors by WHO (Lucas et al., 2020b). Previously, this tumor was known as "intraventricular DNET" or "DNET-like tumor of the septum pellucidum." MGTs are surrounded by prominent myxoid/mucin-rich stroma, mimicking DNET or oligodendroglioma. They might also have neurocytic rosettes in some cases (Chiang et al., 2019; Lucas et al., 2020b; Solomon et al., 2018).

Age, sex distribution, and location

MGTs are found in the septal nuclei, septum pellucidum, lateral ventricles, corpus callosum, and the subcallosal area (Baisden et al., 2001; Kleinschmidt-DeMasters et al., 2022).

Immunohistochemistry

Positive expression of Diffuse OLIG2, GFAP, MAP2, and SOX10 has been observed. Synaptophysin staining has also revealed the neutrophil cores of neurocytic rosettes along with several floating neurons. The Ki67 labeling index has reported to be consistently low, i.e., nearly 1%–4% (Lucas et al., 2020b).

Genetic alterations

Myxoid glioneuronal tumor are characterized as "*PDGFRA* p.K385-mutant" because of a dinucleotide mutation in *PDGF* receptor alpha protein at codon 385 in which lysine is either replaced by isoleucine or leucine (p.K385I/L) (Solomon et al., 2018). Solomon et al. have observed the Trisomy of 12q while another case represents the germline truncating mutation in the tumor suppressor gene *BRCA2* but the contribution of *BRCA2* mutation to MGTs development is uncertain. Kleinschmidt-DeMasters et al. have demonstrated the mutation in *NOTCH1*, resulting in a substitution of single amino acid (p. T1344M) along with *PDGFRA* p.K385L (Kleinschmidt-DeMasters et al., 2022). Genome-wide DNA methylation profiling revealed that the tumor has been closely clustered along with cortically-based dysembryoplastic neuroepithelial tumors (Solomon et al., 2018) (Table 10).

Treatment

Majority of MGTs have been treated by surgical excision with few cases requiring chemotherapy or radiotherapy. For better understanding and determining the appropriate guidelines for the treatment of this new tumor subtype, more research will be needed in future.

Table 10 Summary of the genetic/chromosomal aberrations involved in MGT.

S. no.	Gene/Chromosome	Variation	References
1.	*PDGFRA* Trisomy of 12q Germline *BRCA2* mutation	*PDGFRA* p.K385L/I (exon 8)	Lucas et al. (2020b)
2.	*PDGFRA-NOTCH1*	*PDGFRA* c.1153_1154inv (p.K385L)-*NOTCH1* c.4031C>T (p.T1344M)	Kleinschmidt-DeMasters et al. (2022)

Diffuse leptomeningeal glioneuronal tumor

Diffuse leptomeningeal glioneuronal tumor (DLGNT) is a rare neuronal/glioneuronal neoplasm under WHO classification of CNS tumors, known previously as a disseminated oligodendroglial-like leptomeningeal tumor of childhood (Lakhani et al., 2020). The predominant involvement includes nodular leptomeningeal enhancement which diffuses with no sure intraparenchymal mass with formation of subpial cyst that almost coats the brain (Gardiman et al., 2010; Tiwari et al., 2020). DLGNT patients have frequently been manifested by the signs of increasing hydrocephalus, i.e., headache, ataxia, vomiting, and nausea (Tan et al., 2019). Chludzinsaki et al. have reported the first instance of DLGNT in a 2-year-old cat having progressive ataxia (Chludzinski et al., 2021).

Age, sex distribution, and location

More common toward pediatric group, but can occur rarely in adult with slight predilection toward males (Saez–Alegre et al., 2021). Presents commonly as nodular enhancement and thickening of leptomeninges more around basal cisterns, extending all over the CNS (Gardiman et al., 2010).

Immunohistochemical markers

Positive expression of GFAP, Nestin, OLIG2, and synaptophysin has been observed during the immunohistochemical analysis, along with robust expression of S100 protein (Tan et al., 2019; Dodgshun et al., 2016).

Genetic alterations

The *ERK/MAPK* signaling pathway is thought to be a potential tumorigenesis driver in approximately 80% of all the DLGNT cases along with *KIAA1549:BRAF* fusions (Rodriguez et al., 2015) which constitutively activates the tyrosine kinase domain of *BRAF* and hence permanently activate the MAP kinase (*MAPK*) pathway (Manoharan et al., 2021). Manoharan et al. described a case having a pathogenic somatic *BCOR* truncating mutation (p.Glu519Ter) in exon 4/15 along with CNV study showing 1p/19q codeletion, gain of 1q, 7, losses in 9p arm and *KIAA1549-BRAF* fusion. Another case reported a somatic *RET* variant (p.Ala919Pro) along with a loss of 1p, gain of 1q and 8 with *KIAA1549-BRAF* fusion (Manoharan et al., 2021). Kurozumi et al. reported one fusion gene involving exon 21 of *ARHGEF2* and exon 10 of *NTRK1* fusion or exon 20 of *ARHGEF2* and exon10 of *NTRK1* (Kurozumi et al., 2019). *BRAF* V600E mutations and fusions of NTRK1/2/3 and TRIM33:RAF1 have also been reported in DLGNT, both of which are known to activate the MAPK/ERK pathway (Amatu et al., 2016; Deng et al., 2018). H3K27M-mutant lesions (Navarro et al., 2021) and *TP53* exon 5 (p.147V > I) germline variant (Tan et al., 2019) have also been reported in the literature (Table 11).

Table 11 Summary of the genetic/chromosomal aberrations involved in DLGNT.

S. no.	Gene/Chromosome	Variation	References
1.	1p/19q codeletion, loss of 9p, gain of 1q, 7, 8 and 17 Somatic *BCOR* truncating mutation *KIAA1549: BRAF* fusion Somatic *RET* truncating mutation MAP-kinase pathway gene alteration	*BCOR* c.1555G>T (p.G519Ter) *RET* c.2755G>C (p.A919P)	Manoharan et al. (2021)
2.	*ARHGEF2-NTRK1* fusion	Exon 21-exon 10/ Exon20-exon 10	Kurozumi et al. (2019)
3.	*BRAF*	c.1799T>A (p.*V600E*)	Manoharan et al. (2021)
4.	Fusions of *NTRK1/2/3* and *TRIM33:RAF1*		Amatu et al. (2016) and Deng et al. (2018)
5.	*TP53* Germline variant	c.439G>A (p.V147I), exon 5	Tan et al. (2019)

Treatment

There are no standardized therapy guidelines for DLGNT patients at this time. This is most likely due to the tumor's paucity in the CNS. The *MAPK/ERK* changes identified in this tumor might be used as therapeutic targets, implying that *BRAF* or *MEK* inhibitors could be used instead (Tan et al., 2019).

4. Conclusion

Neuronal and mixed glioneuronal tumors consisting of glial and neuronal components have shown to be benign, although they can also be aggressive. Because they are pathologically and radiographically complicated, detecting a specific genetic mutation may not be enough to accurately identify a tumor type. Some neuronal tumors have demonstrated mutation in MAPK pathway, specifically the alterations in one of the important proto-oncogenes, i.e., *BRAF* either as *BRAF* fusion or as a single nucleotide missense mutation with the incidences observed in gangliocytoma, ganglioglioma, DLGNT and MVNT, respectively. While some cancers, such as DNETs, neurocytoma, and RGNT, show mutations in the *FGFR-1* gene, located upstream of the MAPK pathway. The patients are now being best managed, with the role of adjuvant treatment in the form of chemotherapy and radiotherapy beyond surgery. Ongoing study is focused at trying to improve our understanding of the genetic changes that lead to tumor formation.

References

AbdelBari Mattar, M., Shebl, A.M., Toson, E.A., 2021. Atypical central neurocytoma: an investigation of prognostic factors. World Neurosurg. 146, e184–e193.

Abel, T.W., Baker, S.J., Fraser, M.M., et al., 2005. Lhermitte-Duclos disease: a report of 31 cases with immunohistochemical analysis of the PTEN/AKT/mTOR pathway. J. Neuropathol. Exp. Neurol. 64, 341–349.

Aghajan, Y., Malicki, D.M., Levy, M.L., Crawford, J.R., 2019. Atypical central neurocytoma with novel EWSR1-ATF1 fusion and MUTYH mutation detected by next-generation sequencing. BMJ Case Rep. 12.

Ahluwalia, R., Miles, L., Hayes, L., Scherer, A., 2020. Pediatric septal dysembryoplastic neuroepithelial tumor (sDNT): case-based update. Childs Nerv. Syst. 36, 1127–1130.

Ahmad, F., Hyvarinen, A., Pirinen, A., et al., 2021. Lentivirus vector mediated genetic manipulation of oncogenic pathways induces tumor formation in rabbit brain. Mol. Med. Rep. 23.

Alarifi, N., Del Bigio, M.R., Beiko, J., 2022. Adult gangliocytoma arising within the lateral ventricle: a case report and review of the literature. Surg. Neurol. Int. 13, 11.

Alkadhi, H., Keller, M., Brandner, S., Yonekawa, Y., Kollias, S.S., 2001. Neuroimaging of cerebellar liponeurocytoma. Case report. J. Neurosurg. 95, 324–331.

Amatu, A., Sartore-Bianchi, A., Siena, S., 2016. NTRK gene fusions as novel targets of cancer therapy across multiple tumour types. ESMO Open 1, e000023.

Anghileri, E., Eoli, M., Paterra, R., et al., 2012. FABP4 is a candidate marker of cerebellar liponeurocytomas. J. Neuro-Oncol. 108, 513–519.

Arbuiso, S., Roster, K., Gill, A., et al., 2021. Multinodular and vacuolating neuronal tumor: incidental diagnosis of a rare brain lesion. Cureus 13, e20674.

Baisden, B.L., Brat, D.J., Melhem, E.R., Rosenblum, M.K., King, A.P., Burger, P.C., 2001. Dysembryoplastic neuroepithelial tumor-like neoplasm of the septum pellucidum: a lesion often misdiagnosed as glioma: report of 10 cases. Am. J. Surg. Pathol. 25, 494–499.

Bale, T.A., Rosenblum, M.K., 2022. The 2021 WHO classification of tumors of the central nervous system: an update on pediatric low-grade gliomas and glioneuronal tumors. Brain Pathol., e13060.

Barba, C., Jacques, T., Kahane, P., et al., 2013. Epilepsy surgery in neurofibromatosis type 1. Epilepsy Res. 105, 384–395.

Blumcke, I., Wiestler, O.D., 2002. Gangliogliomas: an intriguing tumor entity associated with focal epilepsies. J. Neuropathol. Exp. Neurol. 61, 575–584.

Blumcke, I., Aronica, E., Urbach, H., Alexopoulos, A., Gonzalez-Martinez, J.A., 2014. A neuropathology-based approach to epilepsy surgery in brain tumors and proposal for a new terminology use for long-term epilepsy-associated brain tumors. Acta Neuropathol. 128, 39–54.

Bonney, P.A., Boettcher, L.B., Krysiak 3rd, R.S., Fung, K.M., Sughrue, M.E., 2015. Histology and molecular aspects of central neurocytoma. Neurosurg. Clin. N. Am. 26, 21–29.

Borekci, A., Kuru Bektasoglu, P., Ramazanoglu, A.F., Gurer, B., Celikoglu, E., 2018. Central liponeurocytoma as a clinical entity. Neurol. Neurochir. Pol. 52, 670–676.

Brat, D.J., Scheithauer, B.W., Eberhart, C.G., Burger, P.C., 2001. Extraventricular neurocytomas: pathologic features and clinical outcome. Am. J. Surg. Pathol. 25, 1252–1260.

Broggi, G., Tirro, E., Alzoubi, H., et al., 2022. Cerebellar liponeurocytoma: clinical, histopathological and molecular features of a series of three cases, including one recurrent tumor. Neuropathology 42 (3), 169–180.

Buffa, G.B., Chaves, H., Serra, M.M., Stefanoff, N.I., Gagliardo, A.S., Yanez, P., 2020. Multinodular and vacuolating neuronal tumor of the cerebrum (MVNT): a case series and review of the literature. J. Neuroradiol. 47, 216–220.

Cai, J., Li, W., Du, J., et al., 2018. Supratentorial intracerebral cerebellar liponeurocytoma: a case report and literature review. Medicine 97, e9556.

Carangelo, B., Arrigucci, U., Mariottini, A., et al., 2015. Papillary glioneuronal tumor: case report and review of literature. G. Chir. 36, 63–69.

Cases-Cunillera, S., van Loo, K.M.J., Pitsch, J., et al., 2021. Heterogeneity and excitability of BRAF V600E-induced tumors is determined by Akt/mTOR-signaling state and Trp53-loss. Neuro-Oncology.

Cerda-Nicolas, M., Lopez-Gines, C., Peydro-Olaya, A., Llombart-Bosch, A., 1993. Central neurocytoma: a cytogenetic case study. Cancer Genet. Cytogenet. 65, 173–174.

Chappe, C., Padovani, L., Scavarda, D., et al., 2013. Dysembryoplastic neuroepithelial tumors share with pleomorphic xanthoastrocytomas and gangliogliomas BRAF(V600E) mutation and expression. Brain Pathol. 23, 574–583.

Chassoux, F., Rodrigo, S., Mellerio, C., et al., 2012. Dysembryoplastic neuroepithelial tumors: an MRI-based scheme for epilepsy surgery. Neurology 79, 1699–1707.

Chatterjee, D., Garg, C., Singla, N., Radotra, B.D., 2018. Desmoplastic non-infantile astrocytoma/ganglioglioma: rare low-grade tumor with frequent BRAF V600E mutation. Hum. Pathol. 80, 186–191.

Chen, X.Y., Lu, F., Wang, Y.M., et al., 2014. PTEN inactivation by germline/somatic c.950_953delTACT mutation in patients with Lhermitte-Duclos disease manifesting progressive phenotypes. Clin. Genet. 86, 349–354.

Chiang, J.C.H., Harreld, J.H., Tanaka, R., et al., 2019. Septal dysembryoplastic neuroepithelial tumor: a comprehensive clinical, imaging, histopathologic, and molecular analysis. Neuro-Oncology 21, 800–808.

Chludzinski, E., Puff, C., Weber, J., Hewicker-Trautwein, M., 2021. Case report: primary diffuse leptomeningeal oligodendrogliomatosis in a young adult cat. Front. Vet. Sci. 8, 795126.

Choi, H., Park, S.H., Kim, D.G., Paek, S.H., 2011. Atypical extraventricular neurocytoma. J. Korean Neurosurg. Soc. 50, 381–384.

Choudhari, K.A., Kaliaperumal, C., Jain, A., et al., 2009. Central neurocytoma: a multi-disciplinary review. Br. J. Neurosurg. 23, 585–595.

Chretien, F., Djindjian, M., Caramelle, P., Ricolfi, F., Christov, C., 2007. A 42-year-old man with a densely vascular spinal mass. Brain Pathol. 17, 119–121.

Colby, S., Yehia, L., Niazi, F., et al., 2016. Exome sequencing reveals germline gain-of-function EGFR mutation in an adult with Lhermitte-Duclos disease. Cold Spring Harbor Mol. Case Stud. 2, a001230.

Cossu, G., Brouland, J.P., La Rosa, S., et al., 2019. Comprehensive evaluation of rare pituitary lesions: a single tertiary care pituitary center experience and review of the literature. Endocr. Pathol. 30, 219–236.

Dahiya, S., Haydon, D.H., Alvarado, D., Gurnett, C.A., Gutmann, D.H., Leonard, J.R., 2013. BRAF(V600E) mutation is a negative prognosticator in pediatric ganglioglioma. Acta Neuropathol. 125, 901–910.

Daumas-Duport, C., 1993. Dysembryoplastic neuroepithelial tumours. Brain Pathol. 3, 283–295.

Daumas-Duport, C., Scheithauer, B.W., Chodkiewicz, J.P., Laws Jr., E.R., Vedrenne, C., 1988. Dysembryoplastic neuroepithelial tumor: a surgically curable tumor of young patients with intractable partial seizures. Report of thirty-nine cases. Neurosurgery 23, 545–556.

Delfino-Machin, M., Madelaine, R., Busolin, G., et al., 2017. Sox10 contributes to the balance of fate choice in dorsal root ganglion progenitors. PLoS One 12, e0172947.

Demierre, B., Stichnoth, F.A., Hori, A., Spoerri, O., 1986. Intracerebral ganglioglioma. J. Neurosurg. 65, 177–182.

Deng, M.Y., Sill, M., Chiang, J., et al., 2018. Molecularly defined diffuse leptomeningeal glioneuronal tumor (DLGNT) comprises two subgroups with distinct clinical and genetic features. Acta Neuropathol. 136, 239–253.

Deng, M.Y., Sill, M., Sturm, D., et al., 2020. Diffuse glioneuronal tumour with oligodendroglioma-like features and nuclear clusters (DGONC)—a molecularly defined glioneuronal CNS tumour class displaying recurrent monosomy 14. Neuropathol. Appl. Neurobiol. 46, 422–430.

Dodgshun, A.J., SantaCruz, N., Hwang, J., et al., 2016. Disseminated glioneuronal tumors occurring in childhood: treatment outcomes and BRAF alterations including V600E mutation. J. Neuro-Oncol. 128, 293–302.

Donson, A.M., Kleinschmidt-DeMasters, B.K., Aisner, D.L., et al., 2014. Pediatric brainstem gangliogliomas show BRAF(V600E) mutation in a high percentage of cases. Brain Pathol. 24, 173–183.

Dougherty, M.J., Santi, M., Brose, M.S., et al., 2010. Activating mutations in BRAF characterize a spectrum of pediatric low-grade gliomas. Neuro-Oncology 12, 621–630.

Ellezam, B., Theeler, B.J., Luthra, R., Adesina, A.M., Aldape, K.D., Gilbert, M.R., 2012. Recurrent PIK3CA mutations in rosette-forming glioneuronal tumor. Acta Neuropathol. 123, 285–287.

Enam, S.A., Rosenblum, M.L., Ho, K.L., 1997. Neurocytoma in the cerebellum. Case report. J. Neurosurg. 87, 100–102.

Eye, P.G., Davidson, L., Malafronte, P.J., Cantrell, S., Theeler, B.J., 2017. PIK3CA mutation in a mixed dysembryoplastic neuroepithelial tumor and rosette forming glioneuronal tumor, a case report and literature review. J. Neurol. Sci. 373, 280–284.

Faria, C., Miguens, J., Antunes, J.L., et al., 2008. Genetic alterations in a papillary glioneuronal tumor. J. Neurosurg. Pediatr. 1, 99–102.

Ferreol, E., Sawaya, R., de Courten-Myers, G.M., 1989. Primary cerebral neuroblastoma (neurocytoma) in adults. J. Neuro-Oncol. 7, 121–128.

Friedrichs, N., Vorreuther, R., Fischer, H.P., Wiestler, O.D., Buettner, R., 2003. Neurocytoma arising in the pelvis. Virchows Arch. 443, 217–219.

Fuller, G.N., Scheithauer, B.W., 2007. The 2007 revised World Health Organization (WHO) classification of tumours of the central nervous system: newly codified entities. Brain Pathol. 17, 304–307.

Gaggiotti, C., Giammalva, G.R., Raimondi, M., et al., 2021. A rare diagnosis of an extraventricular neurocytoma. Surg. Neurol. Int. 12, 88.

Gardiman, M.P., Fassan, M., Orvieto, E., et al., 2010. Diffuse leptomeningeal glioneuronal tumors: a new entity? Brain Pathol. 20, 361–366.

Gelabert-Gonzalez, M., Serramito-Garcia, R., Arcos-Algaba, A., 2010. Desmoplastic infantile and non-infantile ganglioglioma. Review of the literature. Neurosurg. Rev. 34, 151–158.

Gembruch, O., Junker, A., Monninghoff, C., et al., 2018. Liponeurocytoma: systematic review of a rare entity. World Neurosurg. 120, 214–233.

Gessaga, E.C., 1980. Lhermitte-Duclos disease (diffuse hypertrophy of the cerebellum). Report of two cases. Neurosurg. Rev. 3, 151–158.

Gessi, M., Zur Muhlen, A., Hammes, J., Waha, A., Denkhaus, D., Pietsch, T., 2013. Genome-wide DNA copy number analysis of desmoplastic infantile astrocytomas and desmoplastic infantile gangliogliomas. J. Neuropathol. Exp. Neurol. 72, 807–815.

Gessi, M., Abdel Moneim, Y., Hammes, J., Waha, A., Pietsch, T., 2014a. FGFR1 N546K mutation in a case of papillary glioneuronal tumor (PGNT). Acta Neuropathol. 127, 935–936.

Gessi, M., Moneim, Y.A., Hammes, J., et al., 2014b. FGFR1 mutations in rosette-forming glioneuronal tumors of the fourth ventricle. J. Neuropathol. Exp. Neurol. 73, 580–584.

Ghosal, N., Dadlani, R., Murthy, G., Hegde, A.S., 2010. Primary malignant ganglioglioma of the dorsolumbar spine (D11-L1). J. Clin. Neurosci. 17, 1597–1599.

Giulioni, M., Galassi, E., Zucchelli, M., Volpi, L., 2005. Seizure outcome of lesionectomy in glioneuronal tumors associated with epilepsy in children. J. Neurosurg. 102, 288–293.

Giulioni, M., Gardella, E., Rubboli, G., et al., 2006. Lesionectomy in epileptogenic gangliogliomas: seizure outcome and surgical results. J. Clin. Neurosci. 13, 529–535.

Goethe, E.A., Youssef, M., Patel, A.J., Jalali, A., Goodman, J.C., Mandel, J.J., 2019. Recurrent papillary glioneuronal tumor. World Neurosurg. 128, 127–130.

Greer, A., Foreman, N.K., Donson, A., Davies, K.D., Kleinschmidt-DeMasters, B.K., 2017. Desmoplastic infantile astrocytoma/ganglioglioma with rare BRAF V600D mutation. Pediatr. Blood Cancer 64.

Gupte, A., Marupudi, N.I., Mody, S., Kupsky, W., Gorsi, H.S., 2021. BCR-NTRK2 fusion in a pediatric patient with spinal gangliocytoma. Pediatr. Blood Cancer 68, e29029.

Hakim, R., Loeffler, J.S., Anthony, D.C., Black, P.M., 1997. Gangliogliomas in adults. Cancer 79, 127–131.

Hartmann, W., Digon-Sontgerath, B., Koch, A., et al., 2006. Phosphatidylinositol 3′-kinase/AKT signaling is activated in medulloblastoma cell proliferation and is associated with reduced expression of PTEN. Clin. Cancer Res. 12, 3019–3027.

Hassoun, J., Gambarelli, D., Grisoli, F., et al., 1982. Central neurocytoma. An electron-microscopic study of two cases. Acta Neuropathol. 56, 151–156.

Hassoun, J., Soylemezoglu, F., Gambarelli, D., Figarella-Branger, D., von Ammon, K., Kleihues, P., 1993. Central neurocytoma: a synopsis of clinical and histological features. Brain Pathol. 3, 297–306.

Hirono, S., Gao, Y., Matsutani, T., Ikeda, J.I., Yokoo, H., Iwadate, Y., 2021. Metabolic, immunohisto-chemical, and genetic profiling of a cerebellar liponeurocytoma with spinal dissemination: a case report and review of the literature. Brain Tumor Pathol. 38, 257–262.

Hirose, T., Scheithauer, B.W., Lopes, M.B., Gerber, H.A., Altermatt, H.J., VandenBerg, S.R., 1997. Ganglioglioma: an ultrastructural and immunohistochemical study. Cancer 79, 989–1003.

Horstmann, S., Perry, A., Reifenberger, G., et al., 2004. Genetic and expression profiles of cerebellar lipo-neurocytomas. Brain Pathol. 14, 281–289.

Hou, Y., Pinheiro, J., Sahm, F., et al., 2019. Papillary glioneuronal tumor (PGNT) exhibits a characteristic methylation profile and fusions involving PRKCA. Acta Neuropathol. 137, 837–846.

Hu, J.R., Li, J., Lv, G.H., Deng, Y.W., Zou, M.X., 2015. Extraventricular neurocytoma mimicking bone tumor in thoracic spinal column. Spine J. 15, e65–e66.

Huang, C., Li, H., Chen, M., Si, Y., Lei, D., 2014. Factors associated with preoperative and postoperative epileptic seizure in patients with cerebral ganglioglioma. Pak. J. Med. Sci. 30, 245–249.

Hummel, T.R., Miles, L., Mangano, F.T., Jones, B.V., Geller, J.I., 2012. Clinical heterogeneity of desmoplastic infantile ganglioglioma: a case series and literature review. J. Pediatr. Hematol. Oncol. 34, e232–e236.

Huse, J.T., Edgar, M., Halliday, J., Mikolaenko, I., Lavi, E., Rosenblum, M.K., 2013. Multinodular and vacuolating neuronal tumors of the cerebrum: 10 cases of a distinctive seizure-associated lesion. Brain Pathol. 23, 515–524.

Jacob, J.T., Cohen-Gadol, A.A., Scheithauer, B.W., Krauss, W.E., 2005. Intramedullary spinal cord gangliocytoma: case report and a review of the literature. Neurosurg. Rev. 28, 326–329.

Jay, V., Edwards, V., Hoving, E., et al., 1999. Central neurocytoma: morphological, flow cytometric, poly-merase chain reaction, fluorescence in situ hybridization, and karyotypic analyses. Case report. J. Neu-rosurg. 90, 348–354.

Jenkinson, M.D., Bosma, J.J., Du Plessis, D., et al., 2003. Cerebellar liponeurocytoma with an unusually aggressive clinical course: case report. Neurosurgery 53, 1425–1427 (discussion 1428).

Jiang, C., Lu, W.X., Yan, G.Z., et al., 2020. Bilateral dysplastic gangliocytoma with concurrent polyostotic fibrous dysplasia: a case report and literature review. World Neurosurg. 141, 421–424.

Kalyan-Raman, U.P., Olivero, W.C., 1987. Ganglioglioma: a correlative clinicopathological and radiolog-ical study of ten surgically treated cases with follow-up. Neurosurgery 20, 428–433.

Kane, A.J., Sughrue, M.E., Rutkowski, M.J., Tihan, T., Parsa, A.T., 2011. The molecular pathology of central neurocytomas. J. Clin. Neurosci. 18, 1–6.

Kane, A.J., Sughrue, M.E., Rutkowski, M.J., et al., 2012. Atypia predicting prognosis for intracranial extraventricular neurocytomas. J. Neurosurg. 116, 349–354.

Kang, D.H., Lee, C.H., Hwang, S.H., Park, I.S., Han, J.W., Jung, J.M., 2007. Anaplastic ganglioglioma in a middle-aged woman: a case report with a review of the literature. J. Korean Med. Sci. 22 (Suppl), S139–S144.

Karabagli, P., Karabagli, H., Kose, D., Kocak, N., Etus, V., Koksal, Y., 2014. Desmoplastic non-infantile astrocytic tumor with BRAF V600E mutation. Brain Tumor Pathol. 31, 282–288.

Kawaji, H., Saito, O., Amano, S., Kasahara, M., Baba, S., Namba, H., 2014. Extraventricular neurocytoma of the sellar region with spinal dissemination. Brain Tumor Pathol. 31, 51–56.

Khatri, D., Bhaisora, K.S., Das, K.K., Behari, S., Pal, L., 2018. Cerebellar liponeurocytoma: the dilemma of multifocality. World Neurosurg. 120, 131–137.

Killela, P.J., Reitman, Z.J., Jiao, Y., et al., 2013. TERT promoter mutations occur frequently in gliomas and a subset of tumors derived from cells with low rates of self-renewal. Proc. Natl. Acad. Sci. U. S. A. 110, 6021–6026.

Kim, C.Y., Kim, D.G., Joo, J.D., Kim, Y.H., 2015. Clinical outcome and quality of life after treatment of patients with central neurocytoma. Neurosurg. Clin. N. Am. 26, 83–90.

Kleinschmidt-DeMasters, B.K., Chiang, J., Donson, A.M., Borges, T., Gilani, A., 2022. Myxoid glioneuronal tumor, PDGFRA p.K385L-mutant, arising in midbrain tectum with multifocal CSF dis-semination. Brain Pathol. 32, e13008.

Koeller, K.K., Henry, J.M., 2001. From the archives of the AFIP: superficial gliomas: radiologic-pathologic correlation. Armed Forces Institute of Pathology. Radiographics 21, 1533–1556.

Koelsche, C., Wohrer, A., Jeibmann, A., et al., 2013. Mutant BRAF V600E protein in ganglioglioma is predominantly expressed by neuronal tumor cells. Acta Neuropathol. 125, 891–900.

Koelsche, C., Sahm, F., Paulus, W., et al., 2014. BRAF V600E expression and distribution in desmoplastic infantile astrocytoma/ganglioglioma. Neuropathol. Appl. Neurobiol. 40, 337–344.

Koh, H.Y., Kim, S.H., Jang, J., et al., 2018. BRAF somatic mutation contributes to intrinsic epileptogenicity in pediatric brain tumors. Nat. Med. 24, 1662–1668.

Komori, T., Scheithauer, B.W., Anthony, D.C., et al., 1998. Papillary glioneuronal tumor: a new variant of mixed neuronal-glial neoplasm. Am. J. Surg. Pathol. 22, 1171–1183.

Komori, T., Scheithauer, B.W., Hirose, T., 2002. A rosette-forming glioneuronal tumor of the fourth ventricle: infratentorial form of dysembryoplastic neuroepithelial tumor? Am. J. Surg. Pathol. 26, 582–591.

Korshunov, A., Sycheva, R., Golanov, A., 2007. Recurrent cytogenetic aberrations in central neurocytomas and their biological relevance. Acta Neuropathol. 113, 303–312.

Kros, J.M., Delwel, E.J., de Jong, T.H., et al., 2002. Desmoplastic infantile astrocytoma and ganglioglioma: a search for genomic characteristics. Acta Neuropathol. 104, 144–148.

Kulkantrakorn, K., Awwad, E.E., Levy, B., et al., 1997. MRI in Lhermitte-Duclos disease. Neurology 48, 725–731.

Kurozumi, K., Nakano, Y., Ishida, J., et al., 2019. High-grade glioneuronal tumor with an ARHGEF2-NTRK1 fusion gene. Brain Tumor Pathol. 36, 121–128.

Kuten, J., Kaidar-Person, O., Vlodavsky, E., et al., 2012. Anaplastic ganglioglioma in the spinal cord: case report and literature review. Pediatr. Neurosurg. 48, 245–248.

Lakhani, D.A., Mankad, K., Chhabda, S., et al., 2020. Diffuse leptomeningeal glioneuronal tumor of childhood. Am. J. Neuroradiol. 41, 2155–2159.

Lang, F.F., Epstein, F.J., Ransohoff, J., et al., 1993. Central nervous system gangliogliomas. Part 2: clinical outcome. J. Neurosurg. 79, 867–873.

Lee, S.J., Bui, T.T., Chen, C.H., et al., 2016. Central neurocytoma: a review of clinical management and histopathologic features. Brain Tumor Res. Treat. 4, 49–57.

Lok, C., Viseux, V., Avril, M.F., et al., 2005. Brain magnetic resonance imaging in patients with Cowden syndrome. Medicine 84, 129–136.

Louis, D.N., Perry, A., Reifenberger, G., et al., 2016. The 2016 World Health Organization classification of tumors of the central nervous system: a summary. Acta Neuropathol. 131, 803–820.

Lucas, C.G., Gupta, R., Doo, P., et al., 2020a. Comprehensive analysis of diverse low-grade neuroepithelial tumors with FGFR1 alterations reveals a distinct molecular signature of rosette-forming glioneuronal tumor. Acta Neuropathol. Commun. 8, 151.

Lucas, C.G., Villanueva-Meyer, J.E., Whipple, N., et al., 2020b. Myxoid glioneuronal tumor, PDGFRA p. K385-mutant: clinical, radiologic, and histopathologic features. Brain Pathol. 30, 479–494.

Mallick, S., Roy, S., Das, S., et al., 2015. Role of adjuvant radiation in the management of central neurocytoma: experience from a tertiary cancer care center of India. Indian J. Cancer 52, 590–597.

Mallick, S., Benson, R., Rath, G.K., 2018. Patterns of care and survival outcomes in patients with an extraventricular neurocytoma: an individual patient data analysis of 201 cases. Neurol. India 66, 362–367.

Manoharan, N., Ajuyah, P., Senapati, A., et al., 2021. Diffuse leptomeningeal glioneuronal tumour (DLGNT) in children: the emerging role of genomic analysis. Acta Neuropathol. Commun. 9, 147.

Masmoudi, A., Chermi, Z.M., Marrekchi, S., et al., 2011. Cowden syndrome. J. Dermatol. Case Rep. 5, 8–13.

Matsumoto, K., Tamiya, T., Ono, Y., Furuta, T., Asari, S., Ohmoto, T., 1999. Cerebral gangliogliomas: clinical characteristics, CT and MRI. Acta Neurochir. 141, 135–141.

Mhatre, R., Bopanna, K.M., Ganigi, P., Anita, M., 2020. Rare occurrence of gangliocytoma in the medulla oblongata. Childs Nerv. Syst. 36, 447–450.

Mistry, M., Zhukova, N., Merico, D., et al., 2015. BRAF mutation and CDKN2A deletion define a clinically distinct subgroup of childhood secondary high-grade glioma. J. Clin. Oncol. 33, 1015–1022.

Mpairamidis, E., Alexiou, G.A., Stefanaki, K., Sfakianos, G., Prodromou, N., 2009. Extraventricular neurocytoma in a child: case report and review of the literature. J. Child Neurol. 24, 491–494.

Nagaishi, M., Nobusawa, S., Matsumura, N., et al., 2016. SLC44A1-PRKCA fusion in papillary and rosette-forming glioneuronal tumors. J. Clin. Neurosci. 23, 73–75.

Nair, A.R., Gopalakrishnan, C.V., Kapilamoorthy, T.R., Radhakrishnan, N., 2014. Rosette forming glioneuronal tumor of the fourth ventricle in squash cytology smear. J. Cytol. 31, 215–217.

Navarro, R.E., Golub, D., Hill, T., et al., 2021. Pediatric midline H3K27M-mutant tumor with disseminated leptomeningeal disease and glioneuronal features: case report and literature review. Childs Nerv. Syst. 37, 2347–2356.

Niemeyer, B., Marchiori, E., 2018. Anaplastic ganglioglioma involving the entire length of the spinal cord. Eur. Neurol. 79, 125.

Nishimoto, T., Kaya, B., 2012. Cerebellar liponeurocytoma. Arch. Pathol. Lab. Med. 136, 965–969.

Nishio, S., Takeshita, I., Fukui, M., 1990. Primary cerebral ganglioneurocytoma in an adult. Cancer 66, 358–362.

Nishio, S., Takeshita, I., Kaneko, Y., Fukui, M., 1992. Cerebral neurocytoma. A new subset of benign neuronal tumors of the cerebrum. Cancer 70, 529–537.

Nowak, D.A., Trost, H.A., 2002. Lhermitte-Duclos disease (dysplastic cerebellar gangliocytoma): a malformation, hamartoma or neoplasm? Acta Neurol. Scand. 105, 137–145.

Nunes, R.H., Hsu, C.C., da Rocha, A.J., et al., 2017. Multinodular and vacuolating neuronal tumor of the cerebrum: a new "leave me alone" lesion with a characteristic imaging pattern. Am. J. Neuroradiol. 38, 1899–1904.

Pages, M., Lacroix, L., Tauziede-Espariat, A., et al., 2015. Papillary glioneuronal tumors: histological and molecular characteristics and diagnostic value of SLC44A1-PRKCA fusion. Acta Neuropathol. Commun. 3, 85.

Pandita, A., Balasubramaniam, A., Perrin, R., Shannon, P., Guha, A., 2007. Malignant and benign ganglioglioma: a pathological and molecular study. Neuro-Oncology 9, 124–134.

Pekmezci, M., Stevers, M., Phillips, J.J., et al., 2018. Multinodular and vacuolating neuronal tumor of the cerebrum is a clonal neoplasm defined by genetic alterations that activate the MAP kinase signaling pathway. Acta Neuropathol. 135, 485–488.

Pickles, J.C., Mankad, K., Aizpurua, M., et al., 2021. A case series of diffuse glioneuronal tumours with oligodendroglioma-like features and nuclear clusters (DGONC). Neuropathol. Appl. Neurobiol. 47, 464–467.

Prabowo, A.S., Iyer, A.M., Veersema, T.J., et al., 2014. BRAF V600E mutation is associated with mTOR signaling activation in glioneuronal tumors. Brain Pathol. 24, 52–66.

Prabowo, A.S., van Thuijl, H.F., Scheinin, I., et al., 2015. Landscape of chromosomal copy number aberrations in gangliogliomas and dysembryoplastic neuroepithelial tumours. Neuropathol. Appl. Neurobiol. 41, 743–755.

Rak, B., Szlufik, S., Grajkowska, W., et al., 2013. Upregulation of mitogen-activated protein kinase in ganglioglioma. Folia Neuropathol. 51, 283–289.

Rivera, B., Gayden, T., Carrot-Zhang, J., et al., 2016. Germline and somatic FGFR1 abnormalities in dysembryoplastic neuroepithelial tumors. Acta Neuropathol. 131, 847–863.

Rodriguez, F.J., Mota, R.A., Scheithauer, B.W., et al., 2009. Interphase cytogenetics for 1p19q and t(1;19) (q10;p10) may distinguish prognostically relevant subgroups in extraventricular neurocytoma. Brain Pathol. 19, 623–629.

Rodriguez, F.J., Schniederjan, M.J., Nicolaides, T., Tihan, T., Burger, P.C., Perry, A., 2015. High rate of concurrent BRAF-KIAA1549 gene fusion and 1p deletion in disseminated oligodendroglioma-like leptomeningeal neoplasms (DOLN). Acta Neuropathol. 129, 609–610.

Roessmann, U., Wongmongkolrit, T., 1984. Dysplastic gangliocytoma of cerebellum in a newborn. Case report. J. Neurosurg. 60, 845–847.

Rush, S., Foreman, N., Liu, A., 2013. Brainstem ganglioglioma successfully treated with vemurafenib. J. Clin. Oncol. 31, e159–e160.

Saez-Alegre, M., Saceda Gutierrez, J.M., Utrilla Contreras, C., Aracil Santos, F.J., Garcia-Feijoo, P., Carceller, B.F., 2021. Diffuse leptomeningeal glioneuronal tumour: where to biopsy? Case report and literature review. Childs Nerv. Syst. 37, 2405–2408.

Sander, C., Wallenborn, M., Brandt, V.P., et al., 2019. Central neurocytoma: SNP array analyses, subtel FISH, and review of the literature. Pathol. Res. Pract. 215, 152397.

Savardekar, A., Salunke, P., Ahuja, C.K., Rane, S., Singla, N., 2012. Unusual presentation in adult medulloblastomas: imaging features mimicking cerebellar dysplastic gangliocytoma (Lhermitte-Duclos disease). Neurol. India 60, 555–557.

Schmidt, M.H., Gottfried, O.N., von Koch, C.S., Chang, S.M., McDermott, M.W., 2004. Central neurocytoma: a review. J. Neuro-Oncol. 66, 377–384.

Schneider, C., Vosbeck, J., Grotzer, M.A., Boltshauser, E., Kothbauer, K.F., 2012. Anaplastic ganglioglioma: a very rare intramedullary spinal cord tumor. Pediatr. Neurosurg. 48, 42–47.

Selvanathan, S.K., Hammouche, S., Salminen, H.J., Jenkinson, M.D., 2011. Outcome and prognostic features in anaplastic ganglioglioma: analysis of cases from the SEER database. J. Neuro-Oncol. 105, 539–545.

Taruscio, D., Danesi, R., Montaldi, A., Cerasoli, S., Cenacchi, G., Giangaspero, F., 1997. Nonrandom gain of chromosome 7 in central neurocytoma: a chromosomal analysis and fluorescence in situ hybridization study. Virchows Arch. 430, 47–51.

Stupp, R., Hegi, M.E., 2007. Targeting brain-tumor stem cells. Nat. Biotechnol. 25, 193–194.

Sim, F.J., Keyoung, H.M., Goldman, J.E., et al., 2006. Neurocytoma is a tumor of adult neuronal progenitor cells. J. Neurosci. 26, 12544–12555.

Yu, J.H., Yang, L.H., Lin, X.Y., Dai, S.D., Qiu, X.S., Wang, E.H., 2015. Neurocytoma arising from a mature ovary teratoma: a case report. Diagn. Pathol. 10, 171.

Tucker, A., Boon-Unge, K., McLaughlin, N., et al., 2017. Cerebellar liponeurocytoma: relevant clinical cytogenetic findings. J. Pathol. Transl. Med. 51, 335–340.

Zhou, X.P., Marsh, D.J., Morrison, C.D., et al., 2003. Germline inactivation of PTEN and dysregulation of the phosphoinositol-3-kinase/Akt pathway cause human Lhermitte-Duclos disease in adults. Am. J. Hum. Genet. 73, 1191–1198.

Wolf, H.K., Muller, M.B., Spanle, M., Zentner, J., Schramm, J., Wiestler, O.D., 1994. Ganglioglioma: a detailed histopathological and immunohistochemical analysis of 61 cases. Acta Neuropathol. 88, 166–173.

Takahashi, M., Kondo, T., Morichika, M., et al., 2016. Autopsy case of undiagnosed gangliocytoma in the medulla oblongata complicated with cerebral palsy. Legal Med. 19, 119–121.

Wakao, N., Imagama, S., 2012. Intramedullary gangliocytoma with calcification and multiple intramedullary cysts. Neuroradiology 54, 893–895.

Tao, T., Shi, H., Durbin, A.D., Look, A.T., 2021. Targeting ganglioneuromas with mTOR inhibitors. Mol. Cell. Oncol. 8, 1856621.

Wang, H., Krishnan, C., Charville, G.W., 2019. INSM1 expression in peripheral neuroblastic tumors and other embryonal neoplasms. Pediatr. Dev. Pathol. 22, 440–448.

Zhang, D., Henning, T.D., Zou, L.G., et al., 2008. Intracranial ganglioglioma: clinicopathological and MRI findings in 16 patients. Clin. Radiol. 63, 80–91.

Tandon, V., Bansal, S., Chandra, P.S., et al., 2016. Ganglioglioma: single-institutional experience of 24 cases with review of literature. Asian J. Neurosurg. 11, 407–411.

Yano, H., Saigoh, C., Nakayama, N., et al., 2013. Mixed neuronal-glial tumor in the temporal lobe of an infant: a case report. Diagn. Pathol. 8, 164.

Zanello, M., Pages, M., Tauziede-Espariat, A., et al., 2016. Clinical, imaging, histopathological and molecular characterization of anaplastic ganglioglioma. J. Neuropathol. Exp. Neurol. 75, 971–980.

Vlachos, N., Lampros, M.G., Zigouris, A., Voulgaris, S., Alexiou, G.A., 2021. Anaplastic gangliogliomas of the spinal cord: a scoping review of the literature. Neurosurg. Rev. 55 (6), 1377–1392.

Varlet, P., Soni, D., Miquel, C., et al., 2004. New variants of malignant glioneuronal tumors: a clinicopathological study of 40 cases. Neurosurgery 55, 1377–1391 (discussion 1391-1372).

Taratuto, A.L., Monges, J., Lylyk, P., Leiguarda, R., 1984. Superficial cerebral astrocytoma attached to dura. Report of six cases in infants. Cancer 54, 2505–2512.

Zhang, J., Wu, G., Miller, C.P., et al., 2013. Whole-genome sequencing identifies genetic alterations in pediatric low-grade gliomas. Nat. Genet. 45, 602–612.

Xu, J., Yang, Y., Liu, Y., et al., 2012. Rosette-forming glioneuronal tumor in the pineal gland and the third ventricle: a case with radiological and clinical implications. Quant. Imaging Med. Surg. 2, 227–231.

Wilson, C.P., Chakraborty, A.R., Pelargos, P.E., et al., 2020. Rosette-forming glioneuronal tumor: an illustrative case and a systematic review. Neuro-Oncol. Adv. 2, vdaa116.

Thommen, F., Hewer, E., Schafer, S.C., Vassella, E., Kappeler, A., Vajtai, I., 2013. Rosette-forming glioneuronal tumor of the cerebellum in statu nascendi: an incidentally detected diminutive example indicates derivation from the internal granule cell layer. Clin. Neuropathol. 32, 370–376.

Zehir, A., Benayed, R., Shah, R.H., et al., 2017. Mutational landscape of metastatic cancer revealed from prospective clinical sequencing of 10,000 patients. Nat. Med. 23, 703–713.

Sievers, P., Appay, R., Schrimpf, D., et al., 2019. Rosette-forming glioneuronal tumors share a distinct DNA methylation profile and mutations in FGFR1, with recurrent co-mutation of PIK3CA and NF1. Acta Neuropathol. 138, 497–504.

Yuan, J., Sharma, N., Choudhri, H., Figueroa, R., Sharma, S., 2011. Intraventricular dysembryoplastic neuroepithelial tumor in a pediatric patient: is it the most common extracortical location for DNT? Childs Nerv. Syst. 27, 485–490.

Sontowska, I., Matyja, E., Malejczyk, J., Grajkowska, W., 2017. Dysembryoplastic neuroepithelial tumour: insight into the pathology and pathogenesis. Folia Neuropathol. 55, 1–13.

Thom, M., Toma, A., An, S., et al., 2011. One hundred and one dysembryoplastic neuroepithelial tumors: an adult epilepsy series with immunohistochemical, molecular genetic, and clinical correlations and a review of the literature. J. Neuropathol. Exp. Neurol. 70, 859–878.

Slegers, R.J., Blumcke, I., 2020. Low-grade developmental and epilepsy associated brain tumors: a critical update 2020. Acta Neuropathol. Commun. 8, 27.

Stone, T.J., Keeley, A., Virasami, A., et al., 2018. Comprehensive molecular characterisation of epilepsy-associated glioneuronal tumours. Acta Neuropathol. 135, 115–129.

Suh, Y.L., 2015. Dysembryoplastic neuroepithelial tumors. J. Pathol. Transl. Med. 49, 438–449.

Solomon, D.A., Korshunov, A., Sill, M., et al., 2018. Myxoid glioneuronal tumor of the septum pellucidum and lateral ventricle is defined by a recurrent PDGFRA p.K385 mutation and DNT-like methylation profile. Acta Neuropathol. 136, 339–343.

Tiwari, S., Yadav, T., Pamnani, J., et al., 2020. Diffuse leptomeningeal glioneuronal tumor: a unique leptomeningeal tumor entity. World Neurosurg. 135, 297–300.

Tan, G.I.L., Merchant, K., Tan, E.E.K., et al., 2019. A germline variant of TP53 in paediatric diffuse leptomeningeal glioneuronal tumour. Childs Nerv. Syst. 35, 1021–1027.

CHAPTER SEVENTEEN

Therapeutic potential of melatonin in glioblastoma: Current knowledge and future prospects

Nithar Ranjan Madhu[a], Bhanumati Sarkar[b], Paramita Biswas[c], Shubhadeep Roychoudhury[d], Biplab Kumar Behera[e], and Chandan Kumar Acharya[f]

[a]Department of Zoology, Acharya Prafulla Chandra College, New Barrackpore, West Bengal, India
[b]Department of Botany, Acharya Prafulla Chandra College, New Barrackpore, West Bengal, India
[c]Department of Agronomy, Faculty of Agriculture, Uttar Banga Krishi Viswavidyalaya, Cooch Behar, West Bengal, India
[d]Department of Life Science and Bioinformatics, Assam University, Silchar, India
[e]Department of Zoology, Siliguri College, Siliguri, West Bengal, India
[f]Department of Botany, Bajkul Milani Mahavidyalaya, Kismat Bajkul, West Bengal, India

1. Introduction

The difficulties of physically removing a whole tumor and treating persons with gliomas (glioblastoma multiforme—GBM) are very challenging since most GBMs recur after receiving chemotherapy and radiation treatment. Several researchers have focused on creating unique cotherapeutic procedures, preferably based on natural resources, to generate anticancer compounds that may be used in clinical studies. Antioxidant and anticancer properties of melatonin are being shown in several investigations. In addition, GBM therapy with melatonin may overcome multidrug resistance (Moretti et al., 2020; Qazi et al., 2017).

Melatonin (MLT), a hormone, has various effects on cancer cells' apoptotic response. Caspases are cysteine proteases that target aspartates and are members of the IL-1-converting enzyme superfamily. These enzymes are important regulators of the efficacy of apoptotic signals in the body. Caspase-3 expression is raised more quickly, while MLT therapy inhibits activation and overexpression of this enzyme. MLT therapy boosts the levels of p53, a tumor suppressor protein in cancer cells, which enhances apoptosis.

During the night, when the light/dark cycle is regular, humans and other animals release MLT, a pineal gland hormone that regulates circadian rhythms and is produced in large quantities (Madhu and Manna, 2011, 2021; Madhu, 2018). The pineal gland produces MLT throughout the night, and an endogenous clock controls its production in the hypothalamus' suprachiasmatic nucleus (SCN), which also governs the synthesis of melatonin (Claustrat et al., 2005; Madhu and Manna, 2009, 2010; Madhu et al., 2010).

Biomarkers in Cancer Detection and Monitoring of Therapeutics
https://doi.org/10.1016/B978-0-323-95114-2.00002-9

MLT's hydrophilic and lipophilic properties enable it to penetrate almost all tissues and bodily fluids without requiring a specialized receptor to do so. As a result, the hormone MLT stimulates various biological activities, which does so via signaling pathways that are both receptor-dependent and receptor-independent. As a natural chronobiotic medicine, MLT, for example, has immune-boosting properties that make it a good choice. Furthermore, for a long time, it has been recognized that methylated MLT has antioxidant and antiinflammatory characteristics and directly impacts metabolism, sleep, and reproduction (Sánchez-López et al., 2018). In healthy cells, MLT functions as an antioxidant by inhibiting the production of free radicals, yet, in cancer cells, it has a paradoxical pro-oxidant effect, resulting in cell death. Consequently, MLT may delay cancer development by increasing the levels of oxidative stress in tumor cells (Fan et al., 2015; Moretti et al., 2020).

1.1 Gliomas: Types and cause

Gliomas are common primary tumors that develop in the brain and spinal cord and may be either benign or malignant in nature. Gliomas are tumors that develop in the gluey supporting cells (glial cells) and surrounding nerve cells. Glial cells in the brain can grow into tumors, and three types of glial cells may do so. Analysis of the kind of glial cell present in the tumor and its genetic traits allows for predicting how cancer will behave over time and which treatments are most likely to be successful. There are many different forms of glioma—(i) astrocytomas, which include astrocytoma, anaplastic astrocytoma, and glioblastoma, astrocytes, which are star-shaped cells in the brain, are malignancies of the brain. The cerebrum, the biggest portion of the brain in adults, is where this cancer often begins, (ii) epidermomas, including anaplastic ependymomas, myxopapillary ependymomas, and subependymomas, develop on the skin and do not pose a threat to the individual's health, (iii) oligodendrogliomas, which include oligodendroglioma, anaplastic oligodendroglioma, and anaplastic oligoastrocytoma, are malignant tumors of the glial cells of the brain. The capacity of glioblastoma tumors to sustain themselves with blood contributes to their rapid development. They must first enter normal brain tissue, which they do very easily. In primary GBM, males are more likely than females to acquire them.

On the other hand, females have a greater incidence of secondary GBM (Moretti et al., 2020). Grade IV tumors, glioblastomas develop quickly and aggressively. In order to expand swiftly, they must produce new blood vessels to provide themselves with more blood. However, it normally does not spread to other parts of the body. A subpopulation of glioma stem-like cells (GSCs) has been shown to promote the proliferation and self-renewal of GBM (Dirks, 2010). Studies have shown that these GSCs play a significant role in promoting tumor formation and the reinvigoration of the illness (Chen et al., 2012).

It is estimated that almost half of all primary brain tumors are astrocytomas, the most common intra-axial brain tumors. Glial cell tumors develop from astrocytes, cells of the connective tissue. The cerebrum (the large outer portion of the brain) is the most common location, although they may also be found in the cerebellum (located at the base of the brain).

Astrocytomas may affect both children and adults. The most dangerous kind of high-grade astrocytoma is glioblastoma multiforme. Glioblastoma's signs and symptoms are typically the same as those of other types of gliomas. In children, low-grade cerebellar gliomas are common, such as pilocytic astrocytomas. However, adults are more prone than children to acquire astrocytomas, which are benign brain tumors. Occasionally, tumors grow in the brain stem called diffuse infiltrating brainstem gliomas (DIBGs). As a result of their remote location in the brain, where they interfere with the delicate and complex functions this area governs, surgical removal is often impractical. Because they are more frequent in school-aged children, primary brain tumors kill a disproportionately large number of children and adolescents.

Ependymomas are made up of cells from the lining of the ventricles of the spinal cord. Ependymomas, which are rare, account for just 2%–3% of primary brain tumors. These tumors affect between 8% and 10% of children under the age of 10, and they are more prevalent in those under the age of 10. The cerebellum is the most prevalent location of tumor growth in ependymomas. Because of the cerebral spinal fluid flow, this posture raises the risk of increased intracranial pressure (obstructive hydrocephalus). Furthermore, since spinal fluid travels via the spinal cord, these tumors can spread to other parts of the brain or spinal cord (drop-metastases). Tumors containing various glial cell types are "mixed gliomas" or "oligo-astrocytomas." Although their designation as a distinct tumor type is controversial, genetic testing of tumor samples may resolve this issue. Adult men are more likely to develop these tumors found in the cerebrum. A tumor developed from oligodendrocytes, the brain's supporting tissue cells, is known as an oligodendroglioma. Oligodendrogliomas account for roughly 2%–4% of all primary brain tumors. Males are more likely than females to develop them while they are young or middle-aged. Seizures are one of the most common adverse effects of malignant tumors, affecting 50%–80% of patients. Patients with oligodendrogliomas, in general, have a better prognosis than those with other forms of tumors. Optic pathways in the optic nerves and the chiasm, where visual information is sent from the eyes to the brain, are often invaded by low-grade gliomas known as optic pathway gliomas. Patients with neurofibromatosis are more likely to get them. Aside from the visual loss, optic nerve gliomas may cause hormonal imbalances since they are often located around the base of the brain. Gliomas that affect hormone function are hypothalamic gliomas.

DNA alterations are responsible for developing brain tumors and spinal cord tumors such as gliomas. Genetic mutations, or alterations, to the DNA in our genes may cause cells to proliferate in an uncontrolled manner. It is possible to pass on genetic modifications of DNA, which is the cause of glioma.

2. Melatonin's structure, physiology, and functions

MLT is a neurohormone composed of L-tryptophan derivatives that are produced primarily in the brain (cerebral cortex, cerebellum, striate body, and raphe nuclei), spinal cord, lens, retina, skin, cochlea, gastrointestinal tracts (small and large intestine), bones, lymphocytes, platelets, mouse bone marrow, ovaries, and testicles. When it comes to the neuroendocrine system, MLT is a hormone that plays an essential role in energy metabolism. Its synthesis is stimulated by darkness and decreased by light (Khodadadi, 2020). MLT is an endogenous indoleamine with a wide variety of properties and functions (Acuña Castroviejo et al., 2014; Bubenik and Konturek, 2011). MLT can be transported into almost all tissues and fluids because of its lipophilic and hydrophilic characteristics, making it receptor independent. Signaling pathways for MLT are dependent on the *tor* and its receptor. In the family of transmembrane "G" protein-coupled transmembrane receptors, the MLT receptors (MT1), MT2 and MT3 are found (MT3) (Dubocovich et al., 2003; Slominski et al., 2012; Witt-Enderby et al., 2003). It has been shown that breast cancer cells produce higher levels of MT1 than normal cells, which suggests that cancer cells are more responsive to MLT. However, even if MLT receptors are present, the majority of MLT's actions are mediated by non-receptor-based processes, such as antiinflammatory and antioxidant activities, as well as mitochondrial activity (Tan et al., 2002; Cutando et al., 2011; Ghosh et al., 2017; Rusanova et al., 2019).

It is also possible that MLT binding sites exist in the nucleus of certain cells, which function in concert to impact the activity of antioxidant enzymes (Tomás-Zapico and Coto-Montes, 2005; Moretti et al., 2020). Cellular signaling and the messenger system are only a few examples of the many functions it performs, including the production, distribution, and range of effects of various receptors in a specific brain area. As shown by the current study, MLT levels may grow throughout the night, signaling cells and organs to begin their regular homeostatic metabolic cycles (Khodadadi, 2020).

3. Tumor growth suppression and melatonin

Melatonin has been shown to have an inhibitory impact on the apoptotic pathway in C6 glioma cells, which may be advantageous in cancer prevention in the long run, according to the results of this study. MT1 and MT2 receptors are expressed in these cell lines, modulating MLT in glioma treatment. Three genes involved in brain cell differentiation and proliferation were also utilized as indicators of transcriptional regulation in the nervous system's development: Nestin, BMI-1, and Sox2 (Khodadadi, 2020).

According to a study undertaken in the past decade, MLT is a hormone that seems to have a function in immunological modulation, antioxidant activity, and hematopoiesis, as well as other processes (Li et al., 2017). MLT has neuroprotective properties, according

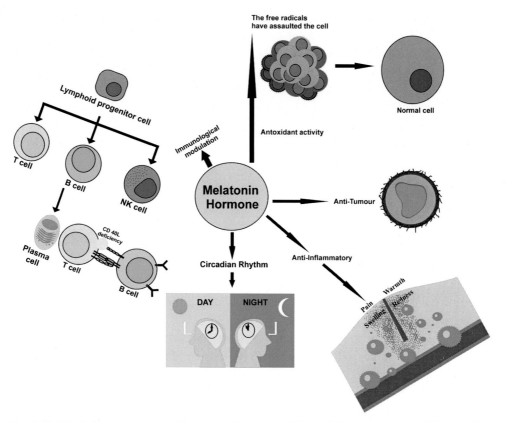

Fig. 1 Melatonin hormone has a wide range of functions. *(The basic idea was taken and developed further from Gurunathan, S., Qasim, M., Kang, M.H., Kim, J.H., 2021. Role and therapeutic potential of melatonin in various type of cancers. Onco. Targets Ther. 14, 2019–2052; Moretti, E., Favero, G., Rodella, L.F., Rezzani, R., 2020. Melatonin's antineoplastic potential against glioblastoma. Cells 9, 599. Figure created using the Corel Draw Graphics Suit program.)*

to data from trials on animal models of brain injury, regardless of whether it is given as a preventive or curative treatment (Olivier et al., 2009) (Fig. 1).

MLT deficiency, which may have a severe influence on normal physiology, can induce malignancy in the brain and ultimately glioma. Consequently, it is generally expected to be used as a cancer treatment adjuvant (Chen et al., 2012). MLT is a naturally occurring hormone used as a cancer treatment adjuvant. MLT is connected to the steroidogenesis of sexual hormones in breast, ovarian, and prostate cancers. Exposure to light at night, on the other hand, may disrupt MLT, an antiestrogenic medication that regulates levels and influences ER and AR transcription activity. Because of MLT's possible synergism with chemotherapy drugs, lower chemotherapeutic agent doses may be employed, and adverse chemotherapeutic side effects may be avoided. Clinical studies have shown MLT's ability to enhance the therapeutic benefits of numerous anticancer medicines and improve cancer patients' quality of life. MLT is an antimetastasis drug that inhibits tumor cell proliferation and autonomous growth while disrupting signal transduction pathways (Tam et al., 2007; García-Navarro et al., 2007; Gurunathan et al., 2021).

MLT's anticancer and antiangiogenic activities in cancer are mediated by membrane receptor-dependent and membrane receptor-independent mechanisms. When it comes to cancer, angiogenesis is a vital phase in the process. The activation of angiogenic factors and the suppression of antiangiogenic factors are two mechanisms by which cancer cells often enhance angiogenesis (Folkman, 1985; Cao, 2005). The presence of VEGF is required for angiogenesis to occur. The growth of tumor blood vessels was prevented in mice treated with MLT, and serum VEGF levels were decreased in the treated animals (Colombo et al., 2016; Cerezo et al., 2007). MLT reduced VEGF protein and mRNA levels in pancreatic carcinoma cells in individuals with cancer metastases, suggesting a direct anticancer mechanism (Lissoni et al., 2001; Lv et al., 2012).

MLT can cause cell death, known as apoptosis. This medication may have the effect of inhibiting tumor cell proliferation and growth, preventing cancer-causing cells from becoming cancer-causing cells, encouraging cellular turnover, and replacing cancer-causing cells with healthy cells, among other things (Fischer et al., 2008; Sánchez-Hidalgo et al., 2012). P21/WAF1 suppressor genes and MLT concentrations at normal levels lowered the tumor cells' quantity and viability by activating pro-apoptotic pathways, therefore stopping cancer cells from reproducing in the first place (Mediavilla et al., 1999; Mełen-Mucha et al., 1998) (Fig. 2).

MLT concentration and cell redox state were shown to affect various anticancer processes, including activation of apoptosis, proliferation and differentiation inhibition, and intracellular redox status changes. Depending on the kind of tumor, creating an antiproliferative or cytotoxic environment is required for tumor demise (Di-Bella et al., 2013). Cell death is triggered by increased ROS and diminished antioxidant defenses, connected with MLT's antiproliferative effects (Sánchez-Sánchez et al., 2011).

Oncostatic activity of MLT is associated with interactions between cells and between cells and the extracellular matrix and cytoskeletal rearrangement and EMT. Angiogenesis is also associated with the oncostatic activity of MLT, as is angiogenesis-mediated extracellular matrix remodeling. A cancerous tumor's spread is one of the most prevalent causes of cancer-related death (Su et al., 2007). As an immunological modulator, MLT exhibits both pro-inflammatory and antiinflammatory actions in the body, despite its antioxidant properties. Isolated cell culture studies or leukocyte-derived cell lines have been extensively studied in the scientific literature for their pro-inflammatory effects. This exercise boosts preventative methods (Mortezaee et al., 2019).

MLT affects the production of interleukin-2 (IL-2), interleukin-10 (IL-10), and interferon-beta (IFN-beta) for the activation of T-helper cells (Th) (Zhang et al., 2019). Th cells have a function in oncostatin production. The nuclear factor-kappa

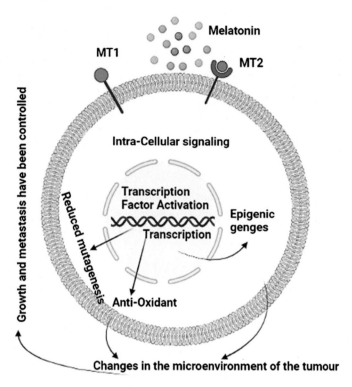

Fig. 2 Melatonin's tumor-inhibitory characteristics on transcription factors, growth, and metastasis have been regulated. *(The basic idea was taken and developed further from Bondy, S.C., Campbell, A., 2018. Mechanisms underlying tumor suppressive properties of melatonin. Int. J. Mol. Sci. 19, 2205; Moretti, E., Favero, G., Rodella, L.F., Rezzani, R., 2020. Melatonin's antineoplastic potential against glioblastoma. Cells 9, 599. Figure created using the BioRender program.)*

B (NF-κB) stimulates the generation of reactive oxygen species (ROS), which causes DNA instability (Hardeland, 2018; Carrillo-Vico et al., 2013). NF-κB is a key player in the inflammatory cascade that leads to OVC (Kumar et al., 2019). Reduced ROS generation may be attributed to MLT's effect on NF-κB phosphorylation (Yang and Lian, 2020). In several investigations, this enzyme, COX2, is over expressed in cancer cells. MLT reduces COX2 activity (Harrington and Annunziata, 2019; Qiu et al., 2019), which limits the inflammatory response and damages DNA (Harrington and Annunziata, 2019) (Sheng et al., 2020). The Akt/ERK/NFB signaling pathway is also regulated by this indolamine, which inhibits H_2O_2-induced OS (Liu et al., 2015). When MLT treatment is used in mice, it has been shown to reduce the NF-B1 and NF-B2 mRNAs (Ortiz-Franco et al., 2017). Tumor necrosis factor-α (TNF-α), an essential inflammatory cytokine, is also decreased due to this treatment. MLT exhibits antiinflammatory effects as a defense (Ramli et al., 2020). Inflammation and cancer may be caused by TNF-, a pro-inflammatory agent (Hardeland, 2014). TNF–alpha expression is increased in OVC cells, which is a pro-inflammatory response (Konturek et al., 2008). TNF–alpha expression is increased in OVC cells, a pro-inflammatory response (Konturek et al., 2008). TNF-α levels in OVC cells are dramatically reduced after treatment with MLT. This is in addition to the fact that it causes inflammation and tumors to form. A cancer cell's chemoresistance is boosted, and its ability to spread is enhanced by the secretion of IL-1 and IL-6, which activate NF-κB and STAT3 signaling activities (Kany et al., 2019). The invasiveness of metastatic impact is prevented by MLT, which prevents the mesenchymal-epithelial transition (Hong et al., 2018). Melatonin also suppresses the expression of Her-2 in invasive tumors, which reduces the Her-2 system's activity. Transformation growth factor-β1 (TGF-β1) is essential in OVC development (Liu et al., 2018). Apoptosis may be inhibited by TGF-β1, which regulates the cell cycle and promotes cell survival. The expression of TGF-β1 and its receptors has been shown to benefit the proliferation of tumor cells (Roane et al., 2019). MLT reduces the expression of TGF-1 in the epithelial cells of OVCs (Zhang et al., 2017; Das and Samanta, 2021).

3.1 Angiogenesis and melatonin

Angiogenesis is critical in cancer development. Due to angiogenesis in healthy and diseased conditions, de novo blood vessels are created due to angiogenesis. Various factors, including both pro- and antiangiogenic, impact the dynamics of vascular regeneration. EGF, NO, VEGF, SDF-1, TGF-1, and TGF-1 and -2 are only a few of the many signaling effectors involved in this process. The oxygen, food, and waste disposal requirements of solid tumors are mostly provided by angiogenesis (Chen et al., 2019). Vascular endothelial growth factor (VEGF) levels are higher in cancer patients (Bu et al., 2020). Carcinogenesis may be facilitated by preventing apoptosis in endothelial cells, maintaining vascular expansion, and speeding up cell proliferation (Lugano et al., 2020). MLT decreased angiogenesis in an OVC animal model by reducing VEGF production and angiopoietins (Hwang and Heath, 2010). Pro-angiogenic growth factors are also activated and overexpressed in the presence of hypoxia (Bhullar et al., 2018). Hypoxia-inducible factor-1 (HIF-1) is a transcription factor that promotes the production of VEGF (González et al., 2021). Several angiogenesis inhibitors are effective in diverse cell lines. In consequence, antiangiogenic factors may be used to treat cancer. Bevacizumab (Avastin), an antiangiogenic medicine approved by the Food and Drug Administration (FDA) in 2004, was a component of this endeavor (Krock et al., 2011). Because of the stabilization of HIF-1 by STAT3, there is an increase in VEGF synthesis, which is required for angiogenesis to occur (Ziello et al., 2007). The progression of certain carcinomas, such as melanoma and OVC, is accelerated when STAT3 is activated. It is necessary for cell survival, proliferation, migration, invasion, and angiogenesis, as well as for angiogenesis (Samanta et al., 2018). In hypoxic settings, MLT suppresses angiogenesis via blocking the transcription factor HIF-1. HIF-1 has been found in cancer cells, and its capacity to link to the native ubiquitin ligase VHL is required for its destruction. MLT may speed up the breakdown of HIF-1 in the body by promoting HIF-1 binding to VHL. MLT improves the binding capacity between VHL and HIF-1 in glioma cells (González et al., 2021). Because of MLT's pleiotropic and multiorgan effects, majority of previously published studies emphasized the role of MLT in preventing tumor angiogenesis. MLT has been shown to induce the production of pro-angiogenic factors by stem cells, immune cells, and ECs. In the infarcted area, injury repair is dependent on producing substances that inhibit apoptosis and promote angiogenesis. According to these studies, MLT may be an anticancer agent in solid tumors with a high density of blood vessels, particularly when paired with KC7F2 (a new tiny molecule of interest HIF-1α is a transcriptional inhibitor).

3.2 Melatonin helps combat glioblastoma in vitro

A study found that glioblastoma cell lines, U251 and T98G, can grow for almost 3 weeks in a stem cell enrichment medium (serum-free, supplemented with B27, bFGF, and EGF) before their tumor-sphere diameters reached 200 m (Zheng et al., 2017). In addition, GSC markers such as CD133 and SOX2 were examined in the glioma cell lines and tumor-spheres produced from the relevant cell line. According to the data, mRNA expressions of CD133 and SOX2 in the tumor-sphere cells were considerably greater. After acute cell dissociation, the effects of MLT alone on cells isolated from human GBM postsurgical tissues were investigated. Treatment with MLT dramatically slowed cancer cell proliferation and induced a decrease in self-renewal and clonogenic capacity, as well as a decrease in the expression of stem-cell markers, such as the transmembrane glycoprotein cluster of differentiation 133 (CD133) (Martín et al., 2014).

It is well-known that the hormone MLT specifically targets mitochondria, which are also the primary source of reactive oxygen species (ROS) (Reiter et al., 2017a, b). As previously documented, when given topically, MLT had a pro-oxidant impact on cancer cells. It's possible that a high quantity of reactive oxygen species (ROS) in the body damages mitochondrial and nuclear DNA and alters oncogene and tumor suppressor gene expression (Luchetti et al., 2010).

Franco et al. (2018) investigated the effects of 3 mM melatonin on human GBM cells to decrease tumor growth. Instead, they noticed that the expression of mitochondrial transcription factor A (TFAM), an important protein that ensures the integrity of mitochondrial DNA (mtDNA), was reduced (Campbell et al., 2012). MLT boosted ROS production in GBM cancer cells while also delaying cell-cycle progression, resulting in surprisingly significant results compared to the control group (Franco et al., 2018). The body needs more MLT in the circulation than it typically produces to inhibit tumor cell proliferation effectively. MLT's anticancer properties are boosted when the cell's MLT concentration is high. MLT at pharmaceutical concentrations provides therapeutic advantages, but only when incubated for a sufficient length of time. There were no changes in cell viability or ROS concentrations when cells were treated for less than 72h (Franco et al., 2018). Only a few studies looked at whether MLT's effects were receptor-mediated or receptor-independent. More investigation into the particular elements of MLT's anti-GBM effects is needed to understand better how it operates. Martín et al. (2006, 2014) employed both pertussis toxin (200 ng/mL), a G-coupled receptor inhibitor, and luzindole (10 Amol/L), an MT1 and MT2 antagonist, to find that MLT was effective in suppressing glioma cell growth, demonstrating that MLT may operate via many molecular routes. The melatonin membrane receptor's dissociation constant (K_d) is determined in this nanomolar range. The rats' glioma cells seem to be unaffected by low amounts of melatonin.

Martín et al. (2006, 2014) further explored whether MLT binding to its membrane receptors caused antiproliferative action at large doses (1 mM) of the hormone and revealed that this was not the case. Furthermore, MLT's direct and indirect antioxidant activities play a significant role in the differentiation of GBM cells. In rat glioma cells, cellular oxidative stress regulates the activation of nuclear factor-κB (NF-κB) and activator protein-1, two transcription factors. The therapy with 1 mmol/L melatonin did not affect the baseline activation of AP-1, although it did reduce NF-kB activity. Patients with GBM may benefit from a treatment that inhibits monocytes' tumor-promoting activities. According to Lai and colleagues, MLT supplementation in GBM lowered monocyte adhesion molecules and the generation of the chemoattractant chemokine CCL2, which reduced monocyte recruitment and activity (2019).

According to Lai et al., MLT therapy also enhanced the expression of sirtuin 1, which lowered the expression of monocyte adhesion molecules (Lai et al., 2019). MLT's potential to impact epigenetic activity is one of the most crucial properties in cancer therapy (Haim and Zubidat, 2015).

MLT's potential to downregulate oncogenes and upregulate cosuppression genes, which interacts with intracellular signaling networks and selectively triggers death in tumor cells, may affect cancer cells (Bondy and Campbell, 2018). MLT-treated cells had a significant increase in mitochondrial membrane depolarization, indicating that cytochrome c and other pro-apoptotic chemicals were released, prompting cell death (Kosar et al., 2016).

MLT can affect transcription factors like the c-Jun N-terminal kinase (JNK) pathway and activate caspase-3, resulting in cell death. MLT treatment may also affect the expression of another important transcription factor, nuclear factor erythroid 2-related factor (Nrf2), which interacts with various antioxidants and antiinflammatory genes (Bondy and Campbell, 2018; Bondy and Campbell, 2018). MLT's inhibitory effect on GSCs may be partly explained by the downregulation of the enhancer of zeste 2 polycomb repressive complex 2 subunits (EZH2). Zheng et al. (2017) discovered that knocking down the transcription factor EZH2 in GBM cells significantly reduced Notch1 expression, which is a transmembrane protein that plays an important role in cell embryonic and postnatal development and is overexpressed in many cancer types including breast, lung, pancreatic, and colon cancer (Shao et al., 2015) (Fig. 3).

The lowering of EZH2 has reduced both the number of GSCs and their self-renewal activity. MLT treatment inhibited the development of GBM cells significantly, showing the role of MLT in regulating the EZH2-Notch1 signaling pathway and its potential therapeutic implications. The conditions influence the qualities of malignant cells in their immediate environs. While hypoxia is a well-known feature of the GBM microenvironment, it also plays a role in tumor aggressiveness and treatment resistance. Zhang et al. (2013) discovered that hypoxia GBM cells were two times more invasive than normoxic GBM cells. MLT had antimigratory and antiinvasive effects on GBM cells in both normoxia and hypoxia. Furthermore, MLT administration altered HIF-1 (a key oncogenic factor that plays an important role in tumor invasion and angiogenesis under hypoxia) and the activity of enzymes that degrade HIF-1 (Zhang et al., 2013).

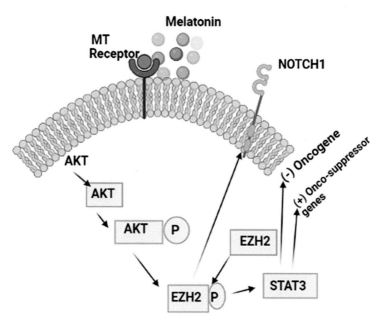

Fig. 3 Melatonin's interaction with its membrane receptors in Akt-overexpressing glioma stem-like cells (GSCs) alters the activity of the protein kinase B (Akt)-enhancer of ZESTE2 polycomb repressive complex 2 subunits (EZH2)-sign transducer and activator of transcription 3 (STAT3) and EZH2-Notch1 pathways (GSCs). To diminish EZH2 pro-oncotic effects such as Notch1 overexpression, melatonin suppresses EZH2 activation. Melatonin's effects on the Akt-EZH2-STAT3 and EZH2-Notch1 pathways are summarized in this diagram. *(This diagram is based on Moretti, E., Favero, G., Rodella, L.F., Rezzani, R., 2020. Melatonin's antineoplastic potential against glioblastoma. Cells 9, 599. This image was created using the BioRender program.)*

4. Conclusion

Several questions about the development of effective GBM therapy remain unresolved in molecular oncology. MLT has been demonstrated to improve therapeutic advantages such as glioma cancer patients' sleep and general quality of life by boosting the efficacy of anticancer drugs in clinical settings. MLT has been shown in many clinical studies to boost the effectiveness of chemotherapy when used in conjunction with other therapies. MLT is a potential agent in anticancer research, and this multitasking indoleamine has a wide range of actions against GBM. MLT has a unique interaction with cancer cells, and it has been proven in experimental animals to reduce GBM proliferative activity and aggressiveness. MLT in conjunction with chemotherapy may increase the cytotoxic effects on cancer while lowering the quantity of chemotherapy given, minimizing side effects and improving quality of life. According to the findings, melatonin has been shown to have an intriguing epigenetic effect against GBM in vitro. Experimental and clinical data show that MLT has anticancer properties against all solid and liquid tumors, including apoptotic, oncostatic, antiproliferative, and antiangiogenic actions. MLT successfully prevents cancer at all progression, development, and metastatic phases. The most distinguishing characteristic of MLT is that it hinders the entrance of cancer cells into the circulatory system and stops them from spreading to other parts of the body. Based on these investigations, MLT is known to have both preapoptotic and anti-apoptotic activities. MLT has an anticancer impact, and experimental studies into the link between autophagy and mitochondrial dysfunctions are conceivable. MLT's low toxicity, several mechanisms of action, and high success in glioma cancer prevention and treatment make it a good candidate for cancer prevention and treatment in general.

The disparity between epidemiological studies and other investigations will need more inquiry in the future. Sufficient human studies, several MLT assessment procedures, and different collection times may be required to perform an extensive study. There are various methods for measuring MLT, and the most reliable ones should be adopted in future studies. In conclusion, more studies are required to better understand MLT's impact on cancer growth and prevention, as well as its therapeutic potential.

Conflict of interest

There is no conflict of interest between the authors and their work.

References

Acuña Castroviejo, D., Escames, G., Venegas, C., Díaz Casado, M.E., Lima Cabello, E., López, L.C., Rosales Corral, S., Tan, D.X., Reiter, R.J., 2014. Extrapineal melatonin: sources, regulation, and potential functions. Cell. Mol. Life Sci. 71, 2997–3025.

Bhullar, K.S., Lagarón, N.O., McGowan, E.M., Parmar, I., Jha, A., Hubbard, B.P., Rupasinghe, H.V., 2018. Kinase-targeted cancer therapies: progress, challenges and future directions. Mol. Cancer 17 (1), 1–20.

Bondy, S.C., Campbell, A., 2018. Mechanisms underlying tumor suppressive properties of melatonin. Int. J. Mol. Sci. 19, 2205.

Bu, S., Wang, Q., Sun, J., Li, X., Gu, T., Lai, D., 2020. Melatonin suppresses chronic restraint stress-mediated metastasis of epithelial ovarian cancer via NE/AKT/β-catenin/SLUG axis. Cell Death Dis. 11 (8), 1–7.

Bubenik, G.A., Konturek, S.J., 2011. Melatonin and aging: prospects for human treatment. J. Physiol. Pharmacol. 62, 13–19.

Campbell, C.T., Kolesar, J.E., Kaufman, B.A., 2012. Mitochondrial transcription factor A regulates mitochondrial transcription initiation, DNA packaging, and genome copy number. Biochim. Biophys. Acta 1819, 921–929.

Cao, Y., 2005. Tumor angiogenesis and therapy. Biomed. Pharmacother. 59, S340–S343.

Carrillo-Vico, A., Lardone, P.J., Álvarez-Sánchez, N., Rodríguez-Rodríguez, A., Guerrero, J.M., 2013. Melatonin: buffering the immune system. Int. J. Mol. Sci. 14 (4), 8638–8683.

Cerezo, A.B., Hornedo-Ortega, R., Álvarez-fernández, M.A., Troncoso, A.M., García-Parrilla, M.C., 2007. Inhibition of VEGF-induced VEGFR-2 activation and HUVEC migration by melatonin and other bioactive indolic compounds. Nutrients 9 (3), 249.

Chen, J., Li, Y., Yu, T.S., McKay, R.M., Burns, D.K., Kernie, S.G., Parada, L.F., 2012. A restricted cell population propagates glioblastoma growth after chemotherapy. Nature 488, 522–526.

Chen, J., Gingold, J.A., Su, X., 2019. Immunomodulatory TGF-β signaling in hepatocellular carcinoma. Trends Mol. Med. 25 (11), 1010–1023.

Claustrat, B., Brun, J., Chazot, G., 2005. The basic physiology and pathophysiology of melatonin. Sleep Med. Rev. 9, 11–24.

Colombo, J., Maciel, J.M., Ferreira, L.C., Da-Silva, R.F., Zuccari, D.A., 2016. Effects of melatonin on HIF-1α and VEGF expression and on the invasive properties of hepatocarcinoma cells. Oncol. Lett. 12 (1), 231–237.

Cutando, A., Aneiros-Fernández, J., López-Valverde, A., Arias-Santiago, S., Aneiros-Cachaza, J., Reiter, R.J., 2011. A new perspective in oral health: potential importance and actions of melatonin receptors MT1, MT2, MT3, and RZR/ROR in the oral cavity. Arch. Oral Biol. 56, 944–950.

Das, N.K., Samanta, S., 2021. The promising oncostatic effects of melatonin against ovarian cancer. World J. Curr. Med. Pharm. Res. 3 (4), 85–93.

Di-Bella, G., Mascia, F., Gualano, L., Di-Bella, L., 2013. Melatonin anticancer effects: review. Int. J. Mol. Sci. 14 (2), 2410–2430.

Dirks, P.B., 2010. Brain tumor stem cells: the cancer stem cell hypothesis writ large. Mol. Oncol. 4, 420–430.

Dubocovich, M.L., Rivera-Bermudez, M.A., Gerdin, M.J., Masana, M.I., 2003. Molecular pharmacology, regulation and function of mammalian melatonin receptors. Front. Biosci. 8, 1093–1108.

Fan, C., Pan, Y., Yang, Y., Di, S., Jiang, S., Ma, Z., Li, T., Zhang, Z., Li, W., Li, X., 2015. HDAC1 inhibition by melatonin leads to suppression of lung adenocarcinoma cells via induction of oxidative stress and activation of apoptotic pathways. J. Pineal Res. 59, 321–333.

Fischer, T.W., Zmijewski, M.A., Wortsman, J., Slominski, A., 2008. Melatonin maintains mitochondrial membrane potential and attenuates activation of initiator (casp-9) and effector caspases (casp-3/casp-7) and PARP in UVR-exposed HaCaT keratinocytes. J. Pineal Res. 44 (4), 397–407.

Folkman, J., 1985. Tumor angiogenesis. Adv. Cancer Res. 43, 175–203. https://doi.org/10.1016/s0065-230x(08)60946-x.

Franco, D.G., Moretti, I.F., Marie, S.K.N., 2018. Mitochondria transcription factor A: a putative target for the effect of melatonin on U87MG malignant glioma cell line. Molecules 23, 1129.

García-Navarro, A., González-Puga, C., Escames, G., 2007. Cellular mechanisms involved in the melatonin inhibition of HT-29 human colon cancer cell proliferation in culture. J. Pineal Res. 43 (2), 195–205.

Ghosh, A.K., Naaz, S., Bhattacharjee, B., Ghosal, N., Chattopadhyay, A., Roy, S., Reiter, R.J., Bandyopadhyay, D., 2017. Mechanism of melatonin protection against copper-ascorbate-induced oxidative damage in vitro through isothermal titration calorimetry. Life Sci. 180, 123–136.

González, A., Alonso-González, C., González-González, A., Menéndez-Menéndez, J., Cos, S., Martínez-Campa, C., 2021. Melatonin as an adjuvant to antiangiogenic cancer treatments. Cancers 13 (13), 3263.

Gurunathan, S., Qasim, M., Kang, M.H., Kim, J.H., 2021. Role and therapeutic potential of melatonin in various type of cancers. OncoTargets Ther. 14, 2019–2052.

Haim, A., Zubidat, A.E., 2015. Artificial light at night: melatonin as a mediator between the environment and epigenome. Philos. Trans. R. Soc. Lond. Ser. B Biol. Sci. 370, 1–7.

Hardeland, R., 2014. Melatonin, noncoding RNAs, messenger RNA stability and epigenetics—evidence, hints, gaps and perspectives. Int. J. Mol. Sci. 15 (10), 18221–18252.

Hardeland, R., 2018. Melatonin and inflammation—story of a double-edged blade. J. Pineal Res. 65 (4), e12525.

Harrington, B.S., Annunziata, C.M., 2019. NF-κB signaling in ovarian cancer. Cancers 11 (8), 1182.

Hong, L., Wang, S., Li, W., Wu, D., Chen, W., 2018. Tumour associated macrophages promote the metastasis of ovarian carcinoma cells by enhancing CXCL16/CXCR6 expression. Pathol. Res. Pract. 214 (9), 1345–1351.

Hwang, C., Heath, E.I., 2010. Angiogenesis inhibitors in the treatment of prostate cancer. J. Hematol. Oncol. 3 (1), 1–2.

Kany, S., Vollrath, J.T., Relja, B., 2019. Cytokines in inflammatory disease. Int. J. Mol. Sci. 20 (23), 6008.

Khodadadi, S., 2020. Melatonin inhibitory effects on forming brain tumor. J. Endocrinol. Thyroid. Res. 5 (3). JETR.MS. ID 555664.

Konturek, P.C., Burnat, G., Brzozowski, T., Zopf, Y., Konturek, S.J., 2008. Tryptophan free diet delays healing of chronic gastric ulcers in rat. J. Physiol. Pharmacol. 59 (Suppl 2), 53–65.

Kosar, P.A., Razirogler, M., Ovey, I.S., Ciq, B., 2016. Synergic effects of doxorubicin and melatonin on apoptosis and mitochondrial oxidative stress in MCF-7 breast cancer cells: involvement of TRPV1 channels. J. Membr. Biol. 249, 129–214.

Krock, B.L., Skuli, N., Simon, M.C., 2011. Hypoxia-induced angiogenesis: good and evil. Genes Cancer 2 (12), 1117–1133.

Kumar, R.N., George, B.P., Chandran, R., Tynga, I.M., Houreld, N., Abrahamse, H., 2019. The influence of light on reactive oxygen species and NF-κB in disease progression. Antioxidants 8 (12), 640.

Lai, S.W., Liu, Y.S., Lu, D.Y., Tsai, C.F., 2019. Melatonin modulates the microenvironment of glioblastoma multiforme by targeting sirtuin 1. Nutrients 11, 1343.

Li, Y., Li, S., Zhou, Y., Meng, X., Zhang, J.J., 2017. Melatonin for the prevention and treatment of cancer. Oncotarget 8 (24), 39896–39921.

Lissoni, P., Rovelli, F., Malugani, F., Bucovec, R., Conti, A., Maestroni, G.J., 2001. Anti-angiogenic activity of melatonin in advanced cancer patients. Neuro. Endocrinol. Lett. 22 (1), 45–47.

Liu, B., Qu, L., Yan, S., 2015. Cyclooxygenase-2 promotes tumor growth and suppresses tumor immunity. Cancer Cell Int. 15 (1), 1–6.

Liu, S., Lee, J.S., Jie, C., Park, M.H., Iwakura, Y., Patel, Y., Soni, M., Reisman, D., Chen, H., 2018. HER2 overexpression triggers an IL1α proinflammatory circuit to drive tumorigenesis and promote chemotherapy resistance. Cancer Res. 78 (8), 2040–2051.

Luchetti, F., Canonico, B., Betti, M., Arcangeletti, M., Pilolli, F., Piroddi, M., Canesi, L., Papa, S., Galli, F., 2010. Melatonin signaling and cell protection function. FASEB J. 24, 3603–3624.

Lugano, R., Ramachandran, M., Dimberg, A., 2020. Tumor angiogenesis: causes, consequences, challenges and opportunities. Cell. Mol. Life Sci. 77 (9), 1745–1770.

Lv, D., Cui, P.L., Yao, S.W., Xu, Y.Q., Yang, Z.X., 2012. Melatonin inhibits the expression of vascular endothelial growth factor in pancreatic cancer cells. Chin. J. Cancer Res. 24 (4), 310–316.

Madhu, N.R., 2018. The Regulatory Role of the Avian Pineal Gland: A Clock for All Seasons. Lambert Academic Publishing, Beau Bassin, Mauritius, Germany, ISBN: 978-613-9-968-19-0.

Madhu, N.R., Manna, C.K., 2009. Seasonal histomorphological study of the pineal gland in relation to gonadal and adrenal gland activities in adult domestic pigeon, Columba livia Gmelin. Proc. Zool. Soc. 62 (1), 13–22.

Madhu, N.R., Manna, C.K., 2010. Pineal-adrenal interactions in domestic male pigeon exposed to variable circadian light regimes and exogenous melatonin. Endocr. Regul. 44, 121–127.

Madhu, N.R., Manna, C.K., 2011. Pineal-adrenocortical interactions in domestic male pigeon exposed to long and short photoperiods and exogenous testosterone propionate. Biol. Rhythm. Res. 44 (4), 349–362.

Madhu, N.R., Manna, C.K., 2021. Ultra-structural changes of the pineal and adrenal gland under effects of photoperiod, melatonin and testosterone propionate in the adult male pigeon. Chettinad Health City Med. J. 10 (1), 1–5.

Madhu, N.R., Sarkar, B., Manna, C.K., 2010. Biochemical, histochemical and immuno-cytochemical changes in the adrenal cortex of adult male domestic pigeon, Columba livia in relation to the annual testicular and environmental cycles. Ceylon J. Sci. 39 (2), 137–146.

Martín, V., Herrera, F., Carrera-Gonzalez, P., García-Santos, G., Antolín, I., Rodriguez-Blanco, J., Rodriguez, C., 2006. Intracellular signaling pathways involved in the cell growth inhibition of glioma cells by melatonin. Cancer Res. 66, 1081–1088.

Martín, V., Sanchez-Sanchez, A.M., Puente-Moncada, N., Gomez-Lobo, M., Alvarez-Vega, M.A., Antolín, I., Rodriguez, C., 2014. Involvement of autophagy in melatonin-induced cytotoxicity in glioma-initiating cells. J. Pineal Res. 57, 308–316.

Mediavilla, M.D., Cos, S., Sánchez-Barceló, E.J., 1999. Melatonin increases p53 and p21WAF1 expression in MCF-7 human breast cancer cells in vitro. Life Sci. 65 (4), 415–420.

Mełen-Mucha, G., Winczyk, K., Pawlikowski, M., 1998. Somatostatin analogue octreotide and melatonin inhibit bromodeoxyuridine incorporation into cell nuclei and enhance apoptosis in the transplantable murine colon 38 cancer. Anticancer Res. 18 (5a), 3615–3619.

Moretti, E., Favero, G., Rodella, L.F., Rezzani, R., 2020. Melatonin's antineoplastic potential against glioblastoma. Cells 9, 599.

Mortezaee, K., Najafi, M., Farhood, B., Ahmadi, A., Potes, Y., Shabeeb, D., Musa, A.E., 2019. Modulation of apoptosis by melatonin for improving cancer treatment efficiency: an updated review. Life Sci. 228, 228–2241.

Olivier, P., Fontaine, R.H., Loron, G., Steenwinckel, V.S., Biran, V., 2009. Melatonin promotes oligodendroglial maturation of injured white matter in neonatal rats. PLoS One 4 (9), e7128.

Ortiz-Franco, M., Planells, E., Quintero, B., Acuña-Castroviejo, D., Rusanova, I., Escames, G., Molina-López, J., 2017. Effect of melatonin supplementation on antioxidant status and DNA damage in high intensity trained athletes. Int. J. Sports Med. 38 (14), 1117–1125.

Qazi, M.A., Vora, P., Venugopal, C., Sidhu, S.S., Moffat, J., Swanton, C., Singh, S.K., 2017. Intratumoral heterogeneity: pathways to treatment resistance and relapse in human glioblastoma. Ann. Oncol. 28, 1448–1456.

Qiu, X., Wang, X., Qiu, J., Zhu, Y., Liang, T., Gao, B., Wu, Z., Lian, C., Peng, Y., Liang, A., Su, P., 2019. Melatonin rescued reactive oxygen species-impaired osteogenesis of human bone marrow mesenchymal stem cells in the presence of tumor necrosis factor-alpha. Stem Cells Int. 2019, 6403967.

Ramli, N.Z., Yahaya, M.F., Tooyama, I., Damanhuri, H.A., 2020. A mechanistic evaluation of antioxidant nutraceuticals on their potential against age-associated neurodegenerative diseases. Antioxidants 9 (10), 1019.

Reiter, R.J., Rosales-Corral, S., Tan, D.X., Jou, M.J., Galano, A., Xu, B., 2017a. Melatonin as a mitochondria-targeted antioxidant: one of evolution's best ideas. Cell. Mol. Life Sci. 7, 3863–3881.

Reiter, R.J., Rosales-Corral, S.A., Tan, D.X., Acuna, C.D., Qin, L., Yang, S.F., Xu, K., 2017b. Melatonin, a full service anti-cancer agent: inhibition of initiation, progression and metastasis. Int. J. Mol. Sci. 18 (4), 843.

Roane, B.M., Arend, R.C., Birrer, M.J., 2019. Targeting the transforming growth factor-beta pathway in ovarian cancer. Cancers 11 (5), 668.

Rusanova, I., Martínez-Ruiz, L., Florido, J., Rodríguez-Santana, C., Guerra-Librero, A., Acuña-Castroviejo, D., Escames, G., 2019. Protective effects of melatonin on the skin: future perspectives. Int. J. Mol. Sci. 20, 4948.

Samanta, S., Dassarma, B., Jana, S., Rakshit, S., Saha, S.A., 2018. Hypoxia inducible factor-1 (HIF-1) and cancer progression: a comprehensive review. Indian J. Cancer Educ. Res. 6 (1), 94–109.

Sánchez-Hidalgo, M., Lee, M., de la Lastra, C.A., Guerrero, J.M., Packham, G., 2012. Melatonin inhibits cell proliferation and induces caspase activation and apoptosis in human malignant lymphoid cell lines. J. Pineal Res. 53 (4), 366–373.

Sánchez-López, A.L., Ortiz, G.G., Pacheco-Moises, F.P., Mireles-Ramírez, M.A., Bitzer-Quintero, O.K., Delgado-Lara, D.L.C., Ramírez-Jirano, L.J., Velázquez-Brizuela, I.E., 2018. Efficacy of melatonin on serum pro-inflammatory cytokines and oxidative stress markers in relapsing remitting multiple sclerosis. Arch. Med. Res. 49, 391–398.

Sánchez-Sánchez, A.M., Martín, V., García-Santos, G., 2011. Intracellular redox state as determinant for melatonin antiproliferative vs cytotoxic effects in cancer cells. Free Radic. Res. 45 (11−12), 1333–1341.

Shao, S., Zhao, X., Zhang, X., Luo, M., Zuo, X., Huang, S., Wang, Y., Gu, S., Zhao, X., 2015. Notch1 signaling regulates the epithelial-mesenchymal transition and invasion of breast cancer in a Slug-dependent manner. Mol. Cancer 14, 28.

Sheng, J., Sun, H., Yu, F.B., Li, B., Zhang, Y., Zhu, Y.T., 2020. The role of cyclooxygenase-2 in colorectal cancer. Int. J. Med. Sci. 17 (8), 1095–1101.

Slominski, R.M., Reiter, R.J., Schlabritz-Loutsevitch, N., Ostrom, R.S., Slominski, A.T., 2012. Melatonin membrane receptors in peripheral tissues: distribution and functions. Mol. Cell. Endocrinol. 351, 152–166.

Su, S.C., Hsieh, M.J., Yang, W.E., Chung, W.H., Reiter, R.J., Yang, S.F., 2007. Cancer metastasis: mechanisms of inhibition by melatonin. J. Pineal Res. 62 (1), e12370.

Tam, C.W., Mo, C.W., Yao, K.M., Shiu, S.Y., 2007. Signaling mechanisms of melatonin in antiproliferation of hormone-refractory 22Rv1 human prostate cancer cells: implications for prostate cancer chemoprevention. J. Pineal Res. 42 (2), 191–202.

Tan, D.X., Reiter, R.J., Manchester, L.C., Yan, M.T., El-Sawi, M., Sainz, R.M., Mayo, J.C., Kohen, R., Allegra, M., Hardeland, R., 2002. Chemical and physical properties and potential mechanisms: melatonin as a broad spectrum antioxidant and free radical scavenger. Curr. Top. Med. Chem. 2, 181–197.

Tomás-Zapico, C., Coto-Montes, A., 2005. A proposed mechanism to explain the stimulatory effect of melatonin on antioxidative enzymes. J. Pineal Res. 39, 99–104.

Witt-Enderby, P.A., Bennett, J., Jarzynka, M.J., Firestine, S., Melan, M.A., 2003. Melatonin receptors and their regulation: biochemical and structural mechanisms. Life Sci. 72, 2183–2198.

Yang, S., Lian, G., 2020. ROS and diseases: role in metabolism and energy supply. Mol. Cell. Biochem. 467 (1), 1–2.

Zhang, Y., Liu, Q., Wang, F., Ling, E.A., Liu, S., Wang, L., Yang, Y., Yao, L., Chen, X., Wang, F., 2013. Melatonin antagonizes hypoxia-mediated glioblastoma cell migration and invasion via inhibition of HIF-1α. J. Pineal Res. 55, 121–130.

Zhang, Y., Alexander, P.B., Wang, X.F., 2017. TGF-β family signaling in the control of cell proliferation and survival. Cold Spring Harb. Perspect. Biol. 9 (4), a022145.

Zhang, X., Hou, G., Liu, A., Xu, H., Guan, Y., Wu, Y., Deng, J., Cao, X., 2019. Matrine inhibits the development and progression of ovarian cancer by repressing cancer associated phosphorylation signalling pathways. Cell Death Dis. 10 (10), 1–7.

Zheng, X., Pang, B., Gu, G., Gao, T., Zhang, R., 2017. Melatonin inhibits glioblastoma stem-like cells through suppression of EZH2-NOTCH1 signaling axis. Int. J. Biol. Sci. 13 (2), 245–253.

Ziello, J.E., Jovin, I.S., Huang, Y., 2007. Hypoxia-inducible factor (HIF)-1 regulatory pathway and its potential for therapeutic intervention in malignancy and ischemia. Yale J. Biol. Med. 80 (2), 51–60.

CHAPTER EIGHTEEN

Genotype influenced pharmacokinetics of anticancer medicine: A connecting link

Monika Kadian[a], Kritika Sharma[a], Kanishka Shrivasatava[a], Shivani Pandita[a], Anusha Rana[b], Preeti Jaiswal[b], Ramica Sharma[b], and Anil Kumar[a]
[a]Pharmacology Division, University Institute of Pharmaceutical Sciences, UGC Centre of Advanced Study, Panjab University, Chandigarh, India
[b]University School of Pharmaceutical Sciences, Rayat Bahra University, Mohali, Punjab, India

1. Introduction

Due to the marked interindividual disparities in treatment outcome and toxicity, cancer treatment is becoming increasingly individualized. Drug-drug interactions, ethnicity, age, renal and hepatic function, comorbidities, nutritional condition, smoking, and alcohol intake are all factors that contribute to interindividual heterogeneity in pharmacokinetics and pharmacodynamics. Genetic factors, on the other hand, may have a higher impact on therapeutic efficacy and toxicity. In oncology, genetic differences can be detected as somatic mutations in the tumor genome, impacting the choice of chemotherapeutic treatment, or as germline alterations, perhaps modifying the pharmacology of specific drugs (Pavlos et al., 2012).

Screening for pharmacogenetics mutations and/or drug-specific phenotyping in cancer patients who are candidates for therapy with prior to the start of anticancer treatment, chemotherapeutic medicine can improve patients response or resistance toward the treatment, the detection of people who are at a higher risk of the development of toxicity would allow for either dose adaptation or dose reduction. Xenobiotic metabolism is commonly classified into three phases: modification (phase I), conjugation (phase II), and elimination (phase III) (most often in urine or bile). Drugs are oxidized, reduced, and hydrolyzed by phase I drug metabolizing enzymes, particularly members of the cytochrome P450 (CYP) family (Lamb et al., 2007). Whereas, phase II drug-metabolizing enzymes, such as glutathione *S*-transferases (GSTs) and uridine diphosphate glucuronosyltransferases (UGTs), use conjugation processes to inactivate or activate compounds (Jancova et al., 2010). Several anticancer medicines pharmacokinetics have

Biomarkers in Cancer Detection and Monitoring of Therapeutics
https://doi.org/10.1016/B978-0-323-95114-2.00013-3

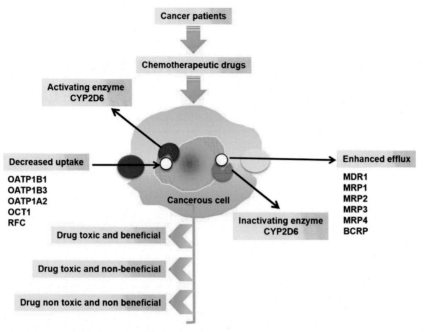

Fig. 1 Schematic view of influence of different enzymes and transporters on the pharmacokinetics of anticancer drugs. *BCRP*, breast cancer resistance protein; *CYP2D6*, cytochrome P450 2D6; *MDR*, multidrug resistance; *MRP*, multidrug resistance-related protein; *OATP*, organic anion transporting polypeptide; *OCT*, ornithine carbamoyltransferase; *RFC*, reduced folate carrier.

been shown to be influenced by polymorphism in these enzymes (Fig. 1). This chapter provides an overview about the types of cancer and their linked genetic mutations, enzymatic influence on pharmacokinetics of anticancer drugs, and how drug transporters and associated genetic variance and other miscellaneous factors affected the pharmacokinetics of anticancer medicine.

2. Cancer types and linked genetic mutations

Cancer can be classified in two ways, according to the International Classification of Diseases for Oncology, 3rd edition, provided international standards for the classification and nomenclature on basis of histology, as in which tissue cancer originates and on basis of location where the cancer first developed. There are hundreds of distinct malignancies from a histology aspect, which are divided into six primary types as shown in Table 1. Here, in Table 1, we are describing about types of cancer and their involved gene mutations.

Table 1 Types of cancer and their linked gene mutations.

Cancer types	Subtypes	Origin	Mutated gene
Carcinoma	*Adenocarcinoma*	Organ or gland	– Activation of proto-oncogenes (K-Ras)
	Squamous cell carcinoma	Squamous epithelium	– Inactivation of at least three tumor suppressor genes, like loss of APC (chromosome region 5q21), loss of p53 (chromosome region 17p13), and loss of heterozygosity for the long arm of chromosome 18
Mesenchymal sarcoma	Osteosarcoma or osteogenic sarcoma	Bone	Mutations in p53, RB, PI3K, and IDH genes and these are the most prevalent mutations identified in sarcomas
	Chondrosarcoma	Cartilage	
	Leiomyosarcoma	Smooth muscle	
	Rhabdomyosarcoma	Skeletal muscle	
	Mesothelial sarcoma or mesothelioma	Membranous lining of body cavities	
	Fibrosarcoma	Fibrous tissue	
	Angiosarcoma or hemangioendothelioma	Blood vessels	
	Liposarcoma	Adipose tissue	
	Glioma or astrocytoma	Brain neurogenic connective tissue	
	Myosarcoma	Primitive embryonic connective tissue	
	Mesenchymous or mixed mesodermal tumor	Mixed connective tissue types	

Continued

Table 1 Types of cancer and their linked gene mutations—cont'd

Cancer types	Subtypes	Origin	Mutated gene
Myeloma		Bone marrow plasma	Mutations in KRAS, TP53, and FAM46C
Leukemia	Myelogenous or granulocytic leukemia	Malignancy of the myeloid and granulocytic white blood cell series	Mutations observed with genes KIT, NPM1, RAS, WT1, BAALC, MN1, DNMT, TET2, IDH, ASXL1, PTPN11, and CBL
	Lymphatic, lymphocytic, or lymphoblastic leukemia	Malignancy of the lymphoid and lymphocytic blood cell series	
	Polycythemia vera or erythremia	Malignancy of various blood cell products, but dominant with red cells	
Lymphoma	Hodgkin lymphoma	Reed-Sternberg cells (present)	Mutation in TP53, MYD88, PIM1, CARD11, BCL6, CREBBP, EZH2 genes
	Non-Hodgkin lymphoma	Reed-Sternberg cells (absent)	

APC, adenomatous polyposis coli; ASXL1, additional sex combs-like 1; BAALC, brain and acute leukemia, cytoplasmic; BCL6, B-cell lymphoma 6 protein; CARD11, caspase recruitment domain family member 11; CBL, casitas B-lineage lymphoma; CREBBP, cyclic adenosine monophosphate response element-binding protein; DNMT, DNA methyltransferase; EZH2, enhancer of Zeste homolog 2; FAM46C, family with sequence similarity 46, member C; IDH, isocitrate dehydrogenase; KIT, receptor tyrosine kinase; KRAS, Kirsten rat sarcoma viral oncogene homolog; MN1, meningioma 1; MYD88, myeloid differentiation primary response 88; NPM1, nucleophosmin; PI3K, phosphatidylinositol 3-kinase; PTPN11, protein tyrosine phosphatase nonreceptor type 11; RAS, rat sarcoma virus; RB, retinoblastoma gene; TET2, Tet methylcytosine dioxygenase; TP53, tumor protein p53; WT1, Wilms' tumor suppressor gene 1.

3. Influence of enzymes on the pharmacokinetics of drugs

The chemical modification of molecules or any chemical entity after they reach the body is known as drug metabolism. Drug metabolism reduces the therapeutic efficacy of medications in general. During drug biotransformation, the majority of medicines' lipophilic centers are changed to hydrophilic centers, which increases their water solubility and allows for urine or bile evacuation. This is significant advancement for medication metabolism since pharmaceuticals' lipophilic nature allows them to remain in the body for extended periods of time, potentially resulting in toxicity.

3.1 Cytochrome P450 (CYP)-mediated phase I-metabolizing enzymes

Drug metabolism is the metabolic breakdown of drugs through specialized enzymatic systems CYPs are involved in more than 90% of the reported enzymatic reactions. Regarding drug metabolism, CYPs are the most well-known drug-metabolizing enzymes and are mainly expressed in the liver, but other organs are also involved such as kidney, placenta, adrenal gland, gastrointestinal tract, and skin. Among the 57 putatively functional human CYPs (Ingelman, 2004), the isoforms belonging to the CYP1, 2, and 3 families are mainly responsible for the metabolism of about 80% of clinical drugs. CYP-mediated drug metabolism converts lipophilic products into hydrophilic products to facilitate elimination and plays a critical role in determining treatment outcomes by influencing drug action, safety, bioavailability, and drug resistance through the metabolism in both metabolic organs and local sites of action. Moreover, CYPs, as the most diverse catalysts known in biochemistry, contribute to interindividual variations in drug responses, resulting from genetic and epigenetic variants, as well as environmental factors, such as gender, age, nutrition, disease states, and pathophysiological factors. In particular, CYPs can be inhibited or induced by concomitant drugs and circulating metabolites, which can influence treatment outcomes through drug-drug interaction, drug-gene interaction, and drug-drug-gene interactions. Further, CYPs have been detected in tumors, as well as cancer cells and cell lines and it was reported that most antitumor agents that exert antitumor efficacy in cancer cells have been observed to be metabolized by the CYP1, CYP2, and CYP3 families (Passot et al., 2013) such as flavonoids by CYP1b1, tamoxifen by CYP2D6, docetaxel, and cyclophosphamide by CYP3A4/5, thalidomide by CYP2C9 and CYP2C19, and paclitaxel by CYP2C8 (Bertholee et al., 2017). Thus, the expression of CYPs in tumor cells may play an important role in antitumor therapy as shown in Table 2.

Table 2 Metabolizing enzymes and their genetic variation influences the pharmacokinetics profile of anticancer drugs.

Involved enzymes	Influenced pharmacokinetic of drugs	Selective target	Polymorphism affecting pharmacokinetic	References
Cytochrome P450 (CYP1)				
Cytochrome P450 CYP1A1	**Alkylating agents:** Dacarbazine	DNA	Unknown	Bertholee et al. (2017)
CytochromeP450 CYP1A2	**Alkylating agents:** Bendamustine, Dacarbazine	DNA	No	Bertholee et al. (2017)
	Antimetabolites: Tegafur	DNA/RNA	Yes	Bertholee et al. (2017)
	Topoisomerase inhibitors: Etoposide	Topoisomerase	Yes	Ekhart et al. (2008)
	Antihormones: Flutamide	Flutamide aromatase	No	Rodriguez-Antona and Ingelman-Sundberg (2006)
	Tyrosine kinase inhibitors: Axitinib, Pazopanib	VEGF-R 1–3 and multitargeted	**No** (Axitinib) **Unknown** (Pazopanib)	Brennan et al. (2012) and Bertholee et al. (2017)
	Immunomodulators: Pomalidomide	Bone marrow	Unknown	Bertholee et al. (2017)
	Other: Bortezomib	Proteasome	No	Quinn et al. (2009)
Cytochrome P450 CYP2E1	**Alkylating agents:** Dacarbazine	DNA	Unknown	Bertholee et al. (2017)
	Antimitotic cytostatics: Vinorelbine	Microtubule	Unknown	Bertholee et al. (2017)
	Others: Cisplatin Trabectedin	DNA	**Yes** (Cisplatin) **Unknown** (Trabectedin)	Gurney et al. (2007) and Bertholee et al. (2017)
Cytochrome P450 CYP3A4	**Alkylating agents:** Cyclophosphamide, Ifosfamide, Thiotepa	DNA	Yes	Rodriguez-Antona and Ingelman-Sundberg (2006), Ekhart et al. (2008), Johnson et al. (2013), and Bertholee et al. (2017)
	Antimitoticcytostatic: Cabazitaxel, Docetaxel, Paclitaxel, Vinblastine, Vinorelbine, Vincristine	Microtubule	**Unknown** (Cabazitaxe, Vinblastine, Vinorelbine, Vinorelbine) **Yes** (Docetaxel, Paclitaxel) **No** (Vincristine)	Ekhart et al. (2008), Guilhaumou et al. (2011), and Bertholee et al. (2017)

Drug class	Target	Metabolized	References
Antitumor antibacterial: Doxorubicin Mitoxantrone	DNA	**Yes** (Doxorubicin) **Unknown** (Mitoxantrone)	Lal et al. (2008) and Bertholee et al. (2017)
Topoisomerase inhibitors: Irinotecan Teniposide Topotecan	Topoisomerase	**Yes** (Irinotecan) **Unknown** (Teniposide) **No** (Topotecan)	Kim and Innocenti (2007), Stewart et al. (2014), and Bertholee et al. (2017)
Antihormones: Anastrozole, Exemestane, Letrozole Tamoxifen, Enzalutamide, Fulvestrant	Aromatase androgen receptor and estrogen receptor	**Yes** (Anastrozole, Exemestane, Letrozole) **Unknown** (Tamoxifen, Enzalutamide) **No, mainly nonenzymatic** (Fulvestrant)	Abubakar et al. (2014) and Bertholee et al. (2017)
Tyrosine kinase inhibitors: Axitinib, Bosutinib, Dasatinib Imatinib, Lapatinib, Pazopanib, Nilotinib, Ponatinib, Crizotinib Erlotinib, Gefetinib Olaparib, Sorafenib, Sunitinib, Regorafeni, Vandetanib	— **VEGF-R 1–3** (Axitinib) — **BCR-ABL/ SRc** (Dasatinib, Imatinib, Lapatinib, Pazopanib Nilotinib, Ponatinib) — **ALK** (Crizotinib) — **EGFR** (Erlotinib, Gefetinib)	**No** (Axitinib, Nilotinib, Ponatinib, Erlotinib, Gefetinib) **Yes** (Bosutinib, Dasatinib, Imatinib, Lapatinib, Sorafenib, Sunitinib) **Unknown** (Pazopanib, Crizotinib, Olaparib, Regorafeni, Vandetanib)	Brennan et al. (2012), Boudou-Rouquette et al. (2012), Kobayashi et al. (2015), Polillo et al. (2015) and Bertholee et al. (2017)

Continued

Table 2 Metabolizing enzymes and their genetic variation influences the pharmacokinetics profile of anticancer drugs—cont'd

Involved enzymes	Influenced pharmacokinetic of drugs	Selective target	Polymorphism affecting pharmacokinetic	References
		— **PARP** (Olaparib)		
		— **Multi** (Sorafenib, Sunitinib, Regorafeni, Vandetanib)		
	Biologicals: Brentuximab	CD30	Unknown	Bertholee et al. (2017)
	Immunomodulants: Pomalidomide	Bone marrow	Unknown	Bertholee et al. (2017)
	Others: Bortezomib, Cisplatin, Trabectedin, Temsirolimus	— **Proteasome** (Bortezomib)	**No** (Bortezomib) **Yes** (Cisplatin)	Gurney et al. (2007), Quinn et al. (2009), and Bertholee et al. (2017)
		— **DNA** (Cisplatin, Trabectedin)	**Unknown** (Trabectedin, Temsirolimus)	
		— **mTOR** (Temsirolimus)		
Cytochrome P450 (CYP2)				
Cytochrome P450 CYP2B6	**Alkylating agents:** Busulfan, Ifosfamide, Cyclophosphamide, Procarbazine	DNA	**Yes** (Busulfan, Ifosfamide, Cyclophosphamide, Thiotepa) **Unknown** (Procarbazine)	Huezo-Diaz et al. (2014) and Ten Brink et al. (2014)
	Antimitotic cytostatics: Docetaxel	Microtubule	Yes	Rodriguez-Antona and Ingelman-Sundberg (2006)
	Antitumor antibacterials: Doxorubicin	DNA	Yes	Ekhart et al. (2008), Lal et al. (2008), and Bertholee et al. (2017)
	Alkylating agents: Busulfan	DNA	Yes	Huezo-Diaz et al. (2014)

Enzyme	Drug class: Drug	Target	Clinically relevant	References
Cytochrome P450 CYP2C9	**Antitumor antibacterials:** Idarubicin	DNA	Unknown	Bertholee et al. (2017)
	Others: Trabectedin	DNA	Unknown	Bertholee et al. (2017)
Cytochrome P450 CYP2C19	**Alkylating agents:** Cyclophosphamide Ifosfamide	DNA	Yes	Ekhart et al. (2008)
	Antihormones: Tamoxifen	Estrogen receptor	Yes	Rodriguez-Antona and Ingelman-Sundberg (2006)
	Tyrosine kinase inhibitors: Axitinib, Lapatinib	**VEGF-R 1–3** (Axitinib) **HER-2** (Lapatinib)	**No** (Axitinib), **Unknown** (Lapatinib)	Mwinyi et al. (2014)
	Immunomodulators: Pomalidomide, Thalidomide	Bone Marrow	**Unknown** (Pomalidomide) **Yes** (Thalidomide)	Brennan et al. (2012) and Bertholee et al. (2017)
	Others: Bortezomib, Trabectedin	**Proteasome** (Bortezomib), **DNA** (Trabectedin)	**No** (Bortezomib) **Unknown** (Trabectedin)	Matsuzawa et al. (2012), Quinn et al. (2009), and Bertholee et al. (2017)
Cytochrome P450 CYP2D6	**Antimitotic cytostatics:** Vinorelbine	Microtubule	Unknown	Bertholee et al. (2017)
	Antitumor antibacterials: Idarubicin	DNA	Unknown	Bertholee et al. (2017)
	Antihormones: Tamoxifen	Estrogen receptors	Yes	Mwinyi et al. (2014)
	Biologicals: Brentuximab	CD30	Unknown	Bertholee et al. (2017)
	Immunomodulators: Pamalidomide	Bone marrow	Unknown	Bertholee et al. (2017)
	Others: Trabectedin	DNA	Unknown	Bertholee et al. (2017)

ALK, anaplastic lymphoma kinase; *BCR-ABL/SRc*, breakpoint cluster region protein–Abelson murine leukemia viral oncogene homolog/protooncogene tyrosine–protein kinase Src; *CD30*, cluster of differentiation 30; *EGFR*, epidermal growth factor receptor; *HER-2*, human epidermal growth factor receptor 2; *mTOR*, mammalian target of rapamycin; *PARP*, poly(ADP–ribose) polymerase; *PD-1*, programmed cell death protein; *VEGFR 1–3*, vascular endothelial growth factor subtypes 1–3.

3.2 Non-CYP phase-II metabolizing enzymes

In the literature, several clinically significant gene polymorphisms linked to phase II drug metabolism and pharmacokinetics of anticancer medicines have been documented and the Glutathione *S*-transferase (GST) enzyme family and uridine diphosphate glucuronosyltransferase (UGT) enzymes have received enormous attention. Glutathione *S*-transferases (GSTs) are a group of enzymes that are involved in the detoxification of xenobiotics, such as platinum compounds. GSTs are classified into numerous groups, each of which is encoded by a separate gene or gene family (Houtsma et al., 2010). When cancer patients are treated with medications like cyclofosfamide, carboplatin, doxorubicin, and cisplatin, polymorphisms in the genes are thought to cause a different impact or toxicity manifestation other than this uridine diphosphate glucuronosyltransferase-1 (UGT-1) is involved in the glucuronidation of bilirubin, as well as a variety of lipophilic medicines for instance irinotecan's active metabolite, SN-38. As irinotecan is a cancer-fighting drug (Hu et al., 2014; Kadakol et al., 2000) and its metabolite SN-38 is mainly cleared by the enzyme uridine diphosphate glucuronosyltransferase-1A1 (UGT1A1). There are different variations of the gene but the most important one is UGT1A1*28 (an insertion of the element TA in the promoter region of the UGT1 gene) and this alteration impairs the enzyme activity and affect irinotecan metabolism. In people who are homozygous for UGT1A1*28 allele, UGT1 activity is decreased by 70%. Furthermore, methylenetetrahydrofolate reductase is an enzyme which participates in 5-FU and methotrexate (MTX) pathway (Houtsma et al., 2010) and it plays an important role in the metabolism of folate and methionine and thus in the synthesis and methylation of DNA. In Table 3, we described about how pharmacokinetics of anticancer drugs linked with non-CYP-metabolizing enzymes along with neoplasms associated.

4. Drug transporters

Polymorphisms in genes encoding drug efflux transporters, such as SLC, MDR 1, and ABC might affect anticancer drug absorption and excretion, resulting in interindividual pharmacokinetic variability and, thus, substantial disparities occurs in treatment response among cancer patients. The sodium-independent glucose transporters have 14 subtypes within humans, as shown in Table 4. Briefly, the SLC2A1 to SLC2A14 genes encodes for GLUT1 to GLUT14 proteins. As hypoxia is a hallmark feature in cancer therefore cancer cells prefer the glycolysis pathway, which yields only two ATP molecules from one glucose molecule however, cancer cells demands more glucose than healthy cells. Further, overexpression of glucose transporters results in increased glucose absorption by cancer cells and increased levels of glucose transporters also promotes carcinogenesis and modulates cancer resilience and intrusiveness on the other end it can be advantageous as well. Additionally, increased level of glucose transporters, for instance, is

Table 3 Pharmacokinetics of anticancer drugs linked with non-CYP-metabolizing enzymes.

Enzymes	Subfamilies	Drugs	Effect	Neoplasma	References
Uridine diphosphate glucuronosyltransferases (UGTs)	UGT1A1, UGT1A1*28, UGT1A1*27, UGT1A1*6	Irinotecan	Toxicity/ADR	Colorectal carcinoma	Houtsma et al. (2010) and Bertholee et al. (2017)
Enzymes of purine and pyrimidine metabolism	DPYD	DPYD (Fluoropyramidines: 5-Fluorouracil (5-FU), Capecitabine, Tegafur)	Efficacy/resistance/toxicity	Colorectal carcinoma, breast cancer, head–neck cancer	Diasio et al. (1988), Hawwa et al. (2008), Kantar et al. (2009), Knights et al. (2014), and Ogungbenro and Aarons (2015)
	DPYS	5-FU			
	UPB1	Tegafur			
	MTHFR	Capecitabine, Methotrexate	Dosage/toxicity/ADR	Acute lymphatic leukemia	
	ARID5B, ABCC2	Methotrexate			
	CDA, CNTN4, ALOX5AP, and HEXD	Gemcitabine			
	TPMT	Azathioprine, Mercaptopirune, Thioguanine			

Continued

Table 3 Pharmacokinetics of anticancer drugs linked with non-CYP-metabolizing enzymes—cont'd

Enzymes	Subfamilies	Drugs	Effect	Neoplasma	References
Glutathione S-transferase (GST)	GSTA	Busulfan	Efficacy/ toxicity/ ADR	Cancer: colorectal, bladder, head and neck, lung, ovarian, and testicular	Houtsma et al. (2010) and Kulkarni (2016)
	GSTA1*B	Melphalan and Chlorambucil			
	GSTM	Platinum compounds			
	GSTP	Cyclofosfamide, Carboplatin			
	GSTP1	Doxorubicin, Cisplatin, Oxaliplatin			
	GSTT	Thiotepa			

ALOX5AP, arachidonate 5-lipoxygenase activating protein; *ARID5B*, AT-rich interaction domain; *CDA*, cytidine deaminase; *CNTN4*, contactin 4; *DPYD*, dihydropyrimidine dehydrogenase; *DPYS*, dihydropyrimidinase; *GST*, glutathione-S-transferase; *HEXD*, hexosaminidase D; *MTHFR*, methylenetetrahydrofolatereductase; *TPMT*, thiopurine–S-methyltransferase; *UGT*, uridine diphosphate glucuronosyltransferase; *UPB*, beta-ureidopropionase.

Table 4 Influence on the pharmacokinetics of drugs due polymorphisms in genes encoding drug efflux transporters.

Transporter	Gene	Location	Types of cancer	Inhibitors	References
GLUT-1 (492 amino acids)	SLC2A1	Cerebral cortex, choroid plexus, erythrocytes, granulocytes, muscle cells, and colon	– **Increased GLUT-1** (Hepatic tumors, renal cell carcinoma, prostate cancer, cervical cancer, ovarian cancer, breast cancer, thyroid cancer, thymic carcinomas, bone cancer and multiple myeloma) – **Decreased GLUT-1** (Hepatoblastomas and non-melanoma skin cancer)	WZB117, Glutor, Fasentin, Oxime-based inhibitors, Polyphenols, STF 31	Mano et al. (2014), Huang et al. (2014a, b), Wei et al. (2017), Meyer et al. (2019a, b), and Reckzeh et al. (2019)
GLUT-2 (524 amino acids)	SLC2A2	Hepatocytes, pancreatic β cells, kidney cells, olfactory bulbs, and brain nuclei	– **Increased GLUT-2** (Hepatocellular carcinoma, biliary intra epithelial neoplasia, liver metastases, gastric tumors and Colorectal cancer) – **Decreased GLUT-2** (Preneoplastic and neoplastic hepatic lesions, neuroendocrine tumor, and renal cell carcinoma)	Gluten, Polyphenols, STF-31	Daskalow et al. (2009), Zheng et al. (2012), and Szablewski (2013)
GLUT-3 (496 amino acids)	SLC2A3	Brain, spermatozoa, placenta, embryos, WBCs, and platelets	– **Increased GLUT-3** (Gastric tumor, kidney cancer, ovarian cancer, brain tumor, thyroid, adrenocortical carcinoma, and non-Hodgkin's lymphoma) – **Decreased GLUT-3** (Multiple myeloma)	Gluten, Adriamycin, Camptothecin, and Etoposide	Watanabe et al. (2012) and Chai et al. (2017)

Continued

Table 4 Influence on the pharmacokinetics of drugs due polymorphisms in genes encoding drug efflux transporters—cont'd

Transporter	Gene	Location	Types of cancer	Inhibitors	References
GLUT-4 (509 amino acids)	SLC2A4	Skeletal muscle cells, adipose tissue, hypothalamus, cerebellum, and hippocampus	– **Increased GLUT-4** (Pancreatic tumor, colon adenocarcinoma, colon cancer, ovarian tumor, glioma tumor, thyroid cancer, multiple myeloma, and chronic lymphoblastic leukemia) – **Decreased GLUT-4** (Pancreatic tumor)	Polyphenol and shRNA	Suganuma et al. (2007) and McBrayer et al. (2012)
GLUT-5 (501 amino acids)	SLC2A5	Spermatozoa, kidney, skeletal muscle, and brain	– **Increased GLUT-5** (Liver carcinoma, renal cell carcinoma, prostatic intra-epithelial neoplasia, breast cancer, and lung cancer)	Antisense oligonucleotide	Mochizuki et al. (2001) and Reinicke et al. (2012)
GLUT-6 (507 amino acids)	SLC2A6	Brain, spleen, peripheral leukocytes, and germinal cells of the testis	– **Increased GLUT-6** (Endometrial cancer)		Oh et al. (2017)
GLUT-7 (524 amino acids)	SLC2A7	Small intestine, colon, testis, and prostate gland	– **Increased GLUT-7** (Benign prostate tumor)		Meyer et al. (2019a, b)
GLUT-8 (477 amino acids)	SLC2A8	Testis, cerebellum, adrenal gland, liver, spleen, and brown adipose tissue	– **Increased GLUT-8** (Multiple myeloma)		Watanabe et al. (2012)
GLUT-9 (GLUT9–540 amino acids and GLUT9b 512 amino acids)	SLC2A9	Liver and kidney	– **Increased GLUT-9** (Papillary thyroid carcinoma) – **Decreased GLUT-9** (Prostate cancer and renal cancer)		

Protein	Gene	Tissue distribution	Cancer association	Substrate/Inhibitors	References
GLUT-10 (541 amino acids)	SLC2A10	Skeletal muscle, heart, adipose tissue, liver, pancreas, placenta, and kidney	– **Increased GLUT-10** (Breast cancer)		Abrantes et al. (2010)
GLUT-11 (496 amino acids)	SLC2A11	Heart, skeletal muscle, kidneys adipose tissue, placenta, and pancreas	– **Increased GLUT-11** (Prostate cancer and multiple myeloma)		Meyer et al. (2019a, b)
GLUT-12 (617 amino acids)	SLC2A12	Heart, skeletal muscle, adipose tissue, prostate gland, kidneys, small intestine, chondrocytes, and placenta	– **Increased GLUT-12** (Malignant prostate cancer) – **Decreased GLUT-12** (Kidney tumor)	Glycoconjugate	Matsui et al. (2017)
GLUT-13 (629 amino acids)	SLC2A13	Brain, white and brown adipose tissue, and kidneys	– **Increased GLUT-13** leads to multiple myeloma		Reinicke et al. (2012)
GLUT-14 (GLUT14-S 497 amino acid and GLUT14-L 520 amino acids)	SLC2A14	Human testis	– **Increased GLUT-14** (Thyroid cancer)		Oh et al. (2017)
ABCB-1 (1280 amino acids)	MDR-1	Breast, blood-brain barrier, liver, pancreas, and kidney	Deletion of abcb1-a and abcb1-b leads to CNS toxicity and reduce intracellular drug levels causes chemo-resistance	Naringenin, Quercetin, Quinine, Berberine, Verapamil, Reserpine	Gameiro et al. (2017) and Zhang et al. (2020)

Continued

Table 4 Influence on the pharmacokinetics of drugs due polymorphisms in genes encoding drug efflux transporters—cont'd

Transporter	Gene	Location	Types of cancer	Inhibitors	References
ABCG-2 (655 amino acids)	ABCG-2	Placenta, prostate, kidney, blood-brain barrier, liver, ovary, small intestine, and seminal vesicle	Influence uric acid transport, which leads to gout, kidney disease, hypertension and its overexpression leads to leukemic CD34+/38-cells	Chrysin, Guajadial, Tariquidar, Fumitremorgin C	Traxl et al. (2019) and Orlando and Liao (2020)
ABCC-1 (580 amino acids)	ABCC-1	Liver, kidney, lung, intestine, blood-brain barrier, and peripheral blood monocellular cells	Overexpression leads to acute myeloblastic, glioma, lymphoblastic leukemia, head and neck, neuroblastoma, melanoma, thyroid cancer	Timosaponine A-3, Chrysin, 3β-acetyl tormentic acid	Dury et al. (2017)

ABC, ATP-binding cassette transporters; *GLUT*, glucose transporter; *SLC*, solute carrier family.

utilized in diagnostic procedures using fluorodeoxyglucose positron emission tomography (FDGPET). The process of cancer resilience and intrusiveness is particularly evident in the case of GLUT1 and GLUT3; hence, GLUT1 or GLUT3 overexpression could be used as a marker for the recognition of carcinogenesis at earliest (Pliszka and Szablewski, 2021). Moreover, multidrug resistance 1 (MDR1) gene encodes for P-glycoprotein or ABCB1 and ABCG2 gene encodes for ABCG2 transporter, in contrast ABCC1 gene encodes for ABCC1 transporter. Furthermore, overexpression of ATP-binding cassette (ABC) transporters facilitates the efflux of a range of medicines from cancerous cells, therefore decreasing intracellular drug concentrations, which ultimately leads to multidrug resistance (MDR).

5. Cancer derived immunoglobulins vs B-cell derived immunoglobulins

Immunoglobulins consist of two types of chain, one is heavy and another is light and they are joined by disulfide bridges to produce a two-fold symmetric structure. The immunoglobulin heavy chain is divided into five isotypes such as Igμ, Igγ, Igα, Igδ, and Igε. Further, the Igγ and Igα comprise four subclasses Igγ1, Igγ2, Igγ3, and Igγ4 and two subclasses Igα1 and Igα2, respectively. In contrast, immunoglobulin light chain has two isotypes such as Igκ and Igλ. Cancer cells have their unique immune system, and they create immunoglobulins that are different from those produced by B-cells (Lee, 2016) and these immunoglobulins are mainly expressed on epithelial cancerous tissue which further accelerate tumor growth (Hu et al., 2011). Given in Table 5, cancers of breast,

Table 5 Clinical significance of cancer derived immunoglobulins.

Type of cancer	Immunoglobulins	Biological function	Clinical significance	References
Colon cancer	IgG	Encourages expansion, migration, and invasion	Differentiation of cancerous cell, infiltration of inflammatory mediators, and lymph node metastasis	Qiu et al. (2003), Geng et al. (2019), and Jiang et al. (2019)
Lung cancer	IgG	Elevate expansion, migration, and invasion	Prognosis and differentiation of cancerous cell, local invasion, and metastasis of lymph node	Lee and Ge (2009)

Continued

Table 5 Clinical significance of cancer derived immunoglobulins—cont'd

Type of cancer	Immunoglobulins	Biological function	Clinical significance	References
Breast cancer	IgG	Promote tumor, immune escape, promote growth	Metastasis and clinical stage	Wang et al. (2020) and Ma et al. (2013)
	IgA	NA	Lymph node metastasis	
Liver cancer	IgG	Inhibits apoptosis, promote growth, and migration	NA	Qiu et al. (2003) and Lei et al. (2014)
Laryngeal cancer	IgM	NA	Prognosis and lymph node metastasis	Wang et al. (2013)
Salivary gland cancer	IgG	Regulates epithelial-mesenchymal transition (EMT), mediates motility, and promotes growth	Prognosis, metastasis, and nerve invasion	Lv et al. (2017)
Oral cancer	IgG and IgA	Regulates EMT, promotes growth, and promotes motility	Prognosis and nerve invasion	Wang and Gan (2021)
Soft tissue tumor	IgG	NA	Differentiation of tumor	Chen et al. (2011)
Pancreatic cancer	IgG	Induces inflammation, inhibits NK cell cytotoxicity, inhibits apoptosis, increases growth, migration, and invasion, and inhibits apoptosis	Chemoresistance, metastasis, prognosis, and differentiation of the tumor	Chen et al. (2019) and Cui et al. (2020)
Cervical cancer	IgG and IgA	Induces inflammation while promoting growth and inhibiting NK cell effector activity	NA	Li et al. (2004), Zheng et al. (2007), and Lee and Ge (2009)
	Igκ	Encourage malignant transformation	NA	
Acute myeloid leukemia	IgG	Inhibition of apoptosis encourages growth	Prognosis and differentiation of tumor	Wang et al. (2015) and Wu et al. (2020)
	IgM	Encourages growth	NA	
	Igκ	Encourages migration	NA	

colon, lung, laryngeal tissue, pancreatic, liver, oral cavity, cervical tissue, salivary gland, soft tissue, and acute myeloid leukemia all have cancer-derived immunoglobulins. With the knowledge that immunoglobulins expressed on the cancer cell surface play a key role in cancer immunology, several reported studies described that the cancer associated immunoglobulins have wide range of protumorigenic actions, including elevating cancer cell malignancy, mediating tumor immune escape, causing inflammation, and triggering platelet aggregation, in contrast to B cell-derived immunoglobulins, which act as an anti-body in the humoral immune response. These cancer-derived immunoglobulins behave as a growth factor, promoting cancer cell malignancies such as multiplication, spread, infiltration, and resistance to cell death (Cui et al., 2021).

6. Concluding remarks

Genetic variations in genes have explained a great deal of interindividual variation in response and toxicity of anticancer drugs. There are multiple factors that have influence on the treatment related to cancer as explained in this chapter and they are very complex to deal with it. Introducing patient genotyping into clinical settings can facilitate decision-making regarding chemotherapy regimens and drug dosages with maximal effect and minimal risk of toxicity. Although many different studies have been conducted so far, therapies targeting genes associated with cancer have shown promising effects in preclinical studies but more information is necessary for personalized medicine to be applied into everyday practice. Furthermore, there has been a substantial success in situations where single genes play a significant role in overall drug response, but the future of cancer treatment lies in whole-genome approaches. Future developments in some key areas will play a critical role in deciding the overall influence of pharmacogenetics data on therapeutic decisions.

Conflict of interest

Authors declare no conflict of interest.

References

Abrantes, A.M., Martins, M., Gonçalves, A.C., Rodrigues, M.C., Mamede, A.C., Tavares, S.D., Lima, J.M., Rodrigues, A., Sarmento-Ribeiro, A.B., Botelho, M.F., 2010. GLUT expression and 18F-FDG uptake in breast cancer cell lines. BMC Proc., 1. https://doi.org/10.1186/1753-6561-4-S2-P21.

Abubakar, M.B., Wei, K., Gan, S.H., 2014. The influence of genetic polymorphisms on the efficacy and side effects of anastrozole in postmenopausal breast cancer patients. Pharmacogenet. Genomics 24 (12), 575–581. https://journals.lww.com/jpharmacogenetics/Abstract/2014/12000/The_influence_of_genetic_polymorphisms_on_the.1.aspx.

Bertholee, D., Maring, J.G., Van, A.B., 2017. Genotypes affecting the pharmacokinetics of anticancer drugs. Clin. Pharmacokinet. 56 (4), 317–337. https://doi.org/10.1007/s40262-016-0450-z.

Boudou-Rouquette, P., Narjoz, C., Golmard, J.L., Thomas-Schoemann, A., Mir, O., Taieb, F., Durand, J. P., Coriat, R., Dauphin, A., Vidal, M., Tod, M., 2012. Early sorafenib-induced toxicity is associated with drug exposure and UGTIA9 genetic polymorphism in patients with solid tumors: a preliminary study. PLoS One. https://journals.plos.org/plosone/article?id=10.1371/journal.pone.0042875.

Brennan, M., Williams, J.A., Chen, Y., Tortorici, M., Pithavala, Y., Liu, Y.C., 2012. Meta-analysis of contribution of genetic polymorphisms in drug-metabolizing enzymes or transporters to axitinib pharmacokinetics. Eur. J. Clin. Pharmacol. 68 (5), 645–655. https://doi.org/10.1007/s00228-011-1171-8.

Chai, Y.J., Yi, J.W., Oh, S.W., Kim, Y.A., Yi, K.H., Kim, J.H., Lee, K.E., 2017. Upregulation of SLC2 (GLUT) family genes is related to poor survival outcomes in papillary thyroid carcinoma: analysis of data from the cancer genome atlas. Surgery 161 (1), 188–194. https://doi.org/10.1016/j.surg.2016.04.050.

Chen, Z., Li, J., Xiao, Y., Zhang, J., Zhao, Y., Liu, Y., Ma, C., Qiu, Y., Luo, J., Huang, G., Korteweg, C., 2011. Immunoglobulin G locus events in soft tissue sarcoma cell lines. PLoS One 6 (6), e21276. https://doi.org/10.1371/journal.pone.0021276.

Chen, Q., Wang, J., Zhang, Q., Zhang, J., Lou, Y., Yang, J., Chen, Y., Wei, T., Zhang, J., Fu, Q., Ye, M., 2019. Tumour cell-derived debris and IgG synergistically promote metastasis of pancreatic cancer by inducing inflammation via tumour-associated macrophages. Br. J. Cancer 121 (9), 786–795. https://www.nature.com/articles/s41416-019-0595-2.

Cui, M., You, L., Zheng, B., Huang, X., Liu, Q., Huang, J., Pan, B., Qiu, X., Liao, Q., Zhao, Y., 2020. High expression of cancer-derived glycosylated immunoglobulin G predicts poor prognosis in pancreatic ductal adenocarcinoma. J. Cancer 11 (8), 2213. https://doi.org/10.7150/jca.39800.

Cui, M., Huang, J., Zhang, S., Liu, Q., Liao, Q., Qiu, X., 2021. Immunoglobulin expression in cancer cells and its critical roles in tumorigenesis. Front. Immunol. 12, 893. https://doi.org/10.3389/fimmu.2021.613530.

Daskalow, K., Pfander, D., Weichert, W., Rohwer, N., Thelen, A., Neuhaus, P., Jonas, S., Wiedenmann, B., Benckert, C., Cramer, T., 2009. Distinct temporospatial expression patterns of glycolysis-related proteins in human hepatocellular carcinoma. Histochem. Cell Biol. 132 (1), 21–31. https://doi.org/10.1007/s00418-009-0590-4.

Diasio, R.B., Beavers, T.L., Carpenter, J.T., 1988. Familial deficiency of dihydropyrimidine dehydrogenase: biochemical basis for familial pyrimidinemia and severe 5-fluorouracil-induced toxicity. J. Clin. Invest. 81 (1), 47–51. https://pubmed.ncbi.nlm.nih.gov/3335642/.

Dury, L., Nasr, R., Lorendeau, D., Comsa, E., Wong, I., Zhu, X., Chan, K.F., Chan, T.H., Chow, L., Falson, P., Di Pietro, A., 2017. Flavonoid dimers are highly potent killers of multidrug resistant cancer cells overexpressing MRP1. Biochem. Pharmacol. 24, 10–18. https://doi.org/10.1016/j.bcp.2016.10.013.

Ekhart, C., Rodenhuis, S., Smits, P.H., Beijnen, J.H., Huitema, A.D., 2008. Relations between polymorphisms in drug-metabolising enzymes and toxicity of chemotherapy with cyclophosphamide, thiotepa and carboplatin. Pharmacogenet. Genomics 18 (11), 1009–1015. https://journals.lww.com/jpharmacogenetics/Abstract/2008/11000/Relations_between_polymorphisms_in.9.aspx.

Gameiro, M., Silva, R., Rocha-Pereira, C., Carmo, H., Carvalho, F., Bastos, M.D., Remião, F., 2017. Cellular models and in vitro assays for the screening of modulators of P-gp, MRP1 and BCRP. Molecules 22 (4), 600. https://doi.org/10.3390/molecules22040600.

Geng, Z.H., Ye, C.X., Huang, Y., Jiang, H.P., Ye, Y.J., Wang, S., Zhou, Y., Shen, Z.L., Qiu, X.Y., 2019. Human colorectal cancer cells frequently express IgG and display unique Ig repertoire. World J. Gastrointest. Oncol. 11 (3), 195. https://www.ncbi.nlm.nih.gov/pmc/articles/PMC6425329/.

Guilhaumou, R., Simon, N., Quaranta, S., Verschuur, A., Lacarelle, B., Andre, N., Solas, C., 2011. Population pharmacokinetics and pharmacogenetics of vincristine in paediatric patients treated for solid tumour diseases. Cancer Chemother. Pharmacol. 68 (5), 1191–1198. https://doi.org/10.1007/s00280-010-1541-4.

Gurney, H., Wong, M., Balleine, R.L., Rivory, L.P., McLachlan, A.J., Hoskins, J.M., Wilcken, N., Clarke, C.L., Mann, G.J., Collins, M., Delforce, S.E., 2007. Imatinib disposition and ABCB1 (MDR1, P-glycoprotein) genotype. Clin. Pharmacol. Ther. 82 (1), 33–40. https://doi.org/10.1038/sj.clpt.6100201.

Hawwa, A.F., Collier, P.S., Millership, J.S., 2008. Population pharmacokinetic and pharmacogenetic analysis of 6-mercaptopurine in paediatric patients with acute lymphoblastic leukaemia. Br. J. Clin. Pharmacol. 66 (6), 826–837. https://doi.org/10.1111/j.1365-2125.2008.03281.x. https://www.ncbi.nlm.nih.gov/pmc/articles/PMC2675766/.

Houtsma, D., Guchelaar, H.J., Gelderblom, H., 2010. Pharmacogenetics in oncology: a promising field. Curr. Pharm. Des. 16 (2), 155–163. https://pubmed.ncbi.nlm.nih.gov/20205661/.

Hu, D., Duan, Z., Li, M., Jiang, Y., Liu, H., Zheng, H., Cao, Y., 2011. Heterogeneity of aberrant immunoglobulin expression in cancer cells. Cell. Mol. Immunol. 8 (6), 479–485. https://doi.org/10.1038/cmi.2011.25.

Hu, R.T., Wang, N.Y., Huang, M.J., Huang, C.S., Chen, D.S., Yang, S.S., 2014. Multiple variants in UGT1A1 gene are factors to develop indirect hyper-bilirubinemia. Hepatobiliary Surg. Nutr. 3 (4), 194. https://doi.org/10.3978/j.issn.2304-3881.2014.08.04.

Huang, X.Q., Chen, X., Xie, X.X., Zhou, Q., Li, K., Li, S., Shen, L.F., Su, J., 2014a. Co-expression of CD147 and GLUT-1 indicates radiation resistance and poor prognosis in cervical squamous cell carcinoma. Int. J. Clin. Exp. Pathol. 7 (4), 1651. https://www.ncbi.nlm.nih.gov/pmc/articles/PMC4014246/.

Huang, J., Sun, X., Gong, X., He, Z., Chen, L., Qiu, X., Yin, C.C., 2014b. Rearrangement and expression of the immunoglobulin μ-chain gene in human myeloid cells. Cell Mol. Immunol. 11 (1), 94–104. https://www.nature.com/articles/cmi201345.

Huezo-Diaz, P., Uppugunduri, R.S., Kumar Tyagi, A., Krajinovic, M., Ansari, M., 2014. Pharmacogenetic aspects of drug metabolizing enzymes in busulfan based conditioning prior to allogenic hematopoietic stem cell transplantation in children. Curr. Drug Metab. 15 (3), 251–264. https://www.ingentaconnect.com/content/ben/cdm/2014/00000015/00000003/art00001.

Ingelman, M., 2004. Human drug metabolising cytochrome P450 enzymes: properties and polymorphisms. Naunyn Schmiedeberg's Arch. Pharmacol. 369 (1), 89–104. https://doi.org/10.1007/s00210-003-0819-z.

Jancova, P., Anzenbacher, P., Anzenbacherova, E., 2010. Phase II drug metabolizing enzymes. Biomed. Pap. Med. Fac. Univ. Palacky Olomouc Czech Repub. 154 (2), 103–106. https://pubmed.ncbi.nlm.nih.gov/20668491/.

Jiang, H., Kang, B., Huang, X., Yan, Y., Wang, S., Ye, Y., Shen, Z., 2019. Cancer IgG, a potential prognostic marker, promotes colorectal cancer progression. Chin. J. Cancer Res. 31 (3), 499. https://www.ncbi.nlm.nih.gov/pmc/articles/PMC6613500/.

Johnson, G.G., Lin, K., Cox, T.F., Oates, M., Sibson, D.R., Eccles, R., Lloyd, B., Gardiner, L.J., Carr, D.F., Pirmohamed, M., Strefford, J.C., 2013. CYP2B6* 6 is an independent determinant of inferior response to fludarabine plus cyclophosphamide in chronic lymphocytic leukemia. Blood 122 (26), 4253–4258. https://pubmed.ncbi.nlm.nih.gov/24128861/.

Kadakol, A., Ghosh, S.S., Sappal, B.S., Sharma, G., Chowdhury, J.R., Chowdhury, N.R., 2000. Genetic lesions of bilirubin uridine-diphosphoglucuronate glucuronosyltransferase (UGT1A1) causing Crigler-Najjar and Gilbert syndromes: correlation of genotype to phenotype. Hum. Mutat. 16 (4), 297–306. https://doi.org/10.1002/1098-1004(200010)16:4%3C297::AID-HUMU2%3E3.0.CO;2-Z.

Kantar, M., Kosova, B., Cetingul, N., 2009. Methylenetetrahydrofolate reductase C677T and A1298C gene polymorphisms and therapy-related toxicity in children treated for acute lymphoblastic leukemia and non-Hodgkin lymphoma. Leuk. Lymphoma 50 (6), 912–917. https://doi.org/10.1080/10428190902893819. https://pubmed.ncbi.nlm.nih.gov/19391036/.

Kim, T.W., Innocenti, F., 2007. Insights, challenges, and future directions in irinogenetics. Ther. Drug Monit. 29 (3), 265–270. https://journals.lww.com/drug-monitoring/Abstract/2007/06000/Insights,_Challenges,_and_Future_Directions_in.1.aspx.

Knights, J., Sato, Y., Kaniwa, N., 2014. Genetic factors associated with gemcitabine pharmacokinetics, disposition, and toxicity. Pharmacogenet. Genomics 24 (1), 15–25. https://doi.org/10.1097/fpc.0000000000000016. https://pubmed.ncbi.nlm.nih.gov/24225399/.

Kobayashi, H., Sato, K., Niioka, T., Miura, H., Ito, H., Miura, M., 2015. Relationship among gefitinib exposure, polymorphisms of its metabolizing enzymes and transporters, and side effects in Japanese patients with non-small-cell lung cancer. Clin. Lung Cancer 16 (4), 274–281. https://doi.org/10.1016/j.cllc.2014.12.004.

Kulkarni, P.S., 2016. Pharmacogenetics in oncology: where we stand today? IJMIO 1 (1), 1–5. https://ijmio.com/view-pdf/?article=068262b578b679e91ad792abda84055dcSjZCw==.

Lal, S., Wong, Z.W., Sandanaraj, E., Xiang, X., Ang, P.C., Lee, E.J., Chowbay, B., 2008. Influence of ABCB1 and ABCG2 polymorphisms on doxorubicin disposition in Asian breast cancer patients. Cancer Sci. 99 (4), 816–823. https://doi.org/10.1111/j.1349-7006.2008.00744.x.

Lamb, D.C., Waterman, M.R., Kelly, S.L., Guengerich, F.P., 2007. Cytochromes P450 and drug discovery. Curr. Opin. Biotechnol. 18 (6), 504–512. https://doi.org/10.1016/j.copbio.2007.09.010.

Lee, G., 2016. Distinct functional roles of cancerous immunoglobulins in cancer immunology. Integr. Mol. Med. 3 (4), 749–754. https://doi.org/10.15761/IMM.1000238. https://www.oatext.com/pdf/IMM-3-238.pdf.

Lee, G., Ge, B., 2009. Cancer cell expressions of immunoglobulin heavy chains with unique carbohydrate-associated biomarker. Cancer Biomark. 5 (4–5), 177–188. https://content.iospress.com/articles/cancer-biomarkers/cbm00102.

Lei, Y., Huang, T., Su, M., Luo, J., Korteweg, C., Li, J., Chen, Z., Qiu, Y., Liu, X., Yan, M., Wang, Y., 2014. Expression and distribution of immunoglobulin G in the normal liver, hepatocarcinoma and postpartial hepatectomy liver. Lab. Investig. 94 (11), 1283–1295. https://doi.org/10.1038/labinvest.2014.114.

Li, M., Feng, D.Y., Ren, W., Zheng, L., Zheng, H., Tang, M., Cao, Y., 2004. Expression of immunoglobulin kappa light chain constant region in abnormal human cervical epithelial cells. Int. J. Biochem. Cell Biol. 36 (11), 2250–2257. https://doi.org/10.1016/j.biocel.2004.03.017.

Lv, W.Q., Peng, J., Wang, H.C., Chen, D.P., Yang, Y., Zhao, Y., Qiu, X.Y., Jiang, J.H., Li, C.Y., 2017. Expression of cancer cell–derived IgG and extra domain A-containing fibronectin in salivary adenoid cystic carcinoma. Arch. Oral Biol. 81, 15–20. https://doi.org/10.1016/j.archoralbio.2017.04.010. https://pubmed.ncbi.nlm.nih.gov/28460248/.

Ma, C., Wang, Y., Zhang, G., Chen, Z., Qiu, Y., Li, J., Luo, J., Huang, B., Jiang, C., Huang, G., Wan, X., 2013. Immunoglobulin G expression and its potential role in primary and metastatic breast cancers. Curr. Mol. Med. 13 (3), 429–437. https://doi.org/10.2174/156652413805076731.

Mano, Y., Aishima, S., Kubo, Y., Tanaka, Y., Motomura, T., Toshima, T., Shirabe, K., Baba, S., Maehara, Y., Oda, Y., 2014. Correlation between biological marker expression and fluorine-18 fluorodeoxyglucose uptake in hepatocellular carcinoma. Am. J. Clin. Pathol. 142 (3), 391–397. https://doi.org/10.1309/AJCPG8AFJ5NRKLLM.

Matsui, C., Takatani-Nakase, T., Maeda, S., Nakase, I., Takahashi, K., 2017. Potential roles of GLUT12 for glucose sensing and cellular migration in MCF-7 human breast cancer cells under high glucose conditions. Anticancer Res. 37 (12), 6715–6722. https://ar.iiarjournals.org/content/37/12/6715.short.

Matsuzawa, N., Nakamura, K., Matsuda, M., Ishida, F., Ohmori, S., 2012. Influence of cytochrome P450 2C19 gene variations on pharmacokinetic parameters of thalidomide in Japanese patients. Biol. Pharm. Bull. 35 (3), 317–320. https://doi.org/10.1248/bpb.35.317.

McBrayer, S.K., Cheng, J.C., Singhal, S., Krett, N.L., Rosen, S.T., Shanmugam, M., 2012. Multiple myeloma exhibits novel dependence on GLUT4, GLUT8, and GLUT11: implications for glucose transporter-directed therapy. Blood 119 (20), 4686–4697. https://doi.org/10.1182/blood-2011-09-377846.

Meyer, H.J., Wienke, A., Surov, A., 2019a. Associations between GLUT expression and SUV values derived from FDG-PET in different tumors—a systematic review and meta analysis. PLoS One 14 (6), e0217781. https://doi.org/10.1371/journal.pone.0217781.

Meyer, H.J., Wienke, A., Surov, A., 2019b. Associations between GLUT expression and SUV values derived from FDG-PET in different tumors—a systematic review and meta analysis. PLoS One 14 (6), e0217781. https://doi.org/10.1371/journal.pone.0217781.

Mochizuki, T., Tsukamoto, E., Kuge, Y., Kanegae, K., Zhao, S., Hikosaka, K., Hosokawa, M., Kohanawa, M., Tamaki, N., 2001. FDG uptake and glucose transporter subtype expressions in experimental tumor and inflammation models. J. Nucl. Med. 42 (10), 1551–1555. https://jnm.snmjournals.org/content/42/10/1551.short.

Mwinyi, J., Vokinger, K., Jetter, A., Breitenstein, U., Hiller, C., Kullak-Ublick, G.A., Trojan, A., 2014. Impact of variable CYP genotypes on breast cancer relapse in patients undergoing adjuvant tamoxifen therapy. Cancer Chemother. Pharmacol. 73 (6), 1181–1188. https://doi.org/10.1007/s00280-014-2453-5.

Ogungbenro, K., Aarons, L., 2015. Physiologically based pharmacokinetic model for 6-mercpatopurine: exploring the role of genetic polymorphism in TPMT enzyme activity. Br. J. Clin. Pharmacol. 80 (1), 86–100. https://doi.org/10.1111/bcp.12588. https://pubmed.ncbi.nlm.nih.gov/25614061/.

Oh, S., Kim, H., Nam, K., Shin, I., 2017. Glut1 promotes cell proliferation, migration and invasion by reg-ulating epidermal growth factor receptor and integrin signaling in triple-negative breast cancer cells. BMB Rep. 50 (3), 132. https://www.ncbi.nlm.nih.gov/pmc/articles/PMC5422025/.

Orlando, B.J., Liao, M., 2020. ABCG2 transports anticancer drugs via a closed-to-open switch. Nat. Commun. 11 (1), 1. https://www.nature.com/articles/s41467-020-16155-2.

Passot, C., Azzopardi, N., Renault, S., Baroukh, N., Arnoult, C., Ohresser, M., Boisdron-Celle, M., Gamelin, E., Watier, H., Paintaud, G., Gouilleux-Gruart, V., 2013. Influence of FCGRT gene poly-morphisms on pharmacokinetics of therapeutic antibodies. mAbs 5 (4), 614–619. https://pubmed.ncbi.nlm.nih.gov/23751752/.

Pavlos, R., Mallal, S., Phillips, E., 2012. HLA and pharmacogenetics of drug hypersensitivity. Pharmaco-genomics 13 (11), 1285–1306. https://doi.org/10.2217/pgs.12.108.

Pliszka, M., Szablewski, L., 2021. Glucose transporters as a target for anticancer therapy. Cancer 13 (16), 4184. https://doi.org/10.3390/cancers13164184.

Polillo, M., Galimberti, S., Baratè, C., Petrini, M., Danesi, R., Di Paolo, A., 2015. Pharmacogenetics of BCR/ABL inhibitors in chronic myeloid leukemia. Int. J. Mol. Sci. 16 (9), 22811–22829. https://doi.org/10.3390/ijms160922811.

Qiu, X., Zhu, X., Zhang, L., Mao, Y., Zhang, J., Hao, P., Li, G., Lv, P., Li, Z., Sun, X., Wu, L., 2003. Human epithelial cancers secrete immunoglobulin g with unidentified specificity to promote growth and survival of tumor cells. Cancer Res. 63 (19), 6488–6495. https://aacrjournals.org/cancerres/article/63/19/6488/510402/Human-Epithelial-Cancers-Secrete-Immunoglobulin-G.

Quinn, D.I., Nemunaitis, J., Fuloria, J., Britten, C.D., Gabrail, N., Yee, L., Acharya, M., Chan, K., Cohen, N., Dudov, A., 2009. Effect of the cytochrome P450 2C19 inhibitor omeprazole on the phar-macokinetics and safety profile of bortezomib in patients with advanced solid tumours, non-Hodgkin's lymphoma or multiple myeloma. Clin. Pharm. 48 (3), 199–209. https://doi.org/10.2165/00003088-200948030-00006.

Reckzeh, E.S., Karageorgis, G., Schwalfenberg, M., Ceballos, J., Nowacki, J., Stroet, M.C., Binici, A., Knauer, L., Brand, S., Choidas, A., Strohmann, C., 2019. Inhibition of glucose transporters and gluta-minase synergistically impairs tumor cell growth. Cell Chem. Biol. 26 (9), 1214–1228. https://doi.org/10.1016/j.chembiol.2019.06.005.

Reinicke, K., Sotomayor, P., Cisterna, P., Delgado, C., Nualart, F., Godoy, A., 2012. Cellular distribution of Glut-1 and Glut-5 in benign and malignant human prostate tissue. J. Cell. Biochem. 113 (2), 553–562. https://doi.org/10.1002/jcb.23379.

Rodriguez-Antona, C., Ingelman-Sundberg, M., 2006. Cytochrome P450 pharmacogenetics and cancer. Oncogene 25 (11), 1679–1691. https://www.nature.com/articles/1209377.

Stewart, C.F., Tagen, M., Schwartzberg, L.S., Blakely, L.J., Tauer, K.W., Smiley, L.M., 2014. Phase I dosage finding and pharmacokinetic study of intravenous topotecan and oral erlotinib in adults with refractory solid tumors. Cancer Chemother. Pharmacol. 73 (3), 561–568. https://doi.org/10.1007/s00280-014-2385-0.

Suganuma, N., Segade, F., Matsuzu, K., Bowden, D.W., 2007. Differential expression of facilitative glucose transporters in normal and tumour kidney tissues. BJU Int. 99 (5), 1143–1149. https://pubmed.ncbi.nlm.nih.gov/17437443/.

Szablewski, L., 2013. Expression of glucose transporters in cancers. Biochim. Biophys. Acta Rev. Cancer 1835 (2), 164–169. https://doi.org/10.1016/j.bbcan.2012.12.004.

Ten Brink, M.H., Zwaveling, J., Swen, J.J., Bredius, R.G., Lankester, A.C., Guchelaar, H.J., 2014. Person-alized busulfan and treosulfan conditioning for pediatric stem cell transplantation: the role of pharmacogenetics and pharmacokinetics. Drug Discov. Today 19 (10), 1572–1586. https://doi.org/10.1016/j.drudis.2014.04.005.

Traxl, A., Mairinger, S., Filip, T., Sauberer, M., Stanek, J., Poschner, S., Jäger, W., Zoufal, V., Novarino, G., Tournier, N., Bauer, M., 2019. Inhibition of ABCB1 and ABCG2 at the mouse blood–brain barrier with marketed drugs to improve brain delivery of the model ABCB1/ABCG2 sub-strate [11C] erlotinib. Mol. Pharm. 16 (3), 1282–1293. https://doi.org/10.1021/acs.molpharmaceut.8b01217.

Wang, L.M., Gan, Y.H., 2021. Cancer-derived IgG involved in cisplatin resistance through PTP-BAS/Src/PDK1/AKT signaling pathway. Oral Dis. 27 (3), 464–474. https://doi.org/10.1111/odi.13583.

Wang, H., Cao, X., Liu, E.C., He, D., Ma, Y., Zhang, T., Feng, Y., Qin, G., 2013. Prognostic significance of immunoglobulin M overexpression in laryngeal squamous cell carcinoma. Acta Otolaryngol. 133 (10), 1080–1087. https://doi.org/10.3109/00016489.2013.799776.

Wang, C., Xia, M., Sun, X., He, Z., Hu, F., Chen, L., Bueso-Ramos, C.E., Qiu, X., Yin, C.C., 2015. IGK with conserved IGKV/IGKJ repertoire is expressed in acute myeloid leukemia and promotes leukemic cell migration. Oncotarget 6 (36), 39062. https://doi.org/10.18632/oncotarget.5393.

Wang, Z., Geng, Z., Shao, W., Liu, E., Zhang, J., Tang, J., Wang, P., Sun, X., Xiao, L., Xu, W., Zhang, Y., 2020. Cancer-derived sialylated IgG promotes tumor immune escape by binding to Siglecs on effector T cells. Cell Mol. Immunol. 17 (11), 1148–1162. https://www.nature.com/articles/s41423-019-0327-9.

Watanabe, M., Abe, N., Oshikiri, Y., Stanbridge, E.J., Kitagawa, T., 2012. Selective growth inhibition by glycogen synthase kinase-3 inhibitors in tumorigenic HeLa hybrid cells is mediated through NF-κB-dependent GLUT3 expression. Oncogene 1 (7), e21. https://www.nature.com/articles/oncsis201221.

Wei, C., Achreja, A., Konen, J., Sica, G., Gilbert-Ross, M., Nagrath, D., Marcus, A., Shanmugam, M., 2017. GLUT4 exhibits a non-canonical role of regulating lung cancer metastasis. Cancer Res. 77, 4904. https://doi.org/10.1158/1538-7445.AM2017-4904.

Wu, L., Xia, M., Sun, X., Han, X., Zu, Y., Jabbour, E.J., You, M.J., Lin, P., Li, S., Xu, J., Han, H., 2020. High levels of immunoglobulin expression predict shorter overall survival in patients with acute myeloid leukemia. Eur. J. Haematol. 105 (4), 449–459. https://doi.org/10.1111/ejh.13466.

Zhang, L., Mao, Y., Gao, Z., Chen, X., Li, X., Liu, Y., Xia, G., 2020. The nonclinical pharmacokinetics and prediction of human pharmacokinetics of SPH3127, a novel direct renin inhibitor. Eur. J. Drug Metab. Pharmacokinet. 45 (1), 15–26. https://doi.org/10.1007/s13318-019-00573-9.

Zheng, H., Li, M., Liu, H., Ren, W., Hu, D.S., Shi, Y., Tang, M., Cao, Y., 2007. Immunoglobulin alpha heavy chain derived from human epithelial cancer cells promotes the access of S phase and growth of cancer cells. Cell Biol. Int. 31 (1), 82–87. https://doi.org/10.1016/j.cellbi.2006.09.009.

Zheng, Y., Scow, J.S., Duenes, J.A., Sarr, M.G., 2012. Mechanisms of glucose uptake in intestinal cell lines: role of GLUT2. Surgery 151 (1), 13–25. https://doi.org/10.1016/j.surg.2011.07.010.

CHAPTER NINETEEN

Emergence of metal-based anticancer therapeutics: A promising perspective

Priyatosh Nath[a,b], Abhijit Datta[c], Tanushree Sen[d], and Suman Adhikari[e]

[a]Faculty of Allied Health Sciences, The ICFAI University Tripura, Mohanpur, Tripura, India
[b]Department of Human Physiology, Tripura University, Suryamaninagar, Tripura, India
[c]Department of Botany, Ambedkar College, Fatikroy, Tripura, India
[d]Department of Chemistry, Jagannath Kishore College, Purulia, West Bengal, India
[e]Department of Chemistry, Govt. Degree College, Dharmanagar, Tripura, India

Abbreviations

2PFM	two-photon fluorescence microscopy
5-FU	5 fluorouracil
A	adenine nucleotide
AG	adenine guanine pair
Ag	silver
ATR	ATM and Rad-3-related protein
Au	gold
BAX	Bcl-2-associated X protein (a protein associated with apoptotic pathway)
Bcl2	B-cell lymphoma 2 (a protein associated with apoptotic pathway)
CHK1	checkpoint kinase 1
CLL	chronic lymphocytic leukemia
c-Myc	a transcription factor
CNTs	carbon nanotubes
CTR	copper transporter proteins (a type of protein channel which help in active transport of molecules in and out of the cell)
Cu	copper
DC	dendritic cell (an immune cell population)
DNA	deoxyribonucleic acid
ECF	extracellular fluid, the fluid present outside the cell examples are plasma, tissue fluid
ERK	extracellular signal regulated kinase
FDA	The Food and Drug Administration, United States of America
G	guanine nucleotide
GG	guanine guanine pair
GI	gastrointestinal (digestive tract of human and animals)
HMG	high mobility group protein
hMSH2	human mutS homolog 2 protein
Hsp90	heat shock protein 90

Biomarkers in Cancer Detection and Monitoring of Therapeutics
https://doi.org/10.1016/B978-0-323-95114-2.00012-1

hUBF	human upstream binding factor
ICF	intracellular fluid, the fluid present within the plasma membrane of a cell
ILCT	intraligand charge transfer
Ir	iridium
IUPAC	The International Union of Pure and Applied Chemistry
IV	intravenous (a route of drug administration)
LLCT	ligand-to-ligand charge transfer
LTMTCT	ligand-to-metal-metal charge transfer
MAPK	mitogen-activated protein kinase
MLCT	metal-to-ligand charge transfer
MMP-9	matrix metallopeptidase 9 (an enzyme protein involved in the breakdown of extracellular matrix)
MoA	mechanism of action
MOFs	metal organic framework
MRI	magnetic resonance imaging
NCI	National Cancer Institute, USA
NHCs	N-heterocyclic carbenes
NIR	near infrared region
NPs	nanoparticles
NSCLC	nonsmall cell lung cancer
OCT	organic cation transporters a type of protein channel which are associated with transport of organic cations in and out of cells
Os	osmium
PD-L1	programmed cell death protein 1 (an inhibitor of immune response)
Pd	palladium
PDT	photodynamic therapy
PEG	poly(ethylene glycol)
PET	photo-induced electron transfer
PET	positron emission tomography
PLL	prolymphocytic lymphoma
PS	photosensitizers
Pt	platinum
Pt-DNA	platinum–DNA adducts
RNA	ribonucleic acid
ROS	reactive oxygen species
Ru	ruthenium
SLL	small lymphocytic lymphoma
SOD	superoxide dismutase
SPECT	single-photon emission computerized tomography
T Cell	T lymphocyte cell (an immune cell population)
TBP	TATA binding protein
TDO	tryptophan-2,3-dioxygenase
TrxR	thioredoxin reductase

UK	United Kingdom
UV	ultraviolet light
ZnO	zinc oxide
γ-H2AX	phosphorylated form of H2A histone family member X, it is a sensitive molecular marker of DNA damage and repair

1. Introduction

Cancer is a primary cause of death globally, instigating approximately 10 million deaths in 2020 (Ferlay et al., 2020). Cancer is a general term for a vast group of ailments which distress different parts of the body. One significant feature of malignancy is the fast formation of abnormal cells that grow in an uncontrolled manner, besides invading neighboring parts of the body as well as get spread into other organs; via a process called metastasis which is the prime source of death from cancer.

Medicinal inorganic chemistry is a promising and rapidly expanding subject that entails a variety of activities, including the introduction (or expulsion) of an ionic metal into (or out of) an organism for diagnostic or therapeutic purposes (Singh et al., 2017, 2018; Adhikari et al., 2020; Bhattacharjee et al., 2022). Metals are abundant, and some are required for cellular functions. Since metals are capable of forming cations when submerged in aqueous solution besides bonding to biomolecules having negative charge, charge manipulation can be attained depending on the coordination environment, imparting influence on the production of a cationic, anionic, or neutral biomolecule. Furthermore, metal ions with a high electron affinity can polarize groups that are coordinated to them, allowing for the formation of hydrolysis processes (Haas and Franz, 2009). Metals were chosen during evolution to boost biochemical processes engaged in cellular functions based on their availability. Because of these properties of metal, medicinal inorganic chemistry's potential therapeutic utility in the development of anticancer drugs has recently gained major interest (Adhikari et al., 2019a; Paprocka et al., 2022; Monro et al., 2019). The use of metal complexes as a lifesaving medicine necessitates a thorough analysis of the proposed drug's fundamental aqueous chemistry, including pharmacokinetics, metabolic destiny in the body, and the specific effects it exerts on the target cell. Coordination compounds come in a wide range of variable oxidation states, coordination spheres, and redox potentials, allowing thermodynamic and kinetic properties of the compounds toward biological systems to be systematically changed. Metallodrugs have various advantages over traditional organic compounds when it comes to the development of new therapeutic drugs. These advantages arise from the ability of metal-containing compounds to integrate ligands within a three-dimensional arrangement, permitting for the functionalization of moieties that can be employed to precise subcellular targets (Frezza et al., 2010). Metal-based compounds provide a well-supplied environment in which formation of a various range of unique molecular architectures with an extensive range of geometries and coordination numbers, as well as kinetic features can be observed, which are not possible with standard organic compounds (Frezza et al., 2010).

Metal-based compounds were once widely employed to cure many diseased conditions, but the lack of a distinctive demarcation between the useful therapeutic and toxic doses posed a significant obstacle. This was principally due to inadequacy of knowledge among the ancient practitioners about the dose-response relationship and toxicity of metal-based drugs (Ji et al., 2009). But at present the rational design of a target specific molecule is much easier using the knowledge of advanced molecular biology and combinatorial chemistry. The observation of biological activity of platinum compounds by Barnett Rosenberg's in the 1960s marked a turning point in the history of metallodrugs used in the treatment malignant disorders (Rosenberg et al., 1969; Nicolini, 1997). This observation laid the foundation for the present era of anticancer drugs based on metals. Barnett Rosenberg discovered the anticancer activity of cisplatin eventually become very popular and first choice for cancer chemotherapy. Even though cisplatin is a potent anticancer medicine, it often mediates severe side effects and with time its efficacy is also restricted by resistance. Platinum medications, such as oxaliplatin, lobaplatin, carboplatin, nedaplatin, heptaplatin, etc. (Fig. 1) are the key metal-based chemo drugs used in cancer treatment. The slow progress as well as delayed medicinal achievements with nonplatinum compounds has hampered research in this arena (Kelland, 2007). Nevertheless, there has been a recent uptick in initiatives based on structural data, aimed at enhancing the number of pharmacologically active metallodrugs and nonclassical platinum compounds with mechanisms of action different from established medications like cisplatin. Many metal-based complexes developed either by altering the existing structures by substitution of ligand or by creating an entirely novel complexes have reduced the toxicity of

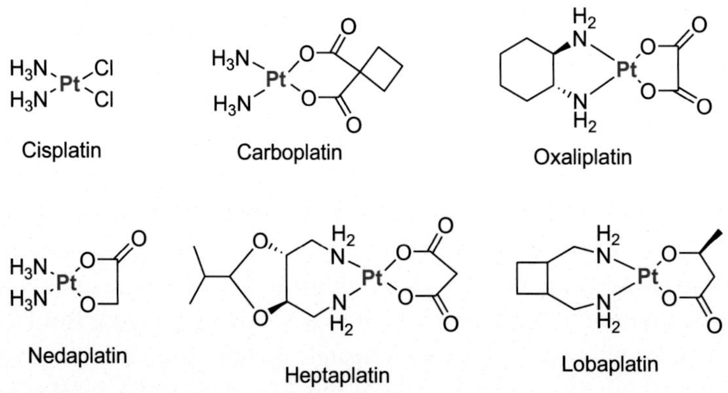

Fig. 1 Clinically approved platinum anticancer drugs.

drugs to a certain extent. Moreover, due to the increased focus on the clinical significance of metallodrugs, a number of these medications are presently in clinical trials, with many more seeking ethical consent to join the trial.

Platinum complexes have a restricted solubility in aqueous media, as well as adverse effects such as ototoxicity, myelosuppression, nephrotoxicity, and low selectivity for healthy cells, even though the fact that platinum complexes provide patients with effective therapeutic treatment. As a result, attempts have been undertaken to find innovative solutions. Nonplatinum complexes (such as Ru, Au, Ir, and others) have been discovered to have anticancer properties (Paprocka et al., 2022; Frezza et al., 2010). Because of its promising cytotoxic and prospective anticancer capabilities, the chemistry of gold and ruthenium-based complexes has recently garnered intense research attention to create a substitute to cisplatin and other platinum-based drugs (Milacic et al., 2008; Bindoli et al., 2009a; Kostova, 2006a; Liu et al., 2018).

Metal-based compounds have recently become more popular in the chemotherapy of cancer. This may be due to the cancer epidemic and, to a lesser extent, the level of in vitro cytotoxicity demonstrated by metallodrugs, particularly those developed in recent years. The incorporation of transition metal ions into rationally designed ligands opens up new possibilities for developing novel metal-containing molecules with improved biological activity, bioavailability, and selectivity. Furthermore, the adoption of new approach of conjugating the metals with bile acid, steroid, peptide, or sugar, etc., other than substitution of ligands and alteration of existing chemical structures can provide better metallodrugs with improved cytotoxic and pharmacokinetic profile as well as easy delivery to target cells population. Metallic nanoparticles have recently been discovered to be especially useful in cancer immunotherapy due to the precise size, shape, and charge. This chapter carefully analyses the advent of metallodrugs along with their mechanism of action as well as the prospects of future metal-based drugs.

2. Platinum-based drugs from past to present

Platinum is the brightest name when the anticancer efficacy of the metals has to be discussed. The pharmacological activity of platinum was not known until the discovery of platinum amine halide complexes (cisplatin) and its biological activity testing by Rosenberg and colleagues in 1965 (Rosenberg et al., 1965; Bertini et al., 1994; Kaim and Schwederski, 1993). In the pioneering study Rosenberg observed inhibition of bacterial growth in presence of platinum amine halide complexes and replicated this study on cancer cell culture just out of curiosity before he came up with this novel discovery. Later, in 1969, the anticancer activity of cisplatin was tested on mice bearing leukemia L1210 and sarcoma 180 (Rosenberg and Van Camp, 1970; Kociba et al., 1970). This study conducted by Rosenberg and coworkers led the cisplatin to enter into phase-I

Table 1 Clinically permitted platinum anticancer drugs.

Generic name	Trade name	Approval granted
Cispatin	Platinol	1978
Carboplatin	Paraplatin	1989
Oxaliplatin	Eloxatin	2002
Nedaplatin	Aqupla アクプラ	1995
Heptaplatin	Sunpla 선플라	1999
Lobaplatin	洛鉑	2010

clinical trial 1971. In 1978, cisplatin got US Food and Drug Administration (FDA) approval for therapeutic application against genitourinary tumors (Smith, 1979). At present it is used for the treatment of number of malignancies including cervical, bladder, testicular, ovarian, head and neck, small-cell and nonsmall cell lung cancers (Ghosh, 2019). It remains first choice for cancer chemotherapy for quite a long time unless its disadvantages and side effects been identified. Some of the potential disadvantages were lack of selectivity against cancerous tissues leading to severe toxicity against many vital organs like kidney, brain and neural tissues, bone-marrow, etc. The mostly noticeable complications include renal impairment, neurotoxicity, vomiting, ototoxicity, and anemia. To overcome these complications the structure of cisplatin has been modified time to time and number of other platinum drugs were synthesized which lead to the development of generations of platinum-based drugs (Kostova, 2006b). Following the introduction of cisplatin into the cancer treatment regimen, many other platinum-based drugs have entered clinical trials and approved for treatment of cancer. Specifically, oxaliplatin and carboplatin got global approval and three others individually in Asian countries like nedaplatin in Japan, lobaplatin in China, and heptaplatin in Korea, gaining approval in single markets (Fig. 1) (Table 1).

2.1 First-generation platinum drugs

The first-generation platinum drug is the conventional platinum anticancer complex cisplatin (*cis*-diammine-dichloroplatinum). The discovery of cisplatin traces back in the mid-19th century in Europe. It was Italian chemist Michele Peyrone, who first described the formula *cis*-[Pt(NH$_3$)$_2$Cl$_2$] for preparation of coordination complex and synthesized Cisplatin (Peyrone's chloride) first in the year of 1844 (Kauffman and Peyrone, 2010). But it remains useless just as many other synthesized chemicals for more than a century until its biological activity was tested and discovered by Rosenberg et al. (1965), Bertini et al. (1994), and Kaim and Schwederski (1993). Started with basic biological activity testing on bacterial cell the cisplatin has revolutionized the chemotherapy of human cancer. As discussed earlier the side effects of cisplatin and subtoxic accumulation of cisplatin within the cell lead to acquisition of resistance by reduced drug influx and increased drug efflux (Alfarouk et al., 2015). Apart from this, cancer cell found to develop tolerance to DNA-cisplatin adducts, modulates cell death pathway, letting the cisplatin ineffective for therapy (Boulikas and Vougiouka, 2003a; Perez, 1998; Kartalou and Essignmann, 2001). These limitations have motivated scientist for synthesis of thousands of cisplatin analogs. This resulted in development of many platinum-based complexes having anticancer attributes with comparatively lesser side effects.

2.2 Second-generation cisplatin analogs

Second-generation platinum drugs in general include the structures which have deviated from the cisplatin template. The only structural difference they have is the presence of mono or bidentate ligands as a substitute of ammine ligands. Presence of these ligands alters the electronic, steric and basicity effects of these platinum drugs. Examples include carboplatin, oxaliplatin, and nedaplatin.

Carboplatin

Carboplatin is the leading second-generation cisplatin analogs. This anticancer drug is sold globally under the commercial trade name of Paraplatin JM 8, Paraplatine Cyclo-platin, Carbomedac, CBDCA, Carbosin, Ribocarbo, etc. (Krishant et al., 2018). The IUPAC name of carboplatin is diammine-[1,1-cyclobutyldicarboxylato-(2-)O,O']) platinum(II)]. Design and development of carboplatin was the result of a collaborative project managed by Johnson Matthey Plc., Institute of Cancer Research, London, UK. The structure of carboplatin differs from traditional cisplatin drug by having a bidentate ligand the cyclobutyldicarboxylato as the leaving group instead of chlorides. Carbaplatin got FDA approval in 1988 for use against ovarian cancer. Although carboplatin is generally used in the treatment ovarian cancer, but its use is not restricted for the treatment of other cancer types such as brain tumors, neuroblastomas, retinoblastomas, and nephroblastomas, as well as head and neck cancer, malignancies of breast, lung, cervix, testes, bladder cancers, etc. Carboplatin in combination with paclitaxel exerts better therapeutic benefit in ovarian cancer patient (Ozols, 2000). It also exerts almost the same antineoplastic activity like cisplatin, for other cancers like lung, head and neck cancers with fewer side effects. The comparative functional study between cisplatin and carboplatin shows better therapeutic result by cisplatin with high toxicity whereas, carboplatin found to have more favorable toxicity profile (Gwo et al., 2016). The presence of the chelating cyclobutane-1,1-dicarboxylate ligand in its structure is supposed to be reason for its lesser organ toxicity (Neidle et al., 1980). Like the other platinum-based drugs, carboplatin mediates its action through DNA binding (Frey et al., 1993). Due to less toxicity profile and other side effects, patients can tolerate much high doses of carboplatin than the cisplatin dosages (Jakupec et al., 2003).

Oxaliplatin

Oxaliplatin was first synthesized by Yoshinori Kidani at Nagoya City University in 1976 (Sharma et al., 2018). Oxaliplatin, also known as platinum oxalate complex formed by oxalate and *trans*-(−)-1,2-cyclohexylamine (DACH) serving as ligands and divalent metal platinum. In oxaliplatin this DACH ligand replaces two ammine ligands of cisplatin (Kelland, 2007). It was first developed for commercial use in 1997 by Debiopharm Ltd., Switzerland. One year after that it was approved for clinical use in France, mainly for the treatment of metastatic colorectal cancer (Bécouarn et al., 1998). Later on, USA in 2002 and Japan in 2005 and many other countries approved this drug for the treatment of colorectal cancer (Sweetman, 2007). It is sold under the trade name of Eloxatin, Dacplat, Dacotin, Elplat, etc. (Krishant et al., 2018). The IUPAC name of oxaliplatin is {[(1R,2R)-cyclohexane-1,2-diamine][ethanedioato-O,O′]-platinum(II)}. Oxaliplatin is the first chemotherapeutic drug which was approved against cisplatin resistance under the commercial brand name of Eloxatin. This drug is known to exhibit stronger antitumor activity against various colon cancer cell lines than its predecessors, cisplatin and carboplatin (Armand et al., 2000). Like all other platinum compounds, oxaliplatin acts primarily by forming interstrand and intrastrand crosslinks in DNA, which cause inhibition of DNA synthesis. Oxaliplatin interacts with DNA differently than cisplatin leads to some functional difference among the both (Boulikas and Vougiouka, 2003b). At similar number of Pt-DNA adducts, oxaliplatin found to be more efficient in inhibiting DNA chain (Woynarowski et al., 2000). It appears to have to distinct mechanism of resistance, which makes it sensitive to cisplatin insensitive cancer cells (Cassidy, 2000). Clinical trials of oxaliplatin made on metastatic gastric, esophagogastric adenocarcinoma, etc., further expanded its spectrum of activity (Lordick et al., 2010). Combination of oxaliplatin with other cytotoxic drugs 5-fluorouracil and AG337 (a thymidylate synthase inhibitor) exerts very good activity against human colon, breast, and ovarian carcinomas (Raymond et al., 1997). Moreover, the reduced toxicity profile of oxaliplatin than cisplatin makes it a more useful chemo therapeutic drug. The presence of oxalate ligand instead of ammine is recognized to cut the side effects of oxaliplatin compared to cisplatin (Cassidy and Misset, 2002).

Nedaplatin

Nedaplatin (*cis*-diammine-glycolatoplatinum), is the third cisplatin analog in our discussion. It was designed and developed to minimize the toxicities and other side effects of cisplatin including the nephron and GI toxicity. It was synthesized by Shionogi Pharmaceutical Company, Osaka, Japan in 1983. The IUPAC name of nedaplatin is diamine [hydroxyacetato (2-)-O,O′] platinum(II). Structurally it holds the same ammine carrier ligands as cisplatin, but presence of a different leaving group. Nedaplatin after uptake by the cell cleaved through hydrolysis to form active species. Like cisplatin these active species it binds with DNA, forms nucleoside–platinum complex, thereby inhibiting DNA replication (Shimada et al., 2013). It is sold under the brand name of Aqupla for treatment of small cell lung cancer, nonsmall cell lung cancer, esophageal cancer, and head and neck carcinoma since 1995 (Alberto et al., 2009; Kawai et al., 2005; Boulikas et al., 2007). Nedaplatin offers better anticancer efficacy over carboplatin with significantly less amount of toxicity and fewer side effects than both cisplatin and carboplatin (Alberto et al., 2009; Kawai et al., 2005; Kuwahara et al., 2009). Promising results have been obtained when nedaplatin used with docetaxel in several Phase I and Phase II investigations against oral squamous cell carcinoma (Kurita et al., 2010). Similarly, the combination of nedaplatin-paclitaxel and nedaplatin-irinotecan drugs against metastatic esophageal carcinoma and nonsmall cell lung cancer (NSCLC), respectively, exerts very good therapeutic result (Oshita et al., 2004). The most commonly seen toxicity which can limit the therapy is myelosuppression, including leukopenia, anemia, and primarily thrombocytopenia (Ota et al., 1992), but no toxicity for kidney and GI tract (Shimada et al., 2013).

2.3 Third-generation cisplatin analogs

Third-generation platinum drugs are the result of scientific attempt to further improve the structure of drugs to minimize their side effects. Some of the third-generation platinum analogs are lobaplatin, heptaplatin, etc. Their activities are written below.

Lobaplatin

Lobaplatin, a third-generation platinum drug, has shown promising therapeutic benefit against a number of malignancies with fewer toxicity outcomes. It is a platinum(II) complex which contains 1,2-bis(aminimethyl)cyclobutane as stable ligand and lactic acid as leaving group developed by ASTA Medica AG company (Frankfurt, Germany). Its IUPAC name is {[2-hydroxypropanoato (2-)-O1,O2] [1,2-cyclobutanedimethanamine-N,N']-platinum (II)} and is sold under the brand name of D-19466(IS) (Krishant et al., 2018). Like the other platinum drugs, lobaplatin interacts with DNA and forms DNA-adducts leading to GG and AG intra strands crosslink formation (McKeage, 2001). Interaction of lobaplatin with the intracellular components found to influence the expression of *c-myc* gene which is associated with the process of oncogenesis, cell proliferation, and apoptosis-related activities (Fliopoulos et al., 1995). Currently, it is used for the treatment of metastatic breast cancer, chronic myelogenous leukemia, and small cell lung carcinoma (Limited, 2003). Lobaplatin's activity in combination with other chemotherapeutic agents was assessed in numerous studies. Lobaplatin in combination with vinorelbine exerts good therapeutic activity in patients of advanced breast cancer (Wheate et al., 2010). The other potential combinations are with 5-FU and leucovorin that can be used for the treatment of recurrent metastatic esophageal cancer. It has much toxicity profile than cisplatin and produces no renal toxicity, neurotoxicity, and alopecia after IV bolus injection (Gietema et al., 1993, 1995; Kavanagh et al., 1995; Degardin et al., 1995; Welink et al., 1999).

Though in many cases lobaplatin gives better therapeutic outcome, a phase 3 trial in patient with phase III–IVB nasopharyngeal cancer the combination of lobaplatin/5-fluorouracil and cisplatin/5-fluorouracil have shown almost same level of benefit (Lv et al., 2021).

Heptaplatin

Heptaplatin is a third-generation platinum drug originally developed and marketed by S.K. Pharmaveutical, Seoul, Korea. Its IUPAC name is {[Propanedioato (2-)-O,O′] [2-(1-methylethyl)-1,3-dioxolane-4,5-dimethanamine-N,N′]-platinum(II)} and sold under the brand name of Sunpla, SKI2053, eptaplatin, NSC644591, NSC-D-644591, etc. (Kostova, 2006b; Krishant et al., 2018). Heptaplatin's high chemical stability in solution (Kim et al., 1995a), less toxicity compared to cisplatin (Kim et al., 1995a) and anticancer activity against cisplatin resistant cancer cells (Choi et al., 2004) make it a molecule of importance for cancer chemotherapy.

Heptaplatin is effective against a large number of human cancer cell lines including gastric cancer with lower toxicity than cisplatin and carboplatin (Kim et al., 1994; Ahn et al., 2002). It was also found highly effective against the growth of cisplatin-resistant L1210 leukemia cells (L1210-CPR) (Kim et al., 1995b). Heptaplatin when used in combination with other chemo agents like 5-fluorouracil or paclitaxel offer very good therapeutic activity against human neck and head cancer (Lee et al., 2006). The combination therapy of heptaplatin/5-fluorouracil and leucovorin was tested against advanced gastric cancer (Lee et al., 2005). The combination of heptaplatin/5-fluorouracil found to exerts better therapeutic benefit for treatment of advanced gastric cancer over the combination of cisplatin/5-fluorouracil. The use of heptaplatin is safer with very few toxic side effects are counted as advantages of using heptaplatin over other platinum drugs (Lee et al., 2009).

Despite the fact that multiple novel platin medications are in preclinical development, just two new platin drugs, LA-12 and dicycloplatin (Fig. 2), have entered clinical trials in the previous decade, indicating a shift in research emphasis from design and development of a novel drug to enhanced formulations of currently licensed platinum drugs. Various

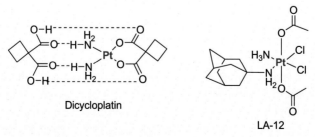

Dicycloplatin

LA-12

Fig. 2 Platinum anticancer drugs under clinical trial.

approaches which are affective to increase the efficacy of drugs include encapsulation, conjugation with nanoparticles. These can effectively slow and prevent degradation of the drug molecules by proteins and peptides; and also increase drug's permeability and retention effect; can give better coordination of drug with important proteins, nutrients, antibodies, and aptamers for active targeting of cancerous cell.

3. Mechanism of action of platinum drugs

The anticancer mechanism of platinum complexes has been studied widely. Here we will discuss the mechanism of action of cisplatin, as a model platinum complex. The extended research carried out globally has revealed a clear picture of cisplatin's cytotoxicity against cancer cells. Cisplatin induced cytotoxicity varies among cancer types in a dose dependent way. Inside the cell cisplatin binds with the DNA which creates problem with DNA replication and transcription mechanism and induces cellular apoptosis by activating various signaling pathways like death receptor signaling, activation of mitochondrial mediated death signaling. Some of the major points in this whole process include cellular uptake of platinum complexes, aquation/activation within intracellular environment, access to the cell nucleus and patination of DNA, and finally affecting the cell signaling necessary for cell survival and apoptosis (Fig. 3).

Let's discuss with the transport of cisplatin into the body and uptake by the cell. Cisplatin is administered in patients intravenously into blood. Owing to its strong reactivity with sulfur of amino acid cysteine it binds with the plasma proteins and rapidly diffuses into the tissues. The binding of cisplatin with plasma proteins leads to inaction of a lion portion of cisplatin molecules and only a little quantity enter the cell after crossing various obstacles. The uptake or cellular internalization of the neutral cisplatin molecule is mainly achieved by passive diffusion and additionally by facilitated or energy driven active transport process. Passive diffusion depends on the SARs profile of the synthesized complex. In recent years the role of copper transporter proteins (CTR1 and CTR2) and organic cation transporters (OCT1 and OCT2) in active transport of platinum complexes was discovered.

Once platinum enters into the cell, the concentration of chloride ion ($\approx$2–30 mM) in the intracellular fluid (ICF) than the chloride ion content ($\approx$100 mM) of extracellular fluid (ECF)/plasma helps in substitution of chlorides in cisplatin with water molecules. The aquation reactions lead to the formation of activated mono and diaqua cisplatin which are very much reactive to nucleophilic center. The activated cisplatin binds with DNA and form adducts. Cisplatin and other platinum compounds primarily interact with N7 of guanine and adenine nucleotide in the major groove of DNA to form DNA-protein as well as DNA-DNA interstrand to intrastrand crosslinks. Intrastrand crosslinks are the main type of adducts with about 60%–65% 1,2-d(GpG) crosslinks and 20%–25% d(ApG) cross-links. The 1,2-intrastrand adducts formed are reported to play key role in

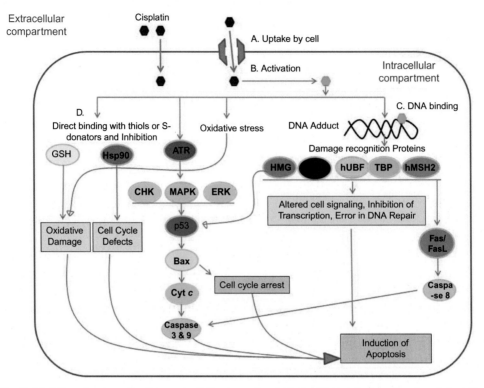

Fig. 3 A brief mechanism of anticancer activity shown by cisplatin. (A) Uptake by cell: entry of cisplatin occurs by passive diffusion as well as by active transport; (B) Activation: a series of aquation reaction cause substitution of chloride by water molecules and activates cisplatin; and (C) DNA binding: active cisplatin interact with N7 of guanine and adenine nucleotide in the major groove of DNA to form DNA-protein as well as DNA-DNA interstrand to intrastrand crosslinks. Various damage recognition protein next identifies and interacts with those adducts and bring about changes in cell signaling regulating cell cycle, controls cell survival a apoptosis, inhibits transcription, and hampers DNA repair. Additionally, cisplatin also inhibits GSH, which is an important antioxidant enzyme thus raising oxidative stress.

cisplatin's anticancer activity. Two important observation in this regard are the specific recognition of 1,2-intrastrand adducts by HMG (high mobility group) proteins and the least efficient nucleotide excision repair for this type of adducts which leads to DNA damage. Proceeding into the cisplatin's mechanism of action, the above mentioned structural distortions in DNA double helix caused by platinum binding is identified by the mismatch repair protein hMSH2 or hMutSα component of mismatch repair complex and many damage recognition proteins including nonhistone chromosomal high-mobility group 1 and 2 (HMG1 & 2), TATA binding protein (TBP), etc., and subsequently transduce DNA damage signals along the various signaling molecules located downstream in this pathway. It has been reported that binding of HMG proteins with cisplatin-DNA adducts cause inhibition of cellular functions vital for survival. Also, exposure to cisplatin found to cause overexpression of HMG1 which interacts with DNA adducts promoting cytotoxicity and hampering DNA repair. Similarly, the binding of hUBF, TBP, 3-methyladenine DNA glycosylase (AAG), etc., sequester their natural activity and prevent them from partaking in transcription. These recognition proteins in this way initiate many such events effecting normal functioning of the cell. The cisplatin induced DNA damage activates number of pathways culminating into cell cycle, activation of p53 and direct cells toward apoptosis. Though activation of p53 is the consequence of DNA damage, multiple other factors are also involved into this. HMG1 & 2 enables the activation of p53 by facilitating its binding with DNA. Cisplatin is reported to cause activation of ATR (ATM and Rad-3-related protein). ATR is a kinase working upstream to the p53 gene and controls its transcriptional activity. Activated ATR causes activation of p53 by phosphorylating serine-15 residues. ATR targets many other downstream targets like CHK1 kinase and MAPK (mitogen-activated protein kinases) and cause their activation which is responsible for phosphorylation of p53 at serine-15, 20, threonine-81 residue, and many. MAPKs are very important signaling molecules involved in most of the cellular processes comprising cell proliferation, differentiation, survival, and apoptosis. Cisplatin treatment activates ERK1/2 which in turn facilitates the phosphorylation and activation of p53. Transactivation of p53 activates a number of genes associated with cell cycle, repair, and apoptosis. The fate between survival and death is decided by the severity of DNA damage. Damage of DNA beyond a critical threshold level, the cellular repair capacity overwhelms and induces apoptosis. Cisplatin induces Bax, increases the ratio of Bax: Bcl-2, and translocation of proapoptotic Bax from cytosol to mitochondria initiating a cascade of events including release of cytochrome-c and activation of caspases which results in apoptosis. Cisplatin also induce apoptosis in tumor cells through death ligand Fas/FasL mediated activation of caspase 8 and 3, which is also assisted by p53. Apart from damaging DNA, cisplatin induces oxidative stress in the cancer cells leading to apoptosis. As mentioned earlier that cisplatin has strong reactivity against the thiols and S-donor biomolecules, glutathione is one of the major targets of cisplatin adversely affecting the antioxidant activities of cell. Cisplatin also inhibits Hsp90 (heat shock protein 90) which have role in cell cycle regulation. Other targets of cisplatin includes telomerase enzyme important for maintenance of telomere ends. Inhibition of telomerase by cisplatin therefore fails to preserve the telomere during successive cell division leading to cell death (Siddik, 2003; Fuertes et al., 2003; Jordan and Carmo-Fonseca, 2000).

4. Toxicity and related side effects of platinum drugs

The platinum-based drugs are among the regularly used chemotherapeutic agents for treatment of tumor. But the uses of platinum drugs are related with many toxic side effects that can lower their therapeutic efficacy. Cancer patient's receiving platinum-based drugs experience one or many specific side effects. Because of their lack of specificity to selectively target cancerous cell and tissue over the normal cells and tissues in the body, maximum chemotherapy drugs exert severe toxic side effects. The dose limiting side effect varies for different platinum compounds. Compounds like cisplatin is mostly nephrotoxic, carboplatin suppresses myelogenesis, and oxaliplatin is mostly toxic to neurons. Other side effects for platinum drugs include anaphylaxis, cardiotoxicity, hematological toxicity causing cytopenias, hepatotoxicity, ototoxicity (ear damage and hearing loss), nausea and vomiting, mucositis, diarrhea, stomatitis, alopecia (loss of hair), cachexia, anorexia, and asthenia. These side effects are mostly due to the lack of specific targeting of tumor cell by platinum drugs. The severity of platinum drugs induced side effects experienced by a patient are measured on a grading scale of 1–5 introduced by National Cancer Institute (NCI), USA. Grade 1 means mild and is used to define asymptomatic or mild symptoms where no medical intervention is required. Grade 2 means moderate side effects and to minimize the complications, local or non-invasive medical intervention is needed. Grade 3 means severe and it defines conditions that are not life-threatening on immediate basis but it requires prolonged medical intervention. Grade 4 defines life-threatening complications that require emergency medical interference. Last is grade 5, which defines death of patients due to the side effects (Oun et al., 2018; Zhang et al., 2020). In addition to systemic toxicity, the efficacy of cisplatin is frequently hampered by malignancies' inherent and acquired resistance. Cisplatin, oxaliplatin, and other platinum compounds used as chemotherapy medicines, have high antitumor activity, but their use is limited due to severe adverse effects. As a result, efforts should be made to produce platinum/non platinum compounds that are less toxic.

5. Ruthenium anticancer compounds

Cisplatin is the most recognized metallodrug, with efficacy in lung, ovarian, head, esophageal, and neck malignancies (Jamieson and Lippard, 1999; Cepeda et al., 2007). Despite the fact that cisplatin and its related platinum anticancer drugs are effective against the most of malignancies, they also cause noncancer cell damage, resulting in serious side effects in patients such as hair loss, peripheral neuropathy, and myelotoxicity (Florea and Büsselberg, 2011; Galluzzi et al., 2012; Zheng et al., 2014; Suntharalingam et al., 2014). Tumor resistance to Pt reduces or completely eliminates the efficacy of Pt-based therapeutics, resulting in treatment failure (Dhar et al., 2008; Fong et al., 2016; Cao et al., 2016). Platinum resistance, both intrinsic and acquired, is becoming a growing clinical problem, especially since Pt metallodrugs are currently utilized in more than half of all chemotherapy regimens (Ai et al., 2016; Shen et al., 2012; Parker et al., 1991). As a result, a novel family of metal-based anticancer drugs with excellent cellular selectivity has been developed and can be used to treat a wide spectrum of cancers.

Ruthenium anticancer compounds have been proved to be a feasible alternative to platinum therapeutics in clinical trials, with similar ligand exchange kinetics and a larger range of available coordination arrangements. In medicinal inorganic chemistry, the Ru(III) and Ru(II) compounds is well documented, and exploration into their potential as anticancer drugs is widespread. Several interesting photophysical and chemical properties are found in Ru complexes, providing new direction for the design and synthesis of novel Ru anticancer drugs. Ru(III) oxidation state compounds are generally thought to be more inert, which is due to the increased effective nuclear charge to some extent. Many Ru(III) derivatives contain ligands that must be activated by the tumor microenvironment (Dragutan et al., 2015). When Ru(III) compounds are reduced to Ru(II) counterparts in vivo, they exhibit anticancer properties. The Ru(II/III) redox potential can be changed by biological conditions such as acidic pH, low concentration of oxygen, and high glutathione levels, allowing Ru(III) complexes to be easily reduced to Ru(II) complexes (Hartinger et al., 2013). For various Ru(III) derivatives, a "activation by reduction" mechanism has been postulated (Schluga et al., 2006), in which cellular reductants such as ascorbate, in amalgamation with the exceedingly reducing environment of a tumor cell, reduce them to their more active Ru(II) counterpart (Wiśniewska et al., 2019). Many ruthenium complexes have an in-cell mechanism of action (MoA) that varies from the DNA-binding mechanism commonly related with Pt therapeutics (Dasari and Bernard Tchounwou, 2014). Ruthenium anticancer drugs have a wider spectrum of intracellular targets, and numerous instances have showed potential in biological systems, in vitro, and in vivo (Dougan et al., 2008; Kandioller et al., 2013; Zhang and Sadler, 2017). Several Ru compounds with various ligands are reported as promising anticancer drugs, and four of them (Fig. 4), including NAMI-A KP1019, KP133910, and the Ru(II)-based anticancer drugs, TLD143311, have progressed to various phases in clinical studies (Fong et al., 2015). However, NAMI-A's low treatment efficacy, several side effects in clinical tests (phase I), and limited retort

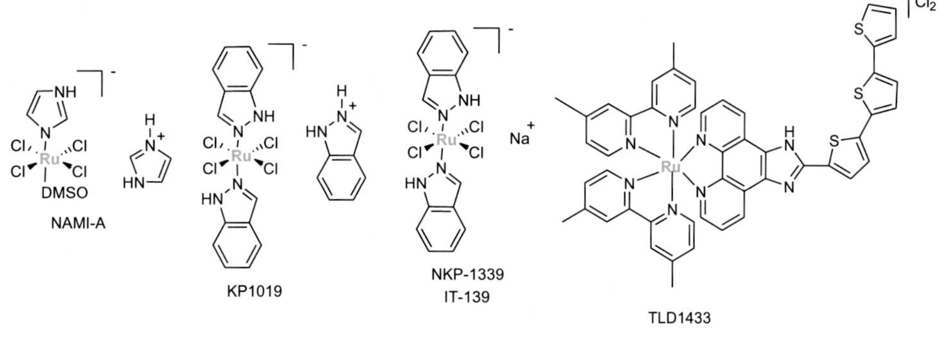

Fig. 4 Ruthenium anticancer drugs under clinical trial.

(phase I/II) restricted its application and resulted in the failure in clinical investigations (Rademaker-Lakhai et al., 2004). Following that, the Keppler group's KP1019 began clinical study (Hartinger et al., 2006, 2008). However, due to its low solubility, further research is hampered, and a more soluble sodium salt, KP1339, is presently being tested in clinical studies (Bytzek et al., 2016). Numerous inorganic Ru(II), organometallic Ru(II), and nanomaterial Ru(II) compounds have recently been developed as anticancer agents with effective curative characteristics (Rodrigues et al., 2016). The usage of Ru photo-sensitizers (PS) to reactive oxygen species (ROS) which induces tumor cell death with one or two photon light activation is a new exciting topic within the study of Ru meta-llodrugs (Zeng et al., 2017). This enables for more accurate regulation of cytotoxicity, which results in less side effects. The excited PS reacts with O_2 at the place of photo-activation within the cell to create radicals that harm the neighboring cell in this type of photodynamic therapy. TLD1433, a mononuclear tris(polypyridyl) Ru(II) derivative, is one PS that has showed potential in this field (Fong et al., 2015). When stimulated at 530 nm, TLD1433 shows a near 100% singlet O_2 quantum yield. In vitro, this compound had a high photodynamic action against glioma and colon tumor tissue, with low dark toxicity in CT26-injected mice models. Premixing TLD1433 with transferrin increases the molar extinction coefficient, which allows for activation of longer wavelengths while reducing dark toxicity and photo bleaching (Kaspler et al., 2016). TLD1433 is now being tested in patients having nonmuscle invasive bladder cancer in phase Ib clinical trials. Gas-ser group has reported that one- or two-photon excitation may be employed in PDT in 3D multicellular HeLa spheroids using tris(polypyridyl) Ru(II) derivatives as PSs (Jeannine et al., 2017). Another Ru(II) derivative that has been found to have clinically useful features is RDC11, an organometallic ruthenium complex (Fig. 5) (Meng et al., 2009). This compound was investigated against U87 glioblastoma cells or xenografted A2780 ovarian cancer cells put into nude mice. Compared to control mice, the tumor volume was reduced by 45%, and the tumor reduction was comparable to cisplatin, but

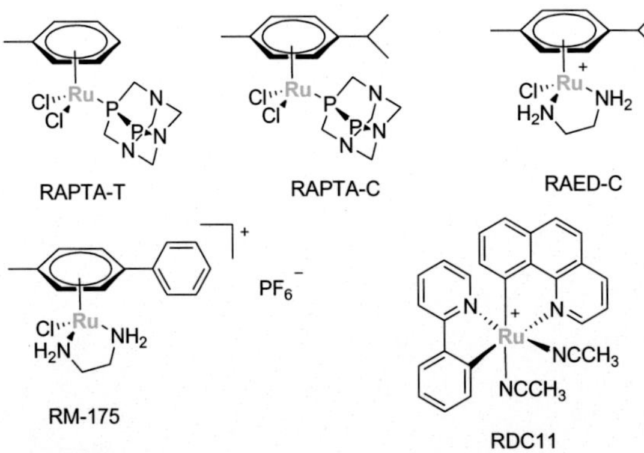

Fig. 5 Ruthenium anticancer drugs.

with less side effects. Ru(II) arene compounds containing the amphiphilic ligand 1,3,5-triaza-7-phosphaadamantane (pta), such as Ru(6-toluene)(pta)Cl$_2$, RAPTA-T and Ru(6-p-cymene)(pta)Cl$_2$, RAPTA-C (Fig. 5), show less toxicity in vivo. In chromatin, RAPTA-C attaches to the histone protein core rather than DNA (Wu et al., 2011; Adhireksan et al., 2014). In vivo, RAPTA-C has a substantial antiangiogenic impact (Nowak-Sliwinska et al., 2011). RAPTA drugs' combined effects appear to be unique, especially when taken in conjunction with other therapeutics. RAPTA-C inhibits tumor growth effectively at relatively low drug doses while avoiding severe side effects (Weiss et al., 2015). Sadler et al. designed and synthesized diamine-based Ru(II)-arenes complexes as a new category of anticancer drugs (Aird et al., 2001; Cummings et al., 2000). The antiproliferative activity of [(η^6-bip)RuCl(en)]PF$_6$ (RM175) (Fig. 5), where bip = η^6-biphenyl, was equivalent to carboplatin. RM175 demonstrated noncross resistance to cisplatin as well as permissibility at high concentration, despite having half the activity of cisplatin. In nonsmall cell lung cancer and breast cancer cell lines, RM175 and its homolog, [RuCl(en)(η^6-tetrahydroanthracene)]PF$_6$ were highly active, with [RuCl(en)(η^6-tetrahydroanthracene)]PF$_6$ showing more activity in vitro (Guichard et al., 2006). Both metallodrugs displayed a considerable delay of tumor growth after i.p. single-dose administration in the A549 in vivo xenograft model. However, when compared to RM175, [RuCl(en)(η^6-tetrahydroanthracene)]PF$_6$ produced higher hepatotoxicity, which was likely due to the polyaromatic arene's more lipophilic character. Furthermore, in the cell-free NCP model, the p-cymene counterpart of RM175, i.e., RAED-C was observed to preferably target DNA (Adhireksan et al., 2014).

For selective and successful cancer therapy, ruthenium compounds must be taken up by cancer cells or other cells. Atoms and molecules must penetrate or cross the cell membrane in order to enter living cells. The cell membrane is made up of a variety of proteins and lipids and is responsible for controlling what enters the cells. Passive diffusion, endocytosis, and active transport are all recognized ways for Ru(II) compounds to enter cells (Gill and Thomas, 2012). Ruthenium compounds have been demonstrated to interact with proteins and nucleic acids in the nucleus through a variety of binding mechanisms (Liang et al., 2014). The synthetic Ru(II) derivative is an excellent compound for the development of nucleoside-targeted therapeutics (Zeng et al., 2017).

Ru complexes have the potential to eradicate several of the fundamental drawbacks of Pt medicines, such as side effects and resistance of drug. Ru metallodrugs have several advantages over Pt-based drugs that make them appealing chemotherapeutic agents, including better tumor cell selectivity, variable oxidation states, ligand exchange kinetics comparable to Pt compounds, and lesser toxicity to regular cells via interaction with transferrin receptors. The vast amount of research and knowledge on the chemical reactivity of ruthenium compounds that has been amassed to date could be useful in determining whether and how the metal can be used to target cancer-causing chemicals. To discover required biological and chemical characteristics allied with an efficacious forthcoming Ru metallodrug, future anticancer research must acquire knowledge from both accomplishments and challenges came across during the synthesis of earlier compounds.

6. Gold anticancer compounds

Following the discovery of cisplatin's anticancer properties, gold(III) complexes were investigated as a potential alternative to platinum-based anticancer agents (Ott, 2009; Zou et al., 2015; Lazarević et al., 2017). The fact that both platinum(II) and gold(III) compounds have the same electronic configuration (d^8) and produce square planar complexes piqued interest. Gold(III) compounds are a novel group of compounds that have excellent cytotoxic characteristics as well as are currently being studied as anticancer agents. Recent investigations have demonstrated that certain gold(III) compounds are stable under physiological environments and have anticancer effects against a variety of human tumor cell lines, which has sparked renewed interest. Gold complexes cause cytotoxicity by blocking thiol-containing enzymes, particularly TrxR, and causing damage to DNA and mitochondrial function, all of which may contribute to their anticancer properties (Shuang et al., 2020; Patel et al., 2013). Gold complexes can prompt destruction of cancer cells by causing the production of proteins on the cell surface, the cytokines secretion, or the disruption of the cell membrane, ensuing in the discharge of intracellular substances. Gold compounds have been shown in numerous in vitro as well as in vivo investigations to stimulate not just direct immune cell-mediated death, but also the T-cell-mediated antitumor immunity cycle through DC. Due to their weaker DNA-binding action along with substantial affinity for the thiol, sulfhydryl, in addition to selenocysteine groups of a number of protein targets, gold complexes having oxidation states of +I and +III have superior selectivity along with effectiveness with respect to cancer cells in comparison to normal cells when compared to platinum-based compounds.

Auranofin (Ridaura) (Fig. 6) containing ligand 1-β-D-thioglucose tetraacetate and a triethylphosphine is now the most advanced drugs in the field of gold research (Sutton et al., 1972; Sutton, 1986; Berners-Price and Filipovska, 2011). Auranofin was used to treat rheumatoid arthritis since it may be taken orally and had superior antiinflammatory effects in vitro. Auranofin's anticancer potential in vitro and in vivo has been thoroughly explored, and it is currently in clinical phase II trials against small lymphocytic lymphoma (SLL), chronic lymphocytic leukemia (CLL), and prolymphocytic lymphoma (PLL) (Roder and Thomson, 2015; Simon et al., 1979; Mirabelli et al., 1985; Dominelli et al., 2018). In contrast to the previously identified cisplatin analogs, Auranofin and similar gold complexes have a "DNA-independent" mechanism of action (Bindoli et al., 2009b). Identifying and developing tailored and multitargeted combination therapy techniques for improvement of the efficaciousness of contemporary immunotherapies

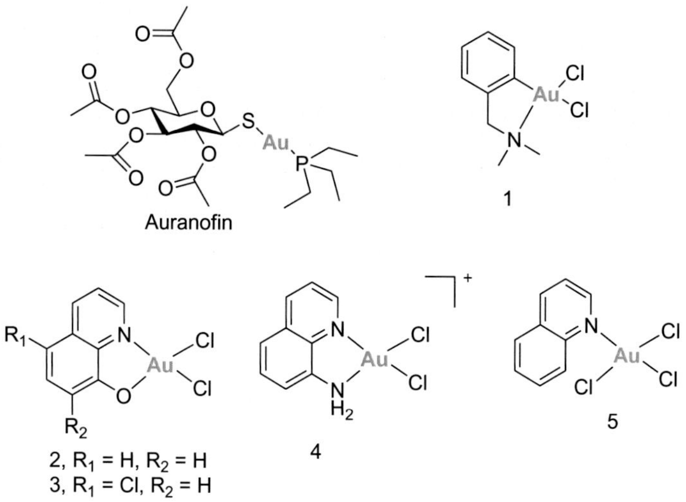

Fig. 6 Gold anticancer drugs.

is a key problem in modern systemic cancer treatment research. Auranofin coupled with an inhibitor of the immunological checkpoint PDL1 showed remarkable anticancer activity in breast cancer cell lines as well as in animals, highlighting intriguing potential of combination immunotherapy dependent on gold derivatives (Raninga et al., 2020). Following the initial discovery of Auranofin as a possible anticancer therapeutics, a number of Au complexes were developed with the goal of improving in vivo stability, cancer cell selectivity, or a novel mode of action. Thiolates-, phosphines-, and N-heterocyclic carbenes (NHCs)-based ligands have been reported as stabilizing ligands for Au(I) complexes. Anticancer characteristics of several Au(III) complexes with cyclometalated complexes or pyridine ligands were also explored. Mirabelli and colleagues investigated the structure-activity relationship of 63 Au(I)-phosphine complexes with the general structure LAuX (L = sulfides, thiolates, amines, pyridines, and phosphines; X = halides, phosphines, nitriles, and thiolates) (Mirabell et al., 1986; Casini et al., 2018). The Auranofin compounds with L = substituted phosphines and X = thiosugars showed the highest in vitro and in vivo activity. Other auxiliary ligands also exhibited high antiproliferative activity, but phosphine ligands were critical for enhanced antiproliferative activity (Mirabell et al., 1986). The presence of chelating phosphine ligands (e.g., 2-bis(diphenylphosphino)ethane (dppe)) in Au(I) phosphine compounds has been found to considerably improve in vivo cytotoxicity due to increased stability against GSH (Berners-Price et al., 1986).

Parish and coworkers' discovery of the antitumor capabilities of the complex [Au-(damp)Cl$_2$], (**1**) (Fig. 6) where damp = 2-[(dimethylamino)methyl]phenyl], and its derivatives [(damp)AuX$_2$] (X = SCN, OAc or X$_2$ = oxalato, malonato) also sparked renewed interest in gold(III) compounds as viable antimalignancy medicines (Parish et al., 1996a, b). Against various human tumor cell lines, these complexes showed similar cytotoxicity to cisplatin, with the acetate and malonato complexes demonstrating the highest efficacy besides selective nature in vitro, along with reasonable anticancer activity in vivo against human carcinoma xenografts (Parish et al., 1996a; Buckley et al., 1996). Various cyclometallated gold(III) complex, having one, two, or three C-Au bond, showed promising anticancer characteristics (Engman et al., 2006). In general, increasing the number of C-Au bonds in a compounds makes it further lipophilic, which improves intracellular absorption. Nevertheless, the capability of interacting with proteins that contain thiols or selenol groups appears to be diminished. Furthermore, $Au(damp)(C_6H_5)Cl$ complex, which has two Au-C bonds, was discovered to be a strong TrxR inhibitor ($IC_{50} = 2.2\,nM$); however, this had no anticancer effect against HT-29 colon cancer as well as MCF-7 breast cancer xenografts (Engman et al., 2006).

Messori et al. designed and synthesized Au(III) complexes with quinolone derivatives ligands (Martín-Santos et al., 2015). These Au(III) derivatives were tested for a range of human tumor cell lines including A427 (lung cancer cell line), LCLC-103H (large cell lung cancer), SISO (uterine adenocarcinoma), and 5637 (uterine adenocarcinoma) (human bladder carcinoma). In almost all cases, complexes 2, 3, and 4 (Fig. 6) outperformed cisplatin in antiproliferative activity. The findings revealed that replacing an oxygen atom with a nitrogen atom had only a minor impact on antitumor action. The quinoline Au(III)-complexes, both neutral and cationic, appear to penetrate cells and inhibit growth. Addition of a chlorine atom to the quinoline ring resulted in a substantial boost in anticancer action against A427 and 5637 cell lines. The nonchelating compound 5 was significantly less effective than the three chelate-ringed compounds. The authors claim that their mechanism of action differs significantly from those of clinically approved Pt(II) compounds.

The alkynyl gold compounds bind to target proteins with excellent selectivity, and they have anticancer and other pharmacological property. Some alkynyl gold compounds exhibit fluorescence property when they enter cells, making distribution easy to determine. Water-soluble phosphine compounds can alter the water solubility of alkyne gold complexes and lower cytotoxicity, but triphenylphosphine or other lipophilic phosphine derivatives can amplify membrane solubility besides affecting the pharmacological profile of the gold compound (Lima and Rodriguez, 2011; Yang et al., 2020).

Because of the broad clinical usage of gold derivatives in the treatment of rheumatoid arthritis and the long-term knowledge of properties of gold, it is possible that gold-based anticancer medications will be more accepted by the medical community than drugs based on other metals. The use of a vast number of ligands characterized by distinct donor atoms (N, O, S, P, and C) has expanded dramatically in the last few years in research on gold (I/III) derivatives as antiproliferative drugs.

7. Fluorescent metal-based complexes: Bioimaging tool

In cancer research and diagnosis, the capability of tracking chemotherapeutic agents intracellularly as well as inside tumors has shown to be extremely useful. Bioimaging and biosensing are two new fields that are becoming increasingly important for gaining a deeper understanding of cellular activities and providing a wide variety of diagnostic criteria for accurate disease diagnosis and therapy. In cancer research, deducing the mechanisms of progress of cancer along with its development, and early-stage detection, are escalated priorities: the development of tools for detection of malignancy has sparked a lot of interest in recent decades. Metal-based complexes have a lot of potential as bioimaging and biosensing probes due to their various physicochemical characteristics. From bench to bedside, a variety of imaging modalities, including optical imaging, positron emission tomography (PET), magnetic resonance imaging (MRI), and single-photon emission computerized tomography (SPECT), are now available, that allows faster progress in pathology, chemical biology, disease diagnosis, drug screening, in addition to therapy (Gao et al., 2017; Choquet et al., 2021; Han et al., 2021). Fluorescent metal-based probes have a number of advantages over conventional imaging instruments, including ease of use, excellent resolution and sensitivity (in the μM range), lower costing, and lack of ionizing radiation, making them one of the most promising imaging techniques in the biomedical arena (Ghosh and Adhikari, 2006a, b, 2008; Adhikari et al., 2019b; Ghosh et al., 2008). Because of their tiny sizes, robust luminosity, large Stokes shifts, extended lifetimes, great photostability, along with tunable toxicity, fluorescent metal-based compounds offer particular potential in optical bioimaging as well as biosensing in vitro and in vivo. Transition metal-based complexes (e.g. Pt(II), Ru(II), and Ir(III)-based complexes) are a well-known class of fluorophores used for cellular/subcellular imaging specifically in imaging of cell organelles like endoplasmic reticulum, lysosomes, mitochondria, as well as nuclei (Ma et al., 2020; Ko et al., 2019). Photosensitizers (PS) are also used in photodynamic therapy (PDT) with fluorescent probes. It occurs in most metal probes as metal-to-ligand charge transfer (MLCT) or ligand-to-metal-metal charge transfer (LTMTCT) from the excited states of the metal complex (LMCT) (Ko et al., 2019). Intraligand (IL) and ligand-to-ligand (LLCT) charge transfer can also take place due to intra- and interligand transitions, correspondingly. Two-photon fluorescence (2PF) is a property of several fluorescent probes (Lim and Cho, 2013). Two-photon excitation in two-photon fluorescence microscopy (2PFM) provides tissue penetration to a deeper extent along with improved resolution of tissues, making these particularly appealing for tissue bioimaging (Denk et al., 1990).

Ruthenium polypyridyl complexes are common fluorescent derivatives as well as antineoplastic drugs, as well as DNA binders, cellular process probes, and PDT agents (Mari et al., 2014; Tsui et al., 2015). Human clinical studies for a Ru(II)-based photosensitizer for nonmuscle invasive bladder cancer began in 2007 (*Intravesical Photodynamic Therapy (PDT) in BCG Refractory/Intolerant Non-Muscle Invasive Bladder Cancer (NMIBC) Patients. NCT03945162, 2020*). Qiu et al. recently studied a set of four lysosome-targeting Ru(II)-polypyridyl compounds with morpholine moieties (Qiu et al., 2019). While the secondary ligands are lipophilic bipyridine derivatives, the complexes' emission is pH-dependent because of the morpholine moiety. In fact, luminescence is suppressed by photo-induced electron transfer (PET) attributable to protonation of the morpholine moiety, with the maximum values ϕ found for pH 6.0 and above. With the highest lipophilicity, ϕ, and toxicity against A549 cells following irradiation, the complex, **6** (Fig. 7), emerged as the most promising. Complex **6** is found in lysosomes, but when exposed to 458 nm light, it is liberated and translocated to mitochondria, generating cellular blebbing. The generation of reactive oxygen species (ROS) following irradiation was confirmed, indicating that lysosome destruction, followed by translocation and damage to mitochondria, is part of the mechanism of toxicity of **6**. This compound also exhibits outstanding two-photon characteristics, making it a promising candidate for two-photon PDT in vivo (Qiu et al., 2019).

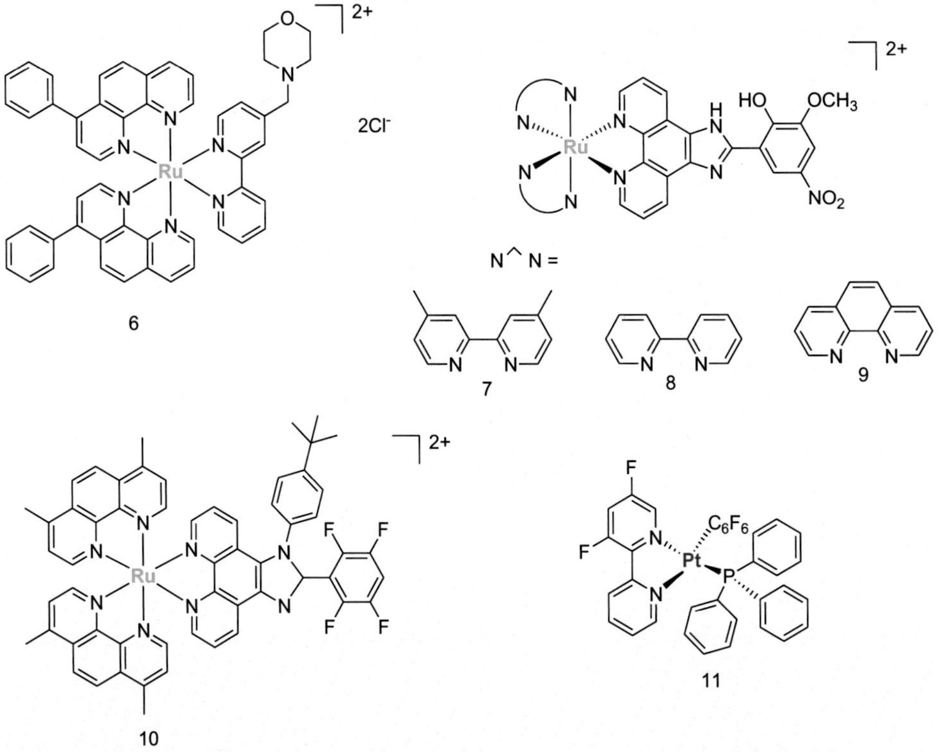

Fig. 7 Ruthenium and platinum anticancer drugs.

Three novel Ru(II) complexes that were attached to distinct polypyridyl moieties have been reported recently (**7–9** in Fig. 7) (He et al., 2019). Except for cytotoxicity after light irradiation, in which every compound demonstrates selectivity for different cell types, the three compounds reveal uniform photophysical traits. The researchers investigated their cytotoxicity mechanism in A549 cells, which were the most cytotoxic to the complexes. All of the complexes had a mild influence on cell cycle, raised ROS levels, and reduced MMP, besides causing release of cytochrome *c*.

Five fluorinated Ru(II) derivatives incorporated with phenanthroline moieties were described as possible PDT agents by Qiu et al. (2017). After 30 min, all complexes were found at the plasmalemma along with induction of cellular damage as well as blebbing after only 4 min of two-photon light irradiation. Higher incubation time, on the other hand, results in increased cellular uptake and mitochondrial localization. With a two-photon IC_{50} of $0.61 \pm 0.11\,\mu M$ against HeLa cells, complex **10** (Fig. 7) turned up as the exceedingly encouraging therapeutics in the series. In vivo investigation of complex **10** in a mouse xenograft model revealed that tumor irradiation with an 800 nm fs laser ($1.18\,W\,cm^{-2}$, for 25 min), 6 h postinjection ($65.8\,\mu g\,kg^{-1}$) resulted in a remarkable 90.5% reduction in tumor volume. These complexes are particularly promising for clinical PDT usage, with submicromolar IC_{50} values after irradiation (460–630 nM) and considerable tumor decrease just 4 h after exposure to the to the complexes.

While ruthenium compounds have showed great promise as theranostics, platinum-based anticancer medicines remain the extensively utilized ones. Millán and colleagues reported cycloplatinated(II) complexes having ligands phenylpyridine (ppy) or difluorophenylpyridine (dfppy) (Millán et al., 2019). The cytotoxicity of **11** of the reported complexes (Fig. 7) was the highest. The complexes are found in the perinuclear area of cancer cells, and **11** causes microtubule depolymerization after 2 h. As a result, cytoskeleton disintegration could be the principal mechanism of this complex's toxicity.

Iridium-based compounds was explored extensively as antiproliferative treatment measure in recent years because they can create ROS, allowing them to catalyze cellular death by their action on mitochondria as well as DNA (Zhang et al., 2019). Because of their photostability and cell permeability, iridium complexes are also used as bio imaging and biosensing agents (Lo and Zhang, 2012). To explore the photo-physical characteristics, a tris-cyclometalated iridium compound **12** with a quaternary ammonium group was synthesized. The complex **12** was found to be less cytotoxic than the precursor amine complex in studies (Fig. 8) (Meksawangwong et al., 2019). Eduardo Palao and associates employed boron dipyrromethene-based ligands to construct biscyclometalated iridium (III) complexes as fluorescent photosentizer agents. When exposed to visible light, the complexes **13** and **14** had increased absorption coefficients, moderate fluorescence emission, as well as singlet oxygen generation efficiency. The compounds are readily absorbed into cells, indicating that they could be used as theranostic agents, according to PDT studies (Palao et al., 2017). An iridium hydride complex **15** was designed, synthesized,

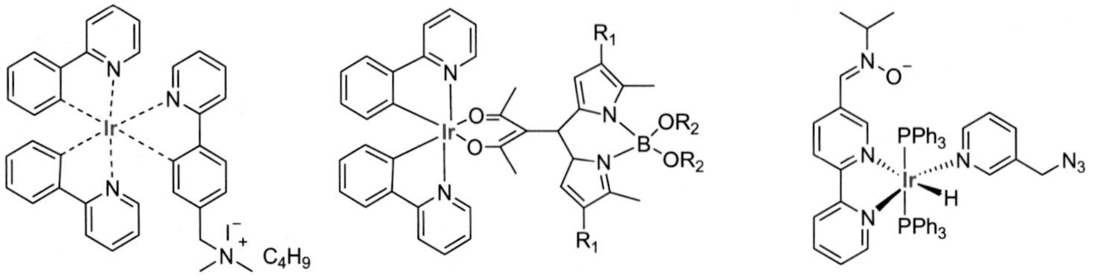

Fig. 8 Iridium anticancer drugs.

and reported by Xiuxiu et al. The compound displays anticancer activity against A2780 cells with an IC_{50} of 0.98 μM and MCF-7 cells with an IC_{50} of 4.46 μM, which is three times higher than cisplatin. This complex is primarily found in mitochondria (50%). Mitochondrial destruction was confirmed by fluorescent microscopy imaging (Wang et al., 2019).

Fluorescent metal-based probes have been successfully and widely used to visualize disease biomarkers noninvasively at all levels, from subcellular to whole-body. The goal of continuing to develop metal-based molecular probes in cancer therapy is to broaden their spectrum of applicability to include things that basic organic molecules cannot, such time-gated luminescence imaging as well as lifetime imaging. Metal-based molecular probes, we believe, will contribute more to bioimaging and biosensing in the coming decade.

8. Metal-based nanoparticles in cancer therapy

Nanoparticles have unique size-dependent features, making them useful in a wide range of applications. Nanoparticles are particularly fascinating for medicine and pharmacology because of the ability to control their properties. They have advantages that larger particles do not have, such as a higher surface-to-volume ratio or better magnetic characteristics (McNamara and Tofail, 2007; Moreno-Vega et al., 2012).

Because of their lack of specificity, most of all antitumor medications have strong systemic toxicity, increasing after effects besides having drug resistance. Metal nanoparticles are unique anticancer medicines that target cancer cells with precise selectivity (Park et al., 2018; Powell et al., 2010). Nanoparticles' physicochemical qualities contribute to their potential anticancer effect, which could be due to intrinsic or extrinsic factors. Its antioxidant action, which slows tumor development, is one of the internal or intrinsic anticancer effects (Porcel et al., 2010). The utilization of metal nanoparticles on tumor growth, formation, and progression has piqued researchers' interest due to their inherent anticancer properties.

8.1 Selective and specific tumor targeting

Owing to their distinctive shapes and increased vascular permeability, metal nanoparticles can be used to target cancer cells (Sperling and Parak, 2010). Metal nanoparticles' tumor targeting selectivity and specificity reduces the toxic effects as well as side effects of chemotherapy agents through distributing multiple medicinal molecules to the precise tumor location even though avoiding biological barriers, reducing chemotherapeutic toxicity and side effects. Despite their permeable vasculature, fenestrations along with inadequate lymphatic drainage, the permeability of cancer tissues to macromolecules is greater than that of healthy tissues, allowing nanoparticles to easily infiltrate into malignant cells and kill them (Minelli et al., 2010; Dinarvand et al., 2012; Ndagi et al., 2017). Gold nanoparticles that are active in the near-infrared (NIR) region and have a size range of 60–400 nm permit tumor specific accumulation due to increased permeability and retention. Gold nanoparticles can be PEGylated onto the surface to prohibit them from being inactivated by the reticuloendothelial system, in addition to passive tumor targeting. As a result, gold nanoparticles are gaining attraction as a possible carrier for tumor targeting that is both selective and specific. In comparison to passive targeting, active targeting has a higher specificity and selectivity for malignant cells while causing little or no harm to healthy cells.

8.2 NPs in drug delivery

Nanotechnology has substantially improved drug delivery systems as well as providing technique for direct delivery of drug to the specific site, avoiding undesired side effects by confining the medication's effect to a specific place while leaving other tissues unaffected. Nanoparticles (NPs) are used in cancer medication to expand bioavailability, in vivo constancy, absorption in the intestinal region, solubility, prolonged as well as targeted delivery, besides therapeutic efficiency (Díaz and Vivas-Mejia, 2013). Most powerful cancer chemotherapeutic drugs show a constricted therapeutic index besides being utilized to treat a variety of tumor types; though, their cytotoxicity actions harm both healthy as well as malignant cells. This made administering metallodrugs in cancer chemotherapy a significant challenge. As a result, the ability of NPs in targeting malignant cells selectively while leaving normal cells alone has piqued curiosity in the development of metal-based chemotherapeutic agents (Aghebati-Maleki et al., 2020).

8.3 NPs in radiotherapy

Metal nanoparticles are widely employed in radiotherapy to increase the specificity of radiations to the targeted spot, reducing radiation dose and preventing toxicity and injury to normal tissues (Chang, 2008). Metal nanoparticles use a variety of ways to improve radiation targeting. Metal nanoparticles boost cellular ROS production from ionizing radiations (AuNPs), enhance oxidative stress in cancer tissue, elevate selective apoptosis, in addition to reduce clonogenic survival (AgNPs) (Zhang, 2012). For radiotherapy, metal nanoparticles like gold, platinum, silver, zinc oxide, titanium dioxide, and others have been employed. Metal nanoparticles have fascinated extensive attention in radio-sensitization nanomedicine due to their intriguing optical, electrical, and conductive capabilities.

8.4 NPs in hyperthermia

Metal nanoparticles cause hyperthermia, which causes the cells to heat up beyond their tolerance limit that is less in malignant cells than healthy tissue attributable to their limited supply of blood, destroying the malignant cell. Malignant tumors have a higher absorption of metal nanoparticles than healthy cells. They use heat to destroy malignant cells by transformation of electromagnetic radiation. Due to their increased radiofrequency and magnetic characteristics, iron oxide nanoparticles are usually utilized in hyperthermia therapy for the treatment of malignancy. Stability, prolonged half-life, attachment of ligand, targeting by coating with various polymers such as dextran, and surface functionalization with PEG molecules are all advantages of iron oxide nanoparticles (Huang and Hainfeld, 2013; Kam, 2005). Photothermal ablation with carbon nanotubes (CNTs) is also utilized to treat cancer (Moon et al., 2009; Burke, 2009). In mouse models, intratumor injection of SWCNTs followed by 3 min of NIR light irradiation results in tumor elimination.

8.5 NPs in diagnosis

Numerous types of extremely specific as well as very profound NP-based optical imaging platforms have been studied for improvement the specificity in the identification of malignancies. When compared to other agents, diagnostic platforms based on NPs provide a significant benefit. These agents can be programmed for targeting tumor cells specifically, that allow imaging as well as chemotherapeutic agents to be administered to particular cells only (Ventola, 2012). Because tumor-precise targeting is accomplished by incorporating the NPs surface with a biomarker or molecule conjugated to the tumor cell receptor, a thorough understanding of tumor-precise receptors, homing proteins, biomarkers, as well as enzymes that allow selective cellular intake of drugs and agents for diagnosis is critical.

8.6 Some important NPs for anticancer therapies

In the presence of nontoxic radiation of wavelength, viz., near-infrared (NIR) or oscillating magnetic fields (MF), iron oxide nanoparticles are changed into toxic reactive oxygen species (ROS) stimuli that destroy tumor cells (van Landeghem, 2009). Because of their magnetic properties, iron oxide nanoparticles decrease harm to normal cells by converting radiant energy to heat or reactive oxygen species (ROS) after being exposed to a local external magnetic field, lowering the risk of cancer therapy side effects. The iron oxide nanoparticles are given as a combination with chemotherapy medications like doxorubicin to boost the therapeutic impact of standard doxorubicin therapy (Silva, 2011). Spherical iron oxide nanoparticles have been approved by the European Union as a medicinal purposes for producing hyperthermia in brain (Johannsen, 2010; Maier-Hauff, 2011) as well as prostate cancer (Kolosnjaj-Tabi, 2014) in a combined treatment with chemotherapy and radiotherapy (Bhattacharyya, 2011).

Gold nanoparticles are emerging as a possible cancer therapeutic adjuvant. Nanoparticles' tiny size permits them to run away from the reticuloendothelial system, resulting in increased permeability and retention, allowing the medication to be continually released over a lengthy period of time (Brown, 2010). A photothermal modulated drug delivery system was demonstrated using gold-gold sulfide nanoshells produced in a hydrogel matrix. After NIR absorption, drug release from hydrogel follows a burst process. When AuNPs coated with PEG were administered to mice with adenocarcinoma and breast cancer, they had a better survival rate when given with ionizing radiations (Hainfeld et al., 2004; Chatterjee et al., 2008). Au-Nanoshells, Au-Nanocages, Au-Nanorods, and other Au-based nanostructures are appropriable for hyperthermia or photothermal therapeutic procedure. Because AuNPs have a trend of accumulation at the tumor site after 4–5 h, they can be used to provide long-term laser hyperthermia therapy (Zhang and Sun, 2004).

TiO_2 nanoparticles can be utilized to replace traditional PS molecules as a direct photosensitizing agent (Çeşmeli and Biray Avci, 2019; Thevenot et al., 2008; Seo et al., 2007). TiO_2 nanoparticles are thought to be particularly promising in cancer therapy due to their increased UV absorption efficacy in addition to improved photocatalytic activity.

ZnO NPs are recently being actively examined in cancer research. ZnO NPs have the greatest result on T98G cancer cells, increasing mitotic and interphase (apoptotic) mortality, while having a modest impact on KB cells and having little or no influence on HEK cells (normal cells) (Baskar et al., 2015). The rate of apoptosis will increase as the concentration of ZnO NPs rises (Colon et al., 2010). They're also utilized as a photodynamic agent, producing a lot of reactive oxygen species (ROS) and inducing apoptotic cell death (Tarnuzzer, 2005). The selectivity, efficacy, and stability of ZnO NPs containing asparaginase, anticancer drug, are very promising (Neri and Supuran, 2011).

Silver nanoparticles (AgNPs) have been shown to induce oxidative stress, affect membrane fluidity, besides promoting tumor cell death by apoptosis (Bagwe et al., 2006; Wang, 2013). The release of silver cations, that absorb electrons as well as cause oxidative stress in the cells, is the process of radiosensitization. They also enhance the production of ROS besides decreasing the quantity of ATP inside the cells.

Plant extracts such as *Ficus religiosa* and *Acalypha indica* are used to make copper oxide nanoparticles. This is known as green nanoparticle synthesis, and it has been observed to be a dependable, simple, nontoxic, as well as environmentally acceptable process. These nanoparticles have a lethal influence on human lung cancer cells, triggering apoptosis and an increase in the generation of ROS. Using B16–F10 cells, copper oxide nanoparticles were utilized in vitro for the treatment of melanoma along with metastatic lung cancers in mice (Sharma et al., 2017; Anselmo and Mitragotri, 2015).

9. Conclusions and future directions

After cardiovascular diseases, cancer is the second biggest cause of mortality, with cancer fatalities expected to rise by 60% in the next 2 decades. Since 2012, the pharmaceutical industry has increased its attention on the research, development, and marketing of novel oncology drug products to meet unmet medical needs, resulting in the approval of 90 new cancer drugs by the US FDA. Since the discovery of cisplatin, there has been a lot of research into the medicinal use of metal-based complexes. The clinical success of cisplatin paved the way for researchers to investigate metals, both nonessential and essential, and metal coordination complexes as anticancer medicines. Thousands of platinum-based compounds have been developed since the discovery of cisplatin's chemotherapeutic properties, with only oxaliplatin and carboplatin seeing extensive clinical use. Cisplatin was the first extensively used metal-based chemotherapy treatment, however due to problems such as acquired and intrinsic resistance, as well as increasing toxicity, researchers are looking for additional metal-based chemotherapy drugs. Oxaliplatin and carboplatin are second- and third-generation platinum medicines that have a significantly more manageable toxicity profile as a result of this. Ruthenium, gold, and iridium among others, have been proposed as nonplatinum-based therapeutics that shows promising anticancer properties. The better features of ruthenium complexes, such as variable oxidation states, low toxicity, great selectivity for cancer cells, antimetastatic properties, and the ability to mimic iron in binding to proteins, are the key reasons that they operate as innovative anticancer medicines. Ruthenium derivatives have a number of advantages over platinum complexes, including lower toxicity, a novel method of action, and variable oxidation states. The exceptional in vitro antiproliferative activity of gold compounds against a vast variety of human cancer cells, frequently at nanomolar levels, has recently sparked increased interest in them.

Fluorescent metal-based probes have several benefits over traditional imaging devices, including ease of use, good resolution and sensitivity, low cost, and the lack of ionizing radiation, making them one of the most promising imaging technologies in the biomedical arena. Transition metal-based complexes (e.g., Pt(II), Ru(II), and Ir(III)-based complexes) are a well-known family of fluorophores utilized for cellular/subcellular imaging, particularly of subcellular organelles such as mitochondria, lysosomes, endoplasmic reticulum, and nuclei. In photodynamic therapy (PDT) using fluorescent probes, photosensitizers (PS) are also employed. The possibility of selectively activating metal complexes in tumor cells using light is also fascinating. The reactions of excited-state metal complexes can differ significantly from those of ground-state metal complexes, posing the risk of highly reactive new species interfering with biological pathways.

Nanomedicine is one of the most exciting fields of study at the moment. In the previous 2 decades, extensive research in this subject has resulted in the filing of 1500 patents and the completion of dozens of clinical trials. Metal nanoparticles have been comprehensively studied in biomedical research due to their remarkable physical and chemical properties. The application of nanomedicine and nanodrug delivery systems is unquestionably the trend that will remain the future arena of research and development for decades to come, by using various types of nanoparticles for the delivery of an exact amount of drug to the affected cells, such as cancer/tumor cells, without disturbing the physiology of the normal cells. Moreover, due to their unique interaction with light, metal nanoparticles provide a reliable means of tracking nanocomplex therapeutic carriers within the body, allowing for a more efficient therapy with a lower chance of side effects than traditional therapies. Furthermore, cancer immunotherapy based on nanoparticles could have a longer-lasting vaccination impact as well as a larger immune response than traditional immunotherapy.

To summarize, the combination of metals such as Ru, Au, and Ir with the versatile class of ligands has permitted the synthesis of new prospective anticancer medicines with high activity, good selectivity, and unique modes of action in the recent decade. Despite several promising in vitro outcomes in terms of antiproliferative activity and selectivity, there are still a few in vivo investigations are yet to be done. Another important challenge to address is determining the appropriate pharmacological combination for each metal-based drug candidate. This, too, can only be addressed if we improve our understanding of these medications' molecular mechanisms and biology. There is still a long way to go before we can replace cisplatin with better, less toxic, and less chemoresistant metal-based medications, but with the right design strategy, this otherwise intriguing family of pharmaceuticals might have a more acceptable outcome. Overall, various metal-based complexes have significant potential for the development of novel anticancer agents with diverse roles and activities, and while their development is still in its early or secondary stages, we believe these metal compounds have a bright future ahead of them.

Acknowledgment

S.A. acknowledges support from Govt. Degree College, Dharmanagar, Tripura (N) 799253, India.

References

Adhikari, S., Bhattacharjee, T., Butcher, R.J., Porchia, M., De Franco, M., Marzano, C., Gandin, V., Tisato, F., 2019a. Synthesis and characterization of mixed-ligand Zn(II) and cu(II) complexes including polyamines and dicyano-dithiolate(2-): in vitro cytotoxic activity of cu(II) compounds. Inorg. Chim. Acta 498, 119098–119110. https://doi.org/10.1016/j.ica.2019.119098.

Adhikari, S., Kar, D., Fröhlich, R., Ghosh, K., 2019b. Pyridine-based macrocyclic and open receptors for urea. ChemistrySelect 4, 12825–12831. https://doi.org/10.1002/slct.201902451.

Adhikari, S., Bhattaharjee, T., Nath, P., Das, A., Jasinski, J.P., Butcher, R.J., Maiti, D., 2020. Bimetallic and trimetallic Cd(II) and Hg(II) mixed-ligand complexes with 1,1-dicyanoethylene-2,2-dithiolate and polyamines: synthesis, crystal structure, Hirshfeld surface analysis, and antimicrobial study. Inorg. Chim. Acta 512, 119877. https://doi.org/10.1016/j.ica.2020.119877.

Adhireksan, Z., Davey, G.E., Campomanes, P.R., Groessl, M., Clavel, C.M., Yu, H., Nazarov, A.A., Yeo, C.H.F., Ang, W.H., Dröge, P., Roethlisberger, U., Dyson, P.J., Davey, C.A., 2014. Ligand substitutions between ruthenium–cymene compounds can control protein versus DNA targeting and anticancer activity. Nat. Commun. 5, 3462. https://doi.org/10.1038/ncomms4462.

Aghebati-Maleki, A., Dolati, S., Ahmadi, M., Baghbanzhadeh, A., Asadi, M., Fotouhi, A., Yousefi, M., Aghebati-Maleki, L., 2020. Nanoparticles and cancer therapy: perspectives for application of nanoparticles in the treatment of cancers. J. Cell. Physiol. 5, 1962–1972. https://doi.org/10.1002/jcp.29126.

Ahn, J.H., Kang, Y.K., Kim, T.W., Bahng, H., Chang, H.M., Kang, W.C., Kim, W.K., Lee, J.S., Park, J.S., 2002. Nephrotoxicity of heptaplatin: a randomized comparison with cisplatin in advanced gastric cancer. Cancer Chemother. Pharmacol. 50, 104–110. https://doi.org/10.1007/s00280-002-0483-x.

Ai, Z., Lu, Y., Qiu, S., Fan, Z., 2016. Overcoming cisplatin resistance of ovarian cancer cells by targeting HIF-1-regulated cancer metabolism. Cancer Lett. 373, 36–44. https://doi.org/10.1016/j.canlet.2016.01.009.

Aird, R.E., Cummings, J., Morris, R., Ritchie, A.A., Sadler, P.J., Jodrell, D.I., 2001. RM175, a novel ruthenium (Ru-11) organo-metallic complex: patterns of resistance in vitro and in vivo. Br. J. Cancer 85, 101.

Alberto, E.M., Lucas, M.F.A., Pavelka, M., Russo, N., 2009. The second generation anticancer drug nedaplatin: a theoretical investigation on the hydrolysis mechanism. J. Phys. Chem. B 113, 14473–14479. https://doi.org/10.1021/jp9056835.

Alfarouk, K.O., Stock, C.-M., Taylor, S., Walsh, M., Muddathir, A.K., Verduzco, D., Bashir, A.H.H., Mohammed, O.Y., Elhassan, G.O., Harguindey, S., Reshkin, S.J., Ibrahim, M.E., Rauch, C., 2015. Resistance to cancer chemotherapy: failure in drug response from ADME to P-gp. Cancer Cell Int. 15, 71–83. https://doi.org/10.1186/s12935-015-0221-1.

Anselmo, A.C., Mitragotri, S., 2015. Nanoparticles in the clinic. Bioeng. Transl. Med. 17, 1041–1054. https://doi.org/10.1002/btm2.10003.

Armand, J.P., Bolgie, V., Raymond, E., Fizazi, K., Faivre, S., Ducreux, M., 2000. Oxaliplatin in colorectal cancer: an overview. Semin. Oncol. 27, 96–104.

Bagwe, R.P., Hilliard, L.R., Tan, W., 2006. Surface modification of silica nanoparticles to reduce aggregation and nonspecific binding. Langmuir 22, 4357–4362. https://doi.org/10.1021/la052797j.

Baskar, G., Chandhuru, J., Sheraz Fahad, K., Praveen, A.S., Chamundeeswari, M., Muthukumar, T., 2015. Anticancer activity of fungal L-asparaginase conjugated with zinc oxide nanoparticles. J. Mater. Sci. Mater. Med. 26, 1–7. https://doi.org/10.1007/s10856-015-5380-z.

Bécouarn, Y., Ychou, M., Ducreux, M., Borel, C., Bertheault-Cvitkovic, F., Seitz, J.F., Nasca, S., Nguyen, T.D., Paillot, B., Raoul, J.L., Duffour, J., Fandi, A., Dupont-André, G., Rougier, P., 1998. Phase II trial of oxaliplatin as first-line chemotherapy in metastatic colorectal cancer patients. Digestive Group of French Federation of Cancer Centers. J. Clin. Oncol. 16, 2739–2744. https://doi.org/10.1200/JCO.1998.16.8.2739.

Berners-Price, S.J., Filipovska, A., 2011. Gold compounds as therapeutic agents for human diseases. Metallomics 3, 863–873. https://doi.org/10.1039/c1mt00062d.

Berners-Price, S.J., Mirabelli, C.K., Johnson, R.K., Mattern, M.R., McCabe, F.L., Faucette, L.F., Sung, C.-M., Mong, S.-M., Sadler, P.J., Crooke, S.T., 1986. In vivo antitumor activity and in vitro cytotoxic properties of bis[1,2-bis(diphenylphosphino)ethane]gold(I) chloride. Cancer Res. 46, 5486–5493.

Bertini, I., Gray, H.B., Lippard, S.J., Valentine, J.S., 1994. Bioinorganic Chemistry. pp. 523–590.

Bhattacharjee, T., Adhikari, S., Datta, A., Daniliuc, C.-G., Montazerozohori, M., Naghiha, R., Hayati, P., 2022. Cadmium(II) coordination polymer based on flexible dithiolate-polyamine binary ligands system: crystal structure, Hirshfeld surface analysis, antimicrobial, and DNA cleavage potential. Polyhedron 211, 115544. https://doi.org/10.1016/j.poly.2021.115544.

Bhattacharyya, S., 2011. Inorganic nanoparticles in cancer therapy. Pharm. Res. 28, 237–259. https://doi.org/10.1007/s11095-010-0318-0.

Bindoli, A., Pia, M., Scutari, G., Gabbiani, C., Casini, A., Messori, L., 2009a. Thioredoxin reductase: a target for gold compounds acting as potential anticancer drugs. Coord. Chem. Rev. 253, 1692–1707. https://doi.org/10.1016/j.ccr.2009.02.026.

Bindoli, A., Rigobello, M.P., Scutari, G., Gabbiani, C., Casini, A., Messori, L., 2009b. Thioredoxin reductase: a target for gold compounds acting as potential anticancer drugs Coord. Chem. Rev. 253, 1692–1707. https://doi.org/10.1016/j.ccr.2009.02.026.

Boulikas, T., Vougiouka, M., 2003a. Cisplatin and platinum drugs at the molecular level. Oncol. Rep. 10, 1663–1682. https://doi.org/10.3892/or.10.6.1663.

Boulikas, T., Vougiouka, M., 2003b. Cis-platin and platinum drugs at the molecular level. Oncol. Rep. 10, 1663–1682. https://doi.org/10.3892/or.10.6.1663.

Boulikas, T., Pantos, A., Bellis, E., Christofis, P., 2007. Designing platinum compounds in cancer: structures and mechanisms. Cancer Ther. 5, 537–583.

Brown, S.D., 2010. Gold nanoparticles for the improved anticancer drug delivery of the active component of oxaliplatin. J. Am. Chem. Soc. 132, 4678–4684. https://doi.org/10.1021/ja908117a.

Buckley, R.G., Elsome, A.M., Fricker, S.P., Henderson, G.R., Theobald, B.R.C., Parish, R.V., Howe, B.-P., Kelland, L.R., 1996. Antitumor properties of some 2-[(dimethylamino)methyl]phenylgold(III) complexes. J. Med. Chem. 39, 5208–5214. https://doi.org/10.1021/jm9601563.

Burke, A., 2009. Long-term survival following a single treatment of kidney tumors with multiwalled carbon nanotubes and near-infrared radiation. Proc. Natl. Acad. Sci. 106, 12897–12902. https://doi.org/10.1073/pnas.0905195106.

Bytzek, A.K., Koellensperger, G., Keppler, B.K., Hartinger, C.G., 2016. Biodistribution of the novel anticancer drug sodium trans-[tetrachloridobis(1H-indazole)ruthenate(III)] KP-1339/IT139 in nude BALB/c mice and implications on its mode of action. J. Inorg. Biochem. 160, 250–255. https://doi.org/10.1016/j.jinorgbio.2016.02.037.

Cao, Z.-T., Chen, Z.-Y., Sun, C.-Y., Li, H.-J., Wang, H.-X., Cheng, Q.-Q., Zuo, Z.-Q., Wang, J.-L., Liu, Y.-Z., Wang, Y.-C., Wang, J., 2016. Overcoming tumor resistance to cisplatin by cationic lipid-assisted prodrug nanoparticles. Biomaterials 94, 9–19. https://doi.org/10.1016/j.biomaterials.2016.04.001.

Casini, A., Sun, R.W., Ott, I., 2018. Medicinal chemistry of gold anticancer metallodrugs. Met. Ions Life Sci. 18. https://doi.org/10.1515/9783110470734-013. books/9783110470734/9783110470734-007/9783110470734-013.xml.

Cassidy, J., 2000. Review of oxaliplatin: an active platinum agent in colorectal cancer. Int. J. Clin. Pract. 54, 399–402.

Cassidy, J., Misset, J.L., 2002. Oxaliplatin-related side effects: characteristics and management. Semin. Oncol. 29, 11–20. https://doi.org/10.1053/sonc.2002.35524.

Cepeda, V., Fuertes, M.A., Castilla, J., Alonso, C., Quevedo, C., Pérez, J.M., 2007. Biochemical mechanisms of cisplatin cytotoxicity. Anti Cancer Agents Med. Chem. 7, 3–18. https://doi.org/10.2174/187152007779314044.

Çeşmeli, S., Biray Avci, C., 2019. Application of titanium dioxide (TiO2) nanoparticles in cancer therapies. J. Drug Target. 27, 762–766. https://doi.org/10.1080/1061186X.2018.1527338.

Chang, M.Y., 2008. Increased apoptotic potential and dose- enhancing effect of gold nanoparticles in combination with single-dose clinical electron beams on tumor-bearing mice. Cancer Sci. 99, 1479–1484. https://doi.org/10.1111/j.1349-7006.2008.00827.x.

Chatterjee, D.K., Fong, L.S., Zhang, Y., 2008. Nanoparticles in photodynamic therapy: an emerging paradigm. Adv. Drug Deliv. Rev. 60, 1627–1637. https://doi.org/10.1016/j.addr.2008.08.003.

Choi, C.H., Cha, Y.J., An, C.S., Kim, K.J., Kim, K.C., Moon, S.P., Lee, Z.H., Min, Y.D., 2004. Molecular mechanisms of heptaplatin effective against cisplatin-resistant cancer cell lines: less involvement of metallothionein. Cancer Cell Int. 4, 6. https://doi.org/10.1186/1475-2867-4-6.

Choquet, D., Sainlos, M., Sibarita, J.-B., 2021. Advanced imaging and labelling methods to decipher brain cell organization and function. Nat. Rev. Neurosci. 22, 237–255. https://doi.org/10.1038/s41583-021-00441-z.

Colon, J., Hsieh, N., Ferguson, A., Kupelian, P., Seal, S., Jenkins, D.W., Baker, C.H., 2010. Cerium oxide nanoparticles protect gastrointestinal epithelium from radiation-induced damage by reduction of reactive oxygen species and upregulation of superoxide dismutase 2. Nanomedicine 6, 698–705. https://doi.org/10.1016/j.nano.2010.01.010.

Cummings, J., Aird, R.E., Morris, R., Chen, H., Murdoch, P.D., Sadler, P.J., Smyth, J.F., Jodrell, D.I., 2000. Novel ruthenium (Ru-II) organo-metallic complexes: in vitro cytotoxicity in wild type and drug resistant A2780 human ovarian cancer cell lines. Clin. Cancer Res. 6, 4494.

Dasari, S., Bernard Tchounwou, P., 2014. Cisplatin in cancer therapy: molecular mechanisms of action. Eur. J. Pharmacol. 740, 364–378. https://doi.org/10.1016/j.ejphar.2014.07.025.

Degardin, M., Armand, J.P., Chevallier, B., Cappeleare, P., Lentz, M.A., David, M., Roche, H., 1995. A clinical screening cooperative group phase II evaluation of lobaplatin ASTA D-19466 in advanced head and neck cancer. Investig. New Drugs 13, 253–255. https://doi.org/10.1007/BF00873809.

Denk, W., Strickler, J., Webb, W., 1990. Two-photon laser scanning fluorescence microscopy. Science 248, 73–76. https://doi.org/10.1126/science.2321027.

Dhar, S., Liu, Z., Thomale, J., Dai, H., Lippard, S.J., 2008. Targeted single-wall carbon nanotube-mediated Pt(IV) prodrug delivery using folate as a homing device. J. Am. Chem. Soc. 130, 11467–11476. https://doi.org/10.1021/ja803036e.

Díaz, M.R., Vivas-Mejia, P.E., 2013. Nanoparticles as drug delivery systems in cancer medicine: emphasis on RNAi-containing nanoliposomes. Pharmaceuticals (Basel) 6, 1361–1380. https://doi.org/10.3390/ph6111361.

Dinarvand, R., Cesar de Morais, P., D'Emanuele, A., 2012. Nanoparticles for targeted delivery of active agents against tumor cells. J. Drug Deliv. 2012. https://doi.org/10.1155/2012/528123.

Dominelli, B., Correia, J.D.G., Kühn, F.E., 2018. Medicinal applications of gold(I/III)-based complexes bearing N-heterocyclic carbene and phosphine ligands. J. Organomet. Chem. 866, 153–164. https://doi.org/10.1016/j.jorganchem.2018.04.023.

Dougan, S.J., Habtemariam, A., McHale, S.E., Parsons, S., Sadler, P.J., 2008. Catalytic organometallic anticancer complexes. Proc. Natl. Acad. Sci. U. S. A. 105, 11628–11633. https://doi.org/10.1073/pnas.0800076105.

Dragutan, I., Dragutan, V., Demonceau, A., 2015. Editorial of special issue ruthenium complex: the expanding chemistry of the ruthenium complexes. Molecules 20, 17244–17274. https://doi.org/10.3390/molecules200917244.

Engman, L., McNaughton, M., Gajewska, M., Kumar, S., Birmingham, A., Powis, G., 2006. Thioredoxin reductase and cancer cell growth inhibition by organogold(III) compounds. Anti-Cancer Drugs 17, 539–544.

Ferlay, J., Ervik, M., Lam, F., Colombet, M., Mery, L., Piñeros, M., 2020. Global Cancer Observatory: Cancer Today. International Agency for Research on Cancer, Lyon. https://gco.iarc.fr/today. (accessed February 2021).

Fliopoulos, A.G., Kerr, D.J., Maurer, R., Hilgard, P., Spandidos, D.A., 1995. Induction of the c-myc but not the cH-ras promoter by platinum compounds. Biochem. Pharmacol. 50, 33–38. https://doi.org/10.1016/0006-2952(95)00085-E.

Florea, A.-M., Büsselberg, D., 2011. Cisplatin as an anti-tumor drug: cellular mechanisms of activity, drug resistance and induced side effects. Cancers 3, 1351–1371. https://doi.org/10.3390/cancers3011351.

Fong, J., Kasimova, K., Arenas, Y., Kaspler, P., Lazic, S., Mandel, A., Lilge, L., 2015. A novel class of ruthenium-based photosensitizers effectively kills in vitro cancer cells and in vivo tumors. Photochem. Photobiol. Sci. 14, 2014–2023. https://doi.org/10.1039/C4PP00438H.

Fong, T.T.-H., Lok, C.-N., Chung, C.Y.-S., Fung, Y.-M.E., Chow, P.-K., Wan, P.-K., Che, C.-M., 2016. Cyclometalated palladium(II) N-heterocyclic carbene complexes: anticancer agents for potent in vitro cytotoxicity and in vivo tumor growth suppression. Angew. Chem. Int. Ed. 55, 11935–11939. https://doi.org/10.1002/anie.201602814.

Frey, U., Ranford, J.D., Sadler, P.J., 1993. Ring-opening reactions of the anticancer drug carboplatin: NMR characterization of cis-[Pt(NH$_3$)$_2$(CBDCA-O)(5'-GMP-N7)] in solution. Inorg. Chem. 32, 1333–1340. https://doi.org/10.1021/ic00060a005.

Frezza, M., Hindo, S., Chen, D., Davenport, A., Schmitt, S., Tomco, D., Dou, Q.P., 2010. Novel metals and metal complexes as platforms for cancer therapy. Curr. Pharm. Des. 16, 1813–1825. https://doi.org/10.2174/138161210791209009.

Fuertes, M.A., Castilla, J., Alonso, C., Pérez, J.M., 2003. Cisplatin biochemical mechanism of action: from cytotoxicity to induction of cell death through interconnections between apoptotic and necrotic pathways. Curr. Med. Chem. 3, 257–266. https://doi.org/10.2174/0929867033368484.

Galluzzi, L., Senovilla, L., Vitale, I., Michels, J., Martins, I., Kepp, O., Castedo, M., Kroemer, G., 2012. Molecular mechanisms of cisplatin resistance. Oncogene 31, 1869–1883. https://doi.org/10.1038/onc.2011.384.

Gao, M., Yu, F., Lv, C., Choo, J., Chen, L., 2017. Fluorescent chemical probes for accurate tumor diagnosis and targeting therapy. Chem. Soc. Rev. 46, 2237–2271. https://doi.org/10.1039/C6CS00908E.

Ghosh, S., 2019. Cisplatin: the first metal based anticancer drug. Bioorg. Chem. 88, 102925. https://doi.org/10.1016/j.bioorg.2019.10292.

Ghosh, K., Adhikari, S., 2006a. Fluorescence sensing of tartaric acid: a case of excimer emission caused by hydrogen bond-mediated complexation. Tetrahedron Lett. 47, 3577–3581. https://doi.org/10.1016/j.tetlet.2006.03.044.

Ghosh, K., Adhikari, S., 2006b. Colorimetric and fluorescence sensing of anions using thiourea based coumarin receptors. Tetrahedron Lett. 47, 8165–8169. https://doi.org/10.1016/j.tetlet.2006.09.035.

Ghosh, K., Adhikari, S., 2008. A quinoline-based tripodal fluororeceptor for citric acid. Tetrahedron Lett. 49, 658–663. https://doi.org/10.1016/j.tetlet.2007.11.139.

Ghosh, K., Adhikari, S., Chattopadhyay, A.P., Chowdhury, P.R., 2008. Quinoline based receptor in fluorometric discrimination of carboxylic acids. Beilstein J. Org. Chem. 4, 52. https://doi.org/10.3762/bjoc.4.52.

Gietema, J.A., Guchelaar, H.J., de Vries, E.G.E., Alenbacher, P., Seifer, D.T., Mulder, N.H., 1993. A phase I study of lobaplatin (D-19466) administered by 72 h continuous infusion. Anti-Cancer Drugs 4, 51–55. https://doi.org/10.1097/00001813-199302000-00007.

Gietema, J.A., Veldhuis, G.J., Guchelaar, H.J., Willemse, P.H.B., Uges, D.R.A., Cats, A., Boonstra, H., Van Der Graaf, W.T.A., Sleijfer, D.T., de Vries, E.G.E., Mulder, N.H., 1995. Phase II and pharmacokinetic study of lobaplatin in patients with relapsed ovarian cancer. Br. J. Cancer 71, 1302–1307. https://doi.org/10.1038/bjc.1995.252.

Gill, M.R., Thomas, J.A., 2012. Ruthenium(II) polypyridyl complexes and DNA—from structural probes to cellular imaging and therapeutics. Chem. Soc. Rev. 41, 3179–3192. https://doi.org/10.1039/C2CS15299A.

Guichard, S.M., Else, R., Reid, E., Zeitlin, B., Aird, R., Muir, M., Dodds, M., Fiebig, H., Sadler, P.J., Jodrell, D.I., 2006. Anti-tumour activity in non-small cell lung cancer models and toxicity profiles for novel ruthenium(II) based organo-metallic compounds. Biochem. Pharmacol. 71, 408–415. https://doi.org/10.1016/j.bcp.2005.10.053.

Gwo, Y.H., Woodward, N., Coward, I.G., 2016. Cisplatin versus carboplatin: comparative review of therapeutic management in solid malignancies. Crit. Rev. Oncol. Hematol. 102, 37–46. https://doi.org/10.1016/j.critrevonc.2016.03.014.

Haas, K., Franz, K., 2009. Application of metal coordination chemistry to explore and manipulate. Chem. Rev. 109, 4921–4960. https://doi.org/10.1021/cr900134a.

Hainfeld, J.F., Slatkin, D.N., Smilowitz, H.M., 2004. The use of gold nanoparticles to enhance radiotherapy in mice. Phys. Med. Biol. 49, N309.

Han, H.H., Tian, H., Zang, Y., Sedgwick, A.C., Li, J., Sessler, J.L., He, X.P., James, T.D., 2021. Small-molecule fluorescence-based probes for interrogating major organ diseases. Chem. Soc. Rev. 50, 9391–9429. https://doi.org/10.1039/D0CS01183E.

Hartinger, C.G., Zorbas-Seifried, S., Jakupec, M.A., Kynast, B., Zorbas, H., Keppler, B.K., 2006. From bench to bedside—preclinical and early clinical development of the anticancer agent indazolium trans-[tetrachlorobis(1H-indazole)ruthenate(III)] (KP1019 or FFC14A). J. Inorg. Biochem. 100, 891–904. https://doi.org/10.1016/j.jinorgbio.2006.02.013.

Hartinger, C.G., Jakupec, M.A., Zorbas-Seifried, S., Groessl, M., Egger, A., Berger, W., Zorbas, H., Dyson, P.J., Keppler, B.K., 2008. KP1019, a new redox-active anticancer agent—preclinical development and results of a clinical phase I study in tumor patients. Chem. Biodivers. 5, 2140–2155. https://doi.org/10.1002/cbdv.200890195.

Hartinger, C.G., Groessl, M., Meier, S.M., Casini, A., Dyson, P.J., 2013. Application of mass spectrometric techniques to delineate the modes-of-action of anticancer metallodrugs. Chem. Soc. Rev. 42, 6186–6199. https://doi.org/10.1039/C3CS35532B.

He, M., Du, F., Zhang, W.-Y., 2019. Photoinduced anticancer effect evaluation of ruthenium(II) poly-pyridyl complexes toward human lung cancer A549 cells. Polyhedron 165, 97–110. https://doi.org/10.1016/j.poly.2019.03.015.

Huang, H.S., Hainfeld, J.F., 2013. Intravenous magnetic nanoparticle cancer hyperthermia. Int. J. Nanomedicine 8, 2521–2532. https://doi.org/10.2147/IJN.S43770.

Intravesical Photodynamic Therapy (PDT) in BCG Refractory/Intolerant Non-Muscle Invasive Bladder Cancer (NMIBC) Patients. NCT03945162. 2021 (accessed 26.02.20).

Jakupec, M.A., Galanski, M., Keppler, B.K., 2003. Tumor inhibiting platinum complexes—state of the art and future perspectives. Rev. Physiol. Biochem. Pharmacol. 146, 1–53. https://doi.org/10.1007/s10254-002-0001-x.

Jamieson, E.R., Lippard, S.J., 1999. Structure, recognition, and processing of cisplatin–DNA adducts. Chem. Rev. 99, 2467–2498. https://doi.org/10.1021/cr980421n.

Jeannine, H., Huaiyi, H., Adrian, K., 2017. Evaluation of the medicinal potential of two ruthenium(II) poly-pyridine complexes as one- and two-photon photodynamic therapy photosensitizers. Chemistry 23, 9888–9896. https://doi.org/10.1002/chem.201701392.

Ji, H.-F., Li, X.-J., Zhang, H.-Y., 2009. Natural products and drug discovery. Can thousands of years of ancient medical knowledge lead us to new and powerful drug combinations in the fight against cancer and dementia? EMBO Rep. 10, 194–200. https://doi.org/10.1038/embor.2009.12.

Johannsen, M., 2010. Magnetic nanoparticle hyperthermia for prostate cancer. Int. J. Hyperth. 26, 790–795. https://doi.org/10.3109/02656731003745740.

Jordan, P., Carmo-Fonseca, M., 2000. Molecular mechanisms involved in cisplatin cytotoxicity. Cell. Mol. Life Sci. 57, 1229–1235. https://doi.org/10.1007/pl00000762.

Kaim, W., Schwederski, B., 1993. Bioinorganic Chemistry: Inorganic Element in the Chemistry of Life: An Introduction and Guide. John Wiley & Sons, Inc., pp. 363–384.

Kam, N.W.S., 2005. Carbon nanotubes as multifunctional biological transporters and near-infrared agents for selective cancer cell destruction. Proc. Natl. Acad. Sci. U. S. A. 102, 11600–11605. https://doi.org/10.1073/PNAS.0502680102.

Kandioller, W., Balsano, E., Meier, S.M., Jungwirth, U., Goschl, S., Roller, A., Jakupec, M.A., Berger, W., Keppler, B.K., Hartinger, C.G., 2013. Organometallic anticancer complexes of lapachol: metal centre-dependent formation of reactive oxygen species and correlation with cytotoxicity. Chem. Commun. 49, 3348–3350. https://doi.org/10.1039/C3CC40432C.

Kartalou, M., Essignmann, J.M., 2001. Mechanisms of resistance to cisplatin. Mutat. Res. 478, 23–43. https://doi.org/10.1016/S0027-5107(01)00141-5.

Kaspler, P., Lazic, S., Forward, S., Arenas, Y., Mandel, A., Lilge, L., 2016. A ruthenium (II) based photo-sensitizer and transferrin complexes enhance photo-physical properties, cell uptake, and photodynamic therapy safety and efficacy. Photochem. Photobiol. Sci. 15, 481–495. https://doi.org/10.1039/C5PP00450K.

Kauffman, G.B., Peyrone, M., 2010. Discoverer of cisplatin. Platin. Met. Rev. 54, 250–256. https://doi.org/10.1595/147106710X534326.

Kavanagh, J.J., Edwards, C.L., Freedman, R.S., Finnegan, M.B., Balat, O., Tresukosol, D., Bunk, K., Loechner, S., Hord, M., Franklin, J.L., Kudelka, A.P., 1995. A trial of lobaplatin (D-19466) in plat-inum resistant ovarian cancer. Gynecol. Oncol. 58, 106–109. https://doi.org/10.1006/gyno.1995.1191.

Kawai, Y., Taniuchi, S., Okahara, S., Nakamura, M., Gemba, M., 2005. Relationship between cis-platinor nedaplatin induced nephrotoxicity and renal accumulation. Biol. Pharm. Bull. 28, 1385–1388. https://doi.org/10.1248/bpb.28.1385.

Kelland, L., 2007. The resurgence of platinum-based cancer chemotherapy. Nat. Rev. Cancer 7, 573–584. https://doi.org/10.1038/nrc2167.

Kim, D.K., Kim, G., Gam, J., Cho, Y.B., Kim, H.T., Tai, J.H., Kim, K.H., Hong, W.S., Park, J.G., 1994. Synthesis and antitumor activity of a series of [2-substituted-4,5-bis(aminomethyl)-1,3-dioxolane]plat-inum(II) complexes. J. Med. Chem. 37, 1471–1485. https://doi.org/10.1021/jm00036a013.

Kim, D.K., Kim, H.T., Tai, J.H., Cho, Y.B., Kim, T.S., Kim, K.H., Park, J.G., Hong, W.S., 1995a. Phar-macokinetics and antitumor activity of a new platinum compound, cis-malonato[(4R,5R)-4,5-bis(aminomethyl)-2-isopropyl-1,3-dioxolane]platinum(II), as determined by ex vivo pharmacodynamics. Cancer Chemother. Pharmacol. 37, 1–6. https://doi.org/10.1007/BF00685622.

Kim, D.K., Kim, H.T., Cho, Y.B., Tai, J.H., Ahn, J.S., Kim, T.S., Kim, K.H., Hong, W.S., 1995b. Antitumor activity of cis-malonato[(4R,5R)-4,5-bis(aminomethyl)-2-isopropyl-1,3-dioxolane]platinum (II), a new platinum analogue, as an anticancer agent. Cancer Chemother. Pharmacol. 35, 441–445. https://doi.org/10.1007/s002800050260.

Ko, C.-N., Li, G., Leung, C.-H., Ma, D.-L., 2019. Dual function luminescent transition metal complexes for cancer theranostics: the combination of diagnosis and therapy. Coord. Chem. Rev. 381, 79–103. https://doi.org/10.1016/j.ccr.2018.11.013.

Kociba, R., Sleiht, S.D., Rosenberg, B., 1970. Inhibition of dunning asciticleukemia and Walker 256 carcinosarcoma with cisdiamminedichloroplatinum (NSC-119875). Cancer Chemother. Rep. 54, 325–328.

Kolosnjaj-Tabi, J., 2014. Heat-generating iron oxide nanocubes: subtle "destructurators" of the tumoral microenvironment. ACS Nano 8, 4268–4283. https://doi.org/10.1021/nn405356r.

Kostova, I., 2006a. Ruthenium complexes as anticancer agents. Curr. Med. Chem. 13, 1085–1107. https://doi.org/10.2174/092986706776360941.

Kostova, I., 2006b. Platinum complexes as anticancer agents. Recent Pat. Anticancer Drug Discov. 1, 1–22. https://doi.org/10.2174/157489206775246458.

Krishant, M.D., Ang, L.D., McGhie, B., Rajamanickam, A., Dhiman, A., Khoury, A., Holland, J., Bjelosevic, A., Pages, B., Gordon, C., Aldrich-Wright, R.J., 2018. Platinum coordination compounds with potent anticancer activity. Coord. Chem. Rev. 375, 148–163. https://doi.org/10.1016/j.ccr.2017.11.014.

Kurita, H., Yamamato, E., Nozaki, S., Wada, S., Furuta, I., Miyata, M., Kurashina, K., 2010. Multicenter phase 2 study of induction chemotherapy with docetaxel and nedaplatin for oral squamous cell carcinoma. Cancer Chemother. Pharmacol. 65, 503–508. https://doi.org/10.1007/s00280-009-1056-z.

Kuwahara, A., Yamamori, M., Nishiguchi, K., Okuno, T., Chayahara, N., Miki, I., Tamura, T., Inokuma, T., Takemoto, Y., Nakamura, T., Kataoka, K., Sakaeda, T., 2009. Replacement of cis-platin with nedaplatin in a definitive 5-fluorouracil/cis-platin-based chemoradiotherapy in Japanese patients with esophageal squamous cell carcinoma. Int. J. Med. Sci. 6, 305–311. https://doi.org/10.7150/ijms.6.305.

Lazarević, T., Rilak, A., Bugarčić, Ž.D., 2017. Platinum, palladium, gold and ruthenium complexes as anticancer agents: current clinical uses, cytotoxicity studies and future perspectives. Eur. J. Med. Chem. 142, 8–31. https://doi.org/10.1016/j.ejmech.2017.04.007.

Lee, W.S., Lee, G.W., Kim, H.W., Lee, O.J., Lee, Y.J., Ko, G.H., Lee, J.S., Jang, J.S., Ha, W.S., 2005. A phase II trial of heptaplatin/5-FU and leucovorin for advanced stomach cancer. Cancer Res. Treat. 37, 208–211. https://doi.org/10.4143/crt.2005.37.4.208.

Lee, J.W., Park, J.K., Lee, S.H., Kim, S.Y., Cho, Y.B., Kuh, H.J., 2006. Antitumor activity of heptaplatin in combination with 5-fluorouracil or paclitaxel against human head and neck cancer cells in vitro. Anti-Cancer Drugs 17, 377–384. https://doi.org/10.1097/01.cad.0000205033.08838.c7.

Lee, K.H., Hyun, M.S., Kim, H.K., Jin, H.M., Yang, J., Song, H.S., Do, Y.R., Ryoo, H.M., Chung, J.S., Zang, D.Y., Lim, H.Y., Jin, J.Y., Yim, C.Y., Park, H.S., Kim, J.S., Sohn, C.H., Lee, S.N., 2009. Randomized, multicenter, phase III trial of heptaplatin 1-hour infusion and 5-fluorouracil combination chemotherapy comparing with cis-platin and 5-fluorouracil combination chemotherapy in patients with advanced gastric cancer. Cancer Res. Treat. 41, 12–18. https://doi.org/10.4143/crt.2009.41.1.12.

Liang, R., Wei, M., Evans, D.G., Duan, X., 2014. Inorganic nanomaterials for bioimaging, targeted drug delivery and therapeutics. Chem. Commun. 50, 14071–14081. https://doi.org/10.1039/C4CC03118K.

Singh, M.K., Sutradhar, S., Paul, B., Adhikari, S., Laskar, F., Butcher, R.J., Acharya, S., Das, A., 2017. A new cadmium(II) complex with bridging dithiolate ligand: synthesis, crystal structure and antifungal activity study. J. Mol. Struct. 1139, 395–399. https://doi.org/10.1016/j.molstruc.2017.03.073.

Singh, M.K., Sutradhar, S., Paul, B., Adhikari, S., Laskar, F., Acharya, S., Chakraborty, D., Biswas, S., Das, A., Roy, S., Frontera, A., 2018. Mixed-ligand complexes of zinc(II) with 1,1-dicyanoethylene-2,2-dithiolate and N-donor ligands: a combined experimental and theoretical study. J. Mol. Struct. 1139, 334–343. https://doi.org/10.1016/j.molstruc.2018.03.073.

Paprocka, R., Szadkowska, M.W., Janciauskiene, S., Kosmalski, T., Kulik, M., Basa, A.H., 2022. Latest developments in metal complexes as anticancer agents. Coord. Chem. Rev. 452, 214307. https://doi.org/10.1016/j.ccr.2021.214307.

Monro, S., Colón, K.L., Yin, H., Roque, J., Konda, P., Gujar, S., Thummel, R.P., Lilge, L., Cameron, C.-G., McFarland, S.A., 2019. Transition metal complexes and photodynamic therapy from a tumorcentered approach: challenges, opportunities, and highlights from the development of TLD-1433. Chem. Rev. 119, 797–828. https://doi.org/10.1021/acs.chemrev.8b00211.

Rosenberg, B., VanCamp, L., Trosko, J.E., Mansour, V.H., 1969. Platinum compounds: a new class of potent antitumour agents. Nature 222, 385–386. https://doi.org/10.1038/222385a0.

Nicolini, M., 1997. Platinum and other metal coordination compounds in cancer chemotherapy. In: Proceedings of the Fifth International Symposium on Platinum and Other Metal Coordination Compounds in Cancer Chemotherapy Abano, 54.

Milacic, V., Fregona, D., Dou, Q.P., 2008. Gold complexes as prospective metal-based anticancer drugs. Histol. Histopathol. 23, 101–108. http://hdl.handle.net/10201/29665.

Liu, J., Zhang, C., Rees, T.W., Ke, L., Ji, L., Chao, H., 2018. Harnessing ruthenium(II) as photodynamic agents: encouraging advances in cancer therapy. Coord. Chem. Rev. 363, 17–28. https://doi.org/10.1016/j.ccr.2018.03.002.

Rosenberg, B., Van Camp, L., Krigas, T., 1965. Inhibition of cell division in Escherichia coli by electrolysis products from a platinum electrode. Nature 205, 698–699. https://doi.org/10.1038/205698a0.

Rosenberg, B., Van Camp, L., 1970. The successful regression of largesolid sarcoma 180 tumors by platinum compounds. Cancer Res. 30, 1799–1802.

Smith, G.H., 1979. New drugs released in 1978. Nurse Pract. 4, 35–41.

Perez, R.P., 1998. Cellular and molecular determinants of cisplatin resistance. Eur. J. Cancer 34, 1535–1542. https://doi.org/10.1016/S0959-8049(98)00227-5.

Ozols, R.F., 2000. Optimun chemotherapy for ovarian cancer. Int. J. Gynecol. Cancer 10, 33–37. https://doi.org/10.1046/j.1525-1438.2000.99508.x.

Neidle, S., Ismail, I.M., Sadler, P.J.J., 1980. The structure of the antitumor complex cis-(diammino)(l,l-cyclobutane-dicarboxylato)-Pt(II): Xray and NMR studies. J. Inorg. Biochem. 13, 205–212. https://doi.org/10.1016/S0162-0134(00)80069-0.

Sharma, G., Anghore, D., Khare, R., Rawal, R.K., 2018. Oxaliplatin for colorectal cancer therapy. Clin. Cancer Drugs 5, 13–27. https://doi.org/10.2174/2212697x05666180905094942.

Sweetman, S.C. (Ed.), 2007. Martindale, the Complete Drug Reference, thirty-fifth ed. Pharmaceutical Press, London.

Woynarowski, J.M., Faivre, S., Herzig, M.C., Arnett, B., Chapman, W.G., Trevino, A.V., Raymond, E., Chaney, S.G., Vaisman, A., Varchenko, M., Juniewicz, P.E., 2000. Oxaliplatin-induced damage of cellular DNA. Mol. Pharmacol. 58, 920–927. https://doi.org/10.1124/mol.58.5.920.

Lordick, F., Luber, B., Lorenzen, S., Hegewisch-Becker, S., Folprecht, G., Woll, E., Decker, T., Endlicher, E., Rothling, N., Schuster, T., Keller, G., Fend, F., Peschel, C., 2010. Cetuximab plus oxaliplatin/leucovorin/5-fluorouracil in first-line metastatic gastric cancer: a phase II study of the Arbeitsgemeinschaft Internistische Onkologie (AIO). Br. J. Cancer 102, 500–505. https://doi.org/10.1038/sj.bjc.6605521.

Raymond, E., Buquet-Fagot, C., Djelloul, S., Mester, J., Cvitkovic, E., Allain, P., Louvet, C., Gespach, C., 1997. Antitumor activity of oxaliplatin in combination with 5-fluorouracil and the thymidylate synthase inhibitor AG337 in human colon, breast and ovarian cancers. Anti-Cancer Drugs 8, 876–885. https://doi.org/10.1097/00001813-199710000-00009.

Shimada, M., Itamochi, H., Kigawa, J., 2013. Nedaplatin: a cisplatin derivative in cancer chemotherapy. Cancer Manag. Res. 5, 67–76. https://doi.org/10.2147/CMAR.S35785.

Oshita, F., Yamada, K., Saito, H., Noda, K., Hamanaka, N., Ikehara, M., 2004. Phase II study of nedaplatin and irinotecan for elderly patients with advanced non-small cell lung cancer. J. Exp. Ther. Oncol. 4, 343–348.

Ota, K., Wakui, A., Majima, H., 1992. Phase I study of a new platinum complex 254-S, cis-diammine (glycolato)-platinum (II). GanTo Kagaku Ryoho 19, 855–861.

McKeage, M.J., 2001. Lobaplatin: a new antitumor platinum drugs. Expert Opin. Investig. Drugs 10, 119–128. https://doi.org/10.1517/13543784.10.1.119.

Limited, A.I., 2003. Drugs R&D 4, 369–372.

Wheate, N.J., Walker, S., Craig, G.E., Oun, R., 2010. The status of platinum anticancer drugs in the clinic and in clinical trials. Dalton Trans. 39, 8113–8127. https://doi.org/10.1039/C0DT00292E.

Welink, J., Boven, E., Vermorken, J.B., Gall, H.E., van der Vijgh, W.J.F., 1999. Pharmacokinetics and pharmacodynamics of lobaplatin (D-19466) in patients with advanced solid tumors, including patients with impaired renal of liver function. Clin. Cancer Res. 5, 2349–2358.

Lv, X., Cao, X., Xia, W.X., 2021. Induction chemotherapy with lobaplatin and fluorouracil versus cisplatin and fluorouracil followed by hemoradiotherapy in patients with stage III–IVB nasopharyngeal carcinoma: an open-label, non-inferiority, randomised, controlled, phase 3 trial. Lancet Oncol. 22, 716–726. https://doi.org/10.1016/S1470-2045(21)00075-9.

Siddik, Z.H., 2003. Cisplatin: mode of cytotoxic action and molecular basis of resistance. Oncogene 22, 7265–7279. https://doi.org/10.1038/sj.onc.1206933.

Oun, R., Moussa, Y.E., Wheate, N.J., 2018. The side effects of platinum-based chemotherapy drugs: a review for chemists. Dalton Trans. 47, 6645–6653. https://doi.org/10.1039/C8DT00838H.

Zhang, Y., Zheng, J., Jiang, Y., Huang, X., Fang, L., 2020. Neglected, drug-induced platinum accumulation causes immune toxicity. Front. Pharmacol. 11, 1166. https://doi.org/10.3389/fphar.2020.01166.

Zheng, Y.-R., Suntharalingam, K., Johnstone, T.C., Yoo, H., Lin, W., Brooks, J.G., Lippard, S.J., 2014. Pt(IV) prodrugs designed to bind non-covalently to human serum albumin for drug delivery. J. Am. Chem. Soc. 136, 8790–8798. https://doi.org/10.1021/ja5038269.

Suntharalingam, K., Song, Y., Lippard, S.J., 2014. Conjugation of vitamin E analog α-TOS to Pt(iv) complexes for dual-targeting anticancer therapy. Chem. Commun. 50, 2465–2468. https://doi.org/10.1039/C3CC48740G.

Shen, D.W., Pouliot, L.M., Hall, M.D., Gottesman, M.M., 2012. Cisplatin resistance: a cellular self-defense mechanism resulting from multiple epigenetic and genetic changes. Pharmacol. Rev. 64, 706–721. https://doi.org/10.1124/pr.111.005637.

Parker, R.J., Eastman, A., Bostick-Bruton, F., Reed, E., 1991. Acquired cisplatin resistance in human ovarian cancer cells is associated with enhanced repair of cisplatin-DNA lesions and reduced drug accumulation. J. Clin. Invest. 87, 772–777. https://doi.org/10.1172/JCI115080.

Schluga, P., Hartinger, C.G., Egger, A., Reisner, E., Galanski, M., Jakupec, M., Keppler, B.K., 2006. Redox behavior of tumor-inhibiting ruthenium(III) complexes and effects of physiological reductants on their binding to GMP. Dalton Trans. 14, 1796–1802. https://doi.org/10.1039/B511792E.

Wiśniewska, J., Fandzloch, M., Łakomska, I., 2019. The reduction of ruthenium(III) complexes with triazolopyrimidine ligands by ascorbic acid and mechanistic insight into their action in anticancer therapy. Inorg. Chim. Acta 484, 305–310. https://doi.org/10.1016/j.ica.2018.09.051.

Zhang, P., Sadler, P.J., 2017. Advances in the design of organometallic anticancer complexes. J. Organomet. Chem. 839, 5–14. https://doi.org/10.1016/j.jorganchem.2017.03.038.

Rademaker-Lakhai, J.M., van den Bongard, D., Pluim, D., Beijnen, J.H., Schellens, J.H., 2004. A phase I and pharmacological study with imidazolium-trans-DMSO-imidazole-tetrachlororuthenate, a novel ruthenium anticancer agent. Clin. Cancer Res. 10, 3717–3727. https://doi.org/10.1158/1078-0432.CCR-03-0746.

Rodrigues, F.P., Carneiro, Z.A., Mascharak, P., Curti, C., da Silva, R.S., 2016. Incorporation of a ruthenium nitrosyl complex into liposomes, the nitric oxide released from these liposomes and HepG2 cell death mechanism. Coord. Chem. Rev. 306, 701–707. https://doi.org/10.1016/j.ccr.2015.03.028.

Zeng, L., Gupta, P., Chen, Y., 2017. The development of anticancer ruthenium(ii) complexes: from single molecule compounds to nanomaterials. Chem. Soc. Rev. 46, 5771–5804. https://doi.org/10.1039/C7CS00195A.

Meng, X.-J., Leyva, M.L., Jenny, M., Gross, I., Benosman, S., Fricker, B., Harlepp, S., Hébraud, P., Boos, A., Wlosik, P., Bischoff, P., Sirlin, C., Pfeffer, M., Loeffler, J.-P., Gaiddon, C., 2009. A ruthenium-containing organometallic compound reduces tumor growth through induction of the endoplasmic reticulum stress gene CHOP. Cancer Res. 69, 5458–5466. https://doi.org/10.1158/0008-5472.CAN-08-4408.

Wu, B., Ong, M.S., Groessl, M., Adhireksan, Z., Hartinger, C.G., Dyson, P.J., Davey, C.A., 2011. A ruthenium antimetastasis agent forms specific histone protein adducts in the nucleosome core. Chem. Eur. J. 17, 3562–3566. https://doi.org/10.1002/chem.201100298.

Nowak-Sliwinska, P., van Beijnum, J.R., Casini, A., Nazarov, A., Wagnières, G., van den Bergh, H., Dyson, P.J., Griffioen, A.W., 2011. Organometallic ruthenium(II) arene compounds with anti-angiogenic activity. J. Med. Chem. 54, 3895–3902. https://doi.org/10.1021/jm2002074.

Weiss, A., Ding, X., van Beijnum, J.R., Wong, I., Wong, T.J., Berndsen, R.H., Dormond, O., Dallinga, M., Shen, L., Schlingemann, R.O., Pili, R., Ho, C.-M., Dyson, P.J., van den Bergh, H., Griffioen, A.W., Nowak-Sliwinska, P., 2015. Rapid optimization of drug combinations for the optimal angiostatic treatment of cancer. Angiogenesis 18, 233–244. https://doi.org/10.1007/s10456-015-9462-9.

Ott, I., 2009. On the medicinal chemistry of gold complexes as anticancer drugs. Coord. Chem. Rev. 253, 1670–1681. https://doi.org/10.1016/j.ccr.2009.02.019.

Zou, T., Ching, A., Lum, T., Lok, C.-N., Zhang, J.-J., Che, C.-M., 2015. Chemical biology of anticancer gold(III) and gold(I) complexes. Chem. Soc. Rev. 44, 8786–8801. https://doi.org/10.1039/C5CS00132C.

Shuang, Y., Miao, L., Huiguo, L., Shuang, W., 2020. Recent advances of gold compounds in anticancer. Immunity 8, 543. https://doi.org/10.3389/fchem.2020.00543.

Patel, M.N., Bhatt, B.S., Dosi, P.A., 2013. Synthesis and evaluation of gold(III) complexes as efficient DNA binders and cytotoxic agents. Spectrochim. Acta A Mol. Biomol. Spectrosc. 110, 20–27. https://doi.org/10.1016/j.saa.2013.03.037.

Sutton, B.M., McGusty, E., Walz, D.T., DiMartino, M.J., 1972. Oral gold. Antiarthritic properties of alkylphosphinegold coordination complexes. J. Med. Chem. 15, 1095–1098. https://doi.org/10.1021/jm00281a001.

Sutton, B.M., 1986. Gold compounds for rheumatoid arthritis. Gold Bull. 19, 15–16. https://doi.org/10.1007/BF03214639.

Roder, C., Thomson, M.J., 2015. Auranofin: repurposing an old drug for a golden new age. Drugs R&D 15, 13–20. https://doi.org/10.1007/s40268-015-0083-y.

Simon, T.M., Kunishima, D.H., Vibert, G.J., Lorber, A., 1979. Inhibitory effects of a new oral gold compound on hela cells. Cancer 44, 1965–1975. https://doi.org/10.1002/1097-0142(197912)44:6%3C1965::AID-CNCR2820440602%3E3.0.CO;2-6.

Mirabelli, C.K., Johnson, R.K., Sung, C.M., Faucette, L., Muirhead, K., Crooke, S.T., 1985. Evaluation of the *in vivo* antitumor activity and *in vitro* cytotoxic properties of auranofin, a coordinated gold compound, in murine tumor models. Cancer Res. 45, 32–39.

Raninga, P.V., Lee, A.C., Sinha, D., Shih, Y.Y., Mittal, D., Makhale, A., 2020. Therapeutic cooperation between auranofin, a thioredoxin reductase inhibitor and anti-PD-L1 antibody for treatment of triple-negative breast cancer. Int. J. Cancer 146, 123–136. https://doi.org/10.1002/ijc.32410.

Mirabell, C.K., Johnson, R.K., Hill, D.T., Faucette, L.F., Girard, G.R., Kuo, G.Y., Sung, C.M., Crooke, S.T., 1986. Correlation of the in vitro cytotoxic and in vivo antitumor activities of gold(I) coordination complexes. J. Med. Chem. 29, 218–223. https://doi.org/10.1021/jm00152a009.

Parish, R.V., Howe, B.P., Wright, J.P., Mack, J., Pritchard, R.G., Buckley, R.G., Elsome, A.M., Fricker, S.P., 1996a. Chemical and biological studies of dichloro(2-((dimethylamino)methyl)phenyl)gold(III). Inorg. Chem. 35, 1659–1666. https://doi.org/10.1021/ic950343b.

Parish, R.V., Mack, J., Hargreaves, L., Wright, J.P., Buckley, R.G., Elsome, A.M., Fricker, S.P., Theobald, B.R.C., 1996b. Chemical and biological reactions of diacetato[2-(dimethylaminomethyl)-phenyl]gold(III), [Au(O$_2$CMe)$_2$(dmamp)]. Dalton Trans., 69–74. https://doi.org/10.1039/DT9960000069.

Martín-Santos, C., Michelucci, E., Marzo, T., Messori, L., Szumlas, P., Bednarski, P.J., Mas-Balleste, R., Navarro-Ranninger, C., Cabrera, S., Aleman, J., 2015. Gold(III) complexes with hydroxyquinoline, aminoquinoline, quinolone ligands: synthesis, cytotoxicity, DNA and protein binding studies. J. Inorg. Biochem. 153, 339–345. https://doi.org/10.1016/j.jinorgbio.2015.09.012.

Lima, J.C., Rodriguez, L., 2011. Applications of gold(I) alkynyl systems: a growing field to explore. Chem. Soc. Rev. 40, 5442–5456. https://doi.org/10.1039/C1CS15123A.

Yang, Z., Jiang, G., Xu, Z., Zhao, S., Liu, W., 2020. Advances in alkynyl gold complexes for use as potential anticancer agents. Coord. Chem. Rev. 423, 213492. https://doi.org/10.1016/j.ccr.2020.213492.

Ma, D.L., Wu, C., Li, G., Yung, T.L., Leung, C.H., 2020. Transition metal complexes as imaging or therapeutic agents for neurodegenerative diseases. J. Mater. Chem. B 8, 4715–4725. https://doi.org/10.1039/C9TB02669J.

Lim, C.S., Cho, B.R., 2013. Two-photon probes for biomedical applications. BMB Rep. 46, 188–194. https://doi.org/10.5483/bmbrep.2013.46.4.045.

Mari, C., Pierroz, V., Rubbiani, R., 2014. DNA intercalating RuII polypyridyl complexes as effective photosensitizers in photodynamic therapy. Chem. Eur. J. 20, 14421–14436. https://doi.org/10.1002/chem.201402796.

Tsui, W.-K., Chung, L.-H., Wong, M.M.-K., 2015. Luminescent ruthenium(II) complex bearing bipyridine and N-heterocyclic carbene-based C∩N∩C pincer ligand for live-cell imaging of endocytosis. Sci. Rep. 5, 9070. https://doi.org/10.1038/srep09070.

Qiu, K., Wen, Y., Ouyang, C., 2019. The stepwise photodamage of organelles by two photon luminescent ruthenium(II) photosensitizers. Chem. Commun. 55, 11235–11238. https://doi.org/10.1039/C9CC05962H.

Qiu, K., Wang, J., Song, C., 2017. Crossfire for two-photon photodynamic therapy with fluorinated ruthenium (II) photosensitizers. ACS Appl. Mater. Interfaces 9, 18482–18492. https://doi.org/10.1021/acsami.7b02977.

Millán, G., Giménez, N., Lara, R., 2019. Luminescent cycloplatinated complexes with biologically relevant phosphine ligands: optical and cytotoxic properties. Inorg. Chem. 58, 1657–1673. https://doi.org/10.1021/acs.inorgchem.8b03211.

Zhang, W., Du, F., He, M., Bai, L., Gu, Y., Yang, L., 2019. Studies of anticancer activity in vitro and in vivo of iridium(III) polypyridyl complexes-loaded liposomes as drug delivery system. Eur. J. Med. Chem. 178, 390–400. https://doi.org/10.1016/j.ejmech.2019.06.009.

Lo, K., Zhang, K., 2012. Iridium(III) complexes as therapeutic and bioimaging reagents for cellular applications. RSC Adv. 2, 12069. https://doi.org/10.1039/C2RA20967E.

Meksawangwong, S., Gohil, B., Punyain, W., Pal, R., Kielar, F., 2019. Synthesis and investigation of a tris-cyclometalated iridium complex bearing a single quarternary ammonium group. Inorg. Chim. Acta 497, 119066. https://doi.org/10.1016/j.ica.2019.119066.

Palao, E., Sola-Llano, R., Tabero, A., Manzano, H., Agarrabeitia, A., Villanueva, A., 2017. Acetylacetonate BODIPY-biscyclometalated iridium(III) complexes: effective strategy towards smarter fluorescent photosensitizer agents. Chem. Eur. J. 23, 10139–10147. https://doi.org/10.1002/chem.201701347.

Wang, X., Zhang, J., Zhao, X., Wei, W., Zhao, J., 2019. Imaging and proteomic study of a clickable iridium complex. Metallomics 11, 1344–1352. https://doi.org/10.1039/c9mt00134d.

McNamara, K., Tofail, A.M., 2007. Nanoparticles in biomedical application. Adv. Phys. X 2, 54–88. https://doi.org/10.1080/23746149.2016.1254570.

Moreno-Vega, A.I., Gomez-Quintero, T., Nunez-Anita, R.E., Acosta-Torres, L.S., Castano, V., 2012. Polymeric and ceramic nanoparticles in biomedical applications. J. Nanotechnol. 2012, 936041–936052. https://doi.org/10.1155/2012/936041.

Park, W., Heo, Y.J., Han, D.K., 2018. New opportunities for nanoparticles in cancer immunotherapy. Biomater. Res. 24, 22–24. https://doi.org/10.1186/s40824-018-0133-y.

Powell, A.C., Paciotti, G.F., Libutti, S.K., 2010. Colloidal gold: a novel nanoparticle for targeted cancer therapeutics. Cancer Nanotechnol., 375–384. https://doi.org/10.1007/978-1-60761-609-2_25.

Porcel, E., Liehn, S., Remita, H., Usami, N., Kobayashi, K., Furusawa, Y., Sech, C.L., Lacombe, C.S., 2010. Platinum nanoparticles: a promising material for future cancer therapy? Nanotechnology 21, 085103.

Sperling, R.A., Parak, W., 2010. Surface modification, functionalization and bioconjugation of colloidal inorganic nanoparticles. Philos. Trans. R. Soc. Lond. A 368, 1333–1383. https://doi.org/10.1098/rsta.2009.0273.

Minelli, C., Lowe, S.B., Stevens, M.M., 2010. Engineering nanocomposite materials for cancer therapy. Small 6, 2336–2357. https://doi.org/10.1002/smll.201000523.

Ndagi, U., Mhlongo, N., Soliman, M.E., 2017. Metal complexes in cancer therapy—an update from drug design perspective. Drug Des. Devel. Ther. 11, 599–616. https://doi.org/10.2147/DDDT.S119488.

Zhang, X.-D., 2012. Size-dependent radiosensitization of PEG-coated gold nanoparticles for cancer radiation therapy. Biomaterials 33, 6408–6419. https://doi.org/10.1016/j.biomaterials.2012.05.047.

Moon, H.K., Lee, S.H., Choi, H.C., 2009. In vivo near-infrared mediated tumor destruction by photothermal effect of carbon nanotubes. ACS Nano 3, 3707–3713. https://doi.org/10.1021/nn900904h.

Ventola, C.L., 2012. The nanomedicine revolution: part 2: current and future clinical applications. Pharm. Ther. 37, 582–591.

van Landeghem, F.K., 2009. Post-mortem studies in glioblastoma patients treated with thermotherapy using magnetic nanoparticles. Biomaterials 30, 52–57. https://doi.org/10.1016/j.biomaterials.2008.09.044.

Silva, A.C., 2011. Application of hyperthermia induced by superparamagnetic iron oxide nanoparticles in glioma treatment. Int. J. Nanomedicine 6, 591–603. https://doi.org/10.2147/IJN.S14737.

Maier-Hauff, K., 2011. Efficacy and safety of intratumoral thermotherapy using magnetic iron-oxide nanoparticles combined with external beam radiotherapy on patients with recurrent glioblastoma multiforme. J. Neuro-Oncol. 103, 317–324. https://doi.org/10.1007/s11060-010-0389-0.

Zhang, A.-P., Sun, Y.-P., 2004. Photocatalytic killing effect of TiO_2 nanoparticles on Ls174-t human colon carcinoma cells. World J. Gastroenterol. 10, 3191–3193. https://doi.org/10.3748/WJG.V10.I21.3191.

Thevenot, P., Cho, J., Wavhal, D., Timmons, R.B., Tang, L., 2008. Surface chemistry influences cancer killing effect of TiO2 nanoparticles. Nanomedicine 4, 226–236. https://doi.org/10.1016/j.nano.2008.04.001.

Seo, J.W., Chung, H., Kim, M.Y., Lee, J., Choi, I.H., Cheon, J., 2007. Development of water-soluble single-crystalline TiO2 nanoparticles for photocatalytic cancer-cell treatment. Small 3, 850–853. https://doi.org/10.1002/smll.200600488.

Tarnuzzer, R.W., 2005. Vacancy engineered ceria nanostructures for protection from radiation-induced cellular damage. Nano Lett. 5, 2573–2577. https://doi.org/10.1021/NL052024F.

Neri, D., Supuran, C.T., 2011. Interfering with pH regulation in tumours as a therapeutic strategy. Nat. Rev. Drug Discov. 10, 767–777. https://doi.org/10.1038/nrd3554.

Wang, Y., 2013. Cuprous oxide nanoparticles inhibit the growth and metastasis of melanoma by targeting mitochondria. Cell Death Dis. 4, 783–792. https://doi.org/10.1038/cddis.2013.314.

Sharma, A., Goyal, A.K., Rath, G., 2017. Recent advances in metal nanoparticles in cancer therapy. J. Drug Target. 26, 617–632. https://doi.org/10.1080/1061186X.2017.1400553.

CHAPTER TWENTY

Nanoparticles for drug delivery in cancer therapy

Adeniyi S. Ohunayo[a], Olusola O. Elekofehinti[b], Olorunfemi R. Molehin[c],
Ajibade O. Oyeyemi[c], and Tiwa M. Ogunleye[d]
[a]Department of Science Laboratory Technology, Faculty of science, Ekiti State University, Ado-Ekiti, Nigeria
[b]Bioinformatics and Molecular Biology Unit, Department of Biochemistry, Federal University of Technology Akure, Akure, Nigeria
[c]Department of Biochemistry, Faculty of Science, Ekiti State University, Ado-Ekiti, Nigeria
[d]Oklahoma State University, Stillwater, OK, United States

Abbreviations

5-Fu	5-fluorouracil
AT	active targeting
AuNPs	gold nanoparticles
CC	cancer cells
CMC	carboxymethylcellulose
DDS	drug delivery system
IoNP	inorganic nanoparticle
LSH	liposome-silica hybrid
NPs	nanoparticles
PT	passive targeting
QSE	quantum size effect
RSA	relative surface area

1. Introduction

Cancers are regarded as the uncontrolled or aberrant cells which can be found in any part of the body. Cancer cells undergo uncontrollable divisions, which in turn result in tumors. Each body cell has specified functions and a well-defined life span, from cell division down to cell death, based on biochemical instructions. Cells receive biochemical instructions to grow, divide and die at a well-specified lifespan. Cancer cells lack what it takes to undergo programmed cell death called apoptosis. However, this failed instruction makes the cell immortal while growth is uncontrolled. A tumor is regarded as an abnormal cell proliferation; from a cancer pathological perspective, they could be classified as benign or malignant. A tumor is benign when it lacks the ability to invade adjacent tissues, remaining localized without any spreading capabilities. Malignant, on the other hand, is capable of

Biomarkers in Cancer Detection and Monitoring of Therapeutics
https://doi.org/10.1016/B978-0-323-95114-2.00017-0
451

invading relatively close tissues, spreading to other regions of the body through metastasis. Malignant tumors are dangerous, costly, and life-threatening which is why it is properly referred to as cancer. Benign cancers can be surgically removed from their localized position in the body, while chemotherapy and radiotherapy are the most widely used treatment for malignant tumors (Cooper, 2000). Biochemically, cancer development has been implicated with mutation—a sudden heritable change in the genetic makeup of an organism, which could affect many body tissues or organs (Fig. 1).

The genetic alteration which happens over time continually results in an inappropriate proteins synthesis and abnormal cell proliferation. Many substances have been identified to cause cancer through DNA damage. Since cancer development is a complex multistep process, substances that trigger tumors' unset have not all been well defined. However, many agents, including chemicals, radiations, lifestyle, and viruses, have been clearly found to cause cancer in experimental models (Cooper, 2000). Cancer is commonly treated by radiation through a process called radiotherapy, by drugs through chemotherapy, and tumor removal through surgery. Cancer chemotherapies are chemical substances or chemical derivatives used to manage, treat and cure cancer. Basically, these chemical agents are targeted against specific processes of cell division in rapidly

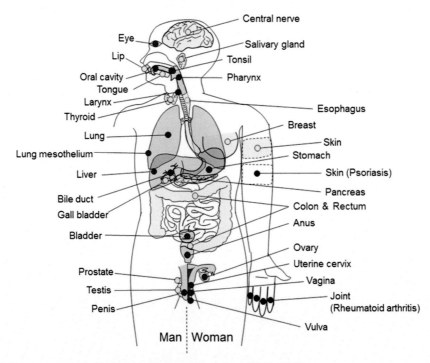

Fig. 1 Most common body part implicated with cancer (CDC, 2016).

multiplying cancer cells. Many of these chemotherapies are sourced from natural products such as plants, while some are synthesized through chemical conversions (Shield, 2017).

Nanoparticles (NPs) are a very wide class of small particulate materials made through the process of nanotechnology. In clear terms, nanoparticles are described as substances sized less than 100 nm. Nanoparticles are structurally different from similar structures, most notably in terms of size and microscopic appearance. Some of these parallel structures include; microparticles, fine particles, and coarse particles, all ranges above 100 nm (Laurent et al., 2008). The appearance of nanoparticles can be seen with different pigments ranging from red, yellow, black, wine, and so on, depending on the physiochemical properties of the substance. Nanoparticles (NPs) have been an integral aspect of medicine since they significantly differ from bulk materials having a great advantage with their increased relative surface area (RSA) and quantum size effect (QSE). These properties have enhanced the medicinal use of these particulates. For example, NPs have a greater relative surface area (RSA) per unit mass compared to bulk or larger molecules, enabling an easy catalytic reaction to occur at their surface, which means that a particular number of NPs will be much more reactive than the same number of materials made up of larger or bulky particles.

2. Limitation of chemotherapy

Anticancer drugs are the most explored means for cancer treatment; this treatment involves the use of chemical compounds or drugs to destroy tumor cells. Medical application of such treatment involving drugs in the treatment of cancer is called chemotherapy. Anticancer drugs or chemotherapy can be broadly classified into; hormones, antimetabolites, natural products, and alkylating agents. However, there exist several chemotherapies used in contemporary medicine which does not belong to the group listed (Rang et al., 2016). Alkylating drugs interrupt replication and transcription processes by binding to DNA. This group of drugs replaces a hydrogen atom with an alkyl radical through an electrolytic process. Antimetabolite's mechanism of action is by inhibiting DNA replication and RNA transcription, which incorporates or induces apoptosis in order to damage the DNA (Abraham et al., 2007). Anticancer drugs present some side effects, ranging from lack of tumor specificity, precise targeting, unknown effective dose and concentration once the molecule gets inside the body, fair of overexpression of functions are common side effects (Song et al., 2014). Patients under chemotherapies may be immunocompromised, they have also been known to experience reduced blood counts, hair loss, heart problems, irritation, diabetes, and diarrhea, among others. 5-Fluorouracil (5-Fu) is one of the most commonly used chemotherapy to treat cancer.

The drug is used in treating breast cancer, head cancer, neck cancer, bladder cancer, and neuroendocrine tumors. This drug uses the facilitated transport system, where its metabolites obstruct RNA synthesis and other key enzymes in transcription processes. As efficient as 5-Fu is, some notable side effect has been associated with it, such as nausea, vomiting, photophobia, and taste change. The effectiveness of chemotherapy has been limited because of some limitations encountered during treatments. One of the significant challenges are targeting delivery and low precision. Also, organ-specified strategy in many chemotherapies has made drug ineffective in providing long-lasting solution against cancer. Many compounds that are more precise with high target system may elicit regression in most tumor cells, however, some cases have been observed where they fail to inhibit cancer growth resulting in tumor redundancy and reoccurrence after chemotherapy has been discontinued (Cardonick and Iacobucci, 2004).

3. Nanoparticle in cancer research

Nanoparticle presents a new aspect of science furnished with more efficient and precise ways of drug delivery system (DDS). Nanoparticles are identified with a large surface area to mass ratio, efficiency, ultra-small size, and high reactivity. These attributes have made nanoparticles more efficient in medicine. The scientific application of nanoparticle in medicine is termed nanomedicine. This field of science has been explored owing to the fact that they possess advantages not found in many existing chemotherapies. Selective toxicity, cost-efficacy, improved half-life, and noninvasiveness are some of the attributes of nanoparticles (Zhang et al., 2008). Conventional chemotherapy without nanostructures, especially those with lower solubilization, have delivery challenges as their bioavailability is significantly reduced during oral or intravenous administration. However, all these restrictions may perhaps be overawed by the application of nanoparticles in the drug delivery system (Golovin et al., 2015) (Fig. 2).

3.1 Organic nanoparticle

Liposomes are one of the widely used organic nanoparticles, the nanostructure consists of lipid layers having bi-layers that are hydrophilic and another hydrophobic in nature. They carry out several functions by imitating biophysical features of lipid of cells, and this improves its drug delivery mechanisms. Organic NPs such as liposomes present good machinery for effective in vivo delivery for anticancer drugs (Cheng et al., 2013). Nanostructure from chitosan has been studied to exhibit high adhesive properties, chitosan-based nanoparticles have gained recent attention due to their compatibility with epithelial cells, enabling an efficient release of drug to the surface membranes. Like liposomes, nanochitosan or nanoparticle-based chitosan enhanced drug life span, nontoxic, and efficient in drug delivery (Artursson et al., 2014). *Alginate is* another organic nanoparticle used as a drug delivery system; they are composed of carboxyl group presenting a greater adhesive strength (Sosnik, 2014).

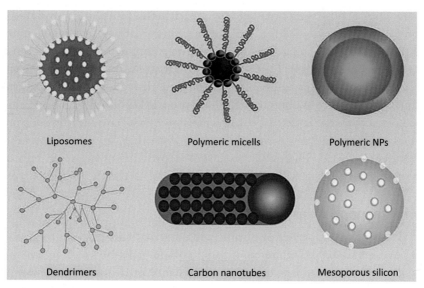

Fig. 2 Structural representation of some types of nanoparticles used as drug delivery system (Cho et al., 2008).

Cellulose and related structures have been extensively used as DDS, especially in the area of drug solubilization. It has been used as a delivery system in many oral chemotherapies. From a chemical point of view, the nanostructure of cellulose origin contains hydrogen bonds enabling the sustained release of the cytopathic effect. Cellulose derivatives such as carboxymethylcellulose (CMC) has been used to deliver 5-fluoroacyl (5-FU) into the colon. CMC enables glueyness in the simulated colonic environment (Sun et al., 2017). Nanostructures of polymeric origin has also been found as drug delivery system, and they are made up of shells that are self-assembling and hydrophobic in nature. The hydrophobicity of the shell has contributed to its solubility and stability in polar solvents (Devarajan and Jain, 2016).

3.2 Inorganic nanoparticle (IoNP)

Element-based nanoparticles such as gold, silicon, silver, and many others have all been explored and currently considered but still in the clinical trial stage. Metal-based (MB) nanoparticles have greater surface plasmon resonance (SPR) than many organic nanoparticles such as liposomes. Inorganic nanoparticles have excellent compatibility and functionality. There is limited information regarding the cytotoxicity of many metal-based nanoparticles and mechanisms of utilization regarding their uptake (Choi et al., 2013). Medications used in cancer treatments can be coupled and fussed into gold nanoparticles (AuNPs) surfaces through chemical bonding and surface absorption and whose release can be controlled biologically. Other advantages of IoNP include its antimicrobial activities. The most widely studied inorganic nanoparticles are gold, carbon, magnesium, with all possessing drug delivery capacity. Gold is the most explored due to its inertness, selective cytotoxicity, and surface functionality. AuNPs are known to enhance drug stimulation and accumulation within tumor cells and help combat drug resistance (Cheng et al., 2013). Carbon-based NPs, because of their inmate properties, have been found to have broad potential in the drug delivery system. Physiochemical and biological properties of carbon have aided their use as DDS in anticancer chemotherapy. Silicon nanoparticles (SNPs) are better understood; they have more proven pharmacodynamics, stability, and treatment efficiency. Hence they are part of the best DDS known (Xu et al., 2019). The stability and biocompatibility of magnetic NPs depend on their subsequent coating with organic materials such as fatty acids and polymers.

3.3 Hybrid nanoparticles

Hybrid NPs combine properties of organic and inorganic nanoparticles to give a more stable and consistent DDS. Combining organic and inorganic NPs to give rise to hybrid NPs systems are commonly explored methods of nanoparticle strategy. Liposome-silica hybrid (LSH) NPs involve silicon core surrounded by lipid bilayer, which has been found to be effective DDS against breast and prostate cancers. The interbreeding of natural biopolymers fused from organic or inorganic NPs is an alternative method for NP fabrication. It has been exemplified in cell membrane covering nanostructures and has currently gained more attention for explorations. This nanotechnology helps to blend the NPs with biological features by directly coating them with NPs, which improves the effectiveness and safety of conventional NPs (Fang et al., 2018).

4. Mechanism of activities of nanoparticle

4.1 Active targeting (AT)

This mechanism involves explicitly direct interaction with the defected cells, they target cancer cells through direct interaction between ligands and receptors, allowing NPs to release therapeutic drugs successfully. AT precisely mark cancer cells via the interactions between ligands and receptors. The ligands on the surface of NPs are designated to mark the particles that are overexpressed on the surface of cancer cells, which permits them to differentiate targeted cells from healthy cells. The interaction between surface and ligands induces endocytosis which allows successful releases of the drug. Moieties of AT include vitamins, carbohydrates, amino acids, peptides, and monoclonal antibiotics, all of which have been suitable for the Nanoparticle drug delivery system (Farokhzad and Langer, 2009).

4.2 Passive targeting (PT)

In passive targeting, the drugs are delivered successfully to the target areas based on the size of the NPs. Passive targeting efficiency deals explicitly with the size of nanoparticles and the behavior of tumor tissue vasculature. The circulation half-life of nanoparticles and the degree of angiogenesis of tumor and normal tissue are required in order to deliver the drug successfully to the targeted area. However, limitations like nonspecific drug distribution and different permeability of blood vessels across various tumors are the major targets of passive targeting. PT is considered to utilize the characteristics of the tumor and normal tissue where the drugs are successfully distributed to the targeted sites in order to play a therapeutic role (Carmeliet and Jain, 2000).

5. Advantages of nanoparticles in cancer therapy

1. It reduces the side effects caused by conventional chemotherapy as it targets the cancer cell leaving the healthy cells around the tumor.
2. It provides a longer shelf life.
3. They are both hydrophilic and hydrophobic in nature.
4. It can be administered through several means.
5. It increases the intercellular concentration of drug either by enhanced permeability or retention effect.

References

Abraham, L.M., Selva, D., Casson, R., Leibovitch, I., 2007. The clinical applications of fluorouracil in ophthalmic practice. Drugs 67, 237–255.

Artursson, P., Lindmark, T., Davis, S.S., Illum, L., 2014. Effect of chitosan on the permeability of monolayers of intestinal epithelial cells (Caco-2). Pharm. Res. 11, 1358–1361.

Cardonick, E., Iacobucci, A., 2004. Use of chemotherapy during human pregnancy. Lancet Oncol. 5, 283–291.

Carmeliet, P., Jain, R.K., 2000. Angiogenesis in cancer and other diseases. Nature 407, 249–257.

Centers for Diseases Control and Prevention, 2016. Casey Research. CDC, DC. Available from: http://www.cdc.gov/cancer/international/statistics.htm.

Cheng, J., Gu, Y.J., Cheng, S.H., Wong, W.T., 2013. Surface functionalized gold nanoparticles for drug delivery. J. Biomed. Nanotechnol. 9, 1362–1369.

Cho, K., Wang, X.U., Nie, S., Shin, D.M., 2008. Therapeutic nanoparticles for drug delivery in cancer. Clin. Cancer Res. 14 (5), 1310–1316.

Choi, S.-J., Lee, J.K., Jeong, J., Choy, J.-H., 2013. Toxicity evaluation of inorganic nanoparticles: considerations and challenges. Mol. Cell. Toxicol. 9, 205–210.

Cooper, G.M., 2000. The Cell: A Molecular Approach, second ed. Sinauer Associates, Sunderland, MA. The Development and Causes of Cancer. Available from: https.

Devarajan, P.V., Jain, S., 2016. Targeted Drug Delivery: Concepts and Design. Springer, Berlin.

Fang, R.H., Kroll, A.V., Gao, W., Zhang, L., 2018. Cell membrane coating nanotechnology. Adv. Mater. 30, e1706759.

Farokhzad, O.C., Langer, R., 2009. Impact of nanotechnology on drug delivery. ACS Nano 3, 16–20.

Golovin, Y.I., Gribanovsky, S.L., Golovin, D.Y., Klyachko, N.L., Majouga, A.G., Master, A.M., Sokolsky, M., Kabanov, A., 2015. Towards nanomedicines of the future: remote magneto-mechanical actuation of nanomedicines by alternating magnetic fields. J. Control. Release 219, 43–60.

Laurent, S., Forge, D., Port, M., Roch, A., Robic, C., Vander Elst, L., Muller, R.N., 2008. Magnetic iron oxide nanoparticles: synthesis, stabilization, vectorization, physicochemical characterizations, and biological applications. Chem. Rev. 108 (6), 2064–2110.

Rang, H.P., Bloom, F.E., Stringer, J.L., Cuthbert, A.W., Thomas, J.A., Scarne, J., 2016. Types of Drugs. Available from: https://global.britannica.com/science/drug-chemicalagent/Types-of-drugs.

Shields, M., 2017. Chemotherapeutics. In: Badal, S., Delgoda, R. (Eds.), Pharmacognosy. Academic Press, pp. 295–313 (Chapter 14).

Song, W., Tang, Z., Li, M., Lv, S., Sun, H., Deng, M., Liu, H., Chen, X., 2014. Polypeptidebased combination of paclitaxel and cisplatin for enhanced chemotherapy efficacy and reduced side-effects. Acta Biomater. 10, 1392–1402.

Sosnik, A., 2014. Alginate particles as platform for drug delivery by the oral route: state-of-the-art. ISRN Pharm. 2014, 926157.

Sun, B., Zhang, M., Shen, J., He, Z., Fatehi, P., Ni, Y., 2017. Applications of cellulose-based materials in sustained drug delivery systems. Curr. Med. Chem. 26 (14), 2485–2501.

Xu, C., Lei, C., Yu, C., 2019. Mesoporous silica nanoparticles for protein protection and delivery. Front. Chem. 7, 290.

Zhang, L., Gu, F., Chan, J., Wang, A., Langer, R., Farokhzad, O., 2008. Nanoparticles in medicine: therapeutic applications and developments. Clin. Pharmacol. Ther. 83, 761–769.

CHAPTER TWENTY-ONE

Near-infrared (NIR) responsive nanomaterial–liposome nanohybrids for cancer photothermal therapy

Animesh Pan[a], Chiranjib Banerjee[b], and Md Golam Jakaria[a]
[a]Department of Chemical Engineering, University of Rhode Island, Kingston, RI, United States
[b]Department of Biological Science, University of Northwestern, Evanston, IL, United States

1. Introduction

Chemotherapeutic medicines are the mainstay of cancer treatment in recent years (Akamatsu et al., 2019). However, because of the low selectivity for tumor tissue, free medicines are retained in normal tissue after injection. Nanomedicine is a rapidly growing discipline with the primary benefit of effectively targeting drug delivery to tumor cells using nanocarriers' increased penetration and retention (EPR) properties (Thakur and Kutty, 2019). Most notably, conventional nanomedicine requires numerous processes to transfer medications to tumor tissue, including circulation, accumulation, penetration, internalization, and release (Dong et al., 2019). Liposomes are a type of nanocarrier that has been used as a possible carrier since the early 1970s (Torchilin, 2005). Liposomes have unique structural features similar to biological membranes. Drug compounds can be put into liposomes depending on their hydrophilic and hydrophobic properties. Liposomes were the first drug delivery method, developed to increase the therapeutic benefits of diverse water soluble and insoluble medications by increasing biocompatibility, solubility, retention time, and lowering system toxicity from theoretical concepts to clinical practice (Luo et al., 2016). However, due of the unpredictable drug release and short in vivo circulation period, typical liposomes have limited therapeutic applicability. As a result, developing smart liposome-based technologies has become a pressing need.

Different external stimuli are employed in the liposomes, such as light, temperature, radiofrequency, and ultrasound, to destabilize the liposomes and allow for the controlled release of liposomal encapsulated pharmaceuticals (Mathiyazhakan et al., 2017). In compared to other stimuli, light offers the advantages for biomedical applications because of its noninvasiveness and its spatiotemporal behaviors. Lights ranging from various wave lengths UV–Visible (200–650 nm) and NIR (650–2000 nm) can be utilized to activate the light response. NIR light has been suited for biological applications due to weakened background signals, and higher penetration depth of biological tissues (Karimi et al.,

2017). In the last decade, the discovery of photothermal treatment (PTT) has piqued the interest of researchers in the fight against many types of cancers and malignant tumors (Liu et al., 2019). Many advantages can be attributed to the use of PTT in tumor ablation: reduced invasiveness, deeper tissue penetration by NIR light, greater tumor selectivity and lower systemic toxicity. Photothermal therapy (PTT) is predominantly relies on the photothermal agents which absorbing light and converts light into heat, resulting rapid increase of local temperature to ablate cancer cells (Jaque et al., 2014). So, the photothermal agents having low toxicity, and high photothermal conversion efficiency could be better candidate for therapeutic study (Zhang et al., 2016).

Photothermal agents based on organic compounds (indocyanine green, IR780, and IR825, among others) and inorganic nanomaterials have been extensively developed, as seen by multiple outstanding reviews (Wang et al., 2021; Zhao et al., 2021a). Inorganic PTAs are now being emphasized by researchers for use in cancer detection and treatment due to their outstanding imaging capacity and photothermal conversion efficiency (He et al., 2016). In this direction, NIR-responsive nanomaterials (NIRNs) have been used in cancer PTT study due to their distinctive size and shape dependent optical and electrical properties (Tao et al., 2020). On the other hand, liposomes offer good biocompatibility and biodegradability. As a result, several studies have concentrated on the usage of NIRN-liposome hybrid nanocarriers (NLHs), which have been shown to overcome NIRN disadvantages (Jia et al., 2020; Wang and Chao, 2018).

2. Strategically design and surface modification of hybrid nanostructures using liposomes

With a better understanding of the interactions between nanoparticles and liposomes, NLHs can be designed with the desired physicochemical qualities. In general, three ways for NIRNs attachment have been established, each of which is based on the feature of NIRNs (Fig. 1). Due to the unique structural properties, hydrophobic

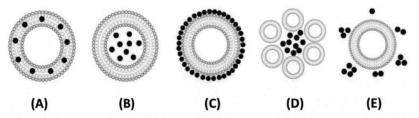

(A)   (B)   (C)   (D)   (E)

Fig. 1 Schematic representation of several types of NLHs: (A) NPs are within the bilayer; (B) NPs are in the liposomes' aqueous core; (C) NPs are on the liposomes' surface; (D) NPs assemble as aggregates with liposomes; and (E) NPs are free in the liposomes' solution. *(Adopted with permission from Mathiyazhakan, M., Wiraja, C., Xu, C., 2017. A concise review of gold nanoparticles-based photo-responsive liposomes for controlled drug delivery. Nano-Micro Lett. 10(1), 10. copyright © Springer Link 2018.)*

NIRNs are enclosed in the aqueous core or conjugated on the outer surface, while hydrophilic NIRNs are placed within the lipid bilayer (Mathiyazhakan et al., 2017). There are several techniques have been employed to design the NLHs. The thin film dispersion approach, however, has irreplaceable benefits in terms of particle size and structural stability (Mathiyazhakan et al., 2017).

However, different factors of nanomaterials (like, size, shape, surface chemistry) also influence the manufacture and application of NIRN-LHs. During the liposome encapsulation procedure, the size of NIRNs should be the initial design consideration. Literature report shows that AuNPs (less than 20 nm in diameter), have high affinity in vitro and in vivo, either in free and targeted form (Hamzawy et al., 2017). Furthermore, other gold nanostructures (gold nanorods with different sizes) can absorb light in the NIR range (650–1000 nm) are good choice for PTT (Mauro et al., 2021). Despite the plasmonic nanomaterials, classical QDs with liposomes nanohybrids and carbon-based nanomaterials (CNT, CDs, GQDs, GO, etc.) have demonstrated great utility in therapeutic studies due to their small sizes and perhaps integrated into the bilayer and encapsulation as well.

The shape of NIRNs has a significant impact as well. In contrast to QDs, gold-based nanomaterials come in a variety of forms, including rod-like, sphere-like, and star-like, each of which has a substantial impact on in vitro and in vivo behavior. Despite the fact that spherical gold nanoparticles are easier to collect in tumor tissue, rod-like nanoparticles have been shown to have a longer life in the blood stream and penetrate tumors more efficiently than spherical AuNPs of similar size due to fewer vascular collisions and a smaller size (Chauhan and Jain, 2013). Spherical AuNPs have a lower thermal capacity than gold-based nanoparticles with pointy or spiky edges (Chatterjee et al., 2018). This is owing to the elongated or branched structures' amplification of laser light, resulting in higher light absorption and heat creation. The polarizability of gold-based nanomaterials is enhanced by their conspicuous shape. But it has been reported that the photothermal conversion efficiency of AuNPs and hollow AuNPs are different. Hollow AuNPs have tunable surface plasmon properties which allow them for tumor photothermal ablation (Li et al., 2018). Similarly, carbon-based materials have tunable properties depending on their size and shapes which influenced the designing the hybrids nanostructures for therapeutic efficacy (Patel et al., 2019).

Surface functionalization or conjugation with targeting ligands has huge impact for nanohybrids in cancer treatment. It has been established that PEGylated modified liposomes have been created to improve circulation time. Folic acid (FA) functionalized RES-loaded PEG-phospholipid coated with reduced GO (rGO) nanomaterials have longer circulation time than free RES (Hai et al., 2017). Several NLHs have been engineered with FA to target a range of cancer cells. DOX is delivered using AuNPs and GQDs encapsulated liposomal nanotheranostics functionalized with FA targeting ligands. Hybrid liposomes given subcutaneously and intravenously demonstrated high

4T1 breast tumor binding ability for at least 48 h, owing to the targeting impact of FA (Prasad et al., 2020). Other than the folic acid, cell penetrating peptides (CPPs) modified liposomes have been widely used to improve cell permeability in recent years. Also, Tf-modified liposomes can greatly improve transport across the blood–brain barrier (BBB) and contribute to imaging and diagnosis, owing to greater Tf-receptor expression on the BBB, which increases receptor-mediated endocytosis (Sonkar et al., 2021). However, particular targeted NLHs for PTT are currently being researched and brought to the clinic. As a result, the in vivo application of NLHs has received little attention thus far.

3. Different kind of nanomaterial–liposome nanohybrids (NLHs)

3.1 Liposomes-gold nanoparticles hybrid (L-AuNPs)

Gold, as one of the unique metals, has a lot of variation in shape, size, and surface chemistry, as well as a lot of resistance to oxidation and degradation (Yang et al., 2015). Different kind of gold nanomaterials (depending on their sizes and shapes) have been created for cancer treatments. In the hybrid nanomedicine delivery system, gold-based nanomaterials have been widely used due their tunable properties. Gold nanoparticles (AuNPs) have a controllable linear NIR absorption that allows them to penetrate deep into tissue (Sailor and Park, 2012). Pure AuNPs are quite stable, but their LSPR extinction coefficient is lower (Zhao et al., 2017). The hybrid liposome system showed a controlled LSPR absorption peak after being coated with gold shells. As a result, integrating gold-based nanoparticles with liposomes to create light-addressable carriers as a generic platform for chemophotothermal therapy has become a hotspot for research. There are several studies based on liposomes-gold nanomaterials hybrid systems for therapeutic application especially for cancer treatment. For example, Jia et al. developed a hybrid system for dual-modal imaging-guided gene and photothermal synergistic therapy for pancreatic cancer. In their system, they used gold nanostar and graphene coated with liposomes (Jia et al., 2020). They demonstrated that the effect of laser power and nanohybrid concentration on temperature increase during irradiation, demonstrating a high photothermal efficiency. Kwon et al. also created GNC-labeled thermosensitive liposomes that induce medication release in the tumor microenvironment when exposed to NIR irradiation from the outside (Kwon et al., 2015). Pradhan et al. (2019) also developed quercetin-encapsulated plasmonic nanoparticles for hepatocellular cancer cell photothermal treatment. Chauhan et al. showed AuNRs supported liposomes nanohybrids for cancer theragnostic (Chauhan et al., 2018). On the other hand, strategically designed plasmon resonance structures with liposomes core and gold shell also show the photothermal efficiency and therapeutic application for cancer therapy (Leung and Romanowski, 2012; Abbasi et al., 2017; Pan et al., 2020).

In vivo studies of liposome-mediated gold nanoshells revealed that they are an effective candidate for in vivo photothermal-mediated cancer ablation (Rengan et al., 2015). However, using the NLHs in clinical trials is difficult.

3.2 Hybrids of liposomes-quantum dots (L-QDs)

Quantum dots are NPs with electrons and holes that are three-dimensionally contained inside the materials' exciton Bohr radius. Unique optical features result from quantum confinement, such as a narrow emission band and size-dependent adjustable photoluminescence. QDs are potential prospects for bioimaging and photodynamic treatment due to their exceptional photostability, huge surface to volume ratio, and large two-photon absorption cross-section (PDT) (Yaghini et al., 2009). In general, classic QDs have been employed in PDT of cancer models, primarily inorganic QDs (e.g., CdSe, CdTe, CdSe/ZnS, and so on). Several studies based on various QDs with liposomes hybrid for cancer therapies have been examined, but there are very few examples of lipid mediated quantum dots for PTT. Other QDs, such as black phosphorus QDs-lipid nanohybrids, exhibit photothermal ablation of tumor cells. The neoantigen peptide Adpgk was developed by Zhang et al. (2020) and coencapsulated with black phosphorus quantum dots into a liposome (Adpgk-BPQDs-liposome) as a therapeutic vaccination. Under 808 nm near-infrared laser irradiation, the heat created by black phosphorus (BP) increases pluronic F127 gel ablation and the release of GM-CSF, which recruits APC cells and primes native T cells. Xu et al. (2020) designed tungsten sulfide (WS_2) and antibiotic vancomycin-loaded liposomes for PTT study.

3.3 Hybrids of liposomes-carbon-based nanomaterials (L-CNHs)

Photothermal transducers based on carbon-based nanomaterials have been developed in the last few years due to their unique properties (Liu et al., 2019). PTT has improved by encapsulating and/or adorning carbon-based nanoparticles in liposomes. By depositing graphene oxide (GO) on the surface of cationic liposomes, Mohadeseh Hashemi et al. created a combined chemophotothermal therapeutic platform (Hashemi et al., 2018). The NIR absorber and heating agent on the liposome is GO. Under NIR laser irradiation, four layers of GO were found to be sufficient to cause the gel to liquid phase transition of liposomes and stimulate cargo release. Hashemi et al. (2019) demonstrated that a novel theragnostic stimuli-sensitive system, consisting of rGO self-assembled into thermosensitive liposome (rGO-Tlip) encapsulating DOX (DOX-rGO-Tlip), as a chemotropic agent, and CQD (CQD-DOX-rGO-Tlip), monitoring drug accumulation and release in the tumorigenic region, can be developed. Prasad et al. (2019) created a stimulus responsive folic acid (FA)–conjugated graphene oxide flakes adorned liposomes (GOF-Lipo-FA) nanohybrid for cancer theragnostic and targeting. They demonstrated a system with improved water dispersibility, rapid photothermal reactions, and a multifunctional (chemo-PTT) therapeutic agent, as well as a prolonged tumor accumulation time (up to 24h). In their study, To achieve high retention and penetrability in tumors, Xue et al. (2018) designed a multifunctional liposome packaging nucleus that targeted CDs. DOX was covalently attached to NLS-CDs through a pH-sensitive hydrazone bond utilizing hydrazinobenzoic acid as a linker, as a chemotherapeutic medication that acts on DNA inside the nucleus. Meanwhile, ICG can interact physically with phospholipids in the liposome membrane, altering its stability and quantum yield while also receiving chemotherapeutic and photothermal therapy. In addition, we demonstrated that ICG can promote phase transition in liposomes under constant near-infrared light and control CDs-DOX release in tumors. They discovered a multistage delivery system capable of carrying, releasing, and delivering two types of NPs into tumor cells.

The thermo-sensitive liposomes loaded with doxorubicin and lysine-modified single-walled carbon nanotube drug delivery system developed by Zhu et al. (2014) was designed to enhance the antitumor effect while reducing the side effects of doxorubicin. When the nanocarrier reaches the tumor target sites, 808nm NIR laser radiation may cause SWNT to produce heat, which could result in tumor therapy effects. Meanwhile, when the temperature rises, DOX is released from the nanocarrier and delivered to the target areas more quickly. Then multimechanism cancer therapy could be realized. Madani et al. (2021) created a drug release system based on DNA-wrapped SWCNTs self-assembling onto model drug (FITC-Dex)-containing liposomes in response to external stimuli. They created an implanted, NIR responsive, targeted drug release device by embedding carbon nanotube liposome complexes (CLCs) into a 3D hydrogel matrix. Zhao et al. (2021b) recently demonstrated temperature-sensitive lipid-coated CNTs for photothermal and gene therapy synergy.

4. Application of NLHs

4.1 Cell death induced by PTT

Cell death processes on PTT remain a matter of debate, despite the fact that this technique is capable of killing and destroying tumors. Because PTT causes cancer cells to undergo numerous changes as the local temperature raises, this property is its most important one. to According to the studies, a temperature of 43°C is adequate for hyperthermia, which causes protein membrane denaturation and destruction, as well as cancer cell death. Heat stress can occur when normal cells are exposed to high temperatures. Protein denaturation is reduced, and apoptosis-related pathways are inhibited because of an increase in heat shock protein expression during this process. Riley et al. also came to a conclusion about the processes of cell death induced by PTT, especially for gold-based nanomaterials (Riley and Day, 2017). Laser power density also influences the photothermal efficiency. Higher laser power–induced necrosis mediated cell death which is beneficial for the tumor ablation. However, this method causes additional tumor

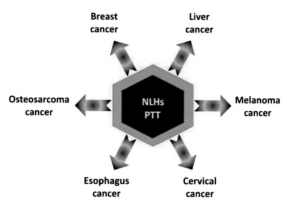

Fig. 2 Recent fabricated NLHs for PTT of different types of cancer therapy (Li et al., 2018; Hai et al., 2017; Prasad et al., 2020; Xue et al., 2018; Alvi et al., 2019).

growth by triggering inflammation caused by cellular waste discharge. PTT with low energy irradiation, on the other hand, promotes apoptosis to decrease inflammation by generating TGF-β and other antiinflammatory chemicals, resulting in a favorable immunogenic response. Photothermal activity and concentration in NIRN tumor tissue, as well as light power, have a major impact on PTT efficacy in this process (Melamed et al., 2015). PTT also generates a lot of reactive oxygen species (ROS) under NIR irradiation, which is one of the important factor for cell death (Prasad et al., 2019; Zhang et al., 2019).

Liposomes loaded with NIR active nanomaterials have been a successful nanohybrid for various tumors in recent studies (represented in Fig. 2) (Li et al., 2018; Hai et al., 2017; Prasad et al., 2020; Xue et al., 2018; Alvi et al., 2019). For example, Liposome-loaded red fluorescent CDs produced from mango leaves, have been shown to be effective for tumor imaging and tumor growth inhibition when exposed to near-infrared light (Ge et al., 2015). Based on recent investigation Pradhan et al. showed that quercetin loaded gold coated liposomes hybrid system which induce apoptosis on PTT for Huh-7 cells (Pradhan et al., 2019). However, using PTT alone to totally ablate a tumor is difficult. As a result, PTT combined with chemotherapy has a higher therapeutic efficacy due to increased drug content at the tumor site due to the heightened temperature. Furthermore, heating the drug molecule may increase its cytotoxicity. This can be compensated for by photo-induced hyperthermia. PTT, which mediated by NIRNs, provides tumor-specific localized heating without the adverse effects of high body temperatures (Riley and Day, 2017). Researchers are focusing for better understanding and application of NLHs toward clinical approach.

4.2 NIR light-triggered drug release

There are several mechanisms have been suggested for NIR light triggered cargo release. Recently, NIR-triggered drug release has been considered as a combine effect of photothermal therapy (PTT) to increase the tumor ablation. Most importantly, for NLHs, the light to heat conversation induces the liposomes permeabilization. Therefore, photothermal conversion efficiency of the NLH systems is an important factor for PPT treatment. Wang et al. provide on-demand drug release while minimizing drug toxicity in normal cells (Wang et al., 2017). They have shown that after 5 min of NIR light irradiation, the release of RES (resveratrol) significantly increased. The phase transition of liposomes bilayer (from gel like state to liquid crystalline state) is attributed to the increase of drug release rate under NIR- light. However, due to the orientation of the phospholipid's hydrophobic tail, drug release is primarily a slow diffusion process below the critical temperature. You et al. showed that the primary role of doxorubicin (DOX) and HAuNS-TSL in triggering DOX release is heat mediated diffusion. As a results, the entire liposome membrane becomes more permeable (You et al., 2014). Few studies have shown the carbon-based materials (e.g., GO, CNTs, and CDs) in NLHs also have comparable effect on the light triggered drug release (Chen et al., 2020; Geng et al., 2018).

4.3 NLHs mediated gene therapy (special focus on photothermal therapy)

Gene therapy is now a therapeutic technique for correcting or compensating for fundamental abnormalities and aberrant genes. Because of their capacity to influence protein production by silencing mRNA, small-interfering RNAs (siRNAs) have gotten a lot of attention (Setten et al., 2019). When NIRNs are combined with PTT, they act as gene delivery carriers, increasing the serum stability of siRNAs and controlling their release. Nanocarriers based on liposomes perform a unique function in siRNA delivery (Sahay et al., 2013). Zhao et al., for example, created a temperature-sensitive CNT-PS/siRNA nanoparticle for cancer cell synergistic PTT and gene therapy (presented in Fig. 3) (Zhao et al., 2021b). Jia et al. (2022) recently demonstrated imaging-guided photothermal and gene synergistic therapy using Prussian blue analog (PBA), an excellent photothermal nanomaterial, the multifunctional carrier liposome-coated Prussian-blue and gold nanoflower linked to targeted cRGD peptides. In summary, all the studies show that an intelligent NIR-responsive nanohybrid system can be used to control the release of therapeutic siRNA both temporally and spatially, which could pave the way for new research into optically regulated antitumor devices for precise, noninvasive, and synergistic therapy in the field of cancer theragnostic.

5. Future perspective and challenges

There is a growing demand for NLH systems that allow for controlled and triggered release in response to light stimulation, leading to more accurate tumor treatment. Therefore, NLHs have been widely used for bioimaging, drug delivery, and different cancer therapies applications over the past decade.

However, several bottlenecks must be overcome before the above-mentioned technology may be made clinically available. The main and most significant

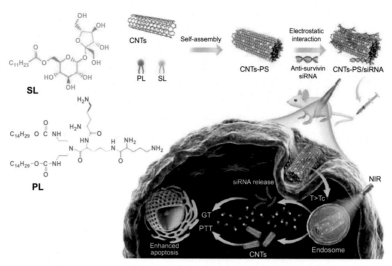

Fig. 3 Temperature sensitive lipid coated carbon nanotubes (CNTs) and siRNA nanohybrid for combination of photothermal therapy (PTT) and gene therapy (GT). *(Adopted with permission from Zhao, Y., Zhao, T., Cao, Y., Sun, J., Zhou, Q., Chen, H., et al., 2021b. Temperature-sensitive lipid-coated carbon nanotubes for synergistic photothermal therapy and gene therapy. ACS Nano 15(4), 6517–29. copyright © American Chemical Society 2021.)*

impediment to successful NLHs is the long-term breakdown mechanism of NIRNs and their probable toxicity in vivo. As previously stated, NIRNs of appropriate sizes should be a predominant factor to provide minimal toxicity and maximum efficacy. With advancing time, usage of nontoxic carbon-based materials has been popular for biological applications instead of traditional inorganic nanomaterials. Clinical research in the future should be well-designed. Second, the structural stability of NLHs should be addressed. Despite a number of promising developments, light mediated tissue penetration is still regarded as a therapeutic constraint in cancer treatment (Hu et al., 2018). Since, photothermal treatment used as an adjuvant therapy as a clinical practice, the combinatorial approaches could be an advanced for cancer treatment. Research is going on for better application of NLHs toward clinical approach. Also, ongoing research aims to engineer NLHs multifunctional systems that can perform drug delivery, bioimaging, and cancer treatment simultaneously. Achieving this goal could pave the way toward a milestone in biomedical research.

References

Abbasi, A., Park, K., Bose, A., Bothun, G.D., 2017. Near-infrared responsive gold–layersome nanoshells. Langmuir 33 (21), 5321–5327.

Akamatsu, H., Ninomiya, K., Kenmotsu, H., Morise, M., Daga, H., Goto, Y., et al., 2019. The Japanese lung cancer society guideline for non-small cell lung cancer, stage IV. Int. J. Clin. Oncol. 24 (7), 731–770.

Alvi, S.B., Appidi, T., Deepak, B.P., Rajalakshmi, P.S., Minhas, G., Singh, S.P., et al., 2019. The "nano to micro" transition of hydrophobic curcumin crystals leading to in situ adjuvant depots for au-liposome nanoparticle mediated enhanced photothermal therapy. Biomater. Sci. 7 (9), 3866–3875.

Chatterjee, H., Rahman, D.S., Sengupta, M., Ghosh, S.K., 2018. Gold nanostars in plasmonic photothermal therapy: the role of tip heads in the thermoplasmonic landscape. J. Phys. Chem. C 122 (24), 13082–13094.

Chauhan, V.P., Jain, R.K., 2013. Strategies for advancing cancer nanomedicine. Nat. Mater. 12 (11), 958–962.

Chauhan, D.S., Prasad, R., Devrukhkar, J., Selvaraj, K., Srivastava, R., 2018. Disintegrable NIR light triggered gold nanorods supported liposomal nanohybrids for cancer theranostics. Bioconjug. Chem. 29 (5), 1510–1518.

Chen, W., Goldys, E.M., Deng, W., 2020. Light-induced liposomes for cancer therapeutics. Prog. Lipid Res. 1 (79), 101052.

Dong, H., Pang, L., Cong, H., Shen, Y., Yu, B., 2019. Application and design of esterase-responsive nanoparticles for cancer therapy. Drug Deliv. 26 (1), 416–432.

Ge, J., Jia, Q., Liu, W., Guo, L., Liu, Q., Lan, M., et al., 2015. Red-emissive carbon dots for fluorescent, photoacoustic, and thermal theranostics in living mice. Adv. Mater. 27 (28), 4169–4177.

Geng, S., Wu, L., Cui, H., Tan, W., Chen, T., Chu, P.K., et al., 2018. Synthesis of lipid–black phosphorus quantum dot bilayer vesicles for near-infrared-controlled drug release. Chem. Commun. 54 (47), 6060–6063.

Hai, L., He, D., He, X., Wang, K., Yang, X., Liu, J., et al., 2017. Facile fabrication of a resveratrol loaded phospholipid@reduced graphene oxide nanoassembly for targeted and near-infrared laser-triggered chemo/photothermal synergistic therapy of cancer in vivo. J. Mater. Chem. B 5 (29), 5783–5792.

Hamzawy, M.A., Abo-youssef, A.M., Salem, H.F., Mohammed, S.A., 2017. Antitumor activity of intratracheal inhalation of temozolomide (TMZ) loaded into gold nanoparticles and/or liposomes against urethane-induced lung cancer in BALB/c mice. Drug Deliv. 24 (1), 599–607.

Hashemi, M., Omidi, M., Muralidharan, B., Tayebi, L., Herpin, M.J., Mohagheghi, M.A., et al., 2018. Layer-by-layer assembly of graphene oxide on thermosensitive liposomes for photo-chemotherapy. Acta Biomater. 1 (65), 376–392.

Hashemi, M., Mohammadi, J., Omidi, M., Smyth, H.D.C., Muralidharan, B., Milner, T.E., et al., 2019. Self-assembling of graphene oxide on carbon quantum dot loaded liposomes. Mater. Sci. Eng. C 1 (103), 109860.

He, C.F., Wang, S.H., Yu, Y.J., Shen, H.Y., Zhao, Y., Gao, H.L., et al., 2016. Advances in biodegradable nanomaterials for photothermal therapy of cancer. Cancer Biol. Med. 13 (3), 299–312.

Hu, J.J., Cheng, Y.J., Zhang, X.Z., 2018. Recent advances in nanomaterials for enhanced photothermal therapy of tumors. Nanoscale 10 (48), 22657–22672.

Jaque, D., Maestro, L.M., del Rosal, B., Haro-Gonzalez, P., Benayas, A., Plaza, J.L., et al., 2014. Nanoparticles for photothermal therapies. Nanoscale 6 (16), 9494–9530.

Jia, X., Xu, W., Ye, Z., Wang, Y., Dong, Q., Wang, E., et al., 2020. Functionalized graphene@gold nanostar/lipid for pancreatic cancer gene and photothermal synergistic therapy under photoacoustic/photothermal imaging dual-modal guidance. Small 16 (39), 2003707.

Jia, X., Lv, M., Fei, Y., Dong, Q., Wang, H., Liu, Q., et al., 2022. Facile one-step synthesis of NIR-responsive siRNA-inorganic hybrid nanoplatform for imaging-guided photothermal and gene synergistic therapy. Biomaterials 1 (282), 121404.

Karimi, M., Sahandi Zangabad, P., Baghaee-Ravari, S., Ghazadeh, M., Mirshekari, H., Hamblin, M.R., 2017. Smart nanostructures for cargo delivery: uncaging and activating by light. J. Am. Chem. Soc. 139 (13), 4584–4610.

Kwon, H.J., Byeon, Y., Jeon, H.N., Cho, S.H., Han, H.D., Shin, B.C., 2015. Gold cluster-labeled thermosensitive liposomes enhance triggered drug release in the tumor microenvironment by a photothermal effect. J. Control. Release 28 (216), 132–139.

Leung, S.J., Romanowski, M., 2012. NIR-activated content release from plasmon resonant liposomes for probing single-cell responses. ACS Nano 6 (11), 9383–9391.

Li, Y., He, D., Tu, J., Wang, R., Zu, C., Chen, Y., et al., 2018. The comparative effect of wrapping solid gold nanoparticles and hollow gold nanoparticles with doxorubicin-loaded thermosensitive liposomes for cancer thermo-chemotherapy. Nanoscale 10 (18), 8628–8641.

Liu, Y., Bhattarai, P., Dai, Z., Chen, X., 2019. Photothermal therapy and photoacoustic imaging via nanotheranostics in fighting cancer. Chem. Soc. Rev. 48 (7), 2053–2108.

Luo, L., Bian, Y., Liu, Y., Zhang, X., Wang, M., Xing, S., et al., 2016. Combined near infrared photothermal therapy and chemotherapy using gold nanoshells coated liposomes to enhance antitumor effect. Small 12 (30), 4103–4112.

Madani, S.Z.M., Safaee, M.M., Gravely, M., Silva, C., Kennedy, S., Bothun, G.D., et al., 2021. Carbon nanotube–liposome complexes in hydrogels for controlled drug delivery via near-infrared laser stimulation. ACS Appl. Nano Mater. 4 (1), 331–342.

Mathiyazhakan, M., Wiraja, C., Xu, C., 2017. A concise review of gold nanoparticles-based photo-responsive liposomes for controlled drug delivery. Nano-Micro Lett. 10 (1), 10.

Mauro, N., Utzeri, M.A., Varvarà, P., Cavallaro, G., 2021. Functionalization of metal and carbon nanoparticles with potential in cancer theranostics. Molecules 26 (11), 3085.

Melamed, J.R., Edelstein, R.S., Day, E.S., 2015. Elucidating the fundamental mechanisms of cell death triggered by photothermal therapy. ACS Nano 9 (1), 6–11.

Pan, A., Jakaria, M.G., Meenach, S.A., Bothun, G.D., 2020. Radiofrequency and near-infrared responsive core–shell nanostructures using layersome templates for cancer treatment. ACS Appl. Bio Mater. 3 (1), 273–281.

Patel, K.D., Singh, R.K., Kim, H.W., 2019. Carbon-based nanomaterials as an emerging platform for theranostics. Mater. Horiz. 6 (3), 434–469.

Pradhan, A., Kumari, A., Srivastava, R., Panda, D., 2019. Quercetin encapsulated biodegradable plasmonic nanoparticles for photothermal therapy of hepatocellular carcinoma cells. ACS Appl. Bio Mater. 2 (12), 5727–5738.

Prasad, R., Yadav, A.S., Gorain, M., Chauhan, D.S., Kundu, G.C., Srivastava, R., et al., 2019. Graphene oxide supported liposomes as red emissive theranostics for phototriggered tissue visualization and tumor regression. ACS Appl. Bio Mater. 2 (8), 3312–3320.

Prasad, R., Jain, N.K., Yadav, A.S., Chauhan, D.S., Devrukhkar, J., Kumawat, M.K., et al., 2020. Liposomal nanotheranostics for multimode targeted in vivo bioimaging and near-infrared light mediated cancer therapy. Commun. Biol. 3 (1), 284.

Rengan, A.K., Bukhari, A.B., Pradhan, A., Malhotra, R., Banerjee, R., Srivastava, R., et al., 2015. In vivo analysis of biodegradable liposome gold nanoparticles as efficient agents for photothermal therapy of Cancer. Nano Lett. 15 (2), 842–848.

Riley, R.S., Day, E.S., 2017. Gold nanoparticle-mediated photothermal therapy: applications and opportunities for multimodal cancer treatment. WIREs Nanomed. Nanobiotechnol. 9 (4), e1449.

Sahay, G., Querbes, W., Alabi, C., Eltoukhy, A., Sarkar, S., Zurenko, C., et al., 2013. Efficiency of siRNA delivery by lipid nanoparticles is limited by endocytic recycling. Nat. Biotechnol. 31 (7), 653–658.

Sailor, M.J., Park, J.H., 2012. Hybrid nanoparticles for detection and treatment of cancer. Adv. Mater. 24 (28), 3779–3802.

Setten, R.L., Rossi, J.J., Han, S., ping., 2019. The current state and future directions of RNAi-based therapeutics. Nat. Rev. Drug Discov. 18 (6), 421–446.

Sonkar, R., Sonali, J.A., Viswanadh, M.K., Burande, A.S., Narendra, et al., 2021. Gold liposomes for brain-targeted drug delivery: formulation and brain distribution kinetics. Mater. Sci. Eng. C 1 (120), 111652.

Tao, Y., Chan, H.F., Shi, B., Li, M., Leong, K.W., 2020. Light: a magical tool for controlled drug delivery. Adv. Funct. Mater. 30 (49), 2005029.

Thakur, V., Kutty, R.V., 2019. Recent advances in nanotheranostics for triple negative breast cancer treatment. J. Exp. Clin. Cancer Res. 38 (1), 430.

Torchilin, V.P., 2005. Recent advances with liposomes as pharmaceutical carriers. Nat. Rev. Drug Discov. 4 (2), 145–160.

Wang, Q., Chao, Y., 2018. Multifunctional quantum dots and liposome complexes in drug delivery. J. Biomed. Res. 32 (2), 91–106.

Wang, M., Liu, Y., Zhang, X., Luo, L., Li, L., Xing, S., et al., 2017. Gold nanoshell coated thermo–pH dual responsive liposomes for resveratrol delivery and chemo–photothermal synergistic cancer therapy. J. Mater. Chem. B 5 (11), 2161–2171.

Wang, Y., Meng, H.M., Li, Z., 2021. Near-infrared inorganic nanomaterial-based nanosystems for photothermal therapy. Nanoscale 13 (19), 8751–8772.

Xu, M., Hu, Y., Xiao, Y., Zhang, Y., Sun, K., Wu, T., et al., 2020. Near-infrared-controlled Nanoplatform exploiting Photothermal promotion of peroxidase-like and OXD-like activities for potent antibacterial and anti-biofilm therapies. ACS Appl. Mater. Interfaces 12 (45), 50260–50274.

Xue, X., Fang, T., Yin, L., Jiang, J., He, Y., Dai, Y., et al., 2018. Multistage delivery of CDs-DOX/ICG-loaded liposome for highly penetration and effective chemo–photothermal combination therapy. Drug Deliv. 25 (1), 1826–1839.

Yaghini, E., Seifalian, A.M., MacRobert, A.J., 2009. Quantum dots and their potential biomedical applications in photosensitization for photodynamic therapy. Nanomedicine 4 (3), 353–363.

Yang, X., Yang, M., Pang, B., Vara, M., Xia, Y., 2015. Gold nanomaterials at work in biomedicine. Chem. Rev. 115 (19), 10410–10488.

You, J., Zhang, P., Hu, F., Du, Y., Yuan, H., Zhu, J., et al., 2014. Near-infrared light-sensitive liposomes for the enhanced photothermal tumor treatment by the combination with chemotherapy. Pharm. Res. 31 (3), 554–565.

Zhang, P., Hu, C., Ran, W., Meng, J., Yin, Q., Li, Y., 2016. Recent progress in light-triggered nanotheranostics for cancer treatment. Theranostics 6 (7), 948–968.

Zhang, W., Ding, X., Cheng, H., Yin, C., Yan, J., Mou, Z., et al., 2019. Dual-targeted gold nanoprism for recognition of early apoptosis, dual-model imaging and precise cancer photothermal therapy. Theranostics 9 (19), 5610–5625.

Zhang, J., Chen, X., Xue, T., Cheng, Q., Ye, X., Wang, C., et al., 2020. Liposomes encapsulating neoantigens and black phosphorus quantum dots for enhancing photothermal immunotherapy. J. Biomed. Nanotechnol. 16 (9), 1394–1405.

Zhao, Y., Zhao, J., Shan, G., Yan, D., Chen, Y., Liu, Y., 2017. SERS-active liposome@ag/au nanocomposite for NIR light-driven drug release. Colloids Surf. B: Biointerfaces 1 (154), 150–159.

Zhao, L., Zhang, X., Wang, X., Guan, X., Zhang, W., Ma, J., 2021a. Recent advances in selective photothermal therapy of tumor. J. Nanobiotechnol. 19 (1), 335.

Zhao, Y., Zhao, T., Cao, Y., Sun, J., Zhou, Q., Chen, H., et al., 2021b. Temperature-sensitive lipid-coated carbon nanotubes for synergistic photothermal therapy and gene therapy. ACS Nano 15 (4), 6517–6529.

Zhu, X., Xie, Y., Zhang, Y., Huang, H., Huang, S., Hou, L., et al., 2014. Thermo-sensitive liposomes loaded with doxorubicin and lysine modified single-walled carbon nanotubes as tumor-targeting drug delivery system. J. Biomater. Appl. 29 (5), 769–779.

CHAPTER TWENTY-TWO

Anticancer activities of macromolecules of marine origin: Clinical evidence

Aryaman Patwardhan[a], Moin Merchant[a], Smit Bhavsar[a], Harpal S. Buttar[b], and Maushmi S. Kumar[c]

[a]Shobhaben Pratapbhai Patel School of Pharmacy and Technology Management SVKM's NMIMS Mumbai, Mumbai, Maharashtra, India
[b]Department of Pathology and Laboratory Medicine, University of Ottawa, Ottawa, ON, Canada
[c]Somaiya Institute of Research and Consultancy, Somaiya Vidyavihar University, Vidya Vihar East, Mumbai, Maharashtra, India

1. Introduction

Since 2008, the focus has shifted in discovering the anticancer compounds from marine sources, with research studies showing growth every year in the number of novel natural products and a drop in the proportion of bioactive synthetic compounds. This provides an impetus and opportunities for developing novel natural products for the treatment of cancer. The purview of this chapter is an in-depth analyses of the classes of anticancer macromolecules derived from the marine origin, which also includes the US-FDA-approved compounds currently undergoing clinical trials (Hu et al., 2015). By convention, the existing anticancer molecules, which are the synthetic chemotherapeutics available commercially, not only show an effect on cancer cells but also on the normal cells in the system targeted which causes the associated toxicity and side-effects for the patient. Such treatments were therefore not meeting the basic therapeutic needs of the patient which led to the search of novel compounds in the natural domain (Fridlender et al., 2015; Greenwell and Rahman, 2015). The biological macromolecules involved in cancer treatment and the various natural anticancer classes are described in Figs. 1 and 2, respectively (Lichota and Gwozdzinski, 2018, b; Tiwari et al., 2022).

2. Anticancer agents—Current scenario

As shown in Table 1, the United States Food and Drug Administration (US-FDA) has approved a few anticancer compounds derived from marine origin, which includes cytarabine (acute myeloid leukemia), trabectedin (advanced soft tissue sarcoma), eribulin mesylate (breast cancer and liposarcoma), brentuximab (refractory hodgkin lymphoma), and midostaurin (acute myeloid leukemia and advance systemic mastocytosis) (Saeed et al., 2021).

Biomarkers in Cancer Detection and Monitoring of Therapeutics
https://doi.org/10.1016/B978-0-323-95114-2.00018-2

Fig. 1 Various bioactive macromolecules possessing significant anticancer properties.

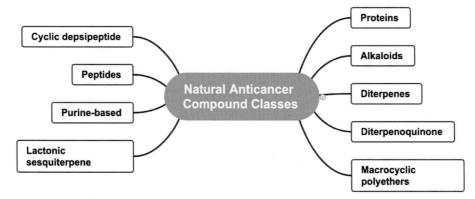

Fig. 2 Different classes of naturally occurring anticancer compound.

Table 1 US-FDA-approved anticancer drugs isolated from marine origin.

Name	Class	Source	References
Cytarabine	Pyrimidine nucleoside analog	*Cryptotheca crypta*	Schwartsmann et al. (2001) and El-Subbagh and Al-Badr (2009)
Trabectedin	Tetrahydroisoquinoline alkaloid	*Ecteinascidia turbinata*	D'Incalci et al. (2014)
Brentuximab	CD30-specific antibody–drug conjugate	A synthetic analog of the natural marine product Dolastatin-10	Younes et al. (2012)
Midostaurin	Indolocarbazole	A derivative of staurosporine	Levis (2017)

As summarized in Table 2, there are 13 compounds of marine origin that are currently undergoing different phases of clinical trials against various cancer types. Out of which, three compounds of marine source will be described specifically, those are being investigated against cancer, and their class actions will also be discussed.

Based on the classification shown in Figs. 1 and 2, the marine source molecules belonging to these different bioactive macromolecule's classes may be described as follows along with further reference to the novel compounds summarized in Table 3.

Table 2 Summary of 13 compounds undergoing clinical trials against different types of cancer (ClinicalTrials.gov).

NCT identifier	Indication	Compound	Source	Study phase	Stage
NCT03886311	Advanced sarcoma	Trabectedin	Sea squirt—*Ecteinascidia turbinata*	Phase 2	Recruiting
NCT04183478	Advanced pancreatic cancer	K-001	Active ingredients isolated from marine microorganisms	Phase 2 Phase 3	Recruiting
NCT04066660	Advanced hepatocellular carcinoma	Fucoidan	Brown algae: – *Fucus vesiculosus* – *Cladosiphon okamuranus* – *Laminaria japonica* – *Undaria pinnatifida*	Phase 2	Recruiting
NCT01653925	Prostate cancer for low-risk prostate cancer patients	Dutasteride	5-alpha reductase inhibitors	NA	Active, not recruiting
NCT01169259	Cancer, heart disease, and stroke	Omega-3 fatty acid	Antilipemic	Phase 3	Active, not recruiting
NCT01661764	Colorectal adenomatous polyps	Eicosapentaenoic acid, docosahexaenoic acid, and oleic acid	Marine-derived *n*-3 PUFAs	Phase 2	Active, not recruiting
NCT02249702	Leiomyosarcoma	Gemcitabine + docetaxel trabectedin	Trabdectin-tetrahydroisoquinoline alkaloid	Phase 2	Active, not recruiting
NCT03661047	Colon cancer	Drug: AMR101 (VASCEPA, icosapent ethyl)	Omega-3 fatty acid	Phase 2	Active, not recruiting
NCT03130829	NSCLC Stage IV NSCLC, Stage III	Oligofucoidan	Polysaccharide	NA	Recruiting

Continued

Table 2 Summary of 13 compounds undergoing clinical trials against different types of cancer (ClinicalTrials.gov)—cont'd

NCT identifier	Indication	Compound	Source	Study phase	Stage
NCT04216251	Reduction in colorectal cancer risk in individuals with history of colorectal adenoma	AMR101 (VASCEPA) – Icosapent ethyl	Omega-3 fatty acid	Phase 1 Phase 2	Active, not recruiting
NCT04597476	Stage III/IV head and neck squamous cell carcinoma	Fucoidan	Long chain sulfated polysaccharide	Phase 2	Active, not recruiting
NCT04066660	Advanced hepatocellular carcinoma	Oligofucoidan	Oligofucoidan, a heparin-like molecule with high percentages of L-fucose and sulfated ester groups and low percentages of D-xylose, D-galactose, D-mannose, and glucuronic acid	Phase 2	Recruiting
NCT04209244	Acute lymphoblastic leukemia	Eskimo-3 pure fish oil	Omega-3 fatty acid	Phase 2	Active, not recruiting

Table 3 Therapeutically promising anticancer macromolecules of marine origin.

Macromolecule class	Macromolecule	Source	Targeted cancer	References
Carbohydrates	(SPUP) sulfated polysaccharide	*Undaria pinnatifida*	Breast cancer	Wu et al. (2019)
	Chitosan	*Procambarus clarkia* (Crayfish)	Breast cancer	Taher et al. (2019)
	SPS-CF	*Capsosiphon fulvescens*	Colon cancer	Choi et al. (2019)
	EPS-CS	*Chlorococcum* sp.	Colon cancer	Zhang et al. (2017)
	Fucoidan	*Undaria pinnatifida*	Pancreatic cancer	Etman et al. (2020)
Proteins	Lyngabyal lectin	*Lyngabya confervoides* MK012409	Breast cancer, colorectal cancer	El-Fakharany et al. (2020)
Nucleic acids–microRNA's (miR's)	miR-34	*Marsupenaeus japonicus*	Breast cancer	Cui et al. (2017)
	miR-331-3p		Nonsmall cell lung carcinoma	Tian et al. (2020)
	miR-22		Colorectal cancer	Cong et al. (2020, p. 22)
	miR-133a-3p		Hepatocellular carcinoma	Han and Parker (2017)

Source: Tiwari, H., Deshmukh, H., Wagh, N.S., Lakkakula, J., 2022. Biological macromolecules as anticancer agents. In: Biological Macromolecules. Elsevier, 243–272.

2.1 Carbohydrates

Under the class of carbohydrates, polysaccharides are the primary macromolecules which show potential as novel anticancer agents. Polysaccharides from marine sources have attracted attention from both the food and pharmaceutical industries due to its promising therapeutic effects. The inclusion of polysaccharides as potential anticancer agents have had a significant increase in recent years as the focus of the research shifted from microbial polysaccharides to plant polysaccharides as the latter contain less toxic (Schepetkin and Quinn, 2006). To illustrate the efficiency of polysaccharides in inducing cytotoxicity in cancer cells, a recent paper made their primary focus on signaling molecules (Alwarsamy et al., 2016). Polysaccharides function against tumor cells in two ways: direct action (inhibition of tumor cell development and induction of apoptosis) and indirect action (induction of apoptosis) (immunostimulating). Several polysaccharides have exhibited direct impact on cancer cells in addition to their indirect function. Many in vitro and in vivo investigations have shown that polysaccharide therapy inhibits tumor cell growth and/or causes them to perish through apoptosis (Fan et al., 2014). Cell cycle arrest and apoptosis are two critical processes in programmed cell death that are largely regulated by cell growth signaling molecules. Several studies have used different cancer cell lines to investigate the impact of polysaccharides in cell cycle activation, prevention of cell proliferation, and induction of apoptosis, as well as the regulatory routes and processes of cell cycle genes and their protein products (Guo et al., 2016; Chu et al., 2016).

Sulfated polysaccharide from Undaria pinnatifida (SPUP)

Sulfated polysaccharide from *Undaria pinnatifida* (SPUP) is considered a prominent study issue, particularly in the realm of cancer therapy. SPUP has shown to have an important role in antibreast cancer treatment by suppressing breast cancer cell proliferation and migration, as well as triggering apoptosis. SPUP regulates the production of apoptosis-related or signal proteins, cell-cycle regulatory proteins, and transcription factors, which can trigger exogenous or endogenous apoptosis pathways in a variety of cancer cell lines (Wu et al., 2019). For embryonic development, the Hh pathway is critical. Activation of the Hh pathway has been linked to the incidence and progression of malignancies, including ovarian cancer (OC), in many prior studies. In OC, the Hh pathway is reported to have a high degree of expression. Inhibition of Hh signals might cause apoptosis, as well as reduce cell viability and motility. Inhibition of the Hh pathway, however, might be a good target for OC therapy (Schmid et al., 2011). The anticancer impact of SPUP in combination with GANT61 was more effective than GANT61 alone, suggesting that SPUP might increase GANT61's anticancer properties. SPUP, like other Hh signal pathway inhibitors, appears to promote OC cell apoptosis and reduce cell proliferation, migration, and invasion by lowering the protein expression of Hh signal pathway components Shh, Ptch1, Smo, and Gli1 (Yang et al., 2021).

Chitosan

Chitosan is a polymer made up of deacetyl-(1,4) glucosamine units that is made by deacetylating chitin with NaOH after the crustacean shells or exoskeletons have been demineralized and deproteinized. The antioxidant activity of 2-phenylhydrazine (or hydrazine) thiosemicarbazone chitosan toxicity in cells is linked to its ability to scavenge cancer-causing free radicals, and oxidative stress caused by an imbalance between antioxidant defense and free radical generation may encourage the etiology of cancer (Zhong et al., 2010). Chitosan-metal complexes have antitumor activity due to their association with deoxyribonucleic acid (DNA) and free radical scavenging behavior. It has been discovered to have anticancer activity with minimal toxicity on noncancer cells, and this activity against different cancer cell lines is influenced by the distribution pattern of -(1,4)-linked *N*-acetylglucosamine and D-glucosamine units along the oligomeric chain, which affects molecular weight and degree of deacetylation. The absorption of chitosan nanoparticles by cultured fibroblasts increased when degree of deacetylation levels increased (Adhikari and Yadav, 2018).

Sulfated polysaccharide from Capsosiphon fulvescens (SPS-CF)

Sulfated polysaccharide from *C. fulvescens* (SPS-CF) was discovered as sulfated glucuronorhamnoxylan, a type of ulvan polysaccharide found in green algae, with a backbone made up of an alternating sequence of 4-linked L-rhamnose-3-sulfate and D-xylose residues (ulvobiose) and monomeric D-glucuronic acid or D-glucuronic acid-3-sulfate on O-2 of some L-rhamnose. SPS-CF, a glucuronorhamnoxylan isolated from the Korean *C. fulvescens*, has been shown to suppress the development of HT-29 human colon cancer cells, suggesting that it may have antitumor properties. SPS-potent CF's anticolon cancer effect was found to be mediated by activation of apoptotic signaling pathway proteins like caspase-3, -8, -9, and PARP, as well as disruption of mitochondrial membrane potential (MMP), and finally by inhibiting HT29 cell growth by arresting the cell cycle at G2/M phase. SPS-CF also significantly inhibited the formation of HT-29 cell xenograft solid tumors in vivo by inducing apoptosis in colon tumor cells.

Microbial extracellular polysaccharides (EPS-CS)

Microbial extracellular polysaccharides (EPS-CS) are carbohydrate polymers that enclose most bacteria's envelope. Bifidobacterium, one of the most common early colonization bacteria in the human intestine, has been shown to influence immunological development, immune modulation, antiinflammation, and anticancer activities. Additionally, bifido-EPS has been demonstrated to have antioxidant activity, which may help to minimize tissue damage even more. Furthermore, EPS has the ability to block DNA synthesis as well as the expression of genes involved in angiogenesis. Apart from immunomodulation and blocking DNA synthesis, extracellular polysaccharides-*Chlorococcum* sp. (EPS-CS) also has antioxidant activity. In the HNSCC cell line, EPS can stop the cell cycle in the G1-S phase. When cells incur DNA damage, PARP is activated, and it is the primary target of caspase 3, whose activation might result in a latent specific proteolytic cleavage during apoptosis. In the treatment group, EPS enhanced caspase 3 expression and the fraction of cleaved-PARP, whereas inferred cell death occurred (Wang et al., 2019a, b). The antitumor impact of EPS might be explained in part by its chemical makeup, which includes rhamnose, arabinose, galactose, glucose, and mannose. It's worth noting that mannose made up the majority of the bifido-EPS, which has been linked to antitumor action. Mannose has the potential to slow tumor development by reducing tumor cell proliferation while boosting cancer cell death. It also demonstrated the presence of chemo-sensitization character (Gonzalez et al., 2018).

Fucoidans

Liver cancer is the fourth leading cause of cancer-related mortality, with the greatest rates in East Asia and Africa. Hepatocellular carcinoma (HCC) is the most frequent kind of liver cancer, accounting for 75%–85% of cases (O'Rourke et al., 2018). Chronic hepatitis B and C virus (HBV/HCV) infection, alcohol consumption, aflatoxin B1 exposure, and metabolic abnormalities are all risk factors. The prevalence of virally linked HCC has reduced as a result of HBV vaccination and anti-HCV drugs 4–6, but non–B non–C (NBNC) HCC is on the rise due to obesity (Jafri and Kamran, 2019; Marengo et al., 2016).

Fucoidan or more specifically oligo–fucoidan (OF), a long chain sulfated polysaccharide has been very recently established to be an anticancer molecule researched and used in treating human malignant glioma cells (Liao et al., 2019). It has also been proven to reduce the occurrence of radiation induced fibrosis and secondary tumors in zebrafish (Wu et al., 2020). And its supplementation in chemotherapy greatly enhances chemosensitivity and renovates the microenvironment such that it prevents the proliferation of aggressive cancer cells and prevents tumor progression in HCT116 colorectal cancer cells (Chen et al., 2020).

3. Clinical trials with fucoidans

Clinical trials have been conducted with oligo–fucoidan in advanced hepatocellular carcinoma (HCC). The reference studies state the advantages of in disease control rate in colorectal cancer patients. The previous studies might help with the development of cancer therapies, especially when natural or herbal items are combined with chemo target drugs.

The primary objective of this study is to test the disease control rate using RECIST version 1.1 and the secondary objectives include the objective response rate, survival rate, progression free survival using RECIST version 1.1 and the quality of life using questionnaire based on EORTC-QLQ30, specific questions evaluated by scores from 1 (not at all), 2 (a little), 3 (quite a bit), 4 (very much); overall healthy and quality of life will be evaluated by scores from 1 (very poor) to 7 (excellent).

3.1 Anticancer proteins of marine origin

Despite sufficient progress in the diagnosis and treatment of cancer, tumor diseases consist of one of the main reasons for deaths worldwide. The side effects of chemotherapy and drug resistance of some cancer types belong to the harsh current therapeutic problems. Hence, searching for new anticancer substances and medicines are very important. Of them, proteins and peptides are a significant group of bioactive compounds and potential anticancer drugs.

Rapid development in molecular biology and sequencing of bacterial and fungal genomes have played a major role in the discovery of new alkaloids in and in the microbial organisms, and good amounts of biosynthetic information for the compounds has been incurred in a number of latest mechanistic studies. Due to which, their role as anticancer agents can be discussed (O'Connor, 2010).

These molecules have been developed from the phenomenon of biodiversity, in which the interactions among various species and with the environment are evolved upon diverse complex chemical entities within the organisms that enhance their survival. The therapeutic area of spreadable diseases and oncology have helped advance greatly from this chemical arsenal and, as with plants, researchers have identified its potential use to inhibit bacteria or cancer cells growth. Incidence of biological activity in compounds coming from marine sources is high, especially with regard to cytotoxicity, where extracts of marine species overcome those of terrestrial origin. Marine natural products are able to interact with desired targets within the cell and are finding increasing use as probes to interfere with biological systems as part of chemical genomics research. Most of the bioactive molecules from the sea are found in invertebrates and, for antitumor agents, several convincing molecules have been isolated from these sea creatures, which are soft bodied and have a sedentary lifestyle demanding chemical means of defense (Imperatore et al., 2014).

Trabectedin therapy in ovarian cancer

Ovarian cancer (OC) represents approximately 10% of gynecological cancers worldwide and 4% of all carcinomas in women (Oberaigner et al., 2012). About 75% of newly diagnosed patients present with advanced disease, with a 5-year survival of 15%–20% (Cannistra, 2003). Except for low-risk disease, the standard approach for the treatment of OC includes surgical resection followed by adjuvant/neoadjuvant platinum-based chemotherapy (Colombo et al., 2019). Although 80% of newly diagnosed OC cases respond to a first-line platinum-based chemotherapy, its effectiveness and clinical benefit reduces in each subsequent line due to the development of platinum resistance and cumulative toxicities (Pujade-Lauraine et al., 2010).

Patients with platinum sensitive disease (i.e., treatment-free interval of platinum, TFIp ≥ 6 months) are usually retreated with a further platinum-based chemotherapy after relapse. Trabectedin has attracted increasing attention for the treatment of OC due to its complex and unique mechanism of action (Larsen et al., 2016). Its structure allows it to bind with the minor deoxyribonucleic acid (DNA) groove, and to protrude outside of the DNA with factors associated with transcription and DNA repair (Ferrandina et al., 2014). As a consequence, trabectedin induces DNA distortion and damage, interferes with the transcription coupled nucleotide excision repair (NER) system, generates double-strand DNA breaks, blocks the cell cycle, and leads to the p53-independent apoptosis.

In addition to direct growth inhibition, trabectedin also affects the tumor microenvironment by inducing depletion of monocytes and tumor-associated macrophages and reducing the production of key inflammatory mediators that promote tumor progression (Ferrandina et al., 2014).

Randomized clinical trials are the golden standard for the approval of therapeutic agents, providing quality data on safety and efficacy (Eisenhauer, 2017). Real world evidence is a consequent step for finishing this information with help from clinical practice, contributing to active pharmacovigilance and to throw some more light on the organic history of disease (Khozin et al., 2017).

Both clinical trials and real-world studies have intrinsic methodological limitations (Sherman et al., 2016; Franklin and Schneeweiss, 2017). For instance, presence of data and deficiency of the fixed timing for evaluating response, which are done with respect to the clinician's usual clinical practice, are the most frequent challenges in real-world studies, which may consist of the surety and credibility of the collected information (Booth et al., 2019). On a different note, original real-world studies usually include a more dissimilar patient population than the population shown in clinical trials, in particular older and/or highly pretreated patients with several comorbidities which may be not presented in clinical trials. With the support of clinical trials, the actual use case of trabectedin has been figured out to fight ovarian cancer.

Anticancer effects of Lyngabyal lectin

In a study, a novel lectin was purified from a recently isolated cyanobacterium, Lyngabya confervoides MK012409 and tested for the antiviral and anticancer activity. Out of 30 isolates, Mabroka-s isolate which identified as *Lyngabya confervoides* MK012409 showed the maximum agglutination titer. Lyngabyal lectin showed the highest and most efficient hemagglutination activity with pigeon/rabbit erythrocytes with little We concentration of 2.4 µg/mL. Physical characterization of Lyngabyal lectin showed ability to keep the activity at a higher temperature up to 80°C with stability over a wide pH range (4–8) as well as its stability toward chemical denaturants. These data show and proves the capacity of Lyngabyal lectin to fight colon and breast cancer, making it an anticancer agent (El-Fakharany et al., 2020).

3.2 Anticancer action of peptidoglycans

The anticancer property of peptidoglycans as a therapeutic molecule came to light with the discovery of its immunomodulating effects through studies carried out on Freund's complete adjuvant (FCA) and peptidoglycan metabolites, such as muropeptides, have proven, by means of animal models, to reduce cancer burden and increase survivability (Stewart-Tull, 1980; Griffin et al., 2019). The synthesis of peptidoglycans is a promising avenue for manufacturing vaccines since the immune response is triggered by lower quantities of antigen in the presence of adjuvant (Stewart-Tull, 1980).

4. Conclusion

In conclusion, natural molecules of marine origin hold a great therapeutic promise as anticancer agents and many have shown positive responsiveness for suppressing the growth and metastasis of cancer cells in animal models and humans. Currently, 13 compounds isolated from marine source are undergoing clinical trials in different phases. However, more experimental and clinical research is warranted in the field of oncology for exploring the anticancer mechanisms of the natural molecules of marine source. At this point in time, the anticancer molecules isolated from marine organisms fall under the broad categories of sulfated polysaccharides, carbohydrates, and proteins, which have emerged as useful tools for treating different types of cancer. Hopefully, the macromolecules of marine origin will turn out as novel futuristic cost-effective and affordable therapies based on their mode of action and lesser adverse consequences.

Acknowledgment

We acknowledge the support of SVKM'S NMIMS in writing this book chapter.

Conflict of interest

The authors declare no conflict of interest.

References

Adhikari, H.S., Yadav, P.N., 2018. Anticancer activity of chitosan, chitosan derivatives, and their mechanism of action. Int. J. Biomater. 2018, e2952085. https://doi.org/10.1155/2018/2952085.

Alwarsamy, M., Gooneratne, R., Ravichandran, R., 2016. Effect of fucoidan from Turbinaria conoides on human lung adenocarcinoma epithelial (A549) cells. Carbohydr. Polym. 152, 207–213. https://doi.org/10.1016/j.carbpol.2016.06.112.

Booth, C.M., Karim, S., Mackillop, W.J., 2019. Real-world data: towards achieving the achievable in cancer care. Nat. Rev. Clin. Oncol. 16 (5), 312–325. https://doi.org/10.1038/s41571-019-0167-7.

Cannistra, S.A., 2003. Progress in the management of gynecologic cancer: consensus summary statement. J. Clin. Oncol. 21 (90100), 129s–1132. https://doi.org/10.1200/JCO.2003.04.003.

Chen, L.-M., Tseng, H.-Y., Chen, Y.-A., Al Haq, A.T., Hwang, P.-A., Hsu, H.-L., 2020. Oligo-fucoidan prevents M2 macrophage differentiation and HCT116 tumor progression. Cancers 12 (2), E421. https://doi.org/10.3390/cancers12020421.

Choi, J.W., Lee, J., Kim, S.C., et al., 2019. Glucuronorhamnoxylan from Capsosiphon fulvescens inhibits the growth of HT-29 human colon cancer cells in vitro and in vivo via induction of apoptotic cell death. Int. J. Biol. Macromol. 124, 1060–1068. https://doi.org/10.1016/j.ijbiomac.2018.12.001.

Chu, B.-F., Lin, H.-C., Huang, X.-W., Huang, H.-Y., Wu, C.P., Kao, M.-C., 2016. An ethanol extract of Poria cocos inhibits the proliferation of non-small cell lung cancer A549 cells via the mitochondria-mediated caspase activation pathway. J. Funct. Foods 23, 614–627. https://doi.org/10.1016/j.jff.2016.03.016.

Colombo, N., Sessa, C., du Bois, A., Ledermann, J., McCluggage, W.G., McNeish, I., Morice, P., et al., 2019. ESMO–ESGO consensus conference recommendations on ovarian cancer: pathology and molecular biology, early and advanced stages, borderline tumours and recurrent disease. Ann. Oncol. 30 (5), 672–705. https://doi.org/10.1093/annonc/mdz062.

Cong, J., Gong, J., Yang, C., et al., 2020. miR-22 suppresses tumor invasion and metastasis in colorectal cancer by targeting NLRP3. Cancer Manag. Res. 12, 5419–5429. https://doi.org/10.2147/CMAR. S255125.

Cui, Y., Yang, X., Zhang, X., 2017. Shrimp miR-34 from shrimp stress response to virus infection suppresses tumorigenesis of breast cancer. Mol. Ther. Nucleic Acids 9, 387–398. https://doi.org/10.1016/j.omtn.2017.10.016.

D'Incalci, M., Badri, N., Galmarini, C.M., Allavena, P., 2014. Trabectedin, a drug acting on both cancer cells and the tumour microenvironment. Br. J. Cancer 111, 646–650. https://doi.org/10.1038/bjc.2014.149.

Eisenhauer, E.A., 2017. Real-world evidence in the treatment of ovarian cancer. Ann. Oncol. 28, viii61–viii65. https://doi.org/10.1093/annonc/mdx443.

El-Fakharany, E.M., Saad, M.H., Salem, M.S., Sidkey, N.M., 2020. Biochemical characterization and application of a novel lectin from the cyanobacterium Lyngabya confervoides MK012409 as an antiviral and anticancer agent. Int. J. Biol. Macromol. 161, 417–430. https://doi.org/10.1016/j.ijbiomac.2020.06.046.

El-Subbagh, H.I., Al-Badr, A.A., 2009. Cytarabine. In: Profiles of Drug Substances, Excipients and Related Methodology. Elsevier, pp. 37–113.

Etman, S.M., Abdallah, O.Y., Elnaggar, Y.S.R., 2020. Novel fucoidan based bioactive targeted nanoparticles from Undaria pinnatifida for treatment of pancreatic cancer. Int. J. Biol. Macromol. 145, 390–401. https://doi.org/10.1016/j.ijbiomac.2019.12.177.

Fan, Y., Lin, M., Luo, A., Chun, Z., Luo, A., 2014. Characterization and antitumor activity of a polysaccharide from Sarcodia ceylonensis. Molecules 19 (8), 10863–10876. https://doi.org/10.3390/molecules190810863.

Ferrandina, G., Mascilini, F., Amadio, G., Grazia Di Stefano, M., Di Legge, A., De Vincenzo, R., Masciullo, V., et al., 2014. Clinical utility of trabectedin for the treatment of ovarian cancer: current evidence. OncoTargets Ther., 1273. https://doi.org/10.2147/OTT.S51550.

Franklin, J.M., Schneeweiss, S., 2017. When and how can real world data analyses substitute for randomized controlled trials?: real world evidence and RCTs. Clin. Pharmacol. Ther. 102 (6), 924–933. https://doi.org/10.1002/cpt.857.

Fridlender, M., Kapulnik, Y., Koltai, H., 2015. Plant derived substances with anti-cancer activity: from folklore to practice. Front. Plant Sci. 6. https://doi.org/10.3389/fpls.2015.00799.

Gonzalez, H., Hagerling, C., Werb, Z., 2018. Roles of the immune system in cancer from tumour initiation to metastatic progression. Genes Dev. 32, 1267–1284. https://doi.org/10.1101/gad.314617.118.

Greenwell, M., Rahman, P.K.S.M., 2015. Medicinal plants: their use in anticancer treatment. Int. J. Pharm. Sci. Res. 6, 4103–4112. https://doi.org/10.13040/IJPSR.0975-8232.6(10).4103-12.

Griffin, M.E., Hespen, C.W., Wang, Y.-.C., Hang, H.C., 2019. Translation of peptidoglycan metabolites into immunotherapeutics. Clin. Transl. Immunol. 8 (12). https://doi.org/10.1002/cti2.1095.

Guo, M., Ding, G.-B., Yang, P., Zhang, L., Wu, H., Li, H., Li, Z., 2016. Migration suppression of small cell lung cancer by polysaccharides from nostoc commune vaucher. J. Agric. Food Chem. 64, 6277–6285 (accessed 28.03.22) https://pubs.acs.org/doi/abs/10.1021/acs.jafc.6b01906.

Han, X., Parker, T.L., 2017. Anti-inflammatory, tissue remodeling, immunomodulatory, and anticancer activities of oregano (Origanum vulgare) essential oil in a human skin disease model. Biochim. Open 4, 73–77. https://doi.org/10.1016/j.biopen.2017.02.005.

Hu, Y., Chen, J., Hu, G., et al., 2015. Statistical research on the bioactivity of new marine natural products discovered during the 28 years from 1985 to 2012. Mar. Drugs 13, 202–221. https://doi.org/10.3390/md13010202.

Imperatore, C., Aiello, A., D'Aniello, F., Senese, M., Menna, M., 2014. Alkaloids from marine invertebrates as important leads for anticancer drugs discovery and development. Molecules 19 (12), 20391–20423. https://doi.org/10.3390/molecules191220391.

Jafri, W., Kamran, M., 2019. Hepatocellular carcinoma in Asia: a challenging situation. Euroasian J. Hepato-Gastroenterol. 9 (1), 27–33. https://doi.org/10.5005/jp-journals-10018-1292.

Khozin, S., Blumenthal, G.M., Pazdur, R., 2017. Real-world data for clinical evidence generation in oncology. J. Natl. Cancer Inst. 109 (11). https://doi.org/10.1093/jnci/djx187.

Larsen, A.K., Galmarini, C.M., D'Incalci, M., 2016. Unique features of trabectedin mechanism of action. Cancer Chemother. Pharmacol. 77 (4), 663–671. https://doi.org/10.1007/s00280-015-2918-1.

Levis, M., 2017. Midostaurin approved for FLT3-mutated AML. Blood 129, 3403–3406. https://doi.org/10.1182/blood-2017-05-782292.

Liao, C.-H., Lai, I.-C., Kuo, H.-C., Chuang, S.-E., Lee, H.-L., Whang-Peng, J., Yao, C.-J., Lai, G.-M., 2019. Epigenetic modification and differentiation induction of malignant glioma cells by oligo-fucoidan. Mar. Drugs 17 (9), E525. https://doi.org/10.3390/md17090525.

Lichota, A., Gwozdzinski, K., 2018. Anticancer activity of natural compounds from plant and marine environment. Int. J. Mol. Sci. 19, E3533. https://doi.org/10.3390/ijms19113533.

Marengo, A., Rosso, C., Bugianesi, E., 2016. Liver cancer: connections with obesity, fatty liver, and cirrhosis. Annu. Rev. Med. 67 (1), 103–117. https://doi.org/10.1146/annurev-med-090514-013832.

O'Connor, S.E., 2010. Alkaloids. In: Comprehensive Natural Products II. Elsevier, pp. 977–1007, https://doi.org/10.1016/B978-008045382-8.00013-7.

O'Rourke, J.M., Mridhu Sagar, V., Shah, T., Shetty, S., 2018. Carcinogenesis on the background of liver fibrosis: implications for the management of hepatocellular cancer. World J. Gastroenterol. 24 (39), 4436–4447. https://doi.org/10.3748/wjg.v24.i39.4436.

Oberaigner, W., Minicozzi, P., Bielska-Lasota, M., Allemani, C., de Angelis, R., Mangone, L., Sant, M., Eurocare Working Group, 2012. Survival for ovarian cancer in Europe: the across-country variation did not shrink in the past decade. Acta Oncol. 51 (4), 441–453. https://doi.org/10.3109/0284186X.2011.653437.

Pujade-Lauraine, E., Wagner, U., Aavall-Lundqvist, E., Gebski, V., Heywood, M., Vasey, P.A., Volgger, B., et al., 2010. Pegylated liposomal doxorubicin and carboplatin compared with paclitaxel and carboplatin for patients with platinum-sensitive ovarian cancer in late relapse. J. Clin. Oncol. 28 (20), 3323–3329. https://doi.org/10.1200/JCO.2009.25.7519.

Saeed, A.F.U.H., Su, J., Ouyang, S., 2021. Marine-derived drugs: recent advances in cancer therapy and immune signaling. Biomed. Pharmacother. 134, 111091. https://doi.org/10.1016/j.biopha.2020.111091.

Schepetkin, I.A., Quinn, M.T., 2006. Botanical polysaccharides: macrophage immunomodulation and therapeutic potential. Int. Immunopharmacol. 6 (3), 317–333. https://doi.org/10.1016/j.intimp.2005.10.005.

Schmid, S., Bieber, M., Zhang, F., et al., 2011. Wnt and hedgehog gene pathway expression in serous ovarian cancer. Int. J. Gynecol. Cancer 21. https://doi.org/10.1097/IGC.0b013e31821caa6f.

Schwartsmann, G., da Rocha, A.B., Berlinck, R.G., Jimeno, J., 2001. Marine organisms as a source of new anticancer agents. Lancet Oncol. 2, 221–225. https://doi.org/10.1016/S1470-2045(00)00292-8.

Sherman, R.E., Anderson, S.A., Dal Pan, G.J., Gray, G.W., Gross, T., Hunter, N.L., LaVange, L., et al., 2016. Real-world evidence—what is it and what can it tell us? N. Engl. J. Med. 375 (23), 2293–2297. https://doi.org/10.1056/NEJMsb1609216.

Stewart-Tull, D.E.S., 1980. The immunological activities of bacterial peptidoglycans. Annu. Rev. Microbiol. 34, 311–340. https://doi.org/10.1146/annurev.mi.34.100180.001523.

Taher, F.A., Ibrahim, S.A., El-Aziz, A.A., et al., 2019. Anti-proliferative effect of chitosan nanoparticles (extracted from crayfish Procambarus clarkii, Crustacea: Cambaridae) against MDA-MB-231 and SK-BR-3 human breast cancer cell lines. Int. J. Biol. Macromol. 126, 478–487. https://doi.org/10.1016/j.ijbiomac.2018.12.151.

Tian, Q.-Q., Xia, J., Zhang, X., et al., 2020. miR-331-3p inhibits tumor cell proliferation, metastasis, invasion by targeting MLLT10 in non-small cell lung cancer. Cancer Manag. Res. 12, 5749–5758. https://doi.org/10.2147/CMAR.S249686.

Tiwari, H., Deshmukh, H., Wagh, N.S., Lakkakula, J., 2022. Biological macromolecules as anticancer agents. In: Biological Macromolecules. Elsevier, pp. 243–272.

Wang, Y., Xing, M., Cao, Q., Ji, A., Liang, H., Song, S., 2019a. Biological activities of fucoidan and the factors mediating its therapeutic effects: a review of recent studies. Mar. Drugs 17 (3), E183. https://doi.org/10.3390/md17030183.

Wang, L., Wang, Y., Li, Q., et al., 2019b. Exopolysaccharide, isolated from a novel strain Bifidobacterium breve lw01 possess an anticancer effect on head and neck cancer—genetic and biochemical evidences. Front. Microbiol. 10, 1044. https://doi.org/10.3390/md17030183.

Wu, J., Li, H., Wang, X., et al., 2019. Effect of polysaccharide from Undaria pinnatifida on proliferation, migration and apoptosis of breast cancer cell MCF7. Int. J. Biol. Macromol. 121, 734–742. https://doi.org/10.1016/j.ijbiomac.2018.10.086.

Wu, S.-Y., Yang, W.-Y., Cheng, C.-C., Hsiao, M.-C., Tsai, S.-L., Lin, H.-K., Lin, K.-H., 2020. Low molecular weight fucoidan prevents radiation-induced fibrosis and secondary tumors in a zebrafish model. Cancers 12 (6), E1608. https://doi.org/10.3390/cancers12061608.

Yang, Y., Zhang, Q., Xu, Y., et al., 2021. Sulfated polysaccharide from Undaria pinnatifida induces apoptosis and inhibits proliferation, migration, and invasion in ovarian cancer via suppressing the hedgehog signaling pathway. Front. Mater. 8, 795061. https://doi.org/10.3389/fmats.2021.795061.

Younes, A., Yasothan, U., Kirkpatrick, P., 2012. Brentuximab vedotin. Nat. Rev. Drug Discov. 11, 19–20. https://doi.org/10.1038/nrd3629.

Zhang, Y., Wu, W., Kang, L., et al., 2017. Effect of Aconitum coreanum polysaccharide and its sulphated derivative on the migration of human breast cancer MDA-MB-435s cell. Int. J. Biol. Macromol. 103, 477–483. https://doi.org/10.1016/j.ijbiomac.2017.05.084.

Zhong, Z., Zhong, Z., Xing, R., et al., 2010. The preparation and antioxidant activity of 2-[phenylhydrazine (or hydrazine)-thiosemicarbazone]-chitosan. Int. J. Biol. Macromol. 47, 93–97. https://doi.org/10.1016/j.ijbiomac.2010.05.016.

CHAPTER TWENTY-THREE

Therapeutic potential of microalgae and their prospects in targeted delivery in cancer management

Dhruv S. Gupta[a], Vaishnavi Gadi[a], and Maushmi S. Kumar[b]
[a]Shobhaben Pratapbhai Patel School of Pharmacy & Technology Management, SVKM's NMIMS, Mumbai, India
[b]Somaiya Institute of Research and Consultancy, Somaiya Vidyavihar University, Vidya Vihar East, Mumbai, Maharashtra, India

1. Introduction

Cancer is a leading cause of mortality across the world, especially in low and middle-income countries, due to a marked increase in lifestyle related risk factors. The most common types of cancer include lung cancer in males, and breast cancer in females (Torre et al., 2016). With a greater number of affected individuals, there has been a steady rise in the extent of care to be provided, greater costs of treatment and an ever-increasing burden on the healthcare system. Conventional approaches for cancer management pose a number of drawbacks, including adverse effects, a high rate of recurrence and the possibility of developing resistance. With the recent advancement in discovering alternative strategies, organisms of marine origin offering numerous bioactive properties have emerged as a promising line of treatment (Zuo and Kwok, 2021). This has led to an increase in the discovery of novel anticancer compounds, and attention has been directed to employing compounds of natural origin for the amelioration and management of the disease.

Microalgae are one of the longest surviving microorganisms, and have been seen to grow across various environmental conditions, owing to the protective effects of the secondary metabolites that they generate. These bioactive compounds have been isolated and employed in various conditions, such as neurodegenerative ailments, cancer, and lifestyle disorders (Saeed et al., 2021). Extensive research has found carotenoids, polyunsaturated fatty acids, vitamins, proteins, and polypeptides to be the major compounds synthesized by these microorganisms. The two most widely produced carotenoids, β-carotene and astaxanthin, have gained clinical interest owing to their antiinflammatory, antitumor, and potent antioxidant properties (Ahmed, 2018). Relevant data obtained from in vitro and in vivo studies has indicated their potential in arresting tumor progression, primarily by inducing apoptosis and cytotoxicity. With the recent advances in research, microalgae-based nanoparticles have been formulated as novel drug delivery

Biomarkers in Cancer Detection and Monitoring of Therapeutics
https://doi.org/10.1016/B978-0-323-95114-2.00021-2

systems, to facilitate targeted drug delivery. The benefits offered include relatively low toxicity, enhancement of surface area and biodegradability of these formulations, offering a significant edge over traditional drug delivery systems (Khavari et al., 2021).

Microalgae can be considered as aquatic photosynthetic microorganisms utilized primarily for their numerous bioactive compounds (Pereira et al., 2020). They are capable of producing numerous advantageous substances such as cosmeceuticals, biodiesel feedstock, nutritional supplements, human food, and animal feed. Their size ranges from a few micrometers to a few hundreds of micrometers (Gügi et al., 2015). It has been said that the existing species are about 2×10^5 to 8×10^5 in number (Venkatesan et al., 2015). Microalgae of many evolutionary sources are generally found in fresh water bodies like rivers and lakes, and saltwater bodies like oceans, providing greater than 45% of primary production in the whole world (Lin and Lin, 2019).

Microalgae have recently gained notable interest globally, mainly because of their substantial application in the renewable energy, biopharmaceuticals, and nutraceutical industries. They are a renewable, economical, and sustainable source of biofuels, medicinal substances, as well as food products (Khan et al., 2018). Some unicellular microalgae, such as *Porphyridium*, *Rhodella*, and cyanobacteria, such as *Arthrospira*, are capable of producing sulfated polysaccharides, which acts as potential antiviral and anticancer agents (De Jesus Raposo et al., 2013). Although a greater number of studies are required to fully understand the mechanisms of antitumor effects of algae, studies conducted on *Chaetoceros calcitrans* and *Chlorella sorokiniana* have demonstrated interesting properties as compared to other commercially available marine anticancer drugs (Ebrahimi Nigjeh et al., 2013). Fucoxanthin, a widely explored bioactive component found in various species of microalgae, has been seen to exhibit antioxidant, antiinflammatory, antitumorigenic, antiobesity, antidiabetic, and cardioprotective effects (Zhang et al., 2015). Silica-based nanoparticles loaded with microalgae and diatoms are used as drug delivery carriers due to their biodegradable nature, simple functioning, low cost, and beneficial properties compared to synthetics, which prepare these agents to be great alternatives for synthetic silica nanoparticles. Fig. 1 encapsulates the structures of major therapeutically beneficial microalgal bioactive. Thus, diatom-based nanoparticles are a feasible choice for the delivery of anticancer agents and for lowering the side-effects of cancer chemotherapy (Khavari et al., 2021). Currently, the anticancer capacity and properties of microalgal carotenoids, microalgal PUFAs, microalgal peptides and microalgal polysaccharides are being extensively studied (Abd El-Hack et al., 2019). Table 1 highlights the sources and therapeutic indications of the major bioactives obtained from microalgae.

The aim of this chapter is to highlight the key pharmacological benefits of these compounds of natural origin, with special reference to lung and breast cancer. In addition to this, the scope of the chapter includes the major limitations to microalgal delivery, formulation-based considerations and methodologies to overcome these barriers, as well as the challenges and future perspectives to be considered.

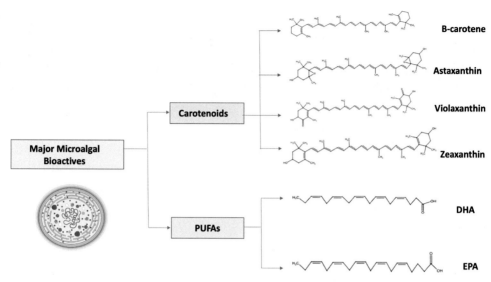

Fig. 1 Classification and structures of some clinically significant microalgal bioactives.

2. Sources and distribution of microalgae

Based on the data obtained from sampling of waters across different marine locations, it was observed that *Chlorophyta* have a significant contribution to the overall microalgal population, with *Mamiellophyceae* making up most of the share of this class. The greatest distribution of this subtype was observed in European coastal waters, while *Pyramimonadales*, ranking second in terms of distribution, were most widespread in Mediterranean waters and North American coastal regions. Other components of the *Chlorophyta* ecosystem, such as *Ulvophyceae*, *Trebouxiophyceae*, and *Chlorodendrophyceae*, were also observed to be highly concentrated in coastal waters across the North Atlantic, North American, and Mediterranean coastline (Tragin and Vaulot, 2018). A study conducted in the Arctic seas revealed the presence of *Mamiellophyceae* and their diversity as tropical microorganisms, represented across 16 algal phylotypes, as determined by high-throughput screening (Belevich et al., 2021).

Research undertaken in the Arctic waters has revealed the elemental composition of microalgae to a great extent, indicating the mineral requirements of these microorganisms, which influences their distribution and higher concentration in areas rich in these nutritional elements (Lobus et al., 2021).

Exploration of coral reefs in the Pacific Ocean has indicated a high concentration of unicellular microalgae belonging to the family *Symbiodiniaceae*, displaying photo

Table 1 Sources and classification of the major bioactives obtained from microalgae.

Class of compounds	Name of the compound	Major microbial source	Therapeutic indications	References
Carotenoids	β-Carotene	*Dunaliella salina*	Antioxidant action, immunomodulatory effects, reduced lipid peroxidation	Guedes et al. (2011)
	Astaxanthin	*Haematococcus pluvialis*	Super antioxidant molecule, reduction of oxidative stress, suppression of reactive oxygen species (ROS) production	Kumar et al. (2021)
	Violaxanthin	*Chlorella ellipsoidea*	Antiinflammatory properties, marked inhibition of nitric acid and prostaglandins	Soontornchaiboon et al. (2012)
	Zeaxanthin	*Dunaliella tertiolecta, D. salina, Chloroidium saccharophilum*	Antiinflammatory effects, arresting of ROS formation, thereby reducing oxidative stress	Ávila-Román et al. (2021)
Polyunsaturated fatty acids (PUFAs)	DHA	*Schizochytrium*	Slowing of cancer progression, enhanced efficacy of chemotherapy, suppression of inflammatory markers and oncogene expression	Doughman et al. (2007)
	EPA	*Schizochytrium* sp., *Cryptocodinium* sp., *Thraustochytrium* sp.	Antiinflammatory effects, marked lowering of IL-6, TNF-α and NF-κB levels	Lenihan-Geels et al. (2013)

symbiosis and engaging in coevolution and a variety of plant-animal interactions. *Zoo-xanthellae* form the largest share of endosymbiotic microalgae belonging to this family (Planes et al., 2019).

In a separate study conducted to assess the antimicrobial properties of bioactives of microalgal origin from the European coast, it was observed that extracts obtained from these microorganisms, chiefly belonging to the families *Chlorophyta* and *Cyanobacteria*, were helpful in exerting a biofilm inhibitory effect and were present in a significant concentration in the marine samples obtained (Cepas et al., 2019).

However, the population of microalgae across different geographies remains scattered, owing to a lowered rate of gene flow and a lack of oceanographic connectivity across different colonies (Sefbom et al., 2018).

3. Molecular pathways of microalgae in cancer management

Bioactive compounds present in various marine microalgae show antiproliferative, radical scavenging, and antimetastatic properties which forms the underlying mechanism of their anticancer activity. Some purified peptides have shown cytotoxic effect on numerous human tumor cell lines like MCF-7, HepG2, and A549 (Kang and Kim, 2013). The anticancer properties can be attributed to their ability of apoptosis induction and cell death by caspase independent or dependent pathways (Abd El-Hack et al., 2019). Table 2 offers an overview of different types of microalgae, with their applications in cancer management. Fucoxanthin shows anticancer action in various types of cancers due to its antioxidant and antiinflammatory properties (Galasso et al., 2019). Its anticancer effects can also be a result of its powerful beta-glucuronidase inhibitory action (Méresse et al., 2020). Microalgae such as *Dunaliella* and *Chlorella* are a vital of source of carotenoids which are being studies extensively for their antiproliferative properties, owing to their antiinflammatory and antioxidant action. Microalgae such as *Euglena tuba* induce intracellular reactive oxygen species and prevent the trigger on ERK1/2 and JNK pathways (Panja et al., 2016). Their anticancer effects are linked to the trigger of intrinsic apoptosis because of downregulation of key regulatory kinases. The antiangiogenetic, antiproliferative, and antiinvasive actions are associated with and lowered by of endothelial growth factors and of matrix metalloproteinases (Le Goff et al., 2019). To better analyze the prospects of microalgae as potential anticancer compounds, we have summarized the results of studies conducted on antitumor properties of certain species of microalgae on breast and lung carcinoma, along with their mechanism of action, in Table 3.

Table 2 The applications of different types of microalgae in cancer management.

S. no.	Microalgae	Bioactive compound	Applications	References
1.	*Dunaliella tertiolecta*	Violaxanthin	Breast adenocarcinoma (MCF-7)	Pasquet et al. (2011)
2.	*Phaeodactylum tricornutum*	Nonyl-8-acetoxy-6-methyloctanoate	Promyelocytic leukemia (HL-60), lung carcinoma, mouse melanoma	Samarakoon et al. (2014)
3.	Dinoflagellate *Gymnodinium* sp.	Polysaccharide GA3P, D-galactan sulfate linked with L-(+)-lactic acid	Notable cytotoxicity against various types of cancer cells	Umemura et al. (2003)
4.	*Synedra acus*	Chrysolaminaran polysaccharide	Colon adenocarcinoma	Gügi et al. (2015)
5.	*Chaetoseros* sp., *P. tricornutum*, *Cylinrotheca closterium*	Fucoxanthin (carotenoid)	Promyelocytic leukemia (HL-60), colon adenocarcinoma, DLD-1, and prostate cancer	Peng et al. (2011)
6.	*Cocconeis scutellum*	Eicosapentaenoic acid	Breast carcinoma (BT20)	Nappo et al. (2012)
7.	*Navicula incerta*	Stigmasterol (phytosterol)	Liver hepatocellular carcinoma (HepG2)	Kim et al. (2014)

4. Nanotechnology to overcome the limitations of microalgal delivery

While microalgae offer a host of useful bioactives, each possessing valuable pharmacological properties, a major drawback of harnessing natural compounds include poor chemical stability and aqueous solubility. This, in turn, is associated with reduced bioavailability in living systems (Yu et al., 2015). In addition to this, these compounds of natural origin require thermochemical treatments, for their isolation and formulation. This poses another challenge, as most microalgal derivatives are thermally unstable and highly susceptible to oxidation (Zanoni et al., 2019). Carotenoids, being lipophilic in nature, possess a poor aqueous solubility profile. This limits their applications in conventional drug delivery systems, raising the need for using novel drug delivery systems and solubility enhancers to facilitate transport across biological membranes (Slonimskiy et al., 2022).

In addition to improving the physical and chemical stability of these agents, there is a need to develop drug delivery systems to improve their organoleptic characteristics. This need is felt most significantly in the case of docosahexaenoic acid (DHA), which has low patient compliance owing to its liquid state of occurrence and a foul odor. Besides, it offers stability and bioavailability challenges as well (Singh et al., 2018).

Table 3 Microalgae bioactive compounds with activity against cancer cells.

Microalgae	Bioactive compound	Lung cancer cell	Molecular mechanism	Observations	References
Dunaliella salina	β-Carotene	A549	Induction of apoptosis, cell cycle arrest	25 μg/mL of EDS significantly lowered A549 cell proliferation by 25.2% ($P<.05$)	Sheu et al. (2008)
Chlorella vulgaris	Flavonoids	H1437, H1299, A549	Inhibition of metastasis, ROS scavenging	The extract (13.40 mg gallic acid/g lyophilized extract) derived from SC-CO_2 showed dual inhibitions to lung cancer cell growth as well as migration (metastasis)	Wang et al. (2010)
Euglena tuba	Phenolics, flavonoids, tannins	A549	Induction of apoptosis and ROS, inhibition of JNK, ERK1/2, P38 mitogen-activated protein kinase pathways	Potent cytotoxicity seen as a reduction in A549 (IC50 92.14 μg/mL) tumor cell growth	Panja et al. (2016)
Chlorella zofingiensis	Lycopene	A549	Inhibition of cell proliferation, tumor invasion, angiogenesis	24 h of treatment with apo-10′-lycopenoic acid (3–10 mM), showed a dose-dependent decrease in endogenous ROS was. The antiproliferative action was mediated by the induced expression of a tumor suppressor gene—RARb receptor	Mein et al. (2008)
Spirulina platensis (SCF extract)	Phycocyanin	A549	Induction of apoptosis, necrosis	SCF showed high cytotoxicity with IC50 value of 26.82 μg/mL	Deniz et al. (2016)
Lyngbya sordida, *Lyngbya majuscule*	Aurilide, Alotmide A	H-460	Induction of apoptosis	Increased cytotoxicity against H-460 cells (IC50 2.6 nM)	Mondal et al. (2020)

Continued

Table 3 Microalgae bioactive compounds with activity against cancer cells—cont'd

Microalgae	Bioactive compound	Lung cancer cell	Molecular mechanism	Observations	References
Euglena tuba	Phenolics, flavonoids, tannins	A549 MCF-7	Induction of apoptosis and ROS, inhibition of JNK, ERK1/2, P38 mitogen-activated protein kinase pathways	Potent cytotoxic activity seen as reduction in the growth of MCF-7 tumor cells (IC50 50.27 μg/mL)	Panja et al. (2016)
Haematococcus pluvialis, *D. salina*	Carotenoids	MCF-7	Regulation of cell signaling, cell cycle progression, cell differentiation and apoptosis	Potent cytotoxic effects seen. 91.2% inhibition and LC50 45.3 μg/mL by the carotenoid fraction and 82.3% inhibition and LC50 62.1 μg/mL by the polar fraction	El-Baz et al. (2018)
Porphyridium cruentum	Sulfated polysaccharides (PcSPs)	MCF-7	Inhibition of cell growth, induction of apoptosis	Cytotoxic effects seen on human breast cancer cells. IC50 value 1089.63 μg/mL. Induction of IL-6 cytokines, majorly TNF-**α**	Casas-Arrojo et al. (2021)
Oscillatoria sancta	Polysaccharides	MCF-7	Induction of apoptosis, cell cycle arrest, free radical scavenging	High anticancer effect seen (IC50 = 15.1 ± 0.7 μg/mL)	Senousy et al. (2020)

Owing to the wide range of therapeutically beneficial compounds sourced from microalgae, various advancements in bioprocessing and formulation processes have been made to ensure that a steady supply of bioactives is achieved, using easily reproducible methods. This is to overcome the barrier posed by low aqueous solubility of these agents, leading to as little as 10% of these compounds being exploited clinically for their therapeutic activities. In addition to this, adoption of nanotechnology has assisted in improved and targeted delivery of these agents to cancer cells. Silver nanoparticles have been employed in conjunction with microalgae for the designing of anticancer formulations, and the efficacy of these is primarily attributed to the triggering of apoptosis of tumor cells, by the exertion of an inhibitory effect on various pathogenic pathways (Khalid, 2020). Encapsulation of microalgae is another strategy that has been adopted to enhance the therapeutic benefits offered by these microorganisms. Astaxanthin, sourced primarily from *Haematococcus pluvialis*, has been most widely exploited for the therapeutic effects offered by the carotenoid. Various nanotechnological systems, such as supercritical fluids, polymeric nanospheres, liposomes, nanostructured carriers (NSCs), and nanoemulsions have been designed as functional foods and pharmaceuticals. The key benefits offered by these formulations include an improved stability under different conditions, greater protection to the active constituents and an improved aqueous solubility, thereby improving the bioavailability of these compounds in biological systems. In addition to this, adopting these novel drug delivery approaches has shown an improvement in the cellular uptake of astaxanthin, leading to an enhanced antioxidant property, which entails an improved free-radical scavenging activity and an enhanced cytoprotective effect to healthy cells (Vieira et al., 2020).

A major advantage of nanoparticle based microalgal formulations is the possibility of usage of a wide variety of carrier materials, both inorganic and organic, as well as an ease of alteration of surface characteristics such as particle size and plasticity. With reference to the activity in biological systems, the usage of nano formulations help to overcome the sequestration of bioactives by the mononuclear phagocytic system (MPS), enhancing their permeability (Bajpai et al., 2018).

Various cyanobacteria, such as *Anabena*, *Calothrix*, and *Spirulina* sp., have been observed to inhibit tumor growth, showing high potency even at very small concentrations. On combining the bioactives from these microalgae with metals such as gold and silver, longer circulation levels of the active constituents are observed, alongside greater specificity, which reduces the possibility of adverse effects. With reference to imaging, green carbon nanotags of cyanobacteria origin have been seen to exhibit satisfactory solubility, and low systemic toxicity. In addition to this, the secondary metabolites produced have been seen to improve the therapeutic index of certain traditional chemotherapeutic medications by exerting a protective effect, thereby reducing organ toxicity and oxidative damage (Qamar et al., 2021).

An in vitro study conducted by Karakaş et al. to study the cytotoxic effects of micro-algae loaded nanoparticles, synthesized via electro spraying and emulsification methods, yielded promising effects on human colorectal cancer cell lines. In comparison with untreated algal extracts, these nano formulations exerted a greater activity and significant cytotoxic effects (Karakaş et al., 2019).

In order to provide an impetus to green chemistry and propel the usage of biodegradable materials, *Amphora subtropica* frustules loaded with chitosan have been utilized as a natural, biodegradable carrier for chemotherapeutic drugs, such as doxorubicin. Key advantages of this design include a greater degree of biocompatibility, a possibility of higher dose loading of the drug, lowered toxicity, and sustained delivery of the therapeutic agent (Sasirekha et al., 2019).

5. Challenges and future perspectives

Microalgae constitute vast varieties of bioactive compounds that are efficient in their crude as well as purified state and show antimicrobial, anticancer, and antioxidant properties. However, one of the most challenging aspects of utilizing these microalgae is the enhancement of microalgae growth rate and product synthesis (Khan et al., 2018). Many microalgal species contain carotenoids as their bioactive constituents and in spite of the notable research and development in this field and engineering algal carotenogenesis, many theories remain to be unexplained (Varela et al., 2015).

Microalgal metabolites have demonstrated promising potential for cancer treatment but there are numerous challenges linked with the formulation of these substances as drugs which require consideration (Mondal et al., 2020). Another challenge is the improper distribution of useful species across various oceans and its lack of accessibility of oceanographers and researchers. Till date, the easily accessible parts were explored and preferred (Fu et al., 2021). Another concern is that the development of a potent molecule needs various resources. There is still less data available on the toxicity studies of these marine bioactive components in normal cells which needs to be addressed (Ávila-Román et al., 2021).

Marine cyanobacteria and microalgae will surely find an enormous potential as anticancer drugs. However, further studies are needed to understand the primary and secondary targets and pathways responsible for the cytotoxicity of these compounds in cancerous cells (Khavari et al., 2021).

Genetic engineering and nanotechnology will play a crucial role in the future of microalgal drug delivery. Microalgae still remain untapped as there are more than 25,000 species out of which less than 20 are approved for use. With the advancement of sophisticated techniques, microalgal biotechnology will be able to meet the challenging demands of pharmaceutical industries in the coming years (Raja et al., 2008). Compounds like polyunsaturated aldehydes, fucoxanthin, stigmasterol may have potential as constituents of pharmaceutical or nutraceutical products or as new drugs in themselves (Martínez Andrade et al., 2018).

Various new biological and molecular studies focusing on such algal-derived anticancerous compounds along with its characterization are still required. Further extensive investigations, in vitro or in vivo, need to be carried out on the bioactive constituents of the various species of microalgae to understand and analyze their potential applications in treating a wide of the cancers (Abd El-Hack et al., 2019).

6. Conclusion

Microalgae and their metabolites contribute to a significant portion of therapeutically beneficial compounds of marine origin. Owing to the wide range of pharmacological actions offered, these agents have been utilized across various therapeutic areas, for disease management. The chapter highlighted the major observed effects of these compounds in the management of lung and breast cancer, along with the limitations and approaches for overcoming them. In addition to the formulation advancements underway, a greater number of preclinical and clinical trials would help to further our understanding of these organisms of natural origin, along with cultivating an understanding of their spectrum of action, adverse effects, if any, and possibilities for concurrent administration with chemotherapeutic and immunotherapeutic agents, widely used in the management of cancer.

Acknowledgment

We acknowledge the support from our institute SPPSPTM and SVKM's NMIMS, Mumbai.

References

Abd El-Hack, M.E., Abdelnour, S., Alagawany, M., Abdo, M., Sakr, M.A., Khafaga, A.F., Mahgoub, S.A., Elnesr, S.S., Gebriel, M.G., 2019. Microalgae in modern cancer therapy: current knowledge. Biomed. Pharmacother. 111 (December 2018), 42–50.

Ahmed, I., 2018. Microalgae as a source of high-value bioactive compounds. Front. Biosci. 10 (1), 197–216. https://doi.org/10.2741/s509.

Ávila-Román, J., García-Gil, S., Rodríguez-Luna, A., Motilva, V., Talero, E., 2021. Anti-inflammatory and anticancer effects of microalgal carotenoids. Mar. Drugs 19 (10), 1896–1897.

Bajpai, V., Shukla, S., Kang, S.-M., Hwang, S., Song, X., Huh, Y., Han, Y.-K., 2018. Developments of cyanobacteria for nano-marine drugs: relevance of nanoformulations in cancer therapies. Mar. Drugs 16 (6), 179.

Belevich, T.A., Milyutina, I.A., Abyzova, G.A., Troitsky, A.V., 2021. The pico-sized Mamiellophyceae and a novel Bathycoccus clade from the summer plankton of Russian Arctic seas and adjacent waters. FEMS Microbiol. Ecol. 97 (2), fiaa251.

Casas-Arrojo, V., Decara, J., de los Ángeles Arrojo-Agudo, M., Pérez-Manríquez, C., Abdala-Díaz, R., 2021. Immunomodulatory, antioxidant activity and cytotoxic effect of sulfated polysaccharides from Porphyridium Cruentum. (s.f.Gray) Nägeli. Biomol. Ther. 11 (4), 488.

Cepas, V., López, Y., Gabasa, Y., Martins, C.B., Ferreira, J.D., Correia, M.J., Santos, L.M.A., et al., 2019. Inhibition of bacterial and fungal biofilm formation by 675 extracts from microalgae and cyanobacteria. Antibiotics 8 (2), 77.

De Jesus Raposo, M.F., De Morais, R.M.S.C., De Morais, A.M.M.B., 2013. Health applications of bioactive compounds from marine microalgae. Life Sci. 93 (15), 479–486.

Deniz, I., Ozgun Ozen, M., Yesil-Celiktas, O., 2016. Supercritical fluid extraction of phycocyanin and investigation of cytotoxicity on human lung cancer cells. J. Supercrit. Fluids 108 (February), 13–18.

Doughman, S.D., Krupanidhi, S., Sanjeevi, C.B., 2007. Omega-3 fatty acids for nutrition and medicine: considering microalgae oil as a vegetarian source of EPA and DHA. Curr. Diabetes Rev. 3 (3), 198–203.

Ebrahimi Nigjeh, S., Md Yusoff, F., Alitheen, N.B.M., Rasoli, M., Keong, Y.S., Omar, A.R.B., 2013. Cytotoxic effect of ethanol extract of microalga, *Chaetoceros calcitrans*, and its mechanisms in inducing apoptosis in human breast cancer cell line. Biomed. Res. Int. 2013, 1–9.

El-Baz, F.K., Hussein, R.A., Mahmoud, K., Abdo, S.M., 2018. Cytotoxic activity of carotenoid rich fractions from *Haematococcus pluvialis* and Dunaliella Salina microalgae and the identification of the phytoconstituents using LC-DAD/ESI-MS. Phytother. Res. 32 (2), 298–304.

Fu, Z., Piumsomboon, A., Punnarak, P., Uttayarnmanee, P., Leaw, C.P., Lim, P.T., Wang, A., Haifeng, G., 2021. Diversity and distribution of harmful microalgae in the Gulf of Thailand assessed by DNA metabarcoding. Harmful Algae 106 (June), 102063.

Galasso, C., Gentile, A., Orefice, I., Ianora, A., Bruno, A., Noonan, D.M., Sansone, C., Albini, A., Brunet, C., 2019. Microalgal derivatives as potential nutraceutical and food supplements for human health: a focus on cancer prevention and interception. Nutrients 11 (6), 1226.

Guedes, A.C., Amaro, H.M., Xavier Malcata, F., 2011. Microalgae as sources of carotenoids. Mar. Drugs 9 (4), 625–644.

Gügi, B., Le Costaouec, T., Burel, C., Lerouge, P., Helbert, W., Bardor, M., 2015. Diatom-specific oligosaccharide and polysaccharide structures help to unravel biosynthetic capabilities in diatoms. Mar. Drugs 13 (9), 5993–6018.

Kang, K.-H., Kim, S.-K., 2013. Beneficial effect of peptides from microalgae on anticancer. Curr. Protein Pept. Sci. 14 (3), 212–217.

Karakaş, C.Y., Tekarslan Şahin, H., İnan, B., Özçimen, D., Erginer, Y.Ö., 2019. In vitro cytotoxic activity of microalgal extracts loaded nano–micro particles produced via electrospraying and microemulsion methods. Biotechnol. Prog. 35 (6), e2876.

Khalid, M., 2020. Nanotechnology and chemical engineering as a tool to bioprocess microalgae for its applications in therapeutics and bioresource management. Crit. Rev. Biotechnol. 40 (1), 46–63.

Khan, M.I., Shin, J.H., Kim, J.D., 2018. The promising future of microalgae: current status, challenges, and optimization of a sustainable and renewable industry for biofuels, feed, and other products. Microb. Cell Fact. 17 (1), 1–21.

Khavari, F., Saidijam, M., Taheri, M., Nouri, F., 2021. Microalgae: therapeutic potentials and applications. Mol. Biol. Rep. 48 (5), 4757–4765.

Kim, Y.S., Li, X.F., Kang, K.H., Ryu, B.M., Kim, S.K., 2014. Stigmasterol isolated from marine microalgae *Navicula incerta* induces apoptosis in human hepatoma HepG2 cells. BMB Rep. 47 (8), 433–438.

Kumar, S., Kumar, R., Diksha, Kumari, A., Panwar, A., 2021. Astaxanthin: a super antioxidant from microalgae and its therapeutic potential. J. Basic Microbiol. https://doi.org/10.1002/jobm.202100391. November.

Le Goff, M., Le Ferrec, E., Mayer, C., Mimouni, V., Lagadic-Gossmann, D., Schoefs, B., Ulmann, L., 2019. Microalgal carotenoids and phytosterols regulate biochemical mechanisms involved in human health and disease prevention. Biochimie 167 (December), 106–118.

Lenihan-Geels, G., Bishop, K., Ferguson, L., 2013. Alternative sources of Omega-3 fats: can we find a sustainable substitute for fish? Nutrients 5 (4), 1301.

Lin, H.Y., Lin, H.J., 2019. Polyamines in microalgae: something borrowed, something new. Mar. Drugs 17 (1).

Lobus, N.V., Kulikovskiy, M.S., Maltsev, Y.I., 2021. Multi-element composition of diatom *Chaetoceros* spp. from natural phytoplankton assemblages of the Russian Arctic seas. Biology 10 (10), 1009.

Martínez Andrade, K.A., Lauritano, C., Romano, G., Ianora, A., 2018. Marine microalgae with anti-cancer properties. Mar. Drugs 16 (5), 165.

Mein, J.R., Lian, F., Dong Wang, X., 2008. Biological activity of lycopene metabolites: implications for cancer prevention. Nutr. Rev. 66 (12), 667–683.

Méresse, S., Fodil, M., Fleury, F., Chénais, B., 2020. Fucoxanthin, a marine-derived carotenoid from brown seaweeds and microalgae: a promising bioactive compound for cancer therapy. Int. J. Mol. Sci. 21 (23), 9273.

Mondal, A., Bose, S., Banerjee, S., Kumar Patra, J., George Kerry, R., Fimognari, C., Bishayee, A., 2020. Marine cyanobacteria and microalgae metabolites—a rich source of potential' anticancer drugs. Mar. Drugs 18, 476.

Nappo, M., Berkov, S., Massucco, C., Di Maria, V., Bastida, J., Codina, C., Avila, C., Messina, P., Zupo, V., Zupo, S., 2012. Apoptotic activity of the marine diatom *Cocconeis scutellum* and eicosapentaenoic acid in BT20 cells. Pharm. Biol. 50 (4), 529–535.

Panja, S., Ghate, N.B., Mandal, N., 2016. A microalga, *Euglena tuba* induces apoptosis and suppresses metastasis in human lung and breast carcinoma cells through ROS-mediated regulation of MAPKs. Cancer Cell Int. 16, 51.

Pasquet, V., Morisset, P., Ihammouine, S., Chepied, A., Aumailley, L., Berard, J.-B., Serive, B., et al., 2011. Antiproliferative activity of violaxanthin isolated from bioguided fractionation of *Dunaliella tertiolecta* extracts. Mar. Drugs 9 (5), 819–831.

Peng, J., Yuan, J.P., Wu, C.F., Wang, J.H., 2011. Fucoxanthin, a marine carotenoid present in brown seaweeds and diatoms: metabolism and bioactivities relevant to human health. Mar. Drugs 9 (10), 1806–1828.

Pereira, A.G., Jimenez-Lopez, C., Fraga, M., Lourenço-Lopes, C., García-Oliveira, P., Lorenzo, J.M., Perez-Lamela, C., Prieto, M.A., Simal-Gandara, J., 2020. Extraction, properties, and applications of bioactive compounds obtained from microalgae. Curr. Pharm. Des. 26 (16), 1929–1950.

Planes, S., Allemand, D., Agostini, S., Banaigs, B., Boissin, E., Boss, E., Bourdin, G., et al., 2019. The Tara Pacific expedition—a pan-ecosystemic approach of the "-omics" complexity of coral reef holobionts across the Pacific Ocean. PLoS Biol. 17 (9), e3000483.

Qamar, H., Hussain, K., Soni, A., Khan, A., Hussain, T., Chénais, B., 2021. Cyanobacteria as natural therapeutics and pharmaceutical potential: role in antitumor activity and as nanovectors. Molecules 26 (1), 247.

Raja, R., Hemaiswarya, S., Ashok Kumar, N., Sridhar, S., Rengasamy, R., 2008. A perspective on the biotechnological potential of microalgae. Crit. Rev. Microbiol. 34 (2), 77–88.

Saeed, M.U., Hussain, N., Shahbaz, A., Hameed, T., Iqbal, H.M.N., Bilal, M., 2021. Bioprospecting microalgae and cyanobacteria for biopharmaceutical applications. J. Basic Microbiol. https://doi.org/10.1002/jobm.202100445 (December).

Samarakoon, K.W., Ko, J.Y., Lee, J.H., Nam Kwon, O., Kim, S.W., Jin Jeon, Y., 2014. Apoptotic anticancer activity of a novel fatty alcohol ester isolated from cultured marine diatom, *Phaeodactylum tricornutum*. J. Funct. Foods 6 (1), 231–240.

Sasirekha, R., Salammal Sheena, T., Sathiya Deepika, M., Santhanam, P., Townley, H.E., Jeganathan, K., Dinesh Kumar, S., Premkumar, K., 2019. Surface engineered *Amphora subtropica* frustules using chitosan as a drug delivery platform for anticancer therapy. Mater. Sci. Eng. C 94 (January), 56–64.

Sefbom, J., Kremp, A., Rengefors, K., Jonsson, P.R., Sjöqvist, C., Godhe, A., 2018. A planktonic diatom displays genetic structure over small spatial scales: small-scale population genetic patterns in a marine diatom. Environ. Microbiol. 20 (8), 2783–2795.

Senousy, H.H., Abd Ellatif, S., Ali, S., 2020. Assessment of the antioxidant and anticancer potential of different isolated strains of cyanobacteria and microalgae from soil and agriculture drain water. Environ. Sci. Pollut. Res. 27 (15), 18463–18474.

Sheu, M.-J., Huang, G.-J., Wu, C.-H., Chen, J.-S., Chang, H.-Y., Chang, S.-J., Chung, J.-G., 2008. Ethanol extract of *Dunaliella salina* induces cell cycle arrest and apoptosis in A549 human non-small cell lung cancer cells. In Vivo 22 (3), 369–378.

Singh, H., Kumar, C., Singh, N., Paul, S., Kumar Jain, S., 2018. Nanoencapsulation of docosahexaenoic acid (DHA) using a combination of food grade polymeric wall materials and its application for improvement in bioavailability and oxidative stability. Food Funct. 9 (4), 2213–2227.

Slonimskiy, Y.B., Egorkin, N.A., Friedrich, T., Maksimov, E.G., Sluchanko, N.N., 2022. Microalgal protein AstaP is a potent carotenoid solubilizer and delivery module with a broad carotenoid binding repertoire. FEBS J. 289 (4), 999–1022.

Soontornchaiboon, W., Soo Joo, S., Moo Kim, S., 2012. Anti-inflammatory effects of violaxanthin isolated from microalga *Chlorella ellipsoidea* in RAW 264.7 macrophages. Biol. Pharm. Bull. 35 (7), 1137–1144.

Torre, L.A., Siegel, R.L., Ward, E.M., Jemal, A., 2016. Global cancer incidence and mortality rates and trends—an update. Cancer Epidemiol. Biomarkers Prev. 25 (1), 16–27.

Tragin, M., Vaulot, D., 2018. Green microalgae in marine coastal waters: the ocean sampling day (OSD) dataset. Sci. Rep. 8 (1), 14020.

Umemura, K., Yanase, K., Suzuki, M., Okutani, K., Yamori, T., Andoh, T., 2003. Inhibition of DNA topoisomerases I and II, and growth inhibition of human cancer cell lines by a marine microalgal polysaccharide. Biochem. Pharmacol. 66 (3), 481–487.

Varela, J.C., Pereira, H., Vila, M., León, R., 2015. Production of carotenoids by microalgae: achievements and challenges. Photosynth. Res. 125 (3), 423–436.

Venkatesan, J., Manivasagan, P., Kim, S.K., 2015. Marine Microalgae Biotechnology: Present Trends and Future Advances. Present Trends and Future Advances. Handbook of Marine Microalgae: Biotechnology Advances. Elsevier Inc.

Vieira, M.V., Pastrana, L.M., Fuciños, P., 2020. Microalgae encapsulation systems for food, pharmaceutical and cosmetics applications. Mar. Drugs 18 (12), 644.

Wang, H.M., Pan, J.L., Chen, C.Y., Chiu, C.C., Yang, M.H., Wei Chang, H., Chang, J.S., 2010. Identification of anti-lung cancer extract from *Chlorella vulgaris* C-C by antioxidant property using supercritical carbon dioxide extraction. Process Biochem. 45 (12), 1865–1872.

Yu, Y., Wu, Y.-H., Zhu, S.-F., Hu, H.-Y., 2015. The bioavailability of the soluble algal products of different microalgal strains and its influence on microalgal growth in unsterilized domestic secondary effluent. Bioresour. Technol. 180 (March), 352–355.

Zanoni, F., Vakarelova, M., Zoccatelli, G., 2019. Development and characterization of astaxanthin-containing whey protein-based nanoparticles. Mar. Drugs 17 (11), 627.

Zhang, H., Tang, Y., Zhang, Y., Zhang, S., Qu, J., Wang, X., Kong, R., Han, C., Liu, Z., 2015. Fucoxanthin: a promising medicinal and nutritional ingredient. Evid. Based Complement. Alternat. Med. 2015, 723515.

Zuo, W., Kwok, H.F., 2021. Development of marine-derived compounds for cancer therapy. Mar. Drugs 19 (6), 342.

CHAPTER TWENTY-FOUR

Prospects of mangrove-derived phytochemicals in cancer research

Sayantani Mitra[a], Nabanita Naskar[b], Arijit Reeves[a], and Punarbasu Chaudhuri[a]
[a]Department of Environmental Science, University of Calcutta, Kolkata, India
[b]Department of Botany, Diamond Harbour Women's University, Kolkata, India

Abbreviations

A2780	ovarian cancer cell line
A549	adenocarcinomic human alveolar basal epithelial cell line
AchE	acetylcholinesterase
AGS	adenocarcinoma gastric cell line
AKT1	protein kinase B
B16F10	murine melanoma cell line
BAX	Bcl-2–associated X factor
BCG-823	human gastric cancer cell line
BEL-7402	human hepatocellular carcinoma cell line
CaCo 2	cancer coli 2 cell (human colon cancer cell line)
DNA	deoxyribonucleic acid
DU145	human prostate cancer cell line
EAC	Ehrlich–Lettre ascites carcinoma
EGFR	epidermal growth factor receptor
FDA	Food and Drug Administration
FITC	fluorescein isothiocyanate
HCT-116	human colon carcinoma cell line
HDAC	histone deacetylases
HEK-293	human embryonic kidney cell line
HeLa	Henrietta lacks
HepG2	human liver cancer cell line
HL-60	human leukemic cell line
IC-50	concentration of a drug that is required for 50% inhibition in vitro
KB	human epithelial carcinoma cells
KT	cytotoxic T cell
LXFA 629 L	lung adenocarcinoma cell line
mAb	monoclonal antibody
MCF-7	Michigan Cancer Foundation-7
MDA-MB-231	breast adenocarcinoma cell line
MRI	magnetic resonance imaging

Biomarkers in Cancer Detection and Monitoring of Therapeutics
https://doi.org/10.1016/B978-0-323-95114-2.00020-0

mTOR	mammalian target of rapamycin
MTT	microculture tetrazolium assay
OAW-42	ovarian serous cystadenocarcinoma
OVCAR3	human ovarian carcinoma cell line
p21	protein 21
P388	murine leukemic cell line
p53	protein 53
PA-1	human ovarian teratocarcinoma cell line
PANC-1	human pancreatic cancer cell line
PET	positron emission tomography
PI3K	phosphoinositide 3-kinases
RT-PCR	reverse transcriptase polymerase chain reaction
SAOS-2	osteosarcoma cell line
SKLU-1	lung adenocarcinoma cell line
SMMC7721	human hepatocarcinoma cell line
SPECT	single-photon emission computed tomography
TS	thymidylate synthase
WHO	World Health Organization
WiDr	colon adenocarcinoma cell line

1. Introduction

Cancer is regarded as the second largest cause of mortality worldwide making it a global health issue of concern. As per an estimate made in 2018, over 17 million new cancer cases had been diagnosed and over half of them were fatal (Rajabi et al., 2021). Reports show that rise in new cases would be up to 27.5 million by the end of 2040 (Ashraf, 2020). The widely accepted theory of carcinogenesis holds that cancer is caused by a series of oncogene and tumor suppressor gene mutations (Hahn and Weinberg, 2002; Heng et al., 2010), which relies on the somatic mutation theory and cell-based gene mutations. According to Hanahan and Weinberg (2000), the six "cancer hallmarks" includes uncontrolled proliferation, refractoriness to proliferation blockers, escaping apoptosis, unlimited proliferation, enhanced angiogenesis, and metastatic spread. According to the World Health Organization (WHO), each year, cancer kills approximately 8.8 million people globally. It is caused by dynamic anomalies in the genome of malignancy cells that modify the expressions of proteins involved in targeting tumor suppressor proteins, growth factors, and transcription factors during cell division. These genetic changes transform normal cells into proliferative malignant cells that can evade apoptosis, avoid detection by immunity, etc. (Cavallo et al., 2011; Akhtar and Swamy, 2018). The variability of the disease at tissue level is a big barrier for its particular diagnosis followed by therapeutic efficacy (Meacham and Morrison, 2013). The most prevalent forms of cancer in men occur in prostate, lungs and bronchus, colon and rectum, urinary bladder whereas in women, majority cases reported are of breast, lung and bronchus, colon and rectum, uterine corpus and thyroid (Siegel et al., 2016; Hassanpour and Dehghani, 2017). Blood cancer, as well as malignancies of the brain and lymph nodes, account for the highest percentage of cancer cases among children (Schottenfeld and Fraumeni Jr., 2006).

Leading causes of cancer mortality, accounting for more than one-third of all cancer deaths globally are obesity, low fruit and vegetable intake, physical inactivity, tobacco, and alcohol consumption. Tobacco smoking alone accounts for nearly 22% of cancer deaths worldwide (Akhtar and Swamy, 2018). Chemical compounds are well known for their function in the formation of gene mutations and cancer cells. Surprisingly, carcinogenic chemicals in the environment affect the cytoplasm and nucleus of cells directly or indirectly, resulting in genetic diseases and gene alterations (Poon et al., 2014; Trafialek and Kolanowski, 2014; Antwi et al., 2015). Other carcinogenic factors include viruses, bacteria and radiation rays that comprise of 7% of all cancers. Cancer, in general, alters cellular relationships and causes vital genes to malfunction. This disruption affects the cell cycle, resulting in aberrant proliferation (Seto et al., 2010). Under normal circumstances, proto-oncogenes are responsible for cell division and proliferation, but when they mutate into oncogenes, they become detrimental for cell survival (Shtivelman et al., 1985). Furthermore, the absence of tumor suppressor genes leads to unregulated cell division (Matlashewski et al., 1984).

Despite considerable advancements in therapeutic and diagnostic approaches, cancer therapy remains challenging. The major roadblocks toward successful treatment of cancer are cancer heterogeneity, tumor hypoxia, and drug resistance (Jaymand et al., 2021). Surgery, radiation therapy, and/or systemic therapies such as chemotherapy, hormone therapy, neoadjuvant therapy, immune therapy, gene therapy, and targeted therapy are currently used to treat various types of cancer (Kerry et al., 2018). Depending on the cancer kind and stage, tumor features, and the patient's age, health, and preferences, the above-mentioned treatments may be administered alone or in combination. Radiation therapy is a viable therapeutic option that is frequently used in conjunction with other cancer treatments including surgery and chemotherapy. Ionizing radiation is used to treat tumors and cancer cells, which destroys their DNA and inhibits further development and proliferation. Radioisotopes have been shown to be effective in the treatment of diseases such as bone metastases, thyroid cancer, liver cancer, brain cancer, neuroblastoma, neuroendocrine tumors, nonlymphoma, Hodgkin's, and bile duct cancer (Orsini et al., 2019; Guidoccio et al., 2017). On the other hand, radionuclide imaging is a noninvasive technique that enables spatial and temporal recording of molecular, subcellular, and cellular processes, as well as imaging of organs and tissue functions. Cancer immunotherapy is the most appealing option to all standard therapies due to improved understanding of the immune system and the discovery of cancer vaccines. A single booster vaccine shot can prevent and eradicate cancer with minimal invasiveness. The most common substances utilized as vaccines in cancer immunotherapy are whole cell lysate, DNA, monoclonal antibody (mAb), or any peptide sequence that can either prevent or eliminate cancer (Lollini et al., 2015). Cancer vaccines are categorized into two types based on their action as preventive and therapeutic vaccine (Lollini et al., 2006). The concept of minimally invasive surgery combined with advanced imaging and diagnostic technology to reduce surgical risks and problems has given rise to a new era of robotic-assisted surgery with enhanced efficacy (Kumar, 2018).

The field of cancer gene therapy is rapidly expanding. Gene therapy is the injection of genetic sequences into the cancer site in order to induce knockdown of a target gene, resulting in tumor shrinkage. Three major types of gene therapy used in current scenario are gene replacement therapy, suicidal gene therapy or prodrug activation therapy and immunomodulatory gene therapy (Kumar, 2018). Another advancement in gene therapy is epigenome therapy. Since epigenetic regulation is reversible, interest in epigenetic-based therapy has surged. DNA methylation and histone modification are two of the most well-studied epigenetic modifications (Jones, 2014). Epigenetics is the study of the inheritable changes in gene expression that occur during cell division but are not caused by changes in gene sequence. Demethylating agents and histone acetylase (HDAC) inhibitors have been licensed by FDA for the treatment of lymphomas (Chahin et al., 2013). Apart from all these therapies discussed, chemotherapy is the most widely used form of medication, which works by interfering with the mechanisms that occur during cell division. The therapeutic potential of the chemotherapeutic drugs arises from their capacity to kill a higher proportion of cancer cells than normal cells (Caley and Jones, 2012). However, better understanding of tumor biology, pharmacology, and resistance patterns is required for effective chemotherapy.

Despite of the effectiveness of all the methods discussed above, they all have substantial flaws, such as low efficiency, nonspecificity, significant side effects, toxicity to healthy cells/tissues, unfavorable pharmacokinetics, poor absorption, etc. Even after the availability of several treatments, many tumors remain incurable, which could be due to delays in diagnosis, sophistication, high treatment costs, etc. The current cancer experimental therapy is very sophisticated, expensive and yields low-satisfactory results. Furthermore, even if FDA approves such therapies due to their serviceability, the exorbitant cost will make them virtually unattainable for ordinary people in low- and middle-income countries. As a consequence, current research is focused on evaluating simpler or greener cancer treatments, such as the utilization of natural products/herbal medicines (Yin et al., 2013). Nature serves as an infinite and inexhaustible natural resource, which may be developed into novel effective drugs, chemotypes, and pharmacophores (Veeresham, 2012). Approximately 54% of anticancer medications licensed between 1940 and 2002 were developed from natural compounds or drugs inspired by knowledge relating to natural products (Yuan et al., 2016). For example, the vinca alkaloids obtained from *Catharanthus roseus* and the terpene paclitaxel generated from *Taxus baccata* are both effective in cancer treatments (Newman et al., 2003; Li-Weber, 2009). Phytochemicals have been in the limelight of cancer research since its emergence, as they were among the first anticancer medications found to have significant effects. Some of the anticancer drugs obtained from natural products are leucovorin, carzinophilin, vincristine, actinomycin D, etc., which emerged in the early 20th century (Newman and Cragg, 2020). It is crucial to highlight that natural substance can be used as both chemotherapeutic agents and adjuvants in cancer treatment (Dehelean et al., 2021). Furthermore, because of their accessibility, recent research has shifted its focus toward identifying anticancer medicines from plants of terrestrial origin (Kerry et al., 2018).

Plants from the mangrove ecosystem are one such promising alternative, due to their rich content of phytochemicals and bioactive compounds, as well as their particular capability to grow in harsh environments and ethnobotanical relevance. Mangrove is a shrub or small tree that develops in muddy or rocky soils in coastal brackish or saline waters. Since mangroves are halophytes, or salt-tolerant plants, they can swiftly adapt to harsh coastal environments. Mangrove plants are rich in natural products and novel chemical compounds. Mangroves have received a great deal of scientific attention because of their powerful activity against a variety of ailments, including cardiovascular disease, diabetes, hypertension, and cancer (Nabeelah Bibi et al., 2019). Attempts have been undertaken in the past to employ in vitro and in vivo models to validate the traditional applications of numerous mangrove trees. This chapter aims to provide a comprehensive insight into the anticancer properties of the mangrove-derived phytochemicals, mangrove-associated microorganisms, in vitro studies on different cancer cell lines and a bibliometric analysis of the global distribution of research of anticancer activity related to mangrove species.

2. Mangrove's distribution and diversity

The diverse and prolific ecosystem of mangroves has always captured the attention of scientists worldwide and the study of this community continues to expand. This salt-tolerant ecosystem is found primarily in the tropical and subtropical intertidal areas around the world (Bandaranayake, 2002). Around 25% of the world's coastline is covered by mangroves, which are found in 112 countries and territories, encompassing ~181,000 km^2 (Spalding et al., 1997). According to Saranraj and Sujitha (2015), the current coverage of mangroves is around 159,041.5 km^2 distributed over 123 countries and territories. Figs. 1 and 2 depicts the global distribution of mangroves. They are among the world's most ecologically productive and diversified wetland ecosystems. They thrive on muddy substratum of varied depth and consistency, which is required for their growth in coastal areas and river estuaries. This coastal halophytic niche serves as a link between the freshwater and marine ecosystems (Chapman, 1976). Asian and African countries have the highest percentage of the world's mangrove ecosystem, followed by America

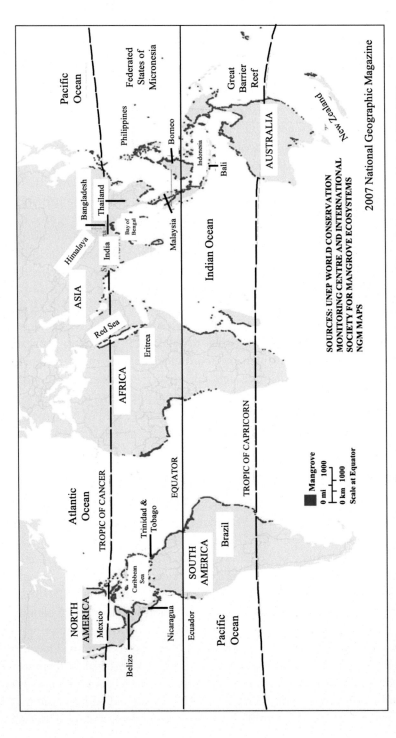

Fig. 1 Global distribution of mangroves (https://i0.wp.com/blog.education.nationalgeographic.org/wp-content/uploads/2014/12/mangrovemap. jpg?ssl=1).

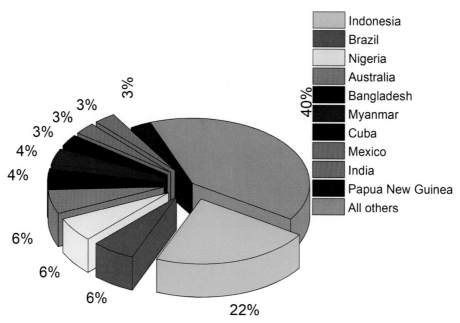

Fig. 2 Mangrove distribution (percentage) among the countries.

(South and Central). The Sundarbans of India and Bangladesh include the world's biggest contagious mangrove forests, covering more than 0.14% of the country's land area (Kathiresan, 2010). Mangroves can be found in West and Central Africa, East and South Africa, Australia and New Zealand, South Asia, North and Central America, South America, Southeast Asia, the Pacific Ocean, the Middle East, and East Asia (Spalding et al., 2010). In South and Southeast Asia, mangroves are found in Indonesia, Malaysia, Myanmar, Papua New Guinea, and Thailand. Fig. 1 depicts the global distribution of mangroves along the coast line. Mangroves distribution in percentage among the countries is shown in Fig. 2. There are 84 mangrove species worldwide, according to Wu et al. (2008), with 70 species being true mangroves and 14 species being semimangroves.

In India, mangrove patches can be found in nine states (West Bengal, Orissa, Andhra Pradesh, Tamil Nadu, Kerala, Karnataka, Goa, Maharashtra, and Gujarat) and four union territories along the Indian coastline (Daman and Diu, Puducherry, Lakshadweep, and Andaman and Nicobar Islands). About 58% of India's total mangroves are found along the eastern shore of the Bay of Bengal, and are known as deltaic mangroves.

Major mangrove species, minor mangrove species and mangrove associates are the three types of mangroves identified by Tomlinson (1986). The major mangrove species are strict or true mangroves, which are found exclusively in mangal (mangrove biome or forest). They play a significant role in community structure, have specialized morphology such as aerial roots and a special mechanism for gas exchange, physiological specialization for salt exclusion, have viviparous reproduction and are taxonomically distinct from terrestrial relatives (Tomlinson, 1986; Kathiresan and Bingham, 2001). True mangrove habitats are typically found in intertidal mangrove ecosystems with salinities ranging from 17.0 to 36.6. Avicenniaceae, Bombacaceae, Combretaceae, Maliaceae, Myrtaceae, Myrsinaceae, Pellicieraceae, Plumbaginaceae, Rhizophoraceae, Rubiaceae, and Sonneratiaceae are true mangrove genus. Semimangrove plants can be found in landward fringe mangrove habitat or terrestrial marginal zones that experience irregular high tides. Semi mangroves include genus such as Acanthaceae, Euphorbiaceae, Lythraceae, Palmae, and Sterculiaceae (Danda et al., 2017; Wu et al., 2008).

3. Bioactivities of mangroves

The enormous floral species of the mangrove environment have traditionally been exploited for medical purposes, since they comprise a valuable source of novel medication compounds, despite the fact that the chemistry and bioactivity of flora are yet unknown (Mitra et al., 2021). Plant-derived medicinal compounds have recently garnered considerable attention in the medical field for treating a variety of health problems and chronic diseases. Mangroves' ability to thrive in the intertidal zone generates different chemo-physiological mechanisms to live and reproduce due to their unique habitat. Secondary metabolites are synthesized via metabolic processes in plants, which could be exploited as therapeutic drugs in the future. Ethnomedicinal usage of mangrove plants are being practiced today, and extracts from mangrove species have been shown to have potent inhibitory effect against plant, animal, and human infections (Saranraj and Sujitha, 2015). Mangrove plants have been intensively researched for antibacterial compounds of pharmacological value, according to literature. Mangroves and mangrove associates have been found to contain metabolites from various chemical classes. Alkaloids, flavonoids, carbohydrates, carotenoids, aliphatic alcohols, amino acids, hydrocarbons, fatty acids, phenolic compounds, tannins, saponins, terpenes, and related compounds are among the metabolites studied (Bandaranayake, 2002).

According to Wu et al. (2008), 349 metabolites have been extracted from mangrove species, with 200 of them being found only in true mangrove plants. Chemicals from basic metabolism, such as amino acids, carbohydrates, and proteins are required for growth, whereas secondary metabolism products, such as alkaloids, flavonoids, phenolics, steroids, and terpenoids, have pharmacological, toxicological, and ecological significance (Bandaranayake, 2002). *Acanthus ilicifolius*, for example, is a rich source of long-chain alcohols, triterpenes and other compounds that are used to treat paralysis, asthma, and rheumatic pains, besides having analgesic and antiinflammatory properties. This plant yielded a novel alkaloid called "acanthicifolin" (Kokpol et al., 1984). Members of the Avicenniaceae, Rhizophoraceae and Sonneratiaceae families are said to be high in tannins

(Bandaranayake, 1995). Rhizophorin, an alkaloid found in *Rhizophora mucronata*, is abundant. *Acrosticum aureum* and *Rhizophora apiculata* have yielded some recognized terpenoids, steroids and a novel terpenoid ester. *Avicennia alba* is said to be a good source of naphthoquinones. *Bruguiera sexangula* bark extracts are found to be effective to both Sarcoma 180 and Lewis Lung Carcinoma (Loder and Russell, 1969). Brugin is another alkaloid isolated from *B. sexangula*. On marine creatures including phytoplanktons, the latex of *Excoecaria agallocha* has a biocidal impact (Reddy et al., 1991; Bandaranayake, 2002). Stigmasterol, a common plant steroid found primarily in *Acanthus ilicifolius*, has been demonstrated to have hypercholesterolemic properties (Kokpol et al., 1984, 1990; Peng and Long, 1994; Firdaus et al., 2013). 2-Benzoxazolin, which is widely utilized as a central nervous system depressant, was derived from this fungus-resistant species (Bandaranayake, 2002). Discussing general bioactivities of mangrove-derived phytochemicals is not the sole aim of this chapter but it may be perceived that compound isolated from mangroves are really important from human health perspective and requires further research to explore the chemical diversity of this ecosystem.

3.1 Anticancer potential of mangrove-derived phytochemicals

With the advancement of technology and growing concern of side effects from drugs of chemical origin, a search for novel metabolites from terrestrial and especially mangroves have gained a considerable attention in recent times. Mangroves are a unique source of secondary metabolites with anticancer properties, such as the tetranor triterpenoids (Xylogranatins A–D) isolated from *Xylocarpus granatum*, among which Xylogranatin B–D was moderately cytotoxic against P-388 murine leukemic cell line and Xylogranatin A-B were found to be cytotoxic against A-549 human lung carcinoma cell line (Yin et al., 2006; Das et al., 2015). In an in vitro cytotoxic experiment, Tian et al. (2009) found that 3′,4′,5,7-tetrahydroxy flavone extracted from *Sonneratia caseolaris* has considerable inhibitory effect against cell growth of SMMC-7721 human hepatoma cells. Patra et al. (2015) investigated the phytochemical profile of *Sonneratia apetala* as well as its anticancer effect in Swiss albino mice using the EAC cell line. In a mouse model, the methanol extract of the leaves exhibited a good response, inhibiting 34% growth of EAC cells. Polyisoprenoids derived from *Nypa fruticans*, according to Sari et al. (2018), have promising anticancer potential. In a mouse model, Prabhu and Guruvayoorappan (2012) tested the antiinflammatory and antitumor activities of a methanolic extract of *R. apiculata* against B16F10 melanoma cells. The presence of 4-pyrrolidinyl, pyrazole, and ketone derivatives in the methanolic extract suggests that they could be used as antiinflammatory and antitumor agents. *Avicennia marina* extracts are high in phenolic and flavonoid content, according to Huang et al. (2016), and can be used to trigger apoptosis in human breast and liver cancer cells. Patil et al. (2011) reported that *E. agallocha* stem extracts can cause cytotoxicity in pancreatic cell lines. *E. agallocha* leaf extracts were found to have anticancer action in another investigation by Batsa and Periyasamy (2013). In particular, an aversion to cancer bioactive chemicals found in *Acanthus ilicifolius* plant extract was proven to be efficient in preventing DNA changes, considerably inhibiting the proliferation of ascites tumor in mice and significantly improving the survival rate (Chakraborty et al., 2007). Khajure and Rathod (2011) used comet assay to evaluate the cytotoxic potential of the same plant's ethanolic acetate extract against KB and HeLa cell lines. They found the results to be quite promising, with cancer cells being inhibited to a greater extent. The alcoholic extract of this plant has cytotoxicity toward lung fibroblast (L-929) cells (Prabhu and Devaraj, 2016). Uddin et al. (2012) identified seven phytocompounds from a methanolic extract of the aerial portions of the mangrove fern *Acrostichum aureum*. Furthermore, a cytotoxicity analysis employing the FITC Annexin V apoptosis assay demonstrated that these biocompounds had the ability to cause toxicity in AGS gastric cancer cell lines by apoptosis and necrosis. As a result of their research, they were able to demonstrate the plant's traditional use in healing peptic ulcers as well as its potential as a source of biocompounds. Smitha et al. (2014) found that an ethyl acetate extract of the leaves and roots of the mangrove plant *Acanthus ilicifolius* had considerable cytotoxicity against two cancer cell lines, MCF-7 and PA-1. At a dosage of 100 g/mL, both leaf and root extracts inhibited MCF-7 and PA-1 cells the most. In Table 1, we have tried to list the anticancer compounds derived from different mangrove species. Figs. 3–11 depict the mangroves species found in Indian Sundarbans along with the anticancer compounds isolated from them. Our research group specializes in Indian Sundarbans, and the pictures provided in this chapter are taken by us during our field study.

Table 1 Anticancer compounds isolated from different mangroves.

Species	Compounds	References
Acanthus ilicifolius	4-Hydroxy-2-benzoxazolone	Boopathy et al. (2011), Khajure and Rathod (2011), and Das et al. (2015)
Avicennia officinalis	Triterpene, betulinic acid	Sumithra et al. (2011) and Das et al. (2015)
Avicennia marina	Naphthoquinones, avicequinones, stenocarpoquinone, iridoid glycosides	Khafagi et al. (2003), Karami et al. (2012), Sukhramani and Patel (2013), and Das et al. (2015)
Avicennia alba	Naphthoquinolines, avicequinones	Ito et al. (2000) and Das et al. (2015)
Bruguiera gymnorrhiza	Brugin	Bunyapraphatsara et al. (2003) and Das et al. (2015)
Bruguiera sexangula	Tropine, benzoic acid, brugin	Kathiresan et al. (2006), Govindasamy and Kannan (2012), and Das et al. (2015)

Table 1 Anticancer compounds isolated from different mangroves—cont'd

Species	Compounds	References
Ceriops decandra	Quinine	Govindasamy and Kannan (2012), Bandaranayake (1998), and Das et al. (2015)
Excoecaria agallocha	Diterpenes, tannins, excoecarin	Subhan et al. (2008a, b, c) and Das et al. (2015)
Heritieria fomes	Phenolic compounds	Patra and Thatoi (2013) and Das et al. (2015)
Cerbera odollam	2′-o-Acetyl cerleaside A, 17b–neriifolin, cerberin	Chan et al. (2016)
Cucumaria frondosa	Frondoside A	Dyshlovoy et al. (2017)
Xylocarpus granatum	Xylogranatins A, B, C, D, Granaxylocarpins A, B, Xylogranatumine A–F	Yin et al. (2006, 2007) and Zhou et al. (2014)

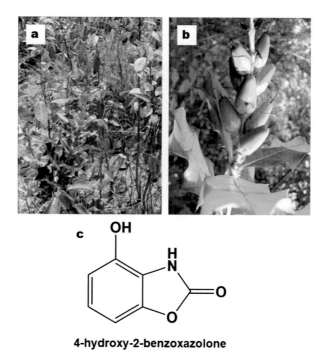

4-hydroxy-2-benzoxazolone

Fig. 3 (A) *Acanthus ilicifolius*—part of the plant, (B) propagule, and (C) 4-hydroxy-2-benzoxazolone (an alkaloid) extracted from *A. ilicifolius*.

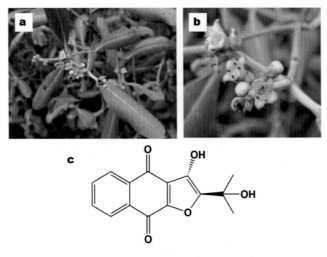

Avicequinone

Fig. 4 (A) *Avicennia alba*—part of the growing plant, (B) flower, and (C) Avicequinone (a naphthoquinone derivative) extracted from A. alba.

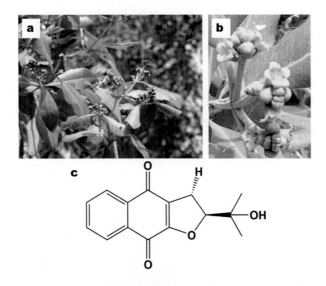

Stenocarpoquinone

Fig. 5 (A) *Avicennia marina*—part of the growing plant, (B) part of the flowering plant, and (C) Stenocarpoquinone (a naphthoquinone derivative) extracted from A. marina.

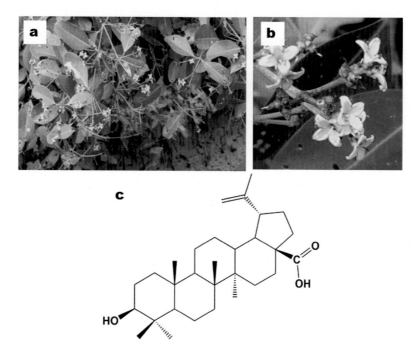

Betulinic acid

Fig. 6 (A) *Avicennia officinalis*—part of the flowering plant, (B) close-up of inflorescence, and (C) betulinic acid (a triterpenoid) extracted from A. officinalis.

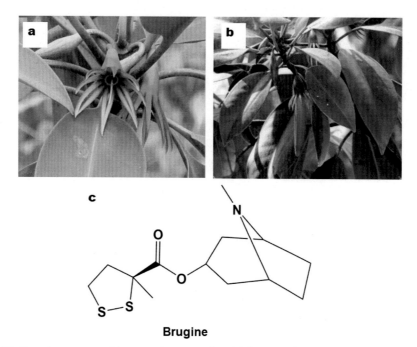

Brugine

Fig. 7 (A) *Bruguiera gymnorrhiza*—persistence calyx, (B) hypocotyle, and (C) brugine (an alkaloid) extracted from *B. gymnorrhiza*.

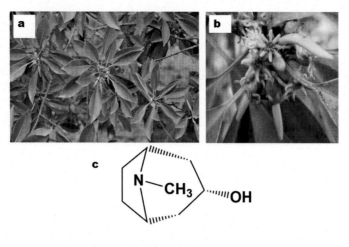

Tropine

Fig. 8 (A) *Bruguiera sexangular*—part of the branch, (B) close-up of inflorescence, and (C) tropine (an alkaloid) extracted from *B. sexangula.*

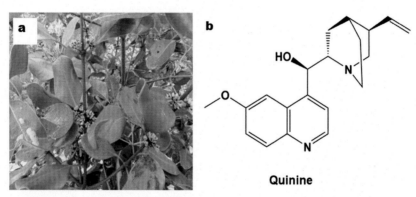

Quinine

Fig. 9 (A) *Ceriops decandra*—part of the growing plant and (B) quinine (an alkaloid) extracted from *C. decandra.*

Acanthus ilicifolius

The evergreen leaves of *Acanthus ilicifolius* L. (Acanthaceae) have spiny edges, and the stem nodes have stipular spines. It is a plant that can be found in marshy areas throughout China's mangroves, as well as India, Burma, and Thailand. *A. ilicifolius* is used to treat inflammation, hepatitis, swollen spleens, asthma, gastralgia, and malignant tumors in traditional Chinese medicine. 4-Hydroxy-2(3*H*)-benzoxazolone, an alkaloid having anticancer property has been separated from the *Acanthus ilicifolius* plant.

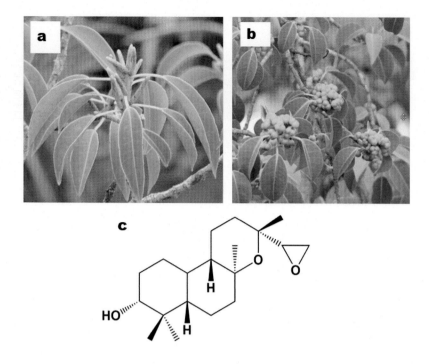

Excoecarin

Fig. 10 (A) *Excoecaria agallocha*—male part, (B) female part, and (C) excoecarin (a diterpene) extracted from *E. agallocha*.

Avicennia alba

Avicennia alba or commonly called Kala Baen is a tall tree up to 25 m. Their roots are pencil-like pneumatophores that emerge above the ground from long shallow underground roots. They grow at the mouth of rivers far away from salt water in tidal forests. Avicequinone belongs to the class of naphthoquinones that are isolated from the stem bark of this plant.

Avicennia marina

A. marina or white mangroves commonly known as Jat Baen are small shrubs that grow up to 4 m. Their roots are pencil-like pneumatophores that emerge above the ground from long shallow underground roots, similar to *A. alba*. They are widely distributed in tropical Asia and Australia. Stenocarpoquinone, a naphthoquinone derivative isolated from *A. marina* showed strong antiproliferative and cytotoxic activities.

Avicennia officinalis

Avicennia officinalis or commonly known as Paira Baen are long trees up to 20 m with branches both spreading and erect. Their roots are pencil like pneumatophores with

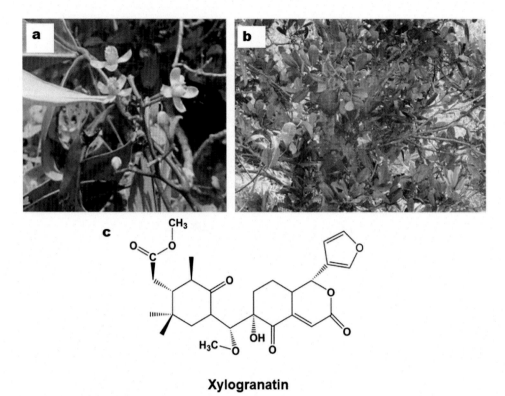

Xylogranatin

Fig. 11 (A) *Xylocarpus granatum*—flower, (B) fruit, and (C) xylogranatin (a limonoid) extracted from *X. granatum*.

occasional stilt roots present. They are widely distributed in tropical Asia and Australia forming pure patches along sea-shores and or muddy flats. Betulinic acid, a triterpenoid was isolated from the stem bark of this plant.

Bruguiera gymnorrhiza

B. gymnorrhiza or Kakra as called in Bengali, they are tall trees up to 30 m with spreading branches. The stem and branches are marked with leaf-scars and stipules. They have short aerial roots thickened at trunk bases. Alkaloid brugine was identified from leaf extract of *B. gymnorrhiza*.

Bruguiera sexangula

B. sexangula or Bakul Kakra are medium sized trees up to 20 m tall, erect and branched. They have underground roots, knee-like buttresses more like *B. gymnorrhiza* and aerial roots with shallow buttresses at the base of the trunk. Tropine has been identified in the crude alkaloid mixtures from the bark of *B. sexangula*.

Ceriops decandra

It is a yellow mangrove commonly called Garan are small shrubs up to 4 m height. They have erect branches turning its canopy into conical. They have aerial roots with shallow buttresses or knee-roots at the trunk bases being mostly distributed in tropical Asia and America. Conventionally parts of this species are used to treat a number of therapeutic conditions like diabetes, hemorrhage, pain, diarrhea, and dysentery. The leaves of *C. decandra* yielded many important bioactive phytochemicals one of which is quinine having anticancer potential.

Excoecaria agallocha

E. agallocha or commonly called Gengwa are evergreen trees with 12 m height widely distributed in tropical Asia, Australia, and Africa. They are found along the sea shore of the mangrove regime. Their barks and woods have traditional medicinal value to combat a lot of therapeutic issues. Excoecarin belonging to diterpene class has been isolated from the woods of this plant.

Xylocarpus granatum

X. granatum are much branched dark green deciduous trees with height up to 20 m or more. They have trunk base with developed buttresses but lacks aerial pneumatophores. This species is mostly distributed in tropical Asia and Africa. Xylogranatin belongs to the class of limonoids that were isolated from the seeds of *X. granatum* has proven anticancer activity.

3.2 Anticancer potential of mangrove-derived microorganisms

Endophytes, which include fungi, actinomycetes and bacteria, are microorganisms that live in harmony with their hosts in the intercellular gaps of plant tissue and several bioactive metabolites can be found in these endophytes. They can produce metabolites that are comparable to those produced by their host plant. They exemplify a wide range of microbial adaptations that have evolved in unique or remote environments. Divergolide D was discovered to have anticancer activity against pancreatic cancer PANC-1, lung cancer LXFA 629 L, sarcoma SAOS-2 and renal cancer RXK 486 L cell lines after being isolated from *Streptomyces* spp. HKI0576 associated with *Bruguiera gymnorrhiza* (Xu et al., 2014). Lam et al. (2014) isolated 52 endophytic actinomycetes from three different kinds of mangroves namely, *Sonneratia caseolaris*, *Sonneratia paracaseolaris*, and *Lumnitzera racemosa*. Only two strains (2E20 and 2E29) were found to have anticancer activity against the cancer cell lines KB, SK-LU-1, HepG2, and MCF7. Polyphenols derived from *Penicillium expansum* 091006 associated with *Excoecaria agallocha*, were found to be cytotoxic toward HL-60 cell lines by Wang et al. (2012). New chitin analogues A–C (Abidi, 2014; Afshar et al., 2021; Akhtar and Swamy, 2018) and one new xanthone derivative were discovered in *Penicillium chrysogenum*, which was isolated from the mangrove *Acanthus ilicifolius*. The anticancer activity of penicitol A–C and penixan acid A was documented in HeLa, BEL-7402, HEK-293, HCT-116, and A549 cell lines (Wenqiang et al., 2015).

Streptomyces cheonanensis VUK-A is a mangrove-derived fungal endophyte that contains two metabolites, 2-methyl butyl propyl phthalate and diethyl phthalate. The former showed cytotoxicity against MDA-MB-231, OAW-42, HeLa, and MCF-7 cell lines (Mangamuri et al., 2016). *Pestalotiopsis neglecta* (endophyte), isolated from the mangrove species *Cupressus torulosa*, was found to possess cytotoxic activity against human embryonic kidney (HEK) cell lines (Sharma et al., 2016). SZ-685C is a physiologically active anthraquinone isolated from the secondary metabolites of *Halorosellinia* spp, a mangrove endophytic fungus with excellent potency against six cancer cell lines originated from human breast cancer (Xie et al., 2010; Hasan et al., 2015). *Pestalotiopsis microspora* is a mangrove-derived endophytic fungus that contains pestalotioprolides C, D–H, and 7-O-methylnigrosporolide, as well as pestalotioprolide B, seiricuprolide, nigrosporolide, and 4,7-dihydroxy-13-tetradeca-2,5,8-trienolide, as well as four recognized analogues. Some of these metabolites have been proven to have anticancer activity in murine lymphoma cell lines and human ovarian cancer cell lines, A2780 (Liu et al., 2016). Mangrove algae are the most prolific producers of anticancer chemicals among marine flora. Many bioactive chemicals (toxins) are produced by cyanobacteria and can be used in medications (Thajuddin, 2005; Uddin et al., 2011). Scytonemin, apratoxin, cryptophycin, stypoldione, coibamide A, largazole, fucoidan, and other anticancer compounds produced by mangrove algae have been investigated.

4. Application of mangroves in in vitro cancer research

Mangroves are the reservoir of novel phytochemicals that are characterized by their unique properties and one of them is anticancer activity. Direct application of mangroves or mangrove based bioactive compounds in cancer therapy is still a budding field with few novel inventions. The current rare quest for anticancer chemicals from mangroves is meant to be vast, but the eye-catching outcomes of traditional, chemically generated therapeutic agents have somewhat blinded the research related to mangroves application in cancer therapy. Chemical theranostics against cancer have expanded significantly in recent decades in comparison to natural therapeutic agents, despite the presumably irreversible side effects. Despite having a significantly greater amount of diverse bioactive chemicals, which is a distinctive trait of mangrove species, the utilization of mangrove species is the least researched among all conceivable natural therapies. Some of the notable works have been mentioned below.

Nypa fruticans is a mangrove palm produces polyisoprenoids, a long chain secondary metabolite (>C50). Polyisoprenoids are made up of polyprenol and dolichol, both of which have anticancer and antimicrobial properties. Istiqomah et al. (2020) studied the anticancer potential of *N. fruticans* leaves in WiDr cells by analyzing the cell cycles of cancer and regulating the expressions of p53, epidermal growth factor receptor

(EGFR), PI3K, AKT1 and mammalian target of rapamycin (mTOR) genes by using the reverse transcription–polymerase chain reaction (RT-PCR). Polyisoprenoids in *N. fruticans* extracts acted as a chemotherapeutic in the G0–G1 cycle at a rate of 79.0%, compared to 88.1% with the positive control 5-fluorouracil and were carried out by specific upregulation of the p53 gene expression and downregulation of the EGFR, PI3K, AKT1, and mTOR genes. This study revealed the ability of polyisoprenoids obtained from *N. fruticans* as a chemotherapeutic option in the treatment of colon cancer. The composition of the secondary metabolites (polyisoprenoid) in the extract is intrinsically linked to the suppression of PI3K/AKT1/mTOR gene expression by *N. fruticans*.

Another study by Istiqomah et al. (2021) analyzed the anticancer effects of dolichol from *Ceriops tagal* and *Rhizophora mucronata* leaves on WiDr cells and cell cycle related cancer. Dolichol is a polyisoprenoid alcohol comprising varying number of isoprene units terminating in an alpha saturated isoprenoid group containing an alcoholic functional group. *C. tagal* dolichol was found to be more effective than *R. mucronata* dolichol, with the efficacy of 87.94% and 82.36% on the G0/G1 cycle, respectively. Both regulated positive control, 5-FU, on the G0/G1 cycle (88.12%), S (9.52%), and G2-M cycles (6.42%). The p53 gene contributes to cellular DNA damage by limiting cell progression and inducing apoptosis if cell DNA damage cannot be repaired. The loss of p53 gene activity and apoptosis regulation results in a lack of cell cycle control, leading in the proliferation of cells with DNA damage and a high risk of becoming malignant. Upregulation (p53) and downregulation (EGFR) of the PI3K, AKT, and mTOR genes led to the contraction of cell cycle in colon cancer cells (WiDr). The cellular accumulation of WiDr with *C. tagal* and *R. mucronata* dolichol in the G0/G1 phase was higher than the cell control, according to the findings. This shows that the mechanism of suppression of the cell cycle in WiDr cells by *C. tagal* and *R. mucronata* dolichol was in the G0/G1 phase. The growth and development of cancer cells were slowed in this situation. In the G0/G1 phase, *C. tagal* and *R. mucronata* dolichol functioned, but not in the S and G2/M phases.

Aegiceras corniculatum is a shrub widely distributed in Asia and Australia. This mangrove species has gained attention as different parts of this plant is traditionally used in treatment of asthma, diabetes, rheumatic, and inflammatory diseases in the local community residing along the coast line. Biochemical investigation of plant extract revealed a plethora of compounds that can scavenge free radicals, produce chelate metal ions, prevent lipid peroxidation, reduce the respiratory burst in cells, and protect cells from oxidative damage (Roome et al., 2008a, b). 5-*O*-ethylembelin and 5-*O*-methylembelin belonging to classes of monohydroxy benzoquinones isolated from this species possess anticancer potential (Xu et al., 2005). Li et al. (2019) reported three new alkylated benzoquinones derived from *A. corniculatum* and analyzed their cytotoxic activities against HL-60, HepG2, BCG-823, NCI-H1650, and A2780 cell lines by MTT assay. The three new compounds showed potent inhibitory effect against HL-60 and

BGC-823 cell lines with IC_{50} value ranging from 7.6 to 10.6 μM. The length of the alkylated chain affected the inhibitory activity, while the length of the alkoxy chain could potentially affect the strength of the activity, according to a preliminary examination of the structure–activity relationships.

Maulana (2021) examined what the IC_{50} value of *Rhizophora apiculata* mangrove leaf extract was on HeLa cell viability and what influence *R. apiculata* mangrove leaf extract dose had on HeLa cell viability. The greatest cell survival value of 46.97% was found in HeLa cell cytotoxicity testing utilizing the MTT technique assay at a dosage of 125 ppm. The percentage of viability at doses of 250, 500, 1000, and 2000 ppm were 42.95%, 37.70%, 35.82%, and 32.12%, respectively. *R. apiculata* leaf extract has an IC50 of 64.42 ppm. The *R. apiculata* extract is harmful to HeLa cells at this concentration.

The ethanol extract of *Avicennia marina* mangrove leaves was found to be cytotoxic to the viability of HeLa cells, with an IC_{50} of 115.345 g/mL (Rahman, 2021). The anticancer activities of *A. marina* leaf extracts on breast, ovarian, and cervical cancer cells are mediated via cell cycle arrest or apoptosis pathways (Afshar et al., 2021). The MTT assay, cell proliferation assay and cell viability assays all revealed antiproliferative action, a decrease in cell population and a decrease in cell viability after treatment with MCF-7, OVCAR3, and HeLa, respectively. In addition, the S phase of the cell cycle increased in MCF-7, according to the cell cycle analysis. Furthermore, Western blot examination revealed an increase in pro-apoptotic cell effectors such as Bax and caspase-1, -3, and -7. Five chemicals in *A. marina* leaves play a role in OVCAR3 and HeLa apoptosis, according to computational results of ligand affinity measured by GC-MS compounds and activated apoptotic effectors found by Western blot.

Eswaraiah et al. (2020) reported that the leaf extract of *Suaeda monoica* had anticancer properties and inhibited MCF 7 and HeLa cell multiplication. *E. agallocha* plant extract suppressed lung cancer cell growth in a dose-dependent manner, causing apoptotic programmed cell death in $p53^{+/+}$ cells and p21-mediated G1 arrest in $p53^{-/-}$ cells. The p53, Bcl-2, and Bax-dependent cell apoptotic pathways are involved in the induction of apoptotic cell death in lung cancer cells (Prabhu and Devaraj, 2016). The ethanolic extract of *E. agallocha* (EEEA) showed cytotoxic potential in terms of antiproliferative activity, apoptosis induction and cell cycle arrest in the breast cancer MCF-7 cell lines (Reddy et al., 2019). MCF-7 cells treated with EEEA extract showed rounding or shrinkage of cells, granulation, and vacuolization in the cytoplasm, confirming phenotypic apoptosis. When compared to untreated cells, the ethanolic extract of *E. agallocha* extract dramatically decreased the gating of cells in the sub-G1 and G0/G1 phases, showing that cell cycle progression is inhibited by decreased DNA content. Six flavonoid glycosides were extracted from the leaves of *E. agallocha* by Rifai et al. (2011) and Abidi (2014) and demonstrated their cytotoxic efficacy against human pancreatic (PANC1), prostate (DU145) and Hep2 cancer cells. The presence of triterpenoids (β-amyrin acetate, epilupeol, epitaraxerol, 3β-[(2E,4E)-5oxodeca-2,4dienoyloxy] olean-12-ene, taraxerol, and taraxerone) in the *E. agallocha* extract may explain its

Table 2 Anticancer activities against specific cell lines of the mangrove-derived compounds.

Species	Compounds	Activity against cell lines	References
Avicennia marina	Stenocarpoquinone B	K562 and HeLa	Han et al. (2007)
Avicennia germinans	3-Chlorodeoxy lapachol	K662 and HeLa	Mahmud et al. (2014)
	Xylomexicanin	Human breast carcinoma and KT cells	
	Gedunin	CaCo-2 colon cancer cell	
Acanthus ilicifolius	Methylapigenin 7-o-β-D-glucuronateflavone Glycosides	MCF-7 and PA-1 cell lines	Smitha et al. (2014)
Acrostichum aureum	Tetracosane	HT9 colon cancer, estrogen-dependent breast cancer (MDA-MB-231) cells, gastric cancer cells	Uddin et al. (2011)
	Kaempfero, patriscabratine	Gastric cancer cells	Uddin et al. (2011)
Curcumaria frondosa	Frondoside A	Urothelial carcinoma cells	Dyshlovoy et al. (2017)
Ceriops tagal	Tagalsins B, C, D, E, F, G, H, W, 9, 10	Hematologic cancer (Human T-cell leukemia), HCT-8, Bel-7402, BGC-823, A549, A2780 cell lines	Yang et al. (2015)
Soneratiia apetala	Mitomycin C	Cancer and diabetes	Patra et al. (2015)
Sonneratia ovata	Sonnercerebroside, dehydroconiferyl alcohol, methoxydehydroconiferyl alcohol	AChE inhibition and cytotoxicity against HeLa, NCI-H460, MCF-7 cell lines, and PHF cells	Nguyen et al. (2015)
Xylocarpus granatum	Xylogranatumine A–F	A549 tumor cell	Zhou et al. (2014)
	Photogedunin	CaCo-2 colon cancer cell	Mahmud et al. (2014)

anticancer potential, according to Zou et al. (2006). Because of the presence of many phytochemicals, the EEEA has the ability to halt cell development and perform the anti-cancer activity. Table 2 summarizes the anticancer activities of bioactive compounds derived from mangroves against specific cell lines.

5. Bibliometric analysis of mangrove-derived phytochemicals in cancer research

To highlight the current status of research in the field of identification of various compounds that have anticancer properties and exhibit the same, extracted from different species of mangroves and its associates, a Bibliometric analysis was conducted.

The analysis was carried out objectively using VOSviewer, which was developed by Ludo Waltman and Nees van Eck at the Centre for Science and Technology Studies at Leiden University (Van Eck and Waltman, 2010). In order to retrieve the relevant bibliometric data from the databases, the Dimensions search engine was used as it possesses the largest dataset of linked research information containing over 124 million publications.

The bibliometric data was retrieved after the search was executed for only published articles on Dimensions with the string ["mangrove" AND ("anticancer" OR "anti cancer")] to match the data in the title and abstracts of the articles. This ensured that only the relevant articles were included in the bibliometric data downloaded from Dimensions. The search returned 159 articles as on December 19, 2021.

Fig. 12 highlights the publication history in this specific field as derived from the above-mentioned search. The first publication was seen in 1999 and the next after a span of 7 years, in 2006. After that, it could be seen to fluctuate every year but its steep rise was seen right after 2017 as publications almost doubled in 2018. The trend, on the other hand, has only been rising exponentially and seems to continue to increase.

The dataset was then used to run two types of analyses. The first is a citation analysis and the other is a term co-occurrence analysis. The former was executed using the retrieved data, with two different units of analysis, namely, countries and organizations. As can be seen from Fig. 13, the first citation analysis was performed keeping the unit of analysis as countries. The analysis was done consisting of the 159 articles of the dataset, which led to the extraction of 32 countries. With a minimum of 1 article published from one country, out of the 32 countries, 28 countries were linked by citations. The 4 exclusions were Jordan, Italy, Canada, and Sri Lanka.

The visualization was done with the weights on the number of documents published from the countries. The citations received were the highest for China followed by India, with the former with about 1000 citations while the latter was around 900. The other countries did not receive half as many citations as them with just over 350 being the highest.

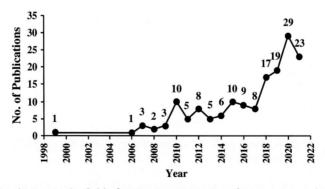

Fig. 12 Publication history in the field of anticancer properties of mangroves and their associates.

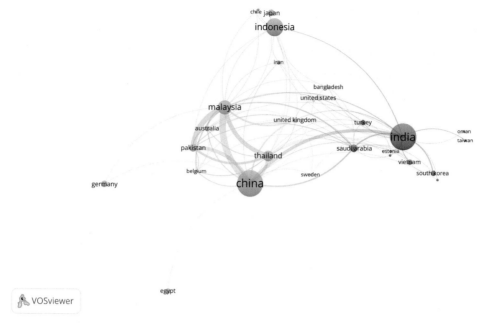

Fig. 13 Citation analysis with countries as the unit of analysis and the number of articles published as the weightage.

This goes on to show that India and China are leading the research in this particular field currently, while the other countries vested in the same research area are quite behind on both the number of articles published as well as the number of citations received. These may be attributed to the specific research questions that these articles were aiming to answer and the reliance of future research on those articles as fundamentals. As can be seen in the same figure, out of the 28 countries, India tops the list of the number of articles that were published with the number at 39 as it claims the largest circle. China closely follows the lead with 38 articles, while Indonesia and Malaysia capture the third and fourth positions with 20 and 14 articles, respectively. Articles from Malaysia can be visualized to be closely and boldly linked to China due to the mutual citations received.

The second citation analysis was performed keeping organizations as the unit of analysis. This was to identify the institutions of the world that were leading in this niche of mangrove research. The same dataset was used to run the analysis and this resulted in the identification of a total number of 158 institutes. The filter of 4 minimum number of published articles showed that there exist 17 institutions, out of which 14 are linked by mutual citations in the network. Fig. 14 highlights these 14 institutes across the world

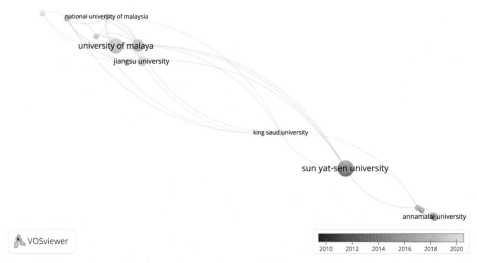

Fig. 14 Citation analysis with organizations as the unit of analysis and the number of articles published as the weightage. The network is in the overlay visualization format with the scores being the average publication year.

in an overlay format. The distribution of the 14 institutions across the nations can be seen in Table 3 along with the number of documents that each have contributed to the scientific community.

From the figure, it can be deduced that the Sun Yat-sen University of China holds the maximum number of documents which is also highlighted in Table 3. This may be due to its average publication per year being around 2010 as compared to the others in the

Table 3 The 14 institutes and their number of published articles alongside the nation they are located in.

Nations	Institutions	Published articles
India	Annamalai University	5
	Biju Patnaik University of Technology	4
	National Centre for Sustainable Coastal Management	4
	Sathyabama Institute of Science and Technology	4
Malaysia	University of Malaya	10
	Monash University Malaysia	8
	National University of Malaysia	4
	University Kebangsaan Malaysia Medical Centre	4
Thailand	Chulalongkorn University	4
	University of Phayao	4
China	Sun Yat-sen University	11
	Jiangsu University	6
Indonesia	University of Brawijaya	4
Saudi Arabia	King Saud University	4

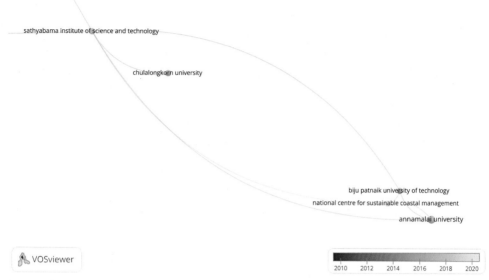

Fig. 15 Cluster harboring the Indian institutes in the network map of the citation analysis with organizations as the unit of analysis as seen in the lower right-hand corner.

network map. The cluster in the lower right-hand corner of Fig. 15 contains the four universities of India, which indicate that Annamalai University, Biju Patnaik University of Technology, and Sathyabama Institute of Science and Technology alongside the Thai institute of Chulalongkorn University take up the spot right after Sun Yat-sen University in terms of the average publication per year. Only the National Centre for Sustainable Coastal Management in India can be seen as a very new player in this field of research.

Similarly, Fig. 16 mostly shows the universities of Malaysia alongside Thailand, Indonesia, and China. These universities can be visualized to have a similar number of articles except the University of Malaysia and Monash University Malaysia, which have 10 and 8 published articles, respectively. All of them are fairly new in this field of research as their average publication per year ranges from 2018 to 2020 as can be seen on the yearly score gradient.

For the term co-occurrence analysis, the dataset was uploaded and allowed to be scanned by VOSviewer for the terms to be extracted. The terms were extracted from both the title and the abstract fields using only the binary counting method. The threshold for the minimum number of terms was set at 10. This extracted a total number of 82 terms which were manually trimmed down to 61 by removing nonrelevant terms. In Fig. 17, it can be visualized that surrounding the term "activity" all the other terms are hovering, re-emphasizing that all the terms are related to discovering and testing the anticancer activity of compounds extracted from mangroves. Furthermore, terms like "hela" and "mcf" refer to the cancer cell lines HeLa and MCF, which are widely used

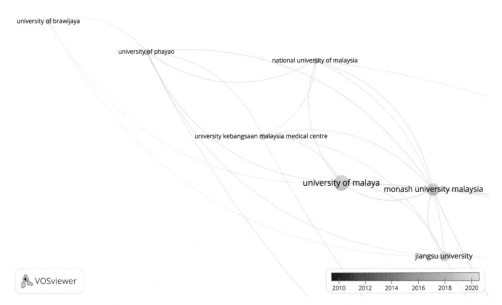

Fig. 16 Cluster harboring the Malaysian, Indonesian and Thai institutes in the network map of the citation analysis with organizations as the unit of analysis as seen in the upper left-hand quadrant of Fig. 15.

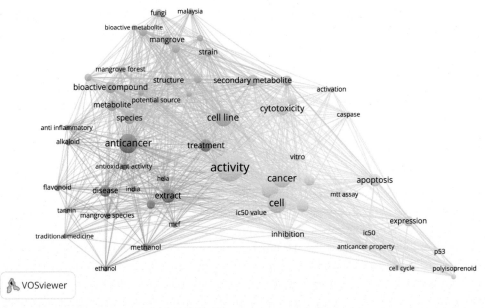

Fig. 17 Term co-occurrence analysis with the binary counting method.

globally, to test out the compounds extracted for their anticancer properties. Another point to consider is the existence of the terms like "flavonoid," "polyisoprenoid," and "alkaloid" which indicate the focus of researchers in this field of mangrove research. The two countries leading the charge in this field are also highlighted in the network, namely, India and Malaysia. Researchers seem to be working on the secondary metabolites as a potential source for anticancer compounds as it is also found to be mentioned in the network map. Finally, caspase has been specifically explored in this field and can also be found in the network map, even though it seems the research on it has been limited.

It can be stated from all of the analyses that this is an emerging field with a very limited amount of scientific information available. As far as separate nations and institutions are concerned, this field is growing and is being led mostly by the South-East Asian Institutions involved in mangrove research. Both India and Malaysia can be predicted to be the top contributors in the coming years based on the current numbers these countries have provided. Thus, this field gives the scientific community huge opportunities to explore and discover ground-breaking contributions in the fields of mangrove research and oncology.

5.1 Limitations of the study

As it goes by saying along with every positive aspect, there are some negative aspects or shortcomings associated. Same is the case for mangroves-derived phytochemicals in cancer therapy. For any natural product to be used in medication, the first priority should be given toward isolation and separation of the respective compound in its pure form. The isolation process and identifying a single compound from the diverse matrix like mangroves is a rigorous procedure requiring high skilled natural product chemistry and sophisticated analytical techniques inquiring exorbitant costs. A lot of research data is published where the anticancer activity is reported for the whole extract (including solvent) so it remains unclear from where the inhibition effect to cancer cells is coming, i.e., whether it is from a single compound or the solvent or in combination of both. The solvents used in extraction of phytochemicals itself are cytotoxic so it is difficult to decipher the effects. Separating the components present in active extracts and isolating a crude product, followed by suitable characterization, is one of the areas that needs to be thoroughly investigated. We have recently published a review on phytochemical extraction, isolation, and separation from mangrove species (Mitra et al., 2021) where we have elaborately discussed the extraction and separation strategies adopted by different researchers worldwide. A generalized plant material extraction technique was discussed, which can be exploited in case of mangrove-based phytochemicals. Precautions are important throughout the extraction process, as many chemicals are thermolabile, pressure-sensitive, and get denatured readily. Also, the yield of the specific compound plays a crucial role. It is seen that in the purification process of a particular compound, the final yield of the product is very low (in milligram range). Following all these limitations, the direct application of mangrove-based phytochemicals in cancer therapy is considerably low.

5.2 Conclusion and future prospects

Mangroves are localized to coastal regions, which have the hostile environment, with alternating tidal and saline regimes. Their biochemical heterogeneity originates from their ability to thrive and survive in this halophytic niche, resulting in the production of novel bioactive compounds that have led to the discovery of numerous herbal and semisynthetic medications. Although many plants from mangroves are widely used in traditional medicine, only a few have been evaluated for biological activities and studied for their possible anticancer qualities. Despite breakthroughs in medicine, molecular biology, and medical physics, cancer diagnosis and therapy pose a significant challenge. Cancer treatment necessitates highly sophisticated, precise, combinatorial, and multifunctional treatment modalities due to its heterogeneity, complexity, and constantly evolving properties. The current practice of innovative drug discovery is based on prior information on varied uses of plants, microorganisms and any other biological or chemical substances. It's not that today's anticancer theranostic phytocompounds are incapable of accomplishing the current measurable aim; rather, target unspecific delivery, low availability and dispersity are some of the stumbling blocks that need to be addressed. However, it is frequently the future that sparks and sets the course for current achievements, leaving behind a glamorous past.

The advancement in nanoscience and nanotechnology in combination with other treatment processes may change and revolutionize the course of medical sciences. Phytosynthesized silver and zinc nanoparticles by using *Heritiera fomes* and *Sonneratia apetala* mangrove plant aqueous extracts as reducing agents, are being employed for the treatment of many types of cancer. These nanoparticles have the potential to be extremely useful in a variety of biomedical applications. Natural bioactive chemicals coupled to nanocarriers can be used instead of synthetic therapies with anticancer action, and they are both effective and have minimal adverse effects. In the approaching decade, advanced cancer treatment will be formulated employing phytocompounds derived from mangroves as nanotherapeutics. These nanocarriers in conjunction with nuclear medicine isotopes may allow the development of more precise and effective radiopharmaceuticals for cancer therapy. The intrinsic property of the nanomaterials provides a vehicle to deliver a variety of radionuclides to the target site. Their high surface-to-volume ratio allows them to be conjugated to a variety of ligands that can detect cancer cells specifically. In addition, nanomaterials can improve the precision and specificity of traditional diagnostic methods including magnetic resonance imaging (MRI), PET, SPECT, and optical and electrochemical biosensors. It is feasible to detect even very low quantities of cancer biomarkers using nanomaterials, which could aid in the early identification of cancer. By following this approach, many neglected mangrove species could be a new source of natural substances that could be successfully employed to treat a variety of human diseases.

In nutshell, more exploration of these natural sources for the discovery of novel cancer therapeutics should be prioritized. Despite this awareness, if the potentiality of mangroves is not put to explicit use in various scientific fields, the apparent credibility of their anticancer activity will continue to remain in the shadows for a long time.

Acknowledgment

This work is a part of Collaborative Research Scheme no UGC-DAE-CSR-KC/CRS/19/RC10/0984 of UGC DAE Consortium of Scientific Research, Kolkata Centre.

References

Abidi, A., 2014. Hedgehog signaling pathway: a novel target for cancer therapy: vismodegib, a promising therapeutic option in treatment of basal cell carcinomas. Indian J. Pharm. 46 (1), 3.

Afshar, A., Khoradmehr, A., Zare, M., Baghban, N., Mohebbi, G., Barmak, A., et al., 2021. Phytochemical analysis, computational modeling and experimental evaluations of Avicennia Marina anti-cancer activity on breast, ovarian and cervical cancer cell lines. Res. Square. https://doi.org/10.21203/rs.3.rs-835233/v1.

Akhtar, M.S., Swamy, M.K., 2018. Anticancer Plants: Properties and Application. Springer, Singapore.

Antwi, S.O., Eckert, E.C., Sabaque, C.V., Leof, E.R., Hawthorne, K.M., Bamlet, W.R., et al., 2015. Exposure to environmental chemicals and heavy metals, and risk of pancreatic cancer. Cancer Causes Control 26 (11), 1583–1591.

Ashraf, M.A., 2020. Phytochemicals as potential anticancer drugs: time to ponder nature's bounty. Biomed. Res. Int. 2020, 8602879.

Bandaranayake, W., 1995. Survey of mangrove plants from northern Australia for phytochemical constituents and UV-absorbing compounds. Curr. Top. Phytochem. 14, 69–78.

Bandaranayake, W., 1998. Traditional and medicinal uses of mangroves. Mangrove Salt Marshes 2 (3), 133–148.

Bandaranayake, W.M., 2002. Bioactivities, bioactive compounds and chemical constituents of mangrove plants. Wetl. Ecol. Manag. 10 (6), 421–452.

Batsa, A., Periyasamy, K., 2013. Anticancer activity of Excoecaria agallocha leaf extract in cell line model. Int. J. Pharm. Biol. Sci. 3, 392–398.

Boopathy, N.S., Kandasamy, K., Subramanian, M., You-Jin, J., 2011. Effect of mangrove tea extract from Ceriops decandra (Griff.) Ding Hou. on salivary bacterial flora of DMBA induced Hamster buccal pouch carcinoma. Indian J. Appl. Microbiol. 51 (3), 338–344.

Bunyapraphatsara, N., Jutiviboonsuk, A., Sornlek, P., Therathanathorn, W., Aksornkaew, S., Fong, H.H., Pezzuto, J.M., Kosmeder, J., 2003. Pharmacological studies of plants in the mangrove forest. Thai J. Phytopharm. 10 (2), 2546.

Caley, A., Jones, R., 2012. The principles of cancer treatment by chemotherapy. Surgery 30 (4), 186–190.

Cavallo, F., De Giovanni, C., Nanni, P., Forni, G., Lollini, P.L., 2011. 2011: the immune hallmarks of cancer. Cancer Immunol. Immunother. 60 (3), 319–326.

Chahin, H., Ekong, B., Fandy, T.E., 2013. Epigenetic therapy in malignant and chronic diseases. J. Pharmacogenomics Pharmacoproteomics 4 (118) (2153-0645).

Chakraborty, T., Bhuniya, D., Chatterjee, M., Rahaman, M., Singha, D., Chatterjee, B.N., et al., 2007. Acanthus ilicifolius plant extract prevents DNA alterations in a transplantable Ehrlich ascites carcinoma-bearing murine model. World J. Gastroenterol. 13 (48), 6538.

Chan, E.W.C., Wong, S.K., Chan, H.T., Baba, S., Kezuka, M., 2016. Cerbera are coastal trees with promising anticancer properties but lethal toxicity: a short review. J. Chin. Pharm. Sci. 25 (3), 161.

Chapman, V.J., 1976. Mangrove Vegetation. Cramer, Vaduz, Liechtenstein.

Danda, A.A., Joshi, A.K., Ghosh, A., Saha, R., 2017. State of Art Report on Biodiversity in Indian Sundarbans. World Wide Fund for Nature-India, New Delhi.

Das, G., Gouda, S., Mohanta, Y.K., Patra, J.K., 2015. Mangrove plants: a potential source for anticancer drugs. Indian J. Geo-Mar. Sci. 44 (5), 666–672.

Dehelean, C.A., Marcovici, I., Soica, C., Mioc, M., Coricovac, D., Iurciuc, S., et al., 2021. Plant-derived anticancer compounds as new perspectives in drug discovery and alternative therapy. Molecules 26 (4), 1109.

Dyshlovoy, S.A., Madanchi, R., Hauschild, J., Otte, K., Alsdorf, W.H., Schumacher, U., et al., 2017. The marine triterpene glycoside frondoside A induces p53-independent apoptosis and inhibits autophagy in urothelial carcinoma cells. BMC Cancer 17 (1), 1–10.

Eswaraiah, G., Peele, K.A., Krupanidhi, S., Kumar, R.B., Venkateswarulu, T.C., 2020. Identification of bioactive compounds in leaf extract of Avicennia alba by GC-MS analysis and evaluation of its in-vitro anticancer potential against MCF7 and HeLa cell lines. J. King Saud Univ. Sci. 32 (1), 740–744.

Firdaus, M., Prihanto, A.A., Nurdiani, R., 2013. Antioxidant and cytotoxic activity of Acanthus ilicifolius flower. Asian Pac. J. Trop. Biomed. 3 (1), 7–21.

Govindasamy, C., Kannan, R., 2012. Pharmacognosy of mangrove plants in the system of unani medicine. Asian Pac. J. Trop. Med. 2, S38–S41.

Guidoccio, F., Mazzarri, S., Orsini, F., Erba, P.A., Mariani, G., 2017. Novel radiopharmaceuticals for therapy. In: Volterrani, D., Erba, P.A., William Strauss, H., Mariani, G., Larson, S.M. (Eds.), Nuclear Oncology. Springer.

Hahn, W.C., Weinberg, R.A., 2002. Modeling the molecular circuitry of cancer. Nat. Rev. Cancer 2, 331–341.

Han, L.J., Huang, X., Dahse, H.M., Moellmann, U., Fu, H., Grabley, S., Sattler, I., Lin, W., 2007. Unusual naphtoquinone derivatives from the twigs of Avicennia marina. J. Nat. Prod. 70, 923–927.

Hanahan, D., Weinberg, R.A., 2000. The hallmarks of cancer. Cell 100, 57–70.

Hasan, S., Ansari, M.I., Ahmad, A., Mishra, M., 2015. Major bioactive metabolites from marine fungi: a review. Bioinformation 11 (4), 176.

Hassanpour, S.H., Dehghani, M., 2017. Review of cancer from perspective of molecular. J. Cancer Res. Pract. 4 (4), 127–129.

Heng, H.H., Stevens, J.B., Bremer, S.W., Ye, K.J., Liu, G., Ye, C.J., 2010. The evolutionary mechanism of cancer. J. Cell. Biochem. 109 (6), 1072–1084.

Huang, C., Lu, C.K., Tu, M.C., Chang, J.H., Chen, Y.J., Tu, Y.H., Huang, H.C., 2016. Polyphenol-rich Avicennia marina leaf extracts induce apoptosis in human breast and liver cancer cells and in a nude mouse xenograft model. Oncotarget 7 (24), 35874–35893.

Istiqomah, M.A., Hasibuan, P.A.Z., Sumaiyah, S., Yusraini, E., Oku, H., Basyuni, M., 2020. Anticancer effects of polyisoprenoid from Nypa fruticans leaves by controlling expression of p53, EGFR, PI3K, AKT1, and mTOR genes in colon cancer (WiDr) cells. Nat. Prod. Commun. 15 (4), 1934578X20918412.

Istiqomah, M.A., Hasibuan, P.A.Z., Nuryawan, A., Sumaiyah, S., 2021. The anticancer compound dolichol from Ceriops tagal and Rhizophora mucronata leaves regulates gene expressions in WiDr colon cancer. Sains Malays. 50 (1), 181–189.

Ito, C., Katsuno, S., Kondo, Y., Tan, H.T.W., Furukawa, H., 2000. Chemical constituents of Avicennia alba. Isolation and structural elucidation of new naphthoquinones and their analogues. Chem. Pharm. Bull. 48 (3), 339–343.

Jaymand, M., Taghipour, Y.D., Rezaei, A., Derakhshankhah, H., Abazari, M.F., Samadian, H., Hamblin, M.R., 2021. Radiolabeled carbon-based nanostructures: new radiopharmaceuticals for cancer therapy? Coord. Chem. Rev. 440, 213974.

Jones, P.A., 2014. At the tipping point for epigenetic therapies in cancer. J. Clin. Invest. 124 (1), 14–16.

Karami, L., Majd, A., Mehrabian, S., Nabiuni, M., Salehi, M., Irian, S., 2012. Antimutagenic and anticancer effects of Avicennia marina leaf extract on Salmonella typhimurium TA100 bacterium and human promyelocytic leukaemia HL-60 cells. Sci. Asia 38 (4), 349–355.

Kathiresan, K., 2010. Importance of mangroves of India. J. Coast. Environ. 1, 11–26.

Kathiresan, K., Bingham, B.L., 2001. Biology of mangroves and mangrove ecosystems. Adv. Mar. Biol. 40, 81–251.

Kathiresan, K., Boopathy, N.S., Kavitha, S., 2006. Coastal vegetation—an underexplored source of anticancer drugs. Nat. Prod. Radiance 5 (2), 115–119.

Kerry, R.G., Pradhan, P., Das, G., Gouda, S., Swamy, M.K., Patra, J.K., 2018. Anticancer potential of mangrove plants: neglected plant species of the marine ecosystem. In: Anticancer Plants: Properties and Application. Springer, Singapore, pp. 303–325.

Khafagi, I., Gab-Alla, A., Salama, W., Fouda, M., 2003. Biological activities and phytochemical constituents of the gray mangrove Avicennia marina (Forssk.) Vierh. Egypt. J. Exp. Biol. 5 (1), 62–69.

Khajure, P.V., Rathod, J., 2011. Potential anticancer activity of Acanthus ilicifolius extracted from the mangroves forest of Karwar, West coast of India. World J. Sci. Technol. 1, 1–6.

Kokpol, U., Chittawong, V., Miles, D.H., 1984. Chemical constituents of the roots of Acanthus ilicifolius. J. Nat. Prod. 49 (2), 355–356.

Kokpol, V., Miles, D., Payne, A., Chittarwong, V., 1990. Chemical constituents and bioactive compounds from mangrove plants. Stud. Nat. Prod. Chem. 7, 175–199.

Kumar, P., 2018. Recent advancement in cancer treatment. In: Design of Nanostructures for Theranostics Applications. William Andrew Publishing, pp. 621–651.

Lam, D.M., Viet, N.D., Mo, T.T., 2014. Screening for anticancer producing endophytic actinomycetes in three mangrove plant species in Nam Dinh province. J. Sci. Hnue 59, 114–122.

Li, Y., Dong, C., Xu, M.J., Lin, W.H., 2019. New alkylated benzoquinones from mangrove plant Aegiceras corniculatum with anticancer activity. J. Asian Nat. Prod. Res.

Liu, S., Dai, H., Makhloufi, G., Heering, C., Janiak, C., Hartmann, R., et al., 2016. Cytotoxic 14-membered macrolides from a mangrove-derived endophytic fungus, Pestalotiopsis microspora. J. Nat. Prod. 79 (9), 2332–2340.

Li-Weber, M., 2009. New therapeutic aspects of flavones: the anticancer properties of Scutellaria and its main active constituents Wogonin, Baicalein and Baicalin. Cancer Treat. Rev. 35 (1), 57–68.

Loder, J., Russell, G., 1969. Tumour inhibitory plants. The alkaloids of Bruguiera sexangula and Bruguiera exaristata (Rhizophoraceae). Aust. J. Chem. 22 (6), 1271–1275.

Lollini, P.L., Cavallo, F., Nanni, P., Forni, G., 2006. Vaccines for tumour prevention. Nat. Rev. Cancer 6 (3), 204–216.

Lollini, P.L., Cavallo, F., Nanni, P., Quaglino, E., 2015. The promise of preventive cancer vaccines. Vaccine 3 (2), 467–489.

Mahmud, I., Islam, M.K., Saha, S., Barman, A.K., Rahman, M.M., Anisuzzman, M., Rahman, T., Al-Nahain, A., Jahan, R., Rahmatullah, M., 2014. Pharmacological and ethnomedicinal overview of Heritiera fomes: future prospects. Int. Sch. Res. Notices 2014, 938543.

Mangamuri, U., Muvva, V., Poda, S., Naragani, K., Munaganti, R.K., Chitturi, B., Yenamandra, V., 2016. Bioactive metabolites produced by streptomyces Cheonanensis VUK-A from Coringa mangrove sediments: isolation, structure elucidation and bioactivity. Biotechnology 6 (1), 1–8.

Matlashewski, G., Lamb, P., Pim, D., Peacock, J., Crawford, L., Benchimol, S., 1984. Isolation and characterization of a human p53 cDNA clone: expression of the human p53 gene. EMBO J. 3 (13), 3257–3262.

Maulana, D.M., 2021. The dose effect of mangrove leaf extract (Rhizophora apiculata) on anticancer activity in HeLa cells. J. Stem Cell Res. Tissue Eng. 5 (1), 1–15.

Meacham, C.E., Morrison, S.J., 2013. Tumour heterogeneity and cancer cell plasticity. Nature 501, 328–337.

Mitra, S., Naskar, N., Chaudhuri, P., 2021. A review on potential bioactive phytochemicals for novel therapeutic applications with special emphasis on mangrove species. Phytomed. Plus 1 (4), 100107.

Nabeelah Bibi, S., Fawzi, M.M., Gokhan, Z., Rajesh, J., Nadeem, N., Kannan, R.R.R., et al., 2019. Ethnopharmacology, phytochemistry, and global distribution of mangroves—a comprehensive review. Mar. Drugs 17 (4), 231.

Newman, D.J., Cragg, G.M., 2020. Natural products as sources of new drugs over the nearly four decades from 01/1981 to 09/2019. J. Nat. Prod. 83 (3), 770–803.

Newman, D.J., Cragg, G.M., Snader, K.M., 2003. Natural products as sources of new drugs over the period 1981–2002. J. Nat. Prod. 66 (7), 1022–1037.

Nguyen, T.H., Pham, H.V., Pham, N.K., Quach, N.D., Pudhom, K., Hansen, P.E., Nguyen, K.P., 2015. Chemical constituents from Sonneratia ovata backer and their in vitro cytotoxicity and acetylcholinesterase inhibitory activities. Bioorg. Med. Chem. Lett. 25, 2366–2371.

Orsini, F., Guidoccio, F., Mariani, G., 2019. Radiopharmaceuticals for therapy. In: Nuclear Medicine Textbook. Springer, Cham, pp. 99–116.

Patil, R., Manohar, S.M., Upadhye, M.V., Katchi, V., Rao, A.J., Mule, A., Moghe, A.S., 2011. Antireverse transcriptase and anticancer activity of stem ethanol extracts of Excoecaria agallocha (Euphorbiaceae). Ceylon J. Sci. 40 (2), 147–155.

Patra, J.K., Thatoi, H., 2013. Anticancer activity and chromatography characterization of methanol extract of Heritiera fomes Buch. Ham., a mangrove plant from Bhitarkanika, India. Orient. Pharm. Exp. Med. 13 (2), 133–142.

Patra, J.K., Das, S.K., Thatoi, H., 2015. Phytochemical profiling and bioactivity of a mangrove plant, Sonneratia apetala from Odisha coast of India. Chin. J. Integr. Med. 21 (4), 274–285.

Peng, X., Long, S., 1994. Chemical constituents in stem of Acanthus ilicifolius. Chin. Tradit. Herb. Drug 7.

Poon, S.L., McPherson, J.R., Tan, P., Teh, B.T., Rozen, S.G., 2014. Mutation signatures of carcinogen exposure: genome-wide detection and new opportunities for cancer prevention. Genome Med. 6, 24.

Prabhu, V.V., Devaraj, S.N., 2016. Natural products from mangrove-potent inhibitors of lung cancer. Malays. J. Biosci. 3 (1), 23–30.

Prabhu, V.V., Guruvayoorappan, C., 2012. Anti-inflammatory and anti-tumor activity of the marine mangrove Rhizophora apiculata. J. Immunotoxicol. 9 (4), 341–352.

Rahman, M., 2021. The effect of dosage of mangrove leaf extract Avicennia Marina on the viability of HeLa cells. J. Stem Cell Res. Tissue Eng. 5 (1), 41–51.

Rajabi, S., Maresca, M., Yumashev, A.V., Choopani, R., Hajimehdipoor, H., 2021. The most competent plant-derived natural products for targeting apoptosis in cancer therapy. Biomol. Ther. 11 (4), 534.

Reddy, T., Rajasekhar, A., Jayasunderamma, B., Ramamurthi, R., 1991. Studies on marine bioactive substances from the Bay of Bengal: bioactive substances from the latex of the mangrove plant Excoecaria agallocha L.: antimicrobial activity and degradation. In: Thompson, M.F., Sarojini, R., Nagabhushanam, R. (Eds.), Bioactive Compounds From Marine Organisms With Emphasis on the Indian Ocean. Oxford & IBH Publishers Co. Pvt. Ltd., New Delhi, pp. 75–78.

Reddy, P.R.K., Durairaj, P., Thiruvanavukkarasu, P., Hari, R., 2019. Effect of ethanolic extract of Excoecaria agallocha leaves on the cytotoxic activity and cell cycle arrest of human breast cancer cell lines—MCF-7. Pharmacogn. Mag. 15 (64), 346.

Rifai, Y., Arai, M.A., Sadhu, S.K., Ahmed, F., Ishibashi, M., 2011. New Hedgehog/GLI signaling inhibitors from Excoecaria agallocha. Bioorg. Med. Chem. Lett. 21 (2), 718–722.

Roome, T., Dar, A., Naqvi, S., Ali, S., Choudhary, M.I., 2008a. Aegiceras corniculatum extract suppresses initial and late phases of inflammation in rat paw and attenuates the production of eicosanoids in rat neutrophils and human platelets. J. Ethnopharmacol. 120 (2), 248–254.

Roome, T., Dar, A., Ali, S., Naqvi, S., Choudhary, M.I., 2008b. A study on antioxidant, free radical scavenging, anti-inflammatory and hepatoprotective actions of Aegiceras corniculatum (stem) extracts. J. Ethnopharmacol. 118 (3), 514–521.

Saranraj, P., Sujitha, D., 2015. Mangrove medicinal plants: a review. Am. Eurasian J. Toxicol. Sci. 7 (3), 146–156.

Sari, D.P., Basyuni, M., Hasibuan, P.A., Sumardi, S., Nuryawan, A., Wati, R., 2018. Cytotoxic and antiproliferative activity of polyisoprenoids in seventeen mangroves species against WiDr colon cancer cells. Asian Pac. J. Cancer Prev. 19 (12), 3393–3400.

Schottenfeld, D., Fraumeni Jr., J.F., 2006. Cancer Epidemiology and Prevention. Oxford University Press.

Seto, M., Honma, K., Nakagawa, M., 2010. Diversity of genome profiles in malignant lymphoma. Cancer Sci. 101 (3), 573–578.

Sharma, D., Pramanik, A., Agrawal, P.K., 2016. Evaluation of bioactive secondary metabolites from endophytic fungus Pestalotiopsis neglecta BAB-5510 isolated from leaves of Cupressus torulosa D. Don. 3Biotech 6 (2), 1–14.

Shtivelman, E., Lifshitz, B., Gale, R.P., Canaani, E., 1985. Fused transcript of abl and bcr genes in chronic myelogenous leukaemia. Nature 315 (6020), 550–554.

Siegel, R.L., Miller, K.D., Jemal, A., 2016. Cancer statistics. CA Cancer J. Clin. 66, 7–30.

Smitha, R.B., Madhusoodanan, P.V., Prakashkumar, R., 2014. Anticancer activity of Acanthus illicifolius Linn. from Chettuva mangroves, Kerala, India. Int. J. Bioassays 3 (11), 3452–3455.

Spalding, M., Blasco, F., Field, C., 1997. World Mangrove Atlas. Okinawa International Society for Mangrove Ecosystems, Japan.

Spalding, M., Kainuma, M., Collins, L., 2010. World Atlas of Mangroves. Earthscan Publisher, London, p. 336.

Subhan, N., Alam, A., Ahmed, F., Shahid, I.Z., 2008a. Antinociceptive and gastroprotective effect of the crude ethanolic extracts of Excoecaria agallocha Linn. Turk. J. Pharm. Sci. 5, 143–154.

Subhan, N., Alam, M.A., Ahmed, F., Shahid, I.J., Nahar, L., Sarker, S.D., 2008b. Bioactivity of Excoecaria agallocha. Rev. Bras. 18 (4), 521–526.

Subhan, N., Ashraful, A.M., Ahmed, F., Abdul, A.M., Nahar, L., Sarker, S.D., 2008c. In vitro antioxidant property of the extract of Excoecaria agallocha (Euphorbiaceae). DARU 16 (3), 149–154.

Sukhramani, P., Patel, P., 2013. Biological screening of Avicennia marina for anticancer activity. Der. Pharm. Sin. 4 (2), 125–130.

Sumithra, M., Anbu, J., Nithya, S., Ravichandiran, V., 2011. Anticancer activity of methanolic leaves extract of Avicennia officinalis on Ehrlich ascitis carcinoma cell lines in rodents. Int. J. Pharmtech Res. 3 (3), 1290–1292.

Thajuddin, N., 2005. Cyanobacterial biodiversity and potential applications in biotechnology. Curr. Sci. 89, 47–57.

Tian, M., Dai, H., Li, X., Wang, B., 2009. Chemical constituents of marine medicinal mangrove plant Sonneratia caseolaris. Chinese J. Oceanol. Limnol. 27 (2), 288.

Tomlinson, P.B., 1986. The Botany of Mangroves. Cambridge University Press, London.

Trafialek, J., Kolanowski, W., 2014. Dietary exposure to meat-related carcinogenic substances: is there a way to estimate the risk? Int. J. Food Sci. Nutr. 65, 774–780.

Uddin, S.J., Jason, T.L.H., Beattie, K.D., Grice, I.D., Tiralongo, E., 2011. (2S,3S)-sulfated Pterosin C, a cytotoxic sesquiterpene from the Bangladeshi mangrove fern Acrostichum aureum. J. Nat. Prod. 74, 1–4.

Uddin, S.J., Grice, D., Tiralongo, E., 2012. Evaluation of cytotoxic activity of patriscabratine, tetracosane and various flavonoids isolated from the Bangladeshi medicinal plant Acrostichum aureum. Pharm. Biol. 50 (10), 1276–1280.

Van Eck, N.J., Waltman, L., 2010. Software survey: VOSviewer, a computer program for bibliometric mapping. Scientometrics 84 (2), 523–538.

Veeresham, C., 2012. Natural products derived from plants as a source of drugs. J. Adv. Pharm. Technol. Res. 3 (4), 200.

Wang, J., Lu, Z., Liu, P., Wang, Y., Li, J., Hong, K., Zhu, W., 2012. Cytotoxic polyphenols from the fungus penicillium expansum 091 006 endogenous with the mangrove plant Excoecaria agallocha. Planta Med. 78 (17), 1861–1866.

Wenqiang, G., Dan, L., Jixing, P., Tianjiao, Z., Qianqun, G., Dehai, L., 2015. Penicitols A–C and penixanacid A from the mangrove-derived Penicillium chrysogenum HDN11-24. J. Nat. Prod. 78, 306–310.

Wu, J., Xiao, Q., Xu, J., Li, M.Y., Pan, J.Y., Yang, M.H., 2008. Natural products from true mangrove flora: source, chemistry and bioactivities. Nat. Prod. Rep. 25 (5), 955–981.

Xie, G.E., Zhu, X., Li, Q., Gu, M., He, Z., Wu, J., et al., 2010. SZ-685C, a marine anthraquinone, is a potent inducer of apoptosis with anticancer activity by suppression of the Akt/FOXO pathway. Br. J. Pharmacol. 159 (3), 689–697.

Xu, M., Cui, J., Fu, H., Proksch, P., Lin, W., Li, M., 2005. Embelin derivatives and their anticancer activity through microtubule disassembly. Planta Med. 71 (10), 944–948.

Xu, D.B., Ye, W.W., Han, Y., Deng, Z.X., Hong, K., 2014. Natural products from mangrove actinomycetes. Mar. Drugs 12 (5), 2590–2613.

Yang, Y., Zhang, Y., Liu, D., Li-Weber, M., Shao, B., Lin, W., 2015. Dolabrane-type diterpenes from the mangrove plant Ceriops tagal with antitumor activities. Fitoterapia 103, 277–282.

Yin, S., Fan, C.Q., Wang, X.N., Lin, L.P., Ding, J., Yue, J.M., 2006. Xylogranatins A–D: novel tetranortriterpenoids with an unusual 9, 10-s eco scaffold from marine mangrove Xylocarpus granatum. Org. Lett. 8 (21), 4935–4938.

Yin, S., Wang, X.N., Fan, C.Q., Lin, L.P., Ding, J., Yue, J.M., 2007. Limonoids from the seeds of the marine mangrove Xylocarpus granatum. J. Nat. Prod. 70 (4), 682–685.

Yin, S.Y., Wei, W.C., Jian, F.Y., Yang, N.S., 2013. Therapeutic applications of herbal medicines for cancer patients. Evid. Based Complement. Alternat. Med. 2013.

Yuan, H., Ma, Q., Ye, L., Piao, G., 2016. The traditional medicine and modern medicine from natural products. Molecules 21 (5), 559.

Zhou, Z.F., Taglialatela-Scafati, O., Liu, H.L., Gu, Y.C., Kong, L.Y., Guo, Y.W., 2014. Apotirucallane protolimonoids from the Chinese mangrove Xylocarpus granatum Koenig. Fitoterapia 97, 192–197.

Zou, J.H., Dai, J., Chen, X., Yuan, J.Q., 2006. Pentacyclic triterpenoids from leaves of Excoecaria agallocha. Chem. Pharm. Bull. 54 (6), 920–921.

CHAPTER TWENTY-FIVE

Impact of pesticides on immune-endocrine disorders and its relationship to cancer development

Tatiane Renata Fagundes[a,*], Aedra Carla Bufalo Kawassaki[b,*],
Virginia Marcia Concato[a,*], João Paulo Assolini[a,*], Taylon Felipe Silva[a,*],
Manoela Daiele Gonçalves[c,*], Elaine da Silva Siqueira[a,*],
Claudia Stoeglehner Sahd[a,*], Fabrício Seidy Ribeiro Inoue[a,*],
Thais Peron da Silva[a,*], Debora Messagi de Lima[a,*], Mariane Okamoto Ferreira[b,*],
Ivete Conchon-Costa[a,*], Wander Rogério Pavanelli[a,*], and Carolina Panis[b,*]

[a]Laboratory of Immunoparasitology of Neglected Diseases and Cancer, State University of Londrina, Londrina, Paraná, Brazil
[b]Laboratory of Tumor Biology, State University of Western Paraná, Francisco Beltrão, Paraná, Brazil
[c]Laboratory of Biotransformation and Phytochemistry, State University of Londrina, Londrina, Paraná, Brazil

Abbreviations

17βHSD	17β–hydroxysteroid dehydrogenase
2,4,-D	2,4–dichlorophenoxyacetic acid
5-HT, serotonin	5HT, 5–hydroxytryptamine
A	adrenaline
ACh	acetylcholine
AChE	acetylcholinesterase
ACTH	adrenocorticotrophic hormone
Akt	protein kinase B
AVP	vasopressin
BMI	body mass index
CAT	catalase
ChAT	choline acetyltransferase activity
CNS	central nervous system
CoQ10	coenzyme Q10
CPF	chlorpyrifos
CPu	caudate-putamen
CRH	corticotrophin-releasing hormone
DA	dopamine
DAP	dialkylphosphate
DDE	dichlorodiphenyl-chloroethylene
DDT	dichlorodiphenyltrichloroethane

*All authors equally contributed to this study.

Biomarkers in Cancer Detection and Monitoring of Therapeutics
https://doi.org/10.1016/B978-0-323-95114-2.00001-7

DLT	deltamethrin
DmCAT	*Drosophila melanogaster* CAT gene
DMT	imethoate
DOPAC	3,4-dihydroxyphenylacetic acid
DPN	2,3-bis(4-hydroxyphenyl)-propionitrile
DREF	DNA replication-related factor
Drp1	dynamin-related protein 1
E1	weakest estrone
E2	17β-estradiol
E3	estriol
EDCs	endocrine-disrupting chemicals
EPA	Environmental Protection Agency
ER	endoplasmic reticulum
ER	estrogen receptor
ERK	extracellular signal-regulation kinase
FSH	follicle-stimulating hormone
GABA	gamma-aminobutyric acid
GH	growing hormone
GSH	glutathione
GWI	Gulf War illness
HDL	high-density lipoproteins
HOMA-IR	homeostatic model assessment for insulin resistance
HPG	hypothalamic-pituitary-gonadal/testicular
IGF-1	insulin-like growth factor 1
IGF-2	insulin-like growth factor-2
IL	interleukin
IMI	neonicotinoid imidacloprid
IP-10	interferon--inducible protein
JNK	JNN N-terminal kinase
LAGDA	larval amphibian growth and development assay
LDH	lactate dehydrogenase
LH	luteinizing hormone
LPO	lipid peroxidation
MC2R	melanocortin 2 receptor
MCF-7	human breast cancer cells
MCP	monocrotophos
MCZ	dithiocarbamatemancozeb
MDA	malondialdehyde
MEOGRT	Medaka Extended One Generation Reproduction Test
MLT	melatonin
MPO	myeloperoxidase
MS	metabolic syndrome
MXC	methoxychlor
NA	noradrenaline
nAChRs	nicotinic agonists of ACh receptors

NE	norepinephrine
NK	natural killer
NO_3^-	nitrate ion
non-DDT	nondichlorodiphenyltrichloroethane derivative
OC	organochlorine
OP	organophosphates
OT	oxytocin
p,p'-DDD	(a DDT-metabolite)
p,p'-DDE	*p,p'*-dichlorodiphenoxydichlorethylene
PC12	rat adrenal gland tumor line
PCP	pentachlorophenol
PD	Parkinson's disease
PERM	permethrin
PH3	phosphine
POEA	polyoxyethylene amine
POMC	pro-opiomelanocortin
PON1	paraoxonase 1
PQ	paraquat
PRL	prolactin
REMSD	rapid eye movement
ROS	reactive oxygen species
SH-SY5Y	human neuroblastoma cells
SOD	superoxide dismutase
STAT5	signal transducer and activator of transcription protein family
T3	triiodothyronine
T4	thyroxine
TAP	total antioxidant performance
TCDD	2,3,7,8-tetra-chlorodibenzo-*p*-dioxin
TGF-β	transforming growth factor beta
TNF-α	tumor necroses factor-alpha
TR	thyroid hormone receptor
Trp	tryptophan
TSH	thyroid hormones
TTM	total thiol molecules
U373-MG	human glioblastoma cells

1. Introduction

Pesticides, also known as agrochemicals, are chemicals used in agriculture as fungicides, herbicides, and insecticides, to protect plantations and guarantee crop production (Jamal et al., 2016). However, the indiscriminate use of agrochemicals in recent years has been linked to an increase of more than 3 million pesticide-induced poisonings, mainly those in the class of paraquat (PQ), rotenone, phosphine (PH3), carbamates, triazines, pyrethroids, organochlorines (OC), and organophosphates (OP) (World Health Organization, 2020), caused through inhalation exposure, food intake and direct skin contact, resulting in allergies, neurological, immunological and endocrine disorders, cancer and even death (Lauretta et al., 2019). According to the US Environmental Protection Agency (EPA), pesticides are considered endocrine-disrupting chemicals (EDCs) that interfere with the physiology of the hypothalamic–pituitary-gonadal (HPG) axis endocrine, and neurological axis (Combarnous, 2017; Mnif et al., 2011). They act directly on the hormone receptors in an agonist or antagonistic ways, altering their production, transport, and regulation without being limited to a single axis or organ (Warembourg et al., 2016). Considering the relevance of this issue, we revised the impact of pesticides on the deregulation of both endocrine and immunological axes and its implications to cancer development.

2. Pesticides as immune-endocrine disruptors
2.1 Effect of pesticides in the insulin axis

Insulin is a hormone synthesized and secreted by the pancreatic beta cells and controls glycemia and storing glucose, especially in the liver and skeletal muscle (Rutter et al., 2015). Due to its systemic effects, deregulation of this axis can result in conditions related to diseases further than diabetes, as obesity and cancer.

Several studies have shown that insulin secretion and function can be altered by exposure to chemical compounds such as pesticides, leading to insulin resistance and type 2 diabetes (Juntarawijit and Juntarawijit, 2018). Besides, these substances also appear to be involved with the onset of obesity and metabolic syndrome (MS) (Rosenbaum et al., 2017), a metabolic disorder involving obesity, dyslipidemia, high blood pressure, and insulin resistance (Mustieles et al., 2017). The effect of pesticides on insulin axis is shown in Fig. 1.

Studies have shown that OP, OC, and imidacloprid pesticides can deregulate the insulin pathway at different stages of life. Debost-Legrand et al. (2016) evaluated a group of pregnant women regarding insulin and adiponectin levels present in umbilical cord blood when exposed to OP pesticides and persistent organic pollutants. The authors demonstrated that the concentration of these hormones was altered in some exposed groups, indicating that these hormonal changes may modify glucose metabolism. For the most part, these alterations are seen and perceived in adolescence and adulthood. Early exposure to glyphosate pesticides in the early years of life increases the risk of developing obesity and MS in adult life (De Long and Holloway, 2017). In addition, Raafat et al. (2012) showed that malathion pesticides in the blood of nondiabetic farmers chronically exposed correlated positively with the appearance of insulin resistance and altered abdominal circumference.

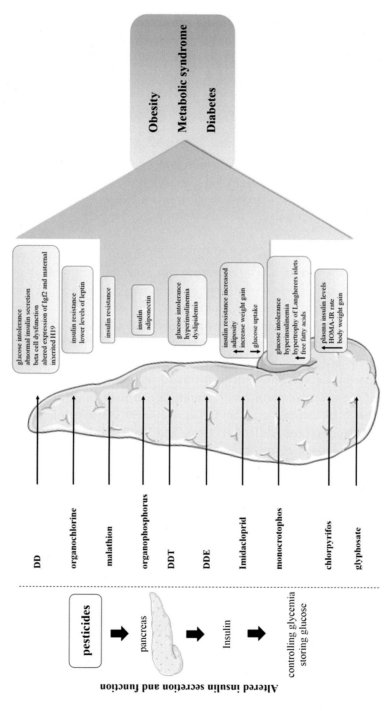

Fig. 1 Pesticides alter insulin function and secretion. Different pesticides deregulate hormone insulin, causing obesity, metabolic syndrome, and diabetes.

Experimental studies with animals corroborate these findings. Male Wistar rats exposed to monocrotophos (MCP) pesticides presented glucose intolerance, hyper-insulinemia, hypertrophy of the Langerhans islets, and increased levels of free fatty acids (Nagaraju et al., 2015; Nagaraju and Rajini, 2016). C57BL/6 N and apoE3 mice exposed to chlorpyrifos (CPF) showed higher plasma insulin levels, HOMA-IR (homeostatic model assessment for insulin resistance) rate, and body weight gain than the control animals, leading to the understanding that this pesticide induces obesity and diabetes (Peris-Sampedro et al., 2015).

In vitro studies showed that NES2Y line cells (human pancreatic beta cells) treated with three sublethal concentrations of dichlorodiphenyltrichloroethane (DDT) and dichloro diphenyl-chloroethylene (DDE) for 1 month showed downregulation of var-ious proteins involved in glucose metabolism, such as cytokeratin 8, 18, actin and alpha-enolase (Pavlikova et al., 2015).

In the animal model, C54BL/6J mice exposed from the eleventh day of gestation to the fifth postnatal day to DDT and its metabolite DDE had the progeny metabolic phenotype analyzed for 9 months. The females of this generation showed a loss in cold tolerance and a higher BMI when compared to the group of nonexposed females. In adulthood, when these females were submitted to a diet rich in fat, they developed glucose intolerance, hyperinsulinemia, dyslipidemia, and increased susceptibility to MS (La Merrill et al., 2014). Moreover, the primary metabolite of p,p'-dichlorodiphenyldichloroethylene (p,p'-DDE), after administered by gavage to pregnant rats, induced glucose intolerance, abnormal insulin secretion, beta-cell dysfunction, altered expression of paternal transcribed insulin-like growth factor-2 (IGF-2), and maternal inherited H19, critical genes for the development of pancreatic beta cells, all of which can be found in later generations (Song and Yang, 2017).

Prepubertal children exposed to OC pesticides have several altered metabolic param-eters, including insulin resistance and lower levels of leptin when compared to nonexposed boys of the same age (Burns et al., 2014). Another study followed 548 adults categorized as exposed or not to OC pesticides, with or without MS, and several other clinical parameters showed a significant association of pesticide exposure and the presence of MS (Rosenbaum et al., 2017). Baudry et al. (2018) observed that people who ate a larger quantity of nonorganic products with pesticides were more susceptible to devel-oping MS, demonstrating that organic foods can be a protective factor. Tomar et al. (2013) measured nine different OC pesticide compounds in blood samples in two adult groups categorized according to the diagnosis of the presence or absence of MS. Although not statistically significant, the levels of the compounds were higher in the group of patients categorized with the MS, presenting the relation of exposure to the pesticides and the alterations in the metabolism.

Imidacloprid, an insecticide of widespread use, can cause insulin resistance and increased adiposity. Kim et al. (2013) demonstrated that this pesticide could induce insulin resistance in three cell models (adipocytes, hepatocytes, and myotubes) when treated for 6 days with the compound, and all showed reduced glucose uptake from the insulin stimulus. The authors proposed that this resistance occurred due to alteration of the insulin signaling cascade, consequently decreasing Akt (protein kinase B) phosphorylation. More recently, Sun et al. (2017) showed that this same pesticide could increase weight gain and adiposity in C57BL/6J mice treated with a high-calorie diet for 12 weeks compared to C57BL/6J mice that were not exposed to imidacloprid.

2.2 Pesticide-induced estrogen deregulation, disease occurrence and cancer development

Estrogen is considered the female sex hormone and has several functions in the human body, such as developing and maintaining sexual characteristics and functions. In addition, to assisting in sexual physiology, estrogens also participate in skeletal homeostasis, cardiovascular system, metabolism of carbohydrates and lipids, central nervous system, and electrolyte balance (Vrtačnik et al., 2014).

Estrogen exists in three forms: the most biologically active 17β-estradiol (E2), the weakest estrone (E1), and the estriol (E3), the less active form. E1 to E2 is catalyzed by 17β-hydroxysteroid dehydrogenase (17βHSD) type 1, while the reverse conversion is due to 17βHSD types 2 and 4. A deficiency in 17βHSD type 2 or an abnormally high E2/E1 ratio in blood and tissues are related to several health problems (El-Hefnawy et al., 2017). This section reviews the influence of pesticides on estrogen (Fig. 2).

In this context, in vitro studies using the reporter gene assay (Blum et al., 2008; Kjeldsen et al., 2013; Vinggaard et al., 1999) have characterized the agonistic and antagonistic activity of fipronil and fipronil sulfone against the estrogen receptor (ER)α and thyroid hormone receptor (TR)β. It was observed in this study that the antiestrogenic activity of fipronil sulfone via ERα did not act as ERα agonists; however, as their antagonistic activity, both pesticides inhibited the estrogenic activity via ERα. It has also been shown that fipronil sulfone binds to TRβ mainly through hydrogen bonds with higher affinity, presenting more significant potential for thyroid interruption activity than fipronil, leading to adverse effects on organisms (Lu et al., 2015).

Astiz et al. (2014) reported that the pesticide dimethoate (DMT) (an OP) (using a sublethal concentration) was able to increase the levels of IL-6, IP10, TNFα, and IL-1β of primary astrocytes derived from male mice. Though, when the hormone estradiol is added to these treated cells, it counteracts the effects of DMT, reducing the inflammatory response. However, female astrocytes were more resistant to treatments and did not differ from the control group. Therefore, estradiol can contribute to the regulation of DMT action in males, beyond the DMT possesses different neurological effects in both sexes.

In vivo studies using Sprague–Dawley female rats (Bertolasio et al., 2011; Cummings and Metcalf, 1995; Metcalf et al., 1996; Ventura et al., 2016) observed that the tissue of

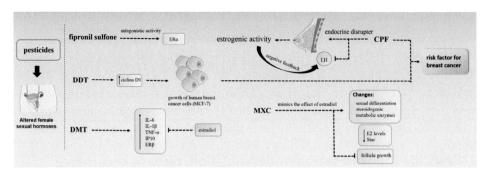

Fig. 2 Pesticides change female sexual hormones. Fipronil sulfone exerts antagonistic activity on ERα receptor. DMT induces the production of proinflammatory cytokines (IL-6, IL-1β, TNF-α, IP10) and ERβ; however, estradiol has the opposite effect. MXC mimics the effect of estradiol, altering sexual differentiation, steroidogenic and metabolic enzymes; reduces levels of E2, STAR; and inhibits follicular growth. DDT induces the proliferation of breast cancer cells (MCF-7), promoting the cell cycle, increasing the synthesis of cyclin D1. CPF acts as an endocrine disruptor in the mammary gland, leading to estrogenic activity, inhibiting LH. Thus, increasing the risk factors for breast cancer.

rats treated with the methoxychlor (MXC), an OC pesticide, or estradiol got an identical pattern, showing that MXC mimics the effect of estradiol on specific synthesis pathways (Cummings and Metcalf, 1995). Similarly, it was observed that the animals treated with high doses of MXC showed altered sexual differentiation during the neonatal period, and these data indicate that MXC was imitating estrogen in the neonatal nervous system (Bertolasio et al., 2011).

In the same way, studies using MXC (Aoyama and Chapin, 2014; Basavarajappa et al., 2011; Craig et al., 2010) investigated their ability to alter steroidogenesis (Basavarajappa et al., 2011; Craig et al., 2010) or the induction of specific anthropic toxicities in the ovarian follicle (Miller et al., 2006). It was observed that MXC inhibits follicle growth at 48, 72, and 96 h, significantly decreasing the E2 levels and the expression levels of StAR (steroidogenic acute regulatory protein—that is crucial for the transport of cholesterol to mitochondria where biosynthesis of steroids is initiated) (Flück et al., 2011), altering steroidogenic and metabolic enzymes (Basavarajappa et al., 2011).

OP pesticides, as CPF, could act as an endocrine disrupter in the mammary glands of female rats using nontoxic and safe doses, ranging from 1 to 0.01 mg/kg/day of the substance. Thus, CPF reproduces the estradiol-induced action local and systemically, inhibiting the increase of luteinizing hormone (LH) induced by ovariectomy. CPF has an estrogenic action in regulating negative feedback of pituitary LH release. These findings suggest that CPF alters the endocrine regulation of the mammary gland and can act as a risk factor for breast cancer (Ventura et al., 2016). In addition, another study showed that DDT stimulates the growth of ER-positive human breast cancer cells (MCF-7) and mimic the effects of both estrogen and estradiol, promoting the progression of the cell cycle through molecular regulators and by increasing the synthesis of the cyclin D1 protein, respectively (Dees et al., 1997).

There are numerous research articles relating occupational exposure to pesticides with fertility problems in men; however, studies among women are scarce. It may be due to higher exposure to pesticides occurring among males, while females are exposed only by reentry activities, i.e., the moment when they come into contact with their spouse's contaminated protective clothing and equipment (Bretveld et al., 2006).

2.3 Pesticide-induced androgens deregulation

Testosterone is the primary reproductive hormone in males, playing a pivotal role in developing during puberty, as sexual maturation, changes in appearance features, behavioral and boosting self-esteem (Freire et al., 2014). This section summarizes the effect of different pesticides on androgenic hormones (Fig. 3).

New testicular cells (Leydig and Sertoli) extracted from healthy adult male albino Sprague–Dawley rats after exposure to glyphosate-based pesticides caused a decrease in testosterone at shallow doses (Clair et al., 2012). In addition, Taxvig et al. (2013) investigated two pesticide blends for their endocrine activity potential. Blend 1 comprised three pesticides: bitertanol, propiconazole, and cypermethrin, and blend 2 included five pesticides: malathion, terbuthylazine, and the three pesticides in blend 1. They observed in vitro that the pesticides of both mixtures affected steroidogenesis, causing an increase in progesterone and decreased testosterone; as for in vivo, there was estradiol depletion and reduced placental testosterone. However, these mixtures did not affect the levels of fetal plasma or testicular hormones, nor the anogenital distance (AGD); this last variable was performed to verify that the size of the fetus could influence the AGD length.

It has been demonstrated in vivo studies that MXC administration causes adverse effects on male reproduction in toxicological doses (Du et al., 2014). MXC doses administration in adult male Sprague–Dawley rats within an interval of 30 to 54 days were

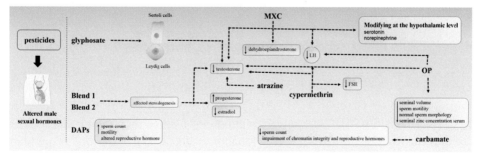

Fig. 3 Pesticides change male sexual hormones. Different pesticides act on male sex hormones, altering the quality, motility, quantity, volume, and morphology of sperm. All these are due to hormonal alteration, mainly in the reduction of testosterone.

responsible for decreasing testosterone and dehydroepiandrosterone levels to 41% and 45%, respectively. Similarly, changes in testosterone secretion alter LH secretion, modifying serotonin and norepinephrine at the hypothalamic level, altering the direct neural pathway between the brain and testes (Lafuente et al., 2008; Murono et al., 2006). The experiments carried out by Friedmann (2002) show that atrazine administration also reduced testosterone serum and intratesticular levels by approximately 50%. Cypermethrin may cause a decrease in epididymal and testis size, daily sperm production; furthermore, testosterone, follicle-stimulating hormone (FSH), and LH serum levels were also reduced (Elbetieha et al., 2001).

In addition, in different world regions, several studies with humans have been conducted due to the growing evidence of increasing reproductive abnormalities among men (Bretveld et al., 2006). The authors analyzed the association of urinary and reproductive parameters of men who attended an infertility clinic with organophosphorus pesticides and observed the presence of six dialkyl phosphate metabolites (DAPs) (used as biomarkers of organophosphorus exposure) in the samples. Decreased sperm counts and motility, with altered levels of reproductive hormones [FSH, LH, Prolactin (PRL), testosterone, and E2] were found, suggesting that OP may play an important role in endocrine functioning.

Venezuelan agricultural workers exposed to OP and carbamate pesticides showed a reduction in sperm count, impairment of chromatin integrity, and reproductive hormones (Miranda-Contreras et al., 2013). Yucra et al. (2006) investigated the exposure of Peruvian workers to the OP pesticide and observed that seminal volume, sperm motility and morphology, seminal zinc concentration, and serum testosterone and LH were low. In the same way, Recio et al. (2005), in their study using Mexican workers, demonstrated that OP exposure disrupts endocrine hypothalamic–pituitary function and indicates that FSH and LH are the most affected hormones.

Other studies involving human exposure to DDT show that it does not entail more severe damage to the hormonal dosages. Nevertheless, subtle changes should not be ruled out, and new studies must be carried out (Gladen et al., 2004; Kamijima et al., 2004).

2.4 Pesticides effect on other reproductive hormones

PRL is a pituitary hormone that has its secretion/production modulated by cholinergic agonists such as serotonin (5-HT) and norepinephrine (NE), which can lead to brain stimulation (Aguilar-Garduño et al., 2013). On the other hand, dopamine (DA) and gamma butyric acid (GABA) negatively regulate PRL since they inhibit the secretion of lactotrophs by the pituitary gland (Mohanty et al., 2017). Exposure to pesticides may alter other reproductive hormones (Fig. 4).

This hormone stimulates mammary gland development in mammals (McKinlay et al., 2008). Increased levels of PRL in the plasma of exposed groups are due to the response to reduced plasma levels of gonadotropins and testosterone and by interruption of the

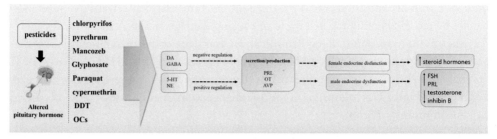

Fig. 4 Pesticides alter pituitary hormone. Chlorpyrifos, pyrethrum, mancozeb, glyphosate, paraquat, cypermethrin, DDT, and OCs act on dopamine (DA) and gamma butyric acid (GABA) regulating negatively the secretion/production of PRL, OT, and AVP, already on serotonin (5-HT) and norepinephrine (NE), act as a positive regulator for the production of these hormones. This change leads to female endocrine dysfunction with increased steroid hormones, and male endocrine dysfunction leads to increased FSH, PRL, and decreased testosterone and inhibin B.

dopaminergic system (Mohanty et al., 2017). Female endocrine dysfunction can result in many reproductive disorders that can affect the menstrual cycle, compromise fertility, lead to the development of endometriosis, polycystic ovary syndrome, and spontaneous abortion (Giulivo et al., 2016). Therefore, long-term exposure to pesticides may cause an inhibitory effect on the hypothalamic–pituitary system and thus reduce the generation of steroid hormones, which reflect on women's physical and sexual development (Bapayeva et al., 2016). Furthermore, pesticide cypermethrin also causes disturbance in the reproductive behavior in fish (Jaensson et al., 2007).

Exposure to CPF affects the levels of neurohypophysis hormones, such as PRL, oxytocin (OT), and arginine vasopressin (AVP) (Tait et al., 2009). In addition, some OP pesticides can also affect the male hormone profile. A study involving 136 floriculture workers from the State of Mexico and Morelos exposed to different concentrations of pesticides OP during two agricultural periods showed increased levels of FSH and PRL and decreased testosterone and inhibin B, a glycoprotein of the transforming growth factor-beta (TGF-β) (Aguilar-Garduño et al., 2013; dos Reis and de Rezende, 2009).

In the same way, a cross-sectional study of 99 rural men and 36 urban men aged 18 to 23 years exposed to herbicides (glyphosate and PQ) and dithiocarbamate fungicides (Mancozeb) showed a reduction of LH and PRL (Cremonese et al., 2017). However, elevated serum concentrations of OC pesticides can increase PRL levels in men and postmenopausal women, triggering an antiandrogenic effect in men and estrogen in women (Freire et al., 2014).

3. Agricultural poisons as immunological disruptors

One of the main long-term effects triggered by agricultural poison is immune response deregulation, and its development depends on the type of chemical, exposition route, duration of exposition, and dose. Immune cells are relatively sensitive to substances that act by either affecting the cell cycle or causing damage to DNA structure. In such a case, the immune response deregulation can be transient or permanent and is a consequence of the immunotoxicity induced by agrochemicals (Mokarizadeh et al., 2015). This event can be measured by either the occurrence of immunosuppression, which causes cancer and spread infections, or immunoenhancement, mainly associated with allergy and autoimmunity (Fig. 5).

The late development and maturation of immunity and the continuous cycling of immune cells in the bone marrow continuously expose the fragility of its regulatory mechanisms to failures induced by chronic exposition to substances capable of targeting the cell cycle. Immune cells are under constant replication and keep in contact with injuring substances in the bloodstream, which can compromise their lifespan in the organism Zhao et al., 2013).

Immune components from adaptive responses as peripheral B cells present a lifespan period of 5 to 6 weeks (Seifert and Küppers, 2016), while peripheral T cells remain resting for very long periods, from months to years. Neutrophils have a short turnover, from 8 h to 5 days on average (Uhl et al., 2016). It means that some cell types are targeted acutely by chemicals that affect the cell cycle, while others as T cells, may be injured by cumulative DNA damage. In both cases, the immune response homeostasis is severely impaired. Neutrophils are in the first line of defense and play a pivotal role in the innate immune response before antigen challenge. Thus, if neutrophilic turnover is compromised, antigen presentation-related functions are probably ruined. The same may occur with lymphocytes since the cumulative DNA damage triggers cell death (Rosales, 2018).

Herbicides and fungicides and their effects on immune components have been extensively studied. The most-known representant of herbicides is glyphosate, a phosphorus-containing amino acid-type herbicide that has been reported to cause immunological damage. Once in contact with immune cells, glyphosate can inhibit the proliferative capacity of human peripheral blood mononuclear cells (which include lymphocytes and monocytes) and affect the production of cytokines like IL-2 and IFN-γ (Nakashima et al., 2002). Further, this compound can be easily inhaled and trigger immune-related respiratory abnormalities because of its low weight. Experiments using glyphosate-rich air samples collected on farms during spraying herbicides or directly inhaled glyphosate have shown significant eosinophilia and mast cell degranulation in mice. This exposition led mice to develop pulmonary IL-13-dependent inflammation promoted by Th2-type cytokines. These data indicate that glyphosate inhalation causes deregulated immune hyperreactivity (Kumar et al., 2014).

Atrazine is another herbicide to which people are constantly exposed. Studies point out that atrazine is also immunotoxic. Experimental data evidence that mice exposition

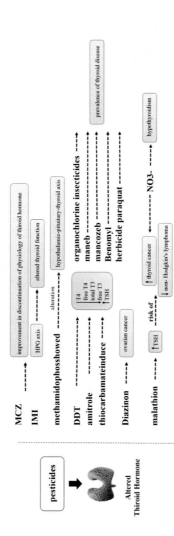

Fig. 5 Pesticides change thyroid hormone. MCZ and IMI improve the discontinuation of the physiology of thyroid hormone and act in hypothalamic-pituitary-gonadal (HPG) axis, altering thyroid function. Methamidophos changes hypothalamic-pituitary-thyroid axis. DDT, amitrole, and thiocarbamate reduce T4, free T4, total T3, and free T3; and increase TSH. Diazinon is associated with ovarian cancer. Malathion induces increased TSH, with a high risk factor for thyroid cancer and low for non-Hodgkin's lymphoma.

to subacute doses of atrazine impairs both thymic and splenic developments, with further alterations in lymphocytes transformation and activity (Zhao et al., 2013).

In vitro studies further indicate that atrazine harms the capacity of human peripheral blood mononuclear cells to produce IFN-γ and TNF-α in a concentration-dependent manner (Thompson et al., 2015). Also, atrazine impairs the in vitro capability of natural killer cells (NK) to deal with tumors, reducing its efficiency to promote the lysis of tumor cells (Whalen et al., 2003). Atrazine exposition further suppresses the capability of NK to proliferate adequately, possibly by induction of cell apoptosis because of the enhanced production of ROS (Chen et al., 2015).

Other widely used herbicides, such as 2,4-dichlorophenoxyacetic acid (2,4-D), are experimentally described as a significant immunosuppressor, probably due to their genotoxicity and inhibition of antibody synthesis (Burns and Swaen, 2012; Smith et al., 2017). Similar results have been observed in farmers after 2,4-D occupational exposure, where effects after the exposition (1–12 days) caused significant diminishment of lymphoproliferative responses and the number CD4+, CD8+ T, and NK cells. The main late effect detected after the exposition (50–70 days) was diminished proliferative response in lymphocytes. These data highlight the need for continuous monitoring of immune response in people chronically exposed to pesticides (Faustini et al., 1996).

Insecticides are significant immune disruptors because they affect pivotal functional pathways of the immune response, directly linked with cancer generation, neurodegenerative pathologies, diabetes, and cardiovascular disease (Gangemi et al., 2016).

Pyrethroids, for example, can affect all stages of the immune response since they induce thymic apoptosis and loss of proliferative capabilities of leukocytes and impair immunoglobulins and cytokines production (Skolarczyk et al., 2017). As pentachlorophenol (PCP) and DDT, others alter NK cells' lytic function and alter TNF-α and IFN-γ secretion (Massawe et al., 2017).

Immunological disturbances induced by agrochemicals can also affect the neuroimmune response. More than 30 years ago, it was proposed that communication among the neuro-immune-endocrine responses suggested the existence of biochemical interactions among them. So, if some substance interferes in one of those axes, the other two may also be affected (Peón and Terrazas, 2018; Rezaei and Saghazadeh, 2019).

One of the primary known evidence regarding this issue is the behavioral and neurological alterations observed in people exposed to poisoning substances during the Gulf War. Most of those substances used in the war were pesticides posteriorly used in agriculture as agrochemicals (for example, pyridostigmine bromide, permethrin, and DEET). It is believed that about 30% of veterans who served the Gulf War presented the Gulf War illness (GWI). GWI has been proposed as a neuroimmune condition characterized by memory and mood dysfunctions associated with specific HLA allele expression. In this context, experiments have been conducted to understand the mechanisms developed after the exposition of pesticides (as sarin nerve agents and pesticides) in people with

GWI (Georgopoulos et al., 2017). Experimental data show that such exposition triggers neuroinflammatory responses in mice, consistent with the behavior-like symptoms observed in the veterans of the Gulf War (Koo et al., 2018). Mitochondrial dysfunctions, in association with genes representative of chronic oxidative stress and cytokines imbalance, have also been reported in the hippocampus of rats exposed to low doses of pesticides used during the Gulf War (Shetty et al., 2017).

Other neuroimmune disorders have also been reported after exposure to pesticides, as PQ. In vitro data evidence that PQ exposition alters neurons' immune environment, affecting the peripheral immune cells infiltration and cytokine secretion (Richardson et al., 2019). These data implicate the neuroimmune response as a putative mechanism for neurodegenerative conditions since the existence of inflammatory priming during the neuronal exposition to toxins modulates its immune profiling. In the same way, experimental data shows that the continuous exposition to low-doses of diquat (similar to those found in food) causes neuroimmune disbalance in the gastric mucosal mast cell proportion and degranulation, causing gastric abnormalities mediated by immune-related cells (Anton et al., 2001). All these findings are summarized in Fig. 5.

4. Implications of pesticide-induced immune-endocrine deregulation in cancer development

The main risk factors for cancer, in general, are age, heredity, and occupations in which there is exposure to toxic agents. Several carcinogenic agents have been researched, among which pesticides have gained prominence as organophosphates, carbamates, organochlorines, organothiophosphates, pyrethroids, and thiocarbamates (Lo et al., 2007).

As already discussed, pesticides can act as endocrine disruptors (EDs), interfere with hormonal homeostasis, from synthesis, secretion, transport, binding to receptors, action or elimination of natural hormones; causing endocrine disruption in humans, animals, and their progeny. It is worth noting that hormones play a crucial role in organogenesis, so endocrine disruption in the early stages of life, such as in the intrauterine and lactation period, can favor the development of cancer in tissues regulated by hormones and other reproductive, immunological, and neurological disorders (Francis and Swain, 2018).

Evidence about the influence of occupational exposure to pesticides and the possible endocrine and immunological disorders associated with hormo ne-dependent tumors and their role in its carcinogenesis and progression are detailed in Table 1.

These studies demonstrated an increased risk of cancer and more aggressive tumors in individuals with occupational exposure to pesticides, although the pathophysiological mechanisms are poorly understood and studies indicate that pesticides can cause oxidative stress, genetic damage, epigenetic changes and endocrine disruption. Most evidence is epidemiological, and some experimental models point out that certain EDs can interact

Table 1 Evidences concerning human exposure to pesticides, immune-endocrine disruption and cancer development.

Author	Primary site of cancer	Study and data description	Pesticides	Endocrine/ immunological disruptors mechanism related	Pesticide exposure, immune-endocrine disorders and cancer: Are they linked?
Pardo et al. (2020)	Prostate (PCa)	An epidemiologic study from the Agricultural Health Study, witch 883 cases of aggressive PCa diagnosed between 1993 and 2015, adjusted for birth year, state, family history of PCa, race, and smoking status was analyzed	Organothioate insecticide dimethoate, triclopyr herbicide	Aggressive PCa risk among users of the organodithioate to never users	Pesticides were associated with aggressive prostate cancer risk in this large cohort of pesticide applicators
Nowak et al. (2019)	Nonspecific	Review article of immunomodulatory effects of synthetic endocrine disrupting chemicals (EDCs) on the development and functions of human immune cells	Tetrachlorodibenzo-p-dioxin (TCDD), Dichlorodifenylotrichloroetan (DDT)	EDCs deregulates adaptive and innate immune mechanisms and interferes with cellular and humoral activities	A direct effect of endocrine disrupting chemicals exposure is the suppression of inflammatory processes, which may lead to an insufficient immune response against bacteria, fungi, viruses, and cancer cells
Prins (2008)	Prostate	A commentary about endocrine disruptors and prostate cancer risk	Methyl bromide, chlorpyrifos, fonofos, coumaphos, phorate, permethrin, and butylate	These compounds may interfere with steroid hormone metabolism by the liver as well as the prostate and, in so doing, alter steroid balance and availability which in turn may contribute to increased prostate cancer risk	There is increasing evidence both from epidemiology studies and animal models that specific endocrine-disrupting compounds may influence the development or progression of prostate cancer

Reference	Cancer type	Pesticide	Description	Findings
Quagliariello et al. (2017)	Prostate	Pesticides, insecticide (endosulfan, lindane, propoxur)	Review article about metabolic syndrome, endocrine disruptors and prostate cancer associations	Endosulfan increase activating phosphorylation of EGFR type 2 and it increases the activity of several oncogenes like MAPK in prostate cancer cells. Endosulfan with other xenoestrogens like lindane and propoxur, act as angiogenesis stimulators both in vitro as well as in vivo models but more molecular and biochemical studies are needed	EDCs may DNA damage and mutagenicity, act as antiandrogen, estrogen agonist, angiogenesis stimulator, induces cellular micronuvlel; increases expression of P21; enhance progression and metastasis of prostate cancer, inhibition of apoptosis
Landau-Ossondo et al. (2009)	Prostate and breast	Organochlorine pesticides	Review about key mechanisms of pesticide-induced prostate and breast cancers	Many xenoestrogens, especially organochlorine pesticides have been shown to disrupt endocrine processes by acting as agonists on era and/or antagonists on erβ and also possibly as antagonists on androgenic receptors (ars)	Pesticides may be causally involved in the growing incidence of prostate and breast cancers in Martinique through a common carcinogenic endocrine disruption mechanism
Koutros et al. (2013)	Prostate	Organophosphate insecticides, an organochlorine insecticide	This study studied the risk of prostate cancer associated with specific pesticides in the Agricultural Health	There was not find significant association between any specific pesticide and risk of total prostate cancer,	Observed significant increases in the risk of aggressive prostate cancer associated with 4 insecticides: fonofos

Continued

Table 1 Evidences concerning human exposure to pesticides, immune-endocrine disruption and cancer development—cont'd

Author	Primary site of cancer	Study and data description	Pesticides	Endocrine/ immunological disruptors mechanism related	Pesticide exposure, immune-endocrine disorders and cancer: Are they linked?
		Study, in a 919 aggressive prostate cancers among 54,412 pesticides applicators		although insecticides were associated with aggressive prostate cancer	(organophosphate), malathion (organophosphate), terbufos (organophosphate), and aldrin (organochlorine)
Lo et al. (2007)	Prostate	The authors tested EDCs for their effect on 5α-reductase activity in vitro test systems; an enzyme assay with human prostate tissue homogenate as 5α-reductase source and an enzyme assay with human Lymph Node Carcinoma of Prostate (LNCaP) cells as a prostate model	Monobutyltin (MBT), dibutyltin (DBT), tributyltin (TBT), triphenyltin (TPT), diuron, fenarimol, linuron, p,p DDE, prochloraz and vinclozolin	5a-reductase activity in human Lymph Node Carcinoma of Prostate (LNCaP) cells and an enzyme assay with human prostate tissue homogenate	Many of the tested pesticides can inhibit the 5a-reductase reactivity and cause reduced dihydrotestosterone (DHT) levels, which might be of clinical relevance
Silva et al. (2016)	Prostate	Systematic review of the literature about exposure to pesticides and prostate cancer. The review included 49 studies published	Pesticides in general	Most studies (32 articles) found a positive association between prostate cancer and pesticides	The evidence provided by the reviewed studies indicates a possible association between the development of prostate cancer and

Reference	Cancer	Study description	Pesticide	Mechanism/findings	Conclusions
		between 1993 and 2015 (15 were case–control studies, and 34 were cohort studies)		agricultural occupations	pesticide exposure and/or agricultural occupations
Fan et al. (2007)	Rodents mammary and prostate cancer	Research about implications for endocrine disruption in wildlife and reproductive cancers in humans. Comparison of steroidogenic factor 1 (SF-1) expression in atrazine responsive and nonresponsive cell lines and transfected SF-1 into nonresponsive cell lines to assess SF-1's role in atrazine-induced aromatase	Atrazine	Atrazine is a potent endocrine disruptor that increases aromatase expression. The mechanism involves the inhibition of phosphodiesterase and subsequent elevation of cAMP	Atrazine bound directly to SF-1, showing that atrazine is a ligand for this "orphan" receptor. The current findings are consistent with atrazine's endocrine-disrupting effects in fish, amphibians, and reptiles; the induction of mammary and prostate cancer in laboratory rodents; and correlations between atrazine and similar reproductive cancers in humans
Xu et al. (2010)	Breast and Prostate	Associations between serum concentrations of OC pesticides and prostate and breast cancers in 1999–2004 National Health and Nutrition Examination Survey data	Organochlorine pesticides (OC)	Serum concentrations of OC pesticides and prostate and breast cancers	OC pesticide exposures may have a significant effect on cancer risk

Continued

Table 1 Evidences concerning human exposure to pesticides, immune-endocrine disruption and cancer development—cont'd

Author	Primary site of cancer	Study and data description	Pesticides	Endocrine/immunological disruptors mechanism related	Pesticide exposure, immune-endocrine disorders and cancer: Are they linked?
Del Mazo et al. (2013)	Testicular cancer (TC)	Literature review regarding various aspects of genetic, transcriptomic and epigenetic changes related to testicular development, exposure to EDCs and the occurrence of germ cell tumors	Pesticides in general	It is likely that these compounds alter the interaction between the mechanisms of gene regulation and functional gene networks in windows of risk, mainly during embryonic development. Moreover, such changes could be transmitted through generations by epigenetic mechanisms	EDCs may trigger disturbances in the regulatory pathways of gene expression, leading to reproductive dysfunctions and pathologies such as testicular cancer. Moreover, such changes could be transmitted through generations by epigenetic mechanisms
Giannandrea et al. (2013)	Testicular cancer (TC)	This review summarize the literature about hormonal factors, endogenous hormones and environmental xenoestrogens, and testicular carcinogenesis	Organochlorine compounds	Summarize published studies to identify risk factors related to TC, with a particular emphasis on endogenous and exogenous hormonal factors that constitute a risk of disease development	Organochlorine compounds mimic the actions of estrogen by binding to estrogen receptors or have antiandrogenic effects. Chronic exposure to organochlorine has been related to pesticides, including cancer, endocrine problems, and reproductive disorders including detrimental effects in the male offspring

| Rochefort (2017) | Breast and prostate | Several complementary approaches have been used: French cancer records, epidemiological studies on cohorts followed over several decades, numerous in vitro experimental studies using cell cultures and in vivo animal studies. | Dichlorodifenylotrichloroetan (DDT), dioxins | DDT on breast cancer after early in utero or perinatal exposure appears much later after puberty. Other eds, dioxins, and certain pesticides are co-carcinogens with a delayed effect on breast and prostate cancer | Converging experimental approaches, both in vitro experiments on cell lines and in vivo on animals, combined with epidemiological studies monitoring cohorts of women exposed to EDCs make a compelling case for their co-carcinogenic effect, an effect that does not become evident until much later in life. These approaches all converge to the same result, strongly suggesting a causal relationship between EDs and precancerous lesions |
| Hall and Greco (2019) | Testicular, breast, endometrial, prostate | Review of experimental, clinical, and epidemiological studies, about the dysregulation of Nuclear Hormone Receptor function by environmental EDCs, | Pesticides in general | Experimental data established a strong causal link between EDCs exposure and disorders of numerous organ systems and metabolic processes. Epidemiological | There is sufficient experimental information on disease risks that can be extrapolated to predict human outcomes, and thus prompt us to limit EDCs exposure, |

Continued

Table 1 Evidences concerning human exposure to pesticides, immune-endocrine disruption and cancer development—cont'd

Author	Primary site of cancer	Study and data description	Pesticides	Endocrine/immunological disruptors mechanism related	Pesticide exposure, immune-endocrine disorders and cancer: Are they linked?
		and the associated pathological consequences including cancers		studies have highlighted the clinical consequences of EDC exposure during various phases of development and adulthood	especially during sensitive developmental periods (i.e., in utero, neonatal, and puberty)
Marotta et al. (2020)	Thyroid cancer	Review of studies with different methodological approaches aiming to define the role of anthropogenic environmental chemicals in thyroid carcinogenesis	Organochlorine and organophosphate compounds	A series of case–control studies, assessing exposure to thyroid-disrupting agents, as measured on biological matrices were explored	Controversial results were reported for pesticides. However, such studies cannot demonstrate the causal link with disease occurrence, as exposure is assessed after tumor development. Such studies cannot demonstrate the causal link with disease occurrence, as exposure is assessed after tumor development
Cohn et al. (2015)	Breast	A prospective study to relate quantitative measures of in utero DDT exposure to risk of breast cancer in	DDT	DDT associated with carcinogenesis by interfering with normal tissue–hormone response	The susceptibility to develop life on exposure to one of future studies was tested in the early stages

Reference	Cancer	Chemical	Description	Findings	Conclusion
			daughters, by a 54-year follow-up of 20,754 pregnancies, resulting in 9300 live-born female offspring in the Child Health and Development Studies (CHDS) pregnancy cohort		of life in humans, moreover, this risk was increased 5 times when exposure occurred compared to greater when the onset of life did not occur later, later in relation to cancer
Kaur et al. (2019)	Breast	Hexachlorocyclohexane (HCH)–α, β, γ, endosulfan, DDT	This case–control study assessed the serum levels of organochlorine compounds (OC) in 42 patients of breast cancer and 42 age-matched controls by performing assays in blood samples for pesticides in North Indian population of young women	Serum DDT levels were higher in breast cancer patients compared to healthy subjects	Exposure to organochlorines may be contributing to the increased incidence of breast cancer in younger women in India
Krigbaum et al. (2020)	Breast	p'-DDT	This was a case–control study nested in a prospective 54-year follow-up of 9300 daughters in the CHDS pregnancy cohort (n=118 breast cancer cases, diagnosed by age 52 y and 354 controls matched on birth year)	DDT associated with carcinogenesis by interfering with normal tissue–hormone response	Mammographic density is considered a marker of breast cancer risk, resulting from a combination of hormonal activity and is important during the development of breast tissue. p,p'-DDT was associated with higher breast density in women with a history of maternal breast cancer

Continued

Table 1 Evidences concerning human exposure to pesticides, immune-endocrine disruption and cancer development—cont'd

Author	Primary site of cancer	Study and data description	Pesticides	Endocrine/ immunological disruptors mechanism related	Pesticide exposure, immune-endocrine disorders and cancer: Are they linked?
Miret et al. (2019)	Breast, thyroid and uterus	This review provides a thorough analysis of results obtained in the last 15 years of research and evaluates data from assays in mammary gland and breast cancer in diverse animal models	Hexachlorobenzene (HCB)	HCB binds to the aryl hydrocarbon receptor (ahr), activating both the membrane (c-Src) and nuclear pathways. In addition, it interacts with other membrane receptors, including estrogen receptor-α, insulin-like growth factor receptor-1, epidermal growth factor receptor, and transforming growth factor beta-1 receptors	Several pathways involved in breast morphogenesis and breast cancer development are modified, inducing tumor progression. HCB thus stimulates the proliferation of epithelial cells, preneoplastic lesions and alterations in the development of the mammary gland, as well as migration and invasion of neoplastic cells, metastasis and angiogenesis in breast cancer
Kim et al. (2014)	Ovarian cancer	This is an in vitro study, who's the potential impact of MXC and TCS on ovarian cancer cell growth and the underlying mechanism was examined following their treatments in BG-1 ovarian cancer cells	Metoxichlor (MXC)	MXC induced the growth of ovarian cancer cells (BG-1) via regulation of cyclin D1, p21 and Bax genes related to cell cycle and apoptosis	MXC can stimulate ovarian cancer growth through an ER-dependent pathway

Lerro et al. (2015)	Breast, thyroid and ovarian cancer	This research evaluated personal use of specific OPs and cancer incidence among female spouses of pesticide applicators in the prospective Agricultural Health Study cohort	Organophosphporous (OP)	Endocrine deregulation	Increased risk with OP use for several hormone-related cancers, including breast, thyroid, and ovary, suggesting potential for hormone-mediated effects
Albanito et al. (2015)	Ovarian cancer	This study evaluated the potential of atrazine to trigger GPER-mediated signaling in cancer cells and cancer-associated fibroblasts (CAFs)	Atrazine	Atrazine stimulated the proliferation of ovarian cancer cells that depend on GPER and Erα	It induced ERK phosphorylation, gene expression and migration in cancer-associated fibroblasts, thus extending its stimulatory role to these key players in the tumor microenvironment

mainly with steroid hormone receptors, thyroid receptors, interfering with carcinogenesis, progression and aggressiveness of hormone-dependent tumors. It is known that tumors of the prostate, testes, breast, uterus, ovaries and thyroid are mostly regulated by hormones, and these remain as essential elements in anticancer therapy (carcinogenesis, evolution and prognosis).

Early life stage exposure to pesticides affects the development, functions, and lifespan of immune cells can influence the development and effector functions of innate and adaptive immunity; are associated in the development of several diseases (Bansal et al., 2018; Nowak et al., 2019). However, to elucidate the action of pesticides such as DEs and their pathophysiological consequences, and to directly link cancer, more in vitro and in vivo research is needed.

Acknowledgments
The authors gratefully acknowledge Ivy Gobeti for helping with the editing of the paper.

Funding
Not applicable.

Authors' contributions
All authors equally contributed to this manuscript. All authors read and approved the final manuscript.

Competing interests
The authors declare that they have no competing interests.

References
Aguilar-Garduño, C., Lacasaña, M., Blanco-Muñoz, J., et al., 2013. Changes in male hormone profile after occupational organophosphate exposure. A longitudinal study. Toxicology 307, 55–65. https://doi.org/10.1016/j.tox.2012.11.001.

Albanito, L., Lappano, R., Madeo, A., et al., 2015. Effects of atrazine on estrogen receptor α- and G protein-coupled receptor 30-mediated signaling and proliferation in cancer cells and cancer-associated fibroblasts. Environ. Health Perspect. 123, 493–499. https://doi.org/10.1289/EHP.1408586.

Anton, P.M., Theodorou, V., Fioramonti, J., et al., 2001. Chronic low-level administration of diquat increases the nociceptive response to gastric distension in rats: role of mast cells and tachykinin receptor activation. Pain 92, 219–227. https://doi.org/10.1016/S0304-3959(01)00257-3.

Aoyama, H., Chapin, R.E., 2014. Reproductive toxicities of Methoxychlor based on estrogenic properties of the compound and its estrogenic metabolite, Hydroxyphenyltrichloroethane. Vitam. Horm. 94, 193–210. https://doi.org/10.1016/B978-0-12-800095-3.00007-9. Academic Press Inc.

Astiz, M., Acaz-Fonseca, E., Garcia-Segura, L.M., 2014. Sex differences and effects of estrogenic compounds on the expression of inflammatory molecules by astrocytes exposed to the insecticide dimethoate. Neurotox. Res. 25, 271–285. https://doi.org/10.1007/s12640-013-9417-0.

Bansal, A., Henao-Mejia, J., Simmons, R.A., 2018. Immune system: an emerging player in mediating effects of endocrine disruptors on metabolic health. Endocrinology 159, 32–45. https://doi.org/10.1210/EN.2017-00882.

Bapayeva, G., Issayeva, R., Zhumadilova, A., et al., 2016. Organochlorine pesticides and female puberty in South Kazakhstan. Reprod. Toxicol. 65, 67–75. https://doi.org/10.1016/j.reprotox.2016.06.017.

Basavarajappa, M.S., Craig, Z.R., Hernández-Ochoa, I., et al., 2011. Methoxychlor reduces estradiol levels by altering steroidogenesis and metabolism in mouse antral follicles in vitro. Toxicol. Appl. Pharmacol. 253, 161–169. https://doi.org/10.1016/j.taap.2011.04.007.

Baudry, J., Lelong, H., Adriouch, S., Julia, C., Allès, B., Hercberg, S., Touvier, M., Lairon, D., Galan, P., Kesse-Guyot, E., 2018. Association between organic food consumption and metabolic syndrome: cross-sectional results from the NutriNet-Santé study. Eur. J. Nutr. 57 (7), 2477–2488. https://doi.org/10.1007/s00394-017-1520-1.

Bertolasio, J., Fyfe, S., Snyder, B.W., et al., 2011. Neonatal injections of methoxychlor decrease adult rat female reproductive behavior. Neurotoxicology 32, 809–813. https://doi.org/10.1016/j.neuro.2011.06.007.

Blum, J.L., James, M.O., Stuchal, L.D., et al., 2008. Stimulation of transactivation of the largemouth bass estrogen receptors alpha, beta-a, and beta-b by methoxychlor and its mono- and bis-demethylated metabolites in HepG2 cells. J. Steroid Biochem. Mol. Biol. 108, 55–63. https://doi.org/10.1016/j.jsbmb.2007.06.004.

Bretveld, R.W., Thomas, C.M.G., Scheepers, P.T.J., et al., 2006. Pesticide exposure: the hormonal function of the female reproductive system disrupted? Reprod. Biol. Endocrinol. https://doi.org/10.1186/1477-7827-4-30.

Burns, C.J., Swaen, G.M.H., 2012. Review of 2,4-dichlorophenoxyacetic acid (2,4-D) biomonitoring and epidemiology. Crit. Rev. Toxicol. https://doi.org/10.3109/10408444.2012.710576.

Burns, J.S., Williams, P.L., Korrick, S.A., et al., 2014. Original contribution association between chlorinated pesticides in the serum of prepubertal Russian boys and longitudinal biomarkers of metabolic function. Am. J. Epidemiol. https://doi.org/10.1093/aje/kwu212.

Chen, J., Huo, J., Jia, Z., et al., 2015. Effects of atrazine on the proliferation and cytotoxicity of murine lymphocytes with the use of carboxyfluorescein succinimidyl ester-based flow cytometric approaches. Food Chem. Toxicol. 76, 61–69. https://doi.org/10.1016/j.fct.2014.11.026.

Clair, É., Mesnage, R., Travert, C., et al., 2012. A glyphosate-based herbicide induces necrosis and apoptosis in mature rat testicular cells in vitro, and testosterone decrease at lower levels. Toxicol. In Vitro 26, 269–279. https://doi.org/10.1016/j.tiv.2011.12.009.

Cohn, B.A., La Merrill, M., Krigbaum, N.Y., et al., 2015. DDT exposure in utero and breast cancer. J. Clin. Endocrinol. Metab. 100, 2865–2872. https://doi.org/10.1210/JC.2015-1841.

Combarnous, Y., 2017. Endocrine disruptor compounds (EDCs) and agriculture: the case of pesticides. C. R. Biol. https://doi.org/10.1016/j.crvi.2017.07.009.

Craig, Z.R., Leslie, T.C., Hatfield, K.P., et al., 2010. Mono-hydroxy methoxychlor alters levels of key sex steroids and steroidogenic enzymes in cultured mouse antral follicles. Toxicol. Appl. Pharmacol. 249, 107–113. https://doi.org/10.1016/j.taap.2010.09.001.

Cremonese, C., Piccoli, C., Pasqualotto, F., et al., 2017. Occupational exposure to pesticides, reproductive hormone levels and sperm quality in young Brazilian men. Reprod. Toxicol. 67, 174–185. https://doi.org/10.1016/j.reprotox.2017.01.001.

Cummings, A.M., Metcalf, J.L., 1995. Methoxychlor regulates rat uterine estrogen-induced protein. Toxicol. Appl. Pharmacol. 130, 154–160. https://doi.org/10.1006/taap.1995.1020.

De Long, N.E., Holloway, A.C., 2017. Early-life chemical exposures and risk of metabolic syndrome. Diabetes Metab. Syndr. Obes. https://doi.org/10.2147/DMSO.S95296.

Debost-Legrand, A., Warembourg, C., Massart, C., et al., 2016. Prenatal exposure to persistent organic pollutants and organophosphate pesticides, and markers of glucose metabolism at birth. Environ. Res. 146, 207–217. https://doi.org/10.1016/j.envres.2016.01.005.

Dees, C., Askari, M., Foster, J.S., et al., 1997. DDT mimicks estradiol stimulation of breast cancer cells to enter the cell cycle. Mol. Carcinog. 18, 107–114. https://doi.org/10.1002/(SICI)1098-2744(199702)18:2<107::AID-MC6>3.0.CO;2-D.

Del Mazo, J., Brieño-Enríquez, M.A., García-López, J., et al., 2013. Endocrine disruptors, gene deregulation and male germ cell tumors. Int. J. Dev. Biol. 57, 225–239. https://doi.org/10.1387/IJDB.130042JD.

dos Reis, F.M., de Rezende, C.P., 2009. Aplicações das dosagens de inibinas em Ginecologia e Obstetrícia. Rev. Bras. Ginecol. Obstet. 31, 621–625. https://doi.org/10.1590/s0100-72032009001200008.

Du, X., Zhang, H., Liu, Y., et al., 2014. Perinatal exposure to low-dose Methoxychlor impairs testicular development in C57BL/6 mice. PLoS One 9, e103016. https://doi.org/10.1371/journal.pone.0103016.

Elbetieha, A., Da'as, S.I., Khamas, W., et al., 2001. Evaluation of the toxic potentials of cypermethrin pesticide on some reproductive and fertility parameters in the male rats. Arch. Environ. Contam. Toxicol. 41, 522–528. https://doi.org/10.1007/s002440010280.

El-Hefnawy, T., Hernandez, C., Stabile, L.P., 2017. The endocrine disrupting alkylphenols and 4,4'-DDT interfere with estrogen conversion and clearance by mouse liver cytosol. Reprod. Biol. 17, 185–192. https://doi.org/10.1016/j.repbio.2017.04.003.

Fan, W.Q., Yanase, T., Morinaga, H., et al., 2007. Atrazine-induced aromatase expression is SF-1 dependent: implications for endocrine disruption in wildlife and reproductive cancers in humans. Environ. Health Perspect. 115, 720–727. https://doi.org/10.1289/EHP.9758.

Faustini, A., Settimi, L., Pacifici, R., et al., 1996. Immunological changes among farmers exposed to phenoxy herbicides: preliminary observations. Occup. Environ. Med. 53, 583–585. https://doi.org/10.1136/oem.53.9.583.

Flück, C.E., Pandey, A.V., Dick, B., et al., 2011. Characterization of novel StAR (steroidogenic acute regulatory protein) mutations causing non-classic lipoid adrenal hyperplasia. PLoS One 6. https://doi.org/10.1371/journal.pone.0020178.

Francis, J.C., Swain, A., 2018. Prostate Organogenesis. Cold Spring Harb. Perspect. Med. 8, a030353. https://doi.org/10.1101/CSHPERSPECT.A030353.

Freire, C., Koifman, R.J., Sarcinelli, P.N., et al., 2014. Association between serum levels of organochlorine pesticides and sex hormones in adults living in a heavily contaminated area in Brazil. Int. J. Hyg. Environ. Health 217, 370–378. https://doi.org/10.1016/j.ijheh.2013.07.012.

Friedmann, A.S., 2002. Atrazine inhibition of testosterone production in rat males following peripubertal exposure. Reprod. Toxicol. 16, 275–279. https://doi.org/10.1016/S0890-6238(02)00019-9.

Gangemi, S., Gofita, E., Costa, C., et al., 2016. Occupational and environmental exposure to pesticides and cytokine pathways in chronic diseases. Int. J. Mol. Med. https://doi.org/10.3892/ijmm.2016.2728.

Georgopoulos, A.P., James, L.M., Carpenter, A.F., et al., 2017. Gulf war illness (GWI) as a neuroimmune disease. Exp. Brain Res. 235, 3217–3225. https://doi.org/10.1007/s00221-017-5050-0.

Giannandrea, F., Paoli, D., Figà-Talamanca, I., et al., 2013. Effect of endogenous and exogenous hormones on testicular cancer: the epidemiological evidence. Int. J. Dev. Biol. 57, 255–263. https://doi.org/10.1387/IJDB.130015FG.

Giulivo, M., Lopez de Alda, M., Capri, E., et al., 2016. Human exposure to endocrine disrupting compounds: their role in reproductive systems, metabolic syndrome and breast cancer. A review. Environ. Res. https://doi.org/10.1016/j.envres.2016.07.011.

Gladen, B.C., Klebanoff, M.A., Hediger, M.L., et al., 2004. Prenatal DDT exposure in relation to anthropometric and pubertal measures in adolescent males. Environ. Health Perspect. 112, 1761–1767. https://doi.org/10.1289/ehp.7287.

Hall, J.M., Greco, C.W., 2019. Perturbation of nuclear hormone receptors by endocrine disrupting chemicals: mechanisms and pathological consequences of exposure. Cells 9 (1), 13. https://doi.org/10.3390/cells9010013.

Jaensson, A., Scott, A.P., Moore, A., et al., 2007. Effects of a pyrethroid pesticide on endocrine responses to female odours and reproductive behaviour in male parr of brown trout (Salmo trutta L.). Aquat. Toxicol. 81, 1–9. https://doi.org/10.1016/j.aquatox.2006.10.011.

Jamal, F., Haque, Q.S., Singh, S., et al., 2016. The influence of organophosphate and carbamate on sperm chromatin and reproductive hormones among pesticide sprayers. Toxicol. Ind. Health. https://doi.org/10.1177/0748233714568175.

Juntarawijit, C., Juntarawijit, Y., 2018. Association between diabetes and pesticides: a case-control study among Thai farmers. Environ. Health Prev. Med. 23. https://doi.org/10.1186/s12199-018-0692-5.

Kamijima, M., Hibi, H., Gotoh, M., et al., 2004. A survey of semen indices in insecticide sprayers. J. Occup. Health 46, 109–118. https://doi.org/10.1539/joh.46.109.

Kaur, N., Swain, S.K., Banerjee, B.D., et al., 2019. Organochlorine pesticide exposure as a risk factor for breast cancer in young Indian women: a case–control study. South Asian J. Cancer 8, 212. https://doi.org/10.4103/SAJC.SAJC_427_18.

Kim, J., Park, Y., Yoon, K.S., et al., 2013. Imidacloprid, a neonicotinoid insecticide, induces insulin resistance. J. Toxicol. Sci. https://doi.org/10.2131/jts.38.655.

Kim, J.Y., Yi, B.R., Go, R.E., Hwang, K.A., Nam, K.H., Choi, K.C., 2014. Methoxychlor and triclosan stimulates ovarian cancer growth by regulating cell cycle- and apoptosis-related genes via an estrogen receptor-dependent pathway. Environ. Toxicol. Pharmacol. 37 (3), 1264–1274. https://doi.org/10.1016/j.etap.2014.04.013.

Kjeldsen, L.S., Ghisari, M., Bonefeld-Jørgensen, E.C., 2013. Currently used pesticides and their mixtures affect the function of sex hormone receptors and aromatase enzyme activity. Toxicol. Appl. Pharmacol. 272, 453–464. https://doi.org/10.1016/j.taap.2013.06.028.

Koo, B.B., Michalovicz, L.T., Calderazzo, S., et al., 2018. Corticosterone potentiates DFP-induced neuroinflammation and affects high-order diffusion imaging in a rat model of gulf war illness. Brain Behav. Immun. 67, 42–46. https://doi.org/10.1016/j.bbi.2017.08.003.

Koutros, S., Freeman, L.B., et al., 2013. Risk of Total and Aggressive Prostate Cancer and Pesticide use in the Agricultural Health Study. (academic.oup.com).

Krigbaum, N., Cirillo, P., Flom, J., et al., 2020. In Utero DDT Exposure and Breast Density Before Age 50. (Elsevier).

Kumar, S., Khodoun, M., Kettleson, E.M., et al., 2014. Glyphosate-rich air samples induce IL-33, TSLP and generate IL-13 dependent airway inflammation. Toxicology 325. https://doi.org/10.1016/j.tox.2014.08.008.

La Merrill, M., Karey, E., Moshier, E., et al., 2014. Perinatal exposure of mice to the pesticide DDT impairs energy expenditure and metabolism in adult female offspring. PLoS One 9. https://doi.org/10.1371/journal.pone.0103337.

Lafuente, A., Cabaleiro, T., Caride, A., et al., 2008. Toxic effects of methoxychlor administered subcutaneously on the hypothalamic-pituitary-testicular axis in adult rats. Food Chem. Toxicol. 46, 1570–1575. https://doi.org/10.1016/j.fct.2007.12.017.

Zhao, S., Liu, J., Zhao, F., Liu, W., Li, N., Suo, Q., Zhao, J., Zhao, L., 2013. Sub-acute exposure to the herbicide atrazine suppresses cell immune functions in adolescent mice. Biosci. Trends. 7 (4), 193–201.

Landau-Ossondo, M., Rabia, N., …, et al., 2009. Why pesticides could be a common cause of prostate and breast cancers in the French Caribbean Island, Martinique. An overview on key mechanisms of pesticide induced cancer. (Elsevier).

Lauretta, R., Sansone, A., Sansone, M., et al., 2019. Endocrine disrupting chemicals: effects on endocrine glands. Front. Endocrinol. https://doi.org/10.3389/fendo.2019.00178.

Lerro, C.C., Koutros, S., Andreotti, G., et al., 2015. Organophosphate insecticide use and cancer incidence among spouses of pesticide applicators in the agricultural health study oem.bmj.com doi:https://doi.org/10.1136/oemed-2014-102798.

Lo, S., King, I., Alléra, A., et al., 2007. Effects of Various Pesticides on Human 5α-Reductase Activity in Prostate and LNCaP Cells. (Elsevier).

Lu, M., Du, J., Zhou, P., et al., 2015. Endocrine disrupting potential of fipronil and its metabolite in reporter gene assays. Chemosphere 120, 246–251. https://doi.org/10.1016/j.chemosphere.2014.07.015.

Marotta, V., Malandrino, P., Russo, M., et al., 2020. Fathoming the link between anthropogenic chemical contamination and thyroid cancer. Crit. Rev. Oncol. Hematol. 150, 102950 (Elsevier).

Massawe, R., Drabo, L., Whalen, M., 2017. Effects of pentachlorophenol and dichlorodiphenyltrichloroethane on secretion of interferon gamma (IFNγ) and tumor necrosis factor alpha (TNFα) from human immune cells. Toxicol. Mech. Methods 27, 223–235. https://doi.org/10.1080/15376516.2016.1275906.

McKinlay, R., Plant, J.A., Bell, J.N.B., et al., 2008. Endocrine disrupting pesticides: implications for risk assessment. Environ. Int. 34, 168–183. https://doi.org/10.1016/j.envint.2007.07.013.

Metcalf, J.L., Laws, S.C., Cummings, A.M., 1996. Methoxychlor mimics the action of 17β-estradiol on induction of uterine epidermal growth factor receptors in immature female rats. Reprod. Toxicol. 10, 393–399. https://doi.org/10.1016/0890-6238(96)00085-8.

Miller, K.P., Gupta, R.K., Flaws, J.A., 2006. Methoxychlor metabolites may cause ovarian toxicity through estrogen-regulated pathways. Toxicol. Sci. 93 (1), 180–188. https://doi.org/10.1093/toxsci/kfl034.

Miranda-Contreras, L., Gómez-Pérez, R., Rojas, G., et al., 2013. Occupational exposure to organophosphate and carbamate pesticides affects sperm chromatin integrity and reproductive hormone levels among Venezuelan farm workers. J. Occup. Health 55, 195–203. https://doi.org/10.1539/joh.12-0144-FS.

Miret, N., Pontillo, C., Zárate, L., et al., 2019. Impact of Endocrine Disruptor Hexachlorobenzene on the Mammary Gland and Breast Cancer: the Story Thus Far. (Elsevier).

Mnif, W., Hassine, A.I.H., Bouaziz, A., et al., 2011. Effect of endocrine disruptor pesticides: a review. Int. J. Environ. Res. Public Health. https://doi.org/10.3390/ijerph8062265.

Mohanty, B., Pandey, S.P., Tsutsui, K., 2017. Thyroid disrupting pesticides impair the hypothalamic-pituitary-testicular axis of a wildlife bird, Amandava amandava. Reprod. Toxicol. 71, 32–41. https://doi.org/10.1016/j.reprotox.2017.04.006.

Mokarizadeh, A., Faryabi, M.R., Rezvanfar, M.A., et al., 2015. A comprehensive review of pesticides and the immune dysregulation: mechanisms, evidence and consequences. Toxicol. Mech. Methods 25, 258–278. https://doi.org/10.3109/15376516.2015.1020182.

Murono, E.P., Derk, R.C., Akgul, Y., 2006. In vivo exposure of young adult male rats to methoxychlor reduces serum testosterone levels and ex vivo Leydig cell testosterone formation and cholesterol side-chain cleavage activity. Reprod. Toxicol. 21, 148–153. https://doi.org/10.1016/j.reprotox.2005.08.005.

Mustieles, V., Fernández, M.F., Martin-Olmedo, P., et al., 2017. Human adipose tissue levels of persistent organic pollutants and metabolic syndrome components: combining a cross-sectional with a 10-year longitudinal study using a multi-pollutant approach. Environ. Int. 104, 48–57. https://doi.org/10.1016/j.envint.2017.04.002.

Nagaraju, R., Rajini, P.S., 2016. Adaptive response of rat pancreatic β-cells to insulin resistance induced by monocrotophos: biochemical evidence. Pestic. Biochem. Physiol. 134, 39–48. https://doi.org/10.1016/j.pestbp.2016.04.009.

Nagaraju, R., Joshi, A.K.R., Rajini, P.S., 2015. Organophosphorus insecticide, monocrotophos, possesses the propensity to induce insulin resistance in rats on chronic exposure. J. Diabetes 7, 47–59. https://doi.org/10.1111/1753-0407.12158.

Nakashima, K., Yoshimura, T., Mori, H., Kawaguchi, M., Adachi, S., Nakao, T., Yamazaki, F., 2002. Effects of pesticides on cytokines production by human peripheral blood mononuclear cells—fenitrothion and glyphosate. Chudoku Kenkyu 15 (2), 159–165. Japanese.

Nowak, K., Jabłońska, E., et al., 2019. Immunomodulatory effects of synthetic endocrine disrupting chemicals on the development and functions of human immune cells. Environ. Int. 125, 350–364 (Elsevier).

Pardo, L.A., Beane Freeman, L.E., Lerro, C.C., et al., 2020. Pesticide exposure and risk of aggressive prostate cancer among private pesticide applicators. Environ. Health 19. https://doi.org/10.1186/S12940-020-00583-0.

Pavlikova, N., Smetana, P., Halada, P., et al., 2015. Effect of prolonged exposure to sublethal concentrations of DDT and DDE on protein expression in human pancreatic beta cells. Environ. Res. 142, 257–263. https://doi.org/10.1016/j.envres.2015.06.046.

Peón, A.N., Terrazas, L.I., 2018. Neuro-immune-endocrine interactions in multiple sclerosis. Adv. Neuroimmune Biol. https://doi.org/10.3233/NIB-170130.

Peris-Sampedro, F., Cabré, M., Basaure, P., et al., 2015. Adulthood dietary exposure to a common pesticide leads to an obese-like phenotype and a diabetic profile in apoE3 mice. Environ. Res. 142, 169–176. https://doi.org/10.1016/j.envres.2015.06.036.

Prins, G.S., 2008. Endocrine disruptors and prostate cancer risk. Endocr. Relat. Cancer 15, 649. https://doi.org/10.1677/ERC-08-0043.

Quagliariello, V., Rossetti, S., Cavaliere, C., et al., 2017. Metabolic syndrome, endocrine disruptors and prostate cancer associations: biochemical and pathophysiological evidences. Oncotarget 8, 30606. https://doi.org/10.18632/ONCOTARGET.16725.

Raafat, N., Abass, M.A., Salem, H.M., 2012. Malathion exposure and insulin resistance among a group of farmers in Al-Sharkia governorate. Clin. Biochem. 45 (18), 1591–1595. https://doi.org/10.1016/j.clinbiochem.2012.07.108.

Recio, R., Ocampo-Gómez, G., Morán-Martínez, J., et al., 2005. Pesticide exposure alters follicle-stimulating hormone levels in Mexican agricultural workers. Environ. Health Perspect. 113, 1160–1163. https://doi.org/10.1289/ehp.7374.

Rezaei, N., Saghazadeh, A., 2019. Biophysics and Neurophysiology of the Sixth Sense. Springer International Publishing, https://doi.org/10.1007/978-3-030-10620-1.

Richardson, J.R., Fitsanakis, V., Westerink, R.H.S., et al., 2019. Neurotoxicity of pesticides. Acta Neuropathol. https://doi.org/10.1007/s00401-019-02033-9.

Rochefort, H., 2017. Endocrine disruptors (EDs) and hormone-dependent cancers: correlation or causal relationship? C. R. Biol. 340, 439–445. https://doi.org/10.1016/J.CRVI.2017.07.007.

Rosales, C., 2018. Neutrophil: a cell with many roles in inflammation or several cell types? Front. Physiol. https://doi.org/10.3389/fphys.2018.00113.

Rosenbaum, P.F., Weinstock, R.S., Silverstone, A.E., et al., 2017. Metabolic syndrome is associated with exposure to organochlorine pesticides in Anniston, AL, United States. Environ. Int. 108, 11–21. https://doi.org/10.1016/j.envint.2017.07.017.

Rutter, G.A., Pullen, T.J., Hodson, D.J., et al., 2015. Pancreatic β-cell identity, glucose sensing and the control of insulin secretion. Biochem. J. https://doi.org/10.1042/BJ20141384.

Seifert, M., Küppers, R., 2016. Human memory B cells. Leukemia. https://doi.org/10.1038/leu.2016.226.

Shetty, G.A., Hattiangady, B., Upadhya, D., et al., 2017. Chronic oxidative stress, mitochondrial dysfunction, Nrf2 activation and inflammation in the hippocampus accompany heightened systemic inflammation and oxidative stress in an animal model of gulf war illness. Front. Mol. Neurosci. 10. https://doi.org/10.3389/fnmol.2017.00182.

Silva, J.F.S., Mattos, I.E., Luz, L.L., et al., 2016. Exposure to pesticides and prostate cancer: systematic review of the literature. Rev. Environ. Health 31, 311–327. https://doi.org/10.1515/REVEH-2016-0001.

Skolarczyk, J., Pekar, J., Nieradko-Iwanicka, B., 2017. Immune disorders induced by exposure to pyrethroid insecticides. Postepy Hig. Med. Dosw. https://doi.org/10.5604/01.3001.0010.3827.

Smith, A.M., Smith, M.T., La Merrill, M.A., et al., 2017. 2,4-dichlorophenoxyacetic acid (2,4-D) and risk of non-Hodgkin lymphoma: a meta-analysis accounting for exposure levels. Ann. Epidemiol. https://doi.org/10.1016/j.annepidem.2017.03.003.

Song, Y., Yang, L., 2017. Transgenerational pancreatic impairment with Igf2/H19 epigenetic alteration induced by p,p'-DDE exposure in early life. Toxicol. Lett. 280, 222–231. https://doi.org/10.1016/j.toxlet.2017.08.083.

Sun, Q., Qi, W., Xiao, X., Yang, S.H., Kim, D., Yoon, K.S., Clark, J.M., Park, Y., 2017. Imidacloprid promotes high fat diet-induced adiposity in female C57BL/6J mice and enhances adipogenesis in 3T3-L1 adipocytes via the AMPKα-mediated pathway. J. Agric. Food Chem. 65 (31), 6572–6581. https://doi.org/10.1021/acs.jafc.7b02584.

Tait, S., Ricceri, L., Venerosi, A., et al., 2009. Long-term effects on hypothalamic neuropeptides after developmental exposure to chlorpyrifos in mice. Environ. Health Perspect. 117, 112–116. https://doi.org/10.1289/ehp.11696.

Taxvig, C., Hadrup, N., Boberg, J., et al., 2013. In vitro - in vivo correlations for endocrine activity of a mixture of currently used pesticides. Toxicol. Appl. Pharmacol. 272, 757–766. https://doi.org/10.1016/j.taap.2013.07.028.

Thompson, P.A., Khatami, M., Baglole, C.J., et al., 2015. Environmental immune disruptors, inflammation and cancer risk. Carcinogenesis. https://doi.org/10.1093/carcin/bgv038.

Tomar, L., Agarwal, M., Avasthi, R., et al., 2013. Serum organochlorine pesticide levels in patients with metabolic syndrome. Indian J. Endocrinol. Metab. 17, 342. https://doi.org/10.4103/2230-8210.119612.

Uhl, B., Vadlau, Y., Zuchtriegel, G., et al., 2016. Aged neutrophils contribute to the first line of defense in the acute inflammatory response. Blood 128, 2327–2337. https://doi.org/10.1182/blood-2016-05-718999.

Ventura, C., Nieto, M.R.R., Bourguignon, N., et al., 2016. Pesticide chlorpyrifos acts as an endocrine disruptor in adult rats causing changes in mammary gland and hormonal balance. J. Steroid Biochem. Mol. Biol. 156, 1–9. https://doi.org/10.1016/j.jsbmb.2015.10.010.

Vinggaard, A.M., Bonefeld Joergensen, E.C., Larsen, J.C., 1999. Rapid and sensitive reporter gene assays for detection of antiandrogenic and estrogenic effects of environmental chemicals. Toxicol. Appl. Pharmacol. 155, 150–160. https://doi.org/10.1006/taap.1998.8598.

Vrtačnik, P., Ostanek, B., Mencej-Bedrač, S., et al., 2014. The many faces of estrogen signaling. Biochem. Med. https://doi.org/10.11613/BM.2014.035.

Warembourg, C., Debost-Legrand, A., Bonvallot, N., et al., 2016. Exposure of pregnant women to persistent organic pollutants and cord sex hormone levels. Hum. Reprod. 31, 190–198. https://doi.org/10.1093/humrep/dev260.

Whalen, M.M., Loganathan, B.G., Yamashita, N., et al., 2003. Immunomodulation of human natural killer cell cytotoxic function by triazine and carbamate pesticides. Chem. Biol. Interact. 145, 311–319. https://doi.org/10.1016/S0009-2797(03)00027-9.

World Health Organization, 2020. The WHO Recommended Classification of Pesticides by Hazard and Guidelines to Classification 2019. World Health Organization. https://apps.who.int/iris/handle/10665/332193. (2020).

Xu, X., Dailey, A.B., Talbott, E.O., et al., 2010. Associations of serum concentrations of organochlorine pesticides with breast cancer and prostate cancer in U.S. adults. Environ. Health Perspect. 118, 60–66. https://doi.org/10.1289/EHP.0900919.

Yucra, S., Rubio, J., Gasco, M., et al., 2006. Semen quality and reproductive sex hormone levels in peruvian pesticide sprayers. Int. J. Occup. Environ. Health 12, 355–361. https://doi.org/10.1179/oeh.2006.12.4.355.

Index

Note: Page numbers followed by *f* indicate figures and *t* indicate tables.

A

Acanthus ilicifolius, 506–508, 509*f*, 512
Acrostichum aureum, 507–508
Actinic cheilitis, 13
Actinobacteria, 94
Acute lymphoid leukemia (ALL), 225–226
Acute myeloid leukemia (AML), 224–225, 226*f*, 267
Adrenal crisis, 206–207
Adrenal hypofunction/Addisonian crisis, 180–184, 183–184*f*
Adrenocortical carcinoma (ACC), 181
Aegiceras corniculatum, 517–518
AGG. *See* Anaplastic gangliogliomas (AGG)
Agricultural poisons, 543–547, 545*f*
Agrochemicals. *See* Pesticides
Aldosteronoma/Conn's syndrome, 181
Alginate, 454
American Association of Cancer Research Workshop, 23
American Dental Association, 2017, 37–38
Anaplastic carcinoma, 187
Anaplastic gangliogliomas (AGG)
 age, sex distribution, and location, 351
 genetic alterations, 352, 352*t*
 glial section, 351
 immunohistochemistry, 352
 incidence rate, 351
 survival rate, 351
 treatment, 353
Anemia, 252
Anticancer drugs, 453
Anticancer macromolecules of marine origin
 bioactive macromolecules, 471
 carbohydrates
  chitosan, 476–477
  fucoidans, 478–480
  microbial extracellular polysaccharides (EPS-CS), 477
  polysaccharides, 475–476
  sulfated polysaccharide from Capsosiphon fulvescens (SPS-CF), 477
  sulfated polysaccharide from Undaria pinnatifida (SPUP), 476
 different phases of clinical trials, 472, 473–474*t*
 lyngabyal lectin, 480
 marine natural products, 479
 naturally occurring anticancer compound, 472*f*
 peptidoglycans, 480
 therapeutically promising anticancer macromolecules, 472, 475*t*
 trabectedin therapy in ovarian cancer, 479–480
 US-FDA-approved anticancer drugs, 471, 472*t*
Anticancer medications, 502–503
Anticancer medicine, pharmacokinetics of
 B-cell derived immunoglobulins, 403–405
 cancer derived immunoglobulins, 403–405, 403–404*t*
 cytochrome P450 (CYP)-mediated phase I-metabolizing enzymes, 391–395, 392–395*t*
 immunoglobulin heavy chain, 403–405
 immunoglobulin light chain, 403–405
 non-CYP phase-II metabolizing enzymes, 396, 397–398*t*
 schematic view of, 387–388, 388*f*
 sodium-independent glucose transporters, 396–403, 399–402*t*
Aplastic anemia (AA), 267
Apoptosis, 451–452, 465–466
Auranofin (Ridaura), 428–429, 429*f*
Avicennia alba, 506–507, 510*f*, 513
Avicennia marina, 507–508, 510*f*, 513, 518
Avicennia officinalis, 507–508, 511*f*, 513–514

B

Basal cell carcinoma (BCC), 321, 330, 331*t*
B-cell derived immunoglobulins, 403–405
Bethesda system, 186–187
Blood–brain barrier (BBB), 461–462
Blood cancer, 500–501
Brain development, 340–341
Bruguiera gymnorrhiza, 507–508, 511*f*, 514
Bruguiera sexangula, 506–507, 512*f*, 514

C

Calcium and bone metabolism disorders
calciumand phosphate product (CaxP), 178
corrected calcium levels, 178
familial hypocalciuric hypercalcemia
(FHH), 178
imaging modalities, 179
MEN-I associated parathyroid hyperplasia, 179,
182*f*
osteopenia, 179
osteoporosis, 179
parathyroid hyperfunction, 176–178
right inferior parathyroid adenoma, 179,
179–181*f*
Cancer and gene mutations, 388, 389–390*t*
Cancer-associated fibroblasts, 26
Cancer chemotherapies, 452–453
Cancer derived immunoglobulins, 403–405,
403–404*t*
"Cancer hallmarks", 500–501
Cancer stem cells, 23–25, 25*f*
Cancer Stem Cells Model, 23–24
Cancer vaccines, 501–502
Candida albicans, 10
Candidal leukoplakia, 10
Carbon-based nanomaterials, 463–464
Carbon-based NPs, 455–456
Carboplatin, 417
Carcinoembryonic antigen (CEA), 136
Carcinogenic factors, 501
CC. *See* Cervical cancer (CC)
CD10 biomarker, 327
Cell-penetrating peptides (CPPs) modified
liposomes, 461–462
CellSearch, 41
Central adrenal insufficiency, 206–207
Central nervous system (CNS) tumors
mixed glioneuronal tumors
anaplastic gangliogliomas (AGG), 351–353,
352*t*
desmoplastic infantile astrocytoma and
ganglioglioma (DIA/DIG), 353, 354*t*
diffuse glioneuronal tumor with
oligodendroglioma like features and nuclear
clusters (DGONC), 358
diffuse leptomeningeal glioneuronal tumor
(DLGNT), 360–361, 361*t*
dysembryoplastic neuroepithelial tumor
(DNET), 356–357, 357*t*

gangliogliomas (GG), 349–351
myxoid glioneuronal tumors (MGTs),
358–359, 359*t*
papillary glioneuronal tumors (PGNT),
353–355, 355*t*
Rosette-forming glioneuronal tumors
(RGNTs), 355–356, 356*t*
origin, 341
pure neuronal tumors
central neurocytomas (CNs), 341–343
cerebellar liponeurocytomas (cLNC), 344–346
dysplastic cerebellar gangliocytoma, 346–347,
347*t*
extraventricular neurocytomas (EVNs),
343–344
gangliocytomas (GCs), 347–348
multinodular and vacuolating neuronal tumors
(MVNT), 348–349, 349*t*
2021 WHO classification, 341
Central neurocytomas (CNs)
age, sex distribution, and location, 342
biological origins, 341–342
genetic alteration, 342–343, 343*t*
immunohistochemical markers, 342
Cerebellar liponeurocytomas (cLNC)
age, sex distribution, and location, 344
genetic alterations, 345, 345*t*
histology and immunological profile, 344
immunohistochemical markers, 344
treatment, 346
Ceriops decandra, 507–508, 512*f*, 515
Ceriops tagal, 517
Cervical cancer (CC)
CA19-9, 316
CA125 levels, 316
epigenetic markers
DNA methylation, 317
histone deacetylation, 317–318
miRNA expression, 318–319
fatality rate, 315–316
GLOBOCON report 2018, 315–316
pap smear, 315–316
predictive genomic markers, 317
serum fragments of cytokeratin, 316
squamous cell carcinoma antigen, 316
survival rate of, 315–316
tumor markers under investigation, 316–317
Chemotherapy, 453–454, 502
medicines, 459

oral squamous cell carcinoma (OSCC)
  adjuvant chemoradiotherapy, 57–58
  adjuvant chemotherapy, 57
  cisplatin/carboplatin, 58–59
  frontline chemotherapy, 59
  induction chemotherapy, 58
  myelosuppression, 58–59
  Panitumumab, 59
  platinum-based combination chemotherapy
    regimen, 59
  primary chemoradiation, 58
Chitosan, 476–477
Chlorella, 489
Chondroitin sulfate proteoglycan 4 (CSPG4), 325
Chromogranin A (CgA), 182
Chronic lymphocytic leukemia (CLL), 227–228,
    228*f*
  chemoimmunotherapy (CIT), 238–240
  13q14 chromosomal region deletions, 240
  clinical staging system, 236, 237*t*
  diagnosis/detection of, 236–237
  epigenomic alterations, 242
  functional implications, 246
  incidence, 235–236
  intratumor heterogeneity (ITH), 244–245
  molecular drivers of
    BIRC3, 241–242
    17p13 chromosomal region, 240
    11q22–23 chromosomal region deletions, 240
    13q14 chromosomal region deletions, 240
    CLL up-regulated gene (CLLU1), 240–241
    immunoglobulin heavy chain gene (IGHV),
      238–240
    murine double minute 2 (MDM2) oncogene,
      240–241
    MYD88 gene, 241–242
    next generation sequencing studies, 238–240,
      239*t*
    NOTCH1 gene, 240–241
    protection of telomeres 1 (POT1) gene,
      241–242
    Richter transformation, 237–238
    SF3B1-K700E mutation, 240–241
    somatic mutations, 237–238
    splicing factor 3b subunit 1 (SF3B1) mutations,
      240–241
    Trisomy12, 240–241
    U2snRNP, 240–241
    whole-exome sequencing, 238–240

molecular mechanisms, 246
  overcrowding condition, 235
  signs and symptoms, 235
  treatment modalities, 242–244
Chronic myeloid leukemia (CML), 226–227
Circulating free tumor DNA (cftDNA), 123
Circulating tumor DNA (ctDNA), 123, 295
Cisplatin, 424
  anticancer activity, 414–416, 421, 422*f*
  complications, 415–416
  first-generation platinum drug, 416–417
  mechanism of action, 421–423
  second-generation cisplatin analogs, 417–419
  third-generation cisplatin analogs, 419–421
CLL. *See* Chronic lymphocytic leukemia (CLL)
cLNC. *See* Cerebellar liponeurocytomas (cLNC)
Clonal Evolution Model, 23–24
CNs. *See* Central neurocytomas (CNs)
CNS tumors. *See* Central nervous system (CNS)
  tumors
Comamonadaceae, 94
Common body part implicated with cancer,
    451–452, 452*f*
Compcyst, 141
Congenital dyserythropoietic anemia (CDA), 266
Corynebacterium, 94–95
Cucurbitacin BE polylactic acid nanoparticles
    (CuBE-PLA-NPs) injection, 60
Cupressus torulosa, 515–516
Cushing's syndrome, 180–181
Cyclooxygenase-2, 327
Cystic fluid, 141–142
Cytochrome P450 (CYP)-mediated phase I-
    metabolizing enzymes, 391–395, 392–395*t*

D

Decipher test, 309
Desmoplastic infantile astrocytoma and
    ganglioglioma (DIA/DIG), 353, 354*t*
Diabetes mellitus (DM), 210–212, 211*f*
Diabetic ketoacidosis (DKA), 210
Diatom-based nanoparticles, 486
Diffuse glioneuronal tumor with oligodendroglioma
    like features and nuclear clusters (DGONC),
    358
Diffuse leptomeningeal glioneuronal tumor
    (DLGNT), 360–361, 361*t*
Discoid lupus erythematosus, 14–15
Divergolide D, 515–516

DNA methylation, 100
DOTANOC scan, 188
Dunaliella, 489
Dysbiosis, 95–96
Dysembryoplastic neuroepithelial tumor (DNET), 356–357, 357*t*
Dyskeratosis congenita, 15
Dysplasia, 266
Dysplastic cerebellar gangliocytoma, 346–347, 347*t*

E

EC. *See* Endometrial cancer (EC)
Endocrine complications with cancer immunotherapy
  immune checkpoint inhibitors (ICIs), 199–200
    antibody-dependent cellular cytotoxicity (ADCC), 203–205
    CTLA-4, 201
    diabetes mellitus (DM), 210–212, 211*f*
    FDA approved ICIs, 203, 204*t*
    hypoparathyroidism, 205
    hypophysitis, 206–207, 208*f*
    ipilimumab (CTLA-4 antibodies), 202
    monoclonal antibody molecules (mAbs), 199
    nivolumab, 203
    PD1 expression, 201–202
    pembrolizumab, 203
    pidilizumab, 203
    prevalence rate, 205, 205*t*
    primary adrenal insufficiency (PAI), 212, 213*f*
    therapeutic strategies, 203
    thyroiditis, 207–210, 209*f*
    tremelimumab, 202–203
  management of
    grade 1 endocrinopathies, 214
    grade 2 endocrinopathies, 214
    grade 3 and 4 endocrinopathies, 214
  physiological symptoms, 213–214
  screening strategies, 212–213
  treatment, 213–214
Endocrine diseases
  basic biomarkers
    adrenal hypofunction/Addisonian crisis, 180–184, 183–184*f*
    calcium and bone metabolism disorders, 176–179, 179–182*f*
    diabetes, 185
    differentiated thyroid cancer (DTC), 176
    gastrinoma, 185

hyperthyroidism, 175
    hypothyroidism, 175
    medullary thyroid cancer (MTC), 176
    neuroendocrine tumors (NET), 185
    pituitary and reproductive glands, 185–186
    thyroglobulin, 176
    total thyroidectomy, 176, 176–178*f*
  modern biomarkers
    adrenal diseases, 193–194, 195*f*
    neuroendocrine tumors (NETs), 194–197
    ovarian cancer, 197
    parathyroid carcinoma (PCa), 188–193
    pituitary carcinoma, 197
    testicular cancer, 197
    thyroid cancer, 186–188, 189–192*f*
Endometrial cancer (EC)
  age standardized incidence rate (ASR), 313
  CA125 tumor markers, 313
  epigenetic markers, 314–315
  estrogen receptor alpha (ERα), 314
  HE4 tumor markers, 313
  microsatellite instability (MSI), 314
  mortality rate, 313
  type I, 313
  type II, 313
Epidermolysis bullosa, 15
Epigenetics, 502
Epithelial–mesenchymal transition, 26–27
Epstein–Barr virus (EBV), 110–111
Erythroplakia, 13
Euglena tuba, 489
EVNs. *See* Extraventricular neurocytomas (EVNs)
Excoecaria agallocha, 506–508, 513*f*, 515, 518–519
Exosome-based spectrometric analysis, 124
Extraventricular neurocytomas (EVNs)
  age, sex distribution, and location, 343–344
  atypical EVNs, 343
  genetic alterations, 344
  immunohistochemical markers, 344
  incidences of, 343
  typical EVNs, 343

F

FA-PEGLip@ rGO delivery system, 462
Fluorodeoxyglucose positron emission tomography (FDGPET), 396–403
Fluorouracil (5-Fu), 453
Folic acid (FA), 461–462
Follicular carcinoma, 187

Fucoidans, 478–480
Fucosyltransferase 8 (FUT8), 125–126
Fusobacterium nucleatum, 34–35

G

Galectin-3, 328
Gangliocytomas (GCs), 347–348
Gangliogliomas (GG), 349–351
  age, sex distribution, and location, 350
  genetic alterations, 350–351
  immunohistochemical markers, 350
  treatment, 351
Gastrointestinal molecular biomarkers
  adenomatous polyposis coli (APC) gene, 106
  AT-rich interaction domain 1A (ARID1A)
      mutations, 106
  AT-rich interaction domain-containing protein
      (ARID) mutations, 106
  CD44 cell surface adhesion molecule, 111–112
  E-cadherin (CDH1), 112–113, 113f
  epithelial growth factor receptor (EGFR),
      109–110
  Epstein–Barr virus (EBV), 110–111
  human epidermal growth factor receptor 2
      (HER2) overexpression, 109
  incidence, 105
  MALTA1-GLT1 fusion gene, 108
  matrix metalloproteinases (MMPs), 113–114
  Met tyrosine kinase inhibitors (Met-TKI), 109
  mismatch repair (MMR), 107–108, 107f
  MSI-high gastroesophageal tumors, 107–108,
      107f
  programmed cell death 1 (PD-1) and 2 (PD-2),
      110
  retinoblastoma tumor suppressor gene 1 (RB1),
      108–109
  RNF43 mutations, 105–106
  TP53 gene, 108
  vascular endothelial growth factor-A (VEGF-A),
      111
Gene therapy, 466–467, 502
Genetically acquired disorders
  actinic cheilitis, 13
  erythroplakia, 13
  leukoplakia, 12
GG. *See* Gangliogliomas (GG)
Glioblastoma multiforme (GBM)
  astrocytomas, 372–373

diffuse infiltrating brainstem gliomas (DIBGs),
    373
  ependymomas, 373
  epidermomas, 372
  glioma stem-like cells (GSCs), 372
  melatonin (MLT)
    Akt/ERK/NFB signaling pathway, 376–378
    angiogenesis, 378–379
    antiangiogenic activities, 376
    anticancer properties, 376, 379–380
    antiestrogenic medication, 375–376
    anti-GBM effects, 379–380
    antimetastasis drug, 375–376
    antioxidant and antiinflammatory
        characteristics, 372
    antiproliferative effects, 376
    apoptosis, 376
    biological activities, 372
    caspase-3 expression, 371
    CD133 and SOX2 markers, 379
    cellular signaling, 374
    deficiency, 375–376
    EZH2-Notch1 signaling pathway, 381
    functions, 374–375, 375f
    Her-2 system's activity, 376–378
    hydrophilic and lipophilic properties, 372
    L-tryptophan derivatives, 374
    membrane receptor's dissociation constant
        (K_d), 379–380
    messenger system, 374
    mitochondrial transcription factor A (TFAM),
        379–380
    MT1 and MT2 receptors, 374, 379–380
    neuroprotective properties, 374–375
    nuclear factor-kappa B (NF-κB), 376–378, 380
    oncostatic activity, 376
    p53 levels, 371
    pro-oxidant effect, 372
    P21/WAF1 suppressor genes, 376
    signaling pathways, 374
    tumor-inhibitory characteristics, 376, 377f
    tumor necrosis factor-α (TNF-α), 376–378
  mixed gliomas, 373
  oligo-astrocytomas, 373
  oligodendrogliomas, 372–373
  optic pathway gliomas, 373
  signs and symptoms, 373
Global Burden of Disease collaboration, 7
GLOBOCAN 2018, 3–4

Glutathione S-transferase (GST), 396
GNS@CTS@RES-Lips, 466
Gold anticancer drugs, 428–430, 429f
Gold nanoparticles (AuNPs), 437, 455–456, 462–463
Gram-negative anaerobes, 93
Graphene oxide (GO), 463–464
Graves' disease, 207–210
Green nanoparticle synthesis, 437–438
Gulf War illness (GWI), 546–547

H

Haematococcus pluvialis, 493
Halorosellinia spp., 515–516
HCs. *See* Hematopoietic cancers (HCs)
Healthy microbiomes, 94–95
Hector Battifora mesothelial cell (HBME-1), 187–188
Hematopoietic cancers (HCs)
  leukemia
    acute lymphoid leukemia (ALL), 225–226
    acute myeloid leukemia (AML), 224–225, 226f
    causes, 224
    chronic lymphocytic leukemia (CLL), 227–228, 228f
    chronic myeloid leukemia (CML), 226–227
  lymphoma
    chromosome translocations, 228–229
    genesis of, 228–229
    Hodgkin lymphoma (HL), 229–230, 230f
    immunosuppressive exposures, 228–229
    non-Hodgkin lymphoma (NHL), 230–231
    symptoms, 228–229
Hepatocellular carcinoma (HCC), 478
Heptaplatin, 420–421, 420f
High-risk human papillomavirus (HPV), 8
Hodgkin lymphoma (HL), 229–230, 230f
Homeostatic model assessment for insulin resistance (HOMA-IR), 538
Homologous recombination gene mutations (HRRm), 307–309, 308t
Human melanoma Black-45 (HMB-45), 325
Hydrolysis processes, 413–414
Hyperprolactinemia, 207
Hyperthyroidism, 214
Hypogonadotropic hypogonadism, 206–207
Hyponatremia, 206–207
Hypophysitis, 206–207, 208f
Hypoxia, 32

I

Idelalisib therapy, 245–246
Immune checkpoint inhibitors
  approved checkpoint inhibitors, 284f, 285, 286t
  cytotoxic T-lymphocyte-associated protein 4 (CTLA-4), 282
  Ipilimumab-a CTLA-4 blocker, 283
  PD1/PD-L1 therapies, 283
  programmed death-1 (PD-1), 281–282
Immune-related adverse events (irAEs), 296–297, 297f
Immune surveillance, 285
Immunotherapy, 501–502
  cytokines, 61–62
  immune checkpoint activators, 63
  immune checkpoint inhibitors, 62–63
  toll-like receptors (TLRs), 62
Inflammatory mediators
  CD8$^+$ T cells, 29
  dendritic cells, 29
  mast cells, 30
  myeloid-derived suppressor cells, 30
  natural killer cell, 30
  platelets, 30
  T-cell regulation, 29
  Tregs (regulatory T cells), 29
  tumor-associated macrophages, 28
  tumor-associated neutrophils, 28
Inorganic nanoparticle (IoNP), 455–456
International Association of Cancer Registries (IACR), 3
International Classification of Diseases for Oncology (ICD-O), 3
Intraductal papillary mucinous neoplasms (IPMNs), 140
Intratumor heterogeneity, 23
Ionizing radiation, 501–502
Iridium anticancer drugs, 433–434, 434f
Iron oxide nanoparticles, 436–437

K

Kingella, 94–95

L

Lactate dehydrogenase (LDH), 327
Lactobacillus plantarum, 34–35
Leucopenia, 252
Leukemia

acute lymphoid leukemia (ALL), 225–226
acute myeloid leukemia (AML), 224–225, 226f
causes, 224
chronic lymphocytic leukemia (CLL), 227–228, 228f
chronic myeloid leukemia (CML), 226–227
Leukoplakia, 12
Lip and oral cavity cancer, 3
Liposomes-carbon-based nanomaterials hybrids (Lip-CNHs), 463–464
Liposomes-gold nanoparticles hybrid (Lip-AuNPs), 462–463
Liposomes-quantum dots hybrids (Lip-QDs), 463
Lobaplatin, 419–420
Low-risk human papillomavirus (HPV), 8
Lymphoma
    chromosome translocations, 228–229
    genesis of, 228–229
    Hodgkin lymphoma (HL), 229–230, 230f
    immunosuppressive exposures, 228–229
    non-Hodgkin lymphoma (NHL), 230–231
    symptoms, 228–229
Lyngabyal lectin, 480

M
Mangrove-derived phytochemicals
    acanthicifolin, 506–507
    Acanthus ilicifolius, 506–508, 509f, 512
    Acrostichum aureum, 507–508
    Aegicerus corniculatum, 517–518
    anticancer compounds, 507–508, 508–509t
    anticancer potential of, 515–516
    anticancer properties, 507–508
    application of, 516–519, 519t
    Avicennia alba, 506–507, 510f, 513
    Avicennia marina, 507–508, 510f, 513, 518
    Avicennia officinalis, 507–508, 511f, 513–514
    2-Benzoxazolin, 506–507
    bibliometric analysis
        citation analysis, 520–522, 521–522f
        cluster harboring, 522–523, 523–524f
        co-occurrence analysis, 520, 523–525, 524f
        HeLa and MCF cancer cell lines, 523–525
        publication history, 520, 520f
    Bruguiera gymnorrhiza, 507–508, 511f, 514
    Bruguiera sexangula, 506–507, 512f, 514
    Ceriops decandra, 507–508, 512f, 515
    Ceriops tagal, 517
    Cupressus torulosa, 515–516

cytotoxicity analysis, 507–508
distribution and diversity, 503–506, 504–505f
ethnomedicinal usage, 506
Excoecaria agallocha, 506–508, 513f, 515, 518–519
Halorosellinia spp., 515–516
metabolites, 506
Nypa fruticans, 507–508, 516–517
Penicillium chrysogenum, 515–516
Pestalotiopsis microspora, 515–516
Pestalotiopsis neglecta, 515–516
phytochemical extraction, isolation, and separation, 525–526
polyphenols, 515–516
Rhizophora apiculata, 518
Rhizophora mucronata, 517
rhizophorin, 506–507
Sonneratia apetala, 507–508
Sonneratia caseolaris, 507–508
Streptomyces cheonanensis, 515–516
Suaeda monoica, 518–519
Xylocarpus granatum, 507–508, 515
Matrix metalloproteinase-7 (MMP-7), 329
MDS. *See* Myelodysplastic syndrome (MDS)
Medicinal inorganic chemistry, 413–414
Medullary thyroid cancer (MTC), 188
Megaloblastic anemia, 266
Melan-A, 325
Melanoma cell adhesion molecule (MCAM), 326
Melanoma-inhibiting activity (MIA), 327
Melanoma skin cancer (MSC)
    cause of, 321
    incidence rate, 321
    types of, 328, 329t
Melatonin (MLT)
    Akt/ERK/NFB signaling pathway, 376–378
    angiogenesis, 378–379
    antiangiogenic activities, 376
    anticancer properties, 376, 379–380
    antiestrogenic medication, 375–376
    anti-GBM effects, 379–380
    antimetastasis drug, 375–376
    antioxidant and antiinflammatory characteristics, 372
    antiproliferative effects, 376
    apoptosis, 376
    biological activities, 372
    caspase-3 expression, 371
    CD133 and SOX2 markers, 379
    cellular signaling, 374

Melatonin (MLT) *(Continued)*
  deficiency, 375–376
  EZH2-Notch1 signaling pathway, 381
  functions, 374–375, 375*f*
  Her-2 system's activity, 376–378
  hydrophilic and lipophilic properties, 372
  L-tryptophan derivatives, 374
  membrane receptor's dissociation constant (K_d),
      379–380
  messenger system, 374
  mitochondrial transcription factor A (TFAM),
      379–380
  MT1 and MT2 receptors, 374, 379–380
  neuroprotective properties, 374–375
  nuclear factor-kappa B (NF-κB), 376–378, 380
  oncostatic activity, 376
  p53 levels, 371
  pro-oxidant effect, 372
  P21/WAF1 suppressor genes, 376
  signaling pathways, 374
  tumor-inhibitory characteristics, 376, 377*f*
  tumor necrosis factor-α (TNF-α), 376–378
Metal-based anticancer therapeutics. *See also* Gold
      anticancer drugs; Platinum-based drugs;
      Ruthenium anticancer drugs
  dose-response relationship, 414–415
  fluorescent metal-based complexes, 431–434,
      432*f*, 434*f*
  medicinal inorganic chemistry, 413–414
  metal complexes, 413–414
  metallodrugs, 413–415
  nanoparticles
    copper oxide nanoparticles, 437–438
    in diagnosis, 436
    in drug delivery, 435
    gold nanoparticles, 437
    green nanoparticle synthesis, 437–438
    in hyperthermia, 436
    iron oxide nanoparticles, 436–437
    in radiotherapy, 435–436
    silver nanoparticles (AgNPs), 437
    targeting selectivity and specificity, 435
    TiO_2 nanoparticles, 437
    ZnO NPs, 437
  toxicity, 414–415
Metal-based (MB) nanoparticles, 455–456
Metallodrugs, 413–414
Metallothioneins, 326
Microalgae

anticancer properties, 489
  astaxanthin, 485–486
  β–carotene, 485–486
  bioactive compounds, 489, 491–492*t*
  carotenoids, 490
  Chlorella, 489
  classification and structures, 486, 487*f*
  cyanobacteria, 493
  cytotoxic effects of, 494
  diatom-based nanoparticles, 486
  Dunaliella, 489
  encapsulation of, 493
  Euglena tuba, 489
  fucoxanthin, 486, 489
  growth rate and product synthesis, 494
  Haematococcus pluvialis, 493
  molecular pathways, 489
  nanotechnology, 490–495
  silica-based nanoparticles, 486
  sources and classification, 486–489, 488*t*
  types of, 489, 490*t*
  unicellular microalgae, 486
Microbial extracellular polysaccharides (EPS-CS), 477
Microphthalmia transcription factor (MITF), 325
Mismatch repair gene deficient (dMMR), 307–309,
      308*t*
MitoChip array-based sequencing, 139
MLT. *See* Melatonin (MLT)
Monocrotophos (MCP) pesticides, 538
MSC. *See* Melanoma skin cancer (MSC)
Mucinous cystic neoplasm (MCN), 140
Mucositis, 96
Multinodular and vacuolating neuronal tumors
      (MVNT), 348–349, 349*t*
Multiple myeloma
  diagnosis, 274, 275*f*
  etiopathogenesis, 273
  histology, 276, 277*f*
  neurological features, 274
  osteoclast activation, 273–274
  prognosis, 277
  radiographic evaluation, 275–276, 276*f*
  recurrent infections, 274
  renal failure, 274
  symptoms, 273–274
  treatment, 278*f*
    initial therapy, 277
    lenalidomide and dexamethasone therapy, 277
    supportive treatment, 277–279

Myelodysplastic syndrome (MDS)
  chromosomal abnormalities, 251, 251t
  classification
    FAB classification, 253
    MDS-U, 258–259, 259t
    MDS with excess of blasts, 256–257, 258t
    MDS with isolated del(5q), 257–258, 258t
    MDS with multiple lineage dysplasia
      (MDS-MLD), 255, 256t
    MDS with ring sideroblasts (MDS-RS),
      255–256, 257t
    MDS with single lineage dysplasia
      (MDS-SLD), 254–255, 255t
    refractory cytopenia of childhood (RCC), 259,
      260t
    WHO classification, 253, 254t
    WHO 2016 update, 253, 254t
  clinical presentation, 252–253
  cytogenetic abnormalities, 249
  diagnosis
    bone marrow biopsy, 264–265, 265f
    bone marrow examination, 262–264, 264t
    complete blood count (CBC), 261–262
    differential diagnoses, 265–268, 268f
    peripheral blood film (PBF), 262, 263f
  ineffective myelopoiesis, 249
  morphological features, 249
  normocellular/hypercellular bone marrow, 249
  pathogenesis, 250–252, 251t, 251f
  peripheral cytopenias, 249, 250t
  scoring system, 269, 269–270t
  treatment of, 270–271
Myeloproliferative neoplasms (myelofibrosis), 267
Myxoid glioneuronal tumors (MGTs), 358–359,
  359t

N

Nano-diagnostics, oral squamous cell carcinoma
  (OSCC), 39–40
Nanomedicine, 454, 459
Nanoparticles (NP)
  active targeting (AT), 456
  advantages of, 457
  appearance of, 453
  copper oxide nanoparticles, 437–438
  in diagnosis, 436
  drug delivery system, 435, 454, 455f
  gold nanoparticles, 437
  green nanoparticle synthesis, 437–438

  in hyperthermia, 436
  inorganic nanoparticle (IoNP), 455–456
  iron oxide nanoparticles, 436–437
  organic nanoparticles, 454–455
  passive targeting (PT), 456–457
  in radiotherapy, 435–436
  silver nanoparticles (AgNPs), 437
  targeting selectivity and specificity, 435
  TiO2 nanoparticles, 437
  ZnO NPs, 437
Near-infrared (NIR) responsive
    nanomaterial–liposome nanohybrids. See also
    NIRN-liposome hybrid nanocarriers (NLHs)
  inorganic PTAs, 460
NIRN-liposome hybrid nanocarriers (NLHs)
  application of
    cell death induced by PTT, 464–465
    gene therapy (photothermal therapy), 466
    NIR light-triggered drug release, 465–466
  carbon-based nanomaterials, hybrids of,
    463–464
  challenges, 466–467
  design and surface modification, hybrid
    nanostructures, 460–462
  gold nanoparticles hybrids, 462–463
  perspectives, 466–467
  quantum dots (L-QDs), hybrids of, 463
NIR-responsive nanomaterials (NIRNs). See also
    NIRN-liposome hybrid nanocarriers
    (NLHs)
  cancer PTT study, 460
  gold-based nanomaterials, 461
Necrosis, 466
Nedaplatin, 418–419
Neisseria mucosa, 95
Neuroendocrine tumors (NETs)
  basic biomarkers, 185
  modern biomarkers, 194–197
NIR light-triggered drug release, 466
NIR responsive nanomaterial-liposome
    nanohybrids (NIRN-LHs)
  cell death induced by PTT, 465–466, 465f
  cell-penetrating peptides (CPPs) modified
    liposomes, 463
  CNT-PS/siRNA nanoparticle, 466–467, 467f
  FA-mediated targeted delivery, 462
  gene therapy, 466–467
  hollow AuNPs, 461–462
  hydrophobic NIRNs, 461

NIR responsive nanomaterial-liposome
    nanohybrids (NIRN-LHs) *(Continued)*
  liposomes-carbon-based nanomaterials hybrids
    (Lip-CNHs), 463–464
  liposomes-gold nanoparticles hybrid
    (Lip-AuNPs), 463
  liposomes-quantum dots hybrids (Lip-QDs),
    464–466
  NIR light-triggered drug release, 466
  photothermal conversion efficiency, 461–462
  photothermal therapy (PTT), 459–460, 465–467
  physicochemical properties, 461
  preparation and application of, 461
  purification technologies, 461
  shape of, 460–462
  size-dependent optical and electrical properties,
    460
  small-interfering RNAs (siRNAs) delivery,
    466–467
  transferrin (Tf) receptor, 463
  types of, 460*f*, 461
4-nitroquinoline-1-oxide (5-NQO), 94–95
NMSC. *See* Nonmelanoma skin cancer (NMSC)
Non-CYP phase-II metabolizing enzymes, 396,
  397–398*t*
Non-Hodgkin lymphoma (NHL), 230–231
Nonmelanoma skin cancer (NMSC)
  basal cell carcinoma (BCC), 321, 330, 331*t*
  squamous cell carcinoma (SqCC), 321, 329–330,
    331*t*
NP. *See* Nanoparticles (NP)
Nuclear factor -Kappa B (NF-κB), 21
Nypa fruticans, 507–508, 516–517

O

Omran's theory, 1–2
OncoDiscover Liquid Biopsy technology, 41
Oncotype DX Genomic Prostate Score test (GPS),
  309
Oral blistering, 15–16
Oral epithelial dysplasia, 16–17, 17*f*
Oral lichen planus, 14
Oral microbiome, 96
  anatomical sites, 90
  COVID-19 infection, 92–93
  HPV infection, 94
  oral diseases, 91–92
  oral hygiene practices, 91–92
  oropharynx, 90

  pathogenic and mutualistic bacteria, 90
  smoking effect on gingival crevicular fluid and
    marginal and subgingival plaque microbial
    flora, 91–92, 93*f*
  smoking effect on subgingival plaque microbial
    flora, 90, 91*f*
  socioeconomic conditions, 91–92
  Streptococcus salivarius, 91
  on tongue, 90
  ventilator-associated pneumonia, 90
Oral squamous cell carcinoma (OSCC)
  cancer stem cells, 23–25, 25*f*
  chemotherapy
    adjuvant chemoradiotherapy, 57–58
    adjuvant chemotherapy, 57
    cisplatin/carboplatin, 58–59
    frontline chemotherapy, 59
    induction chemotherapy, 58
    myelosuppression, 58–59
    Panitumumab, 59
    platinum-based combination chemotherapy
      regimen, 59
    primary chemoradiation, 58
  clinical features, 35–37, 36–37*f*
  definition, 2
  diagnosis
    genomics, 46–47
    lab-on-chip/microfluidics, 40
    liquid biopsy, 41–44, 42*f*
    metabolomics, 47–48
    microarray technology, 44
    nano-diagnostics, 39–40
    next generation sequencing, 44–45
    omics, 45–48
    proteomics, 47
    screening test, 38
    transcriptomics, 47
    visual and tactile examinations, 37–38
  early diagnosis of, 2
  epidemiology, 3–4, 4*f*
  epithelial–mesenchymal transition, 32–33
  genetically acquired disorders
    actinic cheilitis, 13
    erythroplakia, 13
    leukoplakia, 12
  genetically inherited disorders, 15–16
  glucose transporters (GLUT 1), 97–98
  histopathological features
    Broders' system, 51

cellular and nuclear alterations, 51
disease-specific survival, 56
histological grading, 51–52
histologic risk scoring scheme, 53
local recurrence, 54–55
lymphocytic infiltration, 55
lymphoplasmacytic infiltration, 52
molecular and morphological characteristics, 53
tumor differentiation, 55
HPV infection, 94
human glucose transporters, 97
immune-mediated disorders, 14–15
immunotherapy
cytokines, 61–62
immune checkpoint activators, 63
immune checkpoint inhibitors, 62–63
toll-like receptors (TLRs), 62
long-term prognosis, 2
metastasis, 33–34
methylated genes, 98–100
morbidity and mortality, 2
nanotechnology, 59–60
neck nodes management, 57
4-nitroquinoline-1-oxide (5-NQO), 94–95
oral bacterial microflora, 34–35
oral epithelial dysplasia, 16–17, 17f
pathogenesis
autophagy, 20–22, 21–22f
sequential progression, 18, 19f
tumor protein 53 (TP53) mutations, 18
prognosis
clinical factors, 66–67
distant metastasis, 70
histopathological factors, 67–70
lymph node metastasis, 70
lymph node ratio, 70
radiotherapy, 60–61
staging of, 48–50
surgical resection, 56–57
therapeutic markers, 64–65
tobacco-induced disorders
oral submucous fibrosis, 13
palatal keratosis associated with reverse smoking, 14
tobacco smoking
alcohol, 8
carcinogenicity, 6
chronic irritation, 11

ENDS devices, 7
epigenetic modifications, 11
forms of, 5, 5–6f
genetic alterations, 11
human papillomavirus (HPV), 8
microbes/microbial infections, 10
oxidative stress, 6
patterns and trends, 7
prevalence, 8–12
tumor microenvironment, 31f
cancer-associated fibroblasts, 26
cellular component, 25–26
endothelial cells, 26
extracellular matrix, 32
inflammatory mediators, 28–30
Oral submucous fibrosis, 13
Organic nanoparticles, 454–455
Organochlorines (OC) pesticides, 538
Organomegaly, 253, 265–266
Oropharyngeal cancer, 1
OSCC. See Oral squamous cell carcinoma (OSCC)
Osteopontin, 328
Ovarian cancer (OC), trabectedin therapy, 479–480
Oxaliplatin, 418

P
Palatal keratosis associated with reverse smoking, 14
Pancreatic cancer
carcinoembryonic antigen (CEA), 136
circulating tumor cells (CTC), 122–123
cystic fluid, 141–142
DNA and RNA markers, 123–124
DNA methylation changes, 133–134
early detection strategy, 121
endoscopic retrograde cholangiopancreatography (ERCP), 135–136
epigenetic markers, 132–133
epithelial markers, 139
EUS-FNA techniques, 143
extracellular matrix (ECM), 139
FOLFIRINOX, 122
5-FU/leucovorin, 122
gemcitabine-based therapy (NAPOLI-1), 122
germline mutations, 121
glycosylation, 125–126
growth factors and receptors, 137
H NMR analysis, 136
micro RNA modification, 134–135
MitoChip array-based sequencing, 139

Pancreatic cancer *(Continued)*
   mitochondrial mutations, 138
   MRI, 143
   mucins, 126–127
   nanoliposomal irinotecan, 122
   oncogenic KRAS, 127–129, 128*f*
   pancreatic tumor juice markers, 135–136
   precancerous lesions, 140
   pyruvate kinase (PK), 138–139
   risk factors, 121
   screening and diagnosis, 142–143
   serum carbohydrate antigen (CA) CA19-9,
      124–125
   serum markers, 124
   symptoms, 122
   telomerase, 138
   tumor suppressor genes
      CDKN2A, 130
      SMAD4, 131–132
      TP53, 131
Pancreatic ductal adenocarcinoma (PDAC)
   diagnostic biomarker
      carbohydrate antigen 19-9 (CA19-9), 155–156
      cell-free DNA (cfDNA)/circulating tumor
         DNA (ctDNA), 157
      DNA methylation, 158–159
      extracellular vesicles (EVs), 157–158
      leukemia inhibitory factor (LIF), 159
      micro-RNAs (miRNAs), 156–157
      PAM4, 159
   incidence of, 151
   metabolic reprogramming
      aberrant amino acids metabolism, 152
      ADI-PEG20, 154–155
      arginase 1, 155
      arginine, 154–155
      asparagine, 154
      CB-389, 154
      CB-839, 154
      glutamine metabolism, 152
      hexosamine biosynthesis pathway (HBP), 152
      indoleamine 2,3-dioxygenase (IDO), 155
      mammalian target of rapamycin (mTOR), 152
      oncogenic KRAS, 152–154, 154*f*
      pentose phosphate pathway (PPP), 152
      Warburg effect, 152
   prognostic biomarkers
      carbohydrate antigen 19-9 (CA19-9), 159–160
      carboxylesterase 2 (CES2) expression, 163

      cell-free DNA (cfDNA), 160–161
      circulating tumor DNA (ctDNA), 160–161
      deoxycytidine kinase (dCK), 162
      dihydropyrimidine dehydrogenase (DPD),
         162–163
      DNA methylation, 161
      extracellular vesicles (EVs), 161
      FOLFIRINOX regimen, 163
      human concentrative nucleoside transporters 3
         (hCNT3), 162
      human equilibrative nucleoside transporter 1
         (hENT1), 161–162
      microRNA, 160
      ribonucleotide reductase M1 (RRM1), 162
   surgical resection, 151
   targeted therapy
      anaplastic lymphoma kinase (ALK) fusion
         genes, 165
      CDKN2A tumor suppressor gene, 165–166
      gemcitabine plus erlotinib, 164
      gemcitabine plus placebo, 164
      neurotrophic tropomyosin receptor kinase
         (NTRK), 165
      oncogenic KRAS, 164–165
      PD-1 inhibitor, 164
      poly (adenosine diphosphate–ribose)
         polymerase (PARP), 163
Pancreatic intraepithelial neoplasias (PanINs), 140
Papillary glioneuronal tumors (PGNT)
   age, sex distribution, and location, 354
   epigenetics and genetic alterations, 354–355, 355*t*
   immunohistochemical markers, 354
   treatment, 355
Paragangliomas, 182
Parathyroid carcinoma (PCa), 188–193
Paroxysmal nocturnal hemoglobinuria (PNH), 267
Parvovirus B19, 266
PCa. *See* Prostate cancer (PCa)
PDAC. *See* Pancreatic ductal adenocarcinoma
     (PDAC)
Pelger–Huët anomaly, 267
Penicillium chrysogenum, 515–516
Peptidoglycans, 480
Periodontitis, 93–94
Pestalotiopsis microspora, 515–516
Pestalotiopsis neglecta, 515–516
Pesticides on immune-endocrine disruptors
   agricultural poisons, 543–547, 545*f*
   androgens deregulation, 541–542, 541*f*

atrazine, 544–546

cypermethrin, 542–543

early life stage exposure, 558

estrogen deregulation, 539–541, 540*f*

Gulf War illness (GWI), 546–547

herbicides and fungicides, 544

human exposure to, 547, 548–557*t*

imidacloprid, 538–539

insecticides, 546

in insulin axis, 536–539, 537*f*

monocrotophos (MCP) pesticides, 538

organochlorines (OC) pesticides, 538

pesticide-induced poisonings, 535–536

pituitary hormone, 542, 543*f*

pyrethroids, 546

PGNT. *See* Papillary glioneuronal tumors (PGNT)

Phosphatase and tensin on chromosome 10 (PTEN)
    mutation, 187

Photosensitizers (PS), 431

Photothermal agents (PTAs), 459–460

Photothermal therapy (PTT), 459–460, 466, 467*f*

Platelet cloak, 34

Platinum-based drugs, 416*t*, 432*f*

    adverse effects, 415

    cisplatin

        anticancer activity, 414–416

        complications, 415–416

        first-generation platinum drug, 416–417

        second-generation cisplatin analogs, 417–419

        third-generation cisplatin analogs, 419–421

    clinically approved drugs, 414–415, 414*f*

    mechanism of action, 421–423, 422*f*

    pharmacological activity, 415–416

    toxicity and related side effects, 423–424

Porphyromonas gingivalis, 34–35

Posttreatment biomarkers

    blood biomarkers, 293

    C-reactive protein (CRP), 293

    differential blood count markers, 293–294

    exosomes, 295–296

    lactate dehydrogenase (LDH), 293

    liquid biopsy biomarkers, 295

    peripheral T-cell biomarkers, 294

    soluble serum biomarkers (cytokines), 294–295

Primary adrenal insufficiency (PAI), 212, 213*f*

Prolaris, 309

Prostate cancer (PCa)

    antibody–drug conjugates (ADCs), 310

    micro-RNA (miRNA), 310

molecular biomarkers for diagnosis, 306*t*

    blood-based molecular biomarkers, 305–306

    tissue-based molecular biomarkers, 307

    urine-based molecular biomarkers, 306

molecular biomarkers for treatment, 308*t*

    androgen receptor splice variant 7 (AR-v7),
        310

    caretaker-type tumor suppressor genes,
        307–309

    gatekeeper-type tumor suppressor genes, 307

    mRNA-based genomic biomarkers, 309–310

prostate-specific antigen (PSA), 305

p53 tumor suppressor gene, 329

Punctuated equilibrium theory, 20

Pyrethroids, 546

Q

Quantum dots (QDs), 463

R

Radiotherapy, 452–453

Refractory cytopenia of childhood (RCC), 259,
    260*t*

Rhizophora apiculata, 518

Rhizophora mucronata, 517

Rodentibacter pneumotropicus, 94–95

Ruthenium anticancer drugs, 425–426*f*, 432*f*

    "activation by reduction" mechanism, 425–427

    in-cell mechanism of action (MoA), 425–427

    KP1339, 425–427

    NAMI-A KP1019, 425–427

    photophysical and chemical properties, 425–427

    RAED-C, 425–427, 426*f*

    RAPTA-C, 425–427, 426*f*

    RAPTA-T, 425–427, 426*f*

    RDC11, 425–427, 426*f*

    RM-175, 425–427, 426*f*

    Ru(II/III) redox potential, 425–427

    Ru(III) and Ru(II) compounds, 425–427

    TLD1433, 425–427

S

Salivaomics, 45–46

Second-generation cisplatin analogs

    carboplatin, 417

    nedaplatin, 418–419

    oxaliplatin, 418

Serine peptidase inhibitor clade A member 1, 329

Serum carbohydrate antigen (CA) CA19-9, 124–125
Sialadenotrophism, 69
Sideroblastic anemia, 267
Silicon nanoparticles (SNPs), 455–456
Silver nanoparticles (AgNPs), 437, 493
Skin cancer
  diagnostic biomarkers, 325–326
  etiopathogenesis of, 323–324
  immunohistochemical biomarkers, 326–327
  incidence of, 321–322
  international status of, 322–323
  MSC (*see* Melanoma skin cancer (MSC))
  national status of, 323
  NMSC (*see* Nonmelanoma skin cancer (NMSC))
  serologic biomarkers, 327–328
  skin layers, 321–322
  types of skin cancers, 321, 322*f*
SM5-1, 325
Small-interfering RNAs (siRNAs), 466
SN-38 metabolite, 396
Sodium-independent glucose transporters, 396–403, 399–402*t*
Sonneratia apetala, 507–508
Sonneratia caseolaris, 507–508
Squamous cell carcinoma (SqCC), 321, 329–330, 331*t*
Stenotrophomonas, 94
Stool biomarkers, 296
Streptococcus anginosus, 96
Streptococcus infantis, 96
Streptococcus salivarius, 91
Streptomyces cheonanensis, 515–516
Suaeda monoica, 518–519
Sulfated polysaccharide from Capsosiphon fulvescens (SPS-CF), 477
sulfated polysaccharide from Undaria pinnatifida (SPUP), 476
Syphilis, 10

T
Tandem mass spectrometry, 141–142
Targeted next-generation sequencing (NGS), 141
Third-generation cisplatin analogs
  heptaplatin, 420–421, 420*f*
  lobaplatin, 419–420
Thrombocytopenia, 252

Thyroglobulin elevated negative iodine scan (TENIS), 187
Thyroid Imaging Reporting and Data Systems (TIRADS) score, 186–187
Thyroiditis, 207–210, 209*f*
TiO_2 nanoparticles, 437
Tissue biomarkers
  DNA mismatch repair (MMR), 289–291
  host germline genetics, 292
  microsatellite instability (MSI), 289–291
  PD-L1 expression on tumor cells, 285–293
  T-cell exhaustion, 292–293
  tumor-infiltrating lymphocytes (TIL), 291–292
  tumor mutation burden, 287–289
Total thyroidectomy
  for Graves disease, 176, 177*f*
  for nodular Graves disease—Marine-Lenhart syndrome, 176, 177*f*
  for toxic goiter, 176, 178*f*
  for toxic multinodular goiter, 176, 176*f*
Trabectedin therapy in ovarian cancer, 479–480
Transferrin (Tf) receptor, 463
Tumor-associated antigen 90 immune complex (TA90IC), 328
Tyrosinase, 325

U
Uridine diphosphate glucuronosyltransferase (UGT) enzymes, 396
US Drug Administration (FDA), 2011, 199

V
Vascular endothelial growth factor (VEGF), 327

W
Warburg effect, 32, 152
Whipple's triad, 185
2019 World Health Organization classification of tumors, 105

X
Xylocarpus granatum, 507–508, 515

Y
YKL-40 biomarker, 328

Z
ZnO NPs, 437